Also by Anthony Cave Brown

Bodyguard of Lies (1975)
Dropshot: The Third World War (1977)

THE LAST
HERO

THE LAST
HERO

WILD BILL
DONOVAN

The biography and political experience of Major General William J. Donovan, founder of the OSS and "father" of the CIA, from his personal and secret papers and the diaries of Ruth Donovan

Anthony
Cave Brown

Times
BOOKS

Published by TIMES BOOKS, a division of
The New York Times Book Co., Inc.
Three Park Avenue, New York, N.Y. 10016

Published simultaneously in Canada by
Fitzhenry & Whiteside, Ltd., Toronto

Library of Congress Cataloging in Publication Data

Cave Brown, Anthony.
The last hero.

Bibliography: p. 836.
Includes index.
1. Donovan, William J. (William Joseph), 1883–
1959. 2. Intelligence officers—United States—
Biography. I. Title.
UB271.U52D663   1982   940.54′86′730924 [B]   82-50046
ISBN 0-8129-1021-4

Manufactured in the United States of America

In Memoriam
Lieutenant Colonel Otto C. Doering, Jr.
1904–1979

CONTENTS

AUTHOR'S NOTE

In what was his last act of World War II, Major General William J. Donovan, director of the Office of Strategic Services, the first American secret intelligence and special operations service and the organization from which sprang the CIA, spent several nights at OSS headquarters in Washington, D.C., with his executive officer, Lieutenant Edwin J. Putzell, Jr., microfilming the director's files. Doing the work themselves because of the political sensitivity of the documentation, they produced two copies; Donovan took possession of one, Putzell the other. The purpose of this large operation was to provide the basis of a history of Donovan's incumbency when that became politically possible.

Several starts were made on work. Professor Conyers Read, the Harvard historian, produced many draft chapters before Donovan himself asked him to stop work because he felt the director's papers were still too sensitive. Read did not resume his work, for death intervened. One of Donovan's wartime majors, Corey Ford, then began work on the project in the mid-1950's, producing a draft manuscript of what was really a biographical history of Donovan and the OSS, but again death intervened before Ford could complete his volume.

After Donovan's death in 1959, the project was taken over by Whitney Shepardson, Donovan's chief of secret intelligence during World War II. For the third time the author died before completing the work. Then came the fourth attempt, this time by Cornelius Ryan, the author of *The Longest Day*. However, although Ryan had the support of Donovan's friends President Dwight D. Eisenhower and Allen W. Dulles, then director of central intelligence, the work was stopped before it really began; a middle-rank official at the CIA managed to stop the project because he believed the book contemplated by Ryan would be too controversial. When he found himself denied access to the directors files, Ryan was compelled to abandon the project temporarily. Then he, too, died before it was possible to resume work.

In all these attempts none of the authors saw the microfilm, except Read, who saw two or three reels having to do with the OSS's formation. During this time Putzell had been taken so seriously ill that he burned his copy of microfilm rather than leave it unguarded in his estate should he die. Happily Putzell did not die; nonetheless, the only copy of the microfilm outside the CIA (where in 1982 it was still classified) was Donovan's. That was in 1970 in the custody of Donovan's law partner, friend, and wartime executive officer Otto C. Doering, Jr.

Doering tried to engage the interest of several of America's leading authors. He was not successful primarily because the men he wished to do the work were involved in large tasks that could not be put aside. Meantime, Donovan's papers, together with the microfilm, were transferred to a storage room alongside the ice-skating rink at Rockefeller Center, where they remained until late 1977.

In that year, having recently published a work on deception and intelligence operations for the Normandy invasion in 1944, a work entitled *Bodyguard of Lies,* I was invited to give a talk to the Veterans of Strategic Services at their annual meeting at the Biltmore Hotel, New York. I chose for my subject the "Place of OSS in History," and I fear I must have startled those present by stating that in my opinion OSS had no place in history because no history had been written and because the known facts had become so encrusted with legend that the truth concerning its performance had become impossible to divine.

After the talk I was invited with other members of the VSS to a party at the El Morocco nightclub, and there I met William J. Casey, who as a younger man had been Donovan's chief of secret intelligence in Europe. Casey was now a member of the President's Foreign Intelligence Advisory Committee and was soon to become director of central intelligence in the Reagan administration. He suggested that I might like to do the Donovan biography. Immediately I declared that I was not the man for the job because its politics made it work for an American, not a Briton. Casey disagreed, for as he said, "An Englishman is not likely to be either a Democrat or a Republican." I saw his point, I agreed to give the project some thought, and after several months of discussion I agreed to undertake the work, provided I was given complete access to the Donovan papers and complete editorial freedom.

After the passage of many weeks I was introduced to Otto Doering at his law chambers in Rockefeller Plaza. It emerged that Doering had read *Bodyguard of Lies* and had been favorably impressed by it. There was a meeting of minds, and after much discussion I agreed to do the biography on the conditions already presented to Casey. Doering thereupon granted me full access to the Donovan papers and complete editorial freedom.

When I began full-time work on the Donovan biography late in 1978, I had not the slightest idea what the Donovan papers consisted of, and at first Doering's only contribution were very lengthy tape-recorded interviews in which he gave me his recollections of Donovan and service in the OSS. While these constituted unique recollections (Doering was at the heart of the OSS machine throughout the war and had been one of Donovan's few intimates), they were not enough. I said so, and shortly Doering managed to obtain the release of some 1,400 bound volumes of Donovan's papers, which had been given to the CIA for safekeeping during the McCone regime.

The papers were returned almost intact, with perhaps one of 148 archives boxes being withheld by the CIA because they contained British or other foreign material which the agency did not have the power to declassify without the permission of the governments concerned. These documents later proved to be of no importance to the Donovan biography.

The next step was the arrival in the winter of 1979 of two five-drawer metal filing cabinets crammed with Donovan's papers and memorabilia and also a very large collection of Donovan's writings, speeches, newspaper clippings, diaries, letters, and the material so necessary for a biography. Still, I did not know of the existence of the microfilm, which Doering had acquired as Donovan's literary executor at Donovan's death. There was, however, nothing personal in this: Doering wanted to be sure that I intended to complete the biography before he revealed its existence to me.

By the spring of 1979, however, the research had progressed well, and Doering then mentioned the existence of the microfilm. He allowed me to see some of it and to take some of it to my place of work. It became apparent that here was a historical trove of high importance. But then Doering died suddenly in the early summer of 1979. At this point I should state that Otto Doering's sudden death was a heavy blow to this volume, for not only had he studied General Donovan since they met first in 1929, when Doering joined Donovan's law firm, but he was a central figure in the formation, the administration, the operations, and the termination of the Office of Strategic Services. No man knew more than he about the inner politics of the establishment of the service. Moreover, Doering was a man with a truly outstanding mind. His memory and recollections were most impressive, and even in the most intricate matters he talked as if the events he was describing had occurred only the day before.

However, his widow, Lucy Doering, and Doering's career-long friend Ralstone R. Irvine, who had been with Donovan in the Antitrust Division and throughout the existence of Donovan Leisure Newton & Irvine, rallied to the assistance of the work. Both spent many scores of hours completing the reminiscences that Otto Doering had begun. Of the highest importance was the microfilm.

When Doering died, he had not handed over to me all the microfilm. Then Mrs. Doering appeared in Irvine's chambers with a number of Bloomingdale's shopping bags. As she explained to him, she had found the microfilm in the place where it had been deposited by Doering for safekeeping and felt that her husband had intended it to be used for the purposes of the Donovan biography. A check showed that the microfilm included all the records of Donovan's involvement in the campaigns in northwestern Europe, in Southeast and eastern Asia, and in Arabia.

Ralstone Irvine took possession of the microfilm, establishing from Doering's secretary of more than thirty years, Lucy McGuire, that it was indeed intended for the biography. Then he handed the microfilm over to me, still in the Bloomingdale's shopping bags. Also, he took the Donovan project under his wing, spending many weeks of his extremely valuable time, both at the office and outside, helping me with his excellent recollections of Donovan as a lawyer and a man and arranging for me to meet a very large number of Donovan's associates. Irvine introduced me to Doering's deputy during the OSS years, Edwin J. Putzell, of Naples, Florida, who had retired recently after many years as general counsel to Monsanto Chemical Corporation. Putzell, who had been a member of Donovan's law firm before going to the OSS at its formation, placed himself unreservedly at the service of the biography.

Also, Irvine introduced me to a number of his colleagues in the law firm, including Carl Newton, John E. Tobin, T. J. McFadden, David Teitelbaum, Judge Owen McGivern, James Withrow, James Hayes, Theodore Hope, and former partners or associates in the firm such as Judge J. Edward Lumbard, Frank Raichle, Bethuel Webster, and William E. Colby. All these men provided much valuable material concerning Donovan's career before, during, and after his OSS years. Also, William J. Casey, Henry B. Hyde, Geoffrey M. T. Jones, Oliver J. Sands, Franklin O. Canfield, Mrs. Marlys Chatel, General William Quinn, Brigadier Sir Douglas Dodds-Parker, and many, many others provided me with information that enabled me, I think, to fill in the lacunae created by the death of Otto Doering.

As important, through Irvine's work the general's son, David R. Donovan, turned over to me more priceless material: his mother's diaries, which she began in 1908 and which she kept up *every day* until incapacitated by illness in 1973; boxes of letters between Donovan and his wife throughout their marriage; the general's medals (which are now displayed in the board room of Donovan Leisure Newton & Irvine); and a large quantity of family albums and scrapbooks. His intention was, as he stated, to enable me to write the definitive biography of Donovan.

Then, again through Irvine, I learned of the existence of the vanden Heuvel diaries. Ambassador William J. vanden Heuvel had been an associate lawyer in the Donovan law firm and, when Donovan was appointed by Eisenhower to the post of U.S. ambassador in Thailand in 1953, Donovan's special assistant at Bangkok. During the year Donovan was ambassador he and vanden Heuvel had many revealing conversations in which Donovan looked back over his life and allowed vanden Heuvel to record his inner thoughts and feelings about the people he had met and the experiences he had had. In many respects, during these conversations Donovan dotted the *i*'s and crossed the *t*'s in his life, for not long after these conversations he suffered a series of minor and then major strokes that robbed him of much of his memory and lucidity.

Ambassador vanden Heuvel lent me these journals, and his generous gesture completed the research process, one marked by a remarkable spirit of cooperation from all involved. To them all I offer my thanks, for no writer could have asked for greater, more friendly, more hospitable cooperation. In this context I might mention the contribution of Henry Hyde. In order to clarify certain parts of the research, Hyde traveled twice to Washington from New York to spend three days with me in which we went through vital parts microscopically in order to ensure complete accuracy. The Algiers, Bern, and Vatican chapters owe much to his knowledge and his journeys. Robert B. Joyce, Donovan's political officer in the Mediterranean, entrusted his memoirs to me to enable me to tread more surely through the Balkan and Italian minefields. In fact, everyone approached for help gave his or her assistance unsparingly. This was particularly so in the case of Irvine.

After the first draft of the manuscript had been completed, Irvine undertook the difficult and painful task of reading it, commenting upon it, guiding me through the subtleties of the antitrust laws, and in general helping me bring Donovan's fluid, complicated, and elusive personality into sharper focus. Irvine also saw all the other drafts and in doing so saved me from fates worse than death even at the end. He was at once my sternest critic and my greatest encouragement, and I am greatly indebted to him.

The manuscript was also read in its penultimate form by Judge Lumbard, Judge McGivern, Teitelbaum, Samuel W. Murphy, Jr. (who in 1982 became head of the Donovan law firm), James Jesus Angleton, T. J. McFadden, Lucy Doering, E. J. Putzell, William J. Casey, Henry Hyde, William Colby, Franklin O. Canfield, James R. Murphy, and David Donovan. Therefore, if after all this scrutiny errors of fact, interpretation, or selection still exist, the responsibility is mine alone. Furthermore, the opinions expressed are all mine alone, and the fact that men such as Casey of the CIA, Irvine of Donovan Leisure Newton & Irvine, and Hyde of the VSS read the final manuscript and the proofs should in no way be taken as an endorsement of the views expressed in the following pages. Nor should it be thought that this volume necessarily reflects such men's views.

With that in mind, I am bound to deal with the problems created by Donovan's papers. In the first place, the archives were large (a three-ton truck was required to move them from New York to my place of work).

These showed that Donovan's was a rare, crowded life. Since it was plain it would be impossible to deal with every aspect of such a life in one volume, the need to be highly selective in the use of the papers was imposed upon me. I decided, therefore, to dwell on events that were important in the evolution of his career, the realization of his ambitions, and the development of the Central Intelligence Agency.

But there were problems even in realizing that modest policy. In the first place, World War II was half over before the OSS could make any significant contribution. It stands to reason that a large industry such as the OSS could not be, and was not, simply conjured out of the atmosphere and placed upon the world stage, ready to do battle with, and defeat, the Sicherheitsdienst and Abwehr of Germany. A long period was necessary in which men were recruited and training, administrative, communications, and operational procedures were developed, OSS found its place in the government, overseas bases were established, and men were deployed to the four corners of the world. All this took time. Therefore, the OSS's contribution to the war was modest before the summer of 1943. It was true that Donovan played a large and important part in the Anglo-American invasion of French North Africa in November 1942 and that his representatives there did much useful work, preparing the way for the armies. However, the nature of Donovan's operations was eclipsed by two factors: (1) the existence of major sources of cryptanalytical intelligence, such as Ultra and Magic, and (2) the overriding importance of the political situation in French North Africa before, during, and after the landings. These were mainly the concern not of Donovan and the OSS, but of General Dwight D. Eisenhower and the State Department.

Furthermore, even when the OSS was deployed and ready for action, as it was by the summer of 1943, it was an inexperienced service, prone to blunder and defeat. That was particularly pronounced in the Mediterranean in 1943, when Donovan launched what was his main contribution to the war—the large-scale extension of OSS activities into the Balkans and Eastern and Central Europe. And at all times the British Secret Intelligence Service placed very severe constraints on what the OSS could and could not do.

The combined effect of these problems was to give the impression that the OSS did little and that what it did do it did not do well. That impression is enhanced by Donovan's files as director of the OSS. While these are full and frank—much fuller and franker than is usually the case with spymasters' papers—they do constitute a litany of troubles with other government departments and with Allied services and defeat at the hands of the enemy. In fact, that is an insoluble problem, for this volume is not a history of the OSS, it is the story of the experience of its director. For a full, rounded account of the OSS, therefore, the reader is recommended to the *War Report of the OSS*, which was published commercially by Walker of New York and Carrollton of Washington in 1976.

That having been said, it is necessary for me to state what this volume is about—to describe the areas I believe were of importance in the Donovan story. These number five:

1. Donovan's experience and personality before he became America's first intelligence master.

2. His problems in forming the first American secret intelligence and special operations organization—in establishing the embryo of the Central Intelligence Agency—especially in relation to the rest of the government and to America's allies.

3. His contribution toward the success of the Arcadia plan, the strategic plan for the defeat of Germany.

4. The evolution of his campaign against the Soviet Union, particularly in Eastern Europe—a campaign that, with the Soviet operations against the United States, foreshadowed the cold war.

5. The events that culminated in the dismissal of Donovan by President Harry S Truman and in the liquidation of the OSS.

These, then, are the five main themes of this work. Donovan's work in Eastern Europe, Scandinavia, and Asia must await another volume, although it must be said that the work was valorous and important.

One final comment is appropriate. Donovan's predicament was America's, and it was created by successive governments from Woodrow Wilson onward. The country was not prepared for warfare on the dark side of the moon. It had little or no knowledge of what such warfare entailed. Neither the State Department nor the Joint Chiefs were experienced in the darker arts of statecraft. Yet it will be realized that by 1944 Donovan was launching operations every hour on the hour throughout the world, and while his defeats were spectacular and Byzantine, many of the operations were successful, and some of them would rank with the greatest exploits of human daring and bravery in the history of the United States and of World War II. Donovan's war was, indeed: *"Une guerre obscure et méritoire."*

Anthony Cave Brown
Washington, D.C.
March 1982

DONOVAN'S AWARDS

World War I

Medal of Honor, for conduct in action near Landres-et-St.-Georges, France, October 15, 1918.

Distinguished Service Cross, for conduct in action crossing the Ourcq River, France, July 28–31, 1918.

Distinguished Service Medal, for services in Baccarat sector, France, July 28–31, 1918, and the Meuse-Argonne offensive, October 1918.

Purple Heart with two Oak Leaf Clusters, for wounds received in action.

Légion d'Honneur and Croix de Guerre with Palm and Silver Star (France).

Croci di Guerra (Italy).

World War II

Oak Leaf Cluster to Distinguished Service Medal for services as Director of Strategic Services.

Czechoslovak War Cross, 1939.

Order of the Crown of Italy.

Knight Commander of the British Empire.

Commandant de la Légion d'Honneur (France).

Grand Officer of the Order of Leopold of Belgium with Palm.

Lateran Medal (Vatican).

Order of St. Sylvester (Vatican).

Commander of the Polonia Restituta (Poland).

Knight of the Most Exalted Order of the White Elephant (Thailand).

Santi Mali Medal (Siam).

Commander of the Royal Order of St. Olav (Norway).

Commander of the Order of Dannebrog (Denmark).

Grand Officer of the Order of Orange Nassau (Netherlands).

Special Collar Order of Yun Hui (China).

Post-World War II

National Security Medal.

Campaign Medals

Mexican Service Border Medal.

World War Victory Medal with five battle clasps.

Army of Occupation of Germany Medal.

American Defense Service Medal

American Campaign Medal.

Asiatic-Pacific Campaign Medal with arrowhead and two bronze service stars for participation in the Central Burma and China offensive campaigns.

Europe-African-Middle Eastern Campaign Medal with arrowheads and silver service stars for participation in the Rome-Arno, Central Europe, Ardennes-Alsace, Normandy, Rhineland, northern France, southern France, Algiers-French Morocco, Sicily, and Anzio campaigns.

World War II Victory Medal.

Armed Forces Reserve Medal with one ten-year device.

Unit Award

Distinguished Unit Emblem with one bronze oak leaf cluster.

THE LAST HERO

Bill Donovan was the last hero.
—President Dwight D. Eisenhower

PROLOGUE

THE BIRTH OF THE OSS AND THE CIA

On Sunday afternoon, December 7, 1941, Colonel William J. Donovan was in his private box at the New York Polo Grounds, watching the football game between the Giants and the Brooklyn Dodgers. Just after two o'clock Pug Manders broke through the Giants' center on a spinner play, and the crowd roared when he gained twenty-nine yards for a first down on the four-yard line. The loudspeaker message was not, therefore, too audible. But Donovan heard it: "Attention, please! Attention! Here is an urgent message. Will Colonel William J. Donovan call Operator nineteen in Washington, D.C."[1]

Donovan, recently named America's first director of central intelligence by FDR, left his box and made his way to the exit. Fifty-eight years old, very handsome with a mane of silver white hair, five feet ten inches tall, and swaddled in a beautiful Chesterfield, he paused for a minute or two to watch the play. Manders had taken the ball and was plunging across the goal line for the Dodgers' second touchdown—they were to beat the Giants 21–7. At the office Donovan called Operator 19. In a few minutes the President's son James Roosevelt, who worked for Donovan's intelligence organization, came on the line. He told Donovan that the Japanese fleet air arm was attacking the U.S. Pacific Fleet at Pearl Harbor and asked Donovan to return to Washington to see the President. Donovan told young Roosevelt that he would leave immediately.

Donovan then called his New York office, and his assistant, James R. Murphy, answered. There was a brief discussion about the attack, and Murphy suggested that Donovan give some thought to the text of an official announcement to forestall any civilian panic on the East and West coasts. Donovan thought that wise, and he told Murphy to meet him at La Guardia Airport and to get two seats on the first plane to the capital after four o'clock.

Donovan and Murphy boarded the military DC-3 at about 5:00 P.M., and about two hours later they were landing at Gravelly Point, the site of what is now National Airport. Donovan's black chauffeur, Freeman, was waiting with the Lincoln and took them straight to Donovan's headquarters in the National Institute of Health, on the fringes of Georgetown. There Donovan noticed the first sign that America was at war: The building was guarded by an infantry platoon in battle order. He noticed also that their uniform and equipment were those of World War I.

It was now about 8:00 P.M. Donovan called his "College of Cardinals" —as his Board of Analysts was called—and asked it to prepare an estimate of the situation for the President and a Cabinet meeting, which was to be held at 9:00 P.M. in the Oval Office. The board consisted of some of the most distinguished academics in the United States: James Phinney Baxter III (president of Williams College); Edward Mead Earle (professor of the School for Economics and Politics at the Institute for Advanced Study, Princeton); William L. Langer (professor of history, Harvard); Edward S. Mason (professor of economics, Harvard); Donald C. McKay (professor of French history, Harvard); Joseph R. Hayden (chairman of the Department of Political Science, University of Michigan), and Calvin B. Hoover (professor of economics, Duke University).

In fact, the board had been meeting since about 4:00 P.M. for just this purpose, but then, as now, the members were not able to present an opinion on the situation, and they particularly did not feel competent to make a prediction concerning Japanese operations in the near future. The reason: Because Donovan's organization did not yet have its own secret intelligence service, the board was dependent upon the Army and Navy Intelligence services for the bulletins on which to make its estimates. However, because the Army and the Navy had ignored the presidential order that Donovan was to see all intelligence having a bearing on national security, that intelligence was being denied to the board.

Here, then, was the root cause of the intelligence failure that produced the Pearl Harbor disaster. The "College of Cardinals" existed to see all intelligence relating to a problem and then make a judgment about what it meant, yet because the Army and the Navy did not trust the security disciplines of a new civilian organization such as Donovan's, vital intelligence was withheld from the "College" before, during, and after the attack.

Thus, Baxter told Donovan that evening, the "College of Cardinals" felt unable to give an opinion concerning Japanese capabilities and intentions on the basis of the wire service reports, and it was virtually without other sources. Consequently Donovan telephoned Colonel G. Edward "Ned" Buxton, an associate in the Office of the Coordinator of Information (COI) who was visiting Los Angeles, and, in San Francisco, Turner McBaine, a young lawyer serving as a West Coast representative of the COI, to see whether they had obtained any information from their Army and Navy colleagues—although there was, again, ample intelligence available in Washington on which to make the required estimate. Both stated they had received no information from either service, and neither man was able to report anything beyond what was happening locally. Buxton advised that his battalion sergeant major in France in World War I, Toki Slocum, a Nisei with a magnificent fighting record, had called at his hotel and presented Buxton with his two samurai swords. In what was America's first secret intelligence bulletin of the new era, Buxton thought that was significant. In recent years Slocum had cultivated Bushido—the cult of emperor worship, the martial virtues, and unfailing loyalty to the overlords. In surrendering his swords, Slocum had shown that with the outbreak of war between America and Japan his loyalties were with America.

Elsewhere, Buxton reported, all fortifications and coastal and antiaircraft guns were being manned, the National Guard was standing by, and balloon barrages were up over Los Angeles. There were persistent rumors of submarines off the naval base at San Diego, and aerial patrols were up. All aircraft on all airfields were now dispersed. The FBI was putting into effect plans for rounding up all Issei; and there was much disquiet among the civilian population in general. There was something of a run on the food stores and gun shops, and Los Angeles police feared there might be panic after nightfall, particularly if aircraft came over the city and the guns opened fire—as in fact happened, although the aircraft proved to be American. From San Francisco, McBaine sent in a report in beautiful copperplate handwriting over the Thermofax machine. It told a story much the same as Buxton's, except that Naval Intelligence was asserting that unidentified submarines had been sighted off the Golden Gate Bridge. Issei were already being rounded up.

Little here would interest FDR on a night like this, with the entire world now at war, so Donovan canceled his request for an estimate, and the Board of Analysts went home when it became clear that nothing was going to come in from the Army and Navy.

Donovan turned to his other responsibilities—propaganda and information. He called in his chief of propaganda and information, Robert Sherwood, the playwright, who pointed out that most Americans did not know where Pearl Harbor was, and those who did thought it was not part of the United States. Sherwood believed it essential that the American public be made to realize that an *American* fleet had been attacked and sunk in an *American* port. He proposed, and Donovan agreed, that a bulletin go out to all editors requesting all maps show plainly that Hawaii was in the Western Hemisphere, that it was part of the Zone of the Interior, and that America itself had been attacked by the Japanese fleet. The next morning all newspaper maps showed clearly that Pearl Harbor was part of the United States.

Donovan spent the rest of the evening preparing for his meeting with Roosevelt, which was now to take place at the White House at midnight. He received a report on the President's attitude from his old friend Frank Knox, secretary of the navy, who had attended a number of meetings at the White House that day. The President's basic feeling was enormous relief, for FDR had long believed it essential that America get into the war on the side of England, but that it must not fire the first shot.

Knox went on to state that FDR had been very pale but very calm, although he could hardly bring himself to describe what had happened. Twice he had said to Knox, "Find out, for God's sake, why those ships were tied up in rows." The casualties and the losses at Pearl Harbor— which Knox and Donovan had only recently visited during a tour of inspection—had crippled the U.S. Pacific Fleet. And while Knox had been talking with the President, Prime Minister Churchill had telephoned from England to discuss the situation. British possessions in Asia—Hong Kong, Singapore—had been attacked as well, and a Japanese task force was approaching the Kra Isthmus, its clear purpose to land an invasion force against Malaya. "We are all in the same boat now," Knox had heard FDR say to Churchill, who was coming to Washington with his political and military staffs as quickly as possible.

Shortly before midnight Donovan and Ed Murrow, the celebrated CBS radio correspondent, went together to see Roosevelt. The usher's diary at the White House shows that they were shown into the Oval Office a minute or two after midnight and remained alone with Roosevelt for about thirty-five minutes.

The room was in semidarkness when Donovan and Murrow were shown in, and the President sat alone in a pool of light cast by his desk lamp. He had still not recovered from the shock of the attack. "They caught our ships like lame ducks! Lame ducks, Bill!" he exclaimed, as if there were something new in the information. "We told them at Pearl Harbor, and everywhere else, to have the lookouts manned. But they still took us by surprise." The President added: "They caught our planes on the ground—on the ground!"

Yet WJD said later he thought he had the same sense about FDR as had Frances Perkins, the secretary of labor, a shrewd observer. The President's surprise was not as great as that of the other men around him. Nor was the attack unwelcome. It had ended the past months of uncertainty caused by FDR's decision that Japan must be seen to make the first overt move. Furthermore, he had had a note from Professor T. North Whitehead of Harvard, son of the philosopher: "The dictator powers have presented us with a united America." That might not have occurred but for the Japanese attack.

As FDR talked, WJD felt that only the size of the disaster, not the attack itself, had shaken him. If the casualties, both human and material, had not been so heavy, the President might have been in a joyful mood. The position between the Axis and the United States had been clarified once and for all. FDR asked Donovan about the note from Professor Whitehead. Was it true? Would America now support a declaration of war against the Axis Powers, as the coalition of Germany, Japan, and Italy and their allies was called? Donovan thought so, as did Murrow.

At some stage during their meeting FDR made a brief reference to the intelligence aspects of the situation. "It's a good thing you got me started on this [intelligence business]" because, repeating himself, FDR said, "They caught our planes on the ground—on the ground!" But the main business was the mood of the public, whether the effect of Pearl Harbor would prove enough to propel the country into accepting total war with the Axis powers. Also, there was discussion about whether the Germans and the Japanese were acting according to a joint plan. Donovan thought there was such a plan, although he had no real evidence.

Donovan and Murrow then began to withdraw. FDR told Donovan to get a good night's rest, and WJD said he would be staying at his headquarters during the present emergency. When they got out into Lafayette Square, Murrow said he thought he detected an air of siege in the sharp, frosty night.

In this way began Donovan's strange odyssey. While he was a Renaissance man of rare experience, little in his past had prepared him for the next four years, for a special, private war of the type that, as Winston Churchill was to write, was "in every respect equal to the most fantastic inventions of romance and melodrama. Tangle within tangle, plot and counterplot, ruse and treachery, cross and double-cross, true agent, false agent, double agent, gold and steel, the bomb, the dagger and the firing party . . . interwoven in many a texture so intricate as to be incredible and yet true."[2]

This private war would give the agency that WJD had in mind—the Central Intelligence Agency—a shape, luster, and attitude that would influence it for the next four decades.

OSS ON THE EVE OF NEPTUNE

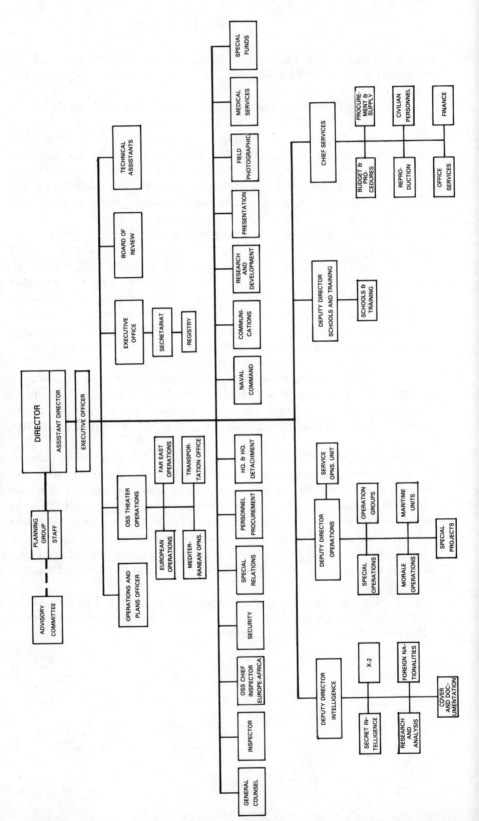

PART ONE

PREPARATION

Being the account of Donovan's youth, education, legal career, military and government service, and how he came to form the Peculiar Service

1

Bill and Ruth

When Thomas Carlyle, the nineteenth-century British author, observed that history was only the biography of great men, the opinion was widely challenged. Yet between 1883 and 1959 there lived an American, William Joseph Donovan, who appeared to many of his countrymen to be the embodiment of that opinion. One such opinion was that of a charter member of the OSS, Edmond Taylor, who was to write that in founding the intelligence agency, Donovan and his organization established "a precedent, or a pattern, for United States intervention in the revolutionary struggles of the postwar age." Moreover, his "influence on U.S. foreign and military policy has continued to be felt even since his death; for good or ill he left a lasting mark on the mind of the nation's power elite. However indirectly, many of our latter-day Cold War successes, disasters, and entrapments can ultimately be traced back to him."[1]

As events will show, that statement was undoubtedly true, if incomplete, for the general belief of those who knew him well, or served with him, is that Donovan was the point man of the force that led to America's emergence as a superpower. Many of his associates would regard him as the greatest living American of his time, his chief accomplishment being that he prodded Washington military and political thought in 1940 from a doctrine established by George Washington into the twentieth century —he introduced the principles of modern war into Washington, conceiving a multipronged method of waging war at every level of human endeavor.

This was substantially correct, although he did not conceive the new doctrines. He adapted to American usage ideas and tactics that had been coming into increasing use in Europe and Asia ever since the Bolshevik Revolution of 1917 and that found their ultimate expression in the tactics and strategies employed by the Communist powers to defeat the United States in Southeast Asia in the 1960's and 1970's.

Donovan may be included in the list of wizards, good and bad, who shaped the theory of warfare in the second half of the twentieth century —the era described in a chapter title of the U.S. Joint Chiefs of Staff's official history as "The Approach to Armageddon"—wizards who included Churchill, Roosevelt, Hitler, Trotsky, Dzerzhinsky, Mussolini, Stalin, Mao, Einstein, Guderian, "Bomber" Harris, Patton, Montgomery, Rommel. Moreover, Donovan's ideas and influence did not evaporate with his death. For he founded a dynasty of American spymasters that still dominated the American intelligence and special operations community as late as 1982. William Casey, the director of central intelligence in the Reagan administration, was one of Donovan's protégés during and after World War II.

Although Donovan was a preeminent figure in the American establishment for nearly forty years, he was not born to the purple. William Joseph "Wild Bill" Donovan was a second-generation Irish Catholic born on January 1, 1883, in Buffalo, then a major port and industrial and railroad center on the Great Lakes in New York State.

The origins of the O'Donovans were obscure, but it is known that they originated in County Cork, the largest of the Irish counties, a place with a long, rocky, stormy coastline on the Western Approaches to the British Isles and Europe—a coastline with wild, boyish names such as Bantry, Roaringwater, Courtmarcherry, Clonakilty, and Youghal bays; an enchanted place of barren purple-colored mountains, and the fertile valleys of the Bride, Blackwater, Lee, and Bandon; a mystical place littered with many remains of prehistory—brooding dolmens, stone circles—and the ruins of medieval abbeys and churches.

Donovan's grandfather was married in the little Catholic church at Goleen, a village not far from the coast, in about 1825. As was the custom the couple signed their names, together with information about their dates of birth, and stations in life, trade, and the church, on the wall of the church. Evidence as that writing might have contained about the O'Donovans was obliterated when the church walls were painted a century later. There is a suggestion, however, that Grandfather O'Donovan owned a tavern and that he was a prominent member of two powerful organizations in Cork: the Ribbonmen, a Catholic secret society, and Father Mathew's Pledge, a temperance movement started by a Franciscan friar, Father Mathew.

The cause of the O'Donovans' decision to leave Goleen for America is far from clear, but it was made at a time of political uncertainties, crop failures, collapsing banks, intermittent civil war, disease, and the belief, fostered by the shipping companies' agents, that life in America was infinitely better than life in Ireland.

Such evidence as there is suggests that the family traveled as most other Irishmen did, in the boats that brought lumber and wood products from North America and picked up a migrant cargo for the return voyage, each fare costing seven pounds if the migrant took his own food and ten pounds if he ate the ship's food. Since the British Parliament regulated conditions aboard these ships, living conditions were a good deal more tolerable and comfortable than the European migrant trade into New York.

The probability is that the O'Donovans sailed in the late winter of 1846–47, to arrive in North America as early as possible during the year, so that they might earn enough money to tide them over the coming winter. They landed at one of the Canadian maritime ports, probably Montreal, and then walked or took the stagecoach down to Buffalo—there is a suggestion that Grandfather O'Donovan was a cut above the cotter peasantry and had a little money from the sale of some land. His reason for heading for Buffalo was the same as that of the rest of the Irish: It had a large Irish community, there was work in the grain ships and on the railroads and the Erie Canal, laborers' wages were rather higher in Buffalo than elsewhere between Buffalo and Baltimore, and the Roman Catholic Church was strong. Also, so it is said, O'Donovan was attracted by the assertion that "God has made Buffalo" and the fact that poets were singing songs about the place, that it was "the Sovereign City of the Lakes, Crowned and Acknowledged," where "Enterprise and Commerce vex the waves," and an

> Enchanted city where the dreaming soul
> Conjures the minarets of far Cathay. . . .[2]

However, when the O'Donovans arrived in Buffalo, these stories of "The New World's grandest marvel" beside Niagara proved very fanciful. Most of the streets were "rolled billows of a shallow storm-tossed sea" of mud. The city was so unhealthy that a branch of sanitation came to be known as Buffalo City Sewage and Sanitary Science. The few sewers, all of which were in or around Delaware Avenue, the central citadel of the ruling Protestants, were described as "but five or six feet deep, constructed of dry brick, with a board bottom," running through the Irish quarter "into the lake and down Niagara River, near shore, washing the Bird Island Pier, close to which our water works sucked into their tunnel the stream that ran to our lips through the [wooden] city pipes." When the city did at last establish a Bureau of Sanitation, it had to deal with "bigoted ignorance, bigoted tradition, bigoted habits, and long indulged recklessness of neglect."

The Irish quarter, known as the First Ward, was a raucous, damp, watery place of shanties where the arctic winds came straight down from Canada, gathering speed and cold from Lake Erie. It was true that, as the poet wrote, at Buffalo "Enterprise and Commerce" vexed the waves— fortunes were being made in Buffalo, but only on Delaware Avenue, a place of stately mansions set amid elms which the residents regarded as the Paris of North America. Down in the First Ward the Donovans (they soon dropped the lordly O') could not have been more unfortunate, even in Ireland. The same prejudices existed, work beyond manual labor was withheld from the Irish, and everywhere such signs were to be seen as:

NIGHT WATCHMAN WANTED—Must be fairly well educated, neat of appearance, able-bodied, and if necessary be ready to furnish bond; none but those who can show absolute proofs of their honesty and sobriety in all senses of the word need apply. . . .

NINA

The "NINA" meant "No Irish Need Apply."

It would not have taken Donovan long to realize that Buffalo was a Protestants' paradise where almost everything was owned or managed by men with names like Orlando Allen, Cyrenius Bristol, Horatio Shumway, Oliver Forward, Elisha Hickox, Thaddeus Weed, Abner Bryant, and Elijah Efner. The Donovans had merely exchanged one determined, impenetrable Protestant hegemony for another.

The theory of Anglo-Saxon Protestant superiority was as firmly entrenched in America as in England. It is pertinent to note that no Anglo-Saxon Protestant, least of all a rich and influential one, would permit a daughter to "walk out with" an Irish Catholic, and formidable forces would have been deployed to wreck love and marriage. For the rest, they were cooped up in the First Ward, with little or no prospect of breaking away from the laboring classes, unless they were wholly exceptional individuals—usually pugilists, priests, performers, or politicians.

On his arrival in the First Ward, Grandfather Donovan got a job first as a scooper in the grain holds of the ships on the waterfront and then at the railroad yards, for it was there that Buffalo was brimming with the American promise of equality and material reward. The city was considered the logical gateway to the American West, so it was at the yards that there was, in the Irish phrase, a bob or two to be made.

By Irish lights the Donovans prospered, although they did not exactly get up to Delaware Avenue—yet. Grandfather Donovan became a lay figure of some importance in the Catholic Church and through thrift and hard work managed to do something most Irish Catholics could not: He bought the small brick cottage at 74 Michigan Street which he was renting from a Protestant on Delaware Avenue. There were, it seems, good hearts even in Mammon. Yet this house was no more than a working-class cottage set amid wooden shanties on a block of unpaved streets and open sewers.

His success apart, Grandfather Donovan was a man of causes, and although the Holy See had forbidden the faithful to join secret societies, Grandfather Donovan, breathing some of the fire and brimstone of a Mathew Pledgeman and feeling the need to help lift his countrymen out of a state of stupor and inertia, formed a branch of the League of the Cross, established "for the purpose of uniting Catholics, both clergy and laity, in a holy warfare against intemperance, and of thereby raising the religious, social, and domestic state of our Catholic people, especially of the working classes."[3]

Through his shining example, and much lecturing on the spiritual perils of poteen, Grandfather Donovan began to rebuild the souls of the members of the league—they could not have numbered more than twenty or thirty—and brought to his own family (how many children he had is not known) a sense of character in the Catholic theological sense: ". . . a spiritual mark indelibly impressed on the soul, by baptism, confirmation, and holy order, which sacraments cannot be reiterated without sacrilege." There was a good deal of WJD in this dogma and discipline —a total lifelong rejection of liquor; strong personal discipline; preoccupation with honor and with "manly," "soldierly," and "honest conduct." All, doubtless, were inherited from that fiercely devout, tough, leathery old Catholic zealot. Nor were they transient characteristics; half a century later WJD would still be telling associates that he was "not much of a religious man" but "I frequently fall on my knees and ask my God to give me humility."[4]

Yet for all his temperance, discipline, reliability, and respectability, Grandfather Donovan remained what he had been in Ireland. Life was an unrelenting struggle with floods, unemployment, disease, drains, crime, the police. Grandfather Donovan's predicament was, therefore, fundamental, and doubtless in that spirit and belief he became connected with the Fenians, a secret revolutionary society organized in Dublin and New York to obtain Ireland's independence from England. This association was important, for plainly it infected WJD. Although the Fenians had a reputation for being little more than boozy intriguers, with little political power, groups of men arguing over poteen among the dolmens, in Buffalo they became something more than a drinking society. They developed into an underground movement that was, from the point of view of British Canada, dangerous. By 1866 they had become so powerful that the British government outlawed them and pressed the United States to do likewise. In June 1866 General John O'Neill led 800 Fenians in an armed military invasion of Canada—an expedition that was thought to have been planned in the First Ward and was stopped only by the American and British armies.

While there is no evidence Grandfather Donovan took part in the expedition, there is evidence he allowed his house on Michigan Street to be used as a way station for Irishmen moving clandestinely between Canada and the United States. One of WJD's law partners, Thomas J. McFadden, himself an Irish Catholic, later stated that Donovan's home was visited by Irish intellectuals and Irish independence leaders long after the Fenians had been drawn into the Sinn Fein ("We, Ourselves") movement, a forerunner of the Irish Republican Army. That, too, was undoubtedly important in the shaping of WJD's political attitudes, for in his dealings with the British during World War II he was to display, occasionally, a Fenian stubbornness and, more frequently, dislike of some of the institutions of the British Empire.

Like most matters concerning the Irish brotherhoods, facts are scarce. What is sure is that Grandfather Donovan produced a family and that one of his sons was Timothy, a tough, rectangular man who also joined the League of the Cross and was so devout that he was employed as a trainbearer when the bishop of Buffalo, John Timon, visited the parish. Timothy Donovan became a "great friend" of the third bishop of Buffalo, James E. Quigley, a pastor who "came prominently before the people by his able defense of the church against the attacks of socialists and anarchists."[5]

As for party politics, Timothy Donovan appears to have been a nonconformist who joined not the Democrats, as was usually the case in Irish communities, but the Republicans. That departure in both father and son was found by many men to be surprising and worrying, for the Republicans were the party of the Protestant landlords. But it was not wholly an unlikely allegiance. The "new" Republicans in Buffalo in 1860 had shown themselves to be hostile to slavery and religious prejudice, especially toward the American, or Know-Nothing, movement, which was anti-Catholic.

In his work, Timothy was plainly a man of consequence. He had begun his career as a greaser on the locomotives of the Erie & Lackawanna Railroad and worked his way up to the position of yardmaster at Black Rock, a main terminal of both passenger and freight trains. In a community such as the First Ward, the yardmaster was king. He allocated track, made up the crews, directed the assembly of trains, and could hire and fire. He had to be tough and fit, for he had to be about the yard in all weather, marshaling the iron horses, tapping wheels, checking couplings and bills of ladings, ensuring cars with cargo for Chicago were not attached to trains going to Atlanta. Furthermore, he had to do his work quickly and efficiently, for there was always some Anglo-Saxon Protestant waiting to take the job.

When Timothy Donovan felt the time had come to marry, he took as his bride Anna Letitia Lennon, an Ulsterwoman but a Catholic and the daughter of a bacon curer. Timothy and Anna, who were married in style at Holy Cross, produced nine children. But while the marriage was a happy one, it was also blemished by tragedy. The first four children all died of meningitis, leaving WJD the eldest, followed by Timothy (1884), Mary (1885), Vincent (1886), and Loretta (1889). Possibly because of the unhealthiness of the First Ward, Timothy decided to move. This took place sometime during WJD's boyhood, when the family moved into a larger, wood-frame house at 44 Prospect Avenue, near what is now the site of the Peace Bridge, the link between America and Canada. Yet there was a trait in the family, a strain of genetic sickness, that cleaner air and more sanitary surroundings could never overcome, and the remaining children except WJD and his brother Vincent were to die prematurely of such complaints as alcoholism or dementia praecox.

Yet that was in the future. From their earliest age Timothy subjected his children to a severe discipline calculated to produce mental, physical, and spiritual fitness. All the children, WJD included, were confirmed into the church at a time when that ceremony shaped a man for life. The Baltimore Catechism, the basic doctrine of the Catholic in America, was drummed into the children, and WJD would remember part of it until the day he died: "To know Him, to love Him, to serve Him in this world, and to be happy with Him forever in Heaven." But these were relatively orthodox rituals. What made the Donovans' upbringing unusual was Timothy Donovan's attention to moral theology, "the science of the laws which regulate duty." Through this preoccupation and through the other aspects of Timothy Donovan's regimen, WJD's concern with God, country, honor, and duty was unusually marked, even for that virtuous era.

For the frame there was much boxing, boating, walking, running, and gymnastics, while for the intellect, Timothy Donovan introduced his children to the Gaelic Revival, then fashionable in Ireland, and he taught them the decisive value of books—"great men are men who read"—in a man's career. Throughout his life, wherever he was, whatever he was doing, WJD always read two or three books a week, often a book a day, almost all of them about military, historical, or political affairs, many of them old volumes, and some of them in Latin or French—WJD learned to read and speak Latin and French well.

Also for the mind was that amazing book in American temporal history, *McGuffey's Eclectic Reader,* which for WJD, as for 70,000,000 to 80,000,000 other Americans between 1836 and 1920, not only assisted the improvement of the mind but also provided an introduction to what one social historian of the times would call "integrity, honesty, industry, temperance, true patriotism, courage, politeness, and all other moral and intellectual virtues."[6] For WJD, to whom patriotism became a guiding light,

McGuffey's became a life force, helping shape his actions as the volumes did for four generations of Americans of all classes. For the object of *McGuffey's,* as a preface stated, was not only to "present the best specimens of style in the English language" and "to impart valuable information" but also to "exert a decided and healthful moral influence."

Of all the qualities that made up Donovan's complicated personality, the most striking was his attitude toward death. In his military, legal, and intelligence careers WJD consistently displayed a fearlessness that was often beyond rationality. Yet to be fearless is to be phenomenal. All men fear something. But in the realm of the ultimate fear—that of death— Donovan certainly appeared to be fearless. This may be explained by Celtic fatalism. As WJD said later, some of the first words he spoke were those of the Introit in the requiem mass: *Requiem aeternam dona eis, domine,* and the open coffin on the trestles in the parlor and the corpse with the pennies in the eye sockets became a familiar sight. Yet the real basis of WJD's fearlessness lay not in a familiarity with death, but in faith.

Donovan had done well at parochial school, his father had caught the eye of the local Catholic hierarchs as a man of the faith, and without difficulty Donovan was received into St. Joseph's Collegiate Institute, another Christian Brothers' school, but one in which the curriculum was wider, the regimen less harsh than the elementary school's, the surroundings less grim. Also, to "give him a little polish, dancing, elocution, dramatics, and the like," Donovan went for a time to the Nardin Academy, a Catholic private day school in Buffalo.[7]

Again he did well, charming the sisters, and at about the time Theodore Roosevelt, WJD's earliest political hero, became President, he went to Niagara College, another Catholic institution, near Niagara Falls. There he paid his way, working during vacations on street repairs, carrying a chain with a surveyor's gang, acting as assistant superintendent in a baking powder factory, and timekeeping on a construction site. Among the subjects he studied were elocution, dramatics, and singing, and he developed an attractive speaking voice. He also displayed some talent as an orator, being awarded the College Medal for his delivery of a paper entitled "On Christian Doctrine," in which he spent much time discussing moral theology and dogma. While receiving the spiritual guidance of Father William Egan, a "Soldier of Christ" and a moral theologian of stature, Donovan decided to enter the Dominicans, the Order of Preachers (OP), a contemplative order in which the friars' lives were devoted to theological study. However, Egan dissuaded him, for as Vincent Donovan, who did become a Dominican friar, believed, Father Egan "saw qualities in my brother that suggested law as more fitting for him than the church: his thoroughness, maybe, and his active mind."[8]

That Donovan's mind was unusually active is apparent from his early notebooks. By the age of eighteen he had begun to keep notebooks in which he collected statements, excerpts from poems, aphorisms, bits of librettos, and lines from plays that interested him. These were written down in beautiful handwriting—far better than the illegible scrawl it became—and one of these notebooks, dated September 1901, has survived to show the sort of matter with which Donovan was filling his mind. On the first page, interestingly, was an aphorism by Disraeli, "Success is the child of audacity," and a similar statement by Desiderius Erasmus, "Fortune favors the audacious." Then came a piece of anonymous wisdom in Latin and English: "Seek not what the future may bring . . . nor as a boy spurn the sweet loves nor while the moroseness of old age is absent, neglect the dance." And then there appeared this interesting statement attributed to R. W. Emerson: "He had read the inscription on the gates of Busyrane—'Be bold;' and on the second gate—'Be bold, be bold, and evermore be bold;' and then again had paused well at the third gate—'But not too bold.' "

In September 1903, when he was twenty, Donovan entered Columbia College on a certificate—a form of scholarship by recommendation, known as the Professional Option and applied to bright scholars—from Niagara. But at Columbia WJD was not to continue to display the early brilliance his spiritual adviser, who had signed the certificate, believed he had shown at Niagara. The best that can be said for WJD's academic performance throughout his stay at Columbia College and Law School is that he emerges as one of the great inspirations for all who fail at school but hope to succeed afterward—a career closely resembling that of Winston Churchill, who was a walking disaster at school but who became one of the three men to make the modern world, along with FDR and Stalin.

Donovan's grades were deplorable throughout his university years—not once was there the bright gleam of an A or a B—and in another day and age he would have been expelled. Despite his poor performance, Donovan was graduated as a Doctor of Laws on May 27, 1908. He always claimed, however, to have graduated in 1907. Why he should have been insistent about this is difficult to understand, for the records show clearly that in May 1908 he was still reading pleading and practice and partnership law. Yet he insisted in all autobiographical statements that he had received his degree in 1907, and despite the evidence of the record, the university, of which he was to become a trustee, decided to defer to his wishes.

As for his poor performance, that is impossible to fathom, and he survived only because he displayed certain characteristics that attracted the attention of Harlan Fiske Stone, dean of the Law School, who was to become U.S. attorney general and later a justice of the Supreme Court. Stone was sure that Donovan could and would do better when he began to practice, as indeed he did. Among the qualities said to have impressed

Stone were Donovan's clarity of thought and speech, his oratorical capabilities, his exceedingly wide general knowledge, his political interests and sense. Moreover, during his two years at Columbia Law Donovan displayed convictions and abilities that were important: his convictions concerning the importance of the law in a democratic society; his thoroughness in preparation; his abilities in examination; his irreproachable personal conduct; his impressive bearing; the fact that he never stopped the process of learning—a characteristic that would remain with him for life, so that by the time he was forty-five he would have become the superior of more gifted rivals. That is the significant aspect of WJD's development intellectually, professionally, and culturally.

At Columbia, Donovan paid his own way by working as house manager for his fraternity, Phi Kappa Psi, and for two summers he acted as tutor to a wealthy family with backward boys. He confirmed his reputation as a formidable public speaker with a paper called "The Awakening of Japan," for which he won an important medal for public speaking instituted by George William Curtis, the editor of *Harper's Weekly,* the reformer of the civil service, and a close friend of Theodore Roosevelt's. In what was a rare glimpse into Donovan's private life, the manuscript was dedicated to a girl, Blanche Lopez.

Born in 1888, Miss Lopez was a member of a family of Asturian aristocrats who left Spain for America earlier in the century and established a well-known tobacco firm, Calixto Lopez and Company, the manufacturers of Eden cigars, which were famous at the turn of the century. She was educated at Sacred Heart Convent, a private school for upper-class Catholic girls, in Manhattan, where the family owned a large house at 716 Saint Nicholas Avenue in Manhattan. Donovan and Miss Lopez met at the Church of the Holy Ghost, not far from Columbia (Donovan lived for a time while at Columbia at 306 West 109th Street), and he spent much time with her and her family at a Lopez-owned mansion in Rumson, New Jersey, one of the wealthiest and most exclusive summer resorts on the northeastern coast. For a time marriage seems to have been in the air; Blanche stated years later to her son, Randall Keator: "But for a misunderstanding you would have been Bill Donovan's son."[9]

Although the association lasted throughout Donovan's stay at Columbia, it appears to have ended when he left after graduation. Then Miss Lopez became engaged to another Columbia man, Randall Moss Keator, a Protestant who converted to Catholicism and had rowed with WJD in the varsity crew.

By all surviving accounts, Donovan was a popular man, so much so that Franklin D. Roosevelt, who was eleven months older than WJD, always claimed that the two had been friends at Columbia, a claim WJD was always careful to deny. Why FDR should make the claim, and WJD deny it, is hard to understand, unless it had to do with Donovan's opposition to the New Deal. But FDR's personality at the time, and his social circumstances, would certainly have made friendship unlikely. The son of prominent Episcopalians, his father a leading lawyer and financier, a product of Groton and Harvard, FDR, so they said at Columbia Law, spoke only to the sons of railway tycoons, not to those of railway gangers and greasers.

The reason for FDR's admiration of WJD is not elusive. At a time in American social history when Ivy League football heroes were stars of their generation, Donovan not only was excellent as a runner and in crew but clawed his way into college lore as a quarterback with the Columbia Lions. Men who succeeded at Columbia's Baker Field became idolized, and the idolatry often lasted for life—as in the case of WJD. "Many a time in your old football days have I watched you play and admired your pluck," wrote one of New York's leading lawyers, T. Ludlow Chrystie, himself a football hero at Columbia before Donovan, in later years. "I have always thought that Billy Donovan was one of the sandiest and headiest men who ever played for Columbia." Referring to an act of gallantry on the battlefield in France, Chrystie went on: "To-day the whole world knows what the old football men of Columbia knew more than a dozen years ago. I am proud of you, Donovan. God bless you."[10]

There is much in this vein in Donovan's papers. The admiration lasted throughout his life and demonstrates why it was conceivable that FDR admired WJD, whose best football season was that of 1905.

That year he led the Lions to three victories and two ties in their first five games. He played a full game against Williams on October 14, 1905, but unfortunately he was injured in the game with Princeton and was sidelined for the rest of the season. However, the Lions did finish with a 4-3-2 record.

Nor can it be said that WJD's performance was transitory. His football record at Columbia became a permanent part of his record: "WJD: soldier, statesman, lawyer, ambassador, presidential agent, intelligence-master, Columbia quarterback." Fifty years later the university was declaring: "Today Columbia honors one of its most loyal, outstanding athletic sons and also one of America's greatest heroes. Today Columbia pays homage again to William Joseph Donovan, '05C, 07L."[11]

Yet for all his striking qualities, in his private life, then and later, WJD was very secretive. Were it not for his future wife's diaries and the papers he left, little would be known about Donovan's life beyond his record as a lawyer and politician. The observer senses that he led a vigorous private life, but it is concealed as if it had not existed. Even that institution with special powers, the Federal Bureau of Investigation, could not penetrate the mask of discretion and obscurity. If it expected to find Donovan in a compromising boudoir (and the FBI and others interested in Donovan's political activities certainly hoped to do so), he was too smart for them, his enemies, his friends, his biographers. As the FBI would be compelled to report primly to President Dwight D. Eisenhower of Bill Donovan's schooldays, "There is nothing of a derogatory nature noted in subject's scholastic record."[12]

Like that famous character of Celtic lore the Shee-an-Gannon, Donovan was arriving in the land of the giants, and his law school certainly believed he was a great man. Seventy years later it dedicated a statue on its grounds to him—the only statue to be dedicated to a former student. It is called "The Tightrope Walker."

As Donovan settled into Miss Frink's Boarding House, an establishment in Buffalo for "nice young men of the city"—young bachelor lawyers, bank and city employees, and the like—Donovan's wife-to-be was "coming out."

In 1891, when Ruth Rumsey was born, the world seemed fair to see, especially when viewed from the family's mansion at 742 Delaware Avenue or the summer house on the American Lake Shore. The only daughter of the third marriage of Dexter P. Rumsey, the richest man in Buffalo, Ruth was a wealthy young woman by any standards, European as well as American. Her mother was a member of Rhode Island's Hazard family, one of the leading families of the Thirteen Colonies, landowners who had had a thousand slaves.

The Rumsey fortunes had been established from nothing by Aaron Rumsey, in the early 1800's in the tannery industry in Buffalo. When Aaron Rumsey died, his two sons, Dexter and Bronson, sold the business and went into railroads and real estate. By the time Ruth Rumsey was born both Dexter, Ruth's father, and her uncle, Bronson, were said to be worth $10,000,000 apiece, owning twenty-two of Buffalo's forty-three square miles,[13] at a time when there was no income tax and, indeed, few taxes of any description.

Although the Rumseys were not an important political family, they were extremely influential, and it was said he who knew a Rumsey knew enough. The influence of the Rumseys extended far beyond Buffalo, for while they were not as rich as the robber barons of New York City, they were very rich by British and French standards, and through their positions as masters of the Genesee Valley Hunt, then the most exclusive hunt in America, they were welcome at the leading meets in England, at a time when the hunt was a political force in world affairs.

The Rumseys traveled constantly and widely, often in that stately procession of retainers and carriages known as the grand tour. As devout Episcopalians they held their spiritual home to be Canterbury in England, to which all members of the family made at least one pilgrimage, and as with all people of their station, the schism between the English Protestants and Irish Catholics was fundamental. Ecumenism was impossible and abhorrent. It was unthinkable, therefore, that Ruth should "walk out" with anyone but a wealthy Anglo-Saxon Protestant's son. That was an unspoken principle of the family. When she grew up, there was much speculation whether she would marry young Eddie Byers, the son of the city's leading grain shipper, or young Newton, whose family had bought some land at a sheriff's sale and harnessed the hydroelectric power of Niagara Falls. But neither was to be her choice; there was a "modern" streak in Ruth Rumsey.

As soon as she could walk, Ruth Rumsey learned to ride, and she remained a horsewoman and huntswoman for life. She went to Rosemary Hall in Connecticut, a school for young ladies of the white Anglo-Saxon Protestant establishment.

Ruth's father died in 1906, and his fortune was placed in trust. Through the terms of the trust, established before inheritance taxes, Ruth's mother received a quarter, and Ruth and her brother each received 12 ½ percent, the principal and interest to be placed to the benefit of whoever survived, which, as the fates later decided, was Ruth. Both children's shares were placed in trust for them until they reached twenty-one, at which time they received what would be a handsome legacy and a substantial income for life. Their mother's annual income from her husband's estate, an enormous sum by the standards of the times, made her a millionairess, and while she gave at least one-third of it to the poor and the needy, both mother and children were in that minute category of humanity that with modest prudence need have no financial worries for the rest of their lives. Assuredly Mrs. Rumsey was able to maintain her viceregal existence in Buffalo, since the estate was not trammeled by creditors.

In June 1908 Ruth set out for Europe "for culture," accompanied by her mother, aunt, and brother, some cousins, three servants, twenty-eight trunks, and a steam-driven Locomobile with a chauffeur. Lasting four months, it was the first of such journeys, which culminated in Ruth's grand tour, which lasted ten months. The purpose of these journeys was to give a young woman final polish before marriage and enable her to meet people of her own age who would, in due course, succeed as leaders of national and international society. Thus, when Ruth set out, she was still a schoolgirl, and her diary was a jewel of schoolgirls' English. Everything was "fine and dandy," each day there was a "dandy ride out in good season," everything she saw "was perfectly grand," and at the end of each day she "retired joyfully," having "fooled around after dinner."[14]

In the Locomobile the group crossed France, Belgium, Luxembourg, Germany, drove alongside the Rhine and the Moselle, inspected castles and cathedrals and churches of Germany, motored across Bavaria and the Alps into Italy, and then returned across France to Paris.

By the thirtieth of August they were on the road from Fontainebleau to Paris, where they stayed at the Hôtel de l'Empire, had "dandy rooms," and thought that "Paris is pretty fine anyway." They then returned to Buffalo before the next legs of their tour, first to the western United States, then to South America. Finally, they embarked on a voyage around the world that lasted from October 14, 1912, to August 6, 1913.

During those ten months of travels she and two school friends, accompanied by a chaperone, a Mrs. Wolcott, visited Egypt, Ceylon, India, Burma, Afghanistan, Malaya, Singapore, Java, Hong Kong, and the Philippines; set foot in China; and returned to Buffalo through Budapest, Vienna, and Paris. While in India Ruth was the guest in turn of the viceroy, the nizam of Hyderabad, the rajah of Jodhpur, the maharajah of Gwalior, and the governor of Lahore, the introduction to the viceroy having been made by Sir Valentine Chirol, director of the foreign department of the London *Times*, then the most influential newspaper in the world, and a man who modernized the Indian Civil Service to ensure that the subcontinent remained a part of the British Empire.

When Ruth arrived back in Buffalo on August 6, 1913, Donovan had been practicing law for almost six years. About this time, he drove a cast-off Locomobile, which puffed between his chambers and his two rooms in a frame house just off Bryant, on the fringes of respectable territory. He was a splendid-looking fellow, fit, charming, ambitious, rising in the world. He had only one vice—he ate vast quantities of food which he had to work off with fierce exercise. Socially he was becoming reasonably well known as a popular sportsman, for as the *Burgee*, the journal of the Buffalo Canoe Club, recorded when Donovan was taken ill:

> It was a great surprise and an occasion of much anxiety to "Bill" Donovan's legion of friends to learn that almost without warning he was stricken with appendicitis early in June. An immediate operation was imperative and he was hurried to hospital where he is still confined. Thanks to his magnificent constitution and physique his recovery has been rapid and uninterrupted. By the time this notice is read, it is not unlikely that he will be among us again.
>
> Appendicitis strikes the weak and strong alike, but we hazard the opinion that those who, like this enthusiastic paddler and athlete, live in the open and take advantage of our sports, are most likely to come safely through the trying ordeal of a major operation.
>
> It will be a glad day for us all when we can shake his hand again and welcome him back to the place he loves so well.[15]

By now Donovan was beginning to prosper, as indeed all Buffalo seemed to be prospering. Donovan's first job was as an associate lawyer with Love & Keating, a small, respectable law firm founded by Thomas C. Love, a local worthy who had been, in turn, judge of the Court of Common Pleas, district attorney of Erie County, congressman, and surrogate of Erie County. "I congratulate Mr. Donovan on getting into so prominent a firm thus early in his legal practice," wrote a journalist in the Buffalo *Express*, "and knowing that a steady head rests upon those broad shoulders, I can see nothing ahead for him but the rewards that almost invariably come from hard work and high intellectual capacity."[16]

WJD earned about $1,800 a year at Love & Keating, a firm consisting of the two partners and five clerks. It was an extremely conservative firm; the partners always wore morning dress to court and always arrived at the office in coaches-and-four. It is likely, therefore, that his days were no more interesting than that of the lawyer in Shakespeare's *Coriolanus:* ". . . you wear out a good wholesome forenoon in hearing a cause between an orange-wife and a fosset-seller; and then rejourn the controversy of three pence to a second day of audience." Donovan was after bigger game, and he did not stay long with Love & Keating. At Columbia, he had become friendly with another young Buffalonian, Bradley Goodyear, the son of Charles Waterhouse Goodyear, a man in the front rank of Buffalo worthies along with the Loves and the Newtons—apart from vast interests in the lumber, railroad, and tanning industries C. W. Goodyear had been Grover Cleveland's law partner in the firm of Cleveland Bissell Sicard & Goodyear.

Bradley Goodyear and Donovan became stout friends, Goodyear putting Donovan up for membership in the Saturn and the Buffalo clubs at a time when the club was the principal venue for politics, business, intrigue, and lobbying. Those clubs may have provided Donovan with what were known at the time as "opportunities for associations that are required for advancement in life." In Buffalo the club was as powerful and influential an institution in a man's professional life as was the church to his spirit, and Donovan became the first Irish Catholic from the First Ward to be admitted to both clubs.

Donovan and Goodyear then established their own law firm, Donovan & Goodyear of Ellicott Square, the best address in town, a development in the business life of the city which a local newspaper viewed with approval:

> The opening of the business and professional season of 1911–12 sees changes here and there. One which is exciting much favorable comment is the new law partnership formed by William J. Donovan and Bradley Goodyear. . . . It has been clear sailing for young Attorney Donovan from the time he carried his book and slate to Miss Nardin's Academy . . . his fluent Celtic tongue and brilliant imagery of mind won from a large class of able contestants [at Columbia] the George William Curtis Medal for Oratory. The world has many thinkers but few who possess that divine gift which can sway an audience, rouse it to enthusiasm, move it to laughter or tears.
>
> Mr. Donovan began the practice of law in Buffalo with the firm of Love and Keating, since which time success has exceeded the best wishes of even his

best friends. But he is too young, too healthy a type of manhood not to delight in something more kin to youth and virile strength than the study of leather-bound tomes.[17]

The author of the article was shrewder than he knew, for the time had come for Donovan to begin his military career. Although he had never ridden a horse, he and a group of young blades at the Saturn Club decided to ask the War Department for permission and assistance to form a cavalry troop. That permission was forthcoming, and on May 7, 1912, forty-two young Buffalonians took the military oath of allegiance to the United States at a ceremony in the 65th Regiment Armory. The group was established as Troop I, 1st Cavalry Regiment, New York National Guard, and in the local press it came to be called the Silk Stocking Boys because of the social prominence of so many of its members. Mr. Donovan became Trooper Donovan, Trooper Donovan became Sergeant Donovan, and on October 12, 1912, the troop elected Sergeant Donovan Captain Donovan, commanding officer of the troop. When Donovan took the troop away to summer camp, the Buffalo *News* exhibited its usual approval:

> Captain William J. Donovan . . . has a right to be proud of his men. He leads them on a summer excursion in full regalia.
> The young men of this troop are so zealous in the service and so genuinely patriotic as to furnish their own mounts and pay their own expenses during the week of their marching and camping. Every military requirement of cavalry is observed during the volunteer trick of this season. . . . When this gallant corps of horsemen comes thundering into the quiet country village on the line of march let none be afraid. They are not Japanese invaders intent on eating the United States up alive. They are at worst only a herd of Buffaloes and at best a company of the finest, most splendid, young men that any city in America can show.
> Captain Donovan, the NEWS salutes you and your magnificent command and wishes you all the best of health and appetite and a safe return from perils of picketing night camps and stampeding mules, to say nothing of saddles that may not be wholly comfortable.[18]

WJD was now to learn that life with the troop was not all rides, flags, shoots, and balls; the National Guard was expected to provide disagreeable service called "aid to the civil power" at times of domestic disturbance; and not long after Troop I was formed, riots broke out at Depew, a suburb of Buffalo, where a company called Gould Couplar made railroad cars. In March 1914 the workers struck for higher wages and better working conditions. The chimney barons who owned Gould Couplar were in no mood for compromise with the strikers, and after days of argument the owners decided to break the strike and the trade union that had organized it. They locked all workers out and arranged to bring in trainloads of nonunion workers to replace the strikers.

The strikers stopped the trains from getting to the works by piling ties and logs across the tracks near the back gates on Transit Road, and when the scabs were stopped from getting into the plant by hails of stones, the owners of Gould Couplar called upon the police to restore order. Sheriff's deputies were sent to the works. In the confusion shots were fired, one of the strikers was killed, and eight were wounded. The mood of the town turned menacing, there was much talk of burning down Gould Couplar, and the governor of New York State ordered in 900 officers and men of the Buffalo National Guard. A curfew was imposed, the Guard arrested those who broke the curfew, and when a procession to bury the dead man in St. Mary's Cemetery seemed likely to become a riot, Donovan and sixty men of Troop I were mobilized and sent to Depew to help.

Donovan and the cavalry were received with great hostility by the workers, especially when it was learned that the Guard had forbidden all public meetings and loitering. A local newspaper noted that the cavalry was known as the Silk Stocking Boys, bringing the specter of class warfare into the disturbances; it was reported that Donovan, Gould, and Couplar were members of the Saturn and the Buffalo clubs; and when on one occasion Donovan ordered the troop to clear the street, he was called the "Cossack" in one of the Depew socialist newspapers, a cognomen that was to stick. Although the troop did not draw swords, and nobody was injured, the incident was to damage Donovan's political career in the future.

At Depew, order was soon obtained and maintained, and the troop returned to more agreeable interests. For Donovan, among those interests was a young actress, Eleanor Robson, who was four years older than he and married to August Belmont, at fifty-seven one of society's most eligible millionaires, a banker, owner of the Belmont racing stables, chairman of the Jockey Club, and founder of the New York Rapid Transit Subway Construction Company.

Donovan appears to have met Miss Robson before she married Belmont in August 1910, probably just after he had parted company with Miss Lopez. In 1910 Miss Robson was in her late twenties and very beautiful. Later she became a leading actress and the founder of the New York Metropolitan Opera Guild. At the time she was on tour, playing in Buffalo, and met Donovan while he was playing the leading role in an amateur performance of Robert Browning's *In a Balcony.* "She was so impressed with his ability that she offered to coach him," Donovan's brother Vincent, who had become a Dominican friar, recalled. "Once a week he would go down to New York for his dramatic lesson."[19]

That friendship now collided with another. During the winter season of 1913–14 Donovan met John Lord O'Brian, a prominent Buffalo lawyer and leading member of the Bar Association, whom Arthur Krock of *The New York Times* later described as "the most distinguished lawyer and classical liberal of our time." Of Irish descent, O'Brian was a Republican, an Episcopalian, and a member of the Buffalo Club when Donovan met him at a social function. O'Brian and Donovan's father, Timothy, had been friendly, so it was natural that O'Brian should take an interest in young Donovan. Just beginning a career of presidential service that would last from Taft to Kennedy, part of that career being concerned with intelligence and security matters, O'Brian invited Donovan and Goodyear to merge their firm with his, and they established the firm of O'Brian Hamlin Donovan & Goodyear, of which Donovan remained a senior partner for the next six years.

On New Year's Eve of 1913–14, when he gave a black-tie dinner at the Buffalo Club, O'Brian included Donovan and Bradley Goodyear among his guests. By arrangement, the party went on after dinner to the annual New Year's Eve party given at the Hoyt mansion on Delaware Avenue, the home of William B. Hoyt, attorney for the Vanderbilts' railroad system and a trustee of Cornell University. At this leading social event of the season in a city that was exceptionally class-conscious, Goodyear introduced Donovan to some friends, Dexter P. Rumsey, Jr., and his sister, Ruth. Donovan and Ruth danced—Donovan was an excellent ballroom dancer all his life—and Ruth was immediately attracted to Donovan. "And why not?" asked Donald Rumsey, the family historian. "Donovan was head and shoulders above anyone else around."[20]

Close to his thirty-first year, Donovan had met the woman he was to marry. She was five feet four inches tall, slim, a pure blonde, and, Rumsey recalled, "truly aristocratic in appearance and bearing, in the best sense of that word. She had a good figure, a good brain, and she was an excellent horsewoman. She had traveled widely for a woman of her years. But her really striking features were her hair and eyes—she was a platinum blonde with startlingly blue eyes which had pronounced black rings around the irises."

Donovan and Ruth Rumsey began to be seen about town, especially at the Genesee Valley Hunt, a hunt so exclusive that it had its own livery, pink with gold piping instead of scarlet and black. If Donald Rumsey is correct, Ruth's mother was strongly opposed to her daughter's association with Donovan, for she was soon aware that he was Irish and Catholic and from the First Ward, while the Rumseys were leaders of the Protestant church in Buffalo. Susan Fiske Rumsey is said to have implored her daughter to end the association. That did not happen, for Donovan and Ruth appear to have felt equally strongly about each other.

Clearly Donovan was conscious of the world into which he had intruded and of its class implications, for in a later letter to Ruth he discussed what he called "the real beginning" of the association that led to their marriage. He described how, during an outing with the Celtic Canoe Club, where Donovan was a member of the crew:

> Most of the time . . . my heart was in my mouth. I wanted you so much and yet thought you would choose rather some one of your own class. I thought you very sweet and liked the unconcern with which you received my informa- tion that you would be obliged to sit on my lap. My restraint in that ride was astounding. . . . I remember thinking of that trip only the other day. That was the real beginning. I remember how I hated to leave you and wanted to keep you [when you had to leave to] go with your beau to the theater.[21]

In April 1914, as rumors of impending war arrived from Europe, Bill and Ruth announced that they were engaged to be married in July. Ruth made it known that she found Donovan's dramatic lessons with Eleanor Robson "not altogether pleasing" and, of course, the lessons were stopped. Suddenly, a month before the marriage, WJD's mother died following an attack of rheumatic fever (her death was followed within the year by that of WJD's father). As she lay on her deathbed, she insisted that the marriage go ahead as planned. And it did. WJD and Ruth were married in a Catholic ceremony, on July 14, 1914, at Old Cathedral, although Ruth was in considerable pain due to a recent appendicitis operation. Part of the marriage agreement between Bill and Ruth pro- vided that any children of the union would be brought up in the Roman Catholic faith.

According to Donald Rumsey, the wedding photograph shows the party standing on the steps of the mansion with Mrs. Rumsey leaning out a window, in tears and wearing white—summer mourning. If that be true, she soon recovered her spirits and came to adore her new son-in-law, making him a trustee of her estate and her legal adviser, thus demonstrat- ing that the American moneyed aristocracy was a good deal less closed as a society than its European counterparts.

But there was little time left for adoration. While the Donovans were on their honeymoon at a ranch in Wyoming, a nineteen-year-old Serbian nationalist political agitator, Gavrilo Princip, assassinated the Archduke Franz Ferdinand and his wife at Sarajevo, capital of Bosnia and Her- zegovina—people and places obscure and unimportant to all save old statesmen. But through that pistol shot, and politics that were Turkish in their complexity, the European cantilever of nations collapsed, and World War I began. However, WJD was not involved, for President Woodrow Wilson declared America's neutrality in the world conflict with the statement "Every man who really loves America will act in the true spirit of neutrality, which is the spirit of impartiality and fairness and friendliness to all concerned."

2

Bugles Call

Donovan's admirers would be unanimous that they had rarely met a man, before or since, in whom the qualities of God, country, duty, honor were so pronounced. There was some truth in this belief, although there was a tendency to disregard the notion that ambition, love of power, and self-interest also played a large part in what he did and said. Nevertheless WJD was a man with deep moral awareness, and in 1914, there occurred an incident in Belgium that offended all his sensibilities—the German sacking of the center of Catholic learning at Louvain in Belgium, during the first days of the German offensive on the western front in 1914.

Such sacrilege was quite enough to make a Catholic intellectual contemplate abandoning career and home for a crusade against the nation that was fast earning the reputation of being the Antichrist. And that is what occurred to WJD. For the time being Donovan's agreeable life in the highest reaches of Buffalo society was disturbed.

On February 23, 1916, while working in his chambers in the Iroquois Building, Donovan received a telegram from the Rockefeller Foundation, inviting him to New York for a meeting. Somewhat mystified—for Donovan was still no more than a provincial corporation lawyer who had yet to make his name beyond Buffalo—he attended the meeting and was invited to go to Europe on behalf of the John D. Rockefeller Foundation, to negotiate with the belligerent governments in London and Berlin for permission to supply the Poles with food to relieve the famine and then to assist in the organization, shipment, and distribution of the supplies.[1]

Plainly, powerful forces were already at work on Donovan's behalf—one of them surely John Lord O'Brian, who was close to Wilson and Rockefeller—and Donovan accepted the mission without compensation. He then obtained his passport, on March 10, 1916, swearing that he required it for no other purpose than the business of the War Relief Commission of the Rockefeller Foundation in Holland, Denmark, Germany, Austria, Turkey, Bulgaria, Norway, and Sweden.

Conscious that the Germans might succeed in making trouble between the United States and Mexico, Donovan advised the War Department where he could be found if the General Staff needed him and his troop and then sailed from New York on March 18, 1916, in the British liner *Olympic,* on his first foreign mission.

On the twenty-sixth Donovan arrived at Southampton, where the ship and all passengers were held while the British security authorities arrested one woman and three men, presumably German or Irish agents. It was twenty-four hours before Donovan was permitted to land. He then took the train up to London with his colleagues, Warwick Greene (director of the Rockefeller Commission), Reginald C. Foster, and Henry D. Topping. Their first duty on arriving in London was to register as neutral aliens at the Vine Street Police Station. Donovan wrote to Ruth of that first encounter with the British intelligence and security services: "We gave name, birth and place of residence as well as occupation—a very pleasant clean cut young Englishman took my records. In the event of our leaving the hotel we have to report to him in writing and upon leaving the country we are to report in person."[2]

In the same letter Donovan also revealed that his mission was over before it had begun: The U.S. ambassador to Britain, Walter Hines Page, advised him that the British War Cabinet would not lift the naval and economic blockade of Germany, a principal weapon of the war at sea, to permit Rockefeller's supplies to get to the Poles. Prime Minister David Lloyd George had been very firm about that, said the ambassador, who felt Donovan had better look for another job. Perhaps Herbert Hoover, whose Belgian famine relief headquarters were in London, would have something for him.

Donovan now encountered for the first time a man who would have a fateful influence on his life and career, and he was not at all sure he liked the man he met. Herbert Clark Hoover, born in 1874 in a humble cottage at West Branch, Iowa, was of Swiss-German ancestry, a Quaker, and an 1895 graduate of Stanford University. His father was a blacksmith and farm equipment salesman. Hoover's first job had been as a mine laborer in California, he had made a fortune as a mining engineer, and he began to walk what he was to call "the slippery road of public life" when he became chairman of the American Relief Committee in London and arranged for the repatriation of some 120,000 American citizens

stranded in Europe at the outbreak of World War I. The Wilson administration had been deeply impressed by his work and generosity, for he had
financed many of the stranded Americans personally. Ambassador Page
was to call him "a simple, modest, energetic man who began his career
in California and will end it in Heaven; and he doesn't want anybody's
thanks."[3]

Then Hoover became director of the U.S. program to feed 10,000,000
Belgians whose provinces had been occupied by the Germans and who
now faced starvation. Donovan saw Hoover in London, and in a letter to
Ruth from Brown's Hotel in Piccadilly on April 5, 1916, he described
Hoover as "a personality, middle-sized, high forehead, large eyes, hands
soft . . . and surprisingly lacking in a capable appearance—but he has a
power—and the loyalty of his men." WJD said nothing about the nature
of his mission beyond the significant statement that he was going to
Belgium to "help see to it that the supplies reach the right hands." But
did more occur to Donovan at this time than met the eye? Did he commence his intelligence career in the service of Great Britain at this time?
That would be one of the riddles deriving from his stay in London.

Later a biographer of William Samuel Stephenson, the British secret
agent known as Intrepid whose work in Washington during 1940 and
1941 was to play an important part in Donovan's appointment as the
American spymaster, claimed that the two men met for the first time in
London in 1916, where Stephenson, a Canadian with an American
mother, was a captain in the British Royal Flying Corps. Whether Stephenson was in or associated with British Intelligence at that time was not
important—all Britons at the time were de facto British spies—but Stephenson's biographer at their meeting asserted the subject of their conversation was "German military and psychological weaknesses."[4]

While Donovan always denied he knew Stephenson before they met in
New York and Washington in the summer of 1940, a letter from Donovan
to Ruth in the Donovan papers does show that while staying at Brown's,
he did meet a Canadian and they dined together. Donovan did not state
what they talked about, nor did he give Ruth the Canadian's name. The
evidence in the Donovan papers to support Stephenson's statement is
slender. Nevertheless, as an American official on famine relief service in
Belgium Donovan was in a position to render British Intelligence services
of great importance—a fact that would not have escaped the officials
whose duty it was to keep an eye on foreigners on British ships and in
London hotels.

Donovan would be entering the German rear areas in Belgium and
northern France and would have comparative freedom of movement at
a critical time for the British—they were preparing to launch their offensive on the Somme, which was to last from June 24 until November 13,

1916, and in which they would make the most extensive use so far of tanks, aircraft, and gas to crack the German line. To the British, knowledge of what was happening in the rear areas as the Germans braced to meet the attack was of the greatest importance, and Donovan would be in a position to supply that information. The size of the casualties the British were prepared to accept in order to break the German line—in any event they lost 420,000 men in killed, wounded, and missing, 60,000 of them on the first day of the offensive—demonstrates that they would have stopped at nothing to get the intelligence they required. And Donovan would have been a very desirable spy, not only because he would have freedom of movement behind the German lines but also because he was a trained cavalry officer of the Reserve with an excellent eye and ear for matters of military importance as well as a man with a lawyer's training in acquiring and setting down facts. But did Donovan work for the British at this time? We do not know the answer for sure, but in 1981 the CIA did reveal that "during World War I" Donovan "probably" received British "military intelligence" training. Moreover, as events early in World War II were to show, the British government displayed unusual confidence in Donovan, without hesitation backing him for one of the most important, sensitive, and influential of Roosevelt's war emergency posts—that of intelligence master of the United States.

A study of Donovan's activities from this period until the end of World War I shows there were only two occasions he could have received such training, and this period in London was one of them. Yet it would seem highly improbable that Donovan, an Irish Catholic, would do anything that would compromise himself, the Rockefeller and the Hoover commissions, and the United States—particularly since it will be remembered that the Easter Rebellion broke out in Dublin on April 24, 1916, while he was still in London.

However, he certainly came to the attention of the British Intelligence and security authorities—aboard the *Olympic* and at Vine Street were but two places where he would have been spotted—and since Donovan kicked his heels in London for three weeks before leaving for the Continent, he had ample time to take a brief course in intelligence matters—an entire basic training course in espionage adopted by the OSS in World War II took no more than thirty-eight one-hour sessions.

Whether WJD collaborated or not with British Intelligence at this time would, in the end, have depended on the strength of his feelings on two issues: the burning of Louvain and his attitude toward the Easter Rebellion. It is not impossible that the sacking of Louvain would have proved to be the stronger force, for there, as WJD said, it was the Antichrist at work.

In any case, when Donovan next wrote to Ruth, he had left London, was in the neutral country of Holland, and was staying at the Hotel Albion at Vlissingen. He wrote from there on April 10, 1916, stating merely that the packet boat had taken two days to cross that large battlefield between the British and the German fleets, the North Sea, and he was going to look at the Van Dycks at The Hague and then start work. While there was not much more Donovan could have told his wife at the time, from that point on all his mail was cautious, brief, and uninformative. He made no mention of the enormous land battles, the ruined cities, the unending columns of refugees, the rights or wrongs of this greatest of all wars. He confined himself to family business, drolleries, and the superficialities of his business—inspections of soup kitchens arriving from the United States, the quality of dried milk and wheat flour, and the like. The immediate reason for his caution was obvious: All his mail was being opened by either British or German censors, and he could ill afford to write anything that would compromise himself or his mission, whether that mission was legal or illegal.

Donovan's mail shows that on April 13, 1916, at Rotterdam he applied for and obtained American and German permission to leave Holland and enter German-occupied Belgium, and for some weeks thereafter he crisscrossed and entered and left Belgium extensively and frequently. But only once is there any reference in any of his official reports to Rockefeller or his private mail to famine relief work—he located a warehouse full of dried milk to the value of $30,000 and sent a telegram to the Rockefeller Commission, recommending its purchase. There is no reference to or correspondence with the Hoover Commission.

On the other hand, his papers and diaries contain much discussion concerning matters connected with the war. He was extremely interested in the case of Nurse Edith Cavell, the Briton who was executed before a German firing squad for espionage and for having helped more than 100 Allied soldiers on the run in Belgium escape to Holland and England.

From Brussels he went to Louvain, immediately in the rear area of the German front. There he certainly engaged in what was an act of political warfare, for he had a meeting with the cardinal bishop of Louvain, Désiré Josèph Mercier, who had in 1914 issued to the world this pastoral letter:

> In this dear city of Louvain, ever in my thoughts, the magnificent church of St. Peter will never recover its former splendour. The ancient college of St. Ives, the art schools, the commercial and consular schools of the University; the old markets, our rich library with its collections, its unique manuscripts, its archives, its gallery of great portraits of illustrious rectors, chancellors, professors dating from the time of the foundation, which preserved for masters and students alike a noble tradition and a spur to emulation—all this accumulation of intellectual, historic, and artistic riches, the fruit of the labors of five centuries—all these are in the dust.[5]

Donovan carried Mercier's appeal for assistance in reconstruction to Rockefeller. And financial help toward the restoration was forthcoming from Rockefeller. But plainly, as with Nurse Cavell, the sack of Louvain had nothing to do with famine relief, and unless his interest in Nurse Cavell and Louvain was mere curiosity, it is impossible to find a reason for Donovan's increasingly odd perambulations behind the Germans' lines on the British sector of the western front—unless he was interested in the dispositions before the Battle of the Somme of the German army. Is it possible WJD had become a spy for Christ? Certainly from now on WJD became increasingly close to the Catholic hierarchs of the United States. And certainly later WJD was made by Pius XII a Knight Grand Cross of the Order of St. Sylvester, the oldest and the most prized of papal decorations, awarded only to 100 knights who "by feat of arms, or writings, or outstanding deeds, have spread the Faith, and have safeguarded and championed the Church"—the so-called Golden Militia.[6] Although the papal citation rarely, if ever, states why a man is admitted to the Golden Militia, there is no reason to doubt the theory that one of the causes was WJD's services to the Holy See in reporting to the Rockefellers on the plight of Louvain.

WJD's movements became no more explicable after he left Louvain than they had before he arrived there—unless he was spying. He went first to Aachen on the Belgian-German border, then to Rotterdam, on to Stockholm, down to Berlin, thence to Vienna, the capital of the Austro-Hungarian Empire, Germany's principal ally. At Vienna he applied for and was refused a visa to enter Bulgaria, another of Germany's allies, went back to Stockholm, then to Rotterdam and London, and then back to Rotterdam and Berlin. During these travels he did see other members of the Rockefeller Commission, but his business with them is nowhere recorded, and again, his movements suggested intelligence rather than good works.

But then, on June 26, 1916 (two days after the British began the preliminary bombardment for the Somme offensive and five days after the great assault opened on those sun-drenched chalk hills), Donovan's mission to Europe was suddenly cut short. Country and duty called. In Berlin he received a telegram from the secretary of war, ordering him to return to the United States immediately. The Silk Stocking Boys had been mobilized, and Donovan had been called to the colors.

On March 9, 1916, a band of 1,500 Mexican soldiers led by the Mexican revolutionary general Pancho Villa had crossed the border into the United States and attacked the small town of Columbus, New Mexico, and the adjacent camp of the 13th Cavalry, killing 9 civilians and 8 troopers. The cavalry had pursued Villa's band back into Mexico, killing 50 of them on American territory and 70 inside Mexico. In announcing Villa's raid, and the fact that the U.S. Army had invaded Mexico to a depth of fifteen miles in the area of the raid, President Wilson told the country on March 15 that this was not the first such act of frontier skirmishing: In three years 76 Americans had been killed in Mexico and 36 had been killed on American territory by Mexican marauders. But as a result of this latest raid, the President announced, he had ordered the Army to mount a punitive expedition into Mexico, under the command of General John J. Pershing, and a mobilization of the National Guard.

Obedient to his orders, by August 1916 Donovan was with the Silk Stocking Boys at McAllen, Texas. For the next six months they trained and rode hard not only in pursuit of Villa but also as part of a toughening-up process for a war that all knew could not now be avoided—war with Germany. To prepare him and the troop for that war, Donovan was quite merciless, a fact that on occasions made him extremely unpopular. He got his men up an hour before anyone else and sent them to bed an hour after everyone else. In between he had them marching, riding, running, crawling through the mesquite in full pack, full bandolier, in the burning heat, the ferocious rainstorms, the bitter cold. He would not let them rest when they were exhausted, and woe betide the man found asleep on sentry duty. He roused them from their sleeping bags when they were too exhausted to move, and in another age he would have been the sort of man who might have been a victim of a fragging. As it was, WJD's insistence that his men be physically fit and mentally alert became so engraved on the minds of his men that the survivors remembered it many years later. "Probably the most vivid memory of Border Days come from those early morning hours when you put us through those damnable exercises," wrote one of Donovan's troopers, Hill Jones, more than fifty years afterward. "But you made us realize what lay ahead of us, you got us to quit playing around at being soldiers." The letter was signed: "From one of those little men who follow along behind, bellyaching at times, of course, but still following."[7]

Yet for all the hardship it was on the Mexican border that Pershing and his staff, always vigilant for promising men, noticed that Donovan possessed moral superiority over all other young officers in the expeditionary force—and moral superiority, a product of *character militaris*, was the hallmark of that rare man, the born leader. Those six months brought Donovan to a peak of physical fitness and mental quickness that he sought perpetually to recover. The weeks and months Donovan and the Silk Stocking Boys hunted Villa's brilliant cavalry, *los Doratos*, among the ravines, hills, and ranches of the Rio Grande were among the happiest of his life, and if the troop saw no action—Villa was too swift, too crafty, too fit—the rabbit, venison, and carrot stews on the mesas under the stars, the banjo parties beside the campfires, the comradeship seemed to compensate for the lack of action.

As for WJD personally, the only thundercloud over those vigorous days was a marital one: Their long separation did not sit well with Ruth, then or later, and as his brother-in-law, Dexter, who had joined the troop under Donovan's command, informed him, she seemed to be suffering from a form of depression. Donovan felt, wrongly, that a stern letter might jolt his wife back to her witty, gracious self:

> Have just come in from drill and I should be on the picket line. I am here to snatch a word with you. Your last letter was much better in that it gave me a little bit of news and told me something of yourself and David [the Donovans' son, born on July 7, 1915]. But it was far from being a love letter and if one does not come within the limit I have already set you, you will have received your last communication from me. Dexter tells me that you look much better. He thinks you should get away and not "mope" around any longer.

Donovan then turned to the matter that was evidently behind Ruth's depression—when he would return to Buffalo, and what then? Would he have to go to war with Germany? On that matter, he advised her: "I have no idea when we are to return. . . . The only safe rule to follow is—arrange your affairs as if we were not returning." He then appended a brief, rare, peremptory expression of affection: "Kiss me Goodnight."

In any event, Donovan and the Silk Stocking Boys were almost the last unit to be withdrawn, not returning until March 12, 1917. That day they paraded before the mayor as part of Preparedness Day, and the Buffalo *Courier* recorded of that stirring event: "Buffalo never before witnessed such a parade. . . . Hats were flying, banners waving, and from a hundred thousand throats came an almost constant cheer. It was a glorious demonstration of the love of our people for their country, and of their unity of purpose. . . ."[8] But Donovan's stay was destined to be all too brief for Ruth.

The troop was mustered out of the service of the United States the next day—the day the government issued orders for the arming of merchant ships. Only three days after Donovan had returned home he received orders to report to the New York National Guard armory at Park Avenue and Thirty-fourth Street in Manhattan, where after a number of staff appointments he was given command of the 1st Battalion of the 69th "Fighting Irish" Infantry Regiment of the New York National Guard, a unit of Irish Catholics with a magnificent fighting record. At about this time Ruth bore WJD a daughter, Patricia Hazard Rumsey, who was baptized "The Daughter of the Regiment" by the padre, Father Francis P. Duffy, at a ceremony before the battalion at Camp Mills. Ruth and WJD spent ten days together while he was preparing his battalion for overseas service.

And then Donovan was gone. For reasons of shipping security and military secrecy, he and his battalion were suddenly ordered to move out during the night of October 25–26, 1917. Not knowing where they were going, they boarded trains that rattled all night across upstate New York until they found themselves at Montreal. There they boarded the transatlantic steamer *Tunisian,* which joined a convoy forming off Nova Scotia. Donovan sounded cheerful enough in a letter dated October 28, 1917, in which he stated:

> Through the courtesy of the Captain this letter will be mailed. He is a short plain agreeable Scot who has been handling troop ships at Salonika and the Dardanelles, a gentleman all over. We are not on a transport, but a passenger ship. There is an Indian Prince on board who looks as old as Indian civilization. He has with him a younger man who at evening mess dresses up in Indian clothes, also a Canadian Brigadier General, a Captain of the British Navy, an English nurse, and many officers returning to England. A young Chaplain, Captain of the Newfoundland Regiment, joined us at Quebec, and I had him say Mass for the men yesterday. . . .

He then spoke of the men, as he did always:

> It is a small ship and it is difficult to drill and discipline the men. I have insisted that the officers give their entire time to the men at the sacrifice of their own. Of course, I am not permitted to say where we are. So far the voyage has been very pleasant, with smiling skies and pleasant seas. . . .

Aware that the smiling skies would soon change, he added a personal word for Ruth: "You are with me always. The more I see your picture the better I like it. It is with me always. Pat is very cute. . . ."

Donovan marched the 1,200 officers and men of his battalion from the steamer *Tunisian* at Liverpool in England on November 11, 1917, exactly one year before the war was to end, and the men began the long journey to the front that freezing November in good spirits. As Donovan told Ruth, their favorite song was an American version of an immortal ditty:

> Oh, Mademoiselle from Armentières, parley-vous?
> Oh, Mademoiselle from Armentières, parley-vous?
> Oh, Mademoiselle from Armentières,
> She hasn't been kissed in forty years,
> Hinky dinky, parley-vous?

Ladies of the YWCA handed out little khaki-bound songbooks containing other, less ribald songs—"On the Banks of the Wabash" and "In the Good Old Summertime"—and a Book of Common Prayer with a waterproof cover. And then the train pulled out to rumble through England for twelve hours heading for a "dark, dirty seaport town"—Gosport—near Southampton. There the battalion got into cross-Channel steamers that heaved and plunged to Le Havre through the black, drizzly night, a "trip that was not soon to be forgotten. Neither moon nor stars. Boat so crowded that it was like walking on a floor of faces to get through the ship."[9]

At Le Havre, which was being turned into a great American entrepôt for the western front, the battalion was met by the Knights of Columbus, the Jewish Welfare Board, the Salvation Army, the YWCA, Traveler's Aid, a representative of the American Library Association with a trolley load of books and magazines, and a French band playing "Men of Harlech." The cold rain was interminable. The Micks—as Donovan had come to call the men of his battalion—were bewildered, "truly overwhelmed," as they "marched through a strange city with queer names in an unknown tongue on all the shop windows," he reported to Ruth. Some "hardy spirits" managed a song or two:

> C-C-C-Cootie,
> Horrible Cootie,
> You're the only b-b-b-bug that I abhor;
> When the m-moon shines over the bunkhouse,
> I will scratch my b-b-b-back until it's sore!

In the main the men trudged "through a heavy fog along dark unlighted muddy streets to our station" silently, drizzle dropping off the brims of their soup-bowl steel helmets, gas capes on to keep out the wet, Springfields carried reversed on the shoulder to keep water out of the barrels, unshaved, cruddy, and miserable. The bands, parades, flags, adoring women of New York were past; the campaign was ahead. Yet Donovan's mass of dull, sodden, silent, steaming men, marching out of step, was translated by the visionaries and propagandists into a flood of joyous manhood marching into battle with springy step. Winston Churchill, then a young statesman, was to record:

> The impression made upon the hard-pressed French by this seemingly inexhaustible flood of gleaming youth in its first maturity of health and vigor was prodigious. None were under twenty, and few over thirty. As crammed in their lorries they clattered along the roads, singing the songs of a new world at the tops of their voices, burning to reach the bloody field, the French Headquarters were thrilled with the impulse of new life. . . . Half-trained, half-organized, with only their courage, their numbers and their magnificent youth behind their weapons, they were to buy their experience at a bitter price. But this they were quite ready to do.[10]

Donovan was full of zest upon his arrival in France. "It does not seem real somehow that I should be here in the land of romance and chivalry, and battle seems highly improbable," he wrote soon after his arrival at his cantonment near a village in the Champagne district. Most soldiers in later life agree that their happiest time was when they commanded a battalion on active service, and Donovan soon came to believe that. "The line is the real place," he wrote to Ruth. "And truly the Major has the best job of the war. It is low enough so that you still have touch with the men and high enough so that you use your intellect." One must be "thinking all the time, besides seeing that men bathe, that each night their feet are examined, that their hair is cut, that they are free from disease. In other words where you have two children I have one thousand." He was very glad he had decided not to remain with the staff, and "I told the colonel that I did not expect promotion, that I was content to serve as a major and that I was going to turn out the best battalion in the entire army."[11]

Donovan pursued "experience" earnestly and dutifully, noting disapprovingly that some officers of the Rainbow Division were quartered in châteaux, but he preferred his room in a little old lady's cottage because "it is better preparation." He wanted to get "experience" into "my fibre and be able to impart it to the battalion";[12] in that spirit he eschewed all thought of leave to Paris. When he did have to go there, his prudery— a quality he was not to lose until he had experienced Washington for a year or two—was outraged. "Stayed in Paris overnight," he wrote to Ruth indignantly. "Almost as many American officers as Belgian and Portuguese officers. To me it was disgraceful. Women in hordes."[13] He could not wait to get back to his billet near the front, and he noted with approval that his men had "learned to wash their clothes at the wash stations in imitation of the women here." He approved even more when the battalion was moved to another town.

It was, he told his wife, "quite interesting to have charge of a town and keeping it clean and sanitary besides looking out for supplies and transportation. Adjustment, transporting and administration. After all four-fifths of war is that and we are still so young in this game." He went on, revealing more about his *character militaris:*

The most important thing is to keep the men healthy. A hundred different human frailties now assert themselves. Jealousies and pettiness and selfishness. And then out of it all stand a few strong figures who are true and patriotic and unselfish. This school should be good to teach us humility. We come here from fairly comfortable billets to a different arrangement all together. We are on the side of a high hill. Mud just as tenacious and much more abundant and long staying predominates. We are in barracks much on the style of the officers' camps only without floors. No light but candle and lanterns. Cots, muddy floors and dampness. I am rather glad of it all myself, because it means a little taste of inconvenience and I was beginning to think it was war de luxe.[14]

As usual, Donovan did not spare the Micks, as he did not spare himself. The days were the unending lot of the dutiful line officer—checking the interior and exterior guards at all hours to make sure none of his men had fallen asleep; checking weapons, food, animals, munitions, feet, armpits, boots, socks, underclothes; marking maps; spotting trails; shooting game for the pot; practicing attack and defense; firing and cleaning weapons; checking the oil, the wagons; forever encouraging, ordering, exhorting, marching; ever vigilant for suspicious body rashes and discharges.

He turned a blind eye to a little wenching among his men, but he was very rigid in his attitude toward drink. There were some ferocious liquors in that part of France, there was little else to do but drink after dark, and the dark came early. Therefore, WJD had decreed that the men "drink light beer and wine," and the "four grog shops in the town" were allowed to sell liquor to soldiers between 4:00 and 8:00 P.M., and then only liquor in sealed bottles with labels. No drinking at all was permitted if the man was on duty or if his unit was engaging in route marching or firing. But although later Donovan would be accused of zealotry in regard to his men, especially in regard to their consumption of liquor, the rules and regulations had been prepared by the Rainbow Division chief of staff, Colonel Douglas MacArthur.

Donovan, in his effort to create the best battalion in the U.S. Army, did not ignore the intellectual side of his work. His main relaxation was reading works of military science, and nobody in the expeditionary force was happier when he found that his Christmas present was a parcel of books: *Wolfe's Instructions to Young Officers* (1768); *An Essay on the Command of Small Detachments* (1766); *Manoeuvres for a Battalion of Infantry, Upon Fixed Principles* (1767); *The Manual of Exercise with Explanations* (1766); and *Manoeuvres for a Battalion of Infantry by a German Officer* (1766). Together, he wrote to Ruth, they were a most valuable, interesting, and delightful present, being "five volumes bound in four, small 12mo, handsomely bound in half levant morocco extra, with gilt backs and gilt tops by H. Wood of London." He was "most delighted."[15]

At the end of the year the Rainbow Division was still in training and had taken part in no fighting. On New Year's Eve Donovan and an American brigadier general were in a dugout forty feet underground where they had dinner of "roast turkey with chestnut dressing and a beautiful cake with a glazed American flag." The only reminders that they were not on maneuvers were the flashes and thuds of howitzer reports on the undersides of the thick clouds far away. On the second day of the New Year Donovan was almost delighted to report that he had just seen "an aeroplane fight, a raid," and had been "under some pretty heavy firing." He was "glad that happened because now I have no fears of being able to stand up under it." He did not "know what a battle is like and of course it has its horrors," but "battles are not fought everyday," and "even so it takes as many bullets to kill a man as it ever has. Have you noticed in the papers that the proportion of casualties is 4 per 1000?"[16]

The reality was that the war was coming closer. The Germans had not been "lying in wait for us," as the Americans had feared, for they had in mind something far more rigorous than an ambush. Ever since the Bolshevik Revolution in Russia the German General Staff had been able to reduce the size of its armies on the Russian front and transfer large numbers of fresh divisions to the western front. Soon the German commander in chief would have 3,500,000 men concentrated in 192 divisions for a series of gigantic offensives—*Kaiserschlachten*—intended to win the war for Germany in the West before the full weight of American industrial might and manpower could be brought to bear upon the battle.

By February 28, 1918, Donovan and his battalion had entered the firing for the first time, taking over a sector of the front at Lunéville, in the trenches at the Forêt de Parroy. Immediately the *Drachen*—observation balloons—rose over the Pomeranian trenches and hung in the dawn sky in sinister fashion, the men in their wicker cupolas watching. There now followed a period of nervous watching and waiting as the Micks and the Pomeranians took the measure of each other. In the next nine days there was a steady dribble of blood from the Micks' firing step: a soldier down with a whiff of mustard gas, another with an ear taken off by a sniper, yet another killed while out in no-man's-land, caught by a Pomeranian raiding party while inspecting the barbed-wire entanglements. But nothing big, nothing to rate more than a sentence in the midnight bulletin to Colonel Douglas MacArthur.

For the time the battalion was up in the line, that midnight report reflected only the mysterious sights and sounds of the battlefield. Donovan had appointed Sergeant Joyce Kilmer, the greatest of the Irish-American Catholic poets of his time and a member of the staff of *The New York Times*, his intelligence clerk, and Kilmer's reports were a nightly essay compounded of fragments of information that were meaningless and valueless to anyone beyond the battlefield, but all of which, no matter how trivial, were deadly in implications: "Hammer blows again heard at night near Leintroy and wagons heard in same direction"; "Locomotives whistling in direction of Blamont"; "Smoke as of burning brushwood observed rising from Clair Bois"; "Many noises in the Bois de Blamont (hammer blows, sounds of irons, sounds of iron plates). Sounds of bells from there about 8 A.M. Thick smoke in Xures. At 11:20 P.M. rockets with 2 white lights and 1 red light observed from the signal of Xousse"; "Red rockets sent up from Niethamer at 12:42 P.M."; "A French patrol in the Près Bois heard noises of the unloading of material near the Fritz horn and the barking of a large dog"; "Comparative artillery fire—French 1642 rounds, German 2188 rounds"; "Subterranean mining noises heard towards La Maison Forestière and the Tellnitz Trench"; "Three men wearing camouflage seen entering Bois de Blamont 4:24 P.M."[17]

There were the raids to nail the Pomeranians to their trenches opposite the Micks' wire. Donovan's description of these forays to Ruth deserves to rank among the best war writing of the campaign:

> The sentry called me at 2:00 A.M. I put on my helmet and gas mask and that completed my dressing. Outside of the door Rohan waited with the horses.
>
> A ride through the night. Just a plain clear night of stars. A rumble of a distant gun. A blockade in the road of excited French drivers whose yelling could be heard in Germany.
>
> A short fine trot and we came to Artillery Headquarters. At 3:00 a breakfast of coffee, oatmeal and eggs with Major Reddin, Battalion C.O. of the 149th. Then in his headquarters where the telephones were busy checking up the batteries and synchronizing the watches. It is the "J" hour minus six minutes and I have an engagement with Colonel Reilley at his observation post. It is impossible to take the horses, and so guided by an orderly who must be a cross country runner—I run and stumble and walk across the field to the Observation Post—a hill top overlooking five miles of German front. Then a sound as if some huge curtain were ripped by giant hands—the artillery opens. It is 4:00 A.M., the "J" hour.
>
> Hundreds of guns echeloned in our immediate vicinity and nearly blew us off the ground. The infantry had left its trenches but we cannot see them with the heavy hanging morning mist. Frantic signal lights calling for help and barrage springs up excitedly along the German front. Forty-two minutes go by during which we see nothing of the movement. We know they are advancing through enemy woods which for three days have been subjected to every manner of artillery smashing. At 5:15 a telephone—the signal man who was to have sent the flare announcing the arrival at objective lost his rockets. A runner is sent back. Then a wait of another hour. In the valley the mist is thickened by the smoke of shells and the church steeple and the tree tops struggle vainly to creep above the mist. The sun comes out and hangs like an up-side-down Chinese lantern. The telephone "they are back." Another wait and "no prisoners." The Germans as was their wont have retired to their rear trenches leaving to be sacrificed four or five watchmen. What is left of their poor broken bodies lie in the woods.[18]

The sequel came in a later letter. When the patrol returned, WJD found that two of the Micks were missing:

> I went to the Colonel and told him that these men had last been seen outside the German wire in No Man's Land. That they might be wounded, that it was

our duty to make a real search for them, that the entire regiment if needs be, officers and men, should turn out to find them, so each man would know however mean or despicable he was if lost in the performance of his duty we would go after him. I insisted that it was vitally important for the morale of the men; also that I should be permitted to conduct the patrol. To all of which he agreed and consented, so last night I went out with two lieutenants and 36 men. That portion of the men that were to remain with me were men I had sentenced on summary court. They were a great looking crew, [and] all of them volunteered to go with me, even though I had taken their money away from them.

I got little Ford cars to take them up to a point near the trenches. From there we went to a dugout in which we 39 crowded, standing in water to our ankles. I took a map and by the light of two candles told them my plan and how we would work. Then we went out, each man taking two grenades. We passed through our wire—the night overcast so you could not see the man ahead of you, though knowing he was there. Into shell holes, under and over and through barb wire. I left one nice wrapped legging and part of another streaming from rusty wire. My nice Brooks Brothers breeches were ripped and muddy. At last the end of the wire and we were in No Man's Land. At the wire I left a Sergeant, a youngster from Buffalo, named Murray,—and two corporals. No Man's Land, once rich meadow land on a hill side, now wet and dotted with huge shell dimples.

You hear the preliminary pop of a Verey [sic] pistol and you hit the ground burying your face in the slime and grateful it is there. The German loves his fireworks party every night and uses an awful lot of them. Then a halt for readjustment and straightening out. The two lieutenants lose each other and I act as liaison and get them started on their combing. Another pause and they come back. Signal lights from the German side which they claim are answered from our lines. But it isn't so, it is from the Germans on our left front. I start them again and go back to my group which is under command of a Sergeant, a Greek who in his knowledge of ground is a wonder. We had just our compasses and we move forward to the reverse side of the hill, then send forward O'Connor and two men to the crest to observe for us. With me are all the others.

It is 11:15 P.M. A misty chill is in the air. We have only a few clothes and try to find a dry spot but there is no such thing. To our left on top of a hill is a bush. I knew it was a bush. I saw it there against the sky. A scout on the left crawls to me. He has seen someone coming to us. I go with him and there sure enough is a figure now erect, now crouching making for us. The word is passed. I turn my head away and blink my eyes, then turn it back. It is the same old bush now swaying in the wind. That is the way in the dark, as you know, one can see whole battalions on manouevre [sic].

1:15 A.M. The flares have ceased. Complete quiet and darkness and the sky begins to clear, a few stars come out. The men are close about me yet I cannot see one of them.

2:10 A.M. The German is signalling again. Grenades on our left and a machine gun playing down the valley. No word yet from our patrol. A pistol shot and then quiet.

I crawl forward to the crest on my elbows, a stream of slime from my chin to toes. I lay beside O'Connor, cheek to cheek, we whisper, but I give it up. His whispering brogue can be heard in Germany. Insensibly it grows lighter and you can distinguish figures. Those patrols must return. Another hour and it will be too late. O'Connor catches figures on our right. We both start towards them—we guess them friendly. Have they the bodies? They move too fast for that. Then a "hiss," the sign of recognition. All back but no luck. Now we get them back. We check each man in as at a turn stile on a boat. A burst of flare. . . . Finally back in the post of command, the names are called and we wander to our new station, the battalion having moved again during the night.

On the road—I was a fine looking Major with half a legging, all mud from head to toe, my breeches in tatters and 36 men behind me in the same way. We met the old Colonel and the new coming to inspect the lines. It was four o'clock. After the first faint grayish streak in the east the day had come with a rush, and with it quietness of guns, but a very melody of bird music in the forest and through it all the sound as of hundreds of cuckoo clocks. Did you know there were so many cuckoo birds here?

A word to the men, then at five to bed until 7. Then I breakfast with the two colonels at nine.[19]

Six days later two men picked up in front of the Alabama Regiment's wire, exhausted and almost unconscious from hunger and fatigue, proved to be Donovan's missing Micks. To increase his sense of joy, Donovan told Ruth, one of his patrols returned without prisoners but brought him "a bouquet of tulips and forget-me-nots gathered in No Man's Land. Incredible, isn't it?"[20]

3

The Ourcq

Between March 21 and July 14, 1918, the German high commander Colonel General Erich Ludendorff launched no fewer than four major offensives on the western front, all intended to win the war for Kaiser Wilhelm. But although the casualties on both sides were more than 1,000,000 men, all the attacks failed to achieve their purpose. With the collapse of the *Kaiserschlachten,* the Allies passed to the offensive. Among the principal tasks was to pinch out the great Marne salient.

As the armies moved into place, Donovan wrote to Ruth:

> I grow prouder of America. She is now magnificent—beyond anything I expected. Her ideals clearer, her purpose higher than all the others. Another thing. Have you considered that before long America will be the strongest nation—with her fleet, her industries, her army, all organized. I wonder if, as all these increase, envious eyes may be cast upon her.

He ended ominously: "I must go now, for the noise outside is increasing and the whole sky is blazing."[1]

In the counteroffensive being mounted, Donovan was to pass from the lists of competent and devoted line officers to the thin ranks of authentic heroes. For as part of the plan the Rainbow Division was to become the spearhead for the operations of the French Sixth Army for the Allied counteroffensive on the Marne front. There was a long break in WJD's correspondence, during which "More of life has been crowded in . . . than

I have ever known before." Donovan had been to a place called Meurcy Farm and was one of the few men to come back.

During the night of July 27–28, Donovan received orders to cross the Ourcq River, one of the tributaries of the Seine, and take Meurcy Farm and Hill 212, neither of which had any importance except as points on the way to other, larger objectives. The orders made it clear that the Rainbow Division's advance would be part of a much larger general operation, the object of which was not only to retake ground held by the Germans for several years but also to destroy enemy power in that sector. Also, as the orders stated, the attack was to be "in the nature of a surprise and, consequently, troops in the attack will not fire *during the assault* but will confine themselves to the bayonet." At ten minutes before the hour of attack the enemy positions would be subjected to "violent artillery preparation . . . of ten minutes duration."[2] The intelligence appreciations about enemy strength in the area were very muddled, but most suggested that the area was only lightly held by the enemy, if he was there at all.

The land before Donovan's line of march from Beauvardes to Meurcy Farm was difficult and dangerous, its principal feature being the valley of the Ourcq River, which lay at right angles to his route, and the little town of Sergy, which consisted of no more than seventy-eight houses, twenty wells, 256 people, and a small umbrella factory. The river was no more than a trout stream at this time of the year—twenty feet wide, twenty inches deep—but the banks on the far side were very steep, high, and afforded little cover. To get to Meurcy Farm, the battalion would have to march down into the valley to the banks of the Ourcq, cross the stream, then climb up the far hillside to the lip of the hill where the farm stood. During the descent and crossing the battalion would be very exposed, and in climbing up toward the farm, it would be equally exposed as the men marched with copses and grainfields on three sides—a perfect trap for determined enemy defenders with machine guns.

It became desirable to find out the nature of the enemy defense in and around Sergy. The intelligence bulletin for July 25 contained the statement "It appears that the enemy is still holding his line with a strong concentration of machine guns," but since the Rainbow Division had not at that time had direct contact with the enemy it was "not possible to form an opinion as to his intentions at that time."[3] But it was noticeable that the enemy was doing his best to shoot down American observation balloons (the balloon at Château Moucheton had been shot down three times in one day, the same observer being forced to his parachute on each occasion, each time landing safely). This indicated the Germans might be trying to conceal an important movement. As for German forces in the area, eight prisoners had been taken, all belonging to low-grade, burned-out units and speaking of having had "much fighting, hard work and little to eat." However, one prisoner did say that a guards division was "in support in rear of the front line." If true, this meant that the Micks were marching toward an elite unit of the Prussian Guards, but little account seems to have been taken of the statement. Furthermore, in the summary of intelligence for the period 8:00 P.M. on July 26 to 8:00 P.M. on July 27, numerous statements seemed to indicate that the Germans had pulled back, not the least in importance being that "The advance of our troops toward the River Ourcq was unmolested by hostile infantry, *indicating a complete withdrawal by the enemy* [author's italics]."

Thus, the intelligence was uncertain and, since men about to go into battle look for hopeful signs, likely to produce optimism and perhaps carelessness among the assault troops.

Donovan now prepared for the advance. He and his company commanders went forward to Beauvardes Woods to spy out the land and ran into "a terrific fight" between an American brigade and a German unit that was "very hot and bloody." Two of WJD's company commanders were wounded, a shell mixed with high explosive and gas hit a roof directly over his head, and the "rain of rocks and dirt and tile fell about my head and I got a beautiful mouthful of gas." For the "next 20 minutes it was very uncomfortable."[4]

Donovan then went to his headquarters in the Château Moucheton to have his eyes, harmed by the German gas, attended to. The doctor gave him some sniffs of ammonia and bathed the eyes with boracic acid, and then Donovan climbed onto a billiard table in the belief that he would be there for the night. But no. Orders were received from division to move up in preparation for the advance on Meurcy Farm. Donovan crawled off the billiard table and got his staff together. The companies were assembled, and in the first hours of the twenty-seventh the battalion began to march the six miles to the French regiment in the Beauvardes Woods. When the relief was effected, Donovan crawled into "a little ditch with a blanket around me for an hour's sleep."

Donovan said afterward he knew there was something wrong, that he might be marching into an ambush, when he made his rounds of the woods at daybreak. There was "an unusual stillness," and he "made report of the fact to Headquarters." The operations officer at division advised him that the Germans were retreating four kilometers ahead. Donovan received orders to advance, and the advance went on throughout that day until about 7:00 P.M., when they came out of the woods and found themselves on a hill overlooking the valley of the Ourcq and the town of Sergy.

Again Donovan's sixth sense spoke. He was to write to Ruth: "This town was on the other side of the Ourcq River and looked very suspicious to me." He halted his battalion and was trying to get in touch with a French unit supposed to be in the town—hamlet would be a more accurate word for Sergy—when a French cavalry patrol appeared at a gallop. Wrote Donovan to his wife:

> [The patrol] disappeared in the sunken road and then reappeared on the bridge crossing the stream. . . . Then we heard a burst of machine gun fire and the patrol came back towards us at a gallop, one riderless horse. We had gained contact [with the enemy]. Then the Lieutenant in command [of the cavalry troop] came back and reported to me, and all of us lay on our stomachs while the shells began to burst all around us. It was a perfect place for a fight. This town lay in a little basin, while up behind it lay high hills. We lay on the forward slope. As darkness was coming over, I moved the Battalion back on the reverse slope where it could be a little freer from the fire, and then tried to get in touch with everyone. That was a horrible night. We had suffered some losses. I had seen a good many youngsters go out that I had counted on for good work. Once kneeling down and talking with two or three officers a shell burst within ten feet of us, killing 7 next to me and smothering us with dirt. We dug in for the night. It was cold, wet and damp, and the shells were pretty uncomfortable. I sat on the ground with my knees huddled up to my chin and managed to sleep 2 or 3 hours.[5]

From this point the battle grew in intensity every hour until it reached a fury that made it an epic American small-unit action of World War I and one of the most heroic incidents in American military history.

The crossing of the Ourcq began at 4:30 A.M., with the intelligence picture of enemy capabilities unchanged since 8:00 the night before—that the far ridge was held by units of a second-string Landwehr division. The reality was very different: Hidden in the corn, the woods, and the farm buildings on the far side of the Ourcq facing the Rainbow's front were machine-gun units of no fewer than three ordinary German divisions and one extraordinary unit—the 4th Guards Division, which, as the Rainbow's intelligence appreciation for July 27–28 admitted ruefully, was "one of the Crack divisions of the German Army," had been put into the line during the evening of the twenty-seventh for the purpose of delivering a counterattack.[6] And the 4th Guards Division's machine gunners were immediately facing Donovan's Micks.

Although they were under heavy medium-caliber shellfire, Donovan's advance began well, with one battalion to the left, the other to the right. He and the Micks passed through the woods on his side of the Ourcq and crossed the stream with the loss of only five men. They started up the slope toward the cornfields and Meurcy Farm on the lip of the hill, and then the machine-gun fire started with a fury that hardly abated for seventy-two hours. It was so intense that the battalions on Donovan's right and left fell back, leaving him and his battalion dug in on the crest of the hill, but surrounded by machine gunners on three sides. Moreover, since the original orders had specified only ten minutes' preparatory artillery fire, the enemy formations were completely intact. Also, the Germans had command of the air, and throughout the seventy-two hours their Fokkers and Pfalzes strafed WJD's positions unmercifully.

Donovan's skills were now put to the test, and they appear to have survived the first onslaught. He managed to save many a life by tucking the men in odd places and folds of ground which the German shells could not reach. The three-sided German crossfire did take a serious toll during that first day, although only one officer was lost. With darkness much of the gunfire subsided, two or three of Donovan's staff dug some small holes, and Donovan's adjutant, Oliver Ames, and Donovan "had a very refreshing 2½ hours sleep, which, with a cup of coffee and a piece of bacon gave us new life."[7]

During the night, however, some of the German machine gunners had wriggled in so close that they made it difficult and sometimes impossible for Donovan to move. Nevertheless, he went back down into the valley to get some artillery assistance, through a "little draw that was just singing with machine gun fire and heavy artillery." Ten men with Donovan were shot as they tried to get across an open space, but he made it to the command post of the 167th Regiment and passed the coordinates for artillery fire on an enemy that was not more than fifty yards from his own troops.

On his way back he met the two other battalion commanders under the Ourcq riverbank. There they discussed the situation, and, Donovan asserted, both "refused to move forward at all without . . . artillery assistance."[8] Donovan told his brother officers that he:

> would go forward in accordance with our orders whether we had assistance or not, or whether our flanks were protected or not. I did not consider that any courage or anything exceptional. It was simply a matter of duty and if a Battalion Commander is lacking in the stomach to tackle a job that looks difficult, we can never win this war.

He waited fifteen minutes to see whether the other battalion commanders would march with him. When it was clear they would not, Donovan gave a runner the order to the battalion to resume the attack and made his way back to his command post.

Abandoning the textbook form of attack, the battalion split up into small parties, Indian fashion, to present as small a target to the scores of light and heavy machine guns playing over the hillsides. The storm of shot and shell was heavy, nonetheless, and in a charge against one machine-gun nest one sergeant with twenty men had only four men standing when he reached the gun—but reach the gun and the seven men serving it he did. And, Donovan was to admit, the Micks took no prisoners. "The men," he wrote, "when they saw the Germans with Red Crosses on one sleeve and serving machine guns against us, firing until the last minute, then cowardly throwing up their hands and crying 'Kamerad,' became just lustful for German blood. I do not blame them." Later when WJD was required to sit in judgment on the German officers' corps for its conduct in World War II, he recalled this incident, realized that if World War I had gone the wrong way, he might have been arrested for having committed war crimes, and he refused to prosecute.

At some time that day—all real sense of time, of cohesion seems to have been lost in the fury of the fighting—Donovan was joined by young Oliver Ames, his adjutant, as Donovan was lying by the side of a stream to talk to a wounded officer. "I ordered him back," Donovan said afterward, "but he just smiled and said he was going to stay with me. He came up and lay beside me. A sniper began to play on us, and machine gun bullets whizzed over our heads. I half turned and as I did a sniper's bullet crossed my shoulder and struck Ames in the ear. He died instantly. I reached for him, and as I did, another bullet struck me in the hand."

There was too little time to mourn Ames's passing; one of America's elite battalions was perishing in this battle—hundreds of men were falling. Donovan's job was to escape the sniper. He rolled "into the creek, worked my way up to a group of men, and with that fire playing over us, stayed there for ¾ of an hour with mud and water above our waists. An aeroplane came over us, saw these troops advancing up the creek, gave its signal to its artillery, and soon shells began to drop all around us and in the creek itself." So it went throughout the day. But by the end of the day "We had advanced some 3 kilometers without any support either on our right or on our left flank, with no artillery preparation and with no auxiliary arms. We had done it with rifles, machine guns and bayonets, against artillery and machine guns—1 machine gun to every four men."[9]

Only at divisional headquarters was the battle seen clearly, and in his intelligence appreciation of July 27–28, MacArthur, now a brigadier general, spoke of "A day of very fierce infantry fighting"—a phrase not often used in the entire war—and then described the part of Donovan's battalion in that fighting:

> When our infantry attempted the crossing of the Ourcq the morning of the 28th they were met with intense rifle and machine gun fire from the heights on the farther side. The crossing was made successfully by elements of [WJD's regiment] and by 10:30 A.M. elements of all four [of the division's] infantry regiments had forced the river. Along our whole front the battle rolled back and forth all day. We took Sergy and moved beyond it. The enemy then launched his counter-attack with a fresh division, the 4th Guard [sic] Division, one of the "aces" of the German Army. Our troops were driven

out of Sergy but returned to the attack and retook the town. They were driven out three times but each time recaptured the ground and at latest reports are still holding it. The enemy was unable to break our line and it is still intact on the north bank of the Ourcq.[10]

Meanwhile, according to Donovan's account of the battle to his family, "All that night we held on and all the next day, with no food, the machine guns which the Germans had placed sweeping us constantly." The divisional commander and MacArthur sent in the Ohio Regiment, but it could not get far enough forward, and Donovan still found himself out in front and flanked on three sides. He suspected that the enemy might be about to launch a counterattack on his machine-gun positions, and he knew that if those positions were swept away, his entire battalion position must collapse. Thus, "just on a poker hunch" he started "a little attack myself against a trench the Germans had, and as luck would have it, found that they had a group of 25 men just ready to rush our machine gun position."[11]

In the fighting the Micks again began to kill their prisoners, and Donovan recorded: "Out of the 25 I was able to save only 2 prisoners, the men killed all the rest." Yet although he had spoiled the German assault, the battalion "had a hard time that afternoon." He did not "know why I was not killed." He was "hit on the chest with a piece of stone or shell which ripped my gas mask," and "another piece of shell hit me on the left heel tearing my shoe and throwing me off balance"—an incident that started a rumor that Donovan had been seen falling, had been killed, and that led to a telegram being sent to Ruth that he was believed killed in action. Within the hour another telegram was received, stating that Donovan was wounded, not dead. Other officers' wives were not so fortunate. "I guess I have been born to be hanged," wrote Donovan, because "All my headquarters officers had been killed or wounded, except Weller." And at some time during that day the Irish-American poet Joyce Kilmer, Donovan's intelligence sergeant, was killed—one of the greatest losses to American letters of World War I. Of Kilmer's death, Donovan wrote to Ruth:

> I had Joyce Kilmer, who is a Sergeant, and whose poetry you have undoubtedly read, acting as my Sergeant Major, my own Sergeant Major having been wounded. Kilmer felt it his duty to look out for me, and got a bullet in his head. We have buried him beside Ames. . . . It just makes me shiver when I think of the devotion and loyalty of these men and young officers immediately about me who have given freely to me in spite of my strictness and sometimes irritability with them.[12]

That night the regimental commander, Colonel Frank McCoy, who was to become one of Donovan's revered friends, managed to get "some food to the men although the Germans were lashing the roads and the trees and the woods with shrapnel and high explosive." MacArthur's nightly bulletin recorded:

> Another day of hard infantry fighting. The enemy machine gun fire is unceasing. The enemy artillery fire was very heavy in the morning . . . the fire in the afternoon was lighter. The enemy aviation was not as active as yesterday. The enemy infantry fought desperately . . . but [the enemy's actions] give the impression that he is still drawing back his artillery and instructing his infantry to resist but to retire slowly when very hard pressed. Meurcy Farm was captured [but not] . . . until the gunners had been killed in hand to hand conflict with our men.[13]

On July 29–30 the entire division was ordered forward to relieve Donovan's battalion, while Donovan was directed to remain in place until the other forces caught up with the Micks. They did not catch up, but he did manage to take some of the woods from which the German guards were firing across the slopes of the Ourcq Valley. Although that action was "rather good fun," with the Micks operating in killing groups of five men, the day was "not without our discomfort," the sting had not gone out of the Germans, and the Micks were still almost beleaguered. It was again a day of hand-to-hand fighting, in which "A few youngsters near me were potted," but they were promised relief that night. That, however, did not materialize, although "on the whole we had a pretty successful night."

That less grim view was not, however, shared by MacArthur, who reported in his intelligence summary:

> A third day of fierce infantry fighting. The enemy took the offensive for the first time and attempted counter-attacks. The artillery fire was heavier than the day before and distributed over wider territory. The machine gun fire was as continuous as usual day and night. Only in the air did the enemy show any diminution of activity. While there was no abnormal amount of artillery in action, the enemy showed no indication of an intention to retire unless forced to do so. . . . During the night the enemy twice attempted to take Sergy but was repulsed both times. He fought fiercely at Meurcy Farm, Bois Brulée and Ferme de Camp [all in the immediate locality of Meurcy Farm] during the morning. His machine gunners hidden along the crest between Meurcy Farm and Sergy . . . stopped our advance in the morning. . . . The enemy made strong efforts to force us back beyond the Ourcq but failed at all points . . . shell fire during the morning was heavier than the day before and a larger proportion of gas was used. The valley of the Ourcq was shelled with high explosive and gas, as were the valleys running down to the river.[14]

With each bulletin, a characteristic became more evident: While the entire division had in general failed to crack the German line on the Ourcq, the exploits of units other than Donovan's were dealt with extensively, despite the failure. Yet Donovan's battalion was never mentioned directly, and the work of the regiment received only scant mention in reports that went up to Pershing—a reflection, no doubt, of the antipathy between MacArthur on the one hand and McCoy, the outstanding regimental commander, and Donovan on the other. Politics, it seems, strayed onto that most desperate of places, the battlefield.

And the battle went on. During the night of July 30–31, Donovan wrote, "I had no more than 1½ or 2 hours sleep all night," and during the daylight hours of July 31 "there was constant heavy bombardment, as if they were going to make a counter-attack. All day long aeroplanes hovered over us, swooping down close to us and firing on us, and at night dropping aerial bombs, the shelling more and more getting on everyone's nerves." It was "surprising, however, how many shells it takes to get a man, and how much ammunition must be expended before a casualty list begins to mount."

By the thirty-first it was clear that the battalion had suffered terrible casualties. How bad the situation was could not be established, but Donovan knew it must be serious because "I had no one in command of the Companies only 2nd lieutenants and it was a real test to keep these youngsters, who were game, but nervous, up to their jobs and make everyone feel that no matter how bad everything looked, we were going to hold on." Hold on they did throughout the day, although there appeared to be no hope of relief getting through on the night of July 31–August 1, as MacArthur reported: "A fourth day of hard infantry fighting" and "The manner of meeting our infantry attack this afternoon shows that the enemy is holding his present line tenaciously and has no intention of retiring further unless compelled to do so."[15]

Yet there is always an angel of mercy on a battlefield, and she appeared in the form of a runner at about 11:00 P.M. on the thirty-first: A relief battalion was on its way and could be expected at about 2:30 A.M. The 3rd Battalion of Donovan's regiment arrived at the killing ground at about 3:00 A.M., and as Donovan put it, "I lay on the ground and slept a very refreshing sleep until 6:00 o'clock." He was awakened by the lieutenant colonel of the incoming battalion and told that the Germans had pulled out and that the 3rd Battalion's patrols were now advancing beyond the farm.

Donovan trudged off down the hillside into Sergy, where the remnants of his battalion had gathered after having been relieved. There for the first time, the full enormity of the losses became apparent to Donovan: In a battalion of about 1,000 men, 600 were killed, wounded, missing. He had lost all but a quarter of his officers. The regiment as a whole had suffered as badly: In the battle on the Ourcq 66 officers and 1,750 of the original 3,000 men—almost the entire fighting strength of the regiment —had been lost. New York's Micks were finished as a regiment.

That frayed remnant of perhaps the best fighting unit in the American Expeditionary Force was awakened, and Donovan took them back up on to the slopes and into the woods and cornfields to find and bury their dead.

> We found 5 Germans for every one of us. There were many pictures that I will never forget. One picture should be done in bronze as typifying the spirit of these men here. He was a big husky middle westerner in full pack. He had evidently just started to make a rush. He had been struck by a piece of shell, and his figure remained fixed in that crouching alert position facing the enemy. As we went over to the position the Germans had abandoned and looked about the valley through which we had come, we wondered how we had done it. . . . We marched that night back through the old farm we had taken, crossed the stream we had crossed some days before, and not a sound from the men. It had its dramatic touch.

Donovan went on to assess the effects of the battle on the battalion and him:

> In 8 days of battle, our Division had forced the passage of the Ourcq, taken prisoners from 6 enemy divisions, met, routed and decimated a crack division of the Prussian Guards, a Bavarian division and one other division and driven back the enemy's line for 16 kilometers. In every day of that fighting our Battalion had participated. It had never retired, it had gone the farthest and stayed the longest. . . . One thing only I am glad of, and that is that the system which I used in the training of these men justified itself. Their discipline and their training, and above all their spirit, held them full of fight in a position which had previously been given up by two other outfits. These men who had all along thought me too strict and felt that I had made them work when others did not work, and I held them to too high a standard, are now convinced that I was right, and that I would ask them to do nothing that I myself would not do. This one tribute is greater than any honor that my superior officers can give me. . . . Lack of sleep and the strain has [sic] pulled me down, but I feel pretty good. I think the Colonel and others thought I would crack under the strain, but the regular life behind me, and the athletic training have certainly been worth while. No one should get into this fight who hasn't the physical endurance and stamina. Courage is the smallest part of it. Physical endurance will give one control of one's nerves long after the breaking point seems to have been reached.[16]

In that statement, Donovan had revealed the special elements in his *character militaris:* dauntlessness; Spartan physical fitness; ruthlessness; a lack of interest in death and physical injury; a sense that to die or excel on the battlefield was man's greatest reward and his highest honor. These were undoubtedly the finest hours of his entire life, for never again would there be an opportunity for him to display the full majesty of his courage.

For his heroism, Donovan received the Distinguished Service Cross and the cognomen "Wild Bill," by which to his chagrin and cost he was to be known for the rest of his life—largely because the words fitted readily into the constricted space of newspaper headlines. Father Duffy related how and when he received that nickname:

I overheard a conversation in the woods which gave me a good story on Major Donovan. The majority of his battalion have always looked on him as the greatest man in the world. But certain numbers were resentful and complaining on account of the hard physical drilling he has continually given them to keep them in condition for just the sort of thing they had to go through last week. As a result of watching him through six days of battle— his coolness, cheerfulness, resourcefulness—there is now no limit to their admiration for him. What I overheard was the partial conversation of the last dissenter. He still had a grouch about what he had been through during the past year, and three other fellows were pounding him with arguments to prove Donovan's greatness. Finally he said grudgingly: "Well, I'll say this: Wild Bill is a son of a b----but he's a game one."[17]

4

The Fortress

As 10,000 American soldiers a day marched ashore at Le Havre, the British launched the first of a series of offensives when 1,000 aircraft, 2,000 tanks, and 300,000 soldiers fell upon the German armies in Flanders on August 8, 1918, an attack so powerful that Ludendorff declared the day to have been the "black day" of the German Army. He began to withdraw his armies into the Hindenburg Line, the last defenses before the Rhine, and he advised the kaiser at Imperial Headquarters to ask for peace.

Donovan spent these epic days near Goncourt, helping rebuild the regiment, but he knew that was impossible: The regiment that had marched from the Thirty-fourth Street armory so cheerfully that bright spring day in 1917 was gone forever. The German machine guns at the Ourcq had not even left a proper cadre on which to rebuild, for the heaviest casualties had been among the officers and noncommissioned officers. The replacements had not the esprit de corps or the training of the dead, and an official account of the regiment contained this withering statement about them: "The men obtained were for the greater part crude and raw, some not knowing how to load their rifles and don their gas masks when they reached us."[1]

Donovan was somewhat more charitable about the new men. He wrote Ruth:

You know I believe that the Americans are rather getting the goat of the Germans. Perhaps this is because [the Germans] are a little tired and weary in looking for the end of the war, and now he sees this husky, ignorant, yet valorous youngster spring in and start hitting him with a club. We cannot outfiness the Germans. His Staff can do in one hour what it takes our Staff [days] to do. . . . But we have, in the language of the street, "the wallop," and if you say to Mr. Boche "We are coming over here and we are going to crack you on the jaw," I think with the present state of his morale, we can pretty nearly keep him going.[2]

By September it was time for the battalion to return to the division to take part in some of the final actions of the war. Donovan, now a lieutenant colonel with operational responsibility for the regiment when in the field, was to win his greatest laurels. They would come to him at a fortress on the Hindenburg Line during the last days of the war. It was after that action—which followed repeated efforts by the army and divisional staffs to get him to accept a desk job, so that he might survive the war—that Ruth received the dreaded telegram, on October 18, 1918:

DEEPLY REGRET TO INFORM YOU THAT IT IS OFFICIALLY REPORTED THAT LIEUT COLONEL WILLIAM J DONOVAN INFY WAS SEVERELY WOUNDED IN ACTION OCTOBER FIFTEENTH FURTHER INFORMATION WHEN RECD

HARRIS THE ADJT GENL

On October 6, 1918, the new German chancellor, Prince Max of Baden, faced with a Bolshevik revolution in Germany and the collapse of the German armies in the field, sent a message to President Woodrow Wilson, requesting an armistice on the basis of Wilson's Fourteen Points. An exchange of messages began as the German armies began to retire into the Hindenburg Line for the defense of the Reich, the purpose of the German General Staff to bleed the Reich's many enemies outside its frontiers while the politicians and diplomats argued about terms.

Stretching from Arras through Quéant, Cambrai, St.-Quentin, and La Fère to the heights of Chemin des Dames, the Hindenburg Line was a very powerful system of field works dug in 1916 and 1917 by the forced labor of civilians and prisoners of war, strengthened by concrete shelters and emplacements, and protected by belts of barbed wire. Villages, small towns, woods, and hills had been leveled to give the German gunners broad fields of unimpeded fire. At points where road communications made the Reich vulnerable, the Hindenburg Line was really several lines of defense, all bearing Wagnerian names; the flanks were guarded by the Michael, Wotan, Hermann, and Kriemhilde lines; and the rear area, including the support lines, was a fortified zone often fifteen to twenty miles deep, with every town and village fortified. A principal feature of the system were the fortresses, of which the Kriemhilde in the Argonne proved to be among the deepest and best constructed, for its fortifications were based on the steep hills and dense forests of the region.

To reduce the Kriemhilde and get to Sedan and into Germany, Pershing had launched 1,250,000 men in the Meuse-Argonne offensive, which began on September 26, 1918, and in which Colonel George C. Marshall, a young officer on Pershing's staff, played an important part in the planning. With a superiority of eight men to one, Pershing hoped to break through the Kriemhilde Line in one sustained rush. But that hope proved illusory. Although Pershing achieved surprise, only one of the three American corps succeeded even in penetrating the Kriemhilde Line, and at a principal fortress known as the Kriemhilde Stellung in the area of the village of Landres-et-St.-Georges the U.S. I Corps was beaten to a standstill in the thick, trackless Argonne Forest after advancing only a little more than a mile. The tanks, then coming into general service as a weapon, were proving mechanically unreliable and unable to march down the muddy roads; the mud and the narrowness of the roads and tracks prevented adequate supply; the American troops proved to be too inexperienced for such difficult operations; and by the end of September 1918 Pershing's grand offensive had been stopped.

Elsewhere the Allied offensive had also foundered, except in one sector of the British front, where imperial troops did break through the Hindenburg defensive system but exhausted themselves in the process. The political effect of the collapse of the general offensive was serious: At precisely the moment the German government was prepared to seek peace after the collapse of the *Kaiserschlachten,* the German success at the Hindenburg Line gave Ludendorff refreshed confidence, and he began to believe that by bloodying the Allied armies he could get the terms he needed to allow the German Army to withdraw into Germany, where the General Staff would reorganize and refit the armies and resist any peace terms considered unacceptable.

That, then, was the situation when Pershing called upon seven experienced divisions, including the Rainbow, to prepare for a fresh assault in the sector of the Hindenburg Line in the general area of Sedan—at the Kriemhilde Fortress.

When Pershing's orders reached the Rainbow to move to face the Kriemhilde, Donovan had returned to the regiment, having left it briefly to prepare to go to staff college—the other occasion after 1916 when he might have taken British intelligence training. He had, therefore, just assumed command of the fighting elements of the entire regiment, not just his own battalion. Convoys of trucks brought the rifle battalions to the Meuse-Argonne sector, where the Rainbow relieved the U.S. 1st Infantry Division—the "Big Red One"—which had been badly bloodied by the Germans during the attack on the Kriemhilde.

Throughout October 13, as Donovan prepared the regiment for the attack on the Kriemhilde Fortress, rumors had swept both the American and the German lines that Germany had surrendered and that the armistice would take effect at 3:30 P.M. on the afternoon of the fourteenth. To an extent, that rumor weakened the resolution of the rifle battalions at precisely the moment the Germans were preparing to give the regiment another bloody nose. WJD did his best to dispel the notion that the regiment was going to take the Kriemhilde without having to fight for it and drew the attention of his staff to an ominous intelligence bulletin: During the day three soldiers of the German 3rd Guards Division who had been captured by American patrols had revealed that the division had taken up positions in the Kriemhilde Fortress. And while Rainbow's Intelligence Section thought that the peace rumors would lessen enemy resistance—nobody on either side wanted to be the last man to die in the war—nevertheless, the captured guardsmen had revealed that their division had received orders to "hold at all costs."[3]

The divisional commander's orders reached Donovan at his post of command on a long ridge facing the Kriemhilde Fortress: time of attack, 5:00 A.M. on the fourteenth. Donovan explained the plan of the attack for Ruth afterward: "There was a multitude of things to do and the orders coming so late they could not be done properly. The brigade on our right was to advance first, all the guns being concentrated to assist it. Then two hours later all the guns being concentrated to help us."[4]

That reference to artillery may have had significance for the long term as well as the short. Although the position regarding WJD's artillery support is far from clear, it does appear that the 129th Artillery Regiment, which had supported the Big Red One, was also to support the Rainbow, the Rainbow's own artillery being elsewhere at the time of the attack on the Kriemhilde. Part of the 129th was Battery D, commanded by Captain Harry Truman, of Independence, Missouri, who was certainly firing at the Kriemhilde during the Big Red One's assault and was also in WJD's sector at least up to the eve of the Rainbow's assault on October 14, 1918. What the record does not show was whether Truman was actually providing fire support on the fourteenth. If he was providing such support, it might explain much about the bad relations in later years between the two men. For the support Donovan received was poor, much of the shellfire falling on the Rainbow's assault troops, and the biographer can easily visualize WJD's telephoning complaints to the Rainbow division commander and the commander of the 129th Artillery Regiment if its guns were responsible—complaints so phrased that Truman, being the sort of man that he was, would not be likely to forget.[5]

The confusion and muddle that led to disaster began as soon as the regiment began the assault. Recorded WJD in a letter to Ruth:

> The party started. I moved to the forward position which [the Germans] were shelling heavily. I could see no advance on our right. Our hour struck and

promptly the leading battalion moved out. The Germans at once put down a heavy barrage and swept the hill we had to climb with indirect machine gun fire. The advance did not go well.[6]

The regiment had still not developed into a coordinated fighting machine after the Ourcq, there were "green company commanders with the companies," there was "not enough punch," confusion developed, the strange artillery brigade's shells began falling within the ranks of the advancing Rainbow troops, and Donovan was forced to lead the attack himself. He had anticipated that might happen and, he told Ruth, "I went out as if I were going to a party, insignia, ribbons, Sam Brown [sic] belt. Foolish, you say, but necessary. New men need some visible symbol of authority." But this was also foolhardy, for German snipers were always looking to pick off officers and noncommissioned officers, and it would not be long before WJD was shot, for if his men could see him, so could the Germans.

Although "resistance was becoming stronger . . . preparation had been hurried, . . . officers had been killed and wounded, N.C.O.'s the same," and while Donovan had "vast quantities of untrained elements," the battalions under his command fought to within 500 meters of the German wire. There the attack stopped. He sent back for another battalion, but because of enemy shellfire, it did not arrive until 8:00 P.M. That unit, too, was beaten back in daylong battles, and when darkness came, Donovan ordered the battalions to "stabilize for the night." He himself then settled down for the night, using a shell hole as a place in which to rest, and "For mess I had an onion which was delicious and raw and two pieces of hardtack."

By now MacArthur had been sent to command a division, and the new chief of staff of the Rainbow was Lieutenant Colonel William N. Hughes. But as at the Ourcq, so chaotic, fierce, and personal was regimental combat that the overall picture of the day's fighting could be obtained only from the divisional intelligence bulletins. Despite the peace rumors, the bulletins spoke somberly of "savage resistance at all points" and stated that "the enemy has continued his resistance with undiminished fury and has at no time showed any tendency to withdraw or surrender." As significant, WJD's regiment was facing not a crack unit such as the guards—they were on the next sector over—but an ordinary, although experienced, infantry division, the 41st. The volume of the enemy artillery fire showed "no lack of ammunition or of guns withdrawn." The Germans had control of the air, and their fighting determination and effectiveness were in no way diminished, although during the day, in support of Donovan's regiment, American artillery had fired no fewer than 23,000 rounds of 75 millimeter ammunition and 2,600 rounds of 155 millimeter—an incredible number of rounds for a narrow sector in one day. The Germans were continuing to use gas extensively, and all that WJD's regiment had achieved for a loss of some 400 men was a very narrow wedge in the enemy's wire, on either side of which the Germans had concentrated "great numbers of heavy machine guns."[7]

On the night of October 14–15, 1918—only twenty-seven days before the end of the war—WJD's problems began to multiply. Shortly after midnight the field telephone at Donovan's side—his only means of communication with the rear except for runners—went out, and he was unable to receive orders and intelligence directly and immediately. He could not know what was happening on the sectors to his right and left, although he knew that the attack would be resumed. But "I did not know how or where it would be launched, what artillery preparation, nothing."[8] The night, he wrote:

> passed all too quickly. I sent back for food but the lieutenant with his party never returned. Ammunition came up and then at 6:20 the orders for an attack at 7:30. With such short notice it was impossible to get proper word to all units and to make the best dispositions. A heavy mist was hanging. I went around to the men and talked to them. All of this was close to the German line. . . . I should not have been there but remained so because it would have had a bad effect on the men if I had taken position further in rear.

In the plan of operations for the day WJD's infantry was to advance behind tanks, which were being sent up to the front for that purpose, and to smash down the German wire defenses. But as he wrote to Ruth later: "Zero hour came but no tanks, so we started anyway." Donovan rose from his shell hole in full dress uniform again. As he was scrambling over the lip of the hole, he was hit. He described the moment for Ruth:

> I had just walked to the different units and was coming back to the telephone when—smash, I felt as if somebody had hit me on the back of the leg with a spiked club. I fell like a log but after minutes managed to crawl into my little telephone hole. A machine gun lieutenant ripped open my breeches and put on the first aid. The leg hurt but there were many things to be done.

The tanks had begun to arrive up a sunken road, but they:

> almost immediately turned back either on account of smashed mechanism or wounded drivers. The situation was bad. There was more defense than we thought and the batallion [sic] was held up. Messengers I sent through were killed or wounded and messages remained undelivered. We were shelled heavily. Beside me three men were blown up and I was showered with the remnants of their bodies. No connection with the rear as the telephone was

still out. Gas was thrown at us, thick and nasty. Five hours passed. I was getting very groggy but managed to get a message through withdrawing the unit on the line and putting another in its place.

Only when the fresh battalion was in place—five hours after he had been hit—did Donovan consent to his removal from the battlefield. A group of the original Micks came to his shellhole, put Donovan into a blanket, and, since he could not walk, took the corners of the blanket and carried him off the battlefield to safety—heroism that earned them the title thereafter of the Blanket Boys. The title was well earned, for even as he was being evacuated, WJD related, "machine-gun bullets passed thru the blankets and one of the bearers was hit. I told them to put me down but they said they were willing to take a chance. It was a tough hike."

What Donovan did not relate in his letter, but emerged only in affidavits by soldiers in the regiment later, was that one of the reasons he insisted in remaining in command for five hours after he had been badly wounded—his knee and all nerve and blood vessels were shattered—was that soon after he was hit, he received news that the Germans were preparing a major counterattack. The size of the German group, the defensive situation, the nature of the enemy artillery bombardment (the Germans were using high explosive mixed with pumice dust impregnated with phosgene poison gas which created pockets of poison gas that did not disperse quickly and which could not easily be detected), and the morale of the regiment—all demanded Donovan's presence.

That decision was wise, for Donovan had just time to deploy his mortar platoon to the front and the flanks when the German infantry, highly charged on schnapps, came dashing out of their smoke barrage, crying, "Für Gott und der Vaterland," and bayoneting, knifing, strangling, clubbing, or shooting all who stood in their way. Such were the violence and suddenness of the attack that the battalion in the line, already badly dispersed by the artillery bombardment, wavered and began to break.

The line would have collapsed altogether had Donovan not remained to encourage his men and to direct the mortar counterbarrage that broke the attack. But he cried through his bullhorn: "They can't get me, and they can't get you." The Micks, not knowing that he was wounded and could not move, believed him. Seizing everything from rifles and pistols to picks and shovels, they smashed the Germans back into the fortress in a glorious burst of battlefield élan that astonished them as much as it did the Germans. Only then, when Donovan was sure the battalion could and would hold, did he permit the Blanket Boys to carry him off the battlefield, and then only when the eddying smoke drifted over the command post and concealed his departure from his troops. Donovan was taken to the battalion aid station where a tag was tied to his right big toe:

> G[un]S[hot]W[ound] Right Knee, Corbet, M.O. Machine gun bullet at the knee just below the joint. Hole in the tibia—a splinter from that hole extending downwards for two and a half inches.[9]

Donovan described the treatment and the hospital:

> . . . they stripped me and rubbed me over with a warm sponge. It being the first in many days it was very welcome. Then the anti-tetanus injection. . . . Placed on the operating table they saw no need for an operation and putting my leg in a splint turned me into a ward. I was put between sheets —think of it. Beside me was an officer shot through the stomach and dying, across two officers coming out of ether and asking the nurse to hold their hands or smooth their brows. In the next ward a bedlam of delirium. . . . Early in the morning the man next to me died still calling for his wife and children. Pancakes for breakfast and then prepared for evacuation. . . . It was in a pouring rain, the road was terrific, I had with me several badly wounded officers who groaned the whole time, and I was not very comfortable myself, so that on the road things were not happy. . . . The nurse was a sister of Rose, the hammer thrower, and looked to me husky enough to handle any of us.[10]

Two days later he was at the American Red Cross Military Hospital No. 3 at the rue de Chevreuse 4 in Paris, on a "floor full of generals and colonels." He was still there on crutches when Senator James W. Wadsworth, a family friend of the Rumseys and an admirer of WJD, came calling. Wadsworth reported to Ruth that:

> Bill looked exceedingly well; in fact, I never saw him look better. He was rapidly recovering from his wound in the leg, had thrown away his crutches and was walking about with only a slight limp. . . . [He] is in the pink of condition, and incidentally enjoys the very highest reputation of any young officer in the A.E.F. I cannot exaggerate to you the esteem in which he is held.[11]

The senator was followed by Herbert Hoover, now the American food administrator, whose duties included provisioning some of the European Allies. Hoover, passing through Paris, heard that Donovan was there recovering from wounds and came to see him, a visit that had established what appeared to be a firm friendship between men who had emerged as two of America's principal military and civilian heroes. And to speed him further to recovery, a letter caught up with Donovan from Theodore Roosevelt, who had been physically and spiritually shattered by the death in action of his youngest son, Quentin, shot down and killed while on flying operations in the general area of the Ourcq—a loss that was soon to kill the ex-President. Making no mention of Quentin's death, Roosevelt wrote:

My dear Colonel Donovan,

It did me good to get your letter of the 9th of September. My own activities here are of no earthly consequence, for all that counts is what is done by you men at the front; but it is hardly necessary for me to say to you that I have been doing everything in my power to have our country insist that we finish this war by you men at the front and not typewriters; and that we beat Germany to her knees . . . and fight the whole combination wherever the fighting can be done most effectively.

Ted [another of Roosevelt's sons in action in France] has just written me saying that he would give anything if only he could be made a full Lt. Colonel in a regiment under you as Colonel. . . . My boys regard you as about the finest example of the American fighting man.

Faithfully yours,
(s) Theodore Roosevelt[12]

Roosevelt's statement about the necessity for the total defeat of Germany reflected exactly Donovan's own thoughts, but in any event the question of Germany was settled by the Germans. The German Navy mutinied, the socialists revolted, the monarchists abdicated, and the militarists accepted the Allies' terms—all during the period that Donovan was recuperating. The end came on November 10, 1918, while he was still in Paris. On that day, he wrote to Ruth: "Rumors of peace today. I believe the armistice will surely be signed."

That afternoon he went to Orly Airfield at Paris to watch an experiment in which men and equipment were parachuted from aircraft—a test that had greater future significance for Donovan than he knew—and in the evening he went to the theater with two brother officers. While he was there, it was announced from the stage that the German emissaries had signed the armistice terms and the guns would go silent on the morrow —at the eleventh hour of the eleventh day of the eleventh month of 1918. And, Donovan wrote to Ruth, "the house was in an uproar. All stood, the band played, and audience roared the Marseillaise."[13]

For Donovan, the war was over. Or was it? Was the armistice no more than an interlude in the long history of conflict between Teuton and Gaul? Those with long vision believed that was the question of that hour.

A week after the armistice took effect on November 11, 1918, Donovan wrote to Ruth: "I am so unsettled I don't feel like writing these days. I am keeping a few notes in my diary and will send it to you. Unsettled because I am going into a new job and my leg is in the way."[14]

Donovan's new work was in the department of the provost marshal general, responsible for law and order in the Army, still a military imperative. The Allies' association with Germany was only a cease-fire, not a peace. Consequently, all the Allied armies closed up to and established bridgeheads on the eastern bank of the Rhine, ready to occupy Germany if the Germans broke the armistice terms or if they resumed general warfare—a possibility that remained politically and militarily possible right up to the ratification of the Versailles Peace Treaty.

To the American fighting men, the issue was more simple: The war was over, it was time to go home, and if they could not go home, they were going to have fun in Paris. Thus, by the end of November 1918 discipline within many American units had broken down, and thousands of the men had taken to the roads, their pockets containing more money than most had had before, and most pointed themselves at Paris—and trouble.

Donovan's ability to command and influence soldiers, and his skill as a lawyer, attracted the attention of his old friend and commanding officer General H. H. Bandholtz, whom Pershing had appointed provost marshal general and who had arranged for Donovan to join him when he was fit for duty. But Donovan disliked the work intensely. Believing it the labor of policemen, not of lawyers and soldiers, he lobbied constantly to return to the Micks, and he explained to Ruth in a letter on November 11, 1918:

> Saw General Bandholtz again early this morning and I appealed to him to be relieved from the order to serve with him. I told him I wanted to stay with the regiment, that I had worked with it from the beginning, that now I could be of real service, and I wanted to stay. To all of this he replied that now that the armistice was signed all my reasons for serving with the regiment were of no force; that I could be of service in the new work; that with new conditions the office of Provost Marshal General was the big one in France; that he needed with him men of energy and intelligence; that no troops would be going home until peace anyway; that he wanted me to have charge of the organization, discipline and inspection of all the different organizations in all parts of the front; that if my work was complete at the time troops were being sent home he might see that I went with the division. This was to be considered not as a promise, but as a possibility. That in any event he had determined to have me and that was an end of it.

Then, suddenly and apparently inexplicably, Bandholtz agreed to return Donovan to his regiment. He arrived on Christmas Eve at Remagen on the Rhine, where the regiment was on occupation duty, and he wrote to Ruth about that first Christmas of the peace:

> . . . at 11:30 P.M. the band came to headquarters and from there, with me at the head of it, marched through the streets of this little town, playing "Onward Christian Soldiers" and "Adestis [sic] Fidelis." As we marched, the

men, Catholic, Jew, and Heretic came hurrying from their billets, and, forming behind, marched to church. The church is a large one—Romanesque in
style—and was impressively lit with many candles. Brown clad men were
everywhere, over flowing aisle and choir and chancel. All of them were neatly
dressed and wore their side arms. A platoon with rifles marched in and
formed about the altar, then the colors—now torn and faded—came in and
were placed at the altar rail. To me the sight was most impressive. Father
Duffy preached, the choir was good, the entire regiment sang the "Te
Deum," and one half hour after the services were over the entire city was
quiet.[15]

But what had occurred to make Bandholtz change his mind and return
Donovan to his regiment? The answer centered on the tall, lean, mystical
padre, Father Duffy, the moral theologian who throughout the campaign
performed an important role in the life of the regiment that was not
always strictly concerned with matters spiritual. The priest at the Church
of Our Saviour in The Bronx, New York, Duffy had acted as a recruiter,
the spiritual and welfare counselor, the regiment's historian, and the
main political force in the regiment, influencing appointments and promotions to make the regiment conform to his notion of what the ideology
of the 69th should be.

While at the end of the war the regiment was a mixture of racial and
religious strains drawn from every part of the United States, including
fifty full-blooded Indians, Duffy appears to have been determined that it
return to New York and a heroic welcome home under Irish Catholic
command as an Irish Catholic regiment. In pursuit of that objective he
was very energetic, for reasons that are not hard to guess. The American
Irish Catholic had long been considered inferior, and here was an opportunity not only to show that the Irish people and Catholic faith were as
vital as any other. Also here was an occasion to offer to the electorate a
crop of warriors that had proved their human worth on that hardest of
all places—the battlefield.

Thus, when Donovan was wounded, Duffy began to try to get him back
to the regiment as the principal Irish Catholic Praetorian—a man fairly
well connected socially and politically, fairly well-to-do, disciplined, devoted, trained, worthy, dependable, highly decorated, whose exploits
were now well known to every newspaper reader in New York State and
to many beyond—a man of *character militaris* worthy of the faith. Here was
a man of perhaps even presidential caliber, for as Duffy probably knew,
Donovan's name was being mentioned widely in New York as Republican
candidate for governor of the state in the 1920 general elections. Donovan himself would say in a letter to Ruth that he wanted no such post,
declaring that his task ahead would be to "try and qualify as your Governor—that is my job."[16]

Moreover, Duffy personally worshiped Donovan. He was to state, examining the joys and sorrows of regimental life: "In a very special degree I am going to miss Donovan." Donovan had made a reputation for "outstanding courage and keen military judgment," he was "a remarkable man," who was always:

> physically fit, always alert, ready to do without food, sleep, rest . . . thinking of nothing but the work in the hand. He has mind and manners and varied experience of life and resoluteness of purpose. He has kept himself clean and sane and whole for whatever adventure life might bring him, and he has come through this surpassing adventure [in France] with honor and fame. I like him for his alert mind and just views and ready wit, for his generous enthusiasms and his whole engaging personality. The richest gain I have gotten out of the war is the friendship of William J. Donovan.[17]

Since the priest bore this conviction of Donovan's moral superiority and the immense potential of his value to America, the Irish cause, and Catholicism, it is not surprising that he began to dislike the new regimental commander, Colonel Charles R. Howland, who had had no previous connection with the regiment. Sure that Howland was arranging matters so that WJD did not return to the regiment from hospital and that he, Howland, would take the regiment back to New York, Duffy began to lobby to ensure that this high honor would be Donovan's. Duffy knew that the homecoming would be a great event in the New York official calendar, with a parade up Fifth Avenue, a reception by the mayor, and the freedom of the city for the commanding officer of the regiment. Therefore, he wrote to Donovan in Paris: "What can you do to keep your fences up? This new man, I know, will drop your name from our rolls as soon as you are officially reported in Base Hosp.—Even though we are up against it for officers, esp. of Battalion size. I'm sick of littleness."[18]

Twelve days later he wrote again:

> Spite of everything, I think this fellow has put the skids under you. But Mag. Gen. McArthur [sic] was here this afternoon, and says he is going to get you back at once to the Division, where he will find something suited to your present strength. I hope you come, even on such terms. This fellow [Howland] is about as big as a pint pot. I don't know how he got by so far, and I think he will stub his toe yet, and you will go back as Col. of the old regiment. There is nobody that wouldn't welcome it, and it is worth taking a chance for. . . . [19]

What action Donovan himself took to get back to the regiment and to obtain its command is not at all clear. He saw Bandholtz regularly during November, asking to be returned to the regiment, and at some stage before November 20, 1918, Donovan saw a young second lieutenant with the regiment's headquarters company, Harold L. Allen, who warned him that Howland had given an order "that the names of all officers sick in hospital be dropped from the regimental rolls." The action had been taken to ensure that Donovan, Howland's principal rival, did not return to the regiment. Donovan then gave Allen a message to give to MacArthur, who was now back with the Rainbow. What the message said is not known, but it is a matter of record that a few days later Allen reported back to WJD that MacArthur had said "it would be wise for you to report to Division at once, where [MacArthur] was confident he would be able to retain you on light duty until such time as you could return to regiment."[20]

Late in November Donovan visited the regiment, as part of his provost marshal's duties, found its morale in a deplorable state, and felt that it was in danger of disintegrating. That fact was conveyed somehow to MacArthur, who, armed with that adverse report, relieved Howland and brought WJD back as a full colonel and commanding officer of the regiment effective February 15, 1919. With that order and that intrigue, the former trooper became a colonel and realized a dream he had had ever since boyhood, when he had been inspired by the lines of James Clarence Mangan:

'Twas there I first beheld, drawn up in file and line,
The brilliant Irish hosts; they came, the bravest of the brave.[21]

While Donovan was in Paris at a conference which led to the establishment of the American Legion—he was a principal organizer of that powerful and enduring group of defenders of the American faith, although he soon resigned his position in protest against the Legion's decision to try to obtain extraordinary benefits for veterans—Duffy began work to obtain for WJD the Congressional Medal of Honor, which, undoubtedly, he deserved richly. However, there was more to Duffy's purpose than a simple desire to see his friend properly recognized for heroism. If that medal could be obtained, Donovan would return the most decorated American officer of the war, for he had received already the Distinguished Service Medal, the Distinguished Service Cross, the Croix de Guerre, and several other foreign decorations and campaign medals. Thus the priest called upon those officers and men who had seen Donovan during the Kriemhilde battle to make affidavits concerning Donovan's conduct on the battlefield. A large number were forthcoming (copies have survived in the Donovan papers) and sent, probably by Duffy, to Major James A. Watson, the adjutant. On the basis of those affidavits Watson then prepared a memorandum for the adjutant general of the Army entitled "Lt. Col. William J. Donovan, 165th Inf., in relation of Medal of Honor,"[22] stating:

I have thoroughly investigated the affidavits of officers and enlisted men hereto attached and am of the opinion that [Donovan] should be awarded the Medal of Honor by reason of exceptional gallantry in action [at the Kriemhilde Fortress].

(a) That he has performed in action deeds of most distinguished personal bravery and self-sacrifice.

(b) Above and beyond the call of duty.

(c) So conspicuous as clearly to distinguish him for gallantry and intrepidity above his comrades.

(d) Which involved risk of life and the performance of more than ordinarily hazardous service.

(e) The omission of which would not justly have subjected him to censure for shortcoming or failure in the performance of his duty.

The paper was then sent to Washington, there were further investigations and inquiries, and a statement was made in WJD's favor by Pershing. There, until 1922, the matter rested. In any event, the decision to award the Medal of Honor would be made, and it would be awarded. But why the decision took so long cannot be explained, and the significance of the delay, if any, is not readily apparent. What is sure is that Pershing received the recommendation favorably and there was no dissent. Thus, it seemed almost certain that Donovan would receive the Medal of Honor when, on March 7, 1919, he received more momentous and gratifying news: The regiment would return home in April, and he would lead it. At the same time he dealt again with the rumors that he would be nominated for governor of New York on his arrival. "I think you would be a very attractive and gracious Lady Governor," he wrote. "But I'm sorry to disappoint you—It cannot be. As I have said before I want to be interested in public life but not hold public office—Not for me, dearest."[23]

So Wild Bill Donovan came home with the regiment aboard the troopship *Harrisonburg,* arriving off the Statue of Liberty on April 21, 1919. The regiment was greeted by flotillas of small ships carrying relatives, friends, and well-wishers, all of which escorted the *Harrisonburg* into Hoboken. Great crowds with bands playing gave the regiment a marvelous welcome which the New York *Herald* described in banner headlines: FIGHTING IRISH OF THE OLD 69TH COME HOME IN A GREAT STORM OF HURRAHS AND BLESSINGS.

Ruth was at the pier with David and Patricia to greet Donovan as he came off the ship, and all around was a mixture of joy, worship, triumph, and sadness—sadness because the regiment had suffered 3,501 casualties, almost the number that had sailed for France in November 1917. Of those, no fewer than 644 men had been killed in action.

The casualties were not forgotten that bright, windy, gay morning of April 28, 1919, when Donovan assembled the regiment by companies at

110th Street. All ranks were in steel helmets and ammunition boots and carried their personal weapons. Donovan elected to march at the head of the regiment, not ride, as was the custom. As he explained to his men about wearing their steel helmets: "They're not going to see your faces —but they'll never forget what you looked like."[24]

To the brave strains of "Garry Owen" and a marching version of "In the Good Old Summertime," the regiment began its march to City Hall to receive the Freedom of the city. The day was a public holiday, there were 1,200,000 people on Fifth Avenue, and among them was a special place for the regiment's crippled and blinded. The bands played American and Irish airs, and when the regiment reached the Gold Star mothers and the wounded, Donovan gave a ringing and moving command of salute.

At St. Patrick's Cathedral the archbishop of New York, Patrick Cardinal Hayes, stood on the reviewing stand with the Knights of Columbus and some 500 priests and 1,800 of the city's and the state's leading Catholics. Wearing clovers in their buttonholes, 6,000 policemen controlled the crowd, and in the aldermanic chamber at City Hall, where Donovan received the keys of the city, the mayor, John "Faithful" Hylan, addressed him and the regiment:

> Colonel Donovan: what you and the men of the 69th Regiment did under your command will be one of the brightest pages of our history. You are not only the idol of your regiment, but of all New York. Your courage and vigor in all the situations confronting the regiment are known to all of us. In congratulating you on your remarkable achievements, I know that I express the gratitude of every race as well as the Irish people in this great metropolis. What a glorious record the 69th has! History will tell of your gallantry and uncalculating indifference to life. . . .[25]

Hylan then spoke of a man and a regiment that had served in more battles and on more fronts than any other in the expeditionary force—Lunéville, Baccarat, Champagne, Château-Thierry, the Ourcq, St.-Mihiel, Argonne-Meuse, Sedan—and with the Army of the Rhine. The chamber gave the regiment and its commanding officer a standing ovation, the band played "The Star-Spangled Banner," and then the men marched away to civilian life to the dashing music of "Garry Owen." They marched into an uncertain future, where heroes were soon forgotten and in the end even the treasured records of ferocious battles, of honor worthy of the Immortals, became no more than paper dust. But Donovan never forgot. That night he and his brother, Vincent, motored out to Camp Mills to make sure that the men of the regiment staying there were comfortable. Having visited the men, having said good-bye to them, Donovan and his brother walked over to the 69th's old lines. They were deserted now, in darkness. Somewhere in the camp a group of men were singing "In the Good Old Summertime," a song that the regiment had roared out while marching up to the Ourcq and that never ceased to haunt Donovan's memories. WJD stood in the gloom for a long time, quite silent, listening to the song, and then he said to Vincent Donovan, "When I think of all the boys I have left behind me who died out of loyalty to me, it's too much."

Then he wept.

5

Saturn

When Donovan came home to Buffalo, he was in his thirty-seventh year and, with General Pershing and Sergeant York, one of the three great American heroes of the war. Aware of his fame and popularity, the Republican party sent his friend Senator James W. Wadsworth to offer him the Republican nomination for governor of New York in the 1920 elections—a nomination that was then a surer path to the presidency than now.

But Donovan was as good as his word to Ruth and his partners. He announced publicly and privately that he did not intend to enter public life. He bought a large Federal-style mansion at 810 West Ferry Street, complete with stables and grounds and close to Delaware Avenue, and rejoined O'Brian's law firm as a senior partner. He acquired a Stearns Knight and a chauffeur, and in dress and manner he seemed to become a member of the Buffalo upper bourgeoisie: five feet ten inches and slightly burly, a man in a dark suit with a gold chain at his waistcoat, a head of strong brown hair carefully brushed back, slightly overweight at about 180 pounds. In manner, he was still watchful and more reserved than he sometimes appeared to be, but he had an agreeable manner, a golden tongue, a nice sense of humor, and a pleasant speaking voice. In short, here was no courtroom thug, all histrionics, elbows, and bullying: Here was the silky charmer, quite deadly, the sort of fellow who knew how to get his way with the jury without bellowing.

First, however, he had to resume married life with Ruth. He had been away for three years, ever since he went off to Europe for Rockefeller early in 1916. As an act of reassurance WJD offered her a second honeymoon, which she accepted, and in June 1919 they left Buffalo for three months to visit the Orient. At the time they left WJD certainly meant well, but just as the outbreak of the war had upset their first years of marriage, so the Russian civil war and his interests in politics and foreign affairs were about to interfere with their lives again.

Donovan plainly felt strongly about Bolshevism at this time. A fragment of a speech by him at about this time shows his early attitude toward the Leninist Revolution:

> . . . the wrongs of the new tyranny have been infinitely worse than those of the old. No Tsar of modern times has ruled so autocratically as Lenin, nor so ruthlessly. Tsars restricted freedom of speech; Lenin abolished it. Tsars suppressed newspapers; Lenin allows none which opposes his views. Tsars put people to death for offenses which existed only in Russia; Lenin has massacred thousands against whom no charge has been brought. The people, he said, were not yet capable of distinguishing between truth and falsehood, so that authority had to decide what they might hear and what they might read.[1]

When the Donovans arrived in Tokyo, they were invited to spend a few days with the U.S. ambassador, Roland Morris, a distinguished lawyer and public servant—he was to become dean of the University of Pennsylvania Law School, regent of the Smithsonian, and trustee of Princeton, the Carnegie Foundation, and the Brookings Institution. Morris was about to leave for Omsk, capital of Russian Central Asia, with the commander in chief of U.S. forces at Vladivostok, General William S. Graves, their purpose to inspect and report on the government of Admiral Aleksandr Vasilyevich Kolchak, who had just appointed himself supreme ruler and commander in chief of all Russia in opposition to Lenin and Trotsky. Would Donovan care to come along and act as a military adviser? That was the end of the Donovans' second honeymoon. Ruth returned to Buffalo, and Donovan took the train to Omsk, to study what Winston Churchill was to call "this thin, cold, insubstantial conflict in the Realm of Dis."[2]

Donovan's fame as a soldier had preceded him, for, as he discovered, the ambassador's secretary, F. C. MacDonald, an assistant professor of English at Princeton, was spending those listless days writing an ode to the last days of Omsk. Donovan appears in the ode:

> What Irish field
> Gave out so rich a yield?
> Leinster nor Connaught grew such grain before;
> Nor Munster held such garner in her store.

Not the Red Branch
Bragged of a soul more staunch;
Nor Brien, crowned in Tara, ever gave
Heroic spoils of war to one so brave.

Boyne water, red,
Among the vanquished dead
Swept no such lover of life; nor the employ
Of wilder geese predestined Fontenoy.

"That's the heroic Donovan," wrote MacDonald as an afterthought in his diary. "Wearer of medals and crosses, now pottering here with notebooks, arguing with His Excellency, reasoning with the General, of great though peaceful service." MacDonald ended the ode to Donovan:

The fields of France
Know of his circumstance,
And war-worn ghosts, set loose at Saint Mihiel,
Come on clear nights his notable deeds to tell.[3]

The secretary of state was, however, less impressed by Donovan and his record. When, at the end of his three-week stay in Omsk, Donovan recommended that the United States provide Kolchak's army with arms and equipment for 600,000 men at a cost of $94,000,000, only silence greeted his recommendation.

By the end of October 1920, having reported to the State Department in Washington upon his return to the United States, Donovan was back in his chambers in Ellicott Square. He remained reasonably stationary at Buffalo for the next five months, to the surprise of his family and the relief of his partners. However, in February 1920 he landed one of the biggest clients on the planet, John Pierpont Morgan, of the House of Morgan, the leading investment bankers in New York.

Here, then, was WJD's first major excursion into the world of big business and its interrelationship with world politics. Donovan's business with Morgan was complex. Having helped finance the war, Morgan now wished to help finance the peace. Establishing the Foreign Commercial Corporation for that purpose, he proposed floating $2 billion worth of the securities of foreign governments and corporations and expanding the House of Morgan's interests widely, promoting mergers and acquiring corporations.

These activities required the best intelligence from the best sources in Europe, especially in England. Donovan and the Rainbow Division's intelligence officer, Grayson Murphy, had been retained through John Lord O'Brian's firm to obtain that intelligence, working in secrecy, for Morgan, like his father, disliked publicity. Morgan was particularly anxious to know whether Europe was going Red, as seemed possible at that time, and how the "new" nations established by the Versailles Treaty out of the ruins of the old Austro-Hungarian Empire—Poland, Czechoslovakia, Yugoslavia—were faring at a time when, as Winston Churchill was writing, "Appetites, passions, hopes, revenge, starvation, and anarchy ruled the hour."[4]

Morgan wished WJD also to pay special attention to the European reaction to the Communist International (Comintern), established on January 24, 1919, to act, proclaimed Lenin, as the "general staff" of the "World Revolution of the Proletariat" against the "rule of bankers and kings," promising the support of the Red Army for any revolution beyond Russia's frontiers. In other days Lenin's proclamation would have been dismissed as an addled nostrum, but in postwar Europe revolutions of the proletariat were a reality. All Europe was disordered. Russia, Germany, Britain, France, Italy, Hungary—almost everywhere there were revolutions or Red disturbances. The reaction of the right was correspondingly apprehensive. "Bolshevism," declared General Max Hoffmann, German commander on the eastern front during the October Revolution, "has ceased to be a regional problem and is now a world problem." Winston Churchill agreed, declaring soon after he became secretary for war and air that civilization was "being completely extinguished over gigantic areas, while Bolsheviks hop and caper like troops of ferocious baboons amid the ruins of cities and corpses of their victims."[5]

Because the times were plainly dangerous for capitalists, Morgan wanted good intelligence before making any plunges. In pursuit of that intelligence, Donovan spent eight months in Europe, returning only occasionally to New York and Buffalo for meetings with his principals. Working extensively through U.S. embassies and consulates and statesmen and politicians such as Churchill and Lloyd George of Britain, Clemenceau of France, Masaryk of Czechoslovakia, and Pilsudski of Poland, Donovan collected every fact he believed material. His files show a rare hunger for exotic intelligence: Herbert Hoover on Polish children's relief; Elihu Root, the U.S. statesman and Cabinet minister, on U.S. policy toward Soviet Russia in 1919; a statement by the last czarist ambassador to the United States, Konstantin Bakhmetiev, on industries of Russia; State Department reports on "The Service of Officers in the Red Army" and "The Inclination of the People to the Soviets Elective Management and the Principle of Equality"; "Comments on German Reparation Payments to Date"; a paper on "The Twelfth Congress of the Communistic Party, Which Is to Be Held in Moscow on 15th April"; Herbert Hoover on "American Relations to [sic] Russia"; a list of foreign loans issued in the United States in 1920; a review of H. G. Wells's book *Russia in the Shadows;* a copy of the diary of Mrs. Claire Sheridan, a British friend of

Leon Trotsky's; a memorandum on finance from the Organizing Committee of the Polish Industrial Credit Corporation; an article on the "sound financial policy" of Czechoslovakia in the Manchester *Guardian;* a U.S. consulate report on the political state of Silesia; reports by the *Times* of London on "Red Policy Towards Poland" and "War Threats as Diplomatic Weapons."[6] And so on and on by the volume. Donovan filled not just single files but scores.

If Aldous Huxley was correct to remark that curiosity is the essence of human intelligence, Donovan was amply endowed: He collected every shred of information he could obtain that might throw light on a problem. On the other hand, at this time in his life he kept little that would throw any light on himself. His diary for August 1920—at which time the Red Army was marching on Warsaw—consists of nothing but the libretto of the opera *Carmen* in Italian and English. His cashbook, which he kept for tax and expense account purposes, contained no entries whatsoever, except a list of books Donovan wanted to get when he returned to London. In some matters Donovan was secrecy and discretion personified. A case in point occurred while he was in Poland.

Only Donovan's mail shows that on August 13, 1920, he met in Warsaw with the Supervising Committee of the Polish Industrial Credit Corporation. What his mail does not show is that on that day the Red Army, which had invaded Poland in retaliation for a Polish invasion of the Ukraine, reached Radzymin, only fifteen miles from Warsaw. We do not know whether the meeting took place in an atmosphere of siege, whether artillery could be heard, whether there was panic in the streets, whether the city was being evacuated, whether General Maxime Weygand of the French General Staff was directing defensive operations, as indeed he was. All we know from WJD's papers was that among the subjects dealt with at his meeting with the Supervising Committee were the number of naphtha distilleries in Galicia and the fact that in 1912 Poland had exported 1,407,000 hectoliters of spirits and that the annual import of bicycles, motor and other vehicles, and musical instruments represented the sum of 31,850,000 francs.

In a few years, this peculiar characteristic—WJD's wizardry at being seen at a place but leaving no trace of his presence there—was to prove one of his most valuable assets.

Donovan's mission for Morgan ended in September 1920, and with his share of the "very comfortable fee"—some say $100,000, others $250,000—in the bank, he resigned his partnership with O'Brian on the friendliest of terms. With Bradley Goodyear and two other Saturn Club members—Frank Raichle, an outstanding young Buffalo trial lawyer, and Ganson Depew, nephew of the Republicans' principal kingmaker, Chauncey M. Depew—WJD established the firm of Donovan Goodyear Raichle & Depew. He set out to build what he firmly believed would be the greatest law firm in the world. "It was a wonderful experiment," Raichle remembered. "There was nothing formal about the partnership or Donovan's method of operating. He was a sage in some ways and naïve in others—a wonderful fellow, full of new ideas. But oh, he was extravagant! For instance, he came back from a meeting with rich clients with the idea that every partner should have a baronial fireplace and baronial doors. For weeks the workmen were in, making law impossible. Expense was never a consideration with Bill."[7]

But the partnership did not last long under Donovan. Suddenly and inexplicably, soon after founding his firm, WJD accepted a warrant from the President to become U.S. attorney for the Western District of New York, which included Buffalo. Donovan took a leave of absence from his firm and began the task of enforcing federal law in that troubled area of the United States.

When Donovan established his law office in Buffalo and then became a U.S. attorney, naturally Ruth hoped that at last the family would be together for more than a few months. It was now 1922, Ruth and Donovan had been married for eight years, and in that time WJD had not been at home for more than eighteen months without extended trips away. Ruth's roots were in Buffalo, particularly with the Genesee Valley Hunt, and the children were reaching an age when they needed their father at home. David, now seven, and Patricia, five, were especially delighted.

David Donovan recalled: "Father at home meant long walks on Sundays. Sometimes we would go exploring in the First Ward, around the railyards and firehouses, where my father seemed to know everyone. Sometimes we would go to the police stations, where my father seemed to know every detective in the city. And on other occasions my father would take us in the car to Lake Shore, while he went to a meeting with some of his informants on the beach—I can see him now, talking with a group of tough-looking men in the distance."[8]

Of all the laws that Donovan had to enforce in his district, the Volstead Act, or Prohibition, occupied most of his time. One of the most peculiar statutes—in both its conception and its consequences—it was a demonstration of the power of puritanism. Simply put, a large number of Americans believed that their compatriots were drinking too much alcohol and that this was affecting the moral fiber of the nation and must be stopped. The demand for such action had been in the background of American politics when the war created wider support for the movement. By 1917 Prohibitionists had succeeded in outlawing the sale, manufacture, and transportation of liquor in nineteen states. The demands of the war added weight to the arguments of moral and social reformers, who began to insist that Congress outlaw liquor throughout the United States in order to conserve food—and also as a patriotic act of condemnation of individuals of German extraction prominent in the brewing and distilling industries.

But from its conception as a major political force Prohibition became entangled in a wide variety of issues unconnected with drink and its effects, extremist politics and religious movements and zealotry of all descriptions. Its protagonists were, for example, closely connected with the anti-Catholic movement. The Volstead Act, named after Andrew Joseph Volstead, of Goodhue County, Minnesota, its begetter in the House of Representatives, was passed by Congress in 1919, was vetoed by President Wilson, was passed over the President's veto, and went into effect at midnight, January 16, 1920, at which hour America became;

> Dry as the bones of Moses,
> Dry as the Dead Sea Shore,
> Dry as the bunch of roses
> that Cleopatra wore.
> Dry as a kippered herring
> that never saw the sea. . . .[9]

If the effects of Prohibition had been confined to poetry, the era would have been a lot less gaudy than it was. The act divided the country as rarely before. There were the wets, who were usually drinkers and deplored the intrusion into their private affairs, and the drys, who vigorously and noisily defended the act as the instrument of a great moral crusade.

It now became Donovan's responsibility to see that the Prohibition law was obeyed. And although he himself was a lifelong teetotaler, he regarded his work as a crusade only insofar as it was his duty to enforce the laws of the land. That he did with energy and devotion. When the Volstead Act became law, he removed all liquors from his home, serving only a brew called near beer. So adamant was he, indeed, that although General Henri Gouraud, Donovan's commanding general on the Champagne front during the war, was known for his appreciation of wines and brandies, he got no liquor when he stayed with the Donovans at North Ferry Street in 1923.

Because of Buffalo's proximity to Canada, where no such law was in force and good liquor of every description was to be had in plenty, Donovan's law enforcement problems were more severe than in most other cities in the United States. On one hand, he had the local unlawful trade to deal with, a matter of complexity, for in the legal machinery set up for enforcement, a distinction had to be made between drinkable alcohol and commercial alcohol. Permits to make commercial alcohol, issuable by the government, became valuable—the more valuable in the cases in which the intent was to turn commercial into drinkable alcohol.

A similar distinction was made between ordinary wine and wine for sacramental use, and permits for wine to be used for communion were sought fraudulently by people whose interest was solely in temporal pleasures. On the other hand, the rumrunners coming in from Canada also kept Donovan awake at nights.

In all, Prohibition enforcement in Buffalo was a dangerous and exhausting business. Donovan's tactics were to capture the small fry running the speakeasies, the illegal cargoes of "dago red"—cheap red wine —on "Rum Row" between America and Canada, and the manufacturers of "orange blossom" and "night-scented stock"—bathtub gin and whiskey—and in return for immunity from prosecution make them reveal the identities of their principals. In turn, against the promise of lighter sentences, the principals were induced to reveal the major suppliers, customers, manufacturers, and shippers.

As Donovan's enforcers penetrated what were really secret societies, there were several threats to dynamite Donovan's home and and to assassinate him. But Donovan was unimpressed. He sent the family out to Walden Farm, the Rumsey estate on Lake Shore outside Buffalo, and continued to pursue his quarry relentlessly. As a result, the legal fraternity on the right side of the law was impressed by WJD's performance. One of them, Peter Bentley, later testified how in 1922, as counsel for the New York Central Railroad, he went to Buffalo to see if a federal criminal prosecution could terminate theft costing the railroad between $2,000,000 and $3,000,000 a year. He had tried before, and the "police department of the railroad, a number of agencies and the police of the City of Buffalo pretended to have endeavored to stop the robberies."[10]

The robberies did not stop, so Bentley went to see Donovan when he was appointed.

> ... within ten weeks after he took over his official office, thirty-six men were indicted, charged with having conspired to and having stolen large quantities of the goods mentioned from the company; ten of these men were convicted and sentenced to Atlanta Penitentiary for periods of from two to ten years. All ten of these men served their sentences until paroled or their terms expired by limitation of law. Of the remaining twenty-six, my recollection is that about sixteen pleaded guilty and the indictments against the remaining were dismissed. Among those indicted were approximately sixteen members of the police department of the New York Central. About ten were employed by the company in other departments.

During Donovan's connection with the case, reported Bentley:

> influence from many sources were [sic] brought to bear upon him to see if certain of the indicted defendants could not be released from prosecution. One man in particular who was captain of police of the company, and a

Catholic, used not only his friends but the church. I know that when the church appealed to Colonel Donovan that it received no consideration. As a matter of fact when one of the representatives of the highest standing in the community, of the church, approached Colonel Donovan on the subject of releasing this man, he was promptly shown the door and told never to return upon such a mission.

Friends of the defendant "even succeeded in having a domestic in the Colonel's house intercede." Donovan "asked the domestic what he ought to do if someone stole the money which the domestic had in a bank." The reply: "The Colonel should send the man to jail." Colonel Donovan "thereupon replied that that was what he was going to do to the man in question. This man was promptly convicted and sentenced to ten years in Atlanta."

In 1923 Bentley returned to Buffalo to represent the International Railway Company in a proposed criminal prosecution against the men responsible for having dynamited one of the company's trains.

> [The] county authorities in Erie County, the police of the City of Buffalo, and special police of the company had done virtually nothing with respect to a criminal prosecution. The dynamiting had taken place because of a labor controversy between the employees of the company and the company. As a result of the Colonel's activities, indictments were found, trials were held and all those defendants whom the Colonel prosecuted were promptly convicted. In this case I know that strenuous endeavors were made to induce Colonel Donovan to depart from his duty. I further know that the efforts had no effect.

A case involving the mayor of Buffalo, Frank X. Schwab, also attracted the attention of the new attorney general in Washington, Judge Harlan Fiske Stone, Donovan's mentor at Columbia. Schwab had just taken office when WJD became U.S. attorney, but Donovan endorsed the prosecution of a case that promised considerable political and social damage if he persisted. Schwab faced charges that while vice-president and general manager of the Buffalo Brewing Company, which existed to make near beer and liquid malt or wort for use by home brewers, he had broken the law. Donovan moved the case for trial and obtained a conviction. Schwab was fined $500 and incurred "civil penalties" totaling $10,000.

Donovan's triumph as U.S. attorney reawakened the Republicans' interest in him, and the inevitable occurred: Donovan at last (but reluctantly) accepted the party's wish to nominate him for lieutenant governor in New York State in the 1922 elections. The announcement was not welcomed by the wets, anti-Catholics, or, in general, the labor vote. But the nomination, which Donovan secured easily, was welcomed by the press, which reported generally, as did the White Plains *Reporter*, that "it is reasonable to believe that the people of New York will consider a military record such as his a decided assurance for complete fitness for the office he has been nominated for. Unless the people have a different viewpoint than what we would expect, they will . . . refuse to scrap his war record at the polls."[11]

But that is exactly what the electorate did do: It rejected Donovan. In this the question of the Medal of Honor, for which he had been recommended by Pershing back in early 1919, played its part. For reasons of sluggish bureaucracy, the decision to award the medal was not arrived at until 1922. To Donovan's embarrassment and annoyance the fact of the decision leaked out *before* the election, although no formal announcement was made, but his political enemies stated immediately that he and the party were using his Medal of Honor to gain political office. Although it was true that Donovan was not awarded the medal under the Democrats, but while a Republican administration was in office, the War Department did not announce that Donovan had been awarded the Medal of Honor until *after* the election.

While the investiture might have influenced the election, Donovan did not countenance this. To the contrary, he arranged that the presentation take place *after* the election at a ceremony at the 69th Infantry Armory at 68 Lexington Avenue, New York, on January 18, 1923. Nobly WJD declined to accept the medal for himself or his family, the first man to win the medal to do so, instead asking the regiment to allow him to:

> deposit with you the Congressional Medal of Honor which was presented to me tonight. This medal was truly won by our entire command at the Kriem-hilde-Stellung in front of Landres-St. Georges October 14–15, 1918—a fight as bitter and as gallant in the annals of the 69th New York as Marye's Heights at Fredericksburg December 13–14, 1862.
>
> A regiment lives by its tradition. The noble tradition we have inherited impels me to ask that this medal remain in the armory, there to serve as recognition of the valor of our regiment, as an incentive to those who enlist under its standard, but most of all as a memorial to our brave and unforgotten dead.

Not surprisingly, Donovan was bitter and angry that the medal had become a matter of party politics, for he had not played up the fact that he was to receive the medal with his family, his law partners, his political associates, and certainly not the electorate. To Donovan, the matter of the medal was sacred, and there it remained. But he had been defeated in his first election, and the reasons were more mundane than glory in battle. There had been a depression, the Republican party had become associated with repressive measures against the left, the state usually voted for a Democratic governor, and he had made small mistakes. He had used his mother-in-law's Delaware Avenue mansion as campaign headquarters at a time when there was a good deal of unemployment in Buffalo; the old controversy of the "Cossack" had come up; some Irish Catholics were jealous of him: In escaping from his class, something very few men managed to do in those days, Donovan had damned himself with the people he had left behind.

Donovan's reaction to his defeat is not clear from his records, but it is evident that his heart was not really in the campaign, and it is plain that at least some of the leaders of the legal community did not regard the defeat as serious. A prominent local lawyer, Hamilton Ward, wrote WJD after the polls:

> I was very much disappointed when you took the nomination for Lieutenant Governor, but now that you have done everything you could for the party, you are free to continue your professional development, and as one of your sincere well-wishers I shall watch this with much interest. We need more high-class lawyers here, and we have seen so many men, fitted to shine in that arduous field, lured away by business, social and political connections. . . . I wish you many years of this kind of life for which I believe you are in the way of becoming qualified.[12]

Donovan's response was interesting:

> I agree with you wholly as to the satisfaction that comes to a lawyer who really works at his profession. That, of course, is the only thing I have ever wanted to do. . . . I had no desire, in fact I absolutely declined, to go into this last fight . . . , but sometimes a man must make a sacrifice, and as soon as it was felt that it was necessary I should play some part, I was willing to do it. For selfish reasons I am glad not to be elected, for I want only to remain a lawyer.[13]

But was it true that all Donovan wanted to be was a lawyer? Or was Donovan, like so many lawyers, using the law as a means to obtain high political office? WJD was to tell William vanden Heuvel at the end of his career, when there was a debate about his becoming chief justice of the United States, that "it would be impossible for him even to consider the Court appointment." He had "no expanded notions about his lawyer's role—he has loved the love [sic], cherished it as a profession," but had "taken only the cases that interested him and continued living a broad life because he felt breadth of experience was equivalent to breadth as a lawyer."[14]

One of WJD's longtime law partners, Ralstone R. Irvine, agreed: "Donovan believed that a lawyer was equipped for public service, he believed that a lawyer had a duty to contribute some of his time to such service, and he encouraged his associates to do so as well. That is why he spent so much time away from the law. But of course, if public service brought with it high office, Donovan was not the sort of man to turn such service down."[15] Moreover, as Donovan confessed to a relative at about this time, his ambition was to become secretary of state.

That, in fact, is what Donovan did: He went back to being U.S. attorney in the short term, but in the long term he had a much more Byzantine future than law.

The Saturn Club stood (as it does in 1982) on Delaware Avenue, a flinty monument to Mammon. One of the first buildings in the United States to be designed as a club, it turned out to resemble, externally and internally, the town house of some late Victorian laird or industrialist in Glasgow or Edinburgh. Its walls were of old red brick and flint, with lots of granite here and there, mock battlements, flagstones on the floors of the corridors, winding stone staircases and some armor, turrets, lots of oak panels and beams and leaded windows. On the walls were heads of stags and a bear or two with yellow eyes, and in certain rooms were stuffed sailfish, swordfish, and salmon. There were several bars, a bullpen, a grillroom, potted plants, leather armchairs, and a large library that was rarely used, except for meetings of the club's officers—more men were said to have been blackballed there than had been there to borrow books.

As with most such clubs, then and now, women were admitted but not allowed to become members and were not allowed to remain after ten at night. Most often the members were either ancient worthies there to nap or to read the newspapers or muscular young Episcopalians of good birth in for squash, a swim, the steam, poker, and backgammon. The Saturn was also an institution much given to politics, racing, cards, business, and hunting and shooting talk. Surprisingly in upper-class Buffalo Jews were admitted—provided they were Sephardic in origin. Certainly most of its members regarded the Volstead Act as an instrument for the good of the poor and believed, therefore, they were not required to observe it. That was the cause of the collision between Donovan and the Saturn Club.

Donovan's law partner Frank Raichle, who was directly involved in the events that now occurred, later related that "during the summer of 1923 there was an extraordinary term of the United States district court and an extraordinary grand jury listening to liquor and dope violations. The routine way of handling those cases was to call in the bootlegger or the dope peddler, give him immunity, and force him under the cloak of that immunity to name his customers." In time "a rather prominent bootlegger was called before the grand jury, and in naming his customers he named the Saturn Club."[16]

For Donovan, that sworn testimony created a brief dilemma. All of Donovan's law partners—Raichle, Depew, and Goodyear—were active members of the club, Goodyear's father had been president, and Goodyear himself was at the time chairman of the house committee. Moreover, almost all of Donovan's friends, wartime associates, the Silk Stocking Boys, clients, city fathers, party leaders, in-laws and their friends and business associates were members.

Obviously he was not in a very enviable position. But Raichle stated: "He had warned the club about the illegal drinking going on there, especially in the grillroom and the men's locker room, and he did state that he would have to act if the drinking did not cease. Moreover, in my presence he told Goodyear that he expected one of his bootleggers would implicate the Saturn Club, and in that event there would have to be official action—there could not be one law for the poor and one for the rich. Bill expected, of course, that Goodyear would warn the club."

But if Goodyear did anything with the warning, the club did not. There was no abatement in either the dispensation or the consumption of liquor because, it was believed, "good old Bill would never raid his own club." There the club was in error. At Donovan's instructions, a search warrant was obtained. Alexander R. Griffin, of the Philadelphia *Record,* who was in Donovan's office at the time, heard WJD tell the local Prohibition enforcement officer and his team, who were also there: "Go ahead, boys. I've warned those fellows three times. For all their prestige, they [the club] are no better than East Side saloons."[17]

At about eight in the evening of August 23, 1923, Raichle was dining alone in the restaurant at the club when he saw Donovan's chief enforcer, a burly man notorious for knocking down doors, pass down the stone corridor in the direction of the locker room and the grillroom. Sensing a raid was about to take place, Raichle abandoned his dinner in some haste and left the club. When he had taken no more than a few steps down Delaware Avenue up drew a number of paddy wagons and police cars, and some thirty men hurried into the club, making for the grill and the locker room, where several members were playing checkers and dominoes and drinking whiskey and gin. They were made to stand in a group in a corner as the bartender was arrested, and, as Raichle recalled, "It then developed that various members of the club had what they called lockers at the back of the bar in which they had their private supplies of liquor. The raiders—that is the correct word to use—used sledgehammers and heavy-handed tactics and in some way or another a list of the members with lockers—a hundred eighteen in all, all of them prominent Buffalonians—was given to the newspapers. Well, you can imagine the interest and consternation that were stirred."

Raichle continued: "What happened next has to be fitted into the context of things as they were. Bill, war hero, great prosecutor, legend in his own time, married to wealth, enjoying a social position some thought he didn't deserve—that divided the city into two camps as it had been rarely divided before. There was a snobbery about him, of course, because he came from a poor side of town, and . . . with this background, with his attractive personality, with his success, he created jealousies."

Raichle went on: "When the Saturn Club episode took place, all the people who were jealous of him, men and women, and there were a lot of women who saw in him what they wished they saw in their husbands, came from under the stones and started to hiss at him. You would not believe the anger and the divisiveness that the confounded raid caused. A delegation called on me from the Saturn Club and told me—and I was then twenty-three or twenty-four—that if I didn't repudiate Bill and leave the firm, then I would never be spoken to at the club again and would never get anywhere as a lawyer. I am not trying to pose as a hero for telling them to go to hell, but that is what I told them. Some of them threatened me physically, and I had two bouts of fisticuffs in the club, one with the town's leading gynecologist, the other with a prominent land-owner, for calling me a bastard and Bill a common mick."

Almost all the most famous names of Delaware Avenue were implicated in the raid. From their lockers, those of their associates, and the club the enforcers confiscated a total of twelve quarts of whiskey, twenty quarts of gin, twenty-three bottles of champagne, five gallons of grain alcohol, and three gallons of miscellaneous alcoholic drinks, such as sloe gin, elder-berry wine, peach brandy, and tequila. "The law is the law and I have sworn to uphold it," Donovan replied when angry members telephoned him at home—contrary to stories that he directed the raid personally, he was at home that evening—to protest. And as the enforcers lugged the liquor out to the paddy wagons, taking the bartender with them, an official of the club, George A. Mitchell, announced to the reporters who had arrived with the federal officers, "The liquor seized by the federal men has evidently been smuggled in by bootlegging employees of the club. The Saturn Club would not countenance the sale of liquors on its premises. As for liquor found in the lockers of members, that is their own affair. The lockers are private property."[18] Mitchell then wrote out a $2,000 personal check with which to pay the bartender's bail.

By midnight that night Donovan's name, once so respected, was being denounced by one end of Delaware Avenue to the other, including his in-laws, the Rumseys. Donovan was unmoved by the rumpus. "I can only say that the Saturn Club's case," he told a reporter on his doorstep, "will be treated in the same manner as any like liquor case." Asked whether he intended resigning from the club, Donovan declared that he saw no reason to deprive himself of the convenience and pleasures of the club simply because some had used it to violate the law—and in fact, Donovan was not blackballed, nor did he resign, remaining a member of the club for many years after.

The next morning, however, there was an unhappy scene at the offices of Donovan, Goodyear, Raichle & Depew in which "very bitterly"[19] Goodyear withdrew from the firm, permanently destroying a friendship Donovan had valued, Goodyear's point being that Donovan should have resigned from the club upon becoming U.S. attorney—a point not without value.

Dexter Rumsey, who deplored the entire affair, maintaining that Donovan should have warned the club the raid was imminent, wandered about glumly, refusing to speak to him. But Mrs. Rumsey took Donovan's side in the argument raging throughout Buffalo society, declaring "Bill has only done his duty."[20] And soon the friendship between Donovan and his brother-in-law was restored.

Although Donovan and Ruth were widely ostracized along Delaware Avenue, Donovan nevertheless prosecuted the Saturn Club, which pleaded guilty as charged and was fined $500. No charges, however, were were brought against any of the 118 members found to have had liquor in their lockers.

Looking back on the entire affair, Raichle assessed the effect of the incident on Donovan's political career: "Bill was a many-sided person, well read, culturally developed, interested in everything and everybody, and my own opinion is that the episode was was not the fault of the mind or the heart, but a misadventure, a case of a fellow simply doing his duty, and with the benefit of hindsight I would have said that the mistake he made was not resigning as a member when he was made U.S. attorney. I do not subscribe to the belief that the incident ruined his political career. I think the incident did him a lot of harm locally but after all, a lot of it was inspired by jealousy, by a lot of people just waiting for him to miss a step."

Meanwhile, the Teapot Dome scandal had broken in Washington, President Warren Harding had died suddenly, his attorney general was implicated in the scandal, and the new President, Calvin Coolidge, had replaced him with Donovan's mentor at Columbia, Harlan Fiske Stone. Immediately Stone asked Donovan to accept the post of assistant attorney general, his main task being to help clean up the mess in the Department of Justice and the Bureau of Investigation.

On August 12, 1924, Donovan's appointment was announced. His salary would be $7,500, a severe reduction in the compensation to which he had become accustomed. However, WJD could not take up his duties immediately, for the Ku Klux Klan was challenging the appointment of Catholics and others to government posts. Although the Klan's objections did not change the situation, and Donovan's appointment was confirmed by Congress, he did not take the oath of office until January 30, 1925, four months later. During that period, the idea of a large international law firm now abandoned, Donovan took Ruth for a holiday in Egypt and Greece. On their return they packed for Washington. The

Buffalo Council of Churches marked Donovan's departure with a luminous testimony:

> The departure of Colonel Donovan for Washington will mean a real loss to
> Buffalo. . . . No man in public life in this city is held in higher regard than
> he. His record is marked by honest dealing and high efficiency. . . . His official
> life in Buffalo has left its influence upon the city. His love of fair play, loyalty
> in the cause of law enforcement and genuine esteem for all men of honorable
> purpose regardless of class or creed, these characteristics have impressed all
> of us who have had dealings with his office. Whatever else the people of
> Buffalo may say . . . , the unanimous word will be "There goes a man.
> . . ." The Department of Justice in Washington is to be congratulated upon
> obtaining a man of such character and ability.[21]

It was noticeable that all the columnists speculated whether, as the
Hamburg *Independent* put it, "the stern daughter of the voice of God" had
summoned "one of Western New York's strongest men" and placed him
on his way to the presidency.[22]

6

Joining the Federal Crowd

Donovan was forty-two when he arrived in Washington in 1925. So far he had had a remarkable run: He had escaped the First Ward; he had become a "high-class lawyer"; he had made powerful friends; he had become an authentic American war hero; he had become the colonel of a famous regiment; he had won America's highest medal for bravery; he had risen fast in the Republican party; he had shown himself to be a fearless and successful federal attorney; he had become an accepted member of one of the sturdiest branches of the Protestant financial aristocracy of America; he had been a member of a presidential mission to Russia; he had successfully carried out an important confidential mission for a major international banking figure. And now, so it seemed, the knight-errant was at the portcullis of that citadel of supreme political power, the White House.

Almost immediately Ruth began to keep a diary, which she continued almost every day for the next half century, a document that served as a spoor for the movements of her elusive husband and also became an interesting testament not only to Donovan's activities but also to some of the inner workings of the financial and political power centers of the United States. Her first entry reflected her earliest reaction to Washington, which amused her but which she did not like, at that time or later:

> Made all my calls on the Cabinet ladies—Mrs. Wilbur the only one in—She is the wife of the Secretary of the Navy—their house very dingy and shabby —and down at the heels—the colored servant sloppy and her toes coming

right out of her shoes—Mrs. Wilbur most unattractive. Looks like a school-marm from some one-horse town—Graying hair with a rat under it I am sure —Glasses with a gold chain, large nose and as she told Bill at luncheon she couldn't eat very fast as she had false teeth—Very proud of her husband apparently. We hear he is doing very well. . . . At one time he seemed hopeless.[1]

Donovan had met President Coolidge, but not socially, when at about six o'clock on Saturday evening, January 24, 1925, immediately after their arrival in the capital, a messenger arrived with a note from the President and Mrs. Coolidge. The Donovans were invited to spend a night aboard the presidential yacht, *Mayflower,* cruising on the Potomac and Chesapeake Bay. Donovan accepted immediately, for, as Ruth recorded with some satisfaction, "An invitation from the President is in reality a command."

The Donovans arrived at the pier in Washington at 12:30 P.M. sharp on Sunday and went on board to find they were part of a party that included Solicitor General Beck and his wife, Assistant Secretary of the Navy and Mrs. Robinson, and C. Carroll Glover, president of the Riggs Bank, and his wife, Marion—who were so wealthy that in 1924 they presented the District of Columbia with 125 acres of woods in the most valuable real estate section of Washington, to serve as a park and nature walk in the center of the city. Ruth and Marion Glover were to become lifelong friends as a result of this meeting. Ruth wrote in her diary:

The President and Mrs. Coolidge arrived shortly amidst bugles and "The Star-Spangled Banner"—they were very cordial and we stood around talking for a time while the *Mayflower* left the pier and made for the river—Presently the President announced luncheon would be ready in fifteen minutes and disappeared. Mrs. C. said she was going to take her hat off and we other ladies could do as we pleased. . . . It was a very gay luncheon. . . . During luncheon as we passed Mount Vernon all went on deck—Taps sounded from the shore and the band on board played "The Star-Spangled Banner." . . . Mrs. C. very nicely switched the ladies about at dinner so that Mrs. Glover and I sat next to the P—He isn't easy to talk to but not so difficult as I suspected and we got along fairly well. After dinner there was a movie performance, Pathé News and all. The play was an old one called *Charlie's Aunt.* Very amusing and quite silly—the P chuckled all thro' it. . . .

The early invitation of the Donovans to the *Mayflower* did not go unno-ticed by the press corps or by those in the power circle. Donovan had been accepted into what was called locally the Federal Crowd, a group whose success had been due largely to presidential favor. If Donovan was ambitious politically, then that preferment was important, for after the Saturn Club raid he had little influence with the Republican machine in his own state.

At first the Donovans lived in a rented house on Hillyard Place, just at the back of Dupont Circle, but soon WJD purchased one of the most handsome private houses in Washington, Walter Lippmann's old home away from home, fourteen rooms, stables, and grounds in Georgetown at 1647 Thirtieth Street, NW. That meant permanency and ambition. And as Ruth Donovan recorded of a conversation she had with her host, Senator David Aiken Reed, of Pennsylvania, during a dinner on the twenty-eighth: "[Reed] has a grand idea that he is going to influence the President to put Bill in as Attorney General. He predicts that within a year Bill will be in the Cabinet due, of course, to his effort entirely. . . ."

Such speculation became fevered when the President and Mrs. Coolidge sent the Donovans a second social invitation in one week, this time to an intimate musicale at the White House. In all, the Donovans were invited to social events at the White House or aboard the yacht no fewer than six times in their first month in the capital. As time would show, these invitations did not arise because the Donovans were new faces in a familiar scene; they continued to be constant guests at the White House throughout the Coolidge presidency, with Ruth there almost as often as her husband, pouring tea for the First Lady. As the socially prominent Washington writer William Hard told Ruth at a dinner party given a few nights after their arrival, Donovan's "charm and personality will conquer Washington."[2]

In examining Coolidge's appointments following Teapot Dome, the press noted that Donovan worked hard. Henry Pringle, in a later critical portrait of Donovan, observed:

> He has extraordinary vitality and can work on a brief until midnight, read for diversion until 3 o'clock in the morning and then be down, fresh and smiling, for a breakfast conference five hours later. . . . Most important of all, perhaps, is Donovan's very real ability as an attorney. Even his envious critics admit that he knows his law and he demonstrates this by appearing before the Supreme Court himself, to argue cases for the government.[3]

Inevitably the marriage between a poor Irish Catholic boy and the rich Protestant landlord's daughter attracted much attention. On the question of the differences in faith, there were problems, although they were temporary. Father Vincent Donovan, now wearing the habit of a Dominican, did attempt to convert Ruth, submitting her to what he called "lectures," long letters devoted to the higher purposes of Catholicism tinctured with thoughts about such divine mysteries as hell and eternal life. The title of one lecture, which survives in the Donovan papers, describes them all: "I Believe in God the Father Almighty, Creator of Heaven and Earth."[4] These lectures ended while the Donovans were in Washington, probably because Donovan believed that conversion was a personal decision, not a matter for the Propaganda Fide. Ruth remained a leisurely Protestant.

More difficult for Ruth was Donovan's predilection for travel. To those outside, the Donovans' seemed to be a marriage on wheels, in which they were constantly in a train, a motorcar, or, soon, an airplane. Ruth's diary tells an extraordinary story of incessant arriving and departing, of Bill and Ruth's meeting briefly and then proceeding. They show Donovan, then as later, unusually restless, rushing off at all hours of the day and night to near and distant parts on government and party business. Ruth herself was also in a form of perpetual motion among the four homes they established during their Washington years: the Georgetown house, their mansion flat in New York at 1 Beekman Place, their summer residence at Nonquitt on Cape Cod, and their country residence in the Virginia horse country.

Moreover, after the first few weeks in Washington they began not to appear in public together, except when attending politically important functions such as those at the White House, those given by the Republican party chairman, Senator William D. Butler, those given by the Glovers, and those of such eminences as Alice Roosevelt Longworth (Teddy Roosevelt's daughter and the wife of Nicholas Longworth, the speaker of the House for many years), and Secretary of Commerce Herbert Hoover, who took an interest in Donovan's career.

What few could understand was that while there was undoubtedly mutual love and esteem in the marriage, by fate and temperament with WJD his career always came first. Ruth was a slave to WJD's duty, whatever it was, throughout their marriage. However, she remained as devoted to Bill Donovan as on the day she married him. As for Donovan, it was inconceivable to the Washington eyes and ears that he was absolutely faithful to Ruth. Yet he was so. He was extremely attentive, especially when she was not well, and telephoned from the four quarters of the globe in a day when a telephone was an instrument of adventure. He was forever buying his wife expensive presents—a Lincoln touring car on one birthday, a mink coat on another—and remembered her birthdays and their wedding anniversaries. He always zoomed (an excellent word for Donovan in motion) in for the family's traditional Christmas Day gathering on Delaware Avenue, but he invariably zoomed out again on Christmas night. Yet they were very separate people, and for Ruth there was a terrible price to pay for that separateness.

She expected more from her marriage than Donovan could ever give her, and one of the things she needed evidently was companionship. When she was deprived of it, she became convinced that she had all manner of illnesses, she was forever "tired" or "discouraged," and for years she complained to her diary about colds and sinus pains. And her fear of some grave illness became complicated by the return of an actual medical condition—a recurrence of trouble she had had at Patricia's birth just before Donovan went to France in 1917—in which Ruth developed a real, painful, and sometimes disabling gynecological complaint.

The affliction became so serious that the only permanent relief lay in surgery, which she wanted to resist for as long as possible. This knowledge, combined with her need for companionship, led her into a close relationship with WJD's brother Timothy, now a leading surgeon in Buffalo, a bachelor, and a handsome and sympathetic man. In time Timothy became Ruth's surgeon, physician, counselor, and companion. More than that he was not, but as Frank Raichle was to say, "They saw a great deal of each other—more than was good for them really. At times Ruth saw more of Timothy than she did Bill. Of course, Donovan's political enemies made the worst of the association, but it was all very platonic, and but for Timothy she would have been sicker than she was. In some odd way Tim kept that marriage together."[5]

That was fortunate for Donovan, for he was soon to find that the political muggers were waiting for him outside his yard.

From the moment Donovan took his oath of office on January 30, 1925, the Washington press corps never ceased to speculate on his political aptitude and future. The New York *World*'s observations on August 10, 1925, were fairly typical. Noting that Governor Alfred E. "Al" Smith, of New York, a Catholic and a wet, was, "with his great personal popularity and his presidential possibilities," a "menacing figure in the Republican councils," the correspondent felt that President Coolidge and the chairman of the Republican National Committee, William D. Butler, were watching Donovan's performance closely and Donovan's high office, "with the Administration backing him, would not be a surprising thing." Donovan himself said very little about his political ambitions, indicating only that he would be honored if one day he became attorney general. However, toward the end of the Coolidge administration there were signs that his ambition had changed, for he confided in a sympathetic and trusted aunt that he would clearly love to become secretary of state—a confession that, given Donovan's interest in foreign affairs, may well have been the truth of his ambitions. For it was the press, not WJD, which saw Donovan as a future President.

Donovan certainly acted as if he intended to remain and succeed in Washington. Judge Harlan Fiske Stone did not remain long as attorney general, being replaced by John Garibaldi Sargent, "a fine old Yankee lawyer from a small country town more or less bewildered by the executive vastness of his job."[6] Donovan's title was somewhat unusual—he was known as first assistant to the attorney general—but he was, in fact, Sargent's deputy at the Department of Justice. Moreover, since Sargent was often absent—he was not a fit man, he disliked Washington and stayed away as often as he could, and even when he was in the city, he is said to have spent much of his time at the White House, playing poker with Coolidge—Donovan was soon made the acting attorney general. But because of the delays in the Senate over his confirmation, Donovan played little part in the work for which Stone had intended him—helping clean up the Department of Justice and the Bureau of Investigation after Teapot Dome. Stone and his team had had almost a year at that task by the time Donovan started work. But to his cost Donovan did become involved in an aftermath of the Harding government scandals. This matter concerned Senator Burton K. Wheeler, Democrat, of Montana.

Wheeler, who was a year older than Donovan, had been a lawyer at Butte, Montana, and a member of the state legislature, and in 1913 he had been appointed U.S. attorney by President Woodrow Wilson. Shortly after his arrival in Washington as senator, Wheeler began to allege on the Senate floor that the Department of Justice was corrupt, allegations that had much substance. The Republican National Committee retaliated with charges, provided by the Bureau of Investigation, that as U.S. attorney Wheeler had permitted Montana to become "a hotbed of treason and sedition."[7]

Wheeler mounted a successful demand for a Senate investigation of the Justice Department, and in response the attorney general in the Harding administration, Harry M. Daugherty, managed to arrange matters so that a federal grand jury in Montana brought an indictment against Wheeler, alleging that he had used his influence to obtain oil and gas leases for a prospector who was a friend and a client.

All this occurred even before Donovan was invited to Washington by Stone. The case was still awaiting trial when Stone arrived to replace Attorney General Daugherty, whose resignation had been demanded by President Coolidge. Daugherty was later prosecuted for engaging in a conspiracy to defraud the U.S. government, along with three other Cabinet officers in the Harding government.

Having taken up his duties as attorney general, Stone examined Daugherty's case against Wheeler and decided that there was a case to pursue. When WJD arrived and saw the file, he, too, decided that the indictment was justified. On that basis the trial proceeded at Butte, Montana. Wheeler was acquitted.

Wheeler then returned to Washington in an angry and bitter mood. He insisted that Daugherty had rigged the evidence in an effort to head off the Senate investigation of the Justice Department and that by their actions Stone and Donovan had become party to the original conspiracy to discredit him. From this point until Wheeler left the Senate in 1947, he became Donovan's main antagonist on the Hill. For part of that time he was supported by a powerful and influential Democrat, Senator Thomas J. Walsh, also of Montana. Since an important Democratic cabal formed around the two Montanans during WJD's stay in Washington, Donovan was to find the group a block to his aspirations to the office of attorney general. Later Wheeler never ceased to attack Donovan when he became Roosevelt's intelligence master in July 1941, becoming an obstacle to all of Donovan's plans throughout WJD's Washington career.

Donovan had made his first important enemy in Washington.

By the time Donovan arrived as assistant attorney general Stone had already supported the recommendation that J. Edgar Hoover be appointed to replace William J. Burns as director of the Federal Bureau of Investigation. Donovan's only relationship with Hoover was, therefore, to supervise and report on Hoover's work before the latter's appointment was confirmed. Hoover is said to have found Donovan's surveillance of his work onerous and to have resented Donovan's using the FBI's lawyers for Justice Department tasks, but the best and the worst that can be said of their relationship at the time was that it was one of master and servant. The severe problems in their relationship did not develop until the Second World War. But then the trouble stemmed not from anything that had been done or said during these early years, but from rivalries that developed when FDR decided to revolutionize the intelligence services of the United States.

In any case, Hoover could not have been displeased, for apparently without reservation Donovan recommended to John Garibaldi Sargent that Hoover's appointment be confirmed. But they were never intimates, and indeed, they seem never even to have lunched together. Yet Donovan was to find later that he had yet another adder at his ankles.

On March 1, 1925, Donovan turned over control of the Criminal Division to a subordinate and took charge of the Antitrust Division. In this work Donovan—who had almost flunked law school—was to become the foremost appellate lawyer of his time. That accomplishment notwithstanding, his conduct of affairs in the Antitrust Division was to be seriously challenged by the man who, from 1925 to 1929, was a close friend and supporter, Herbert Hoover.

Of all of Donovan's work until this time, his activities as head of the Antitrust Division made him at once one of the most powerful and controversial figures in national and international commerce. The reason for this controversy was the nature of the antitrust laws. Introduced in 1890 and supplemented in 1914, the laws were intended to prevent and make unlawful the concentration of economic power in the hands of small groups of individuals called trusts or, in Europe, cartels, for the purpose of enriching or extending the power of the heads of the trusts. The laws were, and remain, a major factor in American economic ideology since they acted, as they were intended to act, as a brake on the abuses of capitalism and to encourage competition in industry.

Their enforcement was in Donovan's time, as now, nationwide business. The preparation of a case was usually complicated and time-consuming, ranging from several months to years. The policy of the Antitrust Division usually being set by the President, the head of the division could adopt one of two policies: He could prosecute the laws vigorously, in which case he would need a large budget and staff; or he could prosecute them without vigor, a policy that would often earn him the gratitude of industry and would require only a small budget and staff. If he pursued the former course, the official usually earned the reputation of being tough on big business; if he pursued the latter, he was soft on big business.

In the case of WJD, to his sorrow, Herbert Hoover later asserted that Donovan's administration of the antitrust laws had been "very bad." By that statement Hoover meant that he had been "soft" on big business, a politically damaging charge at a time when big business was held widely in disrepute and suspicion. The accusation was the more important since it became a factor in Donovan's candidacy for the office of attorney general of the United States in Herbert Hoover's Cabinet. Thus, Donovan's conduct at Antitrust requires more detailed examination, for not only was it the cause of a serious political conflagration at the time, but also it was to contain most of the elements of Donovan's triumph and tragedy in politics. Also, the examination will show where Donovan stood on the perennial question of whether he was the guardian of law and order or the agent of big business at a troubled time in the commercial and social history of the United States.

To help examine Hoover's accusation and the record, Donovan's assistant in the Antitrust Division, Ralstone R. Irvine, later head of Donovan's law firm and one of America's leading antitrust lawyers, prepared a paper entitled "Do the Facts Support the Charge of President Hoover?" Irvine recalled that it was the policy of the Coolidge administration, which Donovan served, "to cooperate with big business and deemphasize politically motivated antitrust action," and that this policy faced Donovan "at every step."[8]

For that reason, Donovan's budget in Antitrust was little more than nominal, or as Irvine put it, "the amounts appropriated by the Congress for the Antitrust Division were woefully inadequate." For fiscal year 1927 Congress allocated $200,000, of which $194,300 was used, and for fiscal year 1928 the amount appropriated had shrunk to $198,000, of which $179,866.48 was used. Irvine maintained that Donovan tried to obtain larger funding to permit more vigorous enforcement of the antitrust laws, but the funds were not granted. And the appropriations that he did receive were in "marked contrast" with those for 1978 and 1979, when $46,377,000 and $48,592,000 were allocated. The reality was, therefore, that Donovan did not have sufficient funds to prosecute five major antitrust cases during his four years in office, let alone the number that he did in fact prosecute—thirteen times that number.

Faced with the dilemma of high operating costs, on the one hand, and a low budget, on the other, "Donovan was forced to reduce the costs of operating the department." He took "many steps to that end." Among them "he transferred to other divisions of the Department of Justice highly paid antitrust lawyers and replaced them with young lawyers, some just out of law school, whose salaries ranged from $1,800 to $6,500 per year." Also, according to Irvine, Donovan was able to act more effectively only as a result of an arrangement with the director of the FBI, J. Edgar Hoover, who was handsomely funded and could therefore afford to permit Donovan to use FBI agents—all of whom were trained lawyers—for antitrust investigations. At the same time, to obtain the maximum result from the resources at his disposal, Donovan made it an act of policy only to investigate those cases where the evidence indicated clear violations of the law. As Irvine was to claim, with these and other economies Donovan was "able to survive and to make a record of vigorous enforcements."

During his four years as head of the Antitrust Division, the reports of the attorney general show, Donovan brought sixty-five cases, rather more than his predecessor, Augustus T. Seymour, and far more than his successor, John Lord O'Brian. This suggests that Donovan was less devoted to the interests of big business and more concerned with the responsibilities of his office. This view is supported by several other facts. In each year of office the fines secured against violators always exceeded Donvan's total budget; and of the total number of cases Donovan instituted, twenty-two were criminal, thus rendering the defendants liable to prison, while the others were "civil cases seeking equitable relief." Also, almost all cases involved major corporations in prolonged and expensive litigation and, in the majority of convictions, in heavy fines. Donovan was personally active in the investigation, trial, and appeal of these and other cases of significance.

At the same time, during his tenure Donovan argued "a substantial [certainly six and possibly eight] number" of antitrust cases before the Supreme Court. That was a remarkable record. Most lawyers never argued one case before the Supreme Court, let alone six or eight in four years and before the advocate was fifty. Moreover, while head of the Antitrust Division Donovan won all his cases, another record that probably has not been emulated, and most of them made what is known as landmark law.

At all times antitrust cases were, and are, cases of great complexity and importance not only to the participants but also to the country. The advocate had to be thoroughly familiar not only with the law but also with the records of the case in the lower courts, which always ran to hundreds of pages and frequently to thousands. Such comprehension cannot be delegated to an assistant, for the advocate must have every fact, every argument, every aspect of the law at his own fingertips. Moreover, only the leader—in this instance, Donovan—must rise with all his facts and arguments assembled.

Thus, each Supreme Court case may be considered a lawyer's supreme mental—and physical—test, especially if he succeeds. But there is more than this. The lawyer must hold the attention of the justices. To do that, he must know his law, he must be intellectually honest, he must be aware of the facts and the precedents; and it is no disadvantage if the advocate is both impressive in appearance and gifted in diction and delivery. For while cases have rarely, if ever, been won through oratory, they have been lost because of their lack of it—failure of the advocate to make his points clearly, simply, comprehensively.

In his arguments, Donovan practiced Machiavelli's dictum: Enemies should be either annihilated or conciliated. It will be recalled that he took elocution lessons as a youngster and that he had some experience as an actor; he therefore knew the power of the spoken word. He had a heroic background, and he was physically impressive, appearing in well-cut morning dress, giving the impression of his being at once cultured, implacable, competent, worth studying carefully. He filled the court with his presence, conveying to all the impression that here was no loutish provincial lawyer, but a gentleman of great powers. He always spoke quietly, gently—but not so softly that the justices could not hear him. Irvine was never able to recall an instance in which WJD raised his voice, anywhere, let alone before the Court. Every word was beautifully produced. There was no hesitancy, no rustling of papers, no searching for phrases. And he knew the value of theater: His main point was always a single point, clearly expressed, incontrovertible. He knew the value of stately pauses as each point, having been delivered, was given the chance to impregnate the minds of the justices. His arguments were never without light and shade, wryly amusing passages, solemn phrases. Invariably Donovan held the attention of the justices, who did not fidget or interrupt. They were usually enraptured by the silver music of this short, powerfully built, ruddy Irish-American's tongue.

But what of the content of these addresses? Did they justify Hoover's contention that Donovan was soft on big business? Donovan appeared in two cases in 1926 and 1927, and his conduct of both seems to indicate that he was his own man. The first was a landmark case, *Trenton Potteries et al.* v. *United States.* Donovan was opposed by two leading members of the Supreme Court bar. The argument was made for the defendants by Charles Evans Hughes, at one time Republican nominee for the presidency and later chief justice of the United States. On the brief for the defendants were Hughes and George Wharton Pepper, nationally esteemed as an appellate lawyer. Despite the great abilities of counsel for the defendants, the Court adopted WJD's views as the fact and the law. Thus, the Trenton Potteries case was of particular importance, for as Donovan stated in his report to the attorney general, a "question long controverted was finally determined." The decision in favor of the government "added strength to the enforcement of the Sherman law [Antitrust Act of 1890] in that it held that an agreement of those controlling over 80 per cent of the business of manufacturing and distributing sanitary pottery in the United States to fix and maintain uniform prices violates the Sherman law, and that this is so whether the prices in themselves are unreasonable."[9]

But in the political context perhaps the 1927 case, *Swift & Company* v. *United States,* was the more significant. Swift & Company had sued the United States, asking to be relieved from the provisions of an antitrust consent decree which imposed drastic restrictions on its future growth and competitive practices. If, in fact, Donovan was "easy" on big business, it would have been expected that this case would have been settled by compromise. But no compromise was effected. Instead, the Supreme Court adopted Donovan's argument that the decree should remain valid and enforceable.

Similarly the other four Supreme Court cases which Donovan argued while at the Department of Justice displayed consideration for the law rather than partiality for big business. They were:

§ *United States* v. *Sisal Sales Corporation,* dealing with the law concerning international cartels.

§ *Arthur C. Brown* v. *United States,* a leading case on the proper scope under the Constitution of a grand jury subpoena.

§ *United States* v. *Journeymen Stone Cutters Association of North America et al.,* dealing with a combination of management and labor to restrict the use within the city of New York of cast stone made in other states.

§ *United States* v. *Goldman et al.,* involving criminal contempt committed by violation of an injunction under the antitrust laws and holding that such contempt was "a criminal offense" within the meaning of the applicable statute.

Irvine thus seems to be justified in his claim that Donovan's "record of success before the Supreme Court was unparalleled" and that his administration of the antitrust laws was concerned wholly with the public interest, not in enabling big business. As Irvine noted, the most important of the cases brought by Donovan were "directed at combinations to increase the price of food at the retail and wholesale levels, international cartels whose unlawful activities were alleged to be injuring American business, the motion-picture industry charging illegal combinations whose overt acts restricted trade and commerce, and numerous criminal and civil cases charging the commission of illegal acts by combinations, some of which involved conspiracies between organized labor and management."

In his defense of Donovan, Irvine was supported by numerous lawyers, among them Allen W. Dulles, himself a corporation lawyer, who was to state that Donovan was "firmly convinced that individual freedom was vitally linked to our system of free enterprise" and therefore "attacked restraints and monopoly with effective enthusiasm." Among the major industries he prosecuted were "oil, sugar, harvesting machinery, motion pictures, water transportation and labor unions." At the same time Donovan "recognized that the uncertainties of our antitrust laws posed serious business problems." Accordingly, "he instituted the practice of passing in advance upon the legality of proposed mergers and certain other business practices which lay in the area of uncertain legality."[10]

Donovan said much the same thing at the time he was head of the Antitrust Division. In a speech in 1927—one demonstrating that his Republicanism was of a reasonable and thoughtful kind, although not wholly in opposition to the economic rough-and-tumble of the old free traders—he made an important statement of the principles guiding him in office.

Too often in the past, WJD contended, corporations had been formed with no inquiry into their organization by governmental agencies. Either by deliberate purpose or by natural result these corporations had attained monopolistic positions, and governmental intervention was invoked only after the concerns had been established and woven into the economic fiber of the country. A long process of inquiry and litigation had followed, but at times, even where evidence had been adduced sufficient to warrant a decree of dissolution of the monopoly, "that decree has proven inadequate to restore the original status, or when effective has resulted in the disruption and dislocation of the industry."[11]

Donovan then presented the novel aspect of his administration of the law:

With that experience in mind the Department of Justice now endeavors to apply what seems to be a practical and intelligent method of meeting the problems presented by proposed combinations. Mergers are inquired into at their inception. Their financial structure, their purpose and their economic background are examined before they enter in the field of business activity and the question of whether they would be violative of the law is considered before a violation has been committed. This method is at once fair to the business men who desire to avoid conflict with the law, and who are entitled to know the attitude of the government towards their effort. It is effective also in preserving the public interest by ascertaining the facts and assuring that illegal combinations shall be dealt with at once.

With one eye on what was going on in Germany, Italy, Russia, and Japan, WJD noted: "The larger the industrial combination the more readily may the transfer to government control be made effective. And there are those who, believing in a socialistic state, are professed advocates of industrial combination in the hope that such a policy may more speedily result in government ownership." The surest method of "avoiding that day is for business men themselves by proper methods of self-regulation to preserve the independence of industry from governmental participation."

In other words, Donovan followed the policy that an hour or two spent in giving industrialists his opinion on the law regarding their business intentions, especially in the realms of proposed mergers and acquisitions, might well prevent a breach of the law, deliberate or accidental, that would consume years of time spent by his own lawyers in investigation and prosecution. What Donovan had in mind for the future, if he succeeded in becoming attorney general of the United States, was a Commerce Court with jurisdiction over all interstate trade and commerce, except public utilities, but free and independent of any other government agency. His view was that such a court would "provide a test which the honest businessman could regard with confidence when he had in view the acquisition of the property of a competitor." It would serve to end the "confusion which now exists in the minds of cautious business men and which may often result in preventing the adoption of constructive measures in the public interest." At the same time "this court could be used as an immediate deterrent to those who would exploit the public by evasion of the Law."[12]

He maintained that the "problems presented in our present industrial age call for some such method." Wisdom dictated that "before we are driven to broader governmental control or participation in business, it is desirable that by furnishing guidance and advice the initiative and the resourcefulness of our industrial life shall be preserved."

At the time WJD's proposal was widely regarded as one of the most sensible and enlightened suggestions to have been made in the history of jurisprudence in the United States since the establishment of the Federal Trade Commission. But it was an idea that was ahead of its time. Before its time came depression and war, and a greater acceptance of certain of the tenets of Fabian socialism intervened to render the idea moribund.

Despite the evidence concerning his administration, Donovan was now to come to trial. The charges against him: a degree of heresy in his administration of the antitrust laws and—of all things—indifferent attitudes to the Prohibition law.

7

The Setback

Four years to the day after he became President, Coolidge announced while on a holiday in the Black Hills of South Dakota that he intended to retire from public life and would not therefore seek reelection in the 1928 election. "It's a pretty good idea," he commented in his simple, mossy way, "to get out when they still want you."[1] That stalwart Quaker Herbert Clark Hoover, who, according to Will Rogers, had "just been resting between calamities," then made it known that he would not reject the nomination.

During their four years together under Coolidge, Hoover, the great civilian war hero of World War I, and Donovan, the great military hero of World War I, seemed to have been close. Consequently it appeared they would make an invincible Republican ticket. The prospect seemed to fascinate the polity and the press, and on May 24, 1928, about three weeks before the convention, *The New York Times* announced that Donovan would be boomed as Vice President at the annual Dandelion Festival at Bemus Point on Chautauqua Lake next day. The *Times* proved well informed, Donovan was boomed, and as the Republican hierarchs had doubtless hoped to establish, the boom was well received, at least at first.

"One of the most enthusiastic political booms in the history of New England has come to life," the Buffalo *News* announced with satisfaction on May 26, 1928, "with the naming of Col. William J. Donovan of Buffalo for the vice-presidency. Never before in the history of this section has such interest been displayed in a possible vice-president candidate." In Connecticut, Maine, and Vermont as well, the "most influential leaders of the Republican party are for the Buffalo soldier. In the Pine Tree State [Maine] . . . Colonel Donovan is linked with Herbert Hoover as the desirable national ticket."

The Washington *News* correspondent agreed,[2] advising his readers that Hoover and Donovan had been "thrown together a great deal in the steps that have been taken to break up foreign monopolies, controlling products such as rubber and potash, upon which the United States must depend for its supplies." But, warned the *News* correspondent, "Political ticket balancers . . . already are out on the tight wire with an umbrella, doing all sorts of tricks," and the truth was that Donovan would probably be more interested in the office of attorney general than in that of the vice presidency.

There seems little doubt that at the time Hoover was sincere in desiring Donovan as Vice President, for Ruth recorded in her diary after talking with Hoover at the convention about Bill's prospects: "There seems no doubt of Hoover. Think Bill might have gotten Vice-Presidency if he wanted it."[3]

Nor was there much doubt among the politicians and the press during the campaign that Donovan was one of Hoover's principal advisers, if not Hoover's Merlin, and that if Hoover won the election, his debt to Donovan would be great. For while Donovan did not appear with Hoover in public and made no speeches on Hoover's behalf, nonetheless he and his legal associate T. J. McFadden, a gentle but nimble Irish spirit, were constantly at Hoover's side from nomination to election. When Hoover secured the nomination, Donovan was the only politician to accompany him on a five-day fishing trip to Brown's Camp on the Klamath River in Oregon, where they sketched out the campaign between killing salmon. Again Donovan was Hoover's only adviser in the writing of Hoover's acceptance speech, a 6,000-word document on which, as the reporter of the New York *World* recorded, Donovan "toiled like a writer on his first novel."[4]

The speech contained much that was clearly Donovan. Its theme was a combination of optimism and warning: optimism that "We in America, are nearer to the final triumph over poverty than ever before," but a warning that in seeking solutions to poverty, the country was venturing away "from those principles upon which our republic was founded and upon which it has grown to greatness"—a reference to Donovan's belief that socialism was beginning to creep into American economic life.

In any event Donovan rejected the vice presidential nomination undoubtedly because he thought he would be more effective elsewhere, particularly in the post of attorney general, which he had occupied in all but title for several years. The nomination for Vice President went to Charles Curtis, a Topeka lawyer who had had one term in Congress and two in the Senate, a man whose chief contribution to Washington political lore, so it was said, was that he had the same initials as Calvin Coolidge.

By election day, however, WJD had only an understanding that Hoover would have him in the Cabinet as attorney general—an understanding that Hoover would claim had not existed except in WJD's mind. Donovan was not the sort of man who had delusions on such matters; and there is no reason to doubt his assertion that Hoover made a definite promise to him soon after election day. In that election, in which for all practical purposes WJD had been Hoover's campaign manager, the Republican party scored one of the biggest victories in its history. Hoover carried all but eight states, the popular vote was 21,392,190 to Alfred E. Smith's 15,016,443, and the electoral vote was 444 for Hoover and 87 for Smith —a victory stemming to an important degree from the desire of the electorate that Prohibition be enforced.

The time had come, therefore, to establish whether Hoover would, or could, carry out his assurances to Donovan. And the question before Hoover was whether, since he had a clear mandate to enforce Prohibition, the man he wanted as attorney general was not too liberal in his attitude toward drink—WJD had always maintained that whether a person drank was for him, not the state, to decide, although he had asserted repeatedly that he would uphold the law whatever it was—an attitude he had demonstrated all too plainly when he authorized the raid on the Saturn Club.

The drama of the end of Donovan's run for a Cabinet post began therefore at exactly the moment when the future looked the most promising.

Hoover, who was at his home in Palo Alto, California, when the results came in, sent for Donovan, and for once Donovan decided to take Ruth with him—the campaign had taken him away more often than was usual, Ruth was "discouraged" by his incessant disappearances, and the trip to California was part of a bout of contrition that he felt in his time of triumph. Moreover, realizing that Ruth might be lonely at Palo Alto, Donovan agreed that she should take Patricia with her.

But of course, there were the usual muddles and turmoil. Both were to go by train, but they would meet at Chicago, Donovan going there from New York, Ruth from Washington. When, as arranged, Ruth arrived at the Blackstone Hotel in Chicago at 2:00 P.M. on November 10, 1928, she found WJD had left at noon by plane. He telephoned apologetically from Moline, Illinois, to make his explanations (Hoover wanted to see him urgently), and as usual Ruth accepted them without complaint. She left with Patricia the next morning for San Francisco aboard the Overland Limited, traveling in the company of the British multimillionaire and yachtsman Sir Thomas Lipton.

When the train reached Ogden, Utah, and stopped to take on water and victuals, there were more apologies from Donovan in the form of a telegram sent when he had landed at Amarillo, Texas, and containing instructions to meet him at the St. Francis Hotel in San Francisco at breakfast time on November 13. However, when Ruth and Patricia arrived at 9:10 A.M. that day, Donovan was not there. Instead, he telephoned from the Hoovers' at Palo Alto to say that he would be at the hotel for lunch—and then arrived for dinner in the company of a stranger called Gregory, a member of Hoover's staff.

Donovan did stay the night at the St. Francis, promising to take his wife and daughter to Chinatown the next day, but at the crack of dawn he changed his mind. He left suddenly for Palo Alto, placing Ruth and Patricia in the hands of Gregory, and vanished for the entire day. The stranger Gregory squired them around Chinatown, and when the day ended with Donovan still away, Ruth recorded in her diary, as she had done so often in the past: "Bill out. Bed early."

At Donovan's instructions, Ruth and Patricia the next day motored down to the Hoovers' for lunch, found the President-elect "very talkative and gay," and after lunch went to the Del Monte Hotel, where Donovan said he would join them later. When he did telephone, he announced that he would be down in three days, and then only for one night, and when he in fact arrived unexpectedly the next night in time for dinner, he announced that he would have to leave on the nineteenth, for Washington. Ruth confided in her diary: "Pat and I walked to the station with Bill. Disgusted he must go back to East. Life with Donovan!" Ruth then spent several days in and around Santa Barbara, and when she next heard from Donovan, he was in New York "but just leaving for Washington."[5]

Nor should it be thought that this record was unusual, brought about perhaps by the pressure of Donovan's duties for the President-elect. Such uncertainties were a constant in his conduct, before, at the time, and later.

In what was one of the last acts of his administration President Coolidge asked Donovan to accept the post of United States commissioner and chairman of the Rio Grande Compact Commission. Donovan received his warrant from President Coolidge and Secretary of State Frank Kellogg on December 15, 1928. The document's terms broadly established WJD's new responsibilities:

> Know Ye, that reposing special trust and confidence in the ability and discretion of William J. Donovan, of New York, I do appoint him Commissioner Representing the United States in the matter of the Rio Grande compact between the States of Colorado, New Mexico and Texas, and do authorize him to attend all conferences of authorized representatives of said States in the negotiation and concluding of such compact to the end that an equitable apportionment of the benefits to be derived from the uses of the waters of

the Rio Grande and its tributaries may be reached between the States, at all times having due regard for the treaties and other obligations of the United States with respect to such waters.

On February 7, 1929, Donovan received a further commission from Coolidge and Kellogg, this time to assume the duties of U.S. commissioner and chairman of the Colorado River Compact Commission, when Herbert Hoover resigned the post upon becoming the President-elect. This commission was worded differently, increasing Donovan's responsibilities greatly:

> Know Ye, That reposing special trust and confidence in the Integrity and Ability of William J. Donovan, of New York, I do appoint him as the Representative of the United States to participate in the negotiations between the States of Arizona, California, Colorado, Nevada, New Mexico, Utah, and Wyoming, contemplated in . . . the "Boulder Canyon Project Act," and make a report to Congress of the proceedings had and of any compact or agreement entered into by said States, and do authorize and empower him to execute and fulfil the duties of this commission with all the powers and privileges thereunto of right appertaining.

Again WJD accepted these heavy, new duties, while continuing as assistant attorney general. But their acceptance caused a good deal of trouble at home. The thought that the two new appointments might once again leave her alone for prolonged periods produced another crisis in Ruth, disturbances that from her diary appear to have been growing in frequency and severity. The pain of her medical condition was crippling on December 11, 1928, as she prayed that Hoover would make Donovan attorney general so that he would, at last perhaps, be tied to his desk. For the next week doctors were in and out of the house, dealing with what was obviously a case of serious depression. Ruth wrote on December 15, 1928: "Cold awful. Went to doctors & back to bed. The president appointed Bill chairman of Rio Grande River Commission in place of Hoover and he had to leave for Santa Fe, New Mexico, at 3. I had a miserable afternoon and night."

Donovan evidently called his brother Timothy from Chicago, for Timothy telephoned Ruth four times during the next three days and as usual seemed to work his magic with Ruth's morale, for she wrote in her diary on the twenty-second: "Felt much better. Got up and went to doctors. A little wobbly. Rested after luncheon and later poured tea at the White House for Mrs. Coolidge. Went to bed again right after supper. Tim called up." Yet as Tim Donovan and the other doctors recognized, these colds did not really exist: They were symptoms of depression produced by Donovan's departures and absences.

While Ruth was emerging from her latest crisis and preparing for the annual Christmas gathering of the family at Delaware Avenue in Buffalo, Donovan was on the mesa, his capabilities being fully tested. There was enough gunsmoke and buckshot in the problems affecting the division of the waters—for the interested parties were always chasing about the mesa on ponies, shooting at engineers, surveyors, builders, and each other— to make the testing an interesting and lively process. And the cold, the hard riding, the flying in "string bags" and driving about in broken-down pickups were there to rekindle Donovan's memories of the days when he chased Pancho Villa and *los Doratos*. James R. Murphy, Ralstone Irvine, Tom McFadden, and Bethuel Webster (later president of the New York City Bar Association) were with him at various times, and all would testify to Donovan's unusual skill as a negotiator and arbitrator. Murphy thought Donovan's overcoming the problems concerning the waters constituted, professionally, his "finest hour."[6]

In a surprisingly short time, given the complexities of the problems, Donovan had proposed, and the states had accepted, the establishment of compacts between the states, rather than federal legislation to divide the waters. He established a durable and workable system for dealing with disputes that would outlast his chairmanship, and when the agreements were finally ratified, Donovan received large, ornate, and expensive plaques as expressions of the states' gratitude—no mean achievement when previously the ranchers might well have dynamited him back to Washington.

However, Donovan's triumph in the Southwest was not obtained without great political cost to himself during the period that Hoover was choosing his Cabinet—between December 1928 and March 1929. Upon discovering that Hoover was considering the appointment of Donovan as attorney general, the forces of reaction started their work to undermine the President's confidence in Donovan. Here they were assisted by some of the phenomena brought to light by the election.

The fact that Al Smith, the Democratic candidate, was a Catholic and a wet had brought out into the open those forces that had hidden behind the Ku Klux Klan (which had bitterly contested WJD's appointment as assistant attorney general because he was a Catholic), and consequently, the electoral vote of five southern states, hitherto solidly Democratic, had gone to Hoover to stop the election of a Catholic as well as in the belief that he would be vigorous in the enforcement of Prohibition. And, the party hierarchs began to point out to Hoover, Donovan might prove to be as great a liability in the Cabinet as Smith's religion had proved to be to the Democrats in the election.

At the same time the mail brought protests that were astonishing in their malignancy:

I am the Pastor of one of the oldest and most historic Churches in America, the Church whose first Pastor baptized General George Washington—The First Baptist Church of New York City. I am now in the forty fifth year of my pastorate with this church. I supported you for President, as did the other Churches.

You surely know that down underneath all other motives, one of the inspirations for the extraordinary registration that swept you into the highest office in the land was the faith and favor of Protestant hearts.

Should you appoint a Romanist to the office of Attorney General . . . I would feel it a deliberate slap across my face and an unspeakable rebuke to a widely known and greatly honored Protestant minister; and there are thousands on thousands who will feel likewise.

Why fill the minds of a vast multitude with revulsion and a spirit of aggressive bitterness, who are now remarkably unified and ready to give you an abiding and efficient support, such as no other President has ever received?[7]

At the other end of the scale were the Catholics, who wished to see Donovan appointed to the Cabinet. The president of the Father Mathew Total Abstinence Society, Edward R. Fitchfield, writing on Hoover's return from a visit to South America, advised:

The citizens of the United States have eagerly followed all the news of your visit to our South American neighbors with mingled feelings of admiration and anxiety, which led some of them to say a "Pater and Ave" for your safe return to your own native land where they are ready to shower you with congratulations upon the success of your friendly mission and give yourself and family such a welcome home that it will warm the cockles of your loyal American heart.

The newspapers have strongly hinted that you intended to select Col. Wm. J. Donovan of the Department of Justice to be a member of your Cabinet, and judging from all the favorable comment on his ability and fitness and his splendid work in the recent campaign the appointment would be a very popular one. Of course it goes without saying that the Catholics who gave you their loyal support would be very glad if he got it, although they were not looking for political plums. . . .

And there were menacing power brokers such as Congressman W. G. Evans, of California, who wrote to Hoover on January 22, 1929, to state:

There is very pronounced opposition from our friends in the southern border states to the naming of Colonel Donovan to a position in the Cabinet. This comes to me by reason of my connections with these people and the party organizations there. The opposition is based on two points. First, that he is not in sympathy with the theory and principles of the Prohibition Act and for that reason would not be satisfactory to those who are in favor of the law and its bona fide enforcement. The other objection is on account of his religion, and which I am constrained to say does not appeal to me personally as a valid reason why any man should not be appointed to a public position. However, these are the reasons being given by the opposition to Colonel Donovan's appointment, and it is said that if he is named, the southern states, which gave you their support, will be disappointed at the very beginning of your administration.

Throughout Christmas and New Year's of 1928–29, Hoover had had inquiries made about Donovan's suitabilities among men and women whose opinions he respected. Donovan's old friend in the Senate, James W. Wadsworth, was strongly for Donovan's appointment as attorney general:

> . . . as a result of intimate acquaintance I have come to have implicit faith, not only in his abilities but in his motives and judgment. In these respects Col. Donovan stands out among the many men I have known in public life. In a word, I am convinced that your administration and the country would be well served if my friend Donovan were to be entrusted with a position of very first importance after March fourth next.[8]

The editor in chief of the Buffalo *News*, Alfred H. Kirchhofer, writing to "Dear Chief"—as Hoover was often called—on January 12, 1929, declared that his "admiration for Col. Donovan is second only to my loyalty to you."

Then came the letter of the famous U.S. Attorney for the Southern District New York, Emory R. Buckner, who had served under Donovan:

> I began my legal career just twenty years ago as assistant United States Attorney in New York City and only recently I served a short term as United States Attorney here. During all these years I have had a very great interest in the Department of Justice and its administration. The combination of unusual executive ability and sound legal judgment is indeed a rare one. Very few lawyers seem to have executive ability. Unusual executive ability is seldom tempered by straight legal thinking. Donovan combines to a greater degree than anyone I can now think of the executive and legal capacity required for a distinctive administration in the Department of Justice. His five years' experience in the Department is a much greater asset than would be supposed by those unfamiliar with the problem.

More opinions that were very influential came. Hoover's principal assistant, George Akerson, saw Senator William E. Borah, sometimes called the great opposer. A devout Prohibitionist and advocate of strict enforcement of the antitrust laws, Borah was an extremely powerful senator, who stated he had made "a close personal study" of the "Donovan situation" in the Senate and was convinced there would be an "ugly and probably successful fight made against Donovan's confirmation for attorney general." Borah stressed he had "nothing against Donovan but there is [a] combination of circumstances which would make his nomination for attorney general unfortunate." He stated that "the many drys in Senate would fight confirmation," and he was "certain that Donovan's confirmation for Attorney General would be held up for many days and that you would start your administration with [the] ugliest fight on confirmation in years." On the other hand, Borah stated that "there would be no objection to confirming Donovan for Secretary of War or any other post in Cabinet except Attorney General."

The second opinion was that of Mrs. Mabel Willebrandt, the acting assistant to the attorney general in Donovan's absence on Colorado water matters, rendered on February 7, 1929. Warning the President (and underlining her contention for effect) that *"Your Attorney General will make or break your Administration,"* Mrs. Willebrandt, who had been in charge of Prohibition enforcement at the Department of Justice under Donovan, advised that he had "administrative and executive ability, a clear scintillating mind," and was "well trained" with "a most engaging personality." He "uses gate crasher tactics but makes himself so pleasant people are rather glad he crashed in!" He "works well under strong forceful leadership such as Justice Stone furnished," but, she warned, he "possesses boyish unseasoned judgment coupled with overweening personal ambition which makes him extremely risky when unsupervised." His "appointment would be unsuitable from the public standpoint" because, among other matters, he was "risky on Prohibition." Therefore, Mrs. Willebrandt concluded: "Donovan's appointment would be disastrous to the incoming Administration as it would destroy the faith of those who worked hardest for it. In spite, however, of that, I believe his administrative qualifications would put his probable accomplishments at a higher level than those of the much abler lawyer, Mr. Mitchell."

That ambiguous letter was followed by another, written this time by William Howard Taft, the twenty-seventh President of the United States, who was in 1928 chief justice of the United States. In a letter to his son, Robert A. Taft, written just after the 1928 election, a copy of which reached Hoover, Chief Justice Taft offered the opinion that:

> There is one point in [Hoover's] administration that he needs to cover almost immediately. All the administrations back to mine have been short of a good Attorney General. Stone was not there long enough to develop a real policy. . . . They are talking about putting Bill Donovan in. Well we have had Donovan before us a number of times. He is a "short horse," and if Hoover puts him in, he will make his administration mediocre from the standpoint of the most important department in the government. . . .

On January 7, 1929, WJD saw Hoover, who stated briefly, but without elaborating, that he could not make Donovan attorney general but would have Donovan in the Cabinet. Before Donovan could do very much about Hoover's statement, a matter concerning the Colorado waters required Donovan's intervention. The principals refused to come to Washington, and Donovan had no choice but to go to Santa Fe despite the likelihood that severe blizzards might immure him in that remote place—as the city was then—for a prolonged period.

Donovan arrived in Santa Fe on or about January 14, 1929, and sure enough a severe blizzard struck the city the moment he arrived. He was pinned there by a combination of snow and argument until mid-February, with the only method of communication an uncertain telephone—an instrument that, although relatively efficient, was not the best method of communicating on confidential matters of state in a hotel crowded with idle and curious hordes marooned by a storm.

To make matters worse, soon after his arrival Timothy telephoned to warn him that Ruth's gynecological problems might be more serious than had been understood and that "special tests" would be required to establish whether she would have to have surgery. When Donovan called his wife, she was evidently very depressed, for Ruth had learned from one of her visitors that after Donovan's departure Hoover had definitely decided not to make him attorney general. That disappointment was reflected in her diary: "Those who know about Bill not being Atty. Gen. are stunned and can't believe it."9

Donovan was still snowed in at Santa Fe on the twenty-fourth, when he called Ruth to tell her that he could not get back in time for the Army and Navy Reception at the White House, the last one for the Coolidges, and she would have to go alone. Yet there was consolation: Tim Donovan arrived from Buffalo on the twenty-sixth and took Ruth to a number of dinners, plays, and concerts, and by February 2 he had managed to charm her back into such good spirits that she was able to ride her horse, Argonne, in the Washington ring. Also, on February 10 Ruth was much encouraged when Donovan telephoned to tell her that "Controversy still going on as to whether he is to be Atty. Gen. or Sec'y of War."

That reference was the first in the diary to the possibility that Hoover might yet redeem his promise by making WJD secretary of war—an appointment of no great consequence in peacetime since America's army was smaller than Bulgaria's—and it also showed that Donovan had been doing some vigorous telephoning to Hoover's kingmakers.

One of Donovan's young lawyers at the Department of Justice, Bethuel Webster, who was in Santa Fe with him at the time, later recalled: "Bill Donovan fought a very able campaign by telephone that went on for several weeks. I think he realized that there was no way of recovering his position regarding the attorney generalship, but there was the secretary of war open, and while Bill was not keen on the War Department, he was keen to get Cabinet rank and experience. Bill wanted to be President, remember. The trouble with doing such business on the telephone was that everyone within earshot becomes interested, especially when the man in the room is Bill Donovan. For although he had a quiet speaking voice, he had to raise his voice on a number of occasions, and not only because the line was bad."[10]

When Donovan called on February 13 he had bad news for Ruth, who was as ambitious for him as he was for himself. He told her he thought William De Witt Mitchell, whose father had been a member of the Supreme Court of Minnesota, who had himself been Coolidge's solicitor general and was a Protestant and a member of the good capitalist law firm Mitchell Doherty Rumble Bunn & Butler of St. Paul, would be the new attorney general—a lusterless, whiskery man in a lusterless, whiskery Cabinet. That upset Ruth again: "Am disappointed. Couldn't sleep until 3."

Meantime, Ruth had had "all kinds of tests and X-Rays" and there had been a "snow fall of 8 inches & streets awful." Suddenly and without warning Donovan appeared in Georgetown on February 25, 1929, having traveled through the weekend from Santa Fe in a roaring blizzard that had left eight inches of snow on the Washington streets. One of the kingmakers, Lawrence Richey, a former agent of the U.S. Secret Service, a Treasury agent, a journalist with *Everybody's Magazine,* Hoover's office manager during the war, and now the President-elect's secretary, had telephoned him at Santa Fe and asked him to come to Washington to see Hoover, intimating that he was to be offered the post of governor-general of the Philippines.

Donovan told Richey he "didn't want to come East if it were simply to be a discussion over taking the Governor Generalship of the Philippines."[11] But Richey said the President-elect wanted him to come, so he left Santa Fe on Friday night, February 22, and arrived in Washington on Monday, February 25. On his arrival he went straight to Hoover's home in Georgetown, and Hoover said, "I have two things to talk over with you." One was the War Department, and the other was the post of governor of the Philippines, which Hoover said required "harder work and greater ability" and was "more important." He could find "five men for the Cabinet," he said, but he could "get only one for that." What he wanted, he said, was independence for the Philippines in such a fashion that the United States would keep its naval and military bases, while no other power, particularly Japan, would be able to get in there.

Politically the post did carry a special charm, and most of the men who had been governors had become members of the Cabinet. Also, Donovan was in no doubt that his political career was at a crossroads: If he went along with Hoover's wishes, the road to the White House would still be open to him a few years hence. But Donovan's reply was instantaneous: "It is impossible." Hoover then endeavored to persuade Donovan of "the great opportunity it meant for my political future." But Donovan declared: "I have no political future; I don't want any."

Donovan then reminded Hoover of the embarrassing position he had been put in by the present maneuvering. Although Hoover had known that Donovan wanted nothing for himself, he had agreed to come into the Cabinet because Hoover himself told him "here in this room that you wanted me in your Cabinet and needed me there." Donovan had said if that were really the case, then "I would do it." He had wanted only to get back to the private practice of law but had been prepared to forgo that to be of service to the President and the country. Donovan reminded Hoover of a conversation in which Hoover had spoken of how embarrassing it had been for him in the Harding administration "to be in the Cabinet one week and out of it the next." But "this situation in which I have been placed is infinitely more cruel."

Donovan told the President-elect directly, "Now, you have made this offer of the War Department, and if [you] want me to do it, I will do [it]." Hoover then said, "You could work there, but I wouldn't suggest it." Thereupon Donovan told Hoover, "I have got to go back this afternoon [to Santa Fe for the water conference]." Hoover then said, "Before you go back I want you to see these men," naming four or five of them—all of them Hoover stalwarts. Donovan said, "I don't want to see them but if you want me to, I will." Hoover: "Do that."

Donovan lunched with President Coolidge but "felt strained and depressed," thinking "back to the time when I had come into the White House for the first time." Both the Coolidges seemed "quite gay" about leaving, and after lunch Donovan went to Coolidge's study. "The shelves were bare of all his books, which had been sent to his home. He lit a cigar and sat down, where during many nights over a period we had discussed affairs of government." The President "skillfully avoided any reference to Hoover or what was going to happen to me." He "talked on and on, I asking only a few questions. . . . His cigar finished, we got up, I told him how grateful I had been to him for all his courtesies, he replied, 'I was glad to have you in my official family.' I wished him good luck . . . said goodbye, and went out the door feeling it was my last time that I would be in the White House."

Donovan then went to see a principal mugger, Mark Sullivan, a Harvard blueblood and author (*Our Times: The United States, 1900–1925*, in six volumes). A man of immense self-control, but at the same time with a fearful anger, Donovan came close to striking Sullivan when, after a long lecture on the importance of the Philippines to the United States and the opportunity they had afforded to other men's careers in the past, Sullivan stated: "Why, now you can step from them to the Vice Presidency and then the Presidency." Donovan retorted that a man "who would take such a job as a springboard to political office was contemptible" and that he could not "take my wife and children to such a place for four years." He recorded in his diary how he began to "feel more than ever the instability of Hoover," and if he went to the Philippines "with that old-woman [Henry L.] Stimson [former governor-general and now secretary of state] at [Hoover's] ear . . . I would find myself coming back a discredited man." (The reference to Stimson was odd, for he was an immensely respected figure who became one of WJD's supporters. However, he did have a reputation for primness although that concealed a rare sense of humor.)

At Donovan's home Judge Stone, his old friend and mentor, came to see him. Donovan felt on hearing what Stone had to say—according to T. J. McFadden, who was present—*"Et tu, Brute?"* Stone said, "You can't leave public life," and explained that there were matters that Hoover had not told him because of *"his peculiar reticence."* Donovan demanded to know what these were, but Stone declined to tell him. At that Donovan asked Judge Stone to tell the President-elect, "I expected nothing from him but honesty, and that I have not received."[12] After Judge Stone left, Donovan commented in his diary, "Well, then I was sick—that, coming from the President of the United States."

Stone's contribution was to arrange what was likely to be the last meeting between Donovan and Hoover. At the meeting Donovan told Hoover that "I am used to dealing with equals," that "If I have any use at all, it is to stay in America and deal with my equals," and that Hoover's honeymoon with America was soon going to be over "and you will need someone to stay here who can pull the sword for you."

Hoover was confident of his hold on the electorate, for he said, "I don't think so, Bill."

Donovan then said good-bye and left, on the way out running into Mark Sullivan, who announced that the new secretary of war was to be James Good. On hearing that such an obscure figure had been taken into the Cabinet, WJD remarked to Sullivan that Hoover "finds that in a scrap I have been a fine thing but a poor thing in time of peace. . . . He calls me a symbol. You can tell Hoover he need no longer consider my name."

And that was that. With Donovan's presidential and Cabinet aspirations and indeed his political career at an end, the Baltimore *Sun* announced:

> Herbert Hoover, almost upon the eve of his inauguration, finds himself parting political company with one of his closest friends, William J. Donovan, of Buffalo, upon whose counsel he relied heavily in his fight for the Presidency.
>
> Offered the post of Governor-General of the Philippines, the now assistant

to the Attorney-General put it aside with a finality that stood against the most persuasive arguments alike of the President-elect and some of his most trusted advisers.

Colonel Donovan is believed to have thus become the first man to refuse an office which proved a stepping stone to the Presidency for William Howard Taft, which was held by Major-General Leonard Wood after he had barely failed to win the nomination to the Presidency, and from which Henry L. Stimson goes into the Secretaryship of State, the highest office a Chief Executive can bestow.[13]

Still, there was much unanswered and unexplained about this oddly tongue-tied exchange between two of the most articulate men of their times. And perhaps the record would have been incomplete but for the fact that Hoover did not intend to go down in posterity as a bigot, for underlying the exchange was Donovan's conviction that he had been abandoned by Hoover because he was a Catholic, a conviction that contained considerable substance. Aware of this, Hoover wrote a paper called "Reasons Donovan Was Not Taken into Cabinet."[14] He listed seven.

The first was the most curious: that Donovan was a wet and opposed to Prohibition—which Hoover had pledged to enforce—and that therefore, as Hoover wrote, "Any Atty Genl publicly opposed to the laws he was called on to enforce could neither command public confidence nor the support of his own staff in vigorous action."

Hoover's other reasons were equally curious: Donovan had "never had administrative experience"; he was "a soldier before soldiers, not a restraining civilian"; he had refused "to agree that he would accept such re-organization plans as administration called for"; his enforcement of the antitrust laws while head of the Antitrust Division had been "very bad"; he had developed a "vast capacity for intrigue which resulted in starting of opposition press campaigns"; and as a result, he could not be "confirmed in the Senate for above reasons." (The reference to intrigue is surprising. Occasionally WJD did show a capacity for political maneuver, especially in his dealings with the press, but his nature was not that of an intriguer in the usual sense; it was more that of a man who believed absolutely in the wisdom of operating without letting his left hand know too much about what his right hand was doing.)

To explain his decision not to have Donovan in the Cabinet as secretary of war, Hoover found four reasons: Groups had been carrying on campaigns the theme of which was: " 'If you do not appoint Donovan to Cabinet it is evidence of intolerance.' " Hoover found "the insistence upon *Cabinet* in these propogandas [*sic*] is sinister enough, especially when linked with distain [*sic*] for Philippine offer." This was in Hoover's view "an endeavor to force a membership in the *Cabinet.*" Hoover thought also that Donovan's "Experience and mental qualities not adapted to his job," and that on his arrival in Washington he had "Organized a force propoganda [sic]" and "assumed a dictatorial tone which made comfortable Cabinet associations impossible." Lastly, he had shown "immaturity of mind" and needed "to be 10 years older."

As for Donovan, he resigned from the Department of Justice on March 5, 1929. Hoover did make several attempts to mend their relationship, one soon after Donovan left Washington. One of Hoover's associates proposed, and the President accepted the idea: "Would not Col. Donovan make an exceptionally capable Ambassador to France? Because of his brilliant war record he would be well received there. He has the money necessary to maintain the embassy on the expected scale." And "His appointment would smooth over a personal and political situation."[15]

Donovan, however, waved the offer away and advised Hoover he intended to return to the practice of law. As he remarked to his friend Tom McFadden, he did not expect to return to Washington, except on legal business. However, it was noted that he did not sell the Georgetown house.

8

Silk Stocking Lawyer

With $100,000 as working capital and a further $100,000 as a reserve, Donovan began the work of establishing the international law firm with many branches that he had visualized in 1920. The times seemed auspicious, for America was still in the New Economic Era proclaimed by Calvin Coolidge, the stock market was still exceedingly bullish, and even that most impeccable name in high finance J. P. Morgan was launching an investment trust called the United Corporation. However, there were Cassandras and there were ominous portents. For example, late in 1928 the Federal Reserve Board issued a cautious and ambiguous warning that speculation was approaching the danger point, and the *Journal of Commerce* observed that "a market of the kind that has been going on cannot last indefinitely but must undergo a readjustment."[1]

To Donovan, now was the time to get started, whatever the portents. There was talk of a partnership between Coolidge and Donovan, a prospect Donovan found interesting, but it came to nothing when Coolidge accepted a $75,000 book contract for his autobiography, a large magazine contract for the serialization rights, and a one-year contract worth $203,045 for a series of 200-word newspaper articles with the McClure newspaper syndicate. Donovan asked Raichle to join him for the second time and then he turned to his colleagues in the Antitrust Division. By the late summer of 1929 he had put together his firm, although it was really no more than a loose association of lawyers sharing chambers, and the announcement cards went out:

The undersigned announce that they have formed a Partnership for the Practice of Law under the Firm Name of

DONOVAN AND BOND

with offices at 534 Washington Building, Washington, District of Columbia.
They will also have offices at 41 Broad Street, New York City, under the name of

DONOVAN AND RAICHLE

Mr. Clyde Y. Morris, member of the War Loan Staff, Officer of the Secretary of the Treasury, and Formerly Special Attorney in the Office of the General Counsel, Bureau of Internal Revenue, has resigned from the Treasury Department to become associated with The Firm at the Washington Office.

> William J. Donovan
> Henry Herrick Bond
> Rush H. Williamson
> Frank G. Raichle
> George S. Leisure
> Horace R. Lamb.

The deluge came almost immediately. The stock exchange crash began on October 24, 1929, "Black Thursday." In a flash the New Economic Era established by Coolidge was wiped out, taking Donovan by surprise. For although he was not a speculator or gambler, he had invested the $100,-000 he had put up as the firm's reserve. The sum had become worth $600,000, and equally rapidly both the principal and the dividends were wiped out.

The Great Depression had begun, and when the British economist John Maynard Keynes was asked by a reporter whether there had been anything like it before, he replied: "Yes, it was called the Dark Ages and it lasted four hundred years."[2]

Donovan had selected the worst time to open for business. Whereas in the past Donovan's brother-in-law, Dexter P. Rumsey, by now the principal trustee of the Rumsey estate, had been generous in making loans to WJD, he was no longer in a position to help. According to his son, Donald Rumsey, Dexter lost $3,000,000 when the crash revealed the empire of the Swedish match king, Ivar Kreuger, to have been a $100,000,000 swindle. Rumsey was compelled to go to work as a junior executive at the Erie County Savings Bank, of which he later became president. To WJD this loss of a source of capital meant that his firm was dependent on his ability to attract business, which was considerable.

Yet the firm rode the calamity, and by 1934 it was beginning to prosper primarily because of Donovan's remarkable capacity to attract business —a capacity that was attended by an equally remarkable share of the profit. Between 1934 and 1939 he received 56.9 percent of the net, while

Leisure received 20.1 percent, and Carl Newton and Edward Lumbard, two other founding partners, each received 10.05 percent. Thus, in 1934 Donovan earned $84,826.42; in 1935, $143,803.84; 1936, $158,807.50; 1937, $165,642.64; 1938, $336,211.61; 1939, $239,523.91—a total in the six years of $1,125,815.92. Given the purchasing power of the dollar during those years—the ratio was still about 4:1—the total by the standards of the eighties might have been worth $4,000,000 to $5,000,000 —large compensation by any standards.

But for all his large earnings, his account at the firm was almost always in the red, sometimes by as much as $200,000, a sum he was not able to cover. Moreover, it appears that although tax returns were prepared for him each year by his secretary, the devoted Walter Berry, Donovan did not pay the taxes for at least some and perhaps all of those years. As his partners learned, for all his executive genius, he was not a good "detail" man, and in financial matters he was hopelessly vague. Where, therefore, did these large sums go?

There is no doubt that his living expenses were extremely high. Also, a large segment of his income went on travel; he was like a kestrel in a cage, always seeking to escape. Yet his "escapes" were rarely, if ever, for personal pleasure.

Later, when it became necessary to clarify Donovan's expenditures for tax purposes, it would be shown that he gave a great deal of money to outsiders. He had been very generous with Catholic and Irish causes, particulars of which were often impossible to discover. He had made very large gifts to Micks who had fallen on hard times. He had been the sole means of support of his sister Loretta, who had been deserted by her husband and was fighting a losing battle with alcoholism, and of her four children.

He was also personally indulgent, going to only the best tailors, shirtmakers, haberdashers, and cobblers. He traveled in only the highest style —he became one of those men the columnist Russell Baker had in mind when he wrote of luxury express trains that thundered "across the prairies at night in a flash of silver, white tablecloths and crystal gleaming at the dining car windows," that gave "the people of lonely towns a sense of the wealth and power and romance of America and stirred among small boys the restless American's dream of faraway places."[3] WJD frequently chartered planes at a time when that was done only by rich Indian princes; he stayed at the finest hotels and rarely in anything less than a suite. Yet whenever he traveled, he would go to considerable lengths to secure a bargain; for example, he would spend hours telephoning steamship companies to get a favorable price on a stateroom. Still, that sort of thing was no more than attempt at thrift which was never sustained.

A further matter that burned holes in Donovan's pockets was the expensive burden of universal acquaintances. Donovan seems to have gone everywhere and known everybody of the period. His diary for November 11 to December 10, 1935, for example, in a partial listing shows that he lunched, took tea with, dined with, or otherwise met Marion Davies (William Randolph Hearst's mistress), Jack Wheeler (director and general manager of the North American Newspaper Alliance), John Hay Whitney (newspaper owner, industrialist, arts patron), Professor Lowell Read (mathematician and statistician), and F. Trubee Davison (president of the American Museum of Natural History). On November 13 he dined with W. Somerset Maugham (novelist), Edgar Bergen (ventriloquist), and Nelson Doubleday (book publisher) and went on to see Millicent Hearst (William Randolph's wife), Herbert Bayard Swope (publicist and journalist), Martin Flavin (playwright), and Clark Gable and William Holden (film actors).

In succeeding days, among other activities, he lunched with the banker James Warburg, dined with Bob Rubin (counsel for Metro-Goldwyn-Mayer), took tea with Elizabeth Allen (English actress), talked with Claybrook Cottingham (president of Louisiana College), visited his partner George Leisure and played with Leisure's son, Michael. He dined with Frank Knox (publisher of the Chicago *Daily News*), called on Russell Livermore (lawyer) at home, talked with Philip Wagoner (manufacturer). He saw Mark Sullivan (author) and Noble Judah (wartime intelligence officer), lunched with the Catholic bishops in the United States, saw the district attorney for Cook County, Chicago, spent an evening with Charles Burdick (dean of Cornell), talked with the editor of the Buffalo *Evening News*, dined with the earl of Cottinham, went to the theater with the manager of the Ottawa branch of the Bank of Montreal, dined out with his children, saw Lily Pons (opera singer), sailed with Morehead Patterson (industrialist), refused to dine with Lady Mendl (wife of a prominent British diplomat), and went to the theater with Ruth.

He dined with Major Ian Hay Beith, Sir Gerald Campbell, Sir Wilmot Lewis (correspondent of the London *Times*), Sir William Wiseman (chief of the British secret service in America in World War I and at this time a partner with the merchant bankers Kuhn, Loeb), breakfasted with his senior and junior partners, received a young man who wanted to marry Patricia, "had a good visit with" Glenn Anderson (mining engineer), lunched with Senator George Fearon (leader of the New York Senate) and the secretary of the Republican State Committee, dined with the members of Council on Foreign Relations, went to Washington for talks with the Italian ambassador, saw the director of Military Intelligence (Babson) and Kelly (head of the Central European Department of the State Department), had tea with "Doctor McGuire, the economist," went to a bridge party at Senator Tydings', dined with Nicholas Roosevelt (author and journalist), dined with the deans of the schools of economics and of sociology at Lehigh University, got a job for "Sergeant Thomas, who helped carry me off the field at Landres-St.-Georges," lunched and then dined with Marcellus Hartley Dodge (a close friend and large stockholder in Remington Arms), lunched with the Republican chairman in San Francisco, talked to Count Perdiciari and Count Casagrandcame (Italian embassy officials), dined with the editor of the Kansas City *Star*, dined with Condé Nast (publisher), talked with Millicent Hearst, and tried to find Marion Davies (who was on "an awful drunk" and was "finally found by Hearst in Cleveland in her pajamas").

Between times, Donovan carried on his active legal career, which, when combined with his social and family lives, cost a great deal of money. It seems that Donovan's and Ruth's incomes were kept separate and that her income, probably not large at the time, went toward sustaining her in the style to which she was accustomed—and to be fair, she was as frugal as Donovan was extravagant.

There is, therefore, little mystery about how he managed to dispose of such large incomes.

Nor, it seems, had Donovan got politics out of his system. Law was great, but it was not enough, and when the party called in 1932, Donovan's partners witnessed once more an all-too-familiar sight—Donovan rushing off to a political tourney.

Despite the Depression, when in the 1930 elections the Republicans only just lost the House and barely held the Senate, Donovan was encouraged again to enter the unpromising field of politics. He won the Republican nomination for the post of governor of New York State against no fewer than seven influential aspirants, who included a former assistant secretary for war for aeronautics, a former justice of the State Supreme Court, the mayor of Syracuse, the president of the State Senate, and Nathan L. Miller, the governor from 1921 to 1923. It seems therefore that Donovan was still being considered as a possible candidate for the presidency, for the governor's mansion at Albany was well known as the last port of call before the White House: No fewer than seven of New York's forty-four governors had been nominated for the presidency from Albany: Van Buren, Cleveland, and Teddy Roosevelt had succeeded; Seymour, Tilden, Hughes, and Smith had tried and failed.

If Donovan could win New York State, he might well succeed Herbert Hoover as President. But could he win the state? In 1932, the cruelest year of the Depression, the Republicans not only were being blamed for the calamity but had also lost the confidence of the electorate. Yet it was generally believed Donovan stood above the party—immensely popular, irreproachable, tried, tested, successful. Moreover, his Democratic opponent was a banker, Herbert Lehman, and if in the public mind Republicans were fools, bankers were knaves who had marketed securities that had had no more value than losing tickets at a race meeting, thereby contributing to the near collapse of the national banking system and to the crash itself.

Donovan was confident of victory, and his advisers, who included John Lord O'Brian, Frank Raichle, and James Wadsworth, thought he would win simply because he was Donovan, the one figure in an otherwise unhappy Republican cast who might be expected to win, win big, and go on to give the party fresh leadership.

What nobody could assess was the extent to which Donovan was now identified in the public mind with the business class, which had become the ruling class but through a concatenation of scandals—the Insull utilities "empire," the Van Sweringen railroad "empire," and lesser but equally serious revelations of fraud and manipulation—had lost public confidence. The feeling was that Donovan was not contaminated, as indeed he was not. Certainly the Blanket Boys and the Micks thought Donovan would win, and they had commissioned one of their number, Tom Donahue, to write the "Wild Bill Donovan Victory Song." Set in tempo di marcia, with a great deal of cresc. and peco rit e mare, it went:

> Our National Distress,
> Finds the Public and the Press
> Loudly hammering and clamoring
> For someone who will guide us through.
>
> A Rainbow's in the sky
> And again our hopes are high
> It's victory for you and me
> And a man we all swear by.
>
> His name is WILD BILL DON-O-VAN!
> There's magic in the name
> Because 'twas WILD BILL DON-O-VAN who fought
>   his way to fame
> In the trenches of the Argonne and the
>   crossing of the Ourcq.
>
> And he'll fight his way to victory
> As Governor of New York!
> Hurrah for WILD BILL DON-O-VAN!
> A leader tried and true
> We send him from the Sixty Ninth to You!
>
> East-side, West-side, all around the town!
> Up state, down state herald his renown
> And if you want a Governor
> To guide you safely through
> We offer WILD BILL DON-O-VAN to you.[4]

On that cheerful, idolatrous note the campaign opened with Donovan's formal acceptance of the nomination on May 9, 1932, at the Broadway Auditorium in Buffalo. Above the platform was a gigantic banner proclaiming: "WHAT THIS STATE NEEDS IS A TWO-FISTED LEADER." Everywhere were large posters of WJD's old patron, Teddy Roosevelt, announcing: "DEE-LIGHTED, BILL!" Similarly other favorite sons of Buffalo, Millard Fillmore and Grover Cleveland, both, like Teddy, long dead, declaimed: "ONWARDS! UPWARDS! BILL!"

When Donovan entered the auditorium, City Hall burst into light, and fireworks and bombs tore the night sky. He was escorted by the Donovan Doughboys, the Lafayette Republican Women's and the Martha Washington Drum Corps, and detectives who had served him when he was U.S. attorney. There was a large gathering of priests, ministers, and rabbis, and "the blare of trumpets and the thunder of drums bounced from the old brick walls and rattled through the rafters in a scene of wild and joyous disorder."[5] It was a night of good-humored, beery jubilation. However, the campaign was to be very different.

The election would be marked as one of the worst for word-of-mouth slander in modern times. Rumors had flooded Buffalo at the time Donovan's nomination was announced that he and Ruth had separated, that Ruth was seeing more of Donovan's brother Timothy, a prominent local surgeon, than was good for her. That was partly nonsense—but during an election such nonsense could be made to tell. So it did: Considerable attention was paid to Ruth at the acceptance ceremony. The Buffalo *News* told how, for example, "Mrs. Donovan watched her husband gravely. She sat straight and hardly moved for an hour. She wore navy blue crepe with touches of dull blue at the neck and a navy hat. Mrs. Dexter P. Rumsey, her mother, sat on her right. Mrs. Rumsey watched the colonel through black opera glasses and fluttered a black and gold fan."

Given the depressed mood of the country, the desire of the electorate for a change from the rule of moneyed aristocracy, such reporting was not likely to help Donovan's campaign, but the campaign itself was skillfully waged. Donovan's supporting speakers built a picture of a self-made lawyer and public servant, a great war hero, a man in the mold of Teddy Roosevelt—brainy, high-minded, successful, two-fisted, gutsy, vigorous, at the height of his powers, the sort of man the state and the country needed to get things working again.

That picture might be reasonably true, but the country wanted reform, and while it was agreed that Donovan was superior to most Republican leaders, he was a Republican, and the Republican platform was inferior to that of the Democrats. Where was the Republicans' answer to the double promise of reductions in federal expenditures and support for the repeal of Prohibition? Because those promises won millions of voters to the Democrats, nothing Donovan could offer could stem the flow in New

York. To make his prospects worse, some of the mud began to stick. Whispering campaigns depicted Donovan as a "traitor to his class, race and religion," as a "former Cossack," as "anti-Labor and pro-Capitalist." The religious issue, particularly, became so unpleasant and damaging that the *Catholic Union and Times* felt forced to print a two-page editorial headlined THE WHISPERING CAMPAIGN. The substance of the religious charges was that Donovan had married a Protestant, that proof of his anti-Catholicism lay in the fact that he was not having his children educated in the Catholic faith, and that since he had only two children, he must be engaging in contraception. In short, Donovan had run up against the narrow prejudices of the class of his birth. And as is often found in narrow-minded societies, if any one of the allegations were true, all must be true. Such was the case with Donovan during the campaign. Patricia and David were being educated in nonsectarian schools, but Donovan remained a good Catholic. But because one criticism was true, all the rest must have substance, and that tended to undermine Donovan's standing in the large and important Catholic vote in the state.

Indeed, the charges were so damaging that the bishop was compelled to defend him, and the *Catholic Union and Times* assured the diocese that there was "no more question of the standing of Col. William J. Donovan in the Catholic Church than of Lieut. Gov. Lehman's standing in the Jewish synagogue." The newspaper informed all concerned that Donovan was "discharging his obligation in the matter of the education of his children in a manner that meets the approval of his pastor, the Bishop of Buffalo, who knows all the circumstances and raises no objection." Moreover, the newspaper stated, the bishop had confirmed both Donovan children in his private chapel, and Donovan himself was "in all respects" in good membership of his congregation.[6]

Whether the bishop's defense did Donovan much good is open to question, for the congregation was well aware that Donovan rarely appeared at the Old Cathedral in Buffalo except for midnight mass on Christmas Eve. What few knew was that he went to his devotions alone, often early in the morning; he generally stood at the back of the church in the shadows because of his dislike for crowds; and he attended confession whenever he felt the need.

However, the attack was damaging. As damaging was the attack against Donovan from the left. The Central Labor Council at Buffalo, which backed Lehman, resurrected the "Cossack incident" and also alleged that he had used his powers as U.S. attorney in 1922 on behalf of the bosses to break a strike of carmen at Depew. To those indictments the council added a third: that in a famous case known as Appalachian Coals, Donovan had defended thirty-seven mineowners—and mineowners were often considered by labor only a shade less rapacious than the bankers —accused of fixing coal prices in the East. What the council omitted was that Donovan had sought, virtually on a *pro bono publico* basis, to save the industry from collapse as a result of overproduction and to prevent what would surely have been a revolution in the coal fields. It also failed to state that the Supreme Court had upheld the legality of the combination, emphasizing that the government had failed to prove an illegal intent or the use or intended use of overt illegal acts.

As for the Depew carmen's strike, the labor council ignored the fact that Donovan had prosecuted only because the carmen had dynamited track, not because they were striking, and that even when he was presenting the case against the dynamiters, he had appealed to the judge—successfully—for leniency.

Like the Catholic issue, the labor issue was a detail in the campaign. Neither could change the outcome, for the tide of history itself was against Donovan. The country was in revolt against unbridled capitalism, and the people wanted reform. So the noisy, inelegant campaign reached its climax on October 30, 1932, when Hoover and Donovan appeared together on the same platform at Madison Square Garden.

Apparently in friendly accord, they denounced Lehman and Roosevelt for their "ambitions,"[7] while WJD declared his support for Hoover's policy of the status quo in financial policy and a continuation of Prohibition. For his part, Hoover charged that Roosevelt's New Deal would "destroy the foundation of the nation," that through his proposals to cut tariffs "grass would grow in the streets of 100 cities, . . . weeds would overrun millions of farms," and the taxpayer would become "enslaved." On the other hand, Hoover claimed, his policies had averted "25 years of chaos," and through him the nation would work its way out of the slump.

It was a disastrous performance by both men, particularly Donovan, for until now he had been regarded as the one Republican with fresh ideas. Furthermore, compared to Roosevelt's and Lehman's proposals, Hoover's and Donovan's offerings were the same old story—wordage. Roosevelt's program included a five-day work week to spread such employment as there was and federal aid for the unemployed at a time when the Republicans considered that "socialistic." Lehman weighed in with a twelve-point labor program for the state that included unemployment relief, advance planning of public construction, unemployment insurance, an extension of workmen's compensation laws, free employment services, protection for women and children in industry, and provision of jury trials for persons accused of violating labor injunctions.

Those programs were calculated to appeal to the masses, and the calculation succeeded. The result was inevitable. There was a landslide in which Roosevelt carried forty-two states, both houses of Congress, and nearly all the state offices and state legislatures. Donovan's candidacy went down in flames, although it was widely agreed that he had much to offer as a man. And that was that. *The New York Times* announced on November 9, 1932:

ROOSEVELT WINNER IN LANDSLIDE!
DEMOCRATS CONTROL WET CONGRESS;
LEHMAN GOVERNOR, O'BRIEN MAYOR

In New York City, the vote for Lehman was 1,525,510, for Donovan 542,492, giving Lehman a plurality of 983,018. In the rest of the state, where the results were not quite complete when *The New York Times* was put to bed, Donovan defeated Lehman by an indicated plurality of 95,817. The indicated plurality throughout the state was, therefore, a victory for Lehman by 887,201 votes. In Buffalo, Lehman had won narrowly with 109,134 votes to Donovan's 91,467.

Two days later Donovan was back at the office, Ruth at her mother's home in Buffalo. She wrote in her diary: "Disappointed that Bill couldn't win but better for us really." Three days later she added: "Received many wonderful letters and all looking forward to Bill's leadership in the future."[8] That leadership could only be in the far distance, if it was ever to occur, for on the morning of January 31, 1933, *The New York Times* announced: HITLER MADE CHANCELLOR OF GERMANY.

9

The Days of Peace Run Out

Throughout this period Donovan had been developing contacts of a special nature with "certain authorities" in Berlin through the agency of the German consul general in New York, Otto Kiep, who was a dinner guest of the Donovans in the period 1936–39; Kiep's wife, Hanna, was a close friend of Ruth's. Also, WJD had made contact with Dr. Paul Leverkühn, whom he had met when the Berlin lawyer was with the German Reparations Commission in Washington. Leverkühn came to New York frequently. In 1938 he used a pretext to enable him to obtain an exit permit with which to transact other, more secret business: He was representing parties interested in the treasure of Czar Nicholas II, which was supposed to be in the United States.

As Leverkühn explained to Donovan, when Nicholas was murdered by the Bolsheviks in 1918, it was believed the imperial family had been murdered with him. However, a woman who had arrived in Berlin claimed to be, or at least the claim was made that she was the czar's youngest daughter, Princess Anastasia. The imperial family's doctor, Yevgeny Botkin, had been murdered with the family, but his son, Gleb Botkin, was alive and convinced that the woman was Anastasia and therefore the heiress to the czar's American estate, thought to be very large. Botkin had asked Leverkühn to act for Princess Anastasia in establishing (1) that the woman was Anastasia, (2) that an estate existed in the United States, and (3) that the only legitimate claimant was Anastasia, not the Soviet government, which was seeking possession of all imperial assets abroad.

According to Donovan's files, Leverkühn was to establish a corporation in the United States through which Princess Anastasia and Botkin could act to secure control of the imperial fortune. While Donovan's law firm did some work on the case, it was mainly labor for associates; neither Donovan nor Leverkühn appears to have spent much time on the matter. Still, Leverkühn reappeared in New York on Botkin's business in 1937 and again in 1938, staying on both occasions at Beekman Place as Donovan's guest. In the light of other evidence, both Donovan and Leverkühn seem to have used their legal business as cover for another, more weighty matter, concerning Admiral Wilhelm Franz Canaris, chief of the Abwehr, the intelligence and counterespionage service of the German General Staff, in the service of which Leverkühn was a high officer. Canaris, it was to emerge, was plotting to overthrow Hitler.

Under the Treaty of Versailles, by which World War I was ended, Germany was forbidden to have an intelligence service. But within a year certain German naval staff officers began to re-form the German Naval Intelligence service, the Etappesdienst, secretly under commercial cover. One of these officers was a man who, like Leverkühn, would haunt Donovan: Lieutenant Commander Canaris, one of the most interesting men of his time, a man "as wise as a serpent, as pure as a dove."[1]

By training, education, and inclination, Canaris was a conservative monarchist with a vision of a United Europe governed by a European parliament—a vision that WJD was to adopt a little later. The German was never a member of far right, militarist organizations, such as the Freikorps, and was wholly uninterested in rightist revolutionary parties such as the National Socialists, whom he disliked and distrusted as much as the Bolsheviks—to him both represented the gutter in politics. Working toward a return to what Canaris saw were the industrious, orderly, contented days of the Hohenzollerns, he embarked on an intrigue to revive and unite the best of the German racial characteristics of the past with a Pax Europa in the future. His objectives were often misunderstood, and when the intrigue was over, there were as many opinions about him and his ambitions as men capable of assessing his peculiar, elusive, and complicated behavior—opinions ascribing to it everything from homosexual Anglophilia to Jesuitical Russophobia.

Colonel Samuel Lohan, spokesman for the secret agencies of England, later dismissed Canaris as an "inefficient, intriguing, traitorous, lisping queer." Professor Sir John Wheeler-Bennett, the royal historian, a man with special connections to the British secret services and with Donovan, saw him as a "grey fox with a lair on the Tirpitzufer." General Louis Rivet, onetime head of the French services, called him a "trapeze artist," adding somberly that "even the best trapeze artists get killed"; and the Italian military attaché in Berlin, General Efisio Marras, saw him as an "extraordinarily intelligent man [who is] quite without scruples." Otto Skorzeny, a high Nazi storm trooper, was to assert that "Canaris betrayed his country's military secrets directly and wittingly from the beginning of his career to its end"; and one of the most prominent of Hitler's generals, Alfred Jodl, asserted that Canaris had "served the enemy for years." Allen Dulles described him as "one of the bravest men of modern history —gentleman, patriot, visionary of a United States of Europe led by England, France and Germany." One of Canaris's successors, Reinhard Gehlen, held that Canaris was "endowed with intellectual traits not seen in officers since the first half of the nineteenth century." And Canaris's principal British antagonist, Stewart Menzies, declared the German had been "damned brave and damned unlucky." Only Donovan, it seems, kept his own counsel about Canaris.

In 1933 Hitler repudiated the Versailles Treaty, embarked on a course of rearmament, and appointed Canaris chief of the Abwehr with the words: "What I want is something like the British Secret Service—an Order, doing its work with passion."[2] But Canaris did not give Hitler what he wanted. From the moment Canaris established his headquarters at Tirpitzufer 76-78 beside the Landwehr Canal in Berlin, he was concerned as much with the lawlessness of the Hitler regime as he was with providing an intelligence service to guard the Reich against its enemies. Under the cover of conventional operations for the General Staff, Canaris appointed a number of high-level contact men with the Western powers' secret services. A Frankfurt lawyer, Fabian von Schlabrendorff, posing as a historian writing a book about Queen Victoria's German relatives, made contact with officers of the British secret service in London. Hans Bernd Gisevius, a Gestapo lawyer, whispered in Bern with the head of the British secret service in Europe, Claude Dansey. Dr. Josef Müller, a Munich lawyer, appeared at the Department of Extraordinary Affairs at the Vatican, a connection that, when it became known to the Sicherheitsdienst (SD), the Nazi party's intelligence service, resulted in the Nazis' code name for the Canaris conspiracy—the *Schwarze Kapelle,* or Black Orchestra. And Paul Leverkühn made contact with, among others in the United States, Donovan.

The object of these contacts: to keep the Western powers informed of the Nazis' conspiracies against world peace and to avoid war with the Western powers—though not necessarily with the Russians. And with those objectives, it is evident that Canaris and Donovan did meet. It is not possible to say when or where they met, but a personal letter from Frau Canaris to Donovan in 1946 certainly suggests association between Canaris and Donovan, and it is known that immediately after World War II Donovan sought out Frau Canaris, made life easier for her with a financial grant, and made her welcome at the villa at Dahlem, Berlin, which he and his service occupied. All this would not have occurred had there not been contact, for Frau Canaris remained unapproachable to all except the very few people whom her husband had trusted. Moreover, in her letter to Donovan she explained why her husband had conducted his affairs of state as he had, something she certainly would not have done to a stranger:

> Concerning his activity as Chief of Abwehr, and especially concerning details of its structure, I can say little or nothing, since as a woman I was never interested in such things. . . . I lived at home as his wife and the mother of our two children and never interfered in official business. My husband did not want women to know of official affairs. . . . [However] it might be of interest to you to know of the human side of my husband since that will explain to you the true motives of his actions. . . .
>
> I think a good term to describe him would be "Christ in Action," as a friend of humanity in the truest and most beautiful sense of the word, for whom there was no difference among human beings as far as profession, rank, race, or confession was concerned. Many of those he helped will bear witness to this. He was very religious and believed in the supernatural. He had a high feeling of responsibility for the unexpressed duties of life. He was extremely active, did not spare himself, and yet was extremely tender in his emotions. In the office he asked everything of himself, of his collaborators and the people under him. He had sympathy and human understanding for them and was always ready to help.

Of Admiral Canaris's activities as one of Hitler's principal officials, Frau Canaris wrote concerning her husband's use of his special powers:

> He used his powers to oppose as much as possible the growing lawlessness. . . . Many people who were persecuted by the Gestapo came to him, such as Jews, pastors, members of Christian organizations, etc. Often meetings took place in our house with people or their representatives. Often he handled these cases directly in his office in spite of the dangers involved.

Frau Canaris went on to advise Donovan that her husband's assistants in intelligence and conspiracy were General Hans Oster, the deputy chief of the Abwehr, and a departmental head, Hans von Dohnanyi. Another lawyer, Dohnanyi was the son of the celebrated composer and conductor Ernst von Dohnanyi, and his brother-in-law was the equally celebrated theologian Pastor Dietrich Bonhoeffer, whom Canaris attached to the Abwehr in order to protect him from the Gestapo. Dohnanyi himself, before joining the Abwehr, had been attached to the Ministry of Justice, where he was a colleague of a man of importance in Donovan's career as spymaster—OSS Agent 512, Hans Bernd Gisevius.

The origins of Canaris's conspiracy, his wife went on, lay in the election of the Nazis to power in 1933:

My husband immediately recognized the dangers of National Socialism. He hoped that the danger could be mastered. To his sorrow the first and best chance to get rid of the system was not utilized—June 30, 1934, when the Army should have struck [after the murder by Hitler's agents of two prominent General Staff officers, Kurt von Schleicher and the then chief of the Abwehr, Kurt von Bredow, during the Night of the Long Knives]. . . . During the following years many plans of overthrowing the regime were doomed to failure because of the mass psychosis of the people, nourished by the treatment foreign nations accorded to Hitler.

Her husband's "chief aim was to get good intelligence from abroad in order to try to convince the powers that be." He "became extremely unpopular because of his continual warnings" about the latent power of the principal Western democracies, England and America, and as a result of his warnings, which he hoped would deter Hitler from his adventurism, he "made many enemies in the [German Supreme Command, or the Oberkommando der Wehrmacht], in the General Staff, the Foreign Office, Gestapo and other places." But, Frau Canaris continued, her husband "kept on because of the hope for the overthrow of the regime, the hope to be able to help reconstruct a new, better, decent Germany. 'I wanted so much to help them,' he said once, referring to the Western powers." Frau Canaris ended her letter:

I shall always remember the days before the outbreak of war. My husband always prophesied the disastrous end of the mad adventure and never changed his mind even in the face of the victories of [Germany] in the first years. . . . He and his friends suffered so terribly because they had to fight on the German side and loved their fatherland, and yet their sympathies were not on that side and could not be—because their philosophical attitude was so different.[3]

For Ruth and Donovan there was a bittersweet quality about that late autumn and early winter of 1938. Patricia had been born as WJD was getting ready to go to World War I. Now, as World War II was about to start, she was reaching her majority. WJD, himself at the far pinnacles of his profession, wrote to her in haste from some distant part: "I have tried to find something lovely for your birthday, but have not succeeded, so I enclose this check, a dollar for each year of your sweet life, & you can write your name on the back, just as David did, and the Bank will give you the money. . . ."[4]

When he got back from one of his foreign trips, there was a party. According to an unidentified gossip columnist, "Patricia Donovan, youthful daughter of the host, received with poise. 'We still have the canteen I was christened from,' she told Deems Taylor, referring to the hectic day during the last war when she was brought to her father, just before he sailed for France, to be christened by Father Francis P. Duffy."

Yet behind this glittering party given by a rich and successful father for his beautiful daughter was sadness. The Donovans' world was coming to an end, for a number of reasons. If war came—and there was more than a hint of the ball before the Battle of Waterloo about Patricia's twenty-first birthday—Donovan would be recalled for some task or another. The war itself was bound to change their world once again. On more personal, human levels it had already changed irrevocably. Donovan had had a brief fling with a well-known society woman—she was at the party—and he had fallen from grace. He had now wandered around, a tortured man, for months, seeking the advice of his partners and the solace of the confessional. And although he had in effect received the pardon of the faith, he could not forgive himself. Whether this was because Ruth knew of the encounter or because of his devotion to his religion is not known. It was probably a combination of both. The incident—and it was no more—cast a blight upon Donovan from which he found it difficult to redeem himself.

In the spring of 1939 all thoughtful men looked at the world with concern. H. G. Wells spoke of "the failure of Homo Sapiens." As WJD flung himself at his work, seeking information as well as redemption, the British prime minister, Neville Chamberlain, abandoned his policy of appeasing the dictators. He had tried to detach Mussolini from Hitler, and failed; he determined upon a firmer policy toward the dictators, although he had little with which to fight if he had to; he tried to strengthen the Anglo-French alliance against Germany, with little success; the British tried to interest Roosevelt in an alliance, but America was in a remote, disinterested mood, still more frightened of depression than aggression. There were strong fears of German wars against Rumania, Holland, and Poland; of Italian aggression against Egypt, Tunisia, and the Sudan.

During the spring and summer of 1939—the time that Winston Churchill called "the gathering storm"—Donovan made at least three long journeys in Europe. Early in 1939 he joined Generalissimo Francisco Franco's Fourth Army on the heights of the Ebro River for one of the decisive battles of the Spanish Civil War, the conflict in which Germany, Italy, and Russia action-tested their armories and doctrines for the coming struggle. As he explained later, he joined Franco's side not because he admired him but because that was where the new German and Italian weapons were being tested—the 88 millimeter dual-purpose cannon, the Stuka dive bomber, the Mark III tank among much else—and he wanted to see how they performed. During one of the battles on the Ebro the position in which WJD was watching was attacked by Republican forces, and, so it was said later, he came very close to death or injury when a Republican soldier, who was said to have been a future member of the

British Parliament, Bob Edwards, threw a hand grenade into the dugout. WJD escaped harm only because the grenade did not explode.

The second journey came shortly afterward when Donovan was invited to attend maneuvers of the German Army's reserves at Nuremberg. There Donovan's attention was attracted by the report of the multibar-reled mortar and the sound of a new machine pistol, the Schmeisser. Reports were made about these important weapons, and the two trips were entered on Donovan's military documents as having been under-taken for the War Department, and his report on the 88 millimeter gun was commended as the first that such a weapon existed.

Donovan's third journey to Europe came in June and July 1939, a period of great uncertainty and tensions in world affairs. Hitler was threatening Poland, the security of which had been guaranteed by En-gland and France, and Donovan set out in the belief that war was immi-nent and that the Germans would attack in the Low Countries. He spent a good deal of time in France, Belgium, Holland, Germany, and Scan-dinavia. Then, significantly, he saw the British Undersecretary of State for Foreign Affairs, R. A. Butler, who reported of their conversation that Donovan was "an active man, of attractive temperament, who has visited Balbo in Libya, Mussolini in Rome and has many contacts in Berlin with the Foreign Office and General Staff."[5]

It is fairly evident that while in Germany, Donovan saw Canaris through Leverkühn and talked with the state secretary at the German Foreign Office, Baron Ernst von Weizsäcker, and with Count Helmuth von Moltke, all of whom were active at this time in schemes to alert England that this time, over Poland, Hitler wanted war, not peace—a warning that probably resulted in Butler's seeing Donovan. Donovan's main impres-sion, according to Butler, was that "the German Army, as he puts it, is 'set for a fight' to achieve their aims at all costs." At the same time, Donovan said that he was advising his business friends to put their money against war, although he warned that Britain would have "an exciting summer."

On his return from Europe Donovan accepted an invitation from a party friend, General Robert E. Wood, chairman of Sears, Roebuck, to hunt grizzly and Dall sheep in the Yukon. Wood was on the far right of the Republican party and was shortly to lead America First, a movement opposed to America's involvement in European wars and supposedly financed in part by the German government. While on its face this seemed an unlikely association for Donovan, who was supposed to be a liberal Republican, at the time WJD was definitely opposed to American involvement in any European war and said so vigorously in various public speeches.

And so it was that at the appointed time Donovan appeared with his guns and duffle at the gathering point, the lobby of the Chicago Club.

There Donovan and Wood were joined by two other important Republicans, Russell Stearns, a Boston investment banker, and H. Wendell Endicott, a director of Sears, Roebuck and Macy's department store in New York.[6] The party left Chicago on August 6, 1939 (the day Chamberlain warned Hitler that Anglo-French guarantees to Poland would be fulfilled by force if necessary), in a private coach attached to the Great Northern *Empire Builder,* a transcontinental express to Seattle. The European situation dominated all thoughts and conversation on the first day out. But the troubles soon passed into the background as the train steamed westward through the Midwest. It was still the great day of rail travel; the train was very luxurious and stopped from time to time to take on fresh trout and meat. The party spent a good deal of time at the card table, and when Donovan was not playing his favorite game, gin rummy, he was talking with another passenger, Norman Reilly Raine, who was writing the scenario of *The Fighting 69th,* a motion picture of Donovan's exploits in World War I, in which the actor George Brent was to play the part of Donovan and Pat O'Brien that of Father Duffy.

The express arrived in Seattle at breakfast time on August 8, and the Seattle *Daily Times* considered the party of such importance and interest that it sent a reporter, Fergus Hoffman, to record the arrival:

> Perhaps no bugle call sounded on the King Street railway station when the Great Northern Empire Builder pulled into Seattle at 8 o'clock. But the screeching of brakes, the rumble of baggage trucks and the shouts of running redcaps made it seem that half of Uncle Sam's Army was arriving in parade formation.
>
> Or perhaps it was the way Maj. Gen. Robert E. Wood . . . descended from the train and started issuing orders.
>
> "Hurry up and make that New York telephone call," General Wood directed Col. William (Wild Bill) Donovan, famous commander of the "Fighting Sixty-Ninth" Regiment in the World War.
>
> "And get to the dentist and have that tooth filled," the General ordered Russell Stearns, Boston investment banker. "We've got to sail at 9 o'clock."
> . . .
> Major Endicott explained that the party will hunt Dall Sheep, bears and other big game near Lake Kluane in Yukon Territory. They have a special permit from the Canadian Government to make a collection of wild life for the New England Museum of Natural History at Boston.
>
> "Sleep under Sears' tents and on Sears' sleeping bags? How in blazes do we know?" the General demanded. "The Jacquot Brothers at Lake Kluane, our guides, will supply all equipment except the guns. We won't have a thing to say about it. The guides will be in command."
>
> Perhaps the guides WILL be in command. They are famous in the Yukon for making famous men obey orders on the hunting trail. But they haven't met General Wood . . . yet.

Stearns returned after a hasty visit to a dentist's office. The Colonel had completed his telephone calls. The hunters were ready to sail on the Alaska Line steamer *Yukon* in fifteen minutes.

"Let's go," the General ordered, genially.

They went—one, two, three, four.

The foreign news radio headlines aboard the SS *Yukon* had to do with the implications of an obscure controversy over customs between the Polish government and the Danzig Senate, and the party paid little attention as the steamer sailed for Juneau through the beautiful waters of the Strait of Georgia.

On *August 11, 1939,* the *Yukon* arrived at Juneau, where the group was to be flown by the famous Alaskan bush pilot Joe Crosson over the St. Elias Mountains and passes in a Lockheed Electra. Bad weather held the party in Juneau until August 13, when the weather cleared. The aircraft took off over Mendenhall Glacier, flew into Chilkoot Pass, and landed at Whitehorse. There the party was refused permission to proceed by the Canadian authorities because the boss of the local airline, Whitehorse Airways, annoyed that so famous a party should use an American airline, had ordered the local immigration, customs, and police to hold the party until Wood chartered one of his planes. But after Donovan called the Canadian ambassador in Washington the party was allowed to proceed to Burwash landing near Kluane Lake, where the Jacquot brothers had their base camp.

It was *Monday, August 14, 1939,* but nobody took much notice of the radio bulletin: An Anglo-American military mission had arrived at Moscow to begin talks with the Red Army General Staff intended to arrange an Anglo-French-Soviet front against Germany and Italy, and the British were sending another tank brigade out to the Army of the Nile.

For the next fifteen days the party rode on horseback through the St. Elias Mountains, along the valley of the Donjek River and Wade Creek, to hunt bear and sheep. Donovan was the first to secure meat, bringing down a sheep above the timberline with a beautiful shot over 300 yards. On *August 17, 1939,* the party was struck by a gale that lasted two days and made the march dangerous; but by daybreak they were at Big Horn Creek, not far from the Kluane Glacier, the headwaters of the Donjek. The Jacquot brothers, Swiss chefs who had caught gold fever in 1900, made a small fortune, lost it all in wild living, and then come back to start a hunting camp, were excellent cooks who could work miracles with ram and trout.

Endicott wrote of a typical dinner, taken in camp beside the Donjek:

. . . before the guns were cleaned . . . we heard the call for dinner. A nippy of Scotch, a bowl of piping hot soup, seasoned to the "queen's taste," and roast of succulent lamb with all the fixings, a hot fluffy biscuit, an apple pie and a cup of tea, followed by a cigar, changed the gloomy attack of the afternoon to a warm cosy evening under the tent with the musical patter of the raindrops falling on our canvas roof.

Since the camp had no radio, the party had no contact with the outside world. Therefore, nobody beside the Donjek knew that in Berlin Hitler had informed the British government that Germany was "unable to renounce" its interest in Danzig and the Polish Corridor. Nor did they know that on *August 24, 1939,* Roosevelt had appealed again to Hitler and Mussolini to keep the peace, and that the new pope, Pius XII, had done the same a little later that same day.

Friday, August 25, 1939, was, wrote Endicott, who kept the diary of the the expedition:

perhaps the most perfect day of the trip and our little camp at Wolf Creek appeared like a gem in a fascinating setting. The greens of the spruce looked greener than ever. The early frosts were already showing their brilliant touches on the poplar leaves. The mountain slopes were blanketed with snow. The mountain-tops with their jagged peaks were sharply outlined against the solid blue of the sky. Each rocky ridge stood out boldly—each minor or greater canyon showed its precise incision on the mountain side. It was a morning of sharp contrasts and bold colors. The demons of the storm had gone and in their place were gods of laughter and sunshine. It was on that day that I got my best pictures of the packtrain crossing the Donjek.

On *August 26* they broke camp and headed for Teepee Lake, about a two-day ride. Wood and Endicott rode with the Indian guides and the pack train, while Donovan and Stearns hunted over the mountains. During that ride WJD's horse, Gracie, slipped on a narrow trail along the edge of a cliff, throwing Donovan, who almost slid over the lip of the cliff into the river 180 feet below. He was badly bruised, but Stearns and he managed to rejoin the camp near Teepee Lake that night.

On that day Russia and Germany signed the Nazi-Soviet Pact, an agreement that liberated Hitler from the fear that if he attacked Poland, he in turn would be attacked by the combined forces of England, France, and Russia and would be compelled to fight on two fronts. The pact made an attack by Hitler against Poland almost a certainty, and if in the event the British and French honored their guarantees to Poland, England and France would declare war on Germany, and a general European war would result. England and France faced the calamitous confrontation with Hitler.

Monday, August 28, 1939: In Europe the German ambassadors to Belgium, Holland, and Luxembourg announced that the Third Reich would respect the sovereignty and neutrality of those countries. In the Yukon "We all deployed in various directions," recorded Endicott. "Russell had a long hunt—saw one Moose, but no other game. The Colonel saw no game. We had a grand day cruising over the high ridges, enjoying the scenery of the St. Clair River and the Klutlan Glacier."

Tuesday, August 29, 1939: In Europe Queen Wilhelmina of Holland and King Leopold of the Belgians offered to mediate between Hitler and the Poles. In the Yukon Stearns was badly hurt in an accident in which his foot was almost twisted out of its socket. He would have to be confined to camp, but he insisted the expedition continue.

Wednesday, August 30, 1939: In Europe Britain sent Hitler a warning not to attack Poland. In the Yukon Wood bagged a bull caribou, but again Donovan secured nothing. Endicott remained at camp with Stearns, who could not move.

Thursday, August 31, 1939: In Europe Hitler published the terms for a settlement he claimed Poland had rejected. In reality the terms had not been presented. Pope Pius XII appealed again for peace, and Mussolini proposed a European conference designed to avoid general war. In the Yukon both Donovan and Wood shot grizzlies. Endicott recorded:

> Bill's prize bear measured some nine feet. It was the great-grandfather of them all. In fact, it was the largest Bear that the Jacquot Brothers in any of their trips had ever secured. The story of this hunt is wholly thrilling. It seemed that the Colonel was obliged to make a very long and difficult stalk with the Bear hanging constantly to the willows. This gave little or no opportunity for a chance to shoot and it also presented to the Colonel an excellent opportunity to lose his prize entirely. At one place he got so close to the Bear that he could hear him just ahead, but could not see him. When he finally did get a fleeting glance at the Bear, it was some two hundred yards away and still he proceeded on the stalk. . . . Suddenly he saw the willows move just ahead of him, but very close, and the guides moved in, urging him forward. "Of course," whispered Bill, "if you expect me to strangle the Bear I will keep on walking." Within forty steps Bill fired and the Bear dropped. Another two well-placed shots completed the business. The Bear never moved eight feet from where he first fell. You can be sure that there was a grand celebration at camp that night. . . .

Friday, September 1, 1939: In Europe at dawn the German armies invaded Poland. The British and the French governments demanded the Germans' withdrawal. The British began to evacuate all nonessential civilians from London as a precaution against a surprise air attack. Mussolini announced he would "not take the initiative" in military operations. In the Yukon Stearns was now completely unable to move, so, having secured their grizzlies and quota of sheep, Wood decided to return to civilization. The expedition made for Teepee Lake, where they knew another hunting party was to fly in the next day, September 2, 1939. They proposed to fly out on that aircraft. Although in great pain, Stearns managed the five-and-a-half-hour ride to Teepee Lake, where they pitched camp. Donovan and Wood caught thirty to forty one-to-two-pound grayling and arctic trout, which they fried for dinner.

Saturday, September 2, 1939: In Europe the British and French armies mobilized, and advance elements of the British Expeditionary Force began crossing the Channel into France. In the Yukon the weather at Teepee Lake closed in, and it was evident that even if the plane came, it would not be able to land. Since Donovan had not secured his ram, he went hunting, bagging a noble animal with a 700-yard shot. "It was a happy and joyous group of four that sat down after our usual bounteous dinner to a table of bridge. The hands of our watches ticked off the hours. By nine-thirty the whole camp had turned in all was quiet."

Sunday, September 3, 1939: In Europe England and France declared war on Germany. In the Yukon Donovan learned in extraordinary circumstances that World War II seemed about to break out. At about 1:00 A.M.:

> our attention was called to a sort of rustling at our tent flaps. Suddenly they parted and in stepped a perfectly strange Indian. "Me, Indian runner," he said. "Message." And with these words he put his hand in his pocket and pulled out an envelope which he tossed on to the middle of the table. It was addressed to General Wood. . . . The General opened the message—he spoke one word—"War!"
>
> There in those distant mountains of the Yukon, two hundred and fifty miles from the nearest town, some seventy-five or eighty miles away from the nearest inhabited cabin and the outpost radio station of Pacific Alaska Airways, we had been found. The message had been delivered to us out of the distant turmoil of civilization to the unutterable peace of the wilderness.

The message, signed by the manager of Pacific Alaskan Airways, read:

FOLLOWING FROM OUR SEATTLE REPRESENTATIVE QUOTE ACTUAL WARFARE STARTED TODAY BETWEEN POLAND AND GERMANY ALTHOUGH WAR WAS NOT OFFICIALLY DECLARED SITUATION EXTREMELY SERIOUS SIGNED T J CARNEY UNQUOTE PLEASE ACKNOWLEDGE RECEIPT THIS WIRE IMMEDIATELY.
1 SEPT 1939 PAA DELEBECQUE, JUNEAU.

Endicott continued: "When we left Juneau . . . we were all of us convinced that there would be no War and while we had discussed on and off the various international problems and possibilities, not one of us was prepared for the news received at that midnight hour." It was "not hard to picture the tense excitement that permeated our immediate discussion. Before leaving home, the General had been appointed by the President to a committee for the mobilization of industry in case of war. He realized at once the undoubted necessity of his immediate return." Wood sent the runner back to Juneau on a fresh horse to request that Pacific Alaskan send an aircraft to meet the group at Burwash Landing on September 7 or 8.

Monday, September 4, 1939: In London it was announced that the British transatlantic liner *Athenia* had been torpedoed and sunk 200 miles west of the Hebrides *en passage* from England to Canada. Aboard were 1,400 passengers, including 292 Americans. The Royal Navy started the blockade of Germany. In the Yukon, after a tiresome trek through the rain, the party reached Tom Dixon's cabin, where there was a gold prospector with a radio. Endicott recorded that Donovan and the rest of the party learned that "the Germans had almost reached Warsaw . . . Russia was standing in with Germany; that Italy remained neutral and the United States neutral; that several boats had been sunk by German submarines; that Japan was in with England and France. It all seemed too unbelievable." Endicott's last entry in his diary reads:

> On Wednesday, September 13th, we entered the Strait of Juan de Fuca in the Coastguard [*sic*] Cutter *Ingham* and thence on to Seattle. We noticed on the Canadian side of the Strait that several boats passing through the Strait were being inspected by a Canadian military airplane. We ourselves were greeted by one of our own Navy airplanes. At two o'clock in the afternoon we pulled into the wharf at Seattle, and with a hand-shake all around, our group of four broke up—the General and the Colonel flying east, Russell and I taking the "Empire Builder" of the Great Northern Railroad. Our trip was over. We had left the peace, the beauty, the joy and the sportsman's thrills of the Canadian wilderness to come back to a world of trouble and war.

Thirty-six hours later the United Airlines DC-3 that had carried Donovan and Wood across the United States set down at Gravelly Point, the site of National Airport. There bad news awaited Donovan. Ruth had been taken seriously ill.

The evening of Sunday, September 3, 1939, Ruth Donovan was at the summer house at Nonquitt on Cape Cod. It had been a quiet day. She had sunned herself on the beach, she had swum a little, she had watched tennis, and in the early evening she had gone to neighbors for cocktails, intending to go on to a chowder picnic with David and his wife—David had married Mary Grandin, the daughter of a wealthy Pennsylvania family —and Patricia. Then she would play a little bridge and retire early.

Before going to the chowder picnic, she switched on the radio to listen to the news and almost immediately heard British Prime Minister Chamberlain announce that England was now at war with Germany:

> I am speaking to you from the Cabinet Room from 10 Downing Street. This morning the British Ambassador in Berlin handed the German Government the final note stating unless we heard from them by 11 o'clock [6:00 A.M. New York time] that they were prepared at once to withdraw their troops from Poland a state of war would exist between us. I have to tell you now that no such undertaking has been received and consequently this country is at war with Germany. . . . May God bless you all and may He defend the right for it is the evil things we shall be fighting against—brute force, broken promises, bad faith. But I am certain that right shall prevail.[7]

There then followed bulletins from London, Paris, Berlin, Warsaw (which was blazing after a Luftwaffe attack), and Moscow, and when these were completed, the announcer in New York stated that President Roosevelt would make an "extraordinary message" to the nation on the war situation that same night. Ruth decided not to go to the chowder picnic and with David and his wife, Mary, remained at Nonquitt that evening.

The President came on the air to ask for "an adjournment of all partisanship and selfishness" and a substitution of "complete national unity in the United States to the end that the newest world war may be kept from the Western Hemisphere."[8] He declared that a proclamation of neutrality was being prepared. "I trust," the President continued, "that in the days to come our neutrality can be made a true neutrality." This nation, he declared, would remain neutral, but he added pointedly that he "could not ask that every American remain neutral in thought as well. Even a neutral has a right to take account of the facts. Even a neutral cannot be asked to close his mind or his conscience."

There followed a long statement concerning America's place in the world and its responsibilities now that Europe was at war. The President's speech came to an end. David lit a fire, and the family settled down to some desultory bridge. Soon Ruth asked the children to excuse her because she had pain in her abdomen. She went to bed, but not to sleep.

By the middle of the night she was in fairly severe pain and asked Patricia to fetch some aspirin. By daybreak, however, the pain had intensified and Patricia called the doctor. He advised Ruth that she required a curettage. Ruth was admitted to the local hospital at 4:30 P.M. on September 4, 1939, the procedure to be undertaken the following morning.

When he began, the surgeon discovered that Ruth's condition was far more serious than had been foreseen and decided to undertake a full-

scale hysterectomy, a major and, under certain circumstances, a dangerous operation. Ruth came through the surgery satisfactorily, and as she
wrote in her diary that night: "Realized as soon as out of ether I had had
something drastic done—Pretty miserable."[9]

Donovan was advised of the surgery when he called Nonquitt from
Washington on or about September 6. While briefly in the capital Donovan heard a rumor from his close friend Frank Knox, publisher of the
Chicago *Daily News,* that Roosevelt was contemplating the formation of
a coalition Cabinet and Donovan might be asked to serve as secretary of
war. He said no more than that he would think about such a post if an
invitation was received and then flew up to Nonquitt to see Ruth. She
seems not to have known that he was there—she was being kept under
very heavy sedation—and Donovan decided to go down to New York and
his law offices and wait there and attend to the matters on his desk while
she was in hospital. But he was very attentive and sent Ruth masses of
flowers each day.

Not until October 13, 1939, did her doctors give Ruth a clean bill of
physical health, but it was evident that she was depressed and needed a
complete change of air, scenery, and companionship. That she discussed
with David on the twenty-second, when she announced that the schooner
Yankee was sailing for the Pacific and she would like to sail with it. David
tried to dissuade her on the grounds that a world war had broken out and
that such a voyage might be dangerous, but she was adamant, and eventually the family and the doctors agreed that she could go.

Donovan also tried to dissuade her, but she insisted she was doing what
she wanted to do, and with that Donovan gave her a significant address:
that of Paul Leverkühn, in Berlin—Pariser Platz 7—presumably for use
if she was captured by a German warship in the Pacific. With all arrangements made, Ruth left Washington aboard a Pan American Clipper at
9:00 P.M. on November 19 and joined the *Yankee* in the Panama Canal
four days later.

Ruth was on watch when the telegram came in over the merchant
marine voice radio band at dictation speed, while the *Yankee* was off
Samoa in the early hours of April 9, 1940. The telegram from Bill contained the most terrible news: Patricia had died following a road accident
at Fredericksburg, Virginia, on the eighth. Ruth wrote in her diary that
night:

> Tuesday, April 9, 1940. Worse [*sic*] day of my whole life. Had radio in eve
> from Bill saying Pat had had auto accident yesterday at 2:30 near Fredericks-
> burg—She died in hospital 4 hrs later never regaining consciousness. M[a-
> rion] Glover with her at end. Heartbroken and just as soon die.

Now followed a period of unbelievable agony for Ruth, as the *Yankee* put about for Samoa, about four days' distance, where she was to disembark and make her way to Honolulu and Washington.

Donovan, too, was going through his own agony, for he adored Patricia, who was much like him in spirit, vitality, intellect, and her sense of curiosity. He had received the news of her accident at his law offices at 2 Wall Street. At that time Patricia was still alive, and he left New York immediately aboard *The Congressional.* When the express reached Baltimore, there was a Western Union telegram for him, apparently from Marion Glover at the hospital. Patricia had died.

Patricia, who was twenty-two, had been driving back to Washington after a weekend with friends, to resume her studies at George Washington University (she was taking English) and to be with her father while he was in the capital for a few days on legal business. Outside Fredericksburg, a severe spring storm had made the road very slippery, and at a corner she had lost control, the car had turned over, and she had suffered serious head injuries. She had lain unconscious in the road for a time until another car happened by, stopped, picked her up, and took her to the hospital.

Donovan was close to physical collapse when he arrived in Washington. The police asked him to identify the body, but his first reaction was to ask his brother-in-law, Dexter Rumsey, to go in his place. In the end he decided to undertake that awful task himself. It brought him very close to collapse, and indeed, WJD never really recovered from Patricia's death. Later he would say that the agony of her death made him white-haired almost overnight.

Now came the equally awful task of informing Ruth. Uncertain about how to communicate with the *Yankee,* or even which latitude the schooner was in, Donovan gave instructions that Patricia was to be kept in a vault until Ruth's return to Washington. Then, WJD stated later, Roosevelt heard of Patricia's death and directed the naval authorities to find a means of communicating with the *Yankee.* The message from WJD was passed to Ruth, and a Japanese freighter, the *Mariposa,* was asked to meet the *Yankee* at Samoa and take Ruth to Honolulu.

At first Donovan intended to fly to Honolulu to meet Ruth and bring her back to Washington. For some unknown reason he could not go, and David Donovan and his wife therefore went to Honolulu and waited for Ruth to land there. Donovan arranged to meet them at Los Angeles Harbor and bring Ruth home from there.

Ruth reached Samoa in the *Yankee* at 3:00 A.M. on April 15 and was invited to stay with the governor of the island. She learned she would have to wait until May 2 or 3 for the Japanese steamer to arrive because it had a great distance to travel. The wait was agonizing, and the world situation made it worse. During that period the Germans invaded Norway and Denmark, and British and French expeditionary forces landed in Norway to hold the center of the country. There were violent naval battles between the British and German fleets off the Norwegian coast, and Ruth tended to confuse the world tragedy with her personal tragedy as she waited in dread.

At last, the *Mariposa* arrived on May 3, 1940. She sailed almost immediately and arrived at Honolulu on the eighth, a month after Pat's death. David and Mary Donovan were at the pier to meet Ruth with her mail, an account of the accident, and an explanation that they would not be able to fly, only sail, to Los Angeles, where WJD would be waiting. Ruth's only recorded statement during the voyage was that "Letters about Pat shattering me."[10]

Ruth, David, and Mary reached Los Angeles at 9:00 A.M. on May 13, 1940 (three days after Winston Churchill became prime minister of England and Hitler opened his offensive against the French, British, and Belgian armies), and Donovan was at the dock. The family went directly to the transcontinental express and, Ruth recorded in her diary: "He looks badly [*sic*]. . . . In evening Bill told me all about Pat—Can't bear much more—She had been doing so well this winter & had developed so much."

As the train rumbled toward Chicago, the war news worsened. The Luftwaffe burned Rotterdam, and the Dutch Army surrendered on the fourteenth. On the fifteenth the Wehrmacht broke through the French front, crossed the Meuse between Mézières and Namur, and began to hurtle across Flanders and down into northern France—news that, when coupled with the surrender of France and the isolation of the British and the threatened invasion of the British Isles by the Wehrmacht, caused WJD to change his belief that America should stay out of the war. He now believed total American involvement was inevitable.

For Ruth, the end of the ghastly journey arrived on May 16, 1940, with Pat's burial in Arlington National Cemetery, an honor to which she was entitled as the "Daughter of the 69th Regiment" and as the daughter of a holder of the Medal of Honor:

> Arrived Washington 9 A.M. Marion Glover at [Georgetown] house and [Father] Vin [Donovan]. . . . Short service for Pat at vault—Quite a few there —Horrible rainy day—Decided I just had to see Pat—She looked lovely but oh the pain of it—Many, many flowers. . . . Can't ever be happy again.

And when the mourners, the priests, the buglers, and the firing squads had departed on May 20, 1940, the day on which the German panzers reached the old Somme battlefields of World War I, "War news still awful —It is a sad world everywhere."[11]

PART TWO

THE TORCH PERIOD

Being the account of Donovan's principal activities from Pearl Harbor to the completion of the Anglo-American invasion of French North Africa in November 1942

10

Presidential Agent

Six weeks after Patricia's funeral Donovan gave a small dinner party at his duplex in Beekman Place. He cut the dinner short to hear a newscast by the CBS correspondent in London, Ed Murrow, a report of a speech by Churchill in which the new British prime minister made his momentous declaration:

> . . . the Battle of France is over. I expect that the Battle of Britain is about to begin. Upon this battle depends the survival of Christian civilization. Upon it depends our own British life, and the long continuity of our institutions and our Empire. The whole fury and might of the enemy must very soon be turned on us. Hitler knows that he will have to break us in this Island or lose the war. If we can stand up to him, all Europe may be free and the life of the world may move forward into broad, sunlit uplands. But if we fail, then the whole world, including the United States, including all that we have known and cared for, will sink into the abyss of a new Dark Age, made more sinister, and perhaps more protracted, by the lights of perverted science. Let us therefore brace ourselves to our duties, and so bear ourselves that, if the British Empire and its Commonwealth last for a thousand years, men will still say: "This was their finest hour."[1]

Three days later, on June 21, 1940, the British liner *Britannic* docked in New York, and ashore came the new chief of the British secret services in the Americas, William S. Stephenson, whose code name was Intrepid and whose mission came directly from the Foreign Office: Bring America into the war or, if that was not possible, turn it to the status of a neutral hostile to Germany. Immediately upon checking into the St. Regis Hotel in New York, Intrepid set to work: He telephoned Donovan at his offices at 2 Wall Street. Within the hour the two men were together in Stephenson's suite—alacrity that suggests they knew each other well. From that moment there sprang up a rare relationship between Donovan, the anti-imperialist, and Stephenson, a principal representative of the world's leading imperial power.

There would never be an adequate explanation for Stephenson's and the British belief that Donovan was a man of influence who could assist England in its desperate hour. Donovan had not as yet emerged as an associate of President Roosevelt, and in any case he seems to have had considerable political antipathy for FDR. So fundamental was that antipathy that according to WJD years later, when Roosevelt created a coalition Cabinet as an emergency measure just before Stephenson's arrival and offered WJD the post of secretary of war, Donovan rejected the post because "their domestic differences remained." FDR said, " 'Now, Bill, we haven't really been too far apart.' " Donovan replied, " 'But oh, yes, we have, Mr. President,' " and then thanked FDR for his consideration but said he could not serve in the Cabinet.[2] After that, for the time being, the only post for which WJD was considered was that of war bonds organizer in New York State.

Yet Stephenson did regard Donovan as an Anglophile to be courted and promoted. Why? Donovan's public political personality shows he was not an Anglophile; to the contrary, he was a Yankee with a definite Fenian streak in him that, one would have thought, would have made him him antipathetic to British causes. His papers show that he had deplored certain aspects of British capitalism and imperialism after World War I, especially in regard to British rule in India. Also in the late 1930's, Donovan revealed to vanden Heuvel, he had held the view that the British and the French should "take care of Germany, and that America should stay out of Europe's wars."[3]

Now, in a flash apparently, this had changed. All Europe, except for a few small neutrals, had been conquered by Germany. The British Empire, itself in the early stages of disintegration, stood alone against the Fascist powers, and most of the rest of the world's nations were arraying themselves behind the Axis against Britain. What, therefore, had caused this change of attitude? There were probably five reasons at least: (1) his belief that the British Isles were America's first line of defense; (2) his suspicion that if Britain were conquered, the next target would be the United States; (3) the fact that if Germany secured the British and the French fleets, the Reich would be confirmed as the most powerful nation in the world; (4) America's need to control the high seas for its own safety and survival; and (5) the need of the United States to ensure access to its sources of raw materials. In short, with Japan acting menacingly in the Pacific, America was almost as beleaguered as England.

For his part, Churchill believed Britain could defeat the Axis coalition only with the United States as a full ally in the war. As a young statesman he had been impressed, as he was to write, by an observation of Lord Grey of Fallodon, British foreign secretary during the first half of World War I. A statesman who worked effectively to establish good relations with the United States, Grey had told Churchill that the United States was like "a gigantic boiler. Once the fire is lighted under it there is no limit to the power it can generate."[4] Churchill insisted what had been true then was true now. Consequently, in the same spirit that the chief of the British secret services in the Americas in World War I, Sir William Wiseman, had cultivated Woodrow Wilson's confidant, Colonel E. M. House, so Stephenson began to cultivate Donovan.

The main outcome of the St. Regis meeting, and others like it, was that Stephenson invited Donovan to visit England and study the intelligence and war establishments. To accept such a mission when the United States was formally neutral required presidential permission, which was sought through WJD's friend Secretary of the Navy Frank Knox. Roosevelt approved Donovan's journey, but at the expense of the United States government, which gave him credentials and a letter of credit for $10,000. In the course of approving the visit, Roosevelt remarked, "Bill Donovan is . . . an old friend of mine—we were in the law school together—and frankly, I should like to have him in the Cabinet, not only for his own ability, but also to repair in a sense the very great injustice done him by President Hoover in the Winter of 1929."[5]

On July 14, 1940, Donovan left New York in a Pan American Clipper flying boat for Lisbon and London. A few days later he was at his favorite hotel in London, Claridge's, in the charge of a man known to the London bureaucracy only as C. During his stay in London Donovan saw everyone of consequence from the sovereign, King George VI, and Prime Minister Churchill, to the Chiefs of Staff, the War Cabinet, and the commanders in chief. The most important in terms of Donovan's career as first American intelligence master was C—Colonel Stewart Menzies. Menzies, a gentle, charming man, was just fifty, seven years younger than Donovan, and he was the product of very rich parents and friends of Edward VII. He was a colonel in the Life Guards, the sovereign's escort. He and Donovan met first at Menzies's headquarters, 52 Broadway, a grimy office block opposite the St. James's Park tube station, a place guarded by ancient pensioners in blue uniforms with brass buttons bearing the inscription *Honi Soit Qui Mal Y Pense* ("Evil be to him who evil thinks").

Menzies's Secret Intelligence Service (SIS) was a quaint combination of antiquity and modernity. It had been established by Sir Francis Walsingham in the reign of Elizabeth I, and over the centuries the appointment to it had remained a royal prerogative, although the candidates were usually selected by the heads of the armed services and endorsed by the prime minister or foreign secretary.

Responsible to the permanent undersecretary at the Foreign Office, the SIS had many branches and functions, but in general its labors were divided into two parts: acquisition of secret intelligence by all means throughout the world, and counterespionage outside the British Isles. Its activities were protected by a ferocious statute known as the Official Secrets Act, through which those imprudent enough to interest themselves with the affairs of the service, publicly or privately, could be sentenced to death in wartime and to a maximum of fourteen years' penal servitude in peacetime.

Almost always its officers operated overseas under diplomatic or consular cover, most often (as in the case of Stephenson in New York) as Passport Control Officers. Oddly, its budget, known as the Secret Vote, was made public each year, although sensible men did not take the figure seriously since the amount stated did not include the larger sums spent in its support by the foreign, colonial, dominion, and armed services' departments.

From the outset Donovan and Menzies do not appear to have been the sort of men who could become firm friends or allies. Menzies was first and foremost a Praetorian of the British Empire, the sort of High Tory who regarded American republicanism with its notions of self-determination and liberty as highly dangerous. Moreover, he epitomized the first principle of the British secret service: silence about its capabilities and intentions. Yet it is evident that Menzies talked fully and candidly to Donovan about his service in all its aspects, including its most secret activities: the code and cipher-breaking service which operated behind the code name Ultra, and Britain's deception operations—together the most secret of all secret service operations. That was remarkable, for the United States was not yet a belligerent, there was no assurance that it would become one, and Donovan was still no more than a private person on temporary state business.

Donovan returned to New York in the British flying boat *Clare*. He arrived at 7:00 P.M. on Sunday, August 4, 1940. Ruth was at the dock to greet him, and together they took the night sleeper down to Washington. Early on Monday morning Donovan was at Secretary Knox's office to report. That report—which vastly intensified British confidence in Donovan and increased their willingness to impart to him their greatest secrets —amounted to a single sentence: The British would fight on; they would not surrender their fleet; their morale was high, but their equipment was deficient. Donovan stressed Churchill's special need for destroyers, for the British had lost many such vessels in the Norwegian sea battles.

In the next twenty days Donovan did little else but convey that message to Washington. He spent two and a half days with Roosevelt, who had just been renominated for a third term as President, on a railroad tour of New England, their first really close contact. Again Donovan passed on the message he had received in London concerning the urgent need for destroyers, no matter how old they were, to take the place of lost units until new British ships came into service.

But as Donovan learned during that journey, the President had been told by the attorney general, Robert H. Jackson, that he had no power to transfer weapons of war such as destroyers to the British flag. Only Congress had that power, and even if it elected to make the transfer, the debate was likely to be long and noisy when the British predicament demanded speed and silence.

To complicate the question of transferring warships, Donovan learned that an amendment to the naval appropriations bill of June 1940 specified that no war equipment could be transferred to a foreign government without certification by the Army Chief of Staff, General George C. Marshall, or the Chief of Naval Operations, Admiral Harold R. Stark, that it was not wanted for the defense of the United States. Moreover, Stark had testified that the destroyers the British wanted still had value to the United States and could hardly retract that statement. Nevertheless, it was evident to Donovan that the President was seeking a method by which the warships could be transferred, and he sanctioned Donovan's suggestion that "I get some of my bright young men in law" to look into the situation with fresh eyes.

When Donovan's travels with Roosevelt were over, he called at his law offices, saw George Leisure and Ralstone Irvine, explained the difficulties, and Irvine agreed to get one of the firm's ablest younger men, James R. Withrow, to look into the statutes and see whether there was any precedent by which the President could act without going to Congress. Immediately Withrow went to Washington and began burrowing into the statute books in the Library of Congress. In three days—and nights—of work he found the precedents. They involved the emergency powers conferred upon Jefferson and Madison to enable them to carry out certain actions in the Barbary Wars of 1804–15, when the United States found itself in naval warfare with some of the North African states. These powers, Withrow established, had not been repealed and could still be used by the President. He prepared a paper for Donovan to present to Roosevelt, and when the attorney general's team had checked and confirmed Withrow's opinion, the President began to take steps to transfer the destroyers, persuading opponents that he was doing so in exchange for bases on eight British islands in the Atlantic. With the destroyers in British hands, and the bases in those of the United States, American security would be enhanced rather than diminished.

Withrow's work was a triumph of legal inquiry. While none of the destroyers was battleworthy, some were not even seaworthy, and most were more dangerous to the British seamen in them than to the German Navy, the United States had secured use of some of the best real estate available for offshore defense. The entire transaction was little more than a sale of property in bankruptcy, but the British were nonetheless grateful to Donovan.

The British accordingly extended fresh invitations to Donovan to visit England, go on to the Mediterranean war zone, and further familiarize himself with the work of the British secret services. The permanent undersecretary of state, Sir Alexander Cadogan, in a note to the foreign secretary on December 17, 1940, the day after Donovan's arrival, demonstrated what the British thought of WJD:

> [Menzies] tells me that Mr. Stephenson, who travelled over with Colonel Donovan, has impressed upon him that the latter really exercises a vast degree of influence in the administration. He has Colonel Knox in his pocket and, as Mr. Stephenson puts it, has more influence with the President than Colonel House had with Mr. Wilson. Mr. Stephenson believes that if the Prime Minister were to be completely frank with Colonel Donovan, the latter would contribute very largely to our obtaining all that we want of the United States.[6]

While this appreciation of Donovan's influence was exaggerated, the British believed it, for at about the same time the British ambassador in Washington supported Cadogan's advice with a telegram that Donovan was "one of our best and most influential friends here with a great deal of influence both with the Service Departments and the Administration."

Within two days Donovan and Churchill had lunched and spent a good part of the afternoon together at 10 Downing Street. To show Donovan England meant business and could give as good as it was receiving from the Luftwaffe, Churchill ordered Royal Air Force Bomber Command to attack the major German inland port and industrial center of Mannheim on the night that Donovan arrived, on the night before their lunch, and on the night after—attacks that were probably not unconnected with the placing by Britain before the U.S. government of requests for weapons and munitions to a total value of $750,000,000.

Although Donovan left no account of his long conversation with Churchill, he did tell a law partner, Otto C. Doering, that the prime minister discussed at length his strategy for the defeat of Germany. Churchill believed that Britain would surely founder as a world power if it suffered again casualties on the scale of those of World War I, and that to avoid such casualties, he had started to look at the map in other ways.

Churchill showed on a globe in his study how Germany was more vulnerable to an attack from the Baltic or the Mediterranean than from the west across the Channel. Donovan, who recalled the casualties his battalion had suffered at the Ourcq through frontal assault, found much wisdom in Churchill's concepts—much more wisdom than he had encountered in his discussions with the U.S. Chiefs of Staff. He liked especially Churchill's ideas to make all Europe rebel against the Germans, "to set Europe alight," as the prime minister put it, as a precursor to a general attack by the armies.

Thus, Donovan and Churchill began their agreeable wartime relationship; and when the prime minister asked Donovan what he wanted particularly to do and see, and Donovan pointed out that the secret service was to take him out to the Mediterranean theater, Churchill endorsed the visit. The PM gave instructions that a telegram be sent to all commanders in chief requiring them to give Donovan "every facility," as he had "great influence with the President," and informed them that Donovan had been "taken fully into our confidence."

On New Year's Eve 1940, a four-engine Sunderland maritime reconnaissance flying boat carrying Donovan took off in a cloud of spume from Plymouth Sound, climbed over The Lizard, and set course over the Western Approaches out to the ten-degree line to avoid the Focke-Wulf Kondors. At that point the captain turned south toward the first of the Empire's great coaling ports and military bastions, Gibraltar.

To make German interception more difficult, the flight lasted from dusk until dawn at Gibraltar, and to make it more agreeable, Lord Louis Mountbatten had sent a hamper containing Donovan's birthday dinner— he became fifty-eight while flying through cirrus clouds over the western fringes of the Bay of Biscay. The hamper contained three bottles of a Moselle, a flask of hot turtle soup, fresh lobster, cold pheasant, and Stilton cheese and Bath Olivers. It was served beautifully by the orderly in a white mess jacket with gleaming brass buttons and white gloves. Even if the British were at war, they had not abandoned their elegances.

The flight was slow (a Sunderland made no more than 180 knots on these long flights), low (it could not fly more than 8,500 feet without oxygen for passengers), and choppy. But in time the Sunderland made its landfall off Cádiz, flew through the Pillars of Hercules, and landed safely and gently on the smooth waters of the Bay of Algeciras.

At the flying boat dock in Admiralty Harbor, Donovan was received by the governor and a band that played "Old Glory" and "God Save the King" and was then taken by the governor in the state Rolls-Royce, American and British flags flying from the hood, to the Alameda. Donovan, the poor boy from the Irish First Ward of Buffalo, had arrived in a citadel of the realm of "Albert Frederick Arthur George, of the United Kingdom of Great Britain, Ireland, and of the British Dominions beyond the Seas, King, Defender of the Faith, Emperor of India."

He had also arrived in the Mediterranean war zone.

Accompanied by Churchill's personal representative, Colonel Vivian Dykes, and by representatives of Menzies's service, for the next two months Donovan toured the British war stations between Baghdad and Madrid, at a time when the war had begun to widen dramatically.

The Italians, showing that they were no New Tenth Legion, had attempted to invade Egypt, Albania, and Greece but had been hopelessly defeated everywhere and been tossed out of Egypt, Abyssinia, and Somaliland. Now the Germans and the Vichy French were coming to their assistance. A German air corps was arriving in Sicily to begin preinvasion air attacks on the British fortress of Malta and to close the narrows between Tunisia and Sicily. The Vichy French in North Africa were actively helping General Erwin Rommel establish his Afrika Korps in the Western Desert on the Libyan frontier with Egypt, the nation that was "the pivot of the British Empire." In Syria the French were conspiring with German agents to raise an Arab revolt against the British just as the British had raised an Arab revolt against the Germans and Turks in World War I. In Iraq and Persia, not without success, German agents were seeking to close the oil fields to the British Empire, which owned them, and in the Balkans, pessimists predicted accurately, it was only a matter of time before the Germans marched into Greece, Yugoslavia, Bulgaria, Rumania, and Albania, perhaps even into Russia. The British now controlled the Mediterranean, having wrecked the Italian fleet, but German U-boat squadrons had begun to filter through the Pillars of Hercules.

Donovan seemed not to be in any way concerned that he was in a war zone and liable to sudden death. He flew from Gibraltar to Malta, then under intense Italo-German air attack, spent two days inspecting the Maltese defenses, and then flew to British imperial headquarters at Cairo, where he arrived on January 7, 1941. He flew up to the Western Desert to observe the British imperial forces trouncing the New Tenth Legion, returned to Cairo, and then flew across the eastern Mediterranean to Athens, Belgrade, and Sofia. At Sofia he attempted to persuade the Great Unifier, Czar Boris III, not to join the Axis—and failed.

From Belgrade, Donovan flew back to Athens, went up to the Albanian front to watch the Greek Army in action against the Italian Army, and then visited British military, diplomatic, and secret intelligence outposts in Turkey, Cyprus, and Palestine. Donovan then returned to Cairo, flew to Baghdad, back to Cairo, up to Benghazi, back to Cairo, and then home through Malta, Gibraltar, Lisbon, Madrid, London, and Dublin.

It was an exhausting, dangerous journey that would have wrecked the nerves even of younger men, not only because of the military dangers but also because most of the flying was in worn-out planes operating in some of the worst winter flying weather in the world. Much of the time Donovan's aircraft were within range of German and Italian fighters, but he submerged whatever fears he might have had in reading, writing, talking, catnapping, usually curled up in the tail of the aircraft, wrapped in traveling rugs and the long sheepskin trench coat he bought at Cordings in Piccadilly before leaving London.

He was also tireless on the ground, although he did develop conjunctivitis—his system's way of showing that he was overworking it. His sixty days on the ground were an unending procession of generals, admirals, air marshals, spies, politicians, sheikhs, priests, mullahs, princes, colonels, and kings. He inspected tanks, guns, feet, planes, trucks, weapons, troops, supply and signals systems, fortresses, hospitals, palaces, antiquities, fieldworks. And everywhere he went he told everyone he met that Britain was fighting, that it would continue to fight, and that it could and would defeat the Germans as it had defeated the Italians, that America would support it to victory come what may, and that the American people were determined not to permit it to be defeated. When Donovan's journey was over, Churchill was so content with the President's agent that he wired Roosevelt: "I must thank you for the magnificent work done by Donovan in his prolonged tour of Balkans and Middle East. He has carried with him throughout an animating, heart-warming flame."[7]

Donovan's journey was of enduring importance to the outcome of the war in two respects: (1) He became involved in the Yugoslav situation and at least partly through his words and actions had fundamentally and disastrously affected Hitler's timetable for his campaign against Russia, and (2) his reports helped Roosevelt decide upon a strategy for the defeat of Germany and Italy with the minimum cost in blood and treasure.

First the Yugoslav affair.

When the Luftwaffe failed to defeat the Royal Air Force in the Battle of Britain, Hitler abandoned his plans for the invasion of the British Isles and used the raids instead to divert attention from what had become his real objective: the invasion of Russia in the late spring of 1941, the destruction of Russian Bolshevism as a world force, and the establishment of a German Empire in European Russia with its eastern frontier running from Archangel to Astrakhan. In the winter of 1940–41 Hitler quietly withdrew the principal fighting units of the Wehrmacht from the front on the English Channel and positioned them in Poland, Rumania, and Bulgaria.

At the same time operational planning began. Hitler decreed, and his generals accepted, that the Red Army must be defeated and all the principal cities of European Russia, including Moscow and Leningrad, must be firmly in German hands before the onset of winter. The reason was clear:

The Wehrmacht had been built for lightning campaigns, not for protracted or winter warfare, and it was estimated, accurately, that unless the Russians were defeated before the winter, the consequence would be a long campaign—which, perhaps, the Wehrmacht could not win. Consequently after much deliberation Hitler and his generals set May 14, 1941, as D-Day for Barbarossa, as the operation was code-named; and it was understood that the operation would not succeed if, for any reason, that date could not be met.

Hitler and his generals recognized that Barbarossa's flank in Greece and Yugoslavia was particularly vulnerable to a British attack and that if there were such an attack, it would upset the timetable for Barbarossa. With that in mind, German agents in both countries worked throughout the winter of 1940–41 to bring the Yugoslav and Greek governments into the Axis. While they failed in the case of Greece, when Donovan arrived in Belgrade on January 23, 1941, Prince Paul, the Yugoslav regent, had taken steps, under duress, to join Britain's enemies.

That same day, to dissuade the Yugoslav ruler from joining the Axis, Donovan stated at lunch with Prince Paul that it was the "definite policy" of the United States to give every possible assistance to those countries willing to fight for their independence. The hint was clear—that Yugoslavia would receive U.S. aid if Paul elected to fight the Germans. But Paul chose to ignore the hint, for he was much under the influence of his pro-German wife. In any case, almost while Donovan and Prince Paul were lunching, the Yugoslav premier and defense minister were leaving for Berchtesgaden to see Hitler. There was, therefore, little hope in Donovan's mind of deflecting Paul from his alliance with Germany.

After the lunch, consequently, Donovan crossed the Danube to Zemun, the headquarters of General Dušan Simović, commander of the Yugoslav Air Force, who was, Churchill later recorded, "a clandestine center of opposition to German penetration into the Balkans and to the inertia of the Yugoslav Government."[8] Donovan found Simović deeply impressed by Roosevelt's Four Freedoms speech of January 6, 1941, and found it opportune to show Simović a telegram signed by Roosevelt, stating that "the United States is looking forward not merely to the present but to the future, and any nation which tamely submits on the grounds of being quickly overrun would receive less sympathy from the world than the nation which resists, even if this resistance can be continued only a few weeks."[9]

The telegram obviously constituted something less than an inducement to revolution; nevertheless, it was later asserted that Donovan promised military assistance to Simović if he mounted a revolution against the prince and entered into an alliance with Britain. Of that assertion there is no evidence in the Donovan papers, nor, it seems, was any inducement necessary. For as Donovan related later:

[Simović was] emphatic in his determination to resist any German infringement of Yugoslav territory. He said that the people of Yugoslavia, if they needed any further lesson, could now clearly see in Rumania [which the Germans had virtually occupied in preparation for Barbarossa] what happened when a country let itself be occupied without resistance. He stated that Yugoslavia would not permit the passage of German troops through its territory, as . . . the people would not stand for it.[10]

Moreover, General Simović also assured Donovan that the Yugoslav Army would fight the Germans if either Greece or Bulgaria was invaded by the Germans, as such an invasion would constitute "intolerable dangers."

With those stout words ringing in his ears, Donovan left Belgrade on January 25, 1941, expecting, probably, to hear no more of Simović's revolution. But after Prince Paul joined the Axis, Simović proved as good as his word. When four British divisions established a beachhead in Greece, Simović overthrew Prince Paul and his government, renounced the treaty with Germany, installed himself as prime minister, and placed the young king, Peter II, on the throne. At that, Hitler launched a lightning attack on Yugoslavia, using powerful air and tank forces which had been on their way east for Barbarossa. For good measure he marched into Greece to eject the British divisions.

The Germans commanders executed the operations with their usual efficiency and ferocity, and by April 17, 1941, Yugoslavia had been subdued—temporarily. The king and Simović had fled, and 17,000 people lay dead, according to Churchill, in the ruins of Belgrade. In Greece the German campaign ended on April 27, 1941, but the British were not destroyed; they merely withdrew in strength to the island of Crete, and Hitler was forced to mount a second, extremely costly operation, to remove that thorn from his side. That he did not succeed in doing until May 31, 1941, seventeen days *after* the Barbarossa D-Day.

The combined effect of the three operations was to remove key fighting units from the Wehrmacht's service during the preparatory period for Barbarossa and to so run down and disperse other principal forces that the timetable for Barbarossa had to be set back five weeks from May 14 to June 22, 1941. Those weeks were to prove the margin by which Hitler failed to defeat Russia before the ferocious winter set in. It would be believed widely, also, that those were the five weeks by which Hitler lost the war, for in failing to defeat Russia that year, Hitler gave the Allies time to gather strength for a protracted war that Germany could not win.

There would also be a powerful school of thought that the upset in Hitler's timetable was caused by Donovan's assurances to Simović. Donovan always denied that he gave any assurances to Simović; nevertheless, the protagonists of the idea were able to present such formidable evidence to support the case that there is no reason to doubt that Donovan set light to the fuse that led to Simović's coup d'état—the event that led Hitler to march into Yugoslavia and Greece and to postponement of the Barbarossa D-Day.

By February 20, 1941, Donovan was back in Cairo, resting at the Mena House, the stately watering place under the Great Pyramids and the Sphinx. There he composed and transmitted a long telegraphic report to Secretary of State Cordell Hull and Secretary of the Navy Frank Knox.[11] Donovan's principal point was that "England has done a superb job in this area from a strategic, tactical and administrative standpoint," the quality of which could be "truly appreciated only by actually seeing that so much has been done with so little." The main strategical conception —Donovan's second point, which confirmed Roosevelt in his thinking— was that the Mediterranean front was of exceptional importance if that sea was viewed "as a No-man's land between two lines on a strategic front running from Spain to the Black Sea."

Donovan pointed out that if the map were looked at with that in mind, then Germany held the northern, or European, line except at the two ends, while Britain controlled much of the southern, or African, line. It was important, therefore, that Britain receive the help it needed to hold that line and then, at an opportune moment, to strike north—Donovan's version of Churchill's theory that the weakest part of the German "alligator" was not its snout or its tail, but its "soft underbelly."

Having planted Churchill's notion of the southern strategy or the soft underbelly theory in the White House and other important centers of decision, Donovan hastened home. His legal practice called—he was still a practicing lawyer, it will be remembered—and there were urgent matters to attend to, among the most urgent being a major antitrust suit concerning the Cement Institute of America. Also, as he was doubtless aware, powerful forces were at work for and against his plans for an American secret intelligence service.

Donovan arrived at the La Guardia flying boat dock aboard a BOAC amphibian on March 18, 1941, to find Ruth and his daughter-in-law, Mary, waiting for him in the freezing wind. After spending the night at Beekman Place, he traveled on to Washington to report to FDR and the Cabinet and was soon immersed in an unending stream of conferences, lunches, and dinners with the capital's eminences, quite forgetting he had business and private affairs to attend to. Ruth had made some social engagements, but when he vanished with the undersecretary of the navy, James Forrestal, she made a rare expression of exasperation in her diary. "Hopeless to do anything with Bill," she wrote on the twenty-second. "Spent eve. clearing out Mary's old clothes." And when instead of leaving one Sunday morning for Berryville to inspect some costly work started at Chapel Hill Farm while he had been away, he hosted a group of strangers who arrived at the Georgetown house for a dawn meeting, Ruth recorded tartly: "Bill has British Empire for breakfast."[12]

Yet Donovan was not merely politicking; his destiny was being decided. While Ruth was sorting old clothes, a new industry was being created in the United States—secret service, one that would lead to the Central Intelligence Agency. Moreover, while she was worrying about whether she had laid out the boxwoods at Berryville correctly, WJD was facing the beginning of a storm in his career: Military Intelligence had heard from its London representative that Donovan had been seeking advice on the constitutional and legal problems involved in establishment of a clandestine service and information on British financial methods involved in clandestine operations.

Alarmed by the intrusion of a civilian into a military domain, the Army's chief of intelligence, General Sherman Miles, wrote to the Chief of Staff, General George C. Marshall, on April 8, 1941:

> In great confidence ONI [Office of Naval Intelligence] tells me that there is considerable reason to believe that there is a movement on foot, fostered by Col. Donovan, to establish a super agency controlling *all* intelligence. This would mean that such an agency would collect, collate and possibly even evaluate all military intelligence which we now gather from foreign countries. From the point of view of the War Department, such a move would appear to be very disadvantageous, if not calamitous.[13]

To the criticisms from many quarters were to be added the intrigues of J. Edgar Hoover, who had established a Special Intelligence Service for work in South America and had begun to develop what he intended should be a worldwide system of "legal attachés"—FBI intelligence officers. Secretary of War Henry L. Stimson confided to his diary how Hoover "goes to the White House . . . and poisons the mind of the President,"[14] while General Marshall complained that Hoover's actions were "very childish" and "petulant" and reminded him "more of a spoiled child than a responsible officer."[15]

At the same time powerful figures in Washington, among them Secretary of the Treasury Henry Morgenthau, Jr., had been impressed by the knowledge of clandestine service displayed by Donovan in his reports upon his return from the war zone and by the fact that he had been into that zone at all. Morgenthau wrote on March 20:[16]

> Donovan is the first man I have talked to that I would be willing to really back. I saw what he did last summer. . . . [He] has been for a week actually in the trenches up in Albania. He was down in Libya when they took that last town,

whatever the last town was. He was with [General Sir Archibald] Wavell [British commander in the Middle East] for over a week. He was with [Anthony] Eden [British foreign secretary after Lord Halifax] in Cairo. He has been twice in England. He has been in Spain and he has been in Portugal. I think he knows more about the situation than anybody I have talked to by about a thousand per cent.

But for all the fine words that reached him about Donovan, and despite the clever and persistent British lobby on his behalf, when Roosevelt acted to produce order out of the muddle and rivalry of the Washington intelligence community, he gave the first job of intelligence *supremo* in New York not to Donovan, but to Vincent Astor, a boyhood friend, sailing companion, financial supporter, fellow New Yorker from Dutchess County, owner of an oceangoing yacht that he had captained from time to time on missions for Naval Intelligence, and one of Roosevelt's personal spies who provided the President with regular reports on the gun room and salon gossip of Manhattan.

Astor's appointment, which seemed to foreshadow his establishing a national intelligence service, did not quell the perturbation, nor did it produce efficiency. Since all involved recognized that secret intelligence was political power, and intelligence shared was power shared, all involved—and there were many—merely intensified the intriguing to get, or to get their man into, the post of Roosevelt's intelligence *supremo*. Meanwhile, with the U.S. Foreign Service collapsed in Europe, and with virtually no political intelligence service beyond a few attachés anywhere, the principal organ of intelligence about foreign politics became *The New York Times*, which was faster, better informed, more intelligent, and more objective than any government agency—and cost three cents.

Roosevelt could have ended the intrigue and confusion at the stroke of his pen, but he did not, adding to them by debating at length whether or not he should appoint Fiorello "Little Flower" La Guardia, New York City's mayor, chief of American clandestine services, an appointment the President seriously contemplated until May 1941, if Astor declined to accept the larger post. Throughout the period of chaos, Donovan remained aloof, attending to the cement antitrust case, listening to, but not encouraging, Stephenson's importunities, and insisting in Washington that he was interested not in a post in intelligence but, as he told Stimson, in command of "the toughest division in the whole outfit."

Yet WJD may not have been quite as aloof from the maneuvering as he appeared, for on April 26, 1941, he sent Knox a requested report on "the instrumentality through which the British Government gathers its information in foreign countries."[17] The report not only revealed the extent to which WJD had been briefed on British clandestine activities by

Menzies and Stephenson—fully—but was to constitute the formal genesis of American clandestine services as well. The letter also ensured that if its recommendations were carried into effect, there would be a war in the Washington intelligence community, although plainly WJD did not have such a war in mind when he wrote to Knox.

WJD presented his ideas about how a U.S. clandestine service should be established:

> Intelligence operations should not be controlled by party exigencies. It is one of the most vital means of national defense. As such it should be headed by some one appointed by the President directly responsible to him and to no one else. It should have a fund solely for the purpose of foreign investigation and the expenditures under this fund should be secret and made solely at the discretion of the President.

The service should *not*—and here was a vital point—"take over the home duties now performed by the F.B.I., nor [sic] the intelligence organizations of the Army and the Navy." It should "(1) have sole charge of intelligence work abroad, (2) coordinate the activities of military and naval attachés and others in the collection of information abroad, (3) classify and interpret all information from whatever source obtained to be available for the President and for such of the services as he would designate." To "make certain of the full cooperation of all departments," WJD thought the President should appoint an advisory committee "consisting at least of the Assistant Secretaries of State, Treasury, War, Navy and Justice and perhaps a full permanent committee. . . ."

Donovan believed that "Modern war operates on more fronts than battle fronts"—as did Churchill—and that "Each combatant seeks to dominate the whole field of communications." No defense system would be effective, therefore, unless it recognized and dealt with this fact. In particular he meant "interception and inspection . . . of mail and cables; the interception of radio communication [i.e., Ultra or, in the United States, Magic]; the use of propaganda to penetrate behind enemy lines; the direction of active subversive operations in enemy countries."

That letter reached Roosevelt through Knox, but FDR took no action on it for a month, while he mulled over the problems of establishing a clandestine service. In the end, his mind was made up for him not by memorandums or lobbyists but by the appearance of a mighty German battle squadron in the North Atlantic. At a time when no fewer than twenty lend-lease convoys were on the high seas, bound for England, news was received that the heavy German battleship *Bismarck*, accompanied by the heavy cruiser *Prinz Eugen*, was loose. Then a single shell from the *Bismarck* sank the huge British battle cruiser *Hood.* In the same engagement the new British battleship *Prince of Wales* was badly damaged before the German squadron escaped, apparently undamaged.

With the escape acute anxiety descended upon the White House. "The President was not only worried that [the German squadron] might show up in the Caribbean [but] wondering what he should do about it if it did," the presidential speech writer Judge Sam Rosenman was to record. "Should he order submarines to attack it? What would the people say if he did? There would obviously not be enough time to ask Congress." The President decided that to obtain the constitutional powers he needed to deal with the German squadron and other such incidents, he would proclaim a state of unlimited national emergency.[18] Roosevelt considered the *Bismarck*'s escape a major threat to the United States and decided to make such a proclamation. Shortly before it was due to be issued, the British located and sank the *Bismarck* as she was making for a French Atlantic port. Nevertheless, Roosevelt decided to make the proclamation.

On May 27, 1941, a very hot night, the governing board of the Pan American Union and its guests—who included the Donovans—gathered in the East Room of the White House. The President then declared that German sinkings of British merchantmen were more than three times the capacity of the British shipyards to replace them and more than twice the combined British and American output of merchant ships. The President warned that America's safety was being grossly affected by these sinkings and stated that to meet the perils of German naval warfare, he had "tonight issued a proclamation that an unlimited national emergency exists and requires the strengthening of our defenses to the extreme limit of our national power and authority." The nation now expected "all individuals in all groups to play their full parts, without stint, and without selfishness, and without doubt that our democracy will triumphantly survive."[19]

The proclamation was received by an audience that was "tense and apprehensive," and to relieve the tensions, Roosevelt invited those present to a musicale on the South Lawn, occasion made the more memorable by the presence of the Donovans' close friend Irving Berlin, the songwriter, who ripped into "Alexander's Ragtime Band" and tunes from *Yip, Yip, Yaphank*, his 1918 hit.

As part of the process of "strengthening our defenses to the extreme limit of our national power," FDR asked Donovan to prepare a paper for him on the theory and practice of clandestine service. This Donovan did with the help of Britons, including Stephenson, David Eccles, of the British Embassy, and Colonel Rex Benson, of the British Secret Intelligence Service in Washington, at a series of meetings at the Georgetown house. Furthermore, as Stephenson reported to Menzies in London he was "attempting to manoeuvre Donovan into accepting the job of co-ordinating all US Intelligence." He was supplying Donovan with "secret information to build up his candidacy," and he had put staff members to work on intelligence memorandums for Donovan to send up "to the Summit." Donovan had not been "initially taken" with the idea of his directing "the new agency that we envisage," and it was not "by any means a foregone conclusion that he would be offered the appointment." But Donovan was "a natural for the job," for he had "the confidence of the President, Hull, Stimson, and Knox; some understanding of the conduct of secret activities; the vision and drive to build an organization; and a demonstrated willingness to cooperate with [the British secret service] in the United States."[20]

The military and naval intelligence services were not unaware that a new central intelligence service was being considered and that Donovan was being considered for director. Both services warned the Joint Board —forerunner of the Joint Chiefs of Staff (JCS), which would not be established until February 1942—that the Army and Navy would be badly disadvantaged if anyone other than they were put in charge of the new organization.

As a result of these apprehensions, a cabal began to form against Donovan when two major British intelligence figures arrived in the United States to engage in what was later called a "friendly, intelligent conspiracy to hurry on the process of change"[21] in the American intelligence community. They were the chief of British Naval Intelligence, Admiral John Godfrey, and his personal assistant, Lieutenant Commander Ian Fleming, who was to create James Bond, the fictional British secret agent.

Donovan had met Godfrey in London in 1940 during discussions on the destroyers-for-bases deal, and both Godfrey and Fleming stayed at the Georgetown house during the time Donovan was preparing his paper on secret intelligence. But while the paper was prepared, Godfrey did not at first succeed in his main purpose: to tell Roosevelt personally that British Intelligence would welcome the appointment of Donovan as director of American central intelligence. In the middle of June 1941, however, Stephenson contacted a familiar figure from the past, Sir William Wiseman, chief of British Intelligence in America during World War I and Donovan's associate at the Walrus Club.

As a result, Wiseman spoke to his friend Arthur Hays Sulzberger, president and publisher of The New York Times, and explained why Godfrey should be allowed to present personally to Roosevelt the British position on Donovan. Sulzberger telephoned Mrs. Roosevelt and asked if it would be possible to arrange a dinner party at which the President and Godfrey would be able to talk. Eleanor Roosevelt agreed, and the dinner took place. Afterward, while the other guests were watching a movie about snake worship in Cambodia, Roosevelt and Godfrey talked in an adjoining room, and although the President tried to avoid discussing intelligence and Donovan, the British admiral succeeded in getting his message across: Make Donovan intelligence master of the United States.

The conversation seems to have helped form Roosevelt's decisions on the matter. Donovan now produced the paper on his ideas for a secret intelligence service that Roosevelt had asked for. The very long paper was entitled "Memorandum of Establishment of Service of Strategic Information," and its main point was that "Strategy, without information on which it can rely, is helpless." Likewise, "information is useless unless it is intelligently directed to the strategic purpose." Although the United States was facing "imminent peril," it lacked "an effective service for analyzing, comprehending, and appraising such information as we might obtain (or in some cases have obtained), relative to the intention of potential enemies and the limit of the economic and military resources of those enemies." The "mechanism for collecting intelligence is inadequate" since the Army and Navy Intelligence services "cannot, out of the very nature of things, obtain that accurate, comprehensive, long-range information without which no strategic board can plan for the future."[22]

There were scattered through government "documents and memoranda concerning military and naval and air and economic potentials of the Axis which, if gathered together and studied in detail by carefully selected trained minds, with a knowledge both of the related languages and techniques, would yield valuable and often decisive results." Donovan thought it "unimaginable that Germany would engage in a $7 billion supply program [as was the United States] without first studying in detail the productive capacity of her actual and potential enemies." It was because "she does exactly this that she displays such a mastery in the secrecy, timing and effectiveness of her attacks."

Even if America participated no more in the war than it was doing now, it was:

> essential that we set up a central enemy intelligence organization which would itself collect, either directly or through existing departments of government . . . pertinent information concerning potential enemies, the character and strength of their armed forces, their internal economic organization, their principal channels of supply, the morale of their troops and their people and their relations with neighbors or allies.

The basic purpose of this service would be "to constitute a means by which the President, as Commander-in-Chief, and his Strategic Board would have available accurate and complete enemy intelligence reports upon which military operational decisions should be based."

Having read the paper, Roosevelt sent for Donovan. During their meeting Donovan told the President he would take the job—provided (1) he reported only to the President, (2) he could draw his finances from the President's Emergency Fund, and (3) all departments of government were instructed to supply him with the information he needed.

At 12:30 P.M. on June 18, 1941, Roosevelt approved Donovan's conditions and gave instructions that a branch of government to be called the Office of Coordinator of Information (COI) was to be established, with WJD as director. With that order at long last the United States had taken the first step toward the establishment of a central intelligence agency. But Roosevelt had been in no great hurry to form the new agency; of the 136 war emergency agencies he established, the clandestine service was not the first but the thirty-second to be formed.

The formal announcement of the formation of the COI was made in the *Federal Register* on July 15, 1941, when the government was informed that it had been established, that it had the "authority to collect and analyze all information and data, which may bear upon the national security," that it would "correlate such information and data," and that it would make "such information and data available to the President and to such departments and officials of the Government as the President may determine." The announcement included also a provision that permitted the COI to carry out, when requested by the President, "such supplementary activities as may facilitate the securing of information important for national security not now available to the Government"—espionage, sabotage, economic and diplomatic warfare, deception, and those acts of legerdemain that the British called special means. The other branches of government with intelligence responsibilities were directed to "make available to the Coordinator of Information all and any such information and data relating to national security as the Coordinator, with the approval of the President, may from time to time request."

Less publicly, Roosevelt wrote Donovan on July 23, 1941, that he would receive no salary for the work but would be entitled to "actual and necessary transportation, subsistence, and other expenses incidental to the performance of your duties."[23] The government, however, soon showed that it did not intend to be generous; the scrambler telephones put in Donovan's house were installed at his own expense.

The American reaction to Donovan's appointment was submerged in world news, for the Germans had attacked Russia and the British and the French were fighting for Syria. The vague announcement of Donovan's appointment, therefore, warranted no more than a third of a column on *The New York Times'* fifth page. All newspapers reflected great confusion about Donovan's duties, and the speculation about his work ranged from espionage to controlling the supply of gasoline. There was little foreign comment until after Pearl Harbor, when the Germans announced:

> Behind the scenes in Washington, a secret bureau has been created, a bureau to which very few have entrée. This new office is under the personal leadership of Colonel Donovan.
>
> "Wild Bill," as he is known in America, first came to our attention when Roosevelt sent him as his special envoy . . . to the South of Europe, in order to incite the people of those countries to rebellion against Germany. The role Colonel Donovan played in Belgrade is still fresh in our minds, and he can be blamed for the tragic Serbian affair. . . .
>
> A second and *more monstrous meddling* is at present under way, and as usual under the leadership of Colonel Donovan. Roosevelt has named the Colonel Coordinator of Information. Hiding behind this title he is brewing a Jewish-Democratic crisis which is directed at all of Europe. Donovan has unlimited power. He can spend any sum of money he desires. He can have as many assistants as he chooses. And he can get any information he desires.
>
> Colonel Donovan's office . . . has grown into the largest espionage and sabotage bureau that has so far been seen in any Anglo-Saxon country. It is, confessedly, the aim of Donovan to create for Roosevelt a huge fifth column in Europe and South America. Terroristic attempts, acts of sabotage, revolts, corruption, bribery . . . are the main points of the Roosevelt-Donovan program. . . .[24]

On the other hand, both Donovan and the British—especially the British—were very pleased with each other. Major Desmond Morton, Churchill's liaison officer with the British secret services, made an unblushing expression of satisfaction when he informed Churchill's military secretary, Colonel E. I. Jacob, on September 18, 1941:

> Another most secret fact of which the Prime Minister is aware . . . is that to all intents and purposes U.S. Security is being run for them at the President's request by the British. A British officer sits in Washington with Mr. Edgar Hoover and General [*sic*] Bill Donovan for this purpose and reports regularly to the president. It is of course essential that this fact should not be known in view of the furious uproar it would cause if known to the isolationists.[25]

Stephenson shared in that satisfaction, for on the day of Donovan's appointment he cabled Menzies in London: "Donovan accuses me of having 'intrigued and driven' him into the appointment. You can imagine how relieved I am after three months of battle and jockeying for position in Washington that our man is in a position of such importance to our efforts."[26]

But if Stephenson was "relieved," many in Washington were far from pleased by the President's action, and in the days that followed, as Donovan became known formally within the British Secret Intelligence Service as Q, all parties took up positions for a battle royal. Indeed, of all those involved or affected by Donovan's appointment, only Ruth seemed to have no strong feelings about it. On the day of the announcement she wrote in her diary: "Went sailing. Lovely day."[27]

11

Forming the Services

Donovan formally resigned from his law firm on July 21, 1941, to prevent
any conflict of interest between his government and private business. His
name remained on the firm's shingle, he kept his office and personal staff
(which he used frequently for government business), he agreed to return
to the firm at the end of his government service, and he became what is
known in law firms as "of counsel," legal adviser to the firm on nongov-
ernmental matters, a post that was not burdensome but that brought him
about $75,000 a year in fees.

That was a generous gesture on the part of Donovan's colleagues;
nonetheless, his return to public service represented a major personal financial sacrifice. For the next three years he drew virtually no salary,
and during that period he maintained himself and subsidized his new
work with his earnings from the firm. These were substantial: in 1940,
$258,949.93; in 1941, $219,960.40; and in 1942, $84,000. But he was not
able to repay any of the $202,576.86 in accumulated debt to the firm since
its foundation—much of which he had spent to prepare for his wartime
task—and that sum the firm covered with a life insurance policy on WJD,
the firm paying the premiums.

Therefore, WJD was not only sacrificing earnings that in 1982 dollars
would have been worth between $800,000 and $1,000,000 a year but he
had become a substantial debtor. It would not be long before such resources as he had were exhausted, and he would be compelled to begin
borrowing. Worse, for some years he had not paid his income taxes, and
when he became a dollar-a-year man, he thought he did not have to do

so. He maintained his former living standard, and he was heading for grave financial trouble. Although the day of reckoning might be distant, it was going to come. Yet he started his new work with a blithe spirit. "God will provide," he stated with confidence.

The Georgetown house became Donovan's headquarters, and Ruth moved to the Berryville farm. Then his adviser on organizational matters from the Bureau of the Budget, believing WJD needed only small quarters for what was going to be a small organization, found him offices. These were two and a half rooms in the Executive Office Building on Lafayette Square, that astonishing building of 900 columns, pavilions, marble halls, granite staircases, two miles of corridors, 620 charwomen in a mixture of Victorian, Greek Revival, Italian, and French architecture —a building so grotesque that it caused General Ulysses S. Grant to exclaim that "it climaxed all the curious constructions he had seen elsewhere in the world."

The building convinced Donovan's earliest callers of the baroque nature of the coordinator's business. Their next vision convinced them that in all there was something pretty peculiar going on here: Sitting at a desk beneath a bronze tablet commemorating the "services and sufferings" of 243,135 horses and mules used by the U.S. Army in World War I was Donovan's receptionist, "an extraordinary and exotic creature" named Mrs. Cushman, who had "startled New York a few years before by getting married in red, thereby becoming the inspiration for the movie *The Bride Wore Red*,"[1] one of the "shockers" of the period. A woman in her middle years, with a heavily painted face and lips and vividly dyed red hair, she sat in the gloom like Frankenstein's daughter, directing spies, safecrackers, wiretappers, and important men to their various destinations.

Donovan did not remain long at the Executive Office Building. He moved into the Apex Building, at the peak of the Federal Triangle, a building so new that callers not only were confronted by Mrs. Cushman but had also to make their way through crowds of sculptors, masons, and general laborers helping the master sculptor Michael Lantz create the great frieze of heroic figures symbolizing "Man Controlling Trade." There WJD began work as coordinator in earnest, displaying certain characteristics that were to mark his entire incumbency as spymaster. There the budget adviser, William O. Hall, later recorded that he found WJD "bursting with ideas," "a man principally gifted for inspiring rather than organizing," and possessing a "marked tendency to desire to undertake anything he thought was a good idea." The result was that WJD "frequently had to be told 'No' by the bureau."[2]

The earliest collision between Donovan and Hall came over salaries: WJD announced that COI executives would be paid two or even three times the going rate for senior men in government—around $7,500 a year—and would not be considered civil servants. He was told bluntly by the director of the budget, Harold D. Smith, that his top men would be civil servants and would be paid according to government scales—and when Donovan was compelled to agree, several key COI men, including Allen Dulles and William L. Langer, who was about to become head of WJD's "College of Cardinals"—as the Board of Analysts was called—threatened to resign.

Then came the second major problem—the budget. It had been estimated WJD would need only a small organization—perhaps seventy experts and a clerical staff—to carry out the executive order. It would be able to manage on $1,454,700 for the first year, the sum to come from FDR's secret $100,000,000 Emergency Fund. Budget Director Smith sent WJD $450,000 to enable him to get started. But Donovan went through that sum fairly rapidly and forgot to ask for more, doing so only when staff began coming to him with complaints that they had not been paid in ten weeks.

There were, however, no resignations. Recruits accepted that they were part of government, and there was no difficulty in finding people outside government to work inside the COI. The earliest recruit appears to have been the playwright Robert E. Sherwood, whom WJD met in New York in 1940 at the premiere of Sherwood's play *There Shall Be No Night,* for which he was awarded the Pulitzer Prize. After WJD's return from England in August 1940 he began to talk with Sherwood about his ideas for the clandestine service, and Sherwood asked Donovan to "count me in," thinking he might be too old for fighting but young enough to do staff work—Sherwood was forty-four. Instead, Donovan made Sherwood head of his radio propaganda department. Conscious of the military's suspicion of "this bunch of faggots"—as one general described the COI to the Yale professor James Grafton Rogers—Sherwood recommended that his operation be centered in New York. Donovan agreed, and a floor was rented at 270 Madison Avenue. Sherwood would remember looking at the empty, unpartitioned vastness of the floor "with horror and wondering if we could ever fill it up."[3] Sherwood need have had no fears: Within a year 800 journalists, broadcasters, and writers were cramming the floor, fighting the good fight with Donovan's propaganda, and in the manner of Parkinson's law, Sherwood was soon looking for more space.

A large number of similarly interesting people arrived to join WJD: Archibald MacLeish, the Librarian of Congress, acted as recruiter in academe for the men and women who were to form the Research and Analysis Branch; two authors, Edmond Taylor, who had written *The Strategy of Terror,* and Douglas Miller, who was about to become rich and famous with *You Can't Do Business with Hitler;* the New York banker and political writer James P. Warburg; the Chicago *Daily News* correspondent

Wallace Deuel; and the foreign editor of the New York *Herald Tribune*, Joseph Barnes, who was to be ruined by the FBI's charges that he was a Communist. Donovan also recruited recruiters, among them Thomas A. Morgan, of the Sperry Corporation; James Roosevelt, one of FDR's sons; Estelle Frankfurter, the daughter of Supreme Court Justice Felix Frankfurter; diplomat John C. Wiley, lately minister to Latvia and Estonia; Atherton C. Richards, a wealthy landowner and a member of one of the seven founding families of the then territory of Hawaii, who brought a "fascinating" wife to "brighten the horizon" in Washington; John Ford, the Hollywood movie producer who had just finished *The Grapes of Wrath;* Merian C. Cooper, another Hollywood producer, who had startled the world with *King Kong.* At this time, and throughout his career, one of Donovan's gifts was that he was able to attract into government service, to keep, and to win the complete loyalty and devotion of the most brilliant yet motley group of peacocks ever assembled in a Washington agency— a factor that was to cause much trouble with the military.

Almost all his senior men were handpicked by Donovan personally, in a process that often took no more than five minutes, and many of the junior staff were also recruited by him in the same way. Both usually came to him through recommendations from associates whose judgment WJD trusted. And one of the remarkable characteristics was the strong ties of loyalty and devotion that grew up between Donovan and his men. He became the living symbol of their wartime work, which for many of them was to become the pinnacle of their life's work, and the visible symbol of their best years, what Doering was to call "our springtime years."

He became a sort of Leonidas at the Pass of Thermopylae—they the Spartans, the rest of the world the Persians. There grew up between them elitist bonds. As with the Spartans, they felt they were probably doomed but would give an excellent account of themselves while they were able. The phenomenon, rare in modern American society but somewhat more familiar to Europeans, would be difficult to account for. Some would suggest that it was caused by the ferocity of the attacks by other agencies during the formative years of the COI. Others would hold that WJD welded them into a brotherhood. But most would state that WJD embodied all that his men wished for themselves and that this strengthened their relationship. His intense patriotism, his pursuit of fairness, his kindliness —all served further to strengthen the bonds. "He looked after his men," replied the Harvard anthropologist Carleton S. Coon, one of WJD's secret service agents in those early days, when asked why it was that his men worshiped him long after he had gone to Arlington.

As with the British services, the Donovan agency became an order that did its work with passion. Even forty years later, when WJD's men gathered for a banquet in New York to present the William J. Donovan Gold Medal to some famous person for services to the cause of freedom (in

1980 the award was presented to British Prime Minister Margaret Thatcher), an immense photograph of the American Leonidas hung above the survivors of WJD's service, brilliantly lit in the gloom, as if it were the picture of some deity, while the assembly stood reverently in brief remembrance.

Of all the men in his service, only three could be described as intimates, and not even they could really penetrate that wall of reserve. James R. Murphy, who had been WJD's law clerk at Justice and who was now practicing law in Washington, received a telephone call from Donovan to "come around immediately and keep the knives out of my back." Murphy did not get back to his chambers for four years. He became chief of Donovan's counterespionage service, X-2; he took part in several assignments of special confidentiality and came to be rated by his British counterparts as the "best U.S. intelligence officer we met during World War II"; and he was to become the mentor of James Jesus Angleton, the famous CIA spycatcher for many years.

Colonel G. Edward "Ned" Buxton, whom WJD had known as a battalion commander in World War I (he had been Sergeant York's commanding officer and had converted York from a conscientious objector to a war hero), arrived to form a service for the interviewing of ship and aircraft passengers arriving from Europe, the Oral Intelligence Unit. A product of Brown University and Harvard Law School, Buxton had been a war correspondent, treasurer of the Providence *Journal* on Rhode Island, and latterly a prominent New England textile manufacturer. An amiable, fair, gentlemanly fellow, Buxton was to become Donovan's principal deputy until the end of the war when, burned out by the pressures of the work and the intrigues, he was compelled to resign.

The third man soon came. He was Otto C. Doering, Jr., a member of a prominent Chicago family, who had joined Donovan's law firm in 1929. A calm, agreeable, wise man with a sharp mind, Doering had studied engineering and law at Cornell before joining the Donovan law firm. A born chief of staff—which is what he became, although not in title—Doering was in turn general counsel, executive officer, and assistant director of the Donovan agency throughout the war years. He was the perfect complement to Donovan. In character and personality he was all the things WJD was not—patient, sedentary—but certain that the conservative virtues were the best, capable of ruthlessness (which WJD was not, although he seemed to be), outstanding in committee work, and a man who weighed every step and decision, a born counterintelligence man. Doering's presence in Donovan's suite was as responsible as anything else first for the survival of the Donovan agency and then for its emergence as one of the world's leading secret services. While Donovan and the fire in his belly generated the power that led to the formation and survival of the agency, it was Doering who supplied the organizational

talent that enabled Donovan to construct his service in thirty months—
against the thirty years it had taken the European powers.

Like Donovan, Doering was assisted by his ability to pick outstanding
men. Into the service came Edwin J. Putzell, Doering's deputy and successor and, later, general counsel for Monsanto; Charles A. Bane, who
became head of the secretariat and, later, a prominent Chicago lawyer;
Duncan C. Lee, personal assistant to WJD who became chief of the
Chinese Section of Secret Intelligence; Robert Thrun, a leading New
York lawyer; John D. Wilson, who was to become an executive vice-
president of the Chase Manhattan Bank; Turner McBaine, junior partner
(and later senior partner and a director of Standard Oil of California) in
the leading San Francisco law firm of Pillsbury Madison & Sutro.

In such men as these lay the origins of American clandestine services
in the modern era. The hostility for the Donovan agency of the military,
naval, and FBI intelligence services determined its early coloration. Unable and perhaps unwilling to recruit among his rivals, Donovan turned
first to men whom he knew and trusted—bankers, lawyers, industrialists,
conservative academics. In their turn, these men recruited among those
whom they knew and trusted; and this gave the Donovan agency its tinge
of well-to-do, Ivy League, often Republican, socially prominent men and
women. It was the American progression of Menzies's adage that "Intelligence is the business of gentlemen"—a belief, founded out of the need
for security, that people who had been to the same schools, were members of the same clubs, whose fathers had known each other, who were
members of the same political party, who were in the same professions,
and who were comfortably off in life were not likely to commit treason.
The belief was essentially tribal, and as events were to show it was not
always well founded—there were Bolsheviks among the bluebloods as
there were among the bourgeoisie and the proletariat. But in wartime,
when danger is sharper and more omnipresent, all men become tribal,
and Donovan and his colleagues were no exception. Nor was WJD proved
wrong. Although his agency would be expanded rapidly into the largest
dependency of the Joint Chiefs, and although in one role or another—
dollar-a-year men, advisers, consultants, accountants, men on loan from
other services and from industry, and the like—some 60,000 people
would be associated with the Donovan agency, there would be no *proved*
case of treason.

Donovan's personality dominated all. Nor did he change his methods.
He remained the empire builder. For by the end of 1941 Donovan had
begun to show that he had in mind a project far larger than a group of
humble professors studying intelligence reports in order to make intelligence estimates for the President.

When the COI was formed, it had been estimated that he would need
only 92 people to meet his obligations under the President's executive

order. But by December 15, 1941, he had 596 people on his payroll, three weeks later 670, and at the end of March 1942, when the Bureau of the Budget thought the payroll should level off at 631 people, Donovan was aiming at 1,300 (that figure became 1,852). When WJD asked for a new budget of $10,000,000, he got it and thus became the first man to get $10,000,000 out of the U.S. Congress without his having to account for it: Throughout the history of his agency most of his money came in the form of secret funds, for which he accounted only by a signature on a certificate that the money had been spent in the national interest—a system illustrative of FDR's trust in his spymaster.

Then his empire building required other, larger premises. Donovan moved the agency again, this time to the National Institute of Health at the corner of Twenty-fifth and E streets, within sight of the Lincoln Memorial in one direction, a brewery in another, and the municipal gasworks to the south. A laboratory containing live monkeys inoculated with diseases still occupied the top floor of one of the buildings, and, Berlin Radio announced, in that malodorous atmosphere "fifty professors, twenty monkeys, ten goats, twelve guinea pigs, and a staff of Jewish scribblers"[4] were working on a plan for the Judeo-Christian-plutocratic rule of the world.

When Colonel Edwin L. Sibert, who was to become chief of intelligence to General Dwight D. Eisenhower and to General Omar N. Bradley, visited the institute, his impression was that COI headquarters "closely resembled a cat house in Laredo on a Saturday night, with rivalries, jealousies, mad schemes, and everyone trying to get the ear of the director. But I felt that a professional organization was in the making, and I am glad to say that I was right."[5]

The British, too, were pleased with their protégé. They had left Commander Fleming with Donovan and had sent in Colonel Charles H. Ellis, a career officer of the Secret Intelligence Service, to give WJD whatever help he needed in forming his organization. Other British officers, experts in clandestine communications and training, arrived at Donovan's request, and as early as August 1941 Fleming reported to London that WJD was "getting well into the saddle."[6] Stephenson was to record:

> On August 9, 1941, I noted to London that our friend's organization was rapidly taking shape, central offices in Washington had been established and were functioning, understanding with the Chiefs of Staff seemed satisfactory, that he [Donovan] felt confident of their cooperation; he had several competent assistants; he had the beginnings of a working apparatus in Washington and New York, and should be able to safeguard secret documents.[7]

That was a remarkable comment, for only yesterday almost every member of the COI had been in civilian life, and almost none had had any experience of clandestine life or work. Some of them had not even been abroad; few had had any experience of working in government; still fewer had served in the armed services; and it is doubtful if any of them, Donovan included, knew anything about the paraphernalia of secret service—the hidden bank accounts, the meaning and importance of cover, the importance of security, the need for rapid telecommunications, loading a silenced pistol or setting a tire burster, or the difference between codes and ciphers. Certainly none of them knew anything about—beyond what they had read—illegal radio sets, cutouts, plastic explosives, how to kill a man silently, how to lie with conviction under deep interrogation, dummy corporations, lethal tablets, chemicals for throwing tracker dogs off the scent, how to recruit secret agents. And, Doering was to recall, no one knew where to obtain even the simplest requirements of a bureaucracy—things like typing paper, paper clips, and typewriter ribbons.

At the outset Donovan showed little interest in establishing the Secret Intelligence (SI) service and its bodyguard, the counterespionage (X-2) Branch, being more occupied with forming his "College of Cardinals," the Research and Analysis Branch, and the political and propaganda warfare services.

That attitude began to change late in August 1941, when Donovan was approached at his law offices by a strange, balding, hunchbacked American businessman, Wallace Banta Phillips. Phillips announced he was head of an outfit called the K Organization, which was in the Office of Naval Intelligence and ran secret agents. He indicated that he was making the approach to Donovan with the knowledge and permission of the director of naval intelligence and then proposed that Donovan take over his organization as part of the COI. Mystified by the approach and inclined to be cautious of Greeks bearing gifts, Donovan invited Phillips to tell him something about himself.

Phillips had an interesting story. Born of American parents in the United States in 1886, he had been educated at the Sorbonne and had served with U.S. Military Intelligence in France between 1917 and 1919. He then had joined and later became chairman of Pyrene, a London-based company interested in petrochemicals. He had built up a very large circle of European acquaintances with whom he had established a commercial intelligence organization in London. At one time Phillips claimed, his intelligence service "had on its payroll no less than seven ex-Prime Ministers" and his bulletins had "a wide circulation among influential American, British, and Continental financial and commercial companies."[8]

At the outbreak of the European war Phillips had been appointed special assistant to the director of naval intelligence, and when in June

1940 a special committee of State, War, Navy, and FBI representatives decided to establish the K Organization, Phillips had been given the task. However, he continued, the program had not proved satisfactory under joint control, and the question now was: Was Donovan interested in taking over Phillips and his unit?

After much discussion, Donovan acquired Phillips's K Organization, which gave the COI its start in espionage—a start, as Donovan put it, "from minus zero." With Intrepid's deputy in Washington, Colonel Ellis, keeping an eye on the new organization, Donovan appointed Phillips Director of Special Information Service (a title that was likely to cause confusion and annoyance because at the time the FBI had an identical post with a similar purpose)[9] on November 17, 1941. Phillips was "authorized, subject to [Donovan's] approval, to engage and supervise representatives of this agency for service abroad, in obtaining necessary information and data which may bear upon national security and be necessary in the interest of national defense."

The Bureau of the Budget approved Donovan's request for $2,546,000 for Phillips's service on the ground of its "high strategic importance," and with that handsome interim budget Phillips was in business as America's first spymaster. His assets were not, however, as impressive as his budget. At that moment, according to Phillips's records, the K Organization consisted of:

§ Four agents operating in *Lithuania, Latvia, and Estonia*—Soviet territory—with a further four agents in those states operating into Germany. The network was controlled by the assistant naval attaché at Helsinki, but Phillips did not know their names. As for the quality of their work, he related to WJD: "Their reports have been very fragmentary and nothing of any importance has come in for the past six weeks."

§ In the *unoccupied zone of France* Phillips had retained "An American speaking perfect French" who had lived in France for many years and was now traveling in France. "I sent him over on a special trip of investigation and to contact a number of French Underground Groups," Phillips advised Donovan. "He also was to try and establish French Agents along the Mediterranean, primarily for Naval information." This man was expected back in the United States within three weeks.

§ *In Rumania* "through a long chain of negotiations and circumstances Lieutenant Commander Melvin Hall, our Assistant Naval Attaché in Turkey, has been able to establish a very interesting contact with an important Group having headquarters in Romania; from there operating through Switzerland into Germany." This group had "direct connections with a number of important

German Officers and has been instrumental in furnishing the best direct military information that I have seen as coming from any source."

§ In *Bulgaria* Phillips had a "Special Agent, an American who is an old Treasury Agent operating in the Balkans."

§ In *Turkey* his agent was Lieutenant Commander Hall, who was "a personal friend of the President of Turkey."

§ In *Syria* Phillips was "in the process of developing agents."

§ In *Egypt* Major William A. Eddy, U.S. Marines, was naval attaché at Cairo. The son of American missionaries at Sidon, Syria, he had been chairman of the Department of English at Cairo University. He had had a distinguished fighting record in World War I and been president of Hobart College, in New York State, when he returned to service at the outbreak of World War II. Prior to his departure for Cairo in May 1941, "I gave him the names of several Arabic speaking Americans employed by the Vacuum Oil Company and the California Texas Company in Palestine and Saudi Arabia, and asked him to arrange to tie these people into a network that would give us a continuous picture of military activity in Arabia."

§ In *North Africa* was a group of twelve U.S. vice-consuls.

§ In *Afghanistan* the "Foreign Editor of the National Geographic Magazine" was "now in this country," although "no reports have come through from him."

§ In *Iran* the "Assistant Curator of the Metropolitan Museum of Art" was was to represent the K Organization, but "He has only recently arrived and no reports have yet been received."

§ In *Mexico* there were "two leading American representatives. One a business man resident in Mexico City. The second, a former radio station owner now representing NBC who travels throughout the Country. We have five Permanent Agents at strategic points and five others who report from time to time on Naval interest."[10]

That, then, was the extent of the American secret intelligence service nineteen days before Pearl Harbor—at a time when all the other main belligerents, actual and prospective, had embarked upon a full-scale ideological underground war. Most of these agents were to fall by the wayside, but those in French North Africa were to prove of exceptional value, more than justifying this expensive transaction.

No other agency of government maintained a secret intelligence service. The State, War, Navy, and Treasury departments, the FBI, the bureaus of Narcotics and Immigration all maintained intelligence services of sorts, but they were specialist services the talents of which could not readily be turned to the gathering of secret intelligence or political warfare. As for Donovan's agency, by Pearl Harbor it had one agent operational in a place other than London: Armand Dennis, who was on his way to Accra as the representative of "Anthropoid Research Incorporated," his cover to engage in the "capturing, caring, and shipping of a group of gorillas," his fee from the COI $5,000, his mission "to observe German espionage and military activity, the attitude of the native chiefs in the Belgian Congo and French Equatorial Africa, the stability of the Free French, industrial production and development." There had been some difficulty in getting Dennis away because he was involved in a lawsuit in Florida concerning nondelivery of baboons, and at first the judge would not release him from his obligations to the court. In the field Dennis did not prove to be the happiest choice of secret agent. First he complained to WJD that he dare not ask questions for fear of being sent to jail; that the answers to most of the questions he had been told to ask could have been gathered in the United States by "intelligent use of the telephone"; that he was being denied permission to go to Fort Rousset to collect gorillas and chimpanzees and would not proceed without a permit from the Belgians and the French. Then, when he did get permission, he collected a gorilla's disease and had to be shipped home.

In all, therefore, on the eve of Pearl Harbor WJD's assets were few and unreliable. No defensive—counterespionage—service of any kind existed within the COI, only in the FBI. But in those early days there occurred several incidents that ensured its rapid formation. The most important was a case involving a man called Djamgaroff.

In September 1941 an incredible person, George Djamgaroff, of New York, applied for a post as a secret intelligence officer with the COI, stressing that he could speak Russian, Armenian, Persian, Arabic, Turkish, Greek, and several dialects of Hindi. He claimed also to have special connections in Latin America, particularly with Rafael Leonidas Trujillo, president of the Dominican Republic. The Donovans knew Djamgaroff vaguely, having attended a ball at his mansion in Irving Place, New York City, in the early thirties, when he was married to the widow of Marcus Daly II.

When Djamgaroff showed up that September, Donovan felt there was something fishy about the man, and said so to Doering. Doering asked the FBI for information on Djamgaroff, and on September 17, 1941, back came a report entitled "George Jamhar Djamgaroff, with aliases."[11] That document showed Djamgaroff to be exceedingly doubtful.

Hoover reported that Djamgaroff was the subject of a Foreign Agents'

Registration Act investigation, undertaken at the request of the President's adviser on internal security, Adolf Berle, assistant secretary of state. Berle had advised the bureau that "Djamgaroff was receiving a split on oil shipments from Mexico to Santo Domingo, and was in turn splitting his commission with Congressman Hamilton Fish of New York." Djamgaroff was registered with the State Department as "publicity agent for the Dominican Republic," and Berle had "desired the investigation on the theory that Hamilton Fish should also be registered if he was receiving part of the commission of a registered agent."

Hoover went on to report that "considerable investigation has been conducted without substantiating the allegation regarding Djamgaroff and Congressman Hamilton Fish receiving any commission on oil shipments." It had been determined, however, that Djamgaroff had been receiving $50,000 a year "for his services as Advertising and Publications Counsel for the Dominican Republic." It was believed this contract had been canceled. Hoover continued:

> Djamgaroff was naturalized January 6, 1926. In his declaration of intention to become a citizen, he stated he was born September 17, 1897 in Caucasus, Russia. He claimed to have arrived in the United States August 3, 1920, his last previous residence having been Constantinople, Turkey. The declaration of intention was filed under the name George John Jamhar. The certificate of arrival attached to his petition for naturalization attests that Fahmer Koharoumi Kourken arrived in the United States on August 20, 1920. The "New York American" on October 26, 1932, reported that Djamgaroff admitted he entered the United States under forged papers in 1920, and that this was the only way he could get out of Russia and into the United States.

In a check on Djamgaroff's credit, "it was discovered that several judgments have been filed against him in New York City." In 1939 he was "maintaining a moderate four figure bank account at the Guaranty Trust Company in New York City." His salary had amounted to more than $4,000 a month, but his account was practically exhausted at the time of the investigation. He "occupied a suite, normally renting for $375 per month, at the Waldorf-Astoria for fifteen months in 1938 and 1939," obtaining the suite "gratis because he arranged to bring the Trujillo party to the hotel during their visit to the New York World's Fair." He still owed the hotel $200 for services rendered during that period.

Moreover, Hoover reported, Djamgaroff "hired Royce W. Powell, nephew of Ralph W. Snowden Hill, Assistant Legal Counsel of the State Department, to obtain confidential information from the State Department concerning transactions between South American countries and the United States." Hill was "discharged by the State Department for unethical conduct." Then, Hoover advised:

On August 26, 1930, the New York Herald Tribune carried an article which stated that Djamgaroff obtained what amounted to fraudulent affidavits identifying Feodor Ziavkin, head of Amtorg [the Soviet trading agency in New York], as a former agent of the Russian Secret Police. Apparently he did this in behalf of Congressman Hamilton Fish, who was head of a Congressional Committee investigating Communist activities.

In 1932, the Federated Press described Djamgaroff as a Russian Monarchist, plotter and peddler of [discredited documents].

In 1932 he was reported to have married Mrs. Marcus Daly II in London on July 20. She had divorced Djamgaroff at Reno, Nevada, late in 1935. At that time it had been:

> necessary for the Special Agent in Charge at New York City to contact Djamgaroff to warn him about falsely giving the impression that he was connected with the [FBI]. At that time in conversations with acquaintances he was making reference to "Edgar Hoover" as an intimate friend of his. When interviewed he stated he had met the Director, which was not true.

All this was of interest to authorities responsible for law and order, but not those responsible for counterespionage, except for the references to the oil shipments, which might have been intended for German U-boats, and to Amtorg. The question before Donovan and Doering was whether Djamgaroff was a hostile penetration agent and, if he was, what they were going to do about him. Donovan contacted Stephenson of British Security Coordination, who in a "For Q" message produced a highly derogatory report:

> The above-mentioned George Djamgaroff, who claims to be a Russian, is an adventurer who has been "in and out of the money" at various periods in his life, and has often been penniless. He was publicity man for Ganna Walska and later sales representative for "Ganna Walska Perfumes." His latest large position was with General Trujillo of Santo Domingo, from whom he received $50,000 a year for publicity purposes. He was married to and divorced from the widow of the late Marcus Daly, whom he would now like to re-marry for her money, which he says amounts to $20,000,000. It is reported that she has refused him.

Stephenson also reported—using the phrase "our indexes show," which pricked WJD's attention—that "both the Germans and the Japanese have attempted to employ him for intelligence work."[12]

Then, in March 1942 Stephenson advised that he had information that Djamgaroff was operating the "A.B.C. News Bureau and is believed to be associated with one Vonsiatsky, Russian 'Fascist' leader, suspected Japanese agent." Also, Djamgaroff recently had made two trips to Argentina that, given the Nazi penetration of that country from 1939 to 1941, were considered highly suspicious.

Finally, in April 1942, Stephenson reported that it now appeared that Djamgaroff had received $100,000 for his part in the oil deal, that he had not given his share to Hamilton Fish, that the money was banked in Santo Domingo, and that "the oil was 'for an un-named foreign country—an indication that Djamgaroff was indeed supplying U-boats with fuel and, probably, much else besides.' "[13]

In Donovan's and Doering's opinions, therefore, Djamgaroff was more fitted for prison than COI work, and his application was rejected. What became of him is not known. What was significant was that WJD might have given him a job. He did not do so not because there was any derogatory information concerning Djamgaroff at the COI, but because other agencies, particularly the British, had identified him as having had contact with hostile intelligence services. Apart from possibly giving WJD a fright, the only significance of the Djamgaroff incident was that it showed a counterespionage service was essential if Donovan and the COI were to be trusted by other agencies and by the British, especially where supersecret sources of intelligence, such as Magic and Ultra, were concerned. Thus, at Christmas 1941 WJD asked James R. Murphy to get started on the formation of a counterespionage service, drawing his attention to Stephenson's references to "our indexes." What were these indexes? Whatever they were, they could be of the highest importance to the security of the United States.

Donovan and Murphy soon learned that through the Ultra system of cryptanalysis the British had managed to penetrate the Enigma machine ciphers used by Admiral Canaris's Abwehr, as well as the systems employed by Canaris's rivals, the Sicherheitsdienst and the party's police force, the Sicherheitspolizei. With these intercepts, the British had had great success against the German and Italian intelligence services—in the United States, for example, thirty-six of the forty-two German secret agents were apprehended by the FBI up to the late summer of 1942 as a result of that capability.

Also, as Donovan learned on a trip to London, behind that capability lay another signal success: the fact that the British intelligence services had managed to bring the German intelligence service in Britain, and throughout much of the world, under British control. The British were able to use these controlled services, therefore, to feed false intelligence about British capabilities and intentions to the German General Staff.

Through these discoveries it was evident to Donovan that here was an intelligence instrument of high importance to the United States, so he spoke to Stephenson about the possibility of learning more. Stephenson was well aware of its existence—it was known to him as ISOS (Intelligence

Service, Oliver Strachey, the head of the enemy intelligence communications branch of the Ultra service at Bletchley)—and he suggested to Menzies that it would be to Britain's advantage if he and Donovan were able to see whether there was a basis for Anglo-American collaboration in the field of counterespionage. Menzies agreed, for he was beginning to reach the outer limits of his manpower and financial resources, and he needed assistance in his single-handed fight with the German, Italian, and Japanese services. At Murphy's request, Donovan sent a brilliant staff officer, George K. Bowden, a peacetime tax lawyer whose work for Donovan was soon to be cut short by a bursting aneurysm, to London to see the man who controlled the British ISOS service, Major Felix Cowgill, chief of the counterespionage branch of the British SIS.

Bowden spent twelve weeks examining ISOS and its associated CEA— Controlled Enemy Agent—operations and then reported back to Donovan and Murphy.[14] The messages produced by ISOS consisted of "instructions from home centers of the Abwehr to its agents in the field and the reports of such agents to headquarters." Through their ability to break the cipher in which the Abwehr's messages were cloaked, the British had acquired "an extraordinary knowledge of personalities and activities of the German Abwehr and [Sicherheitsdienst]." Consequently, ISOS "had never been furnished to any ally," it was "not even sent to the field officers of British SIS," and its "existence was unknown to the vast majority of the officials and employees of British SIS." Menzies and Cowgill had stated that "under no circumstances" would they "turn this material over unprocessed to the United States"—by "unprocessed" Bowden meant British rewriting of ISOS intercepts to make it appear that the intelligence derived from sources other than cryptanalysis; for example, interrogations of captured enemy personnel or the interception of mail. Bowden advised Donovan and Murphy that ISOS was so secret that "distribution of the decodes is subject to the order of the Prime Minister," only six copies of each signal were made, and the recipients were the prime minister, the foreign secretary, the directors of naval and military intelligence, the head of the British Security Service (MI 5), and Menzies.

Bowden then reported he had been taken to a country estate outside Bletchley and was invited to "inspect the collection and processing of" the ISOS intercepts. They were obtained "in the raw by Radio Security Service, a division of the British Government that monitors wireless communications at home and abroad." The service "maintains three central stations, one located in the north of Scotland, a second in north England and a third near Lands End." Their work was "supplemented by some 1,500 amateur radio technicians who do work at their homes on a voluntary basis" throughout the British Isles. The messages they and MI 5 received were turned over to the "cryptology division of the British

Government. Here, as in the monitoring, there is a unified agency to service the various departments of government."

Yet, Bowden noted, even when deciphered and translated, ISOS intercepts were so riddled with code names, allusions, and technical terms that they were meaningless to all but the experts. However, with the files and card indexes of XB—the counterespionage branch of British SIS, also known as Section V—they became the "pure gold" of counterespionage: names, dates, places, finance, movements and objectives of agents, and the policy of the German services.

Bowden continued his report to Donovan: "After spending several days working on the material I came to the conclusion that without the use of the British files as a background the current intercepts would have little value [to the Donovan agency]." But "with the use of these files the intercepts had great value in exposing the personalities and the activities of the Abwehr and to some extent the [Sicherheitsdienst]."

Further inquiry showed that the British counterespionage files and indexes were a vast collection of information concerning persons and organizations of every nationality and description that had come to the attention of the counterespionage authorities since the turn of the century, usually because they had been engaged in seditious or espionage activities against the Empire. Of particular interest were the files and indexes concerning German and Soviet agents and organizations, for which there were no comparable reference or information systems in the United States. The advantage of access to ISOS and the British card index system to the Donovan agency, therefore, would be immense, if only as a foundation on which the United States could build its own security indexes.

The entire system of ISOS and the counterespionage files and indexes was closely related to the British deception system, which, Bowden reported, was at least in part based upon the system of controlled enemy agents that had been highly developed. But that was an aspect of the British security systems beyond the scope of Bowden's mission.

Donovan took the matter in hand. Having received FDR's approval to establish both a counterespionage service and a system of security indexes, he flew to London, and after much negotiation Menzies received permission from Churchill to allow carefully selected individuals within X-2 to see ISOS summaries, and for those summaries to be transmitted to New York, provided both personnel and ciphers were pronounced secure by Section V. Also, provided these criteria were met, Menzies agreed to give Donovan a copy of the British security files and indexes and allow Donovan's men to work with the British security and counterespionage authorities in London. Lastly, he would allow equally carefully selected men into that most Byzantine of all clubs, the XX Committee, which handled controlled enemy agents.

It fell to Murphy to select the X-2 officers to join ISOS, those to handle the ISOS summaries and the files and indexes to be shipped to New York, and those to join the British counterintelligence war rooms, where operations against the enemy services were controlled, and the XX Committee. All this represented a wholly new dimension of the intelligence game, arcane in its nature and vital in its outcome.

Murphy then went to London to integrate his organization with Section V. While he was on this mission, a minor incident in Murphy's own office demonstrated that the specter of insecurity still lurked about Donovan's headquarters. First, $950 in cash was stolen from his office, his secretary reported the theft, and Putzell was given the task of investigating, for the theft had occurred in an office where secret materials were handled.

Then $800 of the money was returned in an envelope smelling of a perfume worn by one of the girls in Murphy's office, an attempt to throw suspicion on her. But while the thief was not identified, a serious state of insecurity was discovered in the very rooms where the ISOS material was to be handled. The master key to the safe in which top secret materials were held was kept in a pocket chess set, and as Putzell established, far from being a sealed area, the offices had become a center for secretaries engaging in social chitchat.

By the time British security officers visited the premises to be used for the handling of ISOS and checked the staff and the procedures for handling Ice and Pair—as the intercepts came to be code-named in the United States—Doering and Putzell had reestablished the security arrangements. It was only just in time, for if the British had learned of this episode and its attendant insecurity, the flow of ISOS intercepts would at least have been delayed until satisfactory arrangements for their handling could be made.

With the completion by Murphy of his mission to England, it remained for Donovan to consummate his relationship with Menzies's counterespionage service by approving Murphy's selection of one of the country's leading literary dons, Norman Holmes Pearson, as chief X-2 representative in London. Virtually crippled by polio and requiring leg braces to walk, Pearson was a man with an enchanted mind and an enchanted career. Known and loved by many of the leading literary figures of the first half of the twentieth century, Pearson was especially chosen for his task because he had been a Rhodes Scholar at Magdalen College, Oxford, and was therefore well known to several of the heads of the British service, and before being recruited into X-2, he had been professor of literature at Yale. With him went Hubert Will (a future federal judge in Chicago), Robert Blum (professor of European history, who was to become one of the greatest American spy catchers), and Dr. Dana Durand (another Rhodes Scholar). That was the advance guard.

Nothing had prepared Pearson or his colleagues for the world they now entered, a world in which, as Pearson was to record, "the dermal and the subdermal took on a new and nerve-wracking significance." It was a world in which, he wrote, "Nuance became all," in which the Britons with whom he was now to work were the "ecologists of double agency." In their world "everything was interrelated, everything must be kept in balance. Yet in the end there was an enemy to be induced down the wrong path, wrong for them but right for us."[15] It was a world where the creed was, as Pearson defined it:

1. To control the enemy system, or as much of it as we could get our hands on
2. To catch fresh spies when they appeared
3. To gain knowledge of the personalities and methods of the German Secret Service
4. To obtain information about the code and cipher work of the German Service
5. To get evidence of enemy plans and intentions from the questions asked by them
6. To influence enemy plans by the answers sent to the enemy
7. To deceive the enemy about our plans and intentions.

Among those British secret service officers who took the American party in charge was that quaint amalgamation of the bawdy and the holy Malcolm Muggeridge, who was to describe the arrival of his American colleagues:

Ah, those first OSS arrivals in London! How well I remember them arriving like *jeune filles en fleur* straight from a finishing school, all fresh and innocent, to start work in our frowsty old intelligence brothel. All too soon they were ravished and corrupted, becoming indistinguishable from seasoned pros who had been in the game for a quarter century or more.[16]

12

Pearl Harbor

It was not long before WJD was plunged into his first and, in some respects, most intriguing state problem—a curtain raiser to Pearl Harbor and war with Germany. The first glimpse of that task did not emerge until 1980, when the FBI declassified its huge file on Donovan and his agency. In the file was a report from New Haven that a man called Malcolm R. Lovell had told an FBI agent that before Pearl Harbor Donovan authorized him to offer $1,000,000—a fortune at the time—to the German acting ambassador in Washington, Dr. Hans Thomsen, if he would defect to the United States. It seemed, however, that no great weight could be placed on the report because it seemed part of a personal dossier being kept on Donovan by J. Edgar Hoover, director of the FBI, for political purposes. But as events were to unfold, there was more to this report than met the eye[1]—that WJD and Thomsen engaged in an intrigue to overthrow Hitler and seize the power of the German state while the United States was still neutral in the war.

Donovan's personal assistant in the COI days, James Murphy, would state that Lovell was known to both him and Donovan and was a close friend of Thomsen's. A search of the Donovan papers, a large task, unearthed a small file on Malcolm Lovell, which showed a brief, odd association between Lovell and Donovan, with Murphy most often acting as the intermediary.

The file showed that Lovell was WJD's first secret agent. A prominent Quaker of good repute, he described himself in *Who's Who* as a public relations counselor, born at Fall River, Massachusetts, a graduate of the University of Pennsylvania (1914), a Democrat, a member of the Society of Mayflower Descendants, an assistant to the undersecretary of agriculture in the Roosevelt administration in 1933 and 1934, a financial adviser to the Federal Housing Administration in 1934 and 1935, and at various other times a banker in Manhattan. In 1941, when he was in his fifties, he had his own public relations firm and was also executive secretary of the Quaker Service Council.

Lovell had come to Donovan's attention through a letter of introduction from Thomas D. Thacher, of a leading New York law firm, Simpson, Thacher & Bartlett. Thacher, a man prominent in both the law and civic works, advised Donovan in a "Dear Bill" letter on September 5, 1941, that he had known Lovell "for a number of years" through Lovell's friendship with Judge Thomas W. Swan, a federal judge on the Second Circuit and also a former dean and professor of law at Yale Law School.

Thacher stated Lovell had been "very active in connection with the work of the Quakers abroad and in this connection has had much to do with the representatives of foreign governments here." Lovell had told Thacher that he believed he could be useful to WJD, "without any desire to seek employment, compensation or publicity in connection with any service he may render you." Thacher thought also that it would be "desirable for you to meet him some evening and hear his story, of which he has told me a very little."[2]

WJD saw Lovell in Washington on September 9, 1941, on "German matters." The file reveals nothing about what these matters could have been, but they talked again, possibly on the telephone, on September 11, 1941. The same day Lovell wrote a note to WJD stating that he had looked at his records and found that "the date of the start of the negotiations in which I acted as intermediary, was Friday, July 19th, 1940."[3] The note also contained this statement: "In connection with our conversation of this morning, may I suggest that only two, or at the most three, very discreet men besides yourself, ever know of my proposed association with you in the matter we discussed." The letter contained an allusion to living abroad, possibly Berlin.

On September 15, 1941, Donovan sent a two-line letter to Intrepid at the British Passport Control Office (the cover organization for the British Secret Intelligence Service) at 995 Fifth Avenue, showing that they had discussed the Lovell matter. The letter said: "The man to whom I talked to you [about] is Malcolm R. Lovell, 26 East 38th Street, New York."[4] Also, there is in the Donovan papers some slight indication that by this date WJD had spoken with FDR about the Lovell contact.

On September 19, 1941, Lovell apparently had a long conversation with the German acting ambassador in Washington, Dr. Thomsen. In a very long, confidential letter to WJD on that same day, Lovell explained their relationship:

> A close personal friendship over a three year period has grown up between us. I am far closer to him than any other person in the United States. Some time ago we agreed that after the war he would leave the diplomatic service and we would go into business in New York as partners. He said that with his European connections and my American, our firm would be hugely financially successful.
>
> He has many, many times told me that he wishes to live out his life in the United States and Mrs. Thomsen has stated to both my wife and to me that she never wishes to return to Germany.
>
> Dr. T. is more Norwegian in spirit than German. His father was full Norwegian. His mother is German. Mrs. T. is Austrian.
>
> Dr. T. was formerly secretary to Chancellor Hitler and knows him intimately. Dr. T. tells me that due to my peace work of the summer of 1940 I am well known to Hitler, von Ribbentrop and Goering, and am considered one of the important men of the United States (this is obviously absurd but I think Dr. T. may have given them this impression for various reasons of his own).[5]

Then Lovell reported the results of his conversation with Thomsen concerning the matters discussed between Lovell and Donovan on September 11:

> "Money for me is not necessary. I am a rich man by German standards." This is the statement he made to me following my suggestion that money might be available under certain circumstances.
>
> He further said, "It has always been my intention to bring about friendship between Germany and the United States. My efforts in this direction are well known both in Germany and the United States."

He quoted Thomsen as having said, "If the United States had given more political encouragement to Germany against Britain and France, and had backed the German governmental system in 1918, war in Europe today never would have occurred." Lovell continued quoting Thomsen:

> "I have never approved of undercover methods, and I have never taken part in them. I know nothing of them. These undercover operations are run by certain departments under the control of the Army and are not in the slightest degree connected with the embassy under our knowledge or control. The undercover agencies in the United States communicate with Germany directly through their own system, and never through the embassy facilities. I would under no circumstances permit it. I have always believed that such

undercover methods by either side promote ill will and gain little information of value for either."

It is to be presumed only that this comment had been stimulated by some discussion between Lovell and Thomsen of undercover operations or Thomsen's attitude toward engaging in them. Lovell then quoted Thomsen in a statement that alluded to the $1,000,000 offer:

"I might possibly be very interested in financial backing and moral and physical aid in a later effort to gain control of the government, provided internal conditions justified such an attempt. With unlimited funds at my call I might succeed in such an attempt. I would, of course, agree that the government I would set up would pursue a policy consonant with the aims of the United States, and the true interests of the German people."

He went on to state:

Dr. T. made it very clear that the above is not his *decision* [original emphasis]. He must have time to consider all phases of this matter, but he will discuss it with me very shortly again, and I may be able to iron out problems as they occur to him.

Dr. T. fears that word of these talks might leak out. He says that with the invention of the typewriter all secrets became public. He trusts the discretion of no women and few men.

Lovell implied that Thomsen had told him, "I may talk only to two persons, Col. D. and the President":

Should Dr. T decide to explore this matter fully he is willing to meet Col. D. at my home in New York, and later, if it is deemed advisable, drive with me to Hyde Park at night to meet the President and Col. D, with me.

No written memoranda may be made of any of these discussions, and no record of any kind may be kept.

He said, "I fear memoranda may some day be written by Col D. or the President, and I would discuss nothing unless I am given a pledge by each man that no mention will ever be made of these talks, or any decision taken later.

Dr. T. makes emphatic statement that he is a patriotic German, but he feels certain conditions are wrong and while he would personally never be willing to accept any money for himself, he conceivably might for the good of Germany if this [aided?] him to [lead?] his country from disaster and chaos.

That letter constitutes the only discussion by anyone in the Donovan papers of the business between Donovan, Stephenson, Lovell, and Thomsen and possibly FDR. It is possible that, in the context of the FBI report relating to Lovell's assertion that he was authorized by Donovan to offer Thomsen $1,000,000 if he would conspire against Hitler or defect, there were further discussions. However, there was certainly further contact between Lovell and Thomsen and Lovell and Donovan, again usually through Murphy, up to and including Pearl Harbor weekend, when Lovell and Thomsen dined together in New York before and after the attack. But there is no evidence that the matters alluded to in Lovell's letter of September 19 were discussed further. Again it can only be speculated that this was the result of Thomsen's insistence that the matter be held to the minimum number of people and that there be no memorandums.

Only assumption is possible, therefore, about what lay behind this demarche. The text of Lovell's letter plainly indicates that a conspiracy against Hitler, involving large sums of U.S. government funds, was budding. But how did Donovan and Thomsen contemplate overthrowing the Hitler government? In September 1941 Hitler was immured at his field headquarters in the East Prussian forests near Rastenburg, directing the Wehrmacht's drive on Moscow, Leningrad, and Stalingrad. He rarely left the Wolf's Lair, as his headquarters were code-named, and when he did, he usually went only to his home at Berchtesgaden, Bavaria, where a regiment of the SS Liebstandarte Adolf Hitler was quartered at all times. The Army, Navy, and Air Force were completely loyal to him at this time, as were, in general, the German General Staff and the officers' corps. The only organized opposition was the Black Orchestra, centered in Admiral Canaris's intelligence and counterespionage service, the Abwehr. The party, population, press, industry, Reichstag, and foreign ministry—all were loyal at the time.

It is impossible, therefore, to gauge whether WJD was seriously considering anything other than Thomsen's defection in 1941. Thomsen was certainly prominent in the German bureaucracy, and his defection, if accompanied by suitable propaganda, would have been a hard blow to German prestige. But it could not have been a fatal blow, one worth $1,000,000. Nor would Thomsen's establishment of a German opposition government in exile in the United States have been likely to keep Hitler awake at night: Numerous prominent Germans, including one of Hitler's immediate predecessors as chancellor, Heinrich Brüning, were in the United States, and Hitler's socially prominent friend Ernst "Putzi" Hanfstaengl was in detention under WJD's control on the Potomac at Fort Myer, awaiting the summons to help restore Germany to grace and favor.

Whatever the object of their association, what did derive from it in the end was intelligence. Lovell claimed later that Thomsen warned him appreciably before the event that the Japanese intended to attack the United States at Pearl Harbor, but if that was true, there is nothing in the Donovan papers to show that the warning was conveyed in writing to

FDR. Also, Lovell claimed that Thomsen warned him, and he warned WJD, that if war broke out between America and Japan, Germany would honor its commitment under the tripartite pact among Germany, Italy, and Japan and declare war on the United States. That piece of genuinely vital strategic intelligence was received by Donovan, and sent to FDR in writing on November 13, 1941: "The following is the substance of statements made by Dr. Hans Thomsen on Thursday afternoon, November 6, to Mr. Malcolm R. Lovell: If Japan goes to war with the United States, Germany will immediately follow suit."[6]

Plainly there was some scheme afoot in this curious affair. What it was we do not know. When Japan attacked Pearl Harbor, Thomsen was arrested, placed in detention with other German subjects at the Greenbrier Hotel, White Sulphur Springs, West Virginia, and then deported to Germany in the Swedish exchange ship *Drottningholm* when Germany released the staff of the U.S. Embassy in Berlin. Donovan then passed control of Lovell to the FBI, and Lovell passed from COI interest. But WJD did not lose interest in projects to kill or capture Hitler. With Thomsen's departure Donovan's attention was to fasten upon the German ambassador to Turkey, Franz von Papen, a well-known World War I spy in Washington, a member of the German General Staff, the chancellor of Germany just before Hitler, and now an old bisexual fox languishing on the frontiers of the German Empire, awaiting his call to power and glory.

With the wind of danger freshening sharply between America and Japan the late summer of 1941, the relationship between Donovan and Roosevelt became of interest and importance. During the New York gubernatorial campaign Donovan had denounced Roosevelt as "that faker," but whether he still held that opinion was doubtful. To the contrary, by October 1941 it appears that a high degree of respect and trust had developed between FDR and his intelligence master, and their relationship had come to resemble that, in some respects, of Colonel House and President Woodrow Wilson in World War I. The President was WJD's only master, and in those first months of operations FDR remarked to Adolf Berle, the assistant secretary of state, that he thought "Bill was doing a pretty good job on propaganda and something of a job in terms of intelligence."[7]

To the President, Donovan was almost always "Bill," while to WJD FDR was always "Mr. President." Despite their different political beliefs, each appeared to have admired the other. Even so, WJD was careful not to become too friendly with FDR, for as Donovan once remarked to James Murphy, FDR was a conceited man whose moods resembled those of a young girl: They were liable to sudden changes. In consequence, Donovan kept his social visits to the White House to a minimum, limited his business sessions to thirty minutes, and conducted most of his business by telephone or memorandum—Donovan wrote 260 to FDR in the first six months of their relationship.

There was talk about a "peace overture" from the German General Staff; Donovan's budget of $1,800,000 for shortwave broadcasting ($1,500,000 approved by FDR), $2,000,000 for medium wave (approved), $3,800,000 for Research and Analysis, and $1,115,000 for the production of motion pictures on the American war effort ($1,000,000 approved); Donovan's first budget, for 1942—$14,124,508 for secret or special works of all descriptions. FDR asked Donovan to publicize Russia's toleration of religious freedom in Poland, to make lend-lease for Russia more acceptable to the U.S. taxpayer; Research and Analysis reported to the President on losses in Soviet industrial production; there were summaries and analyses of the Germans' shortwave broadcasts to the United States and reports on the use by German intelligence agents of Spanish diplomatic passports and an increase in Spanish consular staffs in the United States; FDR spoke of a letter he was to write to Churchill in which he proposed to state that Donovan had spoken of the "most helpful cooperation from the officers of His Majesty's Government who are charged with direct responsibility for your war work"; Donovan discussed the Nazi map of South America which the British had "purloined" from a German courier and a project for building twelve large radio stations with which to broadcast the U.S. version of events to the world.

Yet the curious aspect about their relationship was at no time do they appear to have discussed the intelligence aspects of the deepening tensions or the possibility of war between America and Japan. At no time does WJD appear to have offered the President intelligence about the situation, and at no time does the President appear to have requested intelligence.

That puzzling lacuna in Donovan's affairs, the apparent absence of involvement in the events that led to Pearl Harbor, undoubtedly involved an intelligence source known within the administration as Magic. For although the executive order establishing the COI plainly stated that WJD was to receive *all* intelligence having a bearing on national security, he was in fact excluded from Magic at the insistence of the man who controlled its distribution, General George C. Marshall, the Army Chief of Staff—an exclusion that constitutes one of the most mysterious and troublesome episodes of the Pearl Harbor maelstrom—for, it is claimed, had Magic been made available to the "College of Cardinals" for collation and analysis, undoubtedly the fact that Pearl Harbor was to be a target for Japanese attack would have emerged beforehand, enabling the U.S. armed forces to have taken more active defensive steps than were in fact taken.

Magic was WJD's first encounter with cryptanalysis, which, along with deception, became the two principal intelligence activities of World War

II. Both these intelligence sciences were to become major preoccupations for WJD, and cryptanalysis and his access to it would run like a steel thread through the history of the organization that he was forming—and contribute materially to his Calvary as U.S. spymaster.

Magic had been in existence since 1938, when, after a superhuman operation involving high mathematics and analysis, William F. Friedman, the leading American cryptanalyst, succeeded in unraveling the highly complicated cipher in which the Japanese Foreign Office encased its most secret telegrams in order to prevent foreign powers from reading their contents. The Army and Navy signal services introduced an interception service to pluck the Japanese signals out of the ionosphere, a communications system to transmit them rapidly to Washington, a machine cipher-breaking system to "unbutton" the system rapidly, a translation service to render the Japanese into English, and a security and distribution system to get the "unbuttoned" telegrams to "the customers" as quickly as possible. This interception system was code-named Magic.

By 1941 Magic was producing a great volume of most secret intelligence about Japanese plans, capabilities, intentions, and instructions, not only in the field of diplomacy but also in intelligence matters, on a current, worldwide basis. These interceptions, the Department of Defense was to state, threw much light on "Japanese secret plans, policies, and activities" and were "undoubtedly of great value to those charged with estimating the trend of future events."[8]

Recognizing that this priceless penetration of Japanese ciphers would last only so long as the Japanese were unaware of the penetration, Marshall drew up what was called the Top List, which limited distribution of Magic to FDR, the secretaries of state, war, and the Navy, and the directors of Military and Naval Intelligence—for the obvious reason that the more people who knew of the existence of Magic, the more probable it was that there would be a leak. The Japanese would become aware of the penetration and would change to a new system of enciphering their telegrams. The Top List was drawn up at the inception of the Magic service, before Donovan's appointment, before the promulgation of the executive order, and before the establishment of the "College of Cardinals" as the main, indeed the only, intelligence analysis bureau in the U.S. government.

However, after the formation of the COI, the record shows, oddly, that FDR gave no instructions to Marshall to include Donovan on the Top List; equally oddly, WJD made no request to be included. Yet he cannot have been ignorant of the existence of Magic; even the Germans and the Japanese were made aware of the penetration, although the Japanese refused to believe it.

The only reason WJD was being excluded from Magic distribution could have been security. But was WJD or the "College of Cardinals" regarded as too insecure, too untested to be entrusted with such a vital source of intelligence? The only clear answer to this question came from the National Security Agency, the U.S. cryptanalytical agency, when it declared in 1981[9] that Donovan's name was never on any Top List. What is only vaguely clear is the reason for the exclusion, when the executive order plainly intended that Donovan be included.

One of the reasons undoubtedly was that Marshall and the other Chiefs of Staff were suspicious of the discretion of a civilian organization such as the COI and would not give Magic to it for analysis by the "College of Cardinals" for that reason. Also, military politics undoubtedly played a role: In Washington at the time Magic was power, and Magic shared was power shared. And it is evident that the directors of Naval and Military Intelligence did not intend to share the power of secret intelligence with Donovan, then or later.

Furthermore, a security failure just before Pearl Harbor may have served to confirm the Chiefs of Staff in their thinking concerning the reliability of the COI. In that case a copy of a highly secret journal called the *Defense Record,* published by the U.S. government and containing much information about defense industrial programs, was leaked to the British. Unaware that the document was confidential, and annoyed by a statement in it, the British complained to the White House, thus revealing that they were receiving the publication. The Chiefs of Staff demanded an investigation, and of all the names of U.S. government officials to whom the document was sent only Donovan's was removed. Donovan protested, but FDR refused to restore his name. It seems evident, therefore, that FDR believed someone in the COI had given a copy of the publication to the British, when that was forbidden, and that the organization therefore must be excluded from distribution.

If it was excluded from Magic because of the incident, as seems possible, the consequences were to be grave, for the country, for the COI, and for Donovan. That would later be acknowledged even by Donovan's principal rival in the Pacific theater of war. General Charles A. Willoughby, chief of intelligence to the supreme Allied commander in the Southwest Pacific, General Douglas MacArthur, having seen the Magic file, would contend:

> The sequence of messages referred to, had they been known to a competent intelligence officer, with Battle Order and tactical background, beginning [with a Magic intercept dated November 14, 1941], would have led instantly to the inescapable conclusion that Pearl Harbor naval installations were a target for attack, with November 25th or November 29th as the deadlines, suggesting irresistibly that elapsed time was involved, for some sort of naval seaborne sortie.[10]

The man who broke the Japanese diplomatic cipher and thereby gave birth to Magic, William F. Friedman, would agree, stating in a paper commissioned by the National Security Agency: "In 1946, and even now [in 1955] when we reread those messages . . . , I realize that it is fantastic that *somebody* in U.S. Intelligence did not or could not see that the blow was being prepared against Pearl Harbor."[11]

Certainly the evidence available to Roosevelt, the Cabinet, and the Chiefs of Staff was impressive. A survey of the Magics tells a revealing story of a battle fleet being set up for destruction.

As Donovan's papers show, the record of Japanese interest in Pearl Harbor began late in 1940 when—on November 11, 1940—twenty-one Swordfish aircraft from the British aircraft carrier *Illustrious* raided the Italian battleship fleet at Taranto, a port and naval base on the Ionian Sea in southern Italy. Anchored in the Mare Grande, the outer harbor, were two new Italian battleships—the *Littorio* and the *Vittorio Veneto*—three older battleships—the *Conte di Cavour,* the *Giulio Cesare,* and the *Caio Duilio* —three cruisers, and seven destroyers. In the Mare Piccolo, the inner harbor, were four more cruisers and four destroyers. The torpedo nets protecting the ships were incomplete, and the balloon barrage had been swept away in a storm. Moreover, the torpedo nets extended only to the bottom of the draft of the battleships, not to the harbor floor. Accordingly the British had perfected a new type of torpedo which could pass under the nets and explode under the keel of the target vessel.

Attacking from only thirty-five feet in altitude, the Swordfish sank the *Cavour* and badly damaged the *Littorio.* A second wave increased the damage to the *Littorio* and torpedoed the *Caio Duilio.* Other aircraft damaged other ships. By daybreak three of the five Italian battleships had been sunk or put out of action, thereby ensuring British naval supremacy in the Mediterranean for the next six months. British losses were small: two aircraft lost, two damaged. More important, the raid marked the arrival of the aircraft carrier and its planes as the principal weapon of naval warfare.

That fact made itself clear to the Japanese Admiralty, who in the new year asked the German intelligence service to send an agent, code-named Artist by the British, to Taranto to report on the raid in all its respects, particularly the state of the defenses. A friend of Artist, Dusko Popov, a German spy under British control, advised his British masters of the mission, and a little later still the German intelligence service ordered Popov to go to the United States. Among his targets were answers to a very long questionnaire, the text of which has survived, concerning the defenses at Pearl Harbor and the habits of the U.S. Pacific Fleet, stationed there. Particular attention was paid to the battleship squadrons.

Popov advised his British controllers of his assignment. In New York

Popov and the questionnaire were turned over to the New York office of the FBI by the British agent controlling Popov, John Pepper, one of Donovan's friends and Stephenson's deputies. The object was to establish *why* the Axis wanted information about Pearl Harbor, and a connection with the Taranto episode was made. But the FBI refused to collaborate in the stratagem, threatened to arrest Popov, and, it is clear, did nothing with the intelligence questionnaire, which, obviously, had been given to the Germans by the Japanese—the two intelligence services had an alliance. J. Edgar Hoover personally directed that Popov not be permitted to go to Pearl, so that the reasons for Axis interest could be established, and at one stage, he threatened Popov's arrest under the Mann Act, which existed to prosecute those who transported women over state lines for immoral purposes.

When the Japanese failed to obtain the Pearl Harbor intelligence they needed from the Germans, they arranged to procure it themselves, and from September 1941 onward Magic began to intercept intelligence instructions from the Japanese Foreign Ministry to the Japanese consul general at Honolulu, a certain Kita. As the "College of Cardinals" would have discovered, *no* similar intelligence procurement instructions were issued by anyone in Tokyo to any other Japanese representative located at any of the other Japanese targets. Thus, plainly, Pearl Harbor would have emerged as a special target. The obvious question would have been the single word "why."

The first Magic intercept, dated September 24, from the Japanese foreign minister to Kita, directed that in future intelligence reports from Hawaii, Pearl Harbor waters were to be divided into five areas in such a manner that, to an expert, it would have been clear that the Japanese naval planners were working on a plan for a bombing and aerial torpedo attack on the fleet and the airfields. At the same time the foreign minister directed him to report back on "warships and aircraft carriers at anchor, and although not so important, those tied up at wharves, buoys, and in docks. The types and classes of vessels are to be designated briefly and special mention is to be made when two or more vessels are alongside the same wharf."[12]

Five days later, on September 29, 1941, the Japanese foreign minister ordered that a special code be used by the Japanese consul in Honolulu when referring to the location of American warships. Thus, "KS" meant the repair dock in the Navy Yard; "FV" was the moorings in the vicinity of Ford Island; "FG" designated the areas alongside Ford Island; and "A" and "B" indicated the east and west sides of "FG" respectively—which would prove to be principal areas of attack on Pearl Harbor day.

Then on November 15 the Japanese foreign minister directed that "in view of the critical relations between Japan and the United States"

Kita was to report on "ships in harbor . . . at the rate of twice a week." Care was to be maintained regarding the secrecy of that instruction.

There followed a series of telegrams in cipher from Japanese Consul Kita in Hawaii to Tokyo which, beginning on November 18, 1941, made such reports as:

> . . . a battleship of the Oklahoma class has entered port and one tanker has left port between Ford Island and the Arsenal. At anchor in the East Loch are 3 heavy cruisers and 1 carrier, the Enterprise or some other vessel, while 2 heavy cruisers of the Chicago class and one of the Pensacola class are tied up at the docks at a point designated "KS." 4 merchant ships are at anchor in the Middle Loch area. 8 destroyers entered Pearl Harbor in single file 1,000 meters apart at 3 knots.

These vessels "changed course at a 30 degree angle 5 times from the entrance of the harbor through the waters between Ford Island and the Arsenal to the buoys in East Loch. 1 hour elapsed during these maneuvers." On the same day Foreign Minister Shigenori Togo requested Kita to make a report "concerning the vessels anchored in 'N' area at Pearl Harbor," abjuring: "Make your investigation with great secrecy."

On November 22, 1941, Togo sent the Japanese ambassador in Washington "a most significant message." He stated there were "reasons beyond your ability to guess why we wanted to settle Japanese-American relations by the 25th." In view of conversations between the ambassador and the American secretary of state the need to obtain a decision was postponed to the twenty-ninth, but at that time, Togo warned, "things are automatically going to happen."

As a result, on November 24, 1941, the U.S. Chief of Naval Operations warned all commanders that "a surprise Japanese aggression could be expected from any direction." The Philippines or Guam—not Pearl Harbor—were thought to be the most probable targets. Then, the same day, Kita sent to Tokyo a very long telegram, in which he gave a detailed description of the movements and moorings of all important warships, including battleships.

By November 26, 1941, it was evident that the U.S.-Japanese diplomatic conversations in Washington were in danger of collapsing, which would almost certainly mean war, but when that information was telegraphed to Tokyo, *the Japanese delegation received instructions not to permit the collapse to take place before December 7.* An intelligence analyst would have deduced from all that had transpired so far that the Japanese carrier fleet was at sea but could not strike before the seventh. Why? What was the significance of December 7—unless it was to be a D-Day? Certainly the U.S. Navy believed a critical situation was at hand, for on November 27,

1941, the Chief of Naval Operations warned all commanders that diplomatic negotiations had ceased and aggression could be expected within a few days. But among the possible targets for a Japanese attack, Pearl Harbor was *not* mentioned. The CNO added: "This is a war warning." At the same time the U.S. commanders in chief in the Pacific were authorized to commence deployments for war in accordance with the prepared war plan, Rainbow 5.

Then on November 28, 1941, Magic provided a most significant intercept: The Tokyo Foreign Ministry advised all diplomatic missions except Washington that peace negotiations with the United States would be broken off, that all portraits of the emperor were to be taken down from all Japanese consulates in the United States, but that Togo's representatives in Washington were to "avoid giving the impression that the negotiations were at an end." Togo also instructed Consul Kita in Honolulu: "Report upon the entrance or departure of capital ships and the length of time they remain at anchor, from the time of entry into the port until the departure."

By November 29, 1941, it was evident from Magic that grave events were in train, for on that day Togo instructed Kita: "We have been receiving reports from you on ship movements, but in future you will also report even when there are no movements." Magic advised the Cabinet the Japanese ambassador in Berlin had informed Tokyo that the Hitler government had stated: "Should Japan become engaged in a war against the United States, Germany, of course, would join the war immediately." Thereupon Togo had advised his ambassador in Berlin: "Say very secretly to them that there is an extreme danger that war may suddenly break out between the Anglo-Saxon nations and Japan through some clash of arms and add the time of the breaking out of this war may come quicker than anyone dreams."

At that the Army and Navy chiefs ordered aerial reconnaissance to begin around the Philippines, but not around the Hawaiian Islands. Roosevelt, away on a brief holiday, suddenly returned to the capital. Then, on December 1, 1941, in a further significant and ominous move, the Japanese fleet suddenly changed all its identifying call signs. However, U.S. Navy traffic analysts were able to read the new system in two days. Still, no aircraft carriers could be located or identified.

Simultaneously Magic revealed that the Japanese ambassador in Washington had been instructed that the Japanese diplomatic missions in London, Hong Kong, Singapore, and Manila were destroying their code and cipher machines and associated equipment—a sure sign that war was imminent. However, the Washington embassy was ordered to keep its cipher equipment operational.

Furthermore, on December 1, 1941, Consul Kita sent more detailed information concerning moorings, movements, and defenses at Pearl. To confirm intense and unusual Japanese interest in Pearl Harbor and the U.S. Fleet there—and it must be stressed that the Japanese displayed no such interest in other ports in the Pacific—on December 2, 1941, Togo wired Kita:

> In view of the present situation, the presence in port of warships, airplane carriers, and cruisers is of utmost importance. . . . Hereafter, to the utmost of your ability, let me know day by day. Wire me in each case whether there are any observation balloons above Pearl Harbor or if there are any indications that they will be sent up. Also advise me whether or not the warships are provided with anti-mine nets.

The same day the Japanese foreign minister ordered its embassy in Washington to *destroy all code and cipher equipment except one copy of each system.* Then the clock started to tick as inexorably as a countdown:

December 5, 1941: Consul Kita advised Tokyo that "(1) During Friday morning, the 5th, three battleships . . . arrived here. . . . (2) The [aircraft carrier] *Lexington* and five heavy cruisers left port on the same day. (3) The following ships were in port on the afternoon of the 5th: 8 battleships, 3 light cruisers, 16 destroyers. Four ships of the Honolulu class and [garbles] were in dock."

December 6, 1941: Consul Kita advised Tokyo: "At the present time there are no signs of barrage balloon equipment . . . the battleships do not have torpedo nets."

Consul Kita advised Tokyo late this day that at nightfall at Pearl Harbor there were in port nine battleships, three minesweepers, three light cruisers, seventeen destroyers. In dock were four light cruisers and two destroyers. The carriers and heavy cruisers were at sea. There was no balloon barrage. [In reality there were in port that evening nine battleships, six light and two heavy cruisers, twenty-nine destroyers, four minesweepers, eight minelayers, three seaplane tenders. Kita had done his work well.]

The Foreign Ministry, Tokyo, instructed the Japanese Embassy, Washington, that the representatives at the conversations with the U.S. government were to expect a long telegram which was to be delivered to the United States government at 1:00 P.M. [7:30 A.M. in Pearl Harbor] December 7, 1941. When the telegram had been received and decoded, the Japanese ambassador was to destroy his remaining code and cipher systems.

At daybreak 360 Japanese aircraft—not 21 as in the case of the British and the Italian fleet at Taranto—appeared over Pearl Harbor. In a short time three battleships—*Arizona, West Virginia, California*—were sunk. The battleship *Oklahoma* capsized, *Nevada* ran aground, and all three remaining battleships—*Maryland, Utah, Tennessee*—were damaged and put out of action. Of the Army's 231 planes, 65 were destroyed, and many more damaged. Of the Navy's and Marines' aircraft, only 54 of 255 were still flyable at the end of the attack. U.S. dead: 2,335 sailors and soldiers, 68 civilians. Wounded: 1,178. Effect: Command of the Pacific passes to the Imperial Japanese Navy.

While it is true that the significance of the evolution of events benefits from hindsight, and while it is also true that this is only a partial transcription of the Magic file, it seems undeniable that if the Magic decryptions had been made available to the "College of Cardinals," and they had done their work correctly, setting the Magics into the context of other diplomatic, naval, military, and technical information available in Washington, the fact that Pearl was *the* target would have emerged with clarity. Certainly Admiral Husband E. Kimmel, the commander in chief of the sunken fleet, who was also excluded from the Top List, believed this to be the case, for the nature of the intelligence available *before* Pearl Harbor was such that he was to write:

> When the information available in Washington prior to the attack was finally disclosed to me long after, I was appalled. Nothing in my experience of nearly forty-two years service in the Navy had prepared me for the actions of the highest officials in our government which denied this vital information to the Pearl Harbor commanders.[13]

To that bitter statement must be added the words of Friedman, who declared in a paper for the National Security Agency that the disaster had occurred because "there was *nobody* in either the Army or the Navy intelligence staffs in Washington whose most important, if not sole duty, was to study the whole story which the MAGIC messages were unfolding." There was "nobody whose responsibility it was to try and put the pieces of the jig-saw puzzle together."[14] The persons cleared to read Magic "had the messages only for so short a time that each message represented only a single frame" in a "long motion picture." They saw only the single frame, not the whole film, and therefore did not understand what the entire film was about. That, essentially, was the cause of Pearl Harbor—the "College of Cardinals" had been ignored because it was a civilian service that consequently could not be entrusted with Magic.

It should not be thought that Pearl was the first and the last of the American intelligence disasters of World War II. It was only the first of them.

A fortnight after Pearl Harbor the British prime minister, Winston Churchill, arrived at Hampton Roads in the new British battleship *Duke of York,* at the head of a large military and political delegation, for the first

of the Anglo-American conferences of grand strategy of World War II—
the Arcadia Conference. On December 22, 1941, Churchill flew up to
Gravelly Point airfield, where he landed after dark to find President
Roosevelt waiting to greet him. "I clasped his hand with comfort and
pleasure," Churchill was to write of their meeting, and "We soon reached
the White House, which was to be in every sense our home for the next
three weeks."[15]

With that meeting what came to be called "the Anglo-American special
relationship" was begun, and while it was not always to be the most
tranquil of associations, it was to last for the next forty years and beyond
and become, therefore, the most enduring alliance of the century. A
single term expressed the nature of the relationship: Donovan and his
colleagues always referred to the British as the Cousins.

That evening Roosevelt gave a dinner party for Churchill and the
British staff. Donovan was among the guests, and he and Churchill
resumed their acquaintanceship. It was a convivial evening, despite the
gravity of events—in the Pacific the Japanese were mounting a full-scale
invasion of the Philippines; in Asia they had just landed at Hong Kong;
in Southeast Asia the British were evacuating Penang; in the Mediterranean Italian frogmen had severely damaged two of the few remaining
British battleships, the *Valiant* and the *Queen Elizabeth;* in Europe the
Royal Air Force was making raids in strength on Wilhelmshaven and
Bremen; on the Russian front Hitler had just assumed supreme command
of the Wehrmacht outside Moscow.

Yet not all the conversation concerned the war. Talking with Churchill,
Donovan happened to mention that as a former cavalryman he had much
enjoyed rereading Churchill's *The River War,* an account of Kitchener's
campaign against the Mahdi and the Dervishes in the Sudan in 1898,
when Churchill served with the 21st Lancers. Churchill and Donovan
talked about the joys of being young cavalry officers. Churchill asked
Donovan about his experiences on the Rio Grande during 1917 with the
Silk Stocking Boys, and by chance both knew and recited together, to the
applause of all present, William Motherwell's cavalry officer's poem:

> A steed! a steed of matchless speed!
> A sword of metal keen!
> All else to noble hearts is dross,
> All else on earth is mean.
> The neighing of the war-horse proud,
> The rolling of the drum,
> The clangor of the trumpet loud,
> Be sounds from heaven that come;
> And oh! the thundering press of knights,
> When as their war-cries swell,

May tole from heaven an angel bright,
And rouse a fiend from hell.

In Winston Churchill's world, men who knew that poem knew a thing
or two, and some indefinable brotherhood—that of the saddle—sprang
up between them. But it was not always to be an agreeable relationship.
As vanden Heuvel was to record, while WJD always "spoke with great
respect for Churchill, although he had many disagreements with him,"
he felt "W.C. knew Britain's interests and always acted accordingly." He
disliked "W.C.'s curtain raising of history habit," although WJD claimed
to be always "convinced of the English soundness psychologically."[16]

The cavalry poem was but a happy interlude; it was the grim business
that counted. On the *Duke of York* Churchill had prepared three papers
on what he thought the Allied strategy should be in the war against the
Axis. As Donovan had foreseen, Churchill's proposals followed the ideas
which the prime minister had offered when the two men had spent the
afternoon together late in 1940. The PM began to present them during
the cocktails and dinner, and the exposition reached full flowering with
the brandy.

Churchill's basic point was that the British planners did not foresee the
need for vast armies of infantry as in World War I. The forces they wished
to employ would be armored divisions with the most modern equipment.
These armored armies would avoid large-scale battles with the full power
of the German military machine but would operate on the periphery of
German-controlled territory. They would strike at the heart of Germany
only when the Germans showed that they were weakening under the
combined weight of blockade, bombing, subversive activities, and propaganda.

As Donovan recorded, Churchill listed five features he considered essential to victory:

§ The realisation of the victory programme of armaments, which
first and foremost required the security of the main areas of war
industry.

§ The maintenance of essential communications, especially those
between England and America.

§ Closing the ring around Germany.

§ Wearing down and undermining German resistance by air bombardment, blockade, subversive activities and propaganda.

§ Maintaining only such positions in the [Asian] theatre as will safeguard vital interests while we are concentrating on the defeat of
Germany.[17]

Churchill saw the war evolving in three stages. The first priority in the first phase must be the early defeat of the U-boat in the North Atlantic, for unless that were done, the United States would not be able to send its armies and air forces to England. As an early measure there must come the occupation of French Morocco and the Atlantic islands—the Cape Verdes, the Azores, and the Canaries—in which to establish bases for the execution of the third phase of Churchill's plan: the invasion of Europe. (The second phase was the Pacific war, which did not concern Donovan at the time.)

The assumption was that after the Battle of the Atlantic against the U-boat had been won and the Western democracies had reestablished naval superiority in the Pacific, the British Isles would have survived Hitler's attacks and be available as a base for the Allied reentry into Europe across the English Channel, or thereabouts. It was also assumed that the coast of Africa and Arabia from Dakar through the Pillars of Hercules to Alexandria and thence to the Turkish frontier with Syria on the Mediterranean would be in Allied hands.

The prime minister's point was: "The war can only be ended through the defeat in Europe of the German armies, or through internal convulsions in Germany produced by the unfavourable course of the war, economic privations, and the Allied bombing offensive." But the Allies must not count on an internal collapse. "Our plans," he declared, "must proceed on the assumption that the resistance of the German Army and Air Force will continue at its present level and that their U-boat warfare will be conducted by increasingly numerous flotillas."[18]

Churchill advocated preparation "for the liberation of the captive countries of Western and Southern Europe by the landing at suitable points, successively or simultaneously, of British and American armies strong enough to enable the conquered populations to revolt." By themselves they would "never be able to revolt, owing to the ruthless countermeasures that will be employed," but if Allied armies were landed in "Norway, Denmark, Holland, Belgium, the French Channel coasts and the French Atlantic coasts, as well as in Italy and possibly the Balkans, the German garrisons would prove insufficient to cope both with the strength of the liberating forces and the fury of the revolting peoples." It would also be impossible for the Germans to have sufficient troops in each of these countries for effective resistance, and their tank units would be hopelessly dispersed. At the same time, to intensify the enemy's discomfiture and to diminish his powers of resistance, immense air fleets would prepare the way for the troops, to support them in their offensive across northwestern Europe, to demolish the enemy's industry, to destroy his will to fight, and to undermine the dominion of Hitler.

For the Allied invasion itself, large numbers of men and great quantities of matériel would not be necessary, Churchill believed. He visualized arms for the uprising of the local people, who would supply the corpus of the liberating offensive. The Allies would put ashore forty armored divisions of 15,000 men each, of which Britain would provide almost half, for a total of 600,000 men. Behind this armor would come a further 1,000,000 Allied soldiers, to "wrest enormous territories from Hitler's domination." These campaigns would require equipment on a lavish scale, but Churchill believed that America's and Britain's war industries would be running at a sufficient scale by the end of 1942.

Churchill's presentation, which was lengthy and lubricated by much brandy, created a blaze of interest among the civilians, but not among the military. The fundamental concept of all American planning for war with Germany had been the need to destroy the power of the German Army at the earliest time. While Donovan admired Churchill's plan, the American Chiefs of Staff did not, for its notion of peripheral warfare—what the British called special means—was contrary to American doctrines of continental land warfare. This difference in concept was to cause Donovan considerable trouble shortly.

Nonetheless, the Arcadia plan went forward for detailed discussion by the Chiefs of Staff of the two powers, who now met at the Federal Reserve Building for twelve days to discuss it and other plans. The decision was taken to re-form the Allied Supreme War Council of World War I, this time as the Combined Chiefs of Staff, with permanent headquarters in Washington, and it soon became an immense institution that resembled not so much a military staff as a great supranational government department the function of which was to marshal and deploy all the resources, human and matériel, of both America and the British Empire, so that the two powers became almost a single state—a state to execute Churchill's Arcadia plan. The Russians were invited to join this new government within two states, but they declined, so the Combined Chiefs worked with them through the American and the British military missions in Moscow and through the Soviet military missions in Washington and London.

With the transmission of the Arcadia plan to the Combined Chiefs for discussion, Donovan and his organization now became directly involved in what was an international command. WJD appears to have recognized both the promise and the danger of the Combined Chiefs to his agency, for while he was responsible only to the President, he anticipated that he would be called upon to carry out operations in support of plans formed by the Combined Chiefs. Immediately, therefore, he made his intention plain to Stephenson. His agency would, of course, collaborate in high degree, but he would continue to insist that the American SIS, like the British SIS, would remain independent of the Combined Chiefs but work in the closest collaboration with them. Donovan's desire that the SIS maintain its complete independence was well understood by both parties, which undertook to collaborate and not to spy on the other.

Donovan and the British representatives got down to the tasks involved in the creation of what they intended should be a series of national insurrections against the Germans as part of the Arcadia plan, what Churchill called "setting Europe ablaze."

From the moment Churchill proposed his combination of orthodox and unorthodox warfare, its only supporter in the American military hierarchy, except Roosevelt, was Donovan. The American Chiefs of Staff made it evident that they were interested not in time-consuming peripheral warfare, which is what they believed the Arcadia plan represented, but only in the development of enormous military power to carry out an enormous land campaign to crush the Germans spiritually and physically. When at Arcadia the British presented a paper called "American-British Grand Strategy," which introduced the "fourth element of warfare," the "wearing down and undermining [of] German resistance by air bombardment, blockade, subversive activities and propaganda" and the "maintenance of the spirit of revolt in the occupied countries, and the organization of subversive movements," it was barely discussed. And it was accepted only by accident.

The subject appeared in the British paper and was intended for detailed discussion, but although the orthodox military aspects of the paper had been thrashed out by the end of the conference, little attention had been paid to unorthodoxy. Although they were uninterested in special means, as the British called that form of warfare, the American Chiefs of Staff accepted the entire paper, rather than argue about a portion of it, one they regarded at the time as of little importance. Thus, special means became part of Roosevelt's armory, and that of future presidents, more or less by accident.

Here then, in the Arcadia plan, was WJD's major task for the next five years. He began work on it immediately.

13

Project George

When Churchill presented his paper "The Campaign of 1943" to Roosevelt during the Arcadia Conference, the prime minister mentioned that the war could be ended only through one of two developments—the defeat in Europe of the German armies or revolution in Germany against Hitler. Speaking on the basis of knowledge obtained from the several contacts between Menzies's service at the Vatican and the Black Orchestra, the Gestapo's code name for the anti-Hitler conspiracy within the German General Staff and its intelligence service, Canaris's Abwehr, Churchill thought a German revolution was always possible, but "we must not count on this."[1] The Allies must be prepared to fight and defeat the Wehrmacht in battle.

Churchill's uncertainty about the nature and strength of the German resistance movement to Hitler stemmed from the Venlo incident, which occurred in November 1939, just after the outbreak of the Anglo-German war. As Donovan knew, the British secret service had given thought to stimulating a revolution against Hitler, and in November 1939 there had been contacts between British secret service officers in Holland and two Germans who represented themselves as being agents of the Black Orchestra.

Arrangements were made to fly the Germans, who produced documents showing themselves to be high officials of the German General Staff, to London for talks with the foreign secretary, Lord Halifax. However, they proved to be agents provocateurs of the Nazi party's intelligence service, the Sicherheitsdienst, endeavoring to establish the identities of real representatives of the Black Orchestra, and the Britons were lured to the Dutch-German border town of Venlo, kidnapped, taken to Berlin for interrogation, and then sent to a concentration camp where they were to spend the rest of the war. Hitler had used the incident as his pretext for the invasion of the Low Countries in 1940.

Humiliated by that trickery and defeat, the British service was reluctant thereafter to trust any German peace emissary. But Donovan believed that he and his service might succeed where the British had failed and encouraged the Black Orchestra to undertake a revolution—after all, his mandate was to locate, nourish, and direct European resistance movements in national insurrections against Hitler.

As is evident, Donovan was aware of the existence of the Black Orchestra through his contacts with Dr. Paul Leverkühn during the Anastasia transactions and with Count Helmuth von Moltke. Now the head of one of Germany's leading families, married to an Englishwoman, a former Rhodes Scholar, and a member of the Inner Temple in London, Count von Moltke was, as Donovan had learned in Berlin in 1939, also the leader of an organization calling itself the Kreisau Circle, after his estate at Kreisau in eastern Germany. Connected to the Black Orchestra through Moltke himself, who was taken on the staff of the Abwehr by Canaris just after the outbreak of war, the circle saw its essential purpose as preparation of a revolutionary all-party policy to be used as an alternative to Nazism.

With the German declaration of war on the United States after Pearl Harbor, Donovan began to encourage the Canaris and Moltke organizations and appears to have hoped to act through the German ambassador in Washington, Dr. Hans Thomsen, a man who was thought by Hitler, Ribbentrop and the American press alike to be an ardent Nazi, but was in fact no more than a passionate German nationalist and anti-Bolshevik who admired American democracy, a man in the mold of Canaris.

The conclusion of the Thomsen affair did not mark the end of Donovan's belief that a revolution in Germany could terminate Hitlerism and that the end of Hitlerism would probably mean the end of the war, as indeed proved to be the case. With that revolution in mind, therefore, at an early date in the history of his agency Donovan began Project George, the real name of which was the Western Continents Corporation.

Western Continents was established by one George H. Muhle on August 14, 1941. Its capitalization was $10,000, all common stock at a par value of $100, its address was Room 829, 30 Rockefeller Plaza, New York City, and its officers described its business as "Research and Analyzation Work and Export and Import." A Dun & Bradstreet report on the corporation showed that Muhle was born on July 17, 1899, at Hamburg, Germany; that he was married; that he had entered the United States as an immigrant on December 9, 1938; that he had filed a petition for naturalization; that he had studied law and economics at Heidelberg University; that he had been a German civil servant of rank and importance but been discharged for anti-Nazi activities; that on his arrival in the United States he had been employed in the business and pension department of the Bank of Manhattan (where Leverkühn once worked for Paul Warburg); that he had left that bank to join the Schering Corporation of New Jersey; and that he was now a consulting economist with Western Continents.

The Dun & Bradstreet report also reported that Muhle's treasurer was one William Diebold, Jr., a native-born American and a professor of economics specializing in international economic problems. It emerged that Diebold had traveled widely to study foreign economic problems, had been a member of the staff of the Council on Foreign Relations, and was the author of a number of publications on economics. Dun & Bradstreet concluded its report with the observation that "The operations of the Corporation are reported to be on a profitable basis, but financial information is withheld."[2]

The vision drawn by the report was, in all, one of a pair of earnest and able economists hard at work in a small but prosperous way of business. And it was a perfectly accurate picture, except that Muhle was not Muhle but George Muhle Mertens, and the corporation was owned by the United Kingdom Commercial Corporation of 30 Rockefeller Plaza, president William H. Stephenson, head of the British secret services in the Americas, and the FBQ Corporation, 52 Wall Street, one of Donovan's business fronts.

The biographical information was also correct, but incomplete. Mertens had withheld the really significant information: Between 1926 and 1927 he had been head of the Bureau of Investigation for Anti-Democratic Activities, a government intelligence organization formed to counter leftist and rightist extremism in Germany, at Königsberg, East Prussia; he had been dismissed from all his posts in the Third Reich personally by the new interior minister, Hermann Göring; he had been arrested for high treason—it was alleged that he was a member of the proscribed militant republican organization Reichsbanner Schwarz-Rot-Gold—while working for the Commerz Bank in Berlin in 1936; and he had been acquitted for "lack of sufficient evidence, not because the trial has proved innocence."[3]

Nor did Mertens, a Protestant, reveal that he had been helped get to the United States by the counselor at the American Embassy in Berlin, Prentiss Gilbert; had joined the Schering Corporation, of Bloomfield, New Jersey, in the belief that its Nazi German owners had sold it to non-German owners; and had soon discovered that the ownership was no more than a cover for Nazi corporations and intelligence services seeking to penetrate the Americas on a large scale.

Mertens certainly did not discuss his activities since 1940. In that year, as a militant anti-Nazi, he decided to act against Schering, sought and was granted an interview with President Roosevelt's adviser on internal security, Adolf Berle, of the State Department, and told Berle that he had "managed early in 1940 to obtain inside knowledge of the complete blueprint according to which the Germans, by means of dummy corporations and supply centers in neutral countries, had organized the maintenance of their overseas business in evasion of blockade and black list controls [by the British government]."

Berle had not "shown much interest," and Mertens then went to the Department of Justice to see Francis McNamara of the Alien Property Office. McNamara, while greatly interested, "did not feel legally able to take action." At that point, Mertens reported in a written statement for Donovan, he contacted Stephenson's organization in New York, which began economic warfare operations to close down secret Nazi and Nazi-related trading corporations throughout the Western Hemisphere.

Then Mertens joined the Stephenson organization as "an expert in German overseas business with particular interest in economic warfare." The Stephenson organization formed Western Continents, putting up the necessary capital, and until March 1942 Mertens worked for Stephenson as a high-grade agent. He also provided Donovan with much information.

Control of Western Continents was passed by Stephenson to Donovan in March 1942, when Senator Kenneth McKellar introduced a bill intended to force the British service to make available to the FBI the identities of its agents and data relating to its activities and finances—a reflection of Berle's and Hoover's anxieties concerning the dramatic spread of British secret activities throughout the Americas. The bill would have put Stephenson out of business, and seriously injured Donovan and the COI, had it become law. To preserve Stephenson's most important assets intact, he transferred them to Donovan's organization, for which they worked for the rest of the war, even after the act was vetoed by Roosevelt on the ground that it was against the national interest and the interests of America's ally Britain.

By the time the transfer was made, however, Mertens had exposed the Nazi commercial structure in the United States, its relationship with the Sicherheitsdienst (SD), and the relationship between both and Nazi interests in South America. All this had been achieved by the simple process of opening and reading German commercial mail and telegrams, which were being intercepted by American, British, and Canadian mail and telegraph intercept bureaus in North and South America. Donovan put Mertens—who was always referred to only as George—to work on similar Nazi activity in South America and other clandestine matters then interesting the OSS chief: the German penetration of Latin America (where in two years, with a staff of only eleven people and a monthly budget averaging $11,000, Mertens provided an impressively detailed and exhaustive exposure of the SD's capabilities and intentions in South America); the personal financial arrangements in the United States of the Fascist French prime minister, Pierre Laval, his associates, and of a Vichy French network of pro-Fascist banks grouped around Banque Worms et Cie in Paris and Vichy; and the Black Orchestra. With that exposure, Mertens was put to work estimating the influence and capabilities of the Black Orchestra and other anti-Nazi organizations in Germany and Austria. The first important source was one Hanfstaengl.

Donovan had displayed the closest interest in Dr. Ernst "Putzi" Hanfstaengl from the moment he heard that Hitler's former friend and financial backer was in British custody. Born in 1887, Hanfstaengl was a leading member of a wealthy Munich family who owned an art publishing company. His mother, Catherine, was a member of an old New England family; he was a graduate of Harvard (class of 1909); and he had lived throughout World War I in New York.

When Hitler entered politics in Munich, Hanfstaengl was much attracted by the power of his oratory and became one of the Führer's acolytes. Even when Hanfstaengl's first wife, Helena, was supposed to be having an affair with Hitler, Hanfstaengl's devotion for Hitler remained untrammeled by the prospects of a painful divorce, and when Hitler's first attempt to seize the power of the state, near the Herrngasse in Munich in 1923, failed in a blaze of police gunfire, "Uncle Alf"—as Hitler was then called—took refuge in Hanfstaengl's country house at Uffing, about thirty-five miles from Munich. There Hanfstaengl stopped Hitler from shooting himself and was at his side when the police came calling and took Hitler away, his face pale and hunted, with a wild lock of hair falling onto it, to the fortress prison at Landsberg am Lech.

A witty, shrewd, and observant companion of no great political consequence, Hanfstaengl had been a frequent and welcome visitor to Hitler's cell throughout the year the Führer was in prison, was at the gates with his cabriolet to collect Hitler when he was released, and remained close throughout the "years of struggle" and Hitler's chancellery until 1936, when he felt that his life was in danger and went into exile.

Hanfstaengl's importance to Donovan lay not in his ideological but in his social knowledge; he knew everybody and had collected a vast store of gossip and minutiae about the Third Reich. As a source of information for the establishment of dossiers, Hanfstaengl was unrivaled outside Germany, and it appeared that he had kept himself informed of the power changes and political developments even while in British custody in Canada.

With Roosevelt's approval, Donovan made contact with Hanfstaengl through a well-known liberal journalist, John Franklin Carter, who ran two columns—"We, the People" and "The Week in Washington"—from rooms at the National Press Building. Although Carter was not employed by Donovan, he was given special authority to negotiate with the British and the Canadian governments on behalf of the COI; the plan was to install Hanfstaengl and his son at Fort Myer, headquarters of the Washington garrison. A letter from Carter to Donovan on March 24, 1942, describes FDR's part in this unusual transaction:

> At the request of the State Department, after consultation with the President, the British Embassy here has asked the Home Office in London to agree to the release of Hanfstaengl to the United States authorities, with a view to accepting Hanfstaengl's offer to assist our propaganda and psychological warfare against Hitler and the Axis. The method of handling Hanfstaengl which has been agreed upon between you and me has also been discussed with the President, who further approves the suggestion that, on his release, Hanfstaengl be given temporary accomodations [*sic*] in Fort Myer, in order to avoid publicity until we have decided on the most effective manner in which we can use the services of this former associate of Hitler.
>
> The idea is that Hanfstaengl shall have the status of a captured officer on parole, perhaps under a temporary pseudonym such as Ernest Sedgewick, with the proviso that he shall not leave Fort Myer except on a pass from the Commandant, certified by either you, David Bruce [chief of OSS Secret Intelligence] or myself.

It was, thought Carter, "essential that at first he should be in a place which will be both accessible to us and not open to the general public."[4]

On the same day Donovan's liaison officer with the War Department, William A. Kimbel, saw Assistant Secretary of War J. J. McCloy, who grumbled a little because "space at Fort Myer is in great demand" and "this proposal will necessitate removing some officer from his house." But under the circumstances he would be "glad to take action."[5] And so it was. Hanfstaengl was driven to Fort Myer under cover of darkness, quartered in a house just down the road from Quarters One, the home of Army Chief of Staff Marshall, and soon German experts from Donovan's George organization began the interrogation, which lasted seven and a half weeks. The results were of great value to a psychiatric profile of Hitler which Donovan commissioned. Also, for a time, Hanfstaengl acted as an adviser in Donovan's schemes to remove the Führer.

Meanwhile, a second major source of intelligence about Hitler had emerged to interest the George organization. Archduke Otto of Hapsburg, pretender to the throne of Austria, was the son of Emperor Charles and Empress Zita, who were forced to flee Schönbrunn Palace in Vienna on the day World War I ended, November 11, 1918, to avoid being seized by Red Guards. But they traveled only as far as the royal hunting lodge at Eckartsau, where for the next year the emperor held court. On March 23, 1919, confronted with a demand by the Communists that he either exile himself or abdicate and become a common citizen of the state, Charles decided to leave the country. With the departure of the imperial family for Switzerland, a dynasty that had existed since the tenth century at last lost the remnants of its authority.

In time, Otto was proclaimed pretender, and while he had not the slightest hope of regaining the throne, in March 1938, when the German army invaded Austria, he appears to have believed that his slender chances would be enhanced if he allied himself with the British, who with a well-established monarchy might look with favor upon a restoration in Austria, provided he could render England some service in the conflict with Hitler. He then accepted a subsidy from the British SIS to help his political activities in Austria and Hungary.

But the relationship did not prosper. The British service expected more for its money than the archduke could render, so he moved to the United States, attended by a small but faithful retinue. He established himself in Washington, where his principal adviser was a Jesuit priest, the Reverend Joseph Cod. Donovan was informed on February 13, 1942, that Otto and the priest lived "in an ample way and strive to maintain a political salon."6 One of the heads of the OSS SI's Foreign Nationalities Branch, Dewitt C. Poole, whose organization existed to keep Donovan and the U.S. government informed on political currents within the European minorities living in the United States, added that the empress Zita was expected in Washington. She was to live in Father Cod's house, and he was to become royal chaplain.

These developments attracted WJD's attention, for he was interested in Austria and Hungary as areas for political mischief-making. Through the intercession of the former U.S. ambassador at Moscow and Paris, William C. Bullitt, on March 23, 1942, Donovan met the archduke Otto at Donovan's home in Washington. There, Donovan later informed President Roosevelt, Otto had made certain requests. He wanted the former Hungarian consul in New York, a certain Megyesy, presently interned at the Greenbrier Hotel, in White Sulphur Springs, West Virginia, to send a message to a mutual friend in Budapest, who was Otto's "personal representative." That man was husband of the sister-in-law of James Gerard, a former U.S. ambassador to Germany and chairman of the finance committee of the Democratic National Committee. Otto thought that his "personal representative" might be able to arrange conversations with the Hungarian premier and interior minister, "in order to prevail upon them to change sides at the acceptable time."7 Also, Donovan informed the President, Otto wished to establish an intelligence service between the United States and Hungary, through Switzerland.

Here, then, was a classic secret intelligence situation, one redolent of those that must have existed during the period of the great pretenders. Otto, head of what had been one of the world's first dynasties and empires, was now impoverished, disgruntled with past secret alliances, presenting complicated schemes for a restoration to men who seemed to promise new secret alliances, and no doubt hoping his new friends would restore him and his family to something of their old grandeur and affluence. Yet Otto's proposals were not without interest. He was a man of influence in Austria, which was now part of the Greater German Reich, and any trouble that Donovan could make there would be of great value to the Arcadia plan. Otto was also an important figure in Hungary, a country that was one of Hitler's principal allies and an important source of oil. Trouble there would certainly be a serious embarrassment to Hitler. And serious trouble in both countries would surely result in a major diversion of the Wehrmacht's strength from the fighting fronts to internal security duties—a major object of the plan. Moreover, Otto might well be an important source of information concerning the German opposition to Hitler in Austria and southern Germany. For several reasons it was desirable, therefore, to cultivate Otto, but not in public, where any official contact might be seen as American support for a Hapsburg restoration.

But could Otto be trusted? Donovan employed Poole (a man not unfamiliar with intrigue—as U.S. consul general in Moscow at the time of the Bolshevik Revolution he had been involved in a plot to murder Lenin that almost succeeded) to find out. Poole reported back on April Fool's Day of 1942 that in conversations Otto had claimed to be "in fairly regular communication with his representatives abroad," that "these representatives appear to exist in fact," and that he "gave an impression of sincerity in discussing his activities." He "seems to believe that if effective collaboration is established [with the Donovan agency] he can be of real use." Poole was "again impressed with his intelligence, poise and tact."[8]

However, Poole continued, Otto had had trouble with the British SIS, which he tried to explain with "a very plausible story of British bungling." Otto's story was that the British had tried to involve him with the "German Freiheit Partie, headed by a retired German General in Munich," but Otto claimed to have seen "a trap" and had refused to have anything to do with the general or the party. That had annoyed the British, but Otto had claimed it was the same story that had resulted in the kidnapping of the British SIS officers at Venlo. But, Otto asserted, the principal cause of friction between himself and British Intelligence was his "categoric refusal to reveal the names of his people on the Continent."

Meanwhile, Donovan had asked Stephenson for an opinion of Otto and his Austrian Freedom Movement. Menzies reported from London:

All movements have, in general, proved disappointing. The people of occupied territories have a certain distrust of more fortunately placed emigrants. In addition, such emigrants are almost invariably persons who in their own country were already repudiated. They are out of touch with their own homelands although they have the virtue of democratic and liberal ideas.[9]

As for Otto personally, he "appeared to be an earnest and keen young man, but a bad judge of character." His aide-de-camp, Count Degenfeld, "was the last word in efficiency and stupidity, and it was clear that Otto clung to him because he kept up all the formulae which would surround an emperor, even when the emperor was sitting in a moth-eaten chair with shaky legs."

Shortly after the German invasion of Austria in March 1938, Menzies went on, "proposals were received from Otto and we agreed to make him a monthly subsidy not far short of £50,000 [$200,000]. This began in 1939." The money was for intelligence, but the information produced by Otto's head of intelligence, a certain Waschnigg, was "very poor," and the arrangement was terminated before war broke out.

Donovan resolved, therefore, to retain the archduke only as a consultant, to assist in Project George's inquiries regarding the Black Orchestra.

Now two other important figures had joined Project George's ring: Paul Hagen, a German émigré living in New York who had founded a Socialist party called New Beginning and was an expert on the personalities and politics of German labor; and Paul Scheffer, a German journalist in New York who had declined to return to Germany after Pearl Harbor and who had an extremely wide knowledge of German political personalities, in both the legal and the illegal German movements. The two men had already begun to supply reports on a modest retainer basis—not more than $400 a month—when the most curious, but also the most promising, character of all emerged in Washington. That man was Father Odo, Duke Charles of Württemberg, head of the family that had ruled the southern German state for centuries, nephew of Queen Mary, the queen mother of England, and now a poor monk of the Benedictine order.

The British SIS knew a great deal about this man, for Father Odo, a man with important connections throughout Europe, had tried on several occasions to interest various British embassies and agencies in "elaborate schemes" to "get in touch with German generals" and "secure their aid in overthrowing the Nazi regime."[10] The bulletin added that "Odo's anti-Hitlerism is beyond question" but that he was "an almost fanatical puritan" and it "makes him difficult to deal with." He was a close personal friend of the former German consul general in New York, Dr. Paul Schwarz, and Odo "usually either stays with him or at least lunches with him when in New York, as Odo is especially fond of pig's knuckles or boiled beef on which Schwarz is New York's outstanding authority." Schwarz was the man in charge of Donovan's project to unearth what was known about the Black Orchestra, Father Odo was a principal informant, and as one of Donovan's early secret agents, Donald Downes, was to state: ". . . between bites of cheese-cake I would hear [from Schwarz] of the dishonesty, perversion, or anti-Nazism of General von Sauerkraut who could be bought or blackmailed or both. Schwarz's information, detailed as it was, never proved unreliable."[11]

Be that as it may, through these and other contacts, by 1942 George had acquired nearly 200 names of German generals, politicians, labor leaders, aristocrats, and diplomats associated with the Black Orchestra. Among them were Colonel Count Klaus Schenk von Stauffenberg (of the General Staff), Arthur Nebe (head of the Criminal Division of the Gestapo), Julius Leber (a leading Social Democrat), Colonel General Kurt von Hammerstein (General Staff), Count Helmuth von Moltke ("the intellectual center of the conspiracy"), Wilhelm Leuschner (labor leader), Ulrich von Hassell (German ambassador in Rome), Colonel General Ludwig Beck (Hitler's first chief of the General Staff), General Baron Alexander von Falkenhausen (military governor of Belgium), Karl Friedrich Goerdeler (civilian leader of the conspiracy and former lord mayor of Leipzig), Albert von Kessel (German Foreign Office), Count Friedrich Werner von der Schulenburg (last German ambassador at Moscow), Hans von Dohnanyi (a principal officer of the Abwehr), Count Peter Yorck von Wartenburg (member of one of the great German families), Adam von Trott zu Solz (Foreign Office), and Otto Kiep (former German consul general in New York).[12]

These men were to be among the leaders of the only serious revolt against the Hitler regime. And with these uncertain first steps into the nervous, intricate world of the counterrevolutionaries, Donovan established an operational principle that would become widely used in both the OSS and CIA: the fostering, not always successfully, of capitalist-democratic movements in authoritarian states. It was a principle that would still be in existence forty years later. They were also to lead Donovan and his men ever more deeply into what may be called the Istanbul imbroglio.

14

Lighting Torch

As James Grafton Rogers, professor of law at Yale and a member of WJD's Board of Analysts, was to record in 1942, WJD went to war in the spirit of a man "spoiling for a general's star and a gun." Few men could resist analyzing Donovan and his character and personality—there would be almost as many opinions of the man as men to make them—but Rogers's opinion was more important than most. He was shrewder than most, less liable to bias in his judgment. And, Rogers continued in his appraisal of Donovan and Washington, "Bill Donovan troubles men. He is so honest, so aggressive, so scattered, so provocative. Day by day I see him getting near elimination because he excites anger." But "he has taught Washington the elements of modern war, and nobody else has even tried."[1]

Rogers was correct. Few generals and admirals in Washington understood the nature of the secret war Donovan had been hired by FDR to fight. The American doctrine of making war had not changed since World War I; it remained the maximum application of brute force, ruthlessly applied, in a direct confrontation, the object being the total defeat of the enemy in the quickest possible time. It was the doctrine of the Ourcq, the Kriemhilde Stellung, and other such battles.

Yet as Putzell, one of the first men to join the Donovan agency, and one of the last out, was to state, Donovan believed that the doctrine required to defeat the German war machine required more subtlety. He understood that after World War I electorates were no longer prepared to suffer bloodbaths in the cause of victory. "Donovan's colleagues at the Pentagon almost always believed in those early days that there was only one way to fight the war—frontal attack," Putzell asserted. "But Donovan tried to show them that there was a second way: the strategy of indirection." In attempting to convert the General Staff to more imaginative ways, Donovan made himself unpopular with it, "which regarded that doctrine as unethical, unsportsmanlike, and distasteful."

On the other hand, Putzell continued, the General Staff was imbued with the American ethic of success. It required an accounting for every action. Yet there was not always a device for measuring whether Donovan had won or lost. Putzell stated: "In our game you could not see what you had achieved as you could in the military—with a body count, or miles gained, men captured, or cities destroyed. The only real victory in our game was a matter of mathematics. Our main task was to force Hitler to disperse his power so that in trying to be strong everywhere he would be weak everywhere. That was WJD's theory. He used to say that if we helped the Combined Chiefs achieve that, and achieved nothing else, then we had earned our keep. But few people understood this, then or afterwards. They thought we were goldbricking."[2]

WJD received his first operational orders directly from FDR, not from the U.S. Chiefs of Staff, only twenty-six days after Pearl Harbor, during a brief, informal talk at the White House. FDR told his spymaster his principal task was, through secret arrangements with the French General Staff, to avoid the war between France and the United States that conceivably could follow an American invasion of French North Africa. Also, he was to ensure that the French fleet did not go over to the Germans and the Italians. Thirdly, he was to ensure that Spain remained neutral, for if it intervened during the period of the invasion, its army in Morocco might tip the scales in favor of the Axis.

To these ends Donovan was authorized to undertake large and expensive clandestine operations in concert with the British secret services. To permit American political and intelligence representatives already in the main centers of French North Africa to keep Washington informed of the attitudes of the French Army and Navy, Donovan was to construct and lay a communications net embracing all the Mediterranean countries. He was to arrange a secure system of providing financial assistance, and war stores when needed, to the elements within French North Africa that were prepared to neutralize French communications at the moment of invasion. He was also to find ways and means of infiltrating the Atlantic islands, to establish whether they were being occupied by the Germans, in such a manner that he did not bring the Spaniards and the Portuguese out against the Allies. At the same time Donovan was authorized to expand his operations in the Iberian Peninsula, his mission there to provide Washington with intelligence about Spanish and German military movements and to be in a position through acts of sabotage—blowing bridges and the like—to impede any such movements. All this WJD did rapidly, but not without cost to himself personally. Although he was fit and tough, the problems of being Roosevelt's spymaster had serious consequences for Donovan in the spring of 1942, reminding him that he was mortal.

As part of the Arcadia plan, $5,000,000 in gold coin was to be sent to Gibraltar to finance secret operations in Iberia, Africa, and France. So that the agent cashier in charge of the shipment, Atherton Richards, could be briefed, Donovan had arranged to see him and Stephenson at the St. Regis Hotel in New York on April 2, 1942. Having worked from just after 5:00 A.M. on April 1, 1942, until just before midnight, he left for Union Station in a staff car driven by his chauffeur, Freeman. Just outside the station a speeding taxi hit the car amidships, and Donovan was badly flung about on the back seat. Nevertheless he hastened to catch the midnight sleeper to New York, which he boarded only just in time. The sleeping car conductor helped him to his stateroom and brought him a cold compress, which Donovan applied to what he thought was a sprained knee. But instead of disappearing, the pain intensified, and with some reason, Donovan complained that it had spread to his chest—there had been a blood clot on his right knee (the knee that had been badly damaged at the Kriemhilde Stellung in 1918), and in the collision the clot had broken loose and had traveled up to his right lung, producing an embolism, a dangerous and sometimes fatal condition, especially in the first twenty-four hours.

Donovan continued the five-hour journey to New York in considerable pain and discomfort. When he reached New York, he went straight to his suite at the St. Regis, and a doctor was called. He diagnosed what had happened. Donovan was confined to bed at the hotel for six weeks, while the body liquidated the clot. He ran his agency as best he could by telephone and messenger, and it was during this period that four of his principal rivals launched their most determined attack on him and on his agency.

On or about April 10, 1942, Undersecretary of State Sumner Welles, Attorney General Francis Biddle, Nelson Rockefeller (head of the Office of Inter-American Activities, which had an intelligence responsibility in South America), and J. Edgar Hoover had gone to the President with a complaint that "Donovan had sent agents into South America in violation of the President's instructions to Donovan to stay out of South America" —that he had defied FDR's order that only the FBI was to conduct secret intelligence operations in the Western Hemisphere.

At the meeting Welles "went over old ground about protecting State," presumably from Donovan's empire building, and declared he wanted "the Donovan organization dissolved." Roosevelt did nothing at the time, although the allegation that Donovan had sent secret agents to operate in Mexico was to prove effective poison. However, Welles was not the sort of bureaucrat who abandoned a cause once it had been started. For as Assistant Secretary of State Breckinridge Long wrote in his diary at the onset of the trouble: " 'Wild Bill' . . . has been a thorn in the side of a number of . . . agencies . . . including the side of the Department of State—and more particularly recently in Welles'." WJD was "into everybody's business," recognized "no bounds of jurisdiction," and did "many things under the *nom de querre* [*sic*] of 'Information.' "

Before going to New York, Donovan had had some indications that a squall was brewing over Mexican agents. Aware that a major factor in the success or failure of Torch—the code name for the Allied invasion of French North Africa, now being prepared—would be the attitude of Fascist Spain—if it declared war, as was possible, or if it allowed Hitler to send an army through Spain and Spanish Morocco to attack the Pillars of Hercules, an extremely dangerous situation might arise—Donovan had decided it was essential to make contact with the anti-Franco Spanish underground in the United States. His objectives were twofold: (1) to create an underground in Spain ready to strike at the German and Spanish communications if Franco permitted the Germans to move through Spain to Gibraltar, and (2) to be fully informed at all times about Franco's capabilities and intentions.

For those purposes, one of Donovan's early secret agents, Donald C. Downes, had made contact with General José Asencio, the former undersecretary of war in the Spanish Republican government at the time of the Civil War, and a former military attaché of the Spanish Embassy in Washington. Now in exile in New York, General Asencio had formed on Masonic lines an underground organization known as the Acción Democrática. Asencio claimed in conversations with Downes that Acción Democrática had links with Spanish Republicans in both Spain and Mexico, its object being to "regain the independence of Spain from German control," to work for the "effective neutrality of Spain in the European war," and to rebuild Spain "after the terrible losses in men and treasure suffered during the civil war."[3] Toward these ends, Acción Democrática had formed "small, secret groups which are in turn in touch with other groups working all over Spain with [Loyalist] leaders in Portugal, England and the Americas." They had "ammunition caches," and "should the Germans try to attack Gibraltar, invade Portugal, or cross into North Africa the organization would give its signal for revolt if it knew that military aid was forthcoming from the democracies, England and the United States." General Asencio then made it known that there was a list of Acción Democrática agents throughout the world at an address in Mexico City, where it could be obtained by Downes if he went and got it himself.

Having cleared his journey with the FBI, which controlled all secret work south of the Rio Grande, and with Donovan's authorization, Downes set out for Mexico City. Almost immediately after his arrival there was trouble in Washington. The rumor spread that despite his promise to the President not to operate in South America at all, Donovan in fact employed ninety secret agents there. On March 25, 1942, Sumner Welles wrote to Donovan to complain:

> The report has reached me today—and I only trouble you in the matter because the source seems to be reputable—that your office has actually some ninety agents operating in Mexico.
>
> You and I agreed some months ago that the office of COI should not send agents to any of the other American Republics unless you and I had a prior understanding with regard to this question.
>
> I was absent in Rio de Janeiro some three weeks during January and it may be that during my absence from Washington an arrangement was entered into which superseded the understanding which you and I had. Will you let me know what the facts may be.[4]

Donovan replied immediately that the agreement still stood and that "the story you refer to is absurd and the source, whoever it is, is entirely unreliable."

A few days later Donovan received a more menacing letter, this time from J. Edgar Hoover:

> I have been advised through Mexican sources that there is presently operating in Mexico one Donald Downs [sic], who is representing himself as being a representative of your organization in Mexico.
>
> Downs is apparently engaged in conducting investigative work upon the representation that he has been empowered by you to do this work. I assume, of course, that Downs has no connection with your organization since the Bureau has received no notification of his employment by you or of the fact that he is operating officially in Mexico. Appropriate steps are, therefore, being taken to bring about a termination of this man's misrepresentation.

The same day Donovan replied from his sickbed that he did employ Downes, who was now back in New York and had gone to Mexico only to "pick up some papers from Spanish and Italian sources," that Downes's trip had been approved by the New York office of the FBI, and that Downes was known to the FBI and had been "of assistance to your people in New York on several occasions." Hoover was not mollified and replied the next day that "this Bureau has made definite arrangements with the authorities in these Latin American countries to arrest any person claiming to represent the American Government, unless he has previously been cleared by the FBI."

Although Donovan had flatly denied that he had any agents south of the Rio Grande, a denial that was quite true, the resolute quartet formally laid their complaint before Roosevelt on April 10, after Donovan had been taken ill and during a period when he was being deeply sedated. Roosevelt made no reference to the allegations in a "get well" message to Donovan on April 13, 1942, but he did mention it to Secretary of the Navy Frank Knox, who relayed it when he called on Donovan on April 26, 1942. Furious, Donovan wrote to the President:

> Frank Knox . . . told me that by now the well worn lie has been retailed to you that I had or have some ninety representatives . . . in Latin America. The repition [sic] of this story makes me angry and indignant, not so much for myself, because I have only contempt for the people who will retail such deliberate falsehoods, but because you should have been annoyed by such stories. . . . You should know me well enough to know that I do adhere strictly to my orders and make no attempt to encroach upon the jurisdiction of anyone else. . . . I assure you that your real concern must be with those who bring such stories to you about men who are trying to serve you loyally, because this tale is a dirty and contemptible lie. . . .

Roosevelt, who was not sure whether his spymaster had disobeyed his orders or not, asked Welles for his opinion, and Welles saw Berle, the man who had begun the rumor of the ninety agents. Berle produced a list of four agents, some informants, a system of "scouts," and vague reports about four more "questionable people." He added that "the FBI has other records, which will take more time to dig up." But he was not able to substantiate his story of ninety agents. Welles, in his reply to the President, tried to cover for Berle by stating that the story had come from "an official high in Colonel Donovan's office," but he was not able to name the individual.

The President (who would have sacked Donovan had the story been true) laid all the "facts" sent him by Welles before Donovan. Donovan answered each allegation and in a covering letter declared: "It is a pity that Mr. Berle could not have been better informed before burdening Mr. Welles with the kind of gossip contained in the latter's letter to you. I hope that the German Army will melt away as rapidly as my alleged force of ninety agents in Mexico melts away under investigation." Referring to Berle's statement that he had first heard about the ninety agents from a high official in the Donovan organization, Donovan assured Roosevelt: "If such an absurd remark was ever made by anyone associated with me, I should be glad to know the identity of such person, because, whatever his motive, he would no longer have any usefulness here."[5]

Donovan then explained how the story had started. When Donovan assumed control of Wallace Banta Phillips's K Organization from the

Office of Naval Intelligence (ONI), Phillips had a unit of four men working for him in Mexico. The FBI knew this and that for a short time the COI had allowed Phillips to maintain control of the agents, until the ONI could find someone else to take over the Mexican organization. After the ONI had found the man it wanted, Donovan returned the agents to its control. In all, Donovan contended, "imagination and conjecture have been too freely exercised," for the simple fact was that "we have scrupulously kept within our jurisdiction."

With that the affair of the ninety agents was closed. They had never existed, and at no time had Donovan had any representatives in Mexico. Certainly he had not disobeyed the order of the President not to operate south of the border. But the attack was symptomatic of the state of affairs within the administration: The state of the turf came before the state of the war, the State Department and the FBI had decided WJD and his agency must go, and the purpose of this attack had been to wreck the only factor that was keeping the COI alive: the relationship between Roosevelt and Donovan. Despite the peril, this episode marked only the start, not the end, of the trouble between Hoover and Donovan.

J. Edgar Hoover, director of the FBI, an appointment for which Donovan had some responsibility when he was assistant attorney general, had emerged over the years as the most powerful bureaucrat—or at least the most feared—in Washington. Wayne Coy of the Bureau of the Budget said it accurately enough: "Nobody dared challenge J. Edgar Hoover, not even Franklin Roosevelt." The secret of that invincibility lay in the FBI archives. Over the years Hoover had had a special system for collecting rumor, gossip, and fact about the private and public lives of leading Americans, especially those likely to become important in government and politics. Among most politicians and bureaucrats the mere thought that such a file existed was enough to ensure that Hoover was neither removed from office nor effectively criticized for his own personal and professional conduct.

Donovan's dossier was begun in 1924 with the report to the Bureau of Investigation by Donovan of the theft of his motorcar. The volume of entries increased only gradually until 1936, when there was a slip from St. Louis to the effect that Donovan had said that if ever the Republicans got back into power, he would have J. Edgar Hoover fired. From that date forward there was a marked intensification of interest by the FBI in Donovan. Hundreds, if not thousands, of snippets of gossip—not intelligence, gossip—were filed away, ready for Hoover's use. The document must have cost a small fortune to compile, and it is evident that somebody must have given instructions to all agents and informants at home and abroad to keep an eye on Donovan and his service, especially in regard to his financial, marital, and political relations and statements.

The existence of the dossier was mentioned for the first time on November 21, 1941, in the column "This Week Any Week" in *Collier's* magazine. In looking into the question of whether Hoover was obeying the executive order to send Donovan all intelligence having a bearing on national security, the columnist reported that an FBI spokesman had declared: " 'Donovan knows everything we know except what we know about Donovan.' "

Aware that Donovan was not a man who took kindly to threats, Hoover wrote to assure him that the dossier mentioned in *Collier's* did not exist and that it was Hoover's earnest wish to cooperate to the fullest extent possible.[6] But that letter was untruthful, and whatever instructions had been given to gather information about Donovan were reissued on several occasions.

Yet for all the energetic inquiry, Hoover was not able to establish a single derogatory fact in Donovan's career: no women, no debts, no drinking, no drugs, no gambling, no mistresses, no peculation. A few samples will serve to show what was gathered at such cost:

§ . . . "A" stated that Colonel Donovan was losing face rapidly with the President and "A" felt that the President would be very receptive to a suggestion that Mr. Hoover take over [the COI] . . . as he felt that the operation of [the COI] had been a miserable failure. . . . It was believed that "A" did not have any particular "Ax to grind," but that he was exceedingly conscientious and that he believed the Donovan organization was a complete failure and a waste of money.[7]

§ On 6/8/43 SAC [Special Agent in Charge] Jerome Doyle at NYC had an informal chat with Mr. Martin Quigley, owner and publisher of the Quigley Publishing Company and an intimate friend of . . . Donovan. Doyle stated that he was convinced that while . . . Donovan had an excellent personality and could individually handle any project given him, that nevertheless Donovan was totally unfit temperamentally to administer any such agency as [the COI].

§ . . . "B" advised a Bureau agent . . . in the strictest of confidence that Gen. Eisenhower had demanded that Col. Donovan's men be withdrawn from Africa, and that Gen. MacArthur had made the same demand with reference to Col. Donovan's men in Australia. . . . "B" summed this matter up from the standpoint of the War Department by saying, "Donovan's past sins are at last catching up with him."

§ A report from "D" dated 11/22/41 refers to a discussion between "D" and "E" . . . at which time the incompetent job being done by [the COI] as well as carelessness of [the COI] in selecting personnel were discussed. "D" said the President did not know what a bad job Donovan was doing. "E" felt sorry for Donovan because [he] felt that Donovan's intentions were good and he was a fine man. . . . "D" said Donovan was paid out of the President's special funds for which no detailed accounting had to be rendered and that "D" had information that a lot of money had been wasted on phonies and worthless information.

§ On 10/14/41 Col. Bennett, a liaison man in the national defense set-up at the White House, advised that Mrs. Edith Randon, owner of the Lentheric beauty shop business of Paris, France, was a personal friend of . . . Donovan.

Hoover was thus keeping his post by what was known as shooting with the files. The onset of war and the intensification of WJD's operations made no difference to Hoover; the opportunities for building up the file were merely enhanced as Donovan, with the knowledge and permission of Roosevelt, began to break the jurisdictional arrangements he had with the FBI not to undertake intelligence operations in the Western Hemisphere and to undertake in Washington some highly illegal operations, not only for God, country, and democracy but also for the Grand Alliance. The first operation concerned the Spanish Embassy.

In the spring of 1942 relations between the Anglo-American alliance and Spain were not tranquil, and as late as May Spanish diplomatic bulletins intercepted by Donovan's agents in Washington showed that the Spanish foreign minister, Ramón Serrano Suñer, a confirmed Fascist, was thinking energetically of joining the Axis in the war and, through a display of what he called in one of his bulletins "the resplendant [sic] and inexorable sword, grasped without hesitation," taking advantage of Allied troubles to restore the Golden Century.

For his part, Donovan, in passing one of the bulletins to President Roosevelt, opined that "it seems clear that you are dealing with an enemy mission located at Washington."[8]

In a combined effort to ensure that Spain remained neutral and did not open its territory to a German expedition against the Pillars of Hercules, America and Britain sent two of their ablest men to Madrid. In June 1940 Sir Samuel Hoare, a former foreign secretary, arrived in Madrid as "Ambassador to Spain on Special Mission," and in May 1942, Carlton J. H. Hayes, a leading historian and Jesuit, and a former captain in U.S. Military Intelligence, arrived for the United States. Both Hoare and Hayes worked closely to maintain Spanish neutrality. But whether they worked together in what appears to have been a British conspiracy with some Spanish generals to keep Spain quiet is a moot point.

The circumstances were reported to Donovan by his chief representative in Iberia, Colonel Robert Solborg, by letter on April 15, 1942. Soon after Solborg's arrival the head of the British secret service in Iberia, Captain Alan Hillgarth, advised him that in the late summer of 1940 he had been authorized by Menzies to "create a hostile attitude in Spanish Army circles toward Spain's entry into the war."[9]

Hillgarth went on to state that the "best means to bring this about was judged to be the suborning of the Spanish generals through gifts of money." The man selected to be the intermediary was well known to Menzies, Juan March, the peasant-turned-capitalist who had provided the finance that had led to Franco's rebellion against the Spanish Republican government in 1936. March had approached some thirty Spanish generals, and, Solborg reported, "his arguments to the generals were supported by a sum of $10,000,000 to be put at their disposal by the British Government."

An agreement was made for six months to expire in May 1941, during which time the Spanish generals "would insist on Spain maintaining her neutrality." The money "was deposited in New York," and "the generals were allowed to draw certain amounts in pesetas which could be discounted against the total amount at an agreed rate when the 'pay off' day would arrive."

Solborg advised Donovan that he was not able to obtain all the names of the generals involved but that they did include the famous defender of Oviedo during the Civil War, General Aranda, now commandant of the War College and an officer with great influence, and General Orgaz, commander in chief in Spanish Morocco and high commissioner of the Canary Islands. Aranda shared "to the extent of $2,000,000 as he is expected to be in charge of the Spanish armed forces when [Franco] was overthrown." In May 1941 "a further $1,000,000 was added to the pool to cover the participation of new members." Then, in the autumn of 1941, "the agreement was further extended until July 1942, and another sum of $2,000,000 was added to the fund, making a total of $13,000,000 devoted to this purpose up until now."

Now, Solborg continued, the Spanish generals involved had suggested to the British government that there be a "definite, written pact," in which the British guaranteed support to them "when they decide to overthrow the present government and throw in their lot with the Allies." Hillgarth had been called to London for a meeting about the proposal with Churchill.

The worth of this surprising report is difficult to assess. There was nothing inherently improbable about such a stratagem, nor was the large sum involved unlikely—if Spain had entered the war, the cost to the Allies would have exceeded that sum by far. Certainly the issues were great enough between the summer of 1940 and the summer of 1942 to warrant judicious bribery, and after the war it became known that a powerful junta of Spanish generals led by Aranda did resolutely block Serrano Suñer's attempts to get Spain into the war.

Nor, it seems, was Donovan uninvolved in similar matters, for on February 24, 1943, he advised the Joint Chiefs that he had received from Aranda, through "confidential sources," a proposal that Aranda should seize the political power of the Spanish state with American assistance in three eventualities:

> (1) If the war should come to an end, so as to maintain law and order, which the military members of the junta did not believe that General Franco would be able to do. (2) If Germany should invade Spain and Franco proved incapable of organizing effective resistance. (3) In the event that Franco refused to resist German aggression against Spain or should permit a German army to pass through Spanish territory to North Africa.[10]

Yet the question of the "Spanish ulcer," as Iberia was known in Eisenhower's campaign, as it had been in Wellington's, was serious enough to warrant any act of legerdemain if it ensured Spanish neutrality during Torch, prevented a German landing in Spanish Morocco at that time, and provided Eisenhower with foreknowledge of Hispano-German capabilities and intentions in the period before the assault. To meet those weighty requirements, Donovan now authorized an act of legerdemain in Washington—and was frustrated by Hoover.

During 1941 the British secret service had successfully burglarized the Spanish Embassy in Washington on several occasions. But following the McKellar Act controversy over British activities in the United States, Stephenson decided the time had come to respect the law of the land rather more than he had been doing. He asked Donovan to accept charge of some of his tasks and agents. Among the tasks: the need to burglarize the Spanish Embassy from time to time, in order to provide the Ultra service with data that would enable Bletchley to keep abreast of the periodic changes in the ciphers introduced by the Spaniards in order to frustrate cryptanalysis. Donovan accepted the task and the agents and placed them in the charge of James R. Murphy.

In July 1942 there arose the need for another burglary of the Spanish Embassy, which had introduced a cipher change that had foxed Bletchley at a critical moment. One of Donovan's agents in Lisbon—probably Solborg—had obtained a copy of war orders to the Spanish mercantile marine, dated July 1, 1942, which showed Spain might be moving closer to war with the Allies, for all ships' masters were informed that if the Spanish minister of mercantile marine had reason to believe that war was imminent, the marine's wireless information service would broadcast this signal: "At 21 degrees 25 minutes north and 5 degrees 10 minutes west are remains of a wreck dangerous to navigation."[11] Thirty minutes later this telegram would follow as confirmation: "Drifting mine at 39 degrees 14 minutes north, 25 degrees 16 minutes west."

On receipt of the telegram the Spanish captains were to open sealed orders, a copy of which had been obtained by the American agent at the same time as the war telegrams—a brilliant stroke. Spanish shipping at sea was forbidden to put into any port other than one under Spanish or Axis control, a statement that showed vividly which way the wind was lying. But did the changes in the keys to the Spanish diplomatic cipher and the issuance of fresh war orders indicating that ships were not to put into Allied ports mean that war was imminent? Only a reading of the diplomatic traffic between Washington and Madrid, and other Spanish embassies and the Foreign Ministry, would make this clear, but this was not possible because, if only temporarily, Bletchley could not read the new Spanish diplomatic cipher. It became imperative, therefore, that the Donovan agency obtain the data on the cipher change as rapidly as possible.

The task fell to Donald Downes. Fat, in his forties, intellectual, liberal, a product of Phillips Exeter and Yale, and a former schoolteacher on Cape Cod, Downes was emerging as one of Donovan's most resourceful and important secret agents.

First it was necessary to plant an agent inside the embassy. That was done easily. The agent, a former school mistress, was taken on by the Spaniards as a replacement for a secretary who had been lured away to a better-paying job by Downes. However, the agent failed in her main task— to get the combination of the safe in which the cipher machine was kept— because she found it impossible to read the combination when the attaché in charge of the safe was working the dials. That failure made it necessary for Downes to introduce a safe expert into the embassy, and that man was located through the former head of the New York Safe Squad.

Downes named the safe expert G. B. Cohen, whose premises were "under the 'el' on West Broadway." There, in a long narrow shop resembling a junk-shop, he found Cohen "at his ancient roll-top desk filing a key." He was "a little pot-bellied Jew with curly gray hair on which his battered derby sat like a chicken on its nest."[12]

Downes recounted later:

> I told him I was from the government, that for the war effort it was necessary to open a certain safe in Washington. Would he do it and how much did he want to be paid.
>
> "Paid!" he screamed. "Paid. You've come into my place to insult me. Don't I have two nephews in the army? Ain't I an American as much as you? Aren't you ashamed? Pay me? You can't even tank me. Even a ticket to Vashington you can't buy me, or a Coca-Cola."

Like a doctor in consultation, Cohen listened to a description of the safe Downes had obtained from the British, and then he recapitulated:

"Two dials, key door inside, Vilton Safe Company—dat is a model of 1925. Vell, you go to Vashington and buy a hard rubber or leather hammer like dey use to beat gold leaf. Tell your sakretary girl [the former schoolmistress] to go early to vork one day vit dat hammer. . . . Tell her to hit dat little dial a smash-banger vit all her might. It von't make no noise."

When the attaché arrived, Cohen continued, he would find that the safe would not open. He would then call the Washington office of the Wilton Safe Company, which would then send Cohen to repair it—" 'dat is if you ask them.' " To repair the safe, he would have to know the combination, which he would get from the attaché, and while he was about it, he would break the lock on the inside of the key door. " 'I vill see vat dat key is like and ve vill also have a key.' "

A week or so later, Downes wrote later, "we had both combinations and a key to the inner door." It was now possible to burglarize the embassy, get into the safe, remove the cipher machine, and establish the key settings being used. For that task the party that would actually enter the embassy had the services of the embassy janitor, a man who was in considerable personal trouble (Downes stated that he had large gambling debts and a paternity suit to think about), and his services had been purchased with dollars from the President's Emergency Fund.

At precisely 11:15 P.M. on July 29, 1942, the party entered the embassy led by one of Downes's subagents, a Spanish Republican called José Aranda, of whom one of Donovan's principal officers later reported: ". . . it is my impression that his 'Republicanism' was of a very liberal kind and that he was motivated in his collaboration with us more by a desire to help overthrow the Franco regime than anything else."[13]

As Aranda and his team worked at the safe in the dark office, the OSS group waited nervously nearby. Downes related: ". . . entering a foreign embassy clandestinely and 'borrowing' code books and coding machinery was full of risks for everyone concerned." Donovan and his associates were "justly nervous," for although the Joint Chiefs had asked Donovan to undertake the burglary in order to get the data required in London, "if we failed, if someone was caught inside the embassy and talked, an international incident of great moment would result." But "While Americans were dying overseas, the calculated risk of our thievery did not seem too great. We had taken all imaginable precautions—except one."

They had never considered "betrayal by someone high enough in the American Government to know what we were doing." J. Edgar Hoover was "out for Donovan's scalp. . . . Not only [the COI], but the British

Secret Intelligence . . . were [sic] constantly being hounded by the FBI"
because only the FBI was allowed to conduct intelligence operations in
the Western Hemisphere. "A friend of ours had warned us that Edgar
Hoover believed we were 'penetrating' embassies and that he was annoyed," wrote Downes afterward. "All these fears and worries raced
round my head as I waited for the three thieves to come back with the
loot."

The operation went brilliantly, and by the hot dawn the team had
acquired 3,400 photographs relating to the system. Those data enabled
the Ultra service to read the Spanish diplomatic wireless traffic throughout August. But because the Spaniards had introduced a complicated,
monthly system of key changes, the operation had to be repeated in
August, September, and October. All went well until the October operation, which was undertaken at the beginning of the month to enable the
cryptanalytical authorities to read Spanish traffic between that date and
Torch D-Day, November 8, 1942.

Then the FBI struck. Just as Aranda and his crew were opening the safe
for the fourth time, two FBI cars pulled up outside the embassy, their
sirens blaring and emergency lights flashing. The performance awoke the
entire street, forcing Aranda and his group to abandon the operation. All,
including Downes, were arrested, together with the code books. They
were then taken to FBI headquarters, where they were kept in guarded
anterooms while each member of the group was interrogated separately.
Downes managed to persuade his interrogators that he was a COI officer
and asked permission to telephone Donovan to prove the fact, although
the FBI officers knew very well who the men were. Downes called Donovan at home—it was now near dawn—and as he was to record:

> I don't believe any single event in his career ever enraged him more. The
> next morning Donovan went to the White House to protest. . . . "Won't the
> President do anything about such near treason?" I asked. "No," said the
> Political Advisor of OSS, "he won't. No President dare touch John Edgar
> Hoover. Let alone congressmen. They are all scared pink of him."

Donovan then telephoned James R. Murphy, who was at home and
asleep, and told him to get down to FBI headquarters and obtain the
release of Downes and his group. At the headquarters Murphy established that the Spanish cipher data were in the possession of the FBI,
having been taken from Aranda as evidence. He dragged a third official
out of bed—this time the liaison officer from the Special Branch of Military Intelligence, which handled cryptographic matters—who came to the
headquarters and took possession of the vital data. Thus, they were still
in the possession of the United States. But the point was: Had the FBI

said anything to the Spanish that would lead them to believe that the object of the burglary had been their cipher systems? If so, they would certainly change the cipher, with possibly the gravest consequences for the intelligence-gathering system on the eve of Torch.

The FBI official who led the attack on Donovan's team said he had talked with no Spanish official, but he was not to be believed. The Joint Chiefs could only wait and see whether or not their source had been compromised. It soon became evident the Spaniards had not discovered that their cipher systems were known to the Allies. They continued with the same system, permitting the cryptanalysts to continue keeping the Combined Chiefs informed about whether the Spaniards would declare war and whether the Germans would be permitted to enter Spain for a march on the Pillars of Hercules.

At the same time it was evident to Donovan that Hoover was seeking to indict Downes, Aranda, and the others involved in the burglary on federal criminal charges. Donovan found it necessary to send all concerned in the burglary out of the country on what Downes's orders stated was a "secret undertaking of great importance to the national war effort."

Through these burglaries the Allied cryptanalytical services were able during the Torch period to read all traffic between Madrid and its ambassadors and other representatives in the United States and throughout Latin America. Before Torch the Spanish telegrams showed that Franco was uneasy and undecided, but that he would not permit Germany to have free passage unless Spanish territory were attacked. Also, while the Spanish were suspicious that the Allies intended some operation in the general area of northwestern Africa, they did not know when or where the attack would be made. That was encouraging for the Allies, for they could assume safely that if the Spaniards were ignorant of the time and place of the invasion, so was the Axis.

The first intercept *after* Torch was, therefore, of great importance, for it would show whether under the impact of the invasion Franco had undergone any change of mind. On November 10, 1942, the Spanish foreign minister telegraphed Washington:

> In re the new military operations in North Africa, H[is] E[xcellency] the Head of State and the Minister for Foreign Affairs have received from the President of the United States and the Government of His Britannic Majesty written guarantees that the continental and insular territories of Spain, and also the colonies and the Protectorate of Morocco will be fully respected, and that they will not be the object of attack nor of any act injurious to our sovereignty and integral independence. In the same way Spanish interests in general will be respected, as also the situation established in Tangier, and the standing of commercial pacts.[14]

Despite the invasion, Spain had every desire to maintain its existing relationship with the Anglo-American governments.

The Madrid official (presumably the foreign minister) then came to matters of vital interest and concern: whether or not Spain would grant passage to the Wehrmacht in an attack on Gibraltar and Tangier. As Madrid explained to the Spanish Embassy in Washington, for several days past there had been conversations with the American ambassador in Madrid, Carlton J. H. Hayes, who had "expressed alarm in the name of his Government at the German pressure for the purpose of securing free passage." He had stated that "this threat" would be "considered by the United States tantamount to [Spain's] entering the war." The Madrid official advised his Washington representative he had "flatly denied any such suppositions, and for Your Excellency's information alone, I should add that such demarches have greatly surprised me as they show that the American Government is badly informed regarding Spanish relations with the Axis countries, because the aforesaid supposition is not only entirely false, but is utterly lacking in verisimilitude."

Madrid advised the Washington representative: ". . . you should try to explain, when occasion arises, that, really and truly, Spain is complete mistress of her sovereignty, and has maintained with [garble] countries such as normally exist between self-respecting nations, and that those Governments have treated Spain in no other than that which is due to a power worthy of entire respect." Of the American supposition that Spain was collaborating with the Axis against the Allied powers, the Madrid official stated:

> The International Policy which Spain has been following cannot in justice be explained as co-operation but only as a natural result of the sympathy for countries which lent us the necessary aid to win our war, and not even in the most pressing moments of that period, were we ever required to pledge anything against our sovereignty, it being worthy of note that time has demonstrated to the full the falsity of the multiple imputations made at that time of cooperation with Axis countries. . . .

These elegant expressions of indignation did not, however, provide the President and the Joint Chiefs with the definite assurance they needed that Franco would not grant free passage to the Wehrmacht, and subsequent messages were awaited with interest. The next message was Madrid's telegram 617, which gave the Washington representative the official Spanish reaction to President Roosevelt's assurances to Spain on the eve of Torch. The President had promised respect for Spanish sovereignty and territory, taken note of Spain's desire to remain neutral, and entirely dissociated the U.S. government from anti-Franco activities *in Spain*—an interesting play on words since at that moment Donovan's agents *in New York* were courting leaders of the Basques, Catalans, Communists, Anarchists, and others against Franco.

In telegram 617 the Washington representative was told to state verbally:

> I accept with pleasure and thank you for the assurances offered . . . that the measures adopted [i.e., Torch] are not, in any way whatever, directed against their interests, nor against any metropolitan territory overseas, or the Protectorate in Morocco; and I confidently hope that the relations between the peoples of both zones [Spanish and French Morocco] will, in future, be maintained in the spirit of peace and reciprocal confidence as they have been up to the present.

He was then asked to secure, in writing if possible, assurances that "the aforesaid declarations cover not only the period in which military operations are carried out in Africa, but the entire duration of the war"—an encouraging sign (unless some charade were being carried on) that Spain would remain neutral.

As Donovan was informed, the communication was presented to the undersecretary, Sumner Welles, on November 16, 1942, by the Spanish representative in Washington, who then advised Madrid by cable (again intercepted and read) that he had requested the assurances in writing as instructed. But Welles had not given him the assurance in writing because, as he had stated, "the statements of the President were clear and final and appeared to be sufficient." However, the Spaniard explained, he had "insisted on my petition, and although I did not obtain a formal promise that I would receive it, he told me that he would see what could be done with a view to satisfying me."

The Spanish representative then raised anew the question of American fears about Franco's granting passage to the Wehrmacht, asking why the American government was so uneasy. Welles had replied that "the uneasiness of the American Government was due to news which he qualified as trustworthy, according to which soundings, or demarches had been made recently" by the German ambassador in Madrid. But Welles stated that "he knew the Spanish Government was maintaining neutrality."

So far the obvious interpretation to be placed on these dainty exchanges was that Spain intended to maintain its neutrality and not to grant free passage. Then, on November 14, came news that the Spanish Army was mobilizing, and while the Spaniards were no great threat, in combination with the Wehrmacht and the arrival in the Mediterranean of a flotilla of twenty-six German U-boats, a grave situation could be arising. Moreover, the Allies had their hands full everywhere, and one more enemy would prove inconvenient.

Therefore, as the Washington representatives explained in a telegram to Madrid on November 19, when he called upon Welles to "insist" upon written assurances that the United States would not attack Spanish Morocco, then and for the rest of the war, Welles used the occasion to ask about the mobilization. The representative reported that Welles had "received pleasantly the memorandum which I had handed [him] explaining the reason for partial mobilization, and underlining the prudent and foreseeing attitude which inspired it, and the intention to maintain Spanish [garbled but probably the word "neutrality"]." The Spaniard reported he himself had taken "advantage of my visit to insist on asking for an extension of the sureties given by President Roosevelt." Welles had repeated that he "considered that the statements of the President were explicit and final and that there is little to add to them," but "he would see in what form he could reply to my letter in order to satisfy me."

On November 23, 1942, when it seemed the Germans were increasing their pressure on Franco to permit the Wehrmacht to pass through Spain to attack Gibraltar and Eisenhower's supply lines, the letter was forthcoming:

> . . . I have presented your request to the President and he has specifically authorized me to notify you for (the information?) of your government that, although he believed that the assurances that this government gave . . . were categorical and so clear as to cover perfectly the point mentioned by your Excellency, he never-the-less is pleased to authorize me in the name of this government to give the assurance, in his name, that the guarantees which he offered to Generalissimo Franco refer not only to the course of present military operations in Africa but likewise to the entire duration of the world war which now involves the United States.

In the absence of any intelligence that the Spaniards or the Germans, separately or together, intended to intrude into French Morocco, and with the anxiety of the Spanish government to obtain Anglo-American sureties, it seemed reasonably clear that Spain would remain neutral, provided nothing was done to provoke it into military action, if only for the time being. But the entire exchange demonstrated afresh the need for human spies—Donovan's—in Spain to ensure that it remained faithful to its high assurances.

That belief was confirmed when an intercept showed that despite the asseverations of the Spanish representative in Washington that German and Italian secret agencies were not being allowed to use Spanish diplomatic communications and embassies and consulates, Spanish diplomats and consuls in truth were making certain accommodations to Axis agents in South America. For example, on November 27, 1942, the Spanish representative at Caracas, Venezuela, confident of the security of his telegrams, wired his foreign minister in Madrid: "Pursuant to instructions received [your?] 91, this Legation has received 1500 Bolivars in compensation . . . for EMITA SCHNELL, Abteistrasse 33, Hamburg. Interested party should be informed and warned not to acknowledge receipt of anything."

A check with the British counterespionage service showed that Emita Schnell was the wife of George Wilhelm Schnell, a known German agent operating in the Caribbean on ship spotting for U-boats. It was evident, therefore, that for all the distinguished protestations, the Spaniards were acting as agents for the Abwehr or the Sicherheitsdienst—a serious violation of the neutrality agreements.

Donovan felt justified, therefore, in conducting major operations in the Iberian Peninsula. And that he began to do.

15

The Noble Puppet

In May 1942 the COI numbered 1,630 people, half of whom worked for the Foreign Information Service (FIS), a press, radio, motion picture, and general propaganda organization formed by Donovan and now headed by the playwright Robert Sherwood under Donovan's command. But in recent months the Donovan-Sherwood friendship had been disturbed by an ideological difference: Donovan thought propaganda should be an instrument with which to baffle and bother the enemy as much as it should be used to inform the world about America's war aims; Sherwood believed that it should be used only to purvey the truth, not to mislead the enemy.

To complicate what became an endlessly complicated rumpus, at a time when Donovan was pressing ardently for the COI to become a division of the Joint Chiefs, the military had made it clear to him that if they did assume responsibility for his agency, they would *not* want to take the Foreign Information Service. Although he was well aware of this, Donovan continued to press not only for transfer to the Joint Chiefs but also to be allowed to keep the Foreign Information Service. Judge Rosenman was to tell how WJD brought "great pressure on the White House," stating that he was not going to stand by "docilely," that he was "trying to hold on to his organization," and that he tried to see Roosevelt "to argue his case."[1]

When he did see Roosevelt on the matter, Donovan's remarks foreshadowed the formation of the direct antecedent of the CIA, the Office of Strategic Services. Donovan stated that he was willing to work under the Joint Chiefs because they "were the ones who would win the war, so that was the place for [the COI] to be." When Roosevelt warned that he'd better stay clear of the Joint Chiefs because "They'll absorb you," Donovan replied: "You leave that to me, Mr. President!" Donovan stated after the war that at the time he was aware of rumors that the Joint Chiefs "wanted to get us under their control and then tear the agency apart piece by piece and scuttle me," but nonetheless, he insisted that the COI should become a dependency of the Joint Chiefs.

Donovan was quite right: Almost every government department with which the COI was in contact had plans to tear it apart. When Marshall asked his advisers for suggestions in mid-May 1942, it was recommended that Research and Analysis go to the Joint Intelligence Committee, Special Operations to Military Intelligence, and the commandos (which Donovan was just forming as part of his agency) to the Marines. However, when the time came, Roosevelt acted in his own fashion to settle what was the dullest, most profitless bureaucratic argument of World War II in Washington.

It happened this way. On June 10, 1942, Donovan had to leave Washington for war talks in London—real war. There he met Brigadier Colin Gubbins, a high officer of the British sabotage and subversion agency, the Special Operations Executive (SOE), of which Gubbins was soon to become director. Formed by Churchill in 1940 with the instruction "Now go out and set Europe ablaze!" the SOE existed to build, arm, and harness the European and resistance movements against the Germans. By 1942 it was becoming a major global industry, directed from an office block next door to Sherlock Holmes's fictional address in Baker Street, London.

Although the SOE was an offshoot of the Secret Intelligence Service, unlike the SIS, it was a paramilitary rather than an intelligence and ideological force. Therefore, Gubbins saw great advantages in an alliance between his SOE and Donovan's Special Operations service. Each had much to offer the other—the British, experience, training, contacts, and special equipment; the Americans, manpower, gold, and political reputation. The war required such an alliance; there were, so to speak, many bridges to be blown, and there was no point in two parties' going in to blow the same bridge.

Moreover, the supply of trained agents, gold, and equipment was not inexhaustible. Therefore, the world had to be divided into British and American theaters of operation. Under the London Agreements, as the SOE-SO accords came to be called, Donovan would be responsible for China, Manchuria, Korea, Australia, the Atlantic islands, and Finland. Gubbins would be responsible for India, East Africa, the Balkans, and the Middle East. Western Europe, where the SOE was operating, but the COI was not, as yet, would remain a British theater of operation controlled by the British in concert with WJD's representatives, but the COI would be allowed to operate in Western Europe as soon as Donovan was able to find the men.

On the other hand, because of Vichy's detestation of Churchill and its admiration of the United States, the Torch area of operations—French North Africa, Spain, Spanish Morocco, and Tangier—would become a COI area of operations. Gibraltar would remain outside COI command, and West Africa would have a COI mission operating through the SOE. But personnel of one power would be permitted to operate in the area, with permission, and there would be a complete interchange of intelligence, finance, equipment, transportation, and plans in order to obtain economy of force.

The agreements were of great importance to Donovan, operationally and politically, for they represented for the first time full acceptance by an established British secret service. Also, they were made at a time when Roosevelt and the Joint Chiefs were deciding whether the COI was to be kept alive, and they signaled that while in Washington Donovan's relationships might not be happy, in London they were excellent. It is significant that Roosevelt decided on Donovan's fate while he was away. After weeks of huffing and puffing by almost all the senior bureaucrats Roosevelt on June 13, 1942, suddenly dissolved the COI and established in its place the Office of Strategic Services (OSS), transferring control of it from the White House to the JCS.

During the reshuffle Donovan lost control of the Foreign Information Service and almost exactly half the COI's staff and established a new agency, the Office of War Information (OWI). The function of propagating America's image of itself to the world was given to the OWI, and Donovan was allowed to keep the darker side of the information trade— so-called black warfare, although the executive order gave the OSS only two functions: the collection and analysis of strategic intelligence for the Joint Chiefs and the planning and direction of such special operations as the Joint Chiefs might require. It was a vague directive, one likely to give rise to further warfare between the Army and Navy Intelligence services and the OSS. But Donovan's enemies had failed in one major respect: They had failed to get rid of him. As the executive order stated the director of the OSS would be William J. Donovan.

When the news reached London, no one appeared more surprised at the development than Donovan. The loss of the FIS was unwelcome news, and the vagueness of the directive troubled him, but he knew at least that his agency was not to be torn to pieces and he himself scuttled —at least for the moment. But if the OSS was to become a military service, Donovan himself was not prepared to be "militarized" at that time. He explained in a letter to his friend General Sir Archibald Wavell, the British commander in chief in India, that for the time being it would be better not to get into uniform as "these admirals and generals might be willing to sit down with citizen Donovan, but not with General Donovan."

With the passage of the agency from the White House to the Munitions Building (the first consequence: Everyone had to change the typewriter ribbon from White House blue to Munitions Building black) the burdens upon Donovan became greater. Rogers wrote in his diary: "People are saying that OSS may never survive control by the soldiers."[2]

As Donovan wrote to his new masters, the Joint Chiefs, in presenting his special means plan for Torch, the occupation of French North Africa by either Axis or Allied forces "would have an important, perhaps decisive effect on the outcome of the war." All preparatory operations must be guided by three imperatives: "to avoid (1) bringing the French fleet into the war on the side of the enemy, or of causing French authorities to invoke German assistance, (2) not to permit the Germans to occupy French North Africa without automatically bringing the French fleet and army into action against them, and (3) the need not to provoke any substantial French military action against American forces."[3]

Donovan was well aware that the diplomacy necessary to prevent French resistance and to avoid thrusting France further into the Axis embrace as an ally would require the diplomatic skills of a Walsingham. But there was no Walsingham in the United States, only Donovan. And, he continued, the greatest problem would be that the French General Staff had been required to swear an oath of personal allegiance to Marshal Henri Pétain, president of France. Given the caste system within the French officers' corps, to renounce that oath would constitute an act of treason against France, one for which the death penalty had been provided. True, Pétain had adopted many of the attributes of a Fascist state, and many of the members of the French officers' corps abhorred his policy. Nevertheless, few of them would commit treason for any reason; they would obey their president's orders, whether they were right or wrong—an attitude particularly pronounced in the French Navy.

However, a few officers believed that the regime was constitutionally illegal, had been imposed upon France by the victorious Germans in what was an act of coercion, and was being kept in place by the Germans because they held 2,000,000 French soldiers prisoner and had made their release conditional upon the loyalty of the French armed forces to Pétain. Also, there was a very small group of officers who did not accept the armistice at all and believed that France was still at war with Germany and that the Germans must be ejected from all French territory.

Donovan looked to these groups for a leader other than General Charles de Gaulle, who was distrusted by President Roosevelt and deemed unacceptable as the steward of France, to rally the French armed forces against the Vichy government of Pétain and its German overlords. It was to be a strange search, in which much depended on the character and affiliations of the searchers. No operation conducted by Donovan during World War II was more secret; none was fraught with more danger; none required more stealth, discretion, and skill; and none carried with it a greater element of potential disaster.

In the early spring of 1942—probably April—Donovan encountered a French Army officer employed at the Vichy French Embassy in Washington who impressed him greatly. The intermediary was almost certainly a COI staff officer, Frederick Dolbeare, who had served with President Woodrow Wilson's deputation to the Versailles Peace Conference, had been an official U.S. adviser to the Siamese government, and would in the future serve as a director of the CIA-funded Free Europe Committee.

Dolbeare and the French officer had met in either Paris or Bangkok, possibly in both, for the French, too, had advisers with the Thai government. Whatever the case, it emerged that, without the knowledge of the ambassador or anyone within the embassy, the French officer, who was always referred to only as Paul, was a high officer of the French secret intelligence service, known in peacetime as the Deuxième Bureau. Although the service had been dissolved by Pétain as part of the armistice agreements with the Germans, it had merely gone underground, its small cadre of top men surviving on funds that had been cached against just such an eventuality as had occurred—the collapse of France. The director of the Deuxième Bureau had succeeded in placing Paul in the French Foreign Ministry at Vichy, and he had been sent to Washington as a member of the staff of Ambassador Gaston Henri-Haye, his task to make contact with the "American secret service."

As Donovan was to inform the Joint Chiefs, this officer had his own ciphers, which could not be used by any other official in the embassy, and their purpose was to permit him to communicate with the head of the Deuxième Bureau in France over the embassy's Washington–Vichy wireless link. Having made contact with Donovan, Paul sent WJD this brief message, probably through Dolbeare:

> May 9—General G, having reached the age limit within the past year goes into retirement. At present he will establish himself with his family in the neighborhood of Lyon.
> He desires no publicity. He wishes to be forgotten as a private citizen. The least publicity given him at present, the better. (s) Paul.[4]

From this point forward Donovan's interest in General Henri Giraud appears to have quickened. Only two days later Donovan received this translation of a letter said by its carrier, a French journalist, Michel

Gordey, arriving in New York on confidential work, to have been written by Giraud, when he was a prisoner of war in Königstein Castle in Saxony:

In Captivity at
Königstein, 1940

To my Children,

I do not know how long I will be here—months, years perhaps. . . . No matter. I give to you . . . sacred work—the restoration of France. I forbid you to resign yourself to defeat. . . . The means don't matter, only the goal is essential, and everything has to be subordinated to it. You will sacrifice your personal interests, your inclinations, your theories, your lives.

At the start, it's not a question of going directly against the enemy who is in possession of our soil, and who has completely disarmed us.

The first urgency, the liberation of the territory inside the frontiers they have left. Then, social, moral reconstruction. Secondly (a) Have children, help those who have them. (b) Raise them as they should be—for France. (c) Guarantee each family a place in the sun.

In third place, always be ready to take advantage of situations that will be offered if there is confidence in us. Consequently remake instantly a modern army. From a distance I present the following principle:

> Minds are made in France.
> Training is done in the colonies.
> Material is made abroad.

In spite of all the controls, such a program is possible, but camouflage is the rule. Nothing so much resembles a military service as Scout training, nothing resembles a military plane as much as a passenger plane. A tractor with treads only needs its carcass to become a tank, etc., etc.

But above all, minds must be equal to the task. . . . No one should hesitate to expatriate himself if he is offered a position abroad where he could be useful to France.

All of you, Pierre, Henri, André, Bernard, and you, my dear daughters: remember that a storm passes but a country remains. A nation lives when it wishes to live. Repeat that around you, force others to think like you, to work like you. We are certain of success if we know how to wish.

Resolution, Patience, Decision
(s) Giraud[5]

Giraud's incitement of his own children to conspiracy and rebellion made a great impression on Donovan, and he sent the letter to Roosevelt, who knew the name Giraud, the reputation, and was impressed. But it was not this letter that persuaded the United States to back Gi-

raud as the steward of France, although it played its part, for the sentiments Giraud expressed were not those of a mere politician. It vibrated
with the only ideas, Roosevelt believed, that could prod the French to
fight and France back to its place of leadership among the nations. Here
was none of the mediocre, selfish, narrow posturing of the average
French officer, of a man anxious only to advance his rank and secure his
pension. Here, it was thought in Washington, was a man prepared to
risk all, including his own family, in the highest task: restoring the grandeur of France.

Donovan's inquiries into Giraud's career seemed to confirm that Giraud was the only man capable of that task. He was the most respected
figure in the French Army, and he had not been contaminated by the
collapse of 1940 or by collaboration with the conqueror. Born in 1879,
he was a product of the Franco-Prussian War, World War I, and World
War II and was likely, therefore, to be passionate in his hatred of the
Germans. A professional army officer who had passed through the École
de Guerre, he had fought with the Army throughout World War I, had
been present at the Battle of Verdun, the greatest and bloodiest battle
of that war—2,000,000 men involved, 760,000 killed in action—and had
been captured by the Germans but escaped back to France to resume
fighting.

Between the wars he had fought for France on the frontiers of the
empire, and in World War II he had commanded the Seventh Army in
northern France until his headquarters were overrun. Then he was captured and taken to Königstein Fortress. For the second time he escaped,
made his way across Germany and the occupied zone of France, and
arrived safely in the provisional capital, Vichy.

There, in an interview with Marshal Pétain, Giraud had undertaken to
abstain from all political associations—an assurance he had had no intention of honoring. While settling down quietly to retirement, in fact, he
began the work he had set his children: creation of the national insurrection against the Germans.

Giraud seemed to be a splendid French officer whom the United States
could, and should, support as the leader of France in bondage until the
French people were liberated and could choose their government. The
decision was not Donovan's; it was Roosevelt's, although as a principal
foreign intelligence adviser Donovan was bound to be deeply involved in
the process of decision—which, as Donovan became increasingly aware
in June 1942, was beset by ambition, ambiguity, and treachery.

Donovan's first attempt to establish contact with Giraud was made
through Paul and the head of the underground Research Section of the
Deuxième Bureau in France, who had expressed the sentiment, according
to a paper on the bureau and its chief by Dolbeare, that "as far as he and

his men are concerned the war is not over and will not be over until the last German has left French territory."[6]

However, the flow of communication between Paul in Washington and his chief at Vichy was small because of technical difficulties and the danger in which both men found themselves. In October, therefore, Dolbeare proposed that the Donovan agency establish a radio station for Paul at one of WJD's posts in or around Washington—probably the Congressional Country Club, which had been turned into a school for the training of agents and was secure and well guarded. Donovan wrote to the Joint Chiefs about this on November 10, 1942, just after Torch D-Day, and the project was almost immediately approved. But by the time the station was established the situation in France and French North Africa had been altered fundamentally. Thus, the principal channel of communication between Washington and Giraud became Donovan's political agent at Algiers, Robert Murphy.

Robert Daniel Murphy was an Irish-American Catholic born in Milwaukee in 1894. He held a Bachelor of Laws from Marquette University, a Jesuit school at Milwaukee, and he had obtained his master's at George Washington University. Murphy had joined the Post Office as a clerk, then transferred to the Consular Service, serving at Bern, Zurich, Munich, Seville, and Paris. In 1941, as chargé d'affaires in Vichy, the famous spa in the Auvergne that had become Marshal Pétain's seat of government when Paris was occupied by the Wehrmacht, Murphy was sent to Algiers to negotiate what came to be called the Murphy-Weygand accords, under which the Roosevelt administration granted the Pétain government licenses to import limited quantities of American food products and manufactured goods into French North Africa.

Roosevelt's condition for granting the licenses was that Pétain allow the United States to station twelve economic vice-consuls in French North Africa as reinforcements for the regular U.S. consular establishment, to ensure that none of the imports passed into Axis hands. There was method in what appeared to be an American gesture of goodwill toward Fascist France: Donovan was anxious to get intelligence and propaganda agents into French North Africa, and the Murphy-Weygand accords provided the means by which the President's requirements could be met: All the economic vice-consuls were connected by radio to Donovan.

The men were stationed under consular cover at Casablanca, Safi, Oran, Algiers, Bizerte, and Tunis, where they began to gather intelligence, keep an eye on the German and Italian armistice commissions, which ran affairs in the French colonies, report the movements of the French fleet, and make contact with anti-Pétain elements. That they did well, and continued to do so when Phillips joined the Donovan agency, bringing them with him. Neither Murphy nor the vice-consuls were, therefore, Donovan employees, and Murphy always remained independent of the OSS, although Donovan provided him with communications, intelligence, and clandestine financial support. A number of the vice-consuls, however, did join the Donovan organization, and most remained with it throughout its existence, becoming majors and colonels and receiving medals for their work.

As what amounted to the American political agent in French North Africa, Murphy was soon in touch with dissidents within the French General Staff and the French colonial administration, both of which had sworn oaths unto death to Marshal Pétain. The connecting link between Giraud in France and the dissidents in French North Africa was Jacques Lemaigre-Dubreuil, who was to prove one of the most mysterious and ambiguous men of his time.

Lemaigre-Dubreuil's motives in conspiracy with Murphy would always be as opaque as his political beliefs. To some men he was a hero, to others he was merely feathering his own nest, and to still others he was a traitor. Even the Donovan agency would be confused about his allegiances, for while Murphy was defending him as an idealist and patriot, Donovan's intelligence service would be denouncing him as a "leading French Fascist and a member of that segment of French society that, fearing bolshevism to be the only alternative, gave Pétain its blessing and support that fateful day, 10 July 1940—the day on which the constitution of the Third Republic was dissolved and full powers were conferred on Pétain, who, promptly, abolished the Republican slogan of 'Liberty, Equality, Fraternity' and replaced it with the French fascist slogan of 'Work, Country, Family.' "[7]

Murphy always insisted that Lemaigre-Dubreuil was not a Fascist, was devoted to American war aims—the Atlantic Charter and the Four Freedoms—and had assumed his political ambiguity so that he might circulate more easily in Vichy French and Parisian Fascist circles, to gather intelligence for the United States. On the other hand, Lemaigre-Dubreuil's dossier asserted that, being the brother-in-law of Pierre Laguionie, of the leading Parisian department store Le Printemps, and husband of Simone Lesieur, member of the Lesieur petroleum family, Lemaigre-Dubreuil was subsidized in his Fascist activities by both and had used those subsidies to create and preside over a French Fascist organization called the League of Taxpayers. That league was affiliated with the Cagoule, a secret society formed by the French synarchists to defend the state against the Comintern.

Donovan himself established through an interrogation of Lemaigre-Dubreuil at the St. Regis Hotel in New York that during the Popular Front from 1936 and 1938 Lemaigre-Dubreuil was appointed a regent of the Banque de France, that citadel of the so-called 200 families of France. There was nothing undesirable about such an appointment until the

French government in May 1940 claimed that he had received German funds for his antigovernment propaganda through the Banque Worms et Cie, which, Donovan had asserted in a memorandum to President Roosevelt, had been the official distributor of Nazi funds in France. Under French wartime law that was treason, and Lemaigre-Dubreuil was placed on the arrest list by the interior minister.

Donovan also established that Lemaigre-Dubreuil was closely associated with the leading right-wing newspapers *Le Matin* and *Le Jour,* had contributed to the Cagoule's finances, and was intimate with synarchists within the French General Staff. All this made it seem to the dossier writer that he was more likely to be a friend of Germany than of America. Yet factors could be taken to show that there might be some truth in Murphy's assertion that Lemaigre-Dubreuil was really a democratic sheep in a Fascist wolf's clothing.

He had fought against the Germans in World War I, not as a staff officer but as a frontline officer, and in World War II he had commanded a machine-gun battalion and had fought with great gallantry until he was taken prisoner by the Germans at Nogent-sur-Seine during the French surrender. It was not clear whether he had escaped from or been released by—the former would have been a sign of honor, the latter ominous—the Germans, but it was "presumed" that his "release was arranged by one of those leading French industrialists whom the Germans believed would contribute to the economic collaboration so necessary for their plans for the New Order."[8]

Instead, according to Murphy, Lemaigre-Dubreuil flew to Algiers and placed himself at Murphy's service, in the belief that "one day America must be the saviour of France." Murphy assured Donovan, who was uneasy about Lemaigre-Dubreuil's associations with Laval and the Banque Worms et Cie, that Lemaigre-Dubreuil was a "courageous patriotic Frenchman who hates the Germans and Italians with an intelligent implacability and favours the Allies." Donovan accepted Murphy's assurances but warned him that the Joint Chiefs were extremely vigilant concerning the security of Torch and that no more than was necessary should be confided to his French associate.

Donovan's concerns were fully justified, for as Lemaigre-Dubreuil's and Murphy's association was maturing, Donovan's men were working with the British secret service in New York, the U.S. Treasury, and the Canadian government on an investigation into the transfer from France to the United States of gold bars and currency, some of which belonged to Laval but most of which seemed to be currency speculation by Banque Worms. That investigation was showing evidence of a financial plot to make vast profits through manipulations of the franc against the dollar and the pound sterling. By June 26, 1942, Donovan felt the plot to be sufficiently serious to bring it to the attention of the President.

In a memorandum entitled "Bank Worms and Synarquisme," Donovan directed FDR's thoughts to a ring in Paris and Vichy that "was very pro-Nazi and could exert great pressure on Marshal Pétain." It was "an association of French financiers and industrialists who have organized themselves into a political pressure group for the maintenance and extension of their economic power in the New Order," Donovan reported. Their political aims were "to prevent Marshal Pétain from introducing paternalistic social reforms," to "advocate maximum political and economic collaboration with Germany," and "to facilitate a negotiated peace between the Axis and the Allies" against Russia.[9]

The political credo of the group was synarchism—rule by a technocratic elite in concert with capital—and, Donovan went on, the group had succeeded in "placing its men in the following positions [in Pétain's government]: Paul Boudouin (minister of foreign affairs), Pierre Pucheu (minister of the interior), René Belin (minister of labor), Jean Berthelot (minister of communications), Jean Bicheloone [sic] (secretary-general for industrial and domestic commerce), Henry Lafond (secretary-general for electric power), Jacques Barnaud (secretary of state for Franco-German economic relations)." The group "thus controls all the truly strategic positions in the Vichy cabinet," and Pucheu "in particular has made the most of the vital post which he commands. He has revamped the entire prefecture and police system of France and has thus built up a personal following of well-entrenched office-holders." It was to transpire that Lemaigre-Dubreuil was, or had been, a close associate of all these men.

As Donovan continued in his paper to FDR, the "fundamental assumption" of the group was that Hitler would win the war, and therefore, its members "patently expect to preserve their economic position by acting as Hitler's faithful apostles of the New Economic Order in France." At the same time there were indications that they hoped to "restore economic connections with the United States." There had been talks between representatives of the group and American diplomats in Africa toward that end, and the ring's representatives had urged upon the diplomats "the advantages to the United States of a negotiated peace." Donovan ended his unusually long paper: "Thus, while [the group] is essentially anti-British in its orientation, it would be only too delighted to facilitate the restoration of amicable relations between the United States and the New Europe."

Later still, after Torch, Donovan would have Lemaigre-Dubreuil investigated even more deeply and find: "Dubreuil, undoubtedly a man of courage and force, is a French oil man and financier, who has maintained association with the 'Cagoulards,' a French Fascist organization, exported lubricating oils to [the Italian Army at] Tripoli [Libya, the main supply port for Axis operations against the British in Egypt], and was considered the principal supplier of French oil to [General Erwin] Rommel [the German commander in chief in Africa]."[10] If that statement was true, the most likely explanation for Lemaigre-Dubreuil's mystery was that he was a man who was playing both ends against the middle.

By his own account of events, Lemaigre-Dubreuil first approached Giraud in June 1942 to convey to the general the sentiments of the French High Command in North Africa concerning an association with the United States against the Pétain government in Vichy and a proposition that Giraud become the leader of the coup d'état taking shape in Algiers. Although joining that conspiracy meant that Giraud would be breaking his oath of allegiance to the Pétain government, the general agreed the time had come to act. Murphy returned to the United States in September 1942, two months before Torch D-Day, when at meetings with Roosevelt, Cordell Hull, Henry Stimson, and Donovan and others it was agreed that Giraud should become America's "noble puppet" and that, acting over Donovan's clandestine communications links with the principal cities in French North Africa, Giraud's coup d'état should be synchronized with the landing of the American Army.

Murphy then returned to Algiers, where, according to Lemaigre-Dubreuil, he recommended that "the first step in the military sense should be a meeting of a high American officer and certain technical experts with certain French general officers, and that this meeting should be held in North Africa." Lemaigre-Dubreuil arranged the meeting, which was to take place "in a native house belonging to a trusted Frenchman at the little town of Cherchel, located on a bay some 115 kilometers to the West of Algiers."[11] Date of the meeting: the night of October 21–22, 1942. Identity of the American representative: General Mark Clark. Identity of the French representative: General Charles Mast, described as the "spokesman for General Giraud" and "the military leader of the dissidents."[12]

Through arrangements made by FDR and Donovan, the wheels were now set in motion for what was a major clandestine diplomatic meeting. Headquarters for the operation were at the British fortress of Gibraltar, where on the night of October 19 Clark boarded the British submarine *Seraph*, accompanied by his staff. It consisted of General Lyman L. Lemnitzer (operations), Colonel Archelaus L. Hamblen (supply), Captain Jerauld Wright (naval, and to give the operation the requisite all-American appearance, the commander of the *Seraph* for this operation, although the crew was British), and Colonel Julius Holmes (interpreter and civil affairs officer).

The mission was under the direct control of the President, working through Donovan's communications with Algiers. An OSS officer, Ridgeway B. Knight (a future European adviser to the Rockefellers and the

Chase Manhattan Bank and U.S. ambassador to Lebanon, Portugal, and Belgium), who was stationed at Algiers under vice-consular cover, would control the lighting system to be used to guide the *Seraph* to her pinpoint off Cherchel, supervise the arrangements to bring Clark's party ashore, and provide the guards around the house during the meeting.

In the event the *Seraph* could not reach the pinpoint at the appointed hour, it was compelled to remain submerged off the Algerian coast throughout the twenty-second. A message that the *Seraph* was delayed did not reach Mast in time, and he went to the rendezvous and stayed there throughout the night of October 21–22. He and his party then returned to Algiers in a state of great nervousness and uncertainty, aware that they were committing high treason. Murphy managed to get the message through to Mast, the meeting was reset for the night of October 22–23, and this time Clark and his party appeared on time. The staff conversations began with Murphy and Lemaigre-Dubreuil present.

Clark announced that "the Allies had decided to send to North Africa a large American force, supported in the air and on the sea by British units."[13] Mast advised Clark to ensure that the Allies prepare for the swiftest possible movement into Tunisia to counterbalance the Axis capability of sending in troops by air within thirty-six hours of the first American landing. He also urged the High Command to establish a bridgehead in southern France. Clark made a noncommittal expression concerning that proposal, for he was aware that such an operation was not being contemplated, although it was dear to Giraud's thinking.

But Clark did advise that he was authorized by Roosevelt to state that the United States would render all assistance to the revolution against the Pétain government. For his part Mast's price for collaboration was high: rearmament for eight infantry and two armored divisions, plus separate tank, artillery, and service units, all ready within one month— a price that included 1,400 aircraft, 5,000 tanks, 3,000 artillery pieces, 30,000 machine guns, and 160,000 rifles with 62,000,000 rounds of ammunition. To that enormous demand, Clark merely responded that he had received authority from the Joint Chiefs to state that "the U.S. will furnish equipment for French forces which will operate against the Axis."

The discussion shifted to the role to be played in the expedition by Giraud. Clark was vague about this, stating only that the general would receive a letter from the American commander in chief setting forth the Allies' intentions and that if he consented to leave France and join the American commander at Gibraltar, an American submarine would be sent for him. Apart from that, the only political commitments were contained in a draft letter that was subject to the ratification of the American commander in chief, General Dwight D. Eisenhower. This, however, assured the French dissidents that France would be restored to its 1939 boundaries; it would be accepted as a member of the Grand Alliance; and Giraud would assume the supreme command in North Africa "at the appropriate time" after the landings—a stipulation that was to cause much trouble later.

At that point Clark was spared the need to discuss in greater detail Giraud's military responsibilities in Torch by the sudden appearance of Knight, who announced that a police raid was imminent and that the representatives should hide. Knight's warning was timely, for shortly the police, who had been made suspicious by the comings and goings at the villa during the past seventy-two hours, entered the house. By that time the building was empty, with Clark and Mast hiding in an empty wine cellar. The search was abandoned, as were the staff conversations. Mast returned to Algiers, and Clark to the beach, where a small boat was waiting to take him out to the *Seraph*.

Back in Algiers, Murphy, who had undertaken at the Cherchel meeting to have the U.S. letter of intent ready by November 2, 1942 (only six days before Torch D-Day), began some hurried telegraphing to Washington and soon had the data he needed for the letter that would, it was hoped, seal the bargain between the United States and Giraud.

In certain important respects, the United States was to regret this letter, for it committed the Allies to recognition of Giraud as Allied supreme commander in French North Africa at an early date. But for the moment a compact had to be arranged, and to that end Lemaigre-Dubreuil left immediately for Marseilles to present the letter to Giraud and arrange his clandestine journey to the headquarters of the Allied commander in chief, General Dwight D. Eisenhower, at Gibraltar.

So far as is known Lemaigre-Dubreuil saw no one in France other than Giraud at Lyons, nor did he have communication with anyone—a matter that would be of great importance shortly. He informed Giraud of the transactions at Cherchel and presented the letter. Giraud undertook to abandon his oath of allegiance to the Pétain government and join Eisenhower's headquarters at Gibraltar. In the belief that he would be made the Allied *supremo* immediately after the landing, he also undertook to make a proclamation to all Frenchmen, calling upon them to resist the Axis and to support the Grand Alliance.

The compact between the United States and Giraud was now arranged, Lemaigre-Dubreuil returned to Algiers, and the *Seraph* departed for the pinpoint off the mouth of the Loup River between Cap d'Antibes and Cros-de-Cagnes, on the French Riviera. At three o'clock in the morning of November 6, 1942, as arranged, the *Seraph* surfaced, and Giraud came aboard, accompanied by his son, Officer Aspirant Bernard Giraud, and two aides-de-camp, Captain André Beaufre and Lieutenant de vaisseau Hubert Vire. The *Seraph* then sailed out into the Mediterranean and met the Catalina flying boat, which sped Giraud and his party to Eisenhower on the Rock.

Giraud arrived at Eisenhower's office during the afternoon before Torch D-Day. As Eisenhower wrote, "General Giraud, though dressed in civilian clothes, looked very much a soldier. He was well over six feet, erect, almost stiff in carriage, and abrupt in speech and mannerisms."[14] But that "gallant, if bedraggled figure" did little to ease the concerns and tensions about Torch inside Eisenhower's headquarters, for upon his arrival Giraud made it evident that he expected to be appointed Allied commander in chief the moment Allied forces landed on French territory.

As gently as possible Eisenhower redefined Giraud's role in Torch. He made it evident that he, Eisenhower, would have to remain commander in chief and that he wanted Giraud to go to Algiers, the capital of French North Africa, as soon as the Allies could guarantee his safety and "there take over command of such French forces as would voluntarily rally to him." Above all things, "we were anxious to have him on our side because of the constant fear at the back of our minds of becoming engaged in prolonged and serious battle against Frenchmen, not only to our sorrow and loss, but to the detriment of our campaign against the Germans."

Giraud proved adamant. He "believed that the honour of himself and his country was involved and that he could not possibly accept any position in the venture lower than that of complete command." Eisenhower thereupon sought to explain why this was impossible. The selection of the Allied commander in chief was an involved process, requiring the agreements of the governments involved in the operation, and therefore, "No subordinate commander in the expedition could legally have accepted an order from General Giraud." Apart from all else, "at that moment there was not a single Frenchman in the Allied Command; on the contrary, the enemy, if any, was French."

Giraud remained insistent, and after several hours of complicated discussion he announced: "General Giraud cannot accept a subordinate position in this command; his countrymen would not understand and his honour as a soldier would be tarnished." At that the conference ended shortly before midnight on the night of November 7–8, 1942, with Giraud departing for bed. "Giraud," he declared as he left Eisenhower, "will be a spectator in this affair." That night, prompted by this incident, Eisenhower dictated a letter to his chief of staff, General Walter Bedell Smith, who was still in London: "It isn't this operation that's wearing me down —it's the petty intrigue and the necessity of dealing with little, selfish, conceited worms who call themselves men. All these Frogs have a single thought—ME."[15]

It was after midnight, zero hour was close, and the assault convoys were approaching the Pillars of Hercules. Apparently the Germans were not aware of what was afoot, for they had concentrated no U-boats across the path of the convoys. The Vichy French did know, however, or at least they suspected but said nothing to their German masters. They had interests in mind other than the military and political mastery of French North Africa and *la gloire de la France.*

16

Donovan and Darlan

On November 8, 1942, at about 6:00 A.M. Gibraltar time, as powerful Allied forces invaded French North Africa between Algiers and Casablanca, Roosevelt's proclamation to the French nation went out on the official American radio transmitters. The object of the broadcast, written by WJD and polished by FDR, was to inform the French people that the United States had no imperial designs on the French Empire and to try to persuade the French armed forces in Africa, and the French people, to rally behind the forces of the Grand Alliance:

> My friends, who suffer day and night under the crushing yoke of the Nazis. I speak to you as one who was with your army and navy in France in 1918. I have held all my life the deepest friendship for the French people—for the entire French people. I retain and cherish the friendship of hundreds of French people in France and outside of France. I know your farms, your villages and your cities. I know your soldiers, professors and workmen. I know what a precious heritage of the French people are your homes, your culture and the principles of democracy in France.
>
> I salute again and reiterate my faith in liberty, equality, and fraternity. No two nations exist which are more united by historic and mutually friendly ties than the people of France and the United States.
>
> Americans, with the assistance of the United Nations, are striving for their own safe future as well as the restoration of the ideals, the liberties, and the democracy of all those who have lived under the tricolor.
>
> We come among you to repulse the cruel invaders who would remove forever your rights of self-government, your rights to religious freedom, and

your rights to live your own lives in peace and security. We come among you solely to defeat and rout your enemies. Have faith in our words. We do not want to cause you any harm.

We assure you that, once the menace of Germany and Italy is removed from you, we shall quit your territory at once.

I am appealing to your realism, to your self-interest and national ideals.

Do not obstruct, I beg you, this great purpose. Help us where you are able, my friends, and we shall see again the glorious day when liberty and peace shall reign on the earth.

Vive la France eternelle![1]

At the same time Carleton Coon and Gordon Browne were with their principal contact agent with the Moroccan tribes, Randolph Mohammed Gusus, drinking beer and eating ham sandwiches in the U.S. consulate at Gibraltar. Coon and his group awaited with special interest the American official broadcast to the Riffs, the warrior tribesmen of Morocco, whom Coon controlled through their religious brotherhood. Coon's, Browne's, and Gusus's interest was proprietorial, for they had written the proclamation for WJD. Their method had been interesting, Coon was to recall. It had been written first in English, and then Browne and Coon had reworded "the English in a more Arabic-sounding way, and Gusus would sing out an Arabic poetical version and then write it down." Every time God was mentioned in the original text, Gusus named Him six times, and "the result was a piece of poetry that might have come out of the Koran."[2]

Then came the proclamation to the Riffs and Berbers:

Praise be unto the only God. In the name of God, the Compassionate, the Merciful. O ye Moslems. O ye beloved sons of the Moghreb. May the blessing of God be upon you.

This is a great day for you and for us, for all the sons of Adam who love freedom.

Behold. We the American Holy Warriors have arrived. Our numbers are as the leaves on the forest trees and as the grains of sand in the sea.

We have come here to fight the great Jihad of Freedom.

We have come to set you free.

We have sailed across the great sea in many ships, on many beaches we are landing, and our fighters swarm across the sands and into the city streets, and into the wide country side, and along the highways.

Light fires on the hilltops; shout from your housetops, and from the high places, and say the sound of the drum be heard in the land, and the ululation of the women, and the voices even of small children. Assemble along the highways to welcome your brothers.

We have come to set you free.

Speak with our fighting men and you will find them pleasing to the eye and gladdening to the heart. We are not as some other Christians whom ye have known, and who trample you under foot. Our soldiers consider you as their brothers, for we have been reared in the way of free men. Our soldiers have been told about your country and about their Moslem brothers and they will treat you with respect and with a friendly spirit in the eyes of God.

Look in their eyes and smiling faces, for they are Holy Warriors happy in their holy work. Greet us therefore as brothers as we will greet you, and help us.

If we are thirsty, show us the way to water. If we lose our way, lead us back to our camping places. Show us the paths over the mountains if needs be, and if you see our enemies, the Germans or Italians, making trouble for us, kill them with knives or with stones or with any other weapon that you may have set your hands upon.

Help us as we have come to help you, and rich will be the reward unto you as all who love justice and righteousness and freedom.

Pray for our success in battle, and help us, and God will help us both.

Lo. The day of freedom hath come.

May God grant his blessing upon you and upon us.—Roosevelt.

As they munched their sandwiches, the question before Coon and Browne was whether the French Army and their Arabs would resist or welcome the invading armies.

Overjoyed that Torch was beginning and overcome with the realization that the long months of clandestinity on hostile territory were over, Lieutenant Colonel William A. Eddy, who had organized the secret operations from the U.S. consulate general at Tangier, sent WJD a telegram from his office in the headquarters of the Allied commander in chief, General Dwight D. Eisenhower, at Gibraltar. Corrupting slightly the words of the French national anthem, "La Marseillaise," he wrote: "THANK GOD, ALL WELL. . . . 'LE JOUR DE GLOIRE, C'EST ARRIVÉ.' "[3]

However, his jubilation was premature. All was not well, and the day of glory had not yet arrived. Neither the French nor the Riffs in the French Army were responding to America's high assurances. The worst had happened: The forces of those ancient allies, America and France, were fighting each other with heavy casualties at all points.

At Casablanca, where nearly half the landing craft in the initial assault were wrecked by the heavy surf, the task force of General George S. Patton, Jr., was being engaged by the French shore batteries. By daybreak French aircraft, warships from Casablanca, and the shore guns all were attacking the transports, the landing beaches, and the surviving landing craft. Furthermore, a French naval squadron had put to sea and was fighting two sharp actions with the American covering warships. In those actions the French cruiser *Primauguet* and six of the seven destroyers were all sunk, disabled, or driven ashore. Of the eight French submarines attacking the invasion fleet, only one would return to her berth undamaged, and three were sunk.

Donovan had spent the night on an iron cot in OSS headquarters, and as messages reaching him before dawn indicated, while the French squadron's shells and torpedoes did little damage to the Americans, the battleship *Massachusetts* and the cruiser *Brooklyn* were nearly torpedoed. In her return fire the sixteen-inch shells of the *Massachusetts* put the new French battleship *Jean Bart* out of action, while three more submarines and many merchantmen and auxiliaries were destroyed within the port of Casablanca. Fierce fighting between American and French troops was taking place in and around Casablanca, where the French generals and colonels had revolted in accordance with Donovan's and Eddy's special means plan but had been overwhelmed by forces remaining loyal to Marshal Pétain. On the credit side, however, American forces landing from two old destroyers had stormed the port of Safi, taking the French by surprise, and now Sherman tanks were rolling ashore without difficulty from the French garrison, although there was some fighting, in which the Americans were to suffer 7 killed, 41 wounded, and 2 missing. On the other hand, Patton was preparing to open a major bombardment of the city of Casablanca if the French commander did not surrender—and he was showing no signs of doing so. In all, the assault troops lost about 100 men dead and 250 wounded, with about 50 missing.

At breakfast Donovan learned that the situation was similarly serious at the major French Algerian port of Oran, where a fleet of more than 70 warships and 32 transports had arrived at midnight November 7–8. The landings were made without opposition, 29,000 men, 2,400 vehicles, and 12,000 tons of stores being put ashore quickly. But within the port itself it was a very different story.

To prevent the French from scuttling ships and destroying the port, a frontal assault was made by two ex-American Coast Guard cutters, the *Walney* and the *Hartland*, commanded by Britons but carrying American assault troops. It was resisted by the French garrison. Although both cutters managed to break through the French boom defenses, the *Walney* was soon totally disabled, most of the Americans were killed or wounded, and the boat sank. The *Hartland* suffered a similar fate: She was disabled, caught fire, and blew up with all in her. Casualties in the frontal assault were very heavy. Of the 17 officers and 376 enlisted men in the American force in the ships, 9 officers and 180 enlisted men were killed or presumed dead, while 5 officers and 152 enlisted men were wounded. Only 3 officers and 44 enlisted men landed unhurt. The Royal Navy lost 113 killed and 86 wounded.

WJD also learned during the course of the morning that the fighting at Oran was likely to be protracted. In fact, the seizure of the port was to be accomplished only after three days of fighting. During that fighting the 1st Infantry Division, the "Big Red One," lost 85 killed, 221 wounded, and 7 missing, while the 1st Armored Division lost 191 killed, 105 wounded, and 9 missing, most of them in the *Walney* and *Hartland.*

By far the most serious situation—apart from that at Algiers—concerned the landing at the Algerian port of Bougie, which was to serve as the advance base for the Allied seizure of Tunisia. In the long term it was the most important of all the Torch landings. The object was to land the British First Army spearheads at the port and then ram them through the Algerian and Tunisian mountains and capture the French naval base of Bizerte and the capital, Tunis, ahead of the Germans and Italians. If this aspect of the Torch plan succeeded, the narrows between Tunisia and Sicily would be open to Allied shipping, the Italo-German Army in Libya could be taken in the rear and destroyed, and the "soft underbelly" of Europe would be open to Allied assault early in 1943.

As the earliest signals reaching WJD indicated, Allied naval and military operations at Algiers had begun well. The ninety-three warships and merchantmen in the invasion task force had arrived on time, the landings on the westernmost sector had taken place punctually, but at the central and eastern sectors there had been some confusion and delay in the assault. Yet the assaults made good progress. A U.S. team captured Maison-Blanche Airfield, the more important of the two fields near Algiers, fighter squadrons began to arrive from Gibraltar almost immediately, and soon afterward the second airfield at Blida was taken.

But the plan had included a frontal assault on Algiers Harbor, similar to that undertaken at Oran. And like that at Oran, the Algiers operation foundered. A total of 24 U.S. officers and 638 enlisted men were to be landed inside Algiers Harbor, to prevent the French from sabotaging the port and scuttling their ships. Again they were in two boats. But when the small force appeared at the mole, French shore batteries engaged it. The *Malcolm* was badly damaged, caught fire, and with serious casualties was forced to withdraw.

The second vessel, the *Broke,* got through the boom defenses, berthed successfully, and landed her troops. Almost immediately strong forces of French colonial troops from Senegal arrived with light tanks and pinned the assault force to its position. There was spirited fighting lasting six hours, but with the arrival of French armored cars to reinforce the tanks, the situation became hopeless, and the American commander surrendered. He and his men were then held prisoner for two days.

The main drama lay in the special operations that had been going on in the meantime in Algiers, affecting the situation throughout French North Africa. As Donovan was instructed during the day, the leaders of a group of some 400 young men trained by Lemaigre-Dubreuil had gathered late in the evening of the seventh in the apartment of Dr. Henri Aboulker, the owner of a large department store in Algiers and an anti-

Pétain conspirator, near the Hôtel Aletti in central Algiers. They all were armed, but, as Murphy, who was present, later remarked, they had "inadequate weapons," and the military capabilities of these "action squads" were "largely symbolic."[4] But these boys were the earliest of Donovan's guerrillas, and that night, according to plans laid by Lemaigre-Dubreuil and approved by Murphy, Eddy, and Donovan, they were expected to seize control of the city from Pétain's soldiers and hold it until relieved by the American Army.

At about midnight the OSS radio in Aboulker's bathroom bleated out code words being transmitted in plain language by the BBC London. These meant that U.S. forces were landing in French North Africa, and one of them—*Ecoute! Robert arrive!*—meant that the Americans would begin to land at Algiers. Only Murphy knew the hour and date, and he instructed Lemaigre-Dubreuil to dispatch the action squads to their targets. The leaders then slipped away into the silent, wet streets to seize the centers of government and communications and toward the beaches to the west and east of the city to act as guides for the invading troops. By about two o'clock in the morning of November 8 the group had succeeded in occupying all its objectives, including the prefecture, Radio Algiers, the military telephone exchange, the headquarters of the commander in chief of the XIX Corps in the area and of the commander in chief of all French armed forces in North Africa, General Alphonse Juin, who had been aware of a conspiracy within his command but had made no commitment to support it. Lemaigre-Dubreuil's action squads encountered some resistance, but it was very light, and the insurgents lost only two men dead and one wounded. Almost all the principal figures in the government were arrested.

When the seizure of the city was complete, Murphy and Vice-Consul Kenneth Pendar went to meet the head of the Deuxième Bureau, Lieutenant Colonel Henri A. E. Chrétien, who then took the Americans out to Les Oliviers, the large yellow palace where Juin lived. According to Donovan's account of events, Murphy's visit at that late hour was not expected, and Juin was apparently not aware that an invasion and revolution were taking place in his dominion, for he was asleep when the three men arrived. When the general appeared, his remarks showed that although he knew that large Allied convoys were crossing the Mediterranean, he did not seem to know their purpose or destinations.

Murphy then informed Juin that "an overwhelming force" of American troops had already started for the beaches of Algiers and the other principal ports in French North Africa, that these forces were acting at the invitation of General Giraud, and that their mission was to assist France liberate itself from the Axis.[5] Murphy recalled that only four days before, Juin had told him the French had had orders to resist if there was an invasion and would certainly do so unless they received an instruction annulling those orders. What Murphy wished to know was whether Juin would issue those orders or there was to be bloodshed between America and France.

Pendar's report[6] to Donovan described how Juin replied emphatically that he was not able to do as Murphy asked, but he did offer to submit the request to Admiral Darlan, who was close by. That astounding information was the first that Murphy received that Jean Darlan, a hated man, was in the city.

With that remark there began an exhausting, intricate discussion in which Murphy tried to persuade Darlan to annul Marshal Pétain's order to resist any foreign power seeking to occupy any part of the French Empire. But Darlan balked at every issue, especially those concerning the British. And when Darlan heard that Giraud had become the "noble puppet," he remarked with emphasis: "He is not your man . . . for politically he is a child."

At about 3:00 A.M. the fortunes of amphibious warfare added a new complication to the political situation caused by Darlan's unexpected appearance. A naval signal reaching Donovan at OSS headquarters showed that in the darkness some of the main forces had landed on the wrong beaches and had become lost. Their arrival in the city had been delayed, the Vichy French forces in the city had recovered from their surprise, and when Lemaigre-Dubreuil's men were not relieved by regular forces, the Vichy troops had recaptured the city, including Juin's residence.

French security troops arrived at Les Oliviers as the Franco-American group was talking, arrested the action squad, and then placed Murphy, Pendar, and Chrétien under arrest in the palace. Nevertheless, Murphy did not permit his changed circumstances to interrupt him. He reminded Darlan of his statement to Admiral Leahy that he would consider collaboration against the Axis when the Americans came to him with 500,000 American soldiers, fully equipped. Those forces, Murphy assured the little admiral, were now approaching. The time for decision had arrived. Darlan's response was that so far he had only Murphy's word that such large forces were on their way. He departed to take command of the French armed forces in North Africa and to consult Marshal Pétain in Vichy. Darlan's first move was to order all French forces to resist the Allied invasion.

In the next few hours Murphy had ample time to speculate on what had brought Darlan to Algiers at this time. The ostensible reason for his visit was to see his son, who was dying in an Algiers hospital, a story that was true inasmuch as Alain Darlan was suffering from a fatal illness. But the fact that Darlan may have received forewarning of the invasion could not be rejected, and an official American account of events that night would observe: "That a man occupying Darlan's position should remain rather

secretly in Algiers while Allied forces crossed the Mediterranean to occupy the city was a coincidence fraught with such impressive consequences that it has been attributed to premeditation and prearrange-
ment."[7]

Signals reaching Donovan from OSS Vichy in the last days before
Torch did in fact indicate that a Dakar cover plan might not be working
and that the French might be revising their early opinion that Dakar
would be the target. However, the signals did not show that the Allies
were expected to land in French North Africa, although a group of high-
ranking French intelligence officers loyal to the Grand Alliance, upon
landing at the Algiers airport after escaping arrest in southern France
during the Torch operation, did claim that they had divined from crypt-
analytic study of Allied wireless traffic that the main French North African
cities would be the target.

Furthermore, shortly Allied financial and shipping experts were to
discover that the masters of French ships at Oran had been warned to
scuttle their vessels in the event of an Allied invasion and not to permit
them to fall into "enemy" hands. Also, in the last week or two before
Torch there had been a flash flood of French francs from the Metropolitan into the French North African banks just before the invasion. That
flood had plainly been caused by the expectation that in the event of a
successful military adventure in French North Africa, the Americans
would peg the French franc at the official rate of exchange against the
dollar, giving great value to money that was otherwise worthless anywhere except within France.

Where had this foreknowledge come from? Had Torch been betrayed
so that French banks might profit? Donovan would learn the answers
shortly, but for the moment Murphy's concern was not to find whether
he had a traitor in his entourage but to stop war between France and
America. The need was to make an immediate cease-fire, not only to
avoid such a war between America and France but also to enable the
British First Army to occupy Tunis and Tunisia ahead of the Germans.

The main hope lay in the power and authority of Giraud, still at Gibraltar. There the situation seemed unpromising. Eisenhower and his advisers spent hours trying to persuade Giraud to fly immediately to Algiers,
make his broadcast to the French nation calling for French support for
the Allies, and take command of the French Army from Darlan and Juin.
But Giraud refused, not because Eisenhower refused to make him the
supreme Allied commander but because he refused to fly to Algiers in any
aircraft that was British or carried British colors. There was, therefore,
a prolonged delay while the theater was searched for an American aircraft
bearing American colors. That was not easy; all aircraft that day were on
operational duties. However, a Lockheed Lodestar with American colors
was found for him, and when it was learned that American troops had

captured Maison-Blanche Airfield at Algiers, Giraud was flown to Africa on November 9, 1942.

So firmly was Darlan in command that Giraud's arrival in Africa made no difference. Mast was "in seclusion," Juin in command of the Army, and the officers were unwilling to accept him: They had decided to remain true to their oath of allegiance to Pétain. Here was another reason for Eisenhower to come to terms with Darlan: The French Army in Tunisia was proving uncertain in its relations with the German and Italian units now arriving, and there was a danger that an alliance would spring up among all three against the Allied forces.

As Donovan was advised by Murphy, Eisenhower was being forced to obtain a cease-fire and French cooperation. Eisenhower sent General Mark Clark to Algiers, and he dealt forcefully with Darlan. If Darlan did not agree to order a general armistice throughout French North Africa, he would be arrested. General Eisenhower would order full-scale military operations against the French armed forces, whose lack of equipment, petroleum, and other essentials of war were well known to the Allies. General Patton at Casablanca had issued a warning that unless the French there accepted his offer of a cease-fire, the city would be flattened—a threat, incidentally, he intended to carry out. Clark assured Darlan that the French armed forces would be destroyed with heavy casualties.

A little later Donovan's agents advised him that Darlan had been impressed by these statements and requested a brief adjournment to obtain legal authority from Pétain. According to the partial text of Pétain's instructions, which became available to WJD, he advised Darlan, "I leave you free to act as you deem best in the interest of France," adding that in view of the German invasion of the unoccupied zone of France, now occurring as a response to the Allied invasion of French North Africa, "Anything I may say from now on is valueless. I am about to become a prisoner."[8]

That telegram constituted a transfer of constitutional power in French North Africa from Pétain to Darlan, or at least that was how Darlan chose to interpret the text. Whatever the legality, just before noon on the tenth Darlan issued an order in Pétain's name requiring all French forces to break off all military operations and to observe complete neutrality. That order was effective, but it came none too soon. In the fighting Eisenhower had lost 1,469 men, 530 of whom were killed, 887 wounded, and 52 missing. All but 4 dead, 50 wounded, and 11 missing—all of them Britons —were American personnel. French casualties were estimated at 4,500 killed, wounded, and missing. As a precaution against a resumption of fighting U.S. troops seized all French armories and ammunition dumps.

Throughout this period of great anxiety—for Donovan loved France and the French—WJD was greatly concerned by the attitude of the French Navy. Soon he was able to advise FDR of the situation: Clark had ordered Darlan to instruct the French fleet at Toulon, which was known to be preparing to sail, to make its way to French North African ports. Darlan had sent his order to Admiral Jean de Laborde, in command of the French fleet at Toulon, although Darlan did warn the Allied naval commander in chief, Admiral Sir Andrew Cunningham, that he doubted his order would be obeyed. That impression had proved correct. WJD advised FDR that although the French minister of marine at Vichy, Admiral Henri Auphan, had agreed that Laborde should sail to Allied ports, Laborde was swamped by indecision, arising mainly from his hatred of the British Navy. By the time he made his decision to sail it had been too late. The Italo-German armies had invaded the unoccupied zone, and to prevent the Axis from seizing the French fleet, Laborde had given the order that his ships were to scuttle. In all, one battleship, two battle cruisers, four heavy and three light cruisers, twenty-four large and small destroyers, and ten submarines sank. Only three submarines succeeded in reaching Allied ports. Left to the Germans and Italians were six destroyers and six submarines, still afloat when the Axis forces arrived at the naval base.

The French fleet, which had been worrying FDR as a power factor, was a factor no longer.

Thus the fighting between the Allied and the French forces came to an end, as did the Torch phase of Donovan's special means—the technical term for the arts and crafts of secret operations. These had not been wholly successful. Still, it is evident that but for the OSS operations the situation would have been much worse. Moreover, throughout French North Africa OSS agents had prevented the situation caused by Darlan's unexpected appearance in Algiers from flaring into prolonged warfare between America and France.

WJD had had his first taste of success. Partially through his work, the Allies now had bases in French North Africa from which to invade Italy and Germany from the south as well as the west. Moreover, strategically Torch had produced a sudden military revolution in the Mediterranean theater. As had been intended, the Axis was forced to undertake new major military commitments between the Pillars of Hercules and the Golden Horn—commitments it could not afford to make. As Hitler would state in a letter to Mussolini on February 16, 1943, the North African battle was "decisive to the success of the war as a whole," for now he had to regard "the Balkan peninsula," the "historic invasion route into the heart of Europe," with the "gravest concern." His "worst nightmare of all" was upon him.[9]

On the other hand, the OSS victory was far from clear-cut. The most serious consequence of its failure to detect, and neutralize, Darlan in Algiers would prove to be the margin between immediate success or failure in getting to Tunis or Bizerte before the Germans and Italians. The arrival of strong German units, matched by the early onset of the rainy season, made it impossible for Eisenhower to get his columns through the Algerian and Tunisian mountains. That meant the Allies were faced by the need for a prolonged campaign before Tunisia could be captured. Also, the speed with which the Wehrmacht built up its forces in Tunisia to the size of an army group brought fresh heart to Franco, meaning that Eisenhower had to watch not only his front in Tunisia but also his rear in Spanish Morocco.

In obtaining the cease-fire, Eisenhower made Darlan high commissioner of French North Africa and Giraud commander in chief of all French forces in northwestern Africa—the so-called Darlan deal. The deal produced great disquiet throughout the Grand Alliance, especially among the resistance forces in occupied Europe. The reaction was very severe in England, where the point was being made that it seemed futile to spend lives and treasure in profusion in a war against Nazism and Fascism if all that was achieved were base and squalid deals with Fascist enemies such as Darlan. Also, in France, as in England, there began to spread the belief that the U.S. government supported the very forces that had brought about the surrender of France. Donovan, in particular, was deeply disquieted by Darlan's appointment, for not only did it undermine the authority of the United States, but it also made his task of raising the French in a national insurrection against the Germans much more difficult.

On December 7, 1942, Donovan wrote a memorandum—to whom is not clear, but it was possibly for FDR, Secretary of State Cordell Hull, and the Joint Chiefs, his usual "customers" in matters such as these—that reflected the gravity of the political state of affairs produced by the Darlan deal. The paper read:

I

The identification of Darlan with our operations in North Africa presents difficulties which cannot be ignored. These difficulties are not changed, whether Darlan foisted himself upon us or was forced upon us by someone else, or whether we made a deal with him on our own.

II

By whatever means we were placed in this position, we have before us the very practical problem of eliminating the political leadership of Darlan with its attendant consequences to the French people and to our own successful prosecution of the war. Our great influence with the people of France has been due not only to our strength but to our straight dealing. It is apparent that the continuance of the present situation will weaken our traditional position. We cannot wait too long to find a solution.

III

While it is essential to prevent the concentration of power in Darlan, it may be impossible for us at this time to repudiate him—at least until Tunisia has been settled. But it is possible to reassure that part of France which has been fighting collaboration and which is now so shocked and stunned as to be incapable of action.

IV

It has been suggested that Deputies of France should be brought out by us and set up in North Africa. I think that has its difficulties—first, it would seem that we were setting up a puppet government. We cannot be placed in the position of selecting either an individual or a group to act for the people of France. There must be some appeal to us by those who are making the basic fight.

V

I therefore suggest the following:

That we stimulate the setting up in Occupied France of a national committee or a coalition government—a coalition of those various elements that have combined together to form patriot armies and to carry on underground the work of resistance to the invader.

Such action would constitute a basis for a democratic form of government and of leadership later on. Such a government would have its strength by reason of its position within the country and it could rely on us for communication and support. Once set up, that government could issue its manifesto, either anonymously or in the name of its signers, asserting its authority over North Africa and asking the United States to accept the trusteeship of that territory until France could be freed to act for itself.

It seems to me that so constituted, it would be an answer to the legitimacy of succession argument of Darlan and the French army, that sanction would be given to our control in North Africa and we would be reestablished in an honest relationship with the French people.[10]

The extent to which this document played a part in the assassination of Darlan, which soon followed, is impossible to estimate with confidence, if indeed it played any part. In the first place, there is no indication to whom the memo went, if it went to anybody, nor is there any evidence of reply or discussion with WJD's "customers." In the second place, while WJD would not have stopped at assassination in wartime if the situation had warranted such an action, there is no evidence in the Donovan papers, which included his cable files, that he contemplated or recommended such action. Certainly there is none that he authorized such a measure. The only reference by WJD before Darlan was murdered was a warning to his chief representative at Algiers, Colonel Eddy, that he had received information from Switzerland the murder was contemplated— a signal that suggests the operation to kill Darlan was not wholly local in its origins, as was suggested after the event.

In any case, Donovan's paper shows he was contemplating political rather than "executive" action to deal with the Darlan problem. Still, there is ample evidence that Donovan was deeply disturbed by the Darlan deal and that he believed that the Grand Alliance had been badly damaged by it, as it had been. He now undertook an action that fully exhibited that anxiety.

Three days after Donovan wrote his paper, Churchill felt compelled to hold a secret session of Parliament, to explain the military and political reasons for the Darlan deal. Aware that great issues—issues such as the integrity and morale of the alliance—were at stake, Donovan directed the OSS chief in London, David Bruce, to obtain an account of the proceedings. Bruce accepted the directive, although such sessions were protected by the Official Secrets Act and he was, strictly speaking, engaging in espionage against an ally. However, it would become a moot point whether or not the OSS actually committed espionage against the sanctity of Parliament, for, as he would state, a young officer of the Secret Intelligence Branch, Lyman B. Kirkpatrick (who was to become a high officer of the CIA and then professor of political science at Brown University), was given a report of the debate for transmission to Donovan. In other words, Kirkpatrick would explain, he did not initiate an espionage operation against the British but, rather, received from them a report of the secret session.[11]

Kirkpatrick refused to name his source, but there is some vague evidence in the Donovan papers that the source was British Foreign Secretary Anthony Eden or his nominee and that Eden's motive was that the British wanted the U.S. government to be in no doubt about the gravity of the attitude of the British government and people toward the Darlan deal. If that evidence is correct, it is difficult to understand why he did not communicate the British viewpoint through the American ambassador in London, whose reports were receiving attention in Washington.

The report of the secret session was received by Kirkpatrick fairly quickly, for he was able to submit it to his branch chief, William P. Maddox, the chief of OSS SI, London, and a former political scientist at Harvard and Yale, two days after the secret session. It was fairly lengthy and detailed, and its principal point was certainly one the British would have preferred to keep a state secret, at least for the time being. For what they planned was to attach a minister of state to Eisenhower's staff as his political adviser and, as Kirkpatrick reported, "to gradually assume administrative control of [French North Africa]"[12] from Eisenhower and his staff. And the British government had "intimated to Mr. Winant [the American ambassador to London] that his Majesty's government would prefer a British Minister of State in view of the greater British experience in colonial administration."[13]

Thus, the material procured by Kirkpatrick was of the highest sensitivity, for, with the French already intensely vigilant for signs of British imperial intentions in French North Africa, the appointment of a British minister of state in Algiers on Eisenhower's staff with authority to "assume administrative control of" French North Africa would, if the minister's authority became known to them, confirm their worst fears and produce serious political reaction.

The American ambassador in London, John G. Winant, considered the British proposal sufficiently important to make a special flight to Washington to report on it and other matters deriving from the Darlan deal. Before he left, Winant, who was shown Kirkpatrick's report, called both Bruce and Maddox to his office and instructed them, as Kirkpatrick recalled, "in no uncertain terms" that this type of intelligence operation was not to be repeated.

The effect of Kirkpatrick's report on American official attitudes cannot be gauged, for it arrived in Washington at about the same time as Winant. But what influence it did or did not have, when a British minister of state was appointed to Eisenhower's headquarters in the person of Harold Macmillan, the British publisher and Tory Member of Parliament, he arrived only with the powers of advice, not those needed to rule.

17

The Assassination

Donovan now found himself remotely but directly embroiled in the quicksand of French politics. At the center of the mysterious events now to occur was a fanatical young Frenchman, Fernand Bonnier de la Chapelle, a youth in his early twenties, variously described as a Gaullist and as a royalist supporting the pretender to the French throne, the comte de Paris, who was in Algiers at this time and led a small, passionate political faction that wished to restore the monarchy to France. Before Torch, Bonnier had joined the Chantiers de la Jeunesse, "the young workmen" led by Henri d'Astier de la Vigerie, whose brother was a prominent Gaullist adherent, but who was himself "a character from the Italian Renaissance, a brilliant, persuasive charmer, fascinated with intrigue, at heart a royalist, who exercised an almost hypnotic influence on the young men he led."[1]

With Murphy's assent, D'Astier and the Chantiers were employed during Torch to help seize Algiers at H-Hour, and several of them were to have been found in Dr. Aboulker's apartment on the night before the landing. In the first hours of the morning of November 8, Bonnier and an action group drawn from the Chantiers surrounded Les Oliviers, General Juin's residence, where Murphy and Pendar met Darlan, until they themselves were overwhelmed by the *gardes mobiles*.

As Donovan was to become aware, when Darlan was made high commissioner, all political prisoners, including Bonnier and the Chantiers, were released from prison, and some twenty or thirty of them joined a military unit called the Corps Franc d'Afrique, which had just been established by Giraud "as a special unit intended to utilize all elements in French North Africa—politically active French subjects, non-French refugees, natives, and Jews under restrictions."[2] There is little doubt that Bonnier was a zealot, a man with clandestine experience in whom political passions ran deeply, a man whose attitudes and skills were not unlike those of Gavrilo Princip of the Black Hand, who murdered the archduke Ferdinand and touched off World War I—a youngster who saw the pistol in his hand as the supreme instrument of political destiny.

Bonnier and the others of the Chantiers who joined the Corps Franc were given quarters at Aïn-Taya, on Cape Matifou about thirty miles west of Algiers, which had just been taken over by the Special Operations Executive (SOE), the British secret service responsible for sabotage and subversion, which recruited agents from among the Corps Franc and gave its recruits small arms and sabotage training at the base. In all other respects the Corps Franc belonged to General Giraud, and its men were paid from the French treasury.

Donovan's agency had no connection with the Corps Franc until, about two weeks after its formation, an OSS secret agent, Carleton Coon, was sent by Colonel Eddy, the OSS chief representative in northwestern Africa, to be OSS representative at Aïn-Taya. There Coon ate and slept at the SOE mess and marked time by acting as an instructor in weapons and explosives to the SOE's Corp Franc recruits, who included Bonnier. Donovan approved of this arrangment, his intention being to use the Corps Franc as a reservoir for spies, saboteurs, and guerrilla leaders.

However, the SOE terminated its association with the Corps Franc and removed its instructors, leaving Coon there alone. Why the British pulled out is not clear, but it is highly probable that they were aware that many, if not all, Corps Franc personnel were involved in dangerous politics. Whatever the reason, Coon thereupon appointed a Frenchman, a certain Sabattier, deputy commander of the unit and tutored six other members of the Corps Franc in clandestine operations so that they might teach those skills to their comrades. Later Coon assured Donovan that at no time was he aware that Sabattier or any of the tutors were involved in a plot to assassinate Darlan or that he knew such a plot existed.

Such a plot did exist. It had its members among Coon's Corps Franc at Aïn-Taya, and behind it stood D'Astier, the former commander of the Chantiers. One of the members of the Corps Franc, Roger Rosfelder, later remarked that at one early meeting between D'Astier and the Corps Franc D'Astier announced that after Darlan's "removal" the comte de Paris would become king of France and he would then call upon General Charles de Gaulle, the British protégé in French affairs outside France, to form a government. As Rosfelder admitted, he and another soldier of the Corps Franc, Mario Faivre, conceived a number of "projects for Darlan's execution," one of which was to:

> form a barrage with two cars: Darlan's car is stopped. I approach and empty my Sten [a British submachine gun] at him. I abandon the Sten (I am covered by another gun) and regain the Boulevard where another car takes me to the Special Detachment of the Corps Franc where I have several witnesses who will recognize that I had spent the day with them.[3]

Rosfelder asserted, however, that while he and his colleagues in the Corps Franc were plotting to kill Darlan, they had not actually decided to do so when that decision was taken by another group in Algiers, which included a French priest, Abbé Cordier of the Church of St. Augustine, a political associate of D'Astier's. Rosfelder indicated he was approached, and on December 23, 1942, he claimed, he took Bonnier to Abbé Cordier, to "hear Bonnier's confession." Almost certainly the meeting in the confessional was to enable Cordier to look Bonnier over.

Coon reported to Donovan that Bonnier evidently satisfied Cordier, for the priest gave him the weapons for the murder—D'Astier's pair of dueling pistols. When Bonnier test-fired the weapons that evening at the Corps Franc's camp, he found that neither was satisfactory. He was then given a third weapon, which Coon stated was a .22 long-barreled Colt Woodsman, a very lethal weapon. Rosfelder did not reveal who gave Bonnier the Colt Woodsman, but it was probably a personal weapon, for the Colt Woodsman was not part of any American or British military armory.[4]

On the morning of December 24, 1942, Murphy and Darlan met at Darlan's room in the Palais d'Été for their regular meeting and then went for lunch, at which Darlan dwelt upon the theme of his retirement and his successor. During that time, according to Rosfelder's account, he, Faivre, and D'Astier's son, Jean, drove Bonnier from Aïn-Taya to the Palais d'Été in Algiers. Bonnier was dressed completely in black for the act of assassination and, Rosfelder stated, had been assured by the Algiers police chief, D'Astier, and Cordier that there would be no risk and that even if he were arrested, no action would be taken and he would be released.

Eddy's reports to Donovan showed that the four young men reached the Palais d'Été at about 2:00 P.M., to find Darlan still at lunch. Without being challenged by the *goumier* ceremonial guard, Bonnier entered the Palais d'Été, went to an anteroom outside Darlan's office, and waited as if a supplicant for Darlan to return from lunch.

Darlan arrived back at about 3:00 P.M., and Bonnier was waiting for him. Bonnier shot Darlan twice at close range, then tried to escape. But he was seized by Darlan's chauffeur and taken to a police station. Darlan died in the hospital later the same afternoon, producing a state of siege throughout Algeria. Although it was Christmas Eve, both Eisenhower and Giraud were at the front in Tunisia. They hastened back to Algiers when news of the assassination reached them.

As Donovan now learned almost immediately from Eddy, events that involved Coon in the murder began to occur. Coon had been in Algiers that day and near the Palais d'Été at the time of the murder. Later, when he was asked what he had been doing there, he explained that while he was training some Corps Franc men in the use of *plastique* explosive, some tiles were blown off a roof and one of them struck him on the head, causing him much pain and some injury. Coon decided to take himself to the U.S. military hospital in Algiers for treatment, then go on to Eddy's home, as previously arranged, for a Christmas meal. He then related how he drove into Algiers and was passing the Palais d'Été when he noticed military activity, stopped, and was told by a goum that Darlan had been murdered.

Coon then stated he was forced to search for Eddy for the rest of the afternoon, finally locating him at a safe house in an apartment block in central Algiers. When Coon arrived at the apartment, he found Eddy profoundly upset and spent the rest of the day trying to calm the OSS chief. Coon explained just before his death: "What had happened was that Eddy had allowed a *Life* correspondent to use an OSS cipher to send a story to New York and thereby avoid the censor—a serious offense. Eisenhower had got to hear about it and had said that he was going to court-martial Eddy. When I got to Eddy's apartment, I found he wanted to commit suicide. I managed to talk him out of that and spent a lousy Christmas calming him down. Eventually, of course, Eisenhower decided not to have him court-martialed."[5]

With Eddy restored to his normal equilibrium, it soon became clear from reports that some people in the French security services in Algiers believed that the OSS knew more about Darlan's murder than it had seemed. It had soon been established that Bonnier was in the Corps Franc and that Coon was its instructor. The police arrested Sabattier, the Frenchman whom Coon had appointed deputy at Aïn-Taya, on suspicion, and all six of Coon's instructors, Coon was to write, "either hid or were jailed."[6]

Then the police inquiries began to involve Coon and the OSS more deeply than Eddy thought desirable. Certainly in the first flush of events after Darlan's assassination, Coon's activities warranted police interest, for not only had the plot to kill Darlan had one of its centers within the small group of the Corps Franc of whom Coon had charge, but as Coon agreed later, he possessed a Colt Woodsman pistol: "I bought the weapon some years before the war and used it for target practice in the

New England woods. I had become used to the weapon and when I was sent out to North Africa by Donovan before Torch I took it with me for use in place of the forty-five weapon regularly issued."

Moreover, as police inquiries soon established, Coon was near the Palais d'Été on the afternoon of the murder and had then disappeared for a considerable period of time. It also became known that Coon shared the hostility for Darlan commonplace in American circles in Algiers at that time and a loathing of Fascism equally commonplace in the American academe before the war. Weighing all the factors and impressed by the acute tensions in Algiers brought about by the assassination, Eddy decided that Coon should leave the city immediately and join an SOE outfit on the Tunisian front near Constantine, in northeastern Algeria, because the Darlan assassination had produced a situation in which "For the sake of others as well as himself, it seemed a good idea for Coon to drop out of sight."[7]

Although it is evident that the French authorities in Algiers regarded Coon and his movements with considerable suspicion, he himself fueled speculation, for when he joined the SOE unit, he began to wear the uniform of a captain in the British Army, stating that he had been given the rank by the commanding officer of the SOE unit, Major Hamish Torrance. Also, as he stated, he "took over the hat of the late Captain Ritinitis," who had "blown himself up." He appears also to have assumed the identity of "Captain Ritinitis." While it was true that Special Operations units in Tunisia were wild affairs, with little regard for regulations, when seen against the assassination, Coon's conduct was strange.

Moreover, Coon was an advocate of political assassination as an instrument of state, for when he returned to Washington and gave Donovan his report on his mission in North Africa, he also handed in an appendix in which he advocated the formation of an elite corps of assassins on the ground that "the world is now too small and too tight to permit a continuation of the process of trial and error" by which the world had been run hitherto. Coon contended, "A mistake made in one quarter will of necessity spread rapidly all over the world, for all our apples are now in one barrel, and if one rots the lot is destroyed."[8]

In what was, it seems, the only paper received by Donovan advocating political assassination, Coon went on:

> . . . we cannot be sure that the clear and objective scholars who study the existing social systems and draw up the blueprints for a society to suit our technology will always be heard, or that their plans will be put into operation. We can almost be sure that this will not be the case. Therefore some other power, some third class of individuals aside from the leaders and the scholars must exist, and this third class must have the task of thwarting mistakes, diagnosing areas of potential world disequilibrium, and nipping the causes

of potential disturbances in the bud. There must be a body of men whose task it is to throw out the rotten apples as soon as the first spots of decay appear.

Coon asserted: "If such a body had existed in 1933 its members could have recognized the potential danger of Hitler and his immediate disciples and have killed this group." That "would have prevented the rise of a Nazi state in the peculiarly lethal form which it has taken." Coon then advised:

> A body of this nature must exist undercover. It must either be a power unto itself, or be given the broadest discretionary powers by the highest human authorities.
>
> The only organizations in existence today which have even the rudiments of what is needed in the formation of such a body of men are the OSS and SOE. Agents of these two organizations are trained to act under cover, to act ruthlessly and without fear. We include objective scientists in our midst, and men of the widest experience in the political, economic and diplomatic fields.
>
> It seems therefore to me not too wild, too visionary, or too improbable a thought to suppose that from these two groups a smaller can be selected; a group of men, sober-minded and without personal ambition, men competent to judge the needs of our world society and to take whatever steps are necessary to prevent this society from a permanent collapse.

Whatever happened to this proposal, Donovan did not include it in his papers, nor did he circulate it within his organization or to other government organizations. Perhaps even in wartime he gauged it imprudent and undesirable to do as Coon advocated and form a special assassination squad.

So Coon left town—always a dangerous matter in a murder case.

As Donovan soon discovered, Giraud also played a strange role. He had been at the French command post at Le Kef, to supervise a forthcoming French attack, when he received news of the murder. He started back to Algiers that night, arriving in the capital on Christmas afternoon. As military commander in chief he ordered an immediate military court-martial for Bonnier, who received no assistance from any of his friends. The court-martial was held the same night. Bonnier was found guilty, condemned to death, and executed by firing squad in the early hours of December 26. D'Astier, who had been arrested during the police sweep after the murder, was sent to prison.

The Imperial Council then met on the twenty-seventh and without delay appointed Giraud high commissioner, an appointment that was the source of intense relief to Eisenhower and Roosevelt, who before the assassination had been pressing Eisenhower and Murphy to remove Darlan and appoint Giraud in his place.

Shortly after these proceedings Bonnier's sentence was annulled posthumously on the ground that after his death documents had been found that "showed conclusively that Admiral Darlan had been acting against the interests of France and that Bonnier's act had been accomplished in the interests of the liberation of France." D'Astier was released from prison and awarded the Croix de Guerre. Thus, in the French fashion, honor and inconvenience had been satisfied. But the speculation about what really lay behind the murder of Darlan was to intoxicate several generations of earnest dons, some of whom sought to show that the American or the British secret services were involved, separately or in combination.

Inevitably public attention fastened mainly upon the United States. The theory was that Roosevelt, concerned at the tempest stirred up by Darlan's appointment as high commissioner and by what appeared to be American recognition of him as the leader of France outside France, had ordered Darlan's assassination as the only means available to extricate the United States from an intolerable political situation. At least part of that theory sprang from a statement made by General Mark Clark, Eisenhower's deputy at the time of the murder, in his memoirs:

> Admiral Darlan's death was, to me, an act of Providence. It is too bad that he went that way, but, strategically speaking, his removal from the scene was like the lancing of a troublesome boil. He had served his purpose, and his death solved what could have been the very difficult problem of what to do with him in the future. Darlan was a political investment forced upon us by circumstances, but we made a sensational profit in lives and time through using him.[9]

But the fact seems to be that there was no official American involvement in the Darlan affair and it was solely the work of a group of hotheads led two by religious, royalist zealots, Cordier and D'Astier, with, perhaps, French connections.

Meanwhile, as the Darlan affair wound its sinister course, a second, lesser but associated affair cast doubt on the reliability of some of Donovan's connections in French North Africa. Fairly soon after Eisenhower had established his headquarters in Algiers, a Treasury official, Lieutenant Colonel Sidney Bernstein, started to look into the currency problems of French North Africa, and a prominent Parisian banker now in Algiers, a certain M. Pose, revealed that just before Torch there had been a sudden massive movement of francs from a number of banks in metropolitan France into the banks of French North Africa. Pose himself admitted that he had "deliberately funnelled off assets" of his bank in France and estimated that in all, the sum transferred by all the banks was about 25 billion francs. He could not state why such currency movements had begun.[10]

It was fairly clear from his statements that the motive had been to take advantage of currency revaluations that would, the Vichy French bankers had anticipated, follow upon American intervention in the area. It was evident, therefore, that some of the French metropolitan banks had obtained knowledge that an American descent upon French North Africa was expected. The question before Eisenhower and Donovan was: How had they obtained such foreknowledge?

The anticipated revaluation did occur on January 24, 1943, when President Roosevelt ordered the rate of exchange to be stabilized at the favorable rate of 50 French francs to the dollar.[11] Since the value of these francs before Torch had been about 250 francs to the dollar, the 25 billion that had flooded French North Africa would have been worth about $100,000,000. At the new rate they would have been worth $500,000,000 representing a profit to be made of $400,000,000. Plainly Secretary of the Treasury Morgenthau believed the French banks had made just such a profit, for he wrote to Donovan it was significant that one of the Darlan government's first requests was that the United States "free all of the blocked and exchange control accounts in the United States of the North African banks."

Some of the exchange controls were removed, and enormous profits were made, for as one of Donovan's senior agent cashiers, Emerson Bigelow, an expert in foreign exchange, advised Donovan, before the invasion the North and West African francs were becoming cheaper and cheaper, going from 43.70 francs to 250 francs to the dollar. But immediately following the invasion, "as a result of pressure by [Darlan] upon our State Department," the rate was stabilized first at 75 and then at 50 francs.[12]

The case received considerable press attention in the United States, where leading columnists stated that the United States had lost tens, if not hundreds, of millions of dollars through the manipulation. Inevitably that disquiet reflected upon Robert Murphy again when it was learned that Lemaigre-Dubreuil had obtained a senior post as economist and financial adviser in the Darlan government. As early as January 1943, when presumably the conversion process was at its height, there was high-level discussion in Algiers and Washington about Lemaigre-Dubreuil and his associates. Fearing the worst, Donovan asked Eddy and Murphy for their opinions.

In a joint telegram Murphy, by now Eisenhower's American political adviser, and Eddy defended Lemaigre-Dubreuil as an honest and patriotic Frenchman whose bad name stemmed from the "deceptive police record" that he had established with Murphy's "knowledge and approval." The record showed that Lemaigre-Dubreuil was a Nazi collaborator, but in reality, Murphy asserted, he had been helping the United States by obtaining information which Murphy had "included in my State Department telegrams." Far from being a French traitor, Murphy stated, "Lemaigre-Dubreuil is known to me as a courageous, patriotic Frenchman who hates the Germans and Italians with an intelligent implacability and favors the Allies." He had "rendered us the most useful service, and I am grateful to him."[13]

However, the rumors proved stronger than Murphy's advocacy, and Lemaigre-Dubreuil was compelled to flee Algiers for asylum in Fascist Spain. He was later admitted to the United States, and by the end of the war he was back in Paris, where he was charged by the Gaullist authorities with "having negotiated with a foreign power." Whether that power was America or Germany was not made clear, nor was a trial held. Murphy persuaded De Gaulle to drop the charges, but they were revived in 1947, and Lemaigre-Dubreuil was arrested and charged with high treason. He was acquitted, left France, and settled in Casablanca, where, on July 12, 1953, he was shot to death by unknown gunmen on the steps of his residence.

The men who murdered Lemaigre-Dubreuil were never apprehended, and no reason for the murder was established. It was stated at the time that he was writing an autobiography that would reveal a good deal about his ordeal, but no manuscript was ever found. The French press always connected the manuscript with the spoils of the landslide of the French franc. Be that as it may, the truth in this case seems to have been that Lemaigre-Dubreuil was indeed all the things that Murphy had claimed for him, except in one regard: He had played both ends against the middle. As for the allegation that Lemaigre-Dubreuil had leaked some indication of the Torch expedition to the banks and, perhaps, even to the Pétain government, that appears reasonable. However, what is also clear is that neither the banks nor the government passed that information to their German and Italian rulers, who were taken completely by surprise by Torch.

18

The Dulles Organization

On the morrow of Torch Allen Dulles arrived at his post in Bern, the Swiss capital, carrying a single suitcase containing two crumpled suits, a $1,000,000 letter of credit, and the rank of "Special Representative of the President of the United States of America." With Dulles's safe arrival—the French were just closing the Franco-Swiss frontier in response to the Torch landings, and for a time there was a danger that Dulles might be arrested and interned by the Vichyites—one of Donovan's most important deployments, which was to affect almost every American operation in the European theater of operations, was completed. For Dulles's main task was, using contacts with Canaris and the Black Orchestra, to report what was happening in the main centers of German power and in the capitals of Germany's allies.

Dulles established his residence in a fine apartment on the garden floor of Herrngasse 23, one of the fine old patrician houses overlooking the Aare River and the Bernese Alps, removed the electric light bulbs from the streetlamp outside the house (and kept them removed throughout the war) so that his guests could arrive and depart after dark without being observed; hired a butler, a chef, and a maid; arranged for an announcement to be leaked to the local press that he was in Switzerland; and then waited, calculating that Canaris's representatives would make contact with him. His confidence was soon justified.[1]

Allen Welsh Dulles was forty-nine when he arrived at Bern, and he was no stranger to either Switzerland or espionage. A man of strong and ruthless personality and ambition concealed by charm and an avuncular

quality that could be misleading, he was a son of the pastor of the Presby-
terian Church in Watertown, New York, who had been almost unfrocked
by the synod because he had cast doubts from the pulpit on the virgin
birth. But that had not occurred, the family had prospered, and Dulles
was able to go to Princeton and George Washington University.

Dulles became a lawyer, a schoolmaster in India, a consular agent and
spy for the United States in Switzerland in World War I, a member along
with David Bruce of President Woodrow Wilson's staff at the Versailles
Peace Conference in 1919, a diplomat in several overseas posts, and a
principal officer at the State Department. When he resigned, he became
a senior partner with Sullivan & Cromwell, the New York law firm. His
brother was John Foster Dulles, who was to become President Dwight D.
Eisenhower's secretary of state.

Dulles had joined the COI quite early, having met Donovan at the
Republican National Convention in Philadelphia in 1940, when WJD
revealed that he was putting together an intelligence service and needed
Dulles's services. Dulles agreed to become head of the COI in New York
in October 1941. He obtained eviction notices against the American
Guild of Organists, the Van Dam Diamond Corporation, and the Rough
Diamond Corporation, all on the twenty-fifth floor of 30 Rockefeller
Plaza and immediately over the United Kingdom Commercial Corporation, president, William Stephenson. Having paid the evicted tenants a
total of $10,000 compensation and signed leases for the then large rent
of $35,737 a year, plus maintenance of $3,532, Dulles began operations
that were "practically unlimited in concept or financial scope."[2]

In the summer of 1942, having performed satisfactorily in New York,
Dulles asked for an overseas assignment, at the time when Donovan was
having great difficulty in establishing a London staff with sufficient experience and authority to be able to resist British attempts at control. He
offered Dulles the post of head of Secret Intelligence with responsibility
for Western Europe, under the command of David Bruce. Dulles declined
because he did not want to work "with a lot of generals looking over my
shoulder."[3]

There was more to Dulles's reason than that. Because he was extremely
ambitious and saw Bruce as his principal rival in the field of intelligence,
he wanted a post where he could operate with as little control as possible.
Also, Dulles's relations with Donovan were complex in that he admired
the director personally but disliked some of his operational and administrative practices. In any event Dulles mistakenly saw himself as Donovan's
successor. (Donovan, at the time of his embolism in 1942, recommended
to Roosevelt that in the event of his death or complete incapacity his
successor should be General Frank McCoy, a brainy soldier who had been
Donovan's regimental commander in World War I.) Nevertheless, Dulles
believed that only he could run an intelligence service, and since he also

believed he would be called upon to do so at some stage, his ambitions might better be served by his being as remote as possible from the Washington or London headquarters.

Indeed, in Bern he could not have been more remote, for following the German occupation of southern France after Torch, Dulles was virtually marooned in the oasis of neutral Switzerland, surrounded by enemy territory. His only communication with Washington until the Swiss frontier was reopened in September 1944 was, for secret material, the telegram and, for nonsecret material, the telephone. There was virtually no mail, for Allied courier aircraft could not land in Switzerland without overflying enemy territory, a highly dangerous and rarely undertaken business, and he had no visitors from Washington or London, except those in Switzerland when the frontiers were closed.

Thus, so it must have seemed to Dulles, he was in that ideal position —chief of the principal European listening post, yet beyond the attentions of other ambitious mortals. However, unknown to him, the Allies had a method of ensuring that through him they were not being victimized by that specter of all intelligence services—planted information intended to cause miscalculation about German capabilities or intentions.

That was Ultra, which, by the time Dulles was operational, was being revolutionized by the introduction of a new machine called the computer. For the first time, intelligence obtained by humans could be measured and tested against intelligence obtained by machines, and Dulles was among the first of the beneficiaries and the victims of that development.

By late 1942 Ultra had become the preeminent source of Allied intelligence about Germany, and in general outperformed humans in most intelligence production except political and social intelligence. No human spy could produce as quickly, economically, and reliably as Ultra, and that superiority was in general assured when the British introduced a series of computerlike machines, culminating in Colossus in the spring of 1944, the start of the most crucial time in Dulles's career as Donovan's spymaster in Switzerland.

A very large contraption described as being "at least a special-purpose program-controlled electronic digital computer," Colossus featured: "Electronic storage registers changeable by an automatically controlled sequence of operations," "Conditional (blanching) logic," "variable programming by means of lever keys which controlled gates which could be connected in series or parallel as required," and "calculated complicated Boolean functions involving up to about 100 symbols."[4]

Although Colossus assured the British of primacy in the intelligence field in the European theater, it did not make the human spy obsolete. It merely made him a second fiddle. Colossus could and did provide humans with the information they needed to break the cipher protecting the enemy traffic's secrets. But obviously it could not act as a human; it could not see, sense, hear, feel, smell, intrigue. Where espionage involving the human senses was concerned, it remained a human undertaking. Colossus could not, for example, supplant the human in the sphere where Dulles excelled—black (or covert) diplomacy. All it could do was provide the intelligence against which the knowledge gained through such activity could be checked to ensure that Dulles was not being tricked by his adversary.

Colossus's first checks of Dulles's intelligence showed that he was not producing acceptable intelligence. The strange machine, which gurgled, winked, blinked, and clicked as it worked, showed that he was either in error or being tricked. Large numbers of Germans, Frenchmen, Italians, Hungarians, Rumanians, Bulgarians, and Swiss began to provide him with intelligence about what was happening within the Axis countries, but because of Colossus, the intelligence community in Washington regarded his product with such suspicion that on April 29, 1943, Donovan felt the need to warn Dulles:

> It has been requested of us to inform you that: "All news from Bern these days is being discounted 100% by the War Department." It is suggested that Switzerland is an ideal location for plants, tendentious intelligence and peace feelers but no details are given. As our duty requires we have passed on the above information. However, we restate our satisfaction that you are the one through whom our Swiss reports come and we believe in your ability to distinguish good intelligence from bad with utmost confidence.[5]

While such highly critical observations were partly the outcome of the intelligence war between Donovan and his colleagues in the other departments of the Washington intelligence community, such comment was obviously damaging to Dulles. Nor, it seems, was this critical opinion confined to the period when he was establishing himself in Bern, when it was obvious that his production would be flawed. In January 1944, fourteen months after his arrival, when the intelligence war in Washington was temporarily quiescent and by which time Dulles should have overcome his beginner's problems, his product was still being seriously attacked in Washington. That month he received no fewer than four rebukes about the quality and content of his reportage, one of which was especially stinging:

> We think it is essential that you be informed at once that almost the entire material which your [telegram 1786/1791] supplied disagrees with reports we have received originating from other sources and parts of it were months old . . . information from other neutral lands indicates . . . that the order has been given [by the enemy intelligence service chiefs] to go all out against our intelligence activities. This possibility appears to correspond with the sudden

degeneration of your information which is now given a lower rating than any other source. This seems to indicate a need for using the greatest care in checking all your sources.[6]

Dulles was not distressed by this criticism, for he was developing an intelligence source that, he believed, was of unprecedented value in this war—George Wood, probably, but not certainly, Fritz Kolbe, a German employed as special assistant to Karl Ritter, an "ambassador for special assignments" at the German Foreign Ministry, who acted as liaison officer between the Foreign Ministry and the German Supreme Command, the Oberkommando der Wehrmacht. Dulles was to describe Wood as "our best intelligence source on Germany," a man who "had the kind of access which is the intelligence officer's dream" and was "one of the best secret agents any intelligence service has ever had."[7] But there were those in Washington who believed, and some who feared, that Dulles was being hoodwinked and that Wood was a particularly clever deception agent involved in a major operation to obtain the two secrets that would decide the outcome of the war in Europe: the time and place of the Allied invasion of Europe, Operation Neptune.

The Wood traffic—in Washington it was code-named the Boston Series —became the subject of one of the most searching intelligence inquiries of World War II. A principal standard by which the Boston Series was measured was Ultra.

Wood had already approached, and been rejected by, the British secret service chief in Switzerland when, on August 23, 1943, a German living in Switzerland, a Fritz Kochertaler, introduced him to a young official at the Office of War Information offices in Bern, Gerald Mayer, who did some work for Dulles. Mayer was sufficiently impressed by Wood's story to arrange for a meeting with Dulles later the same day. Wood advised Dulles that his job was to screen all important incoming telegrams from all German diplomatic and intelligence posts overseas and prepare a digest which Ritter presented to the German Supreme Command. Wood explained that owing to the British bombardment of Berlin, the Foreign Ministry had been evacuated from the capital, and his branch had been sent to Salzburg, fairly close to the Swiss frontier. Since his duties required that he have a special pass permitting free and rapid movement throughout Europe, he was able to visit Switzerland as often as prudence allowed. That meant he would be able, if Dulles wished, to supply the U.S. government with copies or synopses of the materials crossing his desk. Because he had only a short distance to travel, the material would be relatively fresh.

Intrigued by the possibilities of such a remarkable offer, Dulles began to probe the man's motives for committing what was the grossest of

German crimes—*Hochverrat,* or high treason—and Wood claimed to be a member of the Foreign Ministry cell of the Black Orchestra, the anti-Hitler opposition within the German government. To demonstrate the value of the material at his disposal, Wood produced 186 copies and synopses of messages prepared by him. Dulles glanced at the collection and asked for time to study the documents. Wood agreed and left, having arranged to maintain contact with Dulles through Mayer.

In studying the collection, Dulles found that none of the telegrams was more than two weeks old, and most were only a few days old, and he decided that if the entire affair was not a trap, the Wood telegrams were of great importance. They all were highly confidential communications between the German Foreign Ministry and its representatives in twenty-two countries, including all the European neutrals and all of Germany's allies, relating to every aspect of Germany's relationships with those countries.

By Dulles's standards—he knew nothing of Ultra or ISOS—the telegrams were extraordinarily revealing, but he decided before accepting them as gospel to send them for a survey to Washington. There they were subjected to a first analysis that lasted for seven months, from August 1943 to March 1944. The principal analysis was undertaken jointly by the OSS and the Special Branch of Military Intelligence, and to his credit, although Donovan needed victories at the time in order to justify his existence, he did not rush over to the White House with the file in his hands. He waited until he was sure of Wood—and that took a long time.

At the same time the Wood telegrams went to London, where at first the deputy head of the British secret service, Sir Claude Dansey, a man who disliked Americans generally and Dulles particularly, dismissed them as "obviously a plant" and insisted that "Dulles had fallen for it like a ton of bricks."[8] He did not, however, submit Wood's telegram for comparison to Ultra's intercept of the same telegrams, which would have proved conclusively if the traffic was tainted meat.

The comparison was made by others in Dansey's service. The telegrams were then pronounced genuine, although the British withheld an opinion for the moment on what Wood's motives were—a critical factor in the investigation. The information was then passed to OSS Washington, where Dulles's case officer, Ferdinand Lammot Belin, a former ambassador to Poland and vice-president of the National Gallery in Washington, felt able to tell Donovan that the British had advised him: "Both the material and the source had stood the test and are thought to be of great value."[9]

However, that was not quite what the British had said. They had agreed that the telegrams they had been shown were genuine. But they had not given an opinion regarding Wood and his motives. Moreover, although Belin was accurate in his declaration that the British had said they had great value, in fact, that value was to cryptanalysts, not to intelligence officers; in other words, the principal value of the Wood material lay in the technical information they yielded about the ciphers the Germans were employing. They made it possible to widen and deepen the breach in the main German cipher systems by comparing the text of an unsolved intercept with the plain text provided through the Boston Series—a technical point worth a king's ransom to cryptanalysts.

Donovan was not a cryptanalyst and probably did not understand where the true importance of the Boston Series lay. Yet his lawyer's caution obtruded, and he did form a U.S. panel—it consisted of General George V. Strong (head of military intelligence), James Murphy (head of X-2), and Colonel Alfred McCormack (head of MI's Special Branch, which handled Ultra and Magic in the United States)—to provide an opinion. While that preliminary investigation was taking place, Dulles was told to take another look at Wood. That he did, advising Donovan on December 29, 1943: "I now firmly believe in the good faith of Wood and I am ready to stake my reputation on the fact that these documents are genuine."[10]

Only when he had that categoric assurance did Donovan decide to send any of Wood's second consignment to Roosevelt, passing fourteen telegrams to the President on January 10, 1944, but with a guarded opinion on their accuracy and originality:

> We have secured through secret intelligence channels a series of what purport to be authentic reports, transmitted by various German diplomatic, consular, military and intelligence sources to their headquarters. The source and material are being checked as to probable authenticity both here and in London. We shall submit later a considered opinion on this point. It is possible that contact with this source furnishes the first important penetration into a responsible German agency.[11]

Donovan's caution proved wise, for when that considered opinion arrived at OSS headquarters, it was somewhat equivocal. The head of the panel, Colonel McCormack—a prominent lawyer in peacetime—stated that the matters dealt with were of "a very delicate nature" and that the need to "test their authenticity" had been felt, but, the panel noted, even had the documents been found to be completely genuine, as was probably the case, it had to be "clearly recognized" that "the Germans may have the ultimate purpose of using this channel as a means of bringing about an important plant."[12]

McCormack ended his interim opinion by stating: "The Special Branch of MIS has already indicated that it believes the messages to be authentic." A similar view "is expressed by the British." However, "Both feel that the Germans may be employing the technique of disclosing genuine information not particularly harmful to them in order to instil [*sic*], and later to take advantage of, a false sense of confidence" in the Boston Series.

McCormack was then asked to make a fuller investigation, and between February 10 and May 6, 1944, when he rendered his final assessment, he and his colleagues examined 200 telegrams. The panel's conclusion was: "In instances where the same message has been obtained from other sources, as occasionally they have been, the authenticity has been confirmed." In other instances, "external evidence" had permitted the committee to believe them "probably authentic." When authenticity could not be checked, with a few possible exceptions the telegrams " 'sound like' what their originators might send home."[13]

McCormack then turned to the messages' usefulness as intelligence, an important factor in determining whether they might be "chicken feed" for some future enemy plant. Here he noted: "Because of the time lag between date of origin and date of receipt, information that might have been of interest has either been obtained from other sources or has become stale." Secondly, "As is usual with diplomatic communications a good deal of the material is second-hand information upon subjects on which first-hand information is available, or it relays expressions of opinion made for diplomatic purposes or made by persons whose opinions on the particular subjects are of no great consequence." McCormack's implication was clear: The Boston Series might look good, but in general it had no great intelligence value by the time it reached the United States, and therefore, the enemy would run no great risk by playing such information into Allied hands.

With that point established, McCormack then considered such evidence as there was that they were "chicken feed" for a major enemy deception. He drew attention to a message purporting to state what the German commander in chief in Italy, Field Marshal Albert Kesselring, intended to do to Rome if he was forced to evacuate the Italian capital. That message had been "under study for some time" because "It has been puzzling Special Branch, as it has puzzled the British."

Colonel McCormack continued: "Kesselring is said to have issued orders for the destruction of all electric plants in the Rome area except those supplying the Vatican City, all industrial and railroad 'plants' outside 'the city,' all bridges over the Tiber River and the gas and water ducts attached to five of those bridges."

McCormack was pointing to the possibility that this was a plant, inasmuch as knowledge that Kesselring would destroy or severely damage the Eternal City if the Allies tried to take it might cause them to decide not to try. In that event an entire German army could be released for other service, and the city could be held by much smaller forces. The suspicion that the signal was a deception was heightened in McCormack's view because the information, he reported, "conflicts to some extent with such other information as is available on the subject." Therefore, the Special Branch was *not* prepared to say that the message was authentic, "although the British had not yet expressed an opinion." That was an extremely damaging point, for if the one message was a deception, Wood and *all* his material would have to be regarded as deceptive.

McCormack then reported to Donovan on other factors. In view of the limited number of sources of information concerning the Japanese war, it had been "suggested by Special Branch that the OSS attempt to have its representatives in Bern obtain communications addressed to the German Foreign Office from its personnel in Japan and other Asiatic countries." A number of such messages had now been received through the Boston Series, three of which were "purported" to have come from attachés in Tokyo. Two were from the military attaché, Kretschmer, and one from Gronau, the air attaché. Gronau's report and one of the two from Kretschmer "purported" to summarize information and impressions gathered by the two men on an inspection trip they made through Southeast Asia during late January and most of February.

The point for debate here was whether these reports had been manufactured by the Germans as "chicken feed" or whether the attachés had actually made the journeys to which the messages referred. McCormack considered the findings important because it was known from other sources that Kretschmer and Gronau had indeed made the journeys, that Kretschmer had left Tokyo on January 28, 1944, traveled through Singapore, Bangkok, Rangoon, Mandalay, and the Arakan front in Burma, and returned via North Borneo, Makassar, and Davao to Tokyo, where he arrived on February 26, 1944. Gronau had left on a similar trip on January 20, and "there is some reason to believe that" he had returned to Tokyo on February 29. Both had filed their reports to Berlin on March 3, 1944—the detail being a sure sign that there were Magic intercepts of their communications over the Berlin–Tokyo radio link.

The content of their reports was, McCormack advised WJD, what "one would expect to find in such documents." A "good deal" of the information was "quite accurate," and "some of it must have come from a person who was familiar with the situation in the southern areas." There were inaccuracies, and some of the opinions expressed were wrong, but such errors were "not hard to explain" on the basis of knowledge already in the possession of the Special Branch. Taken together, the reports were "of appreciable value," containing "a certain amount of new information which, if true, is useful—notably the identification of a number of divisional commanders in Burma." In addition, they provided "some evidence to confirm reports from other sources," and they were "of interest for what they show about the things that the Germans were permitted to see and know, and the impression that they formed."

McCormack's opinion of the Kretschmer and Gronau reports constituted, therefore, a true bill. While that was important evidence in favor of the opinion that Wood's material was not deceptive in objective, the controllers of Magic and Ultra, the only two sources against which the material could be authenticated, would not accept the Boston Series as a whole and would not circulate all of its messages. The Boston Series was, therefore, frozen as a source. Unless it was accepted, the OSS's principal source of intelligence from within the Third Reich would collapse, and it would suffer a corresponding loss of prestige, at least in the sphere of secret intelligence. Donovan asked Belin to go over the case again, and on April 20, 1944, Belin wired Dulles:

> I am certain that questions have arisen in the minds of all of us relative to the authenticity of this intelligence, which grows more and more interesting, and that we have contemplated the possibility that it is some kind of a plant. Might it be explained, for instance, by a desire to slip in a message a critical moment with the specific intention of misleading us?[14]

Belin then alluded to what may have been behind the Wood affair: an attempt by the German foreign minister, Joachim von Ribbentrop, a trickster to his fingertips, to make trouble between the Russians and the Western Allies, for a feature of Wood's material was that without giving away too much about Germany's plans, intentions, and fears, the largest number of the telegrams pointed to the Red Army's advances into Eastern and Central Europe. Uniformly they told of the chaos and mayhem that accompanied these advances. They skillfully conveyed the impression that the only power capable of stemming the Soviet onrush was Germany, that if the Western powers destroyed Nazi Germany, no power would be left to resist the Russians, and that unless the Russian advances were checked, there would be enormous problems in the future. As Belin observed carefully—for all of Dulles's mild manners he was not a man to be trifled with—in his message of April 20, 1944: ". . . could this [sic] data have been planted with a view to developing a viewpoint which could influence operations in such a way as to affect [Germany] vitally?"

The OSS was encountering a familiar problem in deception in statecraft: It takes a trickster to detect a trickster, and there were not many trained deceivers in statecraft in the United States. Belin was not crafty enough to detect a deception, and he barely understood the special language of the trade—the trade of Mazarin and Churchill. Dulles understood, but he had not the deceiver's supple mind, and anyway he was too close to the case for an objective opinion. Thus, when in his message of the twentieth Belin came to the nub of the question, he did not express Washington's fears strongly enough. Belin stated: "The increasingly significant character of the data impresses us particularly, and at the same time we notice that it becomes proportionately more damaging to the interests of [Germany]." Though "this would appear to be a reason for assuming it is not a plant, it is possible that our enemies might take the position that their only hope lies in taking gambles and that for the purposes of attaining some greater advantage in a more inclusive critical matter they would be justified in taking a chance on any disadvantageous effects which would be of comparatively less importance." That was a good point, but instead of pressing it, Belin ended weakly: "The foregoing is not intended to discourage you in any way but is merely to give oral expression to our thoughts on the subject."

Dulles was able to slip off the hook, and he did in his reply six days later —a delay that showed he was troubled by all these questions about Wood. "I am aware of the risk of becoming so impressed with one's sources that one steps into traps of the kind mentioned in [your] message. [But] from the beginning I have tried to make a critical examination of the [Wood] information with this in mind."[15] His "current opinion" was that "so far" the documents had shown no signs of a plant and that he, too, was convinced of their authenticity.

Dulles reported that "to some extent" Wood was "naïve" and that "in spite of his intelligence," he "seems to lack any of the characteristics which would make him competent to work a doublecrossing scheme." During "hours of interrogation," he had not said anything that would "create a doubt as to his genuineness." Dulles had made "an analysis of the whole arrangement through which the documents have been obtained and transmitted and I find the arrangement reasonable and practical."

As for motive, Dulles stated that Wood had claimed—and Dulles believed him—that he was "working with a group opposed to the Nazis" and that this group included such men as "Leobe, previously president of the Reichstag," "Count Waldersee," and "Dr. Walter Bauer, who was previously the German manager of the Prague-Petchek interests." Dulles agreed that his information about Wood's motives and his associates was "not definitive," but he did believe it was "persuasive." Dulles would continue to subject "the material to critical analysis," although "To date, the only factor creating concern has been indications that Wood has occasionally been reckless." In that regard, Dulles noted, "with illegal plotters this is quite normal behaviour."

Thus, despite his proximity to Wood, Dulles was not able to assure Belin categorically that he was certain Wood was not a participant in a highly dangerous Nazi gambit. Thus, the case was suspended in an atmosphere of uncertainty until Donovan intervened to tell Dulles that the British remained anxious about the affair. But Dulles was not impressed by British anxieties; he explained on May 8, 1944: "I feel that genuine opportunities may be lost to us if we are unduly suspicious." As an instance of this:

> I have the feeling from my dealings with Zulu [Dulles's code name for the British SIS in Switzerland] that their services, because of the leg-pulling they suffered in the gloomy times of 1940–1941, are unaware on occasion of the degree to which the situation has been reversed, even in the field of intelligence. Several of my finest sources would have been lost to me had I pursued their course.[16]

Dulles, at least, believed in his source and defended him to the extent that when Donovan asked him for a list of Germans who might be useful in governing the American zone of Germany, he included Wood. But Donovan and Belin declined to accept the source and his material until after the fall of Rome in June 1944, when it was established that Kesselring had ordered the destruction of the Tiber bridges and public utilities but that Hitler had countermanded the orders. That showed, at least, that the Kesselring signal, which had given McCormack and the British pause, was at least authentic, although, of course, it revealed nothing about the really troubling aspect of the case—Wood's motives for betraying the Reich.

In the end, therefore, the probability is that Wood started out as an attempt by Ribbentrop to frighten the Western powers out of undertaking the aerial and land operations necessary to destroy the Third Reich and into supporting German policy against Russia. But at a certain stage —"when" was the material question—Wood changed his attitude, and the Boston Series became the instrument for his own and his colleagues' reinsurance with the Allies. Be that as it may, Donovan personally came to believe in Wood, and in a paper on Dulles's accomplishments for President Harry S Truman, he stated:

> In August 1943 contact was established with a high German Foreign Office official who made frequent trips to Bern as diplomatic courier and who had use of the German diplomatic pouch. Over a period of 18 months OSS received over 1,600 true readings of secret and top secret German diplomatic correspondence between the Foreign Office and German diplomatic missions in 20 countries. Among the correspondence were reports from the German military and air attachés in Japan and the Far East, data on the structure of the German secret service in Spain, Sweden and Switzerland, and significant items regarding German espionage activities in England and in the British Embassy in Istanbul. Usually skeptical and conservative British intelligence officials rated this contact as the prize intelligence source of the war.[17]

Whether this opinion was justified is open to debate. At the time, no doubt, it appeared correct, but in the light of history and the knowledge of the existence of Ultra, ISOS, and Magic, it does not appear as sound as it did at the time. Yet undoubtedly the Boston Series materially assisted Allied operations, as WJD knew from experience.

There were, however, more formidable, less suspicious sources of intelligence and avenues of covert diplomacy open to Dulles and so to Donovan. The main source lay in Dulles's assistant, Gero von Gaevernitz.

When Donovan was at Columbia Law, he had encountered and become friendly with Ellery C. Huntington, who had been at Yale and was an all-American quarterback. Their friendship had outlasted their university days, and during the interwar years Huntington had joined the Equity Corporation in New York. At the Equity Corporation he had become associated in business—Huntington was a successful business entrepreneur—with a half Jewish, half Quaker German, Gero von Gaevernitz. In his turn Gaevernitz had become friendly at the Equity Corporation with another German, Edward von Waetjen, whose sister had married Godfrey Rockefeller, of the New York banking family.

Huntington and young Gaevernitz had maintained their friendship during the thirties. In 1939 Gaevernitz left Germany at the outbreak of the European war and went to live in Switzerland. Huntington was deeply impressed by his high intelligence and attractive appearance and personality, so that when Huntington was recruited into the COI by Donovan, he recommended that Gaevernitz be recruited as an agent. That was not, however, possible, until shortly before Torch, when Donovan arranged that Dulles go to Bern as the OSS representative. Before Dulles left Huntington gave him a letter of introduction to Gaevernitz, which Dulles presented on his arrival in Switzerland. Dulles, too, found Gaevernitz attractive and intelligent and invited him to join OSS Bern as his principal assistant. Gaevernitz accepted, and the two men worked closely together for the rest of the war.

That letter was to prove one of the seeds of Dulles's success in Bern, for in his turn Gaevernitz was in close contact with Edward von Waetjen, who was one of Canaris's representatives in Switzerland with the Abwehr, operating under German consular cover. In his turn Waetjen had close and ready access to almost the entire German, Finnish, Hungarian, Rumanian, Bulgarian, Croatian, and Japanese intelligence and diplomatic community. At the same time Waetjen was a member of the Black Orchestra, the anti-Nazi German resistance movement. Among that group was a third man, Gisevius.

Hans Bernd Gisevius was six feet four inches tall, heavily built, moonfaced with watchful eyes behind wire glasses, diabetic, balding, ungainly, clever but somewhat reckless, perhaps because he was aware that he suffered from an aneurysm that could burst and kill him at any moment. Politically Gisevius was a devout member of Canaris's most secret circle, and he was in Switzerland on the admiral's behalf as an officer of the Abwehr but for no other purpose than to maintain contact between Canaris and Donovan through Dulles.

A Prussian born in 1903, Gisevius began to beat his path toward the thralldom of *Hochverrat*—the most serious of German crimes—in 1934, when Hitler removed the war minister, Field Marshal Werner von Blomberg, on the ground that he had married a prostitute, and the commander in chief of the Army, General Werner von Fritsch, who was alleged to have been seen committing sodomy with a male prostitute in the Privatstrasse alongside the Wannsee railroad station in Berlin.

As a lawyer working for the Gestapo, Gisevius found the case papers against Blomberg and Fritsch on his desk. He soon saw that the charges against the two officers were fictions created with the purpose of enabling Hitler to get control of the General Staff, which the forces of tradition in Germany regarded as being the watchdogs of the Reich and which then opposed Hitler's plans for war. It also soon became clear to Gisevius why Hitler wanted to control the General Staff: He created a supreme central command of all the armed forces, the Oberkommando der Wehrmacht, in order to wage war against the Versailles treaty powers—a war that would surely broaden into another world conflict which, Gisevius believed, would lead to an even greater calamity for Germany than World War I.

Until that time Gisevius had admired certain aspects of Nazism. But now he revolted against it. At first he decided to leave government service, but a friend, Hans von Dohnanyi, persuaded him to remain with the Gestapo and keep the small group around Admiral Canaris, who had just been appointed chief of the Abwehr by Hitler, informed of the Nazis' intentions and crimes. Gisevius remained with the Ministry of Justice, and that was the start of the conspiracy the Gestapo called the Schwarze Kapelle, or Black Orchestra.

When war came, Gisevius was recruited into the Abwehr by Dohnanyi, and his first assignment was vice-consul in Zurich, his task to develop contacts with the British intelligence service's Z Organization, which operated in Western Europe under the command of Sir Claude Dansey. Soon after Gisevius arrived in Zurich, Canaris's rival service, the Nazi party's foreign intelligence service, called the Sicherheitsdienst (SD), succeeded in kidnapping two senior British officers of the Z Organization, at Venlo on the Dutch-German frontier, where they had gone in the belief that they were to meet a German general plotting against Hitler.

The SD's action precipitated a violent, unrestrained intelligence war that culminated in 1942 with the murder at Prague by the British of the head of the Sicherheitsdienst, Reinhard Heydrich. But for Gisevius in

1939, the immediate consequence of the Venlo incident was that Dansey formed a deep suspicion of him, and on July 31, 1943, OSS London, having talked the matter over with Dansey, warned Dulles:

> It is believed by the British that you should stop seeing 512 [Gisevius's code number] as they think he is untrustworthy. We agree in this except that for future contingencies a contact should be maintained through a cutout who is not known to the Germans. Greatest caution should be observed when sending names, numbers, etc., which have been supplied by this source because of the possible aid to the Germans in cracking our cipher.[18]

But less than two weeks later Dansey received intelligence that caused him to revise his opinion of Gisevius:

> About 512, our British friends now tell us that they have heard he has probably burned his bridges in Germany. His talks may, therefore, be even more interesting and they very much hope the talks will go on. Please cable me your decision and the status of the affair. Your answer anxiously awaited by . . . [Dansey, now vice-chief of the British Secret Intelligence Service].[19]

By the time Dulles received the new British estimate of Gisevius, the German had already demonstrated his trustworthiness with an extraordinary gesture intended to overcome Dulles's suspicion. As Gisevius knew, in February 1941 German cryptanalysts had solved the ciphers used by both the American and British ambassadors at Bern to send their messages to Washington and London. In particular the traffic of the American minister, Leland Harrison, was thought by the Sicherheitsdienst to be very important as a source of intelligence about the members of the Black Orchestra in Switzerland, who trusted Harrison and kept him informed of their plans. Also, when his own circuits were overburdened with work, Dulles used the minister's cipher and communications systems. Gisevius's information, therefore, wrecked a major German source. For good measure, he warned that one of the Reich's cryptographic bureaus had also penetrated the cipher of the British ambassador in Turkey, Sir Hughe Knatchbull-Hugessen.

These warnings served a number of purposes. They did not fail to impress Dulles that Gisevius was a man with great knowledge of the German secret apparatus. They clearly demonstrated Gisevius's good faith toward Dulles and the United States, and they gave Gisevius security in that he could now meet and talk with Dulles without fear that the report of the meeting would be read by the SD. As for Donovan, he, too, was impressed, for much later he would be able to advise President Truman how Gisevius "advised OSS that the Germans had succeeded in deciphering the secret code of the American Legation in Bern and prompt notice to the Minister preserved important State Department reports from falling to the enemy."[20]

That gambit established the firmest association between Dulles and Gisevius, in which the Prussian was able to render important services to the Grand Alliance. For the sake of the security of both, they rarely met. Gisevius communicated with Waetjen, and Waetjen with Mary Bancroft, a Boston socialite whose grandfather had founded *Barron's Weekly* and who was living in Switzerland with her husband, a member of the Freud family. She had been recruited as an informant by Dulles at a salary of $125 per week, although she did not know until the end of the war that she was working for the OSS or even that it existed. All she knew was that she worked for "American intelligence." As she would state, Dulles hired her with the words: "Of course I have millions at my disposal, but because you're you I'm going to be paying you the minimum because later we'll become personal friends"—a prophecy that proved correct.[21] Equally, Mrs. Bancroft became a close friend of Gisevius and his wife.

That friendship began to develop when Gisevius produced the first chapters of what would become a huge manuscript entitled "To the Bitter End," an account of the Nazis' conduct and of the struggle of the German opposition against Hitler until about midsummer 1943, based on the dossiers that Gisevius had kept at the Ministry of Justice and on information given him by Canaris and other members of the Schwarze Kapelle. It became Mrs. Bancroft's job to translate the document into English for Dulles, a job that seemed endless since Gisevius continually added new sections to the report until the second week of July 1944.

In all, Mrs. Bancroft translated some 4,000 pages of closely typewritten material that provided Dulles with the fullest background on the developing plot against Hitler's life inside Germany—a plot Dulles code-named Breakers in his telegrams to Washington. It was also the first major exposé of the world created by the Nazis, and in due course, after much cutting and polishing, Gisevius's report became a book published in New York and London under the title of the report, *To the Bitter End*—a work that ranks among the grimmest accounts of modern political resistance. Unfortunately for the political history of the war, there was no transport from Switzerland to either London or Washington at that stage of the war, the manuscript was too long to send by radio, and it could not be sent out by secret courier for fear that the Germans would intercept it, thereby endangering the lives of all whose names appeared in the document. Therefore, it was not until September 1944, after France had been liberated, that the manuscript could be shipped to New York, and by the time it got there, was read, edited, and put into type most of the men in it were dead and the war was almost over.

Yet it was axiomatic that wars were fought with powder, not paper, and to demonstrate that he was not another woolly idealist hoping to talk the

West into an accommodation with Germany, in the spring of 1943 Gisevius showed that the Schwarze Kapelle was prepared to place large numbers of Germans' lives and important Wehrmacht property on the high altar of understanding with the Western powers. Of this Donovan reported to President Truman later: "This source supplied early information on the preparation of the V-1 and V-2 bombs, which in conjunction with other sources led to the identification of Peenemünde as the Germans' proving ground for new weapons."[22]

By 1943, Gisevius related to Dulles, the Wehrmacht had been experimenting for almost a decade with a number of extremely advanced weapons. Those weapons were the V-1 or pulse-jet-powered cruise missile carrying one ton of high explosive up to 250 miles at a maximum speed of 400 mph. The second weapon was the V-2, a liquid-fuel rocket, forty-six feet long, weighing thirteen tons, and with a one-ton warhead. Both weapons' warheads were a new aluminized explosive with blast power far more powerful than that of any other known explosive. Gisevius's report concluded that almost all research and development, and the scientific staff, for the highly advanced and technical *Vergeltungswaffe* (revenge weapons) program were concentrated at Peenemünde, a town on the Pomeranian coast of Germany, the secret site since 1937 of all German missile and special engines testings.

These were to prove to be dangerous weapons. In all, 30,000 to 32,000 V-1's and 6,000 V-2's were built, of which 20,000 V-1's and 3,000 V-2's were fired operationally, mainly at conurbations in England and Belgium. They killed 8,588 Britons, wounded 47,838, and destroyed nearly 30,000 houses, damaging another 102,000 and blasting the glass out of perhaps another 1,400,000—a bad business in wet and cold weather. On the Continent, they killed about 3,700 people, wounded about 6,000, destroyed about 4,000 houses, and damaged about 110,000.

Production, firings, casualties, and damage would have been, it was estimated, eight times those figures had the German production schedule not been disrupted. But it was disrupted badly when, ten days after Dulles had transmitted Gisevius's information to Donovan, 597 Royal Air Force heavy bombers delivered a shattering, surprise attack on Peenemünde, killing many of the leading scientists and technicians and destroying much of the research, development, and production facility so carefully constructed and concealed over such a long period.

While Gisevius's information was not the first or the decisive intelligence received by the British about Peenemünde and the V weapon program, the intelligence was important, and it showed that the Schwarze Kapelle was not, as had been believed for so long, no more than a group of muddled idealists. The group had teeth, guts, knowledge, purpose. And the courage of its members was the greater, for Dulles could offer them no political rewards. President Roosevelt had proclaimed the policy of unconditional surrender at Casablanca in January 1943, and thereafter all Allied agents could meet Axis agents only for intelligence purposes —not to offer anything that might save Germany from material destruction, invasion, and partition, but only for what the Allied intelligence services could get out of the intermediaries.

Yet from the outset Gisevius provided the most important political information about conditions inside the Greater German Reich. On January 5, 1943, there was remarkable evidence of this when news reached Donovan that:

> General Beck, who was displaced by General Halder as German Chief of Staff, is the leader of the German anti-nazi movement Faderland [sic]. General Beck is under 24 hour surveillance by the Gestapo and is confined to quarters. He will be the military leader of a revolution and is backed by the expatriate, Greek Admiral Canaris [sic].
>
> A movement is on foot headed by a German General (name not disclosed) presently on the Russian front to start a revolution there. This probably will be abortive as was the planned assassination of Hitler on January 1st. March will probably see an attempt by the Junkers to wrest control from the Nazis. . . .[23]

That report proved remarkably prophetic and plainly emanated from the plotters, for who else could have known of the plan in January? For as further intelligence was to demonstrate:

§ Ludwig Beck was displaced by Franz Halder as chief of the General Staff, and he was the military leader of the German anti-Nazi movement, although it is not known that it was called Faderland.

§ A German general on the Russian front in January 1943 was plotting a revolution against Hitler. His name was Henning von Tresckow, and he was chief of staff to the commander in chief on the central front, Field Marshal Günther von Kluge. Tresckow's plan originated with Beck and was known to Canaris.

§ It is not known that there was an attempt to kill Hitler on January 1, 1943. There were, however, several conspiracies against Hitler during that period, all of them stimulated by Beck; all failed because Hitler had the luck of the devil.

§ March was indeed the date set by Tresckow for the culmination of his plot. Tresckow persuaded Kluge to invite Hitler to Kluge's headquarters, Hitler accepted Kluge's invitation and arrived in his personal Focke-Wulf Kondor. While Hitler and Kluge were lunching, Tresckow persuaded a member of Hitler's entourage to take a package that contained, Tresckow claimed, two bottles of Cointreau, a present for a friend at Hitler's headquarters. The officer agreed and placed the package in the tail of Hitler's aircraft, after Tresckow had set the time fuse. The package contained not Cointreau, but *plastique*, enough to blow the tail of Hitler's aircraft away. That did not, however, occur because the pilot, to avoid storms, flew at high altitude, the liquid chemical in the fuse froze, and the detonator, consequently, failed to work.

While at the time the original bulletin was no more than a number of such reports about plots against the life of Hitler, shortly further information confirming the March attempt reached the OSS. Therefore, Donovan had considerable evidence (more than usually available in wartime) that the Schwarze Kapelle was vigorous, determined, and widespread and that the conspiracy had become sufficiently bold, the political situation inside Germany sufficiently desperate, to permit an attempt on Hitler's life.

Plainly, it was desirable to have a talk with Canaris, not to offer him anything, but to see what he planned and what, if anything, could be done to help him. Canaris himself seems to have made the next move. When one of Donovan's colonels, Ulius C. Amoss, arrived in Cairo in February 1943 on business concerning Greece, he received a message from his Greek contacts—in this case King George II of the Hellenes acting through his intelligence master, Stephanos Theofanides, who was also the minister of marine in exile and a close personal friend and collaborator of Amoss. Canaris wished to talk with Amoss. Could a meeting be arranged?

By now, however, there was a standing instruction to all American and British intelligence officers that such overtures must be reported to the State Department and Foreign Office, which had to give their approval before such meetings could take place. In Amoss's case he advised his case officer in Washington, Florimond Duke, an associate of Huntington's. Duke appears to have received authority to proceed with the contact, for there was a good deal of cabling between Duke in Washington and Amoss in Cairo in February 1943 about such a meeting. It is evident from the text of the cables that the Dulles-Gaevernitz-Bancroft-Waetjen-Gisevius-Canaris system was at work, for four of Duke's telegrams to Amoss on the subject of a meeting with Canaris survive in the Donovan papers:

[February 26, 1943:] Canaris is back at Bern after having made a trip through the Balkans last week. He is registered as Dr. Spitz at St. Gotthard Hotel, Bern.
[March 5, 1943:] Canaris made a trip through the Balkans a short time ago, and also visited Turkey. He would like to get in touch with American intelligence. If you think it would be advisable, might be able to make arrange-

ments for his return to Turkey at a time convenient to you.

[March 10, 1943:] It may take some time to execute Canaris' desire to meet you. He is at this time in the south of Spain. As soon as we are able we will forward you information concerning this.

[March 24, 1943:] Canaris has been contacted in France and says that, for the moment, he is under too close a surveillance by Himmler, who suspects he is working for downfall of Hitler and the Party. Therefore Canaris must be extremely careful for his life. Still working on the proposition, though the above confirms your information.[24]

The series showed plainly that OSS Washington had the means to get in touch with Canaris. It showed also a remarkable knowledge of his movements. But whether personal contact was established between Amoss and Canaris is not evident from the Donovan papers. The probability is that no such meeting took place. On the other hand, there were rumors in the OSS that Donovan and Canaris met personally in Spain in March or April 1943 and again in Istanbul in the late summer or early fall of 1943. But we do not know if these meetings actually took place and, if they did, what transpired.

No man was better than Donovan at keeping his own counsel.

PART THREE

THE
ZEPPELIN
PERIOD

Being the account of Donovan's principal operations in the Mediterranean, the Balkans, and Italy in preparation for D-Day in Normandy. The period of the action is 1943, and it is the time at which the OSS became fully operational. At the same time, it suffered severe defeats through inexperience and poor personnel in key operational areas.

19

Donovan at Sixty

Donovan turned sixty on January 1, 1943, and celebrated that milestone in his life with Ruth Donovan and his granddaughter, Patricia, at a breakfast party in the Georgetown mansion before leaving for his headquarters. Ruth gave him a handkerchief as a present, and as she wrote in her diary, "He and Patricia had a cup-cake and one candle for breakfast."

An OSS medical report dated January 18 showed that mentally and organically Donovan was in excellent condition, although appreciably overweight: At five feet ten inches and heavily built, he was 197 pounds when the doctors thought the desirable weight range for a man of his age and build should have been 161 to 175 pounds. His systolic pressure showed a remarkable 115—the enviable blood pressure of the aging athlete. Despite his regimen, there was no sign of any hypertension, and the worst his doctors could do to him was put him on a diet of about 2,400 calories a day—which, naturally, he did not maintain. His hair was not quite silver, his skin had a deep ruddy glow, and his deep blue eyes were clear. As he remarked to Doering, he was in much better shape than most staff officers. Indeed, his indefatigable quality was undiminished, for his records would show that between April 2, 1943, and January 4, 1946, he would make seventeen overseas trips totaling one year, seven months, twenty days outside the United States, against one year, four months, twenty days at his desk or traveling in the United States—a record few, if any, of the members of the staff of the Joint Chiefs could emulate.

In that other important dimension of his personal life—his marriage— WJD and Ruth were readjusting the nature of their life together, especially now that he was in secret war work. When WJD began to use the Georgetown house as a place for his confidential meetings, he asked Ruth to move out to the farm at Berryville. The request caused her considerable heartache. But such was the nature of these meetings that WJD felt unable to explain why it was desirable for her to move—that half the world's statesmen, politicians, intelligence officers, and officials of the armed forces, to say nothing of revolutionaries, spies, and traitors, came there and most of them did not want to be seen by any person other than him.

By now Ruth had accepted that Berryville was her residence for the duration of the war, and she spent half her week working in a nearby military hospital as a nurse's aide and the other half continuing to turn the old house and wild, overgrown fields into a gentleman's residence—landscaping, laying lawns, making rose beds, planting boxwoods and raspberries, putting in elms and firs, supervising the construction of stables and barns, driving tractors, acting as the tree surgeon, and raising steers and hogs. Donovan came down to spend a night about once a month, and Ruth went into Washington to shop and stay a night or two at the house and see movies at the OSS theater in the basement of the National Institute of Health.

The age of passion had gone and the age of companionship had begun. Donovan was reverting to the life he was coming to like the best—the monkish, intense, intricate, austere life of the devoted secret servant of the state. Although he had always appeared to be a gregarious fellow, he was really a rather solitary man, a man with few friends, fewer intimates, and a multitude of acquaintances. At the OSS headquarters he maintained that appearance of friendliness, but it was only an appearance. His office door might always be open, but only men like Ned Buxton, Otto Doering, and James Murphy, whom he trusted absolutely, came through it. The rest of his visitors were on business, and while WJD used his charm to great effect, and everybody thought he was his friend, he was really the able, driving, hard, resourceful, but agreeable, taskmaster.

More than in World War I, he was adored by his men. To Donovan they were "my league of gentlemen." It was a league, Carleton Coon was to recall, made up of "gentlemen volunteers on our honor. We were never under orders. We were always asked, 'Would you like to . . . (e.g., get yourself killed)?' To which we always said 'yes.' " Coon contended that "I never took an oath for the COI or OSS,"[1] and most of the survivors of Donovan's league, especially those who joined in the early days, could not remember doing so either. Putzell, Doering, and others would also speak of the special spirit of the league. "We believed we had an idea," Putzell stated, "we believed it was a good one, we worked hard for it, and while we lost many battles, we did not lose the war."[2] Indeed, WJD managed to develop a spirit that most of his men had not encountered before—that of youth, daring, an elite—and would not encounter again, one that none would forget. For most of the men who served in Donovan's league, it was undoubtedly the high point of their lives—"our springtime years," as Doering was to put it.[3] They had become a secret service, an order, doing their work with passion.

Nor, it seems, were this reverence and this admiration confined to the office. Donovan was a permanent fixture in the affections and esteem of his staff. A Washington society beauty, Marlys Leister, the sole heiress to a fortune made in the Midwest, where her family printed textbooks, married an OSS captain in Special Operations, a foreigner of excellent birth, well educated, extremely handsome, and a former British agent on the Burma Road to China. Such liaisons were not unusual at the time, for the OSS was known locally as "Oh So Social," but what was unusual were Mrs. Leister's powers of observation: "The marriage was rather hurried as Dan was going overseas on operations. His colleagues were at the ceremony, and I was struck by the thought that OSS was a very creamy group. . . . Bill Donovan was there, and I paid great attention to him, because for months before the marriage I had heard little but "Bill says this," and "Bill did that," and he had become a part of our lives. In fact, General Donovan was to become a part of our lives for years to come. The marriage lasted a long time, but not a week would pass without some discussion about General Donovan, not a week. He had entered our lives, and he stayed there.

"When I met General Donovan, he was in civilian clothes and reminded me of being exactly what he was—the very successful corporation lawyer. He was a stunning man, and when he was in the room, everyone was aware. I thought sometimes, Bill Donovan is Bill Donovan's front man, for his great gift was that charm of his. I thought also that another of his great gifts was his ability to read a man's character in a flash and get the best out of him—to put the man before him on track. Perhaps nine-tenths of the men I knew in the OSS would never have done much with their lives . . . but spend their money, but Donovan showed them their path and then made them take it. He engaged their loyalties; the streak of loyalty was never very strong in my husband, for example, but Bill Donovan found it, strengthened it, and made my husband a better man."[4]

While WJD may not have realized this, in the league he was in fact establishing a remarkable dynasty—a dynasty of U.S. intelligence masters that would exist forty years later. Most of the leading names in U.S. Intelligence over the next four decades were joining the league of gentlemen at this time—Magruder, Kirkpatrick, Helms, Colby, Wisner, Angleton, Casey, and Dulles among them, to say nothing of a host of businessmen, lawyers, journalists, and others who were to remain in the service of U.S. secret intelligence long after they had officially left "the firm."

At this time—1943—the roots of secret service had taken hold in the Washington administration. Whether OSS survived remained to be seen, but in some respects WJD's work had been impressive—although so far the service had been tested only against friends, not against enemies, and had barely encountered the Germans. Through what one of FDR's Cabinet advisers called "the work of a man of unlimited imagination and gall," of a man who was "afraid of nobody and nothing, least of all a new concept,"[5] WJD and his assistants had founded what was really a central intelligence agency consisting at that time of five major secret industries:

§ Secret Intelligence (SI) Branch.

§ Research and Analysis (R&A), a branch with a staff of about 400 dons producing estimates and reports of matters concerning the political and military direction of the war.

§ Counterespionage (X-2), which was as yet really no more than a project. But it was a project that would fructify. Its task was to protect OSS against penetration by hostile services.

§ Special Operations (SO), to create and control the national insurrections visualized in the Arcadia plan and to conduct sabotage and subversion on a global scale.

§ Morale Operations (MO), to attack the enemy's will to fight and his belief in his causes.

Behind these branches stood a machine that included a financial division; one for the research and development of special weapons and devices; a communications system now reaching out rapidly to the four corners of the globe; large archival, library, and filing systems; a large recruitment and training division; and a large training system through which no fewer than 4,680 personnel trained in clandestinity before Neptune D-Day in less than fourteen months. There were also thirty-odd sections performing tasks not always concerned with secret service but always related to it.

Donovan's budget stood at about $35,000,000. As for staff, as of April 6, 1943, he would employ 1,651 people; the number rose to 2,063 by October, with an immediate increase approved by the Joint Chiefs for a total of 5,290. That figure would then be revised again so that in twelve months WJD would employ just over 16,000 staff members.

But in one major respect—the secrecy of the OSS—Donovan had failed. He had not succeeded in obtaining legislation intended to protect the security of the agency. The existence of the organization was known to everyone, including the Germans, the Italians, the Japanese, and the Russians, although to a surprising extent the enemy services were not wholly aware of its purposes. And while in theory the OSS was protected

by the wartime emergency acts and the espionage regulations, the restraints were effective only with newspapermen who felt it their patriotic
duty not to discuss its activities in print. Thus, the press could, and did,
discuss the OSS in print occasionally, without fear of legal reprisal. For
example, Drew Pearson, the Washington columnist, dismissed the agency
as "one of the fanciest groups of dilettante diplomats, Wall Street Bankers, and amateur detectives ever seen in Washington." And the Washington *Times-Herald*'s columnist, Austine Cassini, was able to write without
fear of prosecution under any official secrets act:

> If you should by chance wander in the labyrinth of the OSS you'd behold
> ex-polo players, millionaires, Russian princes, society gambol boys, scientists
> and dilettante detectives. All of them are now at the OSS, where they used
> to be allocated between New York, Palm Beach, Long Island, Newport and
> other meccas frequented by the blue-bloods of democracy. And the girls!
> The prettiest, best-born, snappiest girls who used to graduate from debu-
> tantedom to boredom now bend their blonde and brunette locks, or their
> colorful hats, over work in the OSS, the super-ultra-intelligence-counter-
> espionage outfit that is headed by brilliant "Wild Bill" Donovan.[6]

From time to time the British services pressured Donovan to see the
President and his congressional friends and try to enact legislation that
would make it an offense to discuss the OSS in public in wartime, but
while Donovan was being so vigorously challenged and suspected on all
sides, he felt it would be a waste of time. He would have taken steps to
produce an official secrets act had he felt strong enough to do so, but he
never felt confident enough of the permanency of his agency to become
embrangled in the interminable constitutional, legal, and philosophical
problems of the First Amendment, even in wartime. Donovan was to
regret that he had not made such a bill part of his original deal with FDR,
for unrestrained press discussion was to contribute to the ruin of his plans
and, to some extent, his career.

Yet if his relations with his men were excellent, and his service was
blossoming well, Donovan's relations with the rest of Washington were
not enviable. Looking back on the formative years of OSS, Wayne Coy,
a high executive of the Washington *Post* who was made responsible by
FDR for overseeing WJD's finances, would state that the President had
chosen Donovan as his intelligence master because "the traditional intelligence services were wholly inadequate and needed an infusion of new
blood."[7] The traditional services had become "the dumping ground of
a lot of poor, surplus individuals." Donovan "is and was a genius. He has
greater imagination than anyone I have ever known," Coy continued, and
for that reason FDR wanted early in 1943 to amalgamate the OSS and
Naval and Military Intelligence and create a centralized intelligence ser-

vice—a CIA—under his command. But that plan came to naught because "Nobody dared challenge J. Edgar Hoover, not even Franklin Roosevelt," and the plan was "squashed in a very heavy-handed way."

As for WJD, the President believed Donovan "loves power for its own sake," and FDR would say, "We must find a way to harness this guy, because if we don't he will be doing a lot of things other than what we want him to do." Roosevelt "told me in writing that I was to know what every dollar was spent for and what it was going to be spent for, and if we were ever called upon to say where emergency money went, I was the one that would explain it." But Coy admitted that he was never quite able to "harness" Donovan because he was "doing things which the public should not know and it was dangerous for me even to know about them." As a result, Donovan had "a proper reticence in talking to me about [what he was doing], and he always had a running row in the Bureau of the Budget about finances."

Yet Coy admitted that he sympathized with WJD because there would have been "difficulty with the good Lord Himself attempting to do that job," although Donovan's difficulties were "accentuated by Bill Donovan." He did not "share his mind with many people about what he wanted to do or what he was trying to do." Somebody less secretive might have developed more harmonious relationships with the rest of the administration, Coy thought, but "that man would not have been the genius in intelligence that Donovan is." On the whole, he had "made a great contribution in raising the level of intelligence activities through a competitive spirit that he developed out of his own desire to 'grab.' " But the result was that "Bill Donovan is a pretty thoroughly hated guy in a lot of places."

By 1943 the Donovan agency had developed what Deputy Director Buxton would call a reputation for being "a mysterious Midas who exudes as entertainment rare viands, priceless vintages, steam yachts, beautiful women, and collects earth shaking secrets."[8] While WJD rather liked that reputation, most of the rest of Washington regarded the organization with suspicion. It was particularly marked on the Hill, where Senator Burton K. Wheeler, WJD's enemy since Teapot Dome, was now a powerful senator. Wheeler lost no opportunity to attack what he called Donovan's Gestapo. Also, Senator Harry Truman, chairman of the Special Committee to Investigate the National Defense Program, a friend of Wheeler's and a man who may well have been antipathetic since the days of the Kriemhilde Stellung in 1918, was familiar with the gossip about Donovan and the OSS.

Against that formidable background, the rumor following Torch that WJD had spent $40,000,000 in gold on the operation, only to have Darlan in power, caused considerable excitement. In fact, the story was non-sense. It was doubtful whether the entire operation in all countries involved cost more than $1,000,000, and the accounts of the man most likely to have committed large sums of money—Robert Murphy—showed that his disbursements in arranging the revolution of the French Army against Vichy totaled no more than $135,000.

As for Donovan, his expenditures were secret at the time but have survived in his papers. They show that from September 23, 1941, to December 31, 1943, a period that included the Torch expenditures, WJD spent $182,271.78, of which $51,539 was spent on projects connected with Torch. The largest sums disbursed consisted of:

§ $10,500 on May 30, 1941 for "Travel—Expenses of trip to England (William J. Donovan, Preston Goodfellow, and James R. Murphy) and cost of establishment of Special Agents and means of communication. (Polish personnel for laundries, radios, etc, for Gibraltar and North African women agents.)"

§ $10,000 on July 31, 1941, for what he described as "Preparation for North African invasion and development of supply, intelligence, and communications systems. Money for Casablanca and Algiers groups; priest in Azores; airfield watchers; purchase of supplies in U.S. for African agents."

§ $10,000 on October 23, 1941, for the purpose of "Obtaining pilots, agents, spies and saboteurs in preparation for North African invasion."

There were also many smaller payments to agents in the United States, none of which exceeded $400 a month and all of which were connected to operations to obtain information about pro-Axis embassies in Washington, as well as numerous items involving sums between $10 and $1,000 for information and personal expenses.

As one would expect, correspondence in the WJD files shows he was scrupulous about segregating personal from government expenditures; as an instance, there is a dunning letter from the St. Regis Hotel:

Re: $311.61 Past Due Account

Our accounting department has just called attention to the fact that we have not received the payment requested on two recent dates. Frankly, there may be good reasons why a request of this kind is not complied with—but without knowing those reasons, we are obliged to continue writing what may be useless letters.

The amount involved is nominal, and the total of accounts of this size on our books, which for one reason or another are unpaid is considerable. For

that reason, we are compelled to ask that you will either send your check at
this time or advise when we may look for it.

We shall look forward to a reply by return mail.[9]

The best conceivable explanation for the $40,000,000 in gold allegedly
unaccounted for was that someone—probably Wheeler—had become
muddled over a sum being expended by another government department
on the rearmament of the French Army, part of the deal struck between
Mast and Clark at the Cherchel meeting.

Whatever the case, the unorthodox financial activities of the "mysterious Midas" troubled the Washington establishment, even long after
Donovan was able to show that from the earliest days his agency had had
the most comprehensive program for controlling the expenditure of secret funds, preventing fraud and extravagance, and monitoring expenditures of operations and projects taking place—a procedure approved by
the Bureau of the Budget. Much of this difficulty stemmed from a man
called Strong.

Early in the Torch operation a new figure had joined the intelligence
community. General George Veazey Strong was a West Point graduate
and a leading member of the American military establishment. A few
years younger than Donovan, he was slim, smooth-faced, a cavalryman
turned military lawyer. Although he had begun his military career fighting
the Ute Indians, thereafter Strong's career had been a succession of staff
appointments, including that of professor of law at West Point and culminating in the job of chief of intelligence to the War Department and
head of Military Intelligence. Donovan had met his match in Strong,
known throughout Washington as King George on account of his grand
manner. Strong, believing WJD was endeavoring to centralize control of
intelligence in his own person, began to hound him with the same vigor
and determination as Ahab beginning to hunt his big white whale.

Strong was a master of sarcastic memorandums and committee warfare, and his power and influence derived from his place in the Army.
First and most important, he was a personal appointment of the powerful
Army Chief of Staff, General George C. Marshall, whom he served as
adviser and hatchet man. Also, he was chief of the Joint Security Control,
responsible for overseeing the security of military operations and for
integrating American deception operations with those of the British—for
executing those "elements of legerdemain" playing such an important
part in Anglo-American strategy and tactics. The post gave Strong the
right to examine all projects being initiated by the Donovan agency, to
ensure that they contained nothing that would enable the Axis to make
deductions concerning the capability and intentions of the Allies and that
Donovan's operations conformed to the requirements of Allied plans.
Then, as chief of Military Intelligence, he controlled Magic and Ultra, the

most vital intelligence sources of World War II. These sources enabled him to check—and sometimes to denounce—Donovan's intelligence product and operations.

In all, Strong was the most powerful intelligence figure in Washington. He did not like Donovan or his agency, and believing that the country would be better off without WJD and the COI, he set about the task of demolishing the new civilian agency. Strong was not discouraged by his masters, the Joint Chiefs, at least at first, and to assist him, he surrounded himself with a number of highly ambitious colonels who kept him well informed about Donovan and his organization's activities on a global basis. Strong was thereby able to keep the most detailed dossier on Donovan's activities.

The reasons for Strong's dislike of Donovan and his organization are fairly clear: suspicion and anxiety caused by the presence of a civilian agency at the heart of military planning and operations in wartime; WJD's power at the White House and the threat implied by the concept of a central intelligence agency to the military's primacy in secret service; WJD's personality and perhaps his politics; concern about the COI's security; the association between the Donovan agency and Communists; Donovan's empire building; what Strong believed was Donovan's alliance with the British services; what Strong believed was the amateurishness of the Donovan agency; WJD's large, secret financing; and above all, Strong's fears that Donovan was moving in on those most priceless of all intelligence sources, Ultra and Magic, which continued to give the military primacy in the field of intelligence. Strong saw Donovan as his principal rival in the field of intelligence, a candidate for the post Strong wanted—director of the postwar intelligence service, which all knew would develop from the warfare and chaos of the moment.

Strong's malevolence—the word is chosen carefully—seems to have reached a high degree of intensity over Magic. In a clear fabrication of the facts to injure the Donovan agency, Strong reported to General Marshall that in May 1942 some of Donovan's agents had burglarized the office in Lisbon of the Japanese military attaché, stolen his most secret cipher, and then departed, leaving the office in a state that left the Japanese in no doubt that a burglary had taken place and the cipher copied. What made the episode so serious, Strong contended, was: "It appears obvious that the ill advised and amateurish efforts of [Donovan's] representatives in Lisbon have so alarmed the Japanese that it is an even money bet that the codes employed by the Japanese are in imminent danger of being changed."[10] If that was so, "for months we will face a blank wall as far as Military and Naval Intelligence from Japanese sources is concerned, and our present *Magic* summary would cease to exist, with the possibility of catastrophic results as far as the activities of State, War and Navy are concerned."

Strong was successful in communicating his alarm to the President and the Joint Chiefs, for through Magic the Americans had managed to defeat the Japanese at the Battle of Midway, wresting the initiative from and placing them on the defensive in one of the decisive battles of history. In short, Magic had emerged as America's principal intelligence instrument, and misuse or carelessness was regarded as being akin to treason—almost literally.

The Joint Chiefs ordered an investigation of the Lisbon burglary and its effects upon Magic, assigning that task to Colonel C. R. Peck, executive secretary of the JCS. It was not long before Peck established that the facts were not quite as Strong had presented them. Producing the requisite documents to prove his statements, Donovan was able to show Peck that his agency's representatives in Lisbon had employed two agents who worked for the Japanese government. One was a messenger in the office of the Japanese naval attaché; the other, an interpreter-stenographer on the staff of the military attaché. Both were Portuguese, and both had worked secretly for the Donovan agency, their tasks being "to pick up any available information as to Japanese official activities and to report on any callers or conversations."[11]

Donovan asserted that General Strong had been informed in general terms of the existence of these agents and was well aware that the cipher material that had caused the trouble had been "picked up casually by these agents." The material had been sent to Washington, where it was seen by General Strong, who knew that it was no more than copies of the Japanese military attaché's signals extracted from wastepaper baskets. WJD's office had sent the material to the chief signals officer, General Frank Stoner, who also controlled the Army's Cryptanalytical Bureau. All this had been reported to Strong at the time and again when Strong had been informed that Stoner had reported back the messages were in a cipher "used by the Japanese for material of low intelligence value"—so that the material sent to Stoner was not in fact the secret Japanese cipher to which Strong had alluded in his complaint to the Joint Chiefs.

Moreover, WJD continued, a check with the Special Branch, which handled Magic, showed no diminution in the Japanese use of the cipher which Strong said had been compromised through this affair. Therefore, Donovan told Peck, it followed that the Japanese still had confidence in that system and had not been alarmed by events in Lisbon if, indeed, there had been an incident there. Donovan was able to show also that his men had not penetrated the Japanese mission in Lisbon without Strong's knowledge and permission. He had asked the Joint Intelligence Committee for permission to employ the Portuguese, and the British services had been advised of the operation and had not only approved but given it some assistance. The State Department, too, was aware of the penetration, for the chief U.S. diplomat in Lisbon at that time, George F. Kennan, had "congratulated the agent on the operation and encouraged further activities."

Donovan concluded: "It is recognized by [my office] that attempts to penetrate the enemy's cryptographic system should not be made without consultation with those authorities charged with . . . cryptographic operations." However, his office had made no such attempts, and he was sure that "the activities of minor agents such as those in question would not cause alarm to the extent of bringing about a major modification of Japanese cryptographic procedures."

That assertion was true, for surveillance of Japanese secret wireless traffic, the source of Magic, showed that the Japanese were still using the very cipher that Strong had stated had been compromised through OSS stupidity. Magic continued without interruption to provide the U.S. Navy with the intelligence it needed to continue the reduction of the Japanese military and fleet to those of a third-class power.

And that was that. The Magic affair was over. But the struggle with Strong for primacy in the field of national intelligence went on and reached grave proportions, especially in committee debates. Matters of importance to the OSS that should have been settled in an hour took a month, and then the decision was often negative. Even when Donovan's points had merit, he was frequently outvoted. Thus, by late 1942 Strong had so ensnared the OSS in committee problems that Donovan was compelled to disqualify himself from the chairmanship of the Joint Psychological Warfare Committee because he feared his famous self-control might snap and he might hit Strong. And at a meeting on November 2, 1942, Colonel Buxton, who came in as Donovan's representative, found the situation so intolerable that he announced that the "OSS was now almost stopped in its tracks" and was "showing signs of dissolution," and he requested that it be released from its "present entanglement of numerous committees and organizational rivalry."[12]

The situation confronting Donovan was that the OSS could either collapse or triumph, and he played his last card: Dr. James Grafton Rogers, eminent lawyer, educator, scholar, and author who, when he joined the OSS Planning Group, had been professor of law at Yale. A former assistant secretary of state, Rogers was also a man with considerable personal influence with General Marshall.

Rogers later described how Donovan used him to save OSS: "In late 1942 the Army didn't know what to do with OSS." The Army chiefs "claimed that [Donovan] disorganized things, and they were suspicious of his political intentions." Whatever those intentions were, Rogers realized that the OSS was in serious trouble, but he was reluctant to intervene except once because "Marshall [was] death on political influence in the Army. I have seen him, on the very suspicion that an officer intended to write a letter to a congressman, assign him, in twenty minutes, to a far outpost in Alaska." Finally, "things got so bad that Bill said to me one morning: 'Don't you think it's time to call him up?' So I got an appointment next day, just before Marshall's staff meeting." At that meeting "I said, 'OSS is falling to pieces. Especially through the opposition of General Strong, whom you know I feel to be one of the few officers I have known who is unfit for command.' "

Marshall replied: " 'What about Donovan's desire to play politics?' " Rogers declared that he denied that Donovan would use "political pressure" but admitted that he would "freely use contacts." Rogers went on to describe how, after "further discussion," Marshall "was convinced" that Donovan was not applying "political pressure" and asked, "What do you want me to do?" Rogers told Marshall that he wanted him to "take it over yourself" and delegate someone to work out "a new charter for OSS."

At that point Marshall took Rogers into the staff meeting, at which Strong was present, and announced: "Gentlemen, this is Mr. Rogers of OSS, whose judgment, except in the case of General Strong, I have never found to err." Marshall then announced that "I am taking over OSS." After some further discussion, Marshall charged the Vice Chief of Staff, General Joseph McNarney, with the task of seeing what had to be done to put the OSS into business properly. Marshall asked the Chief of Naval Operations, Admiral Ernest J. King, to do likewise, and King assigned Admiral Frederick J. Horne, his vice chief, to work with McNarney. In due course, the Air Chief of Staff, General H. H. Arnold, joined McNarney and Horne, and all three visited Donovan's headquarters and, Rogers claimed, "came away mostly impressed with the degree of organization and planning that had been done."

The appointment of the triad was decisive in the history of U.S. intelligence, for until that moment Strong, Hoover, and Berle had been largely responsible for rendering the opinions upon which Roosevelt and the Joint Chiefs had made their decisions. Both McNarney and Horne, who had been under Strong's influence, were, Rogers stated, "rather surprised to see the magnitude of things over here and the breadth of things." That surprise produced a number of suggestions, not the least of which was one suggesting that Strong and Train be court-martialed.

McNarney made it very plain that there was no further time for argument or discussion. There was a war to be fought, and American combat forces were in action against the Germans in Tunisia and against the Japanese in the Pacific. It was made evident to all concerned, Donovan included, that compromise was necessary, and that if agreements were not reached, those who were recalcitrant would be dismissed.

Donovan and Strong were confronted with a document known as JCS 155/4/D, which was the draft of the OSS's first definitive charter. The

OSS was designated the agency of the Joint Chiefs charged (outside the Americas) with "the planning, development, coordination and execution of the military program for psychological warfare" and with "the compilation of such political, psychological, sociological and economic information as may be required by military operations." The draft invested responsibility with the Joint Chiefs for securing the cooperation of the Office of War Information—a vague division of responsibilities in propaganda that shortly caused serious trouble.

At the same time the OSS was made coequal with Military Intelligence and the Office of Naval Intelligence, causing much protest from those two bodies, and it was given authority to operate in the fields of sabotage, espionage, counterespionage, and raising guerrilla armies in enemy-controlled territory and among foreign nationality groups in the United States. The draft provided also for a planning group to be established within the OSS, to consist of one member from the State Department, two from the Joint Chiefs, two from the U.S. Navy, and four from the OSS. Plans had to be submitted for approval to the Joint Chiefs before execution.

If approved, the draft would remove the committee entanglements that had almost wrecked the Donovan agency. Needless to say, it provoked much protest from the OWI and Strong, but McNarney rammed it through, and it came up before the Joint Chiefs on December 8, 1942—one year after Pearl Harbor and almost eighteen months after the formation of the COI—and it was approved and promulgated on December 23, 1942, under the title "Functions of the Office of Strategic Services."

After twenty-six months of committee warfare it appeared that argument and the intelligence war were over, with Donovan victorious. At the OSS the document came to be called the Golden Directive, for as one of Donovan's inspectors general remarked, it "transformed OSS from a push-cart peddler's to a department store operation."[13] In a spirit of hope and goodwill Donovan and Marshall exchanged Christmas greetings for 1942 that seemed to promise much for the future. Marshall, who had been at least partly culpable for Donovan's difficulties and had done nothing to stop Strong in his campaign to garrote the COI and the OSS, now displayed contrition. Writing to Donovan to thank him for the cooperation and assistance he had given "personally in the trying times of the past year," Marshall added:

> I regret that after voluntarily coming under the jurisdiction of the Joint Chiefs of Staff your organization has not had smoother sailing. Nevertheless, it has rendered invaluable service, particularly with reference to the North African Campaign. I am hopeful that the new Office of Strategic Services' directive will eliminate most, if not all, of your difficulties.[14]

Alas, the wish was not to be fulfilled. A new disturbance in relations with Strong had blown up at the same time that Donovan was defending himself and his agency against attacks from the State Department. The new committee battle had broken out in October 1942, it was to last until May 1943, and it concerned Ultra and Magic. It was a decisive engagement, for within it lay the issue of whether the OSS or Military Intelligence would emerge as the preeminent foreign intelligence service in Washington and would come to control a subject already being discussed in Washington—the postwar intelligence service.

Donovan recognized at an early date—probably soon after becoming director of the COI—that the key to the survival of his concept, and thus the success of his plans for a permanent central intelligence service based upon his agency, was cryptanalysis: Magic and Ultra. In a conversation with Doering late in 1941 Donovan stated that cryptanalysis as an intelligence source so overshadowed human espionage that unless the COI were granted access to the intercept material, his secret intelligence service would be doomed to play only a small, subordinate role in the intelligence war. No human spy could provide intelligence with the same speed, volume, accuracy, and economy as the machine system that plucked the enemy's secret messages out of the ionosphere, broke the cipher in which the secrets were concealed, and then transmitted the intelligence almost immediately to the Allied High Command.

As Donovan knew, the American and British governments had agreed that Ultra and Magic would be handled only by their naval and military staffs. The agreement excluded all other agencies of both governments from handling the raw materials and, in most cases, from even seeing the bulletins produced from the raw intercepts. All this was an effort to ensure that through restriction of distribution to the fewest number of people in both governments, the Axis would not learn that their secret signals were being intercepted and read by their enemies. One of Marshall's reasons for appointing Strong his G-2 was to guarantee that control of all cryptographic intelligence remained with the Joint Chiefs of Staff.

Donovan was not the sort of man who accepted such restrictions. His executive order stated that he was to see *all* intelligence having a bearing on the national security, and he decided, again at an early date, that if he could not obtain Magic and Ultra through the Joint Chiefs, then, in order to discharge his order from the President, he would have to become a producer of cryptanalytical intelligence. Consequently fairly early in the history of the COI Donovan instructed Doering to establish a cover company called the FBQ Corporation. Doering did just that, advising the Commissioner of Internal Revenue that FBQ was "a means or instrumentality by which certain properties and facilities might be acquired and operated in the United States of America without public disclosure."[15] The address of the FBQ Corporation was given as "in care of Lanson and Tamblyn" of 52 Wall Street." As the Donovan papers show, FBQ existed to provide a means through which two commercial wireless listening posts—one at Reseda, California, the other at Bellmore, Long Island— could be purchased by the COI without its seeming involved. If the COI were permitted to enter the cryptanalytical business, the two stations would provide the embryo of a COI cipher-breaking agency. At the same time the services of a leading American cryptographer, Alfred Sheinwold, were retained, ostensibly to check the security of COI ciphers but in reality to establish the incubus for a cryptographic agency.

The purchases having been consummated, Donovan staffed the two stations with personnel experienced in radio monitoring and interception. All were either too old or physically unfit for military service, but all were experienced in the crafts of wireless intelligence, and FBQ was well financed from secret funds to purchase the equipment and the technical capability to intercept maritime communications of the European powers. Donovan also hired interpreters and translators conversant with the Russian, French, German, Dutch, Spanish, Italian, and Japanese languages. Their first task was to intercept voice radio broadcasts of all descriptions, including telephones, emanating from Moscow and Kuybyshev in Russia, Tokyo and Osaka in Japan, New Delhi, Chungking, Shanghai, Manila, Melbourne, Sydney, Brazzaville, Rome, Berlin, Paris, London, Rio de Janeiro, Buenos Aires, and Santiago de Chile. None knew, however, that Donovan intended them to form a cryptanalytical and wireless intelligence service.[16]

The FBQ radio posts operated under Donovan's control throughout the war, providing much interesting and valuable intelligence. A highlight was a yield of twenty-seven unusual messages between Tokyo and Berlin in the period March–May 1944. All were personal messages by American prisoners of war, eighteen of them originating in Tokyo and sent to Berlin, nine originating in Berlin and sent to Tokyo. All were in plain English, and an analysis at Reseda showed that all but one included the *complete* spelling of the state in the American Union from which the prisoner had come. That was unusual because Americans usually employed contractions for their state names, for example, "Va." for Virginia. It was also noted that of the twenty-six telegrams employing full state names, twenty-five were names of active American battleships. The one remaining name was that of a battleship under construction.

To FBQ Reseda this seemed more than coincidence, and an FBQ official advised the Donovan agency of its suspicion that the Japanese were "using messages selected from their extensive files of POW as an open code to inform Tokyo and Berlin regarding movements or whereabouts of capital ships." Despite the "sizeable number of POWs from practically all 48 states, messages thus far intercepted have been addressed only to 13 states, 12 of which are also the names of active battleships, and the 13th is the name of a battleship reported launched and now being commissioned." In other words, the Germans and the Japanese were using POW messages to convey information about the whereabouts of American battleships, what ocean they were in, what part of that ocean, and their state of repair.[17] That, of course, was vital intelligence.

Despite FBQ's excellent work, the call to enter the area of cryptanalysis never came. In circumstances that reflected the bitterness of the Washington intelligence war, Strong saw to it that Donovan did not become a producer of Ultra or Magic, the key to real power and influence in that community. Strong acted to exclude the Donovan agency from access to all cryptographic intelligence and to forbid its production of such intelligence.

After the Pearl Harbor disaster, which was caused by a failure to understand and use cryptographic intelligence correctly, to ensure that such a failure did not recur, the secretary of war, Henry L. Stimson, appointed a leading New York lawyer, Alfred McCormack, a special assistant, his task to study the acquisition and distribution of Ultra and Magic to ensure that the United States obtained the maximum benefit from the two remarkable sources.[18]

The outcome of McCormack's study was that in the early spring of 1942 Strong's Military Intelligence and the Office of Naval Intelligence were confirmed in their control of Ultra and Magic. To secure the fastest handling of that intelligence, Strong formed an organization called the Special Branch, to be under the command of Colonel Carter W. Clarke, one of Strong's colonels in Military Intelligence, and McCormack.

Aware that the COI's weakness was its lack of Magic and Ultra, and aware possibly that WJD intended to produce his own Magic and Ultra through FBQ (Strong had several spies inside the Donovan organization), Strong produced a paper advising Marshall to request that the President, as Commander in Chief, in the interests of the security of the material, formally prohibit a number of government agencies from engaging in cryptanalytical activity and to exclude them from access to intercept intelligence. The three organizations marked by Strong for exclusion were the Office of the Director of Censorship, the Federal Communications Commission, and Donovan's organization.[19]

Donovan filed a formal protest with the Joint Chiefs of Staff on the ground that if approved, Strong's memorandum would "impair the ability of [his organization] to discharge its mission." Without intercept intelligence he could not "operate an organization for the collection of information through espionage," nor could he "execute subversive activities." He insisted that his organization be granted access because "SI representatives in foreign countries are entitled to the protection and assistance derived from knowledge of intercepted enemy messages," such intelligence "frequently constitutes a warning of important events in specific localities," with those warnings "SI representatives can be directed to such localities without delay," and if his organization was excluded, "its services will be less valuable."[20]

Donovan, in a sense fighting for the life of his agency, declared forcefully that his organization:

> by the very nature of its activities, is already charged with a vast amount of most secret material. To exclude this agency from the processed intercepts can imply only that the material is not considered pertinent to the work of [this agency] or that there is a question as to the loyalty, the intelligence or discretion of [this agency] or the manner in which it would guard its security.

If that was so, "This Agency seeks to know which of these points are now raised and to be given an opportunity to meet such an issue."

There now ensued a battle of memorandums in which Strong insisted that the Donovan agency was not secure and should not receive Ultra and Magic because "the intercept material had to be handled with extreme caution," which Donovan's agency was not capable of doing.[21] In this Strong was backed by the Joint Chiefs. Donovan then went to FDR, explained that SI was in danger of collapsing if the Special Branch continued to starve the OSS of intercept material, and Roosevelt intervened as the Commander in Chief.

FDR's handling of the problem was typically deft. He admitted WJD to the Magic and Ultra "clubs," but he excluded Donovan from the production of cryptanalytical intelligence. Also—and here was the damaging part of his decision—he gave the job of deciding what Ultra and Magic material Donovan should see to Strong's Special Branch, while stressing that WJD must see all intelligence bearing on national security. It would be up to the Special Branch to decide what Ultra and Magic was pertinent to the national security, and WJD would have no say.

Donovan had lost the battle of secret intelligence, and his service was not to recover from that defeat. The primacy of Military Intelligence had been confirmed. There seems to be no reason to doubt James Grafton Rogers's belief that some of FDR's reasoning was political. According to Rogers, FDR was "disposed to suppress Donovan and the OSS [which had recently been formed out of the COI] as being too powerful and ambitious." There was also a suspicion, shared by Rogers, that FDR looked upon the OSS as largely Republican in coloration and therefore counted it among his political enemies.[22]

Having delivered one effective harpoon, Strong now sought to stick the entire concept of central intelligence and operations. After almost a year of preparation, early in 1943 Donovan circulated to the Joint Chiefs and other interested authorities his manual of psychological warfare, which contained much about the doctrine and attitudes of the OSS. Marshall sent the manual to Strong for an opinion and recommendation, and Strong produced a vigorous denunciation of no fewer than thirty-four pages in which he contended that the manual was "prepared in bad faith and with the purpose of extending the power of [the OSS] wherever possible."[23]

Describing the Donovan agency as a "hydra-headed organization" that "no one would dream of establishing were he to set out afresh to plan the American organization for war," Strong blasted it as an outfit that "under an ambitious and imaginative Director," and having "large sums of money at its command," had set itself up as "a central intelligence and planning agency" for operations in a wide variety of fields.

Strong related how the Donovan agency was "constantly at war with other Government agencies," had tried to reduce Army and Navy Intelligence to "the status of reporting agencies and research bureaus," and, despite the limitations of its directive, continued to do what it wanted. The manual was "just as objectionable as its authors," for it was "devoid of reference to moral considerations or standards," and its authors had assumed "the ethical color of its enemies in all particulars." They had devised definitions of psychological warfare that were "so synthetic and artificial" that the manual permitted the Donovan agency to "engage in any activity that caught its fancy," and the document was no more than "a lawyer's paper" in which "words were used to accomplish unstated purposes without appearing to do so."

Strong warned that this "legalistic document," with its "little twists of phrases" was really "another, and to date the most ambitious, attempt" by the OSS to "make itself the central planning and intelligence agency of the armed services, with a goodly share of its operations as well." The Donovan agency, he thought, should "forsake its penchant for global thinking," for "the endless collection of vast amounts of information on every conceivable subject," and concentrate, instead, as it had not done, on the "mundane, meticulous and dreary" work of espionage and counterespionage.

The effect of the paper was not damaging, at least to Donovan, but it demonstrated plainly that Strong was a determined opponent and would have to be considered, as would Hoover and Berle, in every major step that Donovan took toward what was now becoming his goal—director of a postwar central intelligence agency. But the concept was secure. Neither the Joints Chiefs nor anyone else required amendments, and so the manual was promulgated.

Donovan was now at last free to embark on what became the most crowded year of his life, the one lasting from July 1943 until July 1944. He began that year by setting out for London to see Menzies, in an effort to establish a *modus vivendi* with Menzies and the British Secret Intelligence Service.

20

Penny Farthing

Donovan's first stop was London. There, as usual, he saw Menzies, hoping doubtless to reestablish with the British Secret Intelligence Service the good relations that he had enjoyed in 1940 and 1941 and that the OSS now enjoyed with the British Special Operations Executive. But it proved impossible. While both Donovan and Menzies might be fighting the same war, each visualized a different peace.

Thinking in terms of a postwar central intelligence agency, Donovan insisted that the OSS should have complete independence, the right to operate wherever and whenever U.S. policy demanded, including the British Empire. Menzies, acting with the confidence and authority of Churchill and Anthony Eden, the foreign secretary, believed that independent OSS operations in the British Empire would ultimately add to the spread of anti-imperialism.

The two points of view were not reconcilable, and that fact began to produce serious tensions between the Secret Intelligence Service of England and the Secret Intelligence Branch of the OSS. Menzies effectively excluded all independent OSS SI operations from the British Isles and to a lesser extent from British territory. He forbade contact in London between the governments in exile there and the OSS SI. And in general he adopted measures that would render the OSS in Britain—the main base outside the United States—subordinate to British command and interests until after the invasion of Europe.

Although the informal relationship between OSS SI and Menzies's SIS was often close and cordial, from mid-1943 onward the official relationship was often icy and sometimes—especially in such British bastions as Cairo, Delhi, and Ceylon—hostile and suspicious. The relationship was one of the most curious features of the Anglo-American alliance, and it derived directly from FDR's and Donovan's anti-imperialist ideas. FDR, in particular, was certain that European colonialism was one of the root causes of the recurrent wars in Europe and was determined to do what he could to end the colonial era. Through Donovan, the OSS became one of the main instruments of that attitude and policy, although the fervor with which the policy was prosecuted by OSS officers abroad depended in great measure upon the ethnic origins of the men concerned: White Anglo-Saxon Protestants tended to be much less fervent, for example, than officers of Jewish or Eastern European and Arabian origins.

There were other reasons for the lack of harmony between the OSS SI and Menzies's service. Henry B. Hyde, Donovan's chief of Secret Intelligence in France and, later, Switzerland, was to explain: "OSS owed everything to the British services. Training curricula, communications systems, operating methods, everything—even such technical matters as suitcase wireless sets, one-time pad ciphers, and all manner of devices used by secret services came to us through Menzies's generosity. But then in mid-1943 Menzies and his officers saw the OSS horde pouring in. Some of our men were much less sophisticated than their British counterparts. There was friction when the OSS found it could not do as it wished when it wanted to do, that it was a cog in the great machine, no more. For their part, I think, the British became afraid—afraid of the spread of American influence, afraid of our money, afraid that we would spoil the market for agents. Furthermore, the British in those days were always very sensitive about the U.S. presence in the Empire, in the Balkans, in Scandinavia, and elsewhere, and disliked what we said when we got into those places. Also, one should never forget that Menzies's world was a Babel in those days: Everybody—Americans, Frenchmen, Poles, Yugoslavs, Greeks, Albanians, Rumanians, Hungarians, Bulgarians, and Uncle Tom Cobbley and all—wanted his help and assistance. We were just some more foreigners who wanted to get into Europe at a time when Menzies had penetrated Europe very nicely and wanted nobody there who was not under his control. All these things had their effect on Anglo-American relations, as I was soon to find out."[1]

The reality of Donovan's relationship with the British in the field of secret intelligence was that he did not have, nor was he to get, the right of independent operations into Western Europe from bases in the British Isles, at least until after the invasion. Displaying his usual resourcefulness, he accepted the London situation and began to concentrate his operational resources for operations into Europe from a base over which the British had no control, Algiers. But if he was to succeed in this design, he needed an alliance, either with the Gaullist intelligence services (which were more or less dominated by the British services) or with Giraud's, the Deuxième Bureau.

However, as was often the case in matters French, passionate and sometimes dangerous politics had to be considered by Donovan in attempting to make his alliance with one or both French services, each in violent rivalry with the other. Aware that the Giraudists might not last forever and that the Gaullists were seeking to supplant Giraud in Algiers, Donovan in London looked into the question of an eventual collaboration with Charles de Gaulle's secret service. Donovan was quickly dissuaded by advice from the U.S. Embassy and the U.S. Navy.

The Gaullists had never been popular at the White House or at the State Department, where their leader, General de Gaulle, was regarded as untrustworthy, insecure, and, after the liberation of France, likely to try to impose on the French people a government they had not elected. Neither the British nor the American secret services believed De Gaulle's following was large, and such following as he had was confined mainly to Frenchmen in London, where in early 1943 he had his headquarters. However, his intelligence service, the Bureau Central de Renseignements et d'Action (BCRA), was regarded by Donovan as proficient and valuable.

Commanded by André Dewavrin, alias Colonel Passy, the BCRA's headquarters were at 10 Duke Street, London, and its agents were to be found wherever there were French colonies and in a large number of other places besides. Dewavrin was not, however, regarded as politically acceptable by the State Department; he was believed widely, and probably wrongly, to have been a cagoulard, a "hooded one."

In January 1943, however, he looked more palatable than the Darlanist and Giraudist intelligence leaders in command at Algiers—until there occurred a bizarre incident which became known in the lore of World War II as the Duke Street Murders. Even as WJD took the first cautious, tentative steps toward association with Dewavrin, he found himself compelled to send this warning to Eddy in Algiers:

1. Absolute censorship has been imposed [by the British] on the following, received from London. The utmost secrecy must be maintained regarding this information. 2. In October [1942] an Alsatian named Paul Manuel [sic] left France, and in Lisbon received provisional approval by the Free French and British, for services with the former in London. He is reported to have broken down under examination in England by both the Free French and the British and to have made the following admissions. *a* Manuel was an assumed name. *b* The Germans sent him here to join the Free French, after training him in a school of espionage. *c* His roles in Free French circles were to be those of spy, saboteur and agent provocateur. 3. Reports received from the Free French state that after the departure of his interrogators, the Alsatian committed suicide by means of a slip-noose fashioned from his belt and placed round his neck.[2]

As Donovan was to learn, there may have been more to the incident than this, and if the allegations against Dewavrin were correct, he was no better than a Sicherheitsdienst thug. Inquiry by WJD showed that in the midsummer of 1942 the BCRA had established what would be called "an inquisitorial chamber" in its headquarters at 10 Duke Street, a block of apartments in Mayfair. Alarmed that allies were using "black methods" of interrogation on British territory, the British services instructed the BCRA to stop the practice and shut the chamber down. It was thought this had been done until a Frenchman named Dufour arrived in London, was interrogated by the British authorities, and pronounced "probably okay." He was then handed over to the BCRA for interrogation at 10 Duke Street.

As Dewavrin was to tell WJD, the interrogators formed the impression that "neither the bars [of rank] nor the many decorations which ornamented Dufour's chest were authentic."[3] He was transferred to the Free French detention center at Camberley, Surrey, to await trial on the serious indictment of having assumed the rank of an officer and wearing decorations to which he was not entitled. Dufour escaped, according to De Gaulle personally, with the assistance of the British Secret Intelligence Service, which was really employing him to spy on the BCRA. Dufour then brought a civil action for damages against De Gaulle, alleging that he had been illegally detained and tortured and producing medical evidence of the tortures he said he had received in the Duke Street "inquisitorial chamber." The case was suppressed by the British.

But as Dewavrin continued in a letter to WJD, in the early autumn of 1942 a certain Paul Manoel arrived in Britain in much the same manner as Dufour—from the Vichy Zone, across Spain, into Gibraltar, thence to Britain. The British interviewed Manoel at their interrogation center in the Royal Patriotic School at Battersea, London, and he announced that he wished to join the Free French Forces of General de Gaulle. But, Dewavrin continued, "The British authorities pointed out to us they had some doubts about him and asked us to interrogate him with particular care."[4] Dewavrin's interrogators succeeded in breaking down his cover story, and when Manoel was examined physically, "he revealed two magnificent swastikas tattooed on his arms." He then admitted that he was an officer of the Sicherheitsdienst and, having been left alone in his cell, hanged himself. He was not murdered by his interrogators, as had been alleged, Dewavrin assured WJD. As evidence Dewavrin produced the certificate of an inquest held into the death of Manoel by the Westminster coroner, W. Bentley Purchase:

> On 13th January 1943, and by adjournment thereafter on 2nd February 1943, I held an inquest upon the body of Paul Manoel at Westminster Coroner's Court, Horseferry Road, London, S.W.1.

On 13th January 1943, I made an order under the Emergency Powers (Defence) Act, 1939, S.6, directing that no disclosure of the fact of an inquest or of the evidence in the matter should be made.

On 2nd February 1943, the following verdict was returned:—"Paul Manoel died at Wigmore House, Duke Street, on 9th January 1943, and the cause of his death was asphyxia due to hanging himself by means of certain pieces of fabric taken from his clothing and suspended from a point in the cell at Wigmore House in which he was then being confined, and I do further say that Paul MANOEL did kill himself.

Such a verdict is one of felo de se.

> (s) W. B. Purchase,
> H. M. Coroner,
> Northern District,
> County of London.[5]

Whatever the case was, the existence of this unpleasant incident so soon after the Darlan affair made it impossible for Donovan to set up an association with the Gaullists at that time, even had he been free to do so—and he was not. The matter was being investigated by both the State Department and the Office of Naval Intelligence representatives in London. Moreover, whether Manoel was murdered or not, De Gaulle's regime was ethically not far removed from that of America's enemies. If that became known, and it became known that Donovan was working with the Gaullists, there would be trouble. And that was the last thing he wanted so soon after the Golden Directive.

Donovan moved on to Algiers, resolved to make a pact with the Giraudists.

Donovan arrived in Algiers to talk with Eddy for the first time late in January 1943, after a particularly perilous light from London. Later he would tell how his British aircraft had lost its way after taking off over the Western Approaches. The pilot strayed over the Channel Islands, which had been occupied by the Germans, and the aircraft came under German antiaircraft gunfire. Donovan, who carried a potassium cyanide capsule manufactured for the OSS by the E. R. Squibb pharmaceutical company, in order to kill himself should he fall into German hands, had taken the capsule out of his special container and was prepared to take it if the aircraft was forced down on enemy-occupied territory. That proved unnecessary when the navigator guided the pilot out of danger.[6]

On his arrival at the OSS headquarters at the Villa Magnol, a nineteenth-century Arab palace in the green hills above Algiers Harbor, Donovan began work with Colonel Eddy. His purpose: to prepare the new command for major operations into southern Europe between the Pillars of Hercules and the Golden Horn, and to seal an alliance with the

Giraudist secret service, the Service des Renseignements (SR). From the outset Donovan was faced with serious problems of command. Not the least of the problems was that of Eddy's personality and his relations with the British services.

"You are a superb soldier," Donovan had wired Eddy immediately after Torch, "and you may have any job you want." After much telegraphing, Eddy elected to become chief of the OSS in the Mediterranean, a theater that gave him operational responsibility for Italy, France south of the Loire, Spain, the Mediterranean islands west of Malta, and the new battlefronts of Tunisia and Spanish Morocco.

Colonel William Alfred Eddy, of the U.S. Marine Corps, was exactly the type of man and soldier Donovan admired the most. Born in 1886 at Sidon, Syria, where his parents were American missionaries, Eddy was that rare combination—a man of action and an intellectual. He was a Doctor of Philosophy of Princeton, a Doctor of Laws of St. Lawrence University, a Doctor of Letters of Wooster College. He had been the head of the English Department at Cairo University, where he had learned not to like the British imperial overlords of Egypt. After that he had been professor of English at Dartmouth College and then president of Hobart College. During this time, as exercise for the brain, he had written *Gulliver's Travels: A Critical Study*, he had edited in two volumes the *Oxford Standard Edition of Jonathan Swift*, and in 1932–33 he had written *Samuel Butler's Erewhon*, an analysis of that classical satire on English social and economic injustices. He spoke Arabic and French and was a first-class rifle and pistol shot. Also, he had had an excellent record in World War I, fighting with the Marines at Belleau Wood in France. He had been so badly wounded that for months he was considered a dying man. He had lost a leg, which had been replaced by a wooden contraption of his own design that accounted for his squeaking when he walked.

Eddy had married well and produced four children; he listed himself in *Who's Who* as a Democrat and Episcopalian; and he had volunteered for service in the Marines at the outbreak of the European war, coming to Donovan from Wallace Banta Phillips's K Organization. During Torch he had controlled all clandestine operations laid on to support Robert Murphy's political stratagems, working from an office in the U.S. consulate general, a small but magnificent Arab palace in the Arab quarter of Tangier—where his security precautions had been badly penetrated by a German agent called Francesca Pinto, a Spanish woman who developed the reputation in the OSS for being the loveliest and most amorous charwoman of World War II. The fact that there was a German agent at work in the consulate general was detected by ISOS and reported to Eddy, who promptly removed an American female secretary, leaving

Señora Pinto to continue to rifle filing cabinets and wastepaper baskets until she was finally detected by X-2, Donovan's counterespionage service, long afterward.

As a personality, Eddy was difficult, a man of pronounced likes and dislikes, trusts and distrusts. He drank heavily and was moody; his colleagues believed that his wooden leg gave him great trouble during periods of high humidity. In his new post he was extremely clannish, preferring to work only with the small group he had worked with during Torch and often proving inhospitable to the newcomers flooding out from Washington, especially if they were in Special Operations—Eddy was a Secret Intelligence man, and the often intense rivalry between the two branches was personified in him. It was alleged that he banished unwelcome SO men to the remotest parts of his fiefdom, on tasks for which they had not been trained, keeping his SI men around him. He disliked organizational and office work, and when, as OSS Algiers expanded rapidly after Torch, he was shown an organization and flow chart by a management man out from Washington, he was said to have exclaimed: "Don't ever bring that fucking thing into my office again!" Eddy, who had powerful vocal cords and was a large, tall football player type, rarely minced words.

Eddy was a man in the mold of Lawrence of Arabia, about as chaotic and temperamentally and emotionally unsuited to the work of higher command as Lawrence. Like Lawrence, he was a man of action, liking life best in the souks among his beloved Arabs, eating sheeps' eyes and couscous. Eddy, aware of this, asked Donovan to appoint someone more suited to running a large establishment and to have him chief of operations. Donovan was sympathetic and promised to do something for Eddy at the earliest moment, pointing out that for the moment he was having difficulty in finding management men skilled in the clandestine arts. Thus, Eddy was stuck with his post and alternated between elation and despair. To increase the disadvantages of his being employed as chief OSS Algiers, Eddy disliked the British SIS and its Praetorians and was forever complaining about their interference with his plans.

The principal business before the two Americans was Donovan's plan for post-Torch operations, which he had submitted to the Joint Chiefs on December 3, 1942. Under the plan—which received the approval of both Eisenhower as theater commander and the Joint and Combined Chiefs —Eddy was to command all secret intelligence, special operations, and counterespionage from French West Africa to and including Libya, southern and southwestern Europe, including the Iberian Peninsula and southern France to the Adriatic coast of Italy. The area included Italy, Sicily, Sardinia, Corsica, France, the Canaries, the Cape Verdes, the Azores, the Madeiras, Spanish Morocco, Río de Oro, and Tangier. The program visualized by WJD would have required 450 new personnel at

Algiers, $25,000,000, aircraft, ships, communications centers, and submarines.

But as Donovan pointed out, the program could work only if Eddy made an effort to work with the British services. Was he prepared to do that? Eddy assured Donovan that he would certainly try, claiming nothing but the best relations with the Special Operations Executive, with which the OSS shared a joint operational base code-named Massingham. However, he declared, relations with the British Secret Intelligence Service was another matter. Even the SOE could not get along with the SIS. Eddy claimed that the SIS was forever trying to prevent him from undertaking independent operations, even though he was obtaining the permission of Eisenhower's headquarters.

Eddy pointed out that the British SIS was controlled not by the Combined Chiefs in Washington, as was the OSS, but by the Foreign Office in London, and it remained an instrument of British imperial policy, which paid only lip service to the provisions of the Atlantic Charter. It was an influential organization among the British component within Eisenhower's headquarters and found it relatively simple to inhibit OSS operations. The British component controlled military operations in Tunisia and with them all the means of transportation, including the aircraft necessary to get OSS agents into France. Moreover, Eddy continued, Eisenhower, acting in the interests of Allied unity, was disposed to accept the British point of view in secret operational matters. Therefore, OSS was bound to play second fiddle to the British. That, he said, he resented, but there was nothing he could do about it except protest—and that merely made the problems worse.

Donovan could only agree. Yet because he could not operate from London to his satisfaction, he remained determined to turn OSS Algiers into his main operating base into Europe. Since the British virtually controlled all sea and air transport available for clandestine operations, he and Eddy held long conversations with the representatives of the Giraudist SR, principally Colonel Louis Rivet. A deal was struck: The French would provide submarine transportation for agents and permit the OSS to recruit French agents, in return for a monthly subsidy of francs to a total value of $70,000. The OSS would also provide the French services with parachute and agent training and with radio equipment. It remained to see if this arrangement would work in practice.

Then Donovan and Eddy turned to the question of the OSS command structure. Here again there were serious problems to be met if the organization was to operate satisfactorily. The principal immediate problem concerned Lieutenant Colonel W. Arthur Roseborough, the chief of Secret Intelligence in Algiers.

Roseborough's principal task, if he was to mount successful clandestine operations into southern Europe, was to establish good working relations with Eisenhower's headquarters and the Giraudists. For that task, it might seem, Roseborough was well endowed. Aged forty-two, he had headed the Western European desk of Secret Intelligence in Washington. He was a Rhodes Scholar, an Oxford hurdles blue, and a former legal secretary to Frank Kellogg at the World Court, and before joining the OSS, he had been a lawyer in the Paris office of Sullivan & Cromwell. By political inclination Roseborough was a liberal. He had supported the Spanish Republicans during the Civil War, and now he regarded the Gaullists, *not* the Giraudists, as the true symbols of nascent France. History was to prove him correct and shrewd, but in January 1943 the Giraudists, not the Gaullists, held the political power in Algiers and within the SR, the organization with which Roseborough had to work. However, Roseborough had demonstrated undisguised disgust at Eisenhower's appointment of Darlan as high commissioner, an attitude that led him into serious conflict with Colonel Julius Holmes, an American officer with executive responsibility for some political operations within Eisenhower's command.

It became evident to Donovan that if the OSS were to achieve anything in Algiers in the near future, Roseborough must go. And so he did. In due course he departed for a high Air Force Intelligence appointment in London. Through the first part of 1943 Henry B. Hyde, a young OSS SI officer, had been at work as chief of the French desk in Algiers, under Roseborough's general command. With Roseborough's departure, his French work descended on Hyde's shoulders.

Henry Hyde was twenty-nine and politically and temperamentally more inclined to work with the Giraudist Deuxième Bureau than Roseborough had been, and Hyde was that rarity in intelligence work: the born spymaster. The grandson of the founder of the Equitable Life Company, Hyde was ideal for the post of chief of OSS SI France. His father had been a passionate Francophile and lived for forty-two years in France, rarely returning to the United States. Hyde was educated at the Collège de Normandie in France, Chillon College in Switzerland, Charterhouse in England, the University of Bonn in Germany, Trinity College, Cambridge, and Harvard Law, from which he was graduated in 1939. In due course he married the daughter of a French baron, who was also a prominent conservative senator.

As a result of this educational process, Hyde had developed a Cartesian mind that was rare in American society. Politically he gravitated from mild liberalism common among youthful intellectuals of the thirties to mild rightism, although he was sometimes thought, mistakenly, to be an admirer of the French pretender, the comte de Paris, who was in Algiers at this time, seeking hopelessly to secure his restoration to the throne of France. Hyde knew, as did few Americans, the nuances of French thought and politics of the period. Being by nature what he called a memorialist, he was a fund of extraordinary detail and minutiae about the French governing, political, financial, and administrative classes. Like most *boulevardiers*, he seemed to know everyone who counted, and everyone who counted seemed to know him.

All this made him invaluable to Donovan as the OSS's principal French spymaster in 1943, and the fact that he had been to Charterhouse and Trinity enabled him also to gauge British attitudes and thus to get along with the British rather more successfully than did those endowed with the average Yankee mind. At once Hyde was familiar with the French, the British, and the American minds in Algiers. That capacity was to stand him in excellent stead during his operations into and within France, at Eisenhower's headquarters in the Hôtel St. Georges and the OSS's in the Villa Magnol.

It was not accidental, therefore, that Hyde's earliest contacts in Algiers included Henri d'Astier de la Vigerie and Abbé Cordier, both of whom had been involved in the murder of Darlan and perhaps had instigated it, and both of whom were advocates of a postwar France in which the comte de Paris would be king and De Gaulle would be prime minister. Although D'Astier and Cordier were involved in the affairs of Lemaigre-Dubreuil, Eddy was not prevented from introducing Hyde to them as contact men for the recruitment of agents. Hyde was aware of the politics of the men with whom he was dealing, but he decided that in the absence of anyone else, he had to collaborate with them. At times he seems almost to have admired both Cordier and D'Astier. The former was, Hyde was to write:

> a quiet-looking Benedictine monk, yet capable of great violence, of whom it was said he had strangled several Germans with his own hands. He was also accused of having been the person who persuaded Darlan's youthful assassin to commit the deed. He was a strong and impressive figure in his white robes and he loathed the Germans with a rare passion.

As for D'Astier (whose brother in early 1943 was leader of an important anti-German resistance network of Gaullist persuasion), he was:

> [a] thin, well-bred looking man whose sensitive El Greco-like face belied the fantastic courage he had already shown and showed later in France at the head of his commandos, when he was well over fifty. One of my agents I met through him later on told me he went to Mass every day at six o'clock whether in combat or at home, and that all weapons actually made him nervous. [He was a] fine representative, by his physique and character, of the old aristocratic French families.[7]

From the passionate group that had formed the Chantiers de la Jeunesse and the Corps Franc d'Afrique, therefore, Hyde recruited his first agent organizers for the penetration of France from the south. And whatever their politics, Hyde and his earliest recruits were to become among the most active and the most successful of all OSS agents.

When Hyde became chief of SI France, he had no previous experience of intelligence work of any kind. All he knew about the game came from his three-week course at OSS schools in and around Washington. Hyde explained:

> In blackboard sessions and agent field trips to penetrate our own military installations or aircraft factories, those of us on the intelligence gathering side had been exposed to the solid body of theory and general rules of intelligence work and to a much lesser extent to its practice. We had also learned such specific things as cipher work, "innocent" letter writing, the use of secret inks and concealment of reports in clothes and personal accessories. At the time most of us graduated, classes for agent organizers in secret radio transmissions had not been established. None of us had been trained in plane or boat drops since, until Algiers was opened up, we had no bases from which to work agents into Europe by air or sea. For the same reason we had not acquired background knowledge of local conditions in Nazi Europe or the documents required there by an alleged "man in the street" nor had our Fake Documents Section in Washington really begun to turn out these documents themselves.

Hyde was compelled to fill out his knowledge of operating agents inside Fortress Europe from what he could glean from the British Special Operations Executive and the French and Polish intelligence services in Algiers, the personnel of which were not always cooperative. His principal tutor in clandestinity was a British captain, John de Guelis, now on duty in Algiers after nine months on operations in the Loire Valley. De Guelis was certainly unusually communicative for a British staff agent organizer:

> John de Guelis was called Le Capitaine Jacques since he was half French and spoke the language perfectly. He even felt and acted like a Frenchman when he switched over to the animation and sometimes agitation of the language of Molière. The rest of the time he was quieter like an Englishman and he always looked like one with his big football player's six foot three frame and his deep base [sic] voice. He was a great epicurean, and managed to have better food, in the plush little Algiers apartment where he would meet and entertain his agents, then [sic] the diplomats and the top brass. He also had a stock of good wines the source of which was about the only thing he would never disclose to me. We had dinner together quite often and after the cigars and brandy would talk way into the night. Apart from French wines he loved French ballad singers and in return for his hospitality I discovered a good

source of Piaf records to pay him back with the French atmosphere he loved. I even got for him "Mon Legionnaire," her hit tune of the phony war period when "La Mome" first started her career. He always talked more evocatively when she was on.

Despite the $70,000-a-month subsidy arranged by Donovan in return for SR assistance in the recruitment of agents and the provision of submarine transportation, Hyde found that the SR was not always cooperative. However, through the Hyde family's association with Colonel André Poniatowski, an officer on Giraud's staff with SR connections, early in 1943 Hyde was permitted to recruit a number of able-bodied Frenchmen of military age. Poniatowski insisted that the OSS must engage not in political espionage against France, but only in military espionage against the Germans and the Italian occupying powers. Hyde assured Poniatowski that if he received any political intelligence from any of his agents, he would tear it up—an assurance he claims to have kept.

As a first installment on the Donovan-Rivet accords, Hyde was allowed to recruit three Frenchmen for operations into France in the first half of 1943. These agents were Truc, Truc's radio operator, and one assistant. These men claimed to have left behind in France an operating intelligence chain of some size, and they had offered to turn this organization over to the OSS. That offer was accepted with the agreement of the SR, and Donovan raised no objection to their use more or less immediately.

A number of factors influenced Hyde's decision: The Truc group claimed to be sufficiently well documented to enter France and get through the police and military controls to rejoin their chain. Also, they had had, they claimed, considerable experience in clandestine movements inside occupied France. With only three weeks' training in OSS procedures, therefore, arrangements were made for Truc and his assistant to proceed by U.S. Navy PT boat to a point outside Spanish waters near the port of Málaga, where they were to transfer to a fishing boat owned by friends. The two men would then be landed and work their way across Spain and the Pyrenees into France. There they would meet up with the radio operator, Bollo, at Toulon. Bollo was to be landed at Cape Lardier on the coast of southern France from the French submarine *Casabianca* and then make his way to Toulon by train.

Unhappily the entire operation ended in disaster. Bollo was captured by the French Fascist police soon after his arrival in Toulon, and in the course of the operation he inadvertently led them to an important OSS Special Operations wireless station code-named Mexico. Bollo was then shot by the Germans. As for Truc and his assistant, twenty-four hours after landing on the Spanish coast, they were captured by the Spanish police, jailed, and questioned. Their cover story—that they were escaping from North Africa because of their anti-American activities, in proof of which they produced false police summonses—held. Both men were released eventually and then turned over to the Allied authorities in Gibraltar without having divulged anything of their mission.

As Hyde was to report to Donovan, the unhappy results of the Truc operation showed that "it does not pay, humanly or practically, to send off agents who are not completely prepared," as was the case in the matter of Bollo. Without complete, tested training, missions were usually not worth undertaking at all, but as Donovan would agree, "a self-assured agent, made psychologically and physically secure by reason of complete technical efficiency and unhurried training in an atmosphere of mutual confidence, could overcome any number of odds in the field."[8]

Hyde resolved to put the lessons learned into practice, although it was May 1, 1943, and the OSS still had virtually no agents of its own in France. Hyde was not to be hurried on what was to be code-named Operation Penny Farthing. For Penny Farthing was intended to be the first major penetration by the OSS of Hitler's Fortress Europe.

Early in May 1943 the French Service de Renseignements, conforming to the Donovan-Rivet accords, handed over to Hyde the control of four agents and three radio operators. With these men Hyde intended to form two-man teams, each consisting of an agent organizer, whose job it would be to establish a chain of subagents, and a radio operator. Each of the three teams would be, Hyde intended, sent to each of the three main areas through which an invading army would have to be moved. These areas were the Rhône Valley from Marseilles to Bordeaux, the Route Napoléon from Marseilles to Lyons, and the Provence coast of France from Marseilles to Menton on the Franco-Italian frontier. As the final report on the operation advised Donovan, "In contrast to the hurried atmosphere in which the first three agents had been dispatched, the next mission was not carried out by [Hyde] until three-and-a-half months later."[9]

Hyde's most promising agents—the Penny Farthing men—were acquired through a lunch in April with Dr. Aboulker, one of the group involved in the assassination of Darlan. Hyde was introduced to three men, all of whom had taken part in the coup d'état at Algiers on the night of Torch. Two of the men were experienced radio operators, and the third, Jacques de Rocquefort, code-named Jacques, was a colorless, tubercular-looking former civil servant with excellent connections in the Lyons area—it was of some importance to Hyde's operations that Rocquefort was married to a niece of Édouard Herriot, a former French Socialist prime minister before the war.

After careful assessment of Rocquefort and a radio operator named Mario Marret, alias Toto, Hyde began their training. This included tutoring in the arts and crafts of espionage in hostile territory, German and

French Fascist police methods, American wireless procedures, the use of small arms, parachute training, codes and ciphers, and methods of recruiting and organizing agents in the field. The training phase of Penny Farthing was so exhaustive that neither agent was ready for active service until June 1943.

While Rocquefort and Marret were completing their training, which lasted twelve weeks against the normal three, Hyde began to search for means by which they could be inserted into France. The obvious method would have been by aircraft, but the OSS had no aircraft; the U.S. Army Air Forces declined to provide one; the British clandestine services had aircraft, but all were committed to British operations for some months to come; and the services of the French submarine *Casabianca* were not available. By mid-May 1943, therefore, Hyde found himself completely frustrated, an agent controller with two excellent men ready for service without the means to get them to France. Moreover, he was aware that each day increased the risk that he would lose the men to the Gaullist service, Dewavrin's BCRA, which had begun to recruit in Algiers.

Hyde approached the head of the Special Operations Executive in Algiers, Colonel A. Douglas Dodds-Parker. On the face of it, Dodds-Parker appeared to be the prototypical British imperialist, a man not likely to assist the OSS in an operation unless he had to. He was a product of Winchester ("Manners Maketh Man") and Magdalen College, a former high officer of the Sudan Political Service, and an officer of the Grenadier Guards, and in the future he would be chairman of the British Empire Producers Organization, a Tory Member of Parliament, and a parliamentary undersecretary of state for foreign affairs. Dodds-Parker had taken a New Yorker as a wife—Aileen Coster had been on the staff of the American ambassador in London, John Winant, when they met—and he was one of those rare men in the British secret services who believed that British primacy in world affairs was over and that the answer to the political menaces of the future lay in an alliance of the English-speaking countries.

Hyde found that the Briton was not able to provide an aircraft from Algiers, for all of Dodds-Parker's aircraft were committed to operations for the foreseeable future. But he did agree to give Hyde's problems some thought. He was as good as his word. Here it should be stated that there was sharp rivalry between the British Secret Intelligence Service and the British Special Operations Executive. Each service meddled in the affairs of the other; in enemy territory the SIS had suffered casualties through the activities of the SOE. They were like water and phosphorous; their operations would not mix without conflagration. It was essential to the safety and success of SIS operations that on the territory where it was working there were no bangs, whispers, or killings to cause a German manhunt. On the other hand, it was the job of the SOE to undertake sabotage, subversion, and assassination operations that, being noisy and impossible to conceal, frequently produced the manhunt that made SIS operations difficult, if not impossible.

To limit the chances of SOE operations' embroiling SIS operations, all clandestine undertakings in enemy territory by both agencies and all other secret bodies had to be cleared through a central committee in London, empowered to rule for or against an operation in the European theater of operations. Moreover, there was a strict ruling that the SIS would not engage in sabotage and subversion, which might endanger SOE agents, while the SOE would not undertake intelligence-gathering operations, lest these interfere with or endanger SIS operations.

When Dodds-Parker next saw Hyde, what he had to offer was, in the light of the tensions between the SOE and SIS, the existence of the central committee, and the agreements between the two services, remarkable—the sort of gesture that could get a man fired. In advising Hyde that SOE London could and would provide airlift to France for OSS SI agents from a base in England, Dodds-Parker, the chief Algiers representative of the SOE, was undertaking a secret intelligence operation in contravention of the SOE-SIS agreements. Also, he would be furthering an OSS SI operation when it was Menzies's policy not to do this. Nevertheless, convinced that Anglo-American relations were at least as important as the relations between the SIS and SOE, Dodds-Parker asked Hyde if he would undertake the operation from a British base. Hyde accepted, Dodds-Parker advised him to get himself and his men to England in time for the July moon—most clandestine operations from England were conducted by moonlight, and if for one reason or another an operation could be not be undertaken by one moon, it was almost always held over until the advent of the next.

However, Hyde discovered it was no simple matter to enter England. The British Isles were governed by emergency powers that prohibited the entrance of foreigners, especially Frenchmen, without permission from the security authorities. Anyone who tried to enter (or leave) without permission was liable to arrest and detention, and to make matters worse for Hyde, all Frenchmen entering the country were invariably detained and sent to the Royal Patriotic School at Battersea, London, where they were submitted to prolonged interrogation about their antecedents, their connections in Continental Europe, and their business in England. The purpose of the interrogation was to detect enemy agents endeavoring to enter the country, and such were the British methods at the Royal Patriotic School that the truth about a man was almost always established. What was more, military and security regulations made it impossible for a man simply to step aboard an aircraft at Algiers. Aerial transportation required a formidable set of travel orders and security clearances, which could not easily be acquired.

Dodds-Parker therefore resorted to subterfuge to get Penny Farthing to England. He provided Hyde and his men with British Army officer uniforms and papers representing Hyde as a British captain and Jacques and Toto as second lieutenants; acquired travel orders representing the group as British secret personnel returning to England on urgent business; and provided them with priority air travel in an American transport aircraft. They left Algiers on June 28, 1943, for Marrakech, Morocco, the U.S. Air Transport base, where they boarded a U.S. plane bound for Prestwick, Scotland, then a main point of entry into the British Isles. In traveling by U.S. aircraft, Hyde felt, as he was to advise Donovan, that:

> this fact made up somewhat for our being in the position of having to beg and intrigue to get British transportation for the [flight into France]. We carried suitcases containing the French clothes and accessories, and the radio sets in British kitbags which, like diplomatic couriers, we never left out of our immediate physical presence. I took along my U.S. civilian passport which I thought might come in handy on arriving in Great Britain, so that at least one of us would be properly documented. . . . We anticipated that entering Great Britain would be quite a different matter from leaving North Africa, and we were right.[10]

At Prestwick the Penny Farthing team found themselves in the presence of a "young and pleasant-looking captain on a stool behind a tall desk," checking the passengers' passports and documentation for undesirables. Hyde waited until all the other passengers had been cleared before he approached the captain and asked if they might have a private word together. The captain then took Hyde into a bare office, and Hyde told Donovan:

> . . . I explained to him that I belonged to O.S.S. and that I and my two French "friends" had been sent up by the S.O.E. unit in connection with a mission involving O.S.S. and S.O.E. headquarters in London. I told him that I was to report to Colonel Bruce, the head of the O.S.S. unit in London, and thereafter get in touch with Colonel [Louis] Franck of S.O.E.

The captain was not impressed and "told me right away that we could not proceed to London immediately and he suggested we have breakfast in the airport restaurant and then wait in the lounge." He stated also that "my men should not leave the airport terminal for the moment." Hyde "noticed that he unobtrusively had failed to return my passport." The three OSS men then had "an excellent breakfast of Scotch porridge and American dried eggs," and Hyde was "not dissatisfied with the first moves of getting my and my companions' feet into the British door." He told Rocquefort and Marret that "the British were always a bit 'sticky' about Frenchmen coming into the British Isles and not to be surprised at being a little delayed in getting to London, due to [*sic*] bureaucratic inefficiency."

For the next three days Hyde and his "boys" kicked their heels in the Prestwick lounge and at a local hotel under Royal Air Force guard and knocked a ball about the world-famous Prestwick golf course—an agreeable detention which concealed the fact that the arrival of Hyde and Penny Farthing had caused great perturbation in the highest secret circles in London. Hyde telephoned Bruce at some point, involving OSS London in the affair, for as Hyde deduced correctly, the telephone was "controlled." Hyde explained to Donovan:

I had decided ahead of time in Algiers that my best chance of flying my team out of England would be not to give advance notice to Colonel Bruce of our arrival lest he be forced to instruct us not to come at all. In my conversation with him I would have to feign surprise that he had not been notified of our trip into his theatre and clear up the deception with him, if possible, later on. I followed this plan on the phone with him, gave him our three assumed names and told him outright that it had been arranged with S.O.E. Algiers to get my two charges into France on an S.O.E. plane in . . . August. He told me he would have to take up the matter with S.O.E. and [SIS] and get us down to London if it were possible.

Hyde recorded: "I clearly sensed from his guarded statements and particularly from the tone of his voice that my mission was going to raise serious problems in London" but that Bruce "would be on our side to try and work them out."

Indeed, three services became involved in the question of this "strange Yank and his two Frogs up at Prestwick." Telegrams flew back and forth between three services and their outposts in Algiers and between OSS London and OSS Washington. There were angry telephone calls between the SIS and the SOE. And some thought was given to putting Penny Farthing on a plane returning to Marrakech. Of most of this, Hyde was unknowing, for as he was to report to Donovan, while the teapot tempest brewed in London, he "engaged in the ancient and honorable Scotch game of golf."

On the third day the British security authorities at Prestwick advised Hyde that the Penny Farthing team would be permitted to proceed to London, and they left by air on the fourth. It was evident, however, that Penny Farthing would get no farther on its mission until "matters had been sorted out" in London and that the British still regarded Penny Farthing with suspicions. In London, Hyde reported to Bruce at OSS headquarters in 70 Upper Grosvenor Street, Mayfair. Hyde recorded that encounter respectfully:

[Bruce] turned out to be his usual unruffled and courteous self. I apologized for any embarrassment my mission might have put him to, explained why I had not given him prior notice of our arrival and indicated that while we were determined at all costs to carry out the mission, he should feel free to repudiate me and send us back to North Africa.

Hyde "admitted to some general knowledge of an agreement between [the OSS] and the British not to carry out independent agent operations out of England," claiming with a lawyer's nose for a loophole that his was not the start of an operation, but the last lap of one. Would Penny Farthing be able to proceed to France? Well, announced Bruce:

> our mission was a temporary "cause célèbre" in the highest British intelligence circles and "C," the chief of the British Intelligence Service, was personally going to decide whether the boys could be dropped by an S.O.E. plane or not. For the moment Colonel Bruce had been able to arrange matters so that until "C" made up his mind about them they could live in a hotel but in the continuous company of either myself or a London O.S.S. man. I was also going to have to write up my reports disclosing the real identity and all available vital statistics concerning the boys and their mission which I was going to have to personally defend later before one of the top British Intelligence Service officers.

Clearly the British wanted neither Hyde nor Penny Farthing in the country, and the OSS France intelligence and special operations chiefs in the British capital, Hyde soon discovered, regarded the operation with "very mixed feelings." They felt "our intrusion into their theatre could endanger their liaison relationships with their British counterparts and lessen the chances of their obtaining independence of action." At the same time there were those who believed, as did Donovan, "that the British had to be forced into recognizing our capacities to operate on other than joint missions with the British, and resented their position of tutelage." At that point Hyde was summoned to the headquarters of the British Secret Intelligence Service the coming Sunday afternoon, to discuss the affair with Sir Claude Dansey, the deputy chief of the British SIS, and Dansey's deputy, General Sir James Marshall-Cornwall—a sure sign that the British intended through sheer weight of brass and authority to keep the OSS from operating from the British Isles.

That Sunday, as Hyde was taken to the headquarters at 52 Broadway, just off Parliament Square near the entrance to St. James's Park underground railway station, he was instructed by his escorting officer, William P. Maddox, chief of OSS SI London, that he was "to forget the location of this holy sanctum and never to refer to it among the uninitated then or thereafter." He found the headquarters to be a "five- or six-story dirty red-brick building in Westminster which had been built as an office building and looked as dingily respectable an edifice as any of the buildings around it. I wondered to myself why the British organization had not moved away from an area fairly close to the Houses of Parliament which the Germans had bombed and seemed likely to want to hit again." He was "considerably awed" when he entered the central citadel of one of the six forces thought to rule the world (the others were said to be Buckingham Palace, the White House, the Bank of England, the Federal Reserve Bank, and the Vatican).

Inside the headquarters Hyde was taken up to the fourth floor "in an encaged elevator" and then led down a narrow corridor to a room facing the front of the building. The room was:

> a medium size office containing two old desks facing one another, a Victorian safe and three or four uncomfortable chairs. The desks were completely bare except for "In" and "Out" boxes and one of the two telephones was green. The only decoration on the walls was a pre-1939 map of Europe which, it seemed to me, had undergone somewhat momentous changes in the interim. . . .[It] was in this unostentatious and innocent appearing room, I thought to myself, that so much skulduggery reaching to the highest levels was thought up and directed. Our own chief's offices in Washington, with its up to date situation map on the wall, the large globe lit up from inside, and the brightly colored relief maps on the working desks, gave quite a different impression.

Whatever the reality behind these fanciful thoughts, Hyde was involved in a conspiracy with the Special Operations Executive against the all-powerful Secret Intelligence Service, the object of which was to parachute two Frenchmen who had not been cleared by the SIS into France contrary to all agreements between the SIS, SOE, and OSS. To make matters worse, no matter who had supplied the uniforms, or why, Hyde and his Frenchmen were wearing British Army officers' uniforms, although they were foreigners who had not taken the king's shilling. Moreover, in furthering his schemes, Hyde was collaborating with the SOE, the mere name of which was likely to bring up the choler in the face of any high-ranking SIS officer. Also Hyde had acted in a manner calculated to mislead even his own superior officers. Not surprisingly, therefore, he expected a difficult encounter with Dansey, who had the reputation of disliking Americans in general and the OSS in particular:

> Sir Claude D[ansey] did not keep me waiting long, and it was he who conducted the one and a half hour conference which General [Marshall-Cornwall] only joined for the last half hour. I noticed as [Dansey] came into the room that he was a tall, spare man of about 60 who carried himself with an

air of authority and who looked as though he were used to having his own way. He greeted us politely but with the air of a man who had other things to do on that particularly beautiful July Sunday afternoon. After a few introductory politenesses . . . he got right down to things by asking me "what was all this business about my bringing agents from North Africa to parachute them through S.O.E. from Great Britain?"

Hyde advised Dansey that Dodds-Parker of the SOE in Algiers—the SIS's rivals—had "had no airlift available to us out of Algiers, that the mission was in implementation of the instructions received from the American Assistant G-2 in the Mediterranean Theatre, and that our S.O.E. friends there with whom we shared a base had agreed to assist us out of Great Britain since they could not do so out of North Africa." Hyde noted later:

[A] look of disapproval came over his face at the mention of S.O.E., but he did not articulate his opinion and instead came to the point by saying: "What is it you people think you can accomplish in France that we and the French are not already doing there?" He went on to use what I later learned was his favorite simile to the effect that he was surprised I did not realise that "one rotten apple can spoil a basket of good apples." He made this statement in a rather crotchety tone so there was nothing I could do but politely disagree with him.

Hyde responded "very courteously" that while "the 'more the merrier' was not an intelligence adage," from what he had learned, intelligence networks on enemy territory were being "continuously blown up and good coverage to date did not ensure good coverage three months hence or even tomorrow," a little Yankee impudence that made Hyde's escorting OSS officer stir uneasily in his chair. Hyde continued:

The American command, while very gratified by the intelligence secured from other Allied sources, particularly from [Dansey's] organization, wanted to have its own sources [of intelligence] to check and supplement and possibly replace the existing sources; . . . in view of the very large contribution in men and material made by the Americans to the prosecution of the war, the U.S. command felt it was only fair and proper that they should have their own sources; and . . . thanks to what we had learned in schools staffed in certain instances by [Dansey's] officers, we had acquired considerable theoretical knowledge augmented by practical up to date experience obtained from S.O.E. personnel in Algiers. I continued by stating that undoubtedly "one rotten apple could spoil a basketful of good ones" but that pre-supposed our apple was bad, which was not the case in my opinion. Finally I stressed that our apple was under explicit instructions under no circumstances to make contact at any time with the already established fruits.

Here, then, was the OSS-SIS disenchantment in a nutshell. Dansey was evidently impressed by the statements of this somewhat pushy American interloper, for he did not continue with his argument that France was so "intensively covered as not to justify further missions there." Instead, he concentrated at length on the qualifications of Hyde's agents. Hyde reported to Donovan:

> I suppose that his purpose in having me do so was to ascertain how much we knew about our business and I deliberately elaborated on the care and foresight I had lavished on my team. One of Sir Claude's interesting reservations which emerged from the questions about the funds I was giving these agents was based on his fear that we would be over-generous in providing financial means to the men. I realized that apart from the poor security of agents living too well in occupied countries, Sir Claude had in the back of his mind that the Almighty Dollar might lure away available talent from the British Intelligence Service. I gave [Dansey] . . . the true figure [the agents] were starting off with and this appeared to be in line with the procedure in his service.

At that point General Marshall-Cornwall strode into the room, exuding that special air of effortless superiority peculiar to officers of the Imperial General Staff who had spent a lifetime serving God, king, and country on the frontiers of the Empire. He intervened with many questions concerning Hyde's several misdemeanors and crimes, declaring that he was not "able to understand why we had been allowed to proceed to Great Britain in view of the agreement arrived at with O.S.S. prohibiting independent O.S.S. operations out of London." That, replied Hyde "rather evasively," was "a matter which was beyond my compass and about which I knew very little."

The meeting now settled down to frosty questions and nimble answers between old and young lions. Hyde, however, carried himself well, and as he had been briefed so to do by Bruce beforehand, in describing the personnel and activities of the OSS at Algiers, Hyde dropped the name Ted Ryan, a grandson of Thomas Fortune Ryan, one of the great American financiers at the turn of the century. Bruce had predicted that mention of the name Thomas Fortune Ryan was likely to temper Dansey's attitude, and he was correct. Hyde related to Donovan: "This led to Colonel Dansey telling us about the period in his life when he had worked for Thomas Fortune Ryan in British West Africa, which appeared to evoke pleasant recollections for him." However, Dansey was not sufficiently defrosted to permit Penny Farthing to go to France.

Three days passed before the liaison officer with the SIS brought news, and then it was favorable. Hyde communicated to Donovan that Dansey " had decided under all the circumstances to allow his mission to proceed as planned." Hyde took the Penny Farthing team to a leading French restaurant, L'Ecu d'Or, for a celebration dinner. As Hyde put it: "For me it was really the celebration of a great occasion, the culmination of four months work and the bringing off of a plot to force the hand of the British to get my first mission into France."

Whatever the truth, Donovan could now state in Washington and Algiers that he had independent agents in place in France—a useful fact when Congress was deciding how much to give the OSS in appropriations and when the Joint Chiefs were making up their minds concerning manpower allotments.

Lastly, of course, OSS London could no longer pester Dansey with requests for permission to insert independent OSS agents into Western Europe. Dansey could turn around and state accurately enough that it already had independent agents in Western Europe.

Such, then, was the state of secret service politics on the eve of Penny Farthing's departure. Through much neat footwork everybody's ambition and susceptibilities had been served, as were the needs of the strategic direction of the war. Shortly, in the charge of SOE London, the men of Penny Farthing left for the Royal Air Force parachute training school at Ringway, Manchester, to complete their training—in Algiers they had been trained in the techniques of parachuting from the side door of a Dakota, not the belly hole of a Halifax. Then they were advised that the mission would be flown by the Royal Air Force from its secret clandestine operations base at Tempsford west of Cambridge on July 17, 1943.

Hyde later recounted for Donovan what occurred in those last days before departure:

> The London OSS Battle Order specialist ran Jacques [de Rocquefort] and Mario [Marret] through the organization of the German Army and the identification of enemy units in the field. Most important of all perhaps they were both checked out by one of our London communications officers on their double transposition system of coding and decoding and in the slurring of certain Morse letters at the end of their messages. All the clothes and personal effects they were taking to France were double checked for British laundry marks, matches or small British coins being in their pockets prior to their being packed in their suitcases. . . . Now that we had some definite departure date, we could also compose personal letters to . . . Jacques and Mario from a wife and girl friend respectively to fill out their wallets and make them look less bare. I used for the actual writing of these letters two native born French girls on the OSS London staff who, coincidentally, came from the same diverse social backgrounds as Jacques and Mario. This meant that their respective handwritings and style fitted perfectly the fictitious writers. I also obtained . . . 1943 season Lyon tramway tickets and cut out from some of his Lyon newspapers one or two articles on sports events for Mario's

wallet, and a wedding and birth announcement from the social page for Jacques.

Hyde spent scores of hours on the minutiae of building up his agents' covers as worthy citizens of Lyons who had lived in and around that city throughout their lives and had never been away from it. They were ready for the first U.S. clandestine intelligence mission by parachute into occupied France by the evening of July 16, 1943, but since none of the Penny Farthing party felt like it, there was no farewell dinner. Instead, they saw a dull movie called *Mission to Moscow*. Hyde collected from an OSS safe their wallets, documents, and cyanide pills—to enable them to commit suicide if they were captured—and then they were driven out of London up the Great North Road.

After about forty miles in the Humber staff car they found themselves "before the imposing gates of an English country estate, and the driver showed his pass to the sentries on guard." At the Tudor mansion they were met by their escorting officer, "a handsome red-haired [woman] who just missed being attractive," Hyde recorded ungallantly, "because of her well-bred British stiffness." She was a member of the First Aid Nursing Yeomanry (FANY), half of whose personnel were in fact engaged on secret duties. She took Penny Farthing up to a room on the second floor, and Hyde explained:

> Her job was to be an escorting officer, friend, and, if necessary, confidante to the departing agents on their last afternoon before leaving England. It was a good thing to have a pretty girl around, the British had learned, at potentially tense moments since it was distracting and most men were ashamed to appear afraid or even concerned in the company of the opposite sex.

Jacques and Toto entered the room as British private soldiers (they were still in their British uniforms) and emerged as gentlemen of Lyons. Their suits, shirts, ties, underclothes, bus tickets, letters, money, official documents, travel permits, identity cards, laundry marks, razors, blades, toothpaste, brushes, combs, brilliantine, eau de cologne—all were exactly what Frenchmen of the class represented by their documentation would be carrying. And to calm the men—a British agent who had been in and out of France many times was to record, "To be dropped in Occupied France was not a great adventure, nor was it an exciting pastime—it was a deadly struggle against a ruthless and savage enemy, most often with death as a reward"[11]—Hyde took his agents for a walk across the flat fields where the children of Alfred the Great had slain the Danish king of East Anglia, Guthrum III.

Hyde described the last supper for Donovan, who had visited Gibraltar Farm—Tempsford's code name—only a few weeks before:

There were about thirty agents going off that night. At dinner, they all sat around a long table with their conducting officer next to each team, a few FANYs scattered among them and the colonel [commanding the base] at the head of the table. There was steak as the main course, which was not so easy to come by in England, an *apéritif*, and half a bottle of Algerian wine for each of them. The agent teams talked among themselves or to the persons assigned to them and there was not much general conversation. At the end of the meal the colonel made a touching little speech about which he obviously felt strongly. He stated that the British greatly respected these patriots present who were going back to their homelands to fight the enemy in a most important manner. He was convinced that they had and would be given all the means to accomplish their various assignments successfully. He ended up by wishing them every success on their brave and valuable undertakings. A bald and paunchy middle aged French agent who looked like a shopkeeper and must have been all of 55 got up in response and toasted the King and S.O.E. A rather homely young French girl, who looked so Jewish that Jacques had not understood her going back to France, stood up and started to sing the Marseillaise. The rest of us got to our feet and joined in. This was as moving as anything else that evening because it was so badly sung and brought tears to all the French eyes. Then the Belgian national anthem was sung lustily by the few Belgians who were going off that night.[12]

The dinner over, the Penny Farthing team and the other agents at the table went off to collect their kits and then prepare to go out to the airfield, where the four-engine Halifaxes of the 183rd Squadron waited in the gathering dusk. Hyde recorded:

We had about an hour after dinner before having to go off to the airport where the boys would put on their parachute camouflage suits and the chutes themselves. On checking through their clothes once more for incriminating objects I found a sixpence in Jacques' trouser pockets and a packet of Bryant & May's English matches in Mario's coat pocket and confiscated these small but deadly giveaways as souvenirs. From then on their cigarettes and matches were removed and it was agreed that I and later on the despatcher would dole out and light cigarettes for them. . . .

[When all the final work was done, Jacques] expressed his appreciation of what I had done for them and said he was leaving confident that I would take care of those he and Mario left behind and in my ability to direct them in the field. Mario said he felt the same way about it. This was my first spoken compliment from my first agents and it made me choke up a little like the first avowals of love for me did. We then joked about our meeting in France when Lyon would be liberated and about the big party we would have the first evening we got together there.

At 8:55 P.M. exactly, Harriet, the escorting officer, came into the room and announced it was time to leave for the airfield. Hyde continued:

As we walked out of the front hall the colonel was standing on the step outside the door, smoking a pipe. He came over to the boys, shook them by the hand, and wished them Godspeed. I checked the two packages in the back of the station wagon to be sure we had the right ones and found the word "Marshmallow"—code name for the operation—painted in white on both of them. Though it was getting dark, the car windows all had drawn shades. It reminded me of well-to-do old English ladies riding shielded from the outside world in their Rolls Royces [*sic*]. In our case the shades were good security for the agents who might have been conspicuous to unfriendly eyes riding in a military vehicle in their civilian clothes. It also protected the departure station and airport for the departing agents not to be able to describe exactly the location from which they flew off in case they were caught and thoroughly worked over as to where the "nest" was. On the ten minute drive to the airport with Miss Harriet, the boys talked of the atmosphere and the procedures of the departure station which had considerably impressed them. . . . They bantered with her about the organizational capacity of the famous "intelligence service brittanique [*sic*]."

The station wagon drove them out to a Nissen hut on the edge of Tempsford airfield. There Hyde and the Penny Farthing team spent an hour checking equipment, weapons, documents, clothing. And then:

The Scots despatcher popped his head through the door to tell us to proceed to the plane. It was a blackout departure with only the lights of the vehicle lighting the way across the forty feet or so of grass to the Halifax. Jacques and I led the way, and Mario and Miss Harriet followed. . . . The despatcher was at the foot of the ladder leading into the belly of plane. He told me I could not come on board because they were a little behind schedule. He would take good care of the men and see that I got a report when the plane got back about six hours later. He started to lift up Jacques's chute so as not to damage it . . . and I just had time to put my arms on his two shoulders and kiss him quickly on both cheeks the way the French do on solemn occasions. . . . I likewise embraced Mario who was smiling and who cockily shouted from the steps that he would be on the air on August 1 as scheduled.

The Halifax door banged shut. The engines, which had been idling, began to roar as the captain put on power. The aircraft disappeared into the darkness, burning no lights. Hyde and Miss Harriet heard the engines run up to takeoff power. There was a flash of green light from the control tower. The aircraft began to roar down the runway, displaying no lights, and in a few moments its black hulk was airborne over the long dark fields of sodden kale.

At that moment Donovan and Hyde were in business as spymasters with "assets" in Europe.

21

The First Star

Having started his operations into Europe, Donovan returned to Washington, to find himself confronted with fresh crises. General Marshall's hopes that the Golden Directive would produce peace in the Washington intelligence and political warfare community soon proved to be illusory. The director of the Office of War Information, Elmer Davis, denounced the directive, which placed propaganda under the Joint Chiefs' jurisdiction, as a violation of the President's principle that propaganda be under civilian control. That assertion reopened old disputes between the propagandists of the OWI and OSS on the boundaries between the two organizations. In a twinkling, a fresh controversy had broken out and, because it involved publicists, was more vociferous than any of its predecessors.

FDR became involved when both sides repeatedly leaked stories about the brawl to the press and radio, thereby violating his rule that no war emergency agencies were to make any statements to the press without permission from the executive branch. When Davis, a peacetime CBS news analyst whose midwestern twang was known to radio listeners throughout America, announced that he would resign if the President did not repudiate the Golden Directive and that most of the OWI staff would resign with him, Roosevelt told him "in the most forceful language" that "he wanted OWI to carry out all the responsibilities assigned to it by the Executive Order."[1]

But the President's intervention did not have the effect of quelling the disturbance. To the contrary, it led to a widening of the dispute between the OSS and OWI, which became so noisy that Secretary of War Henry Stimson remarked he felt like an "innocent bystander in the case of an attempt by a procession of the Ancient and Honorable Order of Hibernians and a procession of Orangemen to pass each other on the same street."[2]

By February 18, 1943, FDR was so exasperated with what seemed to be the inability of Donovan and Davis to settle the dispute themselves that he lunched with General Strong, G-2 of the Army, who had survived the threats to have him court-martialed. After lunch Roosevelt called Strong and Davis into his office and announced that he wanted *all* propaganda run as a civilian activity under Davis—and he told Strong he wanted the OSS transferred from Donovan's to Strong's control.

For good measure, Roosevelt told Strong to draft the transfer order for his signature. Strong lost no time in carrying out the President's order and getting it over to General Marshall for Marshall's approval. The CIA historian recorded:

> Here it must be noted that never had Roosevelt come so close to deserting Donovan as he had in this winter of 1943. In some circles the suspicion was that Roosevelt had concluded that Donovan and OSS had grown too powerful and needed to be abolished. There was also some suspicion that FDR looked upon OSS as largely Republican in coloration and therefore counted it among his political foes. Certainly abolition was the intended and inescapable effect of Strong's memorandum to Marshall.[3]

What now happened is far from clear, but it is known that on February 20, 1943, General McNarney called Donovan to his office and offered him a general's star if he would accept the transfer of the OSS to Strong's department and if he would hand over all propaganda operations to the Office of War Information. Donovan's reaction to this astounding proposition was, Doering recalled, to exhibit "a state of fury such as I had never seen before, and was never to see again. It was controlled fury, but it was real fury, for he felt that the President had betrayed him."[4]

That night Donovan called a staff meeting and announced that it would be impossible for him or the OSS to work under Strong and that he intended to resign. He called another meeting the next day, a Sunday, in order to write his letter of resignation, to advise the Joint Chiefs of the critical situation at hand, and to make a recommendation about a successor.

Donovan's letter of resignation, a document reflecting the degree of his distress, has survived:

> Dear Mr. President,
>
> I have just learned of your instruction [to Strong]. . . . No one could have

convinced me that you would come to that decision upon statements that are untrue and without affording me an opportunity to state the facts.

As you know, the thing I most desired was to take command of a division, and I gave up that opportunity in 1941 in order to do this job. The chief strength of this organization has come from its independence as an arm of the Joint Chiefs of Staff, under your support. The net result of the action now taken will be to dissipate and destroy [the OSS].

In any event, in view of the position which you have taken, I feel that there is no longer any useful purpose for me to serve, and I hope you will accept my resignation.[5]

Donovan scrawled some revision on the letter and then gave it to James Murphy, to have it prepared for the White House. As Murphy was leaving Donovan, he saw Doering. The two agreed the letter should not be sent to the White House until Donovan had been advised formally that the President had signed the order transferring the OSS to Strong's control. That Murphy did, placing the letter in a file—where it remained for the next thirty-nine years.

In that decision, Doering and Murphy were wise, for at the Joint Chiefs' meeting on February 23, 1943, it was decided to go to Donovan's rescue. Admiral Richard D. Edwards denounced the OWI as "a nuisance" while, by contrast, "Colonel Donovan produces valuable results."[6] Admiral Horne declared that "the War and Navy Departments got less help from O.W.I. than from any other government agency" and questioned why "the Joint Chiefs should submit to Mr. Davis' views." He also questioned why the OSS should be turned over to the War Department and thought that it should remain with the Joint Chiefs.

The admirals were backed by the most powerful of their kind, Roosevelt's Chief of Staff, Admiral William D. Leahy, who agreed the OSS should remain with the Joint Chiefs. He counseled that Roosevelt had not yet "reached a definite decision in this matter" and the Joint Chiefs ought to tell him exactly what they wanted. He also declared that he wanted a statement "safeguarding the status and duties of OSS." The generals, too, backed the admirals and the OSS.

The Joint Chiefs then rewrote Strong's draft order, giving some bones to the OWI but keeping the OSS with the JCS, and on March 6, 1943, having wound its way through the Washington labyrinth, and as the capital reverberated with rumors that Donovan, Knox, Stimson, Hull, and others were resigning on the issue, Roosevelt rewrote Leahy's redraft of Strong's draft order.

Because Donovan wanted to know whether "we were guitar players to be put in the baggage of somebody or something," Roosevelt issued some orders to have the Golden Directive slightly revised. With the revision what was called the terrific storm passed. Nobody resigned, and for the first time since Pearl Harbor, fifteen months before, the existence of the Donovan organization was no longer in doubt. After a year of bureaucratic squabbles of such complexity that it took a CIA historian nearly 300 pages of closely packed analysis to get it sorted out, Donovan had obtained for the OSS a secure position within the United States High Command and could concentrate upon fighting the real enemy—the Axis.

Roosevelt showed his contrition by inviting the Donovans to a Service of Intercession at St. John's Church in Lafayette Square, a service which, as FDR explained in a letter, had proved to be "a source of help and inspiration" and which he liked to attend "with certain friends." Noting that FDR had used the term "certain friends," Donovan accepted the invitation "with pleasure."[7]

On that Levantine note, Donovan and FDR resumed their strange relationship. And shortly, as part of the Joint Chiefs' process of "militarizing" the OSS, Donovan was recalled to the colors in the rank of brigadier general.

He began to draw wages and a per diem—$8,400 basic salary, $600 a year marriage allowance, $10 per diem, $120 a month housing allowance, $10,000 life insurance—about what he had been earning each fortnight in his law firm. Nevertheless, the salary was welcome after three years of service without pay, for WJD was beginning to feel an uncomfortable pinch in his fortunes and, recently, had been compelled to write to a friend calling in an $8,000 loan.

He made a hurried visit to Wetzel's in New York, "Military, Mufti, Sporting Tailors and Breeches Maker to the General Staff," and ordered a general's uniform costing $506.46, his coat bearing the single silver star of his new rank. On his breast was the light blue ribbon with thirteen white stars of the Medal of Honor. Ex-Trooper Donovan of the Silk Stocking Boys had become General Donovan of the Office of the Joint Chiefs of Staff. "He loved that gold [sic] on his shoulders," recalled Judge Owen McGivern, formerly one of New York's leading judges, in 1982 counsel to Donovan Leisure Newton & Irvine, and one of WJD's young assistants in the OSS. "He loved that gold on his shoulders as much as anything he had ever achieved."[8]

But his elevation to the exalted rank of general by no means ended the Washington turbulence that attended the emergence of Donovan and the OSS as rivals in the field of foreign intelligence. While he was trying to form and deploy the OSS for war, he was also fighting a running battle with the State Department.

The State Department's antipathy for the Donovan organization stemmed largely from the belief that it existed to usurp the department's traditional function: reporting to and advising the President upon foreign affairs. But there were other elements to the state of extreme hostility that existed between the two organizations between 1941 and 1943. The principal element was the department's fear that, if its men were accorded diplomatic cover, the OSS would bring the U.S. Foreign and Consular services into disrepute with the governments to which they were accredited. And there were other, lesser complaints—that OSS men drew larger salaries and larger expense accounts than diplomats and consuls, and the like.

The frictions were to be encountered at every U.S. foreign post and at every level of officialdom, but nowhere were they were more severe than in Spain. There Ambassador Carlton J. H. Hayes, a Catholic intellectual, had been given the vital task of keeping Spain neutral. For some time before Torch Hayes had shown an intense dislike for OSS men in general, asserting in telegrams to the secretary of state, Cordell Hull, that they were amateurish, clumsy, extravagant, ignorant, and more likely to drag America into a war with Spain than any German agent. He had succeeded in getting rid of one chief representative with a stinging telegram that was probably unprecedented, even in the American bureaucracy:

> . . . the Financial Attaché [the OSS man's cover] here is showing increasing signs of fundamental mental instability, the result of which is to make his presence here a real menace to our security. He distributes money like a drunken sailor; is dangerously indiscreet, and in various ways advertises his special status. Complaints about his indiscretions have been sent to London by his British colleagues [for secret and diplomatic service Spain was a British theater of operations], who refuse to cooperate with him further. I must request that he be asked to return home at once for consultation and that he not be allowed to engage in such work either here or elsewhere.[9]

With the departure of the chief representative there followed an extended period when neither the State Department nor Hayes would permit a replacement to enter Spain, and for a time State even refused to handle OSS telegrams. During that period Hayes evidently kept a dossier on the conduct of other men in Spain, which he unleashed on Washington on March 8, 1943, in what must have been one of the longest telegrams of the war. It was wholly devoted to proving that diplomacy, not secret service, would keep Spain neutral, that if the Donovan agency were allowed to remain in Spain, serious consequences would ensue for the Grand Alliance.

Hayes's principal complaint was that in violation of Roosevelt's Torch pledge of noninterference in Spainish affairs, Donovan's agents were developing associations with the Basques, that powerful clan with septs on both the Spanish and French sides of the Pyrenees that generally had supported the Republicans during the Civil War. Often leftist or Marxist, the Basques wanted no part of Franco's Spain, or anybody else's Spain for that matter, and with a combination of medieval guile and violence that seemed to threaten Franco with permanent guerrilla warfare, sought restoration of the autonomy they had enjoyed under the Republicans.

In addition, Hayes had a large number of complaints about the conduct of OSS officers in Spain. The financial attaché, for example, "became quite a man-about-town. . . . He gave lavish tips to waiters in restaurants, and ran up large bills at tailoring establishments and shirtmakers. He imported large quantities of foodstuffs and merchandise, particularly silk stockings, which he offered freely inside and outside the Embassy."[10] Among those to whom he had presented silk stockings was, Hayes announced with indignation, Madame Franco.

That was not the end of the agent's indiscretions. "He had two automobiles at his disposal, both bearing diplomatic tags. One he lent frequently to a Spanish industrialist, and the other he lent freely to a lady friend. He threw money around like a drunken sailor, even offering it to Spaniards of good family."

As time went by, the agent "gave increasing evidence of a lack of emotional balance. He had fits of impatience and violence, when he would curse at the top of his voice so that it was heard throughout the Embassy. . . . [We] feared that the man was out of his head and would commit acts of personal violence." At the same time "the Embassy had frequent reports that [the agent] was being watched and shadowed by the Spanish police." Also, Hayes had evidence that the agent had tried to bribe the U.S. military attaché's secretary, and "How many other American employees he tried to engage secretly, I can not say, but I do know that he was very generous in offering funds out of his unlimited resources to consuls, consular clerks, et cetera."

Pages of complaints and allegations followed. Hayes concluded: "Altogether, I have little or no confidence in the [Donovan agency] in Spain. . . . [A] few are persons of considerable ability, conscientiousness, and judgment, but the majority are woefully lacking in qualifications for the exacting work they are expected to do." The agency "undoubtedly has excellent facilities for obtaining certain types of information, since it has (1) unlimited funds, (2) adequate transportation, and (3) excellent cover which permits [its staff] to travel freely over the country, investigating petroleum and industrial installations, talk with a variety of persons, and observe a vast deal." However, among the agents who sent in the bulk of the information was "not a single person with any military background or training, and there is not a single person in the organization in a position to give adequate directives to the other members of the organization concerning the kind of information most important from a military point of view." Nor had any of the agents "given any evidence of any political sense or background."

Hayes recommended strongly therefore that the agency in Spain be dissolved, all except its most competent personnel being returned to Washington. Those who remained should be placed under the command of the military attaché, Colonel William Hohenthal, whom Hayes thought a "competent, intelligent, cooperative officer."

Hayes's telegram was handled by Assistant Secretary Adolf Berle, who had shown himself to be no friend of Donovan, and his first step reflected that relationship: He sent a copy to the JCS, where it arrived only days after the Joint Chiefs had issued the Golden Directive. No doubt Berle intended to reinforce Strong's case and to make trouble for Donovan. His covering letter pointed out that Donovan had reapplied to send in a new chief representative, H. Gregory Thomas, but that the department would not agree until the Joint Chiefs had made an "expression of views," and that it was:

> appropriate to note that the ambassador, on a number of previous occasions, has . . . indicated that the presence in Spain of Intelligence men who were not under close and careful direction, or who were inexpert, has been a source of concern to him in the conduct of the very important subject of Spanish-American relations in a delicate and crucial time.[11]

With Donovan at that time just fresh from one of the worst crises of his career, in which Roosevelt had almost handed the OSS over to Strong, the President's Chief of Staff, Admiral Leahy, who was also Chairman of the Joint Chiefs, on April 8, 1943, ordered Donovan to "prepare a memorandum giving a categorical answer to the allegations made by the Spanish ambassador regarding OSS activities in Spain." Also, Donovan was ordered to be present the following day—April 9—in Room 240 of the Public Health Building, where the Joint Chiefs had offices, "to discuss this and allied OSS matters."[12]

Donovan personally presented his defense against Ambassador Hayes's charges at a special meeting of the Joint Chiefs on April 9, 1943. Present were Admiral Leahy, Admiral Ernest J. King, the Chief of Naval Operations, General Marshall for the Army, and General H. H. Arnold for the Army Air Forces.

Donovan's intention was to show that the situation in Spain was not the fault of his agency but the consequences of America's failure to recruit, train, and equip for clandestine warfare before the outbreak of hostilities; that many of the problems in Spain arose from the speed with which he had had to recruit, train, and send his men abroad to meet the emergencies of war; and that other problems arose from the State Department's view, shared by Ambassador Hayes, that the OSS was usurping the Foreign Service's functions. At the outset Donovan declared that Spain had been his "greatest difficulty" and was "the one so-called neutral country where we have failed to establish a firm basis of confidence and a mutually satisfactory working arrangement with the ambassador."[13] He went on: "Although the intelligence material from that country is of great value, we recognize that it could be improved both in content and volume had there been better relations between our organization and Mr. Hayes." Much of the trouble was "a question of personalities rather than procedures" and the difficulties could be overcome immediately if Hayes would admit the OSS's new chief representative, H. Gregory Thomas, for "both the State Department and ourselves believe [Thomas] has both the qualities and personality to correct the present differences."

But, Donovan declared, there was a "more serious aspect of the situation than any criticism of our work or any clash of personalities." That lay in the "evident attitude of the Ambassador that in the calculation of risks he deems it more important to forgo the preparation of adequate communications and organization of resistance groups in the event of Spain's joining the Axis." It was "for the Joint Chiefs of Staff to say which danger is paramount."

As persuasive as Donovan's arguments were, his defense of the OSS was not good enough to avoid a censure. On April 10, 1943, the Joint Chiefs replied to the State Department's complaints, sending a copy to Donovan and instructing Donovan to regard the reply, especially its last paragraph, "in the nature of a Directive." The paragraph stated:

> The Chiefs of Staff are sympathetic to Ambassador Hayes in the trouble he has been given by poorly selected representatives of OSS. They have given instructions that all representatives whose conduct causes embarrassment to the Ambassador or to other officials of the Embassy be summarily withdrawn. They are hopeful that with the arrival of Mr. Thomas in Spain such incidents as those which prompted Ambassador Hayes' protests will be eliminated.[14]

Donovan had received the first censure of his military career.

22

The Balkan Plan

After six months' bitter fighting through the Tunisian mountains, the British First Army entered Tunis, the capital, on May 7, 1943. Shortly afterward the German commander of the Italo-German army group surrendered. The fruits of the victory were very great, materially, psychologically, and strategically.

Although the campaign had cost the Allied armies 70,341 casualties (including 10,290 dead and 21,363 missing), the Italo-German armies had suffered 155,000 casualties during the fighting and surrendered a further 240,000. In the entire North African campaign from 1940 onward they had lost almost 1,000,000 men.

The Allies now controlled North Africa from the Atlantic to the Red Sea, and from their bases at Algiers and Cairo they threatened the southern coast of Europe from the Pillars of Hercules to the Golden Horn, forcing the Germans and the Italians to maintain very large garrisons between those two points—garrisons they could not afford to spare from operations in Russia and in the west. Airfields along the African coast would now permit long-range heavy-bomber missions deep into Fortress Europe, creating another front in the air—which, when coupled with the bombing campaign from England, would compel Hitler to maintain 1,000,000 German soldiers inside Europe, away from the land fronts, doing nothing but provide antiaircraft defense.

Important new bases could be established from which to conduct antisubmarine warfare in areas of the Atlantic where, until now, the U-boats had been safe; the opening of the Mediterranean meant that Allied convoys would no longer have to go around South Africa in order to get supplies to the Russian, Arabian, Indian, and Asian fronts, thus freeing 4,000,000 or 5,000,000 tons of shipping each year for other tasks—and victory would depend on shipping.

Also, the Axis defeats at El Alamein, Stalingrad, and Tunis had left Hitler unable to take the initiative anywhere except in local operations. Thus, strategic control of the war had passed to the Grand Alliance. As important, the American instruments for the making of war had grown in experience and self-confidence through the brutalities of the Tunisian campaign.

In all these triumphs the Grand Alliance owed much to Donovan, for while no single person could or did decide strategy, he had remained almost the sole protagonist of the southern strategy within the U.S. General Staff—Marshall and Eisenhower, for example, had continued to insist that Germany could be defeated only when Allied armies crossed the English Channel and joined battle with the Wehrmacht in France and Western Europe.

At last light at Algiers Harbor on July 9, 1943, as the U.S. command ship *Samuel Chase* was casting off to take her place in the assault convoys forming for the invasion of Sicily, the process of leaving port was suddenly disturbed by a command from the bridge to prepare to receive a visitor. Lieutenant David Donovan, aide to Admiral John L. Hall, the commander of Task Force 81 carrying the 1st "Big Red One" Infantry Division, looked aft and saw a short, portly man with snow white hair—his father—hastening along the weather deck in combat cap, combat overalls, and combat boots. A few minutes later WJD and his aide Ray Kellogg were on the bridge of the *Samuel Chase*, which then cast off.

There had long been a good deal of speculation at the law firm about the relationship between Donovan and his son. It was expected that David Donovan would become a lawyer and then join the firm as a partner, eventually heading it. But David was not interested in the law, and when he told his father that he wished to study agriculture and then become a farmer, there were ructions, which, however, had not lasted long. When Donovan became FDR's intelligence master, there was talk in the agency that it would not be long before David Donovan joined his father. Again, that was not to be, for as David Donovan explained later, "I was not interested in joining OSS, and I never wanted to trade on father's prominence, so to speak." David went off to enlist in the Navy, was rejected once because of poor eyesight, applied again, and was this time accepted for the assault landing branch of the Navy—the branch responsible for transporting and placing the Army on a hostile shore. Nor was David in any way as ambitious as his father. While his father was engaged in matters of grand strategy, high politics, the destruction of enemy governments, and the fomentation of national insurrections against the Axis, David had learned how to handle an assault landing craft. And by the time his father became head of the largest branch of the Joint Chiefs, David had been graduated to the command of a fleet tug—a highly dangerous job in which he was responsible for taking in tow burning, sinking, or otherwise crippled warships and bringing them into port for repair or salvage. But for the moment Donovan father and son were on the *Samuel Chase,* bound for the beaches of Gela, Sicily, in what was to be the U.S. Army's first assault on Fortress Europe—the second major step in the Arcadia plan.

With the *Samuel Chase* packed with staff and assault troops, it was impossible to find Donovan a berth in Officers' Country, although General Clift Andrus, the Big Red One's artillery commander, offered him his cabin. Donovan refused, saying that Andrus was going to need his sleep and he would get a bedroll and bunk out on the weather deck. "That he did," David remembered, "even when a forty-knot gale of wind got up with heavy seas, rain, lightning." His father "loved this sort of thing—generals, admirals, troops, convoys, escort ships darting about, the lash of the guns." He "loved war more than law."[1]

David did not inquire into what his father was doing there or how he had got permission from the commander in chief of the expedition, General Sir Harold Alexander, to join the assault force. The presumption was that he was there "looking for business—looking for customers for OSS wares." But WJD must have been well aware that the rules of his association with the British in ISOS absolutely forbade anyone with knowledge of the existence of that source of intelligence from entering combat areas, where he might be captured and compelled to talk. And although no doubt Donovan felt sure of himself, he was closer to great danger than he knew: Before many hours were out, one of his companions, Lieutenant Colonel Guido Pantaleoni, a young lawyer who was in OSS Secret Intelligence and whose wife, Helenka, was a close friend of Ruth's, was to vanish without trace.

The son of rich Italian immigrants in St. Louis, Pantaleoni had gone to Sicily to establish wireless-equipped agents' chains behind the Italo-German lines. Despite orders not to enter enemy territory himself, he put Sicilian peasants' garb over his uniform. Carrying a small suitcase transceiver and an agents' cipher machine, he hired two peasants with an oxcart and passed into enemy territory at a point where the front line was fluid, probably in the sector of the Hermann Göring Division, one of the roughest units of the Wehrmacht.

Pantaleoni was not seen or heard of again. He was carrying some gold and a good deal of Italian currency, and it was assumed he was captured and executed. If this was so, his killers were not found, and neither was the gold, the money, or the equipment. Nor was any attempt made by the enemy to use the cipher or the transceiver, a fact that suggested he might have been killed by Sicilian peasants for the money he was carrying. It was assumed that he was buried in a common grave, for neither his corpse nor his grave was found. Guido Pantaleoni, one of WJD's brightest young men, had simply vanished off the face of the earth.[2]

None of this deterred Donovan. As he explained to those who questioned the wisdom of his hazarding himself on the battlefield, he felt that he was no chairborne general but a fighting man who met customers, got ideas, and refreshed himself through combat. Menzies did not agree and asked the Chief of the Imperial General Staff, General Sir Alan Brooke, to write to Marshall. That resulted in instructions that Donovan was to stay away from beachheads in the future, yet despite the terms of his warrant as a general officer, his promise to obey the President and his superior generals, that instruction was not effective—Donovan took part in two more assault landings that year.

Yet if it was a customer Donovan was looking for, he certainly ensnared General George S. Patton, the commander of the U.S. Seventh Army in Sicily. H-Hour came at 2:45 A.M. on July 10, 1943. WJD went ashore six hours later and was thus able to tell Marshall, when the Chief of Staff confronted him with Brooke's complaint, that he had not taken part in the assault; all that had happened was that he had gone along for the ride with the task force carrying the floating reserve and the follow-up forces —a statement that was absolutely true in legal terms. But what he did not state was that when he landed, the Hermann Göring Division was putting up a violent counterattack that was knocking the stuffing out of the combat commands of Donovan's old friend General Theodore Roosevelt, Jr. Patton was ashore near the town of Gela, and they had a K ration lunch together. During that lunch, WJD later recalled, "Patton leaned back and roared heartily—'You know, Bill, there are two things in life that I love to do—fucking and fighting!' " Donovan replied: " 'Yes, George, and in that order, too' "—a very rare example of Donovan's appreciating locker-room humor, for he was extremely prudish in personal matters and careful in his speech.[3] Yet the exchange had importance. It was not, perhaps, drawing room, nor was the remark fumed oak, but it was the sort of exchange that is not forgotten, and from that moment Patton became Donovan's staunchest supporter among the army commanders.

Donovan left Sicily for the Château Frontenac at Quebec, where FDR, Churchill, and the Combined Chiefs were to meet for the first great conference on grand strategy since Arcadia just after Pearl Harbor. When Donovan arrived, he found the conference deadlocked in fierce dispute between Field Marshal Brooke and General Marshall, about next moves. Brooke argued for an invasion of Italy, Marshall for a cross-Channel invasion immediately. In the middle of the conference came the news that with Mussolini just overthrown and having been replaced by Marshal Pietro Badoglio, the Italians wished to surrender. That news clarified the issues greatly, and the decision was taken to invade Italy, the principal purpose being to draw German divisions away from the Russian and French fronts. Donovan, too, saw the advantages of the new situation. He knew Badoglio—the Italian had stayed with him in Buffalo during Prohibition and WJD had stayed with Badoglio in Ethiopia in 1936. As news came into the château that Badoglio's representatives had arrived in Lisbon with armistice proposals, WJD found his opportunity to present a plan that had been taking shape for some time—what he called "A Proposal to Accentuate Our Present Subversive Efforts in the Balkans."[4]

The premise of WJD's plan—which was his most ambitious so far—was that "The anticipated collapse of Italy intensifies the fears of the Balkans [sic] ruling class that the Axis will be defeated and that Soviet Europe will dominate Eastern Europe." That being the case, "we propose to capitalize on those fears, and in agreement with Great Britain and the U.S.S.R. to bring to bear upon Bulgaria, Rumania and Hungary certain subversive pressures which may induce those countries to withdraw from the war, or at least to cause difficulties for the Axis." Yugoslavia and Greece were not in Donovan's mind when he wrote this paper, but they came to be included in the plan.

As an illustration of what he had in mind, Donovan outlined what was called the K Project, in which he proposed to "send to Cairo and Istanbul an agent of Bulgarian origin, now a naturalized American citizen," a man who was "the principal private banker in Bulgaria," and a man of "great wealth and ability." This man was "intimately connected with King Boris, Queen Joanna [of Bulgaria], high ranking officers of the Bulgarian Army, the Archbishop and other powerful personalities" and was prepared to "procure Bulgaria's withdrawal from the Axis."

Donovan's scheme revived the memories of those present who recalled that in World War I Bulgaria's defection had led to the crumbling of the German alliance and heralded Germany's collapse, and those present had visions of history's repeating itself to the advantage of the Allies. That prospect, combined with Hitler's predicament as a result of the collapse of Italy, made the Combined Chiefs accept Donovan's paper more readily than they might have done, and on September 7, 1943, to Donovan's delight and no doubt to his surprise, the Joint Chiefs advised him his proposal had been accepted. The only stricture was that Donovan's agents must "show preference among resistance groups or prospective successor governments only on the basis of their willingness to cooperate, and without regard to their . . . political programs." In other words, WJD could subvert both the left and the right, provided that the subversion was to be used against Hitler, not to seize internal power. The stricture was to become of some importance to Donovan later on.[5]

Scarcely able to believe that he had been given a directive so large, so open to so many interpretations, and applicable to so many countries, WJD hastened back to Washington to prepare for yet another trip overseas, this time to Cairo to launch his new plan. What Donovan knew, but what was still secret to all but a few in the OSS, was that the Combined Chiefs had sanctioned his foray into the Balkans because it suited the deception strategy evolved at Quebec: While the Allies prepared in England and the Mediterranean to invade Europe through northeastern and southern France, the Allies were to give the appearance of intending to invade through the Balkans. The plan, Zeppelin, was based on Allied knowledge of German misconceptions, that Churchill favored a Balkan invasion in World War II, as he had in World I. The object of Zeppelin: to force Hitler to defend Fortress Europe everywhere so that on D-Day he would be not be strong enough at the point of actual attack to resist effectively. Zeppelin was the modern application of the Duke of Wellington's reply to Blücher before Waterloo about what his strategy and tactics were to be when they met Napoleon's army: "Sir, my strategy is one against ten, my tactics ten against one."

Donovan knew well the strategic importance of his campaign in the Balkans in helping force the dispersion of the Wehrmacht before the main invasion of Europe. No task was more important. It was a task in which the success or failure of any one of the operations he launched would not really be important, except to those taking part. What mattered was the fiction. It was a stratagem that was not likely to be understood and applauded in Washington, except by the military scientists, and indeed, even years later people would say, "Why did Bill Donovan spend so much time in the Balkans? We didn't intend to land there?" Well, he was pursuing the main task.

Donovan was now facing the trickiest period of his existence. The slightest mistake might ruin Zeppelin and result in the Germans' "reading the stratagem in reverse," thereby divining the truth about Allied intentions for Neptune. At the same time there was Washington's demand for success, success, and yet more success, and all that success entailed for WJD's own ambitions for his service. There were the British and the French to consider, as well as national and his own reputations. But the prospect was actual triumph—victory in World War II—on a scale not hitherto visualized by generals.

Donovan arrived in Cairo on or about September 13, 1943, to set in motion his Balkan plan, his mood much like that of Christ come to cleanse the temple. He relieved the OSS commanding officer, Colonel Gustav Guenther, and then fired everyone ahead of the young supply officer, Major John Toulmin, in peacetime an executive vice-president of the First National City Bank of Boston. He made Toulmin chief of OSS

Cairo, thus completing one of the most rapid promotions in OSS history: In January 1943 Toulmin had been a civilian, in June a captain in the Army, in August the supply major at Cairo, and now in September lieutenant colonel and chief of a large, expanding OSS base. The reason for the promotion: Donovan knew something about Toulmin and liked the way he handled himself, for Toulmin possessed that combination of charm, efficiency, resourcefulness, and daring Donovan admired. With his new team in place Donovan began his operations to "burn the Balkans." A central organization in those operations was the Cereus chain at Istanbul.

When Donovan became coordinator of information in July 1941, one of his earliest recruits was a Republican party associate, Lanning Macfarland of Winnetka, Illinois, an executive of the Northern Trust, one of the leading savings and loan banks in the Midwest, as COI chief representative in Turkey. There was much delay in getting Macfarland out to Turkey, owing wholly to the bureaucratic warfare in Washington during the formation of the COI and the OSS. When Donovan first proposed Macfarland to Adolf Berle in December 1942, Berle refused to grant him diplomatic cover because, he said, "The discovery by the Turkish Government that the Foreign Service was being used as a shield for undercover intelligence could not but have the most unfortunate results."[6]

At that rejection, Donovan approached the director of lend-lease, Harry Hopkins, and although Hopkins was no friend of either Donovan or the OSS, he granted Macfarland lend-lease credentials in Turkey. Even so, as a result of passport, transportation, and accreditation problems with the State Department, the European war was half over before the Macfarland mission arrived in Turkey on May 2, 1943.

Macfarland's mission at first consisted of two other men: Archibald Frederick Coleman, a journalist who had been recruited into Wallace B. Phillips's K Organization and then entered the COI when Phillips brought his unit over from Naval Intelligence in 1941. Coleman worked in Turkey as a correspondent for the *Saturday Evening Post*. The other man was Jerome Sperling, an American archaeologist who had worked for the Turkish government. Macfarland, who alone knew of Donovan's connection with Leverkühn, and Coleman set to work to create the first American secret organization in Turkey, an organization called Cereus, a genus of cactus found in the American West that produced nocturnal flowers. All members of the organization were given the names of flowers as code names, Coleman becoming Snapdragon.

From the start, it was evident that the twin capitals of Turkey, Istanbul and Ankara, were no place for innocents. All the world's intelligence services maintained outposts in Turkey, especially at Istanbul, the chief seaport, the commercial and financial center, the terminus of the Orient

Express from Paris and the Baghdad Express, and the see of the patriarch of the Greek Orthodox Church, of a Latin rite patriarch of the Roman Catholic Church, and of a patriarch of the Armenian Church, and the site of Jewish, Protestant, and Muslim institutions.

Both the Allied and the Axis diplomatic and intelligence services were at work to drag Turkey and its doughty army into the war, while the Turkish intelligence services were vigilant and efficient in protecting Turkey's neutrality. And, so it was said, on every street corner there was a man who would sell his mother for 50 Turkish pounds, the Hagia Sophia mosque for 100. To increase the dangers of entrapment and disaster, before the war Istanbul had been a main point of arrival for the flood of racial, religious, and political refugees leaving Germany. Many of them had settled in Turkey, where large numbers worked as spies and in occupations associated with intelligence services—radio, forgery, illegal currency transfers, smuggling, burglary, special weapons manufacture, thuggery. A number of the best informants proved to be masterful at fabricating intelligence that was almost always convincing and almost always untrue.

To add to the problems of an intelligence officer in Turkey, especially one with little formal training, all the powers used Istanbul to plant deceptions, produced usually by the nimblest brains, which could find their way into official and press dispatches and so influence the policy of the target country. For Istanbul was a dissembler's paradise, and the ablest liars lived handsomely on the proceeds of that lively craft. Certainly Istanbul was very different from Winnetka, for as Macfarland and Coleman (Sperling never became involved in the events that engulfed the Cereus organization) were to discover, friends were almost always enemies and enemies were sometimes friends.

Soon after their arrival in that bewildering place, Macfarland appointed Coleman what the latter called "director of a separate, under-cover unit designed to penetrate Germany, Czechoslovakia, Austria and Hungary."[7] In that work he reported only to Macfarland and enjoyed considerable independence, plodding about Istanbul, "looking for color and stories," while in reality he was establishing his home and espionage headquarters at Babek, a village some eight miles up the Bosporus from Pera, a small town on the Asian side of the Golden Horn. That establishment was "used as a conference room, office, training center upon occasion, personal living quarters, and it was equipped with photographic and communications laboratory." Coleman also turned it into something of a fortress, for, he advised Donovan afterward, "The place was heavily armed and under guard 24 hours a day continuously."

At the same time Coleman had a safe house—a place where he could live and work and to which he could retreat if the Turks or anyone else discovered the existence of the Babek establishment—in a small office

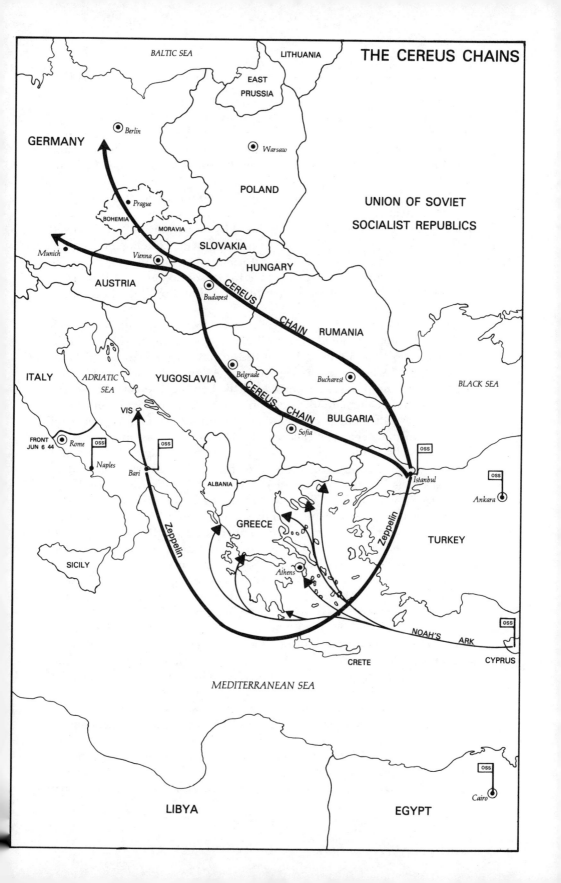

block on the waterfront under the Galata Bridge, on the fringes of the Old City. But as events were soon to show, Coleman was not safe anywhere. Despite his rather elaborate precautions, it was not long before the Istanbul intelligence community knew who he was, where he lived and worked, and began the process of—intellectually speaking—cuckolding him.

The main components of the Cereus organization were two. The Rose chain was headed by an American oilman long resident in Turkey, A. V. Walker. The Dogwood chain was headed by a Czech, who had also lived in Turkey for many years, having been with a British intelligence organization and the U.S. Office of War Information before joining the OSS. Macfarland was principally responsible for Rose, Coleman for Dogwood, with Macfarland carrying executive responsibility for all OSS activity in Turkey.

Coleman established commercial cover for Dogwood, the Czech founding a company called Vestern Elektrik, registering it with the Turkish Fiscal Office, and paying business and payroll taxes to the Turkish government. Its headquarters were on the Asian side of Istanbul, opposite the customs house. Vestern Elektrik became the safe house for Cereus, and as Coleman advised Donovan in his final report of operations: "The staff employees including interpreters, stenographers and general assistants received salaries. Intelligence sources and agents received no salary and only rarely expense accounts." Almost all staff and agents were Germans, Austrians, Czechs, or Hungarians, "and they worked for us because of anti-Nazi or pro-Democratic convictions."

Cereus appears to have been well structured and well financed, with various revolving and personal funds totaling about $500,000 annually. The central, dominating figure in the entire affair was Dogwood himself. His real name is not in the Donovan papers, it has never been revealed anywhere, and he may have died suddenly and mysteriously.

The extent to which Dogwood was assisted in his complex endeavors was never really established, although they were investigated exhaustively later on Donovan's orders, but he did have a number of assistants whose identities became known to the OSS. They were "elderly well-connected individuals resident in Istanbul," including "the president of an Istanbul firm, an Austrian businessman (in radio), a rich and idle Austrian with many social connections in his home country, a German professor of economics—friend of Franz von Papen, the German ambassador in Turkey—another German professor with widespread connections among German Junker families, and a Hungarian nobleman—manager of an American oil firm in Istanbul."

Through these and the many unknown members of the Cereus organization, Coleman continued, Dogwood had contacts in four countries— Germany, Austria, Hungary, and Bulgaria. One of his principal associates was code-named Trillium, that most attractive of wild flowers, which, being said to contain an aphrodisiac, was also called wake-robin. He was the Hungarian military attaché in Turkey, Lieutenant Colonel Otto von Hatz.

Just before Christmas 1943, while Donovan was in Cairo, there arrived in Istanbul the bearer of one of Germany's most illustrious names, Count Helmuth von Moltke, whom Donovan had met in Berlin before the war through Paul Leverkühn, now chief of the Abwehr in Istanbul. Moltke carried a document Donovan would call Plan Herman. The title indicated its importance: "Exposé on the Readiness of a Powerful German Group to Prepare and Assist Allied Military Operations against Nazi Germany."[8]

Count Helmuth von Moltke was the third man to bear that name. The first was the field marshal who defeated France in the Franco-Prussian War, the second was the Chief of the German General Staff at the outbreak of World War I, and the third, who had inherited their titles and estates, was presently engaged in a revolution against Hitler. In his late thirties, Moltke was involved in Canaris's schemes to overthrow Hitler. Moltke's group of co-conspirators was known as the Kreisau Circle, its members being Social Democrats, anti-Nazi officers and civil servants, clergymen, trade unionists, aristocrats, and socially prominent students who, numbering about twenty, were determined opponents of Hitler and representatives of the surviving social and political conscience of Germany. All were anxious for an end to the war with England and America, but they were not, so far as the Project George in New York could tell, prepared to make a similar accommodation with the Soviet Union.

Donovan's files—compiled by George—added other dimensions to the portrait of Moltke. As WJD advised Cordell Hull, the secretary of state, on November 2, 1943, Moltke was a member of the Inner Temple in London as well as of the German bar. His mother was a British subject, the former Dorothy Innes of South Africa, whose family had been associated closely with that of the South African prime minister, world statesman, and close friend of Winston Churchill, Field Marshal Jan Christiaan Smuts. Through his marriage Moltke was related to the Schroeder family of merchant bankers in London, and a brother, an architect, was thought to be serving in the American armed forces. Financially Moltke was not regarded as a wealthy man, although he did live in considerable style at Kreisau. Politically he was, George advised:

Thoroughly Democratic and Liberal; interested in history and politics; outspokenly anti-Nazi; went out of his way to avoid contact with the Nazis and their organizations and made only such concessions as were unavoidable so long as he lived in Germany. He frequently considered leaving Germany but could not make up his mind. Despite his title, he is by nature and inclination anything but a "Prussian," "Junker," or reactionary. Thoroughly European-minded.[9]

He was "well-read and well-educated," "Very quiet and reserved, [with a] strong sense of decency, justice and fairness," and "everyone who knows him agrees about his integrity, his intelligence." In consequence, Donovan felt that Moltke's "close international connections and his genuinely cooperative attitude might be useful in the reconstruction period." Up to the outbreak of war "It was the general opinion that he would risk more than the average German since the Nazis would have hesitated at the time to arrest a man with such a high-sounding name." He was "by conviction anti-Russian and a strong sympathizer with the Anglo-Saxon world."

Moltke's cover at Istanbul had been arranged for him by the Abwehr: He was attached to Papen's staff to examine legal questions for the German Supreme Command, the Oberkommando der Wehrmacht (OKW), concerning Turkish neutrality, and presumably the paper he carried had been approved by Canaris. That document, which was received by Coleman and relayed by him to WJD, reviewed the background and standing of the German opposition groups known to Moltke. One group was in the officers' corps, and the other among senior civil servants, and both were divided into two wings: those oriented toward the West and those toward the East. Of the two, the eastern group was the stronger because of the "strong and traditional conviction of a community of interests between the two mutually complementary powers, Germany and Russia," that had led to the "historical cooperation between Prussia and the Russian monarchy, and between the German Republic and Soviet Russia in the Rapallo Period (1924), when the Reichswehr and the Red Army concluded a far-reaching understanding regarding military collaboration and reciprocal training facilities."[10] Those historical bonds had been reinforced in the present war "by the deep impression wrought by the power and resilience of the Red Army and the competence of its command."

The western group, though numerically weaker, comprised "many key men in the military and civil service hierarchies, including officers of all ranks, and key members of the [OKW]." Furthermore, it was in "close touch with the Catholic bishops and the Protestant Confessional Church, leading circles of the former labor unions and workmen's organizations, as well as influential men of industry and intellectuals." The western group was seeking what Moltke called "a practical basis for effectual collaboration with the Anglo-Saxon Allies."

Moltke, who represented the western group, then presented what he called "Conditions of Collaboration with the Allies." His group recognized that the "Unequivocal military defeat and occupation of Germany" was a "moral and political necessity," and it was also convinced of the justification for the Allied demand for unconditional surrender. It realized also the "untimeliness" of any "discussions of peace terms before this surrender has been accomplished." In short, Moltke's paper accented FDR's dictum that the only terms that would be proffered or accepted would be those of unconditional surrender—an acceptance that was a remarkable departure from all other peace feelers received by the Allies until then.

However, as Moltke continued, the group's "Anglo-Saxon sympathies result from a conviction of the fundamental unity of aims regarding the future organization of human relations which exists between them and the responsible statesmen on the Allied side, and the realization that in view of the natural convergence of interests between post-Nazi Germany and the other democractic nations there must of necessity result a fruitful collaboration between them." Democratic Germans "see in this unity of purpose a far safer guarantee of a status of equality after the War than any formal assurances by the Allies at the present time could give them, provided such assurances were forthcoming."

Continuing what were the first sensible and practical proposals for peace that had been received by any power from any group within Germany until that time, Moltke turned to the ticklish question of Russia. Here he declared that the "important condition for the success of the plan" was the "continuance of an unbroken Eastern front" running no farther west than the line Tilsit–Lemberg. If such a line could be held, the count believed, "Such a situation would justify before the national consciousness radical decisions in the West as the only means of forestalling the overpowering threat from the East."

If that condition was accepted, the western group was "ready to realize a planned military cooperation with the Allies on the largest possible scale, provided that exploitation of the military information, resources, and authority at the Group's disposal is combined with an all-out military effort by the Allies in such a manner as to make prompt and decisive effort on a broad front a practical certainty." And Moltke went on to assure WJD: "This victory over Hitler, followed by Allied occupation of all Germany in the shortest possible time, would at one strike so transform the political situation as to set free the real voice of Germany, which would acclaim the action of the Group as a bold act of true patriots. . . ."

But, he warned, should Allied operations to occupy Germany not be pressed through with the required vigor, military power, and determination, then "any assistance by the Group would not only fail to settle the issue of the War, but would in addition help to create a new 'stab-in-the-back' legend, as well as compromise before the action, and render ineffectual for the future, the patriots who made the attempt." There was "no doubt that half-measures would damage the cause rather than promote it, and the Group is not prepared to lend a hand in any collaboration with limited aims."

Having established the political principle of collaboration between the Schwarze Kappelle and the Allies, Moltke revealed what he had in mind militarily. Dwelling upon the Second Front, as the Allied invasion of Europe from British bases through northern France was called, Moltke declared: "If it is decided to create the Second Front in the West by an unsparing all-out effort, and follow it up with overwhelming force to the goal of total occupation of Germany . . . the Group is ready to support the Allied effort with all its strength and all the important resources at its disposal"—an astounding offer by the political standards of the times.

To that end, the group would "after proper agreement and preparation be ready to despatch a high officer to a specified Allied territory by plane as their fully empowered, informed, and equipped plenipotentiary charged with coordinating the plans of collaboration with the Allied High Command." The only qualification Moltke made to this astounding proposal was: "The readiness of a sufficient number of intact units of the Wehrmacht to follow up the orders given under the Group's operational plan, and cooperate with the Allies, could only be counted upon with a sufficient degree of certainty if the above conditions are fulfilled." But if the Allies did not press their campaign with sufficient vigor, "there would be a grave danger that the orders and operations agreed upon by the commanders and staffs belonging to the Group would at the decisive moment fail to materialize for lack of support, or be executed only with great friction."

While Moltke said nothing about what the group intended to do with Hitler, the National Socialist administration and government, and the Schutzstaffel (SS) which gave the regime its physical grip on the Reich, he did state that "simultaneously with the Allied landing a provisional anti-Nazi Government would be formed which would take over all non-military tasks resulting from the collaboration with the Allies and the political upheaval that would accompany it." The composition of the provisional government would be determined in advance. It may be assumed, therefore, that the group would arrest Hitler and his administration and hold them for trial for crimes against humanity—provided Hitler and the Nazis were not rescued during the civil war that would follow inevitably upon the group's action.

In his next point, Moltke delivered a warning: "The Group, which comprises personages belonging to the most diverse liberal and democratic parties and schools of thought, regards the possibility of the bolshevication [sic] of Germany through the rise of a national communism as the deadliest imminent danger to Germany and the European family of nations." It was therefore "determined to counter this threat by all possible means, and to prevent, in particular, the conclusion of the War through the victory of the Red Army, followed by a Russian occupation of Germany before the arrival of the Anglo-Saxon armies." At the same time the group recognized that it must not "antagonize the strong pro-Russian circles in Germany" but "rally them in a constructive effort and win them over." What it had to avoid "at all costs" was "development of a situation which would lay a democratic government open to the reproach of placing foreign interests above national concerns, and unify against this Government the forces of nationalism, communism and Russophily"—vital if there was not to be a three-way civil war.

Moltke came to his last point. He recommended that the "initial Headquarters" of the "democratic counter-Government would under the postulated circumstances best be South Germany, perhaps Austria." He requested, therefore, that the Allies not "subject the civilian population of this territorial basis" to "indiscriminate air attack" because "experience teaches that bombed-out populations are so exhausted and absorbed by the effort of providing for their bare survival and subsistence that they are out of play so far as revolutionary action is concerned."

Before and during the war there had been several proposals from leading Germans for an anti-Hitler, anti-Soviet coalition with the Anglo-American powers. But none of the proposals so far had contemplated the form that the postrevolutionary German government, politics, and society should take. Almost all had been, in reality, no more than proposals from Canaris to Menzies and Donovan, usually conjointly, for combined conspiracy against Hitler, with little regard for what would occur when the Führer had been liquidated.

Moltke's proposal was very different: He and his principals advocated combined military and political collaboration, and even if Donovan and Menzies had done no more than use it for the purposes of eliminating Hitler, then it warranted close study. Moltke's principal weakness lay in the proposal's anti-Soviet and anti-Communist postulations, but unless the Russians were acquainted with the paper, there was no way of telling whether such plans as Moltke's would be acceptable to them. Nor did the plan take into account the attitude of those powerful elements within Anglo-American society that wished to see the two juggernauts clawing each other to pieces, leaving England and America to reshape humanity in their own image and their own clay.

Sadly for Moltke, Plan Herman did not evoke the attention he wished and perhaps it deserved. It reached the U.S. ambassador in Turkey, Alexander Kirk, through Cereus, and Kirk rejected it, as he wrote to his military attaché, General Richard D. Tindall, "on my own responsibility without consulting anyone."[11] His decision was based not upon any doubt concerning the sincerity of Moltke, whom he had known when he was counselor at the American Embassy in Berlin in 1939, but:

solely on my conviction that the war must end by the military defeat of the German armed forces and not by any dickering on our part with factions within Germany which might entail greater present risks and more serious eventual complications for the United Nations than the problematical advantages would justify. Unconditional surrender is and should remain our slogan and, from my knowledge of the Germans, I fear that any talk with the factions within the country would create the impression that we would be satisfied with something short of that requisite.

With that statement, Kirk asked Tindall to give Moltke his reply: "I would always be glad to see you but I do not see any good purpose would be served by our meeting now as it is my personal conviction that nothing short of the unconditional surrender of the German armed forces will terminate the war in Europe." Thus, Moltke's plan was not transmitted to the State Department for formal consideration.

However, Donovan received a copy from the OSS chief in Turkey, Lanning Macfarland. Since he could see merit in the plan, if only in that through Moltke he might be able to get OSS agents into the Reich, a matter on his mind at the time, he gave it some circulation. Donovan sent the plan to the Joint Chiefs with a covering note that he was "personally acquainted with certain members of this group" and knew them to be "sympathetic to the British and to the Americans."[12] He said he had been "assured by those competent to know" that the group did exist as Moltke had described it, but its weakness "lies in its loose organization, its lack of integration with the great mass of the people, and its failure of proof as to any political strength or ability to carry out the plan."

Donovan assessed the two main points as pivoting upon "two conditions (a) It accepts military defeat and occupation by as well as surrender to the American British Allies," but it was "activated by the fear of Russian invasion," and "(b) The exposé mentions the Tilsit–Lemberg Line as the point where the Russian advance must be stopped as an important condition for the success of the plan." That would mean "that the part to be occupied by British-American troops would include not only all of Germany but also a great part of Poland." This would "seem to show the intention of the Hermann [sic] Group to keep the Russian Army far away from the original German border." The only "fair interpretation" was "to consider it as an anti-Russian proposal."

It was evident to him therefore that the Herman group saw "only one of two alternatives: (a) to negotiate with Russia to prevent an American-British invasion, or (b) to appeal to the American-British forces to prevent a Russian invasion." Moltke sought to "adopt the second alternative."

With these words, the plan was dead so far as Donovan was concerned, and indeed, it made no progress through the Joint Chiefs. As a man, perhaps, Donovan would have liked to come to terms with Moltke, as he would have liked to do with Canaris. An alliance with both would certainly have simplified Donovan's ambition to get OSS men into Germany and operate against the Sicherheitsdienst on its home ground. But as a servant of a state and a member of an alliance with the declared war aim of the unconditional surrender of Germany and the extirpation of German militarism once and for all, plainly nothing could be done without causing a fundamental disturbance within the Grand Alliance—a disturbance that might prove extremely serious, for, it was well understood, the only circumstance in which Hitler could win World War II would be if the alliance collapsed.

Moltke was not to survive much longer. Somebody within the OSS's Cereus organization in Turkey betrayed him to the Sicherheitsdienst. Although Moltke had tentatively agreed to return to Istanbul in January 1944 for further conversations, on his return to Germany he was arrested, and in due course, despite Donovan's efforts through intermediaries to parley for his life, Moltke was found guilty of high treason and was executed on the "Black Widow"—the guillotine at Plötzensee Jail in Berlin.

There was some deadly nightshade in the Cereus.

23

The Morde Incident

While Donovan was in Cairo on his project to detach the Balkan satellites from the Axis, there occurred what was perhaps the most mysterious—and politically dangerous—secret American diplomatic operation of World War II. The M Project, as it was called, resembled the Thomsen affair shortly before Pearl Harbor. There is clear evidence that Donovan and the OSS were involved. But what is impossible to resolve was this question: Who gave Donovan and the OSS orders to undertake the operation?

The Morde case began in July 1943, when Lieutenant Colonel Paul West arrived at Cairo as OSS chief of operations, bringing with him an acquaintance, Theodore A. Morde, then thirty-two. Morde was no stranger to Cairo, having been there as a secret agent first of U.S. Military Intelligence, then of the COI. He transferred to the Office of War Information for a short time before he resigned to become a personal assistant to the ambassador, Alexander Kirk. By profession Morde was an explorer, a journalist, and a well-known prewar cruise lecturer of New Bedford, Massachusetts, who had studied at Brown University. He came back to Cairo in 1943 as Middle East representative of the *Reader's Digest* —which may or may not have been a genuine appointment.

Soon after his arrival Morde saw Colonel Gustav Guenther, OSS chief in Cairo, and placed before him what was, even by the standards of those times, an astonishing project. He had come out to Cairo in order to persuade the German ambassador to Turkey, Franz von Papen, to organize a revolution against Hitler and hand the Führer over to the Allies.

In explanation, Morde revealed that he had made a study of Papen's career, and had concluded that he was not a Nazi. Papen had been a member of the German General Staff and of the Catholic Church, both of which were opposed to the National Socialist party in Germany. The notion that he was a Nazi had been created largely by accident and British propaganda.

Morde, who evidently knew his German politics, pointed out that Papen, a member of the Catholic Center party in the Prussian Parliament, had been appointed chancellor of Germany by President Paul von Hindenburg to stop Hitler from becoming chancellor. Far from assisting Hitler to become chancellor, Papen had opposed him, and Hitler had succeeded only when Papen had failed to keep together the coalition of parties by which he held office. There was some evidence, Morde went on, that Hitler had marked Papen for assassination during the Night of the Long Knives of June 1934, in which Hitler had failed only because Papen had been warned. If Papen had helped Hitler seize Austria during the Anschluss of 1938, that was no crime in Germany, for most Germans and Austrians welcomed the establishment of the Greater German Reich.

While Morde's statements were true, they were simplistic, reflecting little of the intricacies of Papen's association with Hitler and the Nazis. Yet even when Papen appeared before the Allied war crimes tribunal at Nuremberg after the war, he was acquitted of the charges that he had conspired at world dominion with the Nazis. Moreover, a jail sentence of eight years imposed by a German denazification court was found to be unjust and rescinded. Thus, two courts found themselves on weak ground regarding Papen's Nazism.

In any case, Guenther appears to have had orders from someone very highly placed to facilitate Morde's journey to Turkey. The operation also appears to have had the backing of General Patrick Hurley, Roosevelt's special representative to China, in Cairo at that time. Morde saw Hurley and claimed later that Hurley was so enthusiastic about the project that, like Guenther, he wanted to drop everything he was doing and accompany Morde to Turkey. Also, although Toulmin, chief of OSS Cairo, was well aware of the instructions prohibiting the OSS from contact with the enemy without the State Department's approval, he cut Morde's travel orders for Turkey on Hurley's instructions. Toulmin related officially that Hurley "requested orders for Morde to go to Turkey—orders which he could not have obtained otherwise."[1]

Morde arrived in Istanbul by rail, traveling by way of Aleppo and Ankara, during the first week of October (Donovan was in Cairo for much of the period between mid-September 1943 and mid-January 1944) and was met at Ankara by the OSS chief representative, Lanning Macfarland. According to Toulmin, Morde told Macfarland "he wanted to get in touch with von Papen," but Macfarland "did not like the idea," and it was only after after "some discussion" that he "did agree to get him in touch with a person in Istanbul who would put him through to Von Papen." That person was Snapdragon—Archibald Coleman. Coleman was to relate in 1977, after nearly twenty years of trying to persuade the U.S. authorities to let him tell the story, he met Daisy—Morde's code name —at the offices of Vestern Elektrik near the Galata Bridge. Coleman wrote:

> As I went to the door a man half-rose from a back table and waved me over. He was about five-feet-nine, 160 pounds, brown hair, round face with that healthy look, hazel eyes—strictly the all-American type. He was in his early thirties, and he wore a dark Oxford-gray pin-stripe suit, Ivy League, a white button-down shirt with a Third Secretary polka-dot tie, and black shoes— conservative.[2]

Intensely suspicious, Coleman questioned his visitor closely, for, he told his visitor: " 'It shouldn't surprise you to learn that I'm not in the habit of arranging meetings for total strangers who wish to fraternize with the enemy.' " Daisy replied that he understood Coleman's position and produced a visiting card—probably that of either Guenther or Toulmin —on which had been written in pencil: "Introducing [Morde]. Please help him all you can, hold nothing back."

After much pressure by Coleman to get his visitor to name his principals, and much prevarication by Morde, Morde eventually produced from his wallet what Coleman described as "a small sheet of thin tissue with typewritten items on it." He "read it over, hoping that I didn't look as startled as I felt." It was "a list of surrender terms directed to the Axis, but so fantastic as to throw more doubt on Daisy's sanity."

Coleman demanded to know "who in hell sent you on this goddam fool's errand?" That "made [Morde] mad enough to answer me, and he said: 'It's no fool's errand, wise guy, I was sent here by FDR and General Hurley.' " Morde insisted that he was on a presidential mission, with orders given him personally by the President and General Hurley. Coleman recorded his thoughts: "It began to look as if I should re-evaluate this situation. If what Daisy said were true, or if it were a dud, no harm could be done by performance. I doubted that the terms of surrender were sincere, but it might be a device to mislead the Axis. Either way, perhaps we had better do it."

Coleman's first move was to contact Dogwood, the Czech who was, virtually, chief of operations for the Cereus chain—which by now had several scores of spies, some of them prominent men and women, operating from Istanbul into Germany, Austria, Hungary, Rumania, and Bulgaria. Dogwood agreed to bring Magnolia into the case, for Magnolia was on friendly terms with Papen. The true identity of Magnolia was Alexander Rustow, whom Coleman described as an economist and political scientist of note, who had held teaching and lecturing assignments at Tübingen, Heidelberg, Cologne, Kiel, and Berlin universities. At one time Magnolia "had been invited to accept the Ministry of Economics in General von Schleicher's cabinet, but the ill-fated government lasted less than a month." Magnolia "despised Hitler, and he would have done anything to destroy the Nazi hold on his *vaterland* [*sic*], for he was a good and loyal German—devoted to von Papen. He held the chair of economics at the University of Istanbul, and he was a most valuable member of our [Cereus] team."

Magnolia arranged the meeting between Morde and Papen through a second intermediary, whom Donovan named in a memo to FDR as "von Papen's closest friend, a Herr Posth, head of the Deutsche Orient Bank in Istanbul."[3] Magnolia soon advised Coleman that, as luck would have it, Papen was in Istanbul, staying at the German Summer Embassy at Therapia just outside the city. The German ambassador "was interested, even anxious," to receive the intermediary.

As Coleman advised Donovan, in preparation for the meeting between Morde and Papen, Coleman called in a photographic laboratory technician, a Russian who labored under the code name Narcissus. Morde then proceeded to type his proposals on heavy white paper, which was photographed. The negative and two positive prints were given to Morde, and the heavy white paper burned. Coleman then "loaned Daisy a small four-power magnifying glass so he could read the microfilm, and suggested that he carry it with him on the visit to von Papen."[4]

What Narcissus did not state—and Morde had expressly forbidden— was that he had made a third print. He gave that print to Coleman, who placed it in his files.

Many years later Morde's report was located in some of FDR's secret files at the FDR Library at Hyde Park. Except in one important matter— a description of how Morde got to Papen and how he was received, which Morde probably cut in the interests of brevity before giving it to FDR— the document was identical to the one that Morde typed in Coleman's laboratory after his meeting with Papen and that Coleman again succeeded in having copied.

In his report, Morde recorded that he was taken by Professor Rustow, alias Magnolia, for his first meeting with the German ambassador on October 5, 1943:

> At 9:35 this morning Magnolia and I arrived in front of the Osmanli Bank just as a taxi pulled in to the curb. The driver was a husky young German who recognized Magnolia, and he stepped out to open the door for us. Nobody said a word, but since Magnolia raised his hat politely I did the same. The driver, who wore thick dark glasses, turned his head and said some

words in German, and Magnolia replied, but I could detect only the word "Terapia." We went through town, and out a back road at high speed. I looked out the back window a few times, and as far as I could tell we were not being followed.

Morde continued: "After crossing a series of low hills we came out on the boulevard that hugs the shore of the Bosporus all the way to the Black Sea, and at exactly ten o'clock we pulled up at the embassy gate. I had hoped that the car would drive right through, but von Papen had left word to pass the occupants of Taxi No. 1830—not the car." Morde and Magnolia walked up to the embassy and were conducted to Papen's study by a "huge German bodyguard."

[Papen] looked me over for a few seconds and then motioned to a couple of chairs on the other side of the room, suggesting in English that we might sit there. He offered me a Turkish cigarette and a light, then leaned forward in his chair and indicated that he was waiting to hear what I had to say. He speaks English well, hesitating only rarely to find the right word. He apologized for his rusty English, as it had been a long time since he had used it, but I assured him it was good and apologized for not being able to speak German. He was surprised at this, and said, "Nor French either?" When I said "No," he seemed quite pleased. He said it assured him that I was not an intelligence agent.

The windows opened onto the Bosporus, affording a fine view of Asia across the way, and the walls were almost bare. On one side hung a large map of pre-war Europe, devoid of pins, lines or marks of any kind, and on the opposite wall hung a large painting of Hitler in uniform. Beneath the portrait, on a table, sat a framed photograph of Mussolini with three or four lines of his bold script across the bottom.

The political substance of their meeting Morde recorded in Coleman's laboratory immediately after Morde left Papen. The text of the report at Hyde Park and that of Coleman's article are identical. Morde reported to FDR that he told Papen he "had come on a highly secret and important mission from the United States" for the "sole purpose of seeing him."[5] He then assured Papen that he was not an intelligence agent, that "this interview was no trick, and that I came to him in complete good faith. I said that I wanted to speak openly, honestly and frankly and I wanted him to trust me implicitly." Papen asked Morde who he was, and he told him that because of the "delicate nature of this mission," he "carried no credentials other than his passport." Morde showed Papen the passport, and Papen "noted the page which states 'the bearer is Assistant to the American Minister, etc., to Egypt.'" Morde told Papen he was "now traveling under the disguise of a correspondent."

Papen now appeared to be satisfied, "relaxed completely, smiled, offered me another cigarette, lighted it, and gave every evidence that he no longer entertained any suspicions about me." Morde then stated that "I came as a trusted messenger for persons I could not identify to him" and that "I had with me a highly confidential paper which outlined something in which he might be very interested." The paper "in no way represented the official views of the U.S. government," and Morde assured Papen: "*I* had not written it, but . . . was here to find out if he might be interested *if* the aims and details expressed in that document could be worked out." Morde then:

> gave him a magnifying glass and a tiny film—an actual photograph of the paper—and after much difficulty he was able to read it by holding the lens some four inches away from the film. He was tremendously affected. It seemed to me that tears were very close to his eyes. He sat back and closed his eyes for a minute and then whatever reserve he had felt up to that moment broke.

According to Coleman's article, which was based on the print Narcissus managed to obtain, what Papen read was nothing less than an invitation to parley from a person or persons very highly placed in Washington. According to Claudia Coleman, Coleman's daughter—her father had died recently—in 1982 Narcissus's print was still in the family's possession and was in a bank vault.

Coleman's account of the meeting between Papen and Morde claims that the following is "an exact copy" of the document that Morde brought to Turkey and that Papen read with the assistance of the OSS magnifying glass:

> 1. Recognition of the principle that Germany shall dominate the politics, industry and agriculture of Continental Europe, and all that that implies: a. Allies will entertain favorably a proposal that Berlin serve as a seat of parliament comprised of representatives from all the Federated States of Europe. b. Allies will entertain favorably a proposal that Germany's boundaries be re-allocated to include German minority populations, as in Poland, Sudetenland, Austria, etc.
> 2. Germany, USA, and Great Britain shall be the "Big Three Powers:" Germany in Continental Europe; USA on the American Continents and in China; Great Britain overseas generally and in Africa. (Continental Europe to include Poland, Baltic States, and Ukraine.) a. Germany will look to USA and Great Britain for raw materials and give manufactures in exchange. No British or American competition with Germany in the European market.
> 3. Germany NOT to interfere with Allied action against Japan. As *quid pro quo*, Germany to have concessions in Dutch Colonial Empire.
> 4. Lend-lease and direct aid to Russia to cease, provided Germany does not help Japan against Russia or against Allies.

5. USA and Great Britain to guarantee that Russia never will invade inch of German territory; further, to aid Germany by force of arms if necessary in preventing Russia from interfering commercially, politically, or industrially in the new post-war Europe.[6]

Even after almost forty years the document remains astounding. For if it was really by FDR, Hurley, or someone writing on either one's behalf, it constituted an act of monumental treachery and cynical disregard for the Allied compact with the Soviet Union that ranks with Lenin's and Trotsky's decision to end the fighting on the eastern front during World War I. Not surprisingly Papen was deeply affected by the document.

Having read it, he "asked me [Morde] if there could be any hope that what he had read might be true." He said that "the time had come when the war must stop," that "a just peace would come soon," and that "all this horrible bloodshed would stop." Papen declared that "hundreds of thousands of Germans were homeless, with no place to go, because of Allied bombings," and that "all Europe was threatened with Communism."[7]

Morde then came to the point of his visit. In a memorandum which went to Roosevelt, he stated:

I told him that I and every American, like him, wanted this war to stop. But, I said, the war will never stop and the bombings will never stop and the suffering will never end until Hitler and Nazi Totalitarianism have been expelled from Germany.... I said there *was* a chance for peace for Germany, a just peace, a peace that would not again be based on terms like those in the Versailles treaty, but I said Americans felt . . . that it was now up to the Germans to clean their own house, to GET RID of Hitler, and Goebbels, and Goering and Himmler and the rest of the criminals who had brought Germany to the state she was now in.

After some discussion in the same vein, Papen declared that:

our propaganda was wrong, that Americans seem to think *all Germans are Nazis. That, he said, was not true.* He stated that if Americans only hated the Nazis, they should offer some hope to the Germans who were NOT Nazis; that now the Germans are afraid that they will all be included in the revenge that had been promised to them by us and the British.

Morde replied:

I told him we knew very well that not all Germans were Nazis, and that was why I had come to him. I said that it was commonly believed in America that he hated Hitler and the Nazis; that it was believed that he was one of the few great statesmen left in Germany and that if anyone could lead the Germans out of the mess they were in, he alone was the man. . . .

Morde told Papen he was "the one man who can re-form a new Germany" and he now had "the opportunity to hasten that day." Morde went on to tell Papen:

> what America wanted was the immediate elimination of Hitler, either his capture or death. I said I wanted to make myself perfectly clear; that if some way could be found whereby he could help achieve that objective, America was prepared to help in many different ways. I told him that if Hitler should suddenly be flown by plane out of Germany to a spot under American control, like Iceland, or No. Africa, or even No. Ireland, a reaction might set in in the U.S. such as was occasioned when Mussolini was suddenly removed from the Italian scene.
>
> [Papen] asked me what would happen to Hitler, if such a thing should happen as, for instance, Hitler should be delivered into the hands of the Americans. I said I had no idea, but that I thought . . . he would be treated as a prisoner of war in accordance with his former rank as head of a state, and confined in a safe place away from mob violence until such time as he could be accorded justice and tried by a court to be established after the war.

Morde then related that he repeated that "if he knew of any possible way to hasten the fall of Hitler, he could count on every assistance from America. [I] asked him if he fully understood what I was implying, and he replied he did, but that obviously at that moment he was not able to give me any sort of answer." Papen "asked me if I thought Mr. Roosevelt would care to deal with him personally. I said that was something I naturally could not answer, that it was conceivable everything in the future [sic]" but that much would depend upon what Papen "did in our favor to help bring the war to a quick conclusion by ridding Germany of its present government."

Morde's first session with Papen had now ended. The second session took place the next day at Banker Posth's weekend house on Prinkipo Island in the Sea of Marmora. During their talk, which lasted about ninety minutes, Papen showed Morde three pages of "notes" in his own handwriting which, he stated, Morde could not keep, but he was "free to take notes myself on what he had to say, with one reservation: *that I was to show them to no one other than the President.*"

Dealing with the contents of the microfilm which Morde had given him at their previous meeting, Papen stated that he was, "first and foremost, a German patriot," that "his life had been devoted to his country and that his country, not its government, came first." He denied that Germany had ever wished to "dominate" Europe politically and said he "thoroughly approved of a Federation of the European states" in which he felt "Germany should be permitted a role of leadership in the economics of Europe." Economics, he felt, should be "considered as more important than anything political." Moreover, "a Federated government of Europe should have time to give proof that a mutual understanding existed economically," and "later should come any discussion of political disputes or treaties."

Papen declared that "he felt Austria was and is German and must remain German" and that "the people of Austria would so choose if given a chance to decide by themselves." The Sudetenland of Czechoslovakia "should have autonomy, as after Munich." In regard to Poland he believed the 1914 frontiers should be restored and the province of Posen should be returned to Germany. France should be restored to the French intact, but where Alsace-Lorraine was concerned "he felt that some arrangement could easily be effected with France whereby perhaps a division could be made, possibly based on a just plebiscite."

The German had then turned to the Ukraine, which would be "needed by the new Europe as a 'food larder' " and suggested that "the Ukraine should perhaps be made an independent state, allied by common treaty with Europe, but definitely with Europe and not with Russia, or under any Asiatic influence." As for markets, Papen "said that in the postwar Europe" there should be "no fight between Germany and America, or Germany and Britain for markets. . . . Germany needed our products (citing automobiles) and we needed hers, as chemical products, photographic apparatus, etc." But "he dismissed Japan with an expressive wave of his hand, saying Germany had no interest whatever in Japan," adding that the "oil situation was important to Germany" and that "he hoped it might be possible for Germany to get a concession in the Pacific area now under Japanese control." The same applied to rubber, but he "said that the question of colonies should not stand in the way of peace, and that Germany, under a new government, would be prepared to let a just peace conference decide her need in that respect."

Summarizing what might be called his terms, Papen stated that "his interest and that of other leaders of Germany, who were not Nazis and did not approve of the Nazis, was to safeguard the economical [sic], and to whatever extent possible, the political *existence* of the *German people, certainly not the present government of the German people, for the German people could not be included in that government.*" Returning to the question of the federation of Europe, Papen stated "he sincerely believed this was not only possible, but, from Germany's standpoint, desirable." He would "like to see the capital in Berlin, of course, but this was not essential."

Papen moved on to the question of the war itself and Morde's proposals for "getting rid" of Hitler:

He said he himself knew, and that it was known by the German people, that they had no hope of winning the war; further, that even the Nazis knew it. He warned that the Nazis were still capable of tricks, and suggested it was even possible that when Russia reached the point of invading German territory, some "Red" general might try to pull a coup d'état and, salvaging what he could of the German army, make a deal with the Russians and go over to their side in order to share in the Communist sweep of Europe. He said this *"could"* happen one day! That was why they must have an immediate peace, as soon as it could be arranged, to forestall such a catastrophe, that would not only cause ruin to the German people and Europe, but also to America's and England's aims and desires for a lasting peace.

Papen warned that "success breeds success" and that "already some Nazi leaders are gazing admiringly on what Communism had been able to do for Russia, and that they even admired Communism in many respects and felt that it might even be a better system than their own, and worth imitating." For that reason he begged Morde to ask his government to stop the bombing of Germany, which was "doing more to spread Communism inside Germany than anything else." People were beginning to admire Communism and beginning to hate England and America for the bombing, which was achieving nothing militarily.

Papen, in discussing the Allied military occupation of Europe, said he "hoped America and Britain would keep an armed force in Europe for a long enough period to guard against anarchy and to preserve law and order," but "he personally doubted if the democracies could ever be convinced of the necessity for doing this." He said also that "he hoped peace terms would permit Germany to maintain some army to keep guard on her east wall against the Russians," that "such a guard would have to be maintained to save Europe," and that "Germany wanted to do this as her share, and to protect herself."

Morde intervened to state his "visit would be a complete failure if he could not give me a message to take back to America that would show some way whereby he and Germany were anxious to end this war by an act of their own from within." Morde repeated what he had said the day before, that "only one thing would ever satisfy the American people"— "for Hitler to be forcibly ejected from Germany, along with his cohorts, and if possible delivered into the hands of the American people":

> the whole war psychology of the American people would be greatly affected if some day a plane landed in Iceland or No. Africa with Hitler, and perhaps Goering, Himmler and Goebbels on it, signifying the removal from the German scene of the top Nazis. That *only* by their removal could America ever consider discussing a peace with Germany. I told him bluntly that I was there to ask that he bring this about.

Papen replied "very gravely" that:

> this was asking a great deal of him. That he realized it was a job that had to
> be done by the German people themselves. That it had to be done from
> within and could not be done from without. He said, too, not to forget that
> there *were* many Hitler supporters, especially among the youth, and that his
> death or removal would have a great and questionable effect on them. That
> "changing horses in mid-stream" was not easy, and was especially delicate
> in time of war. Finally he said that to overthrow Hitler would be difficult, but
> he thought it could be done. He said this most thoughtfully, and seriously.

But, Papen continued, "for him to stir revolt in Germany and for him
to convince 'his friends' that the time had come to throw out Hitler and
the Nazis," he must "have something to 'offer' to those friends, something definite and 'solid' and based on a sacred understanding." Papen
asked Morde "directly": If "there were to be a new government in Germany, would America and Britain be willing to make peace?" Morde
replied that he could not say; it depended on the nature of the government following the Nazis, and "more than that," it "depended on the
Nazi leaders, including Hitler, being delivered into actual Allied hands."

> . . . unless this were [done], there would always be a suspicion in America
> and England that Hitler and the others were in hiding somewhere, and that
> they might be living, even if they were reported dead . . . that their physical
> persons be in the hands of the Allies before any such story would be believed.
> [Morde] asked him [Papen] directly if he personally were ready to aid the
> Allies in getting rid of Hitler. He said that depended on whether President
> Roosevelt was prepared to offer him a promise of peace that would be
> attractive enough to "his friends" to support him in that effort. He said he
> MUST be able to give them an incentive, something concrete that promised
> a future for Germany that would not be as harsh as unconditional surrender.
> . . . I said, suppose that can be arranged, will you THEN do your utmost to
> get rid of Hitler and the Nazis? He replied very simply, yes.

Papen "said he had the highest respect for the President, and knew he
could trust him to live up to his word." He added he wanted Morde to
tell Roosevelt that "he, von Papen himself, was too old for personal
aspirations, but that he would be honored to be in charge of the new
government of Germany, and that he was looked up to by the German
people and trusted as a leader. That he, however, would be willing to aid
whatever new government was chosen, regardless [of] whether he personally led it."

Morde asked Papen "if he would be willing to meet the President,
supposing that could be arranged, or if he would be willing to meet one
of our highest leaders, and he said he would be *most* willing, if it could

be arranged, but that it would be very difficult. That his life was constantly in danger, and three attempts had been made already." He felt that although he was very conspicuous, he might be able to meet Cordell Hull, the American secretary of state, in Turkey, if Morde would assist.

In conclusion Morde asked:

> [If] I were to meet him again in—say—a month or five weeks, with a definite assurance from the President along the lines he wanted, would he fulfill his part and effect this change of government in Germany. [Papen replied] that he would leave for Germany during my absence in the States, or in any case, would get in touch with his "people" and return to Turkey with a definite plan of action to accomplish what he and we mutually desired. He said: "Tell your President that I will leave to contact my people in Germany. Tell him that I must have something definite to offer them. Tell him that I will do my best and that I believe we will have success."
>
> I told him, if he would do that, I felt my mission had been a success. He smiled and shook hands warmly and said again he must ask my complete confidence as any disclosure of our conversation to anyone other than the President might lead to his death. He said that he trusted me, and that I must be very careful, and that in turn I could trust him without reservation not to disclose to anyone what had taken place between us. He said he hoped to meet me again in four or five weeks.

In a final gesture, Papen gave Morde a secret cipher to enable them to communicate privately by telegram, presumably through Professor Rustow and Herr Posth, if there were any developments after Morde returned to Cairo and Washington.

Morde then returned to Cairo, where, according to Toulmin, he saw the commanding general of United States forces in the Middle East, General Ralph Royce, who gave Morde a "number one priority to [go back to Washington] to talk to the President."[8] Morde left more or less immediately for the United States, and Toulmin recalled later: "Two or three messages did come through from von Papen for Morde, which we could not break. We have no idea what they said, although they were forwarded to him."

In Washington, Morde was received by the President's secretary, General Edwin M. "Pa" Watson, but politically such a matter of high politics was quite beyond that bluff, limited man. He sought the opinion of the playwright Robert Sherwood, head of the OWI.

In a memorandum to Roosevelt, Sherwood related how Morde had been sent to him with an "amazing" story in which, during two interviews with Papen, he had "discussed a possible deal for the overthrow of Hitler and the Nazi Party." Sherwood advised Roosevelt that Morde had been with the OWI but "decided he wanted to resign . . . and join the Cairo office of the Reader's Digest. We agreed to let him go as he had been making a certain amount of trouble." Hurley had disclaimed any connection with Morde's scheme and, "in effect, denounces Morde." Sherwood informed the President he was "going to make a full report of this to the Acting Secretary of State with the suggestion that Morde should not again be given a passport to leave the country."[9]

Alarmed by Sherwood's reception, Morde contacted Donovan through the OSS, and presumably by cable, Donovan arranged that Morde's memorandum be sent directly to Roosevelt, together with a covering message in which Donovan urged the President:

> I beg you to read this carefully. It contains an idea that your skill and imagination could develop.
>
> I don't pretend to suggest what price should be paid by our government for the hoped-for result.
>
> *If* the plan went through, and *if* the culprits were delivered and fittingly tried and executed, and *if* unconditional surrender resulted, it would strengthen your position morally at the peace table.
>
> Russian propaganda is evidently directed to this very purpose.[10]

But Roosevelt refused to see Morde, or to discuss his plan, and gave instructions to the acting secretary of state, Edward R. Stettinius, to withdraw Morde's passport. At that point—shortly before the opening of the Teheran Conference—the Morde affair entered its most troubling phase.

As the triumvirs began to meet to agree on a combined strategy for the Western powers' invasion of Europe in 1944 and a major Red Army offensive to assist that perilous venture, rumors that a representative of Roosevelt's had met with a German representative in Turkey began to spread. The purpose of the meeting, so the rumors stated, had been to agree upon terms between the United States and Germany in the event of a successful coup d'état against Hitler. Plainly the rumors were being spread by German agents, their purpose to disrupt the Teheran Conference. Consequently it was obvious that there had been a leakage concerning the Morde mission. But from where had the information come? Since Papen was not likely to have started rumors against himself, the possibility that there had been a leakage within OSS Istanbul had to be considered as possible and even likely.

What, therefore, is to be made of the contact between Morde and Papen? Who were Morde's principals? Morde took his knowledge to the grave when he died in 1953, and since neither Donovan nor FDR left anything that would throw any light upon the mystery, only speculation and deduction are possible. What seems sure is that FDR could not have written the armistice terms. While internal evidence suggests that these were written in the United States, the terms were such that two possibilities are suggested: (1) Either this was a trick to disrupt or subvert the Third Reich and perhaps even to get Papen to move against Hitler, or (2) the scheme was the product of a group of extreme right-wing influential Americans who regarded Russia, not Germany, as the principal enemy.

FDR's reaction to the Morde operation—withdrawing his passport, etc. —certainly suggests that the President knew nothing about the affair when it was presented to him. The fact that Morde's report was found in FDR's papers is explicable—it was filed along with all other documents read by the President. Certainly the terms were at variance with all of FDR's known attitudes and beliefs. Particularly he deplored the existence of colonial empires and spheres of influence, both of which were prominent geopolitical factors in the terms. Moreover, the Teheran Conference with Stalin and Churchill was about to be held when Morde presented the report, and everything that FDR did and said at Teheran indicated an anxiety to come to terms with Stalin and to achieve the defeat of Germany, Japan, and the other Axis powers at the earliest time. Also, of course, FDR was the architect of the policy of unconditional surrender, and he adhered to that policy resolutely both publicly and privately even when it began to produce stiffened German reaction, heavy American and Allied casualties, and a protracted war with both Germany and Japan.

On balance, therefore, it is not reasonable to suppose that FDR had a hand in the affair—apart from all else, Donovan's memorandum to FDR on October 29, 1943, suggests that to both men the Morde incident was a new development. If so, neither could have had a hand in it. Yet Morde enjoyed powerful support. He was able to leave the United States at a time when all foreign travel was almost impossible, except for people on war emergency business. It is possible, indeed probable, that his *Reader's Digest* credentials would have been sufficient to enable him to get government transport (there was virtually no other way to get to Cairo at that time). But once in Cairo, he must have received considerable assistance to enable him to get to Turkey, forbidden to all but those on official business.

Here such evidence as there is strongly suggests that OSS Cairo was involved. In the first place, the terms were on gelatine, a method adopted by secret services for conveyance of important documents. Gelatine can be eaten, can also be burned without leaving telltale ash. It is difficult to see how the terms could have been transferred to gelatine without the assistance of OSS, for who else would have had the facilities for making a gelatine negative? There is also clear evidence that OSS Cairo placed its services at Morde's disposal, especially in the vital matter of permitting him to leave Egypt and travel across Arabia through innumerable checks designed to apprehend spies and other doubtful individuals on the move.

Unless powerful right-wingers were behind Morde, the most likely scenario was that Morde succeeded in ingratiating himself first with Lieutenant Colonel West, and through West with Guenther, and that both became interested in what was the essence of Morde's plan—to arrange the capture of Hitler through Papen, with the terms as bait. It is entirely possible that Morde intended not only to suborn Papen but also, if the Hitler aspect failed, to arrange for his defection or capture. That would be a prize indeed—one, in fact, that had occurred to Donovan from time to time.

Guenther spoke favorably about the plan to General Hurley, the President's emissary, and Hurley, too, supported the scheme without giving its implications too much thought. Macfarland in Ankara was instructed to give Morde every assistance, as he did, albeit reluctantly. He handed Morde on to Coleman, who was also reluctant and suspicious—until Morde claimed that his principals were Hurley and FDR. In short, Morde's scheme to see Papen was a piece of private enterprise in which he alone was the author and in which he alone was involved. The scheme succeeded because it was bold, because the OSS thought it might work, because Morde was facile, and because he enjoyed a fair measure of good fortune in that he found himself among men who knew him from his previous stays in Cairo—he hoodwinked them, as he hoodwinked everybody else, perhaps with a story that he wanted to go to Turkey to do an article for the *Reader's Digest*.

The weakness in this theory is that one would have thought that far more serious punishment would have been meted out to Morde than the withdrawal of his passport had the mission been entirely unauthorized. That the operation was not entirely unauthorized is evident from a remark made by Lieutenant Colonel Toulmin to the OSS History Board. When asked by the board at the end of the war what lay behind the Morde affair, Toulmin replied that the attitude of OSS to the operation had been: "We wanted OSS involved if Morde was successful, and out of it if he was not."[11] Although it is true that the remark suggests the OSS was not a principal, but a bystander, in the operation, it is also true that the implication is that it was party to the operation.

While this theory is the best one—that the entire affair was an initiative planned and carried out by Morde alone, but aided and abetted by the OSS—the notion that Morde's principals were a group of powerful right-wingers cannot be completely dismissed. There were such Americans, they were the ultra-right-wing remnants of the American Firsters, and in such quarters there was much alarm at the progressive defeat of Germany and even greater alarm at the advance westward of the Red Army. The German defeat at Stalingrad in February 1943, and the even greater German defeat at Kursk in 1943, demonstrated the power of the Red Army and foreshadowed the entry of the Russians into Eastern and Central Europe. That was certainly enough to frighten some Western geopoliticians. Furthermore, such a group would have been able to facilitate Morde's journey.

Yet all this is conjecture. There is no fact to base a judgment upon beyond that of Morde's meeting with Papen—and that Morde's report was found many years later in FDR's papers. Whatever the truth, Morde's discomfiture in Washington did not last long. When the incident was thought buried and forgotten, he was rehabilitated by the OSS. He was enabled to obtain a commission in the United States Naval Reserve and was then employed by the Morale Operations Branch of the OSS. He served with distinction in Europe, and the Mediterranean and the Asian theaters, duly receiving the Legion of Merit for distinguished and meritorious services to the United States. That suggests that WJD, at least, had been involved in the episode.

24

Falling Sparrow

While at Cairo in October and November 1943, continuing his intensification of OSS operations in the Balkans, Donovan put into effect his boldest scheme so far: Sparrow, a plan to produce an anti-Nazi revolution in Hungary, one of Hitler's principal allies. Soon after WJD's arrival at Cairo, Lieutenant Colonel Otto von Hatz, the Hungarian military attaché in Turkey, known as Trillium in the OSS's Cereus organization at Istanbul, intimated to the Czech code-named Dogwood that some of the officers of the General Staff in Budapest wished to desert the alliance with Germany and join the Grand Alliance. Hatz asked Dogwood to speak with his principals and establish whether American officials in Turkey would be prepared to take part in exploratory staff conversations on whether Hungary's defection could be arranged. When Dogwood advised Hatz later that his principals would be prepared to discuss matters with the Hungarians, Macfarland received a message from Dogwood that the "trusted emissary of the Chief of the Hungarian General Staff"[1] would be Hatz himself.

At about the same time other approaches seemed to indicate that Hatz and his principals genuinely desired a peace arrangement with the Allies. Dulles in Bern reported that a Hungarian diplomat, whom he identified only as 645, had presented himself as an intermediary, and in Stockholm the U.S. ambassador, Herschel V. Johnson, reported that R. Taylor Cole of OSS Stockholm and an official of the embassy, H. Francis Cunningham, had had extensive conversations with two Hungarian diplomats, Antel Ullein-Reviczky and Endre Collert. The Hungarians had produced a letter from the Hungarian foreign minister, Ghyczy, stating that Germany had begun a campaign of "cold terror" against Hungary and setting down at length the attitude of the Hungarian administration and Parliament toward a continuation of the war. The letter showed that the peace movement inside Hungary involved not only the General Staff and Foreign Office but also all branches of society. It showed, too, that the Hungarians were prepared to defect, provided two "earnest recommendations" could be met: that the Allies not use the term "unconditional surrender" in the legal documents, although Hungary would in fact surrender unconditionally—a matter, presumably, of Hungarian pride—and that the representatives of the "three principal Allies"—America, Britain, *and* Russia—would send men who had political knowledge of Central and Eastern Europe to meet the Hungarian delegation. The second requirement was not exceptional, for the Allied foreign offices knew enough about the Hungarians to realize that nobody but men skilled in such politics would ever be able to understand, let alone sort out, the territorial, political, and administrative problems that would be produced by Hungary's surrender.

The sum of these diplomatic preliminaries tended to show that the Hungarian peace representatives bore honest faces, and that encouraged Donovan to proceed with Sparrow. However, the appearance was to prove beguiling, for the reality was that all the peace envoys represented different branches of the Hungarian administration, they were not acting in concert, and indeed, they probably knew nothing of each other. Certainly they were not connected with Hatz, who was in Istanbul for a very different purpose.

On October 4, 1943, Dogwood informed Macfarland that he had seen Hatz and had prepared a paper which Coleman could send to Donovan, who appears to have gone to Istanbul to supervise the Hungarian approach there. The document was entitled "Proposed Agreement with Representatives of Hungarian General Staff Concerning Co-operation in the Sphere of Intelligence."[2] The immediate objective was Hungarian intelligence from within the Nazi empire; the ultimate object, the withdrawal of Hungary from the war.

Reading the paper, Coleman noted that there was no mention of the term "unconditional surrender." He told Dogwood that the OSS could not do business with the Hungarians on any other terms. Coleman did, however, agree to this clause: ". . . it is recognized . . . by the Americans that active Hungarian collaboration with the Allies in the sphere of military and political intelligence constitutes a positive contribution by Hungary to the cause of the [Allies]."

Having overcome what was evidently an attempt by Hatz to get the OSS to repudiate unconditional surrender through omission, Coleman agreed to a meeting, which took place, with Macfarland present, on or about

October 27, 1943. Macfarland and Coleman demanded that Hungary provide the Grand Alliance with:

> Unreserved delivery of information about Germany in the sphere of war economy, warfare and Politics, in particular: *a.* regular supply of lists of all German transports of military supplies and troops through Hungary *b.* regular information about the German armament industry, and German war production measures. *c.* current and up-to-date information about Hungarian industries which work for the German war machine *d.* military and political intelligence about Germany received or collected by the Hungarian Intelligence Service *e.* insight into the military and political intelligence material collected by Hungary about Rumania.[3]

Macfarland then "required" that the Hungarian General Staff provide certain other services that would have been of enormous importance to the intelligence capability of the Grand Alliance, and to judge from the tough legalistic nature of the discussions, there is a temptation to believe that Donovan was not far away during the negotiations. Certainly they were momentous enough to warrant his closest attention. For among those services were that the General Staff arrange for the OSS to use "the Hungarian diplomatic and consular representations at Berlin, Vienna, Prague, etc., for the purposes of our communications with agents and collaborators." Macfarland wanted, too, the "Creation of a suitable basis for sending one of our representatives to Budapest to serve as our commissioner with the Hungarian General Staff and our central representative and chief agent in Central Europe." It wished for the creation by "the Hungarian partner" of a "permanent agency [in Istanbul] under a commercial or consular cover to ensure continuous connection with the American intelligence service." And it wanted the "Creation of a suitable basis for the despatch of a senior Hungarian Officer to represent the Hungarian General Staff at our Algiers H.Q."

Macfarland could not have presented these terms without Donovan's knowledge and approval, and there is clear evidence that WJD knew of and approved these transactions. He wrote to the Joint Chiefs on November 20, 1943, relating that OSS Turkey had been in touch with "a Hungarian officer, a Lieutenant Colonel of the Hungarian General Staff," whom "OSS has valid reason to believe . . . personally represents the Hungarian Chief of Staff. . . ." WJD then set down the terms of the proposed agreement, stressing: "In exchange, Hungary asks that the United Nations bear in mind during the peace negotiations that Hungary did make an overt act of assistance to the Allied cause" but that "No commitments, political or military, were asked or given."[4]

In the meantime, Donovan continued, "I have directed our representative . . . to proceed no further until I receive instructions from the Joint

Chiefs of Staff." However, because the Hungarians had said they would be prepared to accept an American liaison officer to the Hungarian General Staff in Budapest he had selected for the operation an American officer who had "the necessary qualifications." That officer was Lieutenant Colonel Florimond Duke—Sparrow, Amoss's case officer during the Canaris contacts.

Two weeks later the Joint Chiefs gave formal authority for the Hungarian operation, including Sparrow, to proceed, with a directive that the OSS was to:

> a. Explore further the possibilities of influencing Hungary to withdraw from the present war on the side of Germany. b. Make no commitment on behalf of the government of the United States of America. c. Transmit to the Joint Chiefs all information, proposals and requests elicited from Hungary, together with your recommendations. d. In the event that Hungary should express a desire to negotiate a separate peace, the proposals will be transmitted as expeditiously as possible to the Joint Chiefs of Staff for transmittal to the Secretary of State.[5]

Thus, Hatz's approach appears to have been accepted as a genuine one. However, during this period fragments of intelligence reaching OSS Washington showed that—to use a British intelligence phrase—some peculiar fish were being fried by Hatz and the Hungarians. The head of French counterintelligence at Algiers, Palling, who had known Hatz before the war, warned Eddy, the head of OSS Algiers, in October 1943, that Hatz might be under the control of the Sicherheitsdienst at Sofia. That cautionary message was quickly followed by another, this time from Whitney Shepardson, OSS SI chief in Washington, advising: "It was just made known to us that the British infiltrated 2 agents into southwestern Hungary about 3 weeks ago. Ninety-four natives who had been in contact with the agents were compromised; furthermore both agents were captured."[6]

Two quesions arose, therefore, from these advices: What evidence was there that Sparrow would meet any more congenial fate? And if the Hungarians were in a mood to desert the Axis alliance, why had they arrested the British agents?

Then, between December 14 and 19, 1943, came several telegrams from Dulles tending to confirm that Hatz's negotiations might be no more than a trap set to catch a sparrow. In the first, Dulles reported that he now had "serious doubts regarding the chances of separating Hungary from the Axis," that "fence-sitting is an art highly developed by the Hungarians," and that through his special contact, 645, he had reason to believe the Hungarians would collaborate only if the Western powers occupied the Balkans and protected Hungary from the Red Army, which was nearing its eastern frontier. The entire affair might be that "Hungary would like to have an anchor to windward with us" and would not take any steps "as might make Nazi occupation [of Hungary] a probability"— and Hitler would certainly occupy Hungary if he believed the Hungarians were about to defect.[7]

To Donovan, Dulles's information was only daunting; it contained no hard intelligence that would warrant cancellation of Sparrow. Thus, by late December 1943 the Sparrow mission had been selected and was being prepared at Algiers for departure by air. It consisted of Duke, forty-nine, from Rochester, New York; Captain Alfred M. Suarez, twenty-nine, wireless operator, from New York City; Captain Guy T. Nunn, twenty-nine, interpreter, from New Orleans.

But on December 29, 1943, there came a definite red light from Dulles. His informant inside the German Foreign Ministry, George Wood, had provided him with diplomatic telegrams from Istanbul that stated Hatz had given the Germans a "very full" report of his negotiations with Macfarland in Istanbul. "Perhaps" Hatz was "pulling our leg," said Dulles, who ended with three words: "I urge caution."[8]

A second telegram conveyed even more sobering intelligence: The SS plenipotentiary at Sofia, Obergruppenführer SS Beckerle, had advised to the German foreign minister, Joachim von Ribbentrop, stating that Hatz had been "in touch with Americans," that the Americans had "made him a proposition," but that he had "declined at once to act in a manner unbecoming to an officer." Moreover, Beckerle had reported the Hungarian General Staff had "come to the conclusion that Hatz should retain his connection with the Americans so that he can secure information for the Germans." If anything "crooked" was planned against Germany, Beckerle stated, "Hatz promised to advise them of it."

Upon that advice WJD grounded Sparrow until the position had become clearer, and he warned Macfarland in a telegram: "We are informed from an enemy source that your man [Hatz] is working under orders to doublecross you. . . . [On] your guard you must be."[9]

Donovan "suggested" Macfarland drop all contacts and meet him in Algiers on or about January 15, 1944. The probability is that WJD wanted a firsthand account of matters, and he may have had ISOS information to impart. That sort of information he would certainly not want to entrust to a radio. But for reasons known only to himself, Macfarland did not obey that "suggestion" (a very dangerous thing to do with WJD) and chose instead to attend another meeting with Hatz. Macfarland did, however, send a note to Donovan in Cairo dated January 12, 1944, in which he stated: "In connection with your warning regarding Colonel H, may I state that he has been known to a principal member of our organization [Dogwood] for eight to ten years as an individual not in sympathy with Nazi ideals and not of German origin."

Macfarland stated that he knew Hatz had been in contact with the chief of German intelligence in Sofia, but "we are inclined to feel that he is only paying lip service to this organization in order to cover up his negotiations." It was known also that Hatz had explained to the Germans that he has "acquaintances among the American and British agencies which he hopes to use for the benefit of the Germans." Macfarland thought again this was "his effort to create a cover for himself."[10]

The letter showed plainly that Macfarland was under Hatz's spell, and when he failed to appear in Algiers, one wonders why Donovan did not relieve Macfarland, as he had relieved others who had failed to obey one of his "suggestions." Almost certainly Macfarland's contact with Leverkühn saved him here, for Macfarland was an intermediary in the Leverkühn connection, which he had handled well, and Donovan had few enough people who could be brought out to replace Macfarland at such a tricky time in the evolution of the Balkan plan.

Thus, Donovan did nothing to stop the meeting that took place among Macfarland, Coleman, Hatz, a person referred to only as WA but who was perhaps the American military attaché in Turkey, and Dogwood's intermediary with Hatz, Magnolia, the Cereus code name for Professor Rustow, the go-between with Papen in the Morde case. Macfarland's report in Donovan's papers shows that he and Coleman presented credentials that showed they were "under military orders of the Joint Chiefs of Staff, through their immediate chief, General Donovan."[11] In his report Macfarland recorded that he told Hatz that it was the policy of the Allied governments to regard the "political leaders of enemy and satellite countries" as war criminals who "without doubt would eventually be brought to punishment," but that if the Axis military leaders "care to avoid the same fate," they "might wish to seize the present opportunity of leading a revolt against Germany, or at least to cooperate to that end." Also, Macfarland advised Hatz that "only the prompt indication of the readiness of the Hungarian General Staff to aid the Allied cause would make further conversations worth while."

Answering Hatz's inquiry regarding the form that collaboration should take, Macfarland "pointed out that it should be possible for the HGS [Hungarian General Staff] to provide complete military intelligence now available to it and jointly work out plans for resisting German occupation [of Hungary] which might involve widespread sabotage and the adoption of a scorched-earth policy" to impede the German occupation. When Hatz stated the Hungarian Chiefs of Staff "might not consider it advisable or ethical to divulge military secrets," Macfarland replied that "ethics were not involved and that the collaboration had to be genuine and complete" if the Hungarians wished to receive Allied recognition.

When Hatz stated that his country and government were "alarmed at the prospect of either German occupation or Russian invasion," Macfarland advised him that it was the duty of the Hungarian Army to resist a German invasion but that the Hungarians had no more to fear from a Russian invasion than it had from an American or a British invasion. The Allies, Macfarland stated, "were committed to a policy of not imposing any form of government on conquered areas, provided the people were allowed to freely choose a form of government not inimical to democratic ideals."

When Hatz continued to seek "clarifications" concerning Hungary's future if it was invaded by Russia, Macfarland terminated that aspect of the conversations with the statement that "the United Nations were not trying to bargain for the services of H, his general staff, or his country." What he was doing was "to provide a means of collaboration, to assist resistance groups in withdrawing from Axis collaboration, and to assist in the defeat of Germany."

Macfarland concluded with a statement that "time was a factor in these negotiations, and that it might be necessary for the American group to interpret further delay or indecision as a rejection by H's general staff of any basis for collaboration; and that the Americans would [then] seek other groups in line with their general directive." Hatz "advised he would return to his country and try to send an answer by the 7th of February, unless communication difficulties intervened."

There was now an interlude of silence, but during that time Dulles's contacts were active. Hungarian contact 684, plainly the Hungarian minister in Bern, emerged on or about January 26, 1944, doubtless impelled by the fresh menaces of the great Russian advances in the east, to "discuss further particulars relative to the Sparrow project." He wished to know whether the Russians would halt their offensive outside Hungarian territory on the line of the Carpathian Mountains if, in in return, Hungary resisted "German assistance" and prevented Germany from "availing herself of any facilities within her borders."[12] Dulles advised that 684 was well aware that such an arrangement between Hungary and the United Nations would produce war between Germany and Hungary, but he hastened to state that, while he knew nothing definitely, he was sure it was "unlikely that this hypothetical question would be placed before the Russians at this particular time."

At that statement 684 hoped "some clue would be forthcoming which would help his country determine her course." As Dulles advised Donovan, 684 was a "trained, discreet man" who made it evident that his people would "risk a break with Germany and try to defend their own frontiers provided they were granted safeguards against an invasion by the Red Army." He had also made it evident that "any Anglo-Saxon occupation would be welcomed by his government."

That telegram, its plea for a "clue," its sober assurances that Hungary would resist in the west if it were spared an invasion in the east, the intimation that Anglo-Saxon occupation would be welcomed may well have been a factor in Donovan's decision to unfreeze the Sparrow operation. In any case, that was done as Hatz reappeared in Istanbul and was seen by Macfarland, Coleman, and Dogwood on February 27, 1944. Afterward Macfarland reported to Donovan that Hatz "assured me at the outset that he had been instructed to work out some method of collaboration with us and that he was to return shortly to his headquarters after he had come to an agreement with us." In particular, the Hungarian General Staff had agreed to commence supplying the OSS with intelligence about the German war machine.[13]

Whether Hatz's statement had any influence on Donovan is not clear; the probability is not. What was decisive was Dulles's message to Donovan of March 3, 1944:

> The following is vital and urgent. We have now secured 684's agreement to a plan which would allow the immediate execution of the Sparrow project under circumstances which, to my mind, curtail the risks attendant on any project of this nature. . . . I am sure our men will reach General Ujszaszy [chief of Hungarian intelligence and Hatz's chief] if they are dropped safely on Hungarian soil. . . .[14]

The Sparrow mission now went forward into its penultimate stage. There was communication with the Hungarian chief of intelligence— probably through Dulles—in which it was agreed that Duke, Suarez, and Nunn were to parachute onto Hungarian territory just over the frontier from Yugoslavia. They were to report to the nearest Hungarian military post and explain that they were members of a military mission to Tito, but that their aircraft had been thrown off course by antiaircraft gunfire and they had landed in Hungary in error. The Sparrow team would be "interrogated" by an officer of Hungarian Military Intelligence, and they would then be taken to Budapest "for further interrogation" by the chief of military intelligence, General Ujszaszy. He would "detain" them at his Budapest headquarters until German suspicions had been allayed, when they would be transferred to more congenial quarters and enabled to begin work extracting and transmitting intelligence about the Germans from Ujszaszy's service and files. They would also, using the wireless Suarez would take with him, act as intermediaries in the negotiations between the Allied governments and Hungary intended to enable Hungary to break its alliance with Germany and join the Allies.

On March 9, 1944, the Sparrow mission was flown to the British special operations squadron at Brindisi in the heel of Italy. There it was discovered that Duke had never before parachuted, so the mission was held up for days while he was given a short course. There, too, Nunn wrote a note to his commanding officer, Major Arthur Goldberg, chief of the OSS SI labor desk and a future secretary of labor and justice of the Supreme Court, that, given the dangers and uncertainties of the mission, was a masterpiece of nonchalance:

> This is a so-long note to you and the gang. We get off tomorrow and hope we can deliver something on the job. . . . I'll wireless out any suggestions that occur to me once we're set up. If nothing is heard from us for, say a month, it should be assumed that we are PWs. . . . Until we are actually in it we'll still be fairly much a shot in the dark, since the Hungarians have given Berne very little notion of what, precisely, they are prepared to do.[15]

Within a few hours Sparrow was in a Royal Air Force Halifax "milk run" to a bonfire on the ground in northern Croatia, where the Halifax dropped war stores to partisans. It flew on to a place near Vienna, where it dropped two British wireless agents. Then the it turned east to Sparrow's pinpoint near the junction of the Yura and Drava rivers, just over the border into Hungary from the frontier with northern Croatia.

At 2:30 A.M. on March 13, 1944, the Sparrow team leaped from the Halifax and landed in a plowed field. After scrambling from their harnesses and shroudlines, they signaled the Halifax to come in again to drop three parachute containers packed with Sparrow's food and extra clothing and such baubles as Parker fountain pens and Zippo lighters—in Europe at the height of World War II gifts that were as valuable to secret agents as glass beads had been to Livingstone and tin trays to Captain Cook.

Then Sparrow vanished, and for a month nothing was heard of them until Doering, on duty late in the evening of April 15, 1944, was handed a telegram from Dulles. The Sparrow team had been arrested and was undergoing interrogation at the headquarters in Prinz Albrechtstrasse, Berlin, of the Sicherheitsdienst.

Shortly after landing just inside Hungary, the Sparrow team buried their radios and parachuting equipment, a task that took until daybreak. Then they walked about one and a half miles through the woods and pastures in the general area of the frontier town of Nagykanizsa, to a small village.

Just after 6:00 A.M. they met their first Hungarian, a former waiter in Paris who spoke French. He took the team to the village hall where a crowd gathered. The men were well treated by friendly Hungarians who brought them breakfast. Duke asked one of the village elders if they could speak to a military official, but there was no telephone in the village, and a peasant had had to be sent to the nearest Hungarian Army camp. The first military official, therefore, did not arrive until about 9:00 A.M., when Duke explained that they "were part of a crew of a large bomber which had been hit by anti-aircraft, and in order to lighten the load so that the plane could return to its base the three of us had jumped."[16]

At about 11:00 A.M. they were approached by a man in mufti who said that he had been waiting for the team for three days and that he was a representative of the chief of Hungarian Military Intelligence, General Ujszaszy. He explained that the team would "have to go through the theater of being examined, etc., but when they had finished he would take us and our equipment along with him." Duke told the representative, an Air Force officer named Kirali, where the radios and stores were buried. The equipment was retrieved, and after spending the night in the officers' quarters, the Sparrow team were driven to the headquarters of the intelligence service in Budapest. There they were placed in cells, but the doors were left open during daylight, and good food was brought in from a restaurant.

It was not until the evening of March 17, 1944, that Major Kirali took the team to see the chief of Hungarian Military Intelligence, General Ujszaszy, who received Sparrow "smoothly and cordially" and, to Duke's surprise, invited them to "state their proposition." So far the arrangements made by Dulles had worked well, but at the use of the term "proposition" Duke bridled and replied that "we had no proposition," that the team had come with "none other than our regular terms of unconditional surrender," and that they were there also "to help and would be interested in learning [about the Hungarians'] plans or ideas."

At that, Ujszaszy announced that the two Cabinet ministers they were to see were out of town—it was a weekend—but they would be back in Budapest on Monday, when a meeting would be arranged. Meantime, the general stated somewhat apologetically they must be held as "prisoners." They spent that Saturday night in their cells, with the doors closed and guarded.

All remained somnolent and unremarkable until nine on Sunday morning, when Kirali came hurriedly to them and announced Ujszaszy wished to see them immediately. The team was taken to Ujszaszy's office, where they found the general "in a very nervous state. He had not slept all night," he was "as white as a sheet," and he "practically had tears in his eyes." The Germans, Ujszaszy announced, had invaded Hungary and were at that moment surrounding Budapest. That development, Ujszaszy stated, meant that Duke and his assistants must now regard themselves, as must all Hungary, as real prisoners. At the news the Sparrow team was sent back to the cells, the doors were locked, and there were no further meals from fancy restaurants.

Later, having had ample time to reflect, Duke reported to Donovan it seemed evident the Germans had invaded Hungary when they learned of the arrival of the Sparrow mission. "The Germans always want to 'justify' their actions," Duke reported. "They wanted to occupy Hungary and in order to justify such action, our mission seemed to be good proof, for it clearly demonstrated that certain members of the Cabinet were endeavoring to double-cross the Germans by negotiating a separate peace." He thought it likely that "the whole scheme might well have been a plan in [sic] which [the Germans] were in on, namely to give them the justification necessary for action such as occupying the whole of Hungary."

Nor was Duke's estimate unsound. The Germans could not permit Allied missions to subvert their grip on Eastern Europe at a time when the Red Army was beginning a major drive on Germany. Furthermore, in 1940 Hitler had used exactly this excuse—that local politicians were dickering with the British secret service to the disadvantage of Germany —to invade Belgium, Holland, and Luxembourg. Lastly, after the war the chief of the Sicherheitsdienst in southeastern Europe, Wilhelm Hoettl, wrote: "I was well informed by Hungarian intelligence officers about all these negotiations [between the OSS and the British and Hungarian dissidents] and particularly about the liaison between Ujszassi [sic] and the American Colonel." He "reported these happenings to Berlin," and "Hitler decided to act. The intention of Hungary to conclude a separate peace must be thwarted, he commanded, if the southern section of the Eastern front were not to be placed in the greatest danger."[17]

In these weighty circumstances, therefore, on March 25, 1944, Duke and his colleagues were turned over to the Sicherheitsdienst. They were taken to the Luftwaffe interrogation center at Pančeva, near Belgrade, where they felt they managed to get their captors to accept their cover story—that "we had intended to join the Yugoslav Partisans in Northern Croatia, but had gone too far and landed in Hungary by mistake." But the Germans did not accept that story: Ujszaszy had made a twenty-page statement on the affair in exchange for his life. Then he had been taken out and shot.

With that document in their possession, Hoettl's men removed Duke and his colleagues to the headquarters in Berlin of the SD. They were placed in solitary confinement for two weeks and then told they, too, were to be shot. Nor did that seem to be an idle threat when Duke and his party were handcuffed and taken to a yard where they were lined up as if they were about to be executed. Instead, they were put into a prison van, taken to one of Berlin's airports, and flown back to Budapest. There the Germans began a detailed interrogation of their prisoners, who, realizing they had no chance unless they cooperated, did so up to a point and, in intelligence jargon for talking nonsense, began "to spin the Germans a load of old fanny."

When Hoettl tried to get them to talk about the OSS, the "fanny" consisted of such statements as Duke's assertion that it was the "well-known organization in America run by Colonel 'Wild Bill' Donovan, specializing in all economic, financial, political problems of all countries in Europe, etc." But Duke stated later, all he really gave his captors was information about the functions and product of the Research and Analysis Branch. Nunn and Suarez did likewise.

When the detailed interrogation was over, Sparrow was removed to Colditz Castle, the medieval fortress near Leipzig used to hold prominent prisoners. There, prevented from escaping by alert guards, high walls, alarm fences, and floodlights, the Sparrow agents spent the rest of the war making raffia baskets and wooden galleons. But a British Intelligence chain with contacts inside Colditz did manage to get to the team, and they sent a message out to Donovan: "Bad treatment by Gestapo in Belgrade, Berlin, Budapest, Vienna. Landed safely and made contact as arranged. General Ujzsassy [sic] turned informant and told all. Propose to return via Budapest. Await instructions."[18]

Thus, the Sparrow fell. But the operation did produce important results. Viewed from Berlin, the operation was a dangerous intrusion into the heart of the German fortress at a critical time. No doubt it caused the greatest anxiety, and it may be remembered that in wartime it is often as useful to worry an enemy as to kill him. Sparrow was at least a catalyst that forced Hitler to invade Hungary with precious armored divisions dragged from other crucial fronts.

Two of the divisions employed by Hitler to subdue Hungary were taken from France, and when they returned, they were neither quite ready nor in quite the right place when the Neptune invasion came from England. For a lengthy period during the 1944 preinvasion period, as Hitler's chief of operations, General Walter Warlimont, would state, the western front was, during the Hungarian operation, "left without a single battle-worthy fully operational armoured division at a moment when the invasion might come any day."[19]

The value of the Sparrow mission to the strategic history of the Neptune campaign was immense, a classic example of what is meant by the theory of contributing to a military victory by unrelenting political pressure. Nor did the end of the mission mean the end of the Hungarian dalliance with the OSS; that continued until the last days of the war and continued to cause Hitler and the Oberkommando der Wehrmacht—and later the Russians—great anxiety.

25

Exit Snapdragon

Throughout the intrigues in Istanbul Donovan had been launching his many plans to "burn the Balkans." The proposal to detach Bulgaria from the Axis had first arisen in November 1942, when Major Murray Gurfein, a former New York assistant district attorney and a future New York judge, presented Donovan with a plan intended to overthrow the Fascist government of the Great Unifier, Czar Boris III of Bulgaria.[1]

Gurfein advised that in New York was a wealthy Bulgarian banker, Angel Kouyoumdjisky, thereafter code-named Kiss for both security and convenience. Kiss was worth between $15,000,000 and $20,000,000 cash, so it was said, he had taken out his first citizenship papers, but he remained influential in Bulgaria, and he was on terms of confidence with Czar Boris and the czarina, Joanna, a daughter of King Victor Emmanuel III of Italy. Kiss was very pro-American and much admired the Four Freedoms, although his record was not spotless: He was thought to be connected with the Macedonian IMRO, a secret society with a good deal of blood on its hands through its dedication to the reestablishment of Macedon, presently divided among Yugoslavia, Bulgaria, and Greece. Nothing had been proved, Gurfein advised Donovan, but Kiss might have been involved in the financing of the assassination at Marseilles in 1934 of King Alexander of Yugoslavia, a possibility that had occurred to the Immigration Department when Kiss applied for first papers.

Gurfein proposed, therefore, that Kiss, who liked the idea, be taken into the OSS as a contract agent, given cover perhaps as a representative of the Board of Economic Warfare on a mission for the United States to buy up raw materials needed by the Germans, and sent to Istanbul. There he would make contact with high personages at the czar's court, including his friend, Ivan Mihailov, who was "secretly a powerful influence with the Macedonian IMRO." Kiss would resume contact with Boris and the Bulgarian General Staff and would reinforce his connections with the "payment of the necessary funds," an exquisite term for bribery.

Requesting an initial budget of $220,000, Gurfein felt that Kiss would be able (1) to obtain secret intelligence about the activities of the Wehrmacht wherever Bulgaria had diplomatic missions and (2) to create a group in Sofia "to aid in the Allied cause by internal activities and, if possible, by overthrowing the government." Donovan took an immediate liking to the project, but not until the Italian collapse did the plan take on fresh importance, for until then Hitler had relied primarily on the Italian and Bulgarian armies to rule the Balkans. With the surrender of the 1,400,000 Italian soldiers, the defense of the Balkans now rested upon 700,000 Bulgarian troops. But they were not sufficiently strong. German forces in large numbers, destined for France and Russia, were being sent in, and if Bulgaria defected, Hitler would have to garrison the entire area with the Wehrmacht—a major diversion of his forces from the active battlefronts.

The prospect of Bulgaria's defection was enhanced shortly before the K Project began when Czar Boris died, the result, it was said by the Germans, of snake poison. There was little doubt that he had been murdered. The only doubt was who had done the murder. The Bulgarians, the Russians, the British, the Americans, the Macedonians, or the Greeks —all had reasons and access. Whatever the case, the czar was dead, and his passing left Bulgaria unstable and uncertain—in a psychological state where the Bulgarian regency and government might find Kiss's proposals more attractive.

Following the Combined Chiefs' approval of Donovan's proposals to "Accentuate our Present Subversive Efforts in the Balkans," Kiss was called to Washington and made a full colonel in the Fiscal Division of the U.S. Army. However, after the commission had been conferred on him Donovan was warned by Allen Dulles, the OSS agent in Bern, Switzerland, that prominent Bulgarians had reacted "violently" when Kiss's name had been mentioned. Dulles quoted one of them:

"I have always enjoyed K's picturesqueness. I have had the opportunity to see him in Sofia and also in London and Paris, but I am sure that it would be a grave error to bring him to the front at the present time in Bulgarian affairs and might readily destroy an understanding. K has a well-founded Bulgarian reputation for vanity and ostentatiousness as well as for buying up people who could aid him in his business. No Bulgarian of any standing would collaborate with K when it comes to the type of thing now being attempted. To have K materialize as an intimate advisor for Washington might create a disastrous impression in the Balkans and Bulgaria."[2]

Donovan might have been well advised to pay attention to the telegram. It would have saved him much trouble later, for Kiss was certainly an unusually ostentatious man. He appeared at the door of an OSS safe house in New York in a silver gray silk suit "built," as the term went, at Pope & Bradley in London, a pink shirt and a violet tie made for him by Sulka in Paris, a Prince Albert hat with a curly brim made at Lock's, St. James's, pearl gray spats, a gardenia from the Pierre in his buttonhole, and he was carrying a black ebony cane with an immense gold top presented to him, so he claimed, by Haile Selassie, the Lion of Judah. As Doering would recall, with his iron gray Prince of Wales whiskers, he made a startling impression. It could be expected, therefore, that he would make an equally startling impression in that fading old tart of a city, Istanbul. That he did.

Colonel Kiss arrived in Istanbul with Major Gurfein "to help the Turkish Government arrange its fiscal reforms," to lend weight to Kiss's real mission—ensuring that the Balkan peoples realized the consequences of not coming to terms with the Grand Alliance. To create the desired mood in Sofia and to demonstrate vividly the perils Bulgaria faced if it maintained its alliance with Germany, the U.S. Fifteenth Air Force launched sharp attacks on Sofia coincidentally with the start of Kiss's work. Two air attacks on January 10, 1944, created "a state of terror," but few casualties. However, in the third and fourth raids, which followed on the fourteenth, there was "general panic," and the Bulgarians claimed 9,000 people were killed, 17,000 were injured, and about 30 percent of the surface area of the city was destroyed.[3]

Yet Kiss's cover did not last too long. At an early date it became evident to the German intelligence service, as to the representatives of the myriad of intelligence agencies in Istanbul, that Kiss was not a colonel in the Fiscal Division of the U.S. Army. How the intelligence community established this became the subject of much anxious inquiry by the OSS. The Germans also soon knew—and the OSS soon knew that they knew—that Kiss was in touch with the metropolitan archbishop of the Orthodox Church, André, and with the Bulgarian minister in Ankara, a certain Balabanoff, who in turn were in touch with the regency in Sofia. Moreover, Dulles was informed by his spy in the German Foreign Office, Source Wood, the Reich plenipotentiary in Sofia, Obergruppenführer SS Beckerle, had informed Berlin that "Kouyoumdjisky is a representative of the capitalists" but was "of limited influence in modern Bulgaria."[4]

That signal seemed to indicate that K's usefulness had collapsed at the outset, for the success of the operation depended upon the Germans' not being aware that Bulgaria was surrendering until it had actually done so.

If they knew prematurely, they could, and would, occupy the country by armed force and change the government to ensure the country's loyalty to the Axis. How, therefore, had the Sicherheitsdienst learned so quickly of the K Project? That was the question that was to haunt Donovan and the OSS.

Donovan could only let the operation proceed, for Major Gurfein pointed out that after the sharp air raids on Sofia the Bulgarians had asked that they be stopped. Kiss had conveyed to Balabanoff the statement that they would be stopped as a precondition of serious conversations, the air raids had in fact stopped, and Balabanoff was now deeply impressed by Kiss's apparent influence with the Allied High Command. Consequently, when Balabanoff went to Sofia to talk over some of the details of the proposed defection, he was able to assure the Regency Council that the raids would not be repeated during the term of the negotiations. And when they were not in fact repeated, the Regency Council, too, became more impressed by Kiss's influence in Washington.

Balabanoff's first move on his return to Istanbul was to send for K, his purpose to impart momentous news: All the regents, the premier, and the chief leaders of the opposition had "consented at last to endeavor to bring about talks with the United States, with a view to joining the United Nations." Balabanoff informed Kiss that the suggestion had been made at his meetings in Sofia that "an exploratory Bulgarian Mission be dispatched to Istanbul with a mandate to outline for us generally the conditions under which the Bulgarian Army would join the Allies on a combatant status."[5]

Gurfein stated at the meeting that Kiss was not empowered to negotiate, only to form contacts, and that as matters stood at the time, the Allies were interested only in Bulgaria's unconditional surrender. Balabanoff replied that was understood by his principals, who wanted only "some kind of a guarantee that the United States does not intend to do away with old Bulgaria"—a reference, perhaps, to Kiss's interest in the reestablishment of Macedonia.

Not surprisingly, Balabanoff's statements produced optimism at OSS headquarters, particularly when Gurfein reported a little later that he had just come from a meeting with Balabanoff, who had informed him that he had a "definite mandate from his Government to discuss this matter."[6] Gurfein added a warning: Balabanoff had stressed the need for absolute discretion and security about the meeting between the OSS and his principals in case the Germans came to hear about it. He was sure that the Bulgarian Army would "follow the government" and would "join forces with the government in expelling the Germans." There would be, Balabanoff had assured him, "no difficulty on that score."

Gurfein then reported that:

the Mission's primary objective has been accomplished, namely, the establishment of direct contact with the Bulgarian Government, the determination that in principle the Bulgarian Government desired to desert the Axis and the provision of a channel through which the arrangements could be made for the dispatch of a Bulgarian Mission to Cairo to meet with British, American, and Russian delegates.

He reported also that "the desire of the Bulgarian Government to join the Allies is sincere" and asked for an extension of the decision not to attack Sofia from the air during the negotiations.

The State Department having been informed of this satisfactory state of affairs on March 2, 1944, it instructed Donovan to direct the K Mission to inform Balabanoff that "representatives of the three Allies are prepared to meet a fully qualified Bulgarian Mission in Cairo." It also requested that Gurfein and Kiss remain at Istanbul to "continue to handle this matter and these negotiations up to the point of the arrival of a qualified Bulgarian Mission at Cairo."

As Donovan moved his pieces for what would have been his first major operational victory—and victory it would have been; despite the smallness of Bulgaria and the mediocrity of its government it *was* the linchpin of the Axis in the Balkans—the lines went dead. Abruptly and inexplicably the K Mission heard no more from Balabanoff, who seemed to have vanished. André, too, had disappeared somewhere deep in the fastness of his church. Everybody began to look for reasons for the collapse.

Toulmin, in an interesting insight into the psychology of the OSS executive, thought the British were involved in some way, warning Donovan: "Personally I think that our cousins are watching the K Mission very carefully and might possibly stoop to attempt a sabotage operation on it."[7] That was not likely.

When that possibility was discounted, the chief in Turkey, Lanning Macfarland, warned Donovan that Kiss's "high-handed and indiscreet manner of handling his contacts" would "retard rather than assist any movement the Bulgarian Government might make to reject its Axis ties or to come over to the United Nations' side."[8] The U.S. Counterintelligence Corps in the Middle East supported this view with the advice that Kiss had become "boastful, talkative and indiscreet." Donovan felt compelled to send him a stern telegram on February 25, 1944:

> Since I had been under the impression that you were aware of the extreme gravity of the undertaking in which you are participating, I have been quite disillusioned and concerned by unfavorable accounts which have come to my ears regarding your want of judgment and your manner of making advances to certain individuals. To preclude the development of additional problems, you will obey absolutely the directions of Mr. Macfarland, who as our Officer

of Strategic Services in that region is to be considered your superior and supervising authority.[9]

In the end, with all lines cold, and with Donovan seriously concerned about Kiss's sense of security, WJD withdrew Kiss to Washington, where he was returned to civilian life. Only later was it to emerge that Donovan, Gurfein, and Kiss had been the victims of what was the most serious OSS intelligence failure of World War II.

The third country in Donovan's plan to accentuate subversive operations against Hitler in the Balkans was Rumania, the principal source of the Wehrmacht's petroleum and a nation with two armies on the Russian front. During 1943 Donovan's planners amply demonstrated the desirability of separating Rumania from the Axis with a study that showed:

> (a) There is at present a serious oil shortage in Germany. (b) Rumanian oil is of vital importance to Nazi Germany. It is estimated that during 1943 Rumania will provide about one-third of the Axis supply of both crude and synthetic petroleum (5,800,000 metric tons of a total of 16,500,000 metric tons). Should this Rumania [sic] supply of oil be cut off Axis military operations would necessarily be reduced in scale.[10]

The planners believed that aerial bombardment could "effectively cripple the oil industry for a considerable period," but not permanently. The only permanent way to stop the oil was to persuade the Rumanian government to desert Germany. There was, the planners reported to WJD, no absence of political contact for use in the process of rupturing the association between Rumania and the Reich.

The observation was correct, for late in January 1943 in New York an OSS agent specializing in Balkan affairs, Bernard Yarrow, began a series of conversations with Edgar Ausnit, a Rumanian who, with his brother Max, had controlled the armaments industry in Rumania for many years and was on terms of confidence with Marshal Ion Antonescu, the Fascist dictator of Rumania.[11]

Edgar Ausnit had transferred $2,000,000 of his assets to New York and then come to America. Max Ausnit, however, was not able to leave and, as the majority stockholder of the Resita Company, which produced most of Rumania's armaments, had been sent to prison. He had now been released and was living in his palace in Bucharest, and the Ausnit brothers were in communication through intermediaries in Lisbon. In that correspondence, Max, who had seen Antonescu recently, had reason to believe that "if a guarantee of the independence of Rumania is secured from the Russian government, and if said guarantee is backed by the United States Government, then Marshal Antonescue [sic] will be ready to join the

United Nations. Furthermore, reported Yarrow, "Edgar Ausnit further believes that his brother . . . would be in an excellent position to help us in this direction." Edgar Ausnit, too, was willing "to do everything in his power to assist us in reaching an understanding with Marshal Antonescu." Yarrow noted that Max Ausnit's eldest boy was now at Harvard and that Max Ausnit's fortune, amounting to "several million dollars," was in English banks, and he felt that "Edgar Ausnit is entirely sincere in his wishes to assist us, and has no other motive except to free Rumania of the enemy and thereby restore his own and his brother's former dominant financial position in Rumania."

Having read Yarrow's paper, Donovan began a large-scale inquiry to establish more definitely the attitude of the Rumanian dictator and government. On February 10, 1943, he wired Dulles in Bern that Marshal Antonescu might be prepared to defect and requested Dulles's advice. Almost immediately Dulles reported that one of his sources had received a letter from Max Ausnit declaring:

> [The] following principles were guiding [Antonescu's] policy: 1. Frontiers of pre-1940 to be preserved. 2. Democratic constitutional program to be immediately produced. 3. Social justice and Christian morals to be reintroduced into public life. 4. System of law and liberty to be reestablished. 5. Confederation of southwestern and central Europe to be realized. 6. Previous orientation of cooperation with democratic governments of the west to be returned. 8. The restoration of the Hapsburg regime to be opposed.[12]

No reference was made to the problem of Russia, where the Rumanian armies had played an important part in the devastation of the Crimea.

At that point Donovan's inquiries were terminated on an order from the secretary of state; Assistant Secretary Berle asserted that OSS was trespassing into the dominion of diplomacy and that he was going to take the matter to Roosevelt. Therefore, Dulles was told on March 10 that the Rumanian matter was "temporarily suspended." Five days later, when Berle had been to see Roosevelt, there was further conversation between Berle and Donovan's representative at the State Department, and Dulles was advised that "although we are not ready to enter discussions, we are interested in information about the line of thought. He adds that of course we are Russia's loyal allies, and without that in mind we could do nothing."

Berle's intervention had the effect of producing a serious interruption in the contact between Donovan and the Rumanian dissidents. The Ausnits dropped out of the picture completely, and between March and September the connection was sustained only with the British Secret Intelligence Service representative at Istanbul. Partly to refresh Antonescu's memory about the danger in which he and his country now stood, the U.S. Army Air Forces sent 177 B-24D's from Libyan bases to attack the facilities at Ploeşti on August 1, 1943. In the attack the Americans lost 532 men killed or captured and 54 aircraft, with almost all aircraft damaged to some degree. But while huge fires resulted, the repair teams soon had the refineries working again, and the United States was to lose more than 350 aircraft, trying to knock the refineries out permanently. They did not succeed, strengthening Donovan's case that political subversion was the only effective means of stopping the flow of Rumanian oil to the Axis.

The first attack, combined with the rapid advance of the Red Army toward the Rumanian frontier during the summer of 1943, did produce a satisfactory change of attitude concerning negotiations. Antonescu sent a new ambassador to Turkey, Alexander Cretzianu, who contacted the chief of the British SIS at Istanbul. There was a conversation between the Rumanian and the Briton which the Briton then communicated to Macfarland of OSS, for transmission to the American ambassador to Turkey, Laurence Steinhardt. The Briton's communication was accompanied by an unusual and significant request: that Macfarland take all precautions as to the security of the message—a sure sign that the British felt OSS Turkey had been penetrated in a manner as yet not established.

In the message Cretzianu stated that King Michael of Rumania and a former premier, Iuliu Maniu, had empowered him to state that "Rumania is prepared to carry out Anglo-American instructions and will even go so far as to revolt if it receives some encouragement from the British and and Americans and is given some guarantee that its boundary problems with Russia receive fair treatment."

The Allied secret services thereupon met in Cairo and decided to act, but, it appears, fears that OSS Turkey might have been penetrated by the enemy played its part in the decision to send only a Briton to Rumania to act as intermediary. As WJD was advised, the British agent was Colonel Gardyne de Chastelain, an Englishman who before the war had been sales manager of the Phoenix Oil and Transport Company in Bucharest and had been close to King Carol II of Rumania and his famous mistress, Magda Lupescu, helping both flee Rumania with all their possessions—including $4,000,000 and some of the palace Rembrandts—when Antonescu forced Carol to abdicate in 1940.

Colonel de Chastelain and a wireless operator were parachuted onto a noble's estate near Bucharest to a reception committee consisting of the guns, the beaters, and the carriages of a hunting party—interesting cover—and both were "arrested" and "imprisoned" in a villa on the outskirts of Bucharest—more interesting cover. The operator then opened communications with MO 4, British secret service headquarters in Cairo, which now worked in close relationship with Toulmin of the

OSS, and conditions of association were arranged with Maniu's representative to enable a high-ranking Rumanian peace envoy to travel to Istanbul and Cairo to talk to a combined Anglo-American-Russian commission.

That "swallow" was Prince Barbu Stirbey, who arrived in Istanbul early in March 1944. He was spirited by the British and American secret services to Cairo, where, on March 17, 1944, he appeared before Ambassador Lincoln McVeagh and Embassy Counselor Harold Shantz for the United States, Lord Moyne for Great Britain, and two Soviet representatives, Solod and Movirev. Although a British secret service officer, Colonel Tom Masterson, attended, OSS representatives were not invited because of the fears of a leak at Istanbul, and the record of proceedings and signals received by the OSS was all British documents obtained "informally" by Macfarland in Istanbul and Toulmin in Cairo. That, perhaps, was unsatisfactory for Donovan, for the arrival of the Rumanian emissary represented the supreme moment in his Balkan plan. Still, the British fears were not unfounded.

At the outset the commission learned that although Antonescu knew of Prince Stirbey's mission, he had a real mandate not from Antonescu, but from the political opposition in Bucharest. However, as Stirbey told the commission, he felt he could arrange Rumania's defection, provided he received assurances:

(A) Rumania would retain its independence. (B) There would be no agreement in advance as to certain territorial adjustments. (C) That his country's status be that of a cobelligerency [with the Allies]. (D) That in the event of an attack by Bulgaria or Hungary on Rumania, the last named shall be given military cooperation by allied forces.[13]

Russian forces would be recognized as Allied forces.

The meeting adjourned in hopeful spirit, for neither Stirbey nor the Russians had mentioned anything during the talks that would show that the Rumanian revolution against the Germans would founder on the ancient rock of Russo-Rumanian antipathies. And then the blow fell.

Although Stirbey's arrival was supposed to have been a state secret, and all precautions had been taken by both the British and American services, British Intelligence reported the Germans knew he was attending peace conversations with the Allies in Turkey. Furthermore, there were leakages in the press. Stirbey's life was, therefore, in the greatest danger, to say nothing of such family as he had left in Bucharest—he had brought his daughter with him. Every effort was made to make the reports appear false, but without success. The Germans, who had 40,000 uniformed men in Rumania, were fully aware of what was happening, and as with Hungary, they were preparing to seize Rumania.

On March 24, 1944, a message reached Macfarland in Ankara from the British secret representative in Turkey:

> With the King of Rumania's permission, Maniu asks that you place the matter below before representatives of the United States and Britain, realizing that every sign points to Rumania being requested, as Hungary was, to accept German troops in their country and that Germany will try to establish still firmer collaboration and will try in every way possible to force Rumania to expend more energy in battling the Russians.[14]

The signal, which was sent immediately to Donovan and Roosevelt, then stated:

> Insofar as it related to Allied interest, Germany's occupation of Rumania on the heels of her occupation of Hungary and to be followed by her occupation of Bulgaria, will indicate the completion of Germany's preparations for Balkan defense. We must know, to give us some basis upon which to organize the possibility of trying to resist German occupation, if we can depend upon a minimum of assistance from Americans and British. We appreciate the fact that we cannot plan immediately upon a military operation of any considerable size. However, limited but prompt assistance from air forces and air borne troops could at least be considered. . . . It is possible that a mass invasion of Rumania by the German forces may be postponed for little while until the Germans are well established in Hungary. Consequently it is not too late even now to make arrangements for military assistance from the U.S. and Britain.

But there could be no saving Rumania from its Nazi ally, even if it was assumed that the telegram was not an attempt to force the commission to make a favorable decision. Relief could have come only from Russia, and Russia's bitterness at the Rumanian rape of the Crimea was paramount. Without agreement at Cairo, there could be no expedition to save Bucharest from the Wehrmacht. In any event, such an expedition was not necessary; Hitler took the country by stealth, using the 40,000 men already there and the Fascist Iron Guard to maintain Rumania as a German ally a little longer.

While that was happening, the Ankara Committee, which controlled British secret service operations in Asia Major and Minor, was sitting to establish who had betrayed Stirbey. During the debate other questions were also asked: Who had betrayed Kiss? And Moltke? And Sparrow? And a legion of men and women throughout Eastern and Central Europe who worked for Cereus and were now vanishing?

Early in February 1944 one of Leverkühn's associates at the Abwehr war station in Istanbul, Erich Vermehren, and his wife, Countess Elizabeth von Plettenburg, suddenly defected to a young official of the Office of War Information, who, puzzled about what to do with them, contacted the OSS. While Vermehren was not an important Abwehr official, Macfarland thought he might have some useful information and spirited him and the countess out to Cairo. Almost immediately three other Abwehr personnel in Turkey, a Dr. Hamburger and a German husband and wife team named Kleczkowski, who had been operating in Turkey under journalistic cover, approached an OSS official and asked for protection. Reluctantly—for both the American and British services had strict orders not to accept defectors, or to encourage defections, without permission from headquarters—the OSS accepted the trio and flew them to Cairo. All five were subjected to detailed interrogation, in Egypt, England, and the United States.

The preliminary interrogations were soon completed and revealed a fact that was important to the OSS: One of its most trusted agents in Turkey had been under Abwehr control. That revelation was considered so important by the British that at a meeting of the Ankara Committee in May "representatives from all British services . . . decided to minimize relations [with OSS Turkey], pending some improvement in security in both business and personal activities."[15]

On June 6, 1944, the chief of Secret Intelligence, Whitney Shepardson, wired Toulmin in Cairo that a "grave situation" that had arisen at Istanbul "not only casts doubt on some of our agents there but . . . may influence the security of our activities and personnel in other places."[16] Donovan's response to the grave situation emerging in Turkey was to order an X-2 inspector, Irving Sherman, to Istanbul to investigate. His first signals served merely to increase the sense of dismay and anxiety. All the cases in which there had been disaster—Kiss, Morde, Moltke, Sparrow, Stirbey—had a common element: Dogwood. A check of his intelligence file also showed a high content of what may have been "chicken feed": Between June 1943 and February 1944 Dogwood had submitted 730 intelligence reports from 58 subagents on the German military, economic, and political machine in Eastern and Central Europe, but the British, who had received copies, considered "about 3%" valuable or interesting. Almost all the rest was either fictitious, did not check against substantiated facts, or was plainly deceptive "chicken feed"— material scattered by the enemy deception service in the hope that the OSS would gobble up and circulate an important deception without noticing it.[17]

The suspicious element in this lamentable record was intensified by Dogwood's refusal, while he was under interrogation by Sherman, to identify his sources. Moreover, a thorough check with the British Security Indexes and the ISOS files in London and New York showed that Hatz was plainly and irrefutably a Sicherheitsdienst penetration agent, "a very clever and a very dangerous one." The fact that Dogwood had consistently defended Hatz to the OSS in the past tended to indicate that he himself was an SD agent and was probably under Hatz's control.

Why, therefore, had it taken so long for suspicions about Dogwood to develop? That was the question before Sherman. In the first place, it was discovered that Dogwood had been retained by Coleman without any check's being run on him in the ISOS files and the Security Indexes, largely because Coleman did not know of their existence—a discovery that led to Donovan's issuing the order to all personnel that data concerning agents about to be employed were to be sent to OSS Washington for checking *before* they were employed and *before* they were entrusted with any confidential task.

There were other reasons for Dogwood's long run of success. As Sherman stated in his report to Donovan, Dogwood was:

> [a] strong-willed, egocentric, domineering individual, who brooked no interference. He was given to outbursts of temperament when contradicted or his authority questioned. He fancied himself to be a practicing psychologist and had the utmost confidence in his ability to make friends and influence people. He was interested largely in grandiose political schemes involving individuals only in high echelon. It is the conviction of those associated with him that he himself has post-war political ambitions.

Sherman found that even when Coleman was joined by an assistant, Lansing Williams, neither "was competent to control a personality as strong as Dogwood's and, in fact, they did not control him."

The chief of mission, Lanning Macfarland, "had personal contact with Dogwood only on very rare occasions," so that supervision of the Czech was almost wholly in the hands of Coleman, but owing to Dogwood's personality, it became Coleman's practice to "turn over to the Dogwood chain for handling *all* contacts which were established in this area for Central European intelligence." For the most part, reported Sherman, "Dogwood talked alone to his agents." He "dictated and edited their reports," and there was "evidence that Dogwood colored intelligence he received to conform to his own ideas." There was also "evidence that he withheld material from us for personal and, perhaps, less obvious reasons. There is evidence that he attributed intelligence subsequently found to be inaccurate, to sub-sources who claim never to have supplied this intelligence."

The reason for Dogwood's behavior was "unclear" at the time Sherman sent in his report, but Sherman found it significant that Dogwood refused to reveal the identities of his agents and contacts and that only a few were known to Coleman, Macfarland, or Williams. Moreover, Sherman continued, "Dogwood was aware of the fact that many of his agents were double agents" employed by the German and Hungarian services. But "so great was his belief in himself that he was confident that his double agents were loyal only to him and paid only lip service to their other employers." The result was that the Cereus chain was "penetrated by individuals of clearly doubtful character and loyalty."

Dealing with Hatz, Sherman described how Dogwood had used him to:

> carry two [OSS] transmitters into Hungary, one destined for the [Hungarian General Staff] and one for Iris. Iris' real name was Fritz Laufer, and he was an important official of the Gestapo in Budapest. There is evidence that Dogwood was warned against Iris, but he ignored the warning and replied that Iris was one of his best agents.

Sherman contended that Dogwood claimed that Laufer was a Cereus informant and "an old personal friend of Dogwood." Furthermore, he advised, another Hungarian agent, Jacaranda, who was well regarded by Dogwood and therefore accepted by Coleman as a member of the Cereus chain, "turned out to have been a British spy since 1941."

Plainly, therefore, the Cereus organization was badly penetrated by the German, Hungarian, and British intelligence services, and perhaps under German control through Dogwood, almost from conception. Less serious, but as embarrassing, were the discoveries that Macfarland's chauffeur was reporting to the Russian secret service in Istanbul and the X-2 representative's chauffeur was reporting regularly to the Turkish secret police. And, it would be conceded ruefully:

> A further notable penetration of OSS was effected by one Mrs. Hildegarde Reilly, reputed to have been the most successful female agent working in Istanbul. . . . Mrs. Reilly came in contact with an OSS officer and, although she was known to be a double agent, [Macfarland] approved the association, hoping that some information on German activity could thus be acquired. The project backfired, inasmuch as Mrs. Reilly is known to have reported to the Germans on OSS personnel and activities. Other similar penetrations were accomplished by various female spies in the city.[18]

The extent and gravity of the German penetration of the Cereus organization became more evident when it was learned that following the capture of Sparrow, the OSS team at Budapest, the Germans arrested the entire Hungarian General Staff. As serious was the loss at the same time of Cassia, an organizer of an Austrian underground called the Committee of 14. Cassia had been assisting the OSS in an operation to land an OSS mission similar to Sparrow near Vienna—Redbird, formed at Algiers by the SI Labor Desk representative, Gerhardt van Arkel. Cassia was a high official of the Semperit Rubber Company of Austria, which operated seven rubber and synthetic rubber plants between Duisburg, Germany, and Cracow, Poland, and as part of his duties he was able to travel between all seven plants. Cassia also had warehouses in twenty centers throughout Europe.

Both the plants and warehouses were staffed by executives he selected because he knew them willing to spy against the Wehrmacht for political reasons, and he traveled between those twenty points. Thus, Cassia had built up what was the OSS's most important espionage network inside Germany. Cassia, who was being controlled by Dulles, had been able to provide Dulles with valuable information about German missile experiments and research and development centers, the fuel and fuel production facilities for the V-2 rocket being prepared for the bombardment of London, the whereabouts of components and assembly plants for the V-2, German synthetic rubber production, and experiments to use rubber plates on German U-boats to neutralize the detecting effect of Allied radar. Over the fourteen months he worked for OSS, Cassia had also provided important information relating to the dispersal of the German aircraft industry and the establishment of "shadow" factors at Ebreichsdorf, Pottendorf, and Vöslau—factories attacked and destroyed by the U.S. Fifteenth Air Force after his information had been verified by photographic missions.

But now Cassia was no more. He had been shot by the Sicherheitsdienst, and, Dulles reported, more than 100 men and women who had worked with him had been arrested by the Gestapo and were suffering some unknown fate. As Irving Sherman, the X-2 inspector, reported to Donovan, the cumulative effect of the German penetration of Cereus was that Macfarland had now lost all the "contacts worthy of the name" in Central and Eastern Europe. Sherman had the sad task also of advising Donovan that the OSS now had "nothing of our own available for secret intelligence from Central Europe" in Turkey because "the organization we set up to handle Central European intelligence was unwisely conceived, badly staffed, and directed in the first instance by mediocrities."[19] Moreover, Sherman went on, "Since all our European eggs had been placed in the Dogwood basket, there was little or nothing that one could salvage."

The full extent of the German control of Cereus was never established. But X-2's chief, James R. Murphy, had to consider it total, an estimate that was probably not far short of the reality. The organizations were, therefore, dissolved. Thought was given to dismissing Macfarland, but he knew too much about the Canaris connection and no risks could be taken. He was withdrawn from Istanbul without fuss and transferred to operations connected with Yugoslavia.

Coleman was brought home, and he left the OSS, having completed his final report. Dogwood simply vanished; it is not impossible that he was "liquidated," although the nationality of his liquidators would forever remain mysterious. Obviously the OSS had the most to gain from his execution, but this possibility was dismissed by James R. Murphy, the head of X-2, as "fanciful." Fanciful or not Dogwood's disappearance was total, so total indeed that another high-ranking X-2 officer felt that Dogwood might have been a Soviet agent. As the X-2 officer explained, "At Istanbul during this period there was a very tough, very dedicated, very astute Soviet agent called Captain Mihailov, whose job it was to penetrate the American, British, and other intelligence services represented in the city. His immediate task was to establish what we and the other services were up to, but he also had a long-range mission. That was to identify Anglo-American agents so that the Soviets would know who they were up against after the war. Mihailov's tactics were interesting: He did not attempt to suborn people already recruited by our intelligence services. What he did was to recruit agents who were not working for any service, indoctrinate them with the glories of Communism, and then feed them to the Allied controllers. In that he was very successful, and the tactic brings to mind Dogwood's recruiting and operating methods. In any case, Dogwood vanished completely, he was not found after the war, and that suggests that he was spirited away to Odessa or some such place."[20]

As for Hatz, he told his associates that he had been relieved as military attaché as a "disciplinary measure" and been "forced to request duty on the Russian front." A few weeks after his departure Budapest Radio announced that he had been tried for high treason and hanged on June 26, 1944—a report that was not true, for Dulles discovered a month later he was serving as aide-de-camp to the Hungarian war minister, Imry Csatay. His final fate was not established, but the thought in the OSS was that the end of the war found him serving the Soviet or Hungarian Communist services with the same diligence that he had served the Hungarian Fascists and German Nazis.

Globally and strategically the consequences of the Vermehren defections were equally serious, although strictly speaking, those consequences could not be laid at the door of the OSS. However, Donovan's enemies were not scrupulous later about deciding who had been responsible for what aspect of the disaster in Turkey. The reality was that the Office of War Information bore responsibility for Vermehren and his wife because one of their employees had encouraged them to defect, unaware that it was the policy of the Anglo-American secret services not to encourage defection. The reason for the policy was simple: The German intelligence services would be much less dangerous to the Allies under Canaris than under a party chieftain; indeed, Canaris had played, and would continue to play, so long as he was able to remain in office, an important role in ensuring the Allied victory.

Therefore, if Canaris were removed from office through, for example, a major defection, he would be replaced by a party official who might be a much more formidable opponent and would so restructure the Abwehr that the advantages the Allies were enjoying through its existence might be lost, with serious consequences upon the outcome of the battle and, perhaps, even the war.

But as Donovan's and his agency's antagonists argued, that downfall was what had occurred through the Vermehren defections. The defections had produced a reaction within the *Führerhauptquartier* out of all proportion to the importance of that collection of small fry. For years the Reichsführer SS, Heinrich Himmler, had been waiting for an excuse to take over the Abwehr and establish a single, unified intelligence and counterespionage service under his control. Such control would complete Himmler's command of the security apparatus of the Third Reich, thus making him the most powerful man in Germany after Hitler. For years Himmler had been frustrated by Canaris's adroit use of the law and of jurisdictions. But now the Reichsführer SS had his excuse. He had reported the defections to Hitler, Hitler had signed the necessary order for unification, Canaris had been dismissed, SS men had begun to replace Abwehr principal officers at all war stations, and a British counterintelligence bulletin issued weekly to advise the Allied Supreme Command on the enemy intelligence situation was cited as an example of what was occurring through "OSS irresponsibility":

> Enemy espionage activities Middle East concerned principally with reorganizing Abwehr in Turkey by replacing all members about whom any suspicion [of] disloyalty exists, tightening Abwehr security, changing ciphers, destroying all Istanbul files, holding families in Germany as hostages and controlling transit into Turkey. Special inspectors have arrived from Berlin to assist new Abwehr head Turkey . . . in reorganization.[21]

And, the opponents of OSS went on, the situation was made the graver because the British had built an immense and extremely effective deception industry around the fact that for some years they had controlled the Abwehr in the British Isles, and through ISOS it was largely under control in the United States, North Africa, and the Middle East. That deception industry was required to mislead Hitler about the two key secrets of the European war—the place and date of Neptune, the cross-Channel attack, the one operation through which the Grand Alliance could lose the war. That operation was now imminent. Until the Istanbul defections the British were sure they could protect the secrets of D-Day and almost sure that it would be possible to obtain strategic surprise by so manipulating the controlled enemy agents that they would mislead the German Supreme Command about the timing and the direction of the immense attack—the unrepeatable attack that would be the emotional and strategical climax of World War II.

What, therefore, was Donovan's position in all this?

The Istanbul affair was undoubtedly a severe blow to the OSS reputation. Just how severe the blow really was depended upon whether the person concerned was for or against the OSS. Those opposed to the service considered it a disaster, produced by WJD's erratic leadership and personnel selection and believed its consequences on the course of the war would be fundamental. The OSS and its supporters argued that the Istanbul incident was a product of two factors: (1) the secret war itself, in which such casualties and collapses occurred to all powers, including those archpractitioners of secret service, the British and the Russians; and (2) the fact that its severity would have been diminished had the United States formed a cadre of trained secret service agents before the war.

Both arguments had truth, but the attitude of the OSS critics was based on a prediction of what was to occur. In fact, the worst fears were not realized. The efficiency of the German intelligence services everywhere was not improved by events at Istanbul. In fact, it was diminished severely at a critical time—on the eve of the invasion when the Germans required a trained, perceptive, skillful service if they were to perceive the truth through the miasma of Allied deception. Many of those trained officials were no longer in the Abwehr, and moreover, the new service visualized by Himmler was in bureaucratic chaos throughout the preinvasion period.

Thus, in the short-term disaster at Istanbul there was long-term success. The German intelligence services had been shattered by the Vermehren defections, and the American intelligence service had not been shattered by the poor performance of Coleman and the Cereus chain. If anything, it had been strengthened by that experience. Just as the American defeat at Kasserine had produced a long-overdue change of attitude in the American military, so the defeat at Istanbul had revolutionized the OSS's attitude toward the secret war. Excellent new men arrived to take up the gauntlet—men such as Frank Wisner—and the battle was resumed.

Moreover, as was soon to be shown, Canaris was not lost to the Black Orchestra conspiracy, relations with the British security services were not permanently affected by the Istanbul affair, and the controlled enemy agents continued to work effectively under the ecologists of double agency—as Norman Holmes Pearson neatly described the practice.

But Snapdragon was still an OSS disaster.

26

Christmas 1943

For Donovan, Christmas 1943 was probably the most extraordinary Christmas of his life. Still in Cairo managing his Balkan plan, on November 22, 1943, he was to be found at the Mena House underneath the Sphinx and Great Pyramids outside Cairo, where Roosevelt, Churchill, and Chiang Kai-shek were to meet for the Sextant Conference on grand strategy. He arranged with Chiang to go to China and with the supreme Allied commander in Southeast Asia, Lord Louis Mountbatten, to Burma, in the first instance to make an alliance with the Chinese secret service and in the second to inspect OSS forces operating in the Burmese jungles and mountains against the Japanese.

Then, on November 25, after the conference, Donovan traveled with FDR's party to Teheran for the Eureka Conference with Churchill and Stalin, the primary purpose of which was to decide upon a joint strategy for the defeat of Nazi Germany, if possible, in 1944. At Teheran, there was the usual debate between FDR, who believed that Germany could be defeated only if the Western Allies crossed the English Channel and destroyed the German armies in France, and Churchill, who clung vigorously to his southern strategy—which would not only enable the Allies to knife into Fortress Europe at its softest point but also have the effect of keeping the Red Army out of Eastern Europe. As usual Donovan supported the Churchillian theory—support that did him little good with the Joint Chiefs.

On December 1, 1943, the military conclusions were embodied in a document signed by the President, the prime minister, and Marshal Stalin. Among the highly secret decisions, the triumvirs announced their decision to launch the cross-Channel attack, Neptune, on or about May 1, 1944. In addition, partially at least upon Donovan's information and recommendations, the triumvirs agreed to support Tito's partisans in Yugoslavia with supplies, equipment, and commando raids. They also made the decision that henceforth the military staffs of the three powers would keep in close touch on the forthcoming operations in Europe—an agreement that gave Donovan the opening he needed to obtain permission to go to Moscow at the earliest date.

Then he set out for Asia. On December 7, 1943, he arrived at Nazira, the site of an OSS base in the Burmese jungle. Donovan thereupon made a journey that some of his colleagues considered not only extremely hazardous but, because he was in possession of the inner secrets of the war as a result of his attendance at the Eureka and Sextant conferences, irresponsible to the point where they doubted whether he was fitted for his high tasks—and they said so at the time.

Detachment 101, the code name of the OSS unit in Burma, had been established on FDR's orders in May 1942 under the command of Colonel Carl Eifler, a tough ex-prison guard and a born guerrilla. For operational purposes Eifler's unit was under the command of General Joseph W. Stilwell. A difficult, complicated man, Stilwell had inherited a difficult and complicated politico-military task involving, mainly but not exclusively, the British, Chinese, Burmese, and Indian administrations and general staffs, and he was called upon to fight with only nominal resources a Japanese Army that was strong, victorious, and resolute. Part of those resources was Eifler's Detachment 101. Stilwell had charged Eifler to disrupt "Japanese communications, shipping, and to bring about Japanese reprisals on the native population which will result in discouraging native aid to the Japanese"—a brutal, heartless assignment no soldier could have relished.[1] The first specific mission was to "deny the use of the Myitkyina aerodrome to the Japanese" and in "the vicinity of the aerodrome [to] destroy the railroad cars, and sink river vessels carrying fuel." Also, Eifler's detachment was to destroy the railroad bridge near Meza.

These assignments were carried out skillfully and ruthlessly. But as WJD was well aware, numerous tensions developed between the officers of the various American and Allied services engaged in the operations. Moreover, probably because they disliked taking action that would bring Japanese reprisals upon the native populations, some of Eifler's men had shown themselves reluctant to make the deep penetrations of enemy territory needed to carry out this aspect of his orders.

Eifler himself had suffered a severe head injury that limited his capacities for command and diplomacy—by nature he was a rough, tough individual, and his injury had markedly shortened his temper—and he was now in sharp conflict with several of Donovan's other executives in the theater. Moreover, there was considerable criticism within Mountbatten's command of Eifler's SI reports.

In September 1943 Donovan had sent out a young staff officer, Captain Duncan C. Lee, who had been an associate in his law firm, to check into the situation. Although Lee was first compelled to bail out of his crippled aircraft into enemy territory and march out of the jungle—a march that took six weeks and in which Eric Sevareid, the CBS correspondent, took part—he was able to confirm that problems existed with Eifler's reportage: "The criticism of Eifler's SI reports is well founded." He believed the trouble was due to the fact that "he [Eifler] does not have on his staff either trained SI staff officers or trained instructors," and that he had started out to "run a [Special Operations] show and is now being called upon by General Stilwell for principally SI work."[2]

Donovan was not satisfied with the state of affairs in Burma, and since he was anxious to impress Mountbatten with the skill of his organization, as part of his campaign to gain acceptance in the Pacific Theater in general, he decided to fly to Burma and deal with the problems personally.

Two hardheaded men met on the airstrip at Nazira. Donovan and Colonel Eifler inspected the 101 base, and Donovan "expressed his satisfaction at how much the detachment was doing with such slender resources" and sent off "messages to Washington directing that more personnel, equipment, and funds be made available to Detachment 101."[3]

At that point Donovan and Eifler went into the war room to confer. Related Richard Dunlop, who served with Detachment 101:

> . . . the general fixed a cold eye on the seven maps hanging on the wall, each depicting a different plan for the location of OSS teams in the field. Donovan sat down on a bamboo chair.
>
> "Well, Eifler," he asked, "what are you doing?"
>
> "General Stilwell told me he might want to approach Burma in seven different ways," replied Eifler. "I was supposed to organize each one of them, and I did."
>
> For a moment Donovan did not comment. He studied the maps. When he spoke, his voice was as soft as ever.
>
> "That's what I mean about you, Carl," he needled. "You are too goddamned ambiguous about organizing. What do you mean by organizing seven different eventualities?"
>
> Eifler suppressed his anger.
>
> "Sir," he said throwing down the challenge, "would you like to go behind Japanese lines and find out for yourself?"

Donovan smiled as if he were accepting a friend's invitation to go for a drive through the Virginia countryside.

"When do we leave?"

"First thing in the morning, sir."

Dunlop was to explain:

Normally, even 101 men would not fly into the forward bases, and yet Eifler was proposing that the director of OSS do just that. The trip might well be called foolhardy. But could Donovan, whose heroism had made him one of the most decorated men in the nation's history, disregard a direct challenge to his bravery? Eifler thought not.

Eifler decided to fly Donovan to Knothead, an OSS base about 150 miles behind Japanese lines and some 275 miles southeast of Nazira. The only aircraft at Nazira was a Gypsy Moth, a light, single-engine aircraft which did not have the range to fly to Knothead and return on one tank of gasoline. It would be necessary to make a fuel drop at Knothead so that the Gypsy Moth could make the return flight.

The night before the flight Donovan shared quarters with Lieutenant Colonel Nicol Smith, who was at Nazira training a group of Siamese for clandestine operations in Thailand. Dunlop recorded:

As the two men got ready for bed in the basha in the middle of the tea gardens, Smith found himself puzzling over why the head of the OSS was risking not only his life but all the critically important secrets he carried around with him in his head. There was little that he did not know about Allied plans all over the world. Smith could restrain himself no longer.

"General, aren't you risking your life?" Smith asked.

"Everything is a risk," replied Donovan. "My boys are risking their lives every day."

Dunlop himself recalled:

Once after the war I asked the general a similar question about the trip behind the lines.

"I was risking my life," he replied with a twinkle, "but I was not risking any secrets. I carried an L pill ready to put in my mouth."

Since I, too, once carried an L [lethal] pill as a necessary precaution, I knew what he meant. The capsule is filled with deadly potassium cyanide. The skin of the capsule is insoluble. Swallow it, and it will go through the digestive system without causing the slightest inconvenience. Chew it, and it means death. We were taught to secrete the capsule beneath the tongue so that it could be taken in an emergency to bring almost instant death, which was unquestionably preferable to torture.

Dunlop then related:

> Smith and the other OSS men at Nazira stayed awake worrying for fear that somehow word of the next day's event might have leaked to the Japanese, but Donovan, in Smith's words, "slept like a babe." In the morning the general gave Nicol Smith his wallet and identification papers for safekeeping.
>
> "If anything goes wrong, it'll be just as well if I'm incognito," he said.
>
> "That's an understatement, General."
>
> After breakfast, [Donovan] refused the parachute offered to him by Eifler as they prepared to go to the airstrip.
>
> "I'll ride the plane down if we crash," he said. "I can't afford to be captured."
>
> Donovan's grandstanding was in character.
>
> "General, if we land within fifteen feet of the enemy, I will bring you back," said Eifler. "Please put on your chute."

Dunlop continued:

> Then the theatricality was at an end. The two men were in the plane and bouncing down the strip cut among the neat rows of tea bushes. Eifler hugged the treetops as he flew over the Naga Hills to avoid Japanese fighters. When the plane reached Knothead, Eifler circled while Kachins raced to pull the simulated bashas off the airstrip.

Eifler landed the Gypsy Moth up the side of the hill. The strip was short, but, Eifler told Dunlop, " 'Gravity helped us to slow down before we reached the far end.' " One of the OSS men watching the landing, Vincent Curl, was to tell how "that day I lived about five lives" before the Gypsy Moth stopped and Donovan and Eifler got out. "I'd met the general in Washington, and he strode right up to me and gave me a real hug. It seemed just as natural seeing him in the middle of the Burmese jungle as it had to see him behind his desk."

Donovan and Eifler "spent the next several hours" talking with the OSS men at Knothead and the Kachin guerrillas they were supplying, training, and leading. Donovan was "plainly impressed" by what he had seen and heard when the time came to depart. The Gypsy Moth was fueled from jerricans dropped for the purpose, and Donovan and Eifler then boarded the aircraft. Eifler then began his takeoff run:

> "Rev it up all you can and then take off," Curl urged Eifler.
>
> The Kachins took hold of the plane and held it back as Eifler revved the engine. At his signal they gave it a push, and the Gypsy Moth went rolling down the field, as Eifler put it later, "like a tumblebug. We were taking off downhill, and we gathered speed slowly because of Donovan's weight."

Eifler failed to mention his own considerable bulk. At the end of the strip the lofty trees of the jungle loomed, and there was little chance that the struggling Gypsy Moth would climb over them. At the last minute Eifler swerved ninety degrees to the left to plunge through a gap in the forest rooftop. The plane cleared the trees by a few feet and then roared down over the river, passing about five feet over the surface. Donovan grinned.

"We haven't got the power on the nose of these planes that we should have," he shouted over the roar of the engine as the plane at last gained air speed.

"I told Carl to give the plane all it got when he took off," says Curl, "but he started off easy. When he banked between those trees, I shut my eyes. I waited for the crash. When the roar of the engine over the river came, I shouted with joy."

Eifler buzzed the strip to say good-bye to Knothead and started back on a tree-hopping journey to Nazira. . . .

When Donovan landed back at Nazira, he found Lieutenant Colonel John Coughlin, 101's executive officer, waiting for him, unimpressed by Donovan's flight behind the lines. Dunlop related:

[Coughlin] never expected to see either of the two men alive again. That night he took the jubilant Donovan aside.

"General, what were you thinking about to go in there with Carl?" he demanded.

One of Donovan's great strengths as a commander was his accessibility to men of all ranks who served under him, and he did not bristle at Coughlin's question.

"I had to," he replied.

"You should have considered more things than your damned honor. If I'd been there, I would have reminded you of every one of them."

Upon leaving Nazira, Donovan took his DC-3 to Sadiya in the Brahmaputra Valley of India, the main point of departure for U.S. aircraft flying over the Himalayas to Kunming. There he caught a C-46 for Kunming, 550 miles away on the other side of the Himalayan range—"The Hump." The C-46 climbed to 14,000 feet to permit it to cross the 10,000-foot Patkai Range and the Chindwin river valley. At that altitude all aboard the aircraft wore oxygen masks. The plane climbed higher to cross a series of 14,000- to 16,000-foot ridges separated by the West Irrawaddy, East Irrawaddy, Salween, and Mekong river valleys—the Hump itself was the 15,000-foot Satsung Range between the Salween and Mekong rivers, and the route was sometimes called the Aluminum Trail because of the crashed aircraft that served as guideposts.

At Kunming Donovan inspected the OSS bases built there to supply and train some 25,000 Chinese guerrillas each year. He sorted out a number of complex staff problems with his executives on the field, presented General Tai Li, head of the Chinese secret service, with a check for $5,000—to be used for the construction of a girls' school—and then settled down to fifteen hours of nonstop staff conversations with Tai Li, OSS representatives at Kunming, and State Department and U.S. Navy representatives. The objective: to ensure the efficient implementation of the Sino-American Cooperation Agreement, which had been signed at the White House by FDR, Chiang Kai-shek, Navy Secretary Frank Knox, and Donovan. With those staff conversations at an end—a principal point was to examine and approve operations to make quinine available to the Allies while denying it to the Japanese—Donovan attended a large banquet marked by long, flowery speeches.

Then he was gone again, this time to New Delhi for meetings with Mountbatten and the OSS theater commander, Colonel Richard Heppner, who had been a partner in the Donovan law firm. Donovan examined and approved projects for the OSS's penetration of French Indochina, Thailand, and the Dutch East Indies—operations that marked the real start of thirty years of U.S. involvement in Southeast Asia. He interviewed a number of American and Indian officials and civilians resident in New Delhi, his object to obtain information for a paper he proposed to write on the economics of wartime India.

And yet again he was gone, this time to Moscow. The record shows that he dictated the paper on Indian economics to the then chief of Special Operations in Washington, Lieutenant Commander R. Davis Halliwell, who was accompanying Donovan, on December 14, 1943, with instructions that the paper be sent to Dr. Rogers "for such consideration as he believed was appropriate by the Planning Group."[4]

That paper, which contained the statement "It would seem that the official bureaucracy in India, vested interests in London, maintaining their conception of how India should be ruled, stands in the way of any immediate economic development," marked the start of active OSS espionage against the British in India.

So Donovan arrived in Moscow, his task to establish an alliance between the capitalist and Communist secret services intended to destroy the German secret services and undermine the institutions of the Third Reich.

Throughout his first two years as Roosevelt's intelligence master Donovan had been obedient to FDR's edict that Russia was "the key to the defeat of Germany."[5] As FDR had directed, there was to be no spying on Russia or Russians, an order that Donovan had observed scrupulously —to the extent that when the OSS developed a contact close to Madame Petrovna, private secretary to the Soviet ambassador in Washington, Maxim Litvinov, Donovan gave orders that the contact was to be broken.[6]

Similarly, when *Harper's* magazine announced plans to publish excerpts from Leon Trotsky's *Life of Stalin,* a bitter attack on Stalin, William L. Langer, chief of OSS Research and Analysis, who had had a hand in the Trotsky project with the Harvard University Library, wrote WJD to ask whether publication should be stopped because it "might have some detrimental effect upon our relations with the present Russian government."[7] Donovan was saved from having to make an awkward decision only when Trotsky's widow (Trotsky had just been murdered in Mexico City by Stalin's agents) brought an injunction to restrain *Harper's* from publishing.

With the Russians' destruction of a German army at Stalingrad, and the first successful Soviet summer offensive in 1943, when the Red Army succeeded in liberating much of occupied Russian territory and began to approach Eastern Europe, the London and Washington governments and the Combined Chiefs began to reexamine their attitude toward Russia. The effect was, on the one hand, to obtain a closer alliance with the Russians and, on the other, to prepare to stem Russian imperialism.

In reflection of that changing attitude, at the Quebec Conference, as part of his presentation to support his Balkan plan, Donovan presented a paper to the Joint Chiefs entitled "Strategy and Policy: Can America and Russia Cooperate?"[8] Prepared jointly by Donovan and Dr. Gerard T. Robinson, professor of history at Columbia University, the paper was important for several reasons. It declared there was a "crisis in the relations of the United States and Great Britain with Soviet Russia," which "calls most urgently for a re-examination and definition of the strategy and policy that will give shape to the post-war settlement," and it set forth America's war aims in terms devoid of sentiment and emotion:

> [The] fundamental aims of the United States in this war are, in the interest of American security, (1) to destroy the German domination of Europe, and (2) to prevent the domination of Europe in the future by any single power (such as the Soviet Union), or by any group of powers in which we do not have a strong influence.

If "we do not achieve *both* these aims, we may consider that we have lost the war."

Donovan and Robinson's conclusions were that the United States must invade Europe in the greatest possible strength, to confront Russia's power, and then obtain a compromise peace settlement. Meanwhile, the greatest vigilance concerning Russian capabilities and intentions must be maintained. But that could not be accomplished while the OSS languished under the President's ban concerning intelligence operations against the Soviet Union. WJD intimated he would like the ban to be relaxed. Whether he received an actual directive from the Joint Chiefs to begin intelligence operations against Russia is not clear—the probability is that he received only verbal permission—but in any case he began to lay his plans. To WJD a nod was always as good as a wink.

Donovan had been examining the intelligence penetration of Russia since January 1943. At that time he instructed his representative at the State Department to obtain the department's views on such a penetration. On January 23, 1943, William A. Kimbel reported back:

> 1. Russia has reputedly the best counter-espionage system in the world. Any undercover representative would probably be disclosed upon arrival.
> 2. The movements of any stranger would be so restricted as to make it impossible to obtain observations and results of value.
> 3. Our relations with Russia are such that if any undercover agent were disclosed, the repercussions could be serious both from a military point of view and politically. Such repercussions could have a serious effect on relations with Russia in this country, in that the State Department has taken a firm stand on prohibiting the activities of any agents of Russia or other Allied nations in the United States. Any indication that we were resorting to such methods in the territory of an Allied nation could therefore be serious.
> 4. [The] State Department would therefore be opposed to our undertaking this undercover activity and would not provide necessary cooperation.[9]

Referring to suggestions that the OSS might work with the British Secret Intelligence Service, Kimbel pointed out that the "representatives of England in Russia are even more restricted in their activities than are those of the United States," and any "association which we might have with the British in such activities would therefore be more of a handicap than an advantage." Even if the OSS were to get an agent into Russia, Kimbel continued, "it would still be practically impossible to maintain communication with him."

However—and this must have been a surprise for WJD—Kimbel advised that "State concurs in the opinion that representation for OSS purposes in Russia is urgently needed," and it would "cooperate with us if the designated individual went openly." Also, if the official went openly, the U.S. ambassador in Moscow would cooperate. State had emphasized the need for "a man of outstanding ability, preferably one who is conversant with Russian conditions and people." Kimbel continued:

> This same conclusion might be achieved through having some representative proceed to Russia openly as attached to the Lend-Lease Mission. This latter method would in all probability be more acceptable to the Russians. With this status our representative would be less restricted in his travels and activities than if actually attached to the Embassy. A representative in this position could establish his own connections among the local people for expanding his means of observation and accumulating information.

The next move came from the British. In the late summer the SOE representative in Moscow, Colonel E. H. Hill, who was persona grata in Moscow, even though in 1918 he had been one of those British secret service men mixed up in an attempt to assassinate Lenin, a conspiracy that had very nearly succeeded, wrote to WJD:

> For a considerable time I have felt that to have an American colleague in Moscow would be of great value in dealing with the NKVD—particularly in (a) questions concerning the Far East (Siberia, Vladivostok) and possible development of cooperation in China with the Russians, and (b) general questions concerning the U.S.S.R.
>   If the matter is approved of in principle by the U.S.A. organisation, I consider that they could find no better representative in Moscow than:
>
> Mr. Lewellyn E. Thompson, Junr.
>
> who is secretary of the Embassy of the United States of America. Thompson has been in U.S.S.R. for some years, is alive and a go-getter.
>   He has an idea of the general liaison work that I do with the N.K.V.D., and has expressed views on the desirability of his own country's having a similar representative. He has also met our chief contact socially at our flat. . . . Personally I could not wish for a better colleague with whom to collaborate.[10]

WJD sent this idea to the State Department, which promptly advised against association with the British services:

> The Department of State agrees that Mr. Thompson is entirely qualified for these duties. However, it is their belief that in view of the existing relations with the Russians and conditions in Moscow, better results could be obtained through the establishment of direct contacts with the Russians rather than through a secret liaison with the British. . . . British-Russian relations are inherently not friendly and the . . . British are therefore finding increasing difficulty in obtaining information from the Russians. Any liaison which we might establish and endeavor to maintain on a basis of secrecy with the British would be discovered by the Russians [and] would therefore tend to destroy our purpose.

On the other hand, "Relations between the Russians and Americans have improved in the recent past, and the Department therefore believes that we would gain more information by openly advising the proper Russian authorities of our intentions." Lastly, "the Department of State would be appreciative if they [sic] could be advised of any information which we succeed in obtaining from the Russians."[11]

Aware now of the attitude of the Joint Chiefs and the State Department, and presumably having been given a nod by FDR, Donovan acted in two ways to get men into Russia. The first was covert.

Donovan's—America's—first secret intelligence operation against the

Soviet Union was launched in September 1943, shortly before he left for Cairo to manage his Balkan operations. As Colonel O. C. O'Conor advised WJD in a memorandum dated September 4, 1943, "an arrangement"[12] had been made with R. E. McCurdy, of E. G. Badger and Sons, a large engineering firm, who was going to Russia to supervise the erection of six oil refineries being given to Russia under lend-lease.

McCurdy, with a staff of three men, expected to leave shortly for Moscow, which would be his headquarters, and he would be followed by thirty more men. "This organization," reported O'Conor, "will be spread over six different locations in Russia known to us, and will remain 18 months or longer." The relationship with McCurdy was "strictly informal"; he had "not been engaged by OSS, in order to protect him and his company." But "he has been indoctrinated along lines which his activities in Russia may encompass." O'Conor was satisfied that "we have a first key-man for the collection of information." O'Conor had limited his instructions to "industrial, agricultural, cultural, and a small amount of political intelligence." With "his organization spread widely in Russia, supplying him with information as employee to employer, I believe we have a safe set-up."

To permit McCurdy to communicate, "We are planning to establish OSS personnel at Vladivostok, at Teheran, at Wusu in Sinkiang province, China, and in Afghanistan." Also, "McCurdy is to be free to acquaint our Embassy with certain current information, and to pass to them publications or data for transmission by State pouch." He was "placing a man at Vladivostok to receive and check all incoming material for his projects, and will accept an assistant whom we will furnish. This latter is an American who speaks Russian, has been engaged in the same activity in the Orient previously."

In addition, "at Wusu on the Russia-China border, it is our intention to locate several OSS men for geological survey in connection with oil development at Urumchi." At Teheran "we are hoping to supplement our present limited staff, using several Army officers in General [Donald H.] Connolly's [Persian Gulf] command." O'Conor assured Donovan:

> As the refinery facilities are being financed by Lend-Lease, and approved by the Russians, ample protection will be given for the movement of the men. The enterprise will be without expense to OSS, will therefore not be a formal project, and not on OSS books as such. This activity should continue for about two years.

Then, with the assistance of the new ambassador in Moscow, W. Averell Harriman, Donovan succeeded in inserting a representative of OSS Research and Analysis, Thomas Porter Whitney, a Russian specialist, who was described on the embassy list as being a member of the Auxiliary

Foreign Service. His salary: $4,600 basic with a $12 per diem. His mission: ". . . to assist the work being carried out in the [Moscow] Embassy along two lines: research, and the collection and forwarding of printed materials for the United States Government."[13] Both these tasks constituted, under Russian law, espionage.

Then came Donovan's overt attempts to get men into Moscow. Donovan arrived in Moscow on Christmas Eve 1943, accompanied by Colonel John H. F. Haskell, West Point graduate, vice-president of the New York Stock Exchange, son of one of Donovan's commanding officers in World War I, and later, in turn, chief of the Marshall Plan mission to Sweden, U.S. defense adviser to NATO, and Paris representative of the Bankers Trust Company. The reason for Haskell's presence: If Donovan could make an alliance with the Russians, Haskell would take the OSS team to Moscow.

Donovan and Haskell moved into the U.S. Embassy as guests of Harriman and prepared for the usual interminable wait. But to the surprise of the ambassador and Donovan, on Christmas Day, the Soviet foreign minister, Vyacheslav Molotov, invited Donovan over to the Kremlin and there stated that the Russian services "were prepared for prompt, serious discussions, even though Stalin was out of the city."[14] The embassy was flabbergasted; usually it took six weeks to arrange a meeting, but acting through Harriman, Donovan had been received, and preliminaries started, within six hours of his arrival.

Two days later Donovan, accompanied by his friend General John R. Deane, lately secretary to the Joint Chiefs and now chief of the U.S. Military Mission to Moscow, and Charles E. "Chip" Bohlen, of the embassy, who acted as interpreter, went to the Commissariat of Internal Affairs, headquarters of the Soviet service the NKVD. There they met a man who was described as the chief of the external intelligence service, General P. N. Fitin, and the official said to be responsible for special operations in enemy territory, General A. P. Ossipov. Both officers received Donovan "cordially," and he spent some time describing the structure, functions, and policy of the OSS.

Harriman later recorded that the "shop talk among spymasters went briskly" as the Russians questioned Donovan "about the particular methods of spying, American style." They were interested "to know how the Americans introduced their agents into enemy territory, how these men were trained and what special equipment they carried." Although the Russians volunteered no information about their methods, "Donovan succeeded in piquing their interest by describing some of the special equipment the OSS had developed, including suitcase radios and plastic explosives."

After several hours' conversation Donovan made the offer he had flown to Moscow to make: The OSS was prepared to exchange intelligence about the enemy with the NKVD if the Russians were agreeable, and if they were, he would designate an American liaison officer to serve as a member of General Deane's military mission. In return, the OSS would welcome warmly a Soviet official in Washington.

The prospects and problems of a formal intelligence alliance between those archenemies—the secret services of capitalism and of Communism, united only by the menace of Nazism—did not seem to disconcert the Russians:

> [General Fitin] responded warmly, offering an example of the kind of situation in which liaison officers could be helpful. Suppose, he said, that Soviet agents were preparing to sabotage an important industrial installation or a railroad in Germany. It would then be most desirable to inform the American government in advance so that it could avoid unwitting interference with the Soviet plan.

Donovan agreed, offering some ideas of his own but, of course, avoiding any hint of discussion about what the NKVD were doing in the United States at that moment—they were, in fact, engaged in one of the largest intelligence operations in history, its objective to steal the secrets of the American atomic bomb.

To the astonishment of the Americans, who were used to dealing with a vast, mysterious, inefficient machine that made decisions almost always in weeks and even months or frequently produced nothing but silence, agreement was reached there and then—something that had not happened before in major matters and would not happen again. It was proposed and accepted that Donovan should send John Haskell to the NKVD; the NKVD would send one of its colonels, A. G. Grauer, to the OSS. Almost as startling was the fact that Fitin gave Donovan and Deane a telephone number where he could be contacted with Military Intelligence during the period before Haskell took up his duties. It was Deane's first unofficial telephone number in Russia, where there was no such thing as a telephone directory, and he "felt I had achieved a tremendous victory."[15]

Harriman was to record:

> The arrangements went forward swiftly after that first meeting at NKVD headquarters. Molotov assured [me] on New Year's Eve that the exchange of intelligence officers would certainly be approved at the Soviet end because, he said, it was such a sensible move. Colonel Grauer and his staff of six assistants were all set to leave for Washington. . . . Colonel Haskell had already drawn an organization chart for the staff of nineteen he would bring to Moscow. General Fitin even called on Donovan at the embassy, an unheard-of event.[16]

But the old Communist suspicion of capitalists bearing gifts was still there. "There was one tense moment," Harriman recorded, "when Fitin asked Donovan whether his sole purpose in coming to Moscow was to offer cooperation or whether he had something else in mind"—a round-about way of asking whether Donovan was in the process of establishing an OSS espionage cell in Moscow. Donovan was not spying on the Russians—at least he was not spying on them at the time—the sally passed, and Fitin and WJD parted in a blaze of comradeship.

His business completed, Donovan prepared to leave Moscow in Harriman's personal B-24. Donovan's skill in winning the Soviet services over to his plans had been remarkable. But as he was leaving, he experienced one of those nasty shocks reserved for foreigners who think they have achieved something in Moscow. For reasons known only to themselves, the Russians refused to let the aircraft leave, they kept refusing for twelve days, and then just as mysteriously they let him leave on January 14, 1944.

Donovan sped to Cairo to put the alliance to work. An early measure was to check with the Joint Security Control in Washington to establish what intelligence material should be given to the Russians. The advice he received resulted in the issuance of a memorandum, "Intelligence to be Furnished the U.S.S.R.," to all branches of OSS on February 4, 1944. The basic principle was that Russia "may be given intelligence which is of distinctive OSS origin and which may be of aid to that country in prosecuting the war against Germany."[17]

Documents, special equipment, secret intelligence—all began to flow in considerable quantities from the OSS to the NKVD. Few categories of intelligence or equipment were withheld, and the United States sent expensive equipment such as miniature cameras, miniature microdot-manufacturing systems, and microfilming cameras and projectors—all of which were of use in the large-scale NKVD espionage operations then going on in the United States. Donovan even sent intelligence that was of great value to the United States, including cryptographic materials. This consisted of some 1,500 pages of German intelligence relating to Soviet ciphers, which had been captured by U.S. troops in Italy. The ciphers were copies of those in use at that time between NKVD headquarters and NKVD representatives with the Soviet armies and were therefore of great interest and importance not only to the NKVD but also to those responsible for Magic.

Donovan sent copies to the Special Branch and advised Fitin that the cipher material was in the OSS's possession, asking that "some trusted Russian come to our Washington office and let us give this material to him." He also advised Deane that Fitin should be told that "Both the President and [the secretary of state] approved and directed that General Donovan take the contemplated action at once." Moreover, "It will . . . be apparent to you and General Fitin that General Donovan took the only course open to a loyal ally in accepting this material as soon as he found it procurable. He furthermore felt that the documentary proof would be of more assistance to our ally than would a mere statement that we were reliably informed that such codes existed in enemy hands."[18]

At length—six weeks passed before the Russians reacted—Donovan's deputy director, Ned Buxton, received a telegram that Deane had asked for the documentation to be taken by safe hand to the Soviet ambassador in Washington, Andrei Gromyko, and that was done by Doering personally about seven months after the documentation originally came into OSS possession. Donovan received a note from Fitin to thank him "for the aid given us . . . in this very essential business."[19]

What made the exchange and courtesy the more remarkable was that Donovan and Fitin's plan to exchange representatives had been killed by Roosevelt, acting on the advice of J. Edgar Hoover, who felt "the NKVD has far too many representatives in this country already." But the Russians did no more than express their regrets when, just as Grauer, his six assistants, and their wives were about to leave Moscow for Washington, Donovan had the difficult task of advising Fitin that the exchange had been "deferred because of timing." Harriman protested to Roosevelt that the exchange was the "first tangible evidence of the spirit of cooperation voiced at the Moscow and Teheran conferences." And, Harriman continued, the U.S. Embassy had "unsuccessfully attempted for the last two and half years to penetrate sources of Soviet information and to get on a basis of mutual confidence and exchange. Here, for the first time, we have penetrated one intelligence branch of the Soviet Government and, if pursued, I am satisfied this will be the opening door to far greater intimacy in other branches." If "we now close the door on this branch of the Soviet Government after they have shown a cooperative spirit and good faith, I cannot express too strongly my conviction that our relations with the Soviet Government in other directions will be adversely affected."[20]

However, J. Edgar Hoover prevailed, and as Donovan was soon to learn, to his chagrin, there were indeed already too many NKVD officers in the United States.

27

Noah's Ark

On his return to Cairo from Moscow, Donovan resumed work on his Balkan plan, despite pouch letters from Buxton and Doering warning him that work requiring his attention was piling up at home and that these prolonged trips were causing unrest in the senior staff. Donovan paid little attention to the warnings, continued to run his far-flung empire by telegram, and turned to the problems of Greece and Operation Noah's Ark.

Under John Toulmin's stern direction, the affairs of the OSS Greek desk in Cairo had been placed in excellent hands. Dr. Rodney Young, a Princeton archaeologist who had spent several years at the American School of Classical Studies in Athens, arrived to command the Secret Intelligence desk, and Lieutenant Colonel Paul West, a journalist, was in charge of Special Operations. But something in the air of Cairo made Greek operations especially complicated and difficult.

Captain G. F. Else, of the U.S. Marine Corps, who worked with OSS SI in Cairo, was to report, all SI and most SO activities were carried on in an atmosphere of furious controversy, in which "events that had never happened were narrated in detail by responsible members of the [Greek] government, with all the exact circumstances and a convincing array of sources."[1] Else's opinion was to be confirmed by Allied Forces Headquarters in Algiers. "The intense political color of the guerrilla forces in Greece made special operations very unsatisfactory . . . the Greeks were too busy fighting among themselves to fight the Germans."[2] Yet there were in Greece and on the Greek islands in late 1943 seven divisions of

Axis troops, most of them Germans and some of them divisions that would be valuable on the Neptune beaches. Somehow they had to be pinned to the Aegean until after the invasion. Therefore, in the late fall of 1943 Donovan turned to the Greek Communist and Socialist guerrilla armies inside Greece—reluctantly but "out of military necessity." Apart from the need to keep German forces idle but expectant in parts of Europe remote from the main battlefields, Donovan and his British colleagues had conceived a plan called Noah's Ark that required, if it was to be effective, the support of the ELAS (Greek People's Army of National Liberation), military arm of the Greek Communist movement inside Greece.

The purposes of Noah's Ark were several. Its first and major purpose was to help maintain the fiction that the main Allied armies would attack Germany not from the west across the Channel, but from the south through the Balkans from bases in the Mediterranean, so that Hitler would maintain his large garrison in the eastern Mediterranean. Noah's Ark's second purpose was to prevent the Wehrmacht in Greece from withdrawing to the Russian or the French fronts. Its third purpose was to unify the guerrilla forces—royalist, Communist, and religious—for the national insurrection that, under the Arcadia plan, would break out just before and at D-Day in France. Fourthly, as the Germans were leaving, the guerrillas were to prevent them from destroying the remnants of the Greek infrastructure—electricity, sewerage, telephone centrals, railway turntables and tunnels, waterworks, bridges, jetties, and the like.

But given the political complexity and rivalries in the Greek scene, the Allies in liberating Greece might unleash anarchy, a state of affairs that would benefit only the Communists. It became essential, consequently, that the Communist political and military movement be brought under the orders of the supreme Allied commander in the Mediterranean, Field Marshal Sir Henry Wilson, representative of the Combined Chiefs of Staff.

To bring about the desired control, Donovan asked Toulmin to send a reliable one-man mission to Featherbed, Allied code name for the headquarters of the ELAS in the Greek mountains. His task would be to advise the Greek Communist commanders of Noah's Ark, to obtain their support for it, to extract from them assurances that they would not act without the orders of the Allied supreme commander—against promises of arms and gold.

After much discussion, the chief of SO, Lieutenant Colonel Paul West, was selected for the task, and Toulmin applied to MO 4 CAIRO, British secret headquarters which controlled all Allied secret operations in Greece, for the neccessary clearance and transportation. The British immediately refused permission, for Greece was in a theater of operations they controlled—they had so many scholars in the country that it was said Oxford ruled northern Greece while Cambridge ruled the south. They continued to refuse permission despite all the charm, persuasion, and guile WJD could bring to bear. Their reason: As a staff officer on secret work Colonel West knew too much about the Allied secret infrastructure in the eastern Mediterranean, the Levant, and North Africa to risk his capture. However, WJD felt that U.S. national interests were paramount and decided to send West despite the British objection—a decision that was not likely to enhance Anglo-American accord in Cairo, where such relationships had never been tranquil.

How WJD managed to get West aboard a British DC-3 going to Featherbed is not known, but he probably used an argument he used frequently when launching missions into territory from which the OSS had been excluded—the fact that U.S. airmen required food and medical assistance or evacuation. In any case, West set out for Featherbed in the first minutes of October 21, 1943.

The DC-3 reached Featherbed safely at about 4:00 A.M., the Greek Communist guerrillas—Andartes—lit the flare path, and the plane landed and taxied over to the emergency takeoff position at the end of the strip, a precaution in case German aircraft arrived and the DC-3 was compelled to make a rapid takeoff. At that point the mission ran into trouble. The aircraft became bogged down in heavy mud, and even when the Andartes unloaded the 4,800 pounds of equipment in it, the pilot still could not move it. To make matters worse, a second DC-3 coming in from Egypt with war stores landed safely but then bogged down with both wheels in the center of the runway, thus preventing any movements until it was moved. By daybreak both aircraft were immobilized, visible and vulnerable in the heart of German territory, with an enemy fighter base only forty minutes away.

West ordered both aircraft to be covered with camouflaged netting, undergrowth, and trees. The aircraft's tracks were concealed in the same way, and then the Americans from the DC-3, the British crews, and the Andartes withdrew to Featherbed headquarters, a deserted summer resort in the mountains consisting of about twenty stone houses, a few of which had water but none of which had heat, light, or furniture. In one of these houses West found the American airmen "in rather poor condition, under-clothed and under-nourished."[3] The temperature was about forty degrees, but the airmen had no more than summer flying suits and had only straw on a stone floor on which to rest. They had received just one meal a day for five weeks—bread and cheese—from the Andartes and an occasional extra meal a day from the British in the area. None was lively, and some were in very poor condition and needed hospital treatment. West resolved to evacuate them at the earliest moment.

Having established the technical reason for his presence in enemy territory, West then began political conversations concerning Noah's

Donovan's favorite picture of himself, taken just after his epic action at the Ourcq River in France in 1918 — the action in which his battalion of the New York 69th Regiment of "Fighting Irish" was practically wiped out. *(Photo courtesy of Donovan Leisure Newton & Irvine)*

The five faces of Donovan: above, the
football star at Columbia, 1905; above
right, as a major in the "Fighting" 69th;
below, as acting attorney general of the
United States in 1929; below right, as a
major general in command of the OSS in
Washington in 1945; far right, in the
late 1950's as a prosperous and influential New York corporation lawyer.
Almost until the end Donovan remained
astoundingly fit and active and traveled
the world ceaselessly. *(Photos courtesy of
Donovan Leisure Newton & Irvine)*

RECEIVED AT ELLICOTT SQUARE BUILDING, MAIN AND SWAN STREETS, BUFFALO, N. Y.
294 W CJ 44 GOVT

WASHN DC 1012P DEC 11

MRS WM J DONOVAN

826 DELEVAN AVE   BUFFALO NY

DEEPLY REGRET TO INFORM YOU THAT IT IS OFFICIALLY REPORTED THAT
LIEUT COLONEL WILLIAM J DONOVAN INFY WAS SEVERELY WOUNDED IN ACTION
OCTOBER FIFTEENTH FURTHER INFORMATION WHEN RECD
                        HARRIS THE ADJT GENL
                                    1057PM

Above, the telegram to Ruth Donovan announcing that her husband had been badly wounded in action on the Hindenburg Line. It was in receiving this wound that Donovan won the Congressional Medal of Honor.

Left, Donovan just before the action on the Hindenburg Line in which he won the Congressional Medal of Honor. *(Photo courtesy of Donovan Leisure Newton & Irvine)*

Donovan as a major in the New York "Fighting" 69th Infantry Regiment in France in 1918. With him is his spiritual mentor and the battalion padre, Father Francis Duffy. *(Photo courtesy of Donovan Leisure Newton & Irvine)*

Donovan's band—the band of the New York 69th Regiment—aboard a troopship off Hoboken, New Jersey, on the return of the regiment, with Donovan as colonel, in 1919 after active service with the Rainbow Division in France. The band's signature tune—"In the Good Old Summertime"—came to haunt Donovan for the rest of his life because it never failed to remind him of the very heavy casualties the "Fighting Irish" suffered in their two epic actions, on the Ourcq River and at the Hindenburg Line in 1918. Donovan never forgot his men and spent a small fortune helping those in need during the Depression years.

Donovan, now the colonel of the regiment, leads the "Fighting" 69th along Fifth Avenue in 1919 to receive the Freedom of the City of New York.

Donovan at the Supreme Court. In many ways a traditionalist, Donovan always wore morning dress when at the Court. One of the leading advocates of his time, he had argued and won no less than five cases before the Supreme Court before he was fifty—although as a student he had almost flunked out of Columbia Law School. In his time he was regarded as one of America's most effective lawyers in the Supreme Court. His specialty was corporation and industrial law.

Left, Ruth Rumsey after her marriage to Donovan. The heiress of a wealthy Protestant family in Buffalo, Ruth was married in the Catholic cathedral in Boston and agreed to rear the children of the union in the Catholic faith. Donovan's family attempted to convert her to Catholicism, but Ruth remained a Protestant throughout her life, although she honored faithfully her commitment to bring up their children, David and Patricia, in the Catholic faith. Her husband was what may be called an "occasional Catholic" throughout his life. *(Photo courtesy of David R. Donovan)*

Below left, the Donovans on their second honeymoon in Peking in 1919. The holiday was terminated when Donovan left for Omsk to report on the Russian Revolution in Siberia for the Woodrow Wilson government. *(Photo courtesy of David R. Donovan)*

Below, Ruth Donovan was an excellent horsewoman and had what the family historian called "a truly aristocratic appearance and bearing in the best sense of that word." A blonde, she had, like Donovan, startling blue eyes. However, fairly early in the marriage, her hair turned silver. *(Photo courtesy of David R. Donovan)*

Right, the Donovans in 1932 at
about the time that Donovan ran for
governor of New York State. He had
been acting attorney general and
head of the Antitrust Division at the
Department of Justice in the Coolidge
administration. Later, when Herbert
Hoover became the Republican President-elect, he agreed to appoint
Donovan attorney general of the
United States. The new President
reneged on his promise, however,
although Donovan had served him
loyally as campaign manager.

Donovan realized that he had been
passed over because Hoover did not
want a Catholic attorney general.
Donovan left government and established the law firm that became
Donovan Leisure Newton & Irvine.
While forming his firm, Donovan suc-
cumbed to Republican pressure to
run for the governorship of New York
State, then a sure road to the White
House. However, Donovan was defeated in the Roosevelt landslide of
1932.

Below, Patricia Donovan in the
summer of 1936, at the age of eighteen, and, below right, again in 1938,
at the age of nineteen. She was killed
in a motoring accident in Virginia
just after her twenty-first birthday.

Donovan's dynasty I. Otto C. Doering, Jr., Donovan's law partner, confidant, and executive officer of the OSS. A quiet-mannered man, Doering was the "glue that held the OSS together." He ran the organization when Donovan was absent, he defended it and Donovan against many enemies, and he was responsible for supervising the internal security of OSS headquarters. It was Doering who detected that it was probably Attorney General Francis Biddle who leaked Donovan's plans for the postwar CIA to the press.

Colonel David Bruce, chief of the OSS in Europe and a member of the Mellon family.

Henry B. Hyde, a New York international lawyer with many connections in France, who was chief of Donovan's Secret Intelligence headquarters at Algiers, the OSS's main base of operations into France. Hyde formed and operated the Penny Farthing espionage chains in France. Later Hyde became chief of OSS SI in Switzerland in succession to Allen W. Dulles.

Donovan with his daughter-in-law, the former Mary Grandin, and Captain James J. Angleton leaving the Vatican in 1945 after an audience with Pope Pius XII. The subject of Donovan's meeting with the Pope was among the most intriguing of his career. In 1944 the OSS, which Donovan then commanded, had developed a most secret intelligence source who claimed to have access to the documentation of the Pope's inner cabinet. This information appeared to be of great value, especially concerning Germany, Russia, and Japan, and was distributed in Washington only to FDR and his Cabinet under the code name Source Vessel. However, in an investigation conducted by Captain Angleton it was found that the intelligence was forged and fabricated.

Donovan toward the end of his life. Covered with honors already, he is visiting Pope Pius XII to receive the Medal of St. Sylvester, the Vatican's highest award, for a lifetime of public and secret services to the Catholic Church.

Donovan's dynasty II. Allen Welsh Dulles, Donovan's spymaster in Switzerland in World War II, who was director of the CIA in President John F. Kennedy's administration. *(Photo courtesy of CIA)*

Richard Helms, one of Donovan's young case officers in the OSS, who became President Nixon's director of central intelligence. *(Photo courtesy of CIA)*

William E. Colby, who served behind the lines for Donovan in France and Norway in World War II and became director of the CIA in the Nixon and Ford administrations. *(Photo courtesy of CIA)*

Donovan's influence in the CIA was still very great even as late as 1982, when William J. Casey, who had been Donovan's chief of Secret Intelligence in London, became President Reagan's director of central intelligence. *(Photo courtesy of CIA)*

Donovan's dynasty III. Donovan had a remarkable ability to attract some of the finest legal talent in the United States. In this photograph, taken in 1953, are the name partners of Donovan Leisure Newton & Irvine, the great Rockefeller Plaza law firm. From left to right: Carl E. Newton and George S. Leisure, two of the leading advocates of the period; General Donovan; and Ralstone R. Irvine, the leading antitrust lawyer, who was head of the firm until his retirement in 1970. *(Photo courtesy of Donovan Leisure Newton & Irvine)*

Donovan with his granddaughter, Patricia. Throughout his life Donovan was away from home more frequently than he was present, although he was a devoted family man. He was shattered when his daughter, Patricia, was killed in a motoring accident in 1940 and transferred his paternal affection to his daughter-in-law, the former Mary Grandin, the daughter of a prominent Pennsylvania family. But in time his granddaughter became the apple of his eye. His daughter-in-law died in tragic circumstances at the family's home at Nonquitt on Cape Cod. *(Photo courtesy of David R. Donovan)*

Donovan at his law offices shortly before his death in 1959.

Ark, accompanied by Captain Jules Ehrgott, OSS representative at the headquarters of Lieutenant General Stephanos Sarafis, commander in chief of the ELAS. Certainly the mission was worth trying, for an SOE mission had succeeded in uniting the Greek Communists and royalists (EDES) in November 1942, and together they had blown up the Gorgopotamos Viaduct on the Athens–Salonika railroad line, thus hampering the movement of reinforcements and supplies to Rommel's Afrika Korps in Libya. Also, in the summer of 1943, before the landing in Sicily, a whole series of joint British-ELAS-EDES (royalist guerrilla) operations against railways and bridges had caused the Germans to fear a landing in Greece, as a result of which they kept an entire panzer brigade in the Peloponnesus, when the brigade might have made the difference against Patton at Gela.

But internal political events had shattered the alliance. Thus, when West reached the headquarters in the mountains of the old brigand, Sarafis, he found the commander in chief more interested in fighting the "six colonels" who commanded the royalists and in politics. Sarafis had inveigled Ehrgott, who was no more than a simple soldier, into accepting command of a Communist regiment, an action that was unimportant in itself but one that the Communist propagandists were turning into an American endorsement of the entire Communist movement in Greece.

Having ordered Ehrgott to break his connection with the Communist regiment publicly and immediately, West reported to Donovan:

> I made it very clear that no American officer attached to the Allied Mission in Greece could command any unit at any time, that all our officers were serving in the capacity of military advisers, instructors, and as liaison and intelligence officers. I thanked [Sarafis] for his confidence in Capt. Ehrgott and said that the Captain would be honored to serve as an *honorary* commander of this unit, only.

But Sarafis knew his military politics. He thereupon held a parade to salute West, announcing that he intended to present the American with what West called "cavalry standards which consisted of the [Communist] emblem together with an American flag." Sarafis had mounted the ELAS's hammer and sickle on the face of Old Glory, in the belief that he was flattering West. But West was not flattered. He refused the standard when it was presented to him by bearers in the presence of drawn ranks of guerrillas because, he explained to Sarafis, "we cannot and would not be affiliated in any way with any political organization." If Sarafis wished to fly a standard in West's honor at the parade, "the American flag could fly on his standards with the Greek national [royalist] emblem." Fresh flags were then fetched, and the American and the Greek flags were flown separately as Sarafis's shirtless patriots marched past in honor of the visiting American colonel—a small point in a large war, perhaps, but one with immense significance in Greece.

West then inspected one of Sarafis's regiments, and there was "much forced clapping of hands and 'vivas' for the American officer." Then Sarafis tried another trick with political implications. His interpreter whispered to West during the ceremony that it would make "a very fine impression if I presented the General with my Marlin submachine gun." West was removing the weapon from his shoulder when he noticed the Communist photographer moving forward and realized what was afoot. Sarafis would claim that the weapon was a token of American arms shipments to the Greek Communist guerrillas, placing upon the weapon an unwarranted significance. West thereupon informed Sarafis that he would get the Marlin, and many others like it, when he re-formed the alliance with the royalists that had led to the destruction of the Gorgopotamos Viaduct—an exploit that was becoming a sort of modern *Iliad* in guerrilla lore.

Sarafis shrugged and said he would do what he could, and the parade continued. However, the point was not lost upon Sarafis. That night Sarafis promised to re-form the alliance with the royalists if West would give him his Marlin. With that promise West turned the weapon over, but as he was to learn later, the promise was not kept, and the Communist propagandists used the episode to establish a picture of the weapon being handed over at a "banquet," the Marlin being a token of American recognition of the ELAS and of large-scale arms shipments. In fact, the "banquet" had been a rough-and-ready supper in which all concerned had sat or sprawled on the floor of a cave, munching hunks of roast lamb torn away from the carcass with their hands, and where the only beverage had been 100 proof ouzo.

Yet West did obtain one promise which Sarafis was to keep: The ELAS would provide all necessary support for Noah's Ark, acknowledging that although it would damage the country seriously, such an operation was necessary if Greece was to be liberated. The guerrillas also accepted the authority of the supreme Allied commander in the Mediterranean, provided he authorized arms deliveries to them, to permit them to defend themselves and to arm more men against the inevitable German reprisals.

In general, the mission was a success, well executed and fruitful. West decided to return to Cairo immediately, and with a warning to Ehrgott to be careful about making gestures to Sarafis, he left for the airfield. There one DC-3 had managed to take off, but West's aircraft was still bogged down. He would have to stay the night while primitive chain blocks were brought from a nearby town to winch out the aircraft and some 600 women and children were put to work to dig drainage ditches. West did not get away until shortly before daybreak on the twenty-fourth, three days after arriving.

Shortly after West's DC-3, crowded with the sick airmen, had taken off, a flock of Junkers 88's and Me-109's came in to blast the strip—a sure sign that the Germans had learned that West was there. In that action eight Greek civilians were killed and more than forty were wounded.

It was fortunate for West that Donovan was expected back at Cairo when he returned, for he encountered the full wrath of the British security authorities for having gone into enemy territory. Toulmin advised Donovan in a note on November 5, 1943: ". . . it was certainly a worthwhile expedition except for the fact that the British have put in a rule that no staff officer should risk capture when he knows as much as West does." The commanding general of U.S. forces in the Middle East, General Royce, had "raised Hell with West for taking the trip," although "in the next breath he told me [Toulmin] personally that he thought we ought to recommend him for a decoration." Toulmin's "own opinion is that no staff officer should make trips such as this without written permission of the Commanding Officer here." But the matter had blown over, although "a repetition by West or anyone else could cause us a great deal of trouble."[4]

The affair was regarded by the British as another example of OSS irresponsibility and more justification for the British refusal to permit OSS officers into the central policy and planning sessions—and it was not forgotten that in some way West had been involved in the Morde affair. West was not sent home, he was spared to fight fresh battles, and with Donovan's return West was given *written* orders for what was to be OSS Cairo's greatest undertaking in Greece—Noah's Ark.

For all operations West had at his disposal no more than 15 officers, 159 enlisted men, and some 160 Special Operations agents. Yet the damage they were to do to the Germans was phenomenal, and the exploits of these tiny forces resembled the work of the hypaspists of Philip II of Macedon—heavily armed but fleet troops. A large, classic guerrilla campaign, it began in January 1944 with the first of a total of seventy-six operations that ended in September 1944, all of which Donovan planned with West the winter of 1943–44. They were, in the vast panorama of the war, minute actions, but even at a range of forty years the war diary has an heroic ring:[5]

§ April 23, 1944: Captain George W. Verghis leads Operational Group One to Epirus, the operational zone of the EDES guerrilla chieftain Napoleon Zervas. Verghis raids the Bulgarians until malaria grips all but three of his men; that and malnutrition force him to return to Cairo. Group One casualties: 0. Enemy casualties, killed and wounded: 76. Material destroyed: 19 trucks. Date of exfiltration: September 5, 1944. Number of days in Greece: 136.

§ May 16, 1944: Group Seven enters Greece commanded by Captain J. A. Rogers, leaves June 21, 1944, returns July 16, leaves November 20. First operational area: Peloponnesus, near Corinth, to blow the Patris–Corinth–Athens railway escape route. They blow a section of the line off a mountainside into the Gulf of Corinth and then withdraw. Second mission: Macedon, birthplace of Alexander the Great. Task: Close down the Salonika–Skopje railroad. Result: successful. Total days in Greece: 164. Enemy casualties, killed and wounded: 127. Number of operations participated in: 16. Group Seven casualties: 0. Material destroyed: 16 trucks, 1 locomotive, 1 railroad car, 1 highway bridge, 1 culvert, 1 railroad bridge, 1 fieldpiece.

§ May 21, 1944: Group Five, commanded by Lieutenant George Papazogleu, arrives in Greece by sea, marches for one month across Greece to its operational base on Mount Paiken. Number of days operational: 163. Target: main railroad to central Europe. Results: 574 enemy killed and wounded, 104 captured. Group Five casualties: 5 wounded. Material destroyed: 2 locomotives, large number of cars, 7 bridges, 1,000 yards of rail, 2 power plants, 2 mine shafts, 1 blockhouse.

§ June 18, 1944: First Lieutenant John Giannaris commands Group Two until June 18, 1944, when he is exfiltrated owing to severe wounds and is replaced by First Lieutenant Nick Pappas. Group Two enters Thessaly to raid the Athens–Salonika railroad. Group One strikes most frequently in the area between mountains known as the Five Mile Run. Group Two blows 7,400 yards of rail, cutting the railroad several times, mining the road in the valley once. It ambushed five enemy troop trains, taking very heavy toll of enemy life. [Operational Groups] casualties: 1 OG killed, 1 officer and 6 OGs wounded. Enemy casualties counted; 675 killed and wounded. Material destroyed: 3 locomotives, 31 boxcars, 7,400 yards of rail, 1 twenty-foot railroad culvert, 40 telegraph poles, 6 trucks. Number of days in Greece: 134.

§ July 19, 1944: Group Three enters Greece, Lieutenant Michael P. Manusos commanding. Number of days on operations in Greece: 112. Group Three lands at a cove called Parga on the west coast of Greece, marches for sixteen days across the country until it reaches its operational base at Deskhati [Deskate], near Larissa; mules carry equipment and supplies. In operations against enemy convoys on the highways enemy casualties, killed and wounded, total 201. Group Three casualties: 0. Material destroyed: 31 trucks, 1 bridge, 1 road cratered for 60 meters, 1 road wall blown onto road.

§ July 19, 1944: Group Six, commanded by Lieutenant George Chumas, lands at Parga, marches across Greece to Mount Olympus. Total number of days operational: 116. Target: rails and roads. Enemy casualties: 200 killed and wounded, 1 prisoner. Material destroyed: 2 armored cars, 3 pillboxes, 5 locomotives, unestimated number of railroad cars, 1,500 yards of track, large number of telegraph poles and lines, 2 bridges.

§ September 19, 1944: Group Four enters Greece by parachute, commanded by Captain Robert E. Eichler. Group commences operations along the old Roman road near Larissa. After sixty-four days operations terminated by the enemy's surrender. One railroad bridge destroyed.

Multiplied a thousandfold each day, as it was by special forces and guerrillas throughout Europe, Noah's Ark was a reflection in miniature of the general nightmare that the *Feldgrau*'s life had become inside the walls of Fortress Europe. Each operation was like the gadfly Io sent Hera to make her mad, and such was the effect of these operations that Hitler rarely spent less than half an hour of his noon conference—his main military conference of the day—discussing these operations and their implications. Nor will it be doubted that a three-man commando raid on a cliff top machine-gun post on the coast of France, in which one or two throats were slit, could, and very frequently did, have the effect of placing the entire German defensive system for northwestern Europe on an alert which lasted all night and which kept scores of thousands of German soldiers sleepless, fearful and expectant of other, larger attacks.

Donovan reveled in these operations and on occasions had to be restrained from going on them. Frequently he read his OGs' action reports aloud, poetically, at luncheon and dinner parties for distinguished guests at the Georgetown house, exhibiting the utmost pride. One of the Noah's Ark operations impressed him greatly, not because the exploit was any more important than the others, or because it achieved more, but because he believed it reflected the cheerful spirit of his OGs in action. He was so pleased with the report that he sent it to FDR, Marshall, Hull, and others. Called the Staircase operation, it was written up by a captain of OSS, J. Andy Rogers, in peacetime a journeyman linesman from Porterville, California:

On the night of 26 March 1944, the 1st Group, Unit A, 3rd Contingent, Operational Groups, OSS, left Taranto, Italy, by destroyer, to be infiltrated through the German lines into the Peloponnessus [*sic*], Greece. Due to enemy activity, bad weather and a broken rudder, we were forced to turn back. On the night of 8–9 May 1944, the 1st Patrol consisting of 9 enlisted men, 1 Officer and myself made an unsuccessful attempt to be infiltrated by air; again due to enemy activity around the dropping point. Another unsuccessful attempt was made on the night of 11–12 May 1944. This particular night much fire was drawn from the enemy who were obstinately sitting on our dropping point. On the night of 14–15 May 1944, we successfully landed with the Huns two hours away. There were no casualties but much equipment was destroyed due to low dropping.

We were met by a reception party of the Allied Mission [to Greece], who very thoughtfully had laid on bread, boiled eggs, and ouzo, which I must say put the life back into one's cold body. We gathered our equipment and just before the break of dawn moved, via mule, into the cover of the trees on the nearest mountain. In this vicinity, we remained for eight days, moving occasionally because of Hun activity and collecting supplies, mules, and carrying out extensive reconnaissance.

We planned to use the same dropping point for the other two patrols. Therefore, we decided to get the one patrol out of the area so as not to blow the pinpoint. 1st Lieutenant Darr and his 9 men were sent southeast toward the interior to collect intelligence and harass the enemy where possible. I remained at the Allied Mission for four days expecting the balance of my men every night, because of the telegrams from Cairo. On the 26th of May word was received that the Staircase operation must be done around the 4th, 5th, or 6th of June [immediately before and on Neptune D-Day in France]. I immediately ordered Lt. Darr's patrol to cut back to the North where we would rendezvous with the British and make necessary preparations for the job. Here the men were given 2 days much needed rest and on the afternoon and evening of the 3rd of June, Lt. Darr, two British officers and myself made a daylight reconnaissance of the site; the plan generally being to cut the road bridge and railway and dropping them into the sea where it would take the Germans approximately one month to repair it. Also to blow up the road bridge and railway bridge one mile away making it necessary to either use boats or shuttle by mule between the two cuts. The Air Force was to join in, generally keeping Jerry busy.

The situation was perfect. Our good friends, the Italians, when in power, had prepared a demolition chamber underneath the roadbed extending almost back to the railway, which ran parallel to the road around the cliff and [was] large enough to place sufficient explosives to do a good job. The site was accessible from the mountains by a trail that ran down from the top. There was good concealment all around and the site could be covered well by our security because of the perfect lay of the land, for example, an L.M.G. [light machine gun] was set up 200 yards away where grazing fire was perfect, covering the site.

We decided to fill the chamber full of ammanol [sic], which was 2200 pounds. The only way we could get it down was by mule. This presented some problem because from the time the mules left the covered side of the mountain, they could be seen from the road. The mules had to come down the trail, which was quite steep, move along the road for 300 yards, go over the bank and back along the water's edge 100 yards. We decided it would take 20 minutes to bring four mules down, unload, and return, and all the time they would be conspicuous to anyone on the road. Incidentally, there were occasional night patrols of from 30 to 40 men that moved between the two nearest towns. But luck was with us this night and Jerry slept. Little attention was given to the bridges, one mile away, for it was a simple job only to place the charge, set it off and move.

On the afternoon of the 5th of June, our party left the hideout, high in the mountains, with destruction on our minds. It was a motley crew, consisting of my 10 Americans, 3 British, 1 Canadian, 1 Australian, 20 odd Greek faithfuls and 28 mules loaded. My men were the covering party and we moved in advance, among, and at the rear of the party. Everything went according to schedule and just as the sun slipped over the mountains and darkness was close at hand, we moved down into our final assembly area which was 500 yards from the Big Job. I moved my men into position and the bridge party moved on down to their job.

The first mules came down at 2100 hours and we sat with our hearts in our mouths for 1 hour 20 minutes until the last mule was whipped back up the hill into cover—17 in all. Then it was a long wait for the sandbagging, priming, and moving out of the working party and then word to pull out the security. All this time we were anxiously peering into the darkness with our glasses, guns pointed and triggers ready; but little did Jerry know what was going on, although 300 were 3½ miles away. By prearranged signal, my security came in, collected, and we moved up to cover the party on the return. Two men and myself remained as rearguard and to see the results.

At 0145 the Big Job went off and I'll bet it jarred the Huns out of bed, even at Athens. Fifteen minutes later the two bridges went up and it was music to my ears to hear the echo from the mainland mountains across the Bay. The cuts were so covered with smoke that a good check could not be made, however, both roadbeds had slid into the sea leaving a sheer cliff several hundred feet high and a cut some 70 feet wide. Both bridges were destroyed and the mission was a complete success.

We moved back to our hideout, ate, slept out the day and night, broke camp and moved for three days into the area where we were dropped. A piece of paper, an American flag and a British flag were placed on a board and left on the road for the Huns. On the paper was written something to this effect, "This is definitely an Allied military operation by American and British troops and please do not take spite out on the poor village people who were not aware of our intentions." As yet no reprisals have been taken. The next day several hundred Germans drove up in armored cars and looked the cuts over. An engine was run into the river where the bridge was blown. Shuttling of supplies was started between the cuts.

After arriving at our destination, we picked a good camp site and prepared to spend a few days resting and gathering ourselves and equipment together. On the third day, I was told part of the British Mission was to be evacuated and my men were wanted for a covering party. It was three days journey to where the operation was to take place by sea. We arrived one day in advance and checked the area.

The night of the operation, my men were all posted and we were afraid the operation might fail as there was a German [manhunt] headed our way and only four hours away. Just 1½ hours before the operation I received word the Americans would be evacuated. Our kit was several hours away and impossible to get before the ship came in, so we came out with our weapons and what we had on our backs. Need I say happy to be on the evacuating destroyer and able to report mission successful.

In conclusion, I might say a volume could be written about what we saw, the experiences my men and I had, how the poor people of Greece are suffering, barefooted and hungry. Also if the good Greek people of America knew the conditions in Greece, the misery, hunger, disease, filth and terrorism not only by the Germans but also by Greek organizations as well, they would do some deep thinking.

> (s) J. Andy Rogers,
> Captain, C.E.[6]

Donovan's idea for the making of unorthodox warfare was that (1) his Morale Operations organization existed to destroy the will to resist of the enemy forces; (2) his Secret Intelligence branch was there to keep the commander in chief informed of the enemy's capabilities and intentions; (3) his Special Operations existed to destroy or disturb the enemy's lines of communication before, during, and after the main attack; and (4) his Operational Groups would prepare the way for the main forces. The novelty of this conception existed in two factors: (1) Nobody in the United States had thought to adopt such "ungentlemanly" practices as a weapon of war and, if anyone had, nobody in the United States had the political power necessary to persuade, or force, the President as Commander in Chief and the Chiefs of Staff to adopt the concept, and (2) the entire organization was under one roof. In Britain, Germany, and Russia, both the concept and the means for waging such wars had existed for some years, but for constitutional, political, budgetary, and organizational reasons the responsibility had been placed in a number of different ministries or military organizations. What WJD had formed was what may be called the Department of Ungentlemanly Warfare.

Yet although it seemed in 1941 to be a desirable force to have at America's disposal, by late 1943 it was evident to WJD that there would be few, if any, opportunities to test his department *as a whole*. The field was too crowded, the realities of warfare waged by a coalition of powers too complex, for any one national organization to be able to conduct such a large share of a single operation. Thus, whether Donovan's theory was the correct one, whether the complex bureaucracy needed to sustain so many functions could work as a single harmonious entity, or whether the British theory of small departments, each carrying out a single function of special means, the whole linked through a high-ranking committee, was the most practical system of waging war was not to be established in World War II.

However, with rumblings of trouble and discontent among his executives in Washington continuing to reach him—the substance being this very question of the OSS concept—Donovan undertook an operation that was not only singular in itself, and important, but demonstrated that three of his principal branches—Secret Intelligence, Research and Analysis, and Special Operations—could be brought to bear successfully on a single project under the command of a single coordinator. This operation, Peoria II, showed that the OSS was passing from the stage of trial and error to proficiency in intelligence, analysis, communications, special operations, mature decisions related directly to the strategic prosecution of the war, harmonious working with other branches of government, technical ability, and collaboration with the British.

Peoria II began in September 1943, when the Allied economic warfare agencies detected signs that the Germans were beginning to suffer from severe shortages of chrome, a vital element in the manufacture of special alloys used in aircraft production, a constituent of several important steel alloys in tanks and warships, and a component in the production of steel-cutting tools and wear-resistant metal surfaces. It became the mission of the OSS to intensify the German shortage and thereby increase distress in the war metals industries.

When Donovan heard that the OSS, not the British services, might receive the mission, he asked Research and Analysis to give him a paper on chrome. The document showed there were no chrome deposits available to Germany anywhere in occupied Eurasia except Greece and Yugoslavia, where the deposits not only were small but, as a result of the war and guerrilla labor, were almost impossible to find, while transportation was almost always interrupted.

Also, although Germany had had large chrome stockpiles at the outbreak of war, by mid-1943 these were badly run down. Germany's principal supplier since the war had been Turkey and, Research and Analysis estimated, if Turkish supplies could be stopped, or even only delayed, the Reich's metals industries might well be unable to meet their production schedules at a critical time.

As R&A went on to report, in the early months of the war the British and French had obtained an agreement in which the Turkish government agreed to sell the Allies all their surplus chrome production for three years up to January 15, 1943, in return for military equipment and munitions. When the agreement came up for renewal in 1943, the Germans managed to persuade the Turks not to continue with the British and to ship 90,000 tons a year to Germany in 1943 and 1944. All efforts of the American and British ambassadors failed to persuade the Turks not to fulfill the agreement, as did operations of the Anglo-American economic warfare organizations to seal the leakage through what was called preemptive buying—offering prices the Germans could not match.

But, the authors of the brief advised, "The German chrome position at the present time is tight even including the . . . receipts from Turkey. Without the Turkish supply German receipts of chrome will fall considerably below basic requirements, since chrome has been used all along as a substitute for ferro-alloys in shorter supply." Thus, the loss of Turkish chrome "would almost certainly affect the level of munitions production (especially aircraft and tanks) within six months."[7]

Thus, early in 1943 Secretary of State Cordell Hull and Lauchlin Currie, deputy administrator of the Foreign Economic Administration, asked Donovan to see if special means could be used to interrupt Germany's supplies from Turkey. In turn, Donovan asked the chief of Research and Analysis, Dr. William L. Langer, to look at the rail routes being used to ship the chrome and see if there were any bridges or tunnels that the OSS might blow up.

Langer shot Donovan's hopes into the Potomac with his first paper. There were bridges to blow, he wrote, notably the big one over the main channel of the Maritsa, one of the Balkans' chief rivers, and the Orient Express railway route across the Arda River, near the northern Greek-Turkish frontier. But, Langer wrote, while the destruction of both bridges might be spectacular, it could not decisively stop or even delay the shipment of chrome by rail. There were too many alternative routes, and even if there were not, it was the opinion of the railway experts that the Germans could throw up replacement bridges within a month and place pontoon bridges across the rivers in less than a week. Moreover, even if for any reason they were unable to do either, since the ore loads passing over the railroads in those sectors at any one time were small, the ore could be transferred from freight cars to trucks and reloaded into freight cars on the other side. Langer concluded:

> There is no doubt that the Maritsa Bridge is an exciting target. But higher authorities apparently are convinced that its destruction would stop the chrome ore shipments. I believe it is necessary to disabuse them of this idea. If the psychological effect is still considered worthy of the expenditure of resources involved then plans should proceed, but on that basis alone.[8]

Donovan found no compelling reason to proceed against such advice, at least for the moment, and the project was shelved until February 26, 1944, when he received a note from the State Department, reopening the matter in encouraging terms:

> During the last three months there has been a notable increase in the amount of chrome exported to Germany and a decrease in the amounts being made available to the British. Strong representations have been made to the Turkish Foreign Office by the British and American Ambassadors regarding this matter.

After careful consideration the British Ambassador and our own have agreed to renew the recommendation made on the 18th of October 1943, for the interruption of the railways between Istanbul and Sofia. In renewing these recommendations no reserve is being made. . . . It is now desired that communications be disrupted anywhere that will affect interruption of traffic for the longest period.[9]

Very rarely had the OSS received an invitation to blow up a bridge from not one but two ambassadors; usually such operations were conducted in the teeth of resolute ambassadorial opposition. Donovan therefore sent for a second opinion on the Maritsa bridge, going around Langer to an expert in Balkan railroads, Edward T. Dickinson. Dickinson's opinion was much more to Donovan's liking:

The most effective means of interfering with exports to the Reich is by destroying transportation carrying Turkish goods through the Balkans. In 1943, about 53% of the 170,000 tons of all goods exported to the Axis and about 60% of the 46,000 tons of chrome were shipped by rail over the Maritsa river just a few yards on the Greek side of the Turkish frontier. The destruction of any of the four spans of the Maritsa bridge would be a simple task for a trained saboteur and would break the single rail line for a considerable period of time. At the same time direct action could be taken against the Turkish chrome and copper mines and the transport facilities carrying the ores through Turkey. Sabotage against the current production of chrome would result in immediate reduction of the quantities of chrome which the Germans can receive from Turkey.[10]

By mid-March 1944 orders had been cut and were with West, the Special Operations officer at OSS Cairo. West selected as leader of the party a young former engineer cadet from Yorkville, Ohio, Captain James L. C. Kellis, who had been trained in leadership, wireless, and demolition. Kellis set out for the target as a request for cooperation went out to the OSS Pericles team at the Communist EAM (political)/ELAS (military) headquarters in the mountains of central Greece. Kellis beat the well-worn path for OSS agents from Cairo going into Greece: up to Alexandria to embark in a fifty-ton caïque, a small fishing and cargo boat run by the OSS Maritime Unit; up to Karavostasi on the northwestern coast of Cyprus, to revictual and take on extra crew; then across to the secret OSS base on the Turkish coast at Kusadasi. There, a change of craft at Rema Bay for the last leg of the journey through the Sporades to Lemnos and then across the Aegean to Alexandropoulis on the Aegean coast of Greek Thrace. There Kellis was met by Communist Andartes with mules that carried the party and explosives up into the mountains near the target area of Svilengrad in Bulgaria.

Then there was the usual long, anxious silence.

Donovan was in London when the telegram arrived from West on June 2, 1944:

> Guerrillas and SO enlisted personnel and officers successfully blew up the railroad bridges designated as *Joliet* and *Milwaukee*. . . . This took place on the nights of May 29th and May 30th. It is thought that there will be a substantial interruption of traffic. This complies for the time being with the request from State and JCS to interrupt exports from Turkey.[11]

Donovan then informed Roosevelt on June 18, 1944:

> You will recall that the Secretary of State asked us to undertake operations to interrupt shipments of chrome. The first operations have been undertaken with the result that on May 29th and 30th, two railway bridges across the Maritsa River were destroyed by representatives of our organization. One of these bridges was near Svilengrad in Bulgaria and is described as the largest bridge over the Maritsa in that area. The other was 12 kilometers east of Alexandropoulis (Dede Agach) in Greece. The main railway line from Istanbul to Sofia passes through Svilengrad; the only alternative rail route passes over the Alexandropoulis line.[12]

The secretary of state's letter to Donovan was a masterpiece of smooth satisfaction at the success of Peoria II. That dry old lawyer Cordell Hull wrote:

> I am sure Ambassador Steinhardt [at Ankara] appreciates the significance of these operations, in view of the recommendations he has made from time to time in relation to such a project and that he, like the Department, will follow with particular interest reports of further interruptions in rail traffic in that general area.[13]

Even diplomatists, it seemed, on occasions liked big bangs.

It was not until almost two months after the attack that Kellis returned to Cairo, heavily bearded, looking like an Aegean fisherman, a duffel bag over his shoulder, still wearing his Greek sailor's cap and blue dungarees, to make his report. That report was then telegraphed to WJD, who then informed General Marshall, that after landing, Kellis and his team "proceeded to the mountain headquarters of the ELAS Andartes where they found, instead of an organized guerrilla unit, a virtual state of civil war."[14] Since Kellis needed the Andartes for his mission, he and ten former Greek army officers "took steps to terminate hostilities and stiffen the attitude of the Andartes toward the enemy."

They were successful, and "shortly thereafter the enemy, quick to notice the change in the attitude of the Andartes due to the presence of the Americans, invoked repressive measures, including the execution of seven Greek hostages and the reinforcement of their troops with 1,000 additional men." Captain Kellis countered by "ascertaining through the Andartes the name of the German political Governor of Evros," Donovan reported. He continued:

> [Kellis] then composed a note to the Governor warning that if reprisals were taken against the Greeks because of American operations, his name would be turned over to the Allies as a war criminal and that on termination of hostilities he would be dealt with accordingly. We are informed that the Germans did increase their security measures following the demolition of the bridges but it is interesting to note . . . that there has been no report of any reprisals against the Greeks.

Preparations for the attacks on the bridges, Donovan went on, were made "in the face of strong German efforts to wipe out the OSS team. At one time the anti-guerrilla reconnaissance battalion succeeded in surrounding Captain Kellis and 13 men who escaped only after seven hours of bitter fighting. Three of the men were slightly wounded." In the attack on the bridge at Alexandropoulis, the twenty-five Greek gendarmes guarding the structure—it was 100 feet long and 45 feet high—joined the fifty Andartes guarding the OSS demolition party. Mining of the bridge lasted about forty minutes, and demolition occurred at 11:30 P.M. on May 30, 1944.

As for the main bridge near Svilengrad, which was attacked by Kellis, the OSS party was accompanied by 170 Andartes, who carried the 1,400 pounds of explosives. Mining began at 10:50 P.M. on May 29 without interference from the enemy guards, who slept until ten minutes past midnight, when, disturbed, they opened fire. By that time the mining had been completed and the fuse was burning. Within five minutes the bridge, 210 feet long and 12 feet high, had vanished in a mighty explosion.

In making their getaway, Kellis and his party were, Donovan wrote, hard pressed for several days by a German reconnaissance battalion, but they escaped, and the Greeks accompanying Kellis ambushed and killed the German battalion commander and his staff. Donovan ended his report to Marshall: "After making his report [in Cairo], Captain Kellis returned to Greece for further operations."

What WJD did not state, perhaps because he did not know, was the effect this resourceful and heroic action had upon the supply of Turkish chrome to Germany. Langer had been correct: The demolitions had no permanent or even long-term effect on the flow at all. Through superb emergency engineering, the Germans threw up pontoon bridges, and in each case shipments were resumed within a month. The best that can be said for the strategic effect of Peoria II was, therefore, that though temporary, the interruptions in chrome shipments were achieved at a time of acute shortage in Germany and that small forces of American special troops tied up large numbers of German troops for many weeks in fruitless work, at a time when they might have been employed in Normandy.

As was often the case at this time, Donovan had overruled his experts in the wider interest of the future of American Intelligence; after the run of failures that had attended his Balkan plan he and his service badly needed a victory, and the raids on the Maritsa and Alexandropoulis bridges provided him with the sort of ammunition he needed. For that was the way the Joint Chiefs worked—they applauded little but success. In the event, therefore, Germany's supplies of chrome were terminated not by *plastique* and heroism, but by vigorous diplomacy: Turkey was compelled to break all pacts, diplomatic as well as economic, with Germany.

One other political factor of importance was involved in Peoria II. The attack had shown that sabotage was at least as effective as aerial bombardment as a method of inhibiting rail traffic over bridges and that saboteurs could be more accurate than bombardiers; it was a more economical method of securing the desired aim (only a few men were needed against the many men needed to launch a bomber mission); and the probability was that casualties were fewer by far than those that would have been suffered in a low-level air attack. That important theoretical point was being debated continuously between the airmen and the saboteurs.

28

Audrey

Exasperated by recurrent British attempts to control the OSS in all key theaters of war, Donovan, as part of his Balkan plan, had been contemplating the establishment of what he called an "Independent American Military Mission to Marshal Tito," his object to break the British hammerlock on intelligence and operations in Yugoslavia. With that operation in mind, he received with considerable interest a proposal for a remarkable piece of OSS private enterprise: Operation Audrey.

The operation had begun when Donovan was in Algiers in September 1943 and two young OSS officers, Hans Tofte and Robert E. S. Thompson, arrived at the Villa Magnol from Cairo. Tofte, a former China hand with coastal shipping experience, and Thompson, a former reporter with a Philadelphia newspaper, stated they had reason to believe that when the port of Bari was captured, as was then imminent, many small Adriatic coastal ships would be found there. Tofte proposed that the OSS should get possession of the ships and then use them not only to supply the Yugoslav guerrillas but also to infiltrate OSS men into Yugoslavia, thus ending the OSS's dependence upon the British at Cairo and Algiers for air and sea transportation—which was, they claimed, rarely provided.

Donovan leaped at this idea, for while he had no authority from the Joint Chiefs to commence independent operations into Yugoslavia, the question of intensifying the supply of warlike stores to the Yugoslavs had been debated favorably by the Combined Chiefs at Quebec in August. No final decision to proceed had been made, but Donovan felt entitled to "prepare" for such operations, since he had good information that the project would receive formal approval when the American, British, and Russian heads of state and staffs met at Cairo and Teheran shortly.

Donovan instructed Tofte and Thompson to accompany him on the night shuttle from Algiers to Cairo, and the three men spent most of the night discussing the scheme. Thompson claimed later that Donovan became so enthusiastic about the prospect of the OSS's running war stores to the Yugoslavs in bulk and getting his own men into Yugoslavia that he promised Thompson and Tofte the Distinguished Service Cross if they did get the "Trans-Adriatic Shipping Line" started.[1]

Whatever the truth of that statement (and it was hotly disputed by Doering), on his arrival in Cairo Donovan met with Tofte's and Thompson's commanding officer, Major Louis Huot, acting chief of Special Operations at Cairo. He instructed Huot to get the operation started, and Huot himself took charge of it, being appointed "chief of the OSS advance base at Bari." He sent Tofte to Palestine for parachute training, in case *parachutage* was necessary. Huot and Thompson arrived in Algiers and began work on or about October 5, 1943.

At Algiers, Huot and Thompson claimed later, they received authority to establish an OSS base at Bari and to proceed with supply operations from all the responsible officers from Eisenhower downward, including representatives of the British secret and military services. Huot maintained that the British arranged for him to receive 400 tons of war stores at Bari and that his authority to act was endorsed by the commanding general of American forces in the Middle East, General Royce, when he passed through Algiers and saw Thompson at the airport. Also, according to Huot and Thompson later, Colonel Gustav Guenther, lately OSS chief in Cairo, who was traveling with Royce, stated specifically that:

> Major Huot and Lt. Thompson were to proceed to Southern Italy with all possible speed, establish a base, make necessary reconnaissance, and begin operations. Major Huot was authorized to requisition personnel, material and funds, sufficient to insure the success of the operations. . . . [Guenther] said that there was a great opportunity to hit the Germans hard on the Dalmatian coast and that he expected results quickly.[2]

Whatever the truth of those claims, later the British contended that Huot had had no authority to act as he did and had exceeded all his orders. It is impossible to reach the truth of what happened, who authorized what, and to what extent corners were cut on an alarming scale. For the moment all that is important is that Huot traveled much faster than staff officers normally traveled, and when Donovan passed through Algiers in mid-November, he appears to have done nothing to terminate the operation.

Accompanied by two stray partisans who had shown up in Algiers,

Serge Makiedo and Jozo Poduje, Huot and Thompson thumbed a ride in a British air vice marshal's aircraft to Taranto. There Huot fast-talked his way past the Allied naval officer commanding the Adriatic, Admiral Sir Arthur Power, who Huot claimed gave him verbal permission to take charge of all coastal shipping at Bari in the name of the supreme Allied commander, Eisenhower. Then the party sped on to Bari.

There Huot's run of cooperation was temporarily interrupted, for he found that Admiral Power had omitted to transmit written orders to the British naval officer in charge of the port, which was being used by Montgomery's Eighth Army as its principal entrepôt in the drive up the Adriatic coast of Italy. This officer "requested written confirmation" of Power's permission, and when Huot was not able to supply such orders, he became "hostile"—not surprisingly since the Briton needed the port and all its facilities to supply a major army on active service.

However, when Huot promised to obtain Power's order at the earliest date, the naval officer in charge "thereupon granted permission to make use of berth #2 for loading, provisioning, watering and fueling the Partisan vessels." Huot then went to see a British civilian who represented the North African Shipping Board and who, on the strength of Huot's report of his conversation with Power, formally endorsed the handing over to Huot of all the Yugoslav ships in the port, thirty or forty vessels, some with crews and ranging from 50 to about 1,200 tons.

Displaying great energy—Tofte was to recall that "Huot was like a whirling dervish in his efforts to get guns to Tito"—Huot began to organize the OSS's first large-scale guerrilla supply operation, and his achievements would generate great admiration later within the organization. With the minimum of paper, fuss, and words, Huot and Thompson had crossed two theaters of war and had obtained authority to act from one field marshal, one supreme commander, at least three generals and one admiral, and several colonels and majors and lesser officers. They had been promised 400 tons of war stores from one officer, 250 from another. They had acquired seventeen ships with crews, berths, and the necessary fuel to operate them, and were in the process of acquiring a further twenty-three. In short, they had acquired control of all the coastwise shipping of a major Italian port through a combination of blandishment and judicious name-dropping. Tofte was to remember: "Huot was forever making statements such as 'General Eisenhower directs . . . ,' 'Admiral Power orders . . . ,' and 'General Bedell Smith requests. . . .'" And Huot was soon to obtain the assistance of General Sir Bernard Montgomery's services of supply to shift the materials and of the Royal Navy, the Royal Engineers, and the Royal Air Force to guard the ships at sea and the crews on land.

Taking the fullest advantage of the confusion that existed in the heel of Italy following the Italian surrender and the chaos often found in the rear of a large army engaged in a major operation, Huot was able formally to begin operations to supply the partisans on October 11, 1943, when Admiral Power, believing Huot was acting for General Eisenhower, sent up a special train laden with 210 tons of supplies. A British minelayer then arrived from Algiers with 400 tons of stores, and by one means or another Huot acquired 200 tons of coal, some claim by playing poker for them. All this pleased Huot greatly, and he wrote in his diary for October 12, 1943:

> . . . everywhere you go for help there is a smile and a crisp order. 2,500 gallons of gasoline were turned over in five minutes and arrived at the berth an hour later. 2,500 gallons of diesel oil and four lorries to truck it were arranged for delivery within an hour. Here, at last, was a whole army of men, Army and Navy, with a single purpose . . . get the stuff up to the men who will fight for it!

But soon Huot began to experience that most uncomfortable of human sensations—finding oneself on the outer edge of the whirlpool of power politics—while he was at the Yugoslav island of Vis aboard a British torpedo boat, surveying Tito's facilities for handling large quantities of supplies and for hiding them from the Luftwaffe. As yet neither the heads of state of the Grand Alliance, the Combined Chiefs, the Joint Chiefs, nor the British Chiefs of Staff had made the decision to commence large-scale supply operations to Tito. Nor had any of these authorities issued any directives to Donovan that gave the slightest legality to Operation Audrey —an operation that was code-named after Huot's British wife.

Therefore, when an SOE survey party arrived at Bari under Lieutenant Colonel Samuel Lohan, its mission to establish a base for supply operations into Yugoslavia, the discovery that the OSS had begun such an operation caused the greatest surprise. As Lohan advised Huot, both the Adriatic and Yugoslavia had been declared British theaters of war by the Combined Chiefs of Staff in Washington, and the port of Bari was under British control for all purposes. Moreover, the coastal shipping fleet had been assigned to the SOE to enable it to commence supply operations to Tito when orders were received to do so from the supreme Allied commander.

Lohan then ordered Huot to cease operations and turn himself, his organization, and all ships and war stores over to the SOE. When the order was promptly rejected by Huot, Lohan sent an angry signal to the head of Eisenhower's clandestine services in Algiers, a Briton in charge of a largely British organization. Huot was then ordered to subordinate himself and his mission to Lohan, an order he ignored. To make matters worse, a Major Sato of the SOE, who was an official with Lohan's party, alleged that the 400 tons of supplies which had arrived in the British minelayer were intended for the SOE and that Huot had "stolen" them —a contention that almost produced a roughhouse between the two groups. From this point forward the controversy widened and relations worsened.

Without authority from the head of the Allied Military Mission in Yugoslavia, Brigadier Fitzroy Maclean, an appointee of Churchill's, Huot visited the Yugoslavian Adriatic islands, making arrangements for the wharfing and warehousing of stores. He entered into extensive negotiations with Tito's representatives on the island of Vis regarding priorities, promising to do what he could to obtain light tanks, trucks, mountain artillery, and other such weapons from captured Italian war matériel dumps in Tunisia—promises that were to embarrass Maclean, who had no authority to give the partisans other than light weapons. Moreover, Huot's promises seriously embarrassed both the State Department, which continued to recognize Draža Mihailović, the royalist leader in Yugoslavia, and FDR, who was on father-and-son terms with King Peter II and also in sympathy at the time with the reestablishment of the monarchy in Yugoslavia after the country was liberated.

In consequence, urgent telegrams concerning Operation Audrey began to flow between Cairo and Washington, and OSS Cairo decided to relieve Huot while he was on Vis. In an attempt to restore Allied amity, OSS Cairo ordered Major Carleton S. Coon, the Harvard anthropologist, to Bari to assume command of Operation Audrey. Claiming that his orders from Eisenhower et al. authorized him to act and had not been rescinded and that until they were, he would continue to operate as chief of OSS Bari, Huot refused to hand over command of the shipping line unless ordered to do so by Donovan. To make matters worse, and ensuring that Huot remained in command, Coon was taken seriously ill soon after his arrival and had to be returned to the United States.

When the British discovered that Huot was still in command and had not been relieved by OSS Cairo, they moved in a business friend of Donovan's and now a senior SOE officer, Lieutenant Colonel the Lord Harcourt, a powerful British banker. When Huot returned from yet another mission aboard the torpedo boat, he was informed by Lord Harcourt that the OSS could continue to operate the "Trans-Adriatic Shipping Line," but only under SOE command. Huot's reaction was not evident from his report, but Tofte thought Huot told Harcourt to "go and f—— himself,"[3] and on October 20, 1943, only a few hours after Harcourt's arrival, to depart in his torpedo boat to see Tito at his headquarters in the Yugoslav mountains. Until now Huot's actions had brought him into conflict only with junior representatives of an Allied service in what might well have been a misunderstanding regarding orders, but now he became involved in a matter of the highest power politics. Without authority, he went to see Tito in the mountains to discuss with the Yugoslav Communist leader what arms and equipment Tito needed—at a time when Tito was beginning a civil war with Mihailović for control of Yugoslavia.

Compounding his mistake, on landing on the Yugoslav mainland Huot made no attempt to see Maclean, who was nearby at Korčula, and pay the usual courtesies to a superior officer, and became involved in a dispute between the British and the partisans in which it was evident that the partisans were seeking to play both the British and the Americans against the middle to obtain maximum supplies from both. Also, he seems not to have understood or cared that even in wartime diplomatic and political niceties had to be observed, if only to avoid trouble later.

Huot reached Tito's headquarters at about 6:00 P.M. on October 23, 1943, being received by Tito at the door of his shed under some cedars. Tito gave him "a warm welcome" and invited Huot for "schnapps and dinner." However, Huot may have been mistaken about the warmth of his reception, for Tito's official biographer, Vladimir Dedijer, was to write in *With Tito:*

> One day a rather strange man appeared on Partisan territory. He was an officer of the United States Army, a major, who said his name was Huot. He asked to see Tito, but inquired all the time whether there were any British officers in the vicinity. At that very moment, a British officer came along. The American immediately asked the town major to hide him another room so that the Englishman should not see him. The town major did as he was asked, but was at a complete loss to understand what the American officer was after. The facts were simple, however. Major Louis Huot had not obtained permission from the Allied command to come to Yugoslavia. He had come on his own initiative to assist the Partisans.[4]

Captain Melvin O. Benson, the OSS liaison officer at Tito's headquarters and one of the OSS members of Maclean's staff, expressed considerable surprise at seeing another American officer at Tito's headquarters, for he had not been told by his base at Cairo that Huot was coming or was authorized to come. Benson advised Huot to inform the British of his mission in Yugoslavia, but Huot would not do that for some time, agreeing only when Benson pointed out that the partisans might misinterpret his reluctance and think there was some trouble between the American and British members of the alliance.

Huot spent eighteen hours at partisan headquarters, much of that time with Tito, taking down details of the supplies Tito needed, together with priorities, engaging in conversations concerning the political composition of the partisan movement, and making estimates concerning the strength, morale, disposition, and equipment of the partisan forces—unaware perhaps that Maclean had been sent by Churchill to make that estimate for the Allied governments.

On the basis of these inquiries, Huot produced a seven-page paper describing the composition, tactics, weapons, locations, and strengths of the eight corps that constituted Tito's principal units; the partisans' training methods and the methods used to select and train officers; a history of the partisan movement; its political and ethnic composition; its attitude toward the king; and Tito's ideas on postwar Yugoslavia.

He made a list of the supplies needed, together with priorities, and covered the partisans' attitudes toward Mihailović; their relations with Russia and the British; and extensive German order-of-battle intelligence. He was not to be faulted as an intelligence reporter, but he did convey a somewhat idealistic view of Tito, who was in fact engaging in as much butchery as Mihailović, and a deprecating opinion of British supply operations to the partisans.

All this was, no doubt, admirable and useful. But then Huot behaved tactlessly once again. Before leaving Tito's headquarters, Huot, without authority, removed two of the OSS representatives with Maclean's mission. He sent Benson to the coast to look after the Yugoslav end of the "Trans-Adriatic Shipping Line" and took the second, Major Lynn Farish, back to Bari with him "to prepare a full report, and perhaps continue on to Cairo and Washington to report to the interested departments of the Government of the United States on his experiences and significance." Huot added: "I realized that this course would inevitably require lengthy and painful explanations with Brigadier Maclean," but the Yugoslavs were "most eager" that Farish should go, Farish himself thought it was "the wisest course," his own impression was that it was "certainly the line of action most expedient in the interests of the war effort," and, moreover, "I was sure the Brigadier would be in Bari within a week and that however difficult it might be, it should be possible to square the situation with him then." Thus "expediency carried and I decided to bring the Major with me."[5]

Not surprisingly, therefore, when Huot arrived back in Bari late in the afternoon of October 27, 1943, he found himself in a hornets' nest. General Colin Gubbins, chief of the SOE, had arrived from London to inspect his base at Bari and found his operations, without his knowledge and consent, being run by the OSS. There were some "frank conversations" between General Gubbins and Major Huot. Then, according to Lieutenant Thompson, Gubbins authorized Huot to continue operations and congratulated Huot "warmly upon his mission," stating that he had done "an incredibly fine job." So he had, but he had also broken every regulation and agreement between the OSS and SOE.

When Maclean returned to Tito's headquarters and found that Huot had visited Tito without his permission or knowledge, had conducted supply and staff conversations without his permission, and had then spirited away his American advisers, the Briton filed a vigorous protest with MO 4, the controlling authority at Cairo for all operations into Yugoslavia. When Maclean passed through Bari within a few days, on his way to be with Churchill at the Cairo Conference with Roosevelt and the Combined Chiefs, he made a number of statements to Huot that were amiable. But the truth was that in Maclean, Huot had made a powerful enemy, one almost as powerful as Lord Harcourt, who was now Huot's commanding officer.

At Huot's meeting with Harcourt, during which there were more "frank discussions," Huot announced very sharply: "For some time there had been in some quarters a tendency to elbow OSS out of the picture, and that unfair and untrue rumors were being circulated regarding the manner in which we had obtained stores from SOE." The time had come, he announced, to settle the matter once and for all. Thompson recorded that Huot informed Harcourt:

> The OSS represented the United States of America. It did not intend to be elbowed out. It had demonstrated its right to be an equal partner in operations from Italy. It would be acutely embarrassing to SOE in its relations with the Partisans if SOE did anything to disrupt the warm relations which exist between Tito and the OSS.

Huot advised Harcourt that it was "a fact which cannot be disputed, that a state of mistrust existed between the Partisans and SOE."

According to Thompson, Harcourt apologized to Huot, agreed that the relationship between the OSS and the SOE was a partnership, and "volunteered to put a stop to the things which had caused the friction." On that basis, Thompson wrote, "Major Huot agreed that we could proceed with the main job as partners."

The partnership was not to last very long. Huot had promised Tito 1,000 trucks, and he asked Harcourt's permission to go to Algiers and arrange their transportation to Vis. Where Huot obtained the notion that Eisenhower had 1,000 trucks to spare, who would drive and service them, and how trucks would operate on the goat trails used by Tito were not clear. Nonetheless, Harcourt saw a chance to rid himself of his troublesome American lieutenant and authorized Huot's journey—properly this time. At Algiers Huot was received as a minor hero—until the staff received Harcourt's complaint about his conduct at Bari. Then he was ordered to Cairo to report to his commanding officer, Lieutenant Colonel Toulmin, who had just been appointed to that post and was determined to bring discipline and order to the Cairo base, its personnel, and its missions after the freewheeling days of Colonel Guenther.

At Cairo, although his achievement had not gone unrecorded, Huot might reasonably have expected a better reception than he got from

Toulmin. For while he was there, Donovan had sent the Joint Chiefs a note that fully explained Huot's excellent services:

> The guerrilla forces [in Yugoslavia] are in great need of supplies but the lack of air and sea transport has made possible the delivery of a ridiculously small supply between July and September [of 1943]. The latest figures available show that between those dates the stores dropped by air to Mihailovitch [*sic*] were 107 tons, to the Partisans 82½ tons. . . . This was done by means of 213 air sorties to Yugoslavia of which 139 were successful. . . .

But between "12 October to 5 November, when we had available to us by the North African Shipping Board small caiques with a total tonnage of 3,000 tons net, we were able to deliver to Tito 1,000 tons of supplies from a base set up in Bari."[6]

While such statements did seem to foreshadow a process in which the Huot matter might be allowed to drop, Maclean's protests soon extinguished the roseate glow of triumph that surrounded Huot. The simple truth was that Harcourt and Maclean were more powerful in high places than Huot, and Huot's career as an outstanding founding member of OSS field operations began to come to its end. There was a quarrel between Huot and Toulmin, who complained to Washington that Huot was "out of control." Huot then received a fatherly telegram from the acting director of Special Operations, Joseph Scribner, warning him that while he was much admired as a fighting man, he ought to try to be more diplomatic. Huot ignored the advice at a time when there were rumors of serious peculation at the Bari base—peculation for which he bore no responsibility—so he was brought home. He mooched about headquarters for a time, writing a book and an official pamphlet about the "Trans-Adriatic Shipping Line." After a brief conversation between Donovan and Huot, the nature of which was not recorded, Huot left the OSS, receiving no official commendation for his exploits, having paid what was altogether too high a price for what was little more than exuberance, excessive elbow work, enthusiasm, and a dash of Anglophobia. And neither Huot nor his colleagues received the Distinguished Service Cross.

Three days after he left Cairo for Washington, Roosevelt, Churchill, Stalin, and their staffs, meeting to decide upon the nature of military operations in 1944, promulgated their military conclusions. These contained a directive to all concerned that henceforth the Allies would intensify guerrilla actions in the Balkans and supply operations to Tito. Huot's main crime had been, therefore, to jump the gun.

Late in 1943 and early in 1944 Donovan returned to his campaign to break finally what he believed was a British stranglehold on intelligence coming out of Yugoslavia. While he was fully prepared to go along with the Teheran decisions to increase support to Tito, he was not prepared to bend to British pressure to terminate intelligence coverage at Mihailović's headquarters. Donovan remained determined to have *independent* American coverage from *both* headquarters. But that required the authority of the Joint Chiefs, so on November 26, 1943, he formally requested that permission.

In a letter to the Joint Chiefs he asserted that the "course of action in the Balkans . . . has been directed by the [British] Foreign Office" and, in a reference to Maclean, stated that in some cases, this policy was being directed by "Foreign Office representatives in uniform and ostensibly under SOE orders but in reality (as we have actually experienced) responsive not to SOE but only to the Foreign Office."[7]

Consequently, the "policy of dealing with the situation has been dictated by the considered long-range political necessity of the British in the Balkans rather than the immediate and vital military problem here or its relation to over-all Allied operations." The governments in exile of Greece and Yugoslavia, both in Cairo, "assert that they have been ignored, communications with their forces in the field denied them, and not consulted in matters affecting their country's sovereignty with resultant impairment of their position." That had resulted in "bitterness and suspicion and distrust of both the British and Americans."

Following that singeing criticism of his begettors and mentors, at a series of meetings with the British in Cairo and Algiers in January 1944 Donovan declined courteously but "frankly" to participate further in Maclean's work in Yugoslavia and intimated that he was considering the formation of an independent American mission to Tito, just as the Russians were now doing. In short, Donovan indicated, he intended to have American intelligence officers at both Tito's and Mihailović's headquarters, using their own wireless and ciphers.

There seems no reason to doubt that Donovan's strong reaction against the British services, his demand for independent American reportage from both Tito's and Mihailović's headquarters, and his sympathy for Mihailović derived not only from who he was but also from the nature of the reports he began to receive with growing frequency from his other officers in Yugoslavia. Still, Donovan was well aware that he was no more than an officer of the Grand Alliance and that one of his duties was to the alliance. With that in mind, therefore, he flew to London on or about February 5, 1944, for a talk with Churchill and Foreign Secretary Eden.

Having lunched with and spent the afternoon with Churchill, Donovan reported to Deputy Director Buxton by telegram that Churchill had stated that where Yugoslavia was concerned, "he must have complete freedom of action and would not consult with the Joint Chiefs on every political aspect of the situation."[8] Donovan had replied that "the propriety of the political situation was a matter for the President and himself alone" and the OSS "had no desire to pass judgment on it."

However, Donovan continued, he had explained to Churchill that the agreements between the OSS and the SOE had provided only that a liaison mission be sent to Tito. Because the mission sent under Maclean had been given political tasks, while the OSS was forbidden to engage in political activity, the agreements between the OSS and the SOE had been broken. Therefore, Donovan had told Churchill that "it seemed only just to tell him that I would recommend a separate mission for the United States." Churchill had replied "he thought it was necessary to have a separate American mission from our point of view and that it was probably a good idea from a general point of view."

Donovan then told Buxton he had gone to see Eden, who had the responsibility in the War Cabinet and Parliament for the British Secret Intelligence Service, and Eden had shown him reports from the SIS claiming there was a "splendid relationship" between the OSS and the SIS. Donovan said that he agreed except in one important matter— British attempts to control or limit OSS operations. Donovan evidently did not mince words, for he "told Eden that if they maintained their short-sighted policy, it would, in the first place, attempt an infringement on our national rights and finally would influence the relationship between Britain and the United States." Eden, Donovan stated, had "concurred."

Having informed the British leaders most concerned about what he was contemplating, Donovan took his problems to Roosevelt, Hull, and the Joint Chiefs. In response Roosevelt wrote in a "Dear Bill" letter on March 22, 1944: "I completely approve of the plan which I understand you have proposed, and in which the State Department agrees, that we should continue to obtain intelligence from [the Mihailović] area, by sending in a new group for this purpose."[9] Moreover, the President continued, "In order that there should be no misunderstanding, it should be made clear to the British that, in accordance with the established policy and practice, we intend to exercise this freedom of action for obtaining independent American secret intelligence." At the same time the OSS officers going to Mihailović's headquarters "should be instructed, and they should make this clear to Mihailović, that they are not to become involved in political questions or permit political functions to be attributed to them."

By the spring of 1944, as Donovan began to flood both the Mihailović and Tito zones of Yugoslavia, the British grip on the OSS had begun to crumble, and now it broke altogether. Following up in the spirit of the

President's letter, the Joint Chiefs informed the American commanding generals in Cairo and Algiers that "OSS-British combined activities will be limited to those pertaining to Special Operations in connection with the supply of resistance and guerrilla forces and to physical subversion activities with respect to such forces"[10] and that "In the organization and conduct of OSS-British combined activities nothing will operate to jeopardize the independence of American Secret Intelligence (SI) or Morale Subversion (MO)."[11]

For Donovan and the OSS these messages, and the President's letter, marked the point at which American Intelligence achieved emancipation, although there were still serious problems with the British in the British Isles and Southeast Asia. Never one to miss an opportunity, Donovan wrote to Buxton on April 7, 1944: "You've got to move on [this] and we must have a good man for it"—speaking of the new post of chief of the "Independent American Military Mission to Marshal Tito" and to the expanded Mihailović mission.

The Tito post went to Donovan's old football friend Colonel Ellery C. Huntington, who was to be in charge of a mission totaling 26 officers and 33 enlisted men, all specialists—a formidable team. The British response was not to increase the size of their mission in Yugoslavia (by August 1944 the British had more than 200 officers and other ranks there) but to pack their mission with lustrous names likely to overshadow the American mission. These included Churchill's son, Major Randolph Churchill, of the Queen's Own Hussars, on duty with the SOE; the novelist Captain Evelyn Waugh, of the Royal Horse Guards, also with the SOE; and many luminaries of Oxford and Cambridge—many of whom were killed when their aircraft crashed and exploded while landing on an OSS-managed airstrip at Gajevi. Churchill and Waugh were pulled clear by Lieutenant Nels Benson, OSS, before the DC-3 exploded.[12]

Huntington and the OSS mission proceeded to their base in stately fashion. They went by ship to Vis, having submitted a list of supplies considered "indispensable" to the mission's operations: jeeps, weapons carriers, insect sprays, "Peanuts, PX Issue," large quantities of nails and lumber, twenty cots, "salad bowls, glasses for cocktails and wine, plates, cups and saucers, frying pans, metal; pan, dish-washing; bowl, egg-beating; ladle, soup, perforated; typewriter, standard, Underwood or Royal," and such miscellaneous items as "skirts, khaki, women's waist 30"," "shirts, khaki, women's bust 38"."[13]

Huntington explained in his covering letter that the clothing was required for the mission's waitresses and:

> The item of glasses, plates, etc., are not needed for the mission itself but for the entertainment of guests. Such entertainment is lavishly done by the

British and Russian missions and by Marshal Tito himself. We must conform. In connection with entertainment, it would be highly desirable—almost essential—to have special foods such as hams and meats. We cannot expect to entertain on C Rations which constitutes the mission diet.

Times were changing in the secret war.

29

Was Tito Betrayed?

Of all the countries named in the Arcadia plan where insurrections could be created against the Germans, Yugoslavia was the place where the class warfare between monarchists and Communists was sharpest and most violent. Moreover, the warfare there was complicated by religious and racial power struggles, producing a situation resembling Hobbes's war of every man against every man.

During his travels in the fall and winter of 1943–1944, Donovan had formed the conviction that only the Americans possessed the moral authority necessary to end the troubles in Yugoslavia. At some stage he communicated that opinion to FDR, who agreed and proposed to Churchill that Donovan become the Allied guerrilla *supremo* for both Yugoslavia and Greece:

> The chaotic conditions developing in the Balkans causes [*sic*] me much concern. I am sure you are also worried. In both Yugoslavia and Greece the guerrilla forces appear to be engaged largely in fighting each other and not the Germans. If these forces could be united and directed towards a common end they would be very effective. In the present confused condition the only hope I see for immediate favorable action is the presence of an aggressive and unqualified officer. The only man I can think of now who might have a chance of success is Donovan.[1]

The President continued: "I do not believe he can do much harm and being a fearless and aggressive character he might do much good." Referring to Donovan's meetings in Belgrade in February 1941 with the regent, Prince Paul, and the commander in chief of the Air Force, General Dušan Simović, which culminated in the German attack on Yugoslavia, Roosevelt went on:

> He was there once before and is given some credit for the Yugoslavs entering the war against the Germans. If we decided to send him, all agencies of ours now working in the Balkans should be placed under his direction and the resources we put into this effort should be at his disposal. I understand that your General Gubbins [of SOE] is now in the Middle East. Donovan could consult with him en route. I feel this is an urgent matter. If you are inclined to agree to my idea I will discuss the possibilities with Donovan at once.

However, Roosevelt had reckoned without the British imperial strategists. Yugoslavia and Greece were important to Britain because they looked down upon the British maritime communications between England, the Suez Canal, and the Empire east of Suez. The British did not want an American guerrilla *supremo* in the Balkans, least of all a highly independent Irish-American who admired neither imperialism nor colonialism. Moreover, to ensure British primacy in the Balkans after the war, Churchill had already created and dispatched a large number of highly trained agents to the region.

The prime minister hastened to reply to Roosevelt's message. "I have a great admiration for Donovan," he telegraphed. "But I do not see any centre in the Balkans from which he could grip the situation. It would take a long time to move from one of the many centres of guerrilla activity to another." Meanwhile, Britain had "many very capable men already with the Yugoslav and Greek guerrillas," and while they were reporting fighting that was "of the most cruel and bloody character with merciless reprisals and execution of hostages," the enemy was "also suffering very heavily and is consuming not less than twenty-five German and eight Bulgarian divisions in the theater without being able to control more than key points and with increasing difficulty in maintaining railway traffic." Churchill sought to kill the Donovan appointment with the information that he hoped his government would soon "compose the Greek quarrels," although the "differences between Tito's Partisans and Mihailović's Serbs are very deep-seated."

For the moment, Churchill assured himself of British Intelligence leadership in the Balkans. Against that political background now occurred one of the most mysterious episodes of World War II.

On May 22, 1944, a German reconnaissance bomber appeared over the Yugoslav town of Drvar, where Tito had his headquarters, and, a British officer reported subsequently, "obviously photographed the area, particular attention being paid to that part of the town occupied by the British Military Mission of Brigadier Fitzroy Maclean." The officer, Lieutenant Colonel Vivian Street, who was acting chief of the British Mission in Maclean's absence, concluded that a German bombing attack was probably imminent, he warned Tito's headquarters, and then the mission left the town.[2]

That move had been completed when at 6:30 A.M. on May 25, 1944, fifty German bombers attacked the town, the weight of the attack being directed at the area which the Maclean mission had just evacuated, presumably in the belief that where Maclean was Tito would be located. Immediately after the bombardment fifteen Junkers 52 transports came over and dropped several scores of paratroopers, who seized landing grounds for about thirty gliders that were being towed by another wave of aircraft following close behind.

The first operation was carried out with practically no opposition from the partisans, who appeared to have been dazed by the opening bombardment and had been taken by surprise when the airborne troops landed. At noon another bombing attack further paralyzed the defenses, and other airborne squadrons arrived to bring the total of German paratroopers up to about 1,000 men. The German force quickly cleared the town and secured some hills dominating the area.

When the attack started, Tito and his staff were in a cave overlooking Drvar, and, as Street reported, "It was clear that the Germans knew the exact location of this cave for soon after the attack started a party attempted to reach it but were driven back." The Germans then covered the path leading to the cave with machine-gun fire which made it impossible for anyone to enter or leave the cave by the normal route. However, Tito and his men had dug an escape route through the back of the cave, and he escaped through that tunnel during the afternoon, making off in the northeasterly direction toward the village of Potoci.

For the next eight days Tito, his staff, and some Allied liaison and intelligence officers, including Donovan's representatives, were pursued by the Germans and forced deeper and deeper into the forests and mountains of Bosnia. Elements of four German divisions hunted his partisan units as German air squadrons harried Tito's every move. Tito, marching 100 miles in 100 hours over some of the most difficult mountainous country in Europe, kept ahead of the Germans and out of sight of the aircraft, although Tito's party was strafed from time to time.

With the passing of each mile Tito lost a little more control over the partisan movement, for he had lost his best radio equipment in the first attacks. The British liaison officer, Colonel Street, sent Major Randolph Churchill, the prime minister's son, to the Adriatic coast to pass a message to the Allied supply base at Bari in the heel of Italy, and the Allies mounted very powerful air attacks on the Germans and many supply missions to the partisans. Few of the supplies reached Tito, and none included the vital wireless sets without which he could not maintain contact with his corps commanders.

By June 2, 1944, it was clear to Tito that his capture by the Germans might be inevitable unless he were evacuated by air to the Allied base at Bari. He talked with Colonel Street about his predicament and asked for an American or British airplane. Street had wireless contact with Bari, and the Royal Air Force agreed to attempt Tito's evacuation from the landing strip at Kuprus Polje at about nine that night. Tito arrived at the strip in time, as did a DC-3, but it proved to be Russian, part of a small flight maintained by the Red Air Force at Bari to supply the Soviet Military Mission to Tito. Why the Allied authorities had sent a Soviet aircraft was never fathomed, for it gave the Russians the chance to claim that they, not the Western Allies, had rescued Tito—a claim they exploited to the full then and later.

The Soviet DC-3 being all there was, Tito and his staff hastened aboard, and before midnight they were landing at Bari, where a Soviet delegation, to the annoyance of the Anglo-American delegation, whisked the Yugoslav leader away to a villa. Tito elected not to remain in Italy longer than was necessary but to reestablish his headquarters on Vis, where he arrived on June 9, 1944, in the British destroyer *Blackmore*.

The same day in Washington—June 9—the question of the German attack on Tito's headquarters took a sinister turn when an informant, described only as Mr. P., called on a British officer at British Security Coordination, Lieutenant Colonel K. M. Bourne, who then reported what Mr. P. had told him to Colonel Doering at OSS headquarters. "A few weeks" before the attack on Tito's headquarters at Drvar the military attaché at the Royal Yugoslav Embassy in Washington, Lieutenant Colonel Zivan L. Knezević, an ardent supporter of Mihailović, had learned from OSS officers of the location of Tito's headquarters, which was secret. Mr. P. alleged that Knezević "cabled in code to the Yugoslav representative in Cairo of Mihailović" and that it was Mr. P.'s belief that "Mihailović passed on this information [to the Germans] and thereby enabled the Nazis to carry out this successful attack."[3]

Lieutenant Colonel Bourne also told Doering that Mr. P. claimed he knew "the Military Attaché, Lt. Col. Knezević, obtained his information from a daughter of Ruth Mitchell, with whom he is very intimate"—Ruth Mitchell being the sister of General William "Billy" Mitchell, the "father of American air power." Ruth Mitchell's daughter had obtained the information in the first place from "a senior officer in the United States Military Intelligence." Mr. P. did not know this officer's name, but he had "no doubt whatever as to this officer being the source of the information."

These allegations provoked an immediate and exhaustive investigation at OSS headquarters. In the course of the investigation, which was conducted by the executive officer, Colonel Doering, Doering's inquiries disclosed that Knezević was an ardent royalist who had played a major role in the coup d'état of March 27, 1941, that brought the young king, Peter II, to power and resulted in the German invasion of Yugoslavia. During that period Knezević had been secretary to the Yugoslav War Cabinet when Mihailović was defense minister, and there seemed no reason to doubt that in Washington Knezević had been a leading figure in the pro-Mihailović lobby.

Further inquiries then showed that the location of Tito's headquarters had been referred to by an OSS officer, Major Richard Weil, Jr., who had been at Tito's headquarters at Drvar between February 27 and March 20, 1944. A New York lawyer in peacetime, Weil had been ordered back to Washington by Donovan to prepare a chronological survey of events in Yugoslavia and had presented Doering with a special report on his mission upon his arrival in Washington on April 17, 1944. That document was then sent to Roosevelt, Hull, the Joint Chiefs, and Army and Navy Intelligence, but an examination of the document showed that Weil had not revealed the whereabouts of Tito's headquarters. He had, however, stated in the chronological survey that while at the headquarters, which he described as being "in the neighborhood of Drvar," the Germans bombed and machine-gunned "the GHQ" almost every day "for the next three weeks." Weil stated also in the chronology that Tito was in a cave "1½ miles away."[4]

Although Weil's statement indicated the Germans had knowledge that Tito's headquarters were in a cave at Dvrar before the date on which Mr. P. alleged that Knezević transmitted the information to Mihailović's representative in Cairo and that therefore, the OSS could not have been held responsible for an incident in which Tito was almost killed or captured and his movement decapitated, the evidence that the Germans knew beforehand was not proved. In any event if Mr. P.'s story was in any way correct, there had been a leakage of highly secret information inside OSS —and in wartime that was a grave matter.

As the investigation unfolded, Donovan, Doering, and several other high executives within the OSS were concerned to discover that the deputy director of OSS intelligence services, Lieutenant Colonel Oliver J. Sands, in peacetime a leading Virginia banker and railway owner, might have been Knezević's point of contact within OSS. But according to Doering's interim report, Weil's chronological survey was seen only by Donovan and the head of Secret Intelligence, Whitney Shepardson, and there was "no record in OSS of its having been seen by the alleged informant (Col. S.)." Moreover, Doering noted that Weil's report showed Germans knew the whereabouts of Tito's headquarters before Sands was alleged to have imparted the information to people in contact with Knezević.

Doering went on to report, however, that on May 2, 1944, twenty-three days before the German attack on Tito's headquarters, there was a "Conference on Weil's report, attended by Col. S., Weil and numerous officials," including representatives of the White House and Army and Navy Intelligence. Doering then authorized a discreet investigation of the connection, if any, between Colonel Sands and the Royal Yugoslav Embassy which disclosed a number of connections and meetings between the colonel and embassy officials and various American supporters of Mihailović, including Ruth Mitchell.[5] OSS security officials presented Doering with the following information found in Sands's office:

§ *November 9, 1943:* Letter from Knezević to Colonel Sands enclosing coded telegram from General Mihailović as proof the embassy was in touch with the general. (From Sands's files.)

§ *November 10, 1943:* A reply from Sands to Knezević containing the statement "with kindest personal regards and looking forward to see you in the very near future. Cordially yours." (In Sands's files.)

§ *December 28, 1943:* Letter from Knezević to Sands, in Sands's files, enclosing certain material pertaining to Yugoslavia.

§ *January 7, 1944:* In Sands's files, acknowledgment of Knezević's letters in which Sands states he is "looking forward to seeing" him "next Saturday night at Miss Mitchell's."

§ *March 23, 1944:* Colonel [Albert] Seitz [OSS representative at Mihailović's headquarters] returns to the United States.

§ *April 1, 1944:* Seitz states he attended a lunch given by the Yugoslav minister, Konstantin Fotić, also attended by Madame Fotić, Colonel Sands, Captain Borislav Todorović [assistant military attaché and close associate of Knezević], and the chief counselor at the embassy.

§ *April 5, 1944:* "Note on S's desk pad, "Fotić material—Get Seitz."

§ *April 14, 1944:* "Dinner at house of Colonel Knezević, the Military Attaché with Colonel Jadwin [of Military Intelligence], Col. S., Captain Walter Mansfield [OSS officer lately returned from Mihailović's headquarters], Captain Todorović, Dr. Roco Ruzić of OWI, 'Mrs. Yon' [Ruth Mitchell's daughter] and other women. Mrs. Yon escorted by Captain T[odorović]. . . ."

§ *April 29, 1944:* "Note on S.'s desk pad, 'Weill [*sic*] (presumably conference)."

§ *June 10, 1944:* "Dinner at Dr. Ruzić's apartment with his wife, Seitz and wife, American Major Gen. who was 'ex-head of 26th Division,' Captain Todorović and Miss M[itchell] (escorted again by

T[odorović]. Tito discussed because the General brought with him an issue of *Yank* [a military magazine of the period] containing article on him."[6]

The security staff's information showed plainly, therefore, that Sands had had a close connection with Knezević. Doering decided the charge serious enough to warrant the taking of a sworn statement by Colonel Sands on June 17, 1944, in the course of which Sands stated that he had been a personal friend of General Mitchell but had never met any members of his family until June 1942, when he was ordered to Portugal as the representative of Military Intelligence, his mission to interview passengers on the returning Swedish prisoner of war and refugee exchange liner *Drottningholm*.

Colonel Sands stated: "Miss Ruth Mitchell, sister of General Mitchell, was to be aboard the vessel; she had been released from a German prison camp, where she had been imprisoned after service under General Mihailović."[7] Her name having been given to Sands at General Strong's headquarters for "particular questioning," he flew to Lisbon to join the ship and "conversed with her on several occasions during the trip home, to obtain information regarding current events in Yugoslavia and in the German prison camp. The information thus elicited was incorporated in my report to G-2."

Colonel Sands heard no more of Miss Mitchell until the fall of 1942, when "she called me on the telephone to request that I arrange a meeting with some person in G2 to whom she could give information about Yugoslavia." He arranged lunch for her with the head of the southern European section of G-2, and at the lunch Miss Mitchell was accompanied by her daughter, Mrs. Yon. Between that lunch and the present date he had seen Miss Mitchell on "four or five occasions and [Mrs. Yon] on perhaps ten or fifteen occasions." These all were social affairs in which Miss Mitchell's guests had included high-ranking officers of the Army, the Marine Corps, Army Intelligence, and such officials as Attorney General Francis Biddle and Assistant Secretary of State Adolf Berle.

Sands's wife had "occasionally met Mrs. Yohn [sic] for a social lunch or horseback riding," but his wife had "little or no knowledge of or interest in foreign politics and I, of course, never discuss with her any information which may come to my attention in the course of my work." Sands then stated:

I wish to make certain unqualified statements with respect to every occasion on which I have met Miss Mitchell or Mrs. Yohn [sic]. I have never discussed with them any information which I received from anyone (either while on duty in the office or elsewhere) relating to Tito, Mihailovitch [sic] or any matter of possible military or political significance. I have never mentioned to either of them the fact that Major Weil visited Tito's headquarters or even that there are such individuals as Major Weil. . . . Since I did not have, at any of the foregoing times, any knowledge of the location of Tito's headquarters . . . I could not, of course, have spoken of this with them or with anyone else. Realizing the nature of Miss Mitchell and the extreme views which she has expressed at times, I have carefully refrained from ever saying anything in the presence of her or of her daughter which they might possibly transmit to anyone or even an incidental piece of information relating to the Mihailovitch-Tito controversy.

Colonel Sands declared his contacts with the Yugoslav Embassy had been "relatively few," advising that "Colonel Knezević . . . speaks no English and I speak no foreign language. We have thus never discussed any subject." From time to time he had "received formal dissemination letters from the Embassy, signed by Colonel Knezević, containing the usual propaganda material which the Embassy forwards to all interested agencies in Washington." They had been sent to him personally because Knezević happened to know his name and address, and for no other reason. Every time he had received one of these documents he had sent the information to the "proper channels within OSS," and he had no recollection of having read the material forwarded with Knezević's letters because "they did not bear upon my specific duties."

Turning to his relations with Knezević's deputy, Captain Todorović, Sands stated they had met on only three occasions, at social affairs given by Yugoslav embassy officials, and he had never discussed any subject with him. In fact, Sands stated, the only person at the embassy with whom he had had "real acquaintance" was a Mr. Sarić, whose wife was an American with friends known to Sands's wife. He had played tennis and ridden with Sarić, but with him, as with other Yugoslav officials and the Mitchells, he had "scrupulously refrained from expressing my opinion with respect to the merits of either faction in the Tito-Mihailović controversy, and I have carefully avoided saying anything which could be construed as an informational item concerning the Yugoslavian situation."

On two occasions he had taken OSS officers recently back from Yugoslavia to the embassy, at the instructions of Assistant Director John Magruder. He stated that he had had no conversations with anyone at the embassy on either visit. The talking had been done by the officers concerned, Colonel Seitz and Captain Walter Mansfield. At those conversations there had been "no reference made to the headquarters of Tito." In general, Sands declared:

> In my work at OSS, it is only occasionally and incidentally that Yugoslav material is directed to my attention. I read few cables relating to that area and my discussions within or outside the agency concerning Yugoslav matters have been relatively infrequent. . . . While I knew that Lt. Col. Weil's

report was available in the office of my chief, General Magruder, I never read that report. Until today I had no knowledge that any separate chronological summary of Weil's trip even existed. I never discussed with Weil the details of his journey, and I know him very slightly. Further, I have no recollection of ever discussing the details of his journey with anyone, within or outside OSS. I am not aware of any information within or outside OSS concerning Tito's headquarters to which I might even have had access. I never knew the location of Tito's headquarters at any time and I do not believe that specific information concerning the location of Tito's headquarters has ever been available to me.

He ended his statement:

I have sought to set forth every fact relating to this matter which might be considered to be relevant. I wish to state unreservedly that any statement or implication that I may have communicated any information to Mrs. Yohn, to Captain Todorović, or to anyone else, is not only wholly unfounded in fact but totally absurd. If there is the slightest ground for any suspicion of my having been implicated in this matter, I must respectfully demand that a complete investigation be immediately made and that I be openly confronted by anyone making any charges against me.

No such investigation was made, nor did anyone involved feel one was necessary. Colonel Sands was exonerated on his own statement and continued his work at the OSS with great distinction. Years later, when he was asked the question "Who betrayed the whereabouts of Tito's headquarters," Sands replied: "I thought it was the British." Was Sands pro-Mihailović? "Certainly I was pro-Mihailović," he stated emphatically. "And so were a lot of other people inside OSS. But we did not play politics with secret intelligence, I assure you. The only politics we played were those that we were told to play by the Joint Chiefs of Staff." Why should the British have betrayed the whereabouts of Tito's headquarters? What had they to gain? Sands stated: "I don't know. But that was the suspicion at the time. There were a lot of British Intelligence people in Washington who didn't like Tito any more than I did."[8]

At the time, however, it was recognized at Donovan's headquarters that Mr. P.'s information might be sound and that Knezević had sent a telegram such as the informant described, although it was by no means clear that the telegram had reached the Germans and had precipitated the attack on Dvrar.

Accordingly, Donovan wrote to the chief of Military Intelligence, General Clayton Bissell, on June 19, 1944:

Following our discussion concerning a possible breach of security on the part of Lt. Colonel Oliver J. Sands, Jr., on duty with this agency, I immediately directed that an investigation be made to determine what information has existed within concerning the location of the headquarters of Tito and whether Lt. Colonel Sands had access to such information.[9]

Donovan reported the facts developed by Doering's inquiry and concluded:

While I have undertaken no general investigation of the reported security breach, I recommend that it be determined which agencies possessed the information, what persons within the agencies had access to it, and which of those persons have had any contact with Miss Mitchell, her daughter [Mrs. Yon] or officials in the Yugoslav embassy.

That vast task was not undertaken. The war was at its height, and the investigatory and analytical brainpower of the United States was stretched to the outer limits in the ordinary day-to-day tasks of fighting the war. Moreover, such an investigation would have developed a breeze that the press would have caught—miraculously the affair never reached any newspaper—and the result would have been only to embarrass the United States in its relations with Tito.

Nevertheless, a security problem plainly existed. The Royal Yugoslav Embassy was running not only a strong lobby but also an intelligence service, and that was against the law in wartime. The decision was made, therefore, to decapitate that service, which proved a simpler undertaking than Doering's quiet investigation. Both Knezević and Todorović, the heads of the intelligence service in Washington, had expressed a desire to visit the Allied base at Bari. That was arranged, they were flown to Bari in a United States transport in August 1944, and when they arrived there, they were—at British, not American, instructions—quietly held incommunicado until it was felt they could no longer intervene effectively in Allied interests.

30

Italian Maelstrom

Throughout this period of cut and thrust in the Balkans, Donovan had been supporting the Zeppelin plan with major clandestine works in Italy, where more than 1,000,000 Allied fighting men were fighting to pin down German armies away from the French and Russian fronts. These OSS operations had begun the moment Donovan arrived at Algiers from Quebec in September 1943 to begin work on the Balkan plan. The first target had been the Italian bastion of Sardinia.

At an operational planning conference at Algiers on the morning of September 13, 1943, the decision was made to capture Sardinia, one of the main Italo-German centers for air attacks on Allied shipping in the central Mediterranean. Would Donovan care to take the job on, for Eisenhower was reluctant to employ regular forces, all of which were needed for the invasion of Italy at Salerno and Taranto? The problem was, Donovan was advised, that there were more than 300,000 Italian soldiers in Sardinia, many still loyal to Mussolini, and parts or all of the Hermann Göring Division might be there. Nobody was sure.

Without hesitation, Donovan volunteered the services of his Operational Groups (OGs), his commandos, and the operations committee accepted. WJD obtained letters from Eisenhower and the king of Italy, calling upon the Italian commander in chief in Sardinia to surrender unconditionally. WJD then selected as commander for the operation Lieutenant Colonel Serge Obolensky, a cornet of the Chevalier Guards Regiment of Moscow during World War I who had started World War II as a private in the 17th Regiment, New York National Guard.

Obolensky and his small party left that same evening from Blida Airfield in an RAF Halifax. At about thirty minutes before midnight the Halifax skirted cumulonimbus over Cape Spartivento, descended to 6,000 feet, and picked up the silver ribbon of Cagliari. To slow the aircraft to parachuting speed, the pilot dropped his landing gear and bomb doors, and a few minutes later Obolensky and his men—an American, Michael Formichelli, and two Britons, James Russell and William Sherwood—tumbled into the sky. Their parachutes opened, and they landed near the village of Siliqua, in the foothills about fifteen miles from Cagliari. Obolensky and Formichelli began to walk down through the vineyards toward Cagliari as Russell and Sherwood remained to set up and guard the wireless. In the valley Obolensky came upon a railway line and three Italian soldiers. Obolensky could speak no Italian, but Formichelli could, and he asked the soldiers to direct them to the headquarters of the Italian commander in chief, General Alberto Basso. Startled by these foreigners in strange uniforms and blackened faces, the soldiers took them instead to the railway carabinieri at Decimomannu, and they, as nonplussed as the soldiers, telephoned Decimomannu Airport.

After argument, imprecations, telephoning, and shouting which lasted all day, Obolensky and his party found themselves at Basso's headquarters near Macomer, at 5:00 P.M. on the fourteenth. Obolensky presented Basso with his letters of credence and the instructions from the king of Italy and the supreme Allied commander, announcing that "the Allied headquarters expected him to press the Germans relentlessly and in every way try and destroy them during their evacuation" from northern Sardinia into Corsica.[1]

With great courtesy, Basso invited Obolensky to remain indoors while his army, which numbered 276,000 men, dealt with the Germans, and on September 16, 1943, Obolensky was informed that all Germans had departed Sardinia for Corsica and that the Army of Sardinia was now at the disposal of President Roosevelt. Having signaled that news to Algiers, Obolensky and his men proceeded to march with General Basso and his staff and representatives of the regiments of his army, to attend a solemn mass at the Cathedral of Sassari "for the deliverance of Italy from the Germans." Obolensky recorded in his final report that "we received many ovations everywhere we went," with many shouts of " 'Viva l'America!' and 'Viva la Liberta.' " After the service the OGs "lunched at the residence of the Prefect with all the Italian Staff," there were many speeches concerning the Army of Sardinia's fidelity to the Grand Alliance, and then Obolensky announced that he was "heading north"—a term used to convey that he was proceeding to enemy territory—to take part in the liberation of French Corsica.

The OSS had captured its first large enemy territory, an important outpost of Fortress Europe.

Tactically, operations into Italy began immediately after Obolensky had captured Sardinia. Both Sardinia and Corsica were important because if the Allies acquired the ports and airfields on the two islands, they could, if they chose, gravely embarrass the rear areas of the German armies in Italy. As important, on Corsica they would be within hit-and-run distance of what was now part of the front line of Fortress Europe, the coast between Nice and Leghorn.

With the German evacuation of Sardinia—25,000 troops, 2,300 vehicles, 5,000 tons of supplies—the German force in Corsica had become formidable, and in view of Corsica's special position in the Ligurian Sea the Germans might be expected to resist any Allied landing and suppress ruthlessly any Corsican uprising. To provide support for the underground, a French expeditionary force of about 15,000 men was raised at Algiers under the command of General Henri Martin. Donovan was asked to send intelligence officers and an operational group with the force. The OSS group was formed and was placed under the command of a familiar figure, Carleton Coon, now a major and a fearful figure with white hair and a great black, piratical beard.

Coon was packing for a parachute mission into Albania when, at six o'clock on Saturday, September 11, General Donovan called him to the OSS headquarters in the Villa Magnol. Coon took his baggage for Albania with him, for he expected that Donovan had asked him around to say good-bye. Instead, he reported, Donovan "asked me how I would like to go to Corsica." Coon replied that he would like to go very much but felt he ought to remind Donovan he was already on his way to Albania and he did not know how the Corsican trip would "affect the plans previously made for the Middle East Theatre." Donovan replied such decisions were up to him, and if he wanted Coon to go to Corsica, the Middle East mission would be taken care of. In reply Coon said he was ready to go to Corsica, and Donovan said: "The ship leaves tomorrow at 6 P.M."[2]

Now followed a period that was incredible even by Coon's standards. His account of his mission to Corsica reflected the confusion, haste, and high drama of those first days after the Italian collapse, when Donovan ran the Mediterranean operations with the motto "*Vitesse! Vitesse!* And yet more *Vitesse!*"—a corruption of what one of Napoleon's generals had once cried at the height of Waterloo. Coon had just turned in for the night when he was awakened by the chief of SI France, Henry B. Hyde, and told that his ship would now be sailing at 6:00 A.M. and he had better get up and get ready. By now Coon was incapable of being surprised by anything, but when going on difficult and dangerous missions, he did like time to prepare his men and their equipment and to inform himself of the situation when he "arrived north."

He recorded that night after Hyde's visit:

This meant staying up all night to get prepared. It was a very hectic night and we could hardly expect to make complete preparations in that time. We did not know what we would need in Corsica. We did not know where the two French battleships were going, whether they would land in the dark, or whether we would have to jump in the water; whether we would be met by Germans, Italians, patriots, or whom; whether we would have to 'take to the Maquis,' or enter the town. In other words, we were in complete ignorance of the military situation in Corsica.

Coon's party assembled before daybreak. It consisted of a Lieutenant Harris, John Ffoulke, Charles Ffoulke, and three French agents, Christopher, Félix, and Claude. Claude and Félix had four radio sets equipped with batteries and two charcoal-burning chargers. Almost immediately one of the sets was taken away for another mission and Claude was removed for another job. Coon and his party were driven down to Algiers Harbor.

[We] presented ourselves at the dock at 6 o'clock, and prepared to go on board the 'Fantasque,' a French light cruiser or heavy destroyer which was to take us to Corsica. The dock was crowded with soldiers of the 'Bataillon de Choc,' who were also to go along. These were dressed in American uniforms with mostly British equipment, and the 'Bataillon de Choc' sewn on their shoulders so that everyone could see who they were. They all carried British Commando knives, and stored their explosive, including such secret materials as booby trap releases, plastic [explosive], and so forth, in open boxes on the dock where everyone could see them.

Although "they themselves did not know where they were going, or at least they had not been told, practically everyone in Algiers did, because a good many of them were Corsicans and speculation was rife, while Corsica was the obvious place for them to go. Security on the dock was nil." Since there were several German stay-behind agents in Algiers, Coon and his party were fearful of being intercepted in the Mediterranean, for the entire loading process should have been done quickly, under cover of darkness, and then the ships should have sailed immediately.

As it was, it was not until nine o'clock on September 13, 1943, that at long last and with great flourish the *Fantasque* and her sister ship, *Terrible*, sailed. Both ships got up to and maintained the "terrific speed of 32 knots all day" until nightfall, when both were recalled to Algiers. They turned about, developed 32 knots again, and then were told to proceed with the mission—the recall message had been for another ship, but the captain was warned "the Germans had heard of our trip and had 45 Stukas waiting for us in Sardinia." The *Terrible* then developed engine trouble, "and so we had to slow down," but at midnight "we came in sight of

Corsica and the Mountains of the Bay of Ajaccio loomed on either side. From afar we could see great fires burning on the mountains."

The whole island seemed to be ablaze, and Coon was puzzled to explain this. Some of the men who knew Corsica said this was an old custom to burn the *maquis*—the undergrowth—during the dry season. However, they said that none of them had seen it done so extensively. Only when they had landed did Coon discover that the Germans had that day set fire to the whole countryside by means of incendiaries, so that these fires were not only annoying the inhabitants but were also setting off Italian gasoline and ammunition dumps, which for the next few days exploded every few hours all over that part of the island.

There was no rapid debarkation and preparation for battle with a determined enemy. To the contrary, there were speeches, bands, parades. And as Coon later reported to WJD: "They were shooting off pistols and shot guns in the air, singing the Marseillaise, yelling, screaming, and dancing with joy." Houses were "lit up, and there was no attempt at black-out or any other form of anti-aircraft security." Coon "fully expected at any moment to have the Germans come in force from the air and wipe us and the docks out of existence. Why they did not do so is a mystery which I cannot explain, since everybody in Corsica must have known what was going on by that time."

When Coon and the OSS team disembarked, last, "We tried to be as quiet and inconspicuous as possible, and loaded our baggage on to a small wooden truck alongside the railroad station." But certain of Coon's agents were recognized immediately, and "their cover lasted for about five minutes." Their Corsican assistants "greeted us in a demonstrative manner and volunteered to pull our waggon [*sic*] for us, since no horse was available." He described the next few minutes:

> [With] our small group of carriage pullers, we proceeded down the main street, whereupon a small procession formed of local civilians who wanted to march along with us. Before we had gone two blocks, we had formed the nucleus of a parade. One fat woman rushed out waving a British flag and proceeded at the head of the procession in front of us prominently displaying it. No one had the heart to inform her that she had brought out the wrong flag for our group, but after a few blocks she turned back and went home.

Although when he set out Coon was told that his mission was secret, primarily because he might have to take to the *maquis* if the French failed to eject the Germans, it soon became evident to all Corsica that Coon and his men were agents of the "American secret service." As such they were not welcomed by the French authorities. There was little but pettiness for WJD's liberators:

I asked Commandant Clipet for the right to requisition some cars for my own group, and he said that I would have to go to Colonel Deleuse. I went to the latter who said that there were no cars and that we could not have any. Knowing therefore that without transport we would be completely useless in Corsica, I proceeded to buy cars in the name of the American Government and obtained receipts for all of them. I bought an excellent Hotchkiss for [about $3,600], a Renault for [about $2,800], a Chenault-Walker for [$2,000], and a Peugeot for [$1,600]. One week after we had bought the last of these cars, the French headquarters passed a decree that it was illegal for Americans or British personnel to purchase motor vehicles in Corsica. . . . When I went to get gasoline through the French, they made all sorts of difficulties, and told me that I would have to get a [ration book], which I did. When I took this to the garage, I was told that no gasoline could be issued on Colonel Deleuse's orders, but that such orders had to come from the Bataillon de Choc. When I went to the latter's headquarters I was told that the gasoline belonged to them and that we had no right to it. After considerable discussion I was given fifty liters as a special favor. This was a drop in the bucket in view of our needs. . . . After this we began buying gasoline on the Black Market, and getting it from the Italians. I went to the Italian colonel who lived in the Hôtel des Etrangers and he telephoned an order to the Italian barracks to give us what we wanted. After that Antoine [an associate of Coon's] made a deal with the Italian captain in charge to get gasoline for us in return for a small bribe . . . and Antoine produced one big drum of gasoline which we used. They then bought five drums which they brought up to the house and set in the back yard. While we were away, French soldiers came and took this away, saying we had no right to it.

As Coon's account of his campaigning in Corsica showed, the secret war was not always one of grim purpose. On occasions it had elements of grim carnival, and frequently afterward in lectures at Harvard on Mediterranean anthropology he referred to the peculiar behavior he had encountered during Vesuvius, as the French code-named the liberation operations. Corsica was not liberated by the Allies, he would contend, and "Far from being the great victory which the occupation of Corsica has been painted in the papers," it was "largely an act of occupying territory which the Germans did not want." All the French, the Italians, and the OSS did was to "annoy them on their way out." The Germans "left as early as, if not actually when, they wanted to leave, and the French moved in afterward."

But there was fighting, and there were casualties. One of Donovan's bright young men, Peter Karlow, had a leg blown off when the torpedo boat in which he was entering Bastia Harbor struck a mine, killing everyone else—eight persons—on board. And then there was what became known in Corsican legend as the Battles of Barqueta, of which there were two.

In the first battle, two battalions of Italians under the command of a colonel marched toward Barqueta, a fishing port useful for torpedo boat operations against the Italian coast, but eight Germans in a machine-gun nest at the entrance to a tunnel near Ponte Alban opened fire. Coon reported:

> The Italians fled. The Colonel returned to our headquarters full of fear stating that all his men with their guns could not proceed down the road because there was a German in front of them. After this they left the region. At the time they left, the only Allied troops between Barqueta and Corte were our thirty men, for which reason we slept with our shoes on.

Then came the Second Battle of Barqueta, a more serious affair. The French general called up his goums and the thirty OGs, who had just arrived from Algiers. Between the goums and the OGs and Barqueta was the German machine-gun nest. This time the goums went around one side of it, the OGs around the other, and while the eight Germans in the nest were looking at their flanks and rear, other goums with knives came up to their front and killed, wounded, or captured all of them. It was now possible to get through to Barqueta, but in doing so, two OG technicians, Sam Maselli and Rocco T. Grasso, were killed by mortar fire. An OG officer, Lieutenant Thomas L. Gordon, hearing armored vehicles approaching, stood up and attacked two of the vehicles with plastic grenades, destroying one tank or armored car and one armored truck. Gordon was killed, it was thought, by the back blast from one of his own grenades.

But Barqueta was taken, the way was open to Bastia, and after several ugly skirmishes such as those at Barqueta the Germans evacuated the island at their leisure across the Ligurian to Leghorn. Reliberation of France had begun. Obolensky arrived from Sardinia to accept the surrender of the 85,000 Italians in Corsica, and with the departure or surrender of all Axis forces in the island it now became Donovan's advance base for maritime and commando operations against the Germans in France, Piedmont, and Liguria.

Immediately after Major Coon signaled OSS Algiers that Corsica had been freed of the enemy, the chief of Donovan's OGs in Italy, Lieutenant Colonel Russell Livermore, a New York lawyer whom Donovan had worked with in peacetime, flew to L'Île Rousse and made his headquarters in a castle the foundations of which were laid in the First Punic War between the Romans and the Carthaginians. Behind Livermore came the new hoplites, in preparation for WJD's campaign along the Ligurian coast of Italy. Formed by Donovan as the American counterpart of the British SAS and the German SS, the operational groups (OGs) were made up of volunteers who were "willing to undertake unusual and dangerous risks."[3] All OGs were told frankly and fully what they could expect, and only men who gave evidence of "a real desire for such duty were chosen." Most of the men spoke the language of the country in which they were to operate, and all were specialists in demolitions, special weapons, scouting, wireless, fieldcraft. They had to meet the same physical standards as those required of paratroopers (many were paratroopers), and special attention was paid to character: "While the risks involved tend to make OG work appeal to young men, the success of OG assignments is not the result of daring and bravado alone. Accordingly, candidates were selected whose past records, civilian and military, gave evidence of stability and good judgment."

Their principal purpose was to "execute prescribed missions in enemy or enemy-occupied territory." Each operational group was an "efficient, mobile, self-sufficient unit" capable of raising guerrillas, organizing their supply, and coordinating their operations with those of the main forces; gathering intelligence; conducting hit-and-run operations; rescuing prisoners of war; and countering the enemy's guerrilla, sabotage, and subversion operations. For those missions, the OGs were the best-equipped fighting men in America. Officers were called not officers, but leaders, and soldiers were called not soldiers or men, but scouts or by such technical terms as the weapons NCO, the medical technician, or the demolitions NCO.

OGs operated secretly away from main battlefields, but on tasks closely connected with the battlefield. As often as not they were the personal troops of the supreme commander, although they acknowledged only Donovan as their leader. Such was the nature of their work that a document known as the Hitler Commando Order was deemed by the Oberkommando der Wehrmacht to apply to OGs as it applied to all other Allied special forces, particularly those who arrived in enemy territory by air. Although the order was itself illegal under the Geneva Convention, it had originated in 1942, when British commando raids were proving so effective at sapping the nervous strength of German troops on coastal duty along the French Channel shores that Hitler decided they must be deterred. A group of British commandos apparently executed a German prisoner whose hands they had bound with wire—so the Germans alleged—during an attack on the German garrison at Sark in the Channel Islands, and as a result, Hitler decreed: "In future, all terror and sabotage troops of the British and their accomplices, who do not act like soldiers but rather like bandits, will be treated as such by the German troops and will be ruthlessly eliminated in battle, wherever they appear."[4]

This communiqué was followed by a secret order to all Wehrmacht forces that all sabotage and "terror troops," whether armed or unarmed, in or out of uniform, who fell into German hands were to be "slaughtered to the last man" by the first troops that encountered them. Those who were arrested by the police were to be handed over to the Sicherheits-dienst—and few men had any doubt about what that meant. It was known that OGs were no longer protected by the Geneva Convention, but few, if any, resigned, although all were given an opportunity to do so.

While Donovan was at Algiers, the Allied tacticians on Eisenhower's staff made a plan that would force the German commander to garrison both the Tyrrhenian and Adriatic coasts of Italy. All special forces such as the OGs were to embark upon a program of gadfly attacks on the Germans to make it seem that the Allies intended to launch a series of major amphibious landings on both coasts, thereby compelling the German commander to garrison both at the expense of the fighting front to the south of Rome.

That campaign began soon after Livermore was installed in his castle at Bastia. The islands of Gorgona and Capraia were seized in a series of sharp, piratical thrusts, the real purpose of which was to "manipulate the islands as a feint attack at the enemy's flank." In a nerve-racking business for both Americans and Germans, night after night small parties of Allied special troops crept ashore. In these operations the OGs were very active. Polar I nicked the German supply railway south of Leghorn, and Polar II and Polar III went in two or three nights later to finish the job.

Neptune Minor hit the Tyrrhenian beaches between Leghorn and Civitavecchia; Neptune II, III, IV, and V kept the Germans awake every night for a fortnight along the coast between Le Fornaci and Cape Fortul-lino; Neptune VI hit the bridge carrying the Via Aurelia over a coastal ravine near Le Fornaci; and Polar IV went back to cruise noisily and menacingly about the mouth of the Arno in the small hours of January 8–9, 1944; the Valentine-Livingstone OGs tried to blow the Roccamurata Tunnel on the Genoa–Piacenza–La Spezia railway; and in the Chicago operation eighteen OGs struck at the German-held island of Pianosa. Chicago II went back a month later to cut three throats and finish the job —and when the job was not quite finished, the Balkis party went in and blew up the German gun emplacements with 1,000 pounds of *plastique.*

An OG called Walla-Walla parachuted north of La Spezia to serve and operate a partisan group against the Germans near Rezzoagbio; Captain Joseph J. Benucci of the OGs took Aztec to work with the 7th Alpine Brigade and the Piave partisans around Val Morel. Omaha, Ford, Cayuga, Lafayette, Nancy, Peedee, Santee, Seneca, Roanoke, Spokane, Helen, Choctaw—operation after operation was mounted to fix German attention on some place or beach remote from intended operations, to blow a bridge or arm a partisan battalion, sink a ship, derail a train, or block a tunnel. The operations were incessant; the British conducted even more of them; and the effect was to tear to shreds the nerves of the Germans along the Ligurian Sea.

Then came Ginny.

The basis of the Ginny mission was that, although the Italian mountainous terrain favored the German defense, the same mountains—the Apennines—made the German supply system highly vulnerable. Most of the main railways and roads ran down the narrow coastal plains of Italy, so were accessible to raiders coming in from the sea, especially along the Ligurian coast. The rail and road system was also heavily punctuated with tunnels, bridges, and culverts which, if destroyed, would block the southward flow of German supplies for as long as these were impassable.

Among the most vulnerable and the most important was the railway tunnel at Stazione Framura on the Ligurian shore, through which passed the main line from La Spezia and Genoa to the German front south of Rome. That tunnel was given to the Ginny mission—two officers, thirteen OGs—to destroy just before or during the great Allied landing at Anzio, when any disruption of the German supply lines would be of maximum benefit to the assaulting forces.

Aerial reconnaissance of the target was undertaken, and surprisingly it was found that both entrances to the tunnel were only lightly guarded by Italian Fascist troops. There was, however, a German infantry unit in the area on coastal defense—Brigade Almers. The target was accepted, planning was completed, and Donovan remained at Bastia another day, to be present when the mission left. That night Livermore and the OGs gave Donovan a baronial K ration dinner at which "my hoplites" sang a song written for the occasion. It was not the best of the OSS songs, but sung to the tune of "The Battle Hymn of the Republic," it certainly captured the spirit of those wonderfully fit, confident men:

> "Is everybody happy?" cried the Sergeant looking up,
> Our hero feebly answered, "Yes,"
> and then they all stood up,
> He jumped right out into the blast,
> his static line unhooked,
> And he ain't gonna jump no more.
>
> Gory, gory, what a helluva way to die,
> Gory, gory, what a helluva way to die,
> Gory, gory, what a helluva way to die,
> And he ain't gonna jump no more.
>
> He counted long, he counted loud,
> he waited for the shock,

> He felt the wind, he felt the clouds,
> he felt the awful drop,
> He jerked the cord, the silk spilled out,
> and wrapped around his legs,
> And he ain't gonna jump no more. . . .[5]

However, Donovan was not present for the departure of the Ginny team: A storm blew up in the sea, delaying departure, the operation could not be mounted again until the night of January 6–7, 1944, and by that time Donovan had hurtled on. The operation was abandoned again on two occasions because of bad weather and suspicious ships in the area where the team was to be landed. It was not, therefore, until the night of March 21–22, 1944, that Ginny was successfully mounted. Then the team consisted of Lieutenant Vincent Russo (commanding), Lieutenant Paul J. Traficante, Technical Sergeant Livio Visceli, Sergeant Alfred L. DeFlumeri, Sergeant Dominic C. Mauro, Technical Fives Liberty J. Fremonte, Joseph M. Farrell, Salvatore DiSclafani, Angelo Sirico, John J. Leone, Thomas N. Savino, Joseph A. Libardi, Joseph Noia, Rosario F. Squatrito, and Santaro Calcara.[6] All the men were from New York City or adjacent areas.

The mission left Bastia in two torpedo boats at 6:00 P.M. on March 21, 1944, arriving off the pinpoint at about 11:00 P.M. All personnel were in American uniform, although the officers wore no insignia. All wore dog tags, and all their equipment was plainly American in manufacture. There could be no doubt that they were uniformed troops of the United States, not secret agents. They were, therefore, lawful combatants entitled to the protection of the Geneva Convention if they were captured.

The torpedo boats went to silent running and had approached to within 300 yards of the shore when the OGs departed in rubber assault boats. The boats withdrew and lay to, listening and watching to ensure that the mission was not intercepted. The only sounds heard from the shore came at about 11:15 P.M. when a radioman in one of the torpedo boats received a garbled message from the shore that he could not understand. At 11:40 P.M. Russo and Traficante were heard talking with each other on their walkie-talkies; their conversation indicated that all was well and that they were making their way inland to the station house on the railroad at the mouth of the tunnel.

But the reality was that Ginny had never been a lucky operation, and now its luck ran out altogether. Shortly before midnight a small convoy appeared on the torpedo boats' radar, heading in their direction. The convoy evidently detected the torpedo boats on their radar, for one of the ships fired off first illumination flares and then some shells. Since plans had been laid for such eventualities as this, the torpedo boat commanders, satisfied that Ginny was safe, decided to withdraw.

As shore lights were switched off and on, and more flares were shot off, the torpedo boats left the area at high speed to return to Bastia. There Livermore asked the Air Force to run a photographic mission over Stazione Framura, to see whether the tunnel mouth had been blown. If it had been blown, it could be presumed that the Ginny team would be waiting to be taken off at a preset hour and place. However the tunnel was found intact.

As Donovan was now advised, Livermore assumed that the Ginny party had heard the gunfire at sea and, when the coastal defenses were alerted, had gone to ground, as the plan provided. In that case, as the plan also provided, the team was to stay under cover until the evening of March 23, 1944, when it would place the charges in the tunnel, setting the fuse to blow at 2:30 A.M. on the twenty-fourth. The men would then withdraw to the pinpoint, be taken off, and the entire party would be clear of Italy by the time the charges exploded.

Two torpedo boats returned to the pinpoint on the twenty-third to evacuate the party, but when they arrived, the sixth sense peculiar to men engaged in this work told the captains something was wrong. Their sixth sense was correct. The boats approached on silent engines to within voice range of the beach. Russo's light signal was not seen, although visibility was good. Furthermore, no radio message was received. There was only silence and darkness until the torpedo boats' radar picked up three large boats just off the pinpoint, heading toward the torpedo boats. The commander of the evacuation party decided this might be a trap and retired at high speed to Bastia.

After the return to Bastia, Livermore sent over another photographic reconnaissance flight on the afternoon of the twenty-fifth, but again the photography showed the tunnel intact, with trains entering and emerging from the tunnel during the twelve minutes the aircraft were overhead.

Once more obedient to the plan, Livermore sent out a further evacuation mission that evening, and the torpedo boats closed the pinpoint without incident. Watch was kept for the prearranged shore signals, and some signals were seen at the pinpoint. They did not, however, correspond to the plan. One white light appeared, blinked indecipherably briefly as if someone were trying to send Morse, and then went out. Other lights appeared thirty to forty yards on either side of the pinpoint, and in the first minutes of March 26 another blinking light was seen at Point Moneglia nearby. It, too, was not decipherable.

The captain of the lead torpedo boat, D. B. Wentzel, was sure this was a trap. No member of the Ginny party was known to have a white light —blue was the color of the mission—none of the lights gave the correct signal, and the night was dark enough to conceal lurking German E-boats. Wentzel said he thought an attempt was being made to entice them inshore. If that was true, it meant that the enemy at least knew of Ginny and had probably captured the party. He ordered the boats to return to Corsica; later his decision proved wise. For the OGs had been caught, the shore lights were a trap, and the Germans and Italian Fascists had been holding fire until the boats closed to within voice range of the beach. Then they planned to open fire with the intention of sinking or capturing the torpedo boats.

The fate of the Ginny party did not become known for some time. But the facts as established were that when he landed, Russo found that the party was about one and one-half miles from the pinpoint. That made it impossible to get to the tunnel mouth, destroy it, and then get back to the beach in time for exfiltration. Russo decided, consequently, to find a place to hide, lie up during the day, blow the tunnel on the night of March 23–24, 1944, and then go on to the pinpoint for evacuation.

Russo and his men found a barn near a peasant's house on the outskirts of the fishing village of Bonassola. At about 9:00 A.M. on March 23, 1944, two of the OGs went foraging for food—why would not be known, for they carried K rations with them, but perhaps they had left them at the beach with the rubber boats.

During the forage they encountered the owner of the cottage, Lagaxo Franco, a local carpenter and fisherman, who invited them into his kitchen to warm themselves before his fire. When they had warmed themselves, they asked Franco if he knew where the station house was. Franco said he knew where it was, and he took them there. It proved to be the wrong building, and tiring and feeling hungry, the two Americans asked Franco to let them rest in front of his fire for a short time. He agreed and, with their money, went off to the village to buy fish, eggs, and wine. Franco then made the OGs some polenta. After they had eaten, the Americans left, arranging to return at about 3:00 P.M. to go with Franco to the station house, obviously to reconnoiter the area for the night's attack.[7]

Franco then went fishing. When he returned to the shore, he saw a local Fascist, Vittorio Bertoni, standing with some other men, examining something—the OGs' rubber boats, which had been imperfectly hidden in some rocks. Franco saw Bertoni go off to the village, and a little later he reappeared with some German soldiers. They began to search the shore and the area around Franco's cottage and, as luck would have it, the two Americans suddenly appeared for the meeting with Franco. Bertoni shouted, "What are you doing here, ugly pigs?"

One of the Americans shouted back in Italian, "We are Italians."

Bertoni shouted, "You are traitors," and threw a hand grenade.

The Germans then opened fire with their weapons, and the Americans, who had no choice unless they wanted to be shot, came out of the olive grove with their hands up.

As Donovan learned much later, other Fascists and Germans meanwhile had found two more boats and three large cases of explosives, a sure sign that more than two men had come ashore. A larger search was mounted, and twelve more Americans were found asleep or resting in the barn near Franco's cottage. One of the Americans attempted to persuade the Germans that they were escaped prisoners of war, but the rubber boats and explosives soon destroyed that claim and were taken as evidence that the Americans were sabotage troops—and therefore liable to execution under Hitler's Commando Order.

Russo, Traficante, and the OGs were taken by truck to the castle nearby where the German Brigade Almers had its headquarters.[8] Almers placed the OGs in the cellars and informed his higher headquarters, LXXV Corps, commanded by General Anton Dostler, near La Spezia. Dostler was told the facts concerning the rubber boats, the explosive, that the Americans were in uniform, but that the officers had no insignia of rank. Dostler ordered the Americans to be closely interrogated about their mission. That done, the interrogations were sent to Dostler, who then considered the "disposition of the prisoners." On the morning of March 25, 1944, he teleprinted back a message signed by himself that the Americans were to be shot immediately in accordance with the Commando Order.

The Americans' interrogator, Lieutenant Georg Sessler, of the German Navy, by that time had no doubt that the Americans were commando troops but had formed a certain sympathy for his captives. Apart from his belief that the Commando Order was illegal, as it was, he recognized one of the OGs as a New York Italian who used to deliver ice to the Hamburg-Amerika Line ships on Piers 84 and 86 in New York when Sessler worked for the line in 1936. On occasions Sessler visited the man's home as a guest at spaghetti dinners. The OG recognized Sessler immediately, crying out, "Here's mud in your eye!" They conversed for a time, and then, pointedly, Sessler hung a pistol on a nail behind the door—for what purpose is not clear, but Sessler uttered the admonition "Don't kill any Germans."

Meanwhile, Almers had given the order for the grave to be dug when he received a second teleprinter message from Dostler, directing that the Americans be shot by 7:00 A.M. on March 26. At that, a member of Almers's staff telephoned Dostler's chief of staff, a Colonel Kraehe, to ask for a stay of execution. Dostler, who was listening to the conversation, interrupted to state: ". . . we cannot change anything. You know the [Hitler order] contains a clause according to which the officers who do not execute the order are to be tried by court-martial." Almers was informed and ordered the officer in charge of the firing squad to have the grave and the Americans ready by 5:00 A.M.

A naval commander, Klaps, then intervened to ask for a stay on the grounds that the Hitler order might not affect the Americans, and in any event, he wished to interrogate the prisoners much more closely "for vital military intelligence." Dostler responded that Klaps was to place his views regarding the applicability of the Hitler order in a teleprinter message, but he refused to stay the execution beyond 7:00 A.M. on the twenty-sixth.

As WJD was to learn, with that declaration a considerable battle developed between Klaps, Sessler, and certain officers of Almers's staff, the object of which was to spare the Americans, and Dostler, who intended that they should be executed in accordance with the *Führerbefehl.* Sessler and Klaps prepared their argument for Dostler but included in the list of addressees the German supreme commander in Italy, Field Marshal Albert Kesselring. They obtained written proof of transmission and reception at Dostler's and Kesselring's headquarters, and they began deliberately to dawdle over the interrogations—Klaps was clearly playing for time in the hope that a reprieve would be forthcoming from Kesselring's headquarters. From Dostler there was only a bleak teleprinter signal at 4:00 P.M.: "The order of shooting must be executed as directed."

But it was a Sunday, and perhaps Kesselring was not at his headquarters. Certainly no order for a reprieve or a stay of execution was received during the night, so the Americans were brought to the killing ground at 7:00 A.M. During the brief ride there was a commotion when, although his hands were tied behind his back with wire, Traficante tried to get at a pistol hidden in his clothing—Sessler's. He was immediately disarmed.

Shortly after seven on the twenty-sixth, still with their hands bound behind their backs, all the OGs were shot to death by the German firing squad. A German officer gave each man the coup de grâce, and the corpses were then placed in the common grave. Grass sods were placed on the top of the grave to conceal its whereabouts.

To his bitter regret, WJD learned afterward that late on the day of the killings a message was received from Kesselring's headquarters in reply to Klaps's message requesting clemency: The commander in chief granted a stay of execution pending further investigations and consideration of the facts. Of course, the message was too late, and when word of the executions reached Kesselring's headquarters, orders went to Brigade Almers to destroy all evidence of the killings, while a Wehrmacht communiqué was issued on March 28, 1944: "Along the Oriental Coast of the Gulf of Genoa, a North American 'Commando' Unit, composed of 2 officers and 13 men, landed northwest of La Spezia and was annihilated in combat."

But the truth could not be concealed. Shortly after the Wehrmacht communiqué the Ultra service at Bletchley intercepted and decrypted part of a signal from Kesselring's to Hitler's headquarters, indicating that American "terror troops" in Italy had been "liquidated" in accordance with the Commando Order. Then a priest resident in the area of Brigade Almers came through the lines, was arrested by American counterintelligence, and under interrogation revealed that he had heard machine-gun fire that day, that it was rumored that a group of American soldiers had been executed, and that when he investigated, he found a grass mound, the geographical coordinates of which he was able to give to his interrogators. Also, Klaps reported to the Abwehr chief in Italy, Helferich, who had been anxious to keep the Ginny mission alive so that he might learn more about the operational groups. In some way information—possibly an ISOS intercept, but possibly from Sessler, who had connections with British Intelligence—leaked to the British. The information implicated Dostler, and Donovan gave the order that Dostler was to be taken alive and tried for what the signal called "violation of the laws and usages of war."

That could not be done for some time, but eventually Dostler was captured and indicted. The indictment read:

> In that Anton Dostler, then General, commanding military forces of the German Reich, a belligerent enemy nation, to wit the 75th Army Corps, did, on or about 24 March 1944, in the vicinity of La Spezia, Italy, contrary to the law of war, order to be shot summarily, a group of United States Army personnel . . . which order was carried into effect on or about 26 March 1944, resulting in the death of the fifteen members of the Army of the United States identified as follows. . . .

When the trial opened at the Royal Palace in Caserta, then the headquarters of the supreme Allied commander, Dostler pleaded not guilty and argued that he had done no more than obey a military order handed down to him by the chief of state and commander in chief of the Wehrmacht, Hitler. As an officer of the Reich he had a duty not to debate the legitimacy of his orders, but to carry them out, as in all armies.

Although the argument carried much truth, Dostler was found guilty and was sentenced to death by musketry. Then followed painful attempts to intervene on Dostler's behalf. Kesselring's successor as commander in chief in Italy, General Heinrich von Vietinghof, wrote to the highest Allied military authorities, asking for mercy in Dostler's case, because Dostler was "well known as an excellent regular soldier, who has paid the strictest attention to the carrying out, without questioning, of all orders."[9]

At the same time Dostler addressed an appeal to Pope Pius XII to intercede, and on the eve of execution day—December 1, 1945—the

Pope's Department of Extraordinary Affairs sent a letter to Harold Titt-mann, assistant to the personal representative of the U.S. President, declaring:

> The Secretary of State of His Holiness . . . takes the liberty to refer to the attention of the competent Allied authorities a plea for clemency which, as is known to those authorities, has been addressed to the Holy Father by General Dostler.
>
> His Holiness in accordance with those sentiments of Christian charity and mercy with which he regards all men cannot but bring this appeal to the attention of the competent authorities. The Secretary of State is directed to inform the Assistant to His Excellency the Personal Representative of the President of the United States to His Holiness that should it be found possible to exercise a measure of clemency in this case and to commute the sentence of capital punishment His Holiness would be grateful since the mitigation of a death sentence is always a source of satisfaction and comfort to Him.[10]

Among the mass of other, lesser letters there arrived one addressed to the Allied commander in chief from Dostler's wife and daughter, couched in piteous terms. The plea, which was in Donovan's papers, read:

> *PLEA FOR MERCY*
> *for the*
> *GENERAL ANTON DOSTLER*
>
> Who is pleading?
> His wife, misses Margot Dostler
> his daughter, miss Annemarie Dostler
> They are pleading on account of their natural right. His wife on account of the union, by which she has tied herself to her husband for the whole life and by which she is obliged to assist him up to the last hour.
>
> His daughter on account of her duty to be grateful to whom—besides God —she owes her life, growth and education. May that demand by the wings of God's help be carried into the hearts of the judges, that are bound to save or to annihilate our husband's and father's life.
>
> Why are we pleading?
> We are pleading out of the holy conviction and of the best knowledge, that he, who is standing before the judges is not a criminal, not a worthless or wicked man. We know him, our husband and father, who has sheltered and protected us with self-denying love, who, with tender regardfulness has removed the stones out of the way of his family's life, who made honesty and the good the first law for his family, who has banished the wrong from the hearth of his and who has chosen love and faithfulness the tutors of his house:
>
> as a soldier, to whom oath and duty were to contence [sic] of his life, fairness and loyalty the guides in his service, simplicity and privations the

companion in his work, self-denying and self-sacrifice for his fellowmen. Inexorably just and correct in his attitude, he made his way as a man, completely unpolitical, a soldier of the ancient german army. Untouched by the political waves of the last years, he kept his hands clean from gathering money and goods and was and remained a soldier, nothing but a soldier:

as the man to whom belief in the eternal creator, loyalty to the divine commands, respect for the moral laws were supreme command.

What are we pleading for?

We are pleading that this our knowledge and these our experiences may be thrown into the skales of justice, when guilt and fate are being weighed;

that humanity and love may be pleading, when our father's and husband's life will be decided;

that hatred may be silent and mercy have her way.

Bayreuth, 27. of october 1945.

[s] Margot Dostler
[s] Annemarie Dostler

Mercy did not have her way. General Matthew B. Ridgway read the Dostlers' letter when he reviewed the case and its petitions on November 27, 1945, and then pronounced the fateful words "In the foregoing case of Anton Dostler, formerly General commanding 75th German Army Corps, the sentence will be carried into execution on or before 1 December 1945, at or in the vicinity of Aversa, Italy."

And so it was. Dostler was executed by musketry a minute or two after daybreak on December 1, 1945, the highest-ranking German officer to be executed by the Allies in the Italian theater of operations.

31

Fettucine with the General

Peter Tompkins, the American author, who once served as chief of WJD's agent chains in Rome, later wrote:

> There is an old joke, retold among veterans of the OSS, about a young subaltern who died in World War II and found himself swimming in a sea of ordure—a sort of *lorda pozza* of the fifth ring of the Inferno. After several attempts to recover his breath he spotted a friendly officer of field grade from a rival branch of the same organization and realized it must be an OSS hell. "Oh, it's not so bad," spluttered the ranking sleuth, "once you learn to tread water." There was a pause while he demonstrated the finesse of his own technique to the admiring subaltern, then added with a sigh: "Except, of course, when Donovan comes by on a tour of inspection. Churns up the stuff like mad with his speedboat!"[1]

And so it was that January 1944 shortly before the great Allied amphibious landing at Anzio and Nettuno, south of Rome. Tompkins was gently treading the ordure-laden waters of Naples when Donovan sped up in his motorboat to create for Tompkins a "circle of hell, undreamed of even by Dante."

On January 15, 1944, Tompkins was at his headquarters in Naples—"a démodé four-story palazzo with a dilapidated garden on a back street belonging to a dispossessed Neapolitan duke"—when he received a sudden visit from Donovan, who announced he would like to stay for dinner and the night. Tompkins gave instructions to his cook to prepare his mess's specialty—fettucine made from GI powdered eggs and flour.

As Tompkins recorded, when dinner was ready, "Donovan took a quick glance at the candle-lit table and frowned his approval. 'You are the host,' he said, 'I shall sit at your right.' " Tompkins continued: "This intimacy with individuals of his vast and chaotic organization was, in my opinion, the most likely of the general's many qualities to assure him of the loyalty of a subordinate under the worst conditions of injustice, corruption, ineptness and political back-stabbing which marked the growing pains of OSS."

During the fettucine, Donovan announced somewhat casually that the British had given Rome to the OSS to cover, as the city was on the American front. He was looking for someone to go there and, he said in so many words, to bring the Roman resistance under OSS control and then, at a moment suitable to Allied military operations, to capture the Italian capital in the name of the OSS and the Grand Alliance. Tompkins then remarked that should be an interesting assignment for someone, hoping Donovan was about to put his mark on him—Tompkins had been offered the post of SI Italy and wanted field experience before taking command. That is what happened. As if it were the most normal prospect in the world, Donovan asked Tompkins if he would go capture Rome.

Tompkins, who saw himself rather as a John Reed or a Byron, not a Trotsky or an Antonov-Ovseyenko in the Winter Palace, avoided making a commitment during the rest of the dinner. But as he was taking Donovan to the airfield in his jeep next morning, Tompkins announced he would accept the mission. He was to record:

> Pacing up and down the muddy runway while his plane warmed up, the general outlined what he wanted of the mission; then he shook me by the hand, climbed into the hatch and took off into the chill north wind, leaving me alone on the airstrip with that feeling of dedication which comes when one has been entrusted with a mission by a superior being.

Weeks later, Tompkins was put ashore from a Royal Navy motor torpedo boat near Civitavecchia, a town on the coast about sixty miles from Rome, on the night of January 20–21, 1944, in an operation launched from the OG base on Corsica, which was now being called Camp Coon. For a short time he found himself alone on the beach, carrying papers that represented him to be a Roman prince, with thirty miles of coastal plain between him and the Eternal City. But he soon found that he had not been abandoned; a reception committee consisting of Italian resistance workers with horse, carriage, and driver arrived to take him inland to a car. By dawn, after some bribery, the car dropped him near the Piazza di Spagna in the heart of the capital. There he disappeared into a warren and arrived at a frescoed house called the Piazzetta Ricci. He was received happily by the ancient servants once employed by the Tompkins family, and after breakfast and a little sleep Tompkins began to get in touch with the Roman underground.

Shortly a "small man, well dressed, with olive skin and dark mustache" called for the *commandante americano* at the villa, "nodding his head in greeting" and giving Tompkins a little bag of fake almond sweets. That man was Topolino, who took Tompkins in a Fiat car, also called a Topolino, to apartments near the Littorio airfield. There, in Topolino's apartment, Tompkins attended a family lunch, was given some orange brandy, and then was invited to rest in an armchair. Tompkins awakened from that nap and was given a great fright when he found himself "face to face with a police officer in full uniform, highly polished boots, [Fascist] arm band and revolver." Believing Topolino had betrayed him, Tompkins went for his pistol, but the policeman begged him to be calm and explained that he was Maurizio Giglio, alias Cervo ("Stag"), of the Roman mounted police and controller of the OSS wireless station, Vittorio. When Tompkins proved his identity, status, and mission, Giglio was joined by three other officers of the Roman underground: Clemente Menicante, alias Coniglio ("Rabbit"); Franco Malfatti, a sharply dressed Socialist who was Giglio's chief of intelligence; and Elio Gambareri, Menicante's paymaster and a man with numerous connections with Roman industrialists, bankers, right-wing politicians, monarchists, and the American, British, and Italian royalist intelligence services.[2]

As Tompkins soon signaled Donovan, he had had immediate and serious reservations about Menicante and Gambareri, although he liked Giglio and Malfatti. Nevertheless, his orders directed him to reveal to these men that a major Allied military operation was imminent and that it would affect Rome. He announced that he had been sent by General Mark Clark to "coordinate intelligence, sabotage and countersabotage" in Rome coincidentally with that operation and asked Menicante as the leader to "get in touch with all the forces at [his] disposal, as soon as [he] possibly could." Menicante agreed to call a "meeting of the various resistance group leaders for early the following morning."

The meeting broke up, and Giglio invited Tompkins to stay at his apartment, on the ground that nobody would expect "to find an American OSS agent in a Fascist policeman's bed." Tompkins, who had formed a good opinion of Giglio, an opinion that was to prove well founded, accepted the invitation, and together they roared off in Giglio's police Fiat to an apartment in the Prati, one of the drabber quarters of Rome.

Over dinner that night Tompkins learned an essential piece of information about Menicante from Giglio: Menicante had visited OSS Naples recently and been appointed "chief OSS clandestine agent in German-occupied Italy" by Tompkins's commanding officer, Colonel Ellery C. Huntington—who had not communicated that fact to Tompkins during his briefing. The appointment was to cause unending and dangerous trouble for Tompkins, who had been appointed "chief of OSS in Rome," a title and position Menicante now refused to recognize.

Furthermore, Tompkins learned there was a third individual in the Roman underground with an OSS title that made him chief of OSS Rome. That man was one Enrico Sorrentino, who claimed to have been appointed "chief political agent in Rome of General Mark Clark," a title he, too, had acquired on a surreptitious visit to Allied headquarters in Naples, where he had been fired by Tompkins as unfit for operations.

To complicate the prospect further, Tompkins learned from Giglio that Menicante commanded not the Roman resistance movement, as he had claimed at the meeting at Topolino's, but an unrepresentative group called the Democratic Union which, through Gambareri, existed to seize power in Rome when the Germans left and the Americans arrived, for and on behalf of the right wing. Lastly, to complete the picture of imminent trouble, while Tompkins had brought with him only limited funds, Menicante and Gambareri were endowed with millions of lire by both the Democratic Union and its banking associates and by the various intelligence services, which had given Menicante a great deal of gold while he was in Naples.

That same night, as Tompkins slept in Giglio's flat, an immense Allied invasion fleet appeared off Anzio and Nettuno, to the south of Rome, and deposited a large army commanded by General John P. Lucas. Aboard one of the ships was Donovan, who in a signal that day reported with satisfaction to Ned Buxton in Washington that surprise had been absolute. Indeed it was. With only two weak German battalions in the neighborhood during the assault by 50,000 American and British troops, Lucas lost only 13 dead, 97 wounded, 44 missing. No German formations of any size lay between the beachhead and Rome, while to the south the German Gustav Line of fortifications, which had held the Allied armies back for months, was cracking under the strain of a combined Allied offensive.

Although Tompkins could not be sure that the Allies were landing that night, he knew the outlines of the operation, and had he known of the situation at the beachhead, he would have been entitled to believe that his Roman mission was over before it had begun. But, sadly, something went wrong with Lucas at the beachhead. A gentle man, he lost his nerve, thought the Germans were about to launch an overwhelming counterattack that would catapult his army back into the sea, and ordered his troops not to strike for the Alban Hills and Rome but to dig in and prepare for the German attack.

Flabbergasted at their good fortune, for they had been taken completely by surprise, Hitler and his generals reacted with their usual speed, efficiency, and ferocity, assembled a complete army—the Fourteenth— and shot it down to the pretty little seaside resorts before Lucas could recover his confidence. Within a few days the Anzio beachhead had been transformed into a second Verdun that was to last for almost five months and consume men at the rate of 2,000 a week. Throughout the period Tompkins was pinned to Rome, which soon became what the French called *un panier à crabes*—a basket of crabs.

When Tompkins awoke on the morning of January 22, 1944, and prepared for his meeting with Menicante's committee, he could not be sure that the great attack had begun. He breakfasted well and in gentlemanly fashion, and then, as arranged, he was taken to a bare, dusty, and unoccupied apartment at the Via d'Ara Coeli 9, a narrow street climbing toward the Capitoline Hill. In one of the empty rooms he found several men standing around in overcoats. "No names were exchanged, just a series of formal handshakes." Tompkins did, however, detect that there was "something curious about these men that was far from reassuring."[3]

As Tompkins reported to WJD, with Menicante present, Tompkins outlined what was expected of the Roman underground, and there was some discussion about establishing headquarters and communications for the operations. As the meeting proceeded, however, it became clear to Tompkins that "these individuals were not particularly informed about the nature of the various forces available in Rome, nor of the technicalities of the operations involved."[4] He suspected that there were no representatives of the military committee of the Committee of National Liberation present, a suspicion that proved correct, and that they were no more than committeemen of the Democratic Union, a suspicion that also proved correct.

Therefore, Tompkins gave those present only the vaguest outline of his orders and suggested a further meeting when they had had a chance to discuss them. The meeting broke up, but as it did, a youngish man came up and said he had been sent by Franco Malfatti, who had been at Topolino's and had asked Tompkins to go at once with the young man. In the street, as they made their way toward the Piazza Venezia, where in happier times Mussolini had delivered powerful orations about Italy's new greatness, Tompkins saw roaring convoys of paratroopers passing by. He concluded from the speed of the convoys and the fact that the paratroopers were in full battle order that the landings had begun.

Tompkins asked Malfatti to arrange a meeting with the military committee of the Committee of National Liberation and then found Giglio and asked him to take him to Station Vittorio, the OSS radio station in Rome, to see whether any messages had been received. Giglio took

Tompkins to an apartment opposite the Hotel Plaza, where the radio was hidden, but no signals relating to the landings had been received at the time. Tompkins then received word of a meeting with representatives of the military committee, to take place immediately at Giglio's flat.

When Tompkins arrived at Giglio's, he saw that the left wing was much more businesslike than the right:

> Partisans were posted for blocks round [Giglio's] house with submachine guns, hand grenades and automatics wrapped in newspaper to look like parcels. . . . As I watched these operations from behind the curtain of the window of my room I knew that I was dealing with reasonably serious organizations.[5]

When he came face-to-face with the committeemen, he found that he was in the presence of the military junta of the Roman Committee of National Liberation—Socialists, Communists, and the centrists' Party of Action. He discovered also that they were in a state of potential armed conflict with the Democratic Union and the other organizations of the right. Yet Tompkins's personal sympathies were with these rough men, for he believed they represented the "only really effective underground." Be that as it may, he had also to consider the OSS's standing edict that agents were not to engage in political activity and were to support resistance movements only on the basis of their effectiveness, irrespective of their political coloration. Therefore, he told the military committee that his job was purely military and what "they did politically was their own damn business." On that basis, he reported later to Donovan, "they all agreed to cooperate to the best of their ability."

Nothing in Rome was quite that straightforward, however, for, Tompkins claimed later, Menicante had begun to intrigue against him, and to make his position tenable, he had to denounce Menicante's maneuvers as "being entirely his own responsibility, in no way supported by either OSS or the Commanding General of the Fifth Army." But once he had made that declaration, his "position with the various resistance groups as an American Intelligence Officer was firmly established, if at the expense of [Menicante's] sympathy and support."[6]

In a world already rife with denunciations to the Germans and the *fascisti*, with that statement Tompkins markedly increased his chances of betrayal—Menicante was not the sort of man who permitted youth to stand between himself and the political and financial power of a great capital that would be his once the Americans arrived.

At Tompkins's second meeting with the military committee Giglio arrived with a telegram from OSS Naples, received over Station Vittorio: The Allies had landed at Anzio and Nettuno, but the march on Rome had been delayed; he was to concentrate on intelligence gathering and abandon the sabotage operations in his instructions. Tompkins changed his plans and asked the military committee if it would establish an intelligence organization, and it agreed. The organization came to be called the Socialist Intelligence Service, its chief was Franco Malfatti, and its headquarters was in the back rooms of a German bookshop opposite the Hotel Excelsior. From that moment forward Tompkins did not use Menicante's professionals because "Personally, I did not have much faith in professional spies, and eventually proved pretty conclusively that for reasons of their own, they often invented large portions of their intelligence, or gathered it from the recesses of their boudoirs, their convents or the back corridors of the Vatican."

On the other hand Tompkins wrote later to WJD:

> . . . there were socialist eyes and ears in practically every office, on every street corner, in the farms and villages between Rome and the beachhead, on the carts and trucks that jogged along the country roads; among the laborers who built the military installations for the Germans; among the fisherfolk and sailors—everywhere in fact that human beings lived and worked, and where the Germans had to pass.[7]

Malfatti's organization did excellent work, providing great quantities of detailed intelligence on the movement of the Wehrmacht, its supply and fuel dumps, its concentration areas and vehicle depots, and the arrivals and departures of trains and motor vehicle and shipping convoys. "All this information," Tompkins reported later, "was boiled down to the bare facts and was brought to me daily at about noon. It then took me about two hours to check it all with past information, find localities on our maps, and draw up the cables of the most urgent information for transmission to the beachhead."

The completed cables were written on tissue paper, "tightly folded and carried by special messengers, inside their socks, or slipped through a ring on their finger where it could be easily swallowed." The messengers took the signals to a man "waiting at a prearranged rendezvous a few blocks away. This man, who didn't know where I was or where I lived, carried the message across town to meet another prearranged rendezvous, who in turn took it wherever the radio station happened to be hidden." The location of Station Vittorio was changed constantly by Giglio, and only he and one or two operators knew where it was at any given time. "Thus the central messenger knew neither where the message came from, nor where it went. If [the Germans] found the radio there would be absolutely no way they could trace the message back to us—or vice versa."

Yet there were severe casualties. Tompkins himself acknowledged: "Why they continued to work for us God only knows. . . . Dozens were arrested, and over twenty were shot."[8] And to increase the probabilities of betrayal there was Menicante's activity. This was investigated later by the OSS agent cashier at Algiers, David C. Crockett, who recorded:

A large proportion of the sums [spent] undoubtedly . . . were used [by Menicante] in a manner in no way connected wth our activities. There is no question in my mind but that the political strength of [Menicante] in Rome . . . was partly due to the fact that [he] was a powerful political figure because of the millions he had at his disposal with which he could support, in the case of OSS, either one group or the other, or one against the other as he saw fit. . . . [Menicante] is a very rough, ruthless "gangster" type.[9]

Tompkins tried to resolve his dangerous relationship with Menicante by asking OSS Naples for two documents: a telegram stating plainly that Tompkins, not Menicante, was head of OSS Rome and a telegram ordering Menicante out of Rome and into northern Italy until the position cleared in Rome. Both telegrams were transmitted as requested and were received by OSS Naples. But they came too late. The telegram to Donovan on April 5, 1944, explained the nature of the disaster: "We have lost Vittorio Station in Rome. One agent has been executed. Arrangements are being made to get Pietro [Tompkins's code name at OSS] out. He is safe."[10]

In one important respect the telegram was in error: Tompkins was not safe. He was in great danger and being hunted by the SD.

Maurizio Giglio, alias Cervo, the lieutenant in the Roman mounted police who ran Station Vittorio, went to the houseboat near the Risorgimento Bridge, intending to move the radio to a new address, at 2:30 P.M. on March 17, 1944. With Giglio was his orderly, whom he left with the motorcycle while he went into the houseboat to get the transceiver. Immediately both men were arrested by an official of the Sicherheitsdienst, a Dr. Koch, and his assistant, a man known only by a work name, Valter.

Giglio and his orderly were taken to the SD interrogation center on the Via Principe Amedeo, near the Termini Station, for questioning about their activities, and they were still there on March 21, 1944, when a powerful charge exploded under a German truck on the Via Rasella, killing thirty-two German soldiers. The bomb had been planted by partisans, and the Germans reacted to the attack with a savagery that Giglio's orderly captured in his diary of his and Giglio's interrogation.[11] The diary was later sent to WJD in Washington:

First interrogation, 17 March 1944, 6:30 P.M. I was interrogated. I insisted I did not know Cervo. They began beating me. Koch, Valter, and three others . . . were all armed with pistols and sharp knives. They took turns in pricking my mouth, temples, ribs, and kidneys with the knives. They then punched me on the chest and on the jaw as though I were a punching bag. They confronted me with Cervo. At his orders, I told them that I knew him and that I worked for him. My mouth and nose were bleeding. . . .

Second interrogation, midnight, 17/18 March 1944. Cervo was interrogated first. I heard Valter and his pals beating him in the corridor. I was then interrogated. Koch, Valter, and from ten to fifteen henchmen were present. Koch wanted to know if Cervo gave me messages to bring to the English, and whether I had arms, ammunition, and hand grenades hidden. I was silent. They beat me more severely than the first time. . . . At 2 A.M. on the 18th Cervo was asked by Koch to sign a confession. Cervo was . . . bleeding at the mouth, nose, his face was swollen and livid with bruises; he had lost several teeth.

Third interrogation, 18 March 1944, 9:30 to 10 P.M. Cervo was interrogated first. He was tortured for twenty minutes and . . . he was in bad shape; he complained especially of pains in his side. . . . I was then called. For half an hour they asked me to talk. In order to persuade me to do so, they pulled out the hairs of my mustache, and by means of screws and a steel bar, they compressed my temples until I thought my eyes were going to burst out. When I began to lose consciousness, they would release the screws. They wanted me to tell them everything, but I told them nothing—The feed consisted solely of a small dish of overcooked rice diluted with a stinking broth; there was no bread. . . .

Fourth interrogation, 20th of March from 8 to 9:15 P.M. Cervo was interrogated first for 40 minutes. Then, ten minutes later, it was my turn. Like Cervo, I was bleeding all over when I returned . . . they made me sit on a chair where they passed an electric current through my body: I was in a cold sweat, pale as a ghost, and in a fainting condition. . . . I was dragged [back to my] cell and chained by the wrists to an iron bar about 5 feet 8 inches above the ground. [Cervo] found the strength to give me a little water and a few slices of potato. . . .

Fifth interrogation, 2 A.M. on the 21st of March. The interrogation lasted about half an hour. They would point pistols at my mouth and temples, and tell me to talk under penalty of death. I was resolute. . . . I told our hangmen that it was an injustice to torture a man in that way. In order to intimidate me, a few shots were fired out of the window into the courtyard.

In view [of] my determination, Koch suggested the application of a new cruelty. In fact, a large frame, supported by a wooden plank, about 30 centimeters wide and almost a meter long, covered with rows of sharp, long nails was brought into the room. I was stripped and placed with my shoulders on this "weaver's loom." . . . I was pressed painfully upon the nails. Excited by sadism and fury, Valter and others closer to me slapped me and pulled my mustache and eyebrows; they fired a few pistol shots; they punched me on the jaw, tossing me right and left. Blood and flesh remained attached to the points of the nails. . . . [Later] as much as my strength would allow me to, I told the lieutenant what had happened. As always, sadly . . . he ran his hands through his hair and said to me "poor fellow, how much you are suffering because of me." . . . About 6 P.M. on the 23rd the door suddenly opened and about eight of Koch's policemen burst into the cell. They notified us of the events of Via Rasella, where 32 of their "German comrades" had been killed. Savagely they attacked everyone with punches and kicks, and spit on us and dealt out abuse generally. . . .

   Sixth interrogation, March 23 from 10 to 10:40 P.M. The lieutenant was interrogated for about ten minutes. When he returned, his face was disfigured and he staggered with exhaustion. . . . He called softly for his mother, almost unconscious. In that moment, Valter, like a wild beast, stood on one leg, and brought the other down with all his might and the weight of his body, kicked the lieutenant in the pubic regions.

   [Cervo] in a weak voice, almost finished, exclaimed "mother of mine, they have killed me." While he turned weakly on his side Valter heeled him again violently between the kidneys and the scrotum. The lieutenant, transfigured and white as snow, encouraged me, always seeking forgiveness for the suffering I would always have to undergo because of him. . . . They kept after me to reveal the activities of the patriots, saying that I had passed pamphlets and advised the Allies of German concentrations and positions to be bombarded, etc.

   The lieutenant hovered between life and death during that night and the next day. . . . He [had] suffered as much as it is humanly possible to suffer. I accompanied him to the water closet, where he passed blood. . . . A serving woman . . . out of compassion, brought the lieutenant a glass of milk, but drinking it was a crisis for him, and he fainted. Then he was taken by the arms out of the cell [by SS men].

Lieutenant Giglio was not seen alive again, for he was taken by the SS to the Catacombs of St. Calliste in the Ardeatine caves near Rome. There, on March 25, 1944, with 319 other Italians, most members of the Roman underground and some members of Tompkins's organization, he was machine-gunned to death as a reprisal for the killing of the 32 Germans on the Via Rasella. Giglio died as he had behaved throughout the interrogation—silently, without mentioning the names, addresses, work names, or assignments of any his colleagues in Tompkins's underground.

   Yet the Germans knew all they needed to know about Tompkins's organization and had begun a drive against it when Giglio was killed. In the first *ratissage*—in secret service terms, the word for manhunt—against the Socialist Intelligence Service, Franco Malfatti reported that he had lost forty-seven helpers, including several women, "many of them with written information on them."[12] There were signs that the Germans were sending their own agents to join Malfatti's organization, the object to expose and destroy it from within. Moreover, Menicante's behavior had become increasingly enigmatic. He had begun to submit openly that

Tompkins had "no authority whatsoever and was in fact nothing but a cheap impostor!"[13] It had also become evident to Tompkins, as he was to signal WJD, that:

> [Menicante's] whole approach to the problem had never been to furnish the Fifth Army with intelligence—his sources weren't providing any and he wasn't even getting his agents into contact with the base—and it looked more and more as if he and Gambareri and Company were in effect political agents sent to infiltrate, not the enemy, but the OSS, so as to assure control of the various intelligence organizations in Italy.[14]

To Tompkins, the really curious matter was that although OSS Naples knew there was serious and possibly dangerous trouble between Tompkins and Menicante, nothing was done to order Menicante to obey Tompkins or to terminate his association with the OSS. That was due possibly to the difficulty of sending politically complicated messages by wireless, but it seemed to Tompkins that headquarters actually welcomed rivalry between the two groups, even though headquarters must have been aware that such rivalry would cause casualties.

By the third week of March Tompkins's operation was oppressed by the sense of inevitable disaster, from either the Germans or Menicante or both. The first sign that disaster had actually struck came when Giglio advised Tompkins that one of Station Vittorio's operators had been arrested by the Germans. That operator knew Giglio's identity, and it was he who betrayed Giglio and the whereabouts of the radio set to the Germans. But Tompkins knew nothing of Giglio's arrest until a telephone call on the evening of March 17, 1944. The caller stated: "The sister wants to know if I have bought her any honey!" Tompkins told the woman who took the call: "Say I will let her know." Then he said: "They've got Cervo. That was the conventional phrase."

Tompkins was forced on the run, moving from address to address, staying as long as his welcome lasted, and then looking for new lodgings, with the Sicherheitsdienst not far behind. He had little money, few helpers, no radio, no chance of exfiltration, political enemies who wanted him dead, and at his heels an utterly merciless enemy who had his photograph and his description. For a young man of only twenty-four his situation was not enviable, but he displayed astonishing boldness. Realizing he could not survive unless he secured fresh cover, he volunteered for service in the Italian African Police, which still existed, although Italy had long since lost its African empire, and, oddly, was still recruiting. He signed the necessary papers and was inducted at the police barracks, drawing arms, ammunition, boots, uniform, rations, and bedding (which smelled "strongly of brilliantine and urine") and then deserting when he had become Corporal Roberto Berlingieri.

Yet that resourcefulness did not end Tompkins's Calvary on the eve of his twenty-fifth birthday on April 29, 1944. During much of his work in Rome Tompkins had made his headquarters and home in an apartment on the Palazzo Lovatelli, which had been lent to him by one of his subagents, Emmanuele de Seta, while his mother, Princess Pignatelli, was away. Tompkins stated later in his formal report to WJD:

> Franco [Malfatti] produced a really startling piece of information. Emanuele had confided in him that, through a German agent in Rome, he had learned that his own mother, who had decided some time back to cross the lines to the Allied side, had, in fact done so as an agent for the Germans. I had long been confused by the De Seta-Pignatelli household, but now learned from Franco that Emanuele's mother had remarried a Pignatelli, who as an adventurer, novelist and Fascist had, after the defection of the greater part of Mussolini's Grand Council, decided to accept the unfillable position of Party Secretary in the Fascist Republic of Saló. . . . But looked at objectively, our situation was pretty peculiar. Here was an American agent living in the house of a German agent . . . whose children were actively but unwittingly aiding him in spying for the Allies! There was no question about its being time to decamp.[15]

Tompkins and three associates set out from Rome in a Topolino, intending to pass through the German Tenth Army into the lines of the British Eighth Army in the general area of Sulmona, a town in the Apennines in the center of the Italian peninsula. They were traveling on Tompkins's police credentials obtained for them by Malfatti. When they reached Aquila, they found the region infested with German SS troops on antipartisan operations, so they went to Ancona on the Adriatic in the hope of finding a boat. There was none, and they were forced to return to Rome—and Princess Pignatelli's apartment in the Palazzo Lovatelli.

Meanwhile, at last the Allies broke out of the Anzio beachhead, and the U.S. Fifth Army arrived in Rome on June 4, 1944, thus relieving Tompkins of further fears for his future. He emerged from hiding to witness the American arrival in the Piazza Venezia, and was mortified to observe that Menicante's men, not his, were there to welcome General Mark Clark. However, WJD advised FDR and the Joint Chiefs that Tompkins' intelligence had saved the beachhead, especially during the main counterattack of February 16, 1944, which Hitler had directed personally.

32

The Inquests

The reckoning for the Rome disaster—an aborted mission, wrecked agent chains, heavy casualties—fell not on Tompkins, but on OSS headquarters in Italy. As Tompkins's story leaked out at Allied Supreme Headquarters, throughout the intelligence community, and at OSS headquarters, Donovan ordered a special investigating committee to examine the entire affair. That committee sat as General Jacob L. Devers, commander in chief of American forces in Italy and the deputy supreme commander, also demanded a thorough investigation into the affairs of OSS Italy. The two inquiries were separate but linked.

The Special Investigating Committee sat in Rome under the chairmanship of the chief of OSS Special Funds in the Mediterranean, David C. Crockett, one of the ablest men in Donovan's administration. Putzell was flown out from Washington to report upon the inquiries.

Crockett's inquiry took testimony from about thirty survivors of the Rome intelligence chains, and he and four colleagues looked into every aspect of Tompkins's operations, his complaints about Menicante, and his allegations of inefficiency at base. They also looked into the financial operations and compensation for the living and the relatives of the dead who had served OSS.

In an interim report Crockett reported that about 20,000,000 lire—at the going rate about $100,000—had been advanced to all OSS groups in in Rome, including Tompkins's and Menicante's, but most of it to Menicante. Some of this money had been advanced by the OSS's arrangements with the Banca Commerciale Italiana, the Innocente Corporation, and various industrialists. Of that sum 6,500,000 lire had been sent to Milan, 2,000,000 had been returned as unexpended funds, and a complete accounting had been received from Innocente for 10,000,000. But, as Crockett stated as "a purely personal observation in this entire matter, there was . . . no question but that a sizeable amount of the above sums was used only indirectly to assist OSS and 5th Army, either in the procurement of intelligence or organized sabotage behind the lines." It was "impossible to determine as no one tells the truth, and probably no one actually knows, what proportion of the sum was actually used in this fashion."[1]

In general, "A large proportion of the sums undoubtedly fell into the hands of the different political groups and were used by them in a manner in no way connected with our activities." In that regard:

> There is no question in my [Crockett's] mind but that the political strength of [Menicante] in Rome . . . was partly due to the fact that [he] was a powerful political figure because of the millions he had at his disposal with which he could support, in the name of OSS, either one group or the other, or one against the other, as he saw fit.

Crockett drew attention to the fact that while the Badoglio government had appointed as military governor of Rome a certain General Armellini, Menicante was able to "sabotage" that appointment, place his own nominee, General Bencivenga, in the post, and ensure that Bencivenga was accepted by all political groups.

The committee passed to the question of relations between Tompkins and Menicante. Complimenting Peter Tompkins on his "tremendous courage," the committee found that the "internecine row" between him and Menicante was due to these factors: (1) Both Tompkins and Menicante were appointed to posts that meant that they both were chief of OSS Rome; (2) "as each one thought he was the chief, neither one would make concessions to the other"; (3) because of German security operations, they had to deal entirely through intermediaries, who "naturally misinterpreted somewhat the point of view of each man, as they too had interests in the final outcome"; and (4) Tompkins's dependency upon Menicante for money "put him in a secondary position to Menicante."

> There is no question in my [Crockett's] mind of the great courage and sincerity of Tompkins and that he acted intelligently and to the best of his knowledge to promote the work as he knew it. But he was dealing with [Menicante] who was [a] very rough, ruthless, "gangster" type, who had been chief of OSS without any doubt up to the time that Tompkins arrived. . . .

Crockett pointed out that Menicante had "nothing but Tompkins' word to tell him that he was not still chief, which, under the circumstances, I can easily see the reason he did not believe." Crockett recommended that Menicante be paid his salary and then his services be terminated. Tompkins should receive the Legion of Merit and return to Washington and the Research and Analysis Branch.

On the question of compensation for the living and the dead, there was likely to be discontent because many of Menicante's agents had been under contract which provided death benefits of $5,000, while the contracts for Tompkins's agents provided for death benefits of only $1,000. Furthermore, while most of Menicante's agents had signed contracts, such was not usually the case with Tompkins's men and women.[2]

Crockett advised that of twenty-two agents who had lost their lives but not been under contract, $1,000 compensation had been requested and settlement for $500 had been made in each case—not a very generous settlement. Rather more generous settlements were reached in the cases of persons of rank or social position who had not been under contract. For example, 1,000,000 lire ($5,000 at the official rate) had been paid to the marchese Giacomo Medici del Vascello, and Senator Parodi received 5,000,000 ($25,000 at the official rate). Moreover, in general, agents of rank received what was demanded, even when the demand was in much more valuable foreign currency.

On the other hand, the demands were not always large: Count Carlo Carlotti asked for and received 115,000 lire ($575 official rate), as did Camillo Angelini Rota, who wanted 11,300 lire ($56). Menicante asked for only $1,800 in American currency, but since that was forbidden by exchange regulations, he received 5,800 Swiss francs and 55 gold pieces. The estate of Maurizio Giglio received only 620,000 lire ($3,100), less than that received by the estate of Paolo Poletti, who was shot by British Field Security Police as a suspected double agent attempting to escape. By contrast, American-born agents resident in the United States at the time of enlistment received $10,000 insurance compensation.

OSS Italy was no more generous with the salaries of its subagents, the men and women—and children—employed by Tompkins and Menicante. The usual salary by contract was $60 a month, with bonuses of $100 a month for outstanding work, and compensation of personal losses— clothing, personal jewelry, and the like. But compensation was not always paid automatically. One of Tompkins's best agents, Gabriele Crespi, claimed $2,000 compensation for the loss of his motorcar; Crockett haggled about it for months and in the end disallowed the claim.

It cannot be said, therefore, that OSS agents and subagents on active service in Italy ended their careers much the richer. Tompkins tried to extract more generous wages and settlements for his agents, but Crockett was imbued with the first principle of the Special Funds Branch: thrift.

Nor did Tompkins's career with the OSS prosper after this somber excursion to Rome. He resisted the proposal that he be sent back to Washington and a desk job with Research and Analysis. However, a number of factors made it seem unwise to return him to operations in Italy. (Later, though, Tompkins had the immense satisfaction of being among the first SI officers to arrive in Berlin.)

When X-2, commanded by Major Alexander Berding, seized a major German stay-behind wireless post in Rome, it found evidence that the Germans had had a complete description of Tompkins and regarded him as dangerous. Consequently, when Colonel Roger Pfaff of X-2 was asked for his opinion about the wisdom of sending Tompkins back into the field, he advised Donovan that:

> it is quite obvious that the Germans have considerable information regarding Peter Tompkins; the fact that he is connected with OSS and that he has participated in intelligence activities. As a result of this, it would seem almost impossible for him to establish adequate and secure cover in any area where the Germans are able to carry out any intelligence activities. Moreover, the cover, communications and operations of any OSS personnel who were even casually connected with Peter Tompkins would be seriously jeopardized by the connections.[3]

Donovan thereupon vetoed a proposal to parachute Tompkins into northern Italy. And for once Donovan was ungenerous in a case in which the man concerned was twenty-four and had spent nearly five months in an enemy capital in circumstances of hideous danger. He wired Buxton: "It is believed by those who know here that Tompkins' life would be in danger if he returned here. As a result of his inexperience and poor handling of people whose lives were lost, he has incurred antagonism of those who are determined to take his life."[4] But it is possible that Donovan's opinion of Tompkins's performance, which was not shared by Crockett, the man who made the investigation, was influenced by an associated case that had troubled the Allied counterintelligence authorities in Italy—and by Devers's complaint.

In March or April 1944, at the time Tompkins was in trouble in Rome, an Italian princess, Maria Pignatelli, managed to cross through the front lines and make contact with Lieutenant Paolo Poletti, an Italian subject employed by OSS Secret Intelligence. Through Poletti the princess was introduced into the highest OSS circles in Naples, and she herself was recruited as an OSS informant, possibly because her family had been closely connected with Mussolini, who now ruled northern Italy through a Fascist Grand Council under German control.

Her association with Donovan—she had been a client before the war —and with Tompkins seems to have weighed in her favor, for she was able to state she had lent Tompkins her apartment in Rome, and her son

Emmanuele was one of his agents. But the British security service, which was powerful in Italy, was not sure about Princess Pignatelli. Largely because the X-2 branch was not yet fully operational in Italy, it kept a watchful but relatively benign eye on OSS activities in Italy, and at some stage the British warned the OSS chiefs in Italy that the princess was a German spy.

The evidence was not conclusive at the time, and the princess was permitted to continue her association with certain OSS officers. But shortly the British case against her hardened, and the British arrested Lieutenant Poletti and another of the princess's associates in the OSS, an Italian identified only as Morris, on suspicion of being German agents or intelligence agents of Mussolini. When Poletti tried to escape, his British guards shot him to death—an incident that caused great anger within OSS Italy. Princess Pignatelli then disappeared.

As Donovan was about to protest the killing to the British authorities, Allen Dulles in Bern related to WJD that he had received information from George Wood, his informant in the German foreign ministry in Salzburg. On or about May 14, 1944, Wood gave Dulles a copy or a summary of a diplomatic message sent by the German ambassador in Rome, Dr. Rudolf Rahn, to Foreign Minister von Ribbentrop, dated May 3, 1944. Rahn had reported: "The Italian princess, Maria Pignatelli, who is the widow of [the Marchese] de Seta, fled from her home in Naples . . . to Rome, in the disguise of a midwife with [Allied military government in Italy] papers which she had bought."[5]

According to Rahn, the princess had seen the German supreme commander in Rome, Field Marshal Albert Kesselring, and gone on to Fascist general headquarters at Fasano, where she had seen Mussolini. The princess had talked with both Kesselring and Mussolini about the "secret Fascist and military organization which has been organized by her husband in southern Italy" and about Sicherheitsdienst plans to use her as "a transmitter of sabotage data." In the meantime, Princess Pignatelli had "probably made her way back to Naples, through the lines from Rome."

Dulles's information was passed by WJD to OSS Italy, where Rahn's information enabled the OSS to arrest Princess Pignatelli as she passed through the front lines for the third time—no mean achievement for a woman in her fifties. She was closely interrogated but maintained she knew nothing of a Fascist sabotage organization in the Allied rear areas. She maintained that she had gone to Rome only to help her son, who was destitute.

While nobody believed the story, nothing could be done except hold the princess, for the major questions were: How much had she known, and how much had she given away? There was some evidence that she might have betrayed to the Sicherheitsdienst data relating to an OSS intelligence team known as the Sweeney-Moscatelli mission, which was feared betrayed and captured.

The fact that the OSS was prepared to hold one of its own agents in no way placated the British, who feared that she had betrayed much valuable intelligence to the Germans. They made the strongest protest to the supreme Allied commander, General Wilson, and all secret intelligence operations behind enemy lines were frozen for a month until it became clearer what, if anything, the princess had known and could have passed to the Germans.

British fears were strengthened when a group of Italian Fascist assassination agents were arrested, and it was established that their mission was to assassinate the army group commander General Sir Harold Alexander, the army commander General Mark Clark, and General Lucien Truscott. The British wanted to know whether these agents were in any way connected with Princess Pignatelli or with the organization referred to in Rahn's telegram.

The Pignatelli case created a crisis of confidence in the OSS by the British, one similar to that occurring over the Cereus affair in Istanbul, where the British were cutting relations with the OSS until it refurbished the security of its operators and operations.

The effect of that crisis, and of the British protest, was to strengthen the hand of James Murphy, chief of X-2, who had been recommending to Donovan that no agent be employed by the OSS in any part of the world who had not first been cleared by X-2. That recommendation was now adopted immediately, although not in time to quiet British concerns about the ease with which Princess Pignatelli had penetrated the OSS. Nor were the British concerns unjustified about both Princess Pignatelli and about the OSS during that phase of the war, for at the end of the war the head of X-2 in Italy, James Jesus Angleton, who was to become head of CIA counterespionage, having seen the German intelligence services' documentation on the Italian campaign, reported:

> Though the name Pignatelli has been the subject of considerable controversy and did result in a most unfortunate death—OSS agent Paul Polletti [sic]— recent information obtained from the captured GIS [German Intelligence Service] officials Herbert Kappler, former police attaché at the German Embassy to the Quirinale in Rome, and Helmut Haeusgen, reveals that Princess Pignatelli in fact did come through the lines on behalf of Polletti and revealed considerable information to [Franz] Land of the GIS, General [Artur] Maeltzer, and proceeded on to Mussolini and [Francesco] Barracu [undersecretary in Mussolini's Fascist government]. . . .[6]

In the end Princess Pignatelli was not reinterrogated and was charged with no crime, although Murphy would state that she had played the major role in the betrayal to the Germans of Tompkins's mission in Rome. The reason is not evident, but it is presumed that by the time action could be taken the Allies no longer had jurisdiction in the case. In any event, with the cold war beginning in Italy the Allies had other, fresher matters to occupy their attentions, thereby permitting the princess to spend the rest of her days in that state of gracious penury peculiar to Florentine princesses of the period.

Too, Angleton's report showed that the British had reason to threaten to cut connection with OSS Italy until its security improved, as they did at Istanbul over the Cereus affair. German intelligence service officers interrogated by Angleton's X-2 detachment claimed the capture during the Italian campaign of some 260 Allied agents—agents of both British and American services—who had been trained in not only espionage but also wireless telegraphy (WT). The Germans captured about fifty wireless sets some of which, they claimed, were successfully doubled and played back to feed false information to the Allied High Command. Also, they claimed to have captured a further 600 agents of the low-grade, line-crossing variety. At least some of the WT agents—the most important—were betrayed to the Germans by Princess Pignatelli, and she certainly contributed to very severe losses.

On the other hand, a chart in the Donovan papers shows that the enemy intelligence services did not escape lightly. Although it does not claim to display solely OSS counterespionage operations, it does claim that 30 enemy agents were executed for espionage by the Allies, a further 675 were apprehended, and 3,575 were identified—an indication of the scale of clandestine warfare that accompanied the military campaign in Italy.[7]

Moreover, even this impressive testament to the skill of OSS X-2 in Italy appears to have been an understatement, probably because the map was drawn before the size of its victory over the German intelligence services had been fully computed. The citation for the award of the Legion of Merit to James Jesus Angleton asserts that between October 28, 1944, and December 4, 1945, while he was commanding officer of the special counterintelligence units of X-2 in the Mediterranean theater, he directed operations which enabled his units "to apprehend over one thousand enemy intelligence agents." That triumph—and triumph it was —was realized through the "dissemination of clear, concise, and comprehensive descriptive material in a form originated by him." While the nature of the "descriptive material" used to capture the enemy agents was not revealed, most, if not all, owed their predicament to ISOS, the cryptanalyzed intercepts of the German intelligence services' secret wireless traffic.

But Angleton's triumph was still in the future. In the short term the Tompkins, Pignatelli, Poletti, and other affairs all produced a miasma of

OSS inefficiency and unreliability that was not ignored by those responsible for the security of operations at Allied forces headquarters. To the contrary, that reputation produced the most serious attack on the OSS since Ambassador Hayes's assaults.

The Tompkins affair revealed a serious state of affairs within Secret Intelligence in Italy, for it showed that as a result of Eddy's lack of firm control, three different, competing services had been allowed to grow, all intensely involved in the politics of the troubled, defeated country. Donovan was not unaware of this, for Donald Downes, who had commanded one of the intelligence factions, told him at the Salerno beachhead much of what he wrote subsequently: that the OSS command in Italy was confused, inexperienced, and incompetent and that "the quality of those directing OSS *in the field* was appallingly low."[8]

Donovan's reaction to Downes's and others' warnings and complaints was to appoint Colonel Edward Glavin, a military man, to command in the Italian theater, but the appointment did not become effective quickly enough to forestall a most serious attack on OSS. Hitherto the attacks on the agency had concerned its competence; the new attack concerned its competence and its honesty.

On April 15, 1944, ten days after Donovan was informed that the OSS had lost Station Vittorio, Glavin wired him that the deputy supreme commander and commanding general of U.S. forces in Italy, General Jacob L. Devers, had "demanded" a "thorough accounting of unvouchered funds," a "briefing concerning the utilization of funds," and information concerning "the sort of account the men give when they come back of the funds expended in the field." Devers had also "demanded" to see the authority for "every single expenditure" authorized by the OSS in Italy and had asked to "view each voucher." There was talk, Glavin warned Donovan, that the general wanted to call in the Army's inspector general to "peruse the books for checking on the foregoing points" and that for the time being responsibility for the investigation had been given by Devers to General Ben J. Caffey, American head of the Special Operations section at Allied Forces Headquarters, the Allied controlling authority for much of the OSS's work in Italy.[9]

Glavin then reported he had advised Caffey that his orders from OSS Washington "did not allow accounting to anyone other than OSS" and asked Donovan to get the Joint Chiefs, the OSS's controlling authority, to advise Devers that it was known and understood in Washington that "our procedures and activities are utterly unlike the Army setup, are completely and regularly reviewed at your end, where all data of this sort is [*sic*] made accessible to the Joint Chiefs of Staff."

Donovan saw immediately that Devers's demand was a stake aimed at the heart of the OSS, not because there had been any great dishonesty or extravagance in Italy but because if the OSS met his demands, the confidentiality of OSS operations everywhere would be destroyed and the identities of those working for the OSS would be revealed. If met, the demand would also destroy a financial system that had been created with presidential and congressional authority and without which a secret service could not be operated. Donovan told Glavin to tell Devers that the OSS would not permit such an investigation and to provide Devers with a copy of the OSS's authority for maintaining a secret financial system.

Glavin wired back on April 25, 1944, that Caffey had accepted Donovan's point of view in regard to finances but had raised a specific matter that had been troubling the operational and fiscal sections of the OSS for some time: the question of the finances at the OSS base at Bari. Caffey had "requested" detailed information about these finances, but Glavin stated all he had been told was that the total expenditures at the base since its establishment seven months before had been $185,000. That had not satisfied Caffey, who wanted "an account of the controls that were applied in each disbursement." Glavin had assembled the information, but before he turned it over, he wanted Donovan's authority.

Donovan refused. He instructed Glavin again that he was not to show the OSS's books to anyone but authorized personnel. For Donovan the issue was not whether there had been dishonesty, extravagance, currency speculation, or carelessness in the way OSS secret funds had been used; the OSS had the means to check and discipline such conduct. The issue, again, was that to be effective, a secret service had to be secret in all respects to all except those within the government to whom it was responsible.

At length, Glavin succeeded in convincing Caffey and Devers of these points, and Devers made no further demands for the OSS's books. But the deeper issue remained: Why was Devers concerned about OSS finances? Why was he looking for trouble on such a sensitive issue? Or were his concerns legitimate? Devers himself supplied the answers at a meeting with Glavin. He had, he said, formed the opinion that the "OSS was expending greater sums than were warranted by the achievements."[10] He referred to the "numbers of agents, the quantity of vehicles and the installations of San Leuccio [sic] as instances of costly Italian operations whose results were dubious." He complained also that through some of the OSS's Italian agents there had been "leaks of information," and he made the "broad statement" that " 'Everybody is aware that OSS in Italy is extravagant.' "

As a result, Glavin went on to report to Donovan, Devers had made General Lyman L. Lemnitzer, the senior American officer at Allied army group headquarters in Italy, "responsible for OSS in Italy." As for finances, Devers had not made "any concrete allegations that irregularities existed in connection with expenditures" or that he had had "any particular or general suspicions that there had been any fraudulent activities or individual misappropriation," but he "intended to obtain high level control of our Italian operations." He intended also to "provide for authorization of disbursements in advance on the basis of plans which had already been approved, regularizing OSS operations with reference to the choice of agents, personnel, movements, transportation, billets, etc."

Devers had also made the "flat statement" that he believed the War Department had the right to examine OSS expenditures of secret funds. He intended to make another tour of inspection of Italy in about ten days, and while Devers had not been "antagonistic" and had stated he desired to see OSS Italy "function smoothly with sufficient control," his statements were "causing us anxiety." For that reason, Glavin advised Donovan, "we propose to make a careful investigation into the entire situation at once." He asked Donovan's permission to establish a board to "screen disbursements, agents and other operations."

Donovan approved, and after about six weeks Glavin wired that he had "finished an exhaustive survey of all activities of Italian SI and all other intelligence operations by our organization in Italy including a perusal of all report files and records . . . pertaining to security violations, agent chains, agents, political activities, expenditures, Branch and Staff Officer relationships, personnel rosters and plans to cope with future requirements."[11]

In a telegraphic summary of a long report sent to Donovan by pouch, Glavin advised that in effect there were two OSS intelligence services in Italy: the Italian SI section commanded by Vincent Scamporino, which was attached to the army group, and the OSS SI detachment operating with the U.S. Fifth Army. Although the former should have commanded the latter, Glavin stated, the separation had become "sharper rather than weaker as time went on," resulting in "growing confusion in intelligence activities" and "organizational confusion accompanied by progressive suspicion and personal animosity." Each unit performed "some very fine SI activities," although each had "committed errors."

The position was somewhat further complicated by the growth of semi-independent intelligence sections attached to corps and divisions. These often conducted operations into enemy territory without advising Scamporino. Scamporino's organization was "not responsible for the separation" that existed, and the Fifth Army detachment was "just as much responsible for placing Italian SI personnel altogether outside intelligence operations and planning"—Glavin's careful way of referring to the thorny allegations that certain OSS SI staff officers and agents had been meddling in Italian politics.

As for the performance of the Fifth Army detachment, of the three teams sent into enemy territory over a five-month period, one produced fair results, one excellent results, and one team was lost. One of the teams, the so-called Sweeney-Moscatelli group, had clashed with both the Italian Navy and British Intelligence, and the fate of the lost team was bound up in the "Pignatelli-Poletti case . . . which involved the British as much as ourselves." The conclusion to be drawn from these figures was that the Fifth Army detachment had not been very energetic or very successful, although in the month of June—after the investigation had begun—it had improved markedly, with a total of four chains and eleven teams operating in enemy territory.

Scamporino's organization had been more energetic and more successful. Twenty-two teams had been sent out "with Scamporino's people in them," and thirteen Scamporino teams had also been dispatched. Seven of those were "currently reporting, 1 of which is doubtful." They had furnished "helpful intelligence, despite the fact that they were separated from the [Fifth Army detachment] and had no suitable control or guidance." In all, Scamporino's casualties had been two teams "in the custody of" Tito in Yugoslavia and "4 teams were captured."

As for Scamporino's security, "There is no evidence in the records to show that a security problem was created at any time by Scamporino's men," although Glavin did discover "traces of political activities by [his men] as well as by others." There was a continuing problem in that regard, but it was now clear that "immediate disciplinary action, including dismissal in those cases which merit it, would attend any political operations by Italian SI personnel."

Glavin went on to report that Scamporino and the new commander of the Fifth Army detachment, Arthur J. Torrielli, "do not trust each other; however both of them are capable of making important and continuing contributions if combined in essential total coordination and integration." Their problems were "placed before them frankly and bluntly and their respective relationships, responsibilities, and functions" had now been established between them in detail.

In his fuller report, Glavin declared that operational security had been "poor," and what was called secret intelligence sometimes had been little more than information procured from newspapers and proclamations. There had been some evidence of political partiality in the decisions concerning distribution of war stores and money to guerrillas in the north of Italy, and there had been "little semblance of the use of proper command channels either up or down."[12]

On the staff level there had been "considerable bitterness, mistrust and suspicion" between the two principal groups, and there was evidence that some OSS officers had been "engaging in secret intelligence operations calculated to produce political results beyond the scope of OSS functions"—another of those careful remarks of Glavin's intended to draw Donovan's attention to the fact that certain American personnel of the left, right, and center had been trying to influence the political life of the liberated territories.

Glavin believed that Italian SI required closer supervision than before. Consequently, he had decided to move his headquarters from Algiers to Caserta at the earliest moment and control the Mediterranean from Italy rather than Algiers. Meanwhile, he had ordered the "complete integration of all intelligence activities into one clearly defined staff and branch organization," and all political activity had been "strictly forbidden henceforth." Glavin hoped that through these measures "a thoroughly unsatisfactory and potentially dangerous situation has been ended."

He ended by advising that he had not completed his investigation of the agent chains being sent into northern Italy from Bari and Brindisi, the so-called Goff chains, which constituted a third intelligence service. But Doering had seen enough. Acting in Donovan's absence, Doering arranged for Putzell to go to OSS Algiers and OSS Caserta and make a third investigation; it was evident that nobody engaged in operations in Italy could work efficiently and successfully and investigate the organizations with which they had to work at the same time.

Putzell soon cleaned the situation up, although he found considerable evidence that some OSS men were making fortunes, especially on the exchange rates between the Italian lire, the Algerian franc, the U.S. dollar, and the pound sterling. He discovered also that the trouble in Italy was not so much a matter of greed, rivalry, incompetence, and political meddling as of Eddy's poor employment policies just after Torch. To that state of affairs had to be added the consequences of the haste in which the Italian missions were put together. That had arisen because the Joint Chiefs had opposed military operations in Italy until forced to do so at the Quebec Conference in August 1943; and when the decision was made to invade Italy from Sicily, after all, no organization existed within the OSS to give intelligence support to those operations. Lastly, the Italian affair illuminated the practical effects of trying to put together a specialist intelligence service such as that needed after a war had actually broken out and when no cadres existed on which Donovan could have built.

Glavin had inherited a mess, and Tompkins's experiences had illuminated the mess. It remained to be seen how much of the mess had been reported back to departments in Washington that were anxious for a change in the command of the OSS, and were anxious also about the direction the intelligence community was taking under the cut and thrust of war.

33

Palace Revolt

Donovan arrived back in Washington from the Mediterranean front in early February 1944, having been absent with only brief periods back at headquarters ever since mid-September 1943. The prolonged absence, coupled with the news that he would soon be leaving on another protracted journey, this time to China and the Pacific theater, produced severe criticism within the highest ranks of the OSS. The five main critics were Admiral William H. Standley (former U.S. ambassador in Russia and now a member of the OSS Planning Group), General John Magruder (chief of all OSS intelligence services, including Secret Intelligence and Counterespionage), Major Lawrence Lowman (chief of OSS communications), Charles Cheston (the OSS deputy director), and Elmo Roper (a well-known pollster and adviser to Donovan on public opinion). On the fringes of what came to be called the Palace Revolt were also Colonel Ellery C. Huntington (chief of Special Operations) and W. Lane Rehm, head of Special Funds, an excellent man who hitherto had been devoted to WJD, both professionally and personally. Cheston, an ambitious peacetime financier and banker with Smith, Barney and J. P. Morgan, appears to have been the ringleader and tried to recruit Putzell, the assistant executive officer. Cheston was not successful, for Putzell was to recall: "I thought the matter took on some of the aspects of a junta, the object of which was to get rid of Donovan, either completely or by kicking him upstairs. Naturally, Donovan's replacement would have been Cheston."[1]

The Donovan papers show that the palace revolt found its earliest expression in a memo of August 23, 1943, while Donovan was in Quebec, floating his Balkan plan. Written by a humble gnome, George Platt, who was responsible for preparing a monthly report of OSS activities to Major Doering, the memo drew the attention of the OSS executive to what he called "a Deterioration of Morale in OSS." Platt thought there was evidence this was being caused by the fact that "no one in the organization, with the exception of those who are very close to the General, can put his finger on anything concrete that the organization has accomplished." Another reason was the disappearance of the "close family ties" that had bound the organization together at the beginning, when the agency was a "very small, closely knit family bristling with ideas, working at top speed to create a field organization," and doing in "six months what should have been organized 20 years ago."[2]

The new executives coming in, men such as Magruder, had not "grown up" in the OSS and were not aware of the "blood, sweat and tears" involved in the "recruiting, training, dispatching and protection of one single man." They had created an "impervious layer" between the medium-rank executives who had the day-to-day job of running operations and General Donovan. To bypass that "impervious layer" matters were being taken directly to Donovan. This was "bad organization" and caused friction. Also, Platt felt, the staff should be kept better informed of OSS achievements, and there should be a house organ to keep it informed of such achievements as were possible to talk about.

Donovan took this paper to heart, for he believed that staff morale was highly important, and he was especially impressed that a relatively minor figure in the agency thought enough of the organization to write to him about the problems.

The next memo came three days later. This time it came from Colonel Huntington, a person WJD liked and respected—Huntington was one of WJD's squash partners; he had served in World War I in France with the 78th Division's artillery; he was a southerner from Nashville, a product of Colgate and Harvard; and he was what Donovan called a "very high class type. He is a lawyer, a gentleman, and has a fine appearance and mental capacity."[3]

On August 23, 1943, Donovan had circulated a paper stating that he was "Raising our sights on equipment and manpower," that the "peanut whistle won't do when a fog horn is needed," and that the "shipping of 6 or 8 agents' [wireless] sets and 4 or 5 men to a theater now and then is simply not good enough." The declaration was followed by WJD's order to the military procurement authorities for 450 agents' wireless sets, 100 of them for OSS SI London, and 350 for Allied intelligence and special operations services to "strengthen our bargaining position with them."[4]

Commenting on that paper, Huntington explained that he was writing about the Special Operations (SO) position because the "altered military situation" demanded "more and more an 'offensive' attitude of mind" and, therefore, "the speeding up of action" and an understanding of the "increasing importance of political considerations," all of which "seem to warrant changes in OSS organization and technique." As Huntington continued, on April 1, 1943, OSS SO had a staff of 128 and 17 agents in the field, and on August 15, 1943, a staff of 909 and 387 agents in the field—a large expansion by OSS standards but small by those of the British. SO had been "late in having personnel ready for the Tunisian and Sicilian campaigns," but while the manpower position had improved, "a regroupment is necessary at the top" of the OSS, where there was "much duplication of effort" and a "dangerous lack of cohesion." With an organization of 4,500 men and women, rising rapidly to 14,000, Huntington thought these states of affairs must be overcome if the OSS were to become fully efficient. He therefore offered his resignation as deputy director of Special Operations because he felt he had become "supernumerary." In due course it was accepted, and Huntington went out to the Mediterranean to become chief of the OSS mission to Tito. But Huntington's memo did have an effect on WJD.

On August 30, 1943, Donovan brought up the twin questions of morale and operating efficiency at a meeting of his executive staff, whereupon the deputy chief of Special Operations, J. M. Scribner, immediately presented a plan and a chart—somebody was always preparing new charts in the OSS—for a major reorganization of the agency. The objective was to meet the twin needs of large new operational responsibilities and increased operational efficiency. Under this plan Donovan would become director general of the OSS with the actual work of running the agency being performed by a "director of staff" through a "director of theater operations." Donovan had no wish to be made a peer just yet, but he asked his executive committee "to make recommendations intended to improve the actual operations of OSS."[5] The committee was also instructed to look into the utility of creating a new post, director of plans and operations. Putzell was to recall: "The junta would have got the organizational changes they wanted but for the way they went about getting them. You don't catch flies with vinegar, and WJD saw instantly what was afoot when he saw their paper."[6]

The committee sat while Donovan was in Cairo on his Balkan plan, and its terms of reference, set by it, were:

(1) The immediate future usefulness of OSS in shortening the war. (2) The long-time possible usefulness of OSS as a permanent instrument of government. (3) The present size and diversity of OSS efforts. (4) The imperative need of an organization which will put into permanent form what has been found necessary in practice.[7]

The question WJD had asked it to look at—the utility of a director of plans and operations—was not addressed. Instead, it seemed the committee was trying to make as a matter of formal record its dissatisfaction with WJD's regime.

Prudently the authors of this memorandum omitted to sign it, although there is no doubt that they were Roper, Cheston, Standley, Lowman, Scribner, and Magruder—almost all of WJD's top executives, in fact, except Doering. The memo found that the present regime was that of a "holding company" because the agency had a "broad field of operations related to each other chiefly by reason of the fact that all report to the same Director." The authors then recommended that the OSS should *confine its future activities to those of intelligence, special and morale operations, and counterespionage, for it was only by concentrating its resources in this fashion that it "could better perform in the area of shortening this war and much better perform in the post war period"*(author's italics). The "tendency to accentuate the para-military (if not military) activities of the OSS is detrimental to its primary mission of Intelligence." It was believed that "the orthodox armed forces can and should have the responsibility for organized uniformed bodies such as OGs." Moreover, all other organizations now connected to the OSS but not concerned with its primary roles should be given to government departments concerned with their functions.

Referring evidently to allegations that OSS was FDR's private global and internal intelligence service, and to repeated complaints from General Strong at Military Intelligence that it was no more than WJD's intellectual plaything, the group said it believed the OSS "would function most effectively if it would confine itself primarily to intelligence activities of direct use for the military program, plus certain clearly defined subversive activities through S.O. and M.O. of a nature not now undertaken by any other Government agency." SO operations should be concerned only with "contact with an assistance to existing underground resistance groups and guerrilla units." These activities should include "the furnishing of supplies and funds, the organization of resistance activities and certain higher forms of subversion." These would be carried on by a "relatively few individuals of high caliber who would supply the necessary impetus but normally would not themselves directly engage in physical subversion."

Morale Operations "of a highly specialized and delicate nature involving subversion of individuals of prominence and power either through appeals to their patriotic aspirations or through subversive methods of other types, including bribery and morale subversion," should be undertaken. In addition, "certain allied activities of a marginal nature, such as the establishment of unorthodox political contacts," should be taken on, "activities which could not legitimately be carried on by the State Department."

·

If these limitations of functions were adopted, the committee believed:

the following advantages are foreseen: (1) OSS would be a closely knit organization, concentrating its best brains on intelligence and allied functions. (b) It would be operating in fields clearly not preempted by other government agencies, and this would avoid jurisdictional disputes. (c) It would avoid the embarrassment of undertaking operations which may exceed its limitations.

The authors concluded:

We have a morale problem within the agency, largely created by general dissatisfaction over the lack of clearcut lines of authority and responsibility; and we feel that if we are to continue to operate in so many fields, the adoption of such an administrative set-up as we have pictured, accompanied by the authority and responsibility we have outlined, will dissipate causes of the lowered morale, and will also permit the organization to operate in an efficient manner.

There followed a long paper dated October 2, 1943, while Donovan was in Cairo, setting forth a complete plan for the reorganization of the OSS. Again it was unsigned, but this time it appears to have come jointly from Assistant Director Cheston, who was ambitious for WJD's job; Elmo Roper, whose only interest appears to have been that in time and motion efficiency; Admiral Standley, who had lost much of the power and influence he had once enjoyed; and General Magruder, who was not ambitious but believed in the value of intelligence as a war-winning instrument.

The submission constituted brave papers to write, for they supported General Strong's memorandum to Marshall that OSS was a "hydra-headed organization" that no one would have formed if the job were to be undertaken again. It struck at the heart of WJD's concept of unorthodox warfare and sought to demolish the machine he had built. It implied considerable dissatisfaction with Donovan's administration and demonstrated that most of his principal lieutenants were opposed to his theories and practices. All this was serious, hence the term "Palace Revolt." Magruder's presence among the disaffected group was especially embarrassing, for he had been regarded as one of Donovan's stalwarts. At the same time there was nothing personal in this situation: WJD was liked and admired as a man. All that was deplored was his instinct for empire building and the empire he had built.

Magruder sent the paper to Doering, by nature a man of a few wise words. Doering saw the threat and wrote a twelve-page paper which was awaiting Donovan when he returned to Washington briefly in November on this and other business. As Doering pointed out, the principal proposal in the paper was the establishment of a post to be called director of operations. That man would be in reality "the Chief Executive, or President, of OSS," with Donovan acting as chairman and Buxton as vice-chairman.[8] In what was essentially a paper to explain what the junta was driving at, Doering made no recommendations about what Donovan's attitude should be. That was politic, for when WJD arrived back from Cairo in November, he wrote one of his rare, carefully modulated, but stinging retorts to the group's recommendation. Addressing the one-and-a-half page note to Magruder, Donovan began:

> 1. When I left, I asked Col. Buxton to designate a Committee to make recommendations to me concerning the functions and duties of an officer for Plans and Operations.
> 2. While I am glad to have the recommendations of any group or any committee of this organization, I would have preferred, first, that the question I asked would have been answered, and then if the Committee wished, it could go on with other suggestions.[9]

Dealing with the analogy of the holding company, Donovan asserted, "Whoever prepared that analogy knows nothing about a holding company," and then dwelt upon a complaint that the heads of branches had not been given sufficient responsibilities in the carrying out of their missions. "As a matter of fact," he asserted, "this is not true." Whatever "failure there has been has been the failure of the Branch Heads to meet their full responsibilities." As for the proposals, they constituted "one way of running the show, but it is not the way that considered experience over a period of months indicates is the best way to run it." According to Donovan, the OSS was not:

> a bank and should not be run as a bank. It is not a War Department and should not be run as that or as a Naval Department. It is made up of a diversity of units and while certain fundamental principles must be kept in mind the whole organization must be a flexible one to meet any particular ends, and so long as I have anything to say about it, it is not going to be wed to any particular scheme or put in any particular niche.

Donovan continued:

> I am prepared at any time to consider, in the interest of the whole organization, how and to what extent Deputy Directors or Special Assistants or whatever names may be given to highly placed officers who have the responsibility of cooperating with the Director in running the show may serve. But this report does not do it. . . .

Likewise, "under the theory of relieving the Director of detail, there is set up a Director of Operations who is given not only all of the duties previously performed by the Director, but many more besides." Concluding, Donovan found the entire proposal "not healthy" and "a doctrine to which I do not subscribe."

The note ended the Palace Revolt, but only for the moment. What was left unsaid was that Donovan's doctrine of special means would work only if he were at his desk to ensure that it did. It could not work, or at least efficiently, if he were absent half the time, as was the case at present. Then the burden fell upon Buxton. That aspect of the issue soon came to the fore.

One of Donovan's high officers, Hugh R. Wilson, a former ambassador to Germany (1938–39) and adviser to the secretary of state (1940), a career Foreign Service officer who had formed a very high opinion of Donovan, rejected Cheston's invitation to join the revolt. Instead, he wrote a warning letter to Donovan:

> The spirit and devotion of the men are admirable, their energy is beyond praise, but the organization has now grown to such a point that new expedients appear desirable. While you are here the situation is carried off by your genius for juggling ten glass balls in the air with your two hands. You can see innumerable people and thrive on it. You can even take home the papers that you have to read and read them until dawn, and what is more remarkable, you remember them. [However,] you are away constantly, and there is every reason you should continue to be. Each trip is a marked gain for this show which we would never make if you did not take the field.[10]

Donovan's absences left Deputy Director Ned Buxton in command, noted Wilson, and "Ned has none of your ability as a prestidigator [sic]. He thinks more slowly. He thinks honestly and sanely. His final judgment is sound as wheat." The problem with Buxton was that he had not Donovan's energy. "Ned gets dreadfully tired," Wilson went on. "I have seen him late in the evenings when I was deeply concerned for him. He had to see dozens of people during the day. He had to make decisions more quickly than he would have preferred, and to top it—a bale of papers waited to be taken home and mastered."

Wilson "begged" Donovan to form a small staff of men, "each vested with genuine and definite authority in a given area of activities." Then "Ned can hold his conferences, issue his decisions, be sure that they are carried out because each person in the room has the authority to carry them out." Such a system would be "sound military practice, based on centuries of experience in administration and command of men." It was a practice that had "grown from the discovery that most men, the normal men perhaps, function at [their] best when [they deal] with relatively few people in [their] command, no matter how large that command may be."

The pressures on Donovan to change his method of running the OSS were mounting, and he did give much thought to how the directorship should function. But for the moment he issued none of the clear-cut directives for which his staff had been asking.

As Putzell was to recall, the situation contained all the ingredients of the dispute that was to bedevil the United States intelligence community for almost four decades to come: whether the United States should have several small, elitist organizations each undertaking one of the main branches of intelligence. Or whether there should be one large organization for all special means. The junta believed in the former; WJD, in the latter. The issue was beclouded by other, lesser, temporary factors: WJD's restlessness; Cheston's ambitiousness. But that was the principal issue.

While criticism of WJD's administrative capability was implied, the reality was that his organization was beginning to work efficiently, despite his absences. But now WJD embarked on one journey too many.

In April 1944, with D-Day in Europe only eight weeks away and much to be done to make the OSS ready for the supreme venture of World War II, Donovan elected to go out to the Pacific theater for the invasion of Hollandia, Dutch New Guinea, by the forces of General Douglas MacArthur. The purpose of the journey is clear from the Donovan papers. Ever since 1942 WJD and his agency had been excluded from Pacific operations by MacArthur, not because Donovan's old World War I commander and co-founder of the American Legion had anything against Donovan and the OSS, but because his intelligence staff led by General Charles Willoughby and Colonel R. F. Merle-Smith believed there was nothing the OSS could do in the Pacific that their own organization could not do better.

On two occasions Donovan had sent prominent emissaries to MacArthur's headquarters, and each time it had seemed that MacArthur would permit OSS to operate in his theater—until Willoughby and Merle-Smith were consulted. At that point negotiations always collapsed in a welter of prevarication which added up to a single conclusion: Willoughby and Merle-Smith did not want the OSS in their theater, where their authority over all intelligence was absolute. In the case of Willoughby it is probable that his attitude was an offshoot of the 1942–43 quarrels with Strong; in the case of Merle-Smith it was thought in the OSS that there was something personal—Merle-Smith's father had been one of WJD's battalion commanders in the Fighting 69th in World War I.

Now Donovan had decided to go to MacArthur's headquarters personally, at MacArthur's invitation, to see whether he could get the OSS working in the Southwest Pacific theater of operations through man-to-man conversations with the supreme Allied commander. WJD set out on April 2, 1944. He was accompanied as far as Pearl Harbor by Putzell—

and reignited the Palace Revolt as he was leaving. Putzell later recollected: "We were in the train at Union Station at Washington, on our way to Chicago . . . where we were to pick up an aircraft going to Pearl Harbor and Australia. The train was about to pull out when an OSS courier arrived with a pouch. I signed for the pouch, opened it, and inside was a letter for the general. At his request I opened it and it was a letter from Cheston and Magruder and the other members of the junta, *insisting* that the general approve their plan for a reorganization of OSS and that WJD accept the post of director general—chairman of the board, so to speak.

"I gave the letter to Donovan without comment, and he started to read it. There were no fireworks, but I could see him get madder and madder —he was a man who kept his feelings under firm control, but on occasions he would grunt, snort, and his eyes would flash. Then you knew he was mad. Then he put the letter down and announced that he was going to stop the train—we were getting up speed between Washington and Baltimore by this time—and deal with these fellows once and for all.

"Well, I thought that unwise and I said so. The general asked me what I would do about it. I told him I would wait until we got to Chicago and then call and read them the riot act. I might even fire one or two. By now the train was beyond Baltimore and we were in open country, and I wondered how, if the general decided to get off the train, we were going to get transport. He must have thought about that, too, for he said he would do just that—wait until we got to Chicago and then read them the riot act. Then he took his papers and went off to his stateroom.

"Next morning, when we were in Chicago, he went to an office and called the men concerned and gave them both barrels. I don't suppose any of them had received such blasts in their adult lives. But he didn't fire anybody. Instead, he promoted Cheston to the rank of deputy director. After that, when the general and Buxton were absent—and Buxton's absences through sickness were becoming more and more frequent— Cheston became acting director and signed himself as such in letters to the President and the Joint Chiefs.

"The reason for this sudden flare-up was, of course, that D-Day was close, the junta felt that Donovan's place was at his desk and that there was an enormous amount to do, and they felt, too, that the position in the Southwest Pacific could and should be handled by one of WJD's lieutenants.

"But Cheston never became director of OSS."[11]

To counterbalance Cheston, Donovan appointed Doering to new key committees. T. J. McFadden, who was now in the OSS, later stated: "What really happened was that he gave Doering the job of minding the store while he was away. Colonel Doering became Donovan's watchdog, the man responsible for keeping the objectives and mandates of OSS in mind, stopping people from starting operations and making expenditures that were not consistent with the OSS charter, and even, on occasions, acting as the OSS's conscience. And it seemed to us that Doering became the only man Donovan really trusted inside the Kremlin"[12]—the nickname for OSS headquarters.

Donovan also appointed Lieutenant Colonel Oliver Jackson Sands, the officer involved in the Tito headquarters investigation, assistant deputy director; McFadden became acting chief of the Pacific and Far Eastern sections of the OSS; another of Donovan's law partners, James R. Withrow, was appointed Pacific area operations officer; Putzell was readied for the post of executive officer in succession to Doering, who was to become an assistant director; and James B. Donovan, a leading lawyer (and no relative), was made general counsel.

In all Donovan made or confirmed thirty-two appointments, most of them suggested by Doering and all intended to strengthen Donovan's command. The effect was to bring about a degree of smoother, more efficient working and to enable WJD not only to prepare for operations in Europe and Asia but also to help him in what had become his ambition: to establish what he called the postwar central intelligence service.

Yet WJD's action in choosing *this* time to go to MacArthur's headquarters was inexplicable, for OSS SI, the cornerstone of Donovan's empire, was in difficulties everywhere on the eve of what would be the emotional and strategical climax of World War II—Neptune D-Day. Donovan was correct in believing that he alone could persuade MacArthur to allow the OSS to operate in his theater, but such was the influence of Willoughby and Merle-Smith over MacArthur that Donovan achieved no more than the previous emissaries. He was well received aboard MacArthur's headquarters ship at the assault on Hollandia, but the only thing he achieved was to persuade MacArthur to use OSS frogmen. He failed to get MacArthur to use SI, SO, MO, and Research and Analysis at all.

PART FOUR

THE OVERLORD PERIOD

Being the account of Donovan's significant operations in Western, Central, and Eastern Europe, the Balkans, and the Mediterranean in support of Allied military operations in Europe in 1944

34

Neptune*

On May 12, 1944, Ruth Donovan wrote in her diary: "Bill celebrated Patricia's birthday today as Bill is off for overseas again—Ned Buxton here and gave her two silver wings." That was all. Donovan did not say where he was going, nor could he, and he did not say when he would return. He was, in fact, bound for London and Neptune and Dragoon, the Allied invasions of Europe across the beaches of Normandy and Provence, the culmination of the Arcadia plan.

---

*Throughout this volume the author has used the official and actual rather than the popular World War II code words for the Allied invasions of France in 1944. Moreover, for their definitions he has relied on the U.S. official history dealing with the Anglo-American invasion of Northwest Europe in 1944. That volume is: Gordon A. Harrison, *Cross-Channel Attack* (Washington, D.C.: Office of the Chief of Military History, Department of the Army, 1950).

In the glossary Harrison offers the following definitions: "Overlord": "Plan for the invasion of northwest Europe, spring 1944"; "Neptune": "Actual 1944 operations within *Overlord*"; "Anvil": "The planned 1944 Allied invasion of southern France in the Toulon-Marseille area"; "Dragoon": "Allied invasion of southern coast of France, 15 August 1944, planned under the code name *Anvil*."

In his official volume, *Strategic Planning for Coalition Warfare 1943–1944* (Washington, D.C.: Office of the Chief of Military History, Department of the Army, 1959), author Maurice Matloff offers some further elucidation regarding the code names "Anvil" and "Dragoon." "Anvil" was the "Early plan for invasion of southern France," while "Dragoon" was "The final codename for invasion of southern France."

Thus, in *The Last Hero* "Overlord" is used as the code word for the invasion plan, for the concept of the invasion. "Neptune" is used for the actual naval and military operations. "Anvil" is not used at all, its having been superseded by the word "Dragoon."

The author recognizes that a popular misconception has arisen in which "Overlord" was

Well before daybreak the next day Donovan came down to the lobby of the St. Regis Hotel in New York. Waiting for him were Intrepid and one of Donovan's assistants, Lieutenant Charles A. Bane, USNR. The three men were driven out to the Military Air Transport Service terminal at La Guardia Airport. There they joined ATS Flight 107, and by 6:30 A.M. the Skymaster transport was at 5,000 feet over Long Island and setting course for Bluie West 8, Greenland, the first port of call on the eighteen-hour flight. Donovan had brought with him Winston Churchill's great literary work, the biography of his ancestor, John Churchill, first duke of Marlborough, captain general of the forces in the reign of Queen Anne. Donovan discovered a description of the events of the War of the Spanish Succession that paralleled the situation at this moment in the history of the Second World War:

> We have now reached the culmination of the eighteenth century world war, and also of this story. . . . We have witnessed a spectacle, so moving for the times in which we live, of a league of twenty-six signatory states successfully resisting and finally overcoming a mighty coherent military despotism. It was a war of the circumference against the centre. . . . Thus the circle of quaking states and peoples, who had almost resigned themselves to an inevitable overlordship, became a ring of fire and steel, which in its contractions wore down and strangled their terrible foe.

Here in a paragraph were not only John Churchill's strategy and tactics in the war of 1701–14 but Winston Churchill's in the war of 1939–44— the strategy and tactics of which Donovan had been, and remained, the leading American advocate. As in 1701, when the British government and John Churchill raised a coalition of states against Louis XIV of France, so it had been on New Year's Day 1942, when representatives of twenty-

---

believed to be the code word for the Normandy invasion, "Anvil" for the Provence invasion. He recognizes also that even major historical figures of the period—men such as Churchill —used these terms.

Nevertheless, they were used inaccurately. The reason for this modest historical muddle is evident: German intelligence successes against the Allies. Both Overlord and Anvil were compromised late in 1943, the former through the German penetration of the British Embassy at Ankara, the latter through, it is believed, German cryptanalytical successes against Allied ciphers, coupled with a breach of security involving the Gaullist French at Algiers.

The compromises were detected, and "Overlord" and "Anvil" were replaced by "Neptune" and "Dragoon" as code words for actual military operations. However, both "Overlord" and "Anvil" had been so widely used before they were compromised that they continued in use, even at high levels, often with the encouragement of the Allied deception and security agencies working to protect the actual code words. Consequently the terms crept into history and into the terminology of the war.

The far more secret—and accurate—terms of "Neptune" and "Dragoon" were never detected by the Germans, and they were known to far fewer people than "Overlord" and "Anvil." Consequently "Neptune" and Dragoon" did not become part of the invasion terminology.

six states had gathered at the White House to sign the Declaration of the
United Nations, thereby establishing the Grand Alliance against Hitler
and the Axis and pledging themselves to destroy the New Order in
Eurasia and not to make peace separately.

Then, as now, the most powerful fleets and armies had been assembled. Then, as now, the world was in revolt against a "mighty coherent
military despotism." The difference between the two events was that
whether the Grand Alliance would triumph in its "war of the circumfer-
ence against the centre" and whether the Allies would succeed in their
purpose, to wear down and strangle "their terrible foe" were yet to be
decided.

The greatest test would be the greatest operation of the world war,
Neptune, and its associated operation in the south of France, Dragoon.
But Ruth Donovan knew nothing of all this. So secret were the details of
the operation, and even the fact it was taking place, that Donovan had not
been permitted even to tell her where he was going or what he would be
doing. So as Donovan's Skymaster was plodding across the North Atlantic on the mission that would be the supreme moment of his career, Ruth
worked in her garden, wrote checks, played poker with her friends the
Greenhalghs, and retired after having written in her diary: "Heard nothing from Bill."[1]

The same day the Washington columnist Frank C. Waldrop wrote:
"The red hot story going around is that Donovan will soon be promoted
to lieutenant general and given such sweeping powers as to make his
rivals green around the gills."[2] At the moment WJD had few rivals.
Strong, Berle, and Hayes—all had gone, or were going, to jobs unconnected with the Washington intelligence world.

Donovan was supreme.

On the eve of the great battle WJD's staff strength was just under
11,000 men and women; it would reach its peak strength of 16,000 by
November 1944. Of the 11,000, some 2,400 were in the British Isles for
Neptune, with another 2,000 in Cairo, Algiers, and Caserta for Dragoon.
A man who by nature never stopped learning, WJD had learned a great
deal from the troubles during the Zeppelin preparatory operations, and
his command structure—which, it will be remembered, had not existed
three years before—gave the impression of being excellent and tightly
controlled everywhere except OSS SI Italy. Donovan's communications
and financial systems, two of the principal keys to good secret service,
were excellent. Serious flaws had emerged in the recruitment and training program of agents for service in France, and more than half the men
and women sent to London for final preparation for active service had to
be rejected. OSS London thought the quality of the rejects a "national
embarrassment,"[3] but the flaws had been caught in time. New disciplines

and a greater awareness of the responsibilities and dangers of being secret agents on active service were now better understood, and an outstanding crop of agents reached London and Algiers in time for acceptance as operational field agents.

Nationally there seemed to be every confidence in Donovan and his organization. On May 27, 1944, Buxton telegraphed to Donovan the joyful news that the "House of Representatives today voted $57,000,000 appropriation for coming year"—the largest budget so far but one that was really only a third of the annual cost of the OSS in real terms, the balance being paid by the armed services. Buxton reported in the same telegram that "Debate on floor of House revealed full confidence in your leadership."[4] As satisfactory was Buxton's statement that the OSS "is only agency both to receive increase and to be granted entire estimated budget."

Militarily there was also reason for confidence in the future. As Buxton reported in the same wire, the Military Appropriations Committee, which had asked all theater commanders for an opinion about the OSS's usefulness in the field (a matter of potential danger for Donovan's organization in the light of General Devers's recent complaints about OSS extravagance and lack of security in Italy) had received a confidential letter from the vice chief of staff, General Joseph T. McNarney, which stated the theater commanders intended to make "increased and important use" of the OSS in military operations and that it was "now performing essential functions overseas."

For many months during the pre-Neptune period Donovan had fretted at his inability to get arms to the maquis (French resistance) at a time when the British were launching ten sorties to every one launched by the OSS. Much of that imbalance was due to the attitude of the Joint Chiefs toward aircraft: Except for three planes operating from North Africa, the U.S. Army Air Forces were unwilling to embark on a large-scale supply program because, they said, it would divert many aircraft from the more valuable task of bombarding German targets. Indeed, so small was the OSS program that an American political officer at Algiers, Edwin C. Wilson, advised the secretary of state in January 1944 that the "situation was fraught with military, psychological, and political dangers."[5]

With some 50,000 Frenchmen already in the maquis, and perhaps triple that number in the process of joining, the movement represented a reasonably large cadre upon which the forces of the national insurrection could be formed when the time came. With the insurrection in mind the French leader in exile, Charles de Gaulle, complained to Churchill about the Allied supply program.

By February 1944 the British were carrying out their commitment with the utmost vigor and were reported to Donovan as giving very high priority to the undertaking. While the Joint Chiefs had supplied a small number of transport aircraft to Special Forces Headquarters, the Eisenhower organization that was to be the instrument of the national insurrection, Donovan's efforts to get the Joint Chiefs and General Arnold at least to equal the British effort were not successful.

In March 1944 the disproportion between the British and the American efforts was so great—ten to one—that French officials in Algiers and London were reported to believe that not only was the undertaking entirely British, but the United States was opposed to arming the French underground for political reasons—the Joint Chiefs were afraid of providing arms and munitions to the Communists, who might use them in the civil war that all feared would break out in France after Neptune.

Donovan, stung by these baseless allegations, went to see Secretary of State Cordell Hull in Washington, and Hull, perceiving the dangers to Franco-American postwar relations, talked to the Joint Chiefs about the matter. On April 17, 1944, General Marshall sent Hull a memorandum which, he hoped, would dispel "any impression that may exist that the U.S. is less aware than the British of the potential importance of the French Resistance groups, and less willing than the British to utilize the very valuable aid the underground can render to our operations."[6]

Marshall explained, first, that the committee organized in London by Churchill to attend to the problems of arming the French was, according to Eisenhower, working "in full cooperation with and under the general supervision of " Eisenhower. The supplies sent to the resistance were in large part provided by the United States, and Marshall reminded Hull that as part of the Torch agreements the United States had been engaged for some months in equipping a new French Army that was "comparable in size to our own peace-time army." In that undertaking, Marshall reported, the British had made no substantial contribution.

Hull, therefore, expressed satisfaction with America's contribution to the French resistance and armed forces—until, on April 21 in Algiers, De Gaulle made a statement at a press conference in which he publicly thanked the British for their work in supplying arms to the underground, ignoring the contribution made by the United States. The statement drew a letter from Donovan in which he warned that his "operational nuclei" —Jedburghs* and OGs—might lose their authority and thus their ability to command the maquis unless steps were taken immediately to ensure that the United States was seen to be supplying the résistants.

*The Jedburghs' task was to parachute into France before, during, and after D-Day to arm and train the French resistance bands and then, by means of wireless with London, to bring the entire French resistance movement under the orders of the supreme Allied commander, General Eisenhower. There were more than 150 of these three-man teams, the main focus of their operation was in Brittany, and their accomplishments ranked with some of the most valorous episodes of World War II. Approximately two-fifths of the Jedburghs were commanded by Donovan.

Donovan felt that De Gaulle's statement could not go unanswered, and Hull did draft a letter to De Gaulle. But it was not sent when Eisenhower in London wired Marshall that he had taken the matter into his own hands and had allocated thirty-two four-engine aircraft to Special Forces Headquarters, against the twenty-two British—although, as Eisenhower did point out, the British had made a supplementary allotment of aircraft totaling sixty-five machines a month. Thereupon the Joint Chiefs made plans to increase the number of machines allotted to the supply of underground movements to fifty-seven four-engine aircraft.

Under Donovan's prodding, by mid-May the American effort had substantially increased, and the OSS had begun to deliver 500 loads regularly, each load consisting of twelve parachutable containers holding four machine guns with 17,000 rounds, forty-four rifles and 6,600 rounds, fifty-five submachine guns with 17,400 rounds, 144 hand grenades, 140 pounds of plastic explosive with fuses and sabotage devices, 200 first-aid kits, fifty pounds of packaged food, and fifty pounds of clothing, blankets, and shoes.

Donovan had begun to play what was his strongest card: American industrial capacity. But as the arms began to flood into France, he was to learn a fundamental lesson of clandestinity: The wise spymaster does not expect, nor does he receive, gratitude or reward.

The spring of 1944, while Donovan toured OSS establishments in the British Isles as they prepared for Neptune, Britain was a nation of subdued fears. Armed with viceregal powers never before conceded to a foreigner except after the Norman Conquest in 1066, General Eisenhower turned England into a security state to protect the secrets of Neptune. The French Channel coast became a mysterious, a menacing, and, to many, a frightening place known as the Far Shore. All knew that soon the Allied armies would cross the Channel to the Far Shore, but those who knew when the operation would start and where the armies would land were few in number—not more than fifty men in the world. It was prayed that none was German.

The German propaganda services, which were far more competent at planting ideas in minds than the Allies admitted, heightened the sense of mystery and menace by creating the notion that their first lines of defenses, the *Atlantikwall*, were invincible and that they would set the Channel afire when the Allied fleets appeared. They created a specter of terrifying military, technological, and scientific power at their command: armies of nearly 2,000,000, equipped with immense tanks, defended in the air by jet fighters and bombers equipped with rocket-controlled glider bombs and missiles; an armory of terrible weapons that included death rays mounted on Alpine peaks, bacteriological bombs that spread laporides and tularemia, mines that spread radioactive dust, fleets of hydrogen-peroxide submarines, and even nuclear weapons. Churchill was said to have had nightmares in which the Channel became clogged with corpses.

In a letter to a friend, Eisenhower described how "tension grows and everybody gets more on edge. This time, because of the stakes involved, because we have all our chips on one number, the atmosphere is probably more electric than ever before."[7] And the Chief of the Imperial General Staff, Field Marshal Sir Alan Brooke, confided to his diary: "I am very uneasy. . . . At the very best it will fall so very far short of the expectations of the bulk of the people, namely all those who know nothing about the difficulties. At the worst it may well be the most ghastly disaster of the whole war. I wish to God it were safely over."[8]

In that atmosphere of anxiety and fear, when all were hypnotized by the mysterious enemy on the Far Shore, the invincible Wehrmacht, Dulles sent the most important signals of his career as WJD's spymaster at Bern.

In the last weeks before Neptune Agent 512—Hans Bernd Gisevius, Dulles's contact with the German intelligence service and military High Command—delivered a report that showed that the Germans might not be so powerful, so resolute as many people believed and feared. On April 7, 1944, Dulles reported to Donovan that Gisevius had brought a message from the Black Orchestra, in which the conspirators stated that "Germany's position is fast coming to a head and that the conclusion of hostilities in Europe can definitely be seen." Gisevius's principals—Canaris and his colleagues—were therefore "now willing and prepared to start action to oust the Nazis and eliminate the Fuhrer."[9]

Dulles reported that those principals claimed to be "the only group able to profit by a personal approach to Hitler and other Nazi chiefs, and with enough arms to accomplish their ends." They were also "the only ones in Germany with enough power in the army and with certain active army chiefs to make the coup feasible." The condition on which the conspirators were prepared to act was that the "Anglo-Saxon powers give assurances that, once the Nazis have been overthrown, the group may negotiate directly with the Western Powers about practical action necessary." They were "especially anxious" that they should not have to negotiate with Moscow and that "dealings" be confined to London and Washington.

The group was, Dulles continued, "rather conservatively minded, although willing to cooperate with any available elements of the Left, barring the Communists." They were motivated by "an ardent wish to keep Central Europe from coming under the sway of the Soviets, factually and ideologically. They feel certain that in the latter case democracy and Christian culture and all their accompanying benefits would vanish in

Europe, and that there would merely be a switch from the current Nazi totalitarianism to the new totalitarianism of the radical left."

Donovan immediately sent that telegram to the President, the secretary of state, the Joint Chiefs, and Eisenhower. Strangely it produced little interest, although a British contact with the Black Orchestra, Otto John, reported much the same as Gisevius had told Dulles.

Then, in the first half of April, Dulles's principal informant, George Wood, appeared in Switzerland with no fewer than 200 most secret telegrams, consisting of some 400 pages. After interviewing Wood about conditions in Germany and at Hitler's headquarters, Dulles read the documents and found them astonishingly revealing, although the Boston Series committee in Washington had still to endorse Wood as a reliable informant. Nevertheless, Dulles showed his satisfaction with Wood and his information with this radio message to Donovan on April 12, 1944:

> Sincerely regret that you are unable at this time to view Wood's material as it stands without condensation and abridgement [sic]. In some 400 pages, dealing with the internal maneuverings of German diplomatic policy for the past two months, a picture of imminent doom and final downfall is presented. Into a tormented General Headquarters and a half-dead Foreign Office stream the lamentations of a score of diplomatic posts. It is a scene wherein haggard Secret Service and diplomatic agents are doing their best to cope with defeatism and desertion of flatly defiant satellites and allies and recalcitrant neutrals. The period of secret service and diplomacy under Canaris and the champagne salesman [i.e., Ribbentrop] is drawing to an end. Already Canaris has disappeared from the picture, and a conference was hurriedly convoked in Berlin at which efforts were made to mend the gaping holes left in the Abwehr. Unable now to fall back on his favorite means of avoiding disconcerting crises by retiring to his bed, Ribbentrop has beat a retreat to Fuschl and retains a number of principal aides at Salzburg. The remainder of the Foreign Office is strung out all the way between Reisengebirge and the capital. Practically impossible working conditions exist in the latter, and bombing shelters are frequently used for code work. Once messages have been deciphered, a frantic search begins to locate the specific service or minister to which each cable must be forwarded; and, when a reply is called for, another search is required to deliver this to the right place. . . .
>
> The final death-bed contortions of a putrefied Nazi diplomacy are pictured in these telegrams. The reader is carried from one extreme of emotions to the other, from tears to laughter, as he examines these messages and sees the cruelty exhibited by the Germans in their final swan-song of brutality toward the peoples so irrevocably and pitifully enmeshed by the Gestapo after half a decade of futile struggles. . . .[10]

If this was true, Germany was falling apart and, far from the Channel's running red with blood, as Churchill believed it might, the Allies might get ashore with minimal casualties.

Confident of Dulles and Wood, the OSS accorded this highly encouraging and optimistic document an A evaluation (Al was reserved for Ultra and other incontestable intelligence, and the scale ran from A1 to F6). It then circulated the opinion widely, to the President, the Joint Chiefs, the secretaries of state, war, and the Navy, Eisenhower, the entire Allied intelligence hierarchy, and such British government personalities as Churchill and Eden. It was without doubt the most dramatic telegram of the period, but it did not correspond with the British opinion of the situation within Germany. Dulles's telegram was promptly challenged in both London and Washington as giving a dangerously inaccurate and hopeful appreciation of the actual situation within Germany.

Buxton wired Dulles to ask him whether he wished to modify the opinions expressed in his telegram of the twelfth. Dulles wired back, according to Buxton;

(1) He sees no reason to change or modify his earlier message as a description of the current Nazi diplomatic and political scene, and (2) That though his evaluation is derived most immediately from the material recently received by him, and from conversations with one tried informant, he has received other similar reports from other well-proven informants in the same strain, and background data available to him in Berne supports his views.

Dulles did add, Buxton continued in a note to the President, that:

. . . his message should not be read as indicating that the morale of the Nazi army is nearing collapse (except probably the so-called Gross Deutscher, Slav and other non-German elements). Nor does he think that any important Nazi military officials are ready and willing to let us come in through the West unopposed. He believes, rather, that fierce opposition may be given to any invasion attempt. A collapse of Germany might follow, however, a few months after the establishment of a firm toe-hold in the West.

Dulles had concluded:

The timing of the invasion attempt may be all important. The German people are war-weary and apathetic, and even in Nazi circles the same kind of psychological impression can be seen as appeared last August and September. Yet if they could stabilize the Russian front once more, they might catch a second wind, and put up an even stronger defense against invasion.[11]

Dulles was to regret, perhaps, that he was so emphatic about the endorsement he gave his message of the twelfth, especially his declarations that there were probably not any Nazi military officials prepared to come to terms with the Western powers and that an invasion might meet fierce opposition. Dulles had never thought much of the Black Orchestra, but some of the most interesting and important political developments of the war were in train at Berlin to render his opinion premature.

On May 13, 1944, Gisevius followed through with a second, even more dramatic proposal, one resembling that made to the OSS in Istanbul by Count von Moltke at the turn of 1943–44. As Dulles wired a few hours after Donovan had left Washington for London and Neptune, the Black Orchestra stood "ready to help our armed units get into Germany under the condition that we agree to allow them to hold the Eastern Front."[12]

In view of the anxiety and nervousness in London and Washington about the outcome of Neptune, this latest telegram caused considerable interest, for the conspirators proposed:

> (1) 3 allied parachute divisions to land in the Berlin region with the assistance of the local army commanders. (2) Amphibian landing operations of major proportions either at or near Bremen and Hamburg along the German coast. (3) The isolation in Obersalzburg of Hitler and high Nazi officials by trustworthy German units posted in the Munich region. (4) Although the preliminary plans for landings on the French coastline will be difficult to formulate, since they can not count on [Field Marshal Erwin] Rommel [the commander of the German army group on the Channel coast] for any cooperation, the above plan will normally be followed by such landings [sic].

Dulles went on to report:

> This same opposition group is reported to feel that the War has been lost, and that the last hope of preventing the spread of Communism in Germany is the occupation of as large a section of Europe as possible by the Americans and the British, and that helping our armed forces enter Germany before the fall of the East Front is the only possible means of accomplishing this.

But, Dulles advised Donovan, he had done "no more than listen to [the conspirators'] argument," although he had once stressed "the fact that we would abide by our agreement with Russia both literally and in the spirit." He suspected there were "actually some Nazi generals who want to liquidate their responsibility to history by collaborating on the construction of a firm Anglo-American bulwark against a Russian-controlled Europe." Seeking to disabuse those who might suspect the proposal was a fabrication intended to dissuade the Allies from undertaking the dangerous invasion at all, Dulles assured Donovan he was sure that Gisevius was "in touch with such a group," but was "rather doubtful as to whether or not this group would actually have the courage to act effectively when the time comes."

In a later signal Dulles revealed some of the identities of Gisevius's principals: former Chief of the German General Staff Franz Halder, who had been fired by Hitler; General Adolf Ernst Heusinger, one of the chiefs of the Operations Branch of the Army High Command, who was to survive the war and become military adviser to the West German government, chairman of the German Joint Chiefs of Staff, and chairman of the NATO Military Committee 1961–64; and General Friedrich Olbricht, deputy commander of the German Home and Replacement Army. A little later still Dulles reported to Donovan that Gisevius had claimed the German supreme commander in the West, Field Marshal Gerd von Rundstedt, would, under certain circumstances, open the Channel front to the Allied armies, thus rendering Neptune unnecessary and making it possible for the Allies armies to march rather than fight their way ashore.

With the receipt of that weighty intelligence—certainly the most important so far obtained by OSS SI—Donovan cabled Acting Director Buxton on May 15, 1944, and instructed him to have Research and Analysis prepare a paper on the German underground movement. He also asked Buxton to send the paper not to the President, who had shown himself opposed to any arrangement with the German General Staff short of unconditional surrender, but to the secretary of state, who had been somewhat less devoted to the formula of unconditional surrender.

Thus, a document entitled "Overtures by German Generals and Civilian Opposition for a Separate Armistice" went to Cordell Hull on May 17, 1944, twenty days before Neptune D-Day.[13] The paper stated: "Since early 1944 the OSS representative in Bern has been approached periodically" by emissaries of a "German group proposing to attempt an overthrow of the Nazi regime." The group included Wilhelm Leuschner, "socialist leader and former Minister of the Interior in Hesse"; General Hans Oster, "a general formerly the right-hand man of Canaris, arrested in 1943 by the Gestapo, kept under surveillance after his release, and recently discharged from official functions by [Field Marshal Wilhelm] Keitel [chief of the German Supreme Command]; Karl Goerdeler, "former Mayor of Leipzig"; and General Ludwig Beck, a former chief of the German General Staff. Recently, the paper went on, the conspirators had been joined by Field Marshal von Rundstedt and General Baron Alexander von Falkenhausen, the German military governor of Belgium, "who would be ready to cease resistance and aid Allied landings, once the Nazis had been ousted."

The group "thought" a "similar arrangement might be worked out for the reception of Allied airborne forces at strategic points in Germany." But while the group was ready to attempt a revolution, it "did not guarantee success." The condition on which the group expressed willingness to act was that they would "deal directly with the West Allies alone after overthrowing the Nazi regime. . . . However, the group declared their willingness to cooperate with any leftist elements except the Communists. . . . The group feared the political and ideological sway over central

Europe by Bolshevism, with a mere exchange of Nazi totalitarianism for a totalitarianism of the radical left. . . ."

Dulles had told the emissaries of his conviction that America and England would not act regarding Germany without Russia and had expressed his skepticism of the conspirators' ability to remove Hitler because the Gestapo had to be aware that there was such a plot. Outlining and examining Dulles's reports of April and May, Donovan's paper pointed out that one of the emissaries had "acknowledged his lack of confidence in the political courage of the German generals, on the basis of past experience." The paper then passed on Dulles's belief that "the group's activities may be . . . useful to undermine the morale of the top echelon in the Wehrmacht."

But the emissaries had risked their lives for nothing. The means by which the war was to be ended had already been decided. Whatever the Germans offered, World War II in Europe, as in Asia, was to be settled by military, not political, means. Still, these exchanges did show the OSS, as well as the Supreme Command, that savagery and revolution were in the wind in Germany. The principal effect of Donovan's advice to Eisenhower was, therefore, promulgation of this bulletin to all commanders in chief thirteen days before D-Day:

> In the German Army, as in German political life, authority is exercised at the top and almost always obeyed at the bottom. For that reason, political trends among the generals in the German Army are of great significance. Should the *Wehrmacht* suffer severe setback [through Neptune] the generals may play a decisive role in determining the future. There has been some evidence of friction between Hitler and his higher commanders as a result of German retreats [and] . . . when the generals recognize defeat as inevitable, they may be unwilling to fight on until Germany is reduced to chaos. The generals are likely to believe themselves in a position to get better terms from the conquerors than the nazis. . . . If the first weeks of invasion indicate that the [Allies] cannot be stopped, high ranking officers of the German Army, recognizing the war-weariness of the German people, may act quickly against Hitler. Politically and psychologically that would be the moment for them to stage a coup. To a majority of German general officers the future of Germany is more important than the future of Hitler. . . . Trends among the German generals during the first weeks of successful invasion will therefore merit the closest analysis.[14]

More confident, less apprehensive, than before, therefore, on May 29, 1944, Eisenhower joined his battle headquarters, a mansion set in the lip of the hills overlooking the naval base of Portsmouth. There, on June 1, he issued the fateful signal "Hornpipe plus six." It meant that D-Day would be June 6, 1944.

35

D-Day

Donovan learned of the effect of his Balkan plan when he visited General Eisenhower's battle headquarters at Southwick House, near Portsmouth, on May 29, 1944. The figures were the most portentous of his life:

Eastern Front:	122 infantry divisions, 25 panzer divisions plus 1 brigade; 17 specialist divisions plus 1 brigade.
Western Front:	64 infantry divisions plus 1 regiment; 12 panzer divisions plus 2 brigades; 12 specialist divisions.
Southern Front:	37 infantry divisions plus 2 brigades; 9 panzer and 4 specialist divisions.
Reserves:	3 infantry divisions plus 1 brigade; 1 panzer division plus 2 brigades; 4 specialist divisions plus 2 brigades.

The implication of this table was obvious: Through a combination of real and fictional strategies a sixth part of German strength was locked in diversionary battles in Italy or kept idle but expectant in the Balkans by Allied feinting. The situation concerning the disposition of German armor was even more impressive. Of the forty-six panzer divisions, nine —roughly a fifth—were locked up in the south on tasks that could not be decisive to the outcome of the war. Yet according to General Sir Frederick Morgan, the man who planned Neptune, if the Germans had had only one more panzer division in northern France and the Low Countries than the twelve that had been bargained for, the balance of power on the Continent would have rested with the Germans.[1]

Many factors had contributed to this distribution of Wehrmacht power, and Donovan and the OSS were only one of them. Moreover, the size of OSS's contribution cannot be measured. But Donovan's was one of the organizations that had maintained the pressure on the southern front which had been decisive in deflecting an important segment of German power from France. Moreover, the importance of the paramilitary operations in the Mediterranean could not be gainsaid.

Here, then, was the justification for the existence of the OSS. If it never achieved anything else, it could always claim with truth that it had in its way helped obtain a favorable balance of power in Europe on D-Day.

After his meeting with his representatives at Eisenhower's battle headquarters, Donovan flew by light plane to the Home Counties to inspect the men, equipment, and installations assembled for Sussex, a program with the British to drop French-born military intelligence officers at key points in France and the Low Countries—the only pre-Neptune operation the British allowed Donovan to undertake before D-Day. At Station Victor, the new OSS wireless station created for Neptune, in the Chiltern Hills forty miles north of London, WJD pinned Good Conduct medals on thirteen members of the Women's Army Corps serving with the OSS. He watched wireless operations with Sussex agents who had been parachuted into France by the April and May moons. Then he left Station Victor for a country house near Leighton Buzzard, where Sussex teams were held before being sent to France. There he saw Sussex team Charles, composed of observer Joyeuse and radioman Chaloner, both French, leave for their *parachutage* near Le Bourget, where they were to watch out for the movements of the crack German Panzer Lehr Division. Having watched their Halifax transport disappear into an angry sky, Donovan hastened back to London, for he had received the hornpipe message from OSS London.

At Claridge's he saw his son, David, who was leaving that night to join his ship, destined for a beach called Omaha. WJD telephoned the OSS operations officer to learn what had become of Sussex team Charles, to be told that it had arrived safely but its radio had been damaged during the *parachutage*. Until new crystals could be flown to the men, they would be dependent on Ascencion, the special ground-to-air agents' voice radio system, which permitted a spy to dictate his message to a wiretape recorder in a specially equipped aircraft flying overhead.

And then Donovan vanished from London.

Donovan's career as U.S. intelligence master now entered one of its most mysterious phases. According to the diary kept by the chief of OSS

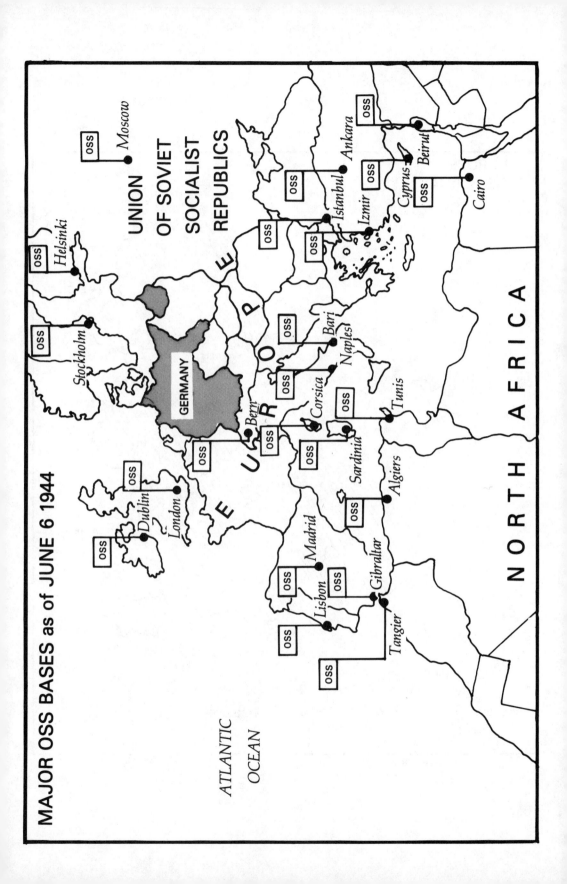

MAJOR OSS BASES as of JUNE 6 1944

EUROPE
JUNE 6 1944

Murmansk

EASTERN
FRONT

NORWAY

SWEDEN

FINLAND

Leningrad

NORTH SEA

Moscow

UNION OF SOVIET

GREAT
BRITAIN

IRELAND

Smolensk

SOCIALIST REPUBLICS

ATLANTIC
OCEAN

DENMARK

London

NETHER
LANDS

Berlin

POLAND

D-DAY LANDINGS

BELGIUM

GERMANY

SLOVAKIA

EASTERN
FRONT

FRANCE

SWITZER
LAND

AUSTRIA

HUNGARY

PORTUGAL

SPAIN

ITALY

DRAGOON

ITALIAN
FRONT

Rome

YUGOSLAVIA

ALBANIA

RUMANIA

Odessa

BLACK SEA

BULGARIA

GREECE

TURKEY

MOROCCO

ALGERIA

TUNISIA

MEDITERRANEAN SEA

London, David K. E. Bruce, and preserved in the Donovan papers, Donovan and Bruce left Claridge's just before midnight on May 30, 1944, their story being that "we were going to make visits to various friends of [WJD's] in British army field units."[2] Obviously they were concealing their movements, but for what purpose? Was it wholly WJD's fear that by his personal travels he might reveal D-Day was imminent? Or was there another reason?

There would lie the mystery. According to Bruce's diary, they drove to Paddington Station in London and caught the 11:30 P.M. train to Plymouth, the British naval base in southwestern England, where they arrived at 7:30 A.M. on May 31 and breakfasted with Admiral Alan G. Kirk, commander of the Western Naval Task Force, in the admiral's flagship, the USS *Augusta*. After touring Plymouth Sound to inspect the vast concentration of shipping assembled for Neptune, Donovan and Bruce boarded the destroyer USS *Davis*. They sailed for Belfast Lough, which the *Davis* reached just before 10:30 A.M. on June 1, 1944. At that hour they boarded the American heavy cruiser *Tuscaloosa*, the flagship of Admiral Morton L. Deyo, commander of the heavy bombardment group of Task Force 87, which was to land the U.S. 36th Division at Utah beach on the base of the Cherbourg Peninsula.

Now WJD and Bruce began to behave very oddly. Until they arrived in Belfast and boarded the *Tuscaloosa*, Donovan and Bruce had conducted themselves with secrecy. But once they were on the cruiser, they did nothing to conceal their presence. Not only did the crew of the *Tuscaloosa* know they were aboard, but so did Deyo's other guests, including Willard Shadel, a CBS correspondent, although he did not report the fact in his radio broadcasts.

After lunching in the *Tuscaloosa* on June 1, Donovan and Bruce took a launch to the port of Belfast, where they were received by the port officer, a Commander Keane, who took them to Belfast Castle to see the flag officer, Admiral Sir Richard Bevan, and the British commander in chief in Ulster, General Sir Alan Cunningham. At both calls Donovan engaged in extensive chitchat. After tea with Cunningham, Donovan and Bruce returned to the *Tuscaloosa* for dinner at 6:30 P.M. and a movie, *Gentleman Jim*, on the life of Gentleman Jim Corbett, the prizefighter.

On June 2, 1944, Donovan's and Bruce's movements were even more public. They went ashore at 9:30 A.M., met Commander Keane again, and, with his driver, Diana Kirkpatrick, at the wheel, drove to the residence of the governor of Northern Ireland, the duke of Abercorn. They lunched with one of General George S. Patton's Third Army division commanders, General S. LeRoy Irwin. From Irwin's command post Donovan and Bruce went to call on the prime minister of Northern Ireland, Sir Basil Brooke, cousin of Field Marshal Brooke, the Chief of the Imperial General Staff. From the premier's they went on to call on the mother of their driver and then visited Clandeboye, the home of the marquess of Dufferin and Ava, where the marchioness "gave us the usual tea, whiskey, jam, cakes and conversation." They returned to the *Tuscaloosa* in time for dinner.

Throughout, Donovan and Bruce had done nothing to keep their presence in Belfast a secret, and it might be thought their movements suggested they were establishing an alibi. But for what purpose? We shall not know for sure, but at precisely this time—according to the French—the OSS and Bruce were involved in the most tragic aspect of the national insurrection, the action the French underground would be called upon to undertake in support of Neptune.

Under arrangements with General Pierre Koenig, commander of Special Forces Headquarters (SFHQ), the division of Eisenhower's Supreme Command responsible for controlling Allied clandestine operations and the French resistance movements, the principal method of controlling the French underground was a system known as personal messages, which were broadcast each night by the BBC after the nine o'clock news. Each resistance group in France had its own code message, allotted by the SFHQ, and only the authors and the recipients were aware of what the message meant.

The personal messages were in pairs. The first half was the alert message, an instruction to the maquis to prepare to carry out their assigned task. When the action message was received they would carry out their mission. Thus, upon receipt of the personal message *"Romeo embrasse Juliette"* the maquis at, for example, Lyons, would call their members together, issue arms and explosives, and await the action message. When the action message *"Juliette embrasse Romeo"* was received, the maquis would set forth to carry out their assigned mission—to blow a bridge, a signal box, a culvert, a telephone exchange, or any one of a score of targets which if destroyed would disrupt German communications or confuse the enemy command.

The very large number of sabotage targets had been carefully plotted by the SFHQ planners. For Neptune's purposes they were mainly targets that would, if sabotaged, interfere with German road, rail, telephone, and telegraphic communications. The principal objective was to confuse and/or delay the German panzers in their movement toward the bridgeheads in that most critical period of the operation—before, at, and immediately after Neptune, when the Allied armies might not be ashore in sufficient strength to withstand a major German armored counterattack. SFHQ had sent scores of organizers equipped with wirelesses to France and Western and Central Europe to see to it that the maquis and the underground movements in general did what they were required to do under the plan, and no more—that the hotheads in the underground did not gain control and launch a premature revolution against the Germans.

Such a revolution would achieve nothing except enormous casualties when the Germans launched ruthless suppressive operations.

To avoid such casualties, an agreement had been made between Eisenhower's and De Gaulle's representatives in London that the French underground should be called into action only zone by zone, partly to conserve the strength of the resistance but also to prevent a premature national insurrection. Orders were taken from London to the underground's central committee in Paris, stressing the need for the underground movement to obey its orders and not to engage in premature and foolhardy operations against the Germans when the Allies landed. The principle to be applied in calling out the maquis was to summon those branches of the underground geographically closest to the invasion area, so that they might be relieved or resupplied rapidly after the action. General Eisenhower himself defined the principle for the supreme Allied commander in the Mediterranean, General Sir Henry Maitland Wilson, on or about May 16, 1944:

> . . . it was the SHAEF [Supreme Headquarters, Allied Expeditionary Forces] policy to restrict general civilian resistance to such covert action as may be possible without inviting mass reprisals against the French from the Germans. Overt action is to be delayed until it can be helpful to tactical operations. Groups organized for resistance throughout France are to do their stuff on receipt of action messages from the BBC which will be issued by the SHAEF authority in London. Their action is intended to delay enemy forces moving by rail and road, to sabotage enemy telecommunications, and to carry out general guerrilla tasks.[3]

However, at conferences after May 16 it became apparent at SHAEF that the Germans might be able to deduce the time and place of the invasion simply by plotting the pattern of resistance activity on a map. Thus the only way to prevent them from making that deduction, or to cause them to make inaccurate deductions, was to order resistance activity throughout France, thereby confusing the Germans about where the invasion would take place and how the campaign would evolve.

This decision produced great anxiety among the OSS and SOE components of General Koenig's headquarters, for if that became accepted strategy, the volume of the messages and their geographical pattern would resemble Vidal, the Allied plan for ordering a national insurrection in France. It was highly probable that the new policy would prove to be the fuse for a general uprising, and all underground movements would commence combat, although they were not armed for anything more than guerrilla activities. Certainly few units could resist German countermeasures. Nevertheless, the order was issued to Brigadier Eric T. Mockler-Ferryman of the SOE and Colonel Joseph Haskell, chief of OSS SO

London, who received their instructions with great misgivings. Aware that the order was likely to produce severe casualties among the French and equally severe reaction from the French leaders, Mockler-Ferryman, the senior British representative at Koenig's headquarters, refused to accept the decision when it was relayed to him verbally and demanded that it be sent to him in writing, as it was.

Because of a standing order that no orders or information relating to the time and place of the invasion were to be given to any Frenchman, the decision could not be conveyed to Koenig until the last possible moment—as it turned out, a sound decision since De Gaulle's communications with his representatives in Washington were among those intercepted and decrypted by the Sicherheitsdienst.

Here possibly is an explanation for Donovan's and Bruce's curious journey, for surely the two senior American Secret Intelligence and Special Operations officers should have been at their headquarters during Neptune, not touring Ulster or joyriding in American warships. Could it be that Donovan realized that if he and Bruce were implicated in such a tragic—but necessary—decision, it would wreck his plans for an alliance with the French intelligence services in France after the liberation, an alliance that would be a cornerstone of postwar American intelligence not only in Europe but throughout the world? We shall not know with any certainty, but it is important that Donovan had had some important, successful conversations with De Gaulle's representatives which augured well for his plans, and if that friendly and promising relationship was to be sustained, it was imperative that both he and Bruce, who was to move his command from London to Paris after the liberation, were seen and known to have had no connection with Eisenhower's decision.

And so it was. On the night of June 5, 1944, the eve of D-Day, personal messages went out to all French underground movements in all parts of France, an act that caused the French historian Robert Aron to write later:

> There is no doubt that the decision for general action was taken by Allied headquarters and communicated *in extremis* to the French. On 4 June 1944, the day before the messages were broadcast, two Allied officers, the British General Gubbins and the American Colonel David Bruce, called on General Koenig—Colonel Passy [code name for André Dewavrin, De Gaulle's chief of intelligence] being present—and inquired whether the French had any objections to messages for a general rising being passed over the air. In fact, this was no more than a polite gesture, for the decision had already been taken and the orders issued.[4]

Although the Communists did accuse Koenig, Bruce, and the American and British governments of unleashing a premature national insurrection that produced little except enormous French casualties, General Koenig and De Gaulle did not protest because "they could not. Nor should they have protested." Aron noted:

> They could not, for the simple reason that they were, in the military hierarchy, subordinate to Allied headquarters; General Koenig was under the command of General Eisenhower. It was [the men at Supreme Headquarters] who were responsible for [Neptune]; and they alone, being in possession of all the facts, were in a position to decide on the appropriate use of the French Resistance on D-Day. If Allied headquarters, at the risk of having certain units of the Maquis prematurely decimated, ordered sabotage and guerrilla warfare throughout France, it was clearly from no casual decision but for overriding strategical reasons. Had [Supreme Headquarters], in order to economize the Resistance forces, broadcast messages applicable only to the regions in which military operations were to take place, it would have meant informing the Germans of the precise localities of the landings and of the areas in which to concentrate their available forces. But Allied tactics were concerned with leaving the Wehrmacht not only uncertain as to where the invasion forces were to land, but also in ignorance of the invasion's true nature. Was it the main operation, or merely a diversion planned to attract the German reserves away from the real battlefield? . . . Furthermore, the broadcasting of all the messages at once was based on two other considerations: "To hinder to the maximum extent, and at one blow, the whole of the enemy's strategic and tactical transport system and to demoralize the enemy to the extent that he could no longer feel secure anywhere in French territory."

General Koenig, in a statement after the war,[5] confirmed Aron's version of events:

> This torrent of [personal messages] could have given some of the agents the impression that [the Allies had ordered] a national insurrection. But [I knew that] if the agents stuck to their orders [this would not occur because] . . . these orders . . . were so arranged (a) to let doubt exist as long as possible on the points where the landing would take place, and (b) to hinder to the maximum and at one blow the assembly . . . of the enemy's army, and (c) to demoralise the enemy, so that he would no longer feel secure at any point on our territory. . . . The resistance was to furnish its maximum effort during the first hours and days which followed H-Hour. That was one of its essential missions. It could not fail at that task.

The only remaining element in the mystery of Donovan's and Bruce's strange journey on the eve of momentous occurrences in the history of the twentieth century was this: Both Aron and Koenig stated that Gubbins and Bruce had informed Koenig of Eisenhower's decision on June 4, 1944. But how could he if Bruce was with Donovan at sea aboard the

Tuscaloosa? The only answer can be that Aron and Koenig were mistaken in the date of the meeting and that the meeting took place probably on the evening of May 30, during the evening before Bruce caught the night train to Plymouth. A check with the *Tuscaloosa*'s log shows that on June 2, 1944, the ship was sealed, and nobody except messengers was allowed on or off her. She proceeded to her battle stations with Donovan and Bruce aboard, and they had no contact with their headquarters during the coming week.

On June 3, 1944, Force Utah, of which the *Tuscaloosa* was part, was at sea, steaming south by east off the Western Approaches to England with a vast concourse of Neptune shipping. The day was bright and clear—the storm that had caused so much trouble with the Neptune timetable had passed on up the Channel—and Bruce recorded something of Donovan's deep pessimism about the outcome of the operation. Donovan had always supported Churchill's notion of a main strike against Germany not across the English Channel but northward across the Mediterranean or through the Balkans, although this proposition had always been resisted bitterly by Donovan's masters, the Joint Chiefs. Bruce wrote:

> General Donovan feels that too easy an optimism over the success of the assault prevails, and that the architects of [Neptune] were lacking in a realization of the actual combat conditions that may confront the Allies. He himself has always favored a thrust from the Mediterranean and through the Balkans, a view shared by many high-ranking British strategists. He told me last night that PM Churchill had not long ago cabled to the British Embassy in Wash a message for transmission to Pres. Roosevelt, denying the allegation that once a cross-channel attack had been decided upon, [Churchill] had expressed discontent over the decision, or pessimism over the result. He did, however, at the same time, again place himself on record as having preferred ever since 1941, when Gen D[onovan] discussed the matter with him, an attack via the Mediterranean, instead of across the English Channel.

On June 4, 1944, Force Utah and the *Tuscaloosa* arrived off Falmouth, a small port in Cornwall at the entrance to the English Channel. There Donovan received news about his son, Lieutenant David Donovan, who was in the command ship *Ancon,* destined for Omaha beach. It was the second time Donovan and David were in a major amphibious attack—the landings at Sicily being the first occasion. At the same time Donovan received news that confirmed him in his pessimism about the outcome of Neptune. Bruce recorded: ". . . owing to bad weather conditions in the Channel, the invasion had been postponed for 24 hours and that if it could not be carried out then it might be further postponed for 2 weeks." Bruce commented:

This incident again highlights what Gen D has so often said about the nature of the tremendous gamble the Allies were making. Only for a few days in each month are the moon, the tides, the light, the weather and sea conditions propitious for a long cross-Channel invasion. On today's choppy seas the landing boats would be tossed about like cockleshells and would probably arrive at the French coast off schedule, partly filled with water, if indeed they were not swamped, and their human freight suffering from the aftermath of seasickness. In the previous landings in which American troops have participated, good luck has played a determining part, nor have any of them been directed against a strong opposition and defenses such as are now to be expected. Underwater obstacles with mines attached, beach mines, light and heavy coastal batteries, machine gun nests, and strong points of every description, supposedly have long been prepared against such an assault, and behind them is a mobile striking force of panzer and infantry divisions, composed of excellent soldiers. The fickle British climate is the true mistress of these seas.

Ordered about, the *Tuscaloosa* and the rest of Force Utah's heavy bombardment squadron sailed around Land's End and back into the Bristol Channel. Bruce noted: "We cruised about all day and went somewhat beyond Bristol before making a turn. This afternoon I counted 76 warships and transports within a radius of a few miles, and it is probable that German reconnaissance planes have done the same." By nightfall the weather cleared again, and "although the sea is still disturbed we are hopeful that the invasion date need not once more be set back." It was not: There was a clear area of weather between two fronts coming in from the Atlantic, and Eisenhower had decided to launch Neptune toward France between them.

On June 5, the eve of Neptune, Bruce noted that they were sailing back to Falmouth, and both he and Donovan were profoundly impressed by the majesty of the great task forces now at sea all around them:

The sight of these cruisers and battleships in line, flanked by destroyers, is majestic. About noon we passed through two large convoys of transports laden with troops; one of them was flying 67 barrage balloons. In this operation there will be about 3,200 ships and thousands of small craft employed against a 90 mile front. Amongst them are numbered six battleships (3 of them American: the *Nevada, Texas* and *Arkansas,* and the other three British; the *Ramillies, Warspite* and *Rodney);* 2 Gunboats (Dutch); 2 Monitors (British); 27 cruisers (21 of them British, 2 French, 1 Polish, and 3 American—the *Tuscaloosa, Augusta* and *Quincy);* 124 Destroyers (mostly British, about 30 being American with some Dutch, Polish and French); 143 minesweepers; 8 Headquarters ships (4 British and 4 American . . .); 9 Assault Group Headquarters Ships (British); 13 PT Boats (American); 150 MTB Boats (British); and a host of other escort and auxiliary craft.

At 9:00 P.M. Bruce noted that:

> the wind has freshened, and the seas instead of quieting down are rising higher. There are heavy cloud banks above us and toward France. However, the authorities who control this expedition must be satisfied over the weather prospects for tonight and tomorrow morning for we have now definitely set our course for the Utah Beaches. . . . Breakfast has been ordered on the Tuscaloosa for 9:30 tonight so it is to be inferred that meals will be very irregular from now on.

And after the BBC newscast at 9:00 P.M. they heard the stream of action messages going out to the maquis throughout France:

> Reeds must grow, leaves rustle. . . .
> I am looking for four-leaf clovers. . . .
> Georges will bring the eglantine. . . .
> *Le chat a neuf vies.* . . .
> *Bénédictine est une liqueur douce.* . . .
> *La vache saute par-dessus la lune.* . . .
> *La lune est pleine d'éléphants rouges.* . . .

In all there were some seventy messages that took thirty-five minutes to pass, against the normal four minutes at that hour. As they were received, the maquis prepared for their tasks throughout France from the Drôme to the Dordogne and Haute-Provence, from the Vienne to the Haute-Loire, Lozère and the Cantal, in the Franche-Comté, the Dauphiné, and the Savoie. The French national insurrection was being created without the knowledge of the French High Command, but as one *maquisard* was to write: "There was nothing scandalous or disgraceful about all this; but one fact emerges and bears repetition: in France's situation in 1944, it was sometimes inevitable that Frenchmen should be sacrificed to effect her liberation."[6]

At 10:30 P.M. Bruce wrote in his diary:

> I feel that something will soon happen, for Gen D, freshly shaven and bathed, has buttoned his trousers about his ankles, put on his rubber soled shoes, taken out his olive wool cap and is calmly eating an apple. Those who have been with him before on similar occasions tell me that when Gen D puts on that costume one should be prepared for trouble. Everyone is now wearing or carrying lifebelts and steel helmets. The cabins have been stripped of glass, and movables had been lashed down. . . . Gen D and I had bacon and eggs.

At 11:45 P.M.: "Ack-Ack fire, probably over land, at airplanes on the starboard side. Lasted about 15 minutes. Strange ships making 25 knots about 11 miles away appear on Radar Screen. Are finally located as friendly. On starboard side four star shells shot into air at great distance, reason unknown."

In the darkness of the bridge, with Barfleur Light flashing on the tip of the Cherbourg Peninsula, Bruce heard Donovan—who knew his Shakespeare—repeat part of Henry V's speech before Agincourt in 1415, on the occasion of another cross-Channel attack:

> He that outlives this day, and comes safe home,
> Will stand a tip-toe when this day is named. . . .
> And gentlemen in England now a-bed,
> Shall think themselves accurs'd they were not here. . . .

Aboard the *Tuscaloosa*, eight bells ushered in D-Day. It was 6:00 P.M. on June 5 at Berryville, Virginia, and Ruth Donovan and David's wife, Mary, had just finished a day of picking cherries and peas to put up for the winter. Neither Ruth nor Mary had the slightest idea that D-Day was at hand.

Nor had the Germans.

Shortly before 3:00 A.M. there was a rattle of chain cable through the hawsepipe and the words "Anchor holding, sir, in seventeen fathoms." The night was black, windy, silent, troubled. Yet 600 warships and 4,000 merchantmen had crossed the Channel and entered the bay of the Seine without encountering enemy opposition. The miraculous had occurred. The Allies had achieved total tactical and strategical surprise largely because the Germans had concluded that the Allies would not and could not invade with the weather in the Channel as bad as it was. And so when Maria von Schmedes closed down the Germans' troop radio service for the night at midnight, as she did always with the song "Another Beautiful Day Draws to a Close," the German General Staff, that most proficient cabal of military monks, had gone to bed and were asleep as the Neptune fleets approached the Norman shore. And as the deputy operations chief at Hitler's headquarters, General Warlimont, would confess in later years: "On 5 June 1944, . . . [the German Supreme Command] had not the slightest idea that the decisive event of the war was upon them."[7]

At 4:05 A.M., two hours before sunrise, with three divisions of paratroopers in the water meadows and low hills just behind the coastline, the assault transports at Utah began to debark their troops into the landing craft. An eighteen-knot wind blew off the Cherbourg Peninsula to kick up the waves; the radar on the masts of the *Tuscaloosa* washed in and out of the low clouds. The landing craft banged against the mother ships' sides, and then set out for the rendezvous points and the run to the shore.

"It is astonishing," wrote Bruce in his diary, "that with this vast force surrounding us such quiet and blackout on the craft can prevail." Overhead the fleets of C-47's were returning from the paradrops, while the undersides of the distant clouds were lit by the flashes from the 4,000 tons of bombs being poured onto the beach defenses by RAF Bomber Command. And just before the dawn more than 1,000 American medium and heavy bombers came over low to take up the work of the night bombers.

At 6:30 A.M.: ". . . our troops start ashore and land at 7." The enemy shore batteries begin to engage the squadron of which the *Tuscaloosa* is part. Bruce wrote:

> When daylight came, the activity was intense. As bomb loads were discharged, great flashes of fire shot towards the sky, followed by columns of dust and smoke, whilst overhead tracers from Ack Ack made golden sparkling showers amid the dark or silver planes. Once a Marauder, in the midst of a tight formation, received a hit, and flamed like a huge Bunsen Burner for a minute before being reduced to a small globule of black soot that hung for a time high in the sky. Throughout the morning, fighters—Spitfires and Lightnings—patrolled above us but no Luftwaffe rose to meet them.
>
> [7:00 A.M.:] . . . there is cannonading on all sides as well as from the shore. Spouts of water rise from near the ships as German long range batteries try to reach them. The [British cruiser] *Black Prince* is bracketed and hit and calls for a smoke screen. 2 planes skim the water and interpose a billowing blanket of cloud between it and the shore. One of the planes, however, is hit and seems to skid along the water's surface until it burst into a glowing red ball and then disappears. Closer in, one sees the darting red tongues of the destroyers [*sic*] guns. Bilious yellow clouds of smoke shoot forth above the mouths of our guns.

Aboard the *Tuscaloosa* "the air is acrid with powder and a fine spray of disintegrated wadding comes down everywhere on us like lava ash. Everywhere there is noise." When she fires, "the decks tremble under our feet, and the joints of the ship seem to creak and stretch. When a whole turret is discharged the teeth almost rattle in one's head."

> [7:10 A.M.:] The U.S. destroyer *Corry* has been hit and may have to be beached. She had previously been hurt on her way to her station by dropping a depth charge in shallow water against a suspected submarine. At the same time a periscope was reported seen 1000 yards from the *Tuscaloosa*. Some landing craft having put their troops ashore are returning—a good sign. . . . The *Corry* has now partially sunk, and will be replaced in her hot spot by the *Butler*.
>
> [8:30 A.M.:] The *Tuscaloosa* has run out of targets for the time being. Four heavy enemy guns are shelling our troops on the beaches, but a landing has been effected and reinforcements are pouring in. The *Hawkins* as well as the

Black Prince received direct hits early in the engagement, but have continued firing and each has knocked out at least two enemy batteries. The most serious casualty thus far on *Tuscaloosa* has been a direct hit by something on Gen D's water closet, adjoining the Admiral's cabin—at any rate it is completely shattered and in ruins on the floor.

[9:50 A.M.:] There is now . . . a complete lull as far as this ship is concerned, and we have not been under enemy fire for some time—the last salvo against us was distant about 2000 yards. The *Tuscaloosa* is beginning to look rather forlorn in the officers' quarters. Repeated concussions have driven screws out of their sockets, shattered light bulbs, thrown articles all over the floors, and generally made an awful mess.

[10:00 A.M.:] We are again being fired upon. The first shell was at 2500 yards and then successively they hit at 2000, 1500, 1000, 500 and 50 yards. After the last, and just in time (for the next shell fell in our anchorage) we shifted position and shelled them back. . . . Both the Omaha and Utah landings are so far successful. German radio announced at 7 A.M. the arrival of American paratroopers in France, which probably means that some of them were captured. Resistance groups were ordered to await further instructions. Broadcasts have been given by Eisenhower, Churchill, Hull, etc. The *Fitch* has been hit, and is now picking up survivors of the *Corry*.

[12:30 P.M.:] Our old enemy, a 3 gun battery which we cannot precisely locate, is keeping after us. It dropped a shell 200 yards away from us, and we got under way. The next shot was exactly correct for range, but off for deflection, which was lucky. When they hit the water near us it feels like depth charges beneath us.

By 4:00 P.M. the *Tuscaloosa* had fired more than 400 shells at the enemy batteries, and at Utah the landings were progressing well. The 4th Division had suffered fewer than 200 casualties in the assault, but some of the paratroop units that had cut a path through the enemy defenses had suffered rather heavily, and at Omaha there had been very heavy fighting, serious casualties, and the bridgehead was far from secure. The probability was that Omaha beachhead would have collapsed if the enemy commander had had just one of the divisions pinned down in the Balkans and Italy. But he did not have that division available so the American V Corps just managed to hold on.

[6:00 P.M.:] Gen. D and I have tea, eggs and marmalade. Men are sleeping all over the decks and corridors, collapsed over their guns, doubled up in corners, constrained into curious and uncomfortable postures. We go above to see the officers and hear the latest news. Our indefatigable officers still carry on unperturbed, but looking drawn and tired. Their usually impeccable uniforms are wrinkled or replaced by rougher garments, they are unshaven (in fact the water pressure is cut off), their eyes are red-rimmed, but they are as considerate and courteous as ever. We have the free run of the ship, and going from the CIC [Combat Information Center] to the chart room, etc. is

like stopping during the afternoon for gossip in a series of men's clubs—
except that there is nothing to drink!

[10:00 P.M.:] More eggs, orange juice and gunfire. Went to bed or rather
lay down shortly after midnight, when battle stations were manned. However, to everyone's surprise the night was quiet. One enemy raider dropped
a bomb near us but we did not open fire, nor was there any activity by shore
batteries. The sky was overcast and the RAF was pounding French airfields,
which may be one reason for their lack of initiative here.

Then, despite the agreement with the British that no American with
knowledge of ISOS would be placed in a position where he might be
captured by the enemy, Donovan and Bruce ignored General Omar Bradley's order that they were not to land in Normandy during the battle. At
four in the afternoon of June 7, 1944, Donovan and Bruce clambered
down a rope ladder over the side of the *Tuscaloosa*, boarded a launch
carrying three fliers, who had been shot down earlier that day, and three
corpses, and went over to a U.S. destroyer escort. That vessel took them
to a landing craft, where Donovan persuaded the commanding officer, "a
swarthy boy from Chicago," to take them into Utah beach. The "swarthy
boy" agreed but then had second thoughts and asked them to go in with
an amphibious truck which took them ashore in the area of St. Germain-
de-Varreville. Bruce recorded:

As we reached the middle of the beach there was the drone of airplane
motors and almost immediately afterwards machinegun fire as they swept
immediately over us down the beach. The General, accustomed to such
emergencies, rolled nimbly off the hood where we were sitting, onto the
sand. I, with slower reflexes, followed, and fell squarely on Gen. D. Two of
the 4 German planes involved, ME 109s, were shot down by anti-aircraft fire,
and we saw one pilot descending by parachute.

While lying in the sand, Donovan remarked to Bruce: "By the way,
David, have you arranged to be buried in Arlington Cemetery?"

Bruce replied: "Why, no."

"Well," said Donovan, as he was getting up and brushing off the sand,
"I have; that's where I want to be buried. David, you've got to get a plot
near mine. Then we can start an Underground together."[8] With that jest
Donovan and Bruce clambered up the seawall, oblivious to the thought
that there might be mines or snipers about, and found the inland road.
After marching about three miles, without escort and without permission,
"We found our soldiers spread over a considerable area, and trucks
passed us containing several German and a number of American
wounded"—a sign that the front was not far away. As they made their way
farther inland, they ran into the American Army commander Bradley and
General Royce, who had been in Cairo during the OSS's wild days and

was now with the Ninth Air Force. Bruce did not record Bradley's reaction to finding Donovan and Bruce in France, but it may be imagined. All Bruce stated was that Bradley and Royce "seemed well pleased with the progress made to date by the invasion. Gen. D. arranged with Gen. Bradley for me to come out soon and spend some time with the First Army."

After much difficulty in getting transportation, Donovan and Bruce returned to the *Tuscaloosa* at 9:00 P.M. that day, as Bruce put it, "in time for a late supper, well content to have touched once more, even if briefly, the soil of France." While they were eating, the ship's intelligence officer, Robert Thayer, informed them that Hitler had just made a broadcast that the Germans would start to use their secret weapons that same night "and that by tomorrow morning there would be no American or British troops left in France"—a statement that heralded the first operational use of cruise and long-range missiles. A little later still Donovan and Bruce learned that the *Rich*, the destroyer escort in which they had made part of their journey to the beach during the afternoon, had been badly damaged when it struck two mines, and the casualties were heavy.

And so D-Day passed. Throughout that day and night the German High Command had been in the utmost chaos, often completely deprived of intelligence about the whereabouts, strength, and composition of the Allied armies as, true to their orders in the personal messages, the maquis throughout France cut the German telephone and telegraph cables, ambushed messengers, and attacked German headquarters. Deeper inland the movement of the panzers toward the beachhead was thrown into disorder by the action of the Franco-European railroad men. Signals, switches, turntables, locomotives—all were interfered with in such a fashion that most of the German alarm units did not move unless they were on their own tracks, and those that did move by rail were bombed. All principal highways and country roads were blocked as the maquis blew culverts and bridges.

The Allied sense of triumph was very great and was conveyed by the "Central Directive of the Political Warfare Executive" for the week beginning June 15, 1944:

> The forcing of the Channel, the first critical phase of the Battle for Europe, has been completed. The most sanguine expectations have been surpassed by the achievements which established and extended the first beachhead of the West.
>
> The years of preparation, production and planning, by which all the skill and resource of modern science and engineering were embodied in the military conception, have dwarfed all German organisation and enterprise, and confounded German military theory.[9]

During D-Day neither Donovan nor Bruce had taken any part in launching and controlling the national insurrection. Throughout that day they both were remote from and unable to communicate with their headquarters, and indeed, the only message Donovan was able to send that day was a four-word advisory to Buxton in Washington: "I am with Deyo."[10] As for Bruce, the chief of the OSS in Europe was not able to send any messages at all since the *Tuscaloosa*'s wireless channels were clogged with naval operational traffic.

Donovan and Bruce returned to Plymouth in the *Tuscaloosa*, which had come in to recharge her ammunition lockers, at 1:30 A.M. on June 10, 1944, running into two submarine attacks during passage. At Plymouth, wrote Bruce, "General Donovan commandeered a Navy automobile. The driver was a former racing man and far more dangerous than any German shells. However, we arrived in London safely at 10 o'clock."

On his arrival at 70 Upper Grosvenor Street, Donovan sent a brief report on his visit to Normandy to Buxton:

> Today I returned from the bridgehead. The whole attack beautifully managed and lodgement obtained in British and one of our sectors with very few casualties, although in another of our sectors our troops suffered severely. The momentum of the landing has been lost and it is hard to get up steam for the succeeding operations. I really believe we have them now, although our mistakes may prolong the War. Bruce and I were on the flagship of Admiral Deyo, who is doing a fine job. His fire support force is giving an excellent example of how a naval force can serve as combined field and railroad artillery. Spent D-Day on the westerly beachhead. Tell [my] family that as I left, David's ship was still untouched.[11]

But WJD was incorrect. The Allied armies had not yet defeated the Wehrmacht. There was to be almost another year of war, another year of anarchy, before his prediction that "we have them" came true.

36

The Uprisings

On landing at Plymouth, Donovan called at the OSS forward headquarters to see that his units were being correctly embarked for Normandy. There he encountered the chief of OSS Morale Operations Europe, Patrick Dolan, a peacetime Irish-American newspaper reporter in his early thirties and one of Donovan's favorites in the group of younger OSS men. Dolan's predicament was much the same as that of all other OSS men attached to the U.S. Army for the assault phase of Neptune: With the OSS-Military Intelligence "war" still going on in Washington OSS men were not welcome at the U.S. First Army; they were generally the first units to be offloaded if the Army needed their space in the ships; and when they reached the far shore, as often as not they found themselves without quarters, without a mess, without transportation, and excluded from First Army headquarters.

As Donovan was to learn later, Dolan (whose mission in France was to engage in psychological warfare intended to break the will and capability of the enemy to resist, usually with propaganda broadcast by loudspeaker across the front lines) had been transported to Normandy on time. But when he got there, he found his special loudspeaker truck had been "borrowed" by the Army and his accreditations to the headquarters of the commanding general of First Army, General Omar N. Bradley, had been invalidated by Bradley's chief of Intelligence, Colonel Benjamin A. "Monk" Dickson, who had been recruited as G-2 First Army by General Strong and was to prove to be the OSS's most resolute opponent in Europe.

Ashore at Utah beach during the first American operations for the seizure of the great port of Cherbourg—the capture of which was a key element in Montgomery's battle plan—Dolan and his assistant found themselves with little more than what they carried. For their mission—psychological warfare against the enemy and spreading the American message of the Four Freedoms—Dolan had no equipment and no transport beyond his bedroll and a little bag containing about 300 gold sovereigns given to him by Donovan because "nobody knows what's going to happen over there."[1]

Dolan claimed that his first action on landing in Fortress Europe was to purchase a horse for fifty sovereigns, with which to follow the U.S. Army in its first major operation on the Continent—capture of the great transatlantic seaport of Cherbourg as a main supply base. The operation reached its culmination on June 21, 1944, a fortnight after the landings, when the officer in command of American operations to take Fortress Cherbourg, General J. Lawton Collins, sent an ultimatum to the German commander in the fortress, General Karl Wilhelm von Schlieben: Surrender by breakfast on June 22 or be annihilated. When the ultimatum was ignored, elements of three Allied air forces commenced an attack on the fortress's strongpoints, Collins opened a major artillery barrage, and three of his most powerful divisions began the task of crushing all resistance.

Collins's attack proceeded well, and by June 24 almost all the port and its fortress—except the great naval arsenal where Schlieben and his command had headquarters—was in American hands. This was important, for the arsenal and its heavy artillery commanded the sea approaches to the port and the port itself, and while there was no doubt that Schlieben and the garrison inside would have to surrender, the fear was that unless special means were employed successfully to force their surrender, the Americans might have to accept very heavy casualties in reducing the fortress—which was protected by a moat and high walls fourteen feet thick and was mounted with antitank, antiaircraft, and machine guns on the parapets. At that point Dolan and his little team of Morale Operations personnel arrived at Collins's headquarters with a suggestion that they be allowed to try to talk Schlieben into surrendering.

Collins agreed to Dolan's proposal, and at 7:30 A.M. on June 27, 1944, Dolan took over from the British some loudspeaker equipment used previously for village election campaigns. The equipment was sited on a truck near a house close to one of the entrances to the arsenal, and as Dolan was to remember, "We got to the frontline units, and everyone thought the thing was ludicrous, the biggest goddamned joke of all time. The West Point colonels could not find even a cup of coffee for us before we started work. They thought we were mad, and I was not so sure that they were not right."

As three battalions of the 47th Infantry Regiment prepared for an assault, accompanied by artillery and air bombardment and assault engineers with satchel charges of TNT, Dolan remembered, "We could not have been more than twenty-five yards away from the entrance. I got some scrap paper, and I wrote out a surrender harangue." The document said in effect: "You've fought very bravely. You are great soldiers, and we are full of admiration for you. But the time has come when you must realize that we must have the port of Cherbourg to land our equipment and material of war, and therefore, we have to have the arsenal. We think as honorable soldiers and good Germans you have fought your battle and you should now live for the new Germany. Therefore, we are giving you this opportunity to quit fighting with honor because you are in an absolutely hopeless position. We are going to give you fifteen minutes. If you do not surrender, you will be subjected to the bombardment of Flying Fortresses, carpet bombing, saturation bombing, naval bombardment, and then storming by infantry." Dolan ended by announcing that he would count off the minutes and that the men inside the fortress should begin to fly white flags when they were ready to surrender.

The note was translated into German, Ukrainian, and Polish—Dolan had such translators on his team and was aware of the nationalities of the men inside the fortress—and broadcast in each language over the truck's loudspeakers. The clock was then set ticking.

At the sixth minute Dolan received a report that a white flag had appeared at one of the casement apertures. He scrambled up onto the roof of the house, and "sure enough there was a white flag. I broadcast back that I could see the flag, but I insisted that there be more flags and restarted the countdown. At the fourth minute there was a blossom of white flags. I then broadcast back that we accepted their word that they were willing to surrender and announced that we were coming out. Here was the moment of truth.

"Since I was the boss, I put my tin hat on, cocked my pistol, and saying a very fervent Hail Mary, I put the tin hat on a stick and poked it around the corner of the wall. There was no firing, so I stepped out into the street. It was littered with bodies from an attempt to take the arsenal the night before." Accompanied by three Morale Operations agents, Dolan walked over to the door of the arsenal and kicked it open. He put his helmet on a stick and poked around the corner. Then, when again there was no gunfire, "we entered a little tunnel, kicked open another door, nothing, went through and found ourselves looking down onto a courtyard. Below were hundreds of German soldiers and sailors milling around, preparing to line up in parade formation. At that point a very elegant German staff officer came up and said that General von Schlieben was waiting on us, and would we come this way? We followed the officer into a heavily guarded office and found Schlieben with an Irish setter dog at his feet and flanked by some naval and army officers."

These officers included General Heinz Sattler, the deputy commander of Fortress Cherbourg, and Admiral Walther Hennecke, a naval officer commanding the Normandy sector of the Channel coast. Dolan recalled: "I saluted and asked Schlieben whether he was ready to surrender. Schlieben replied that 'You appreciate for a German officer who has spent his entire life in the German Army it is difficult for me to surrender to a talking box.' Schlieben paused and then said: 'I wonder if you could use some weapon against us against which we have no defense.' That was a puzzler for me. I said: 'I understand your position, and if I were in your position, I would feel exactly as you do.' We then talked for a moment or two about military honor. I thought very hard and fast . . . and said: 'What about some phosphorus shells?' This was not translated very well, and Schlieben did not seem to know what they were. He asked me what they did, and I said they were explosive incendiary shells and we could lob those in, and 'so long as you give me the exact coordinates, we could have some landing in the fortress in half an hour.' Schlieben thought that that would suffice, and I sent one of my assistants back to the first company command post to get them to telephone General Collins that I had negotiated the surrender but that I wanted four phosphorus shells lobbed into a precise point where they would not cause any casualties.

"Off he scuttles, and twenty minutes later in come the shells. The generals and the admirals were by now on a parapet in front of the arsenal. They saw the shells strike in great clouds of white fire and smoke. Then I said to Schlieben: 'Well, are you ready?' He said: 'I am ready.' We then walked out of the arsenal with Schlieben, one admiral, and the dog, got in the jeep, and then drove into American lines where the Army was absolutely goggle-eyed. The infantry then began to move into the arsenal to make it official."

At U.S. headquarters Dolan introduced Schlieben and Hennecke to Collins, and, as he put it, "I was the hero of the hour." Collins "pinned the Silver Star on me, and a French general pinned the Croix de Guerre on me." Then "they promptly took them back as the medals were the only ones they had. I have never had them since." But "that set up OSS psychological warfare with the Army." However, the OSS Special Detachment with the U.S. First Army headquarters was less welcome than before. Very early in the Battle of Normandy the G-2, Colonel Dickson, ejected the OSS from his headquarters and refused to allow it to return, a position he maintained resolutely until long after the Battle of the Ardennes at Christmas 1944.

As for Donovan, when he heard of Dolan's exploit, he wired: "And what do you propose doing now? Capture Berlin?"

On his return to OSS headquarters in London, it became clear to Donovan that the national insurrection had begun in France, albeit prematurely—ignited by a combination of the arrival of the Allied armies in Normandy, the expectation of other large-scale landings in the Pas de Calais and Provence, the excitement and emotion of the general call to arms implied by the mass release of the *messages personnels,* and fiery statements by De Gaulle. Moreover, all Europe, especially Poland, was rising against the conqueror. Here then was Donovan's finest hour—the hour for which he and his service had been created.

Everywhere in France, except where the Germans were thickest on the ground, the maquis had come down out of the hills and woods; the *sédentaires* had left their work and homes, taking their carefully hidden and oiled weapons with them. Everywhere barricades and officers and soldiers of the old army had appeared, and everywhere the civilian control structure upon which the Wehrmacht rested began to crumble like dry rot. The scale of resistance, ferocity, the determination of the maquis in both towns and countryside surprised both the Germans and the Allies, neither of whom had expected that the French resistance movement would have more than nuisance value. But neither the German nor the Allied commanders had been aware of the depth of the ordinary Frenchman's detestation of the Germans; neither had experienced four weary years of German and Vichy French bureaucratic control and oppression; and nobody had fully estimated the degree of anger, bitterness, humiliation, resentment, or revolutionary spirit in the ordinary market square of France.

Yet as Donovan learned when he returned to his headquarters in Grosvenor Square, the insurrection had only begun. Its full fury might take two to three weeks to develop, and unless the United States and Great Britain sent arms in large quantities—so far weapons for only 140,000 men had been inserted—casualties would become so large they would become a serious political factor in future relationships. A paper to Donovan advised that if the *résistants* were "inadequately armed and supplied large numbers may be slaughtered," and the United States, as the "proclaimed giant of production," would "receive major blame." The size and strength of the maquis were growing rapidly and might, as in Yugoslavia, "provide the basis of effective future government" and also for the "goodwill of French nation" for the United States.[2]

Signals from the field headquarters of the commander in chief of the Allied armies in Normandy, General Sir Bernard Montgomery, supported the opinion found at Koenig's headquarters in London that the maquis had become, unexpectedly, a strategic factor of importance, especially in the delaying of the movement of the German armored army to Normandy. Panzer divisions, brigades, and battalions moving toward the bridgehead from all parts of Europe were proceeding with their ordinary speed and efficiency until they reached the Paris conurbation. There a combination of Allied aerial and *maquisard* activity was causing massive diversions that were eating up not hours, but precious days. Analysis of Wehrmacht movement telegrams showed all German lines of march, fast and slow, to be disordered and, in some parts, chaotic, and when German divisions and brigades set out as entities, they often reached the bridge-head only as companies and battalions.

As Donovan wired the President, General Sir Kenneth W. D. Strong, Eisenhower's chief of intelligence, was crediting the resistance with having caused delays in the movement of German forces toward the beach-head of "up to 48 hours"—a major delay as both sides raced to obtain superiority of power in Normandy. But this was underestimation. Owing to a combination of guerrilla action and bombing in Brittany, the 77th Infantry took thirteen days to make a two-day journey to Normandy; the 165th Infantry Division began to leave Lorient on June 6 but was still not completely at the front by June 16; the 275th Infantry Division, which began to leave the Vannes area on June 7–8, was still arriving on the fourteenth; and one battalion took eight days to make a single day's journey. At a time when the German commander was desperate for infantry to build a dike around the swelling tide of Allied power coming ashore over the Normandy beaches, these were major—if not decisive—delays.

Nor was the opposition encountered only in the area of operations. WJD was informed that "considerable German troops are engaged by resistance movements in the southeast, southwest, and south central portions of France" and that Churchill was so impressed by the size and power of the movement he had ordered "further support" for the maquis, and he "may have either written or spoken to the President in this matter."[3]

With his deep love of France Donovan was anxious about the situation there, and his anxiety was intensified by the political relations between Roosevelt and De Gaulle. Their association was replete with deep animosity that had many origins, but the principal one was Roosevelt's dislike of the schemes De Gaulle had employed to emerge over Giraud as the top political and military figure in France in exile. But Roosevelt could no longer disregard the obvious. De Gaulle was the leader of Free France inside France and outside, and if Eisenhower was to be able to fight the Germans in France with the cooperation of the Fighting French, FDR must come to terms with the Frenchman. Furthermore, many in Washington feared that unless the United States acknowledged De Gaulle's leadership, his position in France at the liberation would be undermined, to the benefit only of a fully armed Communist party that was trained and experienced in clandestinity.

The opportunities and dangers were recognized in secret conversations between De Gaulle's chief of intelligence, André Dewavrin, and

OSS Colonel Glavin, in Algiers in May, and as a consequence, in June De Gaulle's naval representative in Washington, Admiral Raymond Fénard, had a talk with Roosevelt at the White House before flying to London. New factors were beginning to creep into the Franco-American equation —particularly the OSS's activities in Thailand—but Fénard and Roosevelt felt there were reasons and hope for an early meeting with De Gaulle in Washington.

In London, Donovan had secret conversations with both De Gaulle and Fénard concerning both an invitation from Roosevelt to De Gaulle to meet in Washington and a major increase in the supply of munitions to the resistance in France. The results of the conversations were evidently of such high importance that on June 13, 1944, Donovan wired Buxton that he was returning "because I must talk with President Roosevelt regarding General de Gaulle."[4] Bruce also wired to give Buxton WJD's flight number and, because Donovan could not find his house keys, to have him "Call Donovan's home so that he can get in the house"; even spymasters on epic missions lose their front door keys.[5]

Donovan left London for Washington on June 14, as scores, indeed hundreds of Allied missions from both London and Algiers were pouring into France to try to bring the maquis under control. But, as Donovan advised Buxton, complete discipline and obedience to Eisenhower's orders would come only through De Gaulle, and he was complaining about everything, from the rough way that Churchill had talked to him just before Neptune to the quality of the banknotes being printed for use by the Allied forces in France.

"Bill got home at 11 P.M.—on a beachhead in France only three days before," recorded Ruth Donovan in her diary on the fourteenth. And if Donovan had heavy affairs of state and international amity to deal with in Washington, he did not display them on his arrival; he went straight down to the farm at Berryville to see his granddaughter, Patricia. It was not long before the telephone began ringing and Buxton was warning him that the secretaries of war and state were out for his blood; in some way, probably at a Cabinet meeting, word that Donovan had become involved at the center of De Gaulle's visit and armaments for the French resistance had got out, and Stimson and Hull believed both were matters that should properly have been handled by their departments.

Donovan saw Roosevelt on the fifteenth and in the thorny matter of relations between Roosevelt and De Gaulle, Donovan contended that "our intelligence clearly showed that there were many people in France, particularly those in the Maquis resistance groups, who did not like the Algiers set-up"—De Gaulle's Committee of National Liberation. There were many who did not "look with favor upon De Gaulle as a political figure." Nevertheless, in view of the national insurrection, there were many in the resistance groups, whatever their view of De Gaulle as a political leader, who thought it advisable to have him in France now as the main "symbol of resistance."[6]

FDR agreed to receive De Gaulle, and Donovan suddenly shot off to Algiers, presumably to make the arrangements with Dewavrin for De Gaulle's visit to Washington. There is no record of what transpired in Algiers, or whom Donovan saw, but he was back in Washington on or about July 5, 1944, having signaled ahead the news that De Gaulle had agreed to visit Roosevelt between July 6 and 8. Then, on the fifth, WJD received a radiotelephone message from Dulles in Bern that not only demonstrated the violence and power of the national insurrection but also, Donovan noted in another memo to the President, was "the kind of story you may consider represents a common ground on which De Gaulle and yourself may meet in a public condemnation of these atrocities and in a promise to end them."[7]

Describing the dramatic situation at Limoges, the great porcelain and enamel center of France, Dulles, who had many important links to the French resistance, had reported by radiotelephone on July 1, 1944:

> The city is in a virtual state of siege. The center of the city is entirely cut off by barricades and block houses held by the [Fascist] gardes mobiles [security police] and the milice [militia]. The prefect and all the administrative authorities have been deprived of their powers. The person in command is a lieutenant of [the Fascist] Darnand named Vaugelas, former aviator known for his repressive measures against the Haute Savoie maquis. He has installed himself as dictator, forced the young men to enroll in the milice, and requisited [sic] all existing stocks. He arrests anybody he pleases without any judicial procedure. From time to time, in armored trucks, he leads expeditions into the surrounding country.
>
> Thus he went to Guéret at the head of his men to arrest the Secretary-General of the prefecture and a certain number of notables there, and brought them back to prison in Limoges. The Germans, who number about 2,000 in Limoges, are installed in the casernes [barracks]. They patrol the streets and control the city, where the Gestapo is creating a reign of terror.
>
> In the country, the maquis is in control, but it is divided between the FTP [Franc-Tireurs Partisan], of Communist tendencies, the FFI [French Forces of Interior], military elements of the Secret Army, and special groups which obey only their local chiefs. After the invasion, these various elements all wished to make known their presence by various acts of sabotage and even of terrorism.
>
> They proceeded to enroll a large number of people, and, by their disorganized action, brought down terrible reprisals by the Germans. These reprisals have bathed the whole region in blood. Everywhere there are large numbers of civilians who have been executed by the Germans.
>
> After the maquis were driven out of the city, the most serious developments were those which occurred at Tulle and Oradour.

These two small towns lay on the line of march to Normandy of the Das Reich Panzer Division. A colonel of one of the SS regiments vanished, having been killed or captured by the maquis, and the incident, combined with others, produced a murderous state of affairs unequaled even for France at that time. Dulles reported:

[In Tulle] the maquis, after having taken the city, wished to take a small garrison of about a hundred Germans. The inexperience of the men of the maquis cost them heavy losses. When they were finally able to reduce the garrison, they massacred their prisoners. They also executed a certain number of persons suspected of being collaborationists.

The SS *Das Reich* troopers decided to raze the city. On the intervention of the Prefect, and considering that a certain number of German wounded had been saved from the massacre and cared for by the inhabitants, they decided to execute only a part of the population. After days of terror, they ended by hanging from the balconies of the principal street of Tulle 150 hostages taken haphazard throughout the city. Adding to this the number of persons killed at the time of the action and during the razing of the city by the Germans, seven to eight hundred persons were victims of this adventure.

Dulles then turned to the incident at Oradour, where the SS colonel had vanished. Unaware of that factor, Dulles stated that the "savagery of the Germans at Oradour is inexplicable." He continued:

An SS detachment arrived at ten in the morning on the tenth of June. It was market day, and many people from Limoges had gone there to get supplies. There was also a great number of children sent there for their vacation—a total of about twelve hundred persons.

On the pretext of searching for clandestine munitions depots, the SS commander had all the men shut up in two or three barns, and all the women and children in the church. The abandoned village was then pillaged. At two o'clock, the houses were set on fire, then the barns. The Germans machine-gunned all who attempted to escape. At five o'clock the church was set on fire. Here again machine guns were used. One woman only managed to escape.

The German general commanding at Limoges acknowledged before the Prefect that this act dishonored his country. He permitted the bishop and the Prefect to visit the ruins and authorized a funeral service at the cathedral.

Dulles went on:

In the face of these barbarous acts, the whole region trembles. The peasants hide in the woods, and scouts signal the arrival of any German vehicles. [The country has] at one and the same time the violence of the enemy, of the maquis, and of the milice. There is no longer any legal authority. The Prefect is powerless. A wild anger pervades the terrorized people. The fate of Limoges, and that of all the cities in the center of France, is very much the same. At the mercy of this terror—almost impossible to describe. The only comfort in this frightful situation is to be found in the intense patriotism of these people, in their hope of prompt deliverance, and in the reaction which is developing against all violence. It is true that all hope for the constitution of the regular army and the reconstitution of a legitimate authority, but it is high time that these hopes and aspirations are supported by concrete and serious action.

News of these atrocities was imparted jointly to the press by the President and De Gaulle at a press conference on De Gaulle's arrival in Washington, and with it a new name joined the long list of atrocities and savagery of which the Germans now stood accused: Warsaw, Rotterdam, Belgrade, Coventry, the *Athenia,* and now Oradour-sur-Glane, the ruined streets of which De Gaulle decided should be preserved in perpetuity as a monument to the German occupation.

While the Oradour and Tulle massacres did nothing to ease the severe political differences between Roosevelt and De Gaulle, the President spoke cordially of General De Gaulle at a state luncheon given in the Frenchman's honor. "I think," declared the President, "we will all agree that this is an historic occasion we will remember all the rest of our lives." There were "no great problems between the French and the Americans, or between General De Gaulle and myself." Such problems as there were were "all working out awfully well, without exception." They were "going to work out all right, if they will just leave a few of us alone to sit around the table." Therefore, "it has been a great privilege to have General De Gaulle come here to talk about these things."[8] Roosevelt advised Churchill: "The visit has gone very well."

But if De Gaulle's version of the visit was correct, it did not go so well. He did not get what he had come to get: recognition of his committee as the provisional government of France. All he got from Roosevelt was, as the President explained to Churchill, acceptance of the "Committee as temporary de facto authority for civil administration in France provided two things are made clear—first, complete authority to be reserved to Eisenhower to do what he feels necessary to conduct effective military operations, and, second, that French people be given opportunity to make free choice of their own Government."

If Eisenhower was to be made viceroy *ad interim* of France, then at least Donovan's effort was not entirely wasted. For now, largely because of Donovan's quiet words in the lofty rooms of the White House, the French maquis was now being supplied on a vast scale.

At staff conversations with Dewavrin's representatives in Washington during De Gaulle's visit, Donovan announced that he favored the early establishment of a representative of De Gaulle in Brittany as the civil and military power under Allied command and the acknowledgment of the Free French Forces of the Interior (FFI) in France as a fourth arm, part of Eisenhower's command and not a separate entity. All this greatly pleased the French, for it assured De Gaulle of almost uncontested control of France at the liberation. Donovan also assured the French representatives that shortly new, massive airlifts of supplies would eclipse all previous supply operations.

Having arrived from London for the staff conversations, Colonel Haskell presented to the French a paper entitled "Appreciation of the Potentialities of French Resistance," which had impressed SHAEF in England as it was now impressing the Joint Chiefs. The French had already seen something of the power at Donovan's disposal when, in Operation Zebra on June 24, 1944, 176 B-17's of the 3rd Air Division had dropped 2,111 containers to four different maquis in south-central France.[9] All told, that day Donovan's planes had provided arms for 20,000 men. He assured the French that the OSS and the U.S. Army Air Forces were preparing a huge operation, the largest single air supply operation of World War II.

To obtain presidential support, Donovan sent President Roosevelt the longest report of his career so far. On July 6, 1944, Donovan stated that 314 of the 868 rail cuts planned for D-Day by June 16 had been "successfully attacked," with a further 211 "being attacked."[10] These cuts had greatly delayed all rail movement throughout France, and in some regions all rail movement had been stopped. The principal example of the effectiveness of resistance activity was the movement of the 2nd SS Das Reich Panzer Division, which had left the Montauban area for the Normandy front on June 8 and was a unit sufficiently powerful in itself to have disrupted Omaha beachhead. But as late as June 16 its main units had still not been identified as having arrived in Normandy. Also, "reports show that a large number of their heavy tanks had been left behind at Montauban through lack of rail facilities to move them north."

In telecommunications, all long lines from Paris to the provincial capitals, except the Paris–Vichy circuits, had been cut by June 8, and in many instances where repeater stations had been blown the cuts were semipermanent. The short lines from Caen–Rouen, Rouen–Amiens, and St.-Lô–Avranches–Miniac, all of which were close (and vital) to the battle area, were also down. Roads "have been sabotaged in many places and ambushes carried out against troops on the move, staff cars, dispatch riders, etc. Over a thousand bazookas have been placed in the hands of resistance elements in north-east France and are being effectively used in knocking out tanks and other enemy vehicles."

In the north and east of France, Donovan continued, resistance had remained clandestine—small groups executing sabotage missions against selected targets. But in the center, south, and east of France, guerrilla actions had flared out openly, resulting in bitter fighting between German and patriot forces in which the resistance had gained complete control of large areas. The departments of Dordogne, Corrèze, Vienne, Ardèche, Indre, Ain, Jura, and parts of Gers, Drôme, Savoie, Haute-Savoie, and Saône-et-Loire were in a state of general insurrection.

Donovan then converted the national insurrection into matters of strategy, tactics, and politics. By arming and directing the rapidly expanding maquis, he advised the President, the Americans were making the Germans face the alternative of diverting divisions, critically needed elsewhere, to fight the resistance movements or of losing control of northeastern, central, and southern France—their rear areas. They were also being forced to defend not only their communications but also the possibility that the maquis might gain control of ports through which fresh Allied forces could stream or areas which the Allies could use as airheads where airborne armies could be landed in their rear.

Already, Donovan continued, the maquis substantially controlled seven major areas in France, all of which threatened the Germans' communications. To restore Wehrmacht control would require eight German divisions. It was estimated that with the present state of the battle in Normandy and with other large-scale operations threatening on the Provence coast, the Germans could spare no more than three such divisions. Therefore, it could not be long before the German hold on France was totally and irremediably fractured.

The political implications of this situation were great, Donovan asserted. Command at Special Forces Headquarters in London was now truly tripartite, and one of the major results of this integration was "a much greater recognition and appreciation by the French of the scale and scope of American aid to resistance," which previously had been "heavily under-estimated." Since so much of the maquis force had come out into the open, it followed that failure to "support these forces on a sufficient scale to prevent their liquidation by the enemy will not only destroy a valuable military asset but will produce very unfavorable political repercussions." The creation of the "interior" or "4th front" through reinforced American arms supplies "would give large masses of the French people their long desired opportunity of National self-expression" and "produce and give lustre to other military and political leaders." The "net political effect" would be the emergence of alternatives to De Gaulle through the creation of what Donovan called "a larger number of potential leaders for the French people to appraise and select."

The points were not lost on Roosevelt, and on July 14, 1944—Bastille Day, the most important day in the calendar of the French Revolution—the great operation Donovan had promised the French staff took place. In Operation Cadillac, 320 B-17 bombers of the U.S. 3rd Air Division, commanded by General Curtis LeMay, took off from their airfields in eastern England, each bomber laden with twelve parachute containers. The Cadillac force carried 18,379 pounds of explosive, 2,843 submachine guns, 5,069,100 rounds of 9 millimeter ammunition, 6,600 grenades, 555 pistols with 50 rounds per gun, 830 light machine guns and 4,752 rifles with 6,852,368 rounds of ammunition, and 109 rocket launchers of the bazooka type with 2,180 rounds. With such stores sent in, the aerial resupply of the maquis had been transformed.

Escorted by twenty-six squadrons of Thunderbolts, Cadillac reached the seven different large maquis in action against the Wehrmacht in south-central France. Twenty-five miles out the pall from the smoke fires, lit by the maquis to act as beacons for the B-17's, was spotted, and the force began to descend from 17,000 feet to their dropping altitudes of between 500 and 1,125 feet. The planes lowered their flaps, wheels, and bomb doors and throttled back to achieve a dropping speed of 145 knots, bucking and heaving in the currents from the mountains below. Without being intercepted by German fighters or engaged by ground fire, an estimated 90 percent of the aircraft dropped their loads almost directly into the arms of the scurrying figures below.

The dropping operation took twenty minutes longer than estimated, and the escorting fighters were forced to withdraw before relief squadrons could arrive. During that interval twelve Me-109's, which had been lurking about in the cirrus stratus above the bomber force, attacked, damaging a number of B-17's and setting one afire. But the relief escort arrived from England before the Germans could shoot down any of the damaged bombers, and the force climbed back to 17,000 feet and returned to England.

The operation—a sort of Hollywood spectacular of supply operations —was a stunning success, and in the maquis-held areas the organizers were able to report that for the first time since the fall of France in 1940 the resister had become more powerful than the occupier. "Great show!" wirelessed the organizer of the Marksman team in the Cantal, which was being heavily engaged by German and French Fascist troops. "When is the next one?"[11]

The next one took place five days later, and the operations continued until there was no longer any need for them.

No more than a rough estimate of the amount of war stores sent in to the maquis through WJD's efforts is possible, and no estimate at all about the amount delivered jointly by the OSS and the SOE is possible. The French estimated that the maquis came to number about 200,000 men and women, all armed. Most of their arms came from America and Britain, but sizable numbers of weapons and munitions were taken from the Germans and Italians. However, it is known with some precision what was sent from OSS bases in England in the period January–October 1944, most of it between June 6 and October 1944. To these figures must be added perhaps a quarter as much again sent by OSS Algiers, but no precise figures are available. OSS London sent in, among much else, 16,807 .30-caliber rifles, 2,405 Marlin submachine guns, 15,692 .45 automatics, 2,266 bazooka rocket launchers, 1,030,900 rounds of .45 ammunition, 829,000 rounds of .38 parabellum, 5,403,500 rounds of .30 carbine ammunition, 323,029 pounds of *plastique* high explosive, and 43,900 bazooka rockets, as well as 21,000 packages of K and X rations and 11,000 woolen jackets. With the SOE's deliveries—although much of their stores came from OSS depots in England—these figures could be tripled. In making their drops OSS aircraft flew 2,595 missions and lost fifteen aircraft and crews in delivering the stores. They were distributed by a total of 377 agents, a figure that included 200 OGs, sent to France during the insurrectionary period.[12]

When added to the 250,000-man French First Army, equipped at Algiers for Dragoon, the number of men equipped by purely American sources reached just under 500,000. Also, the United States equipped nineteen air squadrons with 1,417 aircraft and supplied 27,000 trucks and 1,400 tanks. In all, the capital cost of the promises made at the Clark-Mast conference at Cherchel was $2,294,000,000 with a further $548,000,000 furnished the French civilian sector up to the end of the world war. All this was paid under lend-lease, except for $232,000,000 paid by France. At the final settlement, it was agreed that France should pay the United States in settlement of all lend-lease debts a further $420,000,000, with interest at 2 percent, commencing July 1, 1952.[13]

37

Cobra

Early in July 1944, while on the mission to Algiers to discuss De Gaulle's meeting with FDR in Washington, Donovan suddenly and unexpectedly left for Rome. There he saw Pope Pius XII in private audience, at which they discussed "Communism, Germany and Russia." WJD took the opportunity of drawing the Pope's attention to the existence of a Japanese espionage transmitter in Vatican City, which was against apostolic law, and it was soon shut down. Also, during the audience, the Pope asked WJD to convey to FDR "All my heart's affection."[1]

That, it seemed from Donovan's papers, was the extent of WJD's business while in Rome. But in fact, he had a meeting with Baron Ernst von Weizsäcker, German ambassador to the Holy See, who was a member of the Black Orchestra and an admirer of Canaris. Weizsäcker referred obliquely to the existence of a plot against the life of Hitler and wished to know what terms could be expected from the Grand Alliance if the German people acted to change their government. Donovan's reply was not recorded, but if he obeyed his instructions from the President and secretary of state, and it is assumed that he did, he could have replied only that he was not empowered to engage in political conversations with enemy representatives but would be prepared to take a message to Washington. Whether that was done is not evident from the record, but Weizsäcker and Donovan did arrange to meet again at the Vatican in August.

At the same time it is not improbable that WJD actively encouraged Weizsäcker to act against Hitler at the earliest opportunity. Whatever WJD did or did not say to the German ambassador, however, a week or ten days later, back in Washington, WJD received this signal from Dulles in Bern, on July 12, 1944: "There is a possibility that a dramatic event may take place up north, if Breakers [Dulles's code name for German resistance movement] courier is to be trusted. We expect a complete account this evening. . . . [Gisevius] has gone north for discussions."[2]

That was electrifying news, for although the Allies had 1,000,000 men ashore in Normandy, with 150,000 vehicles and half a million tons of supplies, the Germans had caught their second wind. A mighty attack by the British Army to take the old Norman city of Caen had been fought to a standstill by the seven panzer and two infantry divisions of Panzer Group West, and Bradley's First Army was entangled in the bocage—the close hedgerow country of the Norman interior—and taking very heavy casualties: 40,000 men a week. Only on the eastern front was the news satisfactory: On June 22, 1944, the Red Army had opened its summer offensive in step with the Normandy battle, and everywhere its armies were victorious. The Russian armies appeared about to break the German line and burst forth into Eastern and Central Europe—a prospect that was regarded with much alarm in London and Washington.

Donovan awaited Dulles's next message anxiously. It arrived on the thirteenth:

> A courier from Breakers, who came here a short time ago, advises that the Soviet victories have given new vigor to the Breakers movement. The success of the Allied movement in Normandy . . . has also contributed to the impetus of this movement. . . . I am not making any forecasts regarding the prospects of success for the Breakers program. . . . Without any doubt, the Gestapo is keeping its eye on developments and it is possible that the Gestapo may get rid of the leaders. Moreover, it is quite probable that the military men, whose action is indispensable to the achievement of these ends, will lack the "intestinal fortitude" to act, just as they have earlier. Furthermore, I am not unaware of the strength of the idea that Germany's defeat must be connected with the criminal program of the Fuehrer and the Nazi clique. Nevertheless, the moral consequences of a display of bravery in taking steps toward setting their own affairs to rights would be valuable to Germany's subsequent status in Europe that will exist after the war.[3]

Only later would Donovan learn that Dulles had been wrong. Conscious that on all six fronts—France, Russia, Italy, the Balkans, the air, and the sea—decisive military operations were afoot, a German staff officer with access to Hitler's person at the daily staff meeting at *Führerhauptquartier* (FHW), in the dark pine woods of East Prussia near Rastenburg, had decided to kill Hitler. Part of the plan—called Valkyrie—included seizure of the power of the state by a group of German officers and civilians, who had at their disposal the Reserve Army in Germany, and the arrest of all members of the National Socialist administration.

Trusted emissaries, who included Gisevius, would then seek an armistice with America, Britain, and Russia.

The officer who was to attempt to assassinate Hitler and then make the revolution was Colonel Count Klaus Schenk von Stauffenberg, thirty-seven, a liberal-minded member of an ancient Württemberg family whose father had been senior marshal and lord privy at the court of Wilhelm II. Stauffenberg had been badly wounded in action with the Afrika Korps in Tunisia in 1942 and was now chief of staff to the commander in chief of the Reserve Army in Berlin, a position that required him personally to make reports to Hitler on the manpower situation within the German Army.

A Catholic, Stauffenberg had never been a member of the Nazi party, and as a General Staff officer he became determined to act when he came to believe, while he was in the hospital at Carthage, in Tunisia, that the war was lost and its continuation was senseless. He joined the Black Orchestra and in the last week of June 1944 saw Canaris's successor, Colonel Georg Hansen. Hansen, too, was in the conspiracy against Hitler, and when Stauffenberg advised Hansen that he would try to kill Hitler at the earliest moment, Hansen sent an official to Switzerland to tell Gisevius.

The official, Theodor Strunck, arrived in Geneva on about July 10, 1944, and saw Edward von Waetjen, one of Hansen's agents and the man with an American mother and a sister who had married David Rockefeller's cousin Godfrey. Waetjen saw Gisevius at Davos, where Gisevius was on holiday. Gisevius contacted Dulles's agent in Geneva, Mary Bancroft, who notified Dulles. Gisevius left for Berlin, where he stayed at Strunck's home at Nürnbergerstrasse 13. There, in close contact with his friend Count Wolf Heinrich von Helldorf, the police president, who was also in the plot, Gisevius became involved in the central planning of the revolution that would follow Hitler's assassination. Thus, Dulles had a trusted agent at the very heart of the conspiracy throughout the next period.

As Donovan gradually became aware, the essence of the plan was Stauffenberg's control of the Reserve Army and the Valkyrie plan, which had been prepared and circulated some months before as a directive to all Wehrmacht units in Germany. Its original purpose was the suppression of disturbances among the 8,000,000 or 9,000,000 foreign and slave workers in the Greater German Reich. Upon receipt of the code word Valkyrie from the headquarters in Berlin of the Reserve Army, which had responsibility for carrying out the plan, all Wehrmacht units were to take over all centers of control in their area, including all means of communication and administration. They were to keep control of these centers until further orders were received from the Reserve Army.

In the original orders neither the Nazi party nor any of its military organizations were mentioned. But supplementary orders, prepared by

Stauffenberg and signed by the commander in chief of the Reserve Army, General Friedrich Fromm, a lazy man who rarely read what he was signing and relied upon his deputy, General Friedrich Olbricht, also a member of the conspiracy, provided for the arrest of the party leaders and the SS —since all SS battle units were at the fronts, no great armed opposition could be offered by party military formations. As for the German Army units in Germany, it was known that their officers would, in general, accept the orders of the new commander in chief, Field Marshal Erwin von Witzleben, also a member of the conspiracy. The conspirators expected their orders to be obeyed everywhere, especially at the headquarters on the western front, where the conspiracy was more powerful than anywhere else except Berlin. Also, Stauffenberg expected no difficulties in seizing all the principal German cities, including Berlin, where the commandant was a prominent member of the conspiracy.

The intention was to seek an immediate armistice in the West and in Italy, with a cessation of the missile bombardment of London, which had started just after D-Day, and a holding of the line on the eastern front pending a final decision regarding eastern policy. Three emissaries were to be used to seek the armistice: Ewald von Kleist in Stockholm, Gisevius in Bern, and Otto John in Lisbon.

The plan was an excellent one, which would work and succeed, provided the conspirators acted expeditiously and with determination. Above all, it was essential that at the outset Hitler's headquarters at Rastenburg were cut off from the outside world, so that generals loyal to Hitler could not issue counterorders. To ensure that all lines between the Wolf's Lair, as the headquarters was code-named, were cut, the chief of the German Army signals service, General Erich Fellgiebel, another conspirator, was there to destroy Hitler's telephone, telegraphic, and radio communications with the outside world.

Meanwhile, the British had received word of the plan, and on the twelfth, Churchill and the deputy premier, Clement Attlee, made parliamentary statements encouraging the Black Orchestra to strike, Churchill going so far on July 12 as to declare that an attack on Hitler now "would be a very well-advised step on the part of the Germans."[4] No such statement was forthcoming, however, from Roosevelt. Dulles telephoned Donovan on the night of July 13 to recommend that the President make such a declaration, and Donovan saw Roosevelt with the latest Breakers news and Dulles's recommendation. However, the President declined absolutely to make such a statement—why he would not say. Nor was he prepared to change his mind, as Donovan tried to get him to do during the evening of the fifteenth, when Donovan either saw Roosevelt at the White House or spoke to him on the telephone concerning more Breakers' intelligence.

On that night Donovan sent the President, the secretary of state, and the Joint Chiefs a paper entitled "Germany: Nazi Opposition Group Reports Progress."[5] The paper was of great importance to the military, for it tended to confirm that an attempt on Hitler's life by powerful elements within the German General Staff was imminent. It stated that Stauffenberg's commanding general, Friedrich Fromm, had joined the conspiracy—indicating that the conspirators might control large bodies of troops—and that the Chief of the German General Staff, General Kurt Zeitzler, hitherto an officer completely loyal to Hitler, might also have done so. Mentioned as involved in the plot was Fromm's deputy, General Friedrich Olbricht, and the paper stated:

> The group is receiving cooperation from another group composed of a number of anti-Hitler elements which are described as working independently of the Gestapo. The former group believes that the next few weeks represent the final opportunity to initiate steps to prove the desire of the German people to overthrow Hitler and his organization and to set up a "respectable government." It is the wish of the group that as much of Germany as possible be kept from falling into Soviet hands.

On the nineteenth—Donovan was to learn—there was a meeting among Stauffenberg, Gisevius, and several others involved in the plot, in the basement of Strunck's home. Stauffenberg announced that he was to report to Hitler personally at Rastenburg on the following morning, at which time he would endeavor to kill the Führer. The meeting confirmed that the conspirators would put into effect the measures already planned for seizing the power of the state, in order to "prove to the world and to future generations that the men of the German resistance movement dared to take the decisive step and to hazard their lives upon it."[6]

That July 20, 1944, Hitler held his noon conference not in the concrete-lined underground bunker at the Wolf's Lair, his headquarters, but in a prefabricated wooden hut on the surface. At about 12:40 P.M. Stauffenberg set the British-made bomb—probably obtained from captured SOE stores in France—and excused himself from the crowded conference room. As he watched from a knoll nearby, a few minutes later the powerful bomb exploded, shattering the building and, Stauffenberg believed, killing everyone inside. He hastened to the airport and took back to Berlin the private aircraft that had brought him from the capital that morning. He was certain that Hitler was dead.

But Stauffenberg was wrong. Some of those present had been killed or mortally wounded, but through a fluke the blast had been deflected away from Hitler, who was suffering from no more than a form of concussion, damage to his inner ear, severe bruising, and a torso peppered with wooden splinters. Aware that Hitler was alive, Fellgiebel lost his nerve and failed to cut the communications links between the Wolf's Lair and

Berlin; thus, when Field Marshal Erwin Witzleben and General Beck, the titular heads of the revolution, announced that the SS had killed Hitler and ordered the Valkyrie plan to be put into effect, Hitler was able to countermand the orders effectively.

While Gisevius watched, the plot thereupon collapsed in a welter of executions and suicides. Stauffenberg was shot summarily by a firing squad that same night, and throughout the Reich there began a Gestapo *ratissage*. Gisevius, one of the few to escape the government quarter of Berlin, went into hiding in one of the suburbs until he could get a message out to Dulles, requesting help in exfiltration to Switzerland. Only at Paris did the plot succeed, and for many hours the SS was effectively immured by the Army High Command. The commander in chief on the western front, Field Marshal Günther von Kluge, at his headquarters in the Château de la Roche Guyon on the outskirts of Paris, came close to issuing orders for the cessation of hostilities in Normandy and of the rocket and cruise-missile bombardment of London—all he wanted was confirmation from Reserve Army that Hitler was dead. Of course, such confirmation never came.

Just before the attempt to kill Hitler on July 20, 1944, Montgomery, perhaps acting on intelligence about the plot from Donovan and the British services, unleashed his left hook to break the German line around Caen. The massive armored operation called Goodwood failed owing primarily to ferocious Waffen SS resistance in and around Caen. Then, just after Valkyrie, came the right hook, Cobra, in which General Omar N. Bradley's U.S. First Army attacked on a narrow front in the area of St.-Lô. The offensive was preceded by one of the greatest bombardments in the history of arms. The German line broke, and by dawn on July 31, 1944, all attention—German as well as Allied—was fixed on Avranches, a hill resort of 7,000 people overlooking Mont-St.-Michel, where there was a single stone bridge over the broad estuary of the Sée River.

Miraculously the Germans had not blown the bridge over the Sée, and the armored spearheads slashed on as towns and villages became bright with tricolors—they were moving so fast that it was not possible to keep track of them on maps, only by reconnaissance aircraft. Where there were tricolors the spearheads had passed by; where there were not, the area was still in the hands of the Germans.

Again miraculously the Germans had not blown the last bridge before Brittany, the old Norman stone bridge with thirteen arches over the Sélune River. Patton rammed the fighting elements of seven divisions— 110,000 men with all arms—over the bridge, and by daybreak on August 1, 1944, his spearheads were at one and the same time turning east toward Chartres, south toward Le Mans, and west toward Brest. "In the next four to eight weeks," announced the G-2 of U.S. First Army, Colonel

Benjamin A. "Monk" Dickson, that day, "the current situation may change with dramatic suddenness into a race to reach a chaotic Germany."[7]

In tankmen's weather—warm, dry, cloudless—one of the two combat commands of General John S. Wood's 4th U.S. Armored Division then made forty miles in an afternoon—faster than Rommel during the fall of France in 1940—across the neck of the Breton peninsula until, in the evening sunset of August 1, 1944, the tankers saw the cupolas of Rennes through the blood red haze created by the setting sun and the dust of a preparatory aerial bombardment by massed Mustangs, Thunderbolts, Lightnings, and Bostons. A German counterattack deflected Wood momentarily, so he sent his tanks darting across the rolling moors to Vannes. With that stroke Patton's army had severed Brittany from the rest of France, along with 70,000 soldiers in the peninsula—110,000 if the Wehrmacht garrison in the Channel Islands was counted. Brest was now 200 miles away up the peninsula, and Wood and General Robert W. Grow, commander of the 6th U.S. Armored Division, both received what would be called "a cavalry mission from a cavalryman."[8]

But Donovan's Jedburghs, now in command of no fewer than 30,000 armed *maquisards*, had already secured most of the principal highways and towns leading to Brest when, on August 3, came the quaint but heroic call to arms over BBC London. That faraway, tinny, hollow voice enunciated the words with great care, like a ghostly train announcer: "*Mes amis, voici le BBC. Voici les messages personnels comme toujours: Le cha . . . peau de Na . . . poléon, est-il tou . . . jours à Perros . . . Guirec? Alors, maintenant: Le cha . . . peau, est-il tou-jours à Per . . . ros . . . Guir . . . ec? Et voilà, ici un autre message personnel . . .*"

General Pierre Koenig, the Frenchman commanding Special Forces Headquarters, went to the microphones of the French service of the BBC to declare formally to call for the French national insurrection:

> French people of Brittany, the hour of your liberation has come! The provisional government of the French Republic calls for the national uprising! French people of Brittany, workers, peasants, officials, employees! The time has come for you to take part, with or without weapons, in the last battle! French people of Brittany! The whole of France salutes you! The whole of France will follow you in the national insurrection![9]

The Arcadia plan now reached its culmination. General de Gaulle went to the microphones to support the call with the words that it was "the simple and sacred duty of every Frenchman" to "take part in the supreme war effort of the country." He cried, "Frenchmen! The hour of liberation sounds! Join the French Forces of the Interior! The national insurrection will be the prelude of liberation! *Français! L'heure de la libération sonne!*"

Like their guerrilla ancestors, the Chouans and the Companions of Jehu, the Bretons rose to a man that day, as the Jedburghs issued a command not heard in France since the French Revolution: *"Formez-vous vos bataillons!"*

Within three weeks the peninsula was secured. Then the Gaullist bureaucrats arrived to plant *le général*'s standard on the soil of France. Mission Aloes—a bitter plant—had come to take control of Brittany from the Jedburghs. Ten Halifaxes towing Waco gliders appeared over the Landes de Lanvaux north of Vannes. The gliders cast off and whistled down with their cargoes of civil servants, armored jeeps, wirelesses, typewriters, safes, mimeograph machines, folding tables and chairs, tents— equipment for De Gaulle's headquarters, which enjoyed the title of *État Major du Commandement Superieur des Forces en la Grande Bretagne et Délégation Militaire du Gouvernement Provisional de la République Française.* Led by Dewavrin, the men of the steward of France, Charles de Gaulle, had come to claim the keys of the Fourth Republic.

But if the general was grateful to Donovan for the singular services rendered by the American and the OSS to the French nation, De Gaulle did not display his gratitude when the time came to bestow the customary honors. Far from receiving the Légion d'Honneur in the highest degree, or even the second degree, Donovan was made a Commander of the Order, the middle grade in the five ranks extending from the Grands Croix to the Chevaliers. This was no more than a routine award, and while it bothered Donovan not at all (he rarely wore any of his many decorations or their ribbons, except for the Congressional Medal of Honor), the lack of distinction and enthusiasm of the Gaullists did not go unnoticed among those who cared in the OSS. The reason for the rather offhand award was, undoubtedly, WJD's close association with Giraud and his intelligence service, the SR, in 1942 and 1943 and his failure to persuade the U.S. government to supply more arms to the French resistance before D-Day.

On the other hand, it was noteworthy, as will be shown shortly, that Donovan pressed his government at risk to himself to award De Gaulle's intelligence master, André Dewavrin, with the Distinguished Service Cross, America's highest award after that of the Medal of Honor.

By August 25, 1944, Donovan's detachment with General Bradley's Twelfth Army Group's tactical headquarters had reached Rambouillet on the outskirts of Paris. There the detachment commander, Lieutenant Colonel Kenneth Downs, interviewed a British secret agent, Colonel Claude Arnould, who with a number of other men had made their way through the lines of battle around Paris. Arnould's mission was to try to arrange the surrender of the German garrison in Paris, which, obedient to orders from Hitler, was preparing to destroy many of the most important buildings in the French capital. On receiving that news, Eisenhower ordered forces under Bradley's command to take the capital, and Bradley's chief of intelligence, General Edwin L. Sibert, ordered Downs to take Arnould back into Paris and provide intelligence needed by the units assigned to the liberation operations.

Lieutenant John Mowinckel, one of Donovan's favorite young officers, was to remember that he was routed out of bed in the Grand Veneur Hotel in Rambouillet at about 3:00 A.M. He wrote later: "We left Rambouillet in a column of four jeeps with me leading the way in my jeep with Colonel Downs and Colonel Arnould. Behind me was my driver with the radio jeep and code sergeant and two back-up vehicles with three men apiece."[10]

Lieutenant Mowinckel's drive to Paris was one of the epic motor journeys of the twentieth century, for at least symbolically the OSS was to represent the United States in the liberation of the French capital. The jeeps leaped out of the courtyard of the Grand Veneur, down to the Rue Grand Lenôtre, on to the Rue Sadi Carnot, and up on to the main road to Versailles and Paris. In the dawn mist there was the Palais de Rambouillet, where Pétain had hunted the stag with *Reichsmarschall* Hermann Göring, during the four years and two months of the New Order in France.

The OSS Phantoms—a service of battlefield intelligence collectors— had affected scarves of orange parachute silk and goggles as protection against the dust, and the bright silk fluttered wildly as the small convoy hurtled across the Chevreuse Valley, with its orchards and vineyards, on past Versailles. Mowinckel was to write:

> We ran into no firefights on our way into Paris and also managed to avoid any mines. The only incident of note occurred shortly before a sharp curve in a forest. Suddenly a group of four armed, bedraggled and fierce-looking civilians sprang out of a ditch and frantically shouted at us to halt. Expecting a German ambush around the corner, I skidded to a stop, whereupon the Frenchmen asked if we would like a glass of wine.

Mowinckel's column sped on to Paris after they had refreshed themselves. They met no trouble on the last miles into Paris. In places German resistance was still fierce, and the French armored division lost 71 dead, 225 wounded, and 21 missing, and 35 tanks, 6 self-propelled guns, and 111 vehicles were destroyed. But when the French tanks rolled down the Rue de Rivoli, poking their 75 millimeter gun snouts into the arcades to force the German guards around the Hôtel Meurice to surrender, the end came rather rapidly.

Accompanied by Mowinckel and one or two other OSS men, some French grenadiers threw smoke bombs and then charged into the lobby of the most distinguished of French hotels. They found the German commander of Paris, General Dietrich von Choltitz, at his desk in his office at the Meurice, smoking a cigarette, and he was so calm that for a moment the young Frenchman leading the party was nonplussed. In his excitement he could shout at Choltitz only: "Do you speak German?" Choltitz replied very calmly, "Probably better than you do," and with those five words Paris fell to the Allied armies.

Choltitz was led downstairs to sign the surrender documents at the prefecture of police, but when the *résistant* who was supposed to drive him there found he had lost the car keys, Choltitz was forced to endure a humiliating and dangerous walk to police headquarters. He arrived there safely, and the surrender document was signed in the prefect's billiard room. Later, when Allied officials came to examine the document, they found that Choltitz had surrendered Paris and France not to Eisenhower, the supreme commander, but to De Gaulle, who had no rank or recognition. And an hour after the signing, De Gaulle himself arrived at the Gare Montparnasse to collect the keys of France. And it was said of Choltitz shortly after the surrender: "He was damn glad to get rid of the job of policing both Paris and Frenchmen, both of whom he apparently detests."[11]

Meanwhile, Arnould, Downs, and Mowinckel had arrived at the Convent of Ste.-Anne, a clinic and death house for the poor run by nuns of the Order of Sisters of Agonie. Headquarters of the British Secret Intelligence Service in Paris, the convent was at 127 Rue de la Santé, directly under the walls of the Ste.-Anne lunatic asylum. Mowinckel recorded: "Colonel [Arnould] directed me through the streets until—at 3 P.M.—we arrived before the large doors of the little convent. [The] Mother Superior . . . peered through the trap-window, shouted a welcome, and with the help of Sister Jean Marie Vianney, opened wide the doors." Four and a quarter years of clandestinity were over. But the termination of that dark period was not without some embarrassment. "Some weeks before," recorded Mowinckel, "I had named my jeep the 'Pet de Nonne,' which is the name of French cream puffs. Literally translated, however, it means 'Nun's Fart.' All the nine nuns broke into laughter as they saw the name painted on my windshield."

With the wireless jeep in the courtyard, Downs and Mowinckel began to transmit their reports to Sibert at Bradley's headquarters, assisted by the contents of a rehoboam of champagne. *This bridge intact, that bridge demined, charges removed from the Palais Bourbon, De Gaulle at the Hôtel de Ville, the Eiffel Tower inspected but no charges found.* . . . They transmitted for almost a week as the reports flooded in about the German evacuation. Then they decided the time had come, as Mowinckel was to describe it, "to proceed into the center of Paris on important business." Signals traffic had stopped, and they were just shutting down when the wireless on the jeep in the yard started to bleat out a fresh message. Mowinckel took down the coded message. Then he decoded it and discovered that it was for him and was signed "Donovan, 7th Army Forward." It stated: "Recently I had the pleasure of lunching with your father at the F Street Club and he is exercised that you have not written to him for some time. As your commanding officer I am therefore ordering you to stop whatever it is you are doing and write a letter to your home without delay."

38

Dragoon

On August 1, 1944, the Donovans took Patricia to the OSS theater for her first movie—the Walt Disney film *Fantasia,* that marvelous experiment with color, music, cartoons, and cameras. Then, as Ruth took the rest of the family up to Nonquitt, Donovan slipped out of the country to Algiers to take part in Dragoon, Eisenhower's right hook, a landing from bases in the Mediterranean by the U.S. Seventh and the French First armies, in the area of St.-Tropez on the Riviera coast of France, its object to capture Marseilles and to advance on Germany from the south.

Dragoon had been mainly an OSS intelligence responsibility, and while the operation was smaller in importance and scale than Neptune, it was one in which Glavin's command had demonstrated proficiency in the intelligence, counterespionage, and special operations fields. That proficiency was displayed when Donovan arrived to join the Dragoon fleet. OSS Algiers X-2 had uncovered what seemed to be potentially the most serious security risk encountered by OSS X-2.

Robert D. Murphy, the U.S. political adviser to the supreme Allied commander in the Mediterranean, Field Marshal Wilson, had had a brilliant professional career. However, the same could not be said about his personal life, which had been blotched by tragedy. Murphy's wife was an incurable manic-depressive, and one of his daughters had committed suicide. The experience had left him vulnerable emotionally. A lonely man, he had early in his work encountered the princess de Ligne, the representative in French North Africa of the comte de Paris, the pretender to the French throne. Their relationship had deepened from one of politics to a matter of the heart. The fact was not in itself exceptional or dangerous, for Murphy knew well how to keep secrets. But associated with the princess de Ligne was David Zagha, a Syrian Jew grown rich as an international dealer in gems and antiques and as the broker and real estate adviser to the princess.

Zagha had come first to the attention of the OSS when he acted as an intermediary in 1941 between Robert Murphy and General Maxime Weygand, the leading French general who had obtained the appointment of governor-general of Algeria in order to resume the war against Germany from French North Africa. When W. Arthur Roseborough became chief of OSS SI in Algiers, he retained Zagha's services, as both an informant and a source for the laundering of OSS funds. Since much could be deduced by hostile intelligence services about OSS intentions from OSS bank dealings, these transactions were handled by Zagha in his own name and through his own banks. Currencies were purchased by Zagha at rates favorable to the OSS, in return for which the OSS reimbursed his wife and family in Buenos Aires. These transactions were handled impeccably. Also, Zagha acted as an informant about salon political gossip in the highest reaches of French North African society. However, at all times Zagha appears to have been motivated by a single ideological interest: himself.

Throughout his association with the OSS, which he served as a dollar-a-year man, he played the OSS and the French intelligence and counterespionage services against the middle, always with great skill. On occasions, he served the OSS, the Giraudist groups, and the Gaullist service simultaneously, providing the OSS with political information about the state of affairs inside French North Africa and the French services with information on the politics, policies, and personalities of the OSS. The probability is that his primary loyalty was to the French services, for Syria was a French mandate, and Zagha maintained large interests in Damascus. On the other hand, only through the OSS could he convert his fortune from worthless francs in French colonial banks to valuable dollars in Buenos Aires.

His politics were never sharply evident. Although he claimed to be a Gaullist in discussions with Roseborough, to the princess de Ligne he claimed to be a royalist and was admitted to her small, influential, and extremely conspiratorial circle, which wanted the reestablishment of the monarchy in France after the war, with the comte de Paris as the king of France. Zagha became closely associated with Lemaigre-Dubreuil and seemed to him to be a Giraudist; to Emmanuel d'Astier de la Vigerie (De Gaulle's commissioner of internal affairs at Algiers after Giraud was toppled) he appeared to be a Gaullist; to Emmanuel's brother, Henri, who had played a part in the murder of Admiral Darlan, he seemed to be a royalist. And behind Zagha lay some formidable intellectual thugs of the

Securité Militaire (SM), who were adept at turning OSS agents against their masters. Among them: le capitaine Dumont, chief of SM 30, the central bureau of the Securité Militaire; Commandant Paillole, chief of the SM; and a mysterious but menacing individual known to OSS Algiers only as le Capelin, who appears to have been head of the section of the SM dealing with the OSS. Most of the time the OSS knew about Zagha's relationship with the SM, tolerated it because the OSS learned much about the politics, policies, and personalities of the SM that might otherwise have eluded it. In any case through the Securité Militaire there was a valuable pipe into the Sicherheitsdienst, whose stay-behind agents still lurked about Algiers, Tunis, Casablanca, and Oran.

Late in 1943 Zagha decided he wished to join his family in Buenos Aires. The OSS transferred to his account there a final payment of $20,000, reimbursement for one of Roseborough's transactions, and with his passage arranged by the OSS, he was flown to New York, not intending to return to Algiers. He was well received by OSS representatives, who did much to enable Zagha to negotiate the purchase for nearly $300,000 of machinery for the manufacture of woolen yarn. Among the men he spent much time with was Colonel H. F. Wanvig, who was leaving for Algiers shortly as X-2 representative. Wanvig was impressed by Zagha, as were most men, and Zagha claimed that Wanvig stated that if he wished to return to Algiers, Wanvig would give him a job in X-2. In return for his services he would be enabled to use OSS facilities to convert French francs into American dollars to a total of $250,000.

Zagha then traveled on to Buenos Aires and was reunited with his wife and children. In Buenos Aires he appears to have rendered an important service to the U.S. military attaché, General John W. Lang, who asked him to speak to Vice President and Defense Minister Juan Perón about some valuable German documents captured by the Argentinian security service, which Perón had refused to give to Lang. However, Zagha succeeded in obtaining the documents and delivered them to Lang—a transaction that not only impressed Lang and Military Intelligence but also strengthened the contact between Zagha and the Washington intelligence community.

Consequently, it was not long before Wanvig in Algiers contacted Zagha in Buenos Aires and, Zagha claimed, not only repeated his offer to convert francs worth $250,000 but also asked Zagha to come to Algiers on X-2 work for two or three months. Anxious to make the conversion —no easy task because of U.S. Treasury controls—Zagha agreed and returned on, he claimed, OSS X-2 travel documents to Algiers. There Zagha resumed contact with the Securité Militaire, almost certainly at Wanvig's request. Wanvig then arranged to buy $250,000 in French francs from Zagha at 75 to $1, a transaction on which Zagha stood to make a very large profit if he bought the francs, as is probable, at the free market rate of about 225–250 to $1; Zagha's $250,000 in U.S. bills would have cost him only about $80,000 in French francs.

But then two matters occurred. Wanvig was transferred from Algiers to another post before the $250,000 deal was completed. His financial affairs were transferred to the agent cashier, the admirable Crockett, who refused to honor the arrangement without authority from Special Funds Washington. Since nobody in Washington knew of the arrangements between Wanvig and Zagha, that authority was not forthcoming. At the same time security officials at OSS Algiers, who were not familiar with the exact nature of Zagha's relationship with the SM, immediately began to suspect him of having become a double agent working for the French against OSS. Those suspicions were heightened when OSS Algiers received a letter from the intelligence officer of the OGs, Lieutenant Colonel David V. Rosen, enclosing a long letter from Zagha to Donovan. Rosen stated emphatically: "We wish to say that we have no desire to make any use of this man or exploit any contacts he may have in North Africa"—a statement that immediately raised the specter that Zagha had been trying to penetrate the operational groups' command.

At that point WJD arrived in Algiers to join the Dragoon expedition. It seems that Donovan was aware only of the relationship between Zagha and the princess de Ligne and between the princess and Murphy. He saw the danger in the relationships and in the OSS's continuing association with Zagha. Moreover, Donovan appears to have seen a danger of a relationship between Zagha and the Sicherheitsdienst, whose agents had become extremely active in their search for intelligence about the destination of the Dragoon convoys—which were then assembling at every major port controlled by the Allies in the Mediterranean.

Donovan acted deftly and swiftly to rid the OSS of its embarrassing associate. Zagha was invited to Washington by the OSS general counsel, James B. Donovan, so that he could state his case regarding the $250,000. As expected, Zagha accepted, and when it was established that he would not have been out of pocket in any way by the refusal of the OSS to honor Wanvig's agreement, he was told that the U.S. Treasury forbade such transactions. He was then offered passage to his family in Buenos Aires, which he accepted. What became of him after his departure was not the OSS's concern; he had already made a great profit on his original currency transactions over a period of years. But of the greatest importance was the fact that at a time when Dragoon was being mounted, Zagha was not present to reveal to his shadowy contacts in Algiers, whoever they were, what, if anything, he had learned about Dragoon's inner secrets.

As a later investigation was to show, that was one of the wisest moves of Donovan's career. For of all the intelligence the SD gathered about Neptune, only one piece revealed where, when, and in what strength the Allies would land in Normandy. That intelligence had originated with a

German agent in Algiers, but mercifully for the Allies the Germans had not believed the intelligence and had filed it away among the dross.

Before joining the USS *Augusta* for the Dragoon assault on the Provence coast, Donovan visited the Villa Magnol. Accompanied by the chief of Algiers OSS SI, Henry Hyde, who had still not reached his thirtieth birthday, Donovan was able to see a major successful OSS human intelligence operation at work—and for the first time learned some of the full, queer details of Penny Farthing, the OSS's first secret intelligence operation into France.

After Jacques and Toto of the Penny Farthing team took off for Clermont-Ferrand aboard the Royal Air Force Halifax from Tempsford, England, in July 1943, Hyde returned to OSS London. He waited there until the RAF dispatcher aboard the Halifax reported on his return to Tempsford that the drop zone had been sighted correctly and that after the jump from the aircraft both Jacques's and Toto's parachutes had opened properly. There had been no antiaircraft gunfire at the *parachutage,* although some searchlights had come on, and one had picked out one of the agents —news that alarmed Hyde. However, the dispatcher went on, the searchlight went out after a split second, and he may not have seen the parachute in the low cumulus at the pinpoint. Hyde had then flown back to Algiers immediately and begun a month of agonizing waiting until August 14, 1943, when the Penny Farthing radio operator, Toto, was to make contact by wireless with the OSS signals station at Cape Matifou, twenty miles east of Algiers.

But when the fourteenth arrived, there was only silence from Toto. Almost beside himself with anxiety, Hyde waited for another period until 9:00 P.M. on the sixteenth when, according to the prearranged signal plan, Toto was to begin transmission if he had been unable to make the first date and time. Again there was silence. This time Hyde had to wait a week for the new date and time. But this time Toto came on the air for Penny Farthing's first transmission. As he explained, he was in Lyons safely with Jacques but had been unable to transmit on either the fourteenth or the sixteenth because that had been the weekend of the Feast of the Assumption. In making their signals plan Hyde and Toto had forgotten that August 14, 15, and 16 were one of the most solemn periods in the Catholic faith and that in France the Feast of the Assumption could not be interfered with by any temporal task. Thus, Toto explained, when he went to his safe house on the fourteenth and the fifteenth, he found it locked and shuttered. Only then did he realize that all his helpers had departed to celebrate the feast.

Relieved that Jacques and Toto had not been captured by the Sicherheitsdienst, as he had feared, Hyde then began traffic with his agents. Thereafter, and for the next eight months, Toto transmitted on schedule,

including in his signals the prearranged idiosyncrasies intended to indicate whether Penny Farthing remained at liberty. In each case the signals
showed that Toto was safe, cheerful, and empire-building—as intended.
As one of his signals indicated, he had established a second wireless post,
this time at Clermont-Ferrand.

On December 13, 1943, that station, code-named Alpina, opened up
from the area of Clermont-Ferrand, the "crossroads of the Massif Centrale" and the capital of the Auvergne—a city on the old invasion route
from the Mediterranean coast to central and eastern France. Furthermore, Jacques, the tubercular-looking little ex-civil servant who was head
of the Penny Farthing chain, in a series of reports to Hyde through Toto,
was able to show that Penny Farthing was multiplying rapidly all the way
across France from Bordeaux on the Biscayan coast to Menton, the seaside resort on the French-Italian border.

Hyde was able to inform Donovan just before Dragoon that Jacques
had about 300 subagents, most of them ex-officers and soldiers of the old
French Army, covering all main Wehrmacht bases south of a line Bordeaux–Clermont-Ferrand–Grenoble. Inside that area was a total of sixteen wireless posts already communicating with Cape Matifou, and their
reportage was being supplemented by intelligence from four wireless
bases set up by OSS Spain. However, casualties had been relatively heavy,
with three of Hyde's twelve-agent teams having been captured on arrival
—a sure sign that the German Sicherheitsdienst and the French milice
were as vigilant as ever. A typical Penny Farthing cable concerning troop
train movements at the time of Neptune read:

> Movement 43 trains. Origin Bayonne. Destination Saintes and beyond. Rate
> at least 12 trains 24 hours. Carrying infantry division. Loaded as follows: 3
> trains at St. Jean de Luz, 3 at Hendaye, 5 at St. Vincent de Tyrosse, 7 at
> Cambo, 7 at Bayonne, 10 at Labenne, 5 at Peyrehorade, 1 at Puyoo, 2 at
> Ustaritz. Codename [of train movement] *Klatschmohn.* [1]

On receiving this information, and the vast quantity like it, Hyde took
it to Force 163, the planning headquarters for Dragoon at Algiers. Force
163 made an aerial survey of the railways and yards mentioned in the
report, and after the report had been confirmed, Allied air squadrons
were sent out to attack the trains, while Allied sabotage agents, several
hundred of whom were available in the zone of operations, attacked
bridges, culverts, signal and switch systems, and locomotives to ensure
that few, if any, of the survivors got to the Normandy bridgehead, at least
on time.

In all, of the 8,000 intelligence messages reaching Hyde from all
sources between May 5, 1943, and September 15, 1944, at least a quarter
emanated from Penny Farthing. The messages concerned the where-

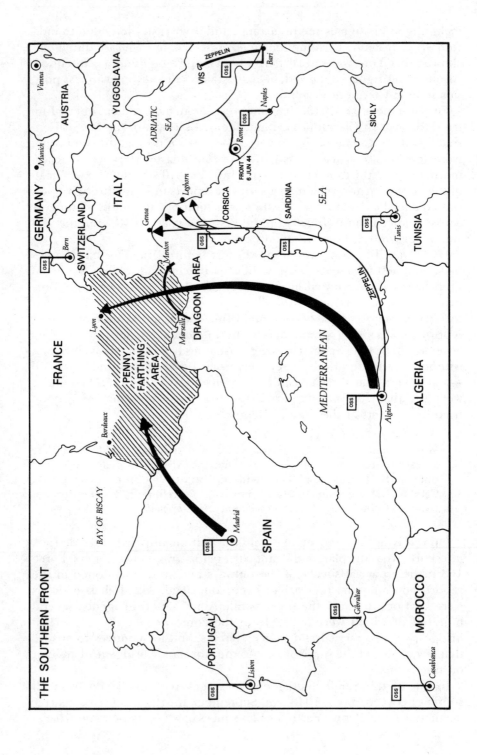

THE SOUTHERN FRONT

abouts and structure of coastal fortifications, minefields, entanglements and traps, roadblocks, antiaircraft guns, searchlights, airfields and the number of aircraft on them, and the number, type, and mission of German troops in a given area. They included also the condition of the Rhône bridges, the construction of submarine pens at Bordeaux, bombing damage to railyards, the capacity of repair shops, the nature of underwater obstacles and antitank walls—all intelligence of the highest value to generals and admirals, literally the stuff of victory.

Of all the information obtained, the most important was news of the arrival in southwestern France of the SS Panzer Division Das Reich, which was thought to be on the Russian front and which constituted one of the most formidable fighting units in the world. That exceptional piece of intelligence was secured by a Penny Farthing spy, Captain Jerome Lescanne, a French professional soldier who had been recruited by Jacques through another Penny Farthing agent, Madeleine Desanges, who owned a brewery in Clermont-Ferrand. Lescanne—who was to receive the U.S. Distinguished Service Cross for his work on Das Reich—covered the region between Bordeaux and Marseilles from a farm near Agen. The great prize was not so much the fact of Das Reich's arrival in his region of operations as securing from subagents working with the French national railways Das Reich's rail movement plan to the Le Havre and Cherbourg areas. This was vital, for when the time came for the division to march to Normandy, Allied air force and guerrilla commanders knew with considerable accuracy beforehand where its units would be and when—and were therefore able to conduct operations to disrupt it in its northward march. That they succeeded became clear in Dulles's dramatic messages to Donovan.[2]

Such triumphs, however, had not come without trouble and tragedy. As Donovan and Hyde were soon to learn, this is what happened.

Fairly soon after commencing transmission to Cape Matifou, Toto reported his radio station was being subjected to German direction-finding operations—which indicated to Hyde that the Sicherheitsdienst knew Penny Farthing was in the area. Hyde sent Toto instructions intended to prevent the Germans from locating Penny Farthing's transmitters: An operator who suspected he was being tracked by a direction finder (DF) should cease operations immediately; the signal plan for each Penny Farthing station must be as dissimilar as possible from any other in the same network; control of more than one transceiver by the same operator must be avoided or disguised by different manipulations of the transmission key; frequencies and transmission times must be changed as often as possible.

These instructions were at first effective, and in any event, Toto was arrested by the SD not by DF work but through treachery. The telegram Hyde received on April 17, 1944, told the first part of the story: "Toto arrested by Gestapo under circumstances that allow no hope. Records codes and most of money saved. Hastings [one of Toto's radio stations near Menton] off air. All traffic henceforth through Carthage [wireless station near St.-Étienne]."[3]

It was then there was yet another of those Byzantine twists that characterized Penny Farthing's operations from the outset. Soon after Hyde learned of Toto's arrest, he received a signal from a strange operator, who proved to be one of Toto's replacements. The message was brief and to the point: It was from Toto, who was in Fort Montluc prison, probably awaiting execution. Some of the guards at the prison were French, and one of them had brought the message from Toto to the radio operator for transmission to Hyde. The message advised that Toto had been contacted by a German intelligence officer, a certain Count Czernin, who had offered to guarantee Toto's life, provided "the American intelligence service in Algiers"—OSS SI—guaranteed Czernin against prosecution for war crimes after the war.

A check with the OSS biographical records center in New York showed that Czernin was an Austrian related in some way to Count Ottokar Czernin, the Austrian foreign minister who had represented the Austro-Hungarian Empire at the negotiations for the Treaty of Brest-Litovsk in World War I, which led to the state of "no war, no peace" between Germany and its allies and the new Bolshevik government of Lenin and Trotsky.

Hyde had no authority to give any such assurance, but he signaled the chief of SI, Whitney Shepardson, who checked Czernin's record and found it clear of war crimes allegations. Shepardson then signaled back the authority Hyde needed before he could close the deal. It was then signaled by Hyde to Czernin at Lyons through Toto's replacement. The results of this unprecedented (for the OSS) transaction were not known for several months. After the Dragoon landings in the south of France, when Hyde and his headquarters reached Lyon, Hyde learned the story of what had befallen Toto and Penny Farthing.

In an operation called Riquet, the head of German counterespionage in Lyons, Lieutenant Colonel Dernbach, alias Mercure, had recruited a particularly devout French Fascist, Speck, to penetrate Penny Farthing, the existence of which had been detected in and around Lyons in November 1943. In turn, Speck had recruited an agent named Rato, a French student from Grenoble, who was in contact with one of Penny Farthing's couriers, Paul Clavier.[4]

By ingratiating himself with some of the fringe members of Penny Farthing, Rato, who had some wireless telegraphy training, obtained an introduction to one of Penny Farthing's wireless operators, a certain Bonvalot of Lyons. Through Bonvalot's help, Rato obtained work as a courier. As such he managed to locate and identify Toto, who by now was chief of all wireless operations, several of the wireless operators and subagents, and the house where much of the OSS equipment was hidden. Some of the equipment included a small box containing the so-called L (for lethal) pills manufactured for the OSS by the E. R. Squibb pharmaceutical company—the same type of pill that Donovan had considered taking when his aircraft lost its way in bad weather near England early in 1943. Death was practically instantaneous the moment the potassium cyanide came into contact with the mucous membranes.

That is what happened with Bonvalot. When Lieutenant Colonel Dernbach thought he had enough information to close Penny Farthing, Rato was instructed to arrange a meeting with the unlocated organizer of the Penny Farthing wireless net, Toto. When Toto arrived at the Café de la Gare on the Place Bellecour in Lyons, he was arrested by the Sicherheitsdienst—the most important American organizer to be arrested in France.

Toto was taken immediately to SD headquarters for the customary detailed interrogation about his associates and the whereabouts of Jacques, who was apparently known to Dernbach. Now Toto rendered the network his greatest service.

When Jacques and Toto arrived in Lyons, they made contact with a schoolmate of Toto, Fernande Robert, who owned a five-story house beyond the Rhône and the Saône on the road to Grenoble. Mlle. Robert agreed to let the Penny Farthing team have an apartment in the building, knowing fully that they were American spies. The team then began to use this apartment as its headquarters and signals center from August 20, 1943, until February 1944, when Toto was arrested. Also the association between Mlle. Robert and Toto ripened into love.

When Toto was arrested, he was on his way to a meeting with other members of the network at the Robert house. There was a standing rule within the organization that if any member of the network was more than thirty minutes late for a meeting, all other members of the meeting must decamp. Remembering the rule, when Toto was taken to Sicherheitsdienst headquarters, he began to play for time until the hour at which the meeting would automatically break up had passed and the other leaders of the network had decamped with as many of the radio sets, radio crystals, gold, cipher and other equipment stored in the Robert house as was possible. According to Hyde, Toto behaved very coolly, bluffing his interrogators and involving them in complicated discussions about American intelligence procedures. Then, suddenly, he went to the telephone and dialed Fernande Robert's apartment. When Mlle. Robert answered, Toto asked: "Is that Mlle. Robert?" As Hyde was to record, "She knew immediately, of course, that something must be wrong since her gentleman friend was unlikely to refer to her thus." Toto then asked Mlle. Robert to confirm to his interrogator that he lived at that address—a request that confirmed in her mind that Toto had been arrested.[5]

Immediately Mlle. Robert rushed upstairs to the Penny Farthing apartment to tell Jacques of the conversation, and the party reported with as much equipment and gold as it could carry to a nearby hospital run by Catholic nuns, the mother superior of which was an aunt of Jacques's. Jacques and his colleagues remained there for a few days and then reestablished their headquarters in the apartment of the proprietor of a black-market restaurant near the Place Bellecour.

Thus, the network—the most important OSS espionage organization in Western Europe at the time—was saved. Nonetheless, there were casualties. In the raid Dernbach captured an OSS store of ten wireless telegraphy sets, a number of crystals, rubber stamps of the prefecture of Lyons used in the production of false papers, and some agents' forged papers. Subsequently he also captured a number of Penny Farthing subagents, perhaps as many as twenty. But Jacques and all the principal figures in the network survived to re-form for Dragoon—except Bonvalot.

Remorseful at having introduced Rato into the network and to prevent himself from talking further, Bonvalot bit into an L pill (lethal pill) as he was being arrested by Mercure and was dead on arrival at the Hôpital Croix Rouge in Lyons—the first and, so far as is known, the only OSS agent to use the L pill purposefully.

Yet despite the disruption and disaster, Penny Farthing was fully operational by Neptune and Dragoon, and the value of the intelligence was attested to by the British colonel of intelligence on the staff of Allied Force Headquarters (AFHQ), H. B. Hitchens, in a rare instance of British Intelligence congratulating OSS:

> Intelligence provided for Dragoon . . . was probably the fullest and most detailed of any provided by G2 AFHQ in a series of combined operations commencing with Torch. . . . A rough estimate of the proportion of accepted ground Intelligence supplied by the three Allied agencies shows that 50% was provided by OSS, 30% by SR (French) and 20% by [the British].[6]

General Alexander M. Patch, commanding general of the U.S. Seventh Army, remarked to Donovan on the "extraordinary accuracy" of the intelligence, a statement supported by Patch's chief of intelligence, Colonel William Quinn, who advised Donovan that the "D-Day dispositions (of German troops) confirmed advance information in every particular."[7] So impressed was Donovan by Penny Farthing's performance, and by Bonvalot's sacrifice, that he recommended and obtained Distinguished Service Crosses for Marret, Rocquefort, Bonvalot, and Lescanne.

Hyde received the Bronze Star Medal, the citation signed by FDR stating:

Mr. Henry B. Hyde, American Civilian, Office of Strategic Services. For meritorious achievement in connection with military operations in North Africa from February 1943 to August 1944. As chief of the French Secret Intelligence Desk, Mr. Hyde was responsible for the collection of all intelligence on enemy forces in occupied France secured from North African bases by the Office of Strategic Services. His duties included the recruiting, briefing and equipping of agents, as well as the selection of drop points and coordination of communications. When he assumed his duties in North Africa only two stations had been established in Southern France, but six months later he was in contact with some twenty independent posts established in France through his efforts. Intelligence provided by his office contributed materially to the success, not only of the United States Seventh Army in South France, but also of the Allied Armies in Northern France.

(s) Franklin D. Roosevelt.[8]

Before leaving to join the cruiser *Augusta* with the assault convoys bound for southern France and Dragoon, Donovan went out to Blida Airport to bid godspeed to Major A. Peter Dewey, son of an old family friend, Congressman Charles S. Dewey. Major Dewey was leaving on a secret mission of great importance, conducted in a fashion typical of the hundreds of secret missions launched that brilliant summer in support of Neptune and Dragoon—with dash, selflessness, high courage, resourcefulness, and initiative. Indeed, Dewey was an excellent example of what Doering meant when recalling the Dragoon campaign. Only weeks before Doering died, he described it as "war in our springtime."

Major Dewey exemplified the faults in the early OSS agent selection process, for on the face of it he appeared to be first-class agent material. His father was an international banker with the Northern Trust Company of Chicago, a man who had played an important part in the establishment of the modern Polish fiscal system after World War I. Major Dewey was born in 1916; had been educated in Switzerland, St. Paul's School (London), Yale, and Virginia Law; had worked in the Paris office of the Chicago *Daily News;* and during the Battle of France in 1940 had served with the Polish Military Ambulance Corps, for which he had received a high decoration. However, when he returned to the United States and volunteered for service in the COI, he was rejected on the vague ground of "unsuitability." Dewey was not the sort of man who could be fobbed off. He took his case directly to Donovan. Donovan looked into it and decided that Dewey was the stuff of which agents are made and hired him despite advice not to do so.

Now, in the summer of 1944, Dewey was leader of the Étoile mission to the *maquisards* of southwestern France, a post fraught with complex political difficulties. Dewey was to parachute with a Gaullist team to enforce the authority of the supreme Allied commander in the Mediterranean over the maquis in that independent, ferocious region—especially over the 40,000 left-wing *maquisards* along the Spanish frontier who, under Spanish Republican command, were plotting the invasion of Franco Spain as soon as the Germans withdrew.

So simply expressed, the objective belied the political delicacy of the task. In the region was a German army, the SS, the SD, Giraudists, Gaullists, many maquis orientated variously toward London, Moscow, and Washington, and innumerable military, political, and religious private armies. SOE and SIS agents were already there, had been for years, and wanted no youthful Americans in their manors. To put Dewey's predicament briefly, Étoile would be in as much danger from forces that were technically friendly as from the Wehrmacht. Moreover, the British element within the Special Operations center at Algiers did not favor the operation, believing that Dewey would not have the authority or experience needed to control the forces the mission would unleash merely by its presence and that his Gaullist lieutenants would take over the mission's political functions and establish the authority of De Gaulle in southwestern France—an action that might well precipitate civil war there.

In that belief the British were not unjustified. One of Algiers's leading Gaullists, André Diethelm, war minister in De Gaulle's Committee of National Liberation, had persuaded Donovan to include in Étoile two aides-de-camp, Major Antoine de Récy, who had lost his right arm in action during the Battle of France, and Lieutenant Gérard de Noblet d'Anglure. Both were ardent Gaullist aristocrats who the British were sure would, at a critical moment, place their allegiance to De Gaulle before their allegiance to the superior Allied commander. However, Donovan dismissed the British protest; such problems were inherent in all such special missions, Dewey would learn how to control such passions, and, he argued, if every mission were abandoned simply because the men undertaking it were young, few missions would be launched.

Donovan was on the tarmac when Étoile gathered for takeoff at Blida Airport, outside Algiers, at 9:30 P.M. on August 10, 1944, five days before Dragoon. The mission consisted of Dewey and three OSS lieutenants, E. Ernouf, J. Russell, and Jack Hemingway, son of Ernest Hemingway, who was talking with him with his trout rod strapped to a leg. With him were five wireless operators supplied by De Gaulle's service, and Récy and Noblet d'Anglure. Donovan bade the team good luck, and then the B-17's took off and vanished to the north.

The mission started badly. Récy's B-17 went up to Périgueux, to the northeast of Bordeaux, to make *parachutages* to a maquis operating in those luxuriant valleys against the German First Army, but when the stores had been dropped, the pilot found that he was lost. He returned to Blida, there to try again. However, Dewey and his party dropped safely near Millau and the Gorges of the Tarn, a thirty-mile wilderness of red and yellow cliffs, trout streams, and underground lakes and rivers whence sprang the Loire. His party's landing and the linkup with Récy's and his team had the full flavor of clandestines on active service:

> *Friday, 11 August 1944:* ... At 03:30 [3:30 A.M.] we jumped. ... At 03:45 [3:45] we assembled. An attempt to take bearings. An impossibility. The region was entirely wooded. We were in a ravine. At dawn we discovered that we were 48 kms from our intended destination, at Castanvielle, 20 kms north of Carcassonne. The country was overrun with the Wehrmacht. We hid the parachutes and equipment in the woods, then looked all day for the radio set which Captain de Noblet discovered about 16:30 [4:30 P.M.]. It could not be used because of the disappearance of the ... codes. ... At 20:30 [8:30 P.M.] our group went to the agreed parachute rendezvous 48 kms northeast where we thought we would find signs of the [Récy party], of whose fate we were ignorant. Night march by compass through woods and mountains covered with briar. The trip was made much more difficult by the complete absence of moonlight and the impossibility of obtaining water during the eighteen hours of the march.

> *Saturday, 12 August 1944:* At Quintance, above Castans, Captain de Noblet met some residents whose farms had been pillaged two days before by a German raid. The farmers did not wish to take us in. We passed the day in the woods and left at nightfall.

That same night Récy's party left Blida again for the original pinpoint, as Dewey and Noblet continued their three-day march to the rendezvous. Dewey resumed the story:

> *Sunday, 13 August 1944:* We walked until daybreak, a gruelling trip which brought us up to Pradelles, occupied by a battalion of German infantry, where we stayed all day at the end of a stream in a wood. Germans were passing in the road 200 m. away. Some P38s came in tight squadrons to bomb in the direction of Toulouse. At nightfall we left for Combe which we reached at three in the morning. We slept in a sheepbarn, awaiting the dawn. During the three days which we used to reach the pinpoint our only food was ... vitamin pills which were in the "escape box" which every aviator has.[9]

Meantime, Récy had landed close to Roqueferre, losing his wireless, which meant that neither Dewey's nor Récy's party could communicate with Algiers. Nor did anyone in Récy's party know where Dewey's party was. At that point, therefore, it seemed Étoile was collapsing. But Récy was a determined and ambitious man, and he knew his peasants; the wireless set was in the area somewhere, and if the local peasants knew the movement of every fox, they would certainly know where the *parachutage* had landed. He was not wrong. Returning to the point where they had landed, Récy went to a farm to try to get information. He soon learned from the farmer that there had been a *parachutage* and a large container had been taken to the mayor of Roqueferre. Dewey heard what happened later and recorded:

> At 1800 [6:00 P.M. on August 13] Major de Récy and radio operator Gély went to see the mayor of Roqueferre and after having revealed his real identity he asked him to give him the radio set. The mayor refused, as he had already made known the existence of the radio set to the German authorities at Carcassonne. . . . Major de Récy then proposed to the mayor that he exchange the packet containing the [wireless] for a package of the same size containing food. . . . The mayor then asked him [Récy] if he were armed, and he replied in the negative. After a long discussion the mayor decided to refer the matter to the Municipal Council, and he asked Major de Récy and his radio operator to wait for the answer on the outskirts of the village, near the cemetery. After half an hour with no one appearing Major de Récy returned to the Town Hall where the mayor announced his decision: he would only give up the radio set under armed duress. Major de Récy answered him: "You will see the armed force as soon as I get back to the forest to get my orders."

At 9:30 P.M. Major de Récy, Lieutenant Ernouf, and radio operator Gély, each armed with a revolver, went back to Roqueferre and met the mayor, who, now impressed with Récy's authority in the requisite degree, took them to where the radio was. With the set in their possession they went to the edge of the wood, reached the summit of a hill, set up the radio, and at 11:44 P.M. sent their first radio message to Algiers, asking for another radio set to be sent to a point designated by coordinates. Having done this, they gave the set back to the mayor of Roqueferre, picked up the supplies they had hidden, and marched all night toward the point they had indicated to Algiers. They arrived there on August 14 at 12:30 A.M. Sure enough, an aircraft appeared at the designated place and time and dropped the replacement radio.

Dewey and Récy did not meet until August 15, Dragoon D-Day, when the Franco-American armies landed on the Provence coast between Hyères and Cannes and began operations to capture Marseilles as a supply port—Donovan was aboard the American cruiser *Augusta* as the assault forces almost walked ashore—total casualties for the Dragoon assault were 183 men killed and wounded, with 49 nonbattle casualties, against the 16,000 killed and wounded in the Neptune assault. Accompanied by Colonel Edward Gamble, peacetime manager of a New York brokerage house dealing in government bonds and now chief of OSS operations for Dragoon, Donovan and the OSS advance party established a headquarters in a house at St.-Tropez with the chief of OSS espionage, Henry Hyde, as 94,000 troops and 11,000 vehicles came ashore for the march on Marseilles and Toulon and up the Rhône Valley to the southern

German border. Almost immediately the St.-Tropez port was attacked by Luftwaffe bombers. Hyde was to recall that Donovan again showed he was unconcerned by personal danger, for although there was no antiaircraft defense as yet ashore, he continued his stroll along the promenade while the shrapnel from the bombs whined and ripped into the jetties and buildings.

The Dragoon invasion marked the start of the prolonged but final phase of the war in Europe—and the beginning of the end of the Arcadia plan as a piece of successful prophecy about how the war was to unfold. On that momentous day, Dewey recorded:

> Major Peter Dewey, Captain de Noblet, and Lieutenant Bourguonais [of the maquis] left on foot across the mountains to find the Corps Franc de la Montagne Noire, in the cantonment of La Galaube. There they made contact with Captain Kervanoel . . . and the priest, the Abbé de Villeneuve. During this time Captain de Noblet sent the radio corporal and a guide to look for Major de Récy on the road which they had presumably taken. We learned of the news of the southern landing. Universal joy. At 17:00 [5:00 P.M.] departure for Villerouat where we had the great pleasure of finding Major de Récy, Lt. Ernouf and Chief Corporal Gély installed with their radio and already having established several contacts with Algiers. . . .

They learned also that their mission had been changed. They were to concentrate on maquis organization and intelligence gathering on the left flank of the Dragoon forces beginning to march up the Route Napoléon toward Paris and the German border—a more satisfactory mission than the purely political work visualized in their original orders. Morever, Mission Étoile was in a position to commence its new work immediately as a result of its contact with the headquarters of the Corps Franc de la Montagne Noire. Its first bulletin was one of its most important: The Wehrmacht was in the process of evacuating the regions of Castres, Mazamet, and Carcassonne by National Routes 112, 113, 118, and "an important ammunition dump (11 trains) was at the Château de Cheminières, near Castelnaudary." This information was transmitted by Hyde's office to the U.S. aircraft carrier *Tulagi*, with the invasion—Peter Mero, OSS communications expert at Algiers, had developed a remarkable system for almost instantaneous transmission of messages from agents in the field to the Dragoon command centers. Hellcat fighter-bomber squadrons were then sent up, and the trains were immobilized or blown up in what the peasants said was the largest explosion in the history of Languedoc.

> *Friday, 18 August 1944:* Organization of intelligence chains and letter boxes. We made plans for the establishment and continuation of other posts of the Etoile mission to branch out towards Aveyron, La Card, and l'Ardèche,

Captain de Noblet installed the [command post] at Co de David. Setting up of boundaries and [aircraft homing] beacons at Terre de Dieu and at Laprade. Telegrams to Algiers: Hun clearing out of Languedoc. Projects for the reception of various parachute drops. We gave notice of the evacuation of Tarn and Aude by infantry columns on National Road 113 between Toulouse and Carcassonne (machine-gunned the next day by pursuit planes—Hell Cat) also Montpelier and Rhône Valley. The 22nd Panzer Division was at Béziers and the 11th Motorized Infantry Division was at Montpelier. Major de Récy and Captain de Noblet went to Mazamet where they had a conference with the regional heads of the [maquis] studying the most efficient means of coordinating the action of the various Maquis groups in liberating the region Albi-Castres-Mazamet and the Montagne Noire. . . .

Then, on August 19, Dewey received dramatic advice from Algiers: The German army group in the south of France was to begin evacuation that day. The intelligence made it clear that the Germans would stand not in the French Alps as expected, but on the German Rhine. At that point Dewey's team made its most valuable acquisition: It captured two German Volkswagen staff cars with which to make its reconnaissances. The men then began a drive 625 miles through enemy territory, operating as OSS Phantoms, risking being shot as spies by the enemy, execution by the maquis, as well as strafing by Allied aircraft. Throughout they radioed their intelligence back to Algiers, which in turn relayed it to the U.S. Seventh or the French First Army. The most important information: the fact that the German First Army in the Biscay region was withdrawing through central France toward the Rhine under the command of General Botho H. Elster. Elster's columns stretched thirty miles between Poitiers and Châteauroux: 750 officers, 18,850 men, 10 women, 400 cars, 500 trucks, 1,000 horse-drawn vehicles. Although it is not clear if Étoile's intelligence about these columns was the first, Jedburgh intelligence resulted in such a major concentration of maquis around the columns that Elster surrendered them to Jedburgh team Frederick, begging for—and receiving—protection from the maquis.

The same day, as the mission was making preparations to leave Co de David, Étoile and its escort of *maquisards* were attacked by three German Mark III tanks. The tanks were engaged by the 6th Squadron of the Corps Franc de la Montagne Noire, and two were destroyed. The third was captured (along with twenty-five prisoners) and presented to the 6th Squadron by Dewey as an armored fighting vehicle to be used in operations.

Sunday, 20 August 1944: With a diversion south of Mazamet the 6th Squadron took part in the capture of Mazamet where it took 104 prisoners. The fight lasted five hours and we took, besides individual equipment, 5 anti-tank and anti-aircraft cannon. We put our tank at the disposition of the [maquis] of Mazamet for the defense of the city.

In the afternoon Major de Récy, Captain de Noblet, and Mr. Reille Smelt, Deputy from Mazamet, went into Castren where 3,000 Germans were still resisting. We must call attention to the actions of Agents de Ville No. 888 and 913, who by their devotion to duty and excellent information facilitated the mission of these two officers by keeping them informed of the disposition of the Germans remaining in the city.

By September 1, 1944, as Dewey reported to Algiers on that day, Mission Étoile had penetrated so far north along the Route Napoléon that it reached the limit of the range of its wireless set. One of Dewey's reconnaissance teams dashed over to the old capital of the French New Order, Vichy, to place a flag on the American Embassy and then struck out through the Burgundian vineyards and Penny Farthing country to find a longer-range radio set at the Vichy Army's radio workshops at Clermont-Ferrand. There the team located a gasoline dump containing 300,000 liters, with which the tanks of the French First Army were re-fueled.

> *3 September 1944:* We had arrived in the sphere of influence of the [British] Intelligence Service and our work became more and more of a delicate nature. We had some difficulty with OSS North [Bruce's organization; OSS South was Gamble's], because we did not know the password of the north zone, the [north] zone suspected us immediately. Several times we ran the risk of being locked up under close custody of our own people.

But they were not locked up. Still with their German staff cars, their tanks, and the 6th Squadron of the Corps Franc de la Montagne Noir as their escort, they sped on to be present at the capture of Villefranche-sur-Saône and of Mâcon, accepting cups of the delicious wines of the region —Fleurie, Moulin-à-Vent, Pouilly-Fuissé—to cut the dust of the hot highway. They hurried to Bourg-en-Bresse, "home of the finest cooking in France," to report *maquisard* intelligence that there were 4,000 to 5,000 Germans in good marching order in a pocket bordered by Moulins—the Canal du Centre-Nevers-Moulins. Then on September 5, Algiers ordered Dewey and his team to meet Donovan, who was at Seventh Army forward headquarters near the famous monastery of the Grande Chartreuse at Grenoble. Donovan, an almost grandfatherly figure with white hair, the crotch of his trousers around his knees, a huge .45 automatic in a leather holster on his hip, his pockets bulging with maps and K rations, greeted Dewey with the words "What mischief have you been up to, boy?"

Donovan promised to make Dewey a lieutenant colonel, and he did— just before Dewey was machine-gunned to death by a Communist Vietnamese soldier at about 11:30 A.M. on September 26, 1945, on a side road near Saigon Airport. Thus, Colonel Dewey was to become the first American soldier killed in action in Vietnam. He would still be working for Donovan when he died. But that was in the future. For the moment these were the happiest of hours, which were spent in the little village of Uriage-les-Bains, where the French Revolution is often said to have begun, where Donovan and Dewey sipped iced cassis sitting on a stone wall watching the Sherman tanks roar through on their way to the German frontier, their pennants flying and their crews with hatches open, giving the V sign.

As for Toto and Count Czernin, Hyde, who was following close behind, was to remember:

> My reunion with Toto was a prosaic one in that he managed to locate me in a town called Bourgoin on the main road from Lyon to Grenoble where I had a temporary headquarters. He arrived in my office there with Czernin, who appeared, as Toto was, emotionally and physically exhausted and drained, for in the last few days before the liberation the Sicherheitsdienst had gone through Fort Montluc where Toto was being held, shooting every French *résistant* they could get their hands on. We arranged special treatment for Czernin in that he lived under constant unobtrusive guard by some of my enlisted men until we were able to turn him over to, I believe, the X-2 people. We wrote a file on him, based on what Toto told us of him, and when I met him later after the war in Salzburg, he told me he was satisfied but not overjoyed by the treatment he had received while in our hands.[10]

39

Crumbling Relationships

The third phase of the Arcadia plan—the march to Berlin—was now to begin. Or so it had been intended. For it was also the time when, Churchill was to record, "the Great Democracies triumphed, and so were able to resume the follies which had so nearly cost them their life."[1]

From Lyons, Donovan flew to the Royal Palace at Caserta, near Naples, there to continue his operations in support of the Allied armies in Western Europe. Almost immediately there was serious trouble between London and Washington over Greece. There, when the Wehrmacht began withdrawing into Central Europe in August 1944, civil war between the Communists and the royalists broke out on an ever-widening scale. The currency collapsed, and there was famine, plague, and general anarchy when Greece awoke to find that because of Noah's Ark, the communications of the country had been destroyed. To complete a scene of severe political trouble, a Soviet Military Mission had parachuted into the ELAS Communist guerrillas.

Under arrangements made by the Combined Chiefs of Staff, Greece was a British theater of operations. Britain was responsible for Greece militarily, politically, and economically. Since the constitutional form of government before the German invasion was a monarchy, Churchill took the position that Britain would restore King George of the Hellenes to Greece, and maintain him, until the Greek people had spoken. This position was not understood by the American press, and only barely by the American administration. There, oddly, sympathies were not with the right or with the forces trying to maintain order, but with the left, which was making civil war on the largest scale.

That attitude now began to show itself violently in OSS Cairo, where Lieutenant Colonel John Toulmin was trying to enforce the OSS's apolitical policy within his large organization of 1,315 men and women. In that task Toulmin was making dangerous enemies for himself as powerful American elements in OSS Cairo worked against his and British policy and tried to throw the power and authority of the OSS behind the Greek Communist movement. Against this background a powerful but unlikely force appeared in the Greek maelstrom, Spyros P. Skouras, president of 20th Century-Fox, the Hollywood mogul.

Donovan had known Skouras through legal business since before the war. He liked the man, and in January 1943 he appointed Skouras a dollar-a-year adviser on Greek-American and Greek politics. Spyros was one of four brothers, sons of a peasant family in Greece, who came to the United States as youths. They were bus boys in a St. Louis restaurant, purchased a bowling alley and then a small movie theater, and got into the movie production business in Hollywood.

Spyros became a leading figure in the industry and a figure of political importance, largely through his connection with Wendell Willkie, Republican nominee for the presidency in 1940, and of his appointment as chairman of 20th Century-Fox. His salary was put at $250,000 a year by the Securities and Exchange Commission. And as WJD was informed in a background memo:[2]

> The Skouras brothers have had no education whatever—not even of the most primitive sort. They were described by a man who is acquainted with them as "socially *very* rough diamonds." They have a very high reputation for integrity in Wall Street. The records disclose only one or two civil legal actions against them which is unusual in the industry. There has never been any complaint taken against any of the brothers by the Bureau of Internal Revenue which is also considered quite unusual in the industry. Spiros is the most active figure in Greek war relief and both of the other brothers are active contributors and organizers of Greek relief projects. . . . They are considered spectacularly successful in the financial world.

Spyros's principal service to the OSS appears to have been to introduce his brother George, a $100,000-a-year officer of 20th Century-Fox, to WJD as a potential secret agent for operations in Greece. For reasons he kept to himself—most likely because WJD felt that George was too involved in Greek politics—Donovan did not hire him. On January 17, 1944, George Skouras, perhaps sensing the reason for WJD's reserve about him, wrote Donovan to state that a year had passed since he had filed his application, the "delay has tortured my patience," and he was taking "the liberty to write you, hoping that you will exercise your authority so that my services may be used for immediate good and advantage."[3]

What Skouras had in mind was that he should parachute into Greece, where he claimed to have many important connections, and use his good offices to bring together the Communists and the royalists, end the civil war, and then, having recently won several championships at skeet shooting, put his "guns to good use." Toward that end he had had "numerous conferences with naval officers and other leaders from [Greece]—leaders in the military, governmental and civil capacity, and other personalities, who have been, and are, part of the country's life, and have accumulated sufficient data and material to become well informed." As for his political involvement in Greek domestic affairs while serving as an OSS officer, Skouras assured Donovan:

> It is inevitable that political participation with ex-members or present members of that Government, or mixing in the politics of that area, is something to be avoided as destructive. Politics in that area is a disease of almost pathological nature. I will not allow myself to be drawn into any political activities or discussions.

This assurance was all well and good, but in the next breath Skouras announced: "Latest reports indicate that conditions [in Greece] have reached a climax. The situation is becoming more desperate every moment and something has to be done about it at once." He added:

> I know the history and modern politics of that nation as well as I know my own children. I know their way of thinking, their customs, habits, and psychological reactions; and aware of their idiosyncrasies, and speak their language fluently.
> I am alert to the dangers.

Again WJD did nothing with Skouras's application, for the last thing he wanted at the time was an influential Greek-American—and Skouras was supposed to be well and favorably known to FDR—becoming involved in Greek politics in Cairo. Donovan had just had to dismiss the head of the Greek Irregular Project, Colonel Ulius C. Amoss, who was also executive officer of OSS Cairo, a man with numerous connections in the Greek court and government, for having become involved in Greek politics in Cairo—he had assisted in the rearrangement of the Greek Cabinet to suit the personal politics and finances of a powerful arms merchant—and WJD had no desire for other such experiences.

But then Donovan found a use for Skouras. In September 1943 the Luftwaffe attacked the invasion fleet putting the U.S. Fifth Army ashore at Salerno, with a new type of radio-controlled glider bomb, causing great damage to several battleships and cruisers and various other ships. When the Germans attacked the Italian fleet, which was steaming toward Malta to surrender to the Royal Navy, one of the bombs sank one new Italian battleship and seriously damaged another. Concerned about the power of the new weapon to disrupt Neptune, the Allied naval commander in chief in the Mediterranean, Admiral Sir Andrew Cunningham, asked WJD if the OSS could do anything to obtain a specimen of the weapon, together with a mother aircraft if possible, so that a countermeasure could be devised. WJD promised to try to put his Special Projects Division, then under the command of Lieutenant Commander John Shaheen, on to what came to be called Operation Simmons. Purpose: Locate and steal one of the glider bombs and its parent aircraft.

By late 1943 all commands had been instructed to make Simmons a main Secret Intelligence project, and in January 1944 OSS SI Cairo claimed to have located a Heinkel III mother ship and a store of glider bombs at the Luftwaffe airfield outside Athens. The OSS chief at Cairo, John Toulmin, advised WJD that for an OG operation to be launched to capture the aircraft and a specimen of the glider bomb, the intelligence would have to be checked. That could be done only by an OSS agent going to the airfield and making inquiries. Toulmin was disinclined to base such an operation on Greek intelligence, which had shown itself not to be reliable. Therefore, an OSS agent, preferably American, would have to go. Donovan agreed, and the task fell to George Skouras. However, Toulmin felt that to employ a Greek-American might not be wise, for Greek-Americans in Greece "stood out like a sore thumb"[4] and might be captured, and the Germans might well force out of him his mission. If that occurred, the whole Simmons project might be neutralized.

But George Skouras it had to be. He was given agent training lasting three weeks, and after several lectures from WJD and others to remain clear of Greek politics, he was flown out to Cairo, where he joined Toulmin's staff. There Skouras began the preparatory operations necessary before parachuting into Greece—studying the intelligence file on the glider bombs and the airfield where they were said to be located. That, however, was not a very lengthy task, and soon Skouras, finding he had much time on his hands, began to meet friends in the Greek political community in Cairo, a city that was the seat of the Greek government in exile of King George II. It was not long before Toulmin determined that Skouras was involving himself in Greek political discussions, including meetings concerning the nature of the postwar Greek constitution and government—whether Greece was to become a republic or remain a monarchy. It emerged that Skouras was a firm advocate of republicanism, an advocacy contrary to British policy and one that brought Skouras to the attention of the British Secret Intelligence Service, which complained to Toulmin that Skouras was being cultivated by the Greek republicans. In short, Skouras was engaging in activity that was contrary to OSS standing orders that no OSS official could engage in any political activity whatsoever, at any time, anywhere, while in OSS service, without the permission of the OSS—orders that were very strictly enforced and contravention of which had led to the dismissal of several excellent men.

On April 10, 1944, while in Washington, Toulmin brought Skouras's conduct in Cairo to the attention of WJD personally, requesting "permission from you that he had no useful purpose in the Middle East Theater." WJD replied that Toulmin could return Skouras to Washington. Toulmin then cabled Cairo, "stating that I had permission to return Skouras to the United States and requested that action be taken."[5] But no action had been taken when Toulmin returned to Cairo on May 12—General Benjamin F. Giles, commander of U.S. forces in the Middle East, including the OSS, had insisted Skouras remain at Cairo on the Simmons operation, either with the OSS or with the USAAF.

Meanwhile, the long-expected civil war had broken out between the left and the right in Greece, producing great effervescence in Greek expatriate communities everywhere. Much of the trouble, Churchill insisted in various statements, including notes to FDR, was caused by Soviet intrigues. FDR himself caused great disquiet in Whitehall by advising Churchill to eschew the re-creation of European spheres of influence, while omitting to make the same point to the Russians.

As the Communist partisan movement began to take over the country, Churchill began to support publicly the government of the radical socialist George Papandreou, whom British secret agents had brought out of Greece in April to become prime minister of the Greek government in exile. The Greek Communists had joined Papandreou's government but had retired when he ordered the dissolution of all resistance movements, directing that the Greek Brigade in Egypt be responsible for the internal security of Greece during the period between the German withdrawal and the holding of free elections.

Then, in July, the Greek world was swept with rumors that the German withdrawal from Greece had begun, rumors that were, like most intelligence from Greece, false. However, the rumors produced intense excitement and discord in Papandreou's Cabinet in Cairo, a group with which Skouras had the closest contact. Skouras then became the OSS's main contact with the Greek Cabinet, although he was not a trained political observer and frequently permitted his deep emotional involvement in Greek causes to get the better of him. Nevertheless, his information, thoughts, and feelings found their way into, and infected the thinking of, the Greek section of OSS Research and Analysis and OSS SI, and some inflammatory analyses and intelligence reached Washington. There they produced a similar result as in Cairo: They were read widely within the administration, and one Greek zealot began to leak OSS reports, despite their high classification, to newsmen such as Drew Pearson.

By July 1944 the effervescence had not abated, and Churchill, who had been responsible for the decision to supply the Communists with gold and arms in the first place, decided that unless the Greek Communists accepted the Papandreou government, he would withdraw all SOE missions and decline to send further assistance—apart from all else, British Foreign Secretary Anthony Eden had decided that the Greek Communists had long since ceased to fight the Germans. Also, at Churchill's instructions, the British government would publicly repudiate the Greek Communist movement and lay evidence of its crimes before the world. General Gubbins of the SOE then sent a message to WJD in Washington through Intrepid in New York, asking Donovan to be ready to pull his teams out of Greece, in order to show the Communists and the Russians that the Western powers were joined in a common front.

But when news of the British decision to invoke the support of the OSS reached OSS Cairo, a group of SI and SO executives led by Stephen Penrose, the chief of SI, sent a message to Donovan: "We are apprehensive that such a move would cause an internal hemorrhage which would seriously endanger the success of our MO, SI and SO missions, plunge organized resistance to the Nazis in Greece into a chaotic state, bar any additional projects, blow up the Noah's Ark project . . . and so forth."[6]

Penrose stated that the British had "forwarded an evacuation alert to American and English representatives on the Allied Military Mission [in Greece]," which declared that "should the denunciation ensue, cooperation between [the leftist forces] and the Allied Military Mission would stop immediately." The British would bring out the American component as well as their own, "demolish" all radio sets, and "obstruct the delivery of all materials of warfare" to the left. Penrose complained that through an inadvertence the American component in the Allied Military Mission had "received this alert without [OSS Cairo's] having been advised that it had been issued."

Springing afresh to his defense of the OSS's right to independent operation, Donovan ordered Toulmin, who was back at Cairo, "to leave things just as they are" and not to "utter a word on the subject and to wait for further instructions. . . . Regardless of action taken concerning operations [in Greece] we shall be firm in defending our right to carry on intelligence and to dispatch groups."[7] Then, Donovan, sure that Churchill was reestablishing Greece as a country in the British sphere of influence, determined to have a showdown with the British once and for all over the question of where the OSS could and could not operate. He wrote to Secretary of State Hull, protesting continual British interference in OSS SI operations, and requesting the views of the State Department on WJD's actions should Churchill order the withdrawal of the Allied Military Mission. Hull replied on July 15, 1944:

> I refer to your memorandum of July 17, 1944, requesting the views of the Department regarding the situation likely to arise in Greece if the British Mission should be withdrawn from that country as a result of possible denunciation of [the left] by the British Government. The Department understands in this connection that: (1) OSS considers it important that intelligence channels remain open to Greece and that OSS activities should not be terminated as a result of purely political decisions to which this Government is not a party; and (2) OSS personnel is working with the British Forces on a combined basis only in limited instances.[8]

Hull then declared that the department agreed that "the interests of the prosecution of the war make it desirable that American personnel remain in Greece at this critical juncture." He went on:

> At the same time it is concerned that no American agencies should become or appear to become involved, directly or indirectly, in Greek domestic politics or factional disputes. The Department accordingly perceives no objection to the continuance of OSS personnel in Greece in the event of British withdrawal, on the following conditions: (1) The OSS officers remaining in Greece should undertake only intelligence work, together with such special operations (including assistance to stranded Allied aviators) as may be specifically approved by [the supreme Allied commander, Mediterranean]; (2) The officers should not be attached to any one Greek faction or operate only in the territory of any one Greek faction; in other words, they should engage in intelligence in respect of the [royalist] and other groups as well as [the left wing]. (3) The officers should explain to the Greeks with whom they come into contact exactly what their functions are and should be instructed to make it clear that: (a) they are not continuing the general liaison or other functions of the British personnel which has been withdrawn; (b) they are not to become involved in political questions or to permit political functions to be attributed to them.

Nothing could be plainer, and WJD relayed Hull's instructions to Toulmin in Cairo. Toulmin, not the sort of man to become emotionally involved in any issue, acted promptly to stop Skouras, who had become a focal point of Greek extremist propaganda inside the OSS. There, meanwhile, early in July 1944 a strange incident had again fastened attention on Skouras's activities in Cairo. On July 4, 1944, a Major Clammer of the Ninth Air Force Communications Section in London, a man associated with the aerial guided missiles project, reported to Lieutenant Commander Lester Armour, of OSS SI London, also involved in the operation, that he had received the following telegram from George Skouras in Cairo to his brother Spyros in London: "Catastrophe is pending and unless someone from there takes action to prevent it all will be lost. See Agnebes."[9] What did it mean? Why had it come over Army, not OSS, communications? Did the telegram refer to the Simmons project? Armour asked George Skouras for an explanation, and George Skouras wired back: "My cable to my brother only dealt with matters pertaining to Greek War Relief or personal matters. OSS rules do not permit the use of OSS channels for personal affairs." Armour then warned Washington:

> Using other than OSS channels, George Skouras is communicating with his brother Spiro [sic] in London according to information we have here. Are you certain he is not engaging in Greek political activities? Advise you investigate contents of messages so that there will be no resulting embarrassment to OSS interests.[10]

Plainly George Skouras had been using General Giles and his Army communications to maintain a correspondence with Spyros Skouras, who was not unknown to Drew Pearson.

Alarmed by this eruption of Skouras at an exceedingly sensitive time in Anglo-American politics, Toulmin decided that he must be returned home before he got OSS Cairo into the gravest trouble with its hosts, the British authorities at Cairo. Toulmin told Skouras there was not sufficient work for him to do in the OSS and he was to be returned to the United States and released from the OSS. He could, however, remain in Cairo as a private person if he wished and continue his activities with the Greek War Relief Commission in Cairo. Skouras then "argued with me considerably on the subject, offering to reduce his pay 90% in order to stay in the theater [with the OSS] until the [Simmons] project was completed." Toulmin remarked also: "I had no doubt that he would take the matter up with General Giles as I was aware of the fact that he saw him quite often."[11]

The following morning General Giles sent for Toulmin, and at the meeting Giles alleged, reported Toulmin:

> (a) That Skouras had been sent from Washington to Cairo for a certain secret project and that this project had not been completed. (b) That Skouras had been briefed in and had knowledge of the project for approximately a year. (c) That he questioned whether OSS had made a full attempt to complete the mission and he doubted if OSS had given Skouras complete cooperation. (d) That he wished to have Skouras remain in the theater as an employee of OSS until the project had been completed and he ordered me to keep him on the OSS roster. (e) [Giles] stated that he thought that I probably didn't realize the influence Skouras had in the United States and that it was perfectly possible if Skouras were to return, (1) I might be removed from my position as Strategic Services Officer, Middle East, (2) that OSS Middle East might be abolished.

Toulmin advised WJD that he was not concerned with Skouras's influence with Giles, or with Giles's threats, and that only because Giles, his superior officer, had given him a direct order to retain Skouras in the theater was he doing so. As for Giles's statement that Skouras had influence in Washington, Donovan was advised by Toulmin that he had replied: "I seriously doubted if Skouras had any real influence in political circles although I had heard rumors that Skouras was friendly with the President." He had remarked also to Giles that it was "relatively unimportant as to whether anyone in Washington could or would have me removed and that I seriously doubted that OSS Middle East would be abolished through the influence of Skouras in any quarter." Then Giles asked if Toulmin had any specific complaints against Skouras, and Toulmin had replied that "in the main I did not although I was continually aware of the fact that Skouras was exceedingly friendly with influential men in Greek political life in Cairo." Then there occurred a sinister event.

Before Toulmin and Donovan could withdraw Skouras, Toulmin collapsed suddenly and for several days lay near death, suffering from a massive disturbance of his central nervous and respiratory systems. At first his affliction defied diagnosis, although he was suffering from what appeared to be almost general paralysis in which his life was in danger. But what had caused that grave illness? Nobody knew immediately, but when forensic samples were flown back to OSS Washington, where the OSS's Medical Services were well equipped and knowledgeable enough to make the necessary tests, it was soon established that Toulmin was suffering from nicotine poisoning—an unusual and crude but effective method of assassination.

The question was how had Toulmin ingested a poison so powerful that fifty milligrams were considered sufficient to cause death within a few minutes? It was true that nicotine was used as a herbicide and could have been taken in through fruit, vegetables, or the Cairene water supply, but when that happened, there were always other cases. But now there had been only one case—Toulmin. Nor, so far as it was known, was the poison in use in Egyptian agriculture.[12]

This strongly suggested that the poisoning had been deliberate. Certainly there were those in Cairo who had much to gain by Toulmin's death. The political situation in Greece, with its noisy reverberations in Egypt, ripened the prospect of assassination for those who, like Toulmin, pursued unpopular political courses or opposed the political plans of extremists. The nicotine had certainly succeeded in that purpose, for the OSS doctors recommended that owing to Toulmin's poor condition (who by now had been flown home), he should not return to Cairo.

Putzell was to recall: "It was certainly a mysterious business, and we looked into the question that Toulmin had been deliberately poisoned. Toulmin was a first-class man, very conscious of his duties and responsibilities, and tried to keep OSS Cairo clear of politics—an almost impossible task. In personality he was a very congenial fellow, but something of a disciplinarian and strict in the New England way. I felt then, as I feel now, that the Greeks in Cairo, who had much to gain by getting Toulmin out of the way, were responsible, but nothing was ever proven. George Skouras was not involved, and he was not questioned, so far as I know. But he was a very emotional, passionate fellow, deeply involving himself in Greek-American politics, something of a lightweight, but very brave and anxious to do something for Greece. But Skouras was not the sort of man who engaged in political assassination; he was far too gentle and kindly. He was the sort of man who would have warned Toulmin had he had any foreknowledge of such action."[13]

There was no doubt at the OSS that Putzell was correct in his estimate of the situation at Cairo, and Donovan took the doctors' advice and sent out a replacement, Colonel Harry S. Aldrich, who took up his duties on August 23, 1944. Aldrich, convinced that Skouras had had nothing to do with Toulmin's illness, kept him on his staff. Skouras then had a distinguished career as a secret agent inside Greece and was often in danger of losing his life.

Yet the situation itself did not change. To the contrary, it worsened, producing a serious fissure in the alliance between England and America. The differences came to a head over a column written by Drew Pearson, and circulated on August 19, 1944, in which the Washington columnist unleashed an insulting attack against Churchill personally, his policy in Greece in particular, and his policy concerning the British Empire in general[14]— an attack that was the most ferocious criticism of any ally by Pearson in the war.

Whatever the truth of Pearson's long and complicated assertions, his report reflected some of the statements made in OSS Cairo SI and Research and Analysis reports. As was to emerge later in another, similar case involving Pearson, he had suborned an OSS official working in Donovan's message center in Washington, and the reports obtained by Pearson from that individual formed the basis of Pearson's attack on Churchill.

Well aware of the attitude of OSS Cairo toward British handling of Greek affairs, Churchill sent Donovan the angriest signal he was known to have sent any official during World War II. Moreover, he sent it to Donovan through Eisenhower's chief of staff, General Walter Bedell Smith, an occasional friend of the OSS and a rival for the post of head of the postwar U.S. intelligence service:

> The Prime Minister to General Donovan, private and personal. Off the Record.
> I must tell you that there is very formidable trouble brewing in the Middle

East against OSS which is doing everything in its power to throw our policy towards Greece for which we have been accorded the main responsibility into confusion. I grieve greatly to see that your name is brought into all this because of our agreeable acquaintance in the past. Drew Pearson's article is a specimen of the kind of stuff that fits in with the campaign of OSS against the British. The OSS activities undoubtedly will have the effect of breeding a local quarrel between them and the British.

I was about to telegraph the president laying out the whole case so that he might have it in mind before we meet in a short time when I realized you were involved. In view of our association I should not like to put this matter on the highest level without asking you whether there is anything you could do to help. If however there is nothing that can be done the whole issue must be raised as between governments. With the great victories we are winning together it would be a great pity to have a lot of public discussion generated about this.[15]

So far as is known, Donovan made no reply to this telegram. Nor did he send any directives to Cairo instructing Aldrich to moderate or in any way change the policy or the reporters. What is evident is that Churchill's complaints concerned not only Pearson's statements but also the political attitude adopted by OSS Cairo, which was supposed to be apolitical. And the central figure in the complaints was the head of R&A's Greek desk, Moses Hadas, professor of Greek at Columbia University, a figure less known for his excellence as a Greek scholar than as the author of a celebrated work of Greek history that proved to be, partly, the fruits of plagiarism. An expert on Greek-Jewish relations in the ancient world, and a political conservative, Hadas seems nonetheless to have been imbued with the anti-imperialism that infected much OSS thinking of the period.

In September 1944 Hadas returned to Washington and handed Dr. W. L. Langer, the chief of R&A, a report entitled "Observations on Greek Affairs in Cairo." The content showed the attitudes of the man who was, to an important degree, responsible for keeping Washington officialdom informed of Greek affairs from May through August 1944—the period of which Churchill complained the most. Hadas opened his report:

Among Greeks in Cairo there is general resentment of the extent and perhaps even more of the manner of British interference in Greek political affairs. This feeling is not limited to liberal elements (for whom "resentment" is an inadequate term), but is shared by conservatives, who also desire a stable regime, but who feel that the British procedure involves an intolerable diminution of Greek sovereignty. The radical position was much more extreme, especially during the month of June. Clandestine publications aimed their attacks not so much at Germans as such but at "fascists," and let it be understood that the term included Greek and British right-wingers as well. Some of the papers warned that a German occupation must not be changed for a British one. [British ambassador to the

Greek government in exile Rex] Leeper was referred to as "the High Commissioner," and the relations between the Cairo Premier Papandreou and the British was [sic] equated to that between the [German puppet Premier] Rallis and the Germans.

Hadas said he had been informed "by a former professor of physics at Athens who had recently escaped from Athens," a man who had worked for EAM/ELAS "who impressed me by his sober intelligence and who seemed not at all the wild-eyed enthusiast" that "if the British persisted in their policy, British occupation of Greece would be opposed as vigorously as the German, and perhaps with greater bitterness, for, whereas the Germans were open enemies, the British were proving treacherous friends." According to Hadas, another informant, well placed in Greek affairs in Cairo and with "substantial social and financial connections," characterized British behavior as "that of a man in a panic. Their arrests of persons in Cairo and Alexandria for security reasons, with no charges preferred, their too patent control over every move of the Greek Government, their distortion of news for press releases, and their extremely severe censorship contributed to such an interpretation."

Hadas alleged that the British had interned "between six and ten thousand men of the Greek armed forces in the Middle East" who had mutinied against the royalist government, that their trials by the British had assumed "a political character," and that EAM believed "the mutineers will one day be looked upon as heroes and the victims of the court martials as national martyrs." Also, the British had "carried out many arrests of civilians for security reasons." He added:

> . . . in order to create a "reliable" Greek army, the British have carried out meticulous political screenings which have resulted in the formation of forces of which the officer cadres at least are outspokenly conservative. . . . An American reporter of Greek origin said that the officers were one and all royalists, and the rank and file at least ostensibly the same. Nevertheless clandestine leftist publications were circulating among the men, and my informant thought that if the Brigade were employed in Greece many might go over to EAM.

In the matter of British press censorship:

> I was present on numerous occasions at information gatherings of press correspondents where the subject was brought up and instances of the censor's severity cited. The deletions noted included not only matter which might imply excessive British interference in Greek affairs, but also comments on Papandreou which might be construed as derogatory, and, in addition, any approval of EAM's position or praise of EAM's achievements.

Turning to a subject which he termed "Disregard of Greek Sensibilities," Hadas advised WJD:

It is not only the extent and the overtness of British interference in Greek politics that have irked the Greeks, but also the apparently contemptuous attitude of the British. On two occasions Mr. Churchill mentioned the death of a single British officer in Greek disturbances, and spoke of the retribution that would be exacted. Greeks of all shades of opinion were annoyed, and recalled the numerous Greek villagers that were killed for sheltering British troops in Greece. The death of one German officer, the saying went, was expiated by the execution of 50 Greeks; but all the Greeks in Greece were not enough to atone for the death of a single Britisher. Whatever moral shortcomings the Greeks may have, by British standards, they are not stupid, and in negotiation with the British they resent the British assumption of superiority and their own treatment as fractious children. In a pension a British lady could not understand why an ex-minister of the Greek Government should not be made to change his more desirable room for the less desirable room of her son, who was "after all, an Englishman." A Greek acquaintance who was very far from radicalism once said to me: "If you would lend us your navy for a few weeks we could talk to these people much better."

Explaining the "Greek View of British Position," Hadas stated: "In the minds of Greek observers the British position has an easy explanation." It was:

A "safe" Greece is of the highest importance to Britain, and the British feel that Greek political behaviour is so unstable, and changes in Greek governments and policies so rapid and unpredictable, that the only means of assuring themselves of a "safe" Greece is to select a politician who will follow their lead, and to ensure that he shall have a firm control over Greece. The answer to this, given by Greeks who are genuinely Anglophile, is that it is more important for the British to possess the good will of the Greeks, allowing them to pursue their national idiosyncrasies in the matter of changing governments, than to retain control through a government which must be unpopular.

As for the British and their relations with the Greek resistance movement, this "seems" to be "cynically opportunist," for "on the surface they have consistently supported a weaker party against one whose strength was becoming dangerous, and have thus sought to maintain an equilibrium by setting Greeks against each other. An unbiased explanation makes the procedure seem less sinister." In the early stages of German occupation, and when supplies were being shipped to Rommel in North Africa through Greece, "the British were anxious to encourage any resistance groups that would hinder the Germans." They found EAM/ELAS the largest and the most effective organization, the only one which possessed the necessary experiences in the techniques of underground activity. They turned their support to EAM/ELAS, which grew to "formidable strength, comprising perhaps some 70% of the total Greek population." They developed a program for postwar Greece. At that point the British came to feel:

> EAM was more interested in attaining its political aims than in fighting Germans, for the Germans would be driven out in any case, whereas the control of Greece was a problem that would outlast the war. The British felt that any additional supplies given EAM would not be used against the Germans, but husbanded . . . for later use in attaining their political aims. They therefore withdrew support from EAM, planned gradually to withdraw their liaison personnel in preparation for an open break, and began giving lavish support to groups hostile to EAM. . . . EAMites feel that this action was responsible for bloody clashes between [the royalist EDES] and ELAS.

Also, the British had adopted an "ambiguous attitude" toward the Fascist Security Battalions in Greece, formed by the Germans to fight Communists and used by them as well to serve "other German interests, such as making arrests and house searches for the Gestapo and keeping guard while German troops were harvesting [stolen] Greek crops." Security Battalion "recruiting officers regularly claimed that while the organization was equipped by the Germans, [their] functions were approved by the British." Hadas commented:

> [The] implication that the British (like the Germans) were willing to use any stick to beat EAM was clear, and was undoubtedly a contributory factor to the frequent rumors that there was an understanding between the British and the Germans for common action against Russia. Only in September 1944, according to an ELAS broadcast, did a British liaison officer openly announce that Greeks remaining in the Security Battalions would be treated as enemies.

He then turned to the question of the "Alleged Bias of British Personnel":

> Exception has been taken to certain leading British liaison personnel in Greece on the grounds that their political and social temperaments and associations render them incapable for forming true judgments of the Greek political situation. The chief offender, because he was senior officer, was [Colonel the Honorable Christopher M. Woodhouse, chief of the Allied Military Mission to Greece in 1943 and 1944]. Woodhouse is perfectly sincere, cultivated and competent, but he was only twenty-two [when] he entered on duty in Greece, and has considerable financial interests there. Despite his previous residence in Greece and his personal integrity, his

CRUMBLING RELATIONSHIPS 609

opponents claim that he is incapable of appreciating Greek problems in their totality.

In general, Hadas reported, all British officials in Cairo except the British Embassy at the Greek government in exile agreed with his opinions.[16]

Not surprisingly the document caused much surprise and anxiety in Washington. Consequently, Donovan sent the originals to the secretary of state and the Joint Chiefs, but a paraphrased version written by himself to FDR. It was faithful to the facts conveyed by Hadas, but their effect was enhanced by the process of paraphrasing. The paper constituted the gravest indictment of the British government and authorities at Cairo, for it would have seemed that America's principal ally was no better in its conduct than the Nazis and the Fascists.

It was this point that Churchill (who was not uninformed about what was happening inside OSS Cairo) resented. And, one of Churchill's principal officers, Colonel Sir Ronald Wingate, later stated: "We had been at war with Germany longer than any other power, we had suffered more, we had sacrificed more, and in the end we would lose more than any other power. Yet here were these God-awful American academics rushing about, talking about the Four Freedoms and the Atlantic Charter, and criticizing us for doing successfully what they would try and fail to do themselves later—restrain the Russians. Donovan was very lucky we didn't send a Guards company to OSS Cairo."[17]

And then, at this point, there occurred an incident on the German frontier that, if only temporarily, wrecked the special relationship in the field of secret intelligence that had been forged at the Arcadia Conference.

At 6:05 P.M. on September 11, 1944, Staff Sergeant Warner W. Holzinger, of the 2nd Platoon, Troop B, 85th Cavalry Reconnaissance Squadron, 5th Armored Division, led his men across the shallow Our River near the little German border village of Wallendorf, climbed a hill to a cluster of farm buildings, and thereby became the first Allied fighting man to enter Germany in World War II.

The OSS was not far behind, and by the fifteenth an X-2 detachment had been established at the Brasseur Hotel, Luxembourg, under the command of Major Maxwell J. Papurt, of Columbus, Ohio, a thirty-seven-year-old expert in penal psychology in New York State who had obtained his Ph.D. at Ohio State University. Papurt, one of the earliest men to join X-2, had played an important part in controlled enemy agent operations, those most secret of all WJD's secret operations. And he was a member of a most exclusive intelligence club—he was cleared to read ISOS. He was, therefore, under strict orders not to place himself in a situation where he might be captured by the Germans.

But as Donovan's papers show, on or about September 25, 1944, he encountered Gertrude Legendre, a prominent Charleston society woman who was with the OSS in charge of David Bruce's message center, and Lieutenant Commander Robert Jennings, a wealthy Texan oilman with OSS SI, both with OSS Paris. Mrs. Legendre had come to the front to see her friend General Patton, and Jennings was escorting her. Their car had broken down, and they were forced to stay at the Brasseur Hotel while it was being repaired. At the hotel they met Papurt, whom Jennings knew, as Papurt was leaving for the Wallendorf area, and Papurt suggested they might like to come along for the ride.

The party, which set out on September 26, consisted of Papurt, Mrs. Legendre, Jennings, and an X-2 driver named Dixon. Just short of Wallendorf, which they believed to be in American hands, their jeep was hit by a bullet. Papurt leaped from the vehicle to hunt what he thought was a sniper—he was armed with a carbine—but shortly afterward the jeep was hit by heavy machine-gun fire, and Papurt was shot through both legs. Another burst of fire also caught Dixon in the legs and in his right hand.

Although badly wounded, Dixon tried to reverse the vehicle back down the road, but the self-starter would not work. All four lay down in the grass verge behind the jeep, burned their papers, and then surrendered by hoisting a carbine with a white handkerchief tied to it. As they waited for the Germans to come get them, they concocted stories that each would tell to conceal the fact that they were with the OSS. Mrs. Legendre was "an interpreter loaned to Jennings and Papurt," Jennings was a "naval observer on a mission to the front," Papurt was "just an ordnance officer," and Dixon was "just a G.I."[18] At this point a group of German soldiers emerged from some bushes, bandaged the wounded, and took the party into captivity, where interrogations began.

The sense of dismay at Menzies's and Donovan's headquarters at Papurt's capture was very great, and both men agreed that all news concerning the capture should be suppressed in England and America. At the same time a special watch was instituted on all German secret service wireless traffic to see whether there was a diminution of such traffic or it ceased altogether. If it did, it was clear that Papurt had revealed that the British counterespionage service was reading the Sicherheitsdienst wireless traffic. In fact, ominously, shortly after the capture there was a diminution in the ISOS yield owing to the sudden introduction by the Germans of a new cipher system.

While only surmise was possible, in a note to the acting chief of OSS London, Colonel Russell Forgan, the head of X-2, Norman Holmes Pearson, thought this could be readily explained by the fact that the SD was switching from the Enigma type of machine-made ciphers to invulnerable one-time pads, as part of the general tightening of security following the bomb attack on Hitler's life on July 20. Pearson insisted: "Until it can be specifically demonstrated that the capture had any definite effect [on the changeover from machine to one-time pad ciphers], little heed should be taken to implications that the capture was responsible."

Pearson also felt sure that "of all our [X-2] personnel Papurt stands the best chance of bluffing his way out [of detailed interrogation]. He possesses a certain natural capacity for this," and if he were forced to talk, he would talk at great length not about X-2 and ISOS, but about the Army's Counterintelligence Corps. For Papurt "uniquely has a wealth of CIC experience in North Africa and Italy on which to draw for detail if any connection is felt by the Germans between him and intelligence work." That might be unfortunate for the CIC's "procedures and resources [but the revelations Papurt had to make] would definitely be the lesser of the two evils." And, Pearson noted hopefully, "It is now approximately one month since the capture and it is possible to believe that we may escape what would have been one of the intelligence disasters of the war."[19]

Pearson warned, however, that Papurt's capture, and the fact that he was cleared for ISOS, were known to Menzies, Eisenhower's chief of intelligence (General Strong), and his American deputy, General Thomas J. Betts. It seemed certain, therefore, that the gravest trouble confronted Donovan, for not only had Papurt violated the OSS X-2 agreements relating to ISOS, but WJD himself had violated those agreements on numerous occasions.

In any event, there was no trouble. Papurt was killed on November 29, 1944, when Allied bombing aircraft hit the camp where he was being held at Diez, Limburg—as it was to be discovered after the war—before the Sicherheitsdienst could make him talk. Nevertheless, the event had occurred to give the British pause in their relations with Donovan's service. To make matters more serious, an incident now took place to disturb his relations with the French intelligence services.

Donovan flew back to Washington on September 14, 1944, to find Ruth and his granddaughter, Patricia, at Nonquitt, cleaning up after a hurricane that had struck Cape Cod that weekend. Donovan flew up to Nonquitt in the OSS's twin-engine Beechcraft, but there was little to be done, and he was soon back at his desk at the Kremlin, as OSS headquarters were called by the staff. There he found his hopes for an alliance with the French services, and his relationship with the Russian Fitin, in danger.

With a badly damaged Anglo-American intelligence relationship in the autumn of 1944, Donovan had high hopes that he might establish an alliance with the SR formed by De Gaulle upon the entry of the provisional government into Paris. Donovan had no reason to believe that such a relationship could not be developed, for the head of the SR had been

De Gaulle's chief of intelligence and counterespionage throughout De Gaulle's exile: André Dewavrin, with whom, despite his reputation for brutality, exoticism, elitism, and mysticism, Donovan had developed a friendly working relationship.

In September 1944 Donovan invited Dewavrin and certain of his staff to the United States as guests of the OSS. To ensure that the visit began well, Bruce, now chief of OSS Paris, put Dewavrin in for the Distinguished Service Cross, America's second highest medal, awarded only for "extraordinary heroism against an armed enemy in circumstances which do not justify the award of the Medal of Honor."[20] It was hoped the medal would be approved in time to be presented to Dewavrin by President Roosevelt in Washington. In a letter supporting Bruce's recommendation, Donovan wrote to Eisenhower on September 15, 1944:

> In connection with the recommendation for the award of a Distinguished Service Cross to Colonel André de Wavrins [sic] (who until recently served under the name of Colonel André Passy) I should like to add a personal endorsement to it. Colonel de Wavrins, and the Services over which he has presided, have to my own intimate knowledge made an outstanding contribution to the Allied war effort. He has risked his life over a considerable period of time when the penalty in case of his capture would have been even more drastic than that imposed on the ordinary secret agent by the enemy. The acts for which he is now cited demonstrated again his unusual qualities of leadership and his high degree of personal courage under extra-hazardous circumstances.

The British Army had awarded him both the Military Cross and the Distinguished Service Cross, he had been similarly decorated by the Norwegians, Dutch, and Belgians, and it was Donovan's "earnest hope that his services to the American Army may be recognized in the manner suggested."[21]

Eisenhower endorsed Bruce's proposal, but not even that most powerful signature could have obtained an American medal for Dewavrin at that time. For the State Department, the Department of Justice, and the Federal Bureau of Investigation all intervened to prevent Dewavrin from coming to Washington and receiving an American medal, on the ground that J. Edgar Hoover had received information that Dewavrin had been involved in one of the Duke Street Murders—the incident at the time of Torch in which Dewavrin was allegedly responsible for the murder in the basement of the Mayfair headquarters of De Gaulle's secret service of a Frenchmen suspected of being a German penetration agent.

When word of this opposition reached Supreme Headquarters, Eisenhower withdrew his endorsement of the Distinguished Service Cross for Dewavrin because, Donovan explained, Eisenhower's chief of staff, General Walter Bedell Smith, had stated that no medal could be awarded "unless prior to the deed for which it was awarded there had been nothing dishonorable in the man's life."[22]

Bruce, who had intimated earlier to Dewavrin that he might receive some high American decoration, now had the difficult, embarrassing task of explaining to the bad-tempered French spymaster that, for the moment at least, such an award could not be given. Dewavrin appears to have accepted the statement with considerable grace. But now worse occurred: The State Department refused to issue a visa to Dewavrin to enter the United States. Donovan wired Bruce that the secretary of state had "temporarily prevented favorable action because [Dewavrin] is one of the few individuals against whom Hull feels most strongly." Donovan told Bruce he had told Hull it was "necessary for us to lay short and long range plans with [Dewavrin] and to cement for the future intelligence relationships which we have effectively developed over past months." But James Clement Dunn, the department's director of European affairs, had replied that Hull's attitude was "based upon series of difficulties encountered by this government with [Dewavrin during the] earlier years of war both in North Africa and London." At one time it was not clear to the department "where [Dewavrin's] sympathies lay."[23]

Donovan fought Hull's decision and won. The visa was granted on condition there would be no publicity, and Dewavrin and his staff officers left Paris for Washington on what was hoped fervently would be a politically tranquil but interesting tour of the United States. That was not to be, for on December 13, 1944, J. Edgar Hoover wrote a long letter to Attorney General Francis Biddle alleging that the real purpose of Dewavrin's visit was to establish espionage rings:

> Sources professing professional experience in the intelligence field and which have proved reliable in the past inform me that Colonel De Wavrin [*sic*] is in the United States to organize and set in operation a secret intelligence organization in behalf of the French Government. While Colonel De Wavrin ostensibly is in this country to reestablish the offices of the French Military Attachés, which he asserts are not concerned with intelligence matters, the sources referred to remain convinced that his visit here as well as his intended tour in the immediate future throughout South and Central America has for its real purpose the organization of a secret foreign intelligence organization in this Hemisphere.
>
> As either the open or secret operation of a foreign intelligence organization on the sovereign soil of the United States cannot but be fraughted [*sic*] with serious danger to the welfare and future safety of this country, I wanted to bring this development to your attention and to furnish you available information about the background of the individual reported to be devoting himself to such a cause. In this connection I am sure you will agree it is obvious that Colonel De Wavrin's background is such as to lend weight and

likelihood to the statements referred to relative to the nature of his real purpose in coming to the United States at this time. His background also would seem to direct particular attention to the probable character of the intelligence organization reportedly being planned by him.[24]

Colonel Dewavrin, Hoover reported, had been appointed "Chief of the French Secret Police" by De Gaulle in 1940. He was said "immediately to have proceeded to form a Gestapo-like organization," and "You may recall that the organization has been responsible for a number of bombings and assassinations of its political enemies in North Africa." Hoover went on:

Indicative of the methods of operation utilized by De Wavrin in achieving his objectives, the New York Times for September 18, 1943, carried an article concerning a court action against Colonel André Passy and others filed by a wounded veteran of the Battle of France who had escaped to Britain in February, 1941, and who alleged he had been unjustifiably beaten and jailed. According to this article when interviewed by Colonel Passy and two of his assistants, who attempted to obtain from this veteran information to which they were not entitled and when the French veteran refused to answer, he was threatened with death and beaten with fists and a steel rod. The veteran further charged in this suit against Passy that he had been confined for ten days to a cellar about three yards long and two-and-one-half yards wide, without furniture or light and with little ventilation. It has been reported that prosecution was suspended on this indictment in the interest of military expediency and political unity until the end of the war.

Hoover then reported that:

an informant had related that following De Wavrin's appointment by de Gaulle to his position as Chief of the French Secret Police certain highly confidential information pertaining to combined British-French operations was revealed without authorization and thereafter two of De Wavrin's principal aides were seized by the British authorities and have been held in custody since.

Colonel Dewavrin himself would have been arrested by the British but for the scandal that would have followed the arrest of "De Gaulle's foremost advisor."

Dewavrin was known as De Gaulle's "Himmler," as his "political hatchet man," and he had "added to his unsavory reputation by his handling of various political purges within the DeGaulliste [sic] regime." Hoover ended his letter to Biddle:

I believe that it is uncontestable that even under the best of circumstances and when dealing with the friendliest and most stable of allies that intelligence organizations of foreign powers must not be permitted to become established on American soil and should be discouraged wherever possible from taking root any place in this Hemisphere. It is obvious that this position is sound, particularly when dealing with an intelligence organization of the government of a country which is provisional in character and within which strange and ruthless forces are at work.

Attorney General Biddle, who was no friend of Donovan and was involved in a new complicated maneuver to terminate the OSS, could hardly be restrained from acting on Hoover's behalf. Attaching Hoover's letter, Biddle wrote to President Roosevelt on December 15, 1944, seeking to show that Dewavrin was a Fascist. Improving on Hoover's telling, Biddle announced:

> I am advised by Edgar Hoover . . . that Colonel De Wavrin is now in this country, ostensibly to reestablish the offices of the French Military Attaché but actually to set in operation a secret intelligence organization in the United States and in Latin America.
>
> De Wavrin has been head of the DeGaulle Secret Police since 1940. He was formerly closely associated with the Cagoule, one of the most ruthless Fascist organizations in France. He is supposed to have been mixed up with several acts of violence, including murder, and is thought to be a dangerous and unscrupulous man.
>
> It is said that the mounting criticism in France against De Wavrin caused DeGaulle to get him out of the way by sending him over here. I do not know who is responsible for bringing him over. In any event, I should think he should not have been brought to America and should now be got out.
>
> I am calling this to your attention as you may wish to make further inquiries about him.[25]

Biddle, of course, knew well who had brought Dewavrin to the United States, as did the President. It was Donovan, and Roosevelt was not prepared to embarrass his spymaster at this time by demanding Dewavrin's return to France. He left the matter until Dewavrin was back in Paris and then requested an investigation of Dewavrin's past, an investigation that could have a bearing only on Donovan's request that the Frenchman receive the Distinguished Service Cross.

With that medal in mind, Donovan asked OSS London to see Menzies and Sir Percy Sillitoe, the chief of the British Security Service, and establish the facts concerning Dewavrin's conduct when he and his service had been quartered in London. On March 3, 1945, Commander Lester Armour, deputy chief of OSS London, signaled that he had seen Sillitoe and the Security Service officer who had investigated the charges against Dewavrin in London after the Duke Street Murders. Both had assured Armour that Dewavrin had had no connection with "black interrogations"—the British term for the third degree—and that interrogations where the third degree had been used had been conducted by a department of the French secret service other than Dewavrin's. The other department was concerned with security, whereas Dewavrin had been wholly concerned with intelligence. The linking of Dewavrin with the Duke Street Murders had been, Sillitoe assured Armour, "political maneuvering." The suspected German agent had been very roughly handled, but he had not died of his injuries. Instead, he had committed suicide, and Sillitoe was able to send Donovan the secret coroner's report testifying that suicide was the cause of death.

However, Sillitoe went on, although there was no evidence that Dewavrin had been involved, black interrogations had taken place, and the British had closed the center and forbidden the practice. An inquiry had shown, Armour reported, that "Other Allied nations similarly involved in methods normal to Continental practice but uncongenial here."[26]

Armour had seen Menzies, he reported, and it was he who had obtained the Distinguished Service Order, a very high decoration and fairly rare, for Dewavrin for gallantry in action. Menzies had warned that he "personally believed [Dewavrin] would be unhappy if not given recognition and felt such naturally useful for possible later cooperation necessary no matter one's personal feelings [sic]."

In the end the assembly by Hoover of a dossier on Dewavrin was really a waste of time. Donovan succeeded in getting Dewavrin's Distinguished Service Cross, for WJD advised President Roosevelt:

> While some of these accusations, stripped of their implications of dictatorship, had some basis in fact and were echoed in the [French] Consultative Assembly, they represented, for the most part, gross exaggerations and mis-representations put forward with the idea of discrediting the Gaullist regime in Allied circles and of creating favor for a more conservative French authority organized under General Giraud.[27]

Yet the damage was done. There had been warnings that the Franco-American intelligence entente might be of only limited use when on August 7, 1944, a principal OSS SI officer at Algiers, Lieutenant Colonel David W. King, who had been watching the French secret scene since before Torch, advised WJD:

> The time has come when [we] are no longer welcome by the French. Had the old French special service chiefs remained in power, we might possibly have developed a useful and cooperative service, but the new chiefs have but one idea: i.e. to clear the country of any sort of American or British special service.[28]

Late in 1944 the French authorities advised SHAEF that a number of U.S. agencies, including the OSS, must leave on the ground that Paris was "too crowded" with Allied personnel. With that complaint Eisenhower's chief of staff, General Smith, "peremptorily" instructed Colonel Bruce, director of OSS Paris, to evacuate the city and find offices in the provinces. The order was successfully resisted by Bruce, who was allowed to retain a reduced staff in Paris. But the intimacy Donovan had hoped to create between the OSS and Dewavrin's services had vanished, and there now began a protracted period of only token collaboration inlaid with fundamental hostility.

But now came excellent news. FDR made WJD a major general, thus increasing his pay by about $2,200. Then the President took a decision regarding the creation of a central intelligence service. The circumstances of the second step were of major importance, and complex.

PART FIVE

THE ECLIPSE PERIOD

Being the account of some of Donovan's final main operations against the Third Reich, the start of his operations against the Soviet Union, the dissolution of his service, his dismissal by President Harry S Truman, and Donovan's return to the practice of the law. Also dealt with are his involvement in the establishment of the Central Intelligence Agency, some of his confidential activities in the opening phases of the cold war, and finally his death.

40

The Betrayal

When Donovan returned to OSS Washington on September 14, 1944, there were numerous signs as a result of the dramatic and tragic episode of the Warsaw uprising that the cold war between East and West had begun. With the Red Army at the eastern gates, the Polish Home Army in Warsaw rose up against the Wehrmacht on August 1, 1944, expecting the Russians to enter the city and join the battle. But that the Red Army did not do. Instead, it remained in place, enigmatically and cold-bloodedly watching the Polish patriots being slaughtered. To make the slaughter greater, when General John Deane and Ambassador Averell Harriman saw Stalin almost immediately on Donovan's behalf, asking for permission for supply flights to land on Ukrainian airfields, permission was refused. Stalin intended that Russia alone should have control of Eastern Europe, and here was the first manifestation of that policy.

When the uprising began, Donovan immediately began signaling FDR, the Joint Chiefs, his staff in London and Caserta, and the commander in chief of the U.S. Army Air Forces. To all he had a single request: Permit the OSS to commence arms supply operations to the Poles on the same scale as to the French after D-Day. From all those Donovan bombarded there came this reply: The political and aeronautical realities were such that no large-scale supply missions were possible unless the USAAF was granted the use of the Red Air Force base at Poltava in the Ukraine, and that had been refused by Stalin and Molotov.

The prohibition remained in force until September 12, 1944, when at last Stalin relented and agreed to permit the U.S. Army Air Forces to use

Poltava, although a Polish historian was to write: "It is not clear whether [Stalin] did so in response to the allies' unremitting pressure, or in order to prolong the insurgents' agony and increase their losses."[1]

Whatever the case, Donovan had ordered Bruce and Glavin to prepare for a mass drop of war stores to Warsaw. They had done their work well, and when FDR issued the necessary permission for the USAAF to commence supply operations, containers were ready for a total of 110 B-17 Flying Fortresses to make the long flight across Europe to Warsaw. During the flight 3 B-17's had to return to England with mechanical trouble. When the 107 B-17's arrived over Warsaw for the drop, they found the city engulfed in flames and smoke, and an accurate drop to the insurgents' bastions could not be made. As a result, of the 1,284 containers carried by the B-17's, only 228 were received by the Poles. A further 32 were in no-man's-land, and 28 had reached the ground in a badly damaged state because of faulty parachute openings. The B-17's then flew on to Poltava to refuel and let the crews rest, and they returned to England via Bari in Italy. Casualties were severe: Between Warsaw and Poltava 1 B-17 was shot down by German fighters, and a further 10 aircraft were badly damaged but managed to limp into Poltava.

A few days later the Home Army in Warsaw surrendered. Hundreds of acres of the city center were then blown up by the Germans as part of a program to remove the city from the map of Europe. When the Red Army did arrive, it found a city of ruins and ghosts—a fact that fundamentally changed Donovan's attitude from the spirit of cooperation that had motivated him up until Warsaw to one of determination to intensify his operations against the Russians. In that new, more aggressive, more determined policy he was encouraged by a paper from Robert B. Joyce, his political officer at Supreme Headquarters in Italy, which had been endorsed by William P. Maddox, Donovan's chief of Secret Intelligence in the Mediterranean theater. Both men urged that because of the worsening situation with the Russians in the Balkans and Eastern Europe, "Washington should speed up its long range plans" for a central intelligence service.[2]

Joyce reported to Donovan in his long paper: "The following represents an endeavor to analyze the present problems confronting us in the Southeastern European area as a consequence of military developments in this region, the result of which has been the dominating position of the Soviet Union in this part of Europe."[3]

After setting forth the OSS position in Rumania, Bulgaria, Albania, Yugoslavia, Greece, and Hungary, Joyce advised Donovan:

> It is apparent from the foregoing situations as they exist in the areas already under Soviet influence that the Russians quite obviously do not desire OSS activities in Southeastern and Central Europe. The opinion is hazarded that

it is perhaps not Russian policy at this moment to appear other than desirous of cooperating with the British and particularly with the Americans, and for this reason the Russians have adopted a policy of temporizing and procrastinating rather than stating flatly and clearly that they do not desire OSS to operate behind Russian military (and political) lines.

At the same time, while "indicating their appreciation of the excellent work OSS has performed . . . in obtaining and reporting primarily political and economic intelligence from the Balkan countries," the State Department's representatives "have recently shown a tendency towards uneasiness and nervousness" about the "existence of an independent American agency in the foreign field not under the full control of the respective Ambassadors."

The quasi-diplomatic American Control Commissions (ACC) in such countries as Rumania and Bulgaria, which were staffed with a combination of State, Army, and OSS personnel under Army politico-military command, had always displayed uneasiness at the OSS's presence in Sofia and Bucharest. This Joyce attributed to "nervousness in the face of Russian displeasure" at OSS operations and "perhaps [to] a lack of understanding as to just what are the functions of American agencies in countries which have fallen almost entirely under Soviet military and political domination."

His conclusion was, therefore: "The Russians do not desire OSS activities in areas controlled by them or under their influence and they are prepared to prevent such activities." As a consequence, the State Department had become "and will probably increasingly become wary of OSS activities and be more and more disinclined to provide the necessary cover and support if we are to continue our operations."

Joyce recommended that in the face of Russian pressure and State Department caution, Donovan should withdraw all OSS units at present operating more or loss openly in Eastern Europe and replace those missions with covert operations. The task of the covert operations would be to "cover the present transitory period" between the end of hostilities in the former enemy territories and the establishment of regular U.S. diplomatic missions in the countries concerned. The matter of the future of the OSS was one of great urgency, for what was also required was "a complete clarification of OSS-State Department-ACC relations . . . in terms of independent reporting and functional and administrative tie-ins." Joyce felt that the time had come when, if the United States were to be correctly informed about Russian activities in the former enemy territories Russia occupied, OSS activities must be placed "on a sound and permanent basis."

Impressed by the reasoning behind this memorandum, Donovan sent it over to FDR and Isadore Lubin, the White House economist. But as action was being taken to commence the necessary preliminaries toward the establishment of a CIA, a tempest that made such steps impossible blew up. Somebody had leaked Donovan's plan to the press.

When Donovan received Joyce's report, he had before him also a paper by Doering, which he had asked for before he left for Dragoon. Doering's paper was entitled "The Basis for a Permanent World-Wide Intelligence Service."[4] Donovan rewrote Doering's paper and sent it to the director of the budget, Harold D. Smith, to comply with Smith's request for Donovan's plans after the war with Germany. That paper was to be the seed from which sprang the CIA.

Donovan contended that:

§ Knowledge of the activities of foreign nations was essential.

§ The collection and analysis of such intelligence must be done centrally.

§ Such an organization must be run by a director appointed by the President.

§ It should be guided by a board of representatives from the State, War, and Navy departments.

§ It should be responsible for all secret activity, including secret intelligence, counterespionage, cryptanalysis, and subversive operations.

§ It should have its own communications systems.

§ It should have access to vouchered and unvouchered funds.

§ "Such a service should not operate clandestine intelligence within the United States."

§ "It should have no police function and should not be identified with any law-enforcing agency, either at home or abroad."

§ There was no need to create a new organization, for it existed already in the OSS.

Doering's paper was presented to Roosevelt by Lubin on or about October 25, 1944, when Lubin sent Roosevelt a note stating: "Bill Donovan's Office of Strategic Services has been doing some swell work. It occurred to me that there will be room after the war for a service in the United States Government which would carry on some of the work now being done under Donovan's auspices."[5]

Plainly Donovan had been doing some clubby brainwashing, for Lubin —a man with a good deal of influence with Roosevelt—felt that after the war there "will be a need for a continuous flow of intelligence which could be used for the development of American foreign policy." The service he had in mind, Lubin hastened to add, "should in no manner encroach upon the duties of the established intelligence services of the Army, Navy and Air Forces" and, he might have added, the State Department and the Foreign Economic Administration.

Lubin had in mind exactly what Donovan had in mind: a service that would "collect, analyze and disseminate intelligence on the policy and strategy levels," that would "objectively and impartially" serve the "needs of the combined diplomatic, military and economic services of the Government." It would be "made up of specialists who were professionally trained in intelligence analysis, with a high degree of competence and knowledge in the economic, social and geographic factors that prevail in different countries throughout the world." It was this "sort of information that we sadly lacked when we entered the war," but happily, "the nucleus of such an organization already exists"—the Office of Strategic Services, which has the "trained personnel, the foreign contacts, the administrative organization and the operating experience."

Obviously in Dr. Lubin Donovan had a powerful friend at court. There were others, however, who felt less kindly toward Donovan and the OSS, and some of them were more influential than Lubin, especially Director of the Budget Smith, whose advice to Roosevelt was to go slow on providing for a postwar intelligence service, and Jay Franklin Carter, a columnist who had done some intelligence work for the President, who saw Donovan's paper and warned Roosevelt to caution because the British secret service had "penetrated" the OSS and was "thoroughly familiar with its methods, plans and personnel." When Donovan saw that comment (he was shown Carter's paper by Roosevelt), he retorted that the OSS had "maintained the integrity of our organization," and "our allies and our enemies know less about our inner workings than we do about theirs."

Whatever the truth of that assertion (and the OSS executive at this stage believed it had clear evidence that the British SIS was cataloguing and indexing OSS operations worldwide), Lubin's influence at the White House seems to have worked. Roosevelt sent a note to Donovan on October 31, 1944, inviting him to give some thought to intelligence in the postwar period. That was the opening for which Donovan had been waiting. He set his executives to work on the preparation of a full-scale proposal and on November 3, 1944, asked Doering to produce a draft presidential directive establishing a central intelligence service. That Doering did, producing a document that, as he stated, would enable the United States to free itself from "our present national dependence upon British intelligence."[6]

By November 18, 1944, the document, with Doering's draft directive, was at the White House. Donovan stated in a covering letter, referring to the Russian situation: "There are commonsense reasons why you may desire to lay the keel of the ship at once."

While the proposals were familiar, Doering's directive was the really new contribution. It proposed:

§ The service would be a new agency designed to coordinate the functions and supplement the work of the departmental intelligence agencies.

§ The service would be placed in the office of the President and the director would work "under the direction and supervision of the President."

§ There would be an advisory board composed of the secretaries of state, war, and navy and "such other members" as the President might appoint. The board would advise and assist, not control, the director of the service.

§ The service would coordinate, collect, and produce finished intelligence, its coordination extended to all government intelligence agencies. Collection would include espionage and counterespionage. The service would also conduct subversive operations abroad and "perform such other functions and duties relating to intelligence" as the President might direct. The production of intelligence would relate to "national planning and security in peace and war," and the new service would have access to the intelligence production of all other services.

§ The service would have control of its own personnel, its own budget, the right to call upon associated intelligence services for such personnel as it needed, and the authority to run its own household and communications.

§ The service would have *no* "police or law enforcement functions, either at home or abroad." It would recognize the right of the departmental agencies to "collect, evaluate, synthesize and disseminate departmental operating intelligence," defined as "intelligence required by such agencies in the actual performance of their functions and duties." In time of war or unlimited national emergency, coordination and/or control would be through the Joint Chiefs or the theater commanders.[7]

The plan produced the most startled reaction of any piece of paper in the intelligence history of the war in Washington, with the exception of the original executive orders establishing the COI and the OSS. The document was widely circulated under highly controlled circumstances, and predictably many attempts were made to destroy its proposals. There was what was called "a series of conferences with gentlemen not too friendly to OSS," who argued it into "stale mutilation." But with a few reservations, it was supported by the civilian agencies and denounced by the military. General Strong, the former Army G-2, who had been relegated to postwar planning when Assistant Secretary of War J. J. McCloy lost confidence in him, rejected the plan when his opinion was sought. It was, he declared, a "new and somewhat cumbersome and possibly dangerous organization." The OSS had been created for the purposes of a war emergency, and when the war was over, it ought to be liquidated, not perpetuated under another name. And, Strong contended, the prewar system had worked "in an eminently satisfactory manner without any advertising, publicity or self-seeking."[8]

However, by the end of the year Donovan's paper and Doering's directive had survived all attempts to destroy the notion that the OSS should be turned into the CIA. The inevitable winter attack began with a vengeance in early February 1945.

On February 9, 1945, the Washington *Times-Herald*, the New York *Daily News*, and the Chicago *Tribune*—all anti-Roosevelt newspapers owned by the McCormick-Patterson empire—unleashed the sensational news under flaring headlines: DONOVAN PROPOSES SUPER SPY SYSTEM FOR POST-WAR NEW DEAL; WOULD TAKE OVER FBI, SECRET SERVICE, ONI AND G2 PROJECT FOR U.S. SUPER-SPIES DISCLOSED IN SECRET MEMO; NEW DEAL PLANS SUPER SPY SYSTEM; SLEUTHS WOULD SNOOP ON U.S. AND THE WORLD; ORDER CREATING IT ALREADY DRAFTED, NEW DEAL PLANS TO SPY ON WORLD AND HOME FOLKS, AND SUPER GESTAPO AGENCY IS UNDER CONSIDERATION.

The author of all three stories was Walter Trohan, a Washington reporter close to J. Edgar Hoover, and he told of the "Creation of an all-powerful intelligence service to spy on the postwar world and to pry into the lives of citizens at home . . . under consideration by the New Deal." The new service would "supersede all existing Federal police and intelligence units," enjoy "a wholesale grant of power," and spy on "good neighbors throughout the world for the purpose of formulating a foreign policy and developing strategy."

Trohan presented Doering's draft directive verbatim (although it was still top secret) and then commented that the director of the new "super spy unit" would have "tremendous power" and could, if he chose, "determine American foreign policy by weeding out, withholding or coloring information gathered at his direction." Trohan did state that the new service would have no police powers at home or abroad, but he contended also that the draft directive would "permit spying at home and employment of the police powers of existing agencies whenever needed." Such agencies could also be stopped from "reporting to their superiors," showing how the director of the new service could "employ the FBI on some task and charge the G-men not to report to J. Edgar Hoover" or even to Attorney General Biddle. Trohan continued:

> . . . in the high circles where the memorandum and draft order are circulat-
> ing, the proposed unit is known as "Frankfurter's Gestapo," because the
> sister of . . . Justice [Felix] Frankfurter is said to hold a confidential personnel
> post in OSS. It is assumed she would pick key personnel, at the suggestion
> of her brother, for Donovan when, as he expects, he would be named spy
> chief. She is Miss Stella Frankfurter.

Furthermore, announced Trohan breathlessly, the Donovan agency would have an independent budget and what he called "secret funds for spy work along the lines of bribing and luxury living described in the novels of E. Phillips Oppenheim."

The next day the entire American polity panted with sensation. In its editorial the Chicago *Tribune* denounced Roosevelt for wanting to "play power politics all around the world" while establishing "a police state at home." Trohan reported that in Congress the "Super-Spy Idea [was] denounced as New Deal OGPU"; Senator Edwin C. Johnson, Democrat of Colorado, announced that the country did not "want any Democratic Gestapo"; Senator Homer Capehart, Republican of Indiana, deplored "any new superduper Gestapo"; Representative John J. Sparkman, Dem-ocrat of Alabama, thought "a great many people would consider it a super Gestapo"; Representative Clare Hoffman, Republican of Michigan, called it "another New Deal move right along the Hitler line." On the twelfth Trohan published more secret documents relating to the debate on the formation of the Donovan agency under these headlines: ARMY, NAVY WANT CONTROL OF "SPY" SETUP; GENERALS, ADMIRALS DECLARE WAR ON OSS. A "pitched battle" had broken out between "the high command of the Army and the Navy" and the OSS for control of the "New Deal's superintelligence agency."

On the other hand, the New York *Herald Tribune* announced more favorably: ROOSEVELT PLANS POST-WAR GLOBAL SECRET SERVICE; DONOVAN MAPS NEW AGENCY TO KEEP U.S. ALERT TO THREAT OF A NEW WAR, while *The New York Times* reported that the comparison of Donovan's agency with the Gestapo was "received with surprise and not a little disapprobation in informed circles." Frank R. Kent of the Baltimore *Sun* ridiculed the "wild charges" hurled at Donovan's plan which he effectively defended point by point, and Edward R. Murrow, of CBS, declared that the plan "wouldn't mean sending a lot of spies into friendly nations or anything of the kind" but would mean that after the fighting ended, "we shall require continuing intelligence of a high order, if the nation is not to be handicapped in conducting its relations with other nations." The Wash-ington *Post,* usually a supporter of Donovan, called him "one of the trail blazers in our war organization" and thought his plan should receive "consideration on its merits as a contribution to our national security." It was "an effort to make a sum out of the parts of our intelligence services," and "Working together they could do an economical, efficient and fundamental service which hitherto has been neglected on the ground that intelligence work is somehow tainted."

Donovan, who was still overseas when the gusher burst, ordered that all OSS stations throughout the world be advised:

> Press here has publicized secret plan for post war Central Intelligence Agency submitted by me to President and referred to JCS for recommendations. This is not an OSS Leak and did not occur from copies of the document prepared originally by OSS. Further details, including photostat copies of newspaper items, being pouched to you. Please keep us informed of any comment in your theater or country.[9]

The responses of OSS representatives showed that Trohan had provoked a worldwide sensation in which friendly and enemy propaganda services and newspapers marveled at the inability of the American "State Secret Police" to protect its own secrets—a point that was humiliating in its accuracy. The *Economist* of London was at one end of the range of comment:

> Inspector Lestrade often swallowed his pride in calling on Mr. Sherlock Holmes. But never in that long partnership was he forced to confess to being stumped by a crime that had taken place inside [Scotland] Yard itself. It is in a position as humiliating as this that the mystery man of Washington, General Donovan, finds himself. The General had drawn up for the President a highly secret memorandum on that most hushed of all subjects, the organization of Intelligence work. Please note, Watson, that fifteen copies only were taken. Presumably, in view of the importance of the subject, they were all marked to persons of consequence.
>
> Yet this document, emanating from an office wrapped in secrecy, and dealing with a matter retailed only in whispers, has been published in full on the front pages of the McCormick-Patterson newspapers, the press most hostile to the Administration. This is Washington's most enthralling "Whodunnit?" "There is a force at work here, Watson, which has its agents in every corner of our city. . . ." Several million readers are now regaled with the plans to co-ordinate the secret services and intelligence units in order to deal with the problems of the peace; and the McCormick press is free to make hay with the slogan of a "New Deal Gestapo."
>
> Once upon a time President Cleveland was asked if he thought a certain secret well kept. "I find the White House cat knew all about it," he said, with a tired smile. The leaks of Drew Pearson are small potatoes compared with this latest burst, which recalls the earlier unhappy results of journalistic enterprise on the part of the *Chicago Tribune.* One cannot help wondering how many more water mains are to be pierced before the United States Congress passes an Official Secrets Act to protect itself and its Allies. Is freedom to blab essential to democracy?[10]

At the other end of the scale was the Nazi *Tagespost:*

A NET OF JEWISH INFORMERS THROUGHOUT THE WORLD
A Super Secret Service Which Is to Perpetuate Germany's Servitude
The U.S. Press publishes in a prominent place the content of a "Secret Memorandum" drawn up by Colonel William J. Donovan by order of the President. It is planned to set up an elaborate organization of informers which, together with the Soviet NKVD, is to envelop and dominate the whole world. The author of this satanic plan is the same man who had staged the Yugoslav "PUTSCH." After having plunged the Balkan peoples into nameless misery, he wants to use his Super Secret Service to hand over the whole world unprotected to the talons of American and Bolshevist Jews. The essential task of that organization will be the permanent surveillance of Germany and Japan in the event of an Allied victory, and is to start when the American occupation is terminated. At the explicit request of Roosevelt that secret service will have special powers and will outrank all other secret service branches including the army's secret intelligence service. That organization, the Jewish-behind-the-scene-wirepullers of Bolshevist Russia and plutocratic U.S. want to forge into a unique tool with which to control the whole world, especially Germany and Japan. The working of that organization is to prevent any country in the world from rising in the slightest respect against the domination of the Bolshevists and Americans. . . ."[11]

Back in Washington on February 7, 1945, Donovan was clearly as angry and bitter at the sabotage of his plans as he had been in 1929, when Herbert Hoover had not appointed him attorney general. He placed Doering in charge of the investigation to identify the source of the leakage and, on February 15, 1945, reporting the matter officially to the Joint Chiefs and citing German radio broadcasts as examples of the damage done, declared: "Such public disclosure of a secret JCS paper strikes at the heart of military security." Unless "this act is speedily investigated and punished," the "future security of JCS documents may be jeopardized."[12]

He went on:

To invade the security of the JCS, by publishing the detailed text of a pending plan, is a serious offense. It is even more serious to disclose to our enemies official expressions of the inadequacies of our intelligence services and the conflicts engendered by an attempt to remedy these deficiencies. . . . Study of the articles leads to the conclusion that the publication was not the result of an accident or a "leak," but a deliberate plan to sabotage any reorganization of the U.S. intelligence services. The falsehood concerning the Frankfurter employment, the characterization of the proposal as a "Gestapo" and "super-spy" scheme of the President, the immediate canvassing of Congress based upon misstatements and distortions of fact, all make clear a design and intent, through the incitement of suspicion and antagonism, to prevent adoption of any proposal.

The past history of the newspapers concerned "may explain their readiness to make a political attack on the President by any means," Donovan declared. Whatever the motive of the newspapers, it was "clear that the producer of the document used these newspapers to create fear of an American Gestapo and to prevent ultimate approval of any plan for a central intelligence service." The disclosures were made "in wilful disregard of consequences to the nation," and the fact that they came at "so critical a moment in the war and in the planning of peace" was "in the nature of a treasonable utterance." He concluded that the matter could be cleared up only by the establishment of "a judicial or quasi-judicial body armed with the power of subpoena and to compel testimony under oath" and recommended that such a body be "designated, and properly empowered," to inquire into and report upon the facts of the leakage. Donovan wrote also to FDR, intimating that he would appreciate presidential support for such an investigation and repeating his assertion that the disclosure was not a "mere leak but a deliberate plan to sabotage" any reorganization of intelligence.[13]

However, no such inquiry was instituted. At first, a decision regarding that request was delayed. Admiral Ernest J. King, commander in chief of the U.S. fleet and a member of the Joint Chiefs, on February 16, 1945, wrote to the secretary of state, J. Edgar Hoover, and the administrator of the Foreign Economic Administration, stating that the Joint Chiefs were "very much concerned with this unauthorized disclosure" and requesting an investigation to establish whether the leakage had occurred in their departments. King stated that a separate investigation was being conducted at the War and Navy departments[14]—as indeed it was, by the inspector general. But when none of these inquiries identified the villain, the matter was permitted to slide into the realm of unfinished business, as did Donovan's proposals for a central intelligence service.

Who was responsible for the leakage? Donovan and Doering believed that J. Edgar Hoover and probably Attorney General Francis Biddle were responsible, although they had no evidence beyond the known fact of Trohan's association with Hoover, Trohan's anti-Roosevelt journalistic and political record, Hoover's intense personal and professional dislike of Donovan, and Hoover's aspirations for his own global intelligence service, the Special Intelligence Service (SIS). In February 1945 that service was already operating on a large scale in South America and expanding into England, France, and Spain, and Hoover was in the process of submitting a proposal to Roosevelt for a global secret intelligence service under FBI control when Donovan's plan arrived on the President's desk. Intended to be the secret intelligence arm of the State, War, and Navy departments, Hoover's service was a major and serious challenge to the OSS. As an instance of Hoover's attitude toward WJD and OSS, the FBI staff overseas appears to have received instructions from

Hoover to keep its eyes and ears open for news about Donovan personally. For in later years there would emerge this "personal and confidential" letter from Hoover's chief representative in London, M. Joseph
Lynch, to Hoover:

> For your information, General William Donovan, head of OSS is presently
> in London, and is preparing to return to the States which trip is expected to
> be made very shortly. He allegedly hopes on his return to the States to catch
> a plane to the South Pacific so that he can "jump off a boat," landing on the
> Japanese mainland in the landings which were apparently to take place in the
> not too distant future.
>
> While here in London, General Donovan informed some members of OSS
> to forward him one copy of everything in the files of OSS so that he could
> peruse same while flying back to the States and that he desired this informa-
> tion immediately. Because of the huge task in assembling this information,
> he was persuaded it would be best for the organization not to assemble this
> information here inasmuch as he could review same in Washington, D.C. at
> OSS headquarters.
>
> General Donovan, while in London, insisted upon seeing many American
> officers, both of OSS and the regular Army, but did not desire to see "any
> damned British." I do not know the reason for his attitude in this last state-
> ment but apparently there is some friction between him and the British
> Intelligence Service. . . .[15]

The letter showed plainly there was no love lost between Donovan and
Hoover, but there was little direct evidence that Hoover actually gave the
Donovan plan to Trohan. There was little more than surmise, then as
later. A CIA historian would opine years later from his position of special
access:

> Donovan's suspicions of Hoover was a measure of the hostility between the
> two. The FBI chief had always been quick to thwart what he considered
> Donovan's design on South America. At the same time, Hoover had sought
> to extend to the rest of the world his own South American SIS which, he
> feared, would be taken away from him under [the Donovan plan]. Hoover
> could well have been alarmed at the prospect—likely to him—of himself as
> the nation's chief investigative officer being subordinated to—of all people
> —"Wild Bill" Donovan as the head of a new, national intelligence system
> with a direct pipeline to the President. With twenty-two years in his job
> behind him and an indefinite future ahead, Hoover had a stake in that job,
> his organization, and its place in American government and society. An
> influential person, he had the motive, the means, and the ability to carry out
> the deed.[16]

The CIA would offer one other solution for the mystery of who had
leaked the document—Trohan's version. Interviewed by the CIA histo-

rian, Trohan stated that he was "called by Steve Early, the President's secretary, given the [Donovan] documents, and told that 'FDR wanted the story out.' "[17] In other words, Roosevelt wanted to test the climate for such a proposal before giving his assent to it.

The best that can be said for Trohan's statement is that such a stratagem would not have been uncharacteristic of Roosevelt on occasions. Whatever the truth was, the effect of the leak was, for the moment, to frustrate Donovan's plans for his central intelligence service. For as General Marshall warned, it would be "inexpedient and undesirable to take action now," for any action would lead to congressional hearings and "endanger our best sources of intelligence"—Ultra and Magic.[18]

41

New Policy, New Targets

With the collapse of the German offensive in the Ardennes in the first weeks of 1945, the ominous and threatening Soviet conduct in Eastern Europe, and the obscurity surrounding British policy toward the Russians, Donovan met at Supreme Headquarters on January 4, 1945, with Robert D. Murphy, U.S. political adviser to Eisenhower, Allen W. Dulles, now chief of OSS Germany, and Colonel Franklin O. Canfield, Donovan's representative at Supreme Headquarters in Europe. His purpose was to outline his proposals for a new, aggressive American secret intelligence policy. The aggressive nature of that policy was demonstrated by one of the minutes of the meeting:

> The subject of secret penetration of the Russian and British sectors by OSS agents was then discussed. It was agreed that OSS should proceed on the basis that the comparable Russian and British services would seek to penetrate the U.S. Sector and that OSS should not limit its secret activities to the U.S. Sector. Such penetration should be exclusive of such arrangements as might be made between OSS and NKVD for exchange of information and missions.[1]

With this wide license—Murphy could not have agreed to it without the permission of Eisenhower and the State Department—Donovan announced in a paper for all senior OSS executives: "The combat phase of the war in Europe is over" and the OSS "must now work to win the peace." That "may prove more difficult than winning the war." Divergent interests of the great powers "must be reconciled and a start must be made toward the reconstruction of a new Europe." Residual elements of the enemy would continue to exist underground and would do all in their power to prevent the Allies from winning the peace. These elements "must be unmasked and destroyed." He warned:

> Neither our Allies nor our enemies will wish us to be in full possession of the information we require for complete understanding of their policies and their activities. This we already know from experience. OSS, working in close collaboration with the State Department, proposes to establish what clandestine organization is necessary in all of these European areas to obtain information essential to a determination and defense of the United States' interests throughout Europe.[2]

In reality Donovan's new, aggressive policy had been in effect for some time, against the Germans, the Russians, and the British.

Its first operational manifestation resulted from the decision that the United Nations Organization, the successor to the League of Nations, was to hold its founding meeting at Veterans' Auditorium in San Francisco. The premiers or foreign ministers of the fifty-two signatory nations (plus Poland, which had no government at the time) would be attending, and the numbers of delegates and their staff would probably number some 4,000 men and women.

Donovan decided that the OSS should attend the conference, although for what purpose is far from clear—presumably he had agent recruitment and intelligence in mind. Thus OSS support personnel going to the conference—telegraphers, stenographers, and the like—were carefully briefed on what they were to say and do. Advised that the "Eyes of the world will be on [the] Conference" and that the "activities of all in San Francisco will be subject to close scrutiny," support personnel were instructed to tell those who asked questions about what they were doing there that they were "on temporary duty in connection with our routine West Coast activities which, of course, are not matters for discussion." To those who knew they were in the OSS, and what it was, they were to say, "We have some experts and scholars who can be helpful" to the delegates. They were to be as "inconspicuous as possible" by leading "a normal life"; they were to "avoid drunkenness"; there were to be "no spendthrifts," no "strained attempts to see and talk with important people," and "No holiday spirit." The association of the OSS with the conference was "not to be exaggerated or dramatized." OSS people were to make "no mysterious references," and they were to "act normal."

However, the Donovan papers show that for the OSS the foundation of the UN was far from a normal event: It was an opportunity to undertake a large-scale multifaceted operation. For that reason, its presence was strongly opposed by those responsible for planning in the State Department presumably because (1) the OSS had no authority to conduct intelligence operations on American territory; (2) the foundation of the United Nations had little to do with the Joint Chiefs, and therefore the OSS would be operating outside its jurisdiction; and (3) there would be political repercussions if it were discovered that it was operating there.

Conscious of the dangers, Donovan did attempt to recruit—as leader of the OSS delegation—one of the most respected and lustrous Americans of the time, Dorsey Richardson, vice-president of the Lehman Corporation, an investment trust closely related to Lehman Brothers, the New York investment bankers. Richardson had had a long and distinguished record as a soldier, a diplomat, a member of American delegations to various international conferences from the Versailles Peace Conference onward, and he was a member of the Washington bar and on the board of a number of leading companies, including the Columbia Broadcasting System.

Dewitt C. Poole, chief of the Foreign Nationalities Branch of the OSS, responsible for reporting on the activities and attitudes of European minority groups and exiles in the United States and the only OSS intelligence organization authorized to operate on U.S. territory, saw Richardson on or about March 16, 1945. Poole—himself a distinguished former member of the U.S. Foreign Service—wrote to WJD on that day that he had explained to Richardson "that a principal OSS function at San Francisco would be diplomatic intelligence."

Richardson had been told also that "general supervision" of the OSS delegation would be exercised by the deputy director, Colonel Buxton, but he would be "busy in part with OSS matters not directly connected with the Conference." Therefore, "some one [sic] of Dorsey's maturity and experience was needed not only for his own contacts, but also to receive, appraise and put into memoranda form for the American Delegation the 'diplomatic intelligence' which would be flowing in from numerous sources." Dorsey had "responded enthusiastically." Poole continued:

> We agreed that Dorsey's ten years or so with the State Department and his excellent personal relations with almost all the officers there were important. If—as we already know to be the fact in one case—misgiving is aroused at the State Department by the idea of OSS being active at San Francisco, Dorsey's name may bring reassurance. He is well known for care and tact and if it were explained that he was to occupy the central point for "diplomatic intelligence" in our little delegation, doubts might disappear.[3]

Poole recommended that Richardson be given the title "Special Assistant to the Director of Strategic Services" or, better still, "Deputy Chief of the Foreign Nationalities Branch."

In the same memo Poole advised Donovan that Malcolm Davis would be attending the conference for the Carnegie Endowment, and the writer André Visson for the *Reader's Digest,* and that these men would act as "antennae." The OSS had undertaken to secure accommodations and servants for Visson and his wife, "expense being no consideration."

Donovan's letter to Robert Lehman, president of the Lehman Corporation, asking for the services of Richardson, caused considerable discomfort in those gentlemanly halls at 1 and 3 South William Street, New York City. Lehman wrote to WJD on March 26, 1945:

> . . . I regret to say that, after having discussed the matter with Dorsey Richardson, we have both come to the conclusion that it would be unwise for him to detach himself from his activities as Vice President of The Lehman Corporation at this time even though it be for a period of a few months only.
>
> However, I want to assure you that this conclusion was arrived at only after very careful consideration. We are naturally anxious to cooperate in any practical way but just at present our organization is severely handicapped due to the absence of many of our important executives because of the war. I trust you will understand this situation.[4]

A day later Richardson himself wrote:

> Dear General Donovan:
> I want to tell you how much I regret the decision of which Robert Lehman notified you yesterday. Your invitation was more than difficult to decline, but under circumstances that exist here, and developments which have occurred since DeWitt [*sic*] Poole first mentioned the matter to me, there was really no alternative. I talked with DeWitt on the telephone last night and explained the situation as best I could.
> It will be a matter of life-long regret to me that circumstances have prevented me having the gratification and distinction that would have come from service in one capacity or another in your organization during the war. You have done a splendid job, of which all your many friends are proud.
>
> With kindest regards and best wishes, I am,
> Sincerely Yours
> [s] Dorsey Richardson[5]

It now fell upon Buxton to end the war as he had begun it—reporting to WJD from San Francisco. On December 10, 1941, he had telephoned WJD to describe how the Pan American Clipper had taken off from Wake Island under rifle fire from Japanese in an assault transport. Now he was to describe how the world was to enter the atomic age. Although exhausted (he had been recently in hospital for extensive pathological tests), he undertook to lead the OSS group, which, the State Department was told, would consist of:

Dr. William L. Langer, Chief, R&A. In civilian life, Coolidge Professor of History at Harvard University. Author of several books and articles on international relations and diplomacy; Dr. G. T. Robinson, Chief USSR Division, R&A. Professor of Slavic History at Columbia University and one of the leading American specialists on Russian affairs; Dr. Sherman Kent, Chief, Europe-Africa Division, R&A. Associate Professor of European History at Yale University and specialist on modern French history and politics; Dr. C. Burton Fahs, Chief of the Far East Division, R&A. Assistant Professor of Oriental Affairs, Pomona and Claremont Colleges and specialist in Japanese language and Japanese affairs; Dr. Maurice Halperin, Chief of the Latin-American Division, R&A. Associate Professor of Training and Research in Romance Languages and Civilizations, University of Oklahoma, and specialist in Latin-American affairs; Mr. Joseph Sweeney, Deputy Chief, British Empire Staff, R&A; Phoebe Morrison, Specialist in International Law.[6]

The note added carefully: "The other OSS people who will be in San Francisco, apart from those who would normally be there in connection with the routine business of our San Francisco office, are some of our Service people concerned wholly with clerical and maintenance duties." That statement was, in fact, superseded; other operational branches of OSS, especially the elite X-2, which engaged in special high-grade espionage as well as high-grade agent recruitment and control, were to be present in force.

Yet except for the existence of interesting evidence in WJD's files—the OSS's groups' liquor bills, paid for out of unvouchered funds—the size and composition of the group would have remained buried forever. But at a time when White Horse scotch whiskey cost $47.80 a case, Colonel E. J. Connely, chief of the San Francisco office of the OSS, paid liquor bills for the OSS group totaling $6,790.77. This was for the period March 21, 1945—April 26, 1945, and all the expenditures were for the "Purchase of liquors to be used for entertainment purposes in obtaining strategic information."[7]

The bills give some idea of the OSS branches represented in the group and their size. The $6,790.77 was broken down into its components, and each component was then debited to the account of the branch. Thus, Secret Intelligence was debited for $2,656.80, Research and Analysis $2051.42, Foreign Nationalities $975.17, Counterespionage (X-2) $754.46, Morale Operations $138.96 and $47.80, and Field Photographic—which engaged in clandestine as well as overt photography—$166.56. It can be seen from the original bills that these sums were the result of large cocktail parties. The bills show that the liquor was purchased a case or two at a time from different stores. Thus, it was used for a large number of small parties rather than one or two large ones. Other bills show that, for example, R&A's component must have been much larger than the handful of men named for the State Department, for at a time when OSS personnel on out-of-town work received a per diem of $6 a day, R&A accounts received itemized expenditures for housekeeping totaling some $2,600.

Nor was the OSS being wholly correct when it advised the State Department that it was sending a small group of analysts, for telegrams from Buxton to WJD show plainly that at least some of the OSS men were there on the business of espionage. For example, the OSS's Bernard Yarrow was there, and so was Tito's new foreign minister, Ivan Subasić, who was known to the OSS by the code name Shepherd.[8]

On April 26, 1945, Buxton reported to "109 only"—Donovan's code number:

> Yarrow has just made this very interesting statement. I had breakfast this morning with Shepherd at my hotel. He informed me that he had talked with Stalin and Molotov who were anxious to get his viewpoint on the situation in Yugoslavia.
>
> Shepherd related to me that he told them frankly that he is having difficulties in Yugoslavia where the prevailing sentiment is that "all the brains are in Moscow and all the power in the Red Army," that furthermore there is a tendency to rely on Soviet only disregarding completely America and Great Britain.
>
> Molotov told Shepherd that the approach is wrong and that although Russia will try to help as much as she can after the war is over, she, Russia, herself will have to seek assistance from the United States to rebuild the devastated cities and the ruined economy, that they themselves will seek loans up to 10 billions to assist in her post-war rehabilitation.
>
> Stalin told Shepherd explicitly not to try to imitate Soviet Russia. Yugoslavia is a small country in comparison with Russia and not to carry on experimentation by establishing a Soviet regime, that they will have to get along with the western democracies and to arrange a democratic regime where the representatives are not appointed but elected by [garble] and expressing the sentiments of the people.
>
> He, Stalin, further told Shepherd that Soviet Russia will act with Great Britain in regard to Yugoslavia in complete harmony and mutual consultation.
>
> Shepherd explained to [Yarrow] that he was having great difficulty at present because of the extreme elements who are trying to rule without having any experience but the important thing is to preserve peace, for the present, and to go slowly, that Tito is very reasonable and he has no difficulties with him because he is first a Yugoslav and then a Communist.
>
> The people in Yugoslavia are so exhausted, said Shepherd, that they are reluctant to have any changes and he was confident the Serbs will fall in line, but expects greater difficulties with the Croats once they are liberated.
>
> Simach, present Yugoslavia Ambassador to Washington, was not Shepherd's choice, nor was Leontich, Ambassador to Great Britain. Shepherd said he will give them a chance to see what they can do but will see to it that they produce the expected results; otherwise, he will act peremptorily.[9]

Plainly this was intelligence of a high order, whether wholly true or not. Furthermore, Buxton's telegram to WJD of May 1,1945, demonstrated that the OSS's task at San Francisco was not only to advise and assist but also to recruit and spy:

I have now heard and seen enough to have some personal opinions which I submit for what they are worth. I find that most of my associates here have the same general opinion.

1. San Francisco is a battleground on which the world's 2 most powerful nations are now feeling each other out. The Russians knew before they came we had the votes. Therefore they are interested at the moment in developing:

A. The strength of international communism and radical labor organizations.

B. Prestige at home and along their bordering satellites. Both Czechoslovakia and Yugoslavia are in the Russian bag and will do as they are told.

Molotov can also bring pressure on other governments containing communistic elements or radical labor organizations.

Russian foreign policy is still obscure in the Far East so far as anything here is indicated. The policy in the West is obvious. All nations bounding Russia on the West must be not only friendly but subservient. Russia will take unilateral action to achieve this purpose. Rumania, Bulgaria, Poland, Czechoslovakia, now Austria, tomorrow Hungary and then Russian occupied Germany if she is not able to dictate the selection of a rubber stamp government in every corner of pre-war Germany.

United States' interest requires us to make what sacrifice is necessary to dominate the 7 seas and the international airways. . . .

Meanwhile, Donovan's new policy was in effect in Europe. There as early as the middle of March 1945 the Russians had shown themselves extremely sensitive about violations of their airspace—a reflection of their deeper concerns about the power of the Anglo-American air forces and, perhaps, the capability of those air forces to position Allied intelligence and subversion agents in their territory. They could, and did, react violently, as an incident on March 18, 1945, had demonstrated. On that day a large force of U.S. heavy bombers over the Soviet bridgehead across the Oder River in eastern Germany was attacked by a wing of Soviet fighters, and although the American aircraft were plainly marked, there was an aerial battle in which six of the Soviet fighters were shot down by the Americans, who suffered no losses, no damage, and no casualties at the hands of the puny Russian fighters. Nothing was said about this incident, but it was followed by others, all occurring along the eastern frontiers of Soviet airspace.

At least part of the reason for Soviet aggressiveness was Casey Jones, an operation which Donovan had conceived in August 1944 but which did not begin until the first days of spring of 1945. Casey Jones, along with its associated operation, Ground Hog, was, according to General Edwin L. Sibert, chief of intelligence first to General Omar N. Bradley at the Twelfth Army Group and then to General Eisenhower as commanding general of United States Forces in Europe, "a project undertaken jointly with the British to use the post war confusion to get photo coverage of all Central and Western Europe, Scandinavia and North Africa. Operation Ground Hog was a similar project for the collection of geological data of military interest."[10]

Under the Donovan-Sibert plan, some 2,000,000 square miles, including parts of Albania, Yugoslavia, and Bulgaria, and all of Russian-occupied Germany, were photomapped. About sixteen squadrons of U.S. and British heavy bombers modified for aerial photography were employed in the operation, which lasted through the spring, summer, and autumn of 1945. Priority was given to those areas occupied by U.S. and British forces that were, by agreement, to be turned over to the Russians.

All U.S. aircraft carried American markings, but there was some evidence that the British used unmarked planes over Albania, Yugoslavia, and Bulgaria, for as Alexander Kirk, American ambassador at Rome, reported in August 1945: "The British Foreign and War Offices have queried [Allied Forces Headquarters in Italy] concerning the feasability [sic] of making aerial photographs of Albania, Yugoslavia and Bulgaria." In reply, the Royal Air Force component at the headquarters recommended that Mosquito aircraft be used "with all insignia removed" to "obtain photographs from 25,000 feet and Governments concerned not be notified."[11]

The purpose of Casey Jones evidently did not escape the Russians, for the operation was almost certainly betrayed to them by one of their spies in either the British or the American intelligence services. Nor did the magnitude of the aerial effort escape their attention, for in one month alone one of the American units involved—the 305th Heavy Bombardment Group—flew about 470 missions, taking 70,000 photographs of about 90,000 square miles. Consequently, the unmistakable nature of aerial photographic flying provoked sharp reaction from the Red Air Force.

On April 2, 1945, General Nathan N. Twining, commanding general of the Mediterranean Allied Strategic Air Force and of the U.S. Fifteenth Air Force, reported no fewer than six engagements with the Russians on that day:

§ Four Mustangs were attacked by between fifteen and twenty Russian LG-5's over western Austria. One Mustang was shot down, but the pilot was thought to be safe. Russian casualties, if any, were unknown.

§ Near Bratislava, Czechoslovakia, ten Soviet Yaks attacked a small group of U.S. Lightnings. The Lightnings avoided combat and did not return fire.

§ Over Neusiedler Lake, near Vienna, four Yaks attacked fifteen Lightnings—a rash thing to do—but the Lightnings refused combat.

§ In the same area, an hour later, six or eight Russian fighters with in-line engines attacked four Mustangs. One of the Russians opened fire, but, as Twining reported, "upon recognition all [Russians] broke off with no damage done."

§ Over Hungary, two LG-5's fired on two Mustangs. The Mustangs replied, but "no damage was inflicted or received."[12]

At the same time the Russians grounded all Allied aircraft in Russia and refused to allow any to enter the country or land, and when the ban was lifted, it was only to the extent of allowing a single DC-3 to carry diplomatic couriers and freight each day between the USAAF base Poltava in the Ukraine and Teheran. To show they meant what they said, the Russians forced down a DC-3 flying on embassy business over the Crimea on June 10, 1945; they forced down an aerial reconnaissance Lightning near the Soviet airfield at Yokheuditz in central Germany; in July 1945 they shot down two RAF Ansons near Klagenfurt; and in August 1945 they made no fewer than 366 complaints of violations of their airspace by Allied aircraft.[13]

Yet Casey Jones continued, and 2,000,000 square miles of Europe and North Africa west of the line 20° longitude were photographed. As Sibert reported, both Casey Jones and Ground Hog were "successful and put us in a good position with respect to any future campaign in Europe."

There could be no doubt the Russians knew what was afoot, for the State Department on three occasions asked for permission to photomap Berlin, Vienna, and Prague, and there can be little doubt that these operations were among the factors that caused the great tensions between the Russian and Western Allies during the last weeks of the war. Yet, Donovan argued correctly, the operation was necessary. During the Neptune period the Allies had suffered greatly from the absence of military maps of Western and Central Europe—the area across which they were to fight. And given the obscure Soviet political attitude, only the imprudent would say that such maps would not again become necessary. What gave the Russians cause for alarm, however, was that only the Americans and the British had strategic air forces, and according to Russian Intelligence, only the Americans and the British had the atomic bomb.

Meanwhile, WJD's new policy had turned to Arabia.

Project Switch reached Donovan's desk on March 26, 1945. Colonel Harry S. Aldrich, now chief of OSS in the Middle Eastern theater of operations, presented what he called a "hot" subject, and "the more I ponder it the more danger it seems to offer to OSS as a project, despite its approval in high quarters at this end."[14]

Outlining the project, Aldrich recalled that FDR had given King Ibn Saud, founder of modern Saudi Arabia and the principal political and religious figure in Arabia, a C-47 Dakota, "to be fitted up as requested by Ibn Saud and supplied with an American Army crew, same to be replaced in the future by S.A." Aldrich had asked General William L. Ritter, deputy commander and chief of staff of U.S. forces in Africa and the Middle East, stationed at Cairo, "if there would be any objection to putting on one or two of our own people [i.e., OSS men] in the crew, if we could find qualified men, for intelligence purposes."

Ritter had agreed, provided the approval of the commanding general, General Giles, was obtained. Aldrich wrote: "I believe he warmed to the idea largely because of the fact recognized out here that the British definitely are 'in' with Ibn Saud and the Americans definitely seem not to be, the president's visit [with Ibn Saud at Cairo late in December 1943] notwithstanding." Ritter and Aldrich had "discussed the difficulties of our getting one or two men in the crew without arousing suspicion in" the headquarters flight at Payne Field, from which the special crew of Ibn Saud's aircraft would be drawn.

Aldrich said that in Cairo he had seen Colonel Eddy, former chief of operations for Torch and now U.S. ambassador at Ibn Saud's court in Riyadh, who said the project "offered real possibilities and he approved of it." Eddy had "suggested a way to solve the difficulties of getting our people on the crew without arousing the suspicion of the regular crew members." The king was "apprehensive of trusting the royal lives to native pilots and crew," and Eddy had suggested that the OSS find Americans who were Muslims and would stay on as the permanent crew paid by the king. "If we could get such men," wrote Aldrich to Donovan, "we would have no difficulty in rationalizing the bringing of 'outsiders' for the crew." It might be possible to "make the whole crew ours."

Aldrich had related this conversation to General Ritter. By that time Ritter had discussed the project with General Giles, who had "approved the project." Ritter stated "we would have to hurry as the plane had arrived and would be ready within 2 weeks." Aldrich felt the plan would have to be approved by Donovan and would "have to be held in the greatest secrecy." However, he warned, "some ten people already knew of the proposal." There the matter stood as of the date on his letter, Aldrich stated.

Obviously there were "outstanding objectives to such a project as well as outstanding intelligence opportunities. . . . Without the president's specific approval, it could be a very dangerous game for our agency, especially in view of the current post-war agency discussion." The project would be "good red meat for our national enemies," Aldrich felt, and "Ditto for our foreign enemies—especially the British."

On April 2, 1945, WJD sent the project over to the chief of OSS SI, Whitney H. Shepardson, for his opinion. Shepardson replied it was "a beautiful project," by far "the most delicate one . . . that we have yet entertained," and "the risks are vast, with all kinds of repercussions unfortunate for OSS if the project is blown." Shepardson thought that "for a dozen reasons" there was "an 85% chance that the project *will be blown.*" He suggested, therefore, that Aldrich be commended "for a brilliant sortie of the imagination," but that Switch be dropped.[15]

Donovan did not agree; he wrote in pencil on Shepardson's letter: "Let us follow this—and get it done." However, for once Donovan's executives overruled him. Buxton and Doering went to see Donovan to try to impress him with the extreme dangers of the project—that ten people already knew about it, some of whom were not inside the OSS. At length WJD agreed, although very reluctantly, and on April 14, 1945, Buxton wrote to Aldrich: "The project was most imaginatively conceived, but as you have observed in your letter, the risks are too great to warrant such an undertaking at this time."

Meanwhile, a third project had been taking shape. This time it concerned India, where the British king, George VI, was emperor.

From his earliest days as director of the COI, Donovan had shown great interest in British India, entertaining Indians lobbying in Washington for independence and writing long memorandums on the political and economic state of affairs on the subcontinent. These memos showed that he viewed British rule of India with distaste, although they were always careful to avoid direct, open criticism of the raj.

During most of the war he conducted no SI operations in India because his agreements with the British services prohibited them. He was permitted to conduct X-2 operations there, but only to protect OSS installations and security, and he stationed a Research and Analysis team at Calcutta, ostensibly to provide studies for the commanders fighting the Japanese in Burma and Southeast Asia. Moreover, in 1943 he initiated a "Special Mid-East Project" called Indian, for which, on November 6, 1943, he signed a paper authorizing a fund of $1,000,000. His memo stated:

1. This will authorize the appropriation of the sum of One Million ($1,000,000) Dollars from unvouchered funds for future operations under the above project.

2. Disbursements from this fund will be made as follows:

(a) Twenty-five Thousand ($25,000) Dollars to be paid to Indian when authorized by Mr. J. M. Scribner [chief of SO at the time].

(b) Periodic accountings will be made as to expenditures, and the $25,000 Working Fund will be replenished from time to time as authorized by Mr. Scribner.

(c) Disbursements in addition to the $25,000 Working Fund will be made as directed by Mr. Scribner, not in excess of $5,000 in each instance; expenditures over $5,000 will be approved by the Director or Assistant Director.

Project Indian was clearly an Arabian project in conception (Arabia being in the British and French spheres of influence at that time), but it began to expand eastward as the war drifted away from the Mediterranean and the Balkans. At least part of the Project Indian funds did become available for operations in Southwest Asia and British India. Whether funds were actually drawn from the Project Indian funds for expenditure on OSS projects in India is not clear. The probability is that they were and that they were kept at Beirut; the OSS was reluctant to use banks in India, all controlled by the British.

Then, on April 21, 1945, the chief of the OSS in the India-Burma theater, Colonel John Coughlin, sent WJD Project Bingo, the "general purpose of which is to obtain economic and political intelligence from India."[16] The author of the plan, Lieutenant Guy Martin, elaborating on his description, stated that Bingo would "undertake to obtain information as to the probable nature of the long-range development of the economy. In the same way, it would undertake to obtain information concerning Indian political activity in India, both of an immediate and long-range nature." It was clear, however, that:

> any attempt to carry out the above objective on a systematic and large-scale basis would be impossible for OSS without a very large trained research staff, a large number of investigators and contact men and perhaps most important of all permission to operate openly in all parts of India. It is therefore essential that some much more narrow and carefully defined objective be used as the basis for the initial investigations. It is suggested that in Bombay, it would be feasible and suitable for a very small staff to investigate the economic and political implications of the interest of what may be termed the Bombay industrial and financial group in the large Sterling credit of the Government of India in London.

The credit, acquired through the war against Japan, was reaching about 2,000 *creres* of rupees, and Martin thought: "Intelligence concerning the proposals for the use of this credit . . . would, it is believed, be of the greatest use to the United States." Three primary interests were competing for control of the credit: the British, the socialist group of the Congress party, and the Bombay industrialists. Martin advised:

The interests of the Indian financial and industrial groups in obtaining control of this credit is [sic] obvious. It would enable them to finance large-scale industrial development without being subject to the financial and economic control which would be entailed by the normal type of foreign investment in India. As the credit is controlled by the Government of India, any use they made of it would be subject only to the control of the Government of India by which they are already largely controlled and restricted. If by proper political agitation and propaganda they were able to exercize [sic] a dominant influence on the Government of India, or at least free themselves from any serious control by it, they would be enabled to finance a large-scale program of industrialization, at the end of which they would themselves have substantial ownership and control of the industrial plant which had been created.

The leaders of all groups interested in the credit were "willing and anxious to talk with Americans." The only problem was the question of cover. In this connection Martin mentioned that an American in Bombay, Henry Robertson, "had a wide range of personal contacts in the business world," and that Martin himself was "assigned to Joint Training Headquarters at the request of the British Military." Because this work did not occupy all his time, "it is only natural that I should meet Mr. Robertson's friends socially." It was also to be expected, "because of my background, that I would have an interest of a personal sort in the financial, legal and cultural activities in Bombay."

Martin's paper provoked considerable interest, and WJD sent it to Richard Hartshorne, professor of geography at the University of Wisconsin and director of research at R&A, for comment. That comment was forthcoming on May 14, 1945:[17]

It seems to us that the justification for the entire OSS establishment in IB [India-Burma] lies in the provision to United States policy making agencies, particularly in Washington, of strategic intelligence on this area. Because of the small United States share in military operations in South East Asia Command [SEAC] the principal strategic intelligence required is that related to long-run political and economic policy for the protection of United States interests and security in Asia.

For this purpose the retention of a strong OSS outpost in IB is of great importance. Its justification is independent of that of other United States military operations in SEAC.

The OSS should "emphasize" in the future "political and economic reporting" not only in India and Burma but also in the other British possessions, such as Ceylon and Malaya. To that end it should participate in city teams entering "newly re-occupied areas for the collection of documents, maps, and strategic intelligence." It should also participate in operations in such places as Tenasserim and Malaya, "thereby to do analytical reporting on political and economic trends growing out of

Japanese occupation and on British, Dutch, French, Japanese, and Communist post-war interests." The program would require between thirty-five and forty of the fifty-two persons presently with the OSS in the India-Burma theater. Most of these personnel were already in the theater.

Martin's paper and Hartshorne's opinion were sent to WJD and Langer. The first of three papers, one that was certainly from Langer's branch and seems to have come from his pen, made the point that it was "presumed that the potential long range plans of OSS for world postwar intelligence take this area into account." If that was so, then there was need for immediate action, because the OSS was there already, although with the war in Southeast Asia coming to an end, its tenure might be short. Both India and Burma were British areas. The "British may naturally be assumed to take a dim view towards intelligence activities directed at these areas" and "further justification for OSS operations from the military point of view will be extremely difficult if not impossible to maintain."[18]

If the Joint Chiefs closed down American representation in the India-Burma theater, as was probable, "valuable intelligence personnel peculiarly well qualified as to India and Burma work will be without cover." Consideration should be given, therefore, to the OSS's securing a policy decision from the Joint Chiefs to maintain itself at Admiral Mountbatten's Supreme Headquarters in Southeast Asia. This would provide the Bingo operation with the necessary cover.

If the problem of cover could be settled, Langer proposed the following program—one that was palpably the committing of espionage against a friendly power:

a. R&A. The preparation of political and economic reports on India and Burma with particular emphasis upon economic reporting such as analysis of Anglo-Indian management trusts, cartels, capital structure, etc. The maintenance of biographical files on political and economic personalities. Political liaison with the Government of Burma regarding postwar reconstruction plans and the re-establishment of civil government.

b. X-2. The preparation of studies showing the structure and organization of the Intelligence Services of India and Burma. The maintenance of biographical files on Intelligence personalities. The maintenance of photographic files on Intelligence personalities. Reporting on possible infiltration of our own intelligence activities.

c. SI. Works completely under cover, principally on orders from Washington. Secures by clandestine means material not possible to obtain except through unorthodox methods. Will act on problems beyond R&A means. Because of operating on British territory it is felt that OSS cover cannot be used for SI operations of political and economic nature and that commercial or diplomatic cover will probably have to be used. This will entail fresh SI personnel from Washington. As long as OWI, FEA, Red Cross, etc., remain in this Theater they offer good cover possibilities.

d. International Document Collection. Collects telephone books, directories, government publications, etc., dealing with political and economic personalities. Continues its routine collection of books and documents on India and Burma.

e. Cover and Documentation. Makes use of its current opportunities to collect Indian and Burmese identity papers, passports, motor car licenses, birth certificates and other papers to aid SI operatives.

f. Intelligence Staff. Coordinates the above activities in terms of Washington and headquarters directives. Act as liaison officers and "contact" men to develop leads as to types and location of intelligence material available. Gathers original intelligence information from targets of opportunity as they arise.

Langer continued:

Consideration has been given as to the location of intelligence "stations" for political and economic work. The following locations are suggested: New Delhi, Bombay, Calcutta, Kandy, Colombo, Madras, Karachi, Simla (as long as the Government of Burma is stationed there), Rangoon, Kabul. With the exception of Simla, Rangoon and Kabul, personnel are already operating at the stations mentioned. To a large extent the personnel is not engaged in this type of activity and a considerable amount of redirection will be necessary consistent with cover.

He warned that the U.S. commander in the India-Burma theater, General Daniel I. Sultan, "has not been advised nor has he approved of political and economic reporting within the Theater by OSS." Sultan's representative at Mountbatten's headquarters, General Thomas S. Timberman, had issued a directive that "copies of all communications between Washington and [Mountbatten's headquarters at Kandy, Ceylon] must be sent to him." Because of the "extreme delicacy from the political standpoint of operations of a political and economic reporting program in this area and the need for well kept cover it is believed that it will be impossible to conform with General Timberman's directive and still carry on a clandestine program of this nature." The author "submitted that consideration should be given by Washington to the exact relationship of the Theater military command and activities of the nature proposed. An alternative more consistent with the nature of the problem would be keeping the American Diplomatic Mission in New Delhi fully advised of activities of this nature, but excluding military channels."

On July 6, 1945, a document entitled "R&A Directive for the India-Burma Theater" was placed in Donovan's files. Classified "Secret/Control," it could not be shown to aliens without Donovan's authority. The document bore the typed signature of Langer, director of R&A, but was not signed by Langer or anyone else. That suggests, as was occasionally custom, that he had dictated a draft directive to be signed and distributed upon WJD's approval. It is not known whether this document became official OSS policy. Its contents nevertheless displayed the spirit of the OSS at the time. The document laid down the "appropriate functions" of Far Eastern Division personnel:

> a. Reporting on political and economic developments in China and surrounding countries and the geographic background thereof insofar as this is possible without undercover operations.
>
> b. Preparation on request from the Commander of the United States Forces in the India Burma Theater or U.S. political missions in Southern Asia of special reports when such reports contribute to strategic planning or policy formulation and utilize R&A techniques of analysis and synthesis.
>
> c. Preparation of memoranda and reports requested by other R&A units in connection with OSS services to the United States Government in other parts of the world.
>
> d. Assistance through analysis of requirements and possibilities to the planning of the strategic intelligence collection programs of SI for covert intelligence, the Map Division for maps, CD for documents, and IDC for publications.
>
> e. Participation in the planning of OSS operational programs, e.g., by analysis of target priorities and the means by which they may be achieved.

This directive was almost a license to engage in every clandestine activity, except actual coups de main, sabotage, and subversion, throughout the Far Eastern Division. All this could not have taken place without WJD's knowledge, permission, and encouragement.

On July 6, 1945—the same date as the directive—Langer sent a letter to Dr. Cora DuBois, an anthropologist interested in European colonialism in Asia and chief of the Far Eastern Division.[19] Langer stated that the OSS had been established as a strategic intelligence agency and that strategic intelligence was "that related to strategy or the planning of campaigns or larger operations rather than to individual engagements." Strategic nonmilitary intelligence "should similarly be pertinent to the formulation and application of policies of broad or long-range scope." He went on:

> Strategic intelligence . . . is urgently needed by OSS in other parts of the world where major consumers are located. Such intelligence should be collected and forwarded even when no local market for it exists. In general, however, effective development of OSS relationships in the field should provide such local outlets and therefore local support for much of the work required for effective support of the position of OSS in Washington and in other Theaters.

By these operations a new era had opened in OSS policy, one likely to prove perilous for U.S. foreign relationships.

42

Secret Missions

As part of the new policy, by the spring of 1945 WJD had established secret agents, and even whole units representing all OSS branches, in every capital of consequence in the world—an astonishing achievement when it is recalled that only four years before he and almost all his men were civilians without clandestine experience. Moreover, WJD had created and honed a clandestine infrastructure—secret communications, finances, and supply organizations—that was now working with considerable proficiency, especially in the areas of X-2 counterespionage, which had become a major industry and which often engaged in sensitive espionage. Also, he had large secret missions in many countries. These extended from the snowfields of northern Norway, where Major William E. Colby, a future CIA director, commanded a large intelligence and sabotage organization, to Germany, where another future director of the CIA, William Casey, was engaged in very large-scale intelligence penetration operations. WJD's network then extended around the world through the lacework of agent chains in northern Italy and the small agent systems in Eastern Europe, the Balkans, and Arabia, into Persia, Afghanistan, India, Ceylon, Burma, China, and the Pacific theater.

Also, Donovan had become energetic in operations intended to penetrate Russian-controlled areas and the areas of operations of the Red Army, especially in Czechoslovakia. There, in March 1945, he launched an operation with special significance in three directions; it involved espionage against the Wehrmacht, the Red Army, and inquiries regarding the plight of European Jewry. The first of these operations involved all three targets but only one OSS operator—Patrick Dolan, the man who had sweet-talked the commander of the German garrison in the Cherbourg arsenal into surrender during Neptune.

During his career as U.S. spymaster Donovan seems not to have made Hitler's program of extermination of European Jewry an intelligence target, although he did declare to key subordinates—notably James Jesus Angleton, the head of X-2—that he deemed it vital for the OSS to obtain all the intelligence needed to prove that this was Germany's war—that the Reich had planned and executed the conflict, that it alone was responsible for it, and that in prosecuting it, its armies and servants had committed atrocities on a very large scale. As he explained to Angleton, the reason for that imperative was that after World War II there must be "no rewriting of history," as there had been after World War I. There must be no opportunity for the re-creation of the belief that the Wehrmacht had been "stabbed in the back by traitors" and that the German Army had not been totally defeated in battle.

With that political attitude in mind, Donovan called Dolan, who had been commanding OSS units engaged in political and psychological warfare against the German enemy, to Paris. Their meeting took place at the Ritz Hotel, which Donovan had made his *pied-à-terre* when in Europe, and over dinner, according to Dolan, WJD stated that "the President was worried, and so was Donovan, about what was going to happen in Czechoslovakia."[1] Then "in his own characteristic way, in his soft and silken way, Bill said it was vitally important to establish what the Czech government in exile was going to do, and whether it had sold out completely to the Soviets. Was Czechoslovakia going to be a vassal of the Soviets? I listened to all this with considerable interest, but political rather than personal interest."

When dinner was over, Donovan said he thought it was "perfectly possible for someone to take a German staff car through the lines—the lines were very fluid, for there was much chaos on both eastern and western fronts—and, traveling only at night, get to Prague, see what was going on there, and then go on east, join up with the Red Army, and then come west with Russians, posing as a liberated American prisoner of war making his way to his own lines." Dolan continued: "Bill, of course, was a consummate lawyer and a great advocate and could really talk the hind leg off a donkey and make the most extraordinary proposal sound very simple and straightforward and reasonable.

"Listening to all this, I said, yes, I thought it was possible, and I said I would go through our staff roster and see if I could dig out some German-speaking Czechs or Czech Russian-speaking fellows who would be prepared to undertake this dangerous mission." Bill then said, no, no, no—he didn't think that was the thing to do. What he had in mind was that I should do it. I protested and said: 'General, first of all, my German isn't very good, secondly, I don't speak Czech, and it seems to me that I was exactly the wrong fellow to do it.' But Donovan said: 'No, Patrick, I've got great confidence in you, and you can take anybody you want, but I don't want to get mixed up with Czechs. They have special axes to grind. What I want to find out, and what the President wants to know, is what the Czechs are going to do.'

"Well, as you can imagine, I was stuck, even though I thought it was pretty mad. But my boss thought it was worthwhile, OK, I thought it was worthwhile. So out of the dilemma I reluctantly agreed that I would take the job on."

Returning to his headquarters on the German border, Dolan saw Omar Bradley, commanding general of Twelfth Army Group, and from him obtained a German staff officer's limousine—a large Daimler-Benz with blinds that could be pulled down—and the services of a German-speaking driver. At that point—the second week in April—Dolan received further instructions from Donovan: While in Czechoslovakia he was to rescue Dr. Leo Baeck, the leading German Jewish theologian and, when he had been arrested by the Gestapo, chief rabbi of Berlin. Baeck, it emerged, was in Theresienstadt concentration camp, to the east of Prague. It then emerged that all OSS and British agents in Czechoslovakia—men who included Lieutenant James Harvey Gaul, son of a well-known organist and composer, and a complete OSS mission called Dawes—had been captured by the Sicherheitsdienst and executed.

Almost certain that he would not return from the mission, Dolan left his headquarters at the old resort town of Bad Nauheim in mid-April, as both eastern and western fronts were crumbling. Traveling with him were two Czechs employed by the OSS, with Dolan posing as a German general, his German greatcoat over a U.S. Army field uniform. They carried with them about $30,000 in gold, Reichsmarks, and Czech currency.

Driving only at night and hiding in woods and abandoned farms by day, they entered the German lines east of Nuremberg and crossed the Danube at Passau, a town near the Austrian border. There, Dolan was to recall, "there was a hell of a mess—the sort of mess always associated with a disintegrating army." They drove on through the southern tip of the Bohemian Forest, across the northern tip of Austria, and entered Czechoslovakia in the vicinity of the small Czech frontier town of Ruda. Taking secondary roads, they circled the southern edges of Prague and, still heading east, encountered a Red Army tank spearhead in Moravia near Brno. During the 200-mile journey behind German lines (which lasted four nights and five days) Dolan's car was stopped three or four times, but each time, believing there was a German general in it, the German police waved it on. Moreover, they obtained all the gasoline they needed. Dolan remembered: "It was all quite simple and straightforward —just as Bill had said it would be."

On sighting the Red Army tank column, Dolan abandoned the car in a wood and then, throwing away the general's greatcoat but making sure that he still had his gold, made his way to the command post of the Russian officer in the column, the party posing as escaped prisoners of war. "The Russian spoke English, thank God," Dolan said, recalling that the officer's "prized possession was a pocket Shakespeare which he read whenever he was not on the march. He was a very nice guy, a highly literate character, and I had a marvelous time with him—I learned a lot about the Russian Army, let me tell you."

Eating from the tank column's rolling kitchens—"everything went in: chickens, cows, pigs, vegetables, fish, so that everything became a huge stew"—they traveled westward for some three or four days. Dolan recalled: "At each town, I discovered, the Russians had two targets: They had lists of Fascists and collaborators in every town, and they collared these people, lined them up, and shot them. The other was to sack the chemists' shops of all drugs and medicaments—their own medical services were as primitive as their system of ration supplies."

When the column neared Prague, Dolan said good-bye, seized a Tatra automobile, and entered the Czech capital. There he contacted a man whose name he had been given, a lovely fellow called Dodo Pispistek, the "Laurence Olivier" of the Czech theater, who hid Dolan and his party in his house. Pispistek's first service was to provide Dolan with a hot bath, his first in a fortnight, and—literally—a bucket of beer. "It was the most delicious drink I had had in my life." Dolan then made contact with the Czech underground, to which he became an adviser in the period when it was street-fighting with an SS police division for control of the capital.

During the chaotic events of the last days of the war, Dolan decided to make his attempt to liberate Dr. Baeck. He assembled a small party of tough Czech Sten gunners, who drove out to Theresienstadt, where they found a vast camp with thousands of emaciated faces at the electrical wire fences. After bursting through the camp gates, they located the SS camp commandant and at the point of the submachine guns demanded that he lead them to Dr. Baeck. The SS man took them to a small house in the middle of the camp, and in a locked and barred room on the top floor they found a small, wispy Jew with a straggly white beard sitting on the edge of an iron cot. Dolan was to remember: "I said: 'Dr. Baeck?' He said: 'That is I.' Then I said: 'Well, I am Patrick Dolan of the Office of Strategic Services, United States Army. I have been sent by the President of the United States to set you free. You must come with me and you must waste no time'—we'd been in the camp only ten minutes, and we could not be sure that the SS guards would not recover from their shock and surprise and engage us. Baeck was astonished, as well he should have been. He demurred for a moment and said that he really ought to remain to look after his ministry—he was the rabbi of the camp as he had been for Berlin.

I told him: 'We do not have much time. Please get your belongings together.' Baeck started to pick up his toothbrush and so on, and I told him not to bother about his toilet things. And so he came out with a red handkerchief containing a Jewish religious book and some religious furniture. Then we hustled him downstairs, into the Tatra, and within a minute or two we had roared out of the camp and were on our way to a safe house in Prague. It was all over in about a minute."

As Dolan recalled, the safe house was at 172 Stalinova, in the center of Prague. But since the Red Army had occupied Prague on the day Baeck was liberated, and since Dolan was aware that the Red political commissars were interested in the rabbi for political purposes, he thought it unwise to try and get Baeck through to American lines. Instead, he decided to wait until the U.S. Control Commission representatives, who had diplomatic privileges, arrived and then to evacuate Baeck under U.S. diplomatic auspices and protection. Thus Baeck was compelled to remain in Prague throughout the immediate posthostilities period, with Dolan, leaving the house only at night and then walking only in the cemetery across the street.

During that long wait Dolan formed the greatest affection for Baeck, who was one of the world's leading Jews. "He was a lovely, gentle, wonderful man, and we became very close friends, partly due to the circumstances. He was one of the great men I have ever met. I don't have many heroes, and certainly Dr. Baeck was one of them. He was an utterly brave, decent, kind man in the midst of what can only be described as a hell on earth."

By now the war was over and the Germans had surrendered. Dolan had established good relations with Dr. Eduard Beneš, the president of the Czech government in exile, who had arrived in Prague, and with the foreign minister, Jan Masaryk. They convinced Dolan that they did not intend to sell out to the Russians, but there were what Dolan called "a number of hard-line Communists in their Cabinet." These men and women convinced Dolan that sooner or later Beneš and Masaryk would fall and that Czechoslovakia would become Communist. To ensure that neither Baeck nor he was captured, therefore, Dolan made a deal with Beneš in which the surgeon general of the Czech Army would warn Dolan if the NKVD, which had now secured the capital, intended to arrest either. Similarly, he made a deal with Beneš's propaganda minister, Vladimir Kopetzky, the *"éminence grise* of the Communist party," in which Kopetzky would also warn Dolan and enable him to escape. The deal: Dolan would return to American lines and bring back several truckloads of drugs and medicines, which were badly needed by the Czech administration.

With much of importance to report concerning the Czech internal situation, therefore, Dolan left for Nuremberg with papers provided by

Kopetzky and the surgeon general. In Nuremberg he sent a long report by teleprinter to Donovan, who in turn asked for and received permission to obtain large surgical and medical stores for the Czech government. The OSS Europe chief, Ed Gamble, provided two U.S. Army trucks loaded with the medical supplies. These then left with Dolan for Prague. There Dolan helped reestablish Prague Radio and the Prague Opera House, browbeating Wieland Wagner, the grandson of Richard Wagner, into giving the Czechs the scenery from Bayreuth for Smetana's *The Bartered Bride*.

That was, it seems, a mistake. Dolan attended the gala reopening of the Prague Opera in U.S. uniform. During the performance Dr. Beneš sent for Dolan to thank him for the drugs and the scenery and, as it happened, introduced Dolan to the principal guest of honor, Marshal Georgi Zhukov. To Dolan's horror, Beneš told the Russian how Dolan had "swiped the scenery for *The Bartered Bride* from Wieland Wagner." The story produced "gales of laughter," but as Dolan was to remember, "I knew at the time Beneš's action was a bad idea, for there was bound to be an NKVD in Zhukov's entourage." And there was.

Within a few days the surgeon general and Kopetzky both warned Dolan that the NKVD was looking for him and that he was to be arrested and expelled. Aware that if he were arrested, Baeck, too, would be arrested, Dolan acted.

While in Nuremberg Dolan had called Donovan in Berlin and arranged a signal which, if received by Gamble, meant that the OSS chief in Europe was to send a Black Widow night fighter to a disused airfield on the outskirts of Prague. Having received the surgeon general's warning at about 1:00 A.M. on or about June 20, 1945, Dolan, who had brought a wireless set back with him, sent the agreed message. He later remembered: "We piled into a Tatra and made for the airstrip. Everything was pitch-black. It was only a few minutes' flight time from the forward air base where the Black Widow was positioned. I switched the car lights on, and happily I heard aero-engines. It turned out to be the Black Widow, which we boarded while the pilot kept his engines running. Then we took off—as NKVD cars came hurtling on to the airfield to arrest Baeck and myself. It was a real movie departure, I can tell you. They flew us back to Paris, and as we crossed the Rhine, I pointed down and said to Baeck: 'Doctor, there's the Rhine—you'll never seen that goddamned place again.' He put a restraining hand on my arm and said to me: 'Patrick, there should be no room for vengeance in your heart. The only thing that is important is that truth and justice should prevail.' "

From Paris Baeck left for the United States to assist in the foundation of the State of Israel. As for Dolan, when he returned home, his reward was to discover that a business partner in a publishing venture had swindled him out of the large sum of money he had accumulated from the business while on active service. Also, it will be recalled, following his capture of the Cherbourg arsenal Dolan was awarded in the field the Silver Star and the Croix de Guerre, although both had been taken away from him immediately afterward because the medals were the only ones the donors had with them. There was, it appears, no record in the files of the investiture, and so those medals were never formally awarded. But this was not quite the end of Dolan's disappointment over medals.

Gamble promised to put Dolan in for a high decoration for his work in Czechoslovakia, for Dolan's political reportage had been excellent, full, and important. But in the turbulence of the end of the war somebody forgot to make out the citation and send it to the adjutant general.

To Donovan, Dolan's operation was immensely successful, one of those likely to help him in his supreme task—the creation of the CIA. But as WJD knew only too well, success was all too rare a commodity in secret service. More often than not there was a high, terrible price to pay for bold operations. Such a price was paid for the Dawes Mission.

During the summer of 1944, through their offensive in support of Neptune, the Russians broke through the German southern front in Russia. By August 1944 the Red Army was at the eastern foothills of the Carpathian Mountains. The Slovak division with the Wehrmacht remained loyal, but the Slovakian partisan forces, which were largely under the control of Moscow, revolted as part of the Europe-wide national insurrections that marked the military campaigns. Hitler detached counterinsurgency forces from other duties to put down the revolt, but the Germans had not met with success when the Red Army failed to get through the Dukla Pass, the main route through the Carpathians. Fierce fighting developed around Banska Bystrica, the insurrectionary capital, in which 25,000 Czechoslovak partisans were said to have been killed or wounded.

But the insurrectionaries at Banska Bystrica were still holding out when, at the end of August or the beginning of September 1944, Donovan ordered the Dawes Mission into the provisional capital. The first segment of the mission consisted of:

Lieutenant J. Holt Green, USNR, of Charleston, South Carolina, chief, OSS Czechoslovakia

Master Sergeant Jerry G. Mican, of Riverside, Illinois, intelligence agent

Staff Sergeant Joseph Horvath, of Cleveland, Ohio, interpreter

Corporal Robert R. Brown, Chicago, radio operator

Specialist Charles Heller, Chicago, radio operator

Private John Swartz, New York City, intelligence agent, with the Houseboat team, which was to make its way to Budapest

Their assignment: to attach themselves to the "Czech Forces of the Interior Headquarters at Banska Bystrica for the purposes of transmitting to Bari enemy order of battle intelligence and situation reports on progress of the campaign, as well as estimating arms, ammunition, and demolition requirements for further resupply to the CFI."[2]

Shortly after Green's team arrived, the German high command, in a special communiqué, reaffirmed the Commando Order of October 18, 1942, under which the Ginny team had been executed the previous Christmas. On the same day—September 23, 1944—WJD advised Roosevelt:

> OSS Secret Intelligence and Special Operations personnel were landed by plane in Czechoslovakia. . . . We have already had word . . . and everything is all right. The operation included as well as the landing of 120 Marlin (submachine guns) and 84,000 rounds of ammunition, 12 Bazooka [antitank rocket launchers] with 16 rounds each. . . . Czech Forces of the Interior prepared the reception and arrangements were made through OSS Secret Intelligence, London, in collaboration with the Czech intelligence service. On the return trip, the planes brought out 2 British ex-prisoners and 13 Americans.[3]

Two weeks later other B-17's brought in reinforcements for Green:

Lieutenant James Harvey Gaul
Photographer's Mate Nelson Paris, of Portland, Oregon, of OSS
    Field Photographic Service
Lieutenant Kenneth Lain, of Champaign, Illinois
Lieutenant William McGregor, Silver Spring, Maryland
Lieutenant Lane H. Miller
Sergeant J. Dunlevy
Captain E. V. Baranski, of Kaysville, Utah
Lieutenant Tibor E. Keszthelyi, of Forest Hill, New York
Lieutenant Francis Perry, of Brooklyn, New York
Sergeant Steve Catlos
Daniel Pavletich, of Rockaway, New York, radio operator
Emil Tomes, of X-2

The aircraft also brought in a correspondent of the Associated Press, Joseph Morton, although the Dawes Mission was a secret mission and he had had no clandestine training of any description. A later inquiry on what he was doing aboard showed that he was the guest of the U.S. Fifteenth Air Force, not of the OSS, which had no idea he would be in the mission until he was found aboard one of the aircraft. Morton explained that he intended to leave when the aircraft returned, but on his arrival at Banska Bystrica he changed his mind and elected to wait for the next incoming aircraft.[4]

All military personnel wore uniform and carried U.S.-made personal weapons, and the civilians "wore G.I. clothing customarily worn by OSS civilians overseas." However, "Heller, Schwartz [sic] and several of the others carried civilian clothes in their baggage."[5] With the party came 100 submachine guns, 99 light machine guns, 150 bazookas, 7 cases of explosives with fuses, 2,800 rounds of bazooka ammunition, and nearly 2,200,000 rounds of small-arms ammunition. The arrival was conducted in a fairground atmosphere in which Keszthelyi of SI, Paris and Morton photographed the entire scene, including the reception committee and the members of the mission.

With arms beginning to pour into Slovakia and eastern Moravia, with an unknown number of British teams operating there, and with at least twenty-three Russian missions in the country, Donovan had little reason to anticipate that the Dawes Mission would run into trouble. He expected, as did the Czech government in exile, that the Red Army would reach Banska Bystrica before the Wehrmacht. But Donovan was wrong. Because of German resistance, the Red Army did not get to Banska Bystrica. The Wehrmacht did, and after very fierce fighting the town fell to the Germans on October 19, 1944. The Red Army did airlift in two light Czech brigades, but these units were no match for the Germans, and Donovan ordered OSS Bari to notify the Dawes Mission that aircraft were being sent to evacuate the party. However, the evacuation proved impossible when Green advised Bari by wireless that the Germans had captured the airfields at Banska Bystrica and Tri Dubny.

With winter coming on—fierce Central European winter—Green decided to split the Dawes Mission into two parts and hide out in the Tatra Mountains until the Red Army arrived. The decision was passed to Bari, and then there was silence until December 6, 1944, when one of Gubbins's SOE majors, Ernst Sehmer, who had been leading a similar mission for SOE but was currently, like Green, on the run from German *ratissages*, advised London that the American and British missions had joined up and thirty people were now hiding on an estate near Dolnialsheta, southeast of Březno. They were in "serious difficulties," with all their equipment lost.

This was the last information received by WJD concerning Dawes, and its fate remained uncertain until January 24, 1945, when Berlin Radio announced:

> . . . Eighteen members of one Anglo-American group of agents, headed by an American named Green and an Englishman named Sehmer, who posed as a major, were caught on Slovakian soil in the hinterland of the German fighting sector, competent German quarters announced. Investigations revealed that they had the task to carry out acts of sabotage in Slovakia and economic and political espionage in Anglo-American interests. Agents, who

wore mufti when arrested, were sentenced to death. They were executed by shooting.[6]

Two days after that announcement a small group of men, led by a girl called Gulovich, stumbled into the headquarters of a Russian patrol in Rumania. In the party was an SOE lieutenant, Stephan Zenopian, who had been with Sehmer and the Dawes Mission as late as Christmas Day, and two members of the mission who had become separated from Green's party. They were Catlos and Dunlevy. They brought with them a terrible story of deprivation, hardship, illness, and shattered hopes.

On October 27, 1944, thirty-seven men and women had been in the Dawes party, including ex-prisoners of war who had attached themselves to the mission pending exfiltration. Green divided the group into four units, commanded by Lain, McGregor, Perry, and himself, and they retreated with the Red Army's 2nd Czech Brigade into the Tatra Mountains near Brasiva, marching in the direction of the Russian lines.

The weather turned very rapidly into blizzards, and many of the Czech soldiers, and some of each of the four parties, became ill from lack of food, exposure, and eating rotten horse meat. On November 6 one member of the Dawes Mission was captured, and the next day Green's group was attacked by German mountain troops and Slovakian Fascist Hlinka militia. Green's group escaped, and on November 15, after nine days' marching in blizzards through and across the Tatras, they reached a mining camp near Doolnia Lehota, where partisan nurses dressed their feet. Then they moved on toward the Russian lines; afterward Green learned that the pursuing Hlinkas had executed the nurses.

On November 26 Major Sehmer, head of the British mission in Czechoslovakia, made contact with Green, and together with Sergeant Horvath and Corporal Brown they went to a British radio post at Polomka to signal Bari. While they were away, the Germans captured Lieutenant Perry, and the rest of the American group only narrowly escaped capture.

As Zenopian went on to report, on December 1 Gaul joined Green and the British party. The combined party then marched by map and compass to the mountain village of Myto, in the hope of finding somebody who could help Photographer's Mate Paris, Lieutenant Miller, and a third man, all of whom had badly frostbitten feet. But the villagers feared German punishment and refused to help any of the fugitives. The party moved on through snow to a hunting lodge near Myto, where they stayed until about December 12, when they were betrayed by the villagers. Keszthelyi and Mican were captured by the German mountain troops, and the rest of the Anglo-American party was forced on the run again. They headed into the mountains north of Polomka and for the next three weeks stayed together in a hunting lodge and an abandoned winter resort hotel called the Velky Bok, which had been an SOE safe house.

On Christmas Eve the Americans and British held a party in the hunting lodge, and on Christmas Day religious services were conducted at the hotel by Gaul. Lieutenant Zenopian wrote Gaul's prayer in his notebook, which he gave to the OSS:

> Oh God, we who are gathered here in Thy name and by Thy name and by Thy blessing, on this day of thanksgiving do offer with deep gratitude our most heartfelt thanks for our deliverance from the blizzards and high winds of the wintry mountains and from the cruel snows fallen upon us, and from the perils of the black night and dark valleys. Gratefully we thank Thee for preserving our group together and for maintaining our physical health and strength and for buttressing our wavering courage and for providing food, even in our darkest days, and we ask Thy blessing on us and our Allies, particularly the Slovak nation, and Thy mercy on our comrades who are missing by enemy action and wintry storms. Amen.[7]

Then, Zenopian went on, they had Christmas dinner.

The Germans surrounded and attacked the hotel on the morning of December 26, 1944. About 250 Germans, Hlinkas, and Ukrainian Fascist troops opened heavy machine-gun fire. The partisan guard with the Anglo-American party resisted for about three hours but were driven off by mountain guns. A Czech who was present told Zenopian, who had left the hotel just before the attack, that "14 persons fully dressed and in complete uniform were marched out alive and taken in the direction of Polomka." As Zenopian explained, he himself, Catlos, Dunlevy, and Miss Gulovich, a Czech girl who worked for the OSS, escaped arrest because they were out scouting for food.

This was all that Zenopian and his colleagues could tell the OSS, except that he drew the organization's attention to the astonishing courage, strength, loyalty, and resource of Miss Gulovich. Nothing more was heard of the Dawes Mission, or of its British colleagues, until OSS X-2 captured by chance a Sicherheitsdienst interpreter, Werner Müller. Under interrogation he told OSS X-2 that on January 7 or 8, 1945, seventeen American and British agents were brought into the Mauthausen concentration camp in Austria. They were in prison clothing, and their interrogations were directed by Standartenführer SS Franz Ziereis, commander of Mauthausen, a Bavarian in his early forties, and Oberkriminalkommissar Habecker. When he entered a room for an interrogation, Müller found Green in a crouched position, his hands tied behind his knees, and with bare buttocks. Standing over him was Untersturmführer SS Arndt, who carried a whip. There was blood on Green's buttocks and forehead which, a member of the interrogation commission, Sturmbannführer SS Schoenenseiffen, joked was "the aureole of Jesus."[8]

In another room Habecker was interrogating Sehmer about the operations conducted at Bari. When Sehmer refused to answer any questions or make any statement, the German stated that he had "means of making him talk—the 'Tibetan Prayer Mill.' " He placed four sticks of wood the size of pencils between Sehmer's fingers and then squeezed the hand, causing unbearable pain. In a third room, Müller continued, a British private soldier, a Palestinian Jew with the work name Wilson, was hanging from the "Chinese Ladder," another of Habecker's methods of making prisoners talk. This time the torture was of a fashion that would, by hanging a man by chains at a certain angle, tear his arms out of their sockets if he were left there.

Then, Müller stated, after three days the interrogations were suspended when a telegram was received from Obergruppenführer SS Ernst Kaltenbrunner, chief of the Sicherheitsdienst: The prisoners were to be executed. According to Müller, the executions were carried out at Mauthausen on January 26, 1945. The prisoners executed were Baranski, Green, Gaul, Perry, Miller, Keszthelyi, Mican, Horvath, Heller, Paris, Brown, Pavletich, Joseph Morton, two OSS civilians, Sehmer, and two British soldiers, Willis and Wilson. Each was taken into a cellar, where he was shot in the nape of the neck by Hauptsturmführer SS Georg Bachnayer. The corpses were then taken to the refrigeration room by a former concentration camp inmate, Willi Ornstein, and a little later still they were cremated by Hauptsturmführer SS Martin Roth, head of the Mauthausen crematorium.

At OSS Washington it was time for an inquest into the cause of the disaster and for explanations to the next of kin. An OSS official report stated:

> The principal difficulty appears to have been incomplete planning on the part of the resistance movement [in Slovakia] and of its Allied supporters. Supplies and a swift advance had been guaranteed by the British and the Russians respectively. As it turned out, the Russians took two months to get through the Dukla Pass, for which they had allotted two weeks. [This failure was not for lack of trying, inasmuch as some 120,000 men were reported lost in the attacks.] Finally, in mid-October, the Russians flew in to Tri Dubny airfields two brigades of Czechoslovaks trained in Russia. Unfortunately these were almost unarmed, and once landed, could only join in the general flight toward the Russian lines. Meanwhile, the British apparently made no effort to help the insurgents. OSS rushed material from Cairo to Bari, but bad weather prevented most of the supply sorties.[9]

Whatever the truth of these contentions—and it is significant that the OSS acknowledged no responsibility—the need for secrecy about the OSS, its assignment, and the mission in Czechoslovakia imposed upon OSS Washington the saddest of duties: Headquarters was required to advise the next of kin without being able to say how the men were killed or what they were doing when they were killed. Consequently, a vast correspondence file developed. The most poignant correspondent was Lieutenant Gaul's mother whom in an ill-considered moment he had listed on his papers as the person to be informed in the event that he became a casualty.

No letters could be sent out until April 5, 1945—they were secret agents with a secret service on a secret mission—and Mrs. Gaul was told, as were all the others, that her son was missing in action. The letter was sent registered mail and marked confidential, and such was Mrs. Gaul's sense of duty that she wrote to WJD on April 18, 1945, to ask if she might have "the privilege of showing it to my husband as it was addressed to me and marked 'confidential.' "[10] Doering's assistant, Robert Thrun, replied on the twenty-fifth that she could show the letter to her husband and that it was intended for the Gaul family, but that "It should not . . . be discussed with others at this time."

When on May 8, 1945, the war in Europe ended, the need for secrecy in the Dawes affair ended also. But when Mrs. Gaul heard nothing about the fate of her son—he was still listed only as missing—she wrote again to Donovan:

> . . . my mind has been racing all over what you called "Central Europe," sifting all newspaper articles, weighing all radio news, unable to focus on the one spot of vital interest to us—where Jim went. I have lost ten pounds and turned grey watching every mail for another letter from you, dreading a boy on a bicycle bearing bad news in a telegram. In human kindness must this suspense continue?

Acting Director Charles Cheston replied on May 30, 1945, that it was known that Gaul and his colleagues had been taken to Mauthausen, but "beyond that we have nothing on which we can base a definite statement concerning him." Cheston did, however, tell Mrs. Gaul about the Christmas party and her son's prayer, enclosing a copy of the prayer. Mrs. Gaul then wrote to Cheston that "in my darkest premonition I did not imagine anything so disheartening as that ambush right after their Christmas party—someone must have betrayed them. Perhaps their own footsteps in the snow." She added there were "a few intimates anxiously waiting for news, and I would like to be allowed to quote Jim's prayer, a message of faith, and perhaps the last word we have from him."

By July 26, 1945, sufficient evidence had been accumulated to show that in Allied law Gaul and his colleagues had been murdered. Cheston said so, and his statement evoked from Mrs. Gaul the most poignant statement:

> The whole thing seems to be a history of narrow margins where things went wrong instead of right—so many ifs. The only thing that I am glad

about is that if Jim had to die for some other country—that it was Czechoslovakia, for that is where his heart was—he was called there—a fate—and
because we sold them down the river—in Chamberlain's day. It wipes out
our shame—we did try—through them—our best and bravest—to do
SOMETHING.

With Tito triumphant in Yugoslavia, Donovan undertook the most
ticklish espionage operation of his career: to attach to the court of King
Peter II of Yugoslavia in London, where Peter enjoyed the protection and
financial support of the British government, an OSS spy who would
report on the constitutional developments affecting Peter and his throne.
This operation was a clear breach of the Arcadia agreements that England
and America would not spy on each other. That it was undertaken reflected the geopolitical fact that at last America had assumed Britain's
place as the leading world power.

The man selected for the Shepherd Project—the operation's code
name—was known to Peter. He was Bernard Yarrow, a Russian-born
lawyer who had been assistant to New York District Attorney Thomas E.
Dewey and was later to become a partner at Sullivan & Cromwell in New
York and then a director of Radio Free Europe. Since it was known that
the king was heavily influenced by his mother-in-law, Princess Aspasia of
Greece, Donovan felt it would be wise to send Yarrow's wife with him—
the first and the only time he allowed an OSS officer's wife to accompany
her husband on a mission.

While Donovan was plainly a principal, it was by no means clear who
had authorized the project. Plainly the State Department had not, for
Cheston advised Donovan in a telegram that the State Department had
declined to accord Yarrow either diplomatic protection or status, on the
grounds of the "extreme delicacy" of the "entire situation" and the
probability that "in the event of political embarrassment arising from
Yarrow's connection or activities" the department "would have to disa-
vow him entirely."[11] Nor is there any evidence in the Donovan papers that
the Joint Chiefs, Donovan's masters, authorized it. The probability is that
since Donovan never undertook an operation without authority, the necessary authority came from FDR verbally.

The State Department's caution was understandable: Yarrow was to
obtain a good deal of secret British state documentation that, in the
wrong hands, could have proved extremely embarrassing to Churchill,
Foreign Secretary Eden, King George VI, Donovan himself, the U.S.
ambassador in London, the secretary of state, and even FDR.

And although Donovan had made an excellent choice of spy in Yarrow,
overriding all of Donovan's considerations at the time was the fact that
in front of Roosevelt were his plans for a postwar central intelligence
agency. It followed that any misadventure in London over the Shepherd

operation would affect Donovan's prospects as first director of central intelligence.

On his arrival in London, Yarrow made contact with the king and the prime minister, Ivan Subasić, a former ban of Croatia, under the extra-vigilant eyes of the British Security Service. Yarrow's first telegram to Donovan—which Donovan sent (as he did almost all of Yarrow's tele-grams) to FDR, the secretary of state, the Joint Chiefs, and various offi-cials at the State Department—set the confidential and intimate tone of this entire secret correspondence:

> On Wednesday, Sept. 27, I saw the King. He gave me a warm welcome and spent an hour with me chatting about the present situation. He told me that he regrets to say that his own mother is working against him by lending support to some Serbian political leaders who are trying to undermine his authority by criticizing his conduct and charging him with neglecting the Serbian people. . . . He told me further that Winston Churchill sent a sizzling telegram to Tito telling him in effect that the British Government has sent supplies and arms to Tito to fight the enemy and not to fight his own people.[12]

The high political drama in which the fate of Yugoslavia was decided began in May 1944, when, under strong Churchillian pressure, the king dismissed Mihailović as war minister. The second stage came when Churchill forced King Peter to dismiss the pan-Serb, antipartisan Cabinet of Premier Bozidar Purić and appoint Subasić, a leading member of the Croat Peasant party. The penultimate stage began when the Red Army entered Yugoslavia on October 1, 1944, and soon afterward Tito as-sumed the duties of political head of state. Peter was not invited to abdicate, but he was forbidden to return to Yugoslavia pending the out-come of a plebiscite on the future of the monarchy. Meantime, he was "invited" to accept a regency to manage his affairs and a government drawn mainly from Tito's Committee of National Liberation.

Peter rejected the proposals as unconstitutional and kept on rejecting them until Christmas 1944, when the Shepherd operation came to full flowering. Throughout that period Yarrow had trod surefootedly through the minefield of Yugoslavian politics. Early in December he obtained a copy of a highly secret letter from Churchill to King Peter and sent it to Washington. The letter, which related to the regency and the British attitude toward the future of the monarchy, caused uneasiness in Washington. Yarrow was immediately advised by Donovan not to tele-graph such documents but to send them through the U.S. ambassador in London. Also, Donovan gave Yarrow friendly advice about the need to remain objective and apart from the politics and emotions at the court of King Peter: "Your role of listening post is difficult since you must be sympathetic to problems of all factions but must avoid giving impression that you, the State Department or I have taken sides and are interfering [in] Jugoslav internal politics."[13]

Yet while Yarrow remained an objective reporter, he continued to accept from the king and Prime Minister Subasić documents of the highest sensitivity. Evidence was to hand when, on December 14, 1944, King Peter went to talk about his troubles with his godfather, King George VI, at Buckingham Palace. At the meeting, according to Yarrow's report, which Donovan sent the President:

> King Peter was told by King George that he himself will have to make his own decision [about ratifying the Tito-Subasić agreement] and that the King would not under the circumstances express his opinion on such a matter. King George, however, added that Peter must be conscious of his responsibilities, and that nobody can compel him to sign the agreement if he does not wish to. King George further said that Peter's idea of seeing Tito personally was not a bad one, and that he, King George, knew that such a meeting between them was at one time contemplated but later abandoned because of various obstacles. King Peter begged King George to intercede on his behalf with Churchill. King George assured him that he will do all he possibly can within his limitations to ask Churchill to take a firm stand on this matter, and that he will speak to Churchill within the next few days. King George further added that Churchill himself is in the habit of making a thorough study and taking all the necessary time before acting on any State matter, and that this is one of his many assets.[14]

At this point Yarrow's operation began to intrude deeply into the troubled and complicated relationship between Churchill and the Yugoslav king. Peter flatly rejected Churchill's impatient demand that he accept the regency, declaring in a letter on December 29, 1944:

> I am a young King but during my reign I pursued a policy and taken [sic] a stand as the King of my country which I can now retrospectively be only proud of. This gives me sufficient right and strength to address myself to my people and unhesitatingly to place myself for their judgment. . . .
>
> Nobody can deny my constitutional right to perform my royal power by myself. If however, general conditions require that I remain abroad for a while, I ask your help, Mr. Prime Minister, so that we may together, in mutual friendship and trust, find a solution which would be in accord with the constitution of my country, and which would guarantee the protection of the right of my people as well as the royal constitutional rights during my absence.[15]

King Peter sent a copy of that letter to George VI, with a note, a copy of which he gave to Yarrow:

Dear Uncle Bertie,

First, let me say again, on behalf of Sandra and myself, all my good wishes to you and Aunt Elizabeth and the girls for a very Happy New Year.

I am sending you a copy of a letter I wrote to Mr. Churchill. Please help me to make him understand my point of view. I cannot act against my oath to the Constitution. I know this is right and wise and will avoid a lot of trouble in the future, and safeguard my people from untold miseries. I feel very hurt at the moment as it does not look as if I am given a fair chance just now.

I did not bargain in the dark days of 1941 when I came in on this side unhesitatingly. I stood by our traditional friend, Great Britain. It is only fair that Great Britain should stand by me now. On my side all my life I will try to be worthy of this friendship and trust in me. With Love,

Peter[16]

According to King Peter in his next talk with Yarrow, on January 5, 1945, he received the first intimation that the British might try to compel him to accept the agreement. The British ambassador to the royal Yugoslav court at London, Sir Ralph Stevenson, called on King Peter and pointed "out all the advantages that will accrue to him if he signs the agreement, that he will be financially well taken care of."[17] If he did not sign, Stevenson "hinted" that the consequences would be to "precipitate the formation of a government of Tito" and Peter would be "finished forever and cut off from all financial support"—it was known that finances were a major consideration with Peter; he was heavily dependent upon the British Treasury, and most of the Karageorgevich dynasty's assets were in real estate in Yugoslavia.

Stevenson stated that Peter's stand was admired and understood, and the reasons for his refusal to sign the document were "irrefutable," but they had lost their significance and value in face of the actual situation. "There is now a revolution in Yugoslavia," Stevenson stated, "and in such times no attention is paid to legalistic arguments." He claimed, truthfully, that the American ambassador, Richard Patterson, "was in complete accord" with these views, and that the United States and Great Britain believed the king's only chance of going home lay in signing.

But Peter remained adamant, stating he had "no intention to legalize by his signing the agreement unconstitutional arrangements entered into by Tito and Subasić without his knowledge and consent." To demonstrate he meant what he said, immediately after his conversation with the British ambassador the king sent Churchill a letter reiterating his refusal to sign, declaring that unless the agreement included "water-tight clauses protecting my people and my constitutional rights, the revolutionary faction represented by [Tito] would have unrestricted legal and factual powers over the whole land. This would be a death-warrant for my people."[18]

A little later the same day by chance Peter met his uncle King George II of Greece, who was in a somewhat similar position with Churchill, and, Yarrow related to Donovan, Peter told him:

> I met Uncle George at Claridge's Hotel and I told him: "Uncle George, I feel awfully sorry for you and I want to express my sympathy to you for the trying days you have had."
>
> King George: "Peter, I had a terrible time. I hope you don't have to go through the same thing. Churchill had me with him from ten o'clock at night until five o'clock in the morning and he certainly gave me the third degree. I was holding out pretty fast in the beginning but towards dawn I weakened and gave in. Better luck to you, Peter."
>
> King Peter: "Uncle, I am dreadfully sorry to hear that but I am a bit younger and I can take it. I will hold firm."[19]

King Peter was, Yarrow advised Donovan, "getting ready for the works and will not give in."

Disturbed by Stevenson's menacing attitude, King Peter and Princess Aspasia went to see Yarrow—for the reality was that the ministers of the great powers were tussling not with a determined young king but with a determined mother-in-law—and, Yarrow reported to Donovan, "the King told me that he wishes to advise the President of the present situation and that he is fearful that the same pressure that was exerted on King George will be applied in his case."[20]

Peter stated: "I know that I shall be given the works and I should like to ask my friend the President, who has always been so kind to me, to speak to Mr. Churchill and ask him to understand my position and to appreciate the fact that I cannot sign the agreement which would bring an end to my reign." He further stated: "I wanted the President to know that I would rather take my chances now of being denounced by Tito and preserve my chances to return to Yugoslavia as King when the situation changes and when normal democratic life is resumed in my country."

Yarrow advised the king and the princess "in a very tactful way" that he "regretted very much indeed" he was "in no position to accept messages for transmission either to the State Department or the President." If he did so, he would exceed his authority. Yet even had Yarrow undertaken to transmit a message to the President, it would have had little effect on Roosevelt, who had already decided not to intervene when he instructed the State Department to advise Ambassador Patterson in London: "As King Peter knows, the President has given much thought to the developments in Yugoslavia, and it is believed that the instructions sent to you and the memorandum already communicated to the British Government reflect his views on the matters in question."[21] Roosevelt's advice: Sign.

Events now began to move more quickly, for Tito had indicated he was not prepared to wait for the king's signature forever. Churchill sent for Peter in the afternoon of January 9, 1945, and as usual, immediately after the audience Peter reported to Yarrow. Churchill was "exceedingly cordial" and received the king in the presence of Ambassador Stevenson and Sir Orme Sargent. Churchill contented himself with the statement "I am an Englishman and a foreigner to Yugoslavia. You are the King, and probably know your people better. My personal advice to you is to sign [the] agreement. Of course I may be wrong in my judgment, but in my opinion by signing the agreement you will preserve the continuity of [the] Royal Yugoslav Government."[22]

If Peter did not sign, Churchill went on, "Your Majesty will probably form a new government which we will formally recognize, but we will continue to deal with Tito. This situation is risky for you, for Tito may proclaim a republic, repudiate you, and put an end to your dynasty." When the king asked Churchill what he thought about his return to Yugoslavia, Churchill replied: "Your Majesty, if you should go back to Yugoslavia, you would be compelled to sign many death warrants at Tito's request, and if you should refuse to sign them you would find that within 24 hours your own name would be added to the list."

When the king tried to insist that he alone be allowed to select the regents, Churchill turned on him sharply for the first time and declared: "You cannot choose them yourself. As a constitutional monarch you must always take the advice of your Ministers." He then warned: "The three great powers will not lift one finger nor sacrifice one man to put any King back on any throne in Europe."

Expressing his sympathy with the king's position, Anthony Eden remarked: "Unfortunately, you are surrounded in London with incompetent politicians who indeed are of little assistance to you. Why don't they go to Yugoslavia, to carry on their political activities over there?" The audience ended with Churchill's statement "I shall always be your personal friend, whether you remain King or not. Make up your mind after careful consideration, and let me know your answer."

As Yarrow hastened to advise Donovan, the king's answer was to reject finally all notion of a deal with Tito. He announced to the press he would sign the agreement only if he were permitted to appoint the regents and only if Tito were not permitted to place "unrestricted legislative powers" in the hands of the Anti-Fascist Committee of National Liberation. The king's action meant that the Tito-Subasić agreements were terminated, and that the rule of kings in Yugoslavia was at an end. But as Peter told Ambassador Stevenson during that day of high tensions, he was taking an "irrevocable position" and he was "aware that my communiqué may cost my throne," but he was "taking full responsibility for my acts. I know

I am right and perhaps I am acting in the words of Mr. Churchill, as Bishop Cameron who held his hand in the fire to become a martyr but I am determined to go through with it."[23]

In a final effort to save his throne, on the fifteenth, King Peter sent Tito a telegram, with a copy for WJD via Yarrow:

> I should be glad to learn whether you share my view that in the highest interests of our people a personal meeting between us in the near future would be desirable. I am sure you will agree that the present junction calls for the fullest concentration of our national forces and in this, I, like yourself, wish to take the utmost possible share. Should the foregoing be in conformity with your own views, I would be grateful to receive your practical proposals for bringing about such a meeting at the earliest possible date. London, January 15th, 1945. Peter II R.[24]

The reply came through Tito's representative in London, General Vlatko Velebit. Tito stated that he would receive messages from the king only through the Yugoslav government. With Tito, kings counted no longer.

Then, Yarrow wired to Donovan, exasperated beyond measure, the British government sent an official communication to the royal Yugoslav government. The British had decided to send the Yugoslav government home and had directed that all members should prepare to leave for Belgrade more or less at once in planes that would be provided free of charge by the Royal Air Force. The British would give Subasić their full support to conclude the agreement with or without the consent of the king. Any government appointed by the king would not be recognized by the British government. Yarrow reported that almost all the 200 Yugoslavs on Subasić's staff had elected to go with him, and Yugoslav guards had been posted throughout the corridors of Kingston House by Subasić to prevent any government formed by King Peter from taking possession of the building.[25]

Having lost the support of Churchill and Eden, Peter now lost the support of his mother, Queen Marie, who, Subasić informed the Cabinet, had "denounced" Peter and demanded that he abdicate in favor of his brother, Prince Tomislav. At that juncture Yarrow advised that Peter "fervently desires help of [the] President and [Donovan]."[26]

Thus, another king had lost his throne. But such were the new politics of the world that Peter's departure was no more than of temporary interest. Of far greater interest was the fact that Donovan had undertaken this operation at all. It had been an act of espionage against America's leading ally, and the fact that such an act had been sanctioned in Washington was of far greater moment than Peter's departure. It meant that the Grand Alliance had disintegrated and that the brilliant Anglo-American comradeship of arms which had produced the Arcadia strategy and Neptune was now at an end. Whether it was to be revived or not would remain to be seen—some would say that the special relationship forged through Pearl Harbor was killed by American pragmatism.

Another operation of almost equal significance reflected the fact that in his last days FDR had been wrenched from his policy of conciliation toward the Communists. The operation occurred in Rumania, and it showed at best that Donovan had learned the dark arts well, at worst that the world was in for a prolonged period of Soviet-American hostility.

In August 1944, after Donovan had landed with Dragoon and was at Allied Supreme Headquarters, King Michael of Rumania overthrew his own pro-German government, replaced it with a pro-Allied government, obtained an armistice from the Soviet Union, declared war on Germany, and started actual air and ground operations on a large scale within the frontiers of Rumania. By September 1, 1944, the Rumanian Home Army —for the two armies Rumania had had in Russia with the Wehrmacht had been destroyed by the Red Army—was advancing with the Soviet Army into neighboring Hungary. The Rumanian Air Force, using German aircraft, was attacking the German Army as it withdrew from Rumania, and the young king had acted promptly to reach an understanding with the Western powers.

On August 27 a Messerschmitt 110 two-seater fighter had landed at the Bari airfield, in the heel of Italy, whence the Allied air forces operated into the Balkans. Piloted by a captain of the Rumanian Air Force, Bazu Cantacuzino, the aircraft carried a passenger, Lieutenant Colonel Bernard Gunn of the U.S. Army Air Forces. Gunn reported to General Charles F. Borne, of the U.S. Fifteenth Air Force at Bari, that he had been shot down while on operations over Rumania, that he had been a prisoner of war in the area of Bucharest, and that there were approximately 1,000 U.S. airmen being held as prisoners of war in the same area. King Michael's new government had stated it was willing to release the airmen and assist in their evacuation. Lieutenant Colonel Gunn and the Rumanian captain had come with a plan to set up the evacuation, and Captain Cantacuzino stated he was also empowered to obtain all possible Allied assistance for the new Rumanian government.

For Donovan, that was the first contact of substance since March 1944, when Prince Stirbey's conversations with a three-power committee at Cairo had broken down as a result of leaks by Dogwood of the Cereus chain at Istanbul.

Sensing that one of the Axis's principal dikes had broken and that the way lay open to the heart of the enemy's intelligence system in the Balkans, Donovan hastened from the headquarters of the supreme commander in Caserta to those at Bari of the commanding general of the U.S. Fifteenth Air Force, Ira C. Eaker. Donovan took command of the planning for what came to be called Operation Gunn.

Borne and Donovan rapidly agreed that a joint OSS-Air Force task force be sent to Bucharest by air to arrange the airlift of the airmen to Bari. At the same time the opportunity should be taken to insert into Rumania Secret Intelligence teams, flying in the B-17's sent to Bucharest to bring the fliers out. "The delicate matter of the [Gunn] mission's relations with the Russians" would be "based on understandings which General Donovan reached with them."[27]

At the planning sessions, which lasted through the night of August 27–28, Colonel Gunn reported that fighting was still going on between the Russo-Rumanian forces and the Wehrmacht in the Bucharest area, and the Luftwaffe was supposed to have twenty to thirty fighters and perhaps forty bombers in the area. But Popeşti Airfield about five miles southwest of Bucharest was in the hands of the Rumanians.

Lieutenant Commander Edward J. Green, of Philadelphia, chief of the OSS at Bari, put together a team to be sent to Popeşti Airfield in B-17's during daylight hours under powerful, long-range Mustang escort. Captain Cantacuzino was to be given cockpit drill and a practice flight on a Mustang on the twenty-ninth, and if he passed the test, he was to fly to Popeşti, land there, contact the Rumanian government and obtain free passage, and then signal to three escorting Mustangs in the air that the Rumanian authorities would permit the main force to land. If the answer was yes, the escorting Mustangs were to climb to a high altitude and contact "Big Fence," the Fifteenth Air Force Communications Center, giving the signal for the remainder of the task force—initially two B-17's with Mustang escort bringing personnel in to establish the airhead at Popeşti—to take off from Bari.

Cantacuzino was to remain at the airfield and warn all Rumanian aircraft to stay on the ground between 2:30 and 4:30 P.M. on the twenty-ninth and also to instruct the antiaircraft gunners to hold their fire during that period. When the USAAF B-17's arrived over Popeşti, they were to receive the all-clear signal from Cantacuzino and land while the Mustangs remained overhead to provide fighter cover.

The OSS team would bring one long-range wireless set and one agent's set and establish communication with Bari. Then the mass evacuation would begin; flights of twelve B-17's would come in at sixty-minute intervals until the entire group had been exfiltrated. At the same time all members of the task force received from General Eaker instructions in which they were "ordered to avoid all political questions and if they were pressed to comment on matters pertaining to the Armistice, they were instructed to say that Britain, America and Russia had agreed to discuss such terms in Moscow and Rumania should send qualified representatives there as soon as possible."[28]

The OSS-Air Force party took off from Bari at 12:10 P.M. on August 29, 1944, in two B-17's. The party consisted of:

Colonel George Kraigher (USAF)
Major Walter M. Ross (OSS)
Lt. (jg) H. J. Forbes (OSS)
2nd Lt. George Bookbinder (OSS)
2nd Lt. Serban Vallimarescu (OSS)
2nd Lt. Nicu T. Hagigogu (OSS)
2nd Lt. Lewis Stavanga (OSS)
2nd Lt. Russell F. Dubes (OSS)
Ens. Beverly M. Bowie (OSS)
S/Sgt. Richard H. Fehrenbach (OSS)

The primary mission of the task force at that stage was to evacuate airmen, but Ensign Bowie was instructed to proceed on to the Ploeşti oil fields and obtain all available intelligence about the German oil situation. Bookbinder, Vallimarescu, Hagigogu, and Fehrenbach were "to remain indefinitely as an intelligence unit to provide military, political, and economic intelligence from that area."

Meanwhile, Donovan had sent an urgent telegram to Istanbul, where one of the OSS's outstanding "new men," Frank Wisner, was in the process of rebuilding the service after the Cereus and Dogwood disasters. A Wall Street lawyer in his mid-thirties, and a Mississippian by birth, Wisner was to come without delay to Bari to take command of the OSS city team in Bucharest, a team enjoying the code name Bughouse.

Wisner was also to take over the Bookbinder mission in Rumania for the evacuation of the airmen. An airplane sent from Cairo to Istanbul collected Wisner and then hedgehopped its way across the Balkans to Popeşti, where it landed safely on September 2, 1944. A second mission had arrived under the command of Colonel John J. Rodrigo of OSS Algiers, who was to take charge of the Ploeşti oil survey. Donovan managed to find (without disrupting other operations) fourteen officers and seven enlisted men, bringing them from all parts of the Mediterranean theater at a moment's notice. They included:

(1) Personnel experienced in evacuating Allied airmen from enemy territory;
(2) five officers from OSS, R&A, who had been attached to the MAAF and US 15th Air Force for target analysis work and were hence thoroughly familiar with the oil bombing program and air force intelligence requirements; (3) several general intelligence officers; (4) a radio communications team; and (5) a field photographic unit. This group was equipped to handle conversations in Romanian, Russian, French and German.[29]

As finally approved by the supreme commander, Field Marshal Wilson, the team's tasks would be threefold: "(1) To evacuate captured Allied airmen. (2) To secure intelligence for the Air Force on the results of the bombings of the Ploeşti Refineries, and on future targets in enemy territory; and (3) To secure general political military and economic intelligence from secret sources."[30]

By the dawn of August 28 Operation Gunn was planned and approved. The rest of the day was spent in assembling the men, briefing them, securing equipment. On the twenty-ninth the operation was begun. Within three days about 1,350 American airmen, some amputees or men wounded, burned, or suffering from serious injuries, were evacuated to Bari. Moreover, during the collection of the airmen the presence of an additional 350 airmen in Bulgaria (which had also just surrendered) was detected. They were exfiltrated to Cairo. During Gunn, therefore, about 1,700 American airmen were rescued—an extraordinary feat—with the help of the Rumanians and without opposition from the Red Army.

The OSS had effectively penetrated a country where Donovan had expected that severe difficulties would be encountered with the Red Army. But through the speed with which he moved his men, the greatest initial difficulty encountered by the Wisner mission was the "considerable difficulty experienced in getting a truck to move the baggage of the group to the Ambassador Hotel" in Bucharest.[31]

The OSS commander in the central Mediterranean, Colonel Glavin, advised Donovan on September 11, 1944:

> The Secret Intelligence group has been in close contact with the heads of Government and has had almost daily interviews with various Ministers. This information is collected every day and as much as possible is sent in a condensed form over the radio to Bari, where it is relayed directly to Washington. We have been getting extremely valuable material of immediate value for AFHQ from the General Staff. . . . G2 is handing us questionnaires daily asking us to secure urgently needed information. . . . We are at the present time the only link between the Allied Forces in the Mediterranean and the Russians. This liaison has been difficult to establish and maintain because of language difficulties, but we hope to improve it with time. . . . The Political Advisor to AFHQ is relying entirely upon us for information from this area and has outlined to us several phases of the work which they would like to see us carry out. Needless to say, our cousins are green with envy at our having gotten there "the fustest with the mostest." . . .[32]

Undoubtedly the OSS had made a brilliant and spectacular penetration of Eastern Europe on a large scale, and WJD received much congratulation from the Joint Chiefs, General Arnold, the chief of staff of the USAAF, and from the chief of the Military Mission to Moscow, General Deane, who wrote on November 4, 1944: "The OSS is certainly doing a great job in the war, and I feel that in the last six months it is beginning to get the recognition it always deserved. Certainly your efforts are paying dividends of which we all may be proud."[33] Neither the Russian nor the British services had reacted to the fall of Rumania with the same speed as Donovan; neither apparently had the same resources, so the laurels went to the OSS, where, promptly, Donovan made arrangements to share the intelligence obtained with the British and Russians.

WJD radioed General Fitin of the NKVD in Moscow on September 29, 1944: "In collaboration with the American 15th Air Force, [the OSS] handled the evacuation of 1900 American airmen up to September 3. Since that time over 300 were evacuated from Bulgaria. This work was greatly helped by the cooperation of local Russian forces."

Donovan outlined the intelligence gathered to that date:

> The following operationally important intelligence was obtained by our organization: identification of chemical works at Moosebierbaum in Austria as manufacturing aviation gasoline; United States air raids reduced oil exports from Rumania to Germany to 38% of normal; destination points of oil shipments to Germany; damage to various refineries in individual raids; total for 1942–1944 of Rumanian oil production and exports; evidence that the fusing on bombs used in raids on oil refineries should be longer than 1/1,000th of second; foil dropping was effectively countered by a special device on the German radar fire control apparatus; the smoke screen at Ploești could be kept up for between 5 and 7 hours; the Dornier Works at Wismar are assembling FW-190 [advanced German fighter aircraft].

He assured Fitin that "we are sending to you documents in connection with the above and other intelligence items on the German air force and oil position." He also advised: "The Office of Strategic Services obtained from the Rumanian General Staff and communicated to our 15th Air Force information on German and Hungarian air order of battle. Because of this, some 200 planes resisting the Soviet advance were destroyed on the ground in Hungary."[34]

That signal was followed by a letter on October 10, 1944:

> My dear General Fitin:
>
> First of all I want to express my appreciation for the spirit of friendly cooperation you have shown us. We have tried to reciprocate.
>
> I think the degree of success we have had so far in our joint enterprises shows what Allies may do together, at least in our field of intelligence. . . .
>
> I am sending you photostatic copies of the following material obtained in Rumania:
>
>> Oil destination points.
>> Report on bomb damage to oil installations in the city and region of Ploești.

A table of aircraft motor manufacturers' numbers (useful for establishing German aircraft production figures and the whereabouts of aircraft manufacturing plants).
List of German spare parts depots.

I am hoping that the photographs taken there will come out well, and if so I will send them to you at once.

As our two forces come together, I hope that there may be an opportunity for us to meet each other in the field.

Sincerely Yours,

(s) William J. Donovan
Director[35]

He wrote again on October 30:

I am most happy to make available to you the first 6 rolls of microfilm covering approximately 1500 pages of material which were obtained in Bucharest and brought to Caserta and later to this country. We have tried to organize the papers according to subject and topic and to prepare brief outlines and introductions to the various types of material included. I think this will make it easier for you to handle.

I have asked General Deane to find out from you your reaction. If you want us to forward more, we shall be happy to do so.[36]

Fitin replied on November 9, 1944—remarkably promptly for the Russians—in a letter that was brief by Western but effusive by official Russian standards:

My dear General Donovan:

I received your letter of 10 October 1944, as well as the material and the photostats attached, which were obtained by your people in Rumania.
I was sincerely pleased on receiving your letter.
I, too, would be just as glad as you to meet with you again.

Sincerely Yours

(s) P. Fitin.[37]

In sending the material on the tenth, Donovan opened as a separate but associated question the matter of establishing a radio station to handle clandestine matters between the OSS and the NKVD, which had been mooted first at the meeting in Moscow between WJD and Fitin at Christmas 1943. Deane raised the matter when he saw Fitin on November 10, 1944, declaring that so far as Donovan was concerned, it was "immaterial" to the United States whether it or the USSR operated the station. As Deane advised Donovan in a telegram on the tenth, Fitin had said he would be "glad to consider the matter but requested that I ask you for a more specific proposal as to the type of communications, the location of the stations that would be in the net, the codes to be used, frequencies, et cetera."[38]

In the same telegram Deane indicated that Fitin was well disposed toward the OSS, for he had used the meeting on the radio station to make two requests:

> (1) Fitin . . . asked me if the OSS has developed a portable microfilm set which agents in the field can carry with them to photograph secret documents which they want to send out of or through hostile territory. I do not know how or why he thought you had such equipment but I told him that I would ask you. (2) Fitin . . . asked that you send your best estimates of the internal situation in Germany—political, economic, military, morale. He seemed to be quite interested in getting what information you have available with supporting data. If you can, you might cable me a brief estimate and follow it with whatever written material is necessary.

Both requests were filled. The microfilm set was shipped, and the estimate of the German situation was transmitted. Meanwhile, WJD had been looking into the question of communications with the NKVD, and on November 17, 1944, he received a memorandum from Colonel Lawrence Lowman, chief of OSS Communications, on the subject:

> It should be entirely feasible to tie in existing OSS and Russian facilities. Russia could designate certain transmitters for direct communication to either OSS Paris/London, or OSS Rome/Caserta, where the traffic would be relayed to Washington.
>
> Arrangements could be worked out in advance as to signal plans, procedures, and ciphers. If possible, ciphers to be held at the seat of the American Mission in Russia and handled by OSS cryptographic personnel, using a one-time pad system.
>
> In addition, information could be transmitted to OSS forward echelons, Bucharest, Budapest, Sophia [sic]—areas under Russian influence—thence via OSS radio circuits to either Rome or Bari for relay to Washington. (With the liberation of Warsaw and the entry of OSS teams there, another relay point could be established to work into OSS London/Paris.)
>
> For your further information, it should be remembered that commercial facilities, Moscow–New York via RCA Communications, are presently available.
>
> Also for your information, the matter of location of stations and frequencies to be used, can be easily worked out after agreement is reached in principle to the tying in of facilities as outlined above.[39]

By mid-November 1944 it seemed that OSS-NKVD relations were developing satisfactorily. But the underlying political relationship between

Russia and America did not favor such collaboration. For grave and sinister events were afoot.

By September 12, 1944, it was evident that the Soviet authorities in Rumania had begun a program of military, political, and economic measures to ensure that the Rumanian Communist party emerged with sufficient strength to seize the power of the state. The Rumanian Army had been disarmed of all antitank weapons and armored fighting vehicles, and the Air Force had been grounded. A Rumanian minister, Buzesti, told Wisner that Soviet delays in signing and implementing the armistice agreements were producing a "desperate" political situation and the "further disintegration of the whole nation's economy."[40] The Russians had "denied the government all means of communication with the outside world." They had ordered the confiscation of all private radios, and the finance minister, Jorda, had stated that the Russians had taken charge of customs. Jorda had suspected that the Russians intended to remove 700,000,000 lei—about $50,000,000 at the official rate of exchange on which the Russians were insisting, as opposed to about $2,500,000 at the free market rate, which they had rejected—in indemnities which, Buzesti had stated, would be a "stern blow to the tottering economic set-up."

Then, on September 14, Wisner wired the text of the first Soviet armistice terms, which he had obtained from the undersecretary of state for national economy, Georgescu. Some of these terms had left the Rumanian government, according to Georgescu, "dumbfounded and confused by certain of the armistice terms and . . . the following terms were especially offensive"[41]: Rumania was to surrender to Soviet control and use "All means of communication, all the Merchant Marine, all utilities and industries, all factories, and all storage depots," and the Russians would "control all publicity and propaganda including the press, radio and public spectacles." Georgescu had commented on these two proposals: "The political and economic life of Rumania will be completely paralyzed by the first of these provisions and the intellectual and spiritual life will likewise be stifled by provision number 2."

He then stated that "what is most inconceivable is the fact that they are far more severe and cannot even be compared with the terms which the Allied Nations proposed to the Rumanian Government in Cairo and later as well." He went on: "At the present time the Rumanian Government is composed for the most part of persons who have been pro-Allied and working in the interests of the Allies for many months. Some have spent time in prison because of their pro-Allied activities. Others have been constantly in danger of imprisonment." Yet the terms being imposed by the Russians were "worse than might have been expected under the terms of unconditional surrender and . . . the present government has no choice but to conclude that it has been abandoned and undercut so that it will fall."

The government, Georgescu had continued, "was not taking exception to" the Russians' demands for very heavy indemnities in cash against Rumania's good behavior, although it was not known how such a sum would be raised, especially now that all industry and commerce were under Soviet control. What was causing the greatest concern was that the Russians had demanded that the Rumanian government and people supply and support the Red Army on Rumanian territory. Already the Russian military authorities had demanded: "(1) More than 2,500,000 tons of grain; (2) 1,700,000 head of cattle; (3) 13,000 horses; (4) Quantities of vegetables, potatoes and cigarettes." These items were estimated to be of the value of 200 billion lei (about $1,160,000 at the official rate, or about $80,000,000 at the unofficial). Moreover, while the government was prepared to accept the Russian demand that Rumania supply twelve divisions with which to fight the Germans, Hungarians, and Austrians, it would have the effect of further diminishing the labor force, making it more difficult than ever to meet the demand for indemnities.

The situation was grave enough, but even more serious intelligence was forthcoming on September 17, 1944. Then Wisner reported that the Russians "have begun to sack [Bucharest] and are already at work undermining the King and Government."[42] At that point Donovan in Washington sent the chief of the U.S. Military Mission in Moscow, General John R. Deane, a long signal summing up Soviet conduct in Rumania since the surrender. The Russians were looting sealed Axis legations in Bucharest, appropriating the ambulances and medical supplies of the Rumanian and International Red Cross organizations in the capital, and effectively placing the blame upon London and Washington for the delay in signing the armistice. The Rumanian government and people were coming to the opinion that America and Britain had betrayed them, and Donovan was so concerned that on September 22, 1944, he advised Wisner:

> Your excellent reports are received with much interest and dissemination given to White House, State Department and also Joint Chiefs when appropriate. [Averell] Harriman [U. S. ambassador at Moscow] is kept informed of their contents.
>
> Please continue sending such material. Also would appreciate full information on trials of the war guilty including procedures adopted and methods of handling as well as parties involved. Let me know if there is any danger that use of your radio will be stopped for we will insist on your right to it.[43]

By September 23, 1944, the situation had become ominous, and Wisner reported, on the basis of a three-hour conversation with the marshal of the court of King Michael, Starcea, that the Rumanian Communist party was being strengthened with former officials of the Comintern, ready to form a government. "Mass recruiting is building up the formerly weak Rumanian Communist Party, 'thug' elements from the former [Fascist] Iron Guard are entering by the score and the 'intellectuals' are even flirting with the Communist cause. Shock forces are being trained and Rumanian Communists are being armed."[44] Soup kitchens were being operated by the Communists for the poor, and medical supplies from the Rumanian Red Cross were being given to the Communists for distribution. "This is being done in an attempt to build up the prestige of the party and to encourage sympathy for the Russian cause."

Russian Communist organizers, among them many Rumanian-speaking women, had entered factories and called mass meetings. They "have urged the workers to establish syndicates and they are making all sorts of inquiries about medical and recreational facilities, wage scales, and working hours." The country houses of the rich were "being burned and looted by the Russian troops and barns and other agricultural installations have likewise suffered."

The railways in Rumania were being changed to Russian gauge so that Rumanian rolling stock could not be used for commercial traffic, and the Russians were tearing down telephone and telegraph lines. Patrascano, the head of the Communist party in Rumania, had just arrived in Bucharest from Moscow and had been admitted into the Cabinet. He had refused to take the oath of allegiance to King Michael. Instead, he had "developed a loud pro-Soviet attitude and is a security problem in cabinet meetings when relations with Russia are discussed."

At that point—around late September 1944—OSS Bucharest began to develop an intelligence contact of the first importance. This was the so-called Bishop Traffic, named after the OSS X-2 officer who handled the case, Major Robert Bishop, who had flown to Bucharest from Istanbul with Wisner. Operating successfully with great skill, care, and stealth— for the NKVD was extravigilant concerning OSS contact—Bishop had managed to connect with the part of the Rumanian Security and Counterespionage Service that, ever since the Bolshevik Revolution, had had for its main task the penetration of the underground Rumanian Communist party. The existence of such a branch of the Rumanian Security Service had not been detected by the NKVD, and neither was Bishop's connection with it, at least for the time being.

Consequently, during the next six months Bishop received all the Rumanian Security Service's intelligence garnered from its penetration of the Rumanian Communist party, which was then in the process, under Moscow's direction, of taking over the power of the state and undermining the present neomonarchical-democratic order. These reports were of the first importance, concerning Soviet and Communist intentions not only toward Rumania but also toward all Eastern and Central Europe.

Bishop transmitted to Washington—he used the virtually unbreakable OSS one-time pad system, addressing his signals personally to the Saint, James R. Murphy—a picture of Russian plans and operations to incorporate the 80,000,000 people and all the nations involved into a pro-Soviet bloc between the Russian western frontier and Western Europe. They showed, also, that when the Russians claimed to have dissolved the old Communist International in 1943, a gesture intended to placate America and to create a political climate wherein the United States would grant Russia even more lend-lease, all they did was change the name. In due time the newly named organization became known: the Communist Information Bureau. But its objective—a world revolution of the proletariat —had remained the same as it had been when the International was established by Lenin in 1919, after the Bolshevik Revolution.

Furthermore, the Bishop Traffic revealed the existence of branches of the NKVD that had not been known, and the traffic alerted the Truman administration to the realities of Soviet political intentions in Europe. The traffic thus became perhaps the most important source on Soviet capabilities and intentions developed by the Donovan agency. It was considered so important that on September 26, 1944, soon after Bishop had begun his transmissions, WJD wired Wisner, warning him that it was vital that the entire OSS unit in Bucharest operate with circumspection. Wisner was able to assure Donovan that so far the NKVD had not identified the Wisner group as OSS and that the reason for the Soviet failure was that OSS Bucharest had been successful "to date in maintaining our cover as an integral part of an American military unit here"—Wisner and his party were, it seems, representing themselves as the advance party of the Allied Control Commission, a quasi-diplomatic entity responsible largely for watching American interests in the armistice process.[45]

The arrival of the American representatives of the Allied Control Commission increased Wisner's and his team's cover, and he succeeded in maintaining his position at Bucharest until March 1945, when he was transferred to even more important duties. During that period he recorded the systematic, ruthless Sovietization of Rumania, the isolation of the king, and the expropriation by the Rumanian Communist party of the wealth and possessions of the former ruling merchant and upper classes. During that period between September 1944 and September 1945, Wisner reported fully and in the greatest detail on this methodical revolution, and although he held frequent meetings with highly placed Rumanians from the king down, he managed it, apparently, without being detected by either the Soviet or the Rumanian Communist authorities. Certainly he did his work without getting his country or his service into trouble, the highest accomplishment of the intelligence master.

Alas, the Bishop Traffic did not survive Wisner's departure. Perhaps the Russians had found a means of decrypting the OSS's one-time pad cipher system, although that was almost, if not completely, impossible. Perhaps there was a betrayal or carelessness in OSS Bucharest, in OSS Bari, or even in OSS Washington. Most likely there was carelessness with the material by one of the OSS's customers. Whatever the case, the NKVD suddenly pounced on the Rumanian Security Service's branch maintaining the contact. All members of the service vanished and were not seen or heard from again. And Bishop's usefulness was terminated.

Yet Wisner had one other source of great importance, an individual known as Source Tonsillitis, and he survived. Tonsillitis's work was remarkable, for he had penetrated the Red Army office at Bucharest handling the daily signals sent by Marshal Rodion Malinovsky, the Soviet commander in chief of the entire southwestern front and of the Second and Third Ukrainian Army Groups. The penetration was achieved by an OSS agent code-named Tonsillitis, who was Theodore Mannicatide, of whom Wisner reported to WJD: "Mannicatide is well known [to me] and is considered to be a highly reliable and accurate informant."[46]

Mannicatide had been in the Rumanian Army until January 1945, serving "for several years" as a staff sergeant and "confidential assistant" to the officers of the Rumanian General Staff's G-2 Section, with special responsibility for order of battle. Wisner continued:

> Since October 1944 Mannicatide has been serving as one of our principal contacts with the Roumanian General Staff, and upon his demobilization he was placed on the OSS payroll. In addition to being a Battle Order expert Mannicatide has many other talents including that of map making. He received his education at Robert College in Istanbul and he speaks fluent English and Turkish. He comes from a respectable upper class family in Constanza and has an unblemished reputation for honesty, integrity and loyalty, traits very rare indeed among Roumanians as a whole. In the opinion of the undersigned and the other officers of his former staff in Bucharest, Mannicatide is thoroughly pro-American in his sentiments.

Wisner explained that Malinovsky sent daily reports to the Red Army High Command in Moscow and to General Susaikov, deputy president of the Allied Control Commission in Bucharest, concerning his own and the enemy's order of battle. The reports were handled in Bucharest by a subsource of Tonsillitis whose identity was known not to Wisner, but only to Mannicatide. Presumably Mannicatide's subsource was a former colleague in the Rumanian Army now working for the Russians in their intelligence, order of battle, or signals sections. In any event, Tonsillitis consistently provided Wisner—whose code name was Typhoid, all members of the Wisner group bearing the code names of serious illnesses— with the highest-grade intelligence about Red Army operations in Malinovsky's theater—one of the most striking penetrations obtained by any spy in any theater in World War II.

The penetration compensated for the espionage at Allied Supreme Headquarters of an NKVD agent on the staff of the Red Army representative with Eisenhower's staff, General P. N. Davidov; it demonstrated that the Iron Curtain was descending on the capitals of Eastern Europe; and it foretold a new and even more bitter intelligence struggle than that with the Axis was in the making, this time between the American and the Russian services.

43

The Vessel Affair

As Donovan was implementing the new policy and FDR was again considering the formation of a central intelligence service with Donovan as its head, there occurred a serious incident that constituted a severe reflection on the value and efficiency of OSS Secret Intelligence.

To make the blunder more serious, it occurred at the Vatican and while Donovan was away from Washington on yet another of his grand journeys —he had flown out to India, Ceylon, and China with a large OSS delegation drawn from all branches to negotiate larger OSS operations with his friend and admirer Admiral Lord Louis Mountbatten, Chiang Kai-shek of China, and Field Marshal Sir Archibald Wavell, the viceroy of India. Donovan's purpose was, now that the German war was ending, to concentrate OSS strength in what he called the "arc of Asia" from Delhi to Hong Kong and to prepare the organization for its posthostilities role. In particular, with one eye on the French, he wished to give his commands in Asia clear instructions on their function in French Indochina, where the Vietnamese Communist nationalist Ho Chi Minh had recently sent Donovan a cordial but threatening demand for independence from the rule of Paris. These tasks were of the highest importance and could not have been undertaken by anyone else in the OSS, for no one else had Donovan's international stature.

Donovan had long had important intelligence connections with the Roman Catholic Church. He was well known to its hierarchy in North America and had been received by Pope Pius XII in July 1944. For their part, the Catholic hierarchs had entered into a friendly but unofficial liaison with Donovan and the OSS. That liaison had begun as early as 1941, when a Father Morlion, founder of a European Catholic anti-Comintern (and then anti-Nazi) intelligence service known as Pro Deo, was evacuated by Donovan from Lisbon to New York after the Germans had overrun Western Europe.

Since that time Donovan had financed Morlion and the Pro Deo service, although Morlion's reports—known within the OSS as the Black Reports—were often little more than dissertations on Catholic dogma in a world at war. Donovan's justification for the expenditure of special funds on such tracts was that they provided a valuable insight into the thinking of the Vatican, an institution of immense global political importance. Also, when the Allies liberated Rome in June 1944 and the Vatican became open to the Western powers, Donovan went to considerable expense, time, and trouble to transport Morlion from New York and establish him at the Holy See. These connections resulted in the Vatican's making available to the OSS the reports of the apostolic delegates in enemy territory, especially in Japan, where the nuncio provided much intelligence useful for the aerial bombardment of targets in the Japanese homeland. There was, therefore, a tendency at OSS SI headquarters to place trust and confidence in Vatican reportage.

Since he was on his way to China when the Vessel case began, Donovan may not have been aware the case had begun. However, his lieutenants at OSS Washington were faithful in repeating to him all telegrams they considered required his attention. Through the excellent OSS communications system the telegrams were almost always in front of Donovan almost instantaneously, except when he was in the air; the communications staff was religious in tracking him down when he was on the move by road; and for the most confidential matters an excellent, fast OSS air courier service could deliver a letter to Donovan wherever he was in the world within a week. Thus, as the Donovan papers show, he was kept well informed about the evolution of the Vessel case. As the papers also show, he did not object to the operation. However, signals and letters are not always completely adequate methods of communicating ticklish matters, and it is possible that the Vessel affair would not have developed as it had —to the cost and embarrassment of Donovan and the OSS—if his deputies had been able to walk down the corridor and talk matters over with him on the spot. Be that as it may, the case began when the OSS SI Italy chief, Vincent Scamporino, whose headquarters were in Rome, received a specimen of intelligence that purported to emanate from the Vatican, at the time an almost closed, impenetrable, mysterious society headed by a remote and enigmatic Pope, Pius XII. Scamporino gave the intelligence the code name Z and sent it for an opinion to his case officer in Washington, Earl Brennan. Neither man was a fool: Scamporino was a young, quick-witted labor lawyer from Connecticut who had been honed in the severe, intricate world of Italian politics—a world where nothing could be trusted at face value—ever since he arrived in Italy late in 1943. Brennan was one of WJD's most trusted and experienced lieutenants, a veteran of the State Department's consular service, a former Republican member of the New Hampshire legislature, and he was experienced in Italian politics—he had worked at the American Embassy during the first years of the Fascist regime and had made a study of the secret police, the *mafiosi,* and the powerful Italian Masonic order. Yet both were deeply impressed by the profuse, detailed intelligence provided by Source Z, especially the reporting on Japan, where OSS SI still had few assets. To Brennan and Scamporino the source represented what seemed to be an intelligence pipe into the heart of the Japanese Empire.

Source Z was quickly accepted as a purveyor of the gospel truth by both Brennan and Scamporino; the number of Washington customers anxious to read his material increased markedly when, with the German war winding down, there was intense need for Japanese intelligence in Washington. Scamporino increased Source Z's retainer from $125 to $500 a month, and Source Z began to assign to his material a system of stars—one star for the least valuable intelligence, seven for the most important. Scamporino also demanded that Angleton hand the case over to OSS SI Italy. When Angleton refused because he was not satisfied the intelligence was not manufactured, Scamporino, acting without Angleton's knowledge, developed his own contact with Dusty, as Angleton had code-named Source Z, and, having no evaluation system of his own (although he did assign a full-time case officer to the source), began to place the raw intelligence into the U.S. system in Washington. Consequently the intelligence was accepted in Washington as true. But, Angleton's suspicions grew when, having examined samples of the intelligence, a U.S. representative at the Vatican, Harold Tittmann, declared he was skeptical about the source and his wares. Scamporino ignored that warning.

By the end of 1944 Dusty had become so important to the OSS that he was taken over by the director of all OSS intelligence services, Brigadier General John Magruder, who was also no fool—before coming to Donovan's staff, he had been at the Command and General Staff School, military attaché at Peking and Bern, chief of Military Intelligence, and chief of the U.S. Military Mission to China (1941 and 1942). Nevertheless, Magruder, too, became deeply impressed by the depth and global range of Dusty's information, and in consequence he wrote to Major General Clayton Bissell, Strong's success as Army G-2, on January 5, 1945:

> The OSS representative in Caserta from time to time transmits information from Vatican sources. For purposes of security the information obtained from this source will be sent in memoranda which bear the code designation

'Vessel' and an identifying number. You of course appreciate the need for the utmost security in the protection of this source.[1]

The OSS's confidence in the Vessel material was, to some extent, understandable, for to men knowledgeable about Vatican signals and bureaucratic procedures, the material appeared to be authentic intelligence emanating from the pens of the Pope, the secretariat, and such key branches of the Vatican administration as the Department of Extraordinary Affairs (the papal Foreign Office) and the Propaganda Fides, the department responsible for propagating the faith. It included what purported to be papal documents, aides-mémoire, transcriptions of highest-level conferences, agenda, and minutes, and it seemed devoid of either propaganda or opinion. Moreover, unlike the Pro Deo material, the intelligence appeared to be directly relevant to the war against Germany and Japan and to political relations with Russia, Great Britain, France, Spain, the Latin American countries and similar matters of high statecraft.

On the other hand, OSS X-2 Rome was not as impressed as SI with it. In the first place, the chief of that organization, James Angleton, was by nature more suspicious of Greeks who came bearing gifts, but that apart, it seemed inconceivable to him that the papal secretariat could be so easily penetrated at such a high level. After all, the Holy See had had centuries of experience in intelligence and counterespionage, and its security, ciphers, staff, administration—all had been thought impenetrable and impervious to common espionage. Beyond that, as a result of the Macfarland-Cereus episode at Istanbul, Donovan had issued a general order directing all OSS personnel at home and abroad not to employ spies or accept their intelligence until they had been checked by X-2 against the British ISOS registry in London and given a clean bill of health. To ensure that X-2 had the means to do this effectively, Donovan had transferred its headquarters from Washington to London, so that the X-2 chief, James R. Murphy, could carry out his assignment.

But as Angleton soon discovered, the cutout in the Vessel traffic, a young Russian emigré named Dubinin, had not been checked by SI against the ISOS registry when Magruder sent out his letter of advice about Source Vessel on January 5, 1945. Therefore, independently of SI, Angleton had instituted inquiries about him. These showed he was a man with no known previous association with any espionage service. At the same time Angleton instituted close OSS surveillance of Dubinin, and it showed that the Russian was in touch with a Jesuit priest, Father Schmeider, who did have a record of espionage *against* the Italians before the war—he had been arrested for having photographed Italian military airfields. What was not known about Schmeider was whom he had been working for when he was spying—it was entirely possible that he had been working for the British or the French, tending to make him somewhat acceptable. However, Angleton regarded this as a warning signal, and he did not recommend to Murphy that Source Vessel be given a clean bill of health by X-2. Angleton's attitude was reinforced by the volume of the intelligence: It was far greater than any one man could handle alone, and therefore, that a ring was at work was clear to Angleton. The question was obvious: Who was in the ring?

In any event, Magruder and his associates in SI won out over X-2's caution, although Magruder did evidence some caution when he telegraphed WJD's political officer at Allied Supreme Headquarters in the Mediterranean, Robert Joyce, that "This series offers great promise," but that "For its full usefulness a careful evaluation of the source or sources is essential. Please give us your considered opinion."[2]

Why Magruder asked Joyce, who was with SI, to make the check, when it was already being conducted by Angleton of X-2, is far from clear. There was certainly a good deal of interservice rivalry between SI and X-2 since Donovan had begun to use X-2 for his supersecret work, and certainly Murphy regarded SI and its academic, rather than cold military, approach toward its work with misgivings. And as Murphy later stated: "Of all the OSS branches, SI was the least professional, the most penetrated. Some of its branches—for example, the Cereus chain and some of the Italian chains—were riddled from top to bottom either by the enemy, the Communists, the Italians, or the British." Furthermore, because "they did not have Ultra or Magic, the work of OSS SI was not in general of a high order."[3]

It is also probable that X-2 may not have reacted to the emergence of Source Vessel quickly enough, for a high officer of X-2 was to state: "At that time all we could spare for the Vessel operation was one lieutenant. You see, we had over a thousand cases of espionage to go after and our first duty was to protect the troops and the security of military operations."[4]

Thus, as a result perhaps of Donovan's absence in Asia, the instructions regarding a check were not given as emphatically as they should have been, and in any case, circulation of the Vessel material to the highest circles in Washington began *before* X-2 had rendered an opinion. Plainly Magruder was more or less sure that his service had succeeded in penetrating one of the greatest centers of world intelligence—the Vatican.

Then in the middle of January 1945, when it became known that Roosevelt, Churchill, and Stalin were to meet to discuss military and political matters concerned with the defeat of Germany and Japan and with postwar political matters of great moment (as they did shortly at Yalta), the Vessel traffic began to take on a new, more imperative, more authoritative tone that could not be, and was not, ignored at OSS SI Washington. The first such report was sent to Roosevelt on January 11, 1945, with a covering note by Acting Director Charles S. Cheston (a man still angling for the directorship of OSS) to the president's private secretary, Grace Tully, pointing to the delicacy of the source and the need for the greatest possible security. The report read:

The following conversation occurred on 25 November between A [the Pope] and B [Pietro Cardinal Fumasoni-Biondi, prefect of the Propaganda Fides].

A: About Japan we already answered that we will study the possibility of mediation. Anyhow it would be advisable for Japan not to make any unfitting gesture, for it would only harm itself.

B: I think that the Russian Government has already decided to renounce the neutrality pact with Japan and that in the coming conference between Stalin, Roosevelt and Churchill the three leaders will just fix the method and the time for the renunciation. However, it will be useful to ascertain the limits of concessions which Japan is willing to make. This could be done by one of our men who is in Tokyo and who is very able.

A: Very well. We will give instructions on it. But it will be necessary to ascertain the peace conditions which would be offered by Great Britain and America, in order that we may be able to see whether the difference between the two stands could be solved by mediation.

B: This will be very difficult, probably impossible, for the Allies want unconditional surrender. They feel sure of Russian cooperation. The news of the resignation of the Polish Prime Minister confirms the belief that the relations between Poland and Russia are evolving in favor of the USSR, and that Moscow on the other hand will comply with the Allies' wishes in the Far East.

A: Perhaps you are right. At any rate we must try to find out what are the conditions of the Allies. We hope the American representative here will help. Please inform your man in Tokyo that it is necessary to know the attitude of the Tokyo Government before determining whether our intervention is opportune. We recommend that he insists that Tokyo keep calm, at least until our answer.

B: I shall follow your orders promptly. But Japanese circles are very excited. They hope that the war in China may definitely turn in favor of Japan before the Allies can seriously intervene.

A: This consideration should favor mediatory action.[5]

The convincing nature of this Vessel transcription, the noble turns of phrase, the beautiful dialogue—all was impressive and of the highest interest to FDR, who had been told by his Chiefs of Staff that he might have to accept 1,000,000 American casualties if he invaded the Japanese homeland. Naturally, he was anxious to obtain all intelligence having a bearing on Japanese morale and political intentions.

By January 15, Vessel had sent a report of another conversation said to have taken place between Pope Pius XII and Cardinal Fumasoni-Biondi. The OSS SI memorandum to President Roosevelt advised:

On 4 January 1945 the highest authority at source conferred with Cardinal Pietro Fumasoni-Biondi . . . who presented a memorandum based on reports from the Apostolic Delegate to Japan and the Consistorial Congregation. The memorandum, dealing with the possible bases of a negotiated peace between the Japanese and the Anglo-Americans, makes the following points:

(1) The Japanese minimum demands for a negotiated peace are the following: Japan will renounce all occupied territories except Hainan and Hong Kong. Manchukuo is to retain its present status. The Philippines are to be independent and sovereign, free from all United States ties. India is to be elevated to dominion status in the British Commonwealth of Nations. The Dutch East Indies are to be elevated to dominion status under Holland. Japan will withdraw completely from China on condition that the Nanking and Chungking governments unite and also sign a treaty of "perpetual alliance" with Japan. England and the United States are to recognize Japan's privileged position in the Far East. Australia is to be opened to Japanese immigration.

(2) It is understood at the source that the minimum Anglo-American demand for a basis of peace discussions is that Japan immediately withdraw from all territories conquered since 1937, when the aggression in China began. The Anglo-Americans want Japan to consider that, in case of a definitive Allied victory, Japan will revert to its status preceding the Sino-Japanese War of 1894.

(3) The Consistorial Congregation expresses its opinion that it is an act of profound generosity on the part of the Anglo-Americans even to consider discussions with Japan in view of the "unheard-of aggression" of Pearl Harbor, the invasion of the Philippines, and the possessions of the Dutch, French, and England in the Far East. Only a "profound sense of humanity" impels the Anglo-Saxons to comply with source's request to furnish minimum demands.

(4) The memorandum notes the wide divergence in the minimum demands of the two belligerent groups and advises that the status of 1937 must be a necessary preliminary. The Japanese demands are regarded as those of a victor, and Japan is warned to consider the tremendous war potential of the Anglo-Americans, to which may be added some Soviet support.

(5) The memorandum cautions the Anglo-Americans that the form rather than the substance of their demands should be tempered and that the psychology of the orientals should be considered. It suggests that, as a basis for an armistice, a neutral zone should be established between the belligerents and that the Philippines should be immediately evacuated by the Japanese and an "independent regime" established there.[6]

Here again was extremely valuable intelligence, if true, for it set forth Japan's minimum demands for a negotiated peace, obtained in secrecy by the apostolic delegate from the Japanese government.

Impressed by the substance of the two reports, on January 16, 1945, Doering asked Putzell, the assistant executive officer, to classify all Vessel traffic "Top Secret/Control," which not only subjected the documentation to all the intense security normally afforded top secret materials but also, as the word "control" implied, made it illegal for anyone other than those on a special list (which excluded aliens) to see the reports without the approval of the President or the secretary of state.[7]

At about the same time Source Vessel changed his reportage slightly, starting to provide intelligence calculated to make his intelligence valuable not only to the American political but also to the military community.

The first of these reports, again purporting to have derived from the apostolic delegate in Japan, was likely to interest the U.S. Navy and the State Department:

> 1. The Japanese have recently put into service a new battleship armed with 9 of the largest naval guns in the world. This warship is commanded by Rear Admiral Yanuchi, a Catholic.
> 2. The warship was probably in the vicinity of Nagasaki on Christmas Eve and 2 days later it was to proceed to join its assigned battle fleet.[8]

Whether this change in the nature of the intelligence produced the desired effect is impossible to tell, but on January 15 the OSS SI chief in Italy, Vincent Scamporino, was able to extend the dissemination of Vessel material significantly when he interested the chief of OSS China, Colonel Richard Heppner, in the product. Heppner was traveling with Donovan on the trip to China and passed through Rome on or about this date. It is possible that WJD learned of the existence of Source Vessel at about this time. If so, there is no evidence that he intervened to establish whether Source Vessel had been cleared by X-2. The probability is that Donovan assumed Source Vessel had been approved at this time, for later he certainly agreed that the OSS should use it.

As Scamporino reported to Magruder, Heppner "expressed keenest interest and stated info would be of inestimable value in contacts with" General Albert C. Wedemeyer, deputy chief of staff to the supreme Allied commander, Mountbatten, and chief of staff to Chiang Kai-shek, and General Patrick Hurley, U.S. ambassador in China. Heppner thought also that the Vessel intelligence would "in some cases be of vital importance [to] Air Force operations" and requested that he be included in the distribution list.[9] OSS Washington agreed the following day, announcing it had established a "special unit" to handle "this precision job" and therefore, the distribution would be done from Washington.[10]

On January 17, 1945, another tidbit, this time for the Joint Chiefs:

> On 10 January the Japanese Emperor attended a secret council meeting during which someone dared to speak about peace feelers. The Emperor was informed that certain Japanese individuals have been attempting to interest [the Pope] in mediating the Pacific War. The Emperor did not express any disapproval of these efforts.
>
> Someone at the meeting declared that such activities might be a useful preparation for a time more opportune than the present. The Council was skeptical of mediation possibilities, evidently believing that only force of arms would settle the conflict.[11]

By January 20, 1945, WJD was in Chungking, negotiating with General Wedemeyer for a larger OSS operational responsibility in the China theater, which he obtained. As Magruder advised Donovan on the twentieth, the following Vessel reports had been received since January 3, 1945:

§ Recent B-29 air raid caused heavy damage to Japanese armored car plant (presumably located in Osaka). Many factory workers killed and many more injured. Production reported suspended for some time.

§ "Japanese industrial workers reported aware of danger to which Japan is exposed. Even most patriotic said to believe that military has deceived Emperor and exposed Japan to great peril."

§ American "indiscriminate and intentional bombing" of Japanese civilians has been protested, maintaining that civilian casualties have been heavier than those of industrial workers.

§ Representatives of Japanese heavy industry and General Staff recently met in Tokyo. They are reported to have agreed to favor aeronautical industry.

§ Japanese industrialists have gained increased influence over the military, owing to recent bombings of Japan and fact that population has been somewhat depressed by recent military defeats, notwithstanding Government efforts to minimize reverses.

§ Although leading Japanese industrialists and other responsible persons in Japan are interested in bringing about peace discussions between Japan and United Nations, some observers believe divergence in viewpoints between military and industrial-commercial elements in Japan is too great to permit the proposal of "reasonable" conditions to Great Britain and United States. They also think that distance between point of view of Allies and that of Japan still too great for negotiated peace.

§ Despite concealment efforts by military, information on Japanese naval losses in Philippines to extent of 4 capital ships has leaked to leading Japanese industrialists who show concern.

§ Japanese are greatly concerned over rising civilian unrest in southern coastal China. News of sweeping American successes in Luzon is reported to be spreading among Chinese population in this area, and anti-Japanese feeling is said to be breaking into open. Japanese have taken severe repressive measures against civil population.

§ Japanese government believes that accord between the three major Allies is impossible before coming [Yalta] conference of Roosevelt, Churchill, and Stalin, and that present Russo-Japanese relations will continue indefinitely. Japanese circles believe Russia has made impossible demands of England and U.S. in return for

Soviet denunciation of pact of non-aggression with Japan. Japanese Ambassador in Moscow informed Tokyo that Russia demands free, independent Poland with no commitments to prevent its possible entrance into Soviet Union, and that Bulgaria, Hungary, and Spain are to be permitted to become Communist if people so decide.[12]

All this indicated that either Vessel was a master spy without parallel —for the Vatican's security was reckoned to be comparable to the Bank of England's—or a faker of documents of majestic ability. Aware of that, and of the Vatican's reputation for impenetrability, Donovan ordered all Vessel intelligence to be placed in a special category, like the Wood intelligence and the Boston Series, and to be submitted to the Reports Board, which existed to weigh and check such intelligence before dissemination. In the case of naval, military, and diplomatic intelligence procured by Vessel and relating to Japan, checking was difficult because of the paucity of intercepts. Nevertheless, in the first testing process Vessel material was regarded as trustworthy, and accordingly, circulation continued to the highest authorities, including the President, the secretary of state, and the Joint Chiefs.

Such was the case when the decision was made on or about January 24, 1945, to send to the President what appeared to be an important discussion between the Vatican's acting secretary of state, Giovanni Cardinal Montini, a future Pope, Hasahide Kanayama (Japanese minister to the Holy See), Monsignor Domenico Tardini (president of the Pontifical Commission for Russia), and Pio Rossignani (private secretary to the Pope). According to Vessel, the discussion took place in Montini's room on January 17, 1945, and "The substance of the conversation is faithfully reported as follows":

> *Kanayama:* The pacifists in Japan have great faith in the Holy See. An attempt by the Holy See to initiate mediation would greatly encourage our pacifists, even if there should be no immediate concrete results.
> *Montini:* It is clear to us that the gap between the viewpoints of the two belligerents is too wide to permit Papal mediation.
> *Tardini:* Japanese adherence to the tri-partite pact [with Germany and Italy, the so-called Axis Pact] seriously hurts the Japanese case in Allied countries. World opinion stigmatizes Japan as an aggressor, and even Soviet Russia concurs.
> *Montini:* The Holy See has striven to soften this world indictment of Japan by emphasizing the differences between the oriental and occidental mentalities.
> *Kanayama:* Your excellencies should consider that our aggression is now justified by the fact that our adversaries are stronger than we. The United

States prepared psychologically for this war in the Pacific as much as did Japan. Books were printed in the United States which predicted war with Japan.

Rossignani: It seems to me that one of these books was written in 1925 by a high American Navy officer, and it predicted a Japanese-American war for 1931 or 1932.

Tardini: My dear son, this is all beside the point. The United States considers Japan the aggressor, and moreover they are certain of victory.

Montini: True enough, but it also seems to me that much depends on Russia.

Kanayama: Our Ambassador in Moscow has informed our Government that the Far East will be discussed when the Big Three meet. The United States, supported by Churchill, will ask for Russian help to crush us completely. The Anglo-Americans will ask that Russia denounce the pact of non-aggression with Japan and that Russia passively participate in the Pacific War and permit Anglo-American use of Russian air bases. Our Government also understands that, before Stalin will agree to this, he will request a wholehearted attempt on the part of the Anglo-Americans to mediate, and that he will even offer to act as mediator. Our Government also understands that the Big Three will discuss European problems first, and that if they are not settled to Russia's satisfaction, especially the Polish question, then Stalin will not discuss the Far East.

Tardini: The United States and England have already made a declaration on Poland. American public opinion is behind Roosevelt.

Kanayama: It is a diplomatic maneuver to draw concessions from Russia. However, Roosevelt and Churchill have another move to make against Russia. Turkey and the countries of the Middle East are ready to enter the war against us. Stalin is opposed to these countries entering either the Pacific or the European War.

Rossignani: In view of all this, would it not be better for the Pope to synchronize his mediation with that of Stalin?

Kanayama: On the contrary, it is urgent that His Holiness come to our assistance before the Big Three meet to discuss Japan, and that this mediation be in full swing at the time. Stalin is interested in close collaboration with the Anglo-Americans, but he wishes to gain the maximum benefits from this collaboration. Stalin knows that the Japanese reaction will be swift when it becomes evident that Russian denunciation of the non-aggression pact is imminent. There may be stiffening of Japanese resistance, or the pacifists may prevail. In this latter case, Stalin would cut a big figure, and he would be able to gain satisfying terms for the Anglo-Americans. And even to the Japanese he might appear as the savior of Japan from destruction. Stalin desires to have De Gaulle at the coming conference, but Roosevelt and Churchill are opposed. However, should De Gaulle be admitted to the conference, then Chiang Kai-shek will be present also.

Montini: Would it not be possible for the Japanese Government to offer terms that would be closer to those of the Anglo-Americans so that the Holy See could begin mediation on more concrete bases?

Kanayama: We will communicate your request to our government at once, together with an account of this conference. Meanwhile, it would be useful if the Holy See would begin mediation attempts.

Rossignani: Very well. This evening I will present Mr. Kanayama's memorandum and the minutes of this conference to His Holiness.[13]

The next day, January 25, 1945, FDR received a brief of the memo to which Rossignani was said to have referred at the Montini meeting:

> At the request of the Japanese Government, the Japanese Ambassador to the Holy See (Harada Ken) has presented the Private Secretary of the Pope (Pio Rossignani) with the following information, which the Japanese ambassador hoped would cause an attempt at mediation to begin immediately:
>
>> The Kremlin has assured the Japanese Ambassador in Moscow that the USSR will continue to define Japan as an aggressor but will take no further step at the coming "Big Three" conference. The Japanese Ambassador in Moscow is negotiating with the Kremlin in an attempt to effect an agreement according to which (1) Russia will respect the non-aggression pact; (2) Japan will denounce the tripartite and anti-Comintern pacts, will break completely with Germany, and will remove all anti-Communist controls in the Japanese islands. The Japanese Government believes Russo-Japanese understanding will expedite Anglo-American willingness to mediate in the Pacific War.[14]

On January 26, Lieutenant Colonel R. Davis Halliwell, WJD's representative at the Hawaiian headquarters of Admiral Chester Nimitz, commander in chief of the U.S. Pacific Fleet, was admitted to the "Vessel Club" in the hope that it would assist him in his task of persuading Nimitz to permit full OSS operations in his area of command. As Acting Director Cheston and General Magruder, chief of OSS intelligence services, advised Halliwell in a telegram, the Vessel code name was "used for material which comes from sources in Vatican which are believed to be highly reliable," and "Great care in handling is essential and you should furnish it only to Admiral Nimitz's Staff Intelligence Officer."[15]

Also on the twenty-sixth, Joyce, who had been checking into the Vessel source at the Quirinale and the Holy See, came up with what must have been an eminently acceptable telegram at OSS Washington. "We are now dealing directly with source," reported Joyce, and "Scamporini is convinced and I am inclined to agree that the material is authentic." Arrangements were being "perfected to test the material and we hope shortly to report definitely that it is genuine." At the same time Joyce suggested that Washington undertake a "careful review of reports already submitted in the light of known developments reported or forecast in this series of reports."

Noting that Vessel had reported that recently, during the papal conversations concerning mediation between America and Japan, Myron Taylor, until lately Roosevelt's personal representative to the Pope, had visited the Holy See, Joyce thought, sensibly, that "an excellent check would be a comparison of Myron Taylor's reports, presumably to the President, against VESSEL reports covering Taylor's activities." Joyce did, however, include one warning signal in his telegram: Vessel had previously made his material available to representatives of two other governments, but Joyce reported, "Scamporino is convinced that we are now receiving it exclusively." Meantime, Joyce stated, he would be returning to Rome in a week and would make a further report.[16]

At that point Angleton's representative approached an official on Taylor's staff at the Holy See to ask for verification of the facts concerning Myron Taylor mentioned in some of Vessel's reports. Certain discrepancies were detected in those reports. They were not, however, serious or conclusive enough to warrant Angleton's branding Vessel as fraudulent. When Taylor was approached directly, he replied that he could not be of assistance to the OSS because what transpired between the Holy Father and one of his flock was a matter of sacred trust—a remark that tended to strengthen the view there was little or nothing wrong with Vessel's reportage.

Meanwhile, in Washington OSS analysts had spent four days checking the report mentioning Taylor's name. Cheston decided to send it to the President. Putzell was deputed to take it to the White House and to try to compare it with any reports Roosevelt might have received from Taylor about the matters discussed. The document read:

> The following is source's account of the conference held on 19 January between the Pope and Mr. Myron Taylor:
> When asked whether he considered Papal mediation in the Pacific war possible, Taylor was skeptical. He stated that recent developments had evidently not brought the Japanese point of view any closer to that of the Anglo-Americans. The Pope asked if he would discuss the situation with the Japanese Ambassador to the Holy See, and Taylor replied that he was neither an official nor a semi-official representative of the United States, and accordingly could speak only as a private individual. Taylor promised to communicate with the President, for which the Pope thanked him, and asked him to explain the sentiments which animated this inquiry.[17]

A number of developments now seemed to warrant OSS confidence in Source Vessel. On the afternoon of January 26 Putzell called on Grace Tully, Roosevelt's private secretary, who was unusually trusted, "to determine whether the subject Vessel report can be confirmed or disproven by communications from Mr. Taylor to the White House." Miss Tully told Putzell that during the evening of the twenty-fifth a telegram was received from Taylor "asking that the President receive a stated individual who has a message for him from Mr. Taylor." Miss Tully "assumed" that the "message concerns the topic outlined in the subject Vessel report" and had sent Taylor's telegram in to the President. Again, the oblique, careful statement tended to lend veracity to the Vessel traffic. But Putzell, being a lawyer, was left quite satisfied with it.

Consequently the same day Putzell made a check with the State Department to see whether anything had been received relating to Taylor's visit to the Pope from the department's representatives at the Holy See. Putzell was mystified to learn that no such telegram had been received, and so he called Miss Tully again. Again all he received was an enigmatic half answer: "The President finds this material most interesting and reads every one carefully. She expressed the same interest on his part in other material that is sent to him from time to time by this office."[18] But that was not quite an answer to Putzell's question, just as Taylor had not quite answered the question put to him by Joyce.

This reaction was odd, for by now Roosevelt, a central figure in the Japanese matters being discussed by Vessel in his reports, must have formed an impression of the veracity of the reports, if only concerning the parts that related to his conversations and communications with Churchill and Stalin on those matters. Whatever his opinion, he kept it to himself, and one is tempted to believe that he did not accept Vessel as a truthful source but was letting the case run before saying so in order to see how the OSS would handle what was becoming the greatest challenge to its judgment, efficiency, and discretion so far. Such a tactic would have been very typical of Roosevelt, who often moved crablike when he was making a major decision.

However, by the thirty-first there had been no further developments in the Taylor report, and Magruder cabled Joyce and Scamporino:

> VESSEL material is greatly valued. It constitutes unique line into Japan. You will appreciate that definitive checks are difficult to elicit in high places. However, we know the President is interested in the material as is State. Have personally had State reaction from [Joseph] Grew [former U.S. ambassador in Japan]. Check from Navy verified plausibility of item re Jap flotilla in Hongkong December 29th.[19]

Then, on February 2, Vessel came on with another important (and checkable) report that seemed to show Roosevelt was secretly negotiating or making some arrangement with the Japanese:

> The Holy See has been informed as follows: A very important White House spokesman advised the Apostolic Delegate to Washington that he could tell the Holy See that President Roosevelt will take account of all the Pope's communications, especially concerning Poland and spheres of influence, at

the "Big Three" [Yalta] conference. The spokesman said the President intends to adhere closely to Dumbarton Oaks policy.[20]

If anything, that report was even more useful as an instrument with which to check the honesty of Vessel's material, for Roosevelt must have known whether he had authorized any such statement to the apostolic delegate or, indeed, whether there had been any contact with the delegate. But if he did say anything to the OSS, there is no record in WJD's papers, and since it seems probable that Roosevelt kept silent, the theory that he was regarding the Vessel affair as a test of OSS statesmanship becomes more tenable. What other reason could FDR have for not advising his intelligence service on the truth or otherwise of this vastly important traffic? It is, of course, always possible that FDR was too preoccupied with the Yalta Conference—he was on his way to the Crimea at this time for the meeting with Churchill and Stalin, due to begin on February 4— to concern himself with the problems of his intelligence service. Nevertheless, while he was en route, the Vessel traffic was relayed to him almost instantaneously over the special naval telecommunications system created for the conference, and it would have been simpler to send a brief signal of advice or warning, whatever the Vessel traffic demanded, than to call an OSS representative to the White House for the same purpose.

Meanwhile, on February 2, 1945, two more Vessel reports had come in and were sent over to the White House. Both had high significance. Report 58A indicated that the United States might now be in for a long and brutal war in the Pacific at the end of the German war if it did not abandon the demand for unconditional surrender:

> Source has been informed by connections in Japan that the Japanese Government is confident that Stalin will categorically refuse to abrogate the non-aggression pact with Japan. The Japanese hope for new Soviet-Japanese pacts strengthening the non-aggression pact.
>
> The Japanese Government feels that Japan can continue the Pacific war indefinitely in view of Russia's certain refusal to enter the war. Japan therefore cannot reduce its minimum terms for a peace settlement.[21]

Report 59A contained intelligence almost as menacing:

> On 25 January, Harada Ken, Japanese Ambassador to the Holy See, made the following assertions to the Pope:
>
> The Japanese Government would be willing to interpret the Vatican's wishes to the Kremlin.
>
> The Kremlin has assured the Japanese Ambassador in Moscow that Russia will ask the Anglo-Americans to attempt to reach a negotiated peace in the Pacific, provided the Japanese Government accepts the Soviet proposal that the Far East peace conference include Russia, China, Great Britain, the United States, France, and Japan.

Then came 60A. This included a statement that, it might have been thought, was an attempt to alarm Roosevelt into a state of mind in which he would accept such suggestions. At a time when the Red Army was actually entering German territory, thus reviving the nineteenth-century Western geopolitical fear of a united Russo-German nation—the so-called Mackinder theory that Russia and Germany united constituted the heartland of the world and that he who controlled the heartland controlled the world—Vessel reported:

> The German Communist Party, with the aid of Social-Democrats and military elements, had formed a German Committee of Liberation (the Free Germany Committee) in Russia. As soon as the Russians have penetrated Germany in depth this Committee will transfer to German soil and pronounce itself the Provisional German Government. Should this occur by the time of the "Big Three" Roosevelt-Churchill-Stalin conference, the Provisional Government will, with the support of the Kremlin, negotiate an armistice with the "Big Three."

Whatever Roosevelt's thoughts were about the Vessel intelligence, these telegrams—58A, 59A, and 60A—were denounced by General John E. Hull, chief of the Operations and Plans Division of the U.S. General Staff, a distinguished strategist, later supreme commander in the Far East, and one of the United States' truly outstanding staff officers. In a telegram of warning on February 4, 1945, to General Marshall, Admiral Leahy, the other members of the Joint Chiefs, and the director of military intelligence, General Bissell, all of whom were in Roosevelt's party on their way to or at Yalta, General Hull declared that the Vessel telegrams were "straight propaganda" and part of "continuing Japanese attempts to cause conflict among the United Nations." It was "likely that the Japanese planted the entire subject matter" of these three telegrams and that the "OSS has happened on a cover [or deception] plan."[22]

The stakes involved in the Vessel traffic had now become large. With such dissemination as General Hull had seen fit to give his opinions, which may have been based on comparison intelligence derived from Magic, the reputation of OSS SI was once more at stake. That was important to WJD. But more important to the Grand Alliance was the growing evidence that attempts were being made, perhaps successfully, given FDR's state of mental health, to influence Roosevelt before and during the Yalta Conference.

Doering now entered the case as an inspector general in the absence of Donovan, who was not due back in Washington from Chungking until the seventh or the eighth. Doering had held the view that Vessel was too good to be true, that the Vatican would never handle its most secret papers of state in such a penetrable manner—after all, it had had a bureaucracy for this purpose since the fifth century. But what had confounded Doering until now was what or who might lay behind the affair. Any one of a number of factors had occurred to him:

§ Genuine Japanese peace feelers.

§ An extremely clever German deception operation intended to make the United States overcommit military strength in the Pacific at the expense of the European theater.

§ A German attempt, as clever, to cause a split within the Grand Alliance.

§ Somebody trying to make money out of OSS with false information.

All were possible. Worse, all were probable.

On February 15, 1945, came the first sign that Doering might have been right in his suspicions. As a result of a warning from Angleton, Joyce, who had been joined in his investigation by the OSS's brilliant signals chief in Italy, Colonel Peter Mero, reported:

We have very good reason to believe that VESSEL service is not exclusive OSS source. It is virtually certain that several other governments have access to this source. These governments include neutrals which, in turn, implies the possibility that said reports reach enemy. This raises the following implications: first our own reports may be subject to plants; second suggest you consider advisability disclosing to your customers that we are aware of this circumstance; third, suggest you also consider appropriately notifying White House and State Department that all activities, reports, and discussions of U.S. officials near the VESSEL source are most probably subject to leakage.

Joyce and Mero concluded that Angleton was "well informed of situation and will take such action at the appropriate time as is deemed necessary."[23]

Despite the red light, Donovan, now back at his desk in OSS headquarters, did not hesitate to send Vessel's next report to FDR. At the same time WJD asked Assistant Secretary of State James Clement Dunn for an opinion, for as Donovan stated, he found the content of Vessel Report 67A "startling." Dated February 16, 1945, it read:

The following is a résumé of the first talk between Myron Taylor and Harada Ken, Japanese ambassador to the Holy See, as reported by Vessel:

Harada declared that Japanese elements desirous of peace are not responsible for the Pacific war, and that those elements might make their will felt if the Anglo-Americans would offer acceptable terms.

Taylor reminded Harada that American public opinion still remembers the unprovoked attack on Pearl Harbor. He promised, however, to initiate a friendly investigation of the possibilities for negotiation.

Taylor and Harada agreed that the terms of the two belligerent groups, as they knew them, were too far apart to permit negotiations.

Harada stated that the United States' chief war aim apparently was a victory that would give Japanese pacifist elements ascendancy over the military and prevent any future militarist aggression. He added that Japan was exhausted by the war she had been fighting since 1937, and that she needs a long period of peace.[24]

Clearly Donovan sent the White House that report, believing that Source Vessel was still trusted by OSS SI. Whatever doubts may have existed about Vessel had not been communicated to Donovan on the sixteenth, for that day Colonel Heppner wired him from Chungking to complain that he was not receiving Vessel's material and asking for his help. Donovan asked Lieutenant Commander Turner McBaine, deputy chief of the Far East division of SI, why Heppner was not receiving Vessel material as arranged, and McBaine advised Donovan that there was "grave doubt as to the validity" of Vessel's reports.[25]

This was apparently the first time WJD was made aware that Source Vessel was tainted meat. Why General Magruder and Whitney Shepardson, the two SI executives most responsible for Vessel, should have taken so long to warn him is mysterious, if not suspicious. Yet WJD could have been in no doubt by the next day, for Magruder and Shepardson sent him a copy of their telegram to Joyce and Angleton in Rome. In that telegram Magruder and Shepardson stated that the entire Vessel series was now judged to be "a mixture of the obvious, the unimportant if true, and plants." For the time being, therefore, they were "withholding the dissemination of most of this material."[26]

Then came Assistant Secretary of State Dunn's information regarding Vessel Report 67A of February 16: "We immediately sent a telegram to Myron Taylor asking him if he had a conversation with the Japanese Ambassador as reported. We have now received a reply from Mr. Taylor which says that he has not seen or talked with [Harada Ken]."[27]

Vessel had invented the entire story of Harada's meeting with Taylor. Vessel was, therefore, a total fraud, a faker, a fabricator. All his intelligence had been, and remained, valueless.

Now seriously embarrassed, Donovan established that among Vessel's past and present customers were OSS SI, OSS X-2, both of which were purchasing the same information, Tass, Reuters, the French news agency, and the Polish, British, American, and Argentinian embassies and that during the German occupation of Rome Vessel had been an informant for German and Japanese newspapers. Other customers had included the British intelligence services.

Donovan now had the difficult and embarrassing task of explaining to the administration that Source Vessel had proved fraudulent. That he did with considerable dexterity, for example, writing to Assistant Secretary Dunn:

> I was glad to have your letter of 2 March relative to the falsity of the statement in the Vessel report I sent to you.
>
> Your statement confirmed us in our suspicion of the source of this material.
>
> For some time we have been inquiring into information coming from a certain source in that institution. As a result of that investigation, we find that a number of persons have been gathering and selling information alleged to have been culled from actual documents there. . . .[28]

General Magruder was given the delicate task of advising the White House, and he did through General Julius Holmes, an assistant secretary of state who was known in FDR's circle. Magruder was also given another painful task: informing Scamporini and Angleton of Donovan's opinion of the Vessel affair. That he did in a telegram on March 3, 1945. Whereas "some unimportant items of Vessel material may be based on factual knowledge of the source, the more important items are believed to be manufactured by the source out of whole cloth or are plants." Consequently, "we are completely withholding dissemination of this material."[29]

That was the end of the matter so far as OSS SI was concerned. OSS X-2 was, however, permitted to continue the case after SI had terminated its connection with Vessel. Angleton continued to receive Vessel material for several months, in return for a retainer of $500 a month. The purpose was not to gather intelligence but to maintain the contact so that surveillance could continue. The hope: It would be established who or what lay behind this affair. In due course Angleton proved successful.

Vessel proved to be Virgilio Scattolini, a short, fat Socratic journalist and writer whose principal claim to fame, until now, was that before the First World War he had written two scorching pornographic books, one entitled *Such Women,* which was about the experiences of Roman prostitutes, the other *Amazons of the Bidet,* which had been a best seller. By birth a Florentine, Scattolini had not, however, remained a pornographer. He had experienced a severe religious conversion, owing largely to the influence of his wife, and he began attending mass each day. Also, he began to study the work of St. Thomas Aquinas—as had Donovan—and became a tertiary, a minor lay officer in the Franciscan order. In that capacity he attained some fresh fame with a set of verses entitled "The Poem of Holy Rome," a work in praise of the papacy.

As a result of this poem, he was taken on the staff of the *Osservatore Romano,* the Vatican's semiofficial daily newspaper, for which he specialized in the cinema and wrote film reviews. However, in 1939 the editor of *Osservatore Romano* discovered that Scattolini was none other than the author of the notorious *Amazons of the Bidet,* and he was fired. To earn his living—by now he had a child as well as a wife—he turned to inventing news, a profitable game at the time. His clients were numerous and rich, and they included news agencies and secret services interested in Vatican intelligence. Such was the excellence of his work that his news stories, all of which proved to be conjecture masquerading as fact, appeared in *The New York Times* and the *Times* of London.

Scattolini's intense religious reversion, his study of St. Thomas, his work with the Franciscans, his post at *Osservatore Romano,* his abiding interest in Vatican politics, his knowledge of the structure and procedures of the Vatican, his gifted pen (or, perhaps more accurately, his imaginative pen), and his remarkable ability for creating dialogue—all served to make his fabrications appear authentic and comprehensive. Neither did he fool just the OSS, the newspapers and wire services, and his many diplomatic subscribers in Rome. He fooled the international academic community as well. After the war his fabrications found their way into a book called *The Secret Documents of Vatican Diplomacy,* which is now (1982) to be found on many eminent shelves—those, for example, of the Library of Congress, Pittsburgh University library, the New York Public Library, the Chatham House library, the Royal Institute of International Affairs, and the Institute of War, Revolution and Peace in the Twentieth Century at Stanford.

But while Scattolini seems not to have been the author of *The Secret Documents of Vatican Diplomacy,* he was treated as if he were. The work told of papist intrigues against world peace, which offended the Roman authorities, and Scattolini was arrested and indicted under an old Fascist law, never before used, that made it an offense to commit hostile acts against a foreign country—i.e., the Vatican. Two CIA officers were said to have attended the trial. Scattolini's defense—that he was a meek, decent individual who was no spy, but only what the court was told "an unrestrained writer"—did not prevail. He was sentenced to seven months and four days in jail. And when he came out of prison, he vanished from the public scene and was not heard from again.

However, in dealing with the central figure in the Vessel case, we have strayed ahead of the narrative and chronology of the case. For in 1945 Angleton had remained on the case and established that Scattolini may not have been quite as innocent of involvement in intelligence matters as he had protested at his trial.

Surveillance led OSS X-2 to "another intelligence service" in Rome, indicating that it was Italian. He maintained that he had evidence that the Vessel operation was run by an element in the Italian Secret Intelligence Service's counterintelligence branch with the object of establishing the identities of officers, agents, subagents, contacts and intermediaries of the American, British, French, Russian, Polish, and Argentinian services in Italy and the adjacent countries—a reasonably acceptable assertion. The Italians, like all other nations, wished to conduct their domestic affairs in private after the war but, as a defeated enemy nation overrun by intelligence services of every description, had little hope of being able to do so unless they could identify at least the principals of the foreign services. Such identifications could be made, so the theory continued, only if those principals were induced to emerge from under their cover, and the only way to bring them out into the open was to dangle juicy papal bait before them. Also, the question of money entered into the case, for the Italian service needed hard currency for its operations. However, the entire affair had not cost the OSS more than $5,000.

Yet this story does not explain the obvious Japanese flavor of the Vessel intelligence before the Yalta Conference. That, presumably, was material planted on Vessel by the Japanese representative at the Holy See and then doctored by Vessel to make it appear to be authentic papal documentation.

Such a theory is perfectly acceptable, for anything and everything could occur in Italy at that time. But if Donovan was in any way concerned with the theological issues implied in OSS espionage against the Holy See, he need not have disturbed himself. WJD was restored to grace, if he had ever departed it, by one final wartime service rendered to Pius XII.

At the end of the war OSS Washington—presumably Donovan—ordered the new chief of OSS Switzerland, Robert Joyce, to the Holy See. He was "to see what, if anything, OSS could do for the Holy Father."[30] Joyce fell ill, could not undertake the mission, and gave the task to his twenty-eight-year-old chief of SI, Henry Hyde, who had distinguished himself with his intelligence operations during Dragoon.

Hyde was granted two political audiences with Pius XII. In 1982 Hyde refused to state what was discussed, but it may be presumed that Pius spoke his mind about the presence of the Red Army in Central Europe and the dangers of that presence. Also, it may be presumed that he conveyed his thoughts about the dangers of a defeated and ruined Germany being left to Soviet mercies—the old Mackinder theory had arisen again. The Pope's statements were then reported to "OSS Washington" —Hyde refused to say that he reported them to Donovan—where Hyde claimed they were "sent over to President Truman." If that was so, there is no record in WJD's papers.

It was now that the OSS rendered its final service to Pius XII. Since the Catholic stronghold in Germany was in the south—Bavaria, Württemberg, the Palatinate—and southern Germany was under American military occupation, could Hyde arrange for a papal envoy to tour that area and parts of Austria? Hyde agreed (he was and remains, by the way, a Protestant) to speak with the American authorities and managed to obtain permission for such a visit. Why the Pope had asked for such assistance then became clear, for the man he had in mind for the mission was a German civilian priest, who could not wander at will through a military zone without running the risk of being arrested. If that had occurred, the OSS and the Pope would be brought into the matter, to the certain embarrassment of the latter. That embarrassment would have been much the greater considering the identity of the man Hyde and his colleagues were to escort around southern Germany and western Austria. Hyde named him as Father Ivo Zieger, a German Jesuit and a teacher of canon law at the Collegium Germanica, who was also the Pope's confessor, his assistant secretary, and head of the Vatican intelligence service. However, Angleton named the priest involved as the famous Father Lieber, one of Pius XII's closest confidants.

Hyde accompanied Zieger to Germany, dressed him in the uniform of a GI, procured false dog tags and papers for the "GI," and traveled with him during part of the pilgrimage in Germany. When Hyde was recalled to Switzerland, two other OSS men were given the task of escorting Zieger until he could return. During the pilgrimage Zieger saw a large number of Catholic eminences, including Cardinal Faulhaber of Munich and Cardinal Innitzer of Vienna. The clear purpose of these meetings was to reestablish papal authority in southern Germany, as a bulwark against Communist and Soviet intelligence and political machinations in the region.

Zieger's mission concerned political matters, which were reported to OSS Washington. What Hyde would not confirm was that the southern German mission left OSS Munich in an excellent position for posthostilities operations against the Werewolf, the Communist party, and the Soviet and other services intruding into the area.

A new game had begun before the old one was barely over, although Donovan and the OSS were not to play it, for the Vessel affair had dealt a fairly serious blow to their prestige. Donovan had had to admit that the OSS had been hoodwinked at precisely the time FDR had been reconsidering his plan for a postwar agency. While such hoodwinking would not in itself have been fatal to WJD's and FDR's aspirations—sensible men realized that such misadventures occur in the life of an intelligence service—when the Vessel affair was associated with other matters (to be related below) FDR's successor, President Truman, concluded that the country would be better served by a new agency with a fresh director.

Furthermore, the Japanese deception did do some damage to genuine Japanese peace feelers in that the Vessel episode created a climate in which, together with other factors, Japanese overtures were received with disbelief. That disbelief, and the prospect of 1,000,000 casualties if the United States was compelled to invade the Japanese home islands, meant that the war could be ended only by military, not political, means. And so it was to be. Hiroshima lay just over the horizon.

44

The Goff Affair

The last offensive opened in Italy on April 1, 1945, with a staggering aerial bombardment of a small sector of the German front before the British Eighth Army positions. Eight hundred heavy bombers laid a lethal carpet of 175,000 twenty-pound fragmentation bombs on the German artillery and reserve positions. The bombardment was followed by another in front of the United States Fifth Army assault sector. Into an area of ten and a half square miles those same 800 heavy bombers poured 148,556 bombs of all sizes, totaling 16,924 tons. Then, behind rolling artillery barrages, both armies began the assault that was to carry them over the Alps into Austria. At the same moment Donovan's and the British operations for a national insurrection in northern Italy reached their culmination: On April 5, 1945, all insurrectionary forces in northern Italy—some 180,000 armed, trained, and Allied-led partisan brigades—rose to attack the German rear.

As that mighty offensive was beginning—it was one of the most brilliant examples of coordinated orthodox and unorthodox warfare in the history of arms—the Allied armies were entering central Germany from the western and eastern fronts. Already there were signs that the Third Reich was disintegrating. Yet in that hour of triumph, especially in Italy, WJD suffered another blow to his hopes to create and command a postwar central intelligence agency out of OSS. Once again it happened in Italy, and it was called the Goff affair.

Shortly after the capture of Naples in late 1943 the chief of OSS SI Italy authorized contact between an OSS officer with left-wing sympathies, Lieutenant Irving Goff, and the Communist party in the city. Complying with his instructions, Goff conducted no negotiations, being responsible only for making the contact. Once it had been made, he turned the contact over to his superior officer, Andre Pacatte, an officer with right-wing sympathies. Pacatte then negotiated an agreement in which the Communists would furnish intelligence, agents, and safe houses for OSS personnel in the north, in return for which the Communist leaders would be allowed to communicate with each other over OSS wireless and pouch systems. But aware that the Communists might use OSS communications for the purpose of seizing power in Italy, Pacatte included various clauses restricting the nature of the signals that might be sent through OSS channels: Those containing materials contrary to Allied political or military policy in Italy would not be transmitted. Since the Communists had no sure communications system of their own, except human couriers who could be intercepted and executed by the Germans, they accepted these stipulations. Goff was then appointed liaison officer between OSS Italy and the Communists.

Donovan approved these arrangements when he visited OSS headquarters in Italy in the autumn of 1943. Goff's operations were placed under the command of Lieutenant Colonel William D. Suhling, a regular soldier from Virginia. For cover purposes, Suhling's headquarters, where Goff worked, were called Company D of the 2677th Regiment (Provisional), and Goff brought in to help him three other left-wingers—Vincent Lossowski, Irving Fajans, and Milton Wolff—who proved themselves to be among WJD's most loyal and devoted men in Italy. With Suhling's permission, Goff began to build all-party agent chains in the north and to establish a radio station to handle the chains' and the Communists' traffic.

Establishing its base near the port of Brindisi in the heel of Italy, and working with energy and efficiency, the Goff organization had seven teams in northern Italy by July 1944, reporting on the Germans, the Italian Fascists, and general social, political, industrial, and military intelligence. By April 1945 Company D had expanded its operations to eighteen teams comprising forty-three agents in the field and an additional twenty-three agents and radio operators ready for insertion into Austria. Almost all communication between Goff and his agents was by wireless, and to overcome Suhling's reservations about giving special handling to Communist party messages, Goff had made a practice of showing him all purely Communist signals for approval before transmission.

In time, the Goff chains proved to be one of the best investments

Donovan made, as Suhling himself acknowledged. "Operational results have been good," he reported to WJD in 1945, "financial costs of these missions has [sic] been below average," and the job of recruiting, training, briefing, dispatching, and field control of the agents had been done by Goff and his three officers and four enlisted men, who had had a "high average" of messages per team and a "good percentage" of intelligence items per message.[1]

Suhling was, however, concerned that Goff was being permitted to transmit and receive Communist traffic, for "Upon assuming command of the Company I was instructed that no activities in support of any political party were to be allowed, this ruling to include support through agents or radio." Consequently, he "kept as close a check as possible on signal traffic as well as on the agents involved." However, he had found none of the traffic exceptional until November 10, 1944, when he was shown a signal from the Comintern leader Ercoli, who had arrived in Italy recently from Moscow to command Communist clandestine operations, to the head of the party in northern Italy, Gallo.

The tone of the message seemed to Suhling to violate the agreements governing the transmission of Communist traffic. Recently the supreme Allied commander—partly because he could not guarantee air supply during the bad weather of the winter and partly because Churchill was anxious to consolidate the authority of the Italian king before initiating a national insurrection in the north—had directed the guerrilla movements in the north to disband for the winter and re-form for spring operations. To Suhling, the Ercoli message seemed to imply a challenge to the supreme commander's directive as well as to be an order not only to maintain but also to intensify operations. If that occurred, the Allies would be forced either to maintain the guerrillas' supplies despite the bad weather or to accept the heavy casualties that would result from German counterinsurgency operations. The message said:

> From Ercoli, 1 November 1944: We call the attention of all the organizations of the party and of all the comrades to our duties at the present moment. The declaration of the leaders of the United Nations during and after the meetings at Quebec and Moscow have underlined the fact that we are in the last months of the war. . . . It is evident that these declarations impose upon all combatants against the Hitlerian Germany the duty of immediate action and greatest effort to . . . make victory as soon as possible. Communists and Italian Patriots must multiply their activities in this moment. If we succeed in forcing the Germans to abandon our country quickly it would be a great victory for us and all the forces of liberty. Collect all your energies, plunge yourself into the struggle with greater decisions, conscious of the fact that it will be the last decisive effort. Arrange then your battle lines and extend it in all manners and forms. Do not give any rest to the Germans and the Fascists. Attack them with all weapons. Destroy them, kill them. Unleash all

possible revolts among the masses in the occupied regions. Forward, for the most rapid complete liberation of our country.[2]

Suhling decided the time had come to stop allowing the Communists to use his wireless links with the north. He wrote to Glavin that "We question the propriety as well as the advisability of continuing to allow the Communist Party to send messages to the field," although he was compelled to admit: "The work the Communist agents are doing for me is excellent in every respect."

But, Suhling also pointed out, producing as evidence a message from an American agent work-named Mercury, the Communists were becoming increasingly cocksure, difficult to manage, and conspiratorial as their power in the north grew. As Mercury warned, the OSS's Communist agents were spreading propaganda, which was preventing union with the center and right of the Committee of National Liberation, the Italian controlling authority of the guerrilla movement in the north, and unless the Communists were placed under his command and he was consulted about the identity and politics of all agents entering and leaving his zone of operations in the north, his mission was "coming out pronto."

Plainly the Communists intended to try to seize power in the north of Italy and were resorting to every means to obtain American arms supplies and gold to enable them to do so, and as Suhling said in his letter to Glavin, their intentions were now so clear that he wanted a ruling from headquarters to enable him to prevent the Communists from sending messages that "run along party lines."

The ruling was not, however, forthcoming. In his reply Glavin expressed the view that Ercoli's message "does not violate the OSS policy of not participating in politics," and Suhling was instructed to continue to afford the Communists use of OSS communications. Glavin did assure Suhling, however, that he would review Goff's back traffic to see whether there had been any violation of the agreements. While that was being done, matters took a serious turn in Washington.

On March 13, 1945, a House military affairs subcommittee announced that it was investigating the loyalty of fourteen soldiers who were Communists, among them Goff, Wolff, and Fajans. Donovan ordered a check of the men in all personnel and security files at OSS headquarters. The files showed only laudatory, not derogatory, references. At the same time he asked Doering for a paper on official policy regarding the employment of Communists.

Doering pointed out that in December 1944 the War Department had issued a directive stating "in effect that membership of the Communist Party will not affect the status of Army personnel if it is established that their loyalty to this country is greater than any other loyalty."[3] The Hatch

Act forbade using any congressional appropriation to pay the salary and wage of any person who advocated the overthrow of the government by force or violence, but the Supreme Court "has recently expressly stated that it has not yet decided whether the Communist Party does in fact advocate the overthrow of the government by force or violence." The attorney general had made "such a ruling as an administrative finding of fact," and since then the Communist party of America had been disbanded. The "principles of its successor do not, so far as can be shown, advocate overthrow of the government by such means."

Doering advised that the "position of OSS is not identical with that of the War Department," in that it "may choose the personnel which it wishes assigned . . . whether they be Army, Navy, or civilians." The OSS was not "compelled to take on any personnel whom for any reason we may regard as unsuitable for work in this agency."

Its policy toward civilians was:

> All Civil Service personnel, if they have not already been approved by the Civil Service Commission, are investigated by that commission and a determination made by it as to the fitness of the employee for government employment. To the best of my knowledge, in each instance where the Civil Service Commission has made a final ruling of ineligibility, that decision has been accepted by OSS. The converse has not always been true. We have at times deemed it in the best interests of the government not to employ civilians who have been ruled eligible by the Civil Service Commission. These decisions are made upon the basis of the individual's qualifications and background for the task which it is proposed he shall perform.

As for service personnel:

> Before taking any action to request the induction or commissioning of civilians or transferring to OSS of any already inducted or commissioned, OSS undertakes an examination of the character, background, and qualifications of each individual with a view to determining whether he is capable of effectively performing his job, both from the standpoint of efficiency and of security. No individual is employed by or transferred to OSS when in our opinion he will acquire information in the course of his duties which will result in future jeopardy to this country, whether by unlawful transmittal of such information to persons who are not authorized to receive it or by any other means.

But, Doering went on, "One point . . . must be made clear":

> In view of the nature of the duties of OSS, it is essential for the performance of particular tasks to use all types of personnel. This does not result in any loss of security. On the contrary it enhances the security of this country by furnishing it with the information necessary to the conduct of the war and

the safety of the country and its institutions. The only possible security in this situation lies in picking the right men for the right jobs, and this is a matter determined in each individual case by the person who is responsible for achieving the necessary results. It cannot be done by public debating in the newspapers as to the merits and demerits of particular individuals who are performing tasks in the intelligence field.

Confident that he and his organizations were well within the regulations and the law of usage, Donovan appeared before the committee. He was not, however, aware of the concerns in certain circles in Italy about the connections between Goff, Fajans, Wolff, and the fourth member of Goff's team, Vincent Lossowski, and the Communists, or that any of these men were being investigated by Army security authorities for allegedly receiving Communist literature in the mail.

Donovan sprang to his men's defense, declaring emphatically that they were loyal, brave, efficient Americans, and informed the subcommittee: "These men I've been in the slit trenches with. I've been in the muck with, and I'd measure them up with any men." He did not "find they were communists. I found that they were not."[4]

Since he usually measured his words very carefully, it is not clear why Donovan was so emphatic about his men's political beliefs. Nevertheless, he was at precisely the moment another element entered a situation that was becoming, in large part without his knowledge, increasingly serious: At that moment Glavin was being informed that the U.S. Army's Counterintelligence Corps had instituted mail surveillance on Goff, Lossowski, Fajans, and Wolff.

This was followed by a notification from the chief of counterintelligence at Allied Forces Headquarters, Colonel Earle B. Nichols, to the head of OSS X-2 Italy, Major Graham Erdwurm, that his headquarters "wished OSS to act quickly on the evacuation of certain officers immediately after [Victory in Italy] Day." The "certain officers" included Goff, Lossowski, Wolff, and Fajans.

No reason was given, but when the chief of OSS SI Italy, Vincent Scamporino, called at Glavin's headquarters in Caserta, he was advised of the concern of the Army counterintelligence people about men who were on his staff and was asked to review and give an opinion on Goff's back traffic. The question was whether the traffic showed that Goff and his colleagues had been abetting a Communist revolution in northern Italy.

Scamporino, unaware evidently that Donovan had already defended the men publicly, read the traffic and declared that the messages he had read contained material outside the Pacatte agreements. He then wrote a memorandum for Glavin and Suhling, setting forth what he considered the evidence for his opinion:

It has been a long-standing OSS rule, and indeed a policy of the Theater Commander, to keep outside Italian political affairs and to lend no aid to any political group. Despite this, it is apparent from the following analysis of cable traffic on the Goff Chain that information of operational interest to the Communist Party in Italy is being transmitted to Communist leaders over OSS communications. In order to appreciate the extent of this misuse of OSS facilities, it is necessary to review briefly the position of the Communists in Italy.

The Communist Party, like all other political parties in Italy, has been confronted with the problem of organizing its movement, both in Liberated and Occupied Italy. Under the leadership of three Moscow-trained Communists—Togliatti, Grieco and Scoccimarro—it has long been its policy to infiltrate all branches of Italian political and economic life. In the government it plays "possom" [sic], waiting for the proper moment when it should strike to seize total power. Communists have succeeded in practically nullifying the Socialist Party by virtue of a pact, and through the Italian Confederation of Labor, now seeks to control the labor movement—thereby the masses—minimizing the competition of the Christian Democrats. The Communist plan has been to obtain control by joining with other parties, under the guise of a "united front." Once the unification is effected the Communists invariably find themselves holding top positions and working astutely to undermine the other members in the so-called "united front." While this work has been proceeding effectively, it has become increasingly important to Togliatti and his colleagues . . . to know what success the Communists are having in Occupied Italy.[5]

Scamporino produced a number of Communist signals passed by Goff, together with his analysis of their true meanings. A fair sample was a message from a Communist agent called Odette to Togliatti on March 11, 1944, which stated: "Our position for transforming the Partisan Formations into regular military units have [sic] been accepted in the most essential points. We can realize it." That was interpreted by Scamporino to mean that Togliatti's policy of infiltrating the Italian Army was succeeding, a matter vital to the Communists since "only with the Army can any insurrection succeed."

Scamporino also took political exception to a number of other signals:

7 March 1945, to Ercoli: The "Giunta of Intesa," in order to strengthen unity of action and to create, in the common fight, the premises for the creation of the single large Marxist-Leninist Party of the working class, has decided to promote a general subscription in favor of the "Avanti" and "Unità," to begin the publication of a common chain of Marxist and Leninist articles, and to publish a bulletin of proletarian unity. This press communiqué was approved at the meeting of the Socialist-Communist Committee on 26 January. [signed] Gallo.

8 March 1945, To his excellency Scoccimarro, Minister for Occupied Italy. The representative of the Democrazia Cristiana has decided [garble] on a separation of the Patriot forces into formations of single parties; in doing so they would break the present unity. The representatives of the Action Party, the Socialist Party and the Communist Party oppose such a proposition which is against the unitarian principle, and they call for your urgent intervention in regard to the Democrazia Cristiana and instructions on the subject. Such a question is of extremely urgent nature due to the developments of the military situation. [signed] For the Action Party, Sergio; for the Socialist Party, Giorgio; for the Communist Party, Mario.

11 March 1945, from Odette for Palmiro Togliatti: The great Soviet victory has facilitated the reactivation of the Partisan movement and also of the masses. Strike at OM. Brescia; elsewhere widespread unrest; successful coups de main on the part of the SAP. Good resistance to the mopping-up operations of Siella, Val Sesia, and Val Dossola; a new influx of forces in the Partisan movement. Germans and Fascists are starting again attempts at compromise. Our intention is surrender or death. Our position for transforming the Partisan Formations into regular military units [sic] have been accepted in the most essential points. We can realize it. We have improved the unitarian work with the Socialists. We are trying to seal our relations with the Christian Democrats. The unit with the [Committee of National Liberation, Italy] has been strengthened. [signed] Gallo.

29 March 1945, for Ercoli: Some elements of minor responsibility of the Veneto C.L. evidence a trend to advance a proposal at the moment of liberation which would take away the authority from the central government and would lead toward secession. We are reacting by supporting the unified authority of the central government, which, in case it did not respond to the situation and the aspirations of the people, could be changed in a normal way as governments can be changed even in our condition.

Little of this, it would seem, was likely to set the Tiber or the Po afire or wreck the march of the Allied Fifteenth Army Group toward the Dolomites. To extremists, perhaps, there were undertones of subversion and power grabbing. Certainly there was a good deal of dull, earnest froth about the dictatorship of the proletariat. At the same time such material was not uninteresting to OSS Research and Analysis specialists in Italian affairs, and there was no other way that such intelligence could be obtained. Nevertheless, some saw political dangers in the content of these messages. Among them was the X-2 Italy chief, Erdwurm, who, on April 9, 1945, having reviewed Goff's back traffic, pronounced: "It is the opinion of the undersigned that [Donovan] should be made fully aware of this traffic, in view of the alleged political sentiments of Lt. Goff."[6]

Erdwurm believed that "this traffic does not reveal . . . any participation by Lt. Goff or his staff in the activities of the Partita Communiste [sic] Italia (PCI) other than serving as technical intermediary for the transmission of same." Moreover, Goff's relations with and use of Communists "merely [parallel] the use of the Socialist Christian Democrat and Action Parties by other OSS personnel for the production of intelligence or other action against the enemy." At one time or another all these parties had "availed themselves of OSS communications or transportation for the relay of messages," although possibly not to the same extent as the Communists.

Erdwurm also advised in a letter for Glavin to be sent on to Donovan and James Murphy: "On the strength of these messages it certainly would not be possible to take action against Goff under any appropriate Article of War." On the other hand, their content did "affirm the necessity" for the "prompt removal of Lt. Goff or any other officer upon completion of active operational duties against the enemy, to insure that he assumes no operational position vis-à-vis the PCI." In short, Goff had done no wrong so far, but he might do, and for that reason he should be relieved, despite an excellent record of loyal and skillful service.

Colonel Nichols, head of Army counterintelligence, supported this view, asserting that "in no case should Goff be permitted continued participation in any OSS post-hostilities program," but agreeing that "it would be impossible to bring charges against Lt. Goff based solely on this cable traffic." He added that "any attempt to prosecute might prove embarrassing to OSS and AFHQ, in view of Communist party participation in the Italian Government."[7]

On April 16, a month after Donovan had testified on the Hill that Fajans and Wolff were to his certain knowledge not Communists, Glavin felt compelled at last to advise Donovan that Allied Forces Headquarters had "requested us" to "evacuate" to the United States "on Victory in Italy Day or before" Goff, Lossowski, Fajans, and Wolff.

Glavin told WJD that AFHQ had "ruled that we cannot delay for debriefing purposes," adding that Scamporino had "reported his belief that Goff had used circuits to relay party messages from Rome to North Italy in direct violation specific orders this Hqs." Glavin declared Suhling had recommended among others Goff, Lossowski, and Fajans for promotion, that the Washington Board of Officers had already approved Goff and Lossowski, and that the promotions of the others were pending. "However," advised Glavin, "in view of above, believed promotions of all 4 should be reconsidered. Your advice would be appreciated."[8] The same day Glavin sent a letter to Suhling, Goff's commanding officer, directing him to "institute rigid check on all traffic on these circuits to prevent transmission of traffic not concerned with our operations against the enemy."[9]

Donovan's reply to Glavin was not long delayed, and it was one of the angriest messages he had sent in some time:

I do not understand why all the facts of this matter were not reported to me before this day. You will have in mind that I appeared before a Congressional Committee inquiring into loyalty of American officers who were charged with having been members of that party. Relying upon my own observations as well as available information from your theatre, I sincerely defended these men and testified as to their loyalty and their efficient service. I want now to have full information including reports of the inquiries, who had charge of the inquiries, etc. With respect to messages to which you refer, give me reason for belief they were passed, what they stated, to whom they were sent, and who was directly or indirectly responsible for them. This is not a matter which can be handled by cable. . . . Pouch direct to me in Washington."[10]

Donovan's position was unenviable. He had only just resoundingly defended his men and stated that they were not Communists. Now he had been told that they were Communists and that the U.S. Army had demanded their return to the United States. He would have to correct his testimony, with the effect not only of drawing attention to the problem but also of making it appear that he was not in complete control of his organization. Furthermore, with the collapse of the Yalta agreements, the gathering belief on the Hill that the U.S. government was riddled with Communist agents, and the first manifestations of McCarthyism beginning to appear, this was likely to affect adversely congressional support for the new agency.

Donovan's stinging message produced a predictable flurry at OSS headquarters. Glavin instructed Goff's commanding officer, Suhling, to investigate the matter fully and report—with speed. The report was soon forthcoming. In July 1944 Goff had behind enemy lines seven teams, almost all of them Communist. By April 1945 the organization had eighteen, with forty-three agents. In addition, there were twenty-three agents and wireless operators being held at base for operations into Austria. Suhling—a gentleman of the right—declared: "Operational results have been good. Recent teams infiltrated have been briefed to stress intelligence as much as operations, this in view of the general military situation as well as general Army directives restricting unlimited organizations of partisans. Financial costs of these missions has [sic] been above average."[11]

Between November 10, 1944, and April 15, 1945, when the Goff chains had ten wireless stations in enemy territory, the stations transmitted 2,232 messages. Suhling reported each message contained an average of 0.86 intelligence items, as against 0.77 per message for non-American stations' traffic, against which Goff's was compared. Goff's was a high average, and the small number of nonintelligence service messages sent and received reflected a high degree of efficiency.

From all the facts before him, Suhling advised Glavin, it appeared:

a. That whether wisely or unwisely agreement was made to use Communist agents for intelligence and operational purposes. b. That the existence of such an agreement was made known to [OSS headquarters] as soon as it was made known to me. c. That [OSS headquarters] concurred in the continuance of said agreement. d. That traffic since [OSS] policy was enunciated has been within the limitations set forth. e. That intelligence has been of a high intelligence and operational value, fully in line with other field stations. . . . g. That advice and instructions given in . . . non-intelligence and non-operational messages has been sound and along the lines desired by all Allied agencies.

In Suhling's opinion:

a. OSS had certain intelligence and operational objectives to obtain, among which was political intelligence, regardless of the color of the intelligence. We have agents from all political parties. The Communist Party is among the stronger in North Italy. To leave out contacts with it would seem disastrous for a balanced intelligence picture.

b. The agreement with the Communist Party opened an avenue to political intelligence not otherwise available and at the same time provided for valuable military and operations intelligence.

c. The price has been cheap for the results obtained.

d. Criticism cannot properly be made of Lt. Goff, etc., for carrying out an agreement concurred in by [OSS headquarters].

e. Revision of the policy or cancelling of the agreement will mean loss of very valuable field missions, which at this date would seem inexcusable from both military and political standpoints.

Suhling's operations officer, Major Judson B. Smith, who had worked closely with Goff and his colleagues, was also directed to make a report. Smith wrote by return that the Goff group had performed its duties in "a very orderly manner," "on a very economical basis," and that its agent chains and the associated training were "well disciplined." The "physical property is clean and orderly as a military establishment should be."[12] When operations were mounted, "they apparently go off with maximum efficiency as I have heard of no cases where, because of the [group's] failure to prepare the personnel or have them properly equipped, the 'snafuing' of an operation resulted." All four men were "unsparing in their time; attend diligently to their duties with every semblance of whole-hearted patriotism in winning the war." The "direction of their missions has been intelligent and in no single case have I observed a signal going to the field that did not deal with straight-from-the-shoulder instructions pertaining directly to the military effort."

Smith went on:

> I have observed practically every message to and from the field and can say that, on the whole, the intelligence traffic [produced by the Goff chains] has been on a par with the over-all traffic coming from all stations in enemy occupied territory, and instructions and briefing of agents in guerrilla and sabotage tactics has [sic] apparently been imparted to the Partisan formations with whom they are operating. . . . They have done good to excellent work against the enemy. . . .

In observing the signals traffic, Smith had noted "a certain amount of 'flag-waving,' indicating that the party was at work and united," but only in the "most rare instances did such messages not convey military intelligence or information along with a sentence or two of flag-waving." The signals file, in fact, showed "an effort on the part of the [Goff] mission to weld together political parties and factions into a common front for action against the enemy." Smith had therefore reached the "definite conclusion" that the "efforts of Lt. Goff, the other officers working for him and the personnel of his missions have rendered a very substantial contribution to the over-all war effort." That "these men are reputed to be of Communistic leaning or outright Communists has not reflected itself in a single instance that has come to my observation that they are interested in the overthrow of the Government of the United States or the undermining of it, nor, for that matter, the overthrow of the existing Italian government." Smith concluded: "The only opinion I would render on their background is that they appear to be men born from the lower walks of life, of considerably more intelligence than men so born, and who, like most in their sphere, felt that there is too great divide between the 'Have Got's' and the 'Have Not's.' "

While nobody could compliment Smith on his syntax, his courage was substantial. And he was supported by no less a personage than Lieutenant Colonel William P. Maddox, a peacetime tutor in international affairs at Princeton and Harvard, whom Glavin asked for an opinion on whether the group's promotions should be stopped. Maddox responded immediately: "I am not satisfied with the interpretation of the messages . . . as offered by Mr. Scamporino. . . . In my view, these messages can be interpreted as part of a morale-building campaign for the military activities of the Communist Party." True, there were political implications to the organization of the Communist military units—the partisans—but "the same may likewise be said of every ounce of support which this headquarters and AFHQ has given to [the Committee for National Liberation], with which the communists are associated."[13]

Maddox said Scamporino had divined in the messages "a cunning design . . . which is aimed at building up Communist domination." Whatever the merits of that argument, there was no evidence in the messages that this was what the Communists intended. Therefore, Maddox did not believe Goff or his associates had violated OSS regulations regarding political activity. Indeed, if there had been such a violation, the "full responsibility" lay with Suhling and Smith, whose job it was to watch the traffic for untoward political content. But, Maddox pointed out, "No two officers in this Regiment would be less likely to countenance activities which had a direct support of the Communist political program than Majors Suhling and Smith." He believed: "The testimony of Major Smith in regard to the unstinting efforts, skillful operations and wholehearted devotion to the establishment of field missions on the part of these officers is so strong that in my judgment it warrants giving favorable consideration to the pending promotions."

With all evidence in, Donovan submitted it to a special investigation committee in Washington. Headed by Major J. J. Monigan, Jr., the committee returned its recommendation on May 10, 1945:

> It is recommended that Col. Glavin be directed to return these officers to the United States if he has not already done so, and that in the absence of a specific assignment suitable for their capabilities and satisfying the necessary elements of security that they be released to the Army or from active duty, whichever appears more appropriate in the individual case.[14]

The following day Monigan gave his opinion on what, if any, action should be taken regarding the transmission of Communist party telegrams over OSS circuits:

> Major Pacatte has stated that there was in fact an agreement by which messages for the Communist Party were transmitted over the communications facilities of this agency. At the time the agreement was made, the intelligence situation . . . was such that the need for agents was acute. The Communist Party had such agents and as part of the price for their working on our behalf, the message arrangement was made. Lt. Goff was in immediate charge of the chain of agents which then began to function.

In view of this evidence "there appears to be no criticism of Lt. Goff for transmitting the messages in accordance with this undertaking." It was, therefore, "recommended that no action be taken concerning Lt. Goff's activity with regard to the transmission of Communist messages."[15]

If Monigan was correct, and he was, why did he recommend the termination of Goff and his colleagues, all of whom had done outstanding work? The answer lay in the changing nature of the war. The question was not whether Goff and Company had performed well against the Nazi and Fascist enemies—there was no doubt about that—but whether they would perform as well against the Soviet Union. That factor led Donovan to bring the men home and discharge them. But he did not do so without genuine regret.

Donovan formally ordered Glavin to send the Goff group back to Washington "at your earliest convenience." To his credit WJD did ensure that the men obtained their promotions. Then their association with OSS was terminated on July 18, 1945. Donovan saw to it that each departing man received a personal letter from him. In Goff's case the letter read:

> I am sorry that, your mission with us having been performed with great credit, you must now return to the Army from which you had originally volunteered to serve with us.
>
> I want you to know that upon the testimony of your immediate commanders, as well as from my own observation of you in action, you have been of the greatest service to our organization.
>
> At all times you have not only shown the discipline and training of a soldier, but a special knowledge in demolition and other skills required in our kind of operation. In addition, you have displayed real ability as an instructor.
>
> More especially, you have been of the greatest assistance to our units fighting with the Partisans in Northern Italy, which won the special commendation of General Clark.
>
> More than anything else, I want to tell you that you have always shown the highest conception of loyalty and devotion to our country.[16]

Only Milton Wolff appears to have replied to Donovan's letter. He wrote WJD on July 28, 1945:

> Will you accept my thanks for your very kind letter. . . . And also for the fine stand you took when I, among others, was the object of a smear campaign. . . .
>
> It is unfortunate that it has become impossible for us to continue on other missions for your organization. Unfortunate because we now have all the experience and training needed to do a really bang-up job without any faltering or blundering around. Unfortunate, too, because we liked working for you and the opportunities to do much for our country appear to abound in OSS.
>
> Should you ever require my services, knowing who and what I am and what my capabilities and limitations are, I gladly offer them.
>
> It is with real regret that I leave your command.[17]

A little later Goff was advised by the adjutant general that he had been awarded the Legion of Merit. The citation read:

> Irving Goff, 02055318, Captain (then 1st Lt), Army of the United States, Hqs 2677th Regiment, OSS, for exceptionally meritorious conduct in the per-

formance of outstanding services in Italy from 19 Sept 43 to 8 May 45. As an officer specially qualified by virtue of previous experience and training, Captain Goff recruited, trained, and placed in the field and directed teams of men whose missions and assignments were of a secret and hazardous nature. These field missions were performed in such a way and in such a superior manner that the Allied Armies received exceptionally valuable intelligence from their actions and reports, thus contributing in a material way to the prosecution of the war. Captain Goff's initiative, untiring effort and efficiency in the handling of his assignment reflected great devotion to duty and highest credit to himself and the Army of the United States.[18]

Meanwhile, on the other side of the lines in northern Italy, a second case had arisen to affect Donovan's plans for the CIA. It was also a case that would haunt him for years to come.

While he was in Italy in the period immediately after Dragoon, WJD arranged with the supreme Allied commander, General Sir Henry Maitland Wilson, a Briton who admired Donovan and the OSS, to undertake very large-scale operations to bring the Italian partisan movement under Allied command. In all Donovan arranged some seventy SI and SO missions to partisan bands, mainly in the north of Italy, their purpose to arm, train, and maintain supplies to the guerrillas. The principal early operational task of the partisans was to destroy German and Italian Fascist communications, particularly telephone and telecommunications lines, on which the Germans were heavily dependent. Then, when the Allied armies launched their final offensive to drive the Germans back across the Alps into Fortress Germany, the OSS and the British services were to unleash a national insurrection.

During their conversation Wilson stressed that the partisan political situation was as complicated and as troublesome as it was in Greece and Yugoslavia, with the left and the right preparing for civil war while fighting the Germans, and that while the partisan movement was controlled by an all-party Committee of National Liberation, the Communists were undoubtedly seeking to take control of the committee. As Wilson revealed, to ensure that the partisan movement, which was wholly financed and armed by the Combined Chiefs of Staff, remained under the control of the Allied theater commander, the SOE was to send General Rafael Cadorna, the son of a famous general in World War I and himself a centrist, to the headquarters of the Committee of National Liberation near Milan. His task would be to establish what would be called a General Headquarters of Volunteers for Occupied Italy.

While Donovan had no quarrel with the SOE's involvement, or Cadorna's appointment, he did believe that the United States should meet a request from the Committee of National Liberation that the OSS station a field grade officer as its representative. Wilson agreed this would be desirable, and the necessary orders were issued by Supreme Headquarters.

At a meeting at Bari, Donovan and Colonel William D. Suhling, the chief of Special Operations in Italy, agreed to launch an OSS mission code-named Chrysler. Its objectives were to "act as liaison with partisan commanders, attempt to guide and control developments [in northern Italy], and create a unified partisan command" under the direction of the supreme Allied commander. But unlike the SOE's mission, the Chrysler team was to have one other task, which was to prove fateful:

> . . . a decision had been made by the American military authorities not to drop so many arms and so much material as formerly to partisan elements because they had already received all they needed to harass and pin down the Germans in the North. These partisan elements now were beginning to quarrel among themselves. This distracted them from using the weapons and material which had been furnished to them against enemy forces. Accordingly, it was decided to curtail further drops in order to discourage internecine strife.[19]

Donovan did, however, intend to continue to supply the partisans with money, clothing, food, medicaments, and arms where necessary, "to keep them in line and maintain their interest in operations against the enemy. This money, in terms of lire, amounted to very substantial sums. However, so far as the OSS was concerned, the money was just paper, which cost nothing and could be used very freely."[20]

Donovan and Suhling also decided that the "special American mission" should be "commanded by an officer of maturity and judgment, particularly one with no interest in local Italian political matters and who, accordingly, would be absolutely impartial in dealing with the various Italian elements and not subject to any influence or control exerted by any Italian faction or group." Donovan's choice fell upon Suhling's executive officer, Major William G. Holohan, a devout Roman Catholic, a graduate of Manhattan College and Harvard Law School, a Wall Street lawyer, a former member of the legal staff of the Securities and Exchange Commission, a bachelor who neither drank nor smoked, and an officer who had already volunteered for just such an operation as Chrysler.[21]

As Suhling explained in later years, he "personally liked Major Holohan," who was "closer to his own age than most of the other individuals assigned to his outfit." Holohan's "background was such that [Suhling and he] were congenial with one another," and Suhling had developed "great confidence" in his executive officer "for his intelligence, discretion, maturity and his tough and aggressive attitude." Suhling's confidence had been enhanced by the fact that "there were a number of queer and strange characters in the OSS, particularly in the Italian operations, and although he [Holohan] got along with them all right, he did not particularly care for most of them and did not associate with them to any extent, apart from his contact in the line of duty."[22]

At the meeting with Donovan (for security reasons, it was conducted in the open air, as they sat on benches on the edge of an airfield), Suhling's nomination of Holohan as special American representative to the Committee of National Liberation met with opposition from Company D's chief of intelligence, Major Max Corvo, who thought "Holohan would not be able to operate effectively inasmuch as he was unfamiliar with the Italian language and was unfamiliar with the local political situation." But Donovan overruled Corvo because he wanted to ensure complete political impartiality.

Holohan was accordingly confirmed as leader of the Chrysler Mission, although the mission itself was composed entirely of Italian-Americans from among SI, SO, and OG personnel. As finally constituted, the Chrysler Mission consisted of:

> Major Holohan (commanding)
> Lieutenant Aldo Icardi (intelligence)
> Sergeant Carl LoDolce (OG wireless operator)
> Tullio Lussi (Italian secret agent)
> One Italian secret agent and 1 Italian wireless operator
> Sergeant Giarmicoli of OG (bodyguard and arms instructor)

Thus, the principal figure other than Holohan was Icardi, a political science major at the University of Pittsburgh and a particularly skilled and experienced agent operator who, at the time of his appointment to Chrysler, was in command of the SI tactical base, infiltrating line crossers on both the Fifth and Eighth Army fronts—a dangerous and bloody business. Previously he had commanded the SI training school in southeastern Italy.

At training, which was conducted by Corvo, the team was warned that security in the zone where they were to land—the Ossola Valley—was extremely fluid, with the partisans controlling the area by night and the Germans in command by day. The political situation was also extremely confused, with Christian and Communist partisan leaders vying for command and some of the partisans desiring to establish an independent republic of Ossola. In all, therefore, Holohan faced anarchy.

The operation was mounted from Blida Airport, Algiers, during the evening of September 26, 1944, and the drop was made near the Lake of Orta, to the north of Milan, at 0030 hours on September 27. Sergeant LoDolce recorded: "The night was a clear one; the ground pattern was well executed; and the right signal was flashed, so that we jumped very soon after reaching the dropping zone."[23] The party was received by representatives of the Liberation Committee and of Enzio Boeri, their right-wing chief of intelligence.

Since the pinpoint was in an area under heavy German and *fascisti* patrol, and a curfew was in effect, the team spent the rest of the night in a cave nearby and then moved into the small town of Coiromonte. There, in his briefing on the political situation in the region, Boeri claimed, untruthfully, that conservative, conservative-socialist, and church partisan bands predominated over the Communist Garibaldi brigades. That information was was not unwelcome to Major Holohan, who began to form "close liaison with proven conservative elements."[24] The reality was that Communist forces under the Comintern-trained clandestine agent Vincenzo Moscatelli were more powerful, more unscrupulous, more clever than their rivals.

Holohan and his men remained at Coiromonte for just over a month. Toward the end of their stay the Germans launched a *restrallemento*—a manhunt—to clean out the partisans and the Chrysler Mission. Holohan and his party were forced to spend the next month moving from village to village, hiding in churches and farms, until Boeri found them the Villa Castelnuovo, an empty house of twenty-two rooms on the shores of the Lake of Orta.

During this period Holohan's signals to OSS headquarters at Bari were routine, except in one important respect, one that seemed to indicate disloyalty among his associates. One of Holohan's principal tasks was to arrange airdrops of fighting stores. These arrangements were always made in the greatest secrecy to ensure the safe delivery of the stores to the correct group, to prevent the Germans and *fascisti* from intercepting them, and to protect the aircraft against attack by the Luftwaffe during the *parachutage.* While betrayal of supply drops by individuals within the receiving party, to either the Germans or rival groups, was not unknown, it had become fairly rare by this late date in the war, because of the improved security of the guerrillas themselves and because guerrilla leaders were left in no doubt that if one *parachutage* were betrayed, there would be no further supply missions until security could be assured.

Thus the betrayal of the first drop called for by Holohan—Pineapple 1 on November 3, 1944, in which machine guns, ammunition, radio sets, and food were dropped to the Di Dio Demo-Christian Partisan Brigade —came as a severe shock to him. The pinpoint was suddenly surrounded by a Communist group called the Sixth Nello Brigade, which claimed the entire drop as its property. An Italian liaison officer between Holohan and Moscatelli, Captain Leto, a man who was immediately and deeply distrusted by Holohan and later proved to be a Soviet agent, was with Icardi at the pinpoint and settled the dispute by giving the demo-Christians and the Communists half the drop. The Communists took their half away immediately, but the Di Dio Brigade buried its in the vaults of a churchyard. The next day the Communists claimed that half as well, at pistol point, claiming that the cemetery was in their area of operations. Again Captain Leto was called in to arbitrate, and again he settled the matter by giving each party one-half of the fighting stores in the vaults —so that the demo-Christians received one-quarter, the Communists three-quarters, of the Pineapple airdrop.

The point was: How had the Communists learned of Pineapple unless there was a traitor in Holohan's or the Di Dio group? With this plunder of Di Dio's stores in mind, Holohan met the Communist leader Moscatelli at the crossroads at Anzo, not far from the Villa Castelnuovo, the purpose to discuss the allocation of airdrops. Holohan took what was to prove a dangerous step: He made it clear that there would be no further deliveries of war stores to the Communists until (1) they placed themselves under his orders as the representative of the supreme Allied commander, and (2) they ceased intriguing against the royalist and demo-Christian partisans. Holohan issued an order to the Chrysler Mission to that effect, making it no secret.

Then, as Donovan soon learned, early in December 1944 the Germans attacked the Villa Castelnuovo, and, according to LoDolce, while everyone else escaped, Holohan was captured. At the same time Chrysler's radio went off the air and was not heard for an extended period—a silence that mystified and worried Donovan and Suhling. And although Chrysler spent six more months in German territory—for a total of eight and a half months—no further word was heard from Holohan.

Donovan's reaction to Holohan's disappearance was to signal all commands, requesting information, for by early 1945 rumors had spread that Holohan had been murdered by either the Sicherheitsdienst or the Communists. There was a general belief that the assassin was Lupo, real name Davide Alessandro, a professional killer who worked for Moscatelli. According to information reaching Donovan and Suhling, Moscatelli's purpose was to kill Holohan, steal the large quantity of gold coin in his possession, and arrange matters with Holohan's successor so that the Communists received the burden of the OSS airdrops of arms, munitions, and fighting stores. But the facts, if any, behind the rumor could not be investigated: Lupo himself had been killed by another of Moscatelli's killers under the orders of Moscatelli, on the ground that he had known known too much about the Communist chieftain's tactics.

That development seemed to end the affair. Then, when Donovan was in Rome early in 1945, he received a copy of a letter sent originally by Landi, the civilian secret agent with Chrysler. The letter, which had been posted from Milan via Dulles in Switzerland, contained a detailed account of the events leading up to the "capture" of Holohan, together with allusions to the relationship between Holohan and Moscatelli, Holohan and Icardi, and Icardi and Moscatelli. Very obliquely Landi suggested that Holohan had been killed not by the Germans, the Fascists, or the Communists, but by an American member of OSS Team Chrysler.

Somewhat later Suhling reported to Donovan in Berlin that LoDolce had arrived from Switzerland and had confirmed the story of the attack on the Villa Castelnuovo. Later still Icardi returned to base and told the exact story in every detail—a similarity that struck Suhling as odd since by their own statements both men had been in different parts of the same locality during the attack.

Meanwhile, the investigation had turned down other channels. At Donovan's direction Murphy had asked the X-2 group with the British ISOS service to examine all decryptions of all German intelligence signals during the period of Holohan's disappearance, especially those during the week after the attack on Villa Castelnuovo. There were a very large number of these, for the German intelligence services' ciphers had been thoroughly penetrated. But none of the signals contained a reference to the capture or death of Holohan. This was odd, for as Donovan advised Suhling, if the Germans had killed or captured such an important official as the major commanding an American mission to the Committee of National Liberation, the fact would have been reported by their intelligence services, and through cryptanalysis or leakage there would have been confirmation of Icardi's and LoDolce's stories from the Germans themselves.

There was, however, one significant ISOS intercept: a report by a German intelligence officer to a higher headquarters of rumors that a senior American officer had been murdered. But the operative word was "officer," *not* "agent," and there was no discussion of any of the circumstances surrounding the rumor. Nevertheless, the ISOS was filed away in the recollections of Lieutenant Colonel Peter Mero, OSS's chief wireless intelligence officer in Italy—a genius at his craft—for future use.

Yet as Suhling himself stated, there was "nothing that he could put his finger on which tended affirmatively to indicate that the accounts given by Icardi and his associates was [*sic*] false." Certainly there were no facts at his disposal to oppose a recommendation that Icardi be given a medal, for he had led an important mission and had spent eight and a half months behind enemy lines, and "it was his [Suhling's] judgment at the time that any man who volunteered for and participated in a mission behind enemy lines was entitled to some special award." The undertaking of such a mission was "in itself a matter of valor, deserving of appropriate recognition."[25] Icardi's eligibility for an award seemed enhanced, moreover, because, according to Corvo, Icardi had been with the partisan bands that captured Milan, the industrial heart of Italy, and it was noted, Corvo recorded, that Icardi had produced "voluminous intelligence unmasking Communist plans for the postwar period."[26]

In due course, therefore, Donovan approved the award to Icardi of the Legion of Merit for "exceptionally meritorious conduct in the performance of outstanding services" during the Chrysler Mission when "on 6 December 1944, upon the capture and disappearance of the mission's chief, 1st Lt. Icardi became the leader of the mission, and in this capacity directed its activities for five months."[27] The mission had operated in the zones of "Novaro, Torino, Vercelli, Milano, Pavia, Brescia, Mantova, Ossola Valley, and Alto Milanese," and under Icardi's direction great quantities of intelligence about the enemy were gathered, the partisans were supplied with "approximately a hundred tons of material composed of food, clothing, arms, and ammunition." That was a major *parachutage*, perhaps fifty planeloads. At the same time Icardi had been in charge of operations in which "over 13,000 enemy troops were captured" and which enabled the U.S. Fifth Army to enter the Ossola Valley without bloodshed.

Only the jealous or the ignorant would quarrel with the decision to award Icardi the Legion of Merit. His operations after Holohan's disappearance had been remarkable, and his bearing full of courage and dash. But these were not normal circumstances. A miasma of suspicion continued to becloud Icardi's and LoDolce's stories. The suspicion hardened at the end of the war or the beginning of the peace, when Tullio Lussi, a highly reliable man and a former economics teacher who had parachuted with Holohan, advised Donovan that there were "unsatisfactory aspects to Holohan's disappearance" and alleged that Holohan had been murdered by the Communists when he refused to arrange the *parachutages* they needed to seize the political power of northern Italy.

At the same time a check of the Wehrmacht's files, which had fallen into Allied hands intact, failed to show any record of any such attack as the one described by Icardi and LoDolce or that an important agent-organizer such as Holohan had been killed or captured on that night or at any other time. That was significant, for the Germans were dutiful keepers of files.

Accordingly, on June 21, 1945, Glavin advised Donovan of developments, indicated suspicions of foul play, and asked for permission to expend secret funds to try to crack the case through bribery. The next day WJD advised Glavin:

> "We are legally authorized to use Special Funds to purchase essential operational information of a confidential character. In light your situation you may spend amount you deem advisable for necessary information in Holohan Case."[28]

Glavin thereupon ordered three highly experienced and trusted OSS officers to the Lake of Orta to investigate and report. They were Captain

Bernard M. W. Knox, a future professor of Hellenic studies at Harvard, and Captains John R. Milodragovich and Donald C. Hays. Knox was to remember: "When we got to [the] Lake [of] Orta, we found an absolute idyll, one of the loveliest places in the world. We interviewed the partisan bands, but there was a conspiracy of silence. We detected that conspiracy but could not penetrate it. We put *plastique* charges into the water where, rumor had it, Holohan's corpse was lying. But nothing came up. One striking thing about the lake, however, was that there were no fish in it. They had all been killed, we were told, by the discharge from a local dye factory some years before the war."[29]

The question of the fish was to prove important later.

45

FDR's Death and the German Surrender

In March of 1945, Donovan's movements, which were always difficult to track, became exceedingly mysterious at a time when the German General Staff was indicating its desire to open the western front to the Western Allies and allow them to occupy all Germany before the Red Army. At least in part these approaches derived from WJD's special connections at the Vatican.

These had opened up in July and August 1944, when Donovan held highly secret conversations with the German ambassador at the Holy See, Baron Ernst von Weizsäcker, an associate of Canaris's. The conversations were arranged by, it is believed, Pope Pius XII, for WJD saw the Pope in July. And following the talks the contact between Donovan and Weizsäcker was maintained, as the Donovan papers show, by Colonel Joseph Rodrigo, a Regular Army intelligence officer who had transferred to the OSS and was stationed in Italy. Rodrigo's contact with Weizsäcker was through Weizsäcker's counselor at the embassy, Albert von Kessel. It was to transpire that both Weizsäcker and Kessel had connections with important members of the German General Staff, including the Chief of the German General Staff, General Heinz Guderian, and Field Marshal von Rundstedt, the supreme German commander on the western front.[1]

While the matter broached by Weizsäcker and Kessel was an attempt to surrender on terms intended to permit the Wehrmacht to maintain the eastern front—terms that were, therefore, totally unacceptable—in Weizsäcker there nevertheless remained a powerful and influential contact with the German General Staff, a replacement for the unfortunate Canaris, who had been arrested after the July 20 bomb attack on Hitler's life and was, it was thought, in an SS concentration camp.

The Weizsäcker contact was still in existence in March 1945, when the Allied armies rolled up to the Rhine for the last offensive against Germany. As a result, the secret war had entered its trickiest stage, one in which the OSS was required to display the most judicial attitudes toward the reports from its representatives overseas if the Grand Alliance was not to be damaged and, perhaps, destroyed at the most critical phase of the war—when the nature of the peace was being decided.

After several real and false attempts at securing an accommodation with the Western powers, on January 24, 1945, as the German panzer armies were withdrawing from the Ardennes, Donovan advised the Joint Chiefs of Staff that the German ambassador to the Vatican, Baron von Weizsäcker, and Kessel had informed a British representative that they were prepared to give important information concerning General der Panzertruppen Heinz Guderian—that Guderian, with Rundstedt, was prepared to open the western front to Eisenhower's armies.[2]

This contact, which appears to have been genuine, led WJD to order that the OSS do nothing until after the Yalta Conference, which was to take place shortly among FDR, Stalin, and Churchill. However, the British did do something with Kessel. He was recruited by the British service as an informant and then, according to an OSS radio to WJD, was taken to somewhere near Allied forces headquarters at Caserta, Naples. There what OSS Italy called exploratory conversations were held between representatives of the British and German military and diplomatic representatives independent of and without the knowledge of representatives of the United States or the USSR. The conversations involved, on the German side, Weizsäcker, Kessel, and an associate of Kessel's at the Vatican embassy, a certain Nostitz, and on the British side a certain Hopkinson, who was described as an official of the British Foreign Office on the political staff of the supreme Allied commander in Italy, Field Marshal Sir Harold Alexander, who had just replaced Field Marshal Wilson as supreme Allied commander in the Mediterranean.

Donovan directed OSS Rome to monitor the Anglo-German conversations, and OSS SI Rome reported that Kessel had told a British intelligence officer that "his primary interest was to do all he could for Germany since events were moving so rapidly that the complete ruin of Germany and Western Europe would soon be effected." By helping Germany, Kessel declared, he would "also benefit Britain and western civilization." Present at this meeting was Baron Siegesmund von Braun of the German Embassy, who declared that "while the present German government was not anxious to make peace, both General Guderian and Field Marshal Gerd von Rundstedt were interested, and were in a position to do so with respect to the western front."

In any event, it was not Kessel but Alexander Constantin von Neurath, another German diplomat, who went to see the German High Command on the western front. There, Neurath advised Dulles, he had received a telephone call from Field Marshal Albert Kesselring, the German commander in chief in Italy, asking him to go to a secret rendezvous. Neurath found himself with General Siegfried Westphal, Kesselring's chief of staff, who was in Germany "recuperating from an illness," and General Johannes Blaskowitz, commander of Army Group G on the western front and a close friend of Rundstedt's.

Neurath told Dulles he knew Westphal well, having served with him for two years as a liaison officer on Rommel's staff in the Libyan desert in 1942 and 1943. As Donovan informed the Joint Chiefs, the "three frankly discussed the possibility of opening the Western Front to the Allies."[3] Neither Westphal nor Blaskowitz made definite suggestions, but they appeared to be working with Kesselring, "to have uppermost in their minds the idea of opening up the Western and Italian Fronts to the Allies," and "to be approaching the point where they might discuss such an arrangement on purely military lines with an American officer." The prerequisites for such discussions would be "adequate security arrangements and personal assurances that they would not be included in the war criminals list but would be granted some basis to justify their action, such as an opportunity to help in the orderly liquidation [of the Nazi government?] and to prevent unnecessary destruction to Germany."[4]

Now events took a most mysterious turn, which seems to have involved Donovan directly.

Donovan left the western front for Washington on February 7, 1945, arrived back in the United States on the eighth, and lunched with Ruth —according to her diary—on the ninth. He then rejoined his headquarters, busying himself with many matters, the most important being his plans for a postwar central intelligence service—the plans that had been so rudely exposed by Trohan in mid-February.

Yet despite the highest importance of the CIA matter, in the third week of February 1945 something made Donovan leave Washington suddenly and very secretly—he went to unusual lengths to cover his tracks. Where he went, whom he saw remain a mystery. His OSS records show he was in Washington throughout this period, but his personnel file with the adjutant general shows that on February 24, 1945, he departed for the European theater of operations, while on February 26, 1945, Ruth recorded: "Bill did leave today for Hawaii."

It seems that WJD's journey was connected with a signal sent on February 27 by Eisenhower to Marshall and the Combined Chiefs that he had "received word via OSS channels of a possible approach by one or more senior German officers with the proposal of facilitating an Allied victory in the west in order to end the war promptly." Eisenhower advised that he had "replied to my informant that, as these reports have gone to my governments, any action on political levels will obviously be taken at their direction, and that so far as any purely military approach is concerned the channels should be those which are recognized by the customs and usages of war." He ended his message by stating he had "no intention of choking off this channel of possible communication with me."[5]

As part of that intention, Donovan's representative at Eisenhower's headquarters, Lieutenant Colonel Franklin O. Canfield, received a request from one of Eisenhower's staff officers to be ready to take part in staff conversations with representatives of the German General Staff intended to realize a surrender of all German forces on the western front. Canfield was to recall that he was not told where the conversations were to be held or with whom they were to be held. He held himself in readiness for several days, and then, "so far as I was concerned, the lines went dead and I heard no more about the conversations."[6]

The question, therefore, was whether WJD flew to Europe to take over the contact. Nobody could be sure because of the mystery that always attended Donovan's journeys. As Robert Joyce was to state: "Donovan was always flying in unannounced, without saying where he had come from. Our long association seems to have been confined to meetings between the two of us between one A.M. and four A.M. on some highly secret political matter. And then he would vanish in his DC-three."[7]

This was by no means the end of the mystery. While it is known that the Rundstedt talks came to naught—Eisenhower was prepared to accept nothing less than unconditional surrender to all members of the Grand Alliance, including Russia—on March 7 there occurred one of the most dramatic and inexplicable incidents of the campaign in northwestern Europe. This was the failure of the German General Staff to destroy the Ludendorff Bridge over the Rhine at Remagen—the bridge over which the U.S. First Army flowed to take over vast areas of central Germany before they were occupied by the Red Army.

In the period after the Battle of the Bulge, the western front was marked by bitter and bloody fighting as General Eisenhower's armies closed up to the Rhine from the North Sea to the Swiss frontier. On the Rhine it seemed probable, even certain, that Hitler had made that mighty river his main line of defense for the Ruhr, the industrial heartland of Germany and the entire Reich. To cross that river, therefore, would require the employment of all arms on the scale of Cobra, the breakout operations in Normandy in August 1944, when four Allied armies were required to crack the German line—a massive, expensive, possibly bloody and unsuccessful operation that seemed unjustified at this late stage in the war if a bridge could be obtained by coup de main or clandestine means. Several attempts to get a bridge using such means were undertaken.

At a time when there was great apprehension that the Red Army might occupy all Germany unless the Allies did so before them, in mid-February Eisenhower began to press upon his commanders what an official U.S. Army historian would call his "intense interest" in seizing a bridge over the Rhine.[8] Donovan, who had been at Eisenhower's headquarters in early February just before returning to Washington, could not have been unaware of this intense interest, for in the period in which the Allied armies closed up to the Rhine there were a number of schemes, some of them involving special means, to seize a bridge.

But all failed—until Remagen. Then, when the U.S. First Army moved up to the Ludendorff Bridge at Remagen, its scouts found the bridge still standing. The German engineers on the bridge had set sufficient explosives to bring the bridge down, but when they tried to activate the explosives they found that, strangely, the wires leading to the detonators had been cut—by, so it was said at the time, shrapnel from exploding shells.

Yet men with suspicious minds in the Allied clandestine services believed there was more to the mystery of the Remagen bridge than that, although it was true they had little evidence to support their beliefs. To them it seemed inconceivable that the Germans, ordinarily so efficient at demolition, did not demolish the Ludendorff Bridge, the last entry into the inner bastion of the Reich.

Certainly Hitler believed there had been treachery: He relieved Rundstedt of command, and flying courts-martial shot everyone involved whom they could get their hands on. And Stalin, too, believed that there had been some arrangement between the Western powers and the Wehrmacht.

In the course of an acrid correspondence among FDR, Stalin, and Churchill, dealing with allegations that the Western powers were secretly negotiating a German surrender that would permit the Wehrmacht to continue operations against the Red Army, Stalin wrote to FDR on April 5, 1945:

> . . . You affirm that so far no negotiations have been entered into. Apparently you are not fully informed. As regards my military colleagues, they, on the basis of information in their possession, are sure that negotiations did take place and that they ended in an agreement with the Germans, whereby the German Commander on the Western Front . . . is to open the front to the Anglo-American troops and let them move east, while the British and Americans have promised, in exchange, to ease the armistice terms for the Germans.[9]

Stalin then made a statement that was not correct but was fairly close to the truth: "And so what we have at the moment is that the Germans on the Western Front have in fact ceased the war against Britain and

America. At the same time they continue the war against Russia, the Ally of Britain and the U.S.A." He concluded threateningly: ". . . I think I must repeat, that I and my colleagues would never in any circumstances have taken such a hazardous step, for we realize that a momentary advantage, no matter how great, is overshadowed by the fundamental advantage of preserving and promoting trust between Allies."

Then, when Roosevelt and Churchill rejected Stalin's accusations, Stalin asserted:

> It is hard to agree that the absence of German resistance on the Western Front is due solely to the fact that they have been beaten. The Germans have 147 divisions on the Eastern Front. They could safely withdraw from 15 to 20 divisions from the Eastern Front to aid their forces on the Western Front. Yet they have not done so, nor are they doing so. They are fighting desperately against the Russians for Zemlenice, an obscure station in Czechoslovakia, which they need just as much as a dead man needs a poultice, but they surrender without any resistance such important towns in the heart of Germany as Osnabrück, Mannheim and Kassel. You will admit that this behaviour on the part of the Germans is more than strange and unaccountable.[10]

Whatever the truth of these assertions, Donovan's movements between February 27 and March 5, 1945, or what is known about them, are troubling. We have seen that there was secret contact between the OSS and Weizsäcker, and there was contact at the same time between Dulles and representatives of the German high command in Italy, the object of which was to realize the surrender of the German armies in Italy. Moreover, since the matter of the Remagen bridge has never been adequately investigated, at least by anyone with any knowledge of clandestine operations, it is at least reasonable for the historian to cast a cold eye on the generally accepted explanation for this remarkable event. Whether Donovan had anything to do with the bridge we shall never know—his papers say nothing about it—but we do know that a group of Polish engineers was at work in the immediate vicinity of the bridge just before the Americans arrived. Since the Poles sabotaged everything else that was German and came within their reach, it is not unreasonable to suppose that they cut the wires. Nor is it unreasonable to suppose that they were asked to do it by someone in the OSS. There were, after all, Polish representatives at Eisenhower's headquarters and a government in exile in London, and no doubt these individuals had the means to contact the Polish underground in Germany.

The mystery attending Donovan's movements between February 27 and March 5, 1945, certainly suggests his involvement in very secret activities, and at the time there was no OSS activity more secret and important than the various contacts with the German high command—which, as we shall soon see, led to the surrender of all German armies in Italy. Indeed, given WJD's personality, it would have been remarkable had he not been directly involved in such a historic matter.

However, there is no record that WJD was at Eisenhower's headquarters, a fact that would suggest, therefore, that he was not in the European theater at this time. On the other hand, there is the statement prepared for the adjutant general as part of a log of WJD's wartime journeys that shows he was *definitely* in Europe, *not* in Hawaii, as he told Ruth. Moreover, the commanding officer of the OSS detachment with the First Army at the time of the Remagen episode, Major Geoffrey M. T. Jones, would have what he called the "clearest recollection of meeting Donovan at First Army just before the capture of the Remagen Bridge."[11]

Certainly the chronology of Donovan's movements, and of the OSS's contacts with the German High Command, suggests some relationship among Remagen, Donovan, and the German desire to surrender. That chronology reads:

> End of January, beginning of February 1945: Weizsäcker attempts to communicate with Joyce.
> February 7: WJD returns to Washington.
> February 24: WJD said to have returned to European theater.
> February 25–28: Eisenhower shows "intense interest" in capturing a Rhine bridge.
> February 26: Ruth states WJD went to Hawaii on this date. WJD advises JCS that Neurath had met with Westphal and Blaskowitz to discuss armistice. Eisenhower advises Marshall that an "OSS informant" had brought word that German emissaries wished to talk peace.
> March 1: WJD reported to have returned to United States on this date. U.S. forces start operations to seize Rhine bridges. Germans blow bridges at Neuss.
> March 3: U.S. forces almost capture bridge at Ürdingen, but it is blown at the last minute by loyal Nazi paratroopers. Ruth's diary: "Bill back in L.A."
> March 4: Ruth's diary: "Bill grounded in Memphis."
> March 5: Ruth's diary: "Bill home for dinner." Germans blow bridges at Rheinhausen, Moers, and Homberg, leaving only one Rhine bridge standing —Remagen. Ruth records Bill back in Washington from Hawaii.
> March 7: U.S. forces capture Ludendorff Bridge from non-Nazi German troops.

Furthermore, the theory that WJD was involved in some way with the Remagen episode gathers some minor strength when it is recalled that he was stationed near Remagen with the Fighting 69th just after World War I, and knew the bridge well. Certainly he knew where the demolition chambers were, for it had been his job to prevent the destruction of the bridge in the event that the Germans failed to honor the World War I armistice terms and the Allies were forced to occupy all Germany. A primary route into Germany would have been across the Remagen bridge into central Germany. The theory gathers some further strength when consideration is given to seven factors: (1) Weizsäcker's anxiety to make an arrangement with the Western powers in order to keep the Red Army out of as much of Germany as possible; (2) Weizsäcker's influence with the German General Staff; (3) the Germans' belief that their negotiating position with the Western powers would be enhanced if Eisenhower were assisted by the German General Staff in the bloodless occupation of Germany; (4) the fact that Weizsäcker plainly had a means of communicating secretly with Rundstedt; (5) enhancement of the OSS's claims for the postwar service if the bridge were seized through a stratagem arranged by Donovan with Eisenhower's knowledge and approval, (6) Donovan's choice of the Remagen bridge out of all bridges to seize by subterfuge; (7) the fact that if WJD had been offered the task by Eisenhower—as it seems he was—he would have found the operation irresistible.

But whatever the truth was we shall not know. For as we have seen, nobody could be more elusive than Donovan, and nobody was better at the craft of not letting his left hand know what his right hand was doing.

The question of the central intelligence service was revived by Dr. Isadore Lubin on April 4, 1945, soon after Donovan returned from the European front. Lubin sent FDR a note calling attention to the fact that WJD's plan was "stalled in one of the subdivisions of the Joint Chiefs of Staff" and suggesting that the world situation required a decision. He recommended that "the ten executive departments, including even the Post Office," meet for a "frank, across-the-table discussion." He attached a note that "might be sent to Bill Donovan."[12] FDR agreed that the subject should be looked at again, initialed the note for WJD, and sent it to OSS headquarters. It said:

> Apropros of your memorandum of November 18, 1944, relative to the establishment of a central intelligence service, I should appreciate your calling together the chiefs of the foreign intelligence and internal security units in the various executive agencies, so that a concensus [sic] of opinion can be secured.
>
> It appears to me that all of the ten executive departments, as well as the Foreign Economic Administration, and the Federal Communications Commission have a direct interest in the proposed venture. They should all be asked to contribute their suggestions to the proposed centralized intelligence service.

Donovan received the President's note on the eve of a twenty-day trip to Europe of great importance—he was to move his main European headquarters from London to Paris—and perhaps in his haste he did not read it carefully enough. The note asked him to call a meeting so that the view of the government could be obtained about Donovan's proposal; instead, WJD prepared twelve letters to the heads of the departments with interests in intelligence and security. He asked each to give his opinion on his plan's "objectives and basic principles" and stated that there would be a conference at a later date, to see how "a consensus of opinion might be obtained."[13]

The letters having gone out, on April 6, 1945, Donovan left Washington for Paris. He was, therefore, away when the replies were received and could do little to prevent what was a unanimous rejection of his plan. The response of Attorney General Francis Biddle was negative to the point of asperity:

> The well-coordinated system for the exchange of intelligence between Naval and Army Intelligence and the FBI has worked well in this country and in Latin America. I should think that system should be built on rather than developing a new organization at this time. I feel strongly that no change ought to be made in the middle of the war, nor do I think it advisable to request any Congressional appropriation for this purpose. I do not believe the Congress would grant it and the intelligence service should be organized quietly and not in the manner suggested.
>
> I approve the plan to appoint an over-all policy committee. This should consist . . . of the services chiefly concerned, namely State, War, Navy, Justice (FBI), and OSS.[14]

But as Lubin told Donovan, he would take up the rejection with the President when he returned from Warm Springs, Georgia. Perhaps he could correct the adverse attitudes at a Cabinet meeting. Alas for WJD, the President would not again intervene on his behalf. At 1:15 P.M. central war time on April 12, 1945, while sitting for Elizabeth Shoumatoff for an oil portrait and wearing a heavy navy cape, Roosevelt was seen to slump forward slightly. He exclaimed to his friend Lucy Rutherfurd: "I have a terrific headache." Then the President began to collapse as Mrs. Shoumatoff ran to the front door of the house and cried to a Secret Service agent: "Call a doctor! Something terrible has happened to the President!" Roosevelt was taken to a bedroom and laid down while his doctor, Lieutenant Commander Howard Bruenn, made his examination. As that began, FDR stopped breathing. Bruenn injected aminophylline and nitroglycerine directly into the arm to expand the arteries and lower the blood pressure. Then papaverine. Then amyl nitrite.

Dr. James Paullin arrived from Atlanta. But the President was in extremis when Paullin got to the bedside. Commander Bruenn had begun artificial respiration, but the President's pulse was barely perceptible. Paullin took a glass syringe, put adrenaline in, and inserted the needle directly into Roosevelt's heart. It was useless, and at 3:35 P.M. Bruenn announced: "This man is dead."

Donovan was shaving in the bathroom of his suite of the Ritz Hotel in Paris (formerly reserved for the exclusive use of *Reichsmarschall* Hermann Göring) when the messenger arrived with the news of the President's death. Mary Bancroft, one of Dulles's agents, who had just arrived in Paris with a letter from Dulles and was waiting for the director in his sitting room, later recorded: "I have the impression of the bathroom door opening and a short man in his trousers and undershirt hastening out, wiping the soap off his throat and ears with a towel and asking someone —Russell Forgan, I think it was—if it would be possible to get a telephone call to Washington."[15]

Because of the time difference between Paris and Washington, Donovan did not hear the news until the thirteenth, and his first reaction was to send a telegram to Buxton asking whether he should return, which did not prove to be necessary. WJD then gave instructions that Washington was to "prepare suitable cable as coming from me and send to Mrs. Roosevelt."[16] The telegram of condolence read:

> Mrs. Franklin Delano Roosevelt, The White House.
>
> Please let me express to you and the members of your family my deep sympathy for the crushing loss which has come to you and the Nation. With my profound respect and personal sorrow.
>
> William J. Donovan[17]

Donovan was well aware that he had lost the principal source of his power in Washington at the worst possible time. Until now he had had little doubt that a CIA would be established under his directorship. Now, with Harry Truman, a man who had been very reserved during Donovan's encounters with him on the Hill and whom Donovan had considered a poor choice for a Vice President in time of war, there was room for doubt. Consequently, Donovan called in some senior colleagues, and they sat in his suite for three hours, discussing the implications of the President's death. He wired Buxton to establish whether protocol required that he resign—he was not required to do so. There was some extensive cabling on the wisdom of sending the head of X-2, James Murphy, who Donovan noted was a "fellow Missourian" and knew Truman slightly, to explain the OSS mission. But if Murphy tried to see the President, he failed, as Donovan was to do.

Donovan decided against returning to Washington for FDR's funeral, and was not pressed to do so, for there was much important business to attend to in Europe now that the war with Germany was in its closing stages.

He held a major conference with his staff in Europe between the twelfth and the fifteenth, the conference was resumed on April 21, and these meetings concerned the nature of German resistance after their surrender—for nobody now doubted they would soon surrender. Dulles had radioed from Bern on April 4, 1945, what was his last signal concerning the mysterious George Wood, a signal that told a story of a government and a nation in collapse:

> Wood arrived last night after laborious trip from Berlin, which he left about March 16. He reports that Foreign Office no longer has importance as regards current developments and that office of his boss, Ritter, which served as contact between FO [Foreign Office] and OKW [Oberkommando der Wehrmacht] is to be liquidated and it seems probable that Wood will be sent to Volkssturm [the German militia]. He has 5 day visa for Suisse [Switzerland] and pending its expiration I must determine his future activity and probably shall either keep him here or, if it can be done with reasonable safety, send him to area where he could be helpful in reporting on German [redoubt].[18]

That remark was significant, for it showed that the OSS was accepting that the German leaders, the Nazi *Apparat* including the Sicherheitsdienst, and as much of the military SS as could be salvaged were concentrating on the Bavarian Alps, which had been turned into an SS fortress where the Nazis intended to hold out with their gold and special weapons such as jet fighters and V-1 and V-2 missiles until the American and the Russian armies came to blows. Indeed, a redoubt had been planned, and some evacuations into its area had taken place, but the speed of the Allied advance across Germany and the linkup between the U.S. and the Red armies at Torgau had made the plan illusory. Nevertheless, the OSS took the position that the U.S. Third, Fifth, and Seventh armies, and the British Eighth, would encounter the redoubt when they reached the Alps, and it planned for a long campaign of sporadic guerrilla warfare.

The tasks before WJD were, therefore, twofold. The first was to assist in the liquidation of the Nazi underground movement, the so-called Werewolf movement, the code name deriving from the creature of lycanthropy that at night changed into a wolf, ate human flesh, and drank human blood, then before daylight returned to a human form. Donovan accepted the existence of such an organization throughout Germany, and the fact that it might be relatively well organized, for it was a dependency of the Reichsführer SS, Heinrich Himmler, who had first referred to its existence in a speech on October 18, 1944:

> Everywhere the enemy steps on the soil of our homeland, whether by an advance on the land or by landings from the air, he must be fanatically attacked, held fast and, wherever possible, eliminated. . . . Every block of

houses in a town, every farm, every ditch, every bush, every forest, will be defended by men, boys and old men and, if necessary, by women and girls. Even in territory which they believe they have conquered the German will of resistance will again and again flare up in their rear and like werewolves the death-defying volunteers will injure the enemy and cut his lifeline.[19]

Then, again in October, the SS journal *Die Schwarze Korps* proclaimed the Nazis' intention to go underground if the Allies occupied the Reich. The journal advised that SS men, who were to be declared war criminals by the Allies, were "particularly suitable for enlistment in the Werewolf," for they were "Hundreds of thousands of the best, cleverest, bravest and most experienced German soldiers" who would "do their duty in this way." They were soldiers who were "most hated by the enemy" and would therefore "risk the utmost as they have the most to lose."

After receiving technical evidence of the existence of the Werewolf, WJD authorized the publication of a bulletin on January 26, 1945:

> Available evidence indicates beyond doubt that the Nazi Party intends to go underground after the German surrender. It will seek (1) to disrupt and compromise Allied Military Government, (2) to discredit and liquidate all German groups and individuals who cooperate with Allied authorities, (3) to organize and carry out guerrilla warfare and sabotage, and (4) to guide political developments within and outside Germany so as to permit the remilitarization of Germany and the continuation of Nazi policies. To achieve these aims, the Nazi underground will probably direct its resistance against both the occupation forces and the democratic elements of a strong anti-Nazi Government.[20]

The rank and file of the Werewolf would include not only the Waffen SS but also the Hitler Jugend and Hitler Mädchen. There was evidence that a Nazi underground elite was being trained in the SD's schools. That bulletin was followed by the receipt of intelligence promulgated on February 22, 1945, that this order had gone out to certain German divisions:

> In order to speed up the establishment of the Werewolf Organization, the above-named divisions will select a number of men whose homes are in territories now occupied by the enemy. These men must be of outstanding ability, experience and courage, to become leaders of Werewolf troops. Men from eastern and western territories are to be considered, with special emphasis on those from the east.

Within a few days the Werewolf showed that it might have teeth. A Werewolf "court" sentenced the U.S.-appointed mayor of Aachen, Franz Oppenhof, to death. An announcement to that effect was made, and on March 22, 1945, Oppenhof was found executed by a single bullet in the nape of the neck—administered at his home that very night.[21]

While X-2 was still investigating Oppenhof's murder, a clandestine radio station calling itself Sender Werewolf began broadcasting on April 3, 1945, with the announcement that Werewolf was now operational as the "exponent of the determination of all Germans who have been subjected to the sword law of an unscrupulous soldiery."[22]

A newspaper called *Appell* declared that the motto of the *Werewolf* was: "Hate Is Our Prayer, Revenge Our Resolve." It declaimed, among much else:

> We know history. We know the fate of the defeated. We know what is at stake. The most sublime examples of resolute steadfastness were furnished by the attitude of Rome during the Punic Wars and of Prussia in the Seven Years War. Therefore, only one course is open to decent people at the front and in the homeland: to learn from history and act accordingly. In particular, deal with the women who desert their Fatherland for a cup of real coffee, just as harlots are dealt with. She who turns enemy's harlot shall be marked as a harlot. Men! Men! Go out into the woods before they deport you as labor slaves. Organize yourself. Join the German Freedom Movement Werewolf, assist the soldiers and the *Volksgenossen* [countrymen] who are being pursued by the enemy. Keep your children away from the alien troops. Punish everyone whose bearing brings dishonor to the sacrifices of our day. Mark him and his possessions with the *Wolfsangel.* Inflict on him a punishment which will reach every traitor.[23]

The proclamation was followed, not long afterward, by what Sender Werewolf proclaimed was its greatest coup de main so far: the assassination in an ambush of Captain John Poston, one of Field Marshal Montgomery's aides-de-camp. Eisenhower's headquarters was to announce in a bulletin on April 29, 1945: "It seems clear that the 'Werewolves' represent more than a mere propaganda stunt. They represent a carefully-prepared plan by which the [Nazi] leaders, and perhaps more particularly Himmler, hope to make Allied military government of Germany a failure."[24]

Having made the OSS's plans and preparations to meet the Werewolf —he intended to use Basque assassin agents employed by OSS Germany for $160 a month—Donovan arrived back in Washington at noon on April 25, 1945, with a gift for Ruth that she had not seen since the summer of 1940: Paris hats, a sure sign that peace, like summer, was coming. Awaiting him was a telegram from Dulles (whom Donovan had just passed over as chief of OSS Europe, because he thought him a poor administrator, making him instead head of German operations) that the Germans had resumed secret negotiations with him intended to arrange the surrender of the German armies in Italy—Operation Sunrise.[25]

Promptly, Donovan contacted General A. J. MacFarland, the American secretary of the Combined Chiefs, but the only advice he received was that instructions would be forthcoming during the night or the next day. At about noon on the twenty-sixth, WJD was informed at the Georgetown house (where he had had a scrambler telephone installed at his own expense because the government would not give him one at Treasury expense) that the Combined Chiefs had authorized Sunrise negotiations. Within a matter of days agreement was reached that all German soldiers in Italy would surrender at noon on May 2, 1945, arrangements approved by the German commanders in Italy. The supreme Allied commander was to state as 1,300,000 German soldiers laid down their arms:

> As a matter of record it may be stated that in great part it was a result of the many initial, preliminary contacts and extraordinarily comprehensive intelligence coverage, effected through the Office of Strategic Services, that the complete and unconditional surrender of the forces of the German Wehrmacht, in Italy and the western areas of Austria, was achieved. In the succeeding stages of negotiations, it was to the Office of Strategic Services that was entrusted complete responsibility for planning and making immediately available various types of services, in particular, all communications, all liaison activity, the establishing of all the necessary safeguards for the security of the operations, and all provisions for interpreters, clerical assistance, transportation, billeting, and cover documentation. Through its early and successful persuasion of Colonel General Heinrich von Vietinghof and SS General Karl Wolff, the two commanders on the Italian front, to ignore Hitler's and Himmler's injunction to fight to the end, the Office of Strategic Services was directly responsible for German troops and installations remaining intact, throughout the long, preliminary stages of negotiations.

For Donovan personally this was an excellent commendation, one likely to help Truman and the Joint Chiefs make up their minds to maintain the OSS as the peacetime secret intelligence service. Then came more laurels from the Italian front. While preparing for a rib roast dinner on May 1, 1945, at the Georgetown house for Victor Cavendish-Bentinck, the future duke of Portland, who had been chairman of the British Joint Intelligence Committee for most of the war, Donovan received excellent news: OSS agents had saved the 24.6 miles of the Simplon Tunnel linking Italy and Switzerland by rail through the Alps, one of the world's greatest engineering achievements, from destruction by the Wehrmacht.

Allen Dulles in Switzerland had learned late in April 1945 that the Wehrmacht had heavily mined the Italian entrance to the tunnel and that the commander of the German engineers was under orders to blow the tunnel the moment Allied forces approached. Donovan wired instructions to Donovan to get the OSS SI Diana team operating in the northern Piedmont near Borgosesia to prevent the tunnel from being blown. Under Diana's command, the 83rd Garibaldi Brigade of partisans, a Communist unit, was prepared for the action.

As the message in Donovan's hand stated, arrangements were made for a priest to "approach leader German garrison and inquire if he willing forego [sic] destruction tunnel for consideration."[26] The German "proposed 7–10 million lira bribe [approximately $34,000 to $48,000 at the official rate of exchange of the dollar to the lira], and priest returned to Diana with tidings." Diana decided, however, that the German would "probably take money and still blow tunnel," so a "military operation was deemed advisable." The 83rd Garibaldi Brigade was ordered to accomplish the task. At 4:00 A.M. on April 25, 1945, the brigade, which consisted of 200 men, split into two. Half, minus shoes to prevent noise, crept down the hillside to the mouth of the tunnel, which was not guarded by the Germans. They found the two-foot shaped charges in the niches in which railwaymen stood when trains passed, for a distance of some 300 yards. They were "wired to go simultaneously" and "would have destroyed whole mouth of the tunnel, blocking it completely."

After all the charges had been neutralized, they were piled up 200 yards from the mouth of the tunnel and set on fire. Awakened by the sound of the exploding fuses, the German garrison at Varzo Station, responsible for guarding the mouth of the tunnel, found itself surrounded by the other half of the Garibaldi Brigade, "fired a few token shots, and then gave up."

Well satisfied with the reports, the Donovans and their guests went in to dinner. During the meal there was cause for many toasts: Mussolini was dead, the Germans in Italy were surrendering, the Fascist government in northern Italy was being swept away, the U.S. Third and Seventh armies and the French First Army had entered the "invincible" Alpine redoubt in Bavaria and Austria, Field Marshal von Rundstedt had been captured, the U.S. First and Ninth armies were on the Elbe, spearheads of Montgomery's Twenty-first Army Group were at Hamburg and Lübeck on the Baltic—and there were strong rumors that peace would be declared that coming weekend. It was marvelous news, and WJD was in high good humor; but nothing in the past four years compared with the news that arrived later the same evening.

After dinner, the Donovans, Cavendish-Bentinck, and the rest of the party went to the OSS theater in the basement of headquarters to see a musical movie. Ruth found it "too long," but happily the show was interrupted. An assistant gave WJD two flimsies, proclamations by the new president of the German Reich, Grand Admiral Karl Dönitz, which stated:

> German men and women, soldiers of the Armed Forces! Our Führer, Adolf Hitler, has fallen! In deepest sorrow and respect, the German people bow! . . .
>
> At an early date he had recognized the frightful danger of Bolshevism and

dedicated his entire existence to this struggle. At the end of his unswerving, straight road of life stands his hero's death in the capital of the German Reich.

His life has been one single service for Germany. His activity in the fight against the Bolshevik storm flood concerned Europe and the entire civilized world.

The Führer has appointed me his successor. Fully conscious of my responsibility, I take over the leadership of the German people at this fateful hour.

It is my first task to save Germany from destruction by the advancing Bolshevik enemy. For this aim alone the military struggle continues. As far and for so long as the achievement of this aim is impeded by the British and the Americans, we shall be forced to carry on our defensive fight against them as well.[27]

Dönitz then addressed the 13,000,000 men and women of the Wehrmacht:

German armed forces! My comrades! The Führer has fallen! Faithful to his great ideal to save the nations of Europe from Bolshevism, he has given his life and has met a hero's death. In him one of the greatest heroes of German history has departed. With proud respect and grief we lower our standards. The Führer has designated me to be Head of the State and Supreme Commander of the Armed Forces.

I am resolved to continue the struggle against the Bolsheviks until our fighting men, until the hundreds of thousands of families of the German East are saved from bondage and extermination. Against the British and Americans I am bound to continue the fight in as far and as long as they impede me in the continuation of the struggle against the Bolsheviks. The situation demands of you . . . who have already achieved such great historic deeds . . . unconditional readiness for action. I demand discipline and obedience. . . .

Whoever evades his duty at this hour is a coward and a traitor, for he brings death or enslavement upon German women and children. For every single one of you the oath of loyalty to the Führer is transferred straight to my person as the Führer's appointed successor.

German soldiers! Do your duty! The existence of our people is at stake!

Donovan asked an assistant to tell the projectionist to shut off the movie. When the lights went on, he handed the flimsies to Cavendish-Bentinck. Then WJD made a brief announcement to the audience. Doering, who was present, remembered: "You would have expected a good deal of rejoicing. But no. There was a rather strange silence. Donovan shook hands with Cavendish-Bentinck. And then everyone went home to bed. I think we were all very tired and, perhaps, exhausted emotionally." Ruth Donovan reflected something of that emptiness in her diary: "Musical too long. Hitler dead. Seems to be authentic. Mussolini, also. Germans in Italy have surrendered. All seems unreal somehow. . . ."[28]

The unconditional surrender of the Third Reich followed six days later. While the announcement was the signal for a great outpouring of rejoicing, Ruth and Bill Donovan dined alone together at the Georgetown house—the first time since 1941.

On May 17, 1945, Donovan left once more for Europe, this time on business connected with the International Military Tribunal, created to try the principal German leaders who had survived the *Götterdämmerung* —the most complete defeat inflicted upon a major power in history. The OSS had been designated the U.S. investigatory unit, and WJD had been appointed special assistant to the U.S. chief prosecutor, Supreme Court Justice Robert H. Jackson.

As Jackson's assistant Donovan had no policy powers, for these had been arranged by a tripartite commission in London long before he began his work. Nor did he attempt to influence Jackson, who was a difficult man. Personally Donovan agreed that the Nazi party and its organizations—the Sicherheitsdienst, Sicherheitspolizei, Gestapo, and the like—should be regarded as criminals. He and his men spent much time attempting to prove there had been a criminal conspiracy to rule the world between the leaders of the Third Reich and Imperial Japan. But the proof eluded Donovan.

He did, however, have a strong opinion about the German General Staff and the corps of officers, both of which had been declared criminal organizations. Donovan thought this indictment wrong, for he subscribed to the view that except where there was evidence of criminal actions in contravention of the Geneva Convention, these organizations were comprised of officers who had obeyed the orders of their government, as he had obeyed the orders of his, right and wrong; perhaps in this he was influenced by the execution by the Micks of the prisoners at the Ourcq in 1918, when, had Germany won the war, he might have been arraigned for war crimes.

The issue caused Donovan's resignation from Jackson's staff, for when Truman agreed that the General Staff and the officers' corps should be regarded as war criminals, Donovan objected, first gently, then forcefully. When Jackson refused to advise the President not to support the Russian demand for the indictment of the General Staff, Donovan decided he should return to the full-time directorship of the OSS.

Therefore, Donovan contributed little to the Nuremberg process, but there is one legacy that must be explored. At one stage Donovan had included in his party an OSS doctor who was known in the medical profession to have conducted experiments into the development of so-called truth drugs. The presence of the doctor in the group led to some speculation in medico-legal circles that the OSS had developed a truth drug, speculation that contained much truth. The question was: Did the

United States permit the use of such drugs on the principal German prisoners at Nuremberg—on such war criminals as Göring, Ribbentrop, and Speer?

For some years before the war scientists and chemists had been experimenting with truth drugs for medical, surgical, criminological, and forensic purposes. But the inquiry was regarded widely as being like the search for the agent that would turn lead into gold—a truth drug was a scientific impossibility. Nevertheless, WJD had authorized a small research program—the budget was $5,000—when, in November 1941, the idea of a truth drug program was presented to the COI by a liberal novelist, Arthur Upham Pope, an expert in Persian art who lived in New York and ran a patriotic organization called the Committee for National Morale.[29]

Doctors associated with Pope on the committee and who had conducted some research in the use of truth drugs in criminology were seen by COI doctors, who expressed an interest in the potential of scopolamine, also known as hyoscine, a drug obtained from plants of the nightshade family. When combined with morphine, the doctors advised the COI, scopolamine produced a tranquilized state similar to twilight sleep. It had been used widely to induce relaxation and calm in obstetrics, and under certain circumstances it could be used to make men talk about matters they would not discuss if they had not been under the influence of a drug.

Pope proved to be an unsatisfactory collaborator, there were certain dangers attached to the use of scopolamine, and the program was for the moment abandoned. It was, however, revived in the remote hope that it might provide some of the intelligence needed to help the Allied navies clear the North Atlantic of enemy submarines in time to give the Torch convoys safe passage to French North Africa.

More research was undertaken into the use of scopolamine mixed with morphine, but the combination proved too dangerous. The program was again abandoned and then revived again in September 1942, under the direction of Stanley Lovell, Donovan's chief scientist, employing only OSS doctors. Lovell was to state that his branch "instituted a search for a drug or narcotic capable of forcing the subject to tell the truth," and "As was to be expected, the project was considered fantastic by the realists, unethical by the moralists, and downright ludicrous by the physicians."[30]

Lovell assured WJD there was no hope whatsoever a drug that would make any contribution to the Torch anti-U-boat program could be found. But he did state some such drug that might prove useful to later operations might be found. Aware that this was going to be a long war, with much naval warfare, Donovan agreed to allow the program to continue and expand. Lovell stated: "The need for such a national weapon was too acute to deny any and every possible attempt to find it." To the need for

U-boat crew interrogations Lovell added the need for the interrogation of prisoners of war of high rank, for use on enemy secret agents, "and for the strategic testing of selected personnel entrusted with the highest secrets of state." Against such people, he asserted, such a weapon would, "if properly secured as to secrecy, be a tremendous national asset."

Lovell and his associates "set down the following simple description of what we wanted: (1) It must be administered without the subject's knowledge. (2) It must induce a talkative mood and if possible a full exposé of the truth, as the subject knew the truth. (3) It must not be habit-forming or physiologically harmful. (4) It must leave no remembrance or suspicion of any kind." However, the "scientific basis of such a search gave only the faintest hope of its realization."

The project was "given the most secret classification," its "whole research [was] limited to four men of known security," and "scores of drugs were tested singly in various combinations [sic], including mescaline, various barbiturates, scopolamine, benzedrine, cannabis indica, etc." Some "were too toxic, others produced hallucinations or sleep, while others were eliminated because of readily detectable odors or tastes."

The team then turned to chemical experimentation and developed eventually a new drug, tetrahydrocannabinol acetate, which could be injected into food or cigarettes but remained "quite undetectable." Lovell continued:

> A few minutes after administration, the subject gradually becomes relaxed, and experiences a sensation of well-being. In a few minutes this state passes into one in which thoughts flow with considerable freedom, and in which conversation becomes animated and accelerated. Inhibitions fall away, and the subjects talk with abandon and indiscretion. During this talkative and irresponsible period, which lasts from one to two hours, skillful interrogation usually elicits information which would not be revealed under other circumstances.

This drug was not habit-forming, and there were no other ill effects, Lovell reported.

All experimentation was done on "volunteer enlisted U.S. Army personnel, under cover of a search for a shell-shock remedy." Lovell ended his report:

> The treatment is by no means a magic key to the secrets of the mind, but it does constitute an assistance to interrogation of inestimable value to the government of the United States. Certain disclosures of the greatest value are in the possession of our military intelligence as a result of this treatment, which it is felt would otherwise not be known. It is believed that use of this method under proper secrecy and only on problems involving the vital interests of our country will further confirm this preliminary conclusion. Properly

employed, with its use known to the smallest possible number of people, perhaps only at the discretion of and request of the Commander-in-Chief [i.e., Roosevelt], it may be a national asset of incalculable importance.

In a further paper to Donovan on the development of tetrahydrocannabinol acetate, Lovell's deputy, Allen Abrams, recorded that on January 1, 1943, the army chief of intelligence, General George V. Strong, requested that "experiments be carried out so that definite recommendations could be made concerning drugs which might be useful in the interrogation of prisoners-of-war."[31] This was after Torch had taken place, and whether the drug was used against the U-boat crews for the purposes of that operation is not known. However, Lovell's paper would suggest that it was put to an important operational use, was successful, and did provide intelligence of what he called "the greatest value." That would certainly suggest U-boat secrets.

At Strong's request there was formed a committee consisting of Dr. Winfred Overholser (director of St. Elizabeths Hospital), Dr. Lawrence S. Kubie (a New York neurologist), E. P. Coffey (director of FBI laboratories), H. J. Anslinger (commissioner of narcotics), Dr. Roger Adams (National Defense Research Council and a specialist in organic reactions), and Stanley Lovell and Allen Abrams of OSS Research and Development.

The committee appears to have started with mescaline tests, conducted at a hospital in Philadelphia on January 30 and 31, 1943. The volunteers to whom the mescaline was administered were Colonel Ainsworth Blogg of the OSS and two noncommissioned officers whose names were given by Abrams as Wagner and Kessler. The tests were a failure, for they did not produce "a proper relaxation of the men," none of whom "divulged any information whatsoever."

The next test involved cannabis indica, administered under the direction of Dr. Kubie. Again the tests were a failure, for as Abrams's report stated, "the men suffered considerable physical discomfort without disclosing confidential information which had been furnished to them." Further tests involving eight men were then carried out at the Neurological Institute, where cannabis was administered by both mouth and cigarette. Again these tests were a failure, and this time one of the volunteers, a certain Simila, "suffered some after effects and was sent to the Walter Reed Hospital." Six weeks later Simila was still in hospital, although it was thought his complaint might be due to causes other than the cannabis.

In subsequent tests, fumes from the new drug, tetrahydrocannabinol acetate, were allowed to percolate into a room, but volunteers were not induced to discuss secret matters, and the tests were abandoned. The panel returned to the program, and members of the committee and

OSS headquarters staff were used as volunteers with "good results in that it appeared possible to administer an amount of the [acetate] which would bring about a state of irresponsibility, causing the subject to become loquacious and free in his impartation of information (some of which it was felt he would certainly not divulge except under the influence of the drug), yet without causing symptoms during, or after, the tests."

At that point the committee authorized a field test of the acetate on a New York gangster, August Del Gaizo, alias Augie Dallas, alias Dell, alias Little Augie. The test was conducted by Captain George H. White, of the OSS, who had been a law enforcement officer before military service and knew the subject and enjoyed his confidence. White stated in his report: "On May 27, 1943 I conducted a field test with cigarettes containing [acetate] upon a subject who did not know he was the subject of an experimentation and who, because of his position, had numerous secrets he was most anxious to conceal, the revelation of which might well result in his imprisonment."[32]

Little Augie was "about 46 years of age, in good health, and is an occasional user of opium. He is known as a 'pleasure' smoker, which means that while he is not addicted to the use of opium he uses it once or twice during a month." The subject was also "a notorious New York gangster" who "in his youth had served prison sentences for felonious assault and murder." In 1936 "he was imprisoned in a concentration camp in Germany for a two-year period on narcotic law charges. . . . For the past 20 years he has been one of the outstanding international narcotic dealers and smugglers." At one time he operated "an opium alkaloid factory in Turkey," and he was "a leader of the Italian underworld in the Lower East Side of New York City, where he resides and owns considerable property." During Prohibition "he engaged in liquor smuggling and at one time had considerably more than one million dollars in cash in his possession."

Since his release from the concentration camp and his return to the United States, Little Augie had been the "object of close investigation and observation by the U.S. Treasury Department." White, who had worked as a Treasury investigator, had arrested Little Augie on several occasions "but was never able to obtain sufficient evidence to warrant a conviction."

White explained:

> In connection with a plan to utilize members of the New York Italian underground in [the OSS] SO and SI operations in Italy, I have had frequent occasion to talk intimately with the subject during the past six weeks. During the course of these conversations, we have frequently discussed the narcotics situation in New York in general terms.

However, "upon no occasion did the subject show willingness to provide any concrete information whatsoever which might be of value to the government as evidence against narcotics law violators." Little Augie prided himself "on the fact that he has never been an informer and that he has been instrumental in killing some persons who have been informants." He was "intimately acquainted with all the major criminals in the New York area."

Captain White then related how much acetate he administered, how he administered it, and its effect upon Little Augie:

> On the day of the experiment, I requested subject to visit me at my apartment in New York on the pretext that I wanted to talk further about plans to utilize his services in Italy. I had previously prepared cigarettes of the same brand I knew him to smoke loaded with both .04 grams of [acetate] and .01 grams of [acetate]. Subject entered the apartment at 2 P.M. and at that time stated that he could not remain long as he had a friend waiting for him in an automobile outside.
>
> After a short conversation regarding the pretext on which he had come to the apartment, I gave him a .04 cigarette at 2:10 P.M. AT 2:30 P.M., having noticed no perceptible effects, I gave him a .01 cigarette. Shortly thereafter subject became obviously "high" and extremely garrulous. He monopolized the conversation and was exceedingly friendly. I turned the conversation into "Enforcement" channels, whereupon with no further encouragement subject divulged the following information:
>
> (1) A prominent enforcement official had been receiving a bribe over a period of years from subject and his associates. This bribe amounted to hundreds of thousands of dollars and eventually included an outside investigator who had been sent in to the city for the purpose of detecting this violation. . . .
>
> (2) Jack Solomon, owner of Gallagher's restaurant, 50th and Broadway in New York, is the contact through which the inspector in the Elizabeth Street Station, N.Y.C., receives bribes. . . . Connected with Solomon in this activity is one Nathan Ulrich, alias "Hawkey," who recently finished serving a prison sentence for narcotic law violation. Solomon and Hawkey also have similar connections with the inspector in charge of the mid-town area.
>
> (3) The place formerly occupied by "Lucky" Luciano in the American underworld has been taken over by a "combination" headed by: Meyer Lansky, Frank Costello, Bugsey Seigal [sic], Longie Zwillman, Willie Moretti.
>
> (4) A man named Benny Silver was a partner with a man named Hans Brown in both the narcotic and the liquor business. Some time past Brown was the subject of a $15,000 extortion plot by two enforcement officers. The subject's brother acted as the collector for this bribe, which was handled through Brown's brother-in-law, Benny Watkins, who retained $2,000 of the bribe for himself.
>
> (5) At one time subject loaned $104,000 to Waxie Gordon. He had a $50,000 interest in a King's brewery in Brooklyn. Subject purchased and still owns a gas station in the Bronx for which he paid $70,000. Subject had more

than one million dollars in cash during the prohibition era. . . . Subject is now working a deal to handle black market whiskey. He has connections with Pennsylvania distillers who are making whiskey in excess of their quota, after regular operating hours. . . .

The information was given to White over two hours, during which time Little Augie apparently did not know that he was under the influence of a drug. Little Augie knew that White had been investigating all the persons he had named for the Treasury over a period of years, but Little Augie's only stricture was: "Whatever you do, don't ever use any of the stuff I'm telling you." He forgot completely the man waiting for him in the automobile, and he left White's apartment at 4:30 P.M. when it had been expected that he would remain only fifteen minutes.

At their second meeting, White reported, he gave Little Augie a cigarette containing 0.04 grams of acetate. When twenty minutes later there was no evidence that it was having any effect, White gave him a second cigarette also loaded with 0.04 grams of the acetate. White recorded:

> At about 4:15 P.M. subject suddenly complained that he felt a "strange" feeling come over him. He had been engaged in playing a game of chess with the writer and suddenly leaned back in his chair and closed his eyes. He said he felt that the "room was going around" and that his scalp, hands and feet felt like they had "pins and needles sticking in them." I suggested subject take a small quantity of brandy. Subject does not drink, but agreed to take the brandy for medicinal purposes. Upon drinking it he then immediately attributed his symptoms to the brandy. He said that he had not eaten for three days and that he had also taken a heavy physic that morning.

During that disturbance, White continued, "subject volunteered that he could arrange to have J. L. Lewis murdered, if I thought that would be helpful to the war effort"—John L. Lewis, the labor leader, founder of the Congress of Industrial Organizations, and president of the United Mine Workers of America, had organized so many strikes during the war that he had earned general public and official disapprobation. White "explained that any such action would merely make Lewis a martyr." Little Augie did not appear to accept White's advice and repeated that he could have Lewis killed "by some employees of Lewis' Union." Only after some difficulty did White "dissuade him from such activity."

At a third session, held while Little Augie was driving White out to Long Island, White gave the gangster a 0.02 cigarette. After he had smoked the cigarette, Little Augie began to give White some extremely interesting information:

> (1) A man by the name of Lindeman, who operates Lindy's Restaurant in New York City, paid Congressman Dickstein $7,000 for Dickstein's services

in bringing Lindeman's family to the United States. On another occasion subject gave Congressman Dickstein $3,000 to assist him in obtaining a passport to Europe in connection with the case for which he was later imprisoned in Germany.

(2) About two years ago he was approached by a man whom he did not know who had started the business of producing opium in Mexico for smuggling into the United States. This man had 300 5-tael cans of opium which he wished to sell for $350 each. Subject stated he did not have the money to handle this deal and arranged for this man to deal with Italians on the upper East Side. This man, according to subject, had been in the narcotics business for many years and is not known to the members of the underworld or to the authorities, and has never been apprehended.

(3) There is a man in California who taught the subject the opium racket. This man was formerly a partner of Oscar Kirshon. He is from San Francisco and is about 75 years of age. He is worth about five million dollars which he made in the drug traffic. In addition to the subject, a man named Hymie Hundred was working for this man.

On that matter-of-fact note White ended his report with this observation: "All of the foregoing information could be damaging to the subject and is a class of information that subject would never give under ordinary circumstances. There is no question but that the administration of the drug was responsible for loosening the subject's tongue."

Upon examining the evidence, including White's reports, the committee agreed in the conclusion that the "cigarette experiments indicated that we had a mechanism which offered promise in relaxing of prisoners to be interrogated."[33] But at that point Donovan again ordered the experiments to be terminated without giving a reason—although it probably had to do with the Geneva Convention's prohibition of the use of such drugs, the effects on Allied prisoners of war in German hands if it became known that the Allies were using, or even planning to use, such drugs against German prisoners, and the serious political dangers inherent in the entire project. But all that was communicated to the committee was that Donovan "apparently did not want to know more about the subject."

However, the question of using truth drugs against the principal German war criminals at Nuremberg—Göring, Ribbentrop, Speer, and the other eight men—was revived when Donovan was appointed to Jackson's staff. According to Donovan's papers on the subject, Jackson gave his approval for the use of the drug. A doctor who had been involved in the program was asked to join Donovan's party, although the doctor concerned had expressed doubts that the drug would have any real value or use. He also pointed to the political dangers involved in both his presence in the party and the use of the drug itself should the fact become known. The papers show that Donovan recognized the dangers, too, and when the party set off for Germany, the name of the doctor was not on the passenger list. Nor was the name of any other doctor associated either with the truth drug program or with the OSS. Although there is no definite statement in Donovan's papers that the project was dropped, it is suggested and is very probable.

Certainly there is no evidence whatsoever that the drug was administered to anyone other than OSS and Army personnel and Little Augie.

Shortly before Donovan's arrival in Nuremberg Ernst Kaltenbrunner, the chief of the Sicherheitsdienst and, therefore, Donovan's principal adversary in the secret war, was found hiding in a mountain cabin high in the Austrian Alps, not far from Altaussee, and surrendered without a struggle. In his kit was one of the three copies of the political and personal testaments written by Hitler just before his suicide in his command post under the Chancellery in Berlin in the last days of the Reich. A very long document, the political testament was dominated by violent polemics against the Jews, by assertions that Hitler had not wanted war with England and America and had done his best to prevent it and that the war had been arranged by the Jews, and by an appeal to the spirit of resistance in Germany: "Centuries will pass, but the ruins of our cities and monuments will repeatedly kindle hatred for the race ultimately responsible, who have brought everything down upon us: international Jewry and its accomplices!"

Kaltenbrunner, a great woodchopper of a man, was to prove no less complaisant than most of his colleagues, for when Donovan went to see him at Nuremberg Prison, on war crimes trial business, he offered Donovan a deal: The SD still had in existence a functioning intelligence network in the Balkans, from which, as Kaltenbrunner apparently knew, the Russians had ejected the OSS. The *centrale* (headquarters) was at Steyr, a small town on the Enns River in Austria, and it had one 240-watt transceiver in Munich and a 100-watt transceiver in Salzburg. The organization was run by Wilhelm Hoettl, head of the Vatican and Balkan sections of Amt VI, the foreign intelligence section of the Sicherheitsdienst, and the main agents in the field were Kurt Auner at Bucharest and Paul Neunteuffel at Budapest, officers of the Sicherheitsdienst, both of whom had been ordered to remain behind and submerge with their networks when the Red Army occupied the Balkan capitals. Both were high-grade intelligence officers with very long experience of field work in the Balkans and Eastern European territories.

The proposition: If WJD arranged that war crimes proceedings be dropped against Kaltenbrunner, on the grounds that it was Hitler, Himmler, and Heydrich, not Kaltenbrunner, who had initiated all the criminal actions carried on by the SD, he would operate the Steyr *centrale* for the benefit of the United States under OSS control. Donovan rejected that deal out of hand, concluded his business with Kaltenbrunner, and then left. He did, however, inform General Bradley's chief of intelligence, General Sibert, of the offer, and Sibert asked OSS X-2 to take the case over for G-2. WJD then gave instructions to Dulles, head of the OSS German mission.

Taking along Hoettl—he had been captured at Altaussee with Kaltenbrunner—X-2 captured the Steyr *centrale* and its transceivers without incident. X-2 operators then activated Auner and Neunteuffel in Budapest and Bucharest, to be sure that they were there and alive and functioning. Contact was established quickly, and both Auner and Neunteuffel volunteered to send intelligence reports. With that, Sibert asked Donovan to advise Fitin of the capture, for Sibert advised G-2 Washington: "Both we and OSS believe nothing could be lost by [informing the Russians], which would have advantage of opening possibly fruitful intelligence contact."[34]

On July 11, 1945, WJD asked Deane, chief of the U.S. Military Mission to Moscow, to advise General Fitin of the existence of the Hoettl network in Eastern Europe. If Fitin was interested in further information, he was to get in touch with Dulles at OSS headquarters at Wiesbaden. Deane contacted Fitin on July 26, 1945, and, he wired to WJD, Fitin "expressed great interest in the suggestion that the Soviets and OSS collaborate in eliminating Dr. Hoettl's organized Balkans Intelligence network."[35] Fitin had submitted a list of questions that, he stated, would assist in "planning concerted measures for suggested collaboration." Among the questions was: Had the OSS "captured other network Chiefs who have similarly worked against Soviets?"

Donovan did not answer this question when he telegraphed Deane from OSS headquarters in London on July 30, 1945, for that would have obligated him to mention certain discussions going on between Sibert, Dulles, and General Reinhardt Gehlen, chief of Hitler's intelligence service on the eastern front during the campaign—discussions that were to lead to an alliance between Sibert and Gehlen and, later, between Gehlen and the CIA. All WJD did say was that if Fitin would send one or more representatives to see Dulles in Berlin, Dulles would "present pertinent material with specific reference to questions presented."[36]

Suddenly and rather strangely the Joint Chiefs stepped in on August 1, 1945, with a sharp wire: They had "misgivings . . . re international implications involved in direct arrangements between Deane Mission and OSS on Soviet Balkan intelligence matters."[37] The reason for this sudden intercession is not clear. A number of possibilities present themselves. First, General George S. Patton, Jr., commanding general of the U.S. Third Army, which captured Hoettl, may well have protested. Hoettl had provided Patton's G-2 with extremely important information about the Red Army in Austria—armies that Patton had faced. Secondly, General Clayton Bissell, the Army G-2 at the Pentagon, may also have complained on the grounds that if a prize such as Hoettl were betrayed to the Russians, and the fact became known, which Germans would work for G-2 again? In the light of the Gehlen negotiations, to liquidate the Hoettl chains might be calamitous. Thirdly, the Joint Chiefs, alarmed at Red Army belligerency in Central Europe and not sure the West might not have to fight the Red Army after all, may well have been debating whether to collaborate with non-Nazi German officers to gather intelligence about Russian capabilities and intentions. Certainly they did their best to stop the exchange between WJD and Fitin, for on August 18, 1945, they wired Eisenhower and Deane: "The action by the Office of Strategic Services, which led to the Russians being informed of the discovery of the Hoettl network, was not coordinated with the War and Navy Departments and has not been confirmed by the Joint Chiefs of Staff."[38] A few days later, however, the chiefs approved the liquidation of the Hoettl network jointly by the OSS and NKVD, probably because the matter had gone too far to stop without incurring the suspicion of the Russians.

Whether the joint liquidation then took place is not clear. Almost certainly Auner and Neunteuffel were captured by the NKVD and suffered the fate usually reserved for SS spies, but Hoettl was not permitted to rot in jail. On September 26, 1945, while at Nuremberg Prison, he wrote a letter to Colonel B. C. Andrus, commanding officer of the U.S. security detachments at Nuremberg, reminded Andrus of his services to the OSS in Switzerland and Italy, of the many hundreds of pages of intelligence he had given Patton, and of the evidence he had given against Kaltenbrunner. Then he advised that for years he had suffered "from an ulcerated stomach, caused by a nervous stomach complaint and am subject to periodical attacks in late spring and autumn."[39] He stated he expected the development of fresh ulcers and under the circumstances should be released from jail. He ended his letter with a request that he be permitted to "report verbally and explicitly, and at the same time to discuss details as to an eventual direct collaboration."

On October 18, 1945, Hoettl received a laissez-passer from Andrus's office. It stated: "Dr. Wilhelm Hoettl is a German citizen and . . . has the permission of this office to go and come anywhere within the confines of Nuremberg, Germany, without police escort or security control. . . ."[40] Yesterday's enemies had become today's collaborators, as yesterday's allies had become today's enemies. The gay deceiver was loose once more.

No such compassion was to be extended to Kaltenbrunner. Appearing at the International Military Tribunal at Nuremberg as a principal war criminal, Kaltenbrunner was indicted and convicted of numerous crimes. In his final statement to the court he insisted he had devoted himself exclusively to the reorganization of the German military and political intelligence services. He protested that he had committed no criminal acts and that if there was a criminal, it was Admiral Canaris, whose "treason" he had established "to the most frightful extent." Canaris, declared Kaltenbrunner, had "collaborated with the enemy for years."[41]

In due course, Kaltenbrunner was taken to the gallows, his executioner being a professional hangman from Texas. His last statement was very brief: "I follow my comrades! I die joyfully for the Reich! Long live the Greater German Reich! Amen!"

Meantime, Donovan had rendered Fitin—a man he had genuinely liked —one final service. In their *ratissages* for the SS, X-2 had captured Hitler's SS dentist, a certain Blaschke, who produced the charts of Hitler's dentition as it had been in April 1945, when he had last treated the Führer. Realizing this evidence might be useful to the Red Army's pathologists in identifying the burned corpse found in the ruins of the Reichskanzlei, WJD sent this message to Fitin:

> Hitler's dentition as April 45 described by personal SS dentist Blaschke: Edge to edge bite, 6 uppers 10 lowers only remaining natural teeth. Upper right: 1 Richman crown, 3, 4 full gold crowns, 2 & 5 dummies. Left: 1 three quarter gold crown, 2 Richman crown, 3 full gold crown, 4 dummy. Single fixed gold bridge over all uppers. Lower right: 1, 2, 4 normal, 3, 5 full gold crowns with lingual bar between. Left: 1 normal, 2 porcelain filling and a pical abscess, 3, 5, 8 full gold crowns, 4, 6, 7 dummies.[42]

That was the last signal of the OSS-NKVD alliance.

46

The Canaris Investigation

When Donovan first arrived at Nuremberg, he lost little time in trying to make contact with, or establishing what had become of, Admiral Canaris, chief of the Abwehr, the German military intelligence and counterespionage service, a man who was at once the cleverest and the most determined of all of Hitler's opponents. It is evident that Donovan had connection with Canaris before the outbreak of war in 1939, and it is also evident that the connection was maintained through intermediaries across the drawn lines of war at least as late as the end of 1943. But neither WJD nor Canaris left much in the way of evidence concerning their communications. Although Donovan had connections with Canaris through King George II of Greece and Ulius Amoss, through Leverkühn and Lanning Macfarland at Istanbul, and through Dulles and Gisevius at Bern, the only formal record of their association was a note by Donovan to President Truman dated June 11, 1945, when he advised that in FDR's time there were "Contacts leading directly into the German *Abwehr* through a key agent [Gisevius] with close connections to high German political circles. Between February 1943, when this contact was established, and 10 July 1944, this source provided the United States with information concerning the plot against Hitler's life . . . early information on the preparation of the V-1 and V-2 [missiles]," and "in conjunction with other sources led to the identification of Peenemuende as the Germans' proving ground for [missile] weapons." In addition, "this source advised OSS that the Germans had succeeded in deciphering the secret code of the American

Legation in Bern and prompt notice to the Minister preserved important State Department records from falling to the enemy."[1]

For reasons known only to himself WJD did not advise Truman that through intermediaries the OSS had obtained a rather detailed picture of German experiments with nuclear fission and the atomic bomb. The irony in this dangerous connection was that much of the intelligence obtained was useless—it had been obtained already through Ultra and other forms of wireless intelligence. Its greatest value had lain in the insight it had given the Allies on conditions inside the Third Reich and the Axis powers, in the trouble it had caused the Sicherheitsdienst, and in the insecurity it had created for Hitler personally—the belief, accurately formed, that he was surrounded by traitors, could not trust his staff and intelligence officers, must rely upon those in the party—who were largely incompetent. That was, undeniably, of immense advantage to the Grand Alliance.

Now came the most remarkable aspect of this interesting association. Into the OSS had come a New York lawyer for whose ability, discretion, and intrepidity Donovan had formed high regard, Otto N. Nordon. WJD set Nordon the task of finding out what had happened not only to Canaris but also to his family—he had a wife and two daughters. This was in March 1945, just after the crossing of the Rhine and the disintegration of the German front. For a time Nordon operated alone, except for a driver and an escort. Then, toward the end of April 1945, he was joined by an expert on the Canaris conspiracy, Dr. Müller.

One of Dulles's "crown jewels," Dr. Josef Müller, a leading Bavarian Christian Democrat and Catholic whose activities at the Vatican in 1939 and 1940 on Canaris's behalf had given rise to the Sicherheitsdienst's code word for the Canaris conspiracy, the Black Orchestra, was one of the avenging angels, one of the few important survivors of the orchestra. He knew well what had happened to Canaris because he had been in the same concentration camp—Flossenburg in Bavaria. Müller told a dreadful story.

Immediately after the attempt to assassinate Hitler on July 20, 1944, Canaris was arrested personally by Brigadeführer SS Walter Schellenberg, head of Amt VI, the Abwehr's rival, and in some queer way Canaris's friend and admirer. Because of that friendship, Schellenberg offered Canaris the "German chance," but Canaris rejected suicide and submitted to arrest.

Eventually Canaris reached the Flossenburg concentration camp for important prisoners, and he was still in a cell there on April 8, 1945, twenty-nine days before the end of the war in Europe and with one of Patton's armored columns less than half a day's drive away. On that day, at Kaltenbrunner's orders, Canaris was taken to a midnight court, charged with high treason and conspiracy to murder Hitler, and sentenced to death. In his final statement he asked to be allowed to go to the Russian front as a common soldier. That was refused.

At some stage during his return to the cell Canaris was severely beaten and his nose was broken. Alone in his cell, awaiting the executioner, he found a spoon and, using prison code, tapped a message out to the man in the next cell, who happened to be the former chief of the Danish intelligence service, Lieutenant Colonel H. M. Lunding:

> I . . . die . . . for . . . my . . . country . . . and . . . with . . . a . . . clear . . . conscience . . . you . . . as . . . officer . . . will . . . realize . . . that . . . I . . . was . . . only . . . doing . . . my . . . duty . . . to . . . my . . . country . . . when . . . I . . . endeavored . . . to . . . oppose . . . Hitler . . . do . . . what . . . you . . . can . . . for . . . my . . . wife . . . daughters . . . they've . . . broken . . . my . . . nose . . . I . . . die . . . this . . . morning . . . farewell.

That was, in effect, Canaris's last will and testament. Just before dawn on April 9, 1945, Lunding, looking through a peephole in his cell door, saw Canaris being dragged naked down the cell block. Müller then stated that an SS officer who had been present at the execution had told him that Canaris was hanged by an iron collar. But the executioner botched the job. He thought Canaris was dead, but when they took him down, they found he was still alive. They hanged him a second time. In all, Canaris had taken thirty minutes to die. His corpse was then incinerated, and his ashes were committed to the winds. The bravest of all the visionaries behind the movement for a United Europe was gone.

With that information, Donovan directed Nordon to find Frau Erika Canaris and her two daughters. Müller was aware that to avoid the bombing of Berlin, Canaris had moved them south early in 1944, and they were thought to be in a house on one of the Bavarian lakes.

By the end of the war Nordon and Müller had not located Frau Canaris, and both were called to Berlin to see Donovan when he arrived there on OSS business on or about May 19, 1945. Nordon was then assigned to WJD's war crimes organization, and the search for Frau Canaris was continued among Nordon's and Müller's other work—WJD felt that Frau Canaris might know where there were copies of Canaris's diaries, which might show evidence of, or leads to, the conspiracy theory. Frau Canaris was not located before October or November 1945, when Nordon and Müller found her in desperate straits with her daughters in the beautiful little village of Niederau, one of the steamer stops on the Ammersee, near Munich. Frau Canaris received both Müller, whom she knew, and Nordon, and at WJD's instructions certain gifts were sent to the Canaris family—probably money, food, and comforts. (Later, it is said, Allen Dulles arranged for her to receive a CIA pension, which was maintained until the formation of the West German government.) Frau Canaris thanked Donovan personally for these gifts in a letter dated November 15, 1945:

> Dear General Donovan,
>
> First permit me to thank you for the human sympathy you have shown me. You were kind enough to send me Captain Nordon to help in some personal difficulties. This [proof] of your kind willingness to help me has done me a lot of good, and I shall never forget it.[2]

At Donovan's request, Frau Canaris wrote a brief exposition of her husband's career and attitudes because she wished "to show him to you in the proper light, and also, perhaps, in order to convince you, General Donovan, that my husband, together with those who thought and lived as he did, represented the decent Germany, which always existed and which will always exist."[3]

In the meantime, through the search for Frau Canaris, Nordon had uncovered important intelligence regarding the Werewolf. In April 1945 Nordon's inquiries showed that there was gold hidden at Ohrdruf in south-central Germany. The information was passed to the OSS detachment with Patton's Third Army, inquiries were made, and the facts proved much more startling than at first seemed probable: In the Kaiseroda salt mine at Merkers, a village near Eisenach, the birthplace of Bach, the SS had hidden almost all of the Reich's gold reserve, an enormous treasury of German and foreign currency, and hundreds of priceless works of art. Immediately Patton gave orders that the village and mine be secured by the nearest sizable unit, which proved to be a battalion of the 90th Division's 358th Infantry Regiment. The battalion could not at first find the mine. It did so as quickly as it did only because a U.S. military policeman, a Private Mootz, happened to pick up a pair of vagabonds on suspicion that they were line crossers. The women protested volubly that they were nothing of the sort, that they were French and on their way to a midwife. Noting that one of the women was very pregnant, Mootz decided to drive them to the battalion aid post. As he was driving them down a road, one of the women pointed to a mine entrance in the side of a high hill and said there was a lot of gold and money there. This information was reported to General Herbert Earnest, commanding general of the 90th Division, who then ordered Lieutenant Colonel William Russell, the division's military government officer, to investigate.

In Merkers, Russell and his guard found Dr. T. O. Rave, the curator and assistant director of the National Gallery in Berlin. What was such a distinguished man doing in a small place like Merkers? Rave glared uneasily at the American infantrymen with their carbines and unshaved faces; then he admitted he was the guardian of the artworks stored in the

Kaiseroda mine. Russell had Rave placed under guard and, shortly, encountered a British sergeant, Walter Farager, who had been captured at Dunkirk. Farager told Russell that he had helped the Germans unload and store the gold and that there were "hundreds of tons" of precious metal and coins in the mine. And how large was the mine? It had five main entrances, said Farager, some thirty miles of passages, and the gold was buried at the 1,400-foot level.

With these statements radioed back to Earnest, the divisional commander sent up fifty tanks of the 712th Tank Battalion of Lieutenant Colonel John Kedrovsky, the entire 358th Infantry Regiment, a Military Police unit, and antiaircraft guns. All mine entrances were placed under guard, and then Earnest made arrangements to enter the mine. When enough steam was raised to provide power for the lifts and ventilators, Russell and some of his officers entered the mine. They encountered the first money—half a billion Reichsmarks with a prewar value of $125,000,000—near one of the entrances to a main passage. Russell demanded to know why the money was there, and Dr. Werner Veick, a Reichsbank official who had been arrested soon after Rave, explained that the money was being moved to Munich when the Americans arrived. Fearing that the movement might be suspected to be part of the Werewolf's financial arrangements, Veick denied this, stating the money was being sent to Munich because the Reichsbank's presses there had broken down and the money was needed for normal circulation—a story that may or may not have been true.

The Americans advanced more deeply into the mine and about a quarter of a mile inside encountered a steel vault door. Farager stated this was where he and his party had put the gold. Russell tried to force the door but was unsuccessful, and army engineers were brought in to blast a hole. The gape revealed a room 75 feet wide and 150 feet deep, and in the gloom Russell saw that the floor was covered with rows of numbered bags—more than 7,000 in all—each containing gold bars or gold coins. Baled paper money was stacked along one wall. At that point, Colonel Sidney Bernstein, a U.S. Treasury official attached to Supreme Headquarters (the same man who investigated the movement of French francs into Algiers at the time of Torch), arrived to organize an inventory.

Some 2.75 billion Reichsmarks were found, $876,600,000 by prewar valuation. The troops counted 8,198 gold bars, each weighing 35 pounds; and 2,474 bags of gold coins, including 711 bags of $10 and $20 gold coins. But that was not all there was in the mine. There were vast quantities of precious stones, platinum, bags of miscellaneous foreign banknotes, including several million dollars and pounds sterling, dies for the printing of five-, three-, and two-mark notes, statuary, pictures, engravings, tapestries, antiques, precious vases, helmets, valuable South Sea native pieces, pharaonic masterworks, costume jewelry, and 120 cases of the Goethe collection, the works of the German genius. There, too, was a special collection of the paintings of Raphael, Rembrandt, Van Dyke, Dürer, and other great artists.

Then, very deep inside the Kaiseroda mine, the existence of a second, grimmer treasure was revealed to OSS Germany by Albert Thoms, chief of the Precious Metals Department of the Reichsbank in Berlin. Upon examination, this proved to consist of 189 containers occupying about 600 square feet. Bernstein noted that each container bore the name Melmer and a shipping tag with the words "Deutsche Reichsbank, Hauptkasse (1) Berlin, C 111." A rough inventory prepared by Bernstein showed that one container held:

> ornamental silver—trays, candlesticks, etc (231 lbs of it in one suitcase alone). Flat silver—knives, forks, spoons. Passover cups and candlestick holders, silver. Gold and silver dental work, some melted down (full bags). Watch chains and cases, gold and silver. Cigarette cases, gold & silver, some with engraved names, some with names scratched out. Powder puff cases. Silver thimbles. Opera glasses. Spectacle frames. Rings, gold and silver and with precious stones—wedding, engagement, anniversary. Necklaces and strings of beads—apparently diamond, pearl, silver, gold. Earrings, bracelets, stickpins, cufflinks, tiaras. Coins and currency of many nations and denomination—including ten and twenty dollar gold pieces, silver pounds sterling, U.S. and British paper money, great amounts of Polish zloty. Silk stockings and laquer [sic]. There were 2,656 gold watch cases listed in one box. There were coins and currency totalling 850,300 Polish zloty in a suitcase. A box with shipping tag dated 15 September 1944 listed 600 pieces of table silver. Silver dental work weighing nearly 22 lbs were [sic] in one suitcase.[4]

Between August 1942, when the Melmer account was opened secretly at the Reichsbank, Berlin, and April 1945, when the Kaiseroda mine was opened by U.S. soldiers, there had been seventy-six shipments such as these. Each shipment had been inventoried by SS and Reichsbank clerks, and the inventories of Shipment 1 and Shipment 16 were found by an OSS flying squad in a bank vault in the town of Hof. The two shipments combined consisted of:

Alarm clocks	7,811.3 pounds
Tableware	18,945.7 pounds
Watches	3,871.9 pounds
Watch repair equipment	73.4 pounds
Fountain pens and pencils	599.1 pounds
Altar ornaments	6,769.4 pounds
Handbags and billfolds	441.1 pounds
Gold coins	70.2 pounds

Other metal coins	5,806.6 pounds
Paper currency	306.7 pounds
Precious and semiprecious stones	353.3 pounds
Gold and other metal rings	765 pounds
Spectacle frames in bone, metal, plastic	532.4 pounds
Gold, silver teeth fillings	689.3 pounds
Silver bars	120 pounds
Gold bars	4 pounds
Stamp collections	20.2 pounds
Shaving razors	332.2 pounds
Metal handbags	88 pounds
Postage stamps	83.6 pounds
Drawing instruments	92.4 pounds
Small tools	165.6 pounds
Novelty jewelry	3,030.8 pounds
Children's toys	134.2 pounds
Dishes and pottery	103.4 pounds
Security bonds	66 pounds
Miscellaneous gold and silver alloy bars	28

All this second treasure proved to have been bric-a-brac taken from concentration camp victims before they were murdered, and with the help of the Reichsbank and the Reich Pawn Shop in Berlin these artifacts were being turned into hard cash to provide a social security fund for SS widows and orphans, and pensions for SS soldiers. Melmer proved to be Bruno August Peter Melmer, an SS Hauptsturmführer. Born on October 7, 1909, at Wiesbaden, he was an official in the auditing department of SS headquarters in Berlin. According to Albert Thoms, Melmer "came as a private individual with truckloads of suitcases, boxes, packages, bags, etc." Thoms understood "the stuff to be ordinary 'booty' or spoils of war from Jews." The treasure was then sold through the Reich Pawn Shop or smelted at home and abroad, and the proceeds were placed in Melmer's account. When the account reached 500,000 marks, Melmer transferred the marks to a second secret account, that of Max Heiliger, whose account also received the proceeds of the clothes of the concentration camp victims, which were sold to the Reich Textile Industry Association.

The entire scheme, Melmer asserted under interrogation, was the creation of Obergruppenführer SS Oswald Pohl, head of the SS Economic and Administrative Office. The Reichsbank received 10 percent of all proceeds, and as Bernstein was to record, it "appears to have acted as the personal agent of Himmler in converting SS loot into orthodox financial assets." In all, according to Thoms, the loot realized was some $10,000,000, a figure that Bernstein challenged immediately on the ground that this sum could not "begin to represent the total extent of the operations of the SS 'economic department' which for 12 years has disposed of the personal and household valuables of millions of racial and political victims of the calculated Nazi policy of extermination."[5] The few caches at Kaiseroda represented the remnants of this industry, and it was reportedly being moved "from Reichsbank, Berlin, by order of Dr. Ernst Kaltenbrunner to be hidden in mountains of southern Germany . . . for purpose of financing Alpine redoubt."[6]

Such was the actuarial and political value of the treasure—Bernstein estimated it represented 96.8 percent of the Reichsbank's gold and hard currency reserves—that Supreme Headquarters realized immediately that in the wrong hands it could be used to finance a revival of Nazism. The treasure became Eisenhower's responsibility, and Bernstein was given the task of evacuating it to a fortress at the junction of the Moselle and Rhine rivers. That was done with the loss of only a few gold coins —taken by troops as souvenirs—in convoys guarded by tanks, armored cars, self-propelled guns, and squadrons of fighter aircraft.

It was a brilliant stroke of intelligence and led to the uncovering of a large number of small troves, established to finance the German underground. With Sibert, WJD now launched the final attack on the last institution of the Third Reich, the Werewolf.

The first major break in the mystery and silence concerning the SS's plans for an underground came on June 13, 1945. On that day security patrols of the U.S. Seventh Army stopped a young man in army uniform whose identity card showed his left ear. For that reason the card was detected immediately as a forgery—the SS had forgotten the German Army rule that the right ear of all personnel must show on the identity photograph. Under interrogation, the prisoner attempted to take a poison vial, which was issued usually only to such organizations as the Sicherheitsdienst. He then broke down and confessed that he was Günther Mannerz, a former member of the SD at Stuttgart, and was now a member of an organization called Elsa, which had its counterparts in the forty-two Gaue—administrative districts—of Germany.[7]

Mannerz, begging his X-2 interrogators not to say that he had talked, for the men of Elsa would kill him and his mother, described what was a national control organization for the Werewolf and other underground organizations. He revealed that the Werewolf plans were circulated by Himmler's office on January 15, 1945, to all Gaue. The courier was able to state from personal knowledge that in Gau Württemberg, the southern German province, there was a meeting in the town of Eglofs, near Wangen, in April called by an Obersturmbannführer SS, a certain Tümmler, attended by some 200 to 300 Gestapo, twenty-four officials of the Sicherheitsdienst, and thirty officers of the Kriminalpolizei. Tümmler's theme was:

The legal military war will last only some fourteen days more, but the illegal political war continues. We await our moment until we may operate openly again, but until that moment the underground must continue to function. Preparations are made for an illegal organization that will take advantage of any conflict between the Western Allies and Russia, and the relaxation of occupation troops.

Of the SS personnel attending the meeting, the older and unfit members were given false papers and sent home. Others were sent with their own papers to the Waffen SS and police units of the Wehrmacht, and anyone could volunteer for "a special undertaking" in Allied-occupied territory. Of the volunteers, only fourteen or fifteen were selected, mainly from Gestapo personnel, with a few Sicherheitsdienst, and these, with others from the Hitler Jugend and the Hitler Mädchen, had formed the nucleus of Elsa. This same type of activity had occurred throughout the Reich, but owing to the speed of the Allied advance into Central Europe, there had been no time for most of these underground organizations to form connecting links with those in adjoining *Gaue*—to form themselves into a nationally controlled organization.

Mannerz went on to relate that Elsa's initial strength was about 120 to 140 men and 40 women, who were organized into groups of 5—Trotsky's principle of the *Fünfergruppen*—with at least one girl attached to each group. "The girls were usually young and attractive and were to be used to obtain information that men could not ordinarily get." The *Fünfergruppen* controlled the "wild groups" of Werewolves on operations.

Within Gau Württemberg was a command post commanded by a Hauptsturmführer SS, a certain Slavinger, which communicated by means of intermediaries to couriers from twenty-two message centers established throughout Württemberg. The courier told the OSS X-2 interrogators that "somewhere in Europe" he believed there was an organization "for the control of all Germany," which communicated with the various command posts through the party chiefs in each *Gau*. None of the groups knew the location of the command post or the whereabouts of any groups or message centers other than their own. Messages were usually verbal but could be camouflaged personal letters—references to bad motorcar batteries, for instance, concealed assassination instructions.

Mannerz was aware of the existence of an organization similar to Elsa in the Black Forest and thought that Tümmler controlled all southwestern Germany, including Alsace and Lorraine. The purpose of the organization was to continue Sicherheitspolizei and Sicherheitsdienst activity "by any means available; at first by espionage, later on by sabotage and the reorganization, coordination and direction of Werewolf groups." Specific tasks were:

to terrorize the people and punish collaborators by murder and burning farms, etc., to gain control of resistance groups and all underground movements, to centralize their orders through *Elsa,* and to organize a communications and news service of a political nature covering the reactions of the people and their dealings with Allied Military Government. It was stressed that the first weeks would be spent in organization, working slowly but thoroughly.

The equipment carried by the informant bespoke an organization that had considerable structure, ingenuity, preparation:

§ *False papers:* Personal, travel, and demobilization papers that were well forged; two false letters addressed to him in his assumed name and character; some photographs (real) of his mother and acquaintances. The X-2 report noted: "He had been well trained in his new identity, personal background, residence and acquaintances—the latter were real people killed in air raids. He was tested on his cover story as if by Allied interrogators."

§ *Equipment:* Pack, blanket, sleeping bag, edibles, cigarettes, first aid, 500 Reichsmarks (new), compass, torch, tube of poison tablets, syringe with morphia and stimulants, and bicycle.

§ *Edibles:* Meat in small cans of 200-gram Kneuchebrot in white paper boxes marked on the back with "125g Kneuchebrot Hersteller Norddeutsche Kneuchebrotwe Hecke Co. Hamburg Work [*sic*] 1." Oblong tins of fish. Sugar, white, granulated in 50-gram sacks. Pressed coffee. Chocolate in orange tins manufactured by Hildebrand Kakea und Schokoladenfabrik GmbH Berlin N 20. Each packet contains two bars. Saccharin in white and blue packets manufactured by Süsstoff GmbH .Berlin N 20. Bandages, three, Wehrmacht type, manufactured by Hauptsanitatspost Berlin.

X-2 advised all commands: "Whilst the possession of the above products individually is no proof of guilt, any person having a number of them together would be under some suspicion of having been equipped by an underground organization of the ELSA type."

Within a week organizations similar to Elsa—with similar products— were identified at Bremen, the principal American port of entry into Germany. There two organizations, Roland and Schuldbruh, had begun operations, and there was gathering evidence that Organization Annaliese existed in Munich, "birthplace of Nazism," and that undoubtedly such units existed in each *Gau.* All the evidence suggested that there were many hundreds of caches of guerrilla equipment and war stores and that the Werewolf was regaining breath after the shattering Allied advance through Germany of April and May. Its principal weakness was that it lacked national control, for that had been swept away with the arrest of Kaltenbrunner, the suicide of Himmler, and the general arrest of the SS and SD, leadership of the Werewolf. But as a bulletin from Twelfth Army Group dated June 14, 1945, warned, it could not be long before the national leadership system—Hitler's *Führerprinzip*—was restored. The most dangerous place: Munich in Bavaria, the place Nazism had been born.

The bulletin was very accurate.

The Bavarian Werewolf was established in April 1945 by Artur Axmann, leader of the Hitler Jugend and the Hitler Mädchen, at a secret meeting at the SS school at Bad Tölz, a small and beautiful town on the Isar River under the Bavarian mountains. A command and communications structure was created along the lines of Organization Elsa, war stores caches were laid away by the scores, and an excellent system of finance was established, on the basis of SS gold hidden on the property of party officials in the small towns around Bad Tölz.

At the meeting, Axmann instructed a Hitler Jugend economist, Willi Heidemann, whose connections with the Nazi party had been very indirect—he was probably a member of the Sicherheitsdienst—to prepare "a systematic plan" to "support Werewolf activities."[8] For that purpose Axmann gave Heidemann Reichsmarks worth $250,000 at prewar valuations, and with the money Heidemann established himself as a coal merchant at Bad Tölz. His overt objective was to ingratiate himself with the American military government when the town was occupied and during the German surrender period. His cover objective was establishment of an organization with the aim of keeping alive the Nazi ideal. The company into which Heidemann bought was Christian Tessmann's in Bad Tölz, and a branch office of a company in Dresden, the Soviet zone, and therefore immune from verification and ideological checks.

When the Americans occupied Bad Tölz, Heidemann lay low until the arrival of the town major, the representative of the U.S. Military Government, a noncombatant officer in late middle age who was noticeably bewildered by the problems of running a Bavarian town. Heidemann made himself known—and useful—to the town major in a number of ways, settling disputes, screening the police force to ensure that Nazis were not employed, advising on the hiring of Germans to help in the civil administration. Heidemann also introduced a Hitler Mädchen to one of the town major's American assistants.

Heidemann sought and obtained the necessary military government papers to operate a number of trucks to make his deliveries and obtain his supplies, and soon he had absorbed four other small businesses in the area. By the end of the summer Heidemann was operating on a rather large scale in the American Zone of Germany. He hired a fairly large

number of drivers, clerks, and laborers, all of whom carried papers showing them to be discharged German Army personnel, but all of whom
were, in fact, connected to the Nazi underground movement in Bavaria,
which included the embryonic movement in Munich.

On July 21, 1945, the U.S. intelligence authorities under the command
of Donovan's friend General Edwin L. Sibert, chief of intelligence in the
U.S. Zone, launched Operation Tally-ho. More than 160,000 U.S. troops
took part in a massive *ratissage* throughout the U.S. Zone to arrest SS men
and other "apprehendables," and more than 85,000 Germans were arrested for offenses ranging from party membership, illegal political activities, black marketeering, currency offenses to the illegal possession of
arms—one Werewolf was found to be in possession of a complete Pan-
ther tank with necessary fuel, ammunition, and spares for operations.
Heidemann and his crew escaped being caught in the net of the *ratissages;*
they had been forewarned by the Hitler Mädchen working in the Bad Tölz
town major's office. Similarly, the Heidemann group was not caught in
Sibert's second operation, Doublecheck. Furthermore, they were now
aware of the importance of the right and the left ears on their *Kennkarten*
—their German Army demobilization identity papers.

However, the effect of the *ratissages* was to convince Heidemann that
"active Werewolf subversion would be foolhardy and might easily end the
Tessmann enterprise." Moreover, "Because Heidemann was the sole
power in the economic branch of the underground movement, he had
little trouble convincing the conspirators to turn to a long-range program, in which he figured as the ultimate hope for rebirth of the Nazi
Party." His plan was to build a large business, through which he would
become influential in the postwar economic life of Germany. When the
Americans had either gone home or relaxed their vigilance, he would
then set to work to rebuild the Nazi party and then, through economic
pressure on the postwar political life of the country, to influence political
thought and action in favor of the Fascist element in German society.
Ultimately Heidemann intended the Nazi party to emerge as the leading
political force in Germany. And, it may be stated, there was little to
prevent Heidemann's plan from maturing: He had survived the intensive
postwar *ratissages;* his organization was expanding rapidly; he had the
intellectual, business, and political acumen for the realization of his plans;
and he was accepted as an uncontaminated businessman.

But during this period the U.S. counterespionage authorities had got
wind of the existence of a Hitler group that met in the bar in the basement
of the bomb-ruined Deutsches Theater in central Munich. The ramifica-
tions of this group were not at all clear when the decision was taken to
use a ferret—a counterintelligence term for an agent whose job it was to
work his way into the suspect organization. In this case the ferret was
Johannes Werner, an American citizen of German birth and education

who was about twenty-three, held a commissioned rank in the U.S. Army, and was employed by OSS SI in Munich. (In 1982 Werner was a wealthy and successful businessman resident in New York and prominent in society.)

Werner, the son of a family of Berliners who were Sephardic Jews, had been educated in Germany during the early years of the Third Reich. He was not "Semitic" in appearance; to the contrary, he was markedly "Aryan." He spoke excellent German and was familiar with the cultism of the Hitler Jugend, the Hitler Mädchen, and the SS. Moreover, he was skilled as a ferret; during the Normandy campaign he had made his way through the tight lines and, dressed as an SS signalman who had been cut off from his own unit, had spent several days in a Wehrmacht signals center, using the mess and the barracks and generally collecting signals intelligence. During the advance into Bavaria he had been attached to the U.S. 45th Infantry Division, working with Turicum, the large anti-Nazi organization in southern Germany on matters concerning SS gold and funds. And he had taken part in the special means that led to the capitulation of the Munich garrison and the surrender of the city.

Now, in Operation Nursery, he was to penetrate the Nazi group meeting in the ruins of the Deutsches Theater. His cover was that of a *Scharführer* SS—a section leader—with the SS 18th Division, which was known to have been on the Czechoslovak front in April and had surrendered to the Red Army. He, however, had been home on leave in Berlin during the collapse and had thus not been captured along with his comrades. To make his cover impermeable, Werner's case officer engaged in a number of tricks of the trade, the most painful of which was the burning off with a glowing cigarette end of Werner's SS number, tattooed near the pit of his left arm—the method used by SS men to remove that telltale mark. Now Werner was ready for Nursery.

Werner was introduced into the Deutsches Theater set by Annalore Axmann, a startlingly beautiful *Münchnerin* who looked like the prototype of the Hitler Mädchen but who was in fact a Sephardic Jewess. (She was no relation to Artur Axmann, head of the Hitler Jugend, Axmann being a fairly common name in southern Germany.) Through her, Werner was introduced to what he later called "an SS baby—fresh from Hitler Jugend, but very brutal and very, very dangerous."[9]

Through this SS man Werner was introduced into a Werewolf forming in a house at the end of an alley in Munich. The house was undamaged, and it provided lodgings for SS men on the run. Werner, at great peril to himself, took a room in the house and began to attend the meetings of the Werewolf. There were, at first, about "twelve or thirteen SS in the group, but it was gradually expanding. All were stupid but devout Nazis." Gradually Werner insinuated his way into the group. His origins were not detected, and they came to trust him. A central factor to emerge from his association with the Werewolf was that it was controlled by other, higher individuals who financed the organization. In due course, Werner learned that the finance, but not the control, came from Christian Tessmann's, the coal and lumber merchants in Bad Tölz. The finances were not large and not sufficient for more than subsistence living, but the group was in no doubt that they would be adequate when the time came to begin operations.

With that information, the U.S. authorities decided to infiltrate Christian Tessmann's at Bad Tölz in an extension of Operation Nursery. Thought was given to using Werner for that purpose, but that was abandoned, for it was felt necessary to keep an eye on the Munich Werewolf. Two other ferrets were used. Since both were Hitler Jugend, one was known to a man already in Heidemann's employment, and with winter coming on Heidemann needed men for his deliveries, both were hired. Their identities are not known, but one must have been fairly influential in the party, for he was present at an important meeting at Christian Tessmann's in October 1945. In that month two men from the British zone, Willi Loehel and Kurt Budaeus, appeared with a proposal that their organization—it may have been the Schuldbruh at Bremen, thought to have been responsible for a bomb explosion in a police station in which some twenty-five people were killed or injured—merge with Tessmann's. According to the Nursery man who was present, Heidemann had rejected the idea with the statement that "he would not consider any consolidation until his cover was fool-proof and the strength of his commercial ventures assured"—a statement that showed fairly clearly that he was engaged in clandestine activities. He did, however, agree to the establishment of Tessmann branches in Bremen, Essen, Hamburg, and Lübeck and to Loehel's and Budaeus's employment as branch managers. The Nursery man learned also that he was opening a branch in the American zone of Austria, that Tessmann's had a list of about 1,000 former Nazis in southern Germany and western Austria, and that the Werewolf in northern Germany had an additional 1,500 names.

The American and British authorities in Austria and northern Germany were contacted and decided to nip the Tessmann organization in the bud. Willi Heidemann and seven of his associates were arrested "for black market offenses"—not political offenses, a far more serious matter. They were sent to prison for a year, during which they were interrogated about their political activities. By April 1, 1946, the occupation authorities in the Anglo-American zones of Germany, and in Austria, had all the information they needed to move. From two o'clock in the morning of that day more than 1,000 people were arrested, and the American account of the Tessmann enterprise stated, "The core of the underground movement had been destroyed. Devoid of its key personnel and its financial support, the remaining portion of the underground was considered helpless."[10]

There remained only the task of cleaning up the Munich Werewolf. That was done at about the same time as the destruction of the Tessmann organization. Werner (accompanied by the harmonica player Larry Adler, who was in Munich for a concert) had his last, long, frightening walk down the dark alley to the SS lodging house. At a given hour the house was surrounded by armed troops, and all approaches were blocked by weapons carriers. Then, with the house bathed in searchlights, the Munich OSS and CIC burst in and arrested sixteen SS men, all of whom were asleep.

The Teuton furor in the twentieth century was at an end. So was the Arcadia plan. It was appropriate that the SS movement ended where it had begun, in Munich. It was also appropriate that its minute, brief revival was terminated by a young Jew and a young Jewess. In the case of Werner, there would be no medals, for the OSS no longer existed. Werner's reward was, therefore, the five remaining points he needed to be shipped home to New York on the next boat.

47

Termination

Three days after the German surrender Robert Joyce, Dulles's successor as chief of OSS Switzerland, cabled Donovan that an OSS secret agent identified only as 673 had reported conversations with Shunichi Kase, the Japanese minister to Bern. In his report, 673 had stated that Kase had "expressed wish to help in arranging for cessation of hostilities between Japs and Allies." Kase "reportedly believes direct talks with Americans and British preferable to negotiations through Russia, as in latter event Russian prestige would so gain that all East would become Communistic." He was "certain that one of few Japan desiderata would be retention of Emperor because without him Japan would turn Communist. He feels that [Joseph] Grew [former U.S. ambassador to Tokyo], whom he considers best USA authority on Japan, shares this opinion."[1]

The approach in Bern evoked no response from Washington, except that on June 1, 1945, Truman sent a special message to Congress entitled "Winning the War with Japan," in which he declared: "The primary task facing the nation today is to win the war in Japan—to win it completely and to win it as quickly as possible." If the Japanese insisted "on continuing resistance beyond the point of reason, their country will suffer the same destruction as Germany."

Furthermore, with the atomic bomb reaching the testing stage in the New Mexican desert, that same day the Interim Committee, a high-level group established to advise the President on how to employ the bomb, recommended: (1) The bomb should be used against Japan as soon as possible; (2) it should be used on a dual target—industrial and civilian buildings—so as to demonstrate the power of the weapon, and (3) it should be used without prior warning about the nature of the weapon.

The next approach came on June 2, 1945, the day after the President's speech, when Joyce in Bern advised that Agent 673 was in touch with Admiral Fujimura, believed to be a high officer of the Japanese intelligence service in Europe. He was "supposed to be in direct and secret cable contact with Jap Minister of Marine and believed to have confidence of Japanese government," reported Joyce. Fujimura "indicates to 673 that he believed Navy circles who now control present Jap Government would be willing to surrender but desire to save some face out of wreckage if possible." In particular, they "stress necessity save Emperor as otherwise communism and chaos will ensue." Fujimura "also stressed that Japan had to retain some of their merchant marine to bring in food imports," as the country was not self-sufficient in its food supplies. Still there was no response from Washington.

It was sixty-seven days to Hiroshima, seventy to Nagasaki.

There was silence until June 21, 1945, when Joyce cabled Donovan and Murphy that "Fujimura, who is in close touch by cable with Tokyo, is insistent that before Japanese surrender they would require assurance that emperor would be allowed to remain." Donovan then explained privately to Truman that 673 was a German national, who had been taken prisoner by the Japanese in World War I and upon his release had remained in Japan and established important commercial relations there. He had placed Japanese orders in Germany, made a substantial fortune, and gained the confidence of high Japanese circles, particularly in the Navy.

As if to confirm that there might be substance in these peace feelers, the U.S. Navy's cryptanalytical branch intercepted a telegram from the former Japanese prime minister, Fumimaro Konoye, to the Japanese ambassador in Moscow, Naotake Sato:

> His Majesty is extremely anxious to terminate the war as soon as possible, being deeply concerned that any further hostilities will not only aggravate the untold miseries of the millions and millions of innocent men and women in the countries at war. Should, however, the United States and Great Britain insist on unconditional surrender, Japan would be forced to fight to the bitter end.

It was twenty-five days to Hiroshima, twenty-eight to Nagasaki.

The next day, July 13, 1945, Allen Dulles, who had been ordered to return to Bern to handle the Japanese contact, advised Donovan that a second channel of communication was developing:

> Per Jacobson [sic], a Swedish national and economic advisor to the Bank for International Settlements (at Bern), has been approached by Kojimo

Kitamura, a director of the Bank, a representative of the Yokohama Specie Bank, and former financial attaché in Berlin. Kitamura indicated to Jacobson that he was anxious to establish immediate contact with American representatives and implied that the only condition on which Japan would insist with respect to surrender would be some consideration for the Japanese Imperial Family. Kitamura showed that he was completely familiar with OSS operations which led to the surrender of German forces in North Italy, and declared that he wished to establish a contact similar to that made by General Karl Wolff.

According to Jacobson, Kitamura is acting with the consent of the Japanese Minister to Switzerland, Shunichi Kase, and is working with Brigadier General Kiyotomi Okamoto, a former Japanese Military Attaché in Bern. (Okamoto is probably the chief of Japanese intelligence in Europe.) Kitamura claims that the Japanese group in Switzerland has direct communications with Tokyo and is in a position to make definite commitments.[2]

But, warned Dulles, the OSS intermediaries who talked with Jacobsson in Basle "believe that the Kitamura approach was initiated locally rather than on the basis of instructions from Tokyo." Hence "it is difficult to assess the seriousness of the approach."

Donovan advised Truman in a report on July 16, 1945—the day the atomic bomb was test-fired for the first time—Jacobsson had had a series of meetings with Yoshimura, another official with the Bank for International Settlements, and Kitamura, who claimed Kase and Okamoto had direct and secret means of communicating with the Japanese Chiefs of Staff. Yoshimura claimed the peace group he represented included the Army Chief of Staff, General Ushijiro Umezu; the minister of the navy, Admiral Kitisumasi Yenai; and the foreign minister, Shigenori Togo. Yoshimura and Kitamura appeared to Jacobsson no longer to question the principle of unconditional surrender, though at one point they asked whether unconditional military and naval surrender might not be sufficient. On his own initiative, Jacobsson had replied that such a proposal would not be acceptable to the Allies but would be considered merely a quibble. Both Japanese officials, Dulles reported, also raised the question of maintaining Japanese territorial integrity, "but they apparently did not seem to include Manchuria, Korea, or Formosa."[3]

At one of their meetings with Jacobsson, Yoshimura and Kitamura prepared a paper for Dulles in which they asked how, if Tokyo were ready to proceed, conversations could be arranged with Allied representatives and what form of authorization would be required—a memorandum that reinforced Jacobsson's strong belief that "these approaches are serious and that the Japanese group in Switzerland is in constant cable contact with Tokyo." But Dulles reminded Donovan that "This conviction appears to be based on impressions only," since Jacobsson's contacts "never stated precisely that they had received instructions from any authorized agency in Tokyo." On the other hand, Dulles agreed with Jacobsson that the Japanese had "taken to heart the consequences which Germany had suffered, including extensive physical destruction and the collapse of all German authority, because it prolonged a futile struggle many months after its hopelessness was wholly apparent."[4] Jacobsson felt that "a tendency is growing in certain Japanese circles to try to terminate the war at any cost, provided that non-militaristic Japanese governmental institutions can be preserved in the Japanese home islands."

Donovan ended his note with the observation that Dulles "expects within a few days to obtain some evidence as to whether these approaches by Yoshimura and Kitamura have any serious backing or represent merely an effort by the Japanese group in Switzerland to start something on their own initiative."[5]

In the meantime, the Potsdam Conference had opened with Truman, Stalin, and Churchill in attendance, the invasion of the Japanese home islands was being mounted by United States armies, and the atomic bomb was successfully detonated in New Mexico. In these circumstances, on July 26, 1945, the triumvirs issued the Potsdam ultimatum to Japan: Surrender unconditionally or face "utter destruction." Japan rejected the ultimatum, and accordingly, without forewarning, operations to atomize two Japanese cities were mounted.

On August 2, 1945, four days before a B-29 was due to drop an atomic bomb on Hiroshima, Donovan advised Truman that Dulles had forwarded a report from Per Jacobsson. The Japanese Chief of Staff had acknowledged a long telegram from General Okamoto, sent from Switzerland on July 19. The Japanese foreign minister had also acknowledged a detailed report from Kase, the Japanese minister at Bern, transmitted on July 21. The substance of both messages to Tokyo was that Japan had lost the war and "must now promptly accept the consequences." The only comment evoked by these two telegrams was from the foreign minister, whose reply to Kase's message contained the question "Is that all you have to say?" That question was taken by Kase to be an invitation to continue peace initiatives. As Kase advised Jacobsson, the Japanese group "emphasizes that it is hoping for some decision within a week 'unless resistance is too great.'" Meanwhile, the Allies should not take "too seriously" what was said on Tokyo Radio regarding the Potsdam ultimatum as this was merely "propaganda to maintain morale" in Japan. The "real reply" would be given through some "official channel," possibly either Minister Kase or General Okamota.[6]

Time had run out. The Bern conversations between the OSS and the Japanese intelligence service were at an end. The Japanese war, like the German and the Italian wars before it, was to be decided by arms. On August 6, 1945, a Superfortress, the *Enola Gay,* appeared over the great

Japanese industrial and population center of Hiroshima and at 8:15 A.M. dropped a 9,000-pound weapon from 31,600 feet. For one ten-thousandths of a second it generated a heat of 300,000 degrees centigrade. Three days later another Superfortress dropped a "Fat Man" bomb on Nagasaki. The Japanese claimed later that 240,000 people were killed in both cities. American figures were substantially lower: 66,000 to 78,000 for Hiroshima and 39,000 in Nagasaki.

At the same time Russia declared war on Japan, and the Red Army began moving into the territory of the Japanese Empire.

The Japanese surrender could not be long delayed. Meanwhile, the fate of Donovan and the OSS still had not been settled.

Through the period of the German and the Japanese surrenders, Truman saw WJD only once and then only for fifteen minutes. The meeting seems to have been unsuccessful, for Truman recorded on his appointments book: "At 9:45 Major General William Donovan came in to tell how important the Secret Service [*sic*] is and how much he could do to run the country on an even basis."[7]

Donovan's proposals, once so flourishing, were being left to dangle on Truman's tree. At the same time at least one of the Cabinet officers arrayed against him—Attorney General Francis Biddle—was engaging in a dangerous scheme to discredit the OSS and Donovan. That scheme began on April 27, with a series of events involving the Washington columnist Drew Pearson. That day Pearson wrote an article that began:

> By the thread of one man's life hung personal relationships which affected nations. Prime Ministers and potentates, once close to Franklin Roosevelt, now must learn how to get along with an unknown gentleman in the White House. Certain Army-Navy officials, who always knew how Roosevelt would react on this and that, now must do business with a man they once criticized. To illustrate how the pendulum of fate has swung, here are some of those who will miss Franklin Roosevelt most. . . .[8]

Pearson then dwelt upon, among others, Donovan and his predicament:

> Gen. "Wild Bill" Donovan—of the Office of Strategic Services, sometimes called the "Cloak and Dagger Club," or "Oh So Social," will miss Roosevelt terribly. Donovan ran the giant espionage outfit which tried to find out what was going on behind enemy lines, and he had accumulated the most bizarre assortment of female spies, social register bluebloods and anti-Roosevelt haters ever seen in Washington. As an old personal friend, Roosevelt gave him free reign [*sic*], including grandiose plans for a postwar espionage service. Truman does not like peacetime espionage and will not be so lenient.

A few days later, describing the American actions that were making the Russians suspicious and uneasy, Pearson declared in his column, "Washington Merry-Go-Round":

> ... the Russians are probably most suspicious of the mysterious United States espionage organization called OSS. The OSS, or Office of Strategic Services, has, strangely, distributed some of the most powerful bankers' representatives in the U.S.A. at key points where they can influence United States policy in occupied Germany.
>
> The roster of OSS men who have been or are operating in Europe reads like a blue-stocking list of the first 60 families. It includes: Paul Mellon, son of Andrew Mellon; Junius and Henry Morgan of the House of Morgan; Alfred du Pont, Lester Armour of the Chicago Armours, Gordon Auchincloss, John Auchincloss, Warwick Potter, Harold Coolidge, William Van Allen of the Astor family, and Allan [sic] Dulles, attorney for various international bankers with previous connections in Germany.
>
> Some of these may not deserve the suspicion focussed upon them. But others more than make up for it. And anyone listening for more than 30 minutes to their conversation about the next war and building up Germany as a partner in that war can understand why the Russians wrongly accused us of a deal to permit the American Army to enter Berlin first.
>
> This is the kind of underlying suspicion which must be killed immediately and permanently if the machinery of San Francisco is to bring about permanent peace.[9]

Then, as the world's statesmen gathered at San Francisco to establish the United Nations, Pearson announced the existence of an OSS plan for an American war against Russia, an accusation that could hardly have improved the atmosphere in which that fateful conference met. This was moonshine, but dangerous moonshine. The fact was that no planning for war with Russia was commenced before March 1946, when the so-called Pincher series was begun, and they were not real war plans. Rather, they were limited to the preparation of strategic studies of particular areas or specific military problems. Planning for war with Russia, including atomic war, would not begin until July 29, 1947, when the Joint War Plans Committee was directed to make Plan Broiler for war forced upon the United States by Soviet aggression within the coming three years. Despite Pearson's attempts to depict Donovan as the power-mad Fascist intelligence master who wanted to atomize Bolshevism out of existence, the war plan for atomic war against Russia was not approved by the Joint Chiefs until January 28, 1949, when Plan Trojan was adopted—in which, incidentally, seventy Soviet cities were on the target list, requiring 133 atomic bombs, of which 8 would be dropped on Moscow and 7 on Leningrad.

Pearson's allegation that WJD was planning for war with Russia was pure fiction, but it was the sort of fiction that confirmed the worst fears of the Russians at a time when they were paranoid about America and the atomic bomb. Despite the clear lack of such planning—apart from all else the Joint Chiefs were as tired of fighting as everyone else—Pearson declared emphatically on the radio:

> Washington: General William J. Donovan, Office of Strategic Services, has just received from his overzealous aides a detailed plan for American war on Russia. I am sure that General Donovan himself and the more responsible members of his super-spy organization had nothing to do with these plans, but I suggest that stupidity like this which, if it leaks to me, will also leak to others, including the Russians, causes distrust between the Allies just as we are trying to end this war and build up a plan to end all wars.[10]

After several other attacks on the OSS in this same vein, Pearson went too far, far too far:

> A series of secret cables sent by General William Donovan, of the Office of Strategic Services (nicknamed "Oh-so-Secret"), to Russell Forgan, former Chicago banker, now in Paris, is intriguing other U.S. officials. Donovan wired Forgan to interrogate directors of the giant Nazi cartel I. G. Farben, now seized by the United States Army.
>
> This is the company which collaborated with Standard Oil of New Jersey and the Aluminum Corporation of America to keep vitally important patents for synthetic rubber, magnesium, and high octane gasoline from the American public at a time when it was essential to use those patents for war.
>
> One cable from Donovan to Forgan in Paris reads:
>
> "I have already asked you to send names of I. G. Farben now in custody. From now on these men should be kept from one another, particularly when the interrogation begins. Files of I. G. Farben should be seized and sent to Paris at once in our custody. This is most important. Essential that we keep control of these men."
>
> What intrigues other U.S. officials is that Donovan's OSS is dominated by actions of the Mellons, the J. P. Morgans and big banking and industrial houses, some of them interested in German patents. . . . Other Government officials are also puzzled as to why the OSS, rather than the Justice Department, should pounce upon I. G. Farben executives. There might be quiet probing of this.
>
> Note—Attorney General Biddle recently told senators: "Many cartel arrangements necessarily disrupted during the European phase of the war are now being resumed. Meetings have been held, plans have been held, plans have been laid [sic], and in some cases agreements already entered into. As to some of these agreements, my department will have something to say before long." Reaction of senators is that big business never learns.[11]

The quoted telegram was important to the OSS, for it constituted almost the exact text of a secret signal Donovan had dictated to the assistant executive officer, Lieutenant Robert Thrun, for transmission over the very secure Telekrypton circuit to Forgan in London during the late afternoon of April 30, 1945. Since the signal had not been declassified—technically it was still secret in 1982—where had Pearson obtained it? Plainly he had obtained it illegally, and if that could be proved, he was in violation of the Espionage Act.

Again Donovan assigned the inquiry to Doering, who, for all his mild-mannered, judicial, unobtrusive, and gentlemanly ways, was a born detective. Doering soon learned that the attorney general, Francis Biddle, had probably obtained the cable from Drew Pearson. That was confirmed by a telephone conversation between Donovan and Biddle on June 15, 1945. Donovan reported of the conversation:

> I said to him, "We have a matter to discuss with you concerning security control bearing upon a cable sent from this office to London, and I would like Colonel Doering, who is inquiring into the matter for us, to talk with you."
>
> He replied, "I know what he wants to ask me—where I got the information concerning the subject matter of that cable. I can't give it to him because I obtained it in confidence and I cannot disclose the source until I get his permission."
>
> I said, "Well, of course, we will have to tell the security control that."
>
> He said, "What would you do if a fellow came in confidentially and gave you the information?"
>
> I said, "So long as it affected, as this does, the welfare of my country I would disclose the information completely."
>
> He said, "Well, I'll have to ask him and I will let you know."
>
> Ten minutes later he called back and said, "Bill, I think I acted a little hastily in talking to you. I was advised three days before publication in Pearson's column."
>
> I said, "Who advised you?"
>
> He replied, "Pearson."
>
> I said, "Did he do it by telephone or did he come over in person?"
>
> He said, "He came to see me on other matters and while here showed me the cable."[12]

To make the evidence against Biddle and Pearson complete, Doering then acquired a letter from the assistant attorney general, Herbert Wechsler, to the assistant secretary of war, John J. McCloy. In the course of asking for McCloy's assistance in stopping OSS from cornering the I.G. Farben documents and personnel, Wechsler revealed that he, too, had read Donovan's telegram to Forgan on that subject; and when Doering questioned Wechsler about where he obtained his information Wechsler said he had no knowledge but felt that the document had come to the attorney general from Pearson.[13]

With the evidence complete, Donovan wrote to the senior member of Joint Security Control, Admiral Hewlett Thebaud, who was also chief of Naval Intelligence, on July 21, 1945. Enclosing "information concerning violation of cryptographic security involved in the disclosure by Drew Pearson of classified messages," Donovan maintained that "The question is much deeper, however, than cryptographic security." This had been apparent "since the disclosure in the Chicago Tribune and the Times Herald of the plan prepared at the request of President Roosevelt for a central intelligence agency." From "that time until now there have been very evident attempts on the part of certain columnists to distort and discredit the work of this agency."[14]

Because of the implications of "such an attack," Donovan continued, it was "not sufficient that Joint Security Control limit its inquiry to the superficial facts in the instant case." Underlying this breach of security were "facts and circumstances which lie at the root of national security." Donovan asserted:

> It has been common gossip that there have been cabinet members who have bought their peace with columnists through furnishing information. Concrete proof of this is found in the present case. The recent Attorney General [Biddle resigned in June 1945 as Doering was in the middle of his investigation] admits that he received from a columnist a copy of the very cable with which we are concerned. The conversation of the ex-public official with Assistant Secretary McCloy as well as his later conversations with me . . . show the sense of public duty held by that official.

He continued:

> No government organization can prevent such penetration if those who purpose doing it have an alliance with officials in government whether within the agency or not. And the facts in this case already admitted raise the suggestion of such an alliance between the former Attorney General of the United States and the columnist who seemingly has access to the most secret files of the government.

Donovan then stated that these questions suggested themselves:

> *a* During his term of office did the Attorney General receive from the columnist governmental secret documents or information from such documents?
> *b* Were the documents or their contents obtained by agents or informants placed with the agency by the columnist acting on his own or were they placed there by the Attorney General or with his knowledge and approval through the medium and with the cover of the columnist? *c* Does the columnist feel free to continue his tactics with impunity because the prosecuting arm of the government has participated in these activities?

If any of these questions had truth, Donovan asserted, "it means no agency can be safe from such 'police state' activities, with resulting important breaches of cryptographic security and disclosure to the enemy."

He requested that Joint Security Control, which through the FBI and Department of Justice had the investigatory and prosecutory powers, take the case over. Meanwhile, Donovan's chief security officer, Archbold Van Beuren, had been looking for the person within the OSS who gave the signal to Pearson in the first place. That person was identified but not until after the officer concerned had left the OSS, making legal action impossible.

Also, Joint Security Control (which was comprised of the leading allies of J. Edgar Hoover in the struggle to prevent the OSS from dominating the CIA) had been advised by the chief signals officer that no violation of cryptographic security could have occurred through the publication of the text of the telegram in Pearson's column. Therefore, Joint Security Control was "withholding submission of its report . . . to the Joint Chiefs of Staff pending your further advice."[15]

Although Pearson was known to have obtained a number—perhaps even a large number—of classified OSS signals there the matter was allowed to rest. It seemed clear to Donovan and Doering that Biddle had been deeply involved in the leakages of not only the Donovan CIA plan but also matters of immediate political and operational interest, but the case died. The matter did not formally reach the Joint Chiefs, who were not therefore required to take any action. Nor had the matter been sent to the White House, probably because Biddle was no longer in the Cabinet.

Satisfied that the OSS was crumbling, Donovan's opponents began their last attack. Just when the House Appropriations Committee was working on the OSS budget for the fiscal year 1946, there came a series of highly damaging accusations: Donovan was employing Communists, the same allegations that led to the collapse of the excellent Goff chains in Italy, and because of the large number of bankers in the OSS, it was conspiring to arrange a "soft peace" with Germany. Then Walter Trohan emerged again to reveal that General MacArthur had forbidden the OSS to enter his theater—a highly damaging statement at the time since the Pacific was now the only active major theater of war. On May 17, 1945, another Times-Herald writer revealed something of the peace conversations at Bern between the Japanese and Dulles through the good offices of Bank for International Settlements. Once again Donovan demanded "a board with power to compel testimony under oath to discover those who are concerned with these disclosures." Once again the demand was ignored.

Then came two terribly damaging Trohan stories: OSS IS BRANDED BRITISH AGENCY TO LEGISLATORS and BRITISH CONTROL OF OSS BARED IN CONGRESS PROBE. In the first story Trohan stated that the OSS had spent more than $125,000,000 "in propagandizing and intelligence work around the world" but was "scarcely more than an arm of the British Intelligence Service." Yet it was now asking Congress for $38,000,000 for the coming fiscal year, although the war in Europe had ended and the organization's services were "not wanted in the Pacific." Also, there was the closest relationship between the OSS and the British, illustrated by the training of OSS agents in England, the use by the British of the OSS to obtain intelligence for them that they would not otherwise be able to get for themselves, a close connection between the OSS and the British Passport Control Office in New York, "the headquarters of British intelligence in the U.S." Finally, on May 20, 1945, Trohan announced that Fleet Admiral Chester W. Nimitz, naval commander in chief in the Pacific, had rejected Donovan's offer of OSS services.[16]

The effect was as calculated: The House Appropriations Committee asked the Joint Chiefs for a statement on the OSS's utility. The Joint Chiefs sent telegrams to MacArthur, Nimitz, Eisenhower, Devers, and the commanding generals in the Arabian, India-Burma, and Chinese theaters, requesting their opinion of the OSS's work. MacArthur and Nimitz confirmed they did not want Donovan's organization. The India-Burma theater (where the fighting was now at an end) found no use for it "under current directives." On the other hand, the China headquarters announced that its value was likely to be "extremely high." Cairo and Caserta reported that the OSS had made a "great contribution" to the Italian campaign, and its presence would remain essential as long as the situation in Italy, Austria, and the Balkans remained unstable. As for the European theater, Eisenhower thought the future value of the OSS to be high and believed that its withdrawal from that theater should not be considered "under any circumstances."[17]

The Joint Chiefs thereupon advised the Appropriations Committee that in their opinion the OSS would "continue to be useful in the conduct of the war," that in the areas where it "has been utilized there is agreement as to the value of its contributions to the war effort," and that it should be permitted to continue its operations in accordance with the desires of the responsible commanders in the field. But they did believe that with the end of the European war the requirements for the next fiscal year "should be appreciably less than those for the past year."[18]

But Trohan's poison had already done its work when the Joint Chiefs' letter was received by Clarence Cannon, the chairman of the Appropriations Committee. The OSS budget had been cut savagely, virtually by half, as the Military Intelligence Service noted with delight. There, OSS and FBI budgets for 1946 were compared:

OSS	
Requested	$45 million
Budget cut to	$42 million
Congress cut to	$38 million
President cut to	$24 million
FBI	
Requested	$49 million
Budget cut to	$46 million
Congress put back to	$49 million
President cut to	$43 million[19]

These cuts represented substantial victories, and encouragement, for Donovan's opposition, still centered in State, War, Navy, and the FBI. They were followed by more damaging stories in the press. In June *Newsweek* reported, for example, that one of the "sensational investigations of war activities will be an inquiry into the use of 'unvouchered funds' " by the OSS and the OWI. These funds had been made available for " 'cloak and dagger' and propaganda operations" but had been used "for buying many diverse things, ranging from whiskey to real estate and radio stations." In the same report *Newsweek* revealed what may have been, if true, at least one of the causes of the personal animosity Truman held for Donovan. The magazine "revealed" that when U.S. Senator Truman was chairman of the Special Committee to Investigate the National Defense Program, he had been deterred from carrying out an investigation of special funds for fear of interfering with the war effort but that he had promised at the time to " 'see to it that the practices were aired after VE [Victory in Europe] Day.' "[20]

There was much else in this tenor in other newspapers and magazines, and by mid-1945, the CIA study of *Donovan and the CIA* later noted:

> While . . . Donovan had certainly not given up he had little reason for optimism. He had been stymied by [State, War, Navy, and FBI], ignored by the President, and was unsupported in the Congress. He had been smeared by the press—he harbored Communists, was controlled by the British, was rebuffed by heroes MacArthur and Nimitz, traveled with self-seeking bankers, financiers, industrialists, and socialites, had squandered money, and was marked for a sensational exposé.[21]

Yet while heading a "hobbled and expiring organization," he "still hoped he could persuade the country and the government of the rightness of his program for a postwar intelligence system." That aspiration was doomed. The intriguers succeeded in 1945 as they had in 1929.

The end of Donovan's career in intelligence came while he was with Ruth at Nonquitt. On August 14, 1945, Japan surrendered unconditionally and Ruth recorded in her diary: "Announcement by Truman of Japan's surrender came at 7 P.M. Horns and whistles blew here in Nonquitt. Marion [Glover] came over. Both of us in tears. Listened to radio. Whole Nation gone mad."

The Donovans were delighted, for David Donovan was now the captain of a fleet tug in the Pacific and was to have taken part in the invasion of Japan. On August 15, 1945, Ruth noted:

> Did flowers. Rain clear in eve. At 6 every one in N[onquitt] to beach. Bishop of Maine read prayers. Flag raised at cliff. More prayers and singing. All ate picnic supper on beach. Later bonfire and singing. Most beautiful sunset and light over bay, and a rainbow. Quite fitting and I hope prophetic.

Alas, Ruth's rainbow was not to prove a happy omen.

Despite a last-minute attempt by the Joint Chiefs to rescue Donovan and OSS, at 3:00 P.M. on Thursday, September 20, 1945, Budget Director Smith presented President Truman with an executive order abolishing the OSS. Smith was to state of that action:

> When I gave the President the Order for OSS for his signature, I told him that this was the best disposition we could make of the matter and that General Donovan . . . would not like it. I showed the President our communication with [Secretary of State] Byrnes and indicated that the State Department was willing to accept certain OSS functions while the rest would go to the War Department. The President glanced over the documents and signed the Order. He commented, as he had done in the past, that he has in mind a different kind of intelligence service from what this country has had in the past.[22]

Donovan's employment as director was terminated with a letter written by Budget Director Smith but signed by Truman. That letter instructed WJD: "Timely steps should . . . be taken to conserve those resources and skills developed within your organization which are vital to our peacetime purposes."[23] The letter ended coldly:

> I want to take this occasion to thank you for the capable leadership you have brought to a vital wartime activity in your capacity as Director of Strategic Services. You may well find satisfaction in the achievements of the Office and take pride in your own contribution to them. These are in themselves large rewards. Great additional reward for your efforts should lie in the knowledge that the peacetime intelligence services of the Government are being erected on the foundation of the facilities and resources mobilized through the [OSS] during the war.

Also, the OSS was to be closed down in fourteen days.

Admiral Ernest J. King, a member of the Joint Chiefs and Chief of Naval

Operations, prepared a letter of appreciation of Donovan's services on behalf of the chiefs, but the letter was not sent on the advice of Admiral Leahy, Truman's chief of staff. Donovan was formally relieved from duty by the adjutant general on January 12, 1946, with ninety-one days' leave —he had taken no leave since his recall to the colors. The last authorization he received from the United States Army was that queer formality —permission to drive an automobile to reach his home. Donovan went quietly to the farm at Berryville, giving Ruth little idea of what had occurred until she noticed that for the first time since he had been made a general officer in the service of the United States he came down to dinner wearing a civilian suit.

48

Farewell the Tranquil Mind

For Donovan the liquidation of the OSS and the aftermath presented him with what appears to have been the greatest moral crisis of his life, at least in the first two years of his return to civilian life. That shrewd observer of mankind Judge McGivern would find the parallel for Donovan's crisis in Othello's when he returned from his campaigns for the doges of Venice:

> Farewell the tranquil mind; farewell content!
> Farewell the plumed troop and the big wars
> That make ambition virtue! O, farewell!
> Farewell the neighing steed, and the shrill trump,
> The spirit-stirring drum, the ear-piercing fife,
> The royal banner, and all quality,
> Pride, pomp, and circumstance of glorious war! . . .
> Farewell! Othello's occupation 's gone!

Judge McGivern's comparison was not exaggerated: Donovan was deeply unhappy at what appeared at the time to be the collapse of his plans for a central intelligence agency. The question is how long that discontent lasted, for it is not certain that he really left the American intelligence community. From 1948 and the Berlin crisis onward, as James R. Withrow, one of the lawyers who were closest to Donovan at this time, stated, Donovan appeared to rejoin it, either formally or informally, remaining associated with the CIA until he was no longer capable of acting. Certainly much in Donovan's activity from 1948 until his death in 1959 suggests that Withrow was accurate.

Be that as it may, for the moment it is necessary to review Donovan's and the OSS's accomplishments. In American society—in global society for that matter—Donovan's greatest accomplishment was undoubtedly to found the American secret intelligence and special operations service, to make it work, and to defend it successfully against a large number of internal domestic and foreign enemies. In thirty months he had created a vast operating service of special means without too much support and assistance beyond FDR's patronage, and he had left the United States an important legacy, one that was to remain a major factor in American and world affairs at least for the next forty years. The nature of the legacy was estimated accurately by one of Donovan's associates in special means, Edmond Taylor, who wrote that:

> [Donovan established] a precedent, or a pattern, for United States intervention in the revolutionary struggles of the post-war age. The Donovan influence on U.S. foreign and military policy has continued to be felt even since his death; for good or ill he left a lasting mark on the mind of the nation's power elite. However indirectly, many of our latter-day Cold War successes, disasters, and entrapments can ultimately be traced back to him.[1]

While Donovan was not a great innovator in the world of secret service —he does not compare with Menzies and Gubbins of England or with Trotsky and Dzerzhinsky of Russia—Taylor was correct in his belief concerning WJD's influence on the American power elite. He introduced it to special means. He made that elite see the need for such activity in a world becoming increasingly politically conscious. Indeed, Donovan created a power elite more conscious of the responsibilities of power than any of its predecessors. Also, he made special means acceptable to the American establishment, and he succeeded in making the ancient game fascinate men. He gave the sons of the power elite a mission. He sent them, as the church had sent missionaries, and the Kremlin its Comintern apparatchiks, to every corner of the globe, to fight the Axis enemy and spread the American gospel of the Four Freedoms. Most of these men and women did very well, as the OSS decorations list shows.

A force of about 16,000 men and women received a total of 2,005 medals for gallantry and proficiency. These included:

Distinguished Service Medals, 3
Distinguished Service Crosses, 51
Navy Crosses, 2
Legions of Merit, 209
Silver Stars, 148
Distinguished Flying Crosses, 76

Soldiers Medals, 72
Bronze Stars, 773
Air Medals, 334
Navy Commendation Ribbons, 4
Medals of Freedom, 9
Purple Hearts, 206
Distinguished Service Order (UK), 1
Orders of the British Empire, 3
Military Crosses (UK), 3
Military Medals (UK), 3
Legions of Honor (France), 4
Croix de Guerre (France), 108

This list was complete only to January 5, 1946; to it must be added perhaps 300 more American and Allied decorations and awards and several hundred certificates of service from foreign governments. In sum, therefore, the number of medals, certificates, and other recognitions awarded to OSS men constitutes a tangible, remarkable testament to the OSS's performance.[2]

Yet it did its work with remarkably few casualties. Despite the magnitude of the worldwide effort engaged in by the OSS, Donovan lost fewer men killed, wounded, and captured in its five years than he had lost on an average week in the trenches during the campaign season of 1918. In all, 143 men and women, excluding subagents, were killed in action, and about 300 men and women were wounded or captured while on active service. Yet the damage Donovan did to the enemy in World War II was far greater than that in World War I. And here was another important demonstration of Donovan's theories: An outpouring of blood was not always necessary in order to cause the enemy severe damage. Two examples will suffice to show what is meant: The OGs who took part in Noah's Ark in Greece suffered no more than 25 dead and wounded (and none was captured). On the other hand, they paralyzed large formations of the Wehrmacht for more than eighteen months and killed or wounded at least 1,400 of the enemy. In Switzerland Dulles's information that the Germans' missile experiments had reached an advanced stage produced a devastating attack by the Royal Air Force. In turn, that attack delayed German production of operational missiles, thereby saving hundreds, if not thousands, of lives and many acres of human dwellings.

Yet the end for the small number of OSS men to meet their Maker was often extremely unpleasant. About half the men who died were killed in circumstances that had not been explained when the list was compiled. For example, David T. Colin (almost certainly a nom-de-guerre) left traces in neither OSS records nor with the men that killed him, the Sicherheitsdienst. Robert N. Anderson and Trygve Berge were "killed in action in European area." There were no records either with the OSS or the SD of Thomas U. Brink's death, as was the case with Harvey J. Dain and V. Darlington. Bernard Gautier of Union City, New Jersey, was "killed in action near France by a German pistol bullet." Elmer Gallovich, 744 West Eighty-first Street, Chicago, was "killed in action in Asiatic area." James H. Green, of Burlington, North Carolina, was listed simply as "Dead." Ernest Knoth was listed as "Dead—No information on our list except the name." The promising young lawyer Guido Pantaleoni, who "went missing" while with WJD during the assault on Sicily, was listed as "Dead." Almost all these men were captured by enemy intelligence services and simply vanished. They were executed and buried where they fell, as with the Ginny team, or executed and cremated, as with the Dawes mission, or died in some concentration camp and were buried in mass graves.

This record, and Donovan's, was recognized belatedly by President Truman when, long after WJD's departure, he approved the award of an oak leaf cluster to WJD's World War I Distinguished Service Medal. In the citation the President noted: "With ability, judgment and foresight he anticipated the need of secret intelligence, research and analysis, and the conduct of unorthodox methods of warfare in support of military operations." Truman went on to observe that Donovan "extended his organization to operate in overseas theaters and neutral areas, and through his many diversified activities gave valuable service in the field of intelligence and special operations to theater commanders, the Joint Chiefs of Staff, the State Department and other government agencies." The President concluded: "Through his successful achievements, General Donovan contributed in a high degree to the success of military operations in the prosecution of the war."[3]

However, as is usual with secret citations, this one was general and vague. It said nothing about what was the most striking quality about Donovan, particularly in the first two years—his indomitability. While he and his service suffered several disasters, he was not conquerable. His service was not defeated by the enemy: it was destroyed by domestic politics of a peculiarly savage quality, which we shall see shortly. But for the moment it is necessary to define Donovan's and the OSS's enduring accomplishments in the operational fields.

Here Donovan's greatest contribution to the war was his recognition of the importance of Churchill's southern strategy, which was rarely understood within the Joint Chiefs. Donovan recognized that through excellent east-west road and rail communications Hitler could switch his armies and divisions rapidly between the French and Russian fronts. But once those divisions had been lured into the mountainous regions of the Balkans and Italy by a combination of the Italian collapse and Allied orthodox and unorthodox military operations, it proved difficult for Hitler to extricate them, unless he was prepared to accept the collapse of his southern front and the appearance of powerful Allied armies on the Danubian plain.

Army Chief of Staff George C. Marshall, the man chiefly responsible for American strategy, could not be brought to understand this. From Pearl Harbor onward Marshall argued that the Mediterranean theater was unimportant, a creation of the British largely to assure their lines of communication with their Empire, and that the Allies must confront the Germans in France.

As early as 1942, only six months after Pearl Harbor, he sent Eisenhower and other representatives to London to try to wean Churchill and the British Chiefs of Staff away from the southern strategy and to invade Europe *that year*. He failed because it soon became apparent that the United States would not then be able to make the necessary contribution to the landings and that even if the men and matériel were available, the Allies would be pinned into their bridgehead and would suffer calamitous losses on the scale of the Somme in 1916. Donovan saw this and spoke at length with FDR about the dangers of a premature head-on confrontation with the Germans. When, in 1943, Marshall again tried to induce FDR to sanction an invasion of France—in a year when the Allies could barely get ashore and stay ashore at Salerno—again Donovan's counsel prevailed.

Tactically Donovan's achievement in the European war again involved the southern strategy. In the first place there was the pressure he helped bring upon Germany from the south following the Italian surrender. Although at this time the OSS did suffer some lurid defeats, these had no effect upon Hitler's strategic considerations. Indeed, they served with the victories to convince Hitler that the Allies intended to invade Europe from the south; once that idea was implanted, there was nothing any of Hitler's military advisers could do to eradicate it.

The consequences for Germany of this dispersal of force were calamitous, for Hitler found himself hoisted on his own strategy, so to speak. There can be little doubt that had the Wehrmacht been permitted to concentrate all its strength in Normandy at the time of Neptune, Montgomery's armies would never have got ashore, and if they had, and if they had succeeded in staying there, the Allies would have faced another vast ex-sanguination such as they had suffered during the war of the trenches in 1914–1918—an ex-sanguination that would have produced severe reactions within the electorate, if not outright revolution. It will not be forgotten that the Red Army, in tackling the Wehrmacht head-on, lost 12,000,000 men dead (say some), or 20,000,000 dead (say others).

Mention must also be made of Donovan's operations in Brittany. Through them he and his Allies denied Rommel the divisions in Brittany at a time when Rommel needed infantry desperately so that he might withdraw his armor from the line and then launch a strategic counter-offensive in the first weeks of the invasion. He had insufficient infantry, he could not withdraw his armor, and there was no strategic offensive in those first precarious weeks.

The OSS's service in World War II was, therefore, gallant, honorable, and valuable. Why, therefore, with this ample evidence of endeavor and capability did Truman dissolve it? Why did he not dissolve the title but preserve the organization? Why did he not adopt WJD's plan for a post-war service? Why did he not keep Donovan as the first director of central intelligence?

The reasons were several, and antipathy played its part. We do not know whether this stemmed from the Kriemhilde Stellung incident in 1918 when WJD was deprived of artillery support, his units attacking the Hindenburg Line suffered severe casualties, and he made a vigorous complaint when he came out of the line. All we know is that Truman and his artillery battery were providing that sector of the front with artillery support on the night before Donovan's attack and that they were with-drawn from that mission soon afterward. What is evident is that Truman had a very long memory and was well capable of harboring intense dis-likes formed even a quarter of a century before.

There are, however, other traces of antipathy at a later date. It will be recalled that when Donovan was appointed assistant attorney general in 1924, the outgoing administration of the Department of Justice had in-stituted criminal proceedings against Senator Burton K. Wheeler, Demo-crat, of Montana, alleging that Wheeler had used his influence to obtain oil and gas leases for a personal friend and client. These accusations were thought widely to have been a Republican fabrication to inhibit Wheeler in his demands for an investigation of the Department of Justice concern-ing the events that came to be called the Teapot Dome scandals.

The charges against Wheeler had been brought by Donovan's pre-decessors, but the case was still awaiting trial when Harlan Stone and Donovan took over at the Department of Justice, their task to purge the department after Teapot Dome. Having reviewed the evidence, Donovan decided that the case must go for trial. It did, at Butte, Montana, but Wheeler was found not guilty. Wheeler then returned to the Hill, and a powerful Democratic anti-Donovan cabal formed around him and his colleague Senator Thomas J. Walsh, also of Montana.

In endorsing the original charges against Wheeler (charges that were, incidentally, justified if only on technical grounds), Donovan had made a very powerful enemy in Wheeler, who thereafter never lost an opportu-nity to attack Donovan. For example, as we have seen the cabal played a part in blocking Donovan's appointment to the post of attorney general in Herbert Hoover's Cabinet. It was an enduring enmity.

When Truman became the junior Democratic senator for Missouri in

1935, he was befriended by Wheeler. Truman acknowledged in his memoirs, "I always remember the cordial reception which Burton K. Wheeler . . . gave me at the beginning of my experience in the Senate," and he related with warm affection how Wheeler brought him onto the Interstate Commerce Committee, Truman's first important committee appointment. "I would not," Truman was to assert, "have been able to obtain this valuable experience without Wheeler," and he was deeply grateful for that help.[4]

From this early association there developed between Truman and Wheeler a strong personal and political friendship that lasted through their careers in the Senate. Wheeler could not have failed to express his dislike and distrust of Donovan during their conversations, especially when Donovan became FDR's spymaster. Certainly Wheeler's antipathy had endured, for in August 1941 the *Congressional Record* shows that Wheeler declared upon Donovan's appointment

> "Wild Bill" Donovan . . . is the man who conducted my prosecution. Mr. Donovan is now head of the Gestapo in the United States. That is the proper place for him, because he knows how such things should be done. He worked with [William J.] Burns, and with all the sleuths in the Department of Justice when they were raiding the offices of the late Senator Caraway, the late Senator Walsh, and old "Battling Bob" LaFollette. So he is a fitting man to head the Gestapo of the United States.[5]

Moreover, it is clear that Truman was antipathetic toward Donovan, for their only meeting between the death of FDR and the dissolution of the OSS lasted just fifteen minutes. It took place on May 14, 1945. For that matter, Donovan's dislike for Truman differed only in that it was more veiled, for as James Murphy later stated: "Truman didn't like Donovan and Donovan didn't like Truman. Period."[6]

There was more to Truman's decision to dissolve OSS than personal likes or dislikes, for the President also refused to see Murphy, who was a Democrat, a constituent, and also a member of the 1,000 Club, which raised campaign funds for Truman. Much more, for, of course, Donovan and the OSS were done in by a clique that had been working on the job since 1942. In the first place, Truman had been excluded by FDR while Vice President from the inner councils of the war. Consequently, he knew little about the world and nothing of intelligence work, except the gossip he had heard on the Hill and during his few visits to the White House— he was consulted only twice by FDR. Secondly, he claimed to have ideas of his own about the nature of the service that he would create to meet the perils of the peace. Also, the OSS was a war emergency agency, a sort of Democratic International, that he might well have thought should be liquidated as soon as possible after the end of the war. Fourthly, he listened to the director of the budget, Harold Smith, who as a mere functionary had formed a poor opinion of the budgetary and administrative procedures of the OSS and thought it wisest to dissolve it and start afresh. Fifthly, Truman distrusted the Republican complexion of the OSS in general and Donovan in particular.

Sixthly, shortly before deciding upon the liquidation of the OSS and the relief of Donovan, Truman received what came to be known as the Park Report. This document was given to Truman by a high officer of Military Intelligence, Colonel Richard Park, in charge of the White House map room for much of the time during the latter stages of FDR's presidency. The report consisted of a fifty-four page paper concerning the conduct of OSS. In a covering letter Park (who owed his appointment to General Strong) explained that on "the day [FDR] departed for Warm Springs [December 18, 1944] he authorized me to make an informal investigation of the Office of Strategic Services and report on my findings and conclusions. Certain information had been brought to [FDR's] attention which made such an investigation both timely and desirable."[7]

The Park Report consisted of

> scores—over 120—of items accusing OSS or its personnel of incompetence, insecurity, corruption, "orgies," nepotism, black-marketing, and almost anything else one could name. While Park cited seven "laudatory comments" on the work of OSS, they did little to lessen the clearness of his recommendations for the replacement of Donovan, the "scattering" of OSS—for instance R&A to G2 or State—and the establishment of a postwar organization modeled on the FBI-ONI-G2 structure in South America.[8]

To a man such as Truman with little experience of the intelligence world, no doubt the Park Report confirmed his own beliefs and suspicions about Donovan and the OSS. Furthermore, while the contents of the report were in general correct, it is evident that it had been compiled not to enhance the security of the United States and its Allies, but to further the ambitions of a few individuals on the U.S. General Staff, including Strong and his successor, General Bissell.

Yet the Park Report is not easily gainsaid. Inevitably the performance of the OSS was compared to the old-line intelligence agencies of the Army and the Navy. Since those agencies controlled Ultra and Magic, the two most important intelligence sources of World War II, it must have seemed to Truman that their performance had been superior to that of the OSS. All that the OSS could offer as a secret intelligence achievement were operations such as Penny Farthing and Shepherd, two of the best of the American human intelligence operations of World War II. Yet even those skillful and valorous exploits were overshadowed by the magic of Magic.

On the debit side there were the disasters. The Cereus affair in Istanbul, the Vessel affair at the Vatican, the Darlan incident, the Spanish problems with the State Department, the incident concerning Tito's headquarters (whether it was the OSS's fault or not), the Italian maelstrom, the grave disturbance with Churchill over the Greek reportage—all served to becloud the OSS's reputation to such an extent that the masterful operations of OSS SI and SO in France could have provided little mitigation for the defeats.

It follows, therefore, that to a man like Truman, Park's report seemed a stunning indictment of Donovan and the OSS. But to men wise and skilled in the ways of intelligence there was nothing exceptional about the contents of the report. Every intelligence service, including the best, encountered trouble of all descriptions. Wise statesmen were aware that ordinary standards of success and failure did not apply in the secret world. Yet clearly Truman neither accepted nor understood Donovan's theory that during a war the smallest success would outweigh the greatest blunder—a theory in which there was much good sense and truth.

So the OSS passed into legend. It was true that its successor organizations employed some of its best men and best intelligence assets—Henry Hyde, of Penny Farthing, for example, became chief of plans for an organization called the Central Intelligence Group. But in general, Truman's peremptory decision left the United States, in intelligence terms, defenseless. His successor organizations were disasters, as will be seen shortly.

Once again America became heavily dependent upon the British Secret Intelligence Service, especially for its European and German secret intelligence. Under the pressures of the Soviet menace, the 1940–41 special relationship between the American and the British services was reestablished, to the great profit and success of both—despite the best efforts of the British traitor Kim Philby, a high officer of the British SIS whose true political affections lay with Russia and Marxism. After brief retirement at the end of the German war Menzies was recalled to active service as head of the British SIS, and he worked harmoniously with WJD's successors.

Donovan himself had not forgotten Menzies's great services to the United States. In September 1944, when Anglo-American secret relations were at their lowest, he put Menzies in for a high American decoration, sending a handsome citation to the adjutant general, recommending that the Briton receive the Legion of Merit "in appropriate degree."[9] Donovan stated that Menzies had:

> made available to this Government the experience of the British in the field of secret intelligence. With his assistance and advice the United States was able to create quickly and effectively an organization capable of obtaining secret intelligence in areas of strategic importance throughout the world.

General Menzies continued his important services to the United States by encouraging a special liaison between the British SIS and its American counterpart, the Secret Intelligence Branch of OSS, performing an outstanding service not only to the Government of this country but to the common cause of Great Britain and the United States in the war against the enemy.

WJD then cited specific examples of the service which Menzies had rendered to the United States:

§ The training of American personnel in schools maintained by SIS in the United Kingdom.

§ Authorizing the arrangement by which British secret intelligence, theretofore unavailable to this country, was furnished by OSS for dissemination to the interested agencies of this Government.

§ Authorizing and effecting the arrangement between British SIS, the Secret Intelligence Branch of OSS, and the French BCRA . . . for a joint training program, as a result of which secret agents were dispatched to France and intelligence of great value to the Allied invasion forces was obtained.

Donovan went on: "Without the cooperation of [Menzies] it would have been extremely difficult for this agency to have undertaken secret intelligence activities in western Europe on behalf of the United States Government." Furthermore, WJD continued:

Throughout the years 1940–44, the period covered by the foregoing, Major General Menzies, whose entire service to this Government has been honorable, has worked diligently and effectively to promote close cooperation between the two nations and their respective agencies. In every possible way he has furthered the development of an organization which could undertake on behalf of the American Government and its Armed Forces the same type of operations so effectively conducted for the British Government by SIS.

In due course Menzies received the Legion of Merit in the degree of Chief Commander, the highest rank. In return Donovan was made a Knight Commander of the Most Excellent Order of the British Empire, which if his government permitted would have entitled WJD to the title "Sir" and the right to wear a cross patonce on a mantle of rose-pink satin.

Thus, at last, all was well in the secret arm of the special relationship, and the high degree of confidence and intimacy was still to be found in existence in the 1980's.

Donovan went back to his firm promptly, for his finances were in a disastrous state. He turned down the post of ambassador to France on the ground that he wanted something more active than garden parties.

In any case, he could not have afforded that post. For as John E. Tobin, a senior partner of WJD's firm, stated, when Donovan came back, "He had not a dime. All he had going for him was the firm and a rich wife."

Donovan went back as head of the firm with greatly reduced percentages—18 percent against the 50 percent he had enjoyed before 1940. That meant he would not be able to settle his debts quickly. Yet those debts were large. Some stated they amounted to $500,000, $300,000 of it in tax delinquencies and interest, $200,000 to the firm. Others contended the debt totaled $600,000, including $100,000 of miscellaneous debt. The result was that Donovan was compelled to sell his assets. Everything went.

The Georgetown house went to the Meyers of the Washington *Post* for $125,000 and became the town residence of Katharine Graham (which it was still in 1982). He sold the flat in Beekman Place, moving to a less expensive apartment at Sutton Place. The farm was sold for $125,000 to the Rumsey Trust, which then held it as Ruth's property, the farm reverting to her when she became the sole beneficiary upon her brother's death. The debt to the firm was covered by a life insurance policy, so that Donovan was just able to meet his obligations. But he was never again as prosperous as he had been and was wholly dependent upon his income from the firm. This was substantial, being in the region of $200,000 a year during the period he remained active in the firm. But when he died, he would be by his standards almost penniless.

Donovan plowed back into his legal career with his usual energy, engaging in a wide variety of other cases all over the United States and the world. But once more he found that the law was not enough. He sought the nomination as senator from New York but failed to get it. That was the last straw, the final humiliation, although the reason why his party would not support his nomination was his old stubbornness—he would not make deals—combined with his poor sense of political timing.

Yet against this general background, Donovan's career entered one of its most interesting phases: the World Commerce Corporation. Whether this organization was an intelligence organization or a corporation engaging in commerce would be debated from time to time.

In May 1945, when the war in Europe had been over but a few days, a small group around William Stephenson—Intrepid—formed a company known as the British American Canadian Corporation S.A., a New York-based company registered in Panama. That title remained in use until April 2, 1947, when BAC changed its name to the World Commerce Corporation, which still had its headquarters in New York and was still registered in Panama. What was remarkable about the corporation was that all but one of its first directors, and almost everyone associated with it, had had intelligence connections with the American and British governments during World War II and that all the officers were former members of Donovan's and Intrepid's services.

They included Sir Charles Hambro (chief of the SOE); George Muhle Merten (who had run WJD's highly secret and exceptionally well-funded Project George, which had been concerned with enemy penetrations of South America); David Mackenzie Ogilvy (one of Intrepid's staff officers); John Arthur Reid Pepper (Intrepid's deputy); and Intrepid himself. In registering their names for tax purposes, all but Hambro used British government addresses in New York and Washington, including the head-quarters of British Security Coordination and the British Embassy.

The officers contemplated at formation were Pepper (president), Ogilvy and Merten (vice-presidents), and Thomas William Hill (secre-tary). Hill gave as his address Room 3606, 30 Rockefeller Plaza, New York City—the same address as that of Intrepid's British Security Coordina-tion organization.

At first Donovan appears to have played no formal part in the establish-ment of either BAC or WCC, although his law firm, at that time known as Donovan Leisure Newton Lumbard & Irvine, acted as legal advisers. Among those legal advisers was Otto C. Doering. Donovan became a director on October 23, 1947, at the same time as Edward R. Stettinius, secretary of state from November 30, 1944, to July 2, 1945, who had substantial financial holdings in the corporation.

In due course a number of other people prominent in intelligence and special operations joined the firm, as directors, officers, or shareholders. They included Russell Forgan, of the Glore Forgan Group of merchant bankers (David Bruce's successor as chief of OSS Europe and Donovan's heir apparent at the end of the war); Lester Armour (former deputy chief of OSS London); Sidney Weinberg (who was to have headed the OSS mission to Moscow); W. K. Eliscu (a member of WJD's OSS staff); Lieu-tenant Colonel Rex L. Benson (of Menzies's staff in the British Secret Intelligence Service and chairman of Robert Benson and Company, of London, merchant bankers); and several persons who had been promi-nent in the Canadian intelligence services.

Also, people with intelligence connections, but not formally members of any intelligence service, took an interest in the corporation. They included Nelson Rockefeller (former coordinator of inter-American affairs, an organization with intelligence responsibilities and associations in South America); J. J. McCloy (former undersecretary at the War De-partment and high commissioner in Germany); Richard Mellon; and Sir Victor Sassoon.

When Frank T. Ryan (of OSS Spain) became president of the World Commerce Corporation in place of Pepper, who remained as executive vice-president, Intrepid arranged for him to see in London a group of men prominent in government, intelligence, and finance. They included

Lord Leathers (wartime transport minister and head of William Cory & Son Ltd., the largest coal, lighterage, general shipping, transportation, and ancillary businesses in the world); Sir William Rootes (the automobile manufacturer); Sir Alexander Korda (head of various motion picture firms); Moir Mackenzie (deputy director of the Federation of British Industries); Lord Selborne (wartime economic warfare minister); Sir Charles and Olaf Hambro (from whom Intrepid hoped to get diamond business for WCC); Richard Fleming (head of Robert Fleming, the merchant bankers); Louis Franck (partner in M. Samuel, largest bullion dealers in the world and one of Intrepid's most important officers); Brigadier W. T. Keswick (head of Matheson and Co., Ltd., the large Far East traders, a director of the Hong Kong and Shanghai Bank, vice-governor of the Hudson's Bay Company, and chief of the SOE in Asia during the war); Sir Harold Wernher (the British industrialist); Geoffrey Lloyd (youngest of Churchill's war ministers and head of the Fuel and Power Ministry); Lord Beaverbrook (proprietor of the London *Daily Express* and the *Evening Standard*); Richard Coit (partner in one of the largest firms of stockbrokers); Ian Fleming (head of the Foreign Department of the Kemsley Press, and second-in-command of British Naval Intelligence); Sir Ralph Glyn (prominent industrialist); Frederic Hudd (Canadian high commissioner in London); Lord Sempill (chairman of the International Chambers of Commerce); Colonel Douglas Dodds-Parker (chief of SOE North Africa and active in the development of German business); George Taylor (Australian Mercantile Company); General Sir Colin Gubbins (chief of the SOE); Sir Campbell Stuart (director of the London *Times*); and Frederick A. Szarvasy (chairman, Anglo-Federal Bank and a leading financier).

All these connections given to Ryan by Intrepid were undoubtedly for purely business purposes. Yet the heavy loading of the World Commerce Corporation with men who had been in intelligence, plus the intelligence connections of their contacts, made them a source of interest, which was not unreasonable or idle. It was to emerge, for example, that a principal contact of WCC in Greece, then under heavy Communist insurgent attack, was a former member of the Greek and British secret services, while in Thailand, which was also threatened, WCC's contact was a prominent OSS secret agent, James Thompson, the "Thai silk king," who was coming to control the Thai silk and brocade industry on finance provided by WCC and who was to be murdered in very odd circumstances in Malaya. What, therefore, was the declared purpose of WCC?

Some clues lie in a letter on the World Commerce Corporation which in November 1947 Donovan forwarded to General Lucius Clay (U.S. high commissioner in Germany), Robert Murphy (U.S. political adviser for Germany), and General Charles E. Saltzman (assistant secretary for occupied areas at the State Department). The letter, written by Ryan, eschewed all political considerations, although the matters dealt with were of immense political importance. Defining the general purposes of the corporation, Ryan wrote:

> In our view the restoration of economic balance in Europe is fundamentally a problem of industrial and agricultural production. The purposes to be served by such production are the maintenance of populations and the creation of internationally exchangeable values which are essential in supporting the continuance of the productive operations. The restoration of production and the continuing processes which involve the international exchange of goods are the fields of primary interest to World Commerce Corporation. In these directions we are prepared to cooperate with private industry and with official bodies.[10]

Ryan advised Clay that WCC had its head office in New York and "close connections in all of the larger centres of the United States." It also had "representation in 47 foreign countries, both through branch offices and direct subsidiaries as well as through agency relationships." There was "thus provided a world-wide network which is intended to serve the purposes of procurement and of distribution as well as to supply reliable and up to date information with respect to markets and products." The "financial resources available to W.C.C. are substantial."[11]

Whether Clay met WCC's request for authority to open an office in Germany is uncertain; the probability is that such an office was opened. But by the end of 1947—as the cold war had developed in intensity, particularly in Germany—the stockholders and associations of WCC had widened greatly. Among the new stockholders were the Atlas Corporation of New York; Bacon, Whipple & Company, of Chicago; David K. E. Bruce; Ellen McHenry and Louise Este Bruce, both of New York; Corporation House of Ottawa; Cudd & Company, of New York; Daniel A. De Menocal, of New York; Thomas G. Drew-Brook, of Toronto; Harold S. Foley, of Vancouver; Charles F. Glore, of Chicago; Joseph C. Grew (former under secretary of state and ambassador to Japan); Hambros Bank (Nominees) Ltd., London; Islands Company Ltd., of Bermuda; Ladenburg, Thalmann & Company, New York; Alan M. Scaife, Pittsburgh; Sarah Mellon Scaife, Pittsburgh; Admiral Lewis H. Strauss (partner in Kuhn, Loeb & Company, New York); Trans America Corporation, San Francisco; Dorothy Reaves Weicker, of New York; Arthur B. van Buskirk, Pittsburgh; Taylor, McDougald & Company, Ltd., Toronto; and Hathaway Watson, Jr., of New York.

In the United States WCC operated through various subsidiaries, buying and selling such merchandise as cement, automobile tires, barbed wire, rice, shoes, and stockings. In England it was engaged in similar procurement activities, operating under agreements with Jardine, Matheson and Company Ltd., and British & Western European Trading Company Ltd., a company in turn associated with the banking firm of Morgan Grenfell.

By late 1947 WCC claimed to have opened trading outlets in Argentina, Uruguay, Peru, Brazil, Chile, Colombia, and Mexico, while through a subsidiary it had outlets in North Africa, India, China, and Ceylon. Through its British associates it operated into France, Holland, Belgium, Spain, Portugal, Switzerland, and Italy. It had acquired the majority stock in the Biddle Sawyer Corporation of New York, which was engaged in worldwide trade in "fine chemicals, pharmaceuticals, botanical drugs, waxes, gums and essential oils." It held also a "number of leading agencies such as surgical instruments, chemical companies, medicinal soaps, cosmetics, food essences and other allied lines." Moreover, it "also acts as purchasing agent in the United States for Messrs. Gordon Woodroffe and Company, Ltd., of London, India, Tunis, Morocco and Algiers and, in this connection, is engaged in exporting such equipment as road-making machinery, excavators, scrapers, tractors, agricultural equipment, motor cars, and general merchandise."[12]

This surely was one of the most interesting corporations in modern U.S. business history—a fine web of the wealthiest, most blue-blooded, and most influential groups in the English-speaking world. Nor, it must be stated, was it financially unsuccessful. In its final financial statement —for the eight months ended August 31, 1962, when it was sold for taxation reasons—World Commerce's balance sheet showed total assets of $16,096,443.62, total liabilities of $6,468,898.89, and total capital of $9,627,544.73. During those eight months its income from trading, commissions, interest, and other sources totaled just under $1,000,000, with administrative and general expenses and taxes of $635,985.65. With the interest income of prior years less taxes, the company earned a further $204,037.80, making a total net income of $513,495.89. Yet in its first year of operations in 1947 it had a $50,000 loss.

What, therefore, was this astonishing company? What was its purpose? Frank Ryan's letter to General Clay provides the underlying philosophy of the World Commerce Corporation. Ever since he had seen Germany in ruins at the end of World War II, Donovan espoused the belief that either a Communist Germany would rise from the ruins or Germany would be rebuilt and restored to the democratic comity. Whether it went left or right would depend to an important extent on the attitude of Anglo-American-Canadian finance and business. World Commerce was, therefore, the outcome of that espousal. It was enlightened capitalism's answer to Communist imperialism. This doctrine is plain from Ryan's letter to Clay:

> W.C.C. is prepared to provide its full cooperation to the Joint Occupying Authority toward the restoration of production in Germany. World market

and price reports, industrial investigations looking toward the development and submission of specific proposals and a general commercial information service are contemplated as proper elements of co-operative activity by W.C.C. in Germany.

In other words, one of the elements of WCC was a commercial intelligence service based on the wartime Anglo-American-Canadian intelligence services, now operating as private, commercial entities with the overt purpose of preventing the economic collapse of a Europe without Germany, and the underlying purpose of preventing Russia from establishing the Russo-German hegemony that would arise from such a collapse. It was the modern progression of the geopolitical theory of Sir Halford Mackinder, who was still alive when WCC was founded. Mackinder had propounded in 1904, in a work entitled *Democratic Ideals and Reality,* that he who controlled Russia and Germany would control the heartland of the world and that the combination of Russian manpower and German industry would create the most powerful combination in the world—the so-called Eurasian hegemony.

World Commerce's plan to frustrate the creation of this hegemony, which would be Marxist, was breathtaking in its magnitude, truly Donovan. For as Ryan advised Clay:

W.C.C. will submit firm offerings of raw materials, supplies or equipment which are required in Germany for the purposes of production.

W.C.C. will submit from bids for products of general commercial usage which may become available for export out of German production.

W.C.C. will develop and submit for co-ordinating the purchases, production and export sales of a specific plant, of a group of plants or of an industry. These proposals will look toward a specifically integrated and self-supporting operation in which the facilities of the German producers on the one hand and W.C.C. on the other will be jointed to accomplish the required result.

He also proposed: "Existing plant and management facilities in Germany will be supplemented by presently unavailable new or additional equipment, by supplies, by raw materials and by technical and sales services to be furnished by W.C.C."

Yet it should not be thought that the majestic scheme for Germany and other war-torn nations in any way benefited Donovan. He owned no stock in the company, no nominees held stock for Donovan, and it is said he even forgot to draw his nominal directors' fees. Be that as it may, World Commerce was Donovan's only hope of restoring his fortunes to their prewar grandeur. But evidently he failed. When Donovan died, he left an estate of $148,000 before probate. He was so heavily in debt that all Ruth received from the estate was a check for $38,000.

While Donovan was engaged in the business of World Commerce, he still practiced law, fighting a Supreme Court case for the Great Atlantic and Pacific Tea Company, flying out to Hong Kong to spend seven weeks examining the legal problems of Claire Chennault's Chinese Air Transport line, and generally running the firm. With the resignation of J. Edward Lumbard, one of the founding partners, to become first a U.S. attorney in New York and then a judge on the Second Circuit Court of Appeals, Irvine became the managing partner. Under him the Donovan firm made its first $1,000,000 in net profits in 1950, when there were twenty-one partners and thirty-four associates. But Donovan became progressively less interested in the practice of law (although he remained extremely active and successful as a business scout) and progressively more interested in the state of United States Intelligence.

With the onset of the cold war, Donovan made a tentative step toward a return to intelligence work in January 1947, at about the same time he became a director of World Commerce. In an address to the New York Young Republicans Club, he declared U.S. Intelligence was once more the "Orphan Annie of the services" and asserted, as he had in 1941, the "security of our nation is dependent on tested knowledge" and "intelligence must be our first line of defense."[13]

Donovan played no part in the deliberations that preceded the passage of the National Security Act and the establishment of the CIA. Yet the CIA was a direct return to the Donovan plan of November 1944, including all of his provisions for a major government department devoted to intelligence at the seat of government, headed by a civilian, serving the President, performing not only intelligence but also all the special means developed by the OSS, and restricted in what it could do within the United States and against American citizens.

For a time WJD hoped that Truman would bring him back as director, and there was considerable lobbying for Donovan toward that end. But WJD was never formally considered as the first director of central intelligence—even assuming that his financial position would have enabled him to accept that post. Instead, Truman appointed Admiral Roscoe H. Hillenkoetter. While it is probably not fair to hold Hillenkoetter responsible, the early performance of the CIA was disastrous, beginning with Hillenkoetter's appointment. While the agency was still a secret matter in Washington, the Paris newspaper *France-Soir* announced the appointment under the headline THE UNITED STATES CREATES A SECRET SERVICE IN TIME OF PEACE. Hillenkoetter, who lately had been naval attaché in Paris, explained lamely: "The French Secret Service seems to find out everything."[14]

A number of major intelligence failures ensued: the Berlin crisis of 1948; the failure to forecast Russia's development of the atomic bomb, at a time when all military-industrial and political planning was being done on the basis that the United States would have the bomb exclusively at least until 1952; the surprise over the Korean War; the surprise over China's entry into that war; the surprise over Russia's establishment of a strategic air force; the surprise over Russia's detonation first of the hydrogen bomb; the chaos created by the failure to gauge accurately France's staying power in Indochina. And so on.

During this period Donovan learned that the CIA was in exactly the same fix as the COI and the OSS before it—despite the existence of laws, none of the other agencies engaged in intelligence work in Washington would work with, or give material to, the CIA, and so it could not fully advise the President what was going on in the world. Again the issue was power—that intelligence was power and intelligence shared was power shared.

In 1948 Donovan was to find out for himself how weak the CIA had become. That year the secretary of defense, James Forrestal, invited him to serve on a small secret committee consisting of Dr. Vannevar Bush, Admiral Sidney Souers, and General Alfred M. Gruenther, to study the problems of defense against unconventional attack against the United States, including clandestine attack employing biological weapons, clandestine delivery of atomic weapons, and propaganda. Donovan was invited to serve on this committee, and he accepted. The subject was divided into seven subjects for investigation:

1. Clandestine attack employing biological weapons.

2. Clandestine delivery of atomic explosives.

3. Attacks on key individuals, groups or installations.

4. Certain special applications of psychological warfare (i.e., thought control or special mode, as it was called).

5. Unconventional methods of economic warfare.

6. Clandestine attack employing chemical weapons.

7. Clandestine attack employing radiological weapons.

In turn, Donovan formed a small committee to study the problems. It consisted of Otto C. Doering, T. J. McFadden, Richard P. Heppner (former chief OSS Southeast Asia), and William E. Colby (a former OSS Jedburgh and a future director of central intelligence). Donovan and his colleagues were cleared to read top secret material, and he called for what the CIA knew about Soviet biological warfare capabilities.

He then learned that the agency knew less about Russia, despite the wartime alliance, than the U.S. intelligence community had known about Germany in 1939. As for biological warfare, all that the Washington intelligence community knew about Russian capabilities was contained in this report dated April 20, 1949:

A. *Organization.*
Limited information from German and Japanese sources indicates that the Russians began conducting BW [biological warfare] research some time in the middle 1930's. The Germans were convinced that the USSR had BW installations on Gradomlya Island in Lake Seliger, Vozrozhdeniya in Lake Aral, and at Schlüsselburg. The Japanese mentioned Vladivostok and Khabarovsk. None of these locations has yet been proved to have BW installations.

Recent reports from a well-informed source in London indicate that [Russian BW] the direction of Col. N. N. Ginsburg. It is believed that the First Chief Directorate of the USSR under Beriya, may be assisting the Red Army in procuring supplies for BW development.

B. *Research and Development.*
Offense: There is no definite knowledge of the kinds of research and development now being undertaken by the USSR; it is certain only that research on BW is in progress. Russian scientists have published purely scientific reports on every pathogenic microorganism and toxin that could possibly be used as a BW agent; therefore, BW research of any kind may conceivably be in progress. Soviet interrogations of German and Japanese scientists demonstrated the Russian interest in plague, anthrax, and the intestinal diseases. The most reliable indication of current Soviet interest is derived from a report of Soviet experiments on the disinfection of wells. Some of these wells have been deliberately contaminated by an agent causing a violent and fatal intestinal disease. A recent unconfirmed report states that the Soviets have bombs for dissemination of biological agents. It is too soon, however, to assert that the Soviets are ready to use BW as a military weapon.

Defense: Practically nothing is known about Soviet research and development on defense against BW. Of course all usual medical research on infectious diseases and on public health facilities for controlling them may be applied to BW defense.

There is only a rumor of the existence of military training for BW. No plans for civilian training are yet known.

C. *National Policy.*
Nothing is known regarding political or military policy with respect to use of BW.[15]

Donovan believed and said that since lack of basic information about Russia was to be found throughout the American system, it followed that the United States was vulnerable to a number of operations in which the Russians had displayed expertise. The United States was easily deceived on Soviet military matters, it could be led into rapid and almost complete demobilization in the belief that the atomic bomb was all that was needed for its defense, and, as Donovan warned, believing that Russia was exhausted by the war, the United States could afford not to undertake expensive programs of weapons research and development.

Thus, the Soviet Union gained a decade in which to regroup its armies and war industries and to prepare for the great ideological battles of the fifties and sixties. Russia's excellent intelligence services expanded rapidly and forcefully into the world being evacuated by the colonial powers, at the same time penetrating all the principal citadels of its ideological adversaries, undermining their institutions and their confidence in themselves.

That irresponsible and dangerous state of affairs was directly traceable to Truman's decision to fire Donovan and dissolve the OSS, and, having done so, his failure to provide the country with effective substitutes.

During this period of turmoil in America's intelligence affairs, the Holohan affair began to filter onto the front pages of the nation's press, giving the OSS and Donovan's stewardship a luridity that obscured their greater achievements and finally destroyed WJD's candidacy for the post of first director of the CIA.

What had occurred between the dissolution of the OSS and the reemergence of the Holohan specter was that the case had been turned over to the U.S. Army's Criminal Investigation authorities at Trieste, which remained under Allied military occupation long after Italy had been handed back to its own people, and assigned to Special Agent Frederick Gardella on or about July 1, 1946, largely as a result of Donovan's prodding in Washington when he learned that the case was rotting on the vine.

Gardella then proceeded to interview a leading partisan leader, Giorgio—Georgi Aminta Migliari—who described Holohan as "an upright man and a true soldier, just but firm." This firmness made Icardi and LoDolce complain, but only as most soldiers do about their commanding officers. A principal cause of complaint was that at first Holohan refused to allow the two to wear civilian clothes. In the first place, the *ordre de mission* specifically excluded the wearing of civilian clothes, and secondly, to have done so would have placed Icardi and LoDolce beyond the protection of the Geneva Convention and, if they were captured, as was very possible, made them liable to execution as spies.[16]

On the other hand, Giorgio believed it had been Lupo, Moscatelli's professional killer, not Icardi and LoDolce, who had murdered Holohan for the gold and because the major had favored the demo-Christian partisans over the Communists.

Gardella's attempts to establish how much money Holohan had been carrying met with little success, for the OSS records were closed. But Icardi did state at some stage that the U.S. value of the gold was $16,000. This was made up of 450 gold marengos, each of six grams and which Holohan valued at 300 Italian lire per gram. Also, he carried a great deal of lire, which had little value anywhere except in Italy, and several thousand Swiss francs and U.S. dollars. At this point Gardella elicited significant information from Giorgio: Before his disappearance Holohan had begun to run short of lire and asked Icardi to exchange some of the gold pieces for lire. Icardi had contacted Giorgio to arrange conversion, stating that Holohan wanted 300 lire per gold gram and if they obtained anything more than that, then they could keep the extra for themselves.

As Donovan's papers show, Gardella established that Giorgio had arranged the exchange through a wealthy industrialist, Allesandro Cancelliere, who changed 450 marengos for 2,600,000 lire. This money had been given to Giorgio in full, except for 97,000 lire used to pay the intermediaries, leaving a sum of 2,503,000. Giorgio and Icardi retained 1,650,000 lire, turning over 853,000 lire to Holohan as finances for the continuance of the Chrysler Mission. Giorgio and Icardi then entered into a business partnership—for, it transpired, the manufacturing of toys. The contract was signed by Giorgio and Icardi and witnessed by a local priest, Don Carlo Murzillo, and Cancelliere. Copies of this contract were furnished Gardella by Giorgio. Shortly after this transaction, on several occasions, Icardi had "approached Giorgio in a confidential manner and proposed getting rid of the major."[17]

But, Gardella warned, Giorgio "was a man of few scruples." It was "known that Georgi used to keep and send home a good portion of the funds that the major gave him weekly to support the mission" and that "The money given him by OSS at the end of the war to pay premiums to partisans that helped the United States Government was also misused by him and in some instances the partisans never received any of it." Giorgio had also "dealt in selling arms to other partisan units."[18]

With that intelligence, Donovan was now inclined to believe that Holohan had been murdered by Icardi, and the belief was reinforced by a further report by Gardella which reached WJD soon after the end of the war. Gardella interviewed Marina Duelli on September 18, 1946. A woman "well liked by Major Holohan in an almost paternal manner," Signorina Duelli had acted as messenger between the partisans' headquarters and Holohan—very dangerous work—and she stated (1) that partisans, not the Germans or the *fascisti,* had been responsible for Holohan's death, (2) there had been friction between Icardi and Holohan, and (3) when she felt that Captain Leto, real name Recapito Pasquale, was working against Holohan on behalf of Moscatelli, she had gone to Switzerland to warn the OSS of her suspicions concerning Holohan's disappearance. At that, Icardi had written a letter, which both Giorgio and Duelli claimed to have seen, to Lupo recommending that she be "put out of circulation." When Gardella saw Duelli, however, she was reluctant to enlarge on this allegation because, she said, "she was afraid that her life would be placed in danger." Agent Gardella did not find Icardi's letter. In other interviews Duelli did add that before he disappeared, Holohan had remarked to her that "he could not rely on anyone, not even Americans."

Agent Gardella then dug up Captain Leto, the agent who had mis-managed the Pineapple airdrop in favor of the Communists. Leto stated that he had heard Icardi make threats against the life of Holohan.

Lastly, as the Donovan files on the case showed, Gardella saw Tullio Lussi, one of the Italian secret agents who had landed with Holohan. Lussi stated that at the time he had regarded the story of Holohan's disappearance in a German-*fascisti restrallemento* on the Villa Castelnuovo as unsatisfactory and investigated the affair then and there. But because of "existing conditions he could not be as thorough as one should be." He had gone to the villa and "found about 90 cartridges and casings of the type used in the Sten guns, which the mission had. He also found the spring from a hand grenade." There had been *no* enemy cartridges lying around, no signs of any enemy dead or wounded, and no signs of a gun battle inside or of forcible entry into the villa. Moreover, there was a caretaker, and he stated that he had heard gunfire and had investigated but had seen no Germans or *fascisti*.

Lussi had reported all this information to OSS Switzerland, but the courier had been captured by the Germans.[19] Then Lussi made a second report for OSS Switzerland and gave it and the cartridge cases and gre-nade spring to Giorgio. But that report, too, had never reached its desti-nation, and when Lussi asked for the cartridge cases and grenade spring, Giorgio "could not produce them."

Gardella then reported that he had located one of Holohan's partisan bodyguards, Giuseppe Mannini, who stated:

> . . . at the time of the incident he . . . was on his way back up the path to the villa. As he was going up, Major Holohan, Lieutenant Icardi, and Sergeant LoDolce were coming down. After he passed them, he heard the noise and the shooting. He immediately answered fire in the direction from where the shots came. Then he retreated, firing as he did. He jumped over the wall near the shore and as he landed there was a loud explosion—the hand grenade. He did not see any of the Americans. He got in the boat and road [*sic*] away. It was rather foggy and he lost his sense of direction and instead of going north he went in a south-easterly direction and ended up near Buccione.[20]

In February 1945, Gardella continued, LoDolce had had a nervous breakdown and had to be exfiltrated to Switzerland. The circumstances of the breakdown were:

> After the incident at Villa Castelnuovo and the subsequent disappearance of the major, Sergeant LoDolce seemed to have become very frightened and nervous. He never wanted to talk about it to anyone. As time passed, his condition grew worse and was noted by everyone. On the 17th of February 1945, he was staying at Quarna with Pupo [a partisan]. There were other partisans in the same house who were talking about killing Fascists, et cetera.

LoDolce understood very little Italian and became nervous. He took Pupo upstairs and told Pupo that these partisans were going to kill them. LoDolce took and tied together his and Pupo's belts, took off his shoes and also told Pupo to do the same. Pupo tried to reason with him but couldn't. LoDolce then started to lower himself out of the window; the belts broke and he fell. Pupo ran downstairs and out and tried to reason with LoDolce and told him to wait while he went to get his shoes. When he returned with LoDolce's shoes, LoDolce was gone.

The next morning a woman brought LoDolce, who had spent the night hiding out and was frozen, to the house, and he was found to be in a nervous condition. They took LoDolce to the priest of Alzo, Don Luigi, who took care of him for several weeks. . . . Lo Dolce's mental derangement was so noticeable that Icardi sent him to Switzerland.[21]

Lastly, during the 1946 investigation it was Gardella's conclusion that:

§ Icardi and LoDolce "made statements at several different times that they wanted to get rid of the major."

§ Icardi and Giorgio "did take and put to their own use 1,650,000 lire of the mission's funds and made up a contract of partnership in reference to said sum on the 21st of November 1944."

§ Icardi was "going about interesting himself in business deals for the future and not letting his superiors know about it."

§ He had "further told certain partisans, if they should get important information, not to let the major know about it, but give same directly to him, and generally had put the mission's security in damage and had been causing the partisans to mistrust the major."

§ It was the opinion of Gardella that "the disappearance of the major was a political move engineered by the Communist group headed by Moscatelli, a man of few scruples, who was capable of weakening the opposite party in order to enrich his own."

§ That "both Icardi and LoDolce did not cooperate with Major Holohan; that Icardi was more interested in personal affairs, and of elevating his position with the mission than carrying out his required duties; that Georgi was the type of partisan who wanted to enrich himself and [was] not primarily interested in his nation's welfare."

§ Mannini was "a mercenary type and also a man of very few scruples, and . . . was quite efficient in carrying out executions of Nazi-Fascist prisoners and of disposing of their bodies in the lake."

Donovan was profoundly alarmed by this report, for it was now clear that one of his key men, the leader of a major mission, had been murdered—in OSS slang "sent to Switzerland without shoes." Moreover, it was not impossible that some of his own men had had a hand in the murder. What concerned Donovan beyond the death of a fine officer was that the facts were becoming known on the Hill and that inevitably such a lurid affair would reflect poorly upon the OSS at a time when the future of American intelligence was becoming a matter of intense public interest.

But for the moment there was little Donovan could do to complete the legal process necessary to secure an indictment.

In 1947 the Holohan case was turned over to the Italian government, who assigned to it an able Carabinieri detective, Lieutenant Elio Albieri. In 1948 Albieri went to see Marina Duelli, the partisan woman whom Holohan had befriended. By now Miss Duelli had returned to Catholicism, and Albieri appealed to her sense of religious duty. Deeply troubled by her knowledge and suspicions, but still afraid of the powerful Communist Moscatelli, she gave Albieri a single broad hint: She mentioned the names of two former partisans who she thought knew more than they had admitted about Holohan's death. The men were Giuseppe Mannini, a worker in a tin factory where he had access to potassium cyanide, and Gualtiero Tozzini, the peasant known to the Communists by the work name Pupo. These men had been part of Holohan's Italian bodyguard and, Duelli stated, Tozzini was particularly likely to talk—the Communists had never succeeded in weaning him from his church. Now, she said, his priest had refused him the comforts of the religion until he told the police what he knew of the events at the Villa Castelnuovo on the night Holohan died.

Albieri's inquiries showed that indeed, Tozzini's divorce from the sacraments was weighing heavily upon his soul and that Miss Duelli was correct: He was the man most likely to break the conspiracy of silence attending those events five years before on that dark, foggy night at the Lake of Orta.

It was now March 1950, and Albieri of the Carabinieri interviewed both Mannini and Tozzini. Neither said much, but their attitude was sufficient to warrant the employment of a U.S. agent, Major Henry L. Manfredi, with the U.S. Army Criminal Investigation Department at Trieste. A special agent of the U.S. Narcotics Bureau before the war and a man who had spent a long career in major crime investigations, Manfredi arrived at Arona to help in the interrogation of Mannini and Tozzini. In due course they both confessed they had taken part with Icardi and LoDolce in the murder of Holohan at the Villa Castelnuovo on the evening of December 6, 1944. They stated that Holohan had been poisoned with cyanide in his minestrone, and when that seemed not to have worked, he was shot twice in the head by LoDolce, using Mannini's 9-millimeter

Beretta, as he lay, sick from the cyanide, on his bed. His corpse had then been taken on Icardi's instructions and placed in the deepest part of the Lake of Orta.

The lake was then dragged at the place where Tozzini stated the corpse had been tipped, and a body wrapped in a heavy canvas sleeping bag was recovered. It was found to be in excellent forensic condition for two reasons: (1) the absence of fish in the lake and (2) the intense cold of the water had preserved the body more or less intact. The corpse was definitely identified as that of Holohan, and two 9-millimeter bullets were removed from the brain. These were compared with bullets fired from Mannini's Beretta, and the markings on the bullets and those test-fired were found to be identical.

But as Donovan's file on the murder was to show, the pathologist failed to detect any traces of potassium cyanide in the corpse, probably either because the lake water had washed away the poison or because, as one of the pathologists stated, Holohan had taken a quantity of sugar or glucose before his death—"as the Rasputin murder case at Petrograd in 1916 had shown, glucose inhibited the effects of potassium cyanide."[22]

News of the discovery of Holohan's corpse soon reached Donovan, who drew the attention of the attorney general, J. Howard McGrath, to the matter. WJD also spoke personally with General George C. Marshall, who was now secretary of defense. To both McGrath and Marshall Donovan pointed out that the evidence of murder against Icardi and LoDolce was substantial. And as WJD indicated, urgency had entered the case since he doubted if the United States had jurisdiction concerning the murder. However, in his view the United States might have jurisdiction in the matter of embezzlement of government funds, provided the government acted rapidly before the statute of limitations ran out. At the same time he wrote to Secretary of State Dean Acheson to ask whether Italy or the United States would have jurisdiction in the question of a murder on Italian territory of a U.S. officer in wartime by U.S. personnel serving under his command. In all, an interesting and rare legal problem attended the case.

Marshall's reaction was to order the assignment of two U.S. agents to the case. They were H. Rex Smith and Harry K. Gisslow, of the Criminal Investigation Department. Because the weakest link was judged to be LoDolce, the ex-sergeant was brought into a Rochester, New York, police station for questioning. There and then he made an eight-page confession in his own handwriting, a document that confirmed the facts related by Tozzini and Mannini, although LoDolce had had no knowledge of what they had said to Manfredi.[23]

LoDolce stated that soon after the Chrysler Mission had landed, friction had developed between Holohan and the representative of the Communist chieftain, Vincenzo Moscatelli, and also between Holohan and

Icardi. They "had never been friendly," and "an air of tenseness and friction developed between them which was felt by myself and the partisans who had contact with us."

Holohan "hardly ever talked to me about what the mission was supposed to do and . . . Icardi would tell me continuously that things were going wrong and how operations should have been conducted and I began to feel that we were all in a situation from which we would not survive." He had begun to feel also, as had Icardi, that "we were being hampered by the Major from performing a useful service. Icardi argued that we could, without the Major, transmit messages of German and Fascist troop movements, armaments, plans, that would save hundreds of American soldiers' lives, instead of sending messages which concerned themselves with partisan's [sic] politics." LoDolce continued:

> It all (the plan to rid ourselves of Major Holohan) began in a joking way. For instance, at times when the Major had been overly authoritative with one of us or one of our partisan attendants and then left the room, someone would say in a joking way, "Should I send him to Switzerland without his shoes?" which meant to kill someone. This expression was used commonly. . . . Somehow, from being just a saying, the thing became serious. Icardi suggested that we give the Major something that would make him sick for a while so that we could get the underground to send him to allied territory via Switzerland, but no one took him seriously.

But then, said LoDolce:

> [Mannini] brought something that looked like sugar in a piece of paper and said that it was poison and could be used to kill the Major. By this date the Major was held in intense aversion by myself, Icardi, [Mannini, and Tozzini], and means of getting rid of him had been discussed. It may have been a means of letting off steam—The fear caused by being in the general situation may have made us want to direct it against something tangible and wild and impossible plans had been discussed and discarded.

During the evening of the "6th of December 1944 things suddenly became serious." Mannini said that " 'he had tried the poison on a cat and that it had died instantly.' " Icardi then said that " 'we would have to use the poison right away—that night.' " Mannini and Tozzini prepared a meal of soup and rice, LoDolce continued:

> . . . and Mannini placed some of the poison in the soup. Major Holohan was then . . . called to dinner, and we all sat down to eat. When the Major had taken a few spoonfuls of the soup he remarked that it burned. Icardi said "Yes, its [sic] hot." [Mannini and Tozzini] were silent (to the best of my memory) throughout the meal. I felt sick and could not bring myself to look

up during the meal, forcing myself to eat. I think the Major ate all his soup and then suddenly rose and left the room. [Mannini] remarked that he probably went upstairs to vomit. The Major came back. I don't remember wether [sic] he ate rice—soon after he came down he said he didn't feel well and was going to bed. When he had left [Mannini] remarked that I had been extremely pale during the meal and that the Major surely knew that something was wrong.

Icardi and I sat in front of the fire-place and wondered what was going to happen. Icardi said something like—"If he lives through this he will send a message to Headquarters, so we'll have to make sure he doesn't live." He asked [Mannini and Tozzini] if they would shoot the Major and they said they absolutely refused, so Icardi said it had to be me or him. I dont [sic] remember clearly my movements from then on. I remember Icardi tossed a coin and I called and lost. [Mannini] gave him a gun, his Beretta. We walked in the Major sat up [sic] and said either "What is it" or "Who is it" or "What's the matter." I walked to the side of his bed and fired two shots. Icardi, [Mannini, and Tozzini] rushed in. Icardi opened the Majors [sic] haversack and removed some money in bills which were rolled up. Im [sic] not sure what was taken because I stood there dazed and weak and couldn't think well.

After the execution, LoDolce went on, Icardi took a piece of cloth and bound the major's head to prevent blood from spilling onto the floor. Then he told Mannini and Tozzini to put the corpse in the sleeping bag and take it out to the boat. LoDolce followed them with his radio equipment while Mannini and Tozzini collected the rest of the headquarter's duffle. Everyone fired his weapon, and a grenade was set off so that "people would think we were being ambushed." Mannini and Tozzini, who knew the lake very well, took the corpse out to deep water and dropped Holohan over the side, having weighted the sleeping bag with some rocks. With that done, the mission split into two sections, Icardi and Mannini traveling by water to the village of Pella; LoDolce and Tozzini walking along the lakeshore to the Villa Maria.

With LoDolce's confession, the U.S. authorities now had testimony from three of the four men known to be involved in Holohan's murder. There remained Icardi, who had been studying for a lawyer's career, was presently employed as a law clerk in Pittsburgh, and who therefore knew something about the legal problems confronting him—and the people seeking to arraign him. By nature tough, intelligent, difficult to catch, and intellectually nimble, Icardi took a number of steps that prolonged the legal process and ensured that the government was prevented from (1) arranging his extradition to Italy, where murder charges had been presented against him, LoDolce, Mazzini, and Tozzini, and (2) that the statute of limitations regarding the embezzlement of government funds ran out.

Donovan now brought Max Corvo, who had been Icardi's commanding officer, into the case. Corvo prepared for WJD a memorandum on the history of the case, which tended still to support the view that Moscatelli's Communists had murdered Holohan. Nevertheless, Corvo recognized that the matter had to be cleared up. "Certain measures"—there is an unsigned note in the Donovan papers using this phrase, without defining what the measures might have been—were undertaken regarding Lo-Dolce. They appear to have been some form of surveillance, possibly by the police in Rochester and Buffalo, on LoDolce.

Whatever the measures were, Donovan was soon informed that Icardi had met LoDolce secretly in the open streets of Buffalo after dark in September 1951. What they discussed was not known, but on February 7, 1952, LoDolce repudiated his confession in letters to Donovan, in which he stated:

> I was a member of Operational Group A first contingent and served under your command for more than two years. As a radio man I took part in at least nine missions into enemy territory, some of which were commando raids lasting part of one night and others which lasted weeks and months. While on these missions I tried hard to be the best radio man in the outfit.
>
> My buddies and I went through enemy attacks, ambushes and strafings and I am proud of their record and of mine. Now, seven years after the end of the war I have been accused of killing one of our own men, Major William Holohan, and my life and my family's has become a nightmare because of an impossible newspaper story of plotting, poisoning, shooting, drowning and robbing. I didn't kill Major Holohan and I do not know who did. I didn't [plot] with any Italians or with Lt. Icardi to kill or rob him of huge sums of money which didn't exist. I am innocent of these crimes.
>
> . . . Please help me, sir. I am fighting a huge and complicated thing and I do not know where to turn for help. . . . [I am told that] the OSS has a fund which is meant to be used for former OSS men in need. If I could draw on this fund I would be able to defend myself without worrying about depriving my family and would repay every penny after I graduate. . . . I have been attending school under the GI Bill at the Rochester Institute of Technology and will graduate from an engineering course this year. I am employed in the engineering department of Sargent and Greenleaf, makers of combination locks. My grades at school are excellent and I have been told that I have the makings of a good engineer, but my present earnings of $54.00 per week barely cover the cost of supporting my wife and two sons. . . .[24]

The Donovan papers do not show that WJD replied to this letter, or that anyone replied on his behalf. Yet LoDolce need not have concerned himself about his future, for the wheels of justice ground very slowly. Neither Icardi nor LoDolce was arrested or even subjected to prolonged questioning; they were allowed to go about their business.

On March 26, 1953, however, Icardi was called before a congressional committee formed to inquire into the circumstances of Holohan's death, and immediately before Icardi gave testimony Manfredi described Icardi for the committee's record:

> Lieutenant Icardi had been described by all those who had occasion to contact him in a business or social manner as a determined individual, energetic, audacious, ambitious and unscrupulous. He liked easy living, to eat well, and to consort with prostitutes. He was intolerant and could not adjust himself to leading a regimented and disciplined life behind the lines. Icardi complained . . . about the major's strictness and rigidness. Mrs. Paola Maria Pozzini, in whose home Icardi was a guest after the death of Major Holohan, stated that one day during dinner Icardi said: "When I return to America, I will either be a national hero or they will send me to the electric chair."[25]

Having been sworn, Icardi then testified that he was appointed assistant and interpreter to Holohan by Corvo in August 1944 and that the object of the missions was liaison between "the Fifteenth Army Group of General [Sir Harold] Alexander, and the National Committee of Liberation Headquarters of Northern Italy, located in the city of Milano."[26] He then explained his financial relationship with Giorgio—the subject of inquiries regarding the embezzlement of government funds and on which the statute of limitations had not quite expired.

At the time of arrival the mission funds, which were in Holohan's possession, had been valued at $16,000 in American money and consisted of $10,000 in Italian lire, $3,000 in gold coins, and $3,000 in U.S. and Swiss paper money. After the mission had landed at Coiromonte, two matters occurred: (1) The Holohan mission had financed two intelligence chains in the region of the Lake of Orta, financing that meant the mission was running short of lire, and (2) Giorgio, upon whom Holohan depended as guide, for provisions, and for safe houses, had approached Icardi and said he had been offered a considerable sum of money to work for La Francha, the British espionage organization in that area. Icardi mentioned Giorgio's offer to Holohan, who asked Icardi what Giorgio wanted to remain with the OSS. Icardi then established that Giorgio would remain if he could, as Icardi explained to the congressional committee, sell the gold for whatever he could get for it, pay the 300 lire a gram required by Holohan, and keep the balance for himself. Icardi claimed that he had taken this deal to Holohan, Holohan had accepted it, and the gold had been turned over to Giorgio for sale.

A few weeks later—in the middle of November 1944—Giorgio had returned, stated that he had sold the gold and was prepared to hand over the 300 lire per gram to the mission, but that in the course of the transaction he had acquired rather more lire than he expected. He did not say how much, but he did say that he might get into trouble with the Italian authorities if it became known that he had acquired such a sum through his wartime activities. Icardi told the committee that Giorgio had felt, therefore, that the best way he could explain the money would be if he were able to show that it had been acquired "in a business venture, with one of the Americans, and therefore he wished either Major Holohan or myself to sign an agreement to that effect." Holohan then stated: "All right, if this is what it is going to take for us to continue the way we have been, which we agree is the proper way to go ahead, you go with Georgi and have this document executed."

Icardi then stated that he and Giorgio had gone to San Giulio, a small island in the middle of the Lake of Orta, where there was a seminary. There, Icardi claimed, for the first time he had learned how much money Giorgio had made on the sale of the gold—1,650,000 lire against 853,000 lire for the mission. Nevertheless, Icardi had signed the paper, a copy of which he produced for the committee:

Private Writing

Between the gentlemen Icardi, Aldo, and Migliari, Aminta, with legal residence, the first in Pittsburgh, Pa., 287 Lelia Street, United States, the second in Gozzano, the suburb Buccione, Italy.

It is agreed and stipulated as follows: the 2 aforementioned agree to form a society with the contribution, capital contribution, of 1,650,000 Italian lire, contributed in equal parts.

The partner Migliari is given the duty of acquiring machinery and eventually land or building production and retaining the management.

At the cessation of hostilities, a legal social contract will be entered into.

In case of the death of one of the contracting parties, the succession to his interest will be according to the laws of succession of families.

Witness, signed Alesandro [sic] Cancelliere, and the coproprietors signed Aldo Icardi and Aminta Migliari, dated Borgo Manero November 21 1944.

Under cross-examination by the committee, Icardi insisted that the form and formality were Giorgio's, not his, but that in any case they conformed to Italian legal requirements. A business—a woodworking and toy factory—had been started after the war, but none of the benefits had come to Icardi, and he had taken no part in the business beyond signing the original contract. He did, however, receive photographs of the work being produced at the factory in the spring of 1946, and a request by Giorgio to see whether the product could be sold in the United States. Icardi had sent a telegram to Giorgio, asking him to send samples, but none came. That was the limit and the end of their business association.

Moreover, Icardi added, following the execution of the instrument, he had "reported to Major Holohan the sum which had been involved. He was surprised, as was I, as to how much money was realized on this gold," for "$3,000 worth of gold had returned $4,500 worth of money" for the mission.

Icardi then turned to the events leading up to Holohan's disappearance. In the third week of November both LoDolce and the Salem radio men (Salem was the code name of one of the two intelligence chains established by Holohan soon after his arrival) had complained that, because of inefficient work at the base station at Bari, both were being compelled to stay on the air for protracted periods, thus rendering them liable to location by enemy radiogoniometrists. On the seventeenth, Icardi informed the committee, four enemy agents had been arrested by partisans on the road near Mottarone, and when the men—they proved to be three Germans and one Swiss—were searched at partisan headquarters, it was found that two were wearing portable radio direction-finding apparatuses around their waists. A third man was carrying a gun, a pistol, and a map in the scale of 1:250,000. The fourth man carried nothing. An examination of the map showed six or seven lines which often converged on one point, which happened to be some 300 yards from the exact location of the Salem radio. "They had been out twice before," Icardi told the committee. "They wanted to be certain that they had this radio pinpointed [in order to capture it]. This was to be their last attempt. We were fortunate in having them captured."

That was the first incident showing that the Germans were trying to locate the Holohan mission and planned a *restrallemento*. The second came soon afterward. An Italian partisan leader, Cesare Cinquanta, betrayed a major daylight aerial supply mission planned by Holohan, but the betrayal was detected by Holohan, who managed to get a message to the aircraft, canceling the operation before the drop was made. As part of the betrayal Cinquanta "met his Fascist and German collaborators, brought them to the place where his men were sleeping, had them captured, and they were taken to a railroad siding, put on a boxcar and sent up to the Brenner Pass, to the German slave-labor camps, and I am told that nearly all of them never returned, and Cinquanta put on the uniform as a captain in the Fascist Guard and strode about the streets of Novara boasting of his feats." The importance of Cinquanta to the Holohan mission was that "he was able to describe, quite vividly, I'm sure, to our enemy, whom we were, how we looked, and whatever he could get from his contact with us concerning our actions, our character, and our probable moves."

Lastly, two nights before the *restrallemento* in which Holohan had been captured, two priests who were friendly, Don Giovanni and Don Carlo, warned that "people in the market place [of Orta] had been chattering that the American mission was located in the Villa Castelnuovo, exactly where we were." The priests had told Holohan and Icardi that "there was a Fascist garrison in that village at that time, and certainly the rumor would get to the enemy in due time, and that it was to our best interests to move as quickly as possible because . . . they would send a patrol over to check."

Holohan had taken the decision to move on the night of the sixth. As the group was doing so:

> . . . machinegun fire broke out up from in the direction or the house, 2 or 3 bursts. All of us always carried our weapons on the ready, safeties off, prepared for any eventuality. It was a dark night there, pitch dark, as a matter of fact. It was overcast, with a light fog. The fog was on the lake surface. And it was cold. It was the first week in December, but there was no snow on the ground. It was bitterly cold that night. And when the machinegun fire broke out up at the house, the rest of us reacted I think as anybody would expect to react. At least, I reacted the way I did react for survival. I immediately fired my pistol, which was a 45-caliber, 4 or 5 rounds, in the direction of the house. I didn't see anybody there. I couldn't have seen them, had there been anyone there. There was shrubbery there and cypress trees, and so forth, between us. I guess I fired because I wanted to make a noise. I can't explain it rationally. I broke to the right of the group and began running, and I ran along a path which skirted the water. I had been over that path the times before that I had gone to Mottarone. And as I ran I saw no one in front of me, I saw no one beside me, and the firing continued with quite a bit of activity for perhaps 45 seconds to a minute. . . . There was a general maelstrom of machinegun fire, and a hand grenade which Major Holohan carried. . . . I don't recall how long I ran along the pathway. I lost track of time. But I know that some time before midnight I found myself in the village of Pella, which is a village located perhaps 2 or 2¼ miles north of our location. I knocked on the door of the house where I knew friends were located, Georgi and other people whom I knew there, the proprietors of the house, and they let me in. They had heard the firing. Everyone else in that area had heard the firing. They asked me what happened, and I told them what I am telling you now.

That account was, of course, completely at variance with the stories of LoDolce in his confession, Mannini, and Tozzini, and it demonstrated that somebody was adding perjury to an already formidable list of crimes. Icardi's statements were recorded by the committee for possible future process, but in any event, neither Icardi nor LoDolce was proceeded against in the United States. In the matter of the allegations of embezzlement, the statute of limitations ran out; in the matter of murder, the attorney general confirmed that the United States had lost jurisdiction in both civil and military law; in the matter of perjury, nothing was done; and Icardi's and LoDolce's lawyers successfully resisted all motions by the Italian government to extradite them for trial on charges of murder.

In the end, therefore, Icardi and LoDolce were only convicted *in absentia*, Icardi being sentenced to death for the murder of Major Holohan,

LoDolce to seventeen years' imprisonment. Both Mannini and Tozzini were acquitted, for their defense counsel stated, "Icardi is a miserable pig —and when one calls Icardi by that name one should apologize to the pig. It was an American crime and the Americans should be made to pay for it."[27]

The case was at an end. It was striking for a number of reasons: It was the worst such incident in the history of the OSS. It demonstrated that the OSS had not overcome a principal weakness—bold, strong, decisive thinking at the command levels, but the unpreparedness of the average Americans for what was essentially complex class warfare. It showed the power of money to weaken the higher motives of clandestine agents, motives such as patriotism and loyalty to a cause and a service. It pointed up that a lawyer's training, good as it may have been, was not intellectual equipment for such intricate struggles of life and death. Holohan was thrown into the breach because he was reliable, not because he was well trained or because he had shown an aptitude for clandestinity. As a result, a fundamental canon of the ideological war was contraverted. That canon was, as the official Armed Forces Headquarters history of the clandestine struggle on the southern front observed:

> It must never be forgotten that special operations in the form of Resistance movements are to a large extent nationalistic in nature and need political guidance. [To deal with the partisans] and effectively control a nationalistic movement firm, tactful staff officers, well versed in special operations tactics and strategy and in the political background of the country, are an absolute necessity.[28]

And to show how rare such men were, of the 4,500 Americans involved in secret operations in the Mediterranean during the war, and the 7,800 Britons, only 20 Americans and 23 Britons were considered to possess the special skills needed to prosecute and survive in these endlessly complicated little ideological wars surrounding the main battle. A list of names of the men so skilled was appended. Holohan was not one of the officers so named. Neither was Icardi.

During the last part of the Holohan drama WJD was ambassador in Bangkok, and there on August 21, 1953, he expressed his private opinion of the affair to his special assistant, William J. vanden Heuvel. As vanden Heuvel recorded:

> On the way home, I questioned the General about the Holohan case. He sent H. into Italy because he feared the growing strength of the Commies around Milan; [Holohan's] mission was to make the monarchists and the partisans work together and allow neither to be superior. H. refused a partisan request for arms and ammunition in a very peremptory fashion, and at that point Lo

Dolce [*sic*] or Icardi began talking of "poisoning his soup." Neither La Dolce [*sic*] or [*sic*] Icardi are thought to have Commie sympathies; it became a matter of intense personal dislike accented by what LaD. and I. thought to be poor judgment by H. They finally shot H. and dumped his body into a fresh water lake which preserved all the evidence of the murder. WJD termed Icardi a "gallant soldier." H. should have taken steps to discipline them earlier but he didn't have enough military experience to sense the situation.[29]

Yet if WJD was inclined to be charitable with Icardi, society was not. The forces of what Donovan called "natural retribution" worked upon his life: He was unable to practice law, and when seen last during the late 1970s, he was operating a taxi in Pittsburgh.

EPILOGUE
LAST JOURNEYS

During the afternoon of December 31, 1951, the vehicles came and went over the long, narrow drive that led from the main road to the main house —the handsome eighteenth-century Federal-style gentleman's residence that Ruth had made out of a ruin—at Chapel Hill Farm. Ruth and Mary were preparing a dinner party for sixty people, who were to see the New Year in and celebrate Donovan's sixty-ninth birthday.

As part of the preparations for those celebrations one of the servants sent a cup of silver polish over to Ruth's house, to enable her to polish some silverware. The cup was placed in a bathroom. There it was found by Donovan's youngest grandchild, Sheilah. Sheilah drank the polish without anyone's being aware until she walked into the kitchen, where Ruth and Mary were working. She asked for some water, and Ruth gave it to her. Within a moment or two Sheilah had collapsed on the kitchen floor.

Soon Sheilah stopped breathing, and Ruth and Mary gave her artificial respiration until the doctor arrived. He sent Sheilah to the hospital, where she was pronounced dead on arrival, producing a sense of terrible sadness in the family similar to that experienced in 1939 when Patricia was killed.

Donovan was as distressed as any member of his family. He adored children, and he had adored Sheilah—he had planned to write a children's book for her. Over the years so many of Donovan's kin and friends had died: Donovan's grandfather, his brothers and sisters, his mother just before his marriage, his father just afterward. There had been Ames and Kilmer killed at his side at the Ourcq; young Roosevelt in a Blériot fighter above it; all the Micks at the Ourcq and the Kriemhilde Stellung; Wadsworth; Pantaleoni during the war and Heppner just after it; a host of lawyers, friends, political associates. For years Ruth's diaries had been a steady stream of deaths of treasured friends and relatives. And now small Sheilah. To Ruth in particular Sheilah's death had been "so avoidable." In "two minutes I would have picked up cup to return to pantry." And, she added in an outburst of despair about life itself, "What is it all about anyway?"[1] It was rare, for usually Ruth concealed all emotion.

As for Donovan, whereas with all the other deaths he had experienced, his reaction had been to stride on as if the people who had died had not existed, this time he began to draw closer to his faith. He had never neglected his devotions, but now he began to make them more often, drawing comfort from the knowledge that he had prayed with Pope Pius XII. He saw much of Francis Cardinal Spellman, who recently had been made the Roman Catholic prelate of America, attending the *Missa privata* —the private mass—Spellman held frequently during the winter months and, in the spring and summer, attending the *Missa parochialis* at least once a week, not always for devotions but as often as not simply to sit quietly in the gloom of the back of the church and gaze upon the altar and its relics.

Also at this time, perhaps because of the implications of Sheilah's death, Donovan began to reflect upon his own life, leaving some of those close to him with the suspicion that he felt that, for all his service and accomplishments, he had not fulfilled himself and his political promise. If this was true, no writing or statement reflects that attitude of mind. Even so, he would not have been human had he not reviewed his career from time to time. That career, it would seem, had been devoted to preparing himself for some high place in government—President, secretary of state, secretary of defense, director of central intelligence. He had devoted his considerable intelligence, abilities, fortunes to developing the national and international range of associations required for effective statesmanship. Had he failed in that career?

Obviously he had not, for he had now emerged as an elder statesman, although one without portfolio. He was known everywhere as a leader of his generation, the great American special emissary of his time. He had become chairman of the American Committee for United Europe, an organization with wide contacts with the future political, industrial, and financial leadership of the Continent. At the European Parliament at Strasbourg, where he sat in the visitors' gallery, he resumed his friendship with Winston Churchill—the friendship ruined by the Greek troubles of 1944 and 1945. They lunched and talked together frequently. Less publicly, Donovan worked intensively but unobtrusively to help obtain the presidential nomination for Eisenhower, who went on to win the presidency in a sweeping victory on November 4, 1952, obtaining 442 electoral votes to Adlai Stevenson's 89. For the first time in twenty years the Republicans held political power, and it is said by Donovan's colleagues that he hoped above all things that he would be asked to become director of central intelligence.

Instead, Eisenhower gave the post to General Walter Bedell Smith, his wartime chief of staff. The appointment eluded WJD again when Smith became undersecretary of state, and Eisenhower made John Foster Dulles the secretary of state and Allen Welsh Dulles the director of central intelligence. Privately Donovan deplored these appointments because he believed that the brothers could not possibly run the two services responsible for foreign intelligence objectively and efficiently. But Donovan was ruled out, so it was said, by some of his associates because of his feud with J. Edgar Hoover.

Yet Donovan's contribution to the CIA does seem to have been substantial, as does the amount of time he devoted to helping ex-OSS men with various problems. A note by Whitney Shepardson, former chief of Secret Intelligence in OSS, in the Donovan papers shows:

> From the end of OSS until 1952, and especially when CIA was under Bedell Smith, WJD was in constant communication and saw B-S frequently. He submitted planning and policy papers on request or on his own initiative— likewise recommendations as to personnel for B-S purposes.
>
> [Shepardson] has looked through the personnel recommendations. They are really of a higher order. The names represent those in OSS whose work was excellent and whose quality has been proved.
>
> In the second (1952–1957) file of [Donovan's] post-war CIA papers, WJD writes chiefly on behalf of old OSS men. They want jobs with CIA, they had claims for injuries, claims for recognition, they want something set right on the record. They want to be able to refer to OSS experience in job applications. . . . It is quite clear that WJD saw scores of such people; was always available to them in his office; and befriended them in every possible way.[2]

In an administrative sense at least Donovan remained closely connected with CIA almost to the end of his life, certainly up until the time he lost his mental faculties in 1957. It is possible also that he participated in certain CIA high-level operations. He took part in meetings and operations that had CIA associations. Moreover, he directed an operation against the Congress of American Women, which had been pronounced subversive by the House Un-American Activities Committee. The FBI also suspected that he had taken some steps toward formation of an anti-Communist intelligence service, not unlike the Better America Bureau at Los Angeles, a private concern financed by oil and industries before the war, and mysteriously microphones were found in Donovan's law offices. Whether they had been placed by the FBI or by some rival law firm was not established. Needless to say, the microphones were removed, and the security of Donovan's law firm was quickly reestablished.

Thus, Donovan seems to have personified the old intelligence adage "Once an intelligence man, always an intelligence man." And while he never formally rejoined the Washington intelligence community, his contact with it became even closer when, on May 15, 1953, while in Oslo attending the wedding of the Norwegian crown prince's daughter, Donovan received a telegram from Bedell Smith: It said: "Extremely urgent General Donovan return immediately (repeat immediately) for conference Washington."[3] Although he was a private citizen, Donovan caught the next plane back to Washington, where Bedell Smith announced he had "a tough dirty job for me."[4] Smith then told Donovan that "I am authorized by the President to offer you the Ambassadorship of Siam." Donovan accepted without condition or hesitation.

On the face of it the position of ambassador at Bangkok was not to be considered after many years of sacrifice and dangerous and devoted service. It was a hard post in the trying, humid climate of a country where there was much travel and great political uncertainties. Why, therefore, did WJD accept Bangkok?

Donovan accepted the Bangkok embassy because it was becoming a frontline post in the cold war. The forces of international Communism had become hyperactive in every country between Rangoon in Burma and Hong Kong, especially in French Indochina and British Malaya, where the British were fighting a major guerrilla war with the Chinese Communist forces. On a number of occasions, in both Korea and Vietnam, the United States had contemplated direct, large-scale military intervention, and Donovan's appointment came at a time when Eisenhower and John Foster Dulles were beginning to espouse the formation of the Southeast Asia Treaty Organization (SEATO), with its headquarters at Bangkok.

As usual Donovan saw his task in larger terms than those that presidents and secretaries of state were prepared to countenance. A few days after accepting the appointment for a year Donovan saw Eisenhower and asked for a directive embodying five points:

(1) In case of necessity the resumption of military in addition to diplomatic status. (2) The establishment of direct communication [to the President]. (3) The designation by me of a staff of at least twelve (12) members. (4) That sufficient funds be made available to me for the purposes of my mission. (5) The right to travel to such areas as in my discretion seems necessary and proper in the accomplishment of the task assigned to me.[5]

In other words, he regarded his mission as that of a warrior-ambassador very similar in conception to that which FDR had had in mind for him in 1943, when the President advocated making Donovan guerrilla *supremo* in the Balkans. WJD argued then and later that all Southeast Asia between Rangoon and Hong Kong was alight with actual guerrilla and political warfare centrally directed by the Communist Politburo. To meet these challenges, the Western democracies must organize themselves centrally.

There was more to Donovan's five demands than this. In the first (and probably the least) place, there was his personal financial position. He was now entirely dependent upon the firm for his income. As a special representative he would be able to continue to accept income from the firm while representing the government. He would not be able to do so as an ambassador; he would have to relinquish his fees if he wished to remain within the law, as he did. Ordinarily, perhaps, that might not have been important, but he had entered into an agreement with the Internal Revenue Service to pay off his back taxes on the basis of his estimated annual earnings as a lawyer. If he became an ambassador, he would earn a greatly reduced income—$740 a month after withholding taxes as against, perhaps, $20,000 a month as a lawyer. It seems fairly evident, therefore, that the IRS would not permit an amendment for the period of WJD's service as an ambassador. Yet it was not for financial reasons alone that Donovan asked to be made a special representative rather than ambassador. Donovan stated to Bedell Smith in his letter of acceptance on May 19, 1953:

> Let me confirm that not only do I believe it my duty to accept the offer you extended, but I deem it an honor to be entrusted with so important a mission in these critical days.
>
> From the enemy's point of view the problem involves a single geographic unit—Burma, Thailand, Malaya, Indonesia, French Indo-China, Hong Kong, the Philippines, Formosa. Within this the organization of Communists in every division permits the enemy to coordinate and operate through unified command centers of political power of varying capacities and speeds of reaction. . . . The situation, therefore, has to be commanded not negotiated into unity. . . . At least for the moment the initiative is with the enemy. Response to that challenge will require irregular improvisation.[6]

Donovan repeated his request to be made not ambassador but "Personal Representative of the President of the United States." He did not wish to press for this title, he declared, but he felt that "it might bring assurance to the Asian peoples that the President has a special interest in their problems. In any case, if it is felt that the term 'Ambassador' must be used, I hope the designation would be 'Personal Representative of the President of the United States with the rank of Ambassador.'"

But this was denied. Eisenhower limited the scope of WJD's mission with a kindly letter dated June 9, 1953:

My dear Bill,

Thank you for your letter. Needless to say, I am deeply appreciative of your continued readiness to serve your country. It is typical of you.

When Foster and I were considering the difficult situation in Southeast Asia, and particularly its possible intensification as a result of events in Korea, we agreed that Thailand was a key point which might be made a bastion of resistance.

One of the immediate desirable moves was to appoint the Military Mission, and this is now in process. Another and more important possibility was to send as Ambassador to Thailand a man with particular experience, knowledge and background who, while serving as Chief of the Diplomatic Mission, would also quietly coordinate the existing means for psychological and economic operations, increase their effectiveness, and possibly prepare them for broader use. You are the man best qualified to do this. However, I want you to do it in the capacity of Ambassador, under the direction of the Secretary of State and within State Department channels of control. I have strongly affirmed the responsibility of the Secretary of State in the field of foreign policy, and I want to maintain his position there.

On the other hand, I realize, as does Foster, the value of your suggestion and we both feel that if events in the East were to take a more adverse turn it is entirely possible that a solution similar to yours would be called for.

This makes it even more important to have on the spot a man capable of carrying it into effect. I do not, however, want to go this far at present, and as I know and appreciate your willingness to serve I propose to appoint you Ambassador to Thailand, as Foster has recommended. He will communicate with you and will amplify the ideas expressed in this letter.

> With warm regard,
> Sincerely
> (s) Dwight D. Eisenhower.[7]

Thus, it was as ambassador to Thailand that Donovan was sworn in by John Foster Dulles on August 12, 1953. He left New York for Bangkok by way of Paris and New Delhi on August 17, 1953. He was disappointed that his recommendation that an extraordinary post—similar in conception to that created by the British when they appointed Malcolm MacDonald high commissioner of Southeast Asia—was not granted. Yet in fairness it should be stressed that WJD's financial considerations played no part in his endeavors to obtain a special status. After all, when before had money played any part in any of Donovan's considerations?

No, his attempts to secure the overlordship of American military and diplomatic representation between Delhi and Hong Kong were purely political—an expression of Donovan's belief that the situation in Asia was extraordinary and required extraordinary responses if it was to be met and mastered.

Donovan's response to Dulles's limitation of his activities was characteristic: He went ahead with what he believed was correct and necessary. He began flying all over Asia, paying his own expenses and those of his assistants, because he believed that the Thai situation was part of a regional problem and that if Thailand was to be secured against Communism, the problem must be tackled regionally as well as locally. It was small wonder that he was, once again, heading rapidly toward penury, for air travel at the time was extremely expensive. And it is interesting to note that there is no record that Donovan was told by Dulles to stay in his own parish.

An early heavy expense came when he flew up to Korea to talk with the new supreme Allied commander, General Matthew B. Ridgway, and the commander of the U.S. Eighth Army, General James A. Van Fleet. Through what he heard and saw he developed a very adverse and pessimistic opinion of America's place in the world, especially of the capabilities of the American armed forces. As he remarked to his assistant, William J. vanden Heuvel, soon afterward: "You're too young to know the feeling, Bill, you have seen our country at times defeated and humiliated, although the ultimate victory has always been ours—but sometimes I long for that feeling I had as a boy that when you waved the flag your enemies shuddered—an incomparable feeling of strength."[8]

To meet the military and ideological problems of the region, Donovan succeeded in getting Allen Dulles to expand greatly Vernon Gresham's CIA organization in Thailand. Donovan was joined by a number of ex-OSS men, among them Carleton Coon and Gordon Browne, who had done such excellent work for Donovan before, during, and after Torch. As vanden Heuvel noted in his diary on September 16, 1953, WJD's Bangkok operations were coming to resemble "a miniature OSS." To inform himself on modern methods of combating insurgents, WJD spent much time with General Sir Gerald Templer, who was fighting a major anti-Communist insurgent campaign in Malaya—again paying his expenses out of his own pocket, since the State Department would only meet those expenses incurred by Donovan inside Thailand.

From Templer, Donovan learned much about the new politico-military counterinsurgency methods evolved for the Malaya campaign, which he adapted for employment in Thailand, particularly land reform, the establishment of fortified villages and village militia, and the introduction of modern agricultural, educational, health, and media methods of preventing Communist subversion. Flying about Thailand in all weather in rickety DC-3's—much of it in turbulent monsoon conditions—Donovan visited scores of villages. The trips took a considerable toll on his health and strength.

At the same time he did not ignore conventional methods of meeting insurgency. He worked to obtain modern arms for the Thai Army, jet fighters for the Thai Air Force, special river craft for the Thai Navy, and reeducation of the Thai police forces. He succeeded in getting the Thai Army to form a Military Intelligence service and in his efforts to persuade the Pentagon and the Thai government to establish a wing of the Strategic Air Command on Thai territory.

Yet, vanden Heuvel noted in his diary, Donovan was not always himself. He began to show occasional torpor, perhaps induced by the heat. He became very irritable and capable of flashes of anger. He was somewhat erratic in keeping social appointments and even in his office hours. Also, he did not conceal his attitude toward the men for whom he worked in Washington, although until now he would never criticize a superior in the presence of a subordinate. He contended that John Foster Dulles was "churchy" and politically dishonest, that Walter Bedell Smith and Allen Dulles had "ruined" the CIA by permitting it to be turned into nothing more than a reporting agency, that Eisenhower was "not a great man," and that he was very surprised that Eisenhower had won the election because of the President's association during the war with his driver, Kay Summersby.

Nor did this behavior end when Ruth and Mary came out to join him. He was as irritable with them as he was, occasionally, with everyone else. Later it was apparent that he had suffered a series of minor strokes, and he was beginning to suffer from an impairment of the blood supply to the brain.

As it became increasingly evident that Donovan was hostile to John Foster Dulles and his policies in Southeast Asia, a development in Washington made it appear possible to vanden Heuvel that WJD might not be in Bangkok for very long. In the middle of September 1953 the chief justice of the United States, Frederick M. Vinson, died. On September 19, 1953, Donovan received a letter from his law partner George Leisure that "told of considerable support, much of it in the midwest, for the General to be Chief Justice in the United States."[9] WJD's assistant, vanden Heuvel, recorded on that day that Donovan felt his age and Eisenhower's political commitments would make such an appointment impossible.

Whether Donovan was ever consulted formally about the post is not clear, but according to vanden Heuvel, at about this time the Senate majority leader, William F. Knowland, of California, arrived in Bangkok on business concerning SEATO, and he and Donovan spent much time together. Knowland stated that Eisenhower had a political debt to Earl Warren, a liberal Republican lawyer and the present governor of California, that meant Eisenhower would have to offer the post to Warren, although he was reluctant to do so because he felt Warren was too liberal. The President intended, therefore, to offer the post to Warren, but if he rejected it, he would offer the post to Donovan, for as vanden Heuvel recorded, "there is considerable pressure on Eisenhower to appoint a Catholic either to the cabinet or to the court."

In the end, as predicted, Eisenhower offered the post to Earl Warren, who accepted it, and so Donovan had been boomed for a major post for the last time. Vanden Heuvel wrote in his diary: "That ends the speculation and I don't think too many people were surprised."[10]

Donovan worked hard throughout the winter, receiving innumerable visitors from Washington, including Vice President Richard Nixon, and on March 2, 1954, he received a telegram from Bedell Smith, inviting him to return to Washington "to discuss a project which WJD 'first suggested.'" Presumably this was WJD's suggestion that he be appointed presidential representative to Asia.

Donovan left Bangkok on March 15, 1954, as the battle for Dienbienphu between the French and the Vietminh forces of Ho Chi Minh was raging at full strength. He flew first to Manila, where, on March 17, 1954, he "wore his best blue suit for St. Patrick's day." He conferred with military and diplomatic representatives and then flew on to Washington that same day. Because he was crossing the international date line, and would therefore live through March 17 twice, he received a cake from the crew of the Pan American airliner inscribed with "To William J. Donovan, the only Irishman to celebrate St. Patrick's Day twice."[11] But Donovan was not well during this journey. One of the diplomats at Manila remarked to vanden Heuvel that "the General had aged some," his "memory had dimmed," and he was not "as quick and as sharp."[12]

Donovan spent two weeks in Washington, saw Eisenhower, the Dulles brothers, and Bedell Smith, and returned to Bangkok on May 4, 1954, without saying much about what had transpired in Washington. He told vanden Heuvel that Bedell Smith did speak of a regional representative, "but nothing definite has come of it," and WJD wondered why he had been recalled. On May 6, 1954, he spent a considerable time with vanden Heuvel, drafting his letter of resignation to President Eisenhower. Vanden Heuvel recorded in his diary: "The financial burden of this position necessitates [WJD's] return to private practice and he has set August 1 as the target date."[13]

Donovan decided to use Marcellus Hartley Dodge, the principal stockholder in the Remington Arms Company and one of his oldest friends, to convey his problems to the President. WJD wrote Dodge on May 7, 1954:

> Because of your close friendship with President Eisenhower and the many kindnesses to me, I would like you to deliver the enclosed letter to the President and use that occasion so that he will understand why I cannot accept an additional period of service in my *present* capacity. You may, if you

think it necessary, show him my financial status which clearly indicates the compelling reasons necessitating my return to private practice. Were there a possibility of service without compensation, or another arrangement as his personal representative which would allow the retention of my private commitments, I would gladly answer his call.

In any event, I want the President to know whatever the circumstances, my experience is at his disposal to serve the best interests of the country.[14]

At least as early as January 1954 Donovan had begun to feel the financial strain of his embassy, as this letter to Allen W. Dulles at the Central Intelligence Agency shows:

Dear Allen:

Thank you for your assurances to me today of the nest egg which I will place in a corner against emergencies. It was thoughtful of you to suggest that this be done.[15]

The existence of such a letter strengthens (but does not prove) the theory that WJD had a strong, unbroken contact with the CIA going back at least as far as Bedell Smith's days, probably as an adviser. If this was so, Donovan evidently felt he did not warrant compensation, for there is no other record of payments to him by the CIA.

Despite the renewed disturbance in Donovan's financial affairs, on May 7, after recording that he had finished writing WJD's letters to Eisenhower and Dodge, vanden Heuvel wrote that Donovan was still willing "to take a personal emissary assignment" because it would permit him to draw income from the law firm and also enable him to work from New York rather than Bangkok.

The fall of Dienbienphu, which occurred on the seventh and led to the collapse of the French in Indochina and to the assumption by the United States of France's responsibilities there, made no difference to WJD: He reaffirmed his intention to resign. Privately he held John Foster Dulles entirely responsible for the French disaster. Vanden Heuvel recorded later: "WJD was particularly vituperative against Dulles, saying that he should resign. He pictures Washington as a center of confusion with Eisenhower playing Chief of Staff with no Staff. He maintains that the U.S. is a party to the conspiracy to lose Indochina."[16]

Whatever the rights or wrongs of this belief, the fact that he uttered such expressions in the presence of a subordinate showed his condition was worsening. In all, therefore, it becomes clear that while WJD's finances were an important factor in his decision not to remain at Bangkok, and while another factor was the question of the special representative, there were third and fourth factors—his decision that he could not work with John Foster Dulles and his health.

Eisenhower's letter accepting Donovan's resignation arrived on June 1, 1954. Eisenhower regretted Donovan's decision to leave, hoped he would continue to be available on a consultative basis, and asked him to remain a few weeks longer while John Foster Dulles sought a replacement. Donovan, not at all sure this was wise, told vanden Heuvel he felt he should leave immediately "to straighten things out personally with Dulles" as "I'm not going to let him determine my position."[17] Donovan made up his mind to go to Washington on June 7 and instructed vanden Heuvel to wire Dulles: "Received President's letter. Would like to talk to you. Request one week author[ization] to visit Washington."[18] He left on the tenth and returned on the twenty-fourth, having made his point that he would remain as special representative, but not as ambassador. Vanden Heuvel noted on June 30: "WJD played tennis and went swimming this morning. . . . He looked much better and seemed his old self, full of energy and imagination."

Donovan's offer to remain as special representative was not accepted, and he left finally for New York by Pan American World Airways on August 21, 1954; Ruth and Mary returned part of the way to the United States aboard the New England schooner Yankee.

Donovan was met at Idlewild Airport by Ralstone R. Irvine, who formed the impression from his appearance that WJD was a very sick man and had had a stroke. Whether this was so or not, Donovan resumed the life of a prominent New York lawyer—a little law, an extensive social life, and constant visitors from all parts of the world. He was practically broke but started energetically to rebuild his fortunes once again. He was seen more frequently about town with Ruth than for years past, and in general he seemed to be happy and fit. This continued until the summer of 1955, when, as usual, the family went to Nonquitt.

Then tragedy struck again.

For years Donovan's daughter-in-law, Mary, had been accepted as a daughter, almost as a substitute for Patricia. Frequently she had acted as Donovan's official hostess, accompanying him on journeys throughout the world. But when Sheilah died from the poison in the silver polish, Mary seemed to become unhinged. She had great difficulty in sleeping, and a doctor prescribed sedatives, which she used carelessly.

On July 25, 1955, Ruth went to Mary's bedroom at Nonquitt and found her dead. Police and pathologists' inquiries showed that the cause of death was an excessive dose of barbiturates. It was believed that before retiring, she had taken liquor and then pills, as usual in the hope that she would sleep more soundly. On several occasions in the middle of the night she must have awakened and in her fuddled state taken more pills in the belief that she had forgotten to take them earlier. As a result, she had taken a lethal dose and had died in her sleep.

Donovan hastened to Nonquitt on hearing of Mary's death, and he was deeply saddened by it, for only recently he had taken her out to California to be with Walt Disney, a client, at the opening of the first Disneyland. Now, to add to her other labors, Ruth had the problem of acting as mother to Mary's five children.

Mary's death drew the Donovans even more closely together, and for most of 1956 WJD rarely left New York, except to go to the farm at Berryville. Then, once more, duty called—for the last time. In November 1956 the Hungarian Revolution broke out, and he spent several grueling months raising $1,5000,000 to help the refugees streaming across the frontier into Austria. He was chairman of the President's Hungarian refugees' relief program and was to be found night after night on the Austro-Hungarian frontier, physically helping refugees coming through the great frozen bulrush swamps as Soviet tanks clanked in the darkness and flares arched across the night sky. Throughout this period he seemed to be fit.

Then came the beginning of the end.

On February 13, 1957, while visiting Dexter Rumsey in Buffalo, Ruth received a telephone call asking her to call George Leisure. Leisure had terrible news, which Ruth recorded in her diary: "Bill is at Mayo Clinic with brain operation necessary." She left Buffalo immediately by air for Rochester, Minnesota. To her astonishment she was met off the plane by Donovan and his close friend Admiral Jack Bergen, and for a moment Ruth was bewildered. But she soon learned the worst: Donovan was in excellent condition physically, but he "had something on the brain."[19]

The doctors spent a week examining Donovan and, in an interim report, advised Ruth that the early tests had revealed a shrinkage of the right cortex, the outer layer of the brain. There was no need to operate; indeed, an operation would not stem the process now going on. Ruth was told the condition might remain as it was or might get worse. If it did, as Ruth put it, "Bill will be sunk."[20]

On the eighteenth the doctors rendered their definitive opinion: WJD was suffering from arteriosclerotic atrophy of the brain. This had been going on for some time (and as like as not explained some of his inexplicable conduct at Bangkok), and nothing could be done to arrest or cure the condition. It was likely to get worse, and Ruth exclaimed hopelessly in her diary: "Of all people to have a brain thing!" Her exclamation was understandable: Donovan was doomed to lose first his mind, then all control over that splendid physique, and finally his life.

At the start Donovan conducted himself as he had always done—up early, a busy day, constant visitors, to bed late. He managed to attend several important functions without revealing that he was incapacitated, among them the visit to the United States of a wartime resistance fighter in France whom the OSS had supported. That was Guy Mollet, prime minister of France in a left-of-center anti-Communist government dedicated, as was WJD, to the concept of a United Europe. Also, he managed to play a great deal of gin rummy with his old friends Albert Lasker, founder of the Lord & Thomas advertising agency of Chicago, and Lasker's wife, Mary—Donovan had introduced the couple on a transcontinental express back in the twenties. When Lasker died, he left Donovan $25,000 in his will as a "small attempt to compensate you for the expenses you have carried on behalf of the country."

Soon WJD's condition worsened. He became more confused and given to prolonged reveries. Frank Raichle, his old friend in Buffalo, came calling at 4 Sutton Place and found Donovan sitting by the window overlooking the East River, humming "In the Good Old Summertime"—the song of the Micks in 1918. Otto Doering called and found Donovan as alert as ever—only to have his attention drawn to the fact that Russian battalions were marching over the Fifty-ninth Street Bridge.

By April 1, 1957, Donovan's condition had worsened, and he required constant nursing attention. When he learned of Donovan's condition, President Eisenhower ordered special quarters—the Pershing Suite—for him at Walter Reed. At the same time Eisenhower (having just recovered from a major heart attack himself) wrote to Donovan:

> Dear Bill:
>
> I have just learned, to my great distress, of your illness. As a veteran of far too many such things in the last couple of years, I know how difficult the enforced period of inactivity must be for you. But—also in my role of "patient"—I do recommend most highly that you cooperate fully with the doctors. I need not tell you that the country needs you back on the active list.
>
> With best wishes for a speedy and complete recovery, and affectionate regard in which I know Mamie joins.
>
> As ever,
> [s] Dwight Eisenhower.[21]

The next day, April 2, 1957, Eisenhower promulgated the following bulletin, making Donovan the only man in the history of the United States to win the country's top four medals for gallantry and public service:

> The President of the United States takes pride in presenting the National Security Medal to
>
> MAJOR GENERAL WILLIAM J. DONOVAN, AUS (Ret)
>
> for service as set forth in the following Citation:
>
> Through his foresight, wisdom, and experience, he foresaw, during the course of World War II, the problems which would face the postwar world

and the urgent need for a permanent, centralized intelligence function. Thus his wartime work contributed to the establishment of the Central Intelligence Agency and a coordinated national intelligence structure. Since the creation of the Agency, he has given to it generously of his experience, making through the postwar years a valuable contribution to the field of intelligence relating to the national security. In 1953 and 1954, as Ambassador of the United States to Thailand, he served in this important diplomatic post with the same tireless energy and skill he had shown in his wartime service. Both in public and private life he has made outstanding contributions to the security and defense of his country.

[s] Dwight D. Eisenhower,

2 April 1957.

As word spread of Donovan's illness, Donovan's colleagues and associates, especially the Micks and the OSSers, wrote by the hundreds. He could read few of the letters he received, but one he did read. It was from Winston Churchill:

Dear General Donovan,

I was indeed sorry to learn of your illness. Pray accept my warm good wishes for an early and complete recovery. I well remember the remarkable services which you rendered to our joint cause in the war years.

I remain,

Yours sincerely,
[s] Winston S. Churchill

At the other end of the scale was this letter from Donovan's secretary, Walter F. Berry, sent on the eve of WJD's seventy-fifth birthday:

Dear General,

For the last twenty-five years I have been your secretary, and I am sure no one could have spent a quarter of a century more enjoyably and interestingly. During that period I probably have been closer to you in your business life than any one else and it is a great satisfaction to me to have been so closely associated with you. Once you autographed a photograph for me—"In remembrance and in gratitude of many good battles together." We did have some constructive "battles" down through the years, and we also had many good times together; I remember so well the many sports events you took me to and the friendly comradeship you always had for me. No secretary could ask for more than you did for me. And I thank you for it.

I am sending you this note on the eve of your seventy-fifth birthday, on which I offer you my sincere congratulations and the fervent hope that before too long you will completely recover your vigorous and vibrant health and resume your distinguished position, not only in this country but in the world; you are sorely needed.

> Sincerely yours,
> [s] Walter F. Berry

But there was to be no recovery. Late in January he was dressed in his major general's uniform and taken by the CIA's general counsel, Laurence Houston, to view the full-length oil painting of him which had just been hung in the lobby of the CIA headquarters at Langley, Virginia. Major Corey Ford was to recall:

> The empty eyes came into focus on the erect figure in Army uniform, the twin stars of rank on each shoulder, the banks of bright ribbons with the blue Medal of Honor at the top. This was the Donovan who had commanded his troops in battle at St. Mihiel and the Argonne Forest, who had led OSS through the Second World War, who had served his country above and beyond the call of duty. The bowed head came up, the jaw hardened, the sagging body stiffened to attention. Straight as a soldier, the General about-faced and strode down the corridor and through the foyer, and climbed without help into the car.[22]

Faithful to the end, Ruth was at his bedside in the Pershing Suite when Donovan was "born into eternity"—in the phrase of the priest—at 1:55 P.M. on Sunday, February 8, 1959. His brother, Vincent, in the robes of a Dominican, gave Donovan the last rites. When he heard the news, Eisenhower remarked to Marcellus Hartley Dodge: "What a man! We have lost the last hero."[23]

Condolences came from every quarter of the globe; among the letters were one from J. Edgar Hoover and one from John Foster Dulles, both to Ruth. Wrote Hoover:

> Dear Mrs. Donovan:
>
> I was distressed to learn of the death of your husband, and I want you to know that my thoughts are with you in deepest sympathy in these trying hours.
>
> There is so little that can be said or done to comfort you at a time like this, but certainly his life's work, devoted as it was to the service of others, should be a source of gratification to all who were honored to know him. If I can be of any assistance, I hope you will let me know.
>
> Sincerely yours,
> [s] J. Edgar Hoover

Wrote John Foster Dulles:

Dear Ruth:

I have just learned with keen regret of the death of your distinguished husband and Janet and I send to you and your family our deepest sympathy.

Bill was a truly great American in every sense of the word. His matchless heroism and courage in wartime have become legendary. His achievements in peacetime are no less imposing and his enviable and patriotic record will be cited and remembered for all time. The nation has lost an outstanding public servant and I, together with the country to which he gave his best efforts, mourn his passing.

Sincerely yours,
Foster

Dressed in his general's uniform, Donovan was buried three days later beside Patricia at Arlington National Cemetery amid a thunder of guns, trumpet calls, and hymns. A signal went out from CIA headquarters to all officials announcing: "The man more responsible than any other for the existence of the Central Intelligence Agency has passed away." The last post was sounded, and Donovan's spirit—the spirit of a rare, superb, vital life—drifted away into memory. Many men who were at the graveside would remember thinking: "We shall not see his like again."

And far away, among the Riffs of the Grand Erg Occidental, the southern slopes of the Atlas Mountains of North Africa, that grand old spy Carleton Coon, still measuring tribesmen's foreheads and tibiae, heard about his chief's death. He sat down in his tent and began writing "Ode on Learning of the Death of Wild Bill Donovan," employing the same dactylic hexameter as Homer in *The Iliad*, the epic of the Trojan Wars:

Wild, people called him, who had heard of his fame
And wild he was in heart and in feyness
But more than wild was the man with the wile of Odysseus
Like the king of Assassins he welded together
An army of desperate, invisible soldiers
Who blew no reveille or taps
Each as bold as himself in single deeds
But none as keen as himself, the leader of all, commander of men
Who would ask, "Jim will you limpet that ship?"
Knowing the answer, for none would refuse him, or
"Carl, a free ride to Albania?" "Yes? Then you're off,
Ten minutes to Zero," and we would all die for him.
Die for him some of us did, but he died for us all.
Some who are left would burn him whole, like a Viking jarl in his ship

Others would cover his bones with a colossal marble cross
Each to his taste, say I, Yankee, Irishman, Italian.
As many tombs will he have in our hearts as the scattered remains of Osiris,
How lucky we were that he came when he did in the long tide of history
Hail to Wild Bill, a hero of men and a name to hang myths on
As American as chowder, Crockett, and Putnam
A free fighter's hero, may God give him peace.

A NOTE
ON SOURCES

The primary source for *The Last Hero* has been General Donovan's own papers. These are a very large collection, consisting of three parts:

1. The files of the office of director of the COI and the OSS, described in the text of the sources and notes as OSSDF. Included also in this collection are OSSDC (Office of Strategic Services' Directors' Cables). These are on microfilm and are described more fully in the Author's Note. The microfilm is not always in good condition.

The reels contained in tins were poorly microfilmed in the first place, have deteriorated greatly since 1945, and require extremely careful handling to avoid tearing. Perhaps one in twenty of the tinned reels is more or less completely illegible, although with patience and cross-referencing the contents can be rebuilt.

The reels in cardboard boxes are, somewhat surprisingly, in much better condition. They were more expertly microfilmed in the first place, and their condition is generally good to excellent. Legibility is almost always excellent, except where the microfilmers' hands and fingers got in the way at the moment of photography.

In general, it may be said that the microfilm in tins consists of those records up to 1943, those in the cardboard boxes from mid-1943 until the dissolution of the OSS.

As with all the Donovan papers, in due course they all will be at the Army War College, Fort Carlisle, Pennsylvania. The date of the public release of these documents is uncertain.

2. What is called the CIA Collection. These were the 148 archives' boxes of bound records given to the CIA by Donovan's law firm for safekeeping. In the boxes are some 1,300 volumes of bound records in generally excellent condition. All are paper records or photostat, and they reflect Donovan's very wide interests.

These volumes would have interest not only to the historian of intelligence and diplomatic matters but also to that of American national and social history. This collection is likely to be opened for public use one year after the publication of *The Last Hero*.

3. What is called the WJD Miscellaneous Collection. This collection consists of documents relevant to Donovan's life but generally not concerning his intelligence activities. The collection consists of two large steel fireproof five-drawer filing cabinets containing memorabilia, bound volumes of documentation concerning Donovan's early years, newspaper clippings, photographs, letters, and so on. One of these filing cabinets is in the care of the author and will be turned over to the Army War College soon after the completion of the manuscript of this volume. The second is with Donovan Leisure Newton & Irvine in New York City, on loan to Geoffrey M. T. Jones, president of the Veterans of Strategic Services. The contents of the cabinet are of less interest than its companion but are nevertheless of importance and interest to those concerned with Donovan's life and the sociology of U.S. intelligence.

Of additional importance to this volume have been Ruth Donovan's diaries and the collection of letters in the possession of the Donovan family. No decision had been made by March 1982 about their fate, but the probability is that they will not be released to the general public since they largely have to do with family personal matters. Also, David Donovan, WJD's son, provided the author with a very large quantity of albums, family letters and memorabilia, and photographs —part of the full, excellent, and hospitable collaboration received by the author from D.D. throughout the history of the preparation of this volume.

Other primary sources have been the records of the Old and Modern Military Records Branches (OMR and MMR) of the National Archives (NA), the Center for Military History (CMH) in Washington, D.C., and, to a very limited extent, those pertaining to Donovan and the OSS in the custody of the FBI. No application was made to, and no assistance was received from, the Central Intelligence Agency in the preparation of this volume, except in two matters: (1) The manuscript of the agency's publication *Donovan and the CIA* was supplied to the author at an early date, as was an early copy of the bound volume deriving from that manuscript, and (2) the CIA did supply a copy of a photograph of the portrait of Donovan hanging in the main hall of the CIA headquarters at Langley, Virginia. The author expresses his gratitude to those who made the arrangements for these contributions.

Mention must be made of the fact that Ralstone R. Irvine, one of the name partners of Donovan Leisure Newton & Irvine, placed at the disposal of the author a small number of important papers he wrote about the early history of his law firm; the author is deeply grateful to Mr. Irvine for these papers. Also, there have been the diaries of Ambassador William J. vanden Heuvel, for which, again, the author is very grateful, and a certain limited number of papers, photographs, and maps from the author's own collection.

Lastly, important material was obtained from the Manuscripts Division of the Library of Congress and from the FDR, Dwight D. Eisenhower, Herbert Hoover, and Harry S Truman libraries. To all involved the author expresses his thanks for the efficiency, rapidity, and knowledge displayed by the curators and librarians during these transactions.

SOURCES
AND NOTES

Prologue
The Birth of the OSS and the CIA

1. Richard E. Goldstein, "Football Sunday, Dec. 7, 1941—Suddenly the Game Didn't Matter," *The New York Times*, December 7, 1980.
2. Winston S. Churchill, quoted by Ian Fleming in foreward to H. Montgomery Hyde, *Room 3603* (New York: Farrar Strauss, 1962).

Chapter 1
Bill and Ruth

1. Edmond Taylor, *Awakening from History* (Boston: Gambit, 1969), pp. 350–51.
2. Henry Wayland Hill, *Municipality of Buffalo, New York: A History, 1720–1923* (Chicago: Lewis Historical Publishing, 1923), vol. 2, 547. All quotations on Buffalo from this source.
3. William E. Addis *et al.*, *A Catholic Dictionary* . . . (New York: Benziger Bros., 1893), p. 554.
4. William vanden Heuvel, diary, August 30, 1953.
5. Hill, *op. cit.*, pp. 2, 645.
6. Mark Sullivan, *Our Times 1900–1925*, vol. 2, *America Finding Herself* (New York: Scribner's, 1927), p. 7.
7. Interview with T. J. McFadden, New York, April 8, 1981.
8. Interview by Corey Ford and O. C. Doering, Jr., of Father Vincent Donovan, probably around 1965.
9. Interview with Randall Keator, Rumson, N.J., August 5, 1981.
10. Letter, T. Ludlow Chrystie to WJD, March 19, 1918, WJD Miscellaneous Collection.
11. Official Program, Homecoming Day, October 15, 1955.
12. FBI loyalty and personal report for Eisenhower, July 15, 1953.
13. Interviews with Donald Rumsey, Berryville, Va., May 9 and 11, 1981.
14. "Ruth Rumsey, My Trip Abroad, Beginning 23 June 1908," David Donovan Collection.
15. Clipping from the *Burgee*, 1911, WJD Miscellaneous Collection.
16. Clipping from Buffalo *Express*, no date, WJD Miscellaneous Collection.
17. Early newspaper clipping, no logo, no date, WJD Miscellaneous Collection.
18. Buffalo *News*, July 16, 1913, WJD Miscellaneous Collection.
19. Ford and Doering, interview with Vincent Donovan, *op. cit.*
20. Interview with Donald Rumsey, Berryville, Va., May 14, 1981.

21. Letter, WJD to Ruth Donovan, postmarked August 16, 1918, WJD Miscellaneous Collection.

Chapter 2
Bugles Call

1. Letter from Flora M. Rhind, secretary, Rockefeller Foundation, April 20, 1959.
2. Letter from WJD to Ruth Donovan, March 28, 1916.
3. Sullivan, *op. cit.*, vol. 5, 406–07.
4. Central Intelligence Agency, *Donovan and the CIA: A History of the Establishment of the Central Intelligence Agency* (Washington, D.C.: CIA Center for the Study of Intelligence, 1981), p. vi. Hereafter called CIA Report.
5. Pastoral Letter by Cardinal Mercier, Christmas, 1914, WJD Miscellaneous Collection.
6. Papal Citation, in Decorations File, WJD Miscellaneous Collection.
7. Letter, Hill Jones to WJD, in file marked "Major General William J. Donovan, 1883–1959," vol. 1, WJD Family Collection.
8. Hill, *op. cit.*, vol. 2, p. 857.
9. Letter, WJD to Ruth Donovan, November 18, 1917.
10. Maurice Matloff, ed., *American Military History* (Washington, D.C.: Office of the Chief of Military History, 1969), p. 392.
11. Letters, WJD to Ruth Donovan, December 15, 1917, January 24, 1918, and February 3, 1918.
12. Letter, WJD to Ruth Donovan, November 24, 1917.
13. *Ibid.*, January 2, 1918.
14. *Ibid.*, November 24, 1917.
15. *Ibid.*, January 7, 1918.
16. *Ibid.*
17. Quotations from Summary of Intelligence, Second Section, General Staff, 42nd Division, AEF, February 21 to November 13, 1918.
18. Letter, WJD to Ruth Donovan, May 3, 1918.
19. *Ibid.*, May 7, 1918.
20. *Ibid.*, May 13, 1918.

Chapter 3
The Ourcq

1. Letter, WJD to Ruth Donovan, July 5, 1918.
2. General Order 51, 9:30 A.M., July 27, 1918, HQ, 42nd Division, AEF.
3. Intelligence Bulletins 110, 111, 112, 113, Second Section, General Staff, 42nd Division, July 25–28, 1918.
4. Letter, WJD to Ruth Donovan, August 7, 1918.
5. Letter, WJD to Ruth Donovan, August 7, 1918.
6. Summary of Intelligence 113, for 8:00 P.M. to 8:00 P.M., July 27–28, 1918, Second Section, General Staff, 42nd Division, AEF.
7. Letter, WJD to Ruth Donovan, August 7, 1918.
8. Ibid.
9. Ibid.
10. Summary of Intelligence 113, *op. cit.*
11. Letter, WJD to Ruth Donovan, August 7, 1918.
12. *Ibid.*

13. Intelligence Bulletin 114, Second Section, General Staff, 42nd Division, AEF, July 28–29, 1918.
14. Intelligence Bulletin 115, Second Section, General Staff, 42nd Division, AEF, July 29–30, 1918.
15. Intelligence Bulletin 116, Second Section, General Staff, 42nd Division, AEF, July 31–August 1, 1918.
16. Letter, WJD to Ruth Donovan, August 7, 1918.
17. Francis P. Duffy, *Father Duffy's Story* (New York: Doran, 1919), p. 220.

Chapter 4
The Fortress

1. *Story of Fighting 69th, 165th Infantry*, unsigned, undated leaflet published on regiment's return to New York, WJD Miscellaneous Collection.
2. Letter, WJD to Ruth Donovan, September 21, 1918.
3. Intelligence Bulletin 141, HQ, 42nd Division, AEF, October 13–14, 1918.
4. Letter, WJD to Ruth Donovan, October 23, 1918.
5. This matter was researched at the Harry S Truman Library by the author and the library staff. However, no light was thrown on the three main questions: (1) Was Truman's battery firing in support of Donovan's attack on October 14, 1918; (2) who was firing if it was not Truman; and (3) if it was Truman firing, did Donovan register the complaint? All that is certain is that Truman was firing in that sector on the thirteenth.
6. Letter, WJD to Ruth Donovan, October 23, 1918.
7. Intelligence Summary 142, HQ, 42nd Division, AEF, October 14–15, 1918.
8. Letter, WJD to Ruth Donovan, October 23, 1918.
9. *Ibid.*
10. *Ibid.*
11. Letter, James W. Wadsworth to Ruth Donovan, January 13, 1919.
12. Letter, Theodore Roosevelt to WJD, October 25, 1918.
13. Letter, WJD to Ruth Donovan, November 10, 1918.
14. *Ibid.*, November 18, 1918.
15. *Ibid.*, December 25, 1918.
16. *Ibid.*, December 22, 1918.
17. Duffy, *op. cit.*, p. 326.
18. Letter, Father Duffy to WJD, November 2, 1918.
19. *Ibid.*, November 14, 1918.
20. Letter, Harold L. Allen to WJD, November 20, 1918.
21. Ford and Doering, Vincent Donovan interview, *op. cit.*, and letter, WJD to Ruth Donovan, February 15, 1919.
22. Memo, commanding officer 165th Infantry to adjutant general of the Army, Remagen, Germany, February 22, 1919.
23. Letter, WJD to Ruth Donovan, March 27, 1919.
24. Vanden Heuvel, diary, August 25, 1953.
25. New York *Mail*, April 29, 1919.

Chapter 5
Saturn

1. Fragment of speech entitled "Russia," two pages, undated, but plainly written from 1919 to 1921, WJD Miscellaneous Collection.

2. Winston S. Churchill, *The Great War* (London: Newnes, 1933), vol. 3, p. 1445.
3. "Omsk Journey," a log kept by F. C. MacDonald, WJD Miscellaneous Collection.
4. Anthony Cave Brown and Charles B. MacDonald, *On a Field of Red* (New York: Putnam, 1981), p. 75.
5. Ibid., pp. 65–67.
6. "Russia, Siberia, Poland," vol. 2, WJD bound files.
7. Interview with Frank Raichle, Buffalo, N.Y., June 5, 1981.
8. Interview with David Donovan, Berryville, Va., October 7, 1981.
9. Anonymous.
10. Letter, Peter Bentley to Herbert Hoover, January 18, 1929, in Pre-Presidential Papers—Appointment, Cab.—Donovan, W. J., in Herbert Hoover Presidential Library.
11. White Plains *Reporter,* no date, WJD Miscellaneous Collection.
12. Letter, Hamilton Ward to WJD, November 9, 1922, WJD Miscellaneous Collection.
13. Letter, WJD to Hamilton Ward, November 12, 1922, WJD Miscellaneous Collection.
14. Vanden Heuvel, diary, September 22, 1953.
15. Interview with Ralstone R. Irvine, Martha's Vineyard, Mass., August 14, 1981.
16. Interview with Frank Raichle, Buffalo, N.Y., March 8, 1981.
17. Letter, Alex. R. Griffin to Herbert Hoover, February 26, 1929, in Pre-Presidential Papers—Appointments, Cab.—Donovan, W. J., Herbert Hoover Presidential Library.
18. Dick Hirsch, Buffalo *Courier-Express,* August 24, 1980.
19. Interview with Frank Raichle, Buffalo N.Y., March 8, 1981.
20. Interview with Donald Rumsey, Buffalo, N.Y., September 5, 1980.
21. Undated clipping from Buffalo newspaper, probably the *News,* WJD Miscellaneous Collection.
22. Hamburg *Independent,* no date, WJD Miscellaneous Collection.

Chapter 6
Joining the Federal Crowd

1. Ruth Donovan, diary, January 23, 1925.
2. *Ibid.,* February 1, 1925.
3. Henry F. Pringle, "Exit 'Wild Bill': A Portrait of William J. Donovan," *Outlook* (January 9, 1929).
4. Letters from Vincent Donovan to Ruth Donovan, undated.
5. Interview with Frank Raichle, Buffalo, N.Y., March 22, 1981.
6. Martin Mayer, *Emory Buckner* (New York: Harper & Row, 1968), p. 176.
7. Sanford J. Unger, *FBI* (Boston: Little, Brown, 1975), pp. 46–47.
8. Memo from Ralstone R. Irvine to author, November 5, 1981.
9. *Report of the Attorney General* (Washington, D.C.: Department of Justice, 1927), p. 21.
10. Allen W. Dulles, Address Before the Erie County Bar Association, March 21, 1960.
11. WJD, speech on "The Antitrust Laws and Foreign Trade," delivered before the National Paint, Oil and Varnish Association, October 28, 1927.

12. WJD, "The Need for a Commerce Court," *The Annal of the American Academy of Political and Social Science* (1930).

Chapter 7
The Setback

1. Margaret Bassett, *Profiles and Portraits of American Presidents* (New York: McKay, 1964), p. 162.
2. Washington *News,* no date, WJD Miscellaneous Collection.
3. Ruth Donovan, diary, October 29, 1929.
4. New York *World,* August 12, 1928.
5. Ruth Donovan, diary, November 8–25, 1928.
6. Interview with James R. Murphy, Washington, D.C. April 7, 1981.
7. Letter, November 14, 1928, Pre-Presidential Papers—Appointments, Cab.—Donovan, W. J., Herbert Hoover Presidential Library.
8. Preceding and following letters from Pre-Presidential Papers—Appointments, Cab.—Donovan, W. J., Herbert Hoover Presidential Library.
9. Ruth Donovan, diary, January 8, 1929.
10. Interview with Bethuel Webster, New York, N.Y., March 16, 1980.
11. WJD, diary, March 2, 1929. All following quotations from this source until otherwise stated.
12. Interview with T. J. McFadden, New York, New York, May 13, 1979.
13. Baltimore *Sun,* February 28, 1929.
14. Herbert Hoover, "Reasons Donovan Was Not Taken into Cabinet," Presidential Index Name File, Herbert Hoover Presidential Library.
15. Presidential Secretaries File, Lockwood, George B., dated August 19, 1929, Herbert Hoover Presidential Library.

Chapter 8
Silk Stocking Lawyer

1. Cabell Phillips, *From the Crash to the Blitz, 1929–1939* (New York: Macmillan, 1969), p. 26.
2. William Manchester, *The Glory and the Dream* (Boston: Little, Brown, 1973), vol. I, p. 35.
3. Quoted in Phillips, *op. cit.,* p. 338.
4. "Wild Bill Donovan Victory Song," words and music by Tom Donahue. New York *Herald Tribune,* October 16, 1932.
5. Buffalo *News,* May 10, 1932.
6. *Catholic Union and Times,* October 13, 1932.
7. *The New York Times,* October 30, 1932.
8. Ruth Donovan, diary, November 9 and 12, 1932.

Chapter 9
The Days of Peace Run Out

1. Eberhard Zeller, *The Flame of Freedom* (London: Woolf, 1967), p. 24.
2. Peter Fleming, *Operation Sea Lion* (New York: Simon & Schuster, 1957), p. 211.
3. Letter from Frau Erika Canaris to WJD, translated at OSS, dated "Riederau, 15 Nov 46," WJD Miscellaneous Collection.

4. Letter, WJD to Patricia H. Donovan, August 12, 1938.
5. CIA Report, p. 39.
6. H. Wendell Endicott, "Personal Records of Alaska and the Yukon Hunting Trip, 1939," WJD Miscellaneous Collection. All quotations from this source until otherwise stated.
7. *The New York Times*, September 3, 1939.
8. *Ibid.*, September 4, 1939.
9. Ruth Donovan, diary, September 6, 1939.
10. *Ibid.*, May 9, 1940.
11. *Ibid.*, May 16 and 20, 1940.

Chapter 10
Presidential Agent

1. Speech, House of Commons, June 18.
2. Vanden Heuvel, diary, September 23, 1953.
3. *Ibid.*, August 22, 1953.
4. Winston S. Churchill, *The Second World War*, vol. III, *The Grand Alliance* (London: Cassell, 1950), p. 540.
5. CIA Report, p. 30.
6. Copy of British Embassy telegram, evidently supplied by Intrepid, WJD Miscellaneous Collection.
7. Churchill, *The Grand Alliance*, p. 97.
8. *Ibid.*, p. 140.
9. Telegram, FDR to WJD, January 20, 1941, WJD Miscellaneous Collection.
10. "Highlights of Conversation Between Col. Wm. Donovan and the Chief of Aviation, Army General Simović," January 24, 1941, Balkans Trip, vol. 1, CIA Collection.
11. Telegram, WJD to secretary of state and secretary of the navy, February 20, 1941, CIA Collection.
12. Ruth Donovan, diary, March 12 and April 6, 1941.
13. CIA Report, p. 42.
14. *Ibid.*
15. *Ibid.*
16. *Ibid.*
17. Letter, WJD to Knox, April 26, 1941, Pre-COI File, WJD Miscellaneous Collection.
18. S. I. Rosenman, *Working with Roosevelt* (New York: Da Capo Press, 1972), p. 283.
19. Ibid., p. 287.
20. CIA Report, p. 57.
21. Donald McLachlan, *Room 39* (New York: Atheneum, 1967), p. 228.
22. "Memorandum of Establishment of Service of Strategic Information," undated, OSSDF. All quotations from this source until otherwise stated.
23. Letter, FDR to WJD, July 23, 1941, OSSDF.
24. "Donovan's Undertaking Roosevelt's Greatest Espionage Organization," *Munchner Neueste Nachrichten*, December 23, 1941, Excerpts from Press and Radio, World War II, OSSDF. Italics in original.
25. CIA Report, p. 68.
26. *Ibid.*
27. Ruth Donovan, diary, July 15, 1941.

Chapter 11
Forming the Services

1. Interview with D. C. McKay by A. M. Wilson, November 13, 1944, OSS History Office interviews, WJD Miscellaneous Collection.
2. Interview with W. O. Hall, December 23, 1944, OSS History Office interviews, WJD Miscellaneous Collection.
3. Interview with R. E. Sherwood, January 10, 1945, History Section, OSSDF.
4. Foreign Broadcasting Intelligence Service intercept, Berlin to North America, December 26, 1941, WJD Miscellaneous Collection.
5. Interview with General Edwin Sibert, Washington, D.C., November 28, 1977.
6. CIA Report, p. 82.
7. *Ibid.*
8. COI Draft History, p. 3.
9. Letter, WJD to W. B. Phillips, November 17, 1941, OSSDF.
10. Memo, W. B. Phillips to WJD, November 18, 1941, OSSDF.
11. Letter, J. Edgar Hoover to WJD, September 17, 1941, OSSDF. All quotations from this source until otherwise stated.
12. Teleprinter for Q re George Djamgaroff, No. 626, apparently originated in January 1942, OSSDF.
13. Teleprinted message for Q, April 2, 1942, OSSDF.
14. George K. Bowden, "British ISOS," March 23, 1943, OSSDF. All quotations from this source until otherwise stated.
15. Norman Holmes Pearson, Foreword, September 1971, to J. C. Masterman, *The Double Cross System in the War of 1939 to 1945* (New Haven, Conn.: Yale University Press, 1972), pp. ix–xvi.
16. Malcolm Muggeridge, "Book Review of a Very Limited Edition," *Esquire* (March 1965).

Chapter 12
Pearl Harbor

1. FBI memo, "Re Malcolm Lowell," March 14, 1946, FBI file 100-25944-47(15).
2. Letter, Thomas Thacher to WJD, September 4, 1941, OSSDF.
3. Letter, Malcolm Lovell to WJD, September 11, 1941, OSSDF.
4. Letter, WJD to W. S. Stephenson, September 15, 1941, OSSDF.
5. Letter, Malcolm Lovell to WJD, September 19, 1941, OSSDF. All quotations from this source until otherwise stated.
6. Letter, WJD to FDR, November 13, 1941, OSSDF.
7. CIA Report, pp. 111–16.
8. Department of Defense, "The 'Magic' Background of Pearl Harbor," declassified in 1977. Hereafter called DoD Report.
9. W. F. Friedman, "Certain Aspects of 'Magic' in the Cryptological Background of the Various Investigations into the Pearl Harbor Attack," NA (MMR) Ultra Collection, *circa* 1955. Hereafter called the Friedman Report.
10. *Ibid.*
11. *Ibid.* Italics in original.
12. All Magic quotations from DoD Report.
13. Husband E. Kimmel, *Admiral Kimmel's Story* (Chicago: Henry Regnery Co., 1955), p. 186.
14. Friedman Report.

15. Churchill, *Second World War,* vol. 3, p. 587 ff.
16. Vanden Heuvel, diary, August 17, 1953.
17. Document fragment, January 31, 1942, WJD Miscellaneous Collection.
18. Churchill, *Second World War,* vol. 3, p. 587 ff.

Chapter 13
Project George

1. Churchill, *The Grand Alliance,* p. 582.
2. Dun & Bradstreet report, dated March 1, 1944, Project George file, OSSDF.
3. George H. Mertens, biography, no date but evidently about March 1944, Project George file, OSSDF. All quotations from this source until otherwise stated.
4. Letter, J. F. Carter to WJD, March 24, 1942, WJD Miscellaneous Collection.
5. Memo, W. A. Kimbel to WJD and David Bruce, March 24, 1942, WJD Miscellaneous Collection.
6. Memo, D. C. Poole to J. C. Wiley and WJD, February 13, 1942, OSSDF. All quotations from this source until otherwise stated.
7. Memo 347, WJD to FDR, March 26, 1942, WJD Main Collection.
8. Memo, D. C. Poole to WJD, April 1, 1942, OSSDF. All quotations from this source until otherwise stated.
9. Memo 353, WJD to FDR, March 26, 1942, WJD Main Collection.
10. "For Q," British Security Council report 639, August 18, 1942, OSSDF.
11. "Memorandum for A.D. [Allen Dulles] concerning Father Odo (Additional Information)," August 21, 1942, OSSDF.
12. Donald Downes, *The Scarlet Thread: Adventures in Wartime Espionage* (New York: British Book Centre, 1953), pp. 71–73.

Chapter 14
Lighting Torch

1. CIA Report, pp. 196 and 202.
2. Interview with E. J. Putzell, Jr., Naples, Fla., November 23, 1981.
3. Roberto Renduelles to James P. Warburg, August 19, 1941, OSSDF.
4. Letter, Summer Welles to WJD, March 25,1942, Donald C. Downes private file, OSSDF. All correspondence relating to this affair is in this file unless otherwise stated.
5. Letter, WJD to FDR, May 9, 1942, OSSDF.
6. Letter, J. Edgar Hoover to WJD, November 24, 1941, OSSDF.
7. FBI dossier item 62-64427-72 (118).
8. Letter, WJD to FDR and secretary of state, May 12, 1942, OSSDF.
9. Letter, Robert Solborg to WJD and Brigadier General R. E. Lee, April 17, 1942, OSSDF.
10. WJD to Brigadier General J. R. Deane, secretary of JCS, February 24, 1943, OSSDF.
11. Letter, WJD to Admiral Ernest J. King, CNO, July 14, 1942, OSSDF. All quotations from this source until otherwise stated.
12. Downes, *op. cit.,* p. 91 ff. All quotations from this source until otherwise stated.
13. Spencer Phenix to WJD, June 13, 1945, OSSDF.
14. Intercept of Madrid to Washington telegram 613, November 10, 1942, Intercepts of Spanish Cables, OSSDF.

Chapter 15
The Noble Puppet

1. CIA Report, p. 146.
2. *Ibid.*, p. 162.
3. WJD to the JCS, September 7, 1942, OSSDF.
4. Message in Frederick Dolbeare private file, dated May 9, 1942 (?), OSSDF.
5. Memo, "Re Giraud," David Bruce to WJD, May 7, 1942, OSSDF.
6. Memo, Frederick Dolbeare to WJD, October 23, 1942, Dolbeare private file, OSSDF.
7. "Jacques Lemaigre-Dubreuil," June 26, 1943, U.S. Government Biographical Records Center, OSSDF. All quotations from this source until otherwise stated.
8. "Memo. of Remarks by Lemaigre-Dubreuil Covering Preparations for the American Campaign in French North Africa," D. C. Poole to WJD, January 21, 1943, OSSDF.
9. Memo 70, WJD to FDR, June 26, 1942, CIA White House Books.
10. Memo, Donald C. McKay to WJD, March 3, 1943, OSSDF.
11. Record of Meeting with Lemaigre-Dubreuil, D. C. Poole to WJD, January 21, 1943, OSSDF.
12. Marcel Vigneras, *Rearming the French* (Washington, D.C.: Government Printing Office, 1957), pp. 1–14.
13. George F. Howe, *Northwest Africa: Seizing the Initiative in the West* (Washington, D.C.: Government Printing Office, 1957), pp. 81–82.
14. Dwight D. Eisenhower, *Crusade in Europe* (London: Heinemann, 1948), p. 162.
15. Stephen E. Ambrose, *Ike's Spies: Eisenhower and the Espionage Establishment* (New York: Doubleday, 1981), p. 30.

Chapter 16
Donovan and Darlan

1. Text of address of FDR to French North Africa, November 8, 1942, Proclamations, OSSDF.
2. Carleton Coon, *A North Africa Story* (Ipswich, Mass.: Gambit, 1980), p. 14.
3. Telegram, William A. Eddy to WJD, November 8, 1942, OSSDF.
4. Robert D. Murphy, *Diplomat Among Warriors* (New York: Pyramid, 1965), p. 149.
5. Howe, *op. cit.*, p. 249 ff.
6. *Ibid.*
7. *Ibid.*, p. 250.
8. Memo, F. L. Belin to WJD, January 23, 1943, OSSDF.
9. F. W. Deakin, *The Brutal Friendship* (New York: Harper & Row, 1957), p. 194.
10. Typed memo with handwritten draft by WJD, in Darlan File, microjob 6, no addressees, dated December 7, 1942, OSSDF.
11. Interview with Lyman B. Kirkpatrick, Providence, R.I., May 5, 1981.
12. Letter, W. P. Maddox to David Bruce, December 14, 1942, OSSDF.
13. Report, Lyman Kirkpatrick to W. P. Maddox, December 13, 1942, OSSDF.

Chapter 17
The Assassination

1. Arthur Funk, *Politics of Torch* (Lawrence, Kan.: University of Kansas Press, 1976), p. 21.
2. Howe, *op. cit.*, p. 615 n.
3. Roger Rosfelder, *Today in France*, no. 99 (January 1972), publication of the Society for French-American Affairs, New York.
4. *Ibid.*
5. Interviews with Carleton Coon, Gloucester, Mass., March 3, 12, 13, 22, 1981.
6. Coon, *op. cit.*, p. 61.
7. *Ibid.*, p. 48.
8. Carleton Coon, from an after-action report, "VIII: Postscript: The World After the War: OSS-SOE: The Invisible Empire." This document is not in WJD's papers, nor was it part of Coon's memoirs, *North Africa Story*. According to Coon, it was excised by his editor. Coon voluntarily sent this segment of his report to the author. All quotations from this source until stated otherwise.
9. Mark Clark, *Calculated Risk* (New York: Harper & Bros., 1950), p. 130.
10. Letter, Secretary of the Treasury Henry Morgenthau, Jr., to WJD, April 23, 1943, OSSDF.
11. Howe, *op. cit.*, pp. 361–62.
12. Memo, Emerson Bigelow to Louis Rehm, February 11, 1943, OSSDF.
13. Telegram 37, Robert Murphy and William Eddy to WJD, February 11, 1942, OSSDC.

Chapter 18
The Dulles Organization

1. Personal details from Mary Bancroft, interview, New York City, January 21, 1981.
2. D. C. Poole to WJD, February 2, 1943, OSSDF.
3. Interview with Otto C. Doering, New York, N.Y., June 11, 1979.
4. B. Randell, "The Colossus: A Paper to Be Presented at the International Research Conference on the History of Computing, Los Alamos Scientific Laboratory, University of California, June 10–15th, 1976."
5. Telegram 8/9, WJD to Allen Dulles, April 29, 1943, OSSDC.
6. Telegram 1148/1149, Whitney Shepardson to Allen Dulles, January 25, 1944, OSSDC.
7. A. W. Dulles, *Secret Surrender* (New York: Popular Library, 1966), pp. 24–25.
8. Kim Philby, *My Silent War* (New York: Grove Press, 1968), pp. 104–06.
9. Memo, F. L. Belin to WJD, October 12, 1943, in Belin Reports 12,784, October 12, 1943, OSSDF.
10. Telegram 1477/79, Allen Dulles to WJD, December 29, 1943, OSSDC.
11. Memo 336, WJD to FDR, January 10, 1944, WJD Miscellaneous Collection.
12. Memo, "Boston Series," October 10, 1944; no file number, but located in Belin 12,784, OSSDF. All quotations from this source until otherwise stated.
13. Boston Series (Evaluation) 13, 836, May 6, 1944, OSSDF.
14. Telegram 1509/9, F. L. Belin to Allen Dulles, April 20, 1944, OSSDC.
15. Telegram 3163/65, Allen Dulles to F. L. Belin, April 26, 1944; telegram 3166, Dulles to Belin, April 26, 1944, OSSDC. All quotations from these sources until otherwise stated.

16. Telegram 337/3379, Dulles to WJD, May 8, 1944, OSSDC.
17. Memo, WJD to Harry Truman, June 22, 1945, OSSDF.
18. Telegram 181, London to Bern, July 31, 1943, OSSDC.
19. Telegram 198, London to Bern, August 11, 1943, OSSDC.
20. Memo, WJD to Harry Truman, June 22, 1945, OSSDF.
21. Interview with Mary Bancroft, New York City, July 16, 1980.
22. Memo, WJD to Harry Truman, June 22, 1945, OSSDF.
23. Memo, Ulius Amoss to David Bruce, January 5, 1943, OSSDF.
24. Telegrams 140, 154 (?), 161, 189 (?), Florimond Duke to Ulius Amoss, February 26, March 5, March 10, March 24, 1943, OSSDC.

Chapter 19
Donovan at Sixty

1. Coon, *op. cit.*, p. ix.
2. Interview with E. J. Putzell, Jr., Naples, Fla., February 2, 1982.
3. Interview with Otto C. Doering, Jr., New York City, June 2, 1978.
4. Interview with Mrs. Marlys Leister, Washington, D.C., November 27, 1981.
5. CIA Report, p. 92.
6. Clipping, Washington *Times-Herald*, no date, WJD Miscellaneous Collection.
7. Interview of Wayne Coy by Conyers Read and Helen T. Linde, July 13, 1945, OSS History Section.
8. Letter, G. E. Buxton to WJD, March 17, 1943, in microjob 66, OSSDF.
9. Letter, Maddox, Credit Department, St. Regis Hotel, to WJD, February 25, 1944, OSSDF.
10. Letter, G. V. Strong to G. C. Marshall, July 6, 1943, OSSDF.
11. Memo, G. E. Buxton to C. R. Peck, July 23, 1943, OSSDF.
12. Interview of Dr. James Grafton Rogers by Conyers Read and A. M. Wilson, October 5, 1944, OSS History Section. All quotations from this source until otherwise stated.
13. Interview with Lieutenant William Applebaum, July 14, 1944, OSS History Section, WJD Miscellaneous Collection.
14. Letter, G. C. Marshall to WJD, December 23, 1942, OSSDF.
15. Letter, WJD to Commissioner of Internal Revenue, January 8, 1943, OSSDF.
16. M. O. Smith to WJD, May 6, 1947, vol. 3, document 116, WJD bound files, OSSDF.
17. Letter, Commander C. S. Perkins to M. H. Easton, May 10, 1944, OSSDF.
18. "Use of CX/MSS Ultra by the U.S. War Dept. (1943–45)", in RG 457, NA (MMR).
19. Letter, G. V. Strong to WJD, October 21, 1942, OSSDF.
20. Letter, WJD to Joint Intelligence Committee, October 22, 1942, OSSDF.
21. John Magruder to WJD, "Discussion of Meeting of JIC on January 7, regarding release of intercept material to OSS," OSSDF.
22. CIA Report, p. 199.
23. *Ibid.*, pp. 204–06.

Chapter 20
Penny Farthing

1. Interview with Henry B. Hyde, Washington, D.C., March 11, 1982.
2. Telegram 205, WJD to W. A. Eddy, January 20, 1943, OSSDC.

3. Letter, Dewavrin to WJD, April 19, 1945, OSSDF.
4. *Ibid.*
5. "Certificate of the Holding of an Inquest," dated April 3, 1943, appended to Dewavrin's letter to WJD of April 19, 1945, OSSDF.
6. Vanden Heuvel, diary, September 7, 1953.
7. Henry B. Hyde, unpublished manuscript of his experiences as chief of OSS SI Algiers. All quotations from this source until otherwise stated.
8. *OSS War Report,* vol. 2, p. 227.
9. *Ibid.*
10. Hyde, *op. cit.* All quotations from this source until otherwise stated.
11. M. R. D. Foot, *SOE in France* (London: HMSO, 1966), p. 78.
12. Hyde, *op. cit.* All quotations from this source until otherwise stated.

Chapter 21
The First Star

1. CIA Report, p. 248.
2. *Ibid.*
3. *Ibid.*
4. Interview with Otto C. Doering, Lake Placid, N.Y., August 6, 1977.
5. The author is grateful to James R. Murphy, of Washington, D.C., for this letter, which for reasons stated does not appear in any of the WJD or government collections.
6. CIA Report, p. 256. All quotations from this source until otherwise stated.
7. Letters, Stephen Early to WJD, February 25, 1943, and WJD to Early, February 28, 1943, FDR File, OSSDF.
8. Interview with Judge Owen McGivern, New York City, October 15, 1981.
9. Copy of telegram from Hayes to Hull, William A. Kimbel to David Bruce, November 13, 1942, OSSDF.
10. "Memorandum on OSS in Spain," March 8, 1943, OSSDF. All quotations from this source until otherwise stated.
11. Letter, Adolf Berle to John Deane, secretary of JCS, March 26, 1943, OSSDF.
12. Letter, Deane to WJD, April 8, 1943, in Intelligence Service 16,083, OSSDF.
13. "Statement by the Director at JCS Meeting re JPS/154," April 4, 1943, OSSDF.
14. Summary of Ambassador Hayes's Complaints, April 10, 1943, OSSDF.

Chapter 22
The Balkan Plan

1. Interview with David Donovan, Berryville, Va., October 22, 1981.
2. Interview with E. J. Putzell, Naples, Fla., September 2, 1981.
3. Vanden Heuvel, diary, October 1, 1953.
4. WJD to secretary, JCS, August 20, 1943, OSSDF.
5. Letter, secretary, JCS, to WJD, September 7, 1943, OSSDF.
6. Memo, "OSS unit to Istanbul," W. A. Kimbel to Lanning Macfarland, December 16, 1942, OSSDF.
7. Archibald F. Coleman, "Report on Field Conditions, Istanbul, for the period 2 May, 1943, to Sept. 14, 1944," dated October 20, 1944, in OSS field report files, OSSDF.
8. OSS German Ops 13, 737, OSSDF. All quotations from this source until otherwise stated. Hereafter called Plan Herman.

9. Memo, "Von Moltke, Helmuth, 14,036," WJD to Cordell Hull, November 2, 1943, OSSDF.
10. Plan Herman.
11. Letter, Alexander Kirk to Richard D. Tindall, January 10, 1944, in Plan Herman file, OSSDF.
12. "Herman Plan," WJD to JCS, April 2, 1944, in Germany 13,733, OSSDF.

Chapter 23
The Morde Incident

1. Interview with Lieutenant Colonel John Toulmin, Washington, D.C., June 5, 1945, OSS History Section. All quotations from Toulmin from this source.
2. A. F. Coleman, "Masterspy Talks—Was FDR Ready to Give Europe to the Germans in 1943?" *Metro: The Magazine of Southeastern Virginia* (May 1977). All quotations from this source until otherwise stated. Hereafter called Coleman Article.
3. Memo, WJD to FDR, October 29, 1943, FDR Library.
4. Coleman Article. All quotations from this source until otherwise stated.
5. WJD to FDR, October 29, 1943, with two attachments. Hereafter called Morde Memorandum. All quotations from this source until otherwise stated.
6. Coleman Article.
7. Morde Memorandum. All quotations from this source until otherwise stated.
8. Toulmin interview, *op. cit.*
9. Robert E. Sherwood to FDR, October 26, 1943, FDR Library.
10. Memo, WJD to FDR, October 29, 1943, FDR Library.
11. Toulmin interview, *op. cit.*

Chapter 24
Falling Sparrow

1. I. R. Sherman, "Report on My Istanbul Mission," to WJD and to Mrs. Hazel Haight, September 26, 1944, in OSS Mission Turkey, 15,049A, OSSDF. Hereafter called Sherman Report.
2. "Report by Cereus and Sub-source Dogwood," October 4, 1943, OSSDF.
3. "Brief on Proposed Collaboration with the Hungarian General Staff on the Basis of the Provisional Agreement, Source Cereus, Sub-source Dogwood," October 27, 1943, OSSDF.
4. "The Hungarian Situation, WJD to Joint Chiefs of Staff, November 20, 1943, in OSS Ops 2196, OSSDF.
5. "Proposal by Hungarian General Staff Officer," from JCS to WJD, December 5, 1943, in OSS Ops 13,196, OSSDF.
6. Telegram 864, W. Shepardson to WJD and Allen Dulles, November 20, 1943, OSSDC.
7. Telegrams 1309–1311, 1312, 1347–1350, 180–182, 1284, Allen Dulles to WJD, December 14–19, 1943, OSSDC.
8. Telegram 1484, A. W. Dulles to WJD, December 29, 1943, OSSDC.
9. Telegram 221, WJD to Lanning Macfarland, January 9, 1944, OSSDC.
10. Letter, Lanning Macfarland to WJD, January 12, 1944, OSSDF.

11. "Minutes of a Secret Meeting Held on January 22, 1944, Present—H, Jacaranda, Cereus, Dogwood, WA & Juniper," OSSDF.
12. Telegram 1875–1878, A. W. Dulles to WJD, January 26, 1944.
13. "Memorandum re My meeting with Colonel 'H' & Jacaranda on the Night of Feb. 27th. Dogwood Was Also Present," March 4, 1944, OSSDF.
14. Telegram 2288-92, A. W. Dulles to WJD, March 3, 1944, OSSDC.
15. Letter, Guy Nunn to Arthur Goldberg, cc to WJD, in OSS Ops Balkan File 13,658A, March 11, 1944, OSSDF.
16. F. Duke, "Report on Field Conditions—Sparrow Mission," July 9, 1945, OSSDF.
17. Wilhelm Hoettl, *The Secret Front* (New York: Praeger, 1954), pp. 195–96.
18. Telegram 110924, Katek (London) to W. Shepardson, February 16, 1945, OSSDC.
19. General W. Warlimont, *Inside Hitler's Headquarters 1939–1945* (London: Weidenfeld & Nicolson, 1964), pp. 411–14.

Chapter 25
Exit Snapdragon

1. Murray Gurfein to WJD and David Bruce, November 30, 1942, in K Project file, OSSDF.
2. Telegram 669-671, A. W. Dulles to WJD, August 29, 1943, OSSDC.
3. "Bulgaria: Public Opinion Prior to 8 March 1944," Report A-24351, April 1, 1944, OSSDF.
4. "Recent Chronology of the 'K' Project," undated, probably originated around March or April 1944, in K Project central file, OSSDF.
5. Telegram In-2417, Lanning Macfarland to WJD, February 6, 1944, OSSDC.
6. Letter, Murray Gurfein to WJD, March 23, 1944, OSSDF.
7. Letter, John Toulmin to WJD, February 7, 1944, OSSDF.
8. Letter, Lanning Macfarland to WJD, February 13, 1944, OSSDF.
9. WJD to Lanning Macfarland, February 25, 1944, OSSDC.
10. "Rumanian Implementation Study," OSS Planning Staff to WJD, February 24, 1943, OSSDF.
11. Memo, "Marshal Ion Antonescu," Bernard Yarrow to WJD, with Dulles attachment, February 8, 1943, OSSDF.
12. Memo, Bernard Yarrow to WJD, April 6, 1943, in OSS Ops Rumania 10, 386A, OSSDF.
13. "Report of Meeting at Cairo Between Prince Stirbey & Allied Representatives," WJD to Joint Chiefs of Staff, in OSS Ops Rumania 14,153, OSSDF.
14. "Istanbul to Donovan," March 25, 1944, relayed to FDR by WJD on March 27, 1944, in Rumania 14,153, OSSDF.
15. *OSS War Report*, vol. 2, pp. 271–72.
16. Telegram 43644, June 6, 1944, OSSDC.
17. Sherman Report. All quotations from this source until otherwise stated.
18. *OSS War Report*, vol. 2, pp. 271–72.
19. Sherman Report.
20. Interview with James R. Murphy, Washington, D.C., March 20, 1981.
21. Memo, "First series weekly information cables summarizing strategic significance enemy espionage previous week and other important general information acquired during week," dated March 12, 1944, OSSDF.

Chapter 26
Christmas 1943

1. "Report by the Theater Officer on the Far East," August 31, 1943, in OSS Ops FETO 12,703, OSSDF. All quotations from this source until otherwise stated.
2. Letter, Duncan C. Lee to WJD, October 20, 1943, OSSDF.
3. Richard Dunlop, *Behind Japanese Lines* (Chicago: Rand McNally, 1979), p. 231. All quotations from this source until otherwise stated.
4. "General Donovan's Notes on India," December 14,1943, in India 13,767, OSSDF.
5. Maurice Matloff, *Strategic Planning for Coalition Warfare, 1943-1944* (Washington, D.C.: Government Printing Office,1968), p. 280 ff.
6. Memo, WJD to JCS, June 29, 1942, in Russia 12,999, OSSDF.
7. Letter, William Langer to WJD, November 6,1941, on microjob 43, OSSDF.
8. Paper and letter, WJD to John Deane, August 20, 1943, OSSDF. All quotations from this source until otherwise stated.
9. Memo, W. A. Kimbel to WJD, January 23, 1943, in Russia 10,020, OSSDF.
10. Letter, E. H. Hill to WJD, undated, in Russia, Reel 47, OSSDF.
11. Memo, W. A. Kimbel to WJD, September 15, 1943, OSSDF.
12. Memo, O. C. O'Conor to WJD, September 4, 1943, in Russia 12,534, OSSDF. All quotations from this source until otherwise stated.
13. Letter, G. E. Buxton to Shaw, February 5, 1944, OSSDF.
14. W. Averell Harriman and Elie Abel, *Special Envoy to Churchill and Stalin* (New York: Random House, 1975), pp. 291–94. All quotations from this source until otherwise stated.
15. John R. Deane, *The Strange Alliance: The Story of Our Efforts at Wartime Cooperation with Russia* (New York: Viking, 1947), p. 53.
16. Harriman and Abel, *op. cit.*
17. "Intelligence to Be Furnished U.S.S.R.," February 4, 1944, OSSDF.
18. Telegram, G. E. Buxton to John Deane, January 5, 1945, in RG334, USMMM OSS Germany, NA (MMR).
19. Note, P. N. Fitin to John Deane, February 15, 1945, in RG334, USMMM OSS, Germany, NA (MMR).
20. FDR to Averell Harriman, March 30, 1944, and Harriman to FDR, in USMMM OSS, NA (MMR).

Chapter 27
Noah's Ark

1. Report by Captain G. F. Else, January 31, 1945, in 16,144D, OSSDF.
2. Allied Forces Headquarters, *Special Operations in the Mediterranean Theatre*, vol. X, p. 3, WJD Miscellaneous Collection.
3. Paul West, "Operation Feather 3," October 25, 1943, in OSS Ops Balkans 13,015, OSSDF.
4. Letter, J. M. Scribner to E. J. Putzell, with "Attached Communication from Paul West to General Donovan," November 6, 1943, in OSS Ops Balkans 13,013, OSSDF.
5. All information and quotes from AFHQ, *op. cit.*
6. Report on Operation Staircase, June 24, 1944, OSSDF.
7. "Interference with the Turkish Chrome Shipments to Germany by Attack on Transportation," in Turkey (Chrome Ore) 13,739, OSSDF.

8. Memo, William Langer to WJD, "Turkish Chrome Ore and the Maritsa Bridge," October 29, 1943, OSSDF.
9. Memo, John Magruder to WJD, February 26, 1944, in Turkey 13,739, OSSDF.
10. Edward T. Dickinson to WJD, February 28, 1944, OSSDF.
11. Telegram 30954, Paul West to WJD, June 2, 1944, in OSS Turkey 13,881, OSSDF.
12. WJD to FDR, June 18, 1944, in OSS Turkey 13,881, OSSDF.
13. Letter, Cordell Hull to WJD, June 24, 1944, in OSS Turkey 13,881, OSSDF.
14. WJD to George Marshall, July 28, 1944, in OSS Turkey 14,262A, OSSDF.

Chapter 28
Audrey

1. Multiple interviews with Hans Tofte and Robert E. S. Thompson, Washington, D.C., and New Haven, Conn., August to October 1979.
2. Robert E. S. Thompson and Louis Huot, "Report of Organization and Activities of Special Operations Branch, OSS-ME, Advance Base, Bari, Italy," November 8, 1943. All quotations from this source until otherwise stated.
3. Interview with Tofte, *op. cit.*
4. Vladimir Dedijer, *With Tito* (London: Hamilton, 1951), p. 197.
5. Louis Huot, attachment: "Advance Base, OSS, Middle East, Bari, Italy: Report of Operations for Period 5 October to 1 November 1943." All quotations from this source until otherwise stated.
6. Memo, "Present Situation in Greece and Yugoslavia—Recommendations and Request for Instructions," WJD to JCS, November 26, 1943, in OSS Ops Balkans 13,301, OSSDF.
7. *Ibid.*
8. Telegram, WJD to G. E. Buxton, February 8, 1944, in OSS Ops Balkans Tito 13,437, OSSDF.
9. Letter, FDR to WJD, March 22, 1944, in Yugoslavia 13,860, OSSDF.
10. Memo, "Relationship, OSS-British North Africa and Middle East," deputy secretary, Joint Chiefs of Staff, to WJD, March 2, 1944, OSSDF.
11. Message 71469, JCS to Jacob Devers and Ralph Royce, March 2, 1944, OSSDF.
12. Field report, by Nels J. Benson, Altmark Mission, October 20, 1944, OSSDF.
13. Letter, Ellery Huntington to Harold G. Lockwood and WJD, August 25, 1944, OSSDF.

Chapter 29
Was Tito Betrayed?

1. Telegram 393, FDR to Winston Churchill, October 22, 1943, and telegram 470, Churchill to FDR, October 23, 1943, OSSDC.
2. Vivian Street, "Operations in Bosnia 25 May to 3 June 1944," Appendix A to "Diary of Movements of Marshal Tito and His HQ from 25 May to 3 June," undated but probably originated about June 24, 1944, in OSS Ops Balkans 14,563, OSSDF.
3. "Report of Interview by Lieutenant Colonel K. M. Bourne with Mr. P.," 11:40 A.M., June 9, 1944, in OSS Ops Balkans 13,563, OSSDF.
4. Memo, "Information with OSS on Tito's Headquarters," June 17, 1944, OSSDF.

5. Memo, "Known Information Concerning Colonel Sands' Relations with Yugoslavia Officials," June 17, 1944, OSSDF.
6. *Ibid.*
7. Oliver Jackson Sands, Jr., statement, "Alleged Breach of Security re Tito," June 17, 1944, in Yugoslavia 14,563. All quotations from this source until otherwise stated.
8. Interview with Oliver J. Sands, Richmond, Va., January 14, 1982.
9. Letter, WJD to Clayton Bissell, June 19, 1944, in Yugoslavia 14,063H, OSSDF.

Chapter 30
Italian Maelstrom

1. "History of Company A, 2671 Special Reconnaissance Battalion," unpublished ms.
2. Carleton Coon to WJD, "OSS Activities in Corsica, September 12th to October 5, 1943," OSSDF. All quotations from this source until otherwise stated.
3. " History of Company A," *op. cit.* All quotations from this source until otherwise stated.
4. Foot, *op. cit.,* p. 187.
5. "Committee for OSS Reduction in Force," August 11, 1944, OSSDF.
6. Report of Ginny Mission; HQ METO, *U.S.* v. *Anton Dostler,* Review of Record of Trial, November 6, 1945; and Livermore Report, in Ginny case file, NA, Suitland, Md.
7. Deposition of Lagaxo Franco, Exhibit O in Ginny case file.
8. *U.S.* v. *Anton Dostler,* Review of Record of Trial by Military Commission, November 6, 1945, in Ginny case file.
9. Letter, General von Vietinghof to General Sir William Morgan, October 12, 1945, in Ginny case file.
10. Letter, Vatican to Harold Pittman, November 30, 1945, in Ginny case file.

Chapter 31
Fettucine with the General

1. Peter Tompkins, *A Spy in Rome* (New York: Avon, 1962), p. 18. All quotations from this source until otherwise stated.
2. "Mission to Rome, 5 March 1945," Peter Tompkins to WJD, in Tompkin's personal file 16,044. Hereafter called the Tompkins Report.
3. Tompkins, *A Spy in Rome,* p. 52.
4. Tompkins Report.
5. Tompkins, *A Spy in Rome,* p. 62.
6. Tompkins Report.
7. *Ibid.*
8. *Ibid.*
9. "2nd Interim Report of Activities of SIC, David Crockett to Edward Glavin July 14, 1944, OSSDF. Hereafter called Crockett Report.
10. Telegram 28814, April 5, 1944, OSSDC.
11. "Maurizio Giglio, Alias Cervo, Report of the Arrest, Detention and Death, by His Orderly," in Final Report of Special Investigating Committee, October 29, 1944, OSSDF.
12. Tompkins, *A Spy in Rome,* p. 149.

13. *Ibid.*, p. 149.
14. *Ibid.*, p. 143.
15. *Ibid.*, p. 256.

Chapter 32
The Inquests

1. Crockett Report. All quotations from this source until otherwise stated.
2. It is not possible to state from the record what casualties the OSS Rome chains suffered during this period. Crockett's report contains a list of some 80 names, but he does not say whether the agents were killed, injured, captured, missing, or had survived but still warranted compensation. The best estimate—only an educated guess—is that during the post-Anzio *ratissages* Tompkins and Menicante between them lost some 80 agents dead and about 250 captured or missing.
3. Memo, subject Peter Tompkins, Roger Pfaff to WJD, March 3, 1945, in Tompkins personal file 16,044, OSSDF.
4. Telegram 24694, WJD to G. E. Buxton, January 10, 1945, OSSDC.
5. Dulles's Kappa message 3465–3466, May 14, 1944, OSSDC.
6. J. J. Angleton HQ X-2 Detachment, 2677th Regiment OSS (Prov.), to Commanding Officer 2677th Regiment (Prov.), July 3, 1945, OSSDF. All quotations from this source until otherwise stated.
7. Photograph of chart entitled "Counter Espionage Italy," marked "660.1," undated, CIAP, WJD Miscellaneous Collection.
8. Donald Downes, preface to Tompkins, *A Spy in Rome, op. cit.*, pp. 11–12.
9. Telegram 30434, Edward Glavin to WJD, April 15, 1944, OSSDC.
10. Telegram 33504, Edward Glavin to WJD, May 9, 1944, OSSDC.
11. Telegram 37357, Dwight Chapin and Edward Glavin to WJD and David Bruce, June 8, 1944, OSSDF.
12. Report, "Investigation of Italian Intelligence Activities," Edward Glavin and Dwight Chapin, June 23, 1944, in SI 14,700, OSSDF.

Chapter 33
Palace Revolt

1. Interview with E. J. Putzell, Naples, Fla., December 4, 1981.
2. Memo, "OSS Morale," George Platt to Otto Doering, August 23, 1943, in OSS 12,367, OSSDF.
3. Report on inspecting SOE London, Ellery C. Huntington to WJD, March 30, 1943, OSSDF.
4. WJD to Communications, August 23 and October 12, 1943, OSSDF.
5. Memo to the acting director, October 1, 1943, in OSS 12,775, OSSDF.
6. Interview with Putzell, *op cit.*
7. Memo to acting director, *op. cit.*
8. "Organization of OSS," Otto Doering to WJD, October 6, 1943, in OSS 12,725, OSSDF.
9. WJD to John Magruder, November 8, 1943, in OSS Org 12,775, OSSDF.
10. Letter, Hugh Wilson to WJD, March 7, 1944, OSSDF.
11. Interviews with E. J. Putzell, Naples, Fla., February 18, 1980, and December 4, 1981.
12. Interview with T. J. McFadden, New York City, March 21, 1981.

Chapter 34
Neptune

1. Ruth Donovan, diary, May 13, 1944.
2. Washington *Times-Herald,* May 13, 1944.
3. Letter, Lieutenant Reeve Shley to WJD, February 3, 1944, OSSDF.
4. Telegram 45494, G. E. Buxton personal for WJD, May 27, 1944, OSSDC.
5. Vigneras, *op. cit.,* p. 301.
6. Memo, George Marshall to Cordell Hull, April 17, 1944, OSSDF.
7. Letter, Dwight Eisenhower to General B. B. Somervell, April 4, 1944, Eisenhower Diary, Eisenhower Library.
8. Arthur Bryant, *Turn of the Tide* (London: Collins, 1957), p. 206.
9. Telegram 2718–22, A. W. Dulles to WJD, April 7, 1944, OSSDC.
10. Telegram 2787–92, A. W. Dulles to WJD, April 12, 1944, OSSDC.
11. Memo, E. G. Buxton to FDR et al., April 18, 1944, OSSDF.
12. Telegram 3423–31, A. W. Dulles to WJD, May 13, 1944, OSSDC.
13. Memo, E. G. Buxton to Cordell Hull, May 17, 1944, in 14,845, OSSDF.
14. G-2 Section. U.S. First Army, Intelligence Summary for May 23, 1944, OCMH.

Chapter 35
D-Day

1. Jordan A. Harrison, *Cross-Channel Attack* (Washington, D.C.: Government Printing Office, 1950), pp. 76–77.
2. David Bruce, typewritten diary for May 30 to June 9, 1944.
3. Harry C. Butcher, *My Three Years with Eisenhower* (New York: Doubleday, 1946), p. 541.
4. Robert Aron, *France Reborn: The History of the Liberation* (New York: Scribner's, 1964), p. 90–91.
5. To author, undated but written summer 1970.
6. Aron, *op. cit.,* p. 95.
7. Warlimont, *op. cit.,* p. 422.
8. Transcript of interview between Major Corey Ford and Father Vincent Donovan, November 1967, WJD Miscellaneous Collection.
9. PWE Central Directive, week beginning June 15, 1944, OSSDF.
10. Telegram 50694, WJD to E. G. Buxton, June 6, 1944, OSSDF.
11. Telegram 52094, WJD to E. G. Buxton, June 11, 1944, OSSDC.

Chapter 36
The Uprisings

1. Interview with Patrick Dolan, Washington, D.C., April 6, 1982. All quotations from this source until otherwise stated.
2. Telegram 53914, Smith to WJD, June 17, 1944, OSSDC.
3. Telegram 54839, David Bruce and Joseph Haskell to WJD, June 21, 1944, OSSDC.
4. Telegram 52534, WJD to E. G. Buxton, June 13, 1944, OSSDC.
5. Telegram 52584, David Bruce to E. G. Buxton, June 15, 1944, OSSDC.
6. Memo, WJD to FDR, June 15, 1944, OSSDF.
7. Memo, WJD to FDR, July 5, 1944, OSSDF. All quotations from this source until otherwise stated.

8. Francis L. Loewenheim, ed., et al., *Roosevelt and Churchill: Their Secret Wartime Correspondence* (New York: Saturday Review Press/Dutton 1975), pp. 550–51.
9. Report on Operation Zebra, July 8, 1944, OSSDF.
10. Memo, "Performance and Potential of French Resistance," WJD to FDR, July 6, 1944, OSSDF.
11. Report on Operation "Cadillac," July 17, 1944, OSSDF.
12. Emerson Bigelow to Charles Cheston, January 27, 1945, OSSDF.
13. Vigneras, *op. cit.*, p. 400 ff.

Chapter 37
Cobra

1. WJD to FDR, July 4, 1944, in WJD's FDR file, OSSDF.
2. Telegram 4085, A. W. Dulles to WJD, July 12, 1944, OSSDC.
3. Telegram 4100–4114, A. W. Dulles to WJD, July 13, 1944, OSSDC.
4. Charles Eade, ed., *The Dawn of Liberation: War Speeches by the Right Honourable Winston S. Churchill* (London: Cassell, 1945), p. 122.
5. Report for White House map room, July 15, 1944, in Reports 14,495, OSSDF.
6. J. W. Wheeler-Bennett, *Nemesis of Power* (London: Macmillan, 1953), p. 627.
7. U.S. First Army, Report of Operations, July 31, 1944.
8. Harrison, *op. cit.*, p. 370.
9. BBC Warnings to Resistance Groups, August 6, 1944, OSSDF.
10. Letter, John Mowinckel to author, February 14, 1981.
11. Harrison, *op. cit.*, p. 618.

Chapter 38
Dragoon

1. *OSS War Report*, vol. 2, p. 237.
2. Letter to author from Henry Hyde, April 7, 1982.
3. *OSS War Report*, vol. 2, p. 230.
4. Memo, "Interrogation Report—Grosskopff, Edmund Unteroffizier, Ast Lyon," May 31, 1945, Norman Holmes Pearson to WJD, OSSDF; and interview with Henry B. Hyde, Washington, D.C., August 16, 1981.
5. Hyde letter, *op. cit.*
6. *OSS War Report*, vol. 2, p. 239, citing memo, "OSS Contribution to Intelligence Collated for Operation Dragoon," H. B. Hitchens to Deputy Assistant Chief of Staff, G2 Allied Forces Headquarters. October 30, 1944.
7. *Ibid.*, p. 238.
8. Hyde family archives.
9. Field report, "Mission Étoile," Albert Peter Dewey to WJD, September 28, 1944, OSSDF; and interview with General William Quinn, G-2 Seventh Army, Washington, D.C., August 28, 1981.
10. Letter to author from Henry Hyde, April 7, 1982.

Chapter 39
Crumbling Relationships

1. Winston S. Churchill, *The Second World War*, vol. VI, *Triumph and Tragedy* (London: Cassell, 1951), epigraph.
2. Memo, "The Skouras Brothers," R. D. Halliwell to WJD, January 9, 1943, in 9925, OSSDF.
3. Letter, George P. Skouras to WJD, January 17, 1944, in 12,653A, OSSDF.

4. Interview with Colonel John Toulmin, Washington, D.C., June 26, 1945, OSS History Section, OSSDF.
5. Memo, "Civilian George Skouras," John Toulmin to WJD, June 28, 1944, in 12,568, OSSDF.
6. Telegram 33854, July 14, 1944, OSSDC.
7. Telegram, WJD to Edward Glavin and John Toulmin, July 19, 1944, OSSDC.
8. Letter, Cordell Hull to WJD, July 25, 1944, in Balkans Basic File, OSSDF.
9. Letter, Lester Armour to WJD, July 4, 1944, in Skouras File 12,568, OSSDF.
10. *Ibid.*
11. *Ibid.*
12. Interview with Colonel Harry Aldrich, July 5, 1946, OSS History Section, OSSDF.
13. Interview with E. J. Putzell, Naples, Fla., December 18, 1981.
14. Drew Pearson, "Washington Merry-Go-Round," August 19, 1944, in the Washington *Post.*
15. Letter, Winston Churchill for General Walter Bedell Smith for WJD, August 24, 1944, in SHAEF SGS 332.01, NA (MMR).
16. Memo, "Observations on Greek Affairs in Cairo," Moses Hadas to William Langer to WJD, September 13, 1944, in Greece 14,817A, OSSDF.
17. Interview with Colonel Sir Ronald Wingate, Bath, England, May 1972.
18. Memo, "Gertrude's Papers," A. Van Beuren to Charles S. Cheston, April 13, 1945, OSSDF.
19. "Papurt Incident," Norman H. Pearson to Russell Forgan, October 23, 1944, to 10,731C, OSSDF.
20. H. Taprell Dorling, *Ribbons and Medals* (London: Phillip, 1960), p. 151.
21. Letter, WJD to Dwight Eisenhower, September 15, 1944, in CIA 1025, OSSDF.
22. Cable, WJD to David Bruce, January 3, 1945, in CIA 1025, OSSDC.
23. Telegram 76499, WJD to David Bruce, October 20, 1944, OSSDC.
24. Letter, "Colonel Andrew De Wavrin, alias Colonel André Passy," J. Edgar Hoover to attorney general, December 13, 1944, in CIA 1025, OSSDF.
25. Letter, Francis Biddle to FDR, December 15, 1944, item 36, CIA 1025, OSSDF.
26. Telegram 14294, Lester Armour to WJD, March 3, 1945, in CIA 1025, OSSDF.
27. Letter, with "Excerpts from OSS R&A Report 2553," WJD to FDR, undated, but in CIA 1025, OSSDF.
28. Report, David W. King to WJD, August 7, 1944, in OSS SX Plan File, OSSDF.

Chapter 40
The Betrayal

1. Jozef Garlinski, *Poland, SOE and the Allies* (London: George Allen & Unwin, 1969), p. 200.
2. Letter, "Re: Memo by Mr. Joyce," William Maddox to WJD, January 4, 1945, OSSDF.
3. Letter, "Analysis of OSS Activities in the Balkans and Central Europe," Robert Joyce to WJD, undated, but around September 1944, in OSS Ops Balkans 16135, OSSDF. All quotations from this source until otherwise stated.
4. Otto Doering, "The Basis for a Permanent World-Wide Intelligence Service," September 26, 1944, in 12,733, OSSDF.

5. "A Permanent United States Foreign Intelligence Service," Isadore Lubin to FDR, October 25, 1944, in 12,733G, OSSDF.
6. Otto Doering to WJD, November 3 and 22, 1944, in OSS 12,733, OSSDF.
7. Memo, WJD to FDR, in "OSS Reports to the White House, November–December, 1944," OSSDF.
8. For an account of these protracted and complicated proceedings, see the CIA Report, Chapter 6.
9. General signal, sent February 17, 1945, OSSDC.
10. The Economist, February 17, 1945.
11. Tagespost, February 10, 1945, OSSDF.
12. Letter, WJD to JCS, February 15, 1943, in OSS 12,733M, OSSDF.
13. Letter, WJD to FDR, February 23, 1945, in OSS 12,733M, OSSDF.
14. Letter, Ernest King to secretary of state, director of FBI, and administrator of FEA, February 16, 1945, in OSS 12,733M, OSSDF.
15. Letter, M. Joseph Lynch to J. Edgar Hoover, in Donovan File, item 94-4-4672-26, FBI.
16. CIA Report, p. 260.
17. Ibid., p. vi.
18. George Marshall to JCS, February 22, 1944, in RG 319 MID 350.09 (April 6, 1945), NA (MMR).

Chapter 41
New Policy, New Targets

1. Minutes of meeting at Supreme Headquarters, January 4, 1945, in file 125, OSS Ops ETO, OSSDF.
2. WJD, "Future Plans," April 28, 1945, in file 127, OSSDF.
3. Memo, D. C. Poole to WJD, March 16, 1945, in SFO Conference 16, 401A, OSSDF.
4. Letter, Robert Lehman to WJD, March 26, 1945, OSSDF.
5. Letter, Dorsey Richardson to WJD, March 27, 1945, OSSDF.
6. Note, list of OSS personnel at San Francisco Conference, OSS to State Department, April 3, 1945, OSSDF.
7. SFO Conference file, 16401, OSSDF.
8. Telegram 0294, E. G. Buxton to WJD, May 1, 1945, OSSDC.
9. Telegram 0139, April 26, 1945, OSSDC.
10. National War College lecture, March 1948, Edwin L. Sibert Collection.
11. Telegram WX-48843, August 13, 1945, in USFET SGS 061, NA (MMR).
12. "Encounters with Red Aircraft 2 April," Nathan Twining to John Deane, April 4, 1945, HQMAAF M-4715, NA (MMR) USMMM.
13. Malinin to Smith, September 7, 1945, in SGS 580/4, Case 17A, NA, U.S. Military Mission Moscow files.
14. Letter, Harry Aldrich to WJD, March 26, 1945, in OSS Ops METO 128, OSSDF.
15. Letter, "Colonel Aldrich's Letter," Whitney Shepardson to WJD, April 2, 1945, in OSS Ops METO, OSSDF.
16. Memo, 'Intelligence Project Bingo," Guy Martin to John Coughlin for WJD, April 21, 1945, in OSS Ops IBT 16,877, OSSDF.
17. Memo, "Needs and Possibilities of R&A in IB," Richard Hartshorne to WJD, May 14, 1945, in OSS Ops IB 16,823, OSSDF.
18. Memo, "The Development of a Program of Political and Economic Intelli-

gence for India and Burma, unsigned, undated, attached to Bingo proposal, OSSDF.
19. Letter, William Langer to Dr. Cora DuBois, "Interpretive Notes on R&A Directive for the India-Burma Theater," July 5, 1945, OSSDF.

Chapter 42
Secret Missions

1. Interview with Patrick Dolan, Ez Haute, near Monte Carlo, June 20, 1982. All quotations from this source until otherwise stated.
2. "Report on Green Mission," in RG 153, U.S. War Crimes Commission Case 8/9/24, Washington National Records Center, Suitland, Md.
3. WJD to FDR, September 23, 1944, in OSS Ops CZ, 19,995D, OSSDF.
4. "Circs. Attending AP Corr. Morton's Presence with Team Green in Slovakia," report to security officer, November 14, 1944, in OSS Ops CZ 19,995D, OSSDF.
5. "Report on Green Mission."
6. Lieutenant Colonel C. E. Williamson, "Capture of Anglo-American Group of Agents," February 13, 1945, in RG 153, U.S. War Crimes Commission Case 8/9/24.
7. WJD to Mrs. Harvey B. Gaul, May 30, 1945, in OSS Ops CZ 19,995D, OSSDF.
8. Captain W. S. Wharton, USNR, "Torture by German Gestapo of U.S. and British Officers," interrogation of H. W. Thost in Team Green File, RG 153, U.S. War Crimes Commission Case 8/9/24, Washington National Records Center, Suitland, Md.
9. OSS War Report, vol. 2, p. 134.
10. Letter, Mrs. H. B. Gaul to WJD, April 18, 1945, Casualties 15,202, OSSDF.
11. Telegram 68274, September 11, 1944, OSSDC.
12. Telegram 79094, Bruce Yarrow to WJD, September 30, 1944, OSSDC.
13. Telegram 86809, WJD to Bruce Yarrow, December 6, 1944, OSSDC.
14. Telegram 95879, Yarrow to WJD, December 15, 1944, OSSDC.
15. King Peter II to Winston Churchill, December 29, 1944, OSSDC.
16. Telegram 0249, Bruce Yarrow to WJD, January 2, 1945, OSSDC.
17. Pouch letter, Yarrow to WJD, January 8, 1945, OSSDF.
18. Telegram 0889, Yarrow to WJD, January 5, 1945, OSSDC.
19. Pouch letter, Yarrow to WJD, January 8, 1945, OSSDF.
20. Ibid., January 9, 1945, OSSDF.
21. Ibid.
22. Telegram 1979, Yarrow to WJD, January 9, 1945.
23. Pouch letter, Yarrow to WJD, January 12, 1945, OSSDF.
24. Pouch letter, Yarrow to WJD, January 15, 1945, OSSDF.
25. Telegram 5199, Yarrow to WJD, January 23, 1945, OSSDC.
26. Ibid.
27. Report by Lieutenants Dorr and Coombs, William Langer to WJD, October 7, 1944, OSSDF. Hereafter called Dorr-Coombs Report.
28. "Evacuation of Air Crew Men from Rumania," Walter M. Ross to WJD, September 16, 1944, OSSDF.
29. Dorr-Coombs Report.
30. Ibid.
31. Memo, "OSS Activities in Rumania," Edward Glavin to WJD, September 11, 1944, OSSDF.

32. *Ibid.*
33. Letter, John Deane to WJD, November 4, 1944, OSSDF.
34. Telegram, unnumbered, September 29, 1944, OSSDC.
35. Letter, WJD to P. Fitin, October 10, 1944, OSSDF.
36. Letter, WJD to P. Fitin, October 30, 1944, OSSDF.
37. Letter, P. Fitin to WJD, November 9, 1944, OSSDF.
38. Telegram 21669, November 10, 1944, OSSDC.
39. Memo, Lawrence Lowman to WJD, November 17, 1944.
40. Telegram 1584, September 12, 1944, OSSDC.
41. Telegram 2064, September 14, 1944, OSSDC.
42. Memo, Robert Joyce to OSS HQ, September 17, 1944, in Rumania 12,120, OSSDF.
43. Telegram 1974, WJD to Frank Wisner, September 22, 1944, OSSDC.
44. Telegram 3824, September 23, 1944, OSSDC.
45 Telegram 4244, Frank Wisner to WJD, September 26, 1944, OSSDC.
46. Memo, "Request for 'Background Information' Concerning Order of Battle Reports from Source Tonsillitis, Bucharest," Frank Wisner to WJD, March 30, 1945, OSSDF.

Chapter 43
The Vessel Affair

1. Letter, John Magruder to Clayton Bissell, January 5, 1945, in Vessel 16,038, OSSDF.
2. Telegram 18984, January 17, 1945, OSSDC.
3. Interview with James R. Murphy, Washington, D.C., February 2, 1981.
4. Interview with high X-2 officer, Washington, D.C., February 2, 1982.
5. Memo, Vessel 7A, Charles Cheston to FDR, January 11, 1945, OSSDF.
6. Vessel Report 20A to FDR, January 15, 1945, OSSDF.
7. Memo, E. J. Putzell to Davenport, January 16, 1945, in Vessel 16,038, OSSDF.
8. Telegram 24434, January 15, 1945, OSSDC.
9. Telegram 25184, January 11, 1945, OSSDC.
10. Telegram 20604, January 16, 1945, OSSDC.
11. Vessel Report 24C, January 17, 1945, in Vessel 16,038, OSSDF.
12. Telegram 4467, January 20, 1945, OSSDC.
13. Vessel Report 42A, January 24, 1945, in Vessel 16,038, OSSDF.
14. Vessel memo 44A, January 25, 1945, in Vessel 16,038, OSSDF.
15. Telegram 3427, January 26, 1945, in Vessel 16,038, OSSDF.
16. Telegram 28519, January 26, 1945, OSSDF.
17. Vessel memo 43A to FDR, January 27, 1945, in Vessel 16,038, OSSDF.
18. "Vessel Report 43-A dated 22 Jan 45," January 27, 1945, in Vessel 16,038, OSSDF.
19. Telegram 22729, January 31, 1945, in Vessel 16,038, OSSDF.
20. Vessel Report 60A to FDR, February 2, 1945, in Vessel 16,038, OSSDF.
21. Vessel Report 58A to FDR, February 2, 1945, in Vessel 16,038, OSSDF.
22. Telegram 32244, February 4, 1945, OSSDF.
23. Telegram 32709, February 15, 1945, in Vessel 16,038, OSSDF.
24. Vessel Report 67A to FDR, February 16, 1945, in Vessel 16,038, OSSDF.
25. Memo, Turner McBaine to WJD, February 20, 1945, in Vessel 16,038, OSSDF.
26. Telegram 25134, February 17, 1945, in Vessel 16,038, OSSDF.

27. Note, James Clement Dunn to WJD, March 2, 1945, in Vessel 16,038, OSSDF.
28. Letter, WJD to J. C. Dunn, March 8, 1945, in Vessel 16,038, Dots 613, OSSDF.
29. Telegram 26864, March 3, 1945, Vessel 16,038, OSSDF.
30. Interview with Henry B. Hyde, New York, N.Y., February 3, 1982.

Chapter 44
The Goff Affair

1. CO, Company D, 2677th Regiment (Provisional) to CO, "Report on Goff Agent Chains," April 24, 1945, OSSDF.
2. Letter, W. D. Suhling to Edward Glavin, cc to WJD, "Communist Agents," date illegible, possibly November 19, 1944, OSSDF. All quotations from this source until otherwise stated.
3. Memo, Otto Doering to WJD, "Basic Principles re Army and OSS Policies re Communists, etc. March 12, 1945, OSSDF.
4. Washington *Times-Herald,* March 13, 1945.
5. "Digest of Memorandum from Vincent J. Scamporini to the Executive Officer, 2677th Regiment, OSS (Prov.) on the Goff Chain, April 10, 1945, OSSDF. All quotations from this source until otherwise stated.
6. X-2 to Exec., "Review of Goff Chains," April 9, 1945, OSSDF. All quotations from this source until otherwise stated.
7. X-2 to Exec., "Goff Affair," April 10, 1945, OSSDF.
8. Telegram 44254, Edward Glavin to WJD, April 16, 1945, OSSDC.
9. Letter, Edward Glavin to W. D. Suhling, April 16, 1945, OSSDF.
10. Telegram 715 (4), April 17, 1945, OSSDC.
11. W. D. Suhling to Edward Glavin, "Report on Goff Agent Chains," April 14, 1945, OSSDF.
12. Judson B. Smith to Edward Glavin, "Report on Lt. Irving Goff, Lt. Vincent Lossowski, Lt. Irving Fajans and Lt. Milton Wolff," April 18, 1945, OSSDF. All quotations from this source until otherwise stated.
13. William Maddox to Edward Glavin, "Reports on Lts. Goff, Lossowski, Fajans & Wolff," April 24, 1945, OSSDF. All quotations from this source until otherwise stated.
14. Special Investigations Committee to WJD, "Report on 2nd Lt. Milton Wolff, 2nd Lt. Irving Fajans, 1st Lt. Vincent Lossowski, and 1st Lt. Irving Goff, May 10, 1945, OSSDF.
15. J. J. Monigan, Jr., to WJD, "Report on Traffic over Circuits to Communist Party Partisan Bands," May 11, 1945, OSSDF.
16. Letter, WJD to Irving Goff, July 15, 1945, OSSDF.
17. Letter, Milton Wolff to WJD, July 28, 1945, OSSDF.
18. Citations File, OSSDF.
19. Memo, "Icardi and LoDolce Treason," of conversations between Victor C. Woerheide, H. L. Manfredi, and Colonel William D. Suhling, November 15–16, 1954, DJ. Victor C. Woerheide, DJ Memo, November 17, 1954, ref. no. 146-28-2201, WJD Miscellaneous Collection. Hereafter called Woerheide Report.
20. *Ibid.*
21. *Ibid.*
22. *Ibid.*
23. "Report of the Chrysler Mission by Sgt. Carl G. LoDolce," OSSDF.

24. Max Corve to WJD, undated, but around June 1945, WJD Miscellaneous Collection. Hereafter called Corve Report.
25. Woerheide Report.
26. Corvo Report.
27. Citation, Aldo L. Icardi, Citations Book, vol. 1, OSSDF.
28. Telegram 37554, June 22, 1945, OSSDC.
29. Interview with B. M. W. Knox, Washington, D.C., December 13,1981.

Chapter 45
FDR's Death and the German Surrender

1. Telegram 29479, Rodrigo to 140, Information 109 and 110, January 31, 1945, OSSDC.
2. Memo, OSS to JCS, January 24, 1945, OSSDF.
3. Memo, "Dot 591," WJD to JCS, February 26, 1945, OSSDF.
4. *Ibid.*
5. Telegram, Eisenhower to Marshall, February 24, 1945, NA (MMR).
6. Interview with Franklin O. Canfield, Southampton, Mass., January 12, 1982.
7. Interview with Robert Joyce, London, January 12, 1982.
8. Charles B. MacDonald, *The Last Offensive* (Washington, D.C.: Office of Chief of Military History, 1973), p. 174.
9. All correspondence between Roosevelt and Stalin derives from (1) the CCS on Crossword and (2) the Moscow Foreign Languages Publishing House's *Correspondence between the Chairman of the Council of Ministers of the USSR and the Presidents of the USA and the Prime Ministers of Great Britain During the Great Patriotic War of 1941–1945.*
10. *Ibid.*
11. Interview with G. M. T. Jones, New York City, January 24, 1982.
12. Note, FDR to WJD, April 14(?), 1945, in OSS 12,733G, OSSDF.
13. Letters and responses are in 12,733G, OSSDF.
14. Francis Biddle to WJD, April 20, 1945, OSS 12,733G, OSSDF.
15. Interview with Mary Bancroft, New York City, June 16, 1980.
16. Telegram 12834, April 13, 1945, OSSDC.
17. FDR file, OSSDF.
18. Telegram 8099, A. W. Dulles to WJD, April 4, 1945, OSSDC.
19. SHAEF G5, "Weekly Journal of Information," number 9, April 19, 1945, in OPD 014.1 ETO, NA (MMR).
20. R & A Bulletin 1934.18, "Nazi Plans to Go Underground," January 26, 1945, WJD Miscellaneous Collection.
21. Office of the Military Governor of the United States in Germany, Weekly Intelligence Summary 4, October 2, 1945, WJD Miscellaneous Collection.
22. Foreign Broadcasting Intelligence Service, (FBIS) study of " 'Join the Were-wolves' Broadcasts from the Reich, April 4, 1945, WJD Miscellaneous Collection.
23. SHAEF G5, Bulletin 5, April 29, 1945, NA (MMR).
24. *Ibid.*
25. AFHQ, *History of Special Operations, op. cit.* All quotations in this segment from this source until otherwise stated.
26. Telegrams, Edward Glavin to WJD, May 1 and 11 and June 2, 1945, OSSDC.
27. Hamburg Radio, May 1, 1945, 9:26 EWT, FBIS intercept.
28. Ruth Donovan, diary, May 1, 1945.
29. Memo, James P. Baxter III to T. G. Early, January 31, 1942, OSSDF.

30. "Preliminary Report: Truth Drug," October 13, 1943, WJD Miscellaneous Collection.
31. Memo, "Development of 'Truth Drug,' " Allen Abrams to WJD, no date, in R&D 11,840A, OSSDF.
32. "Memorandum on T.D.," by Captain George H. White, June 3, 1943, OSSDF.
33. "Employment of 'Truth Drug,' " Allen Abrams to WJD, June 21, 1943, OSSDF.
34. USFET signal 7244, August 3, 1945, in SGS, NA (MMR).
35. John Deane to Edwin Sibert and Allen Dulles, July 26, 1945, NA (MMR), USMMM.
36. Telegram UKX-47035, WJD to Deane, Sibert, and Dulles, July 30, 1945, NA (MMR).
37. Telegram WARX 42306, Adjutant General, War Department, (AGWAR) to John Deane, August 1, 1945, NA (MMR).
38. Telegram WARX 41089, AGWAR to Eisenhower and John Deane, August 18, 1943, NA (MMR).
39. Letter, Wilhelm Hoettl to B. C. Andrus, September 26, 1945, in RG 238, NA (MMR).
40. Pass issued by Office of the U.S. chief of counsel, Nuremberg, October 18, 1945, in RG 238, NA (MMR).
41. Statement of Ernst Kaltenbrunner, *Trial of the Major War Criminals Before the International Military Tribunal Nuremberg*, vol. XXII, NA (German World War II Section).
42. Telegram, WJD to John Deane for P. Fitin, July 28, 1945, OSSDC.

Chapter 46
The Canaris Investigation

1. Memo, WJD to Harry Truman, June 11, 1945, OSSDF.
2. Translation of letter from Frau Erika Canaris to WJD, November 15, 1945.
3. The text of Frau Canaris's letter appears on page 130.
4. Report by Lieutenant Colonel Sidney Bernstein, "Disposition of SS Loot by Reichsbank," May 14, 1945, OMGUS 940.304, RG 260, OMGUS.
5. *Ibid.*
6. Frank C. Gabell letter, "Assets Set Aside for Delivery to IRO," August 19, 1948, OMGUS 940,154, in NA (WNRC).
7. SHAEF Weekly Intelligence Summary, no. 45, June 19, 1945, Annex B, NA (MMR). All quotations from this source until stated otherwise.
8. CMH, *History of the CIC Corps in the European Theater of Operations*, U S. Army, Fort Meade, Maryland, p. 20. All quotations from this source until stated otherwise.
9. Interviews with Johannes Werner, New York, N.Y., August 24, 1977, and September 30, 1981. At Werner's request, the facts about his origins have been rearranged to make his identification impossible.
10. *History of the CIC in the European Theater of Operations, op. cit.*, p. 45.

Chapter 47
Termination

1. Robert Joyce to WJD, May 11, 1945, in Japan Surrender File, OSSDF.
2. Memo, Dulles to WJD to Joint Chiefs, July 13, 1945, OSSDF.

3. Letter, WJD to Harry Truman and JCS, July 16, 1945, OSSDF.
4. *Ibid.*
5. *Ibid.*
6. Telegram, WJD to Harry Truman, August 2, 1945, in OSS Japan Negotiations File, OSSDF.
7. CIA Report, p. 270.
8. Drew Pearson, "Washington Merry-Go-Round," Washington *Post,* April 27, 1945.
9. *Ibid.*, April 27, 1945, OSSDF.
10. Drew Pearson, broadcast, Sunday, May 6, 1945, from San Francisco, OSSDF.
11. Drew Pearson, "Washington Merry-Go-Round," Washington *Post,* May 26, 1945.
12. Transcript of telephone conversation between Francis Biddle and WJD, for J. J. McCloy, June 15, 1945, in OSS 16,810A, OSSDF.
13. Letter, Herbert Wechsler, to J. J. McCloy, May 21, 1945, OSSDF.
14. "Violation of Cryptographic Security," WJD to JCS, July 21, 1945, in 16,810A, OSSDF.
15. Memo, JCS to WJD, August 25, 1945, 16,810A, OSSDF.
16. In *PM,* March 19, 1945, and Washington *Times-Herald,* May 16, 18, 19, 20, 1945, in Publicity File, OSSDF.
17. Outgoing telegrams in RG 165 OPD, case 1028; replies in case 1056, NA (MMR).
18. Letter, William Leahy to Clarence Cannon, May 29, 1945, in RG 165 OPD, case 1049, NA (MMR).
19. RG 165 JCS 334 OSS, case 6-13-42, NA (MMR).
20. CIA Report, p. 284.
21. *Ibid.*
22. *Ibid.*, p. 302.
23. Letter, Harry Truman to WJD, September 20, 1945, in OSS CIA Liquidation 12,733U, OSSDF.

Chapter 48
Farewell the Tranquil Mind

1. Taylor, *op. cit.*, pp. 350–51.
2. Memo, "Decorations Awarded OSS Personnel (including Foreign Nationals) to January 5, 1946," in Citations File, OSSDF.
3. Citation to Oak Leaf Cluster for Distinguished Service Medal, September 21, 1946, WJD Miscellaneous Collection.
4. Harry S Truman, *Year of Decision* (New York: Signet, 1965), p. 145.
5. W. J. Donovan dossier, FBI.
6. Interview with James R. Murphy, Washington, D.C., March 22, 1982.
7. CIA Report, p. 282.
8. *Ibid.*
9. Letter, WJD to adjutant general, September 23, 1944, OSSDF.
10. Letter, Frank T. Ryan to Lucius D. Clay, October 16, 1947.
11. *Ibid.*
12. World Commerce Corporation Report, September 1947.
13. *Republican Review,* January 1947.
14. CIA Report, p. 387.
15. CIA intelligence memo 163, "Foreign Activities in the Field of Biological Warfare (BW)," April 20, 1949, WJD Miscellaneous Collection.

16. Reports File by Special Agent Frederick Gardella, WJD Miscellaneous Collection. Hereafter called Gardella Report.
17. *Ibid.*, p. 50.
18. *Ibid.*
19. *Ibid.*, p. 55.
20. *Ibid.*, p. 57.
21. *Ibid.*, p. 59.
22. "Medico-Legal Report," WJD Personal File on Holohan murder, 3045, WJD Miscellaneous Collection.
23. Statement of Carl George LoDolce, 16 Taft Avenue, Rochester, N.Y., August 3, 1950, in WJD Personal File, 3045, WJD Miscellaneous Collection. All quotations from this source until otherwise stated.
24. Letter, LoDolce to WJD, in WJD Personal File, 3045, WJD Miscellaneous Collection.
25. Hearing Before the Special Subcommittee of the Committee on Armed Services, House of Representatives: Testimony and Confessions Relating to the Disappearance of Major William G. Holohan. U.S. Government Printing Office, 1953, p. 76. Hereafter called Cole Report.
26. Icardi's testimony, Cole Report, pp. 108–59. All quotations from this source until otherwise stated.
27. New York *Sunday News,* December 20, 1953.
28. *AFHQ History of Special Operations, Mediterranean Theater, 1942–1945,* Section XVIII, "Conclusions," p. 1.
29. Vanden Heuvel diary, August 21, 1954.

Epilogue
Last Journeys

1. Ruth Donovan, diary, December 31, 1951.
2. Whitney H. Shepardson, note, "Post-War CIA," undated but obviously written after 1957, WJD Miscellaneous Collection.
3. Telegram 1057, May 15, 1953, WJD Miscellaneous Collection.
4. Letter, WJD to Dwight Eisenhower, June 3, 1953, WJD Miscellaneous Collection.
5. Letter, WJD to Dwight Eisenhower, June 3, 1953, WJD Miscellaneous Collection.
6. Letter, WJD to Walter Bedell Smith, May 19, 1953, WJD Miscellaneous Collection.
7. Letter, Dwight Eisenhower to WJD, June 9, 1953, WJD Miscellaneous Collection.
8. Vanden Heuvel, diary, October 28, 1953.
9. *Ibid.*, September 19, 1953.
10. *Ibid.*, October 1, 1953.
11. *Ibid.*, March 17, 1954.
12. *Ibid.*
13. *Ibid.*, May 4 and 6, 1954.
14. Letter, WJD to M. H. Dodge, May 7, 1954, WJD Miscellaneous Collection.
15. Letter, WJD to A. W. Dulles, January 8, 1954, WJD Miscellaneous Collection.
16. Vanden Heuvel, diary, July 3, 1954.
17. *Ibid.*, June 1, 1954.
18. *Ibid.*, June 7, 1954.
19. Ruth Donovan, diary, February 14, 1957.

20. *Ibid.*, February 16, 1957.
21. Letter, Dwight Eisenhower to WJD, April 1, 1957, WJD Miscellaneous Collection.
22. Corey Ford, *Donovan of OSS* (Boston: Little, Brown, 1970), p. 33.
23. Interview with Otto C. Doering, New York, N.Y., November 1, 1977.

INDEX

Duke, Florimund, 292, 385–386,
　389–393
Duke Street Murders, 318–320,
　612–613
Dulles, Allen W., 100, 129, 170,
　274–293, 385, 407, 500, 634,
　738, 741, 753, 758–759, 821,
　825–828
　background of, 275
　Colossus and, 277
　Donovan on, 285
　Gisevius as source for, 286–292
　Hungarian contacts of, 382, 385,
　　388–389
　in Japanese negotiations, 772–774
　Kiss warned against by, 395–396
　in pre-Neptune Germany, 528–530
　on Rumanian defection, 400
　on Schwarze Kapelle, 527–532
　unreliable information of, 277–278
　on Valkyrie, 566–567
　Wood examined by, 284
Dulles, John Foster, 275, 821–829,
　834
Dunlop, Richard, 413–416
Dunn, James Clement, 613, 699–701
Durand, Dana, 184
Dykes, Vivian, 154

Eaker, Ira C., 671
Early, Steve, 633
Earnest, Herbert, 759–760
Eccles, David, 162
Eddy, William A., 177, 253, 262,
　272–273, 320–325, 385, 503,
　643
　background of, 321
　in Darlan assassination, 266–269
　personality of, 322
　SIS as seen by, 323
Eden, Anthony, 263, 600
　in Yugoslavia situation, 453, 668
EDES (Greek royalists), 429, 431
Egan, William, 18
Ehrgott, Jules, 429–430
Eifler, Carl, 412–416
Eisenhower, Dwight D., 322, 350,
　466, 526–529, 573, 612,
　730–731, 781, 821–829, 831–833
　Darlan assassination and, 268
　Darlan deal of, 261–262

Darlan pressured by, 259
on French resistance, 539
on German commanders, 532
Giraud and, 247–249, 258–259,
　261
in Operation Audrey, 444–446
ELAS (Greek People's Army of
　National Liberation), 427–431,
　439–441
election of 1932, 121–126
　Catholic issue in, 124–125
　Democratic proposals in, 125
　labor issue in, 124–125
　malicious rumors in, 123–125
　outcome of, 126
elections:
　of 1922, 81–83
　of 1928, 102–104
　of 1930, 121
Ellis, Charles H., 174, 176
Else, G. F., 426
Elster, Botho H., 592
Endicott, H. Wendell, 134–139
Enigma machine ciphers, 181
Erdwurm, Graham, 711, 713–714
Ernouf, E., 588–594
Etappesdienst, 128
Étoile, Mission, 587–594
　orders changed for, 591
　rendezvous difficulties of, 588–590
Evans, W. G., 108–109

Fajans, Irving, 707–719
Falkenhausen, Alexander von, 531
FANY (First Aid Nursing Yeomanry),
　338
Farager, Walter, 760
Farish, Lynn, 449
FBI (Federal Bureau of
　Investigation):
　Donovan investigated by, 21–22,
　　821–822
　Donovan's file in, 186, 222–224
　intelligence officers of, 159
　1946 budget for, 782
　see also Hoover, J. Edgar
FBQ Corporation, 208, 310–312
Federal Register, 165
Fellgiebel, Erich, 568–570
Fénard, Raymond, 557
Fenians, 15–16